Household Spending

Who Spends How Much on What

BY THE EDITORS OF NEW STRATEGIST PRESS

Household
Spending

Who Spends How Much on What

BY THE EDITORS OF NEW STRATEGIST PRESS

New Strategist Press, LLC
Amityville, New York

New Strategist Press, LLC
P.O. Box 635, Amityville, New York 11701
800/848-0842; 631/608-8795
www.newstrategist.com

ISBN 978-1-940308-07-4 (paper)
ISBN 978-1-940308-06-7 (hardcover)

Printed in the United States of America

Contents

Chapter 11. Spending on Transportation, 2011

List of Tables

Chapter 3. Spending on Entertainment, 2011

Chapter 4. Spending on Financial Products and Services, 2011

Chapter 5. Spending on Food and Alcoholic Beverages, 2011

Chapter 6. Spending on Gifts for People in Other Households, 2011

Chapter 7. Spending on Health Care, 2011

Chapter 9. Spending on Housing: Shelter and Utilities, 2011

Chapter 10. Spending on Personal Care, Reading, Education, and Tobacco, 2011

Introduction

Welcome to the 18th edition of *Household Spending: Who Spends How Much on What*, your exclusive guide to the spending patterns of American households in 2011. The detailed spending data presented here are not available on any government web site. They were obtained by special request from the Bureau of Labor Statistics. New Strategist has been acquiring and processing these data since 1989 (publishing *Household Spending* every two years through 1999 and annually since 2000), providing a unique and comprehensive analysis of the spending of American households.

Since we published the first edition of *Household Spending*, the economy has cycled through good times and bad. As we publish this edition, we are still recovering from the worst downturn since the Great Depression—popularly dubbed the Great Recession. The spending patterns shown in these pages reveal the struggle by the average household to maintain its standard of living. This struggle began well before the official start of the recession in December 2007. It began many years ago as men's wages stagnated and the cost of housing, health care, education, and energy began to rise much faster than household incomes.

Americans Are Cautious Spenders

To understand spending trends, it is important to distinguish between aggregate consumer spending and average household spending. Aggregate spending is the big picture, the total expenditures of American consumers. Aggregate consumer spending in the United States has been growing fairly steadily for years because of population growth and the aging of the enormous baby-boom generation into the peak spending age groups. Average household spending, in contrast, is the more intimate world of bills and budgets. It shows how individual households allocate their dollars. Over the years, average household spending has grown much less than aggregate spending, and during the Great Recession the decline in spending at the household level was much deeper than at the aggregate level. Between 2000 and 2011, aggregate consumer spending increased by a substantial 24 percent, after adjusting for inflation (see Bureau of Economic Analysis, National Income and Product Accounts, table 2.3.6), whereas average household spending was the same in both years. Aggregate consumer spending reached an all-time high in 2011, while average household spending was still 8 percent below its 2006 peak in 2011. Contrary to popular perception, most Americans are cautious spenders.

In 2011, the average American household spent $49,705, essentially the same as the inflation-adjusted $49,697 of 2000. Average household spending peaked in 2006 at an inflation-adjusted $54,001. Much of the spending growth that occurred in the 2000-to-2006 time period was nondiscretionary—brought about by the ever-larger claim of necessities on the household budget. After adjusting for inflation, the average household spent 21 percent more on mortgage interest in 2006 than in 2000, 24 percent more on property taxes, and 47 percent more on gasoline. Out-of-pocket spending on health insurance increased 27 percent during those years, and spending on education rose 20 percent.

Many discretionary categories experienced declines between 2000 and 2006. Average household spending on women's apparel fell 11 percent. Households cut their spending on new vehicles by 4 percent, and spending on personal care products and services was 11 percent lower in 2006 than in 2000.

Then the Great Recession hit, and spending plunged on most items between 2006 and 2011. Average household spending on mortgage interest fell 24 percent during those years, after adjusting for inflation. Spending on food away from home (mostly restaurant meals) fell 13 percent, furniture 31 percent, and new vehicles 37 percent. Despite the hard times, average household spending on education climbed 6 percent, out-of-pocket spending on health insurance increased 18 percent, and rent spending grew by 5 percent.

Analyzing spending trends at the individual household level, as *Household Spending* does, provides deep insight into the nation's economic ups and downs. Unfortunately, few tackle the household-level data, discouraged by their complexity. Instead, most analysts and reporters take the easy way out, reporting on aggregate consumer spending because it requires an examination of only two figures—today's and yesterday's. In contrast, analyzing spending at the household level requires delving into the who, what, and why of spending—the mindset and motivations of individual consumers. You can find that reality here, in the 18th edition of *Household Spending*. This book is for those who need to know the who, what, and why of American spending patterns.

Consumer spending is the result of a complex mix of wants and needs, hopes and fears. This mix determines the success of individual businesses and the health of our economy. Knowing how consumers spend their dollars is key to understanding where our economy is headed, an insight of immense value as the nation copes with uncertainty.

How the Book Is Organized

Household Spending is based on unpublished data collected by the Bureau of Labor Statistics' Consumer Expenditure Survey, an ongoing, nationwide survey of household spending. The editors of New Strategist start with the average spending figures collected by the Bureau of Labor Statistics and analyze them in a variety of ways, calculating household spending indexes, total household spending, and household market shares. We do this for hundreds of spending categories by age of householder, household income, household type, race and Hispanic origin of householder, region of residence, and educational attainment of householder.

The Bureau of Labor Statistics' Consumer Expenditure Survey is a complete accounting of household expenditures. It includes everything from big-ticket items, such as homes and cars, to small purchases like laundry detergent and video games. The survey does not include expenditures by government, business, or institutions. The data in this book are from the 2011 Consumer Expenditure Survey, unless otherwise noted.

The Consumer Expenditure Survey uses the consumer unit rather than the household as its sampling unit. The Bureau of Labor Statistics defines consumer unit as "a single person or group of persons in a sample household related by blood, marriage, adoption or other legal arrangement or who share responsibility for at least two out of three major types of expenses—food, housing, and other expenses." For convenience, consumer units are referred to as households in the text of this book. For more information about the Consumer Expenditure Survey and consumer units, see Appendix A.

Chapter 1 of *Household Spending* is devoted to summary household spending statistics. These are shown for consumer units by age, income, household type, region of residence, race and Hispanic origin, and education of householder.

Chapters 2 through 11 present detailed spending statistics organized by major product and service category (food, housing, transportation, and so on) and include all typical household expenditures. Within each chapter, spending statistics are shown by age of householder, household income, household type, race and Hispanic origin of householder, region of residence, and educational attainment of householder. For each of the demographic variables, tables show average spending, indexed spending, total (or aggregate) spending, and share of spending.

How to Use the Tables in This Book

The data in *Household Spending* reveal how American households allocate their spending dollars. The starting point for all calculations in *Household Spending* are the unpublished detailed average household spending data collected by the Consumer Expenditure Survey. These are shown in the average spending tables in Chapters 2 through 11. The remaining tables in each chapter were produced by New Strategist's statisticians and are based on the average figures. The indexed household spending tables reveal whether households in a given segment spend more or less than the average for all households (or for all households in that segment), and by how much. The total household spending tables show the overall size of a particular market. The household market share tables reveal how much spending each household segment accounts for. These four types of tables are described in detail below.

• **Average Household Spending Tables.** The average spending tables report the average annual spending of households on each item or category of items in 2011. The Consumer Expenditure Survey produces average spending data for all households in a segment, e.g., all households with a householder aged 25 to 34, not just for those who purchased the item. When reviewing the spending data, remember that by including both purchasers and nonpurchasers in the calculation, the average is diluted—especially for infrequently purchased items. For example, the average household spent $251 on day care centers in 2011. Since only a small percentage of households spend money on day care, this figure greatly underestimates the amount parents spend on day care centers. To provide a more realistic figure of how much buyers spend on an item, Appendix C shows the percentage of households that purchased individual products and services during the average quarter of 2011, and the amount spent by purchasers per quarter. According to Appendix C, only 4.7 percent of households spent on day care centers during the average quarter of 2011. The purchasers spent an average of $1,334 per quarter, for an estimated annual cost of $5,336—a much more realistic figure than the average of $251 for all households.

For frequently purchased items—such as bread—the average spending figures give a fairly accurate account of actual spending. But for most of the products and services examined in *Household Spending*, the average spending figures are less revealing than the indexes and market shares.

Average spending figures are useful in determining the market potential of a product or service in a local area. By multiplying the average amount spent on children's clothing by the number of households in the Dallas metropolitan area, for example, marketers can estimate the size of the market for children's clothing in Dallas. The Dallas media could show those figures to potential advertisers as evidence of the local demand for children's clothing.

Note that because of sampling errors, average values can vary—especially for infrequently purchased items. To examine the standard errors associated with summary average spending figures (Chapter 1), go to http://www.bls.gov/cex/csxstnderror.htm. To examine the standard errors associated with detailed average spending data, contact the Bureau of Labor Statistics Consumer Expenditure Survey statisticians by phone at 202-691-6900 or by email at cexinfo@bls.gov.

• **Indexed Household Spending Tables.** The indexed spending tables compare the spending of each household segment with that of the average household. To compute the indexes, New Strategist's statisticians divide the average amount each household segment spends on a particular item by how much the average household spends on the item and multiply the resulting figure by 100.

An index of 100 is the average for all households. An index of 125 means the spending of a household segment is 25 percent above average (100 plus 25). An index of 75 indicates spending that is 25 percent below the average for all households (100 minus 25). Indexed spending figures identify the best customers for a product or service. Households with an index of 177 for outdoor furniture, for example, are a strong market for that product. Those with an index below 100 are either a weak or an underserved market.

Spending indexes can reveal hidden markets—household segments with a high propensity to buy a particular product or service but which are overshadowed by household segments that account for a larger share of the market. Householders aged 65 to 74, for example, spend 42 percent more than the average household on nonsubscription newspapers and magazines (with an index of 142). This is a higher index than that of any other age group, making householders aged 65 to 74 the best customers of this item. With an index of 100, the spending of householders aged 45 to 54 on nonsubscription newspapers and magazines is just average, but their market share is considerably larger than that of householders aged 65 to 74 (20 vs. 16 percent) because there are almost 11 million more households in the younger age group. Using the indexed spending tables, marketers can see that the older householders are, in fact, the far better customers and adjust their business strategy accordingly.

Note that because of sampling errors, small differences in index values may be insignificant. But the broader patterns revealed by indexes can guide marketers to the best customers.

• **Total Household Spending Tables.** To produce the total (aggregate) spending tables, New Strategist's statisticians multiply average spending figures by the number of households in a segment. The result is the dollar size of the total household market and of each market segment. All totals are shown in thousands of dollars. To convert the numbers in the total spending tables to dollars, append "000" to the number. For example, households headed by people aged 25 to 34 spent more than $10 billion ($10,489,948,000) on alcohol in 2011.

When comparing the total spending figures in *Household Spending* with aggregate spending figures from the Bureau of Economic Analysis, other government agencies, or trade associations, keep in mind that the Consumer Expenditure Survey includes only household spending, not spending by businesses or institutions. Sales data also differ from household spending totals because sales figures for consumer products include the value of goods sold to industries, government, and foreign markets, which may be a significant proportion of sales.

• **Household Market Share Tables.** New Strategist's statisticians produce the market share tables by converting total spending data to percentages. To calculate the percentage of total household spending on an item that is controlled by each demographic segment—i.e., its market share—each segment's total spending on an item is divided by aggregate household spending on the item.

Market shares reveal the biggest customers—the demographic segments that account for the largest share of household spending on a particular product or service. Businesses can reach a large portion of their customers by targeting the demographic segments in control of the largest market shares. Of course, by single-mindedly targeting the biggest customers, businesses cannot nurture potential growth markets. An additional danger of focusing only on the biggest customers is that businesses may end up ignoring their best customers. This is especially problematic because market shares are unstable, thanks to baby booms and busts over the past half-century. For example, householders aged 45 to 54 control a similar share of the market for auto rentals on trips (25 percent) as householders aged 55 to 64 (26 percent), but only because the younger age group is larger. In fact, householders aged 55 to 64 are better customers of vehicle rentals, as they spend 47 percent more than the average household on this item, whereas householders aged 45 to 54 spend just 24 percent more than average. Marketers who ignore their best customers because they are distracted by their biggest customers may end up with no customers.

For More Information

To find out more about the Consumer Expenditure Survey, visit the Bureau of Labor Statistics web site (http://www.bls.gov/cex), where summary average spending figures (as shown in Chapter 1 of this book) are available. The detailed average spending numbers (as shown in Chapters 2 through 11) are available only by special request.

For household spending trends by single product category, see New Strategist's Who's Buying reports. For a detailed look at spending patterns for more than 300 products and services, see New Strategist's *Best Customers: Demographics of Consumer Demand*. To find out more about these books and reports, including tables of contents and sample pages, visit New Strategist's web site at http://www.newstrategist.com. All New Strategist books and reports are available in print or as downloads with links to the Excel version of each table.

Household Spending Trends, 2000 to 2011

As American households struggle with the aftermath of the Great Recession, their spending has declined. Average household spending climbed 9 percent between 2000 and 2006, peaking at $54,001 (in 2011 dollars). Then the recession set in. Average household spending fell 8 percent between 2006 and 2011, to $49,705—essentially the same as the inflation-adjusted $49,697 of 2000.

On many products and services, households boosted their spending between 2000 and 2006 and cut back between 2006 and 2011. Average household spending on alcoholic beverages, for example, grew by a substantial 14 percent between 2000 and 2006, after adjusting for inflation. Between 2006 and 2011, household spending on alcoholic beverages fell 18 percent. Similarly, average household spending on food away from home (primarily restaurant meals) increased 8 percent between 2000 and 2006, then fell 13 percent between 2006 and 2011. Spending on mortgage interest grew by 21 percent between 2000 and 2006 as the housing bubble inflated, then fell 24 percent between 2006 and 2011 as the bubble burst and foreclosures became common.

Despite the recession, the cost of living continued to rise. Consequently, the average household was forced to spend more on necessities such as health care. Average household spending on health care climbed 14 percent between 2000 and 2006 and another 7 percent between 2006 and 2011. Behind the continuing increase was the rise in health insurance premiums, average household spending on health insurance growing by 27 percent between 2000 and 2006 and by another 18 percent between 2006 and 2011. The average household spent 15 percent less on drugs in 2011 than in 2006 as the Medicare prescription drug program kicked in and lowered drug costs for older Americans.

Spending on most discretionary items fell between 2006 and 2011, with one important exception. The average household spent 37 percent more on the category "pets, toys, and playground equipment" in 2011 than in 2006, after adjusting for inflation. Most of the increase was accounted for by much greater spending on pet medicines such as heartworm and flea treatments.

Some spending categories experienced a decline in both time periods. Despite the rising homeownership rate, spending on household furnishings and equipment fell 6 percent between 2000 and 2006 and another 21 percent between 2006 and 2011. Households were devoting so much to mortgage payments that they were forced to reduce spending on items for outfitting their home. Spending on apparel continued its long-term downward trend in both time periods as well.

The sharp reductions in spending on so many items show that American consumers have become not just cautious spenders but penny-pinchers—with enormous consequences for our economy.

Households spent more, then cut back, on many items

(percent change in spending by the average household on selected products and services, 2000–06 and 2006–11; in 2011 dollars)

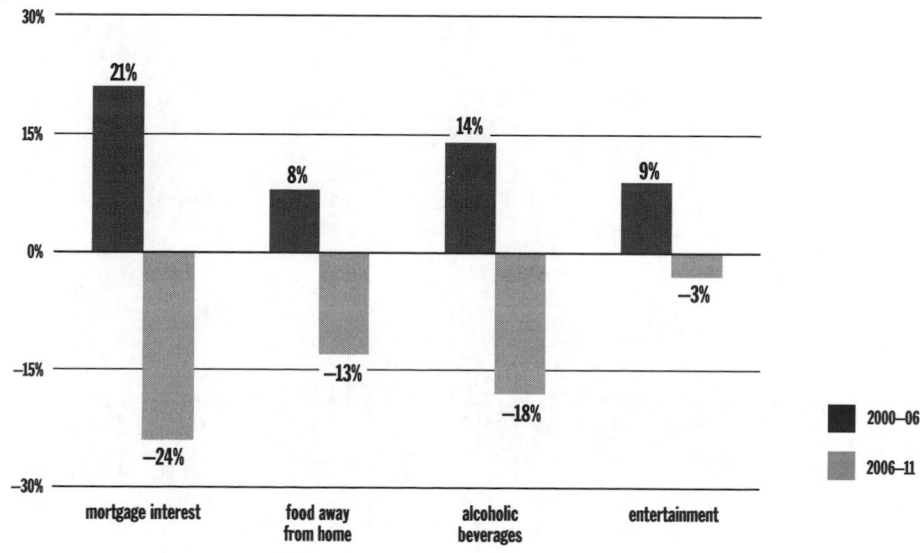

Table 1.1 Household spending trends, 2000 to 2011

(average annual spending of total consumer units, 2000, 2006, 2010, and 2011; percent change, 2006–11, 2000–06, and 2000–11; in 2011 dollars)

	2011	2010	2006	2000	percent change 2006–11	2000–06	2000–11
Number of consumer units (in 000s)	122,287	121,107	118,843	109,367	2.9%	8.7%	11.8%
Average before-tax income of consumer units	$63,685	$64,453	$67,541	$58,323	–5.7	15.8	9.2
Average annual spending of consumer units	**49,705**	**49,628**	**54,001**	**49,697**	**–8.0**	**8.7**	**0.0**
FOOD	**6,458**	**6,322**	**6,818**	**6,738**	**–5.3**	**1.2**	**–4.2**
Food at home	**3,838**	**3,738**	**3,813**	**3,946**	**0.7**	**–3.4**	**–2.7**
Cereals and bakery products	531	518	498	592	6.7	–15.9	–10.3
Cereals and cereal products	175	170	160	204	9.7	–21.7	–14.1
Bakery products	356	348	339	388	5.0	–12.6	–8.2
Meats, poultry, fish, and eggs	832	809	889	1,038	–6.4	–14.4	–19.9
Beef	223	224	263	311	–15.3	–15.3	–28.3
Pork	162	154	175	218	–7.5	–19.7	–25.7
Other meats	123	121	117	132	5.0	–11.2	–6.8
Poultry	154	142	157	189	–2.1	–16.9	–18.7
Fish and seafood	121	121	136	144	–11.1	–5.3	–15.8
Eggs	50	47	41	44	21.1	–7.0	12.6
Dairy products	407	392	411	425	–0.9	–3.3	–4.1
Fresh milk and cream	150	145	156	171	–4.0	–8.7	–12.3
Other dairy products	257	248	254	252	1.0	0.9	1.9
Fruits and vegetables	715	700	661	681	8.2	–2.9	5.1
Fresh fruits	247	239	218	213	13.5	2.2	16.0
Fresh vegetables	224	217	215	208	4.0	3.7	7.8
Processed fruits	116	117	122	150	–4.6	–19.0	–22.8
Processed vegetables	128	128	106	110	20.8	–3.4	16.7
Other food at home	1,353	1,318	1,352	1,211	0.1	11.7	11.7
Sugar and other sweets	144	136	139	153	3.2	–8.7	–5.8
Fats and oils	110	106	96	108	14.6	–11.5	1.5
Miscellaneous foods	690	688	700	571	–1.4	22.6	20.9
Nonalcoholic beverages	361	344	370	327	–2.5	13.4	10.5
Food prepared by consumer unit on trips	48	44	48	52	0.0	–8.2	–8.1
Food away from home	**2,620**	**2,584**	**3,006**	**2,791**	**–12.8**	**7.7**	**–6.1**
ALCOHOLIC BEVERAGES	**456**	**425**	**555**	**486**	**–17.8**	**14.1**	**–6.2**
HOUSING	**16,803**	**17,080**	**18,261**	**16,092**	**–8.0**	**13.5**	**4.4**
Shelter	**9,825**	**10,122**	**10,793**	**9,293**	**–9.0**	**16.1**	**5.7**
Owned dwellings	6,148	6,475	7,270	6,011	–15.4	20.9	2.3
Mortgage interest and charges	3,184	3,457	4,187	3,447	–24.0	21.5	–7.6
Property taxes	1,845	1,871	1,840	1,488	0.3	23.7	24.0
Maintenance, repair, insurance, other expenses	1,120	1,147	1,244	1,078	–10.0	15.4	3.9
Rented dwellings	3,029	2,992	2,890	2,657	4.8	8.8	14.0
Other lodging	648	655	633	624	2.4	1.3	3.8
Utilities, fuels, and public services	**3,727**	**3,776**	**3,790**	**3,251**	**–1.7**	**16.6**	**14.6**
Natural gas	420	454	568	401	–26.0	41.6	4.7
Electricity	1,423	1,458	1,413	1,190	0.7	18.7	19.6
Fuel oil and other fuels	157	144	154	127	2.0	21.5	23.9
Telephone services	1,226	1,215	1,213	1,146	1.1	5.9	7.0
Water and other public services	501	504	443	387	13.1	14.6	29.6
Household services	**1,122**	**1,039**	**1,058**	**893**	**6.1**	**18.4**	**25.6**
Personal services	398	351	438	426	–9.2	3.0	–6.5
Other household services	724	688	619	468	16.9	32.4	54.8
Housekeeping supplies	**615**	**631**	**714**	**630**	**–13.9**	**13.4**	**–2.3**
Laundry and cleaning supplies	145	155	168	171	–13.9	–1.5	–15.3
Other household products	340	339	368	295	–7.7	24.7	15.2
Postage and stationery	130	136	177	165	–26.7	7.8	–21.0
Household furnishings and equipment	**1,514**	**1,513**	**1,906**	**2,023**	**–20.6**	**–5.8**	**–25.2**
Household textiles	109	105	172	138	–36.6	24.1	–21.3
Furniture	358	366	517	511	–30.7	1.1	–29.9
Floor coverings	20	37	54	57	–62.7	–6.8	–65.2

	2011	2010	2006	2000	percent change 2006–11	2000–06	2000–11
Major appliances	$194	$216	$269	$247	−27.9%	8.9%	−21.4%
Small appliances and miscellaneous housewares	89	110	122	114	−26.8	7.0	−21.7
Miscellaneous household equipment	744	678	773	955	−3.8	−19.0	−22.1
APPAREL AND RELATED SERVICES	**1,740**	**1,754**	**2,091**	**2,424**	**−16.8**	**−13.8**	**−28.2**
Men and boys	**404**	**394**	**495**	**575**	**−18.4**	**−13.8**	**−29.7**
Men, aged 16 or older	324	314	394	449	−17.7	−12.3	−27.9
Boys, aged 2 to 15	80	80	102	125	−21.2	−19.0	−36.2
Women and girls	**721**	**684**	**838**	**947**	**−14.0**	**−11.5**	**−23.9**
Women, aged 16 or older	604	580	702	793	−13.9	−11.5	−23.8
Girls, aged 2 to 15	117	104	136	154	−14.0	−11.7	−24.1
Children under age 2	**68**	**94**	**107**	**107**	**−36.5**	**0.0**	**−36.5**
Footwear	**321**	**313**	**339**	**448**	**−5.4**	**−24.3**	**−28.4**
Other apparel products and services	**226**	**269**	**312**	**347**	**−27.7**	**−10.1**	**−35.0**
TRANSPORTATION	**8,293**	**7,919**	**9,493**	**9,689**	**−12.6**	**−2.0**	**−14.4**
Vehicle purchases	**2,669**	**2,670**	**3,817**	**4,465**	**−30.1**	**−14.5**	**−40.2**
Cars and trucks, new	1,265	1,257	2,006	2,097	−36.9	−4.3	−39.7
Cars and trucks, used	1,339	1,360	1,750	2,312	−23.5	−24.3	−42.1
Other vehicles	64	53	60	56	6.2	7.3	13.9
Gasoline and motor oil	**2,655**	**2,199**	**2,485**	**1,686**	**6.8**	**47.3**	**57.4**
Other vehicle expenses	**2,454**	**2,542**	**2,628**	**2,980**	**−6.6**	**−11.8**	**−17.6**
Vehicle finance charges	233	251	332	428	−29.9	−22.4	−45.6
Maintenance and repairs	805	812	768	815	4.9	−5.8	−1.2
Vehicle insurance	983	1,042	989	1,016	−0.6	−2.7	−3.3
Vehicle rentals, leases, licenses, other charges	433	436	538	720	−19.5	−25.3	−39.8
Public transportation	**516**	**509**	**563**	**558**	**−8.4**	**1.0**	**−7.5**
HEALTH CARE	**3,313**	**3,257**	**3,086**	**2,699**	**7.3**	**14.4**	**22.8**
Health insurance	1,922	1,889	1,635	1,284	17.6	27.3	49.7
Medical services	768	745	748	742	2.7	0.8	3.5
Drugs	489	500	574	543	−14.7	5.5	−10.0
Medical supplies	134	123	131	129	2.6	0.9	3.6
ENTERTAINMENT	**2,572**	**2,583**	**2,651**	**2,434**	**−3.0**	**8.9**	**5.7**
Fees and admissions	594	599	676	673	−12.2	0.5	−11.7
Audio and visual equipment and services	977	984	1,011	812	−3.4	24.4	20.2
Pets, toys, and playground equipment	631	625	460	436	37.3	5.4	44.6
Other entertainment products and services	370	375	503	513	−26.5	−2.0	−27.9
PERSONAL CARE PRODUCTS AND SERVICES	**634**	**600**	**653**	**737**	**−2.9**	**−11.4**	**−13.9**
READING	**115**	**103**	**131**	**191**	**−11.9**	**−31.5**	**−39.7**
EDUCATION	**1,051**	**1,108**	**991**	**826**	**6.1**	**20.0**	**27.3**
TOBACCO PRODUCTS AND SMOKING SUPPLIES	**351**	**373**	**365**	**417**	**−3.8**	**−12.4**	**−15.8**
MISCELLANEOUS	**775**	**876**	**944**	**1,014**	**−17.9**	**−6.9**	**−23.5**
CASH CONTRIBUTIONS	**1,721**	**1,685**	**2,085**	**1,557**	**−17.5**	**33.9**	**10.5**
PERSONAL INSURANCE AND PENSIONS	**5,424**	**5,543**	**5,880**	**4,396**	**−7.8**	**33.8**	**23.4**
Life and other personal insurance	317	328	359	521	−11.8	−31.1	−39.2
Pensions and Social Security*	5,106	5,214	5,521	3,874	−7.5	–	–
PERSONAL TAXES	**2,012**	**1,825**	**2,714**	**4,072**	**−25.9**	**−33.4**	**−50.6**
Federal income taxes	1,370	1,172	1,909	3,147	−28.2	−39.3	−56.5
State and local income taxes	505	497	579	734	−12.8	−21.1	−31.2
Other taxes	136	156	225	191	−39.7	18.2	−28.7
GIFTS FOR PEOPLE IN OTHER HOUSEHOLDS	**1,037**	**1,061**	**1,288**	**1,415**	**−19.5**	**−9.0**	**−26.7**

*Recent spending on pensions and Social Security is not comparable with 2000 because of changes in methodology.

Note: Spending by category does not add to total spending because gift spending is also included in the preceding product and service categories and personal taxes are not included in the total.

"–" means data are incomparable.

Source: Bureau of Labor Statistics, 2000, 2006, 2010, and 2011 Consumer Expenditure Surveys, Internet site http://www.bls.gov/cex/; calculations by New Strategist

Spending by Age, 2011

The average household spent $49,705 in 2011, but some spent more and others less. Because spending rises with income, affluent households spend the most. Householders aged 35 to 54 are in their peak earning years, which explains why they spent 15 to 17 percent more than the average household in 2011, the highest level of spending among age groups.

The oldest and the youngest householders spend the least because their incomes are lowest. Householders under age 25 spend just 60 percent as much as the average household, while householders aged 75 or older spend 66 percent as much as the average.

Householders aged 45 to 54 are not far behind, but those aged 35 to 44 spend the most overall, fueled in part by their steep mortgage interest payments, which are 53 percent higher than those of the average household. Other age groups spend more in some categories. Householders under age 35 spend much more than average on rented dwellings, for example, as well as on infants' clothes. Householders under age 25 spent the most on education—over twice the average. Households headed by people aged 65 or older spend the most on health care, including the individual category of health insurance. Americans aged 65 or older also spend more on cash contributions than other age groups.

With millions of baby boomers postponing retirement because of the recession, the two-earner couples of the baby-boom generation may boost the spending of householders aged 55 to 64 in the years ahead.

Table 1.2 Average spending by age of householder, 2011   OVERVIEW

(average annual spending of consumer units by product and service category and age of consumer unit reference person, 2011)

	total consumer units	under 25	25 to 34	35 to 44	45 to 54	55 to 64	65 or older		
							total	65 to 74	75 or older
Number of consumer units (in 000s)	122,287	7,743	20,463	21,699	24,821	21,688	25,873	14,079	11,794
Average number of persons per consumer unit	2.5	2.1	2.9	3.3	2.8	2.1	1.7	1.9	1.6
Average before-tax income of consumer units	$63,685	$27,514	$58,179	$77,376	$78,519	$75,517	$43,232	$52,521	$32,144
Average annual spending of consumer units	49,705	29,912	48,097	57,271	58,050	53,616	39,173	44,646	32,688
FOOD	**6,458**	**4,354**	**6,211**	**7,765**	**7,424**	**6,520**	**5,158**	**5,804**	**4,408**
Food at home	3,838	2,382	3,447	4,594	4,421	3,908	3,309	3,594	2,980
Cereals and bakery products	531	336	479	644	610	515	469	479	458
Cereals and cereal products	175	114	175	218	201	161	142	144	139
Bakery products	356	222	303	426	409	354	328	335	319
Meats, poultry, fish, and eggs	832	527	733	1,006	965	894	671	759	569
Beef	223	137	188	264	267	235	186	218	149
Pork	162	96	133	200	178	183	138	162	110
Other meats	123	63	110	155	157	120	92	102	80
Poultry	154	122	154	190	182	152	108	119	95
Fish and seafood	121	69	103	139	125	152	103	111	94
Eggs	50	38	45	59	55	50	45	49	41
Dairy products	407	244	379	481	475	394	359	387	326
Fresh milk and cream	150	97	144	188	172	137	126	132	120
Other dairy products	257	148	234	293	303	256	233	256	207
Fruits and vegetables	715	424	627	841	803	734	663	713	605
Fresh fruits	247	132	210	291	273	262	237	254	217
Fresh vegetables	224	130	195	254	258	239	206	220	189
Processed fruits	116	80	107	143	128	107	105	111	99
Processed vegetables	128	83	115	154	144	125	115	128	100
Other food at home	1,353	850	1,230	1,622	1,567	1,372	1,147	1,255	1,021
Sugar and other sweets	144	78	112	179	163	152	136	144	128
Fats and oils	110	61	95	126	125	111	106	112	99
Miscellaneous foods	690	454	671	834	779	677	577	626	521
Nonalcoholic beverages	361	236	319	434	442	368	284	310	253
Food prepared by consumer unit on trips	48	20	33	48	58	64	43	62	21
Food away from home	**2,620**	**1,973**	**2,764**	**3,171**	**3,003**	**2,611**	**1,849**	**2,210**	**1,429**
ALCOHOLIC BEVERAGES	**456**	**418**	**513**	**497**	**494**	**468**	**338**	**422**	**241**
HOUSING	**16,803**	**10,282**	**17,026**	**19,979**	**18,782**	**17,173**	**13,706**	**15,105**	**12,046**
Shelter	**9,825**	**6,732**	**10,480**	**12,068**	**11,111**	**9,755**	**7,178**	**7,966**	**6,237**
Owned dwellings	6,148	1,277	4,826	7,844	7,774	7,002	4,953	5,802	3,939
Mortgage interest and charges	3,184	740	3,207	4,873	4,236	3,244	1,419	2,008	716
Property taxes	1,845	306	1,072	1,930	2,300	2,301	2,025	2,243	1,765
Maintenance, repair, insurance, other expenses	1,120	231	547	1,041	1,238	1,456	1,509	1,551	1,459
Rented dwellings	3,029	5,111	5,338	3,714	2,582	1,784	1,480	1,234	1,772
Other lodging	648	345	316	510	756	969	745	929	525
Utilities, fuels, and public services	**3,727**	**1,918**	**3,296**	**4,065**	**4,318**	**4,053**	**3,485**	**3,782**	**3,131**
Natural gas	420	172	341	458	481	461	430	434	426
Electricity	1,423	757	1,256	1,555	1,601	1,555	1,362	1,498	1,199
Fuel oil and other fuels	157	19	77	114	175	197	247	229	267
Telephone services	1,226	777	1,219	1,394	1,502	1,275	921	1,060	756
Water and other public services	501	193	402	544	559	565	525	560	483
Household services	**1,122**	**505**	**1,359**	**1,494**	**969**	**958**	**1,093**	**952**	**1,261**
Personal services	398	174	804	783	188	69	300	110	525
Other household services	724	331	555	710	781	889	793	841	736
Housekeeping supplies	**615**	**268**	**420**	**702**	**691**	**722**	**636**	**695**	**568**
Laundry and cleaning supplies	145	82	117	170	167	151	140	148	130
Other household products	340	141	232	407	368	402	348	379	312
Postage and stationery	130	46	72	125	157	169	148	168	126
Household furnishings and equipment	**1,514**	**858**	**1,471**	**1,650**	**1,693**	**1,685**	**1,314**	**1,711**	**849**
Household textiles	109	37	96	130	107	106	129	183	66
Furniture	358	260	454	404	350	419	229	314	127
Floor coverings	20	5	11	24	21	28	20	31	8

	total consumer units	under 25	25 to 34	35 to 44	45 to 54	55 to 64	65 or older total	65 to 74	75 or older
Major appliances	$194	$82	$160	$219	$209	$246	$175	$214	$129
Small appliances and miscellaneous housewares	89	77	77	93	98	89	92	124	55
Miscellaneous household equipment	744	397	674	781	907	797	668	844	464
APPAREL AND RELATED SERVICES	**1,740**	**1,448**	**1,818**	**2,227**	**1,978**	**1,719**	**1,129**	**1,195**	**1,052**
Men and boys	**404**	**335**	**435**	**559**	**431**	**436**	**210**	**242**	**173**
Men, aged 16 or older	324	309	335	375	353	393	187	213	156
Boys, aged 2 to 15	80	25	100	184	78	43	23	29	16
Women and girls	**721**	**498**	**694**	**842**	**881**	**727**	**545**	**545**	**545**
Women, aged 16 or older	604	468	569	604	733	653	503	477	533
Girls, aged 2 to 15	117	29	125	238	148	74	42	68	11
Children under age 2	**68**	**129**	**146**	**103**	**45**	**29**	**13**	**17**	**8**
Footwear	**321**	**298**	**306**	**449**	**393**	**288**	**189**	**176**	**203**
Other apparel products and services	**226**	**189**	**237**	**274**	**228**	**239**	**173**	**214**	**124**
TRANSPORTATION	**8,293**	**5,474**	**8,860**	**9,700**	**9,505**	**8,991**	**5,751**	**6,962**	**4,309**
Vehicle purchases	**2,669**	**2,068**	**3,203**	**3,434**	**2,624**	**2,953**	**1,588**	**1,858**	**1,267**
Cars and trucks, new	1,265	610	1,243	1,629	1,119	1,671	975	1,190	718
Cars and trucks, used	1,339	1,431	1,855	1,715	1,451	1,212	587	622	545
Other vehicles	64	28	104	90	55	70	26	45	3
Gasoline and motor oil	**2,655**	**1,840**	**2,726**	**3,188**	**3,270**	**2,713**	**1,755**	**2,218**	**1,201**
Other vehicle expenses	**2,454**	**1,265**	**2,402**	**2,565**	**2,985**	**2,746**	**1,994**	**2,343**	**1,581**
Vehicle finance charges	233	128	302	328	269	224	100	144	49
Maintenance and repairs	805	456	718	856	977	950	650	820	449
Vehicle insurance	983	505	957	920	1,201	1,089	894	950	829
Vehicle rentals, leases, licenses, other charges	433	176	425	460	538	483	350	429	256
Public transportation	**516**	**300**	**529**	**513**	**626**	**579**	**414**	**543**	**260**
HEALTH CARE	**3,313**	**841**	**2,094**	**2,762**	**3,411**	**4,048**	**4,769**	**5,038**	**4,449**
Health insurance	1,922	456	1,237	1,581	1,801	2,196	3,076	3,154	2,982
Medical services	768	254	546	694	942	1,013	786	894	656
Drugs	489	93	229	377	515	690	714	791	623
Medical supplies	134	38	82	110	153	149	193	199	188
ENTERTAINMENT	**2,572**	**1,345**	**2,423**	**2,926**	**3,169**	**2,769**	**2,009**	**2,493**	**1,437**
Fees and admissions	594	264	501	810	808	571	400	548	224
Audio and visual equipment and services	977	608	948	1,101	1,111	1,055	808	902	697
Pets, toys, and playground equipment	631	333	599	643	744	759	512	626	380
Other entertainment products and services	370	140	375	372	506	385	289	418	136
PERSONAL CARE PRODUCTS AND SERVICES	**634**	**324**	**570**	**736**	**709**	**695**	**567**	**609**	**517**
READING	**115**	**45**	**74**	**100**	**113**	**149**	**157**	**163**	**148**
EDUCATION	**1,051**	**2,253**	**1,049**	**818**	**1,879**	**866**	**247**	**262**	**229**
TOBACCO PRODUCTS AND SMOKING SUPPLIES	**351**	**256**	**378**	**343**	**465**	**401**	**212**	**289**	**120**
MISCELLANEOUS	**775**	**285**	**606**	**781**	**947**	**931**	**753**	**821**	**674**
CASH CONTRIBUTIONS	**1,721**	**367**	**1,130**	**1,570**	**1,722**	**2,112**	**2,392**	**2,526**	**2,231**
PERSONAL INSURANCE AND PENSIONS	**5,424**	**2,220**	**5,346**	**7,068**	**7,453**	**6,775**	**1,985**	**2,957**	**825**
Life and other personal insurance	317	67	138	308	401	534	280	361	183
Pensions and Social Security	5,106	2,154	5,207	6,760	7,052	6,242	1,706	2,596	643
PERSONAL TAXES	**2,012**	**19**	**1,328**	**1,839**	**3,284**	**3,402**	**907**	**1,360**	**365**
Federal income taxes	1,370	−123	779	1,166	2,407	2,404	595	952	169
State and local income taxes	505	130	477	560	747	786	126	177	65
Other taxes	136	12	72	113	130	211	186	231	131
GIFTS FOR PEOPLE IN OTHER HOUSEHOLDS	**1,037**	**378**	**496**	**711**	**1,553**	**1,535**	**1,025**	**1,269**	**736**

Note: Spending by category does not add to total spending because gift spending is also included in the preceding product and service categories and personal taxes are not included in the total.
Source: Bureau of Labor Statistics, 2011 Consumer Expenditure Survey, Internet site http://www.bls.gov/cex/

(indexed average annual spending of consumer units by product and service category and age of consumer unit reference person, 2011; index definition: an index of 100 is the average for all consumer units; an index of 125 means that spending by consumer units in that group is 25 percent above the average for all consumer units; an index of 75 indicates spending that is 25 percent below the average for all consumer units)

	total consumer units	under 25	25 to 34	35 to 44	45 to 54	55 to 64	65 or older total	65 to 74	75 or older
Average spending of consumer units, total	$49,705	$29,912	$48,097	$57,271	$58,050	$53,616	$39,173	$44,646	$32,688
Average spending of consumer units, index	100	60	97	115	117	108	79	90	66
FOOD	100	67	96	120	115	101	80	90	68
Food at home	100	62	90	120	115	102	86	94	78
Cereals and bakery products	100	63	90	121	115	97	88	90	86
Cereals and cereal products	100	65	100	125	115	92	81	82	79
Bakery products	100	62	85	120	115	99	92	94	90
Meats, poultry, fish, and eggs	100	63	88	121	116	107	81	91	68
Beef	100	61	84	118	120	105	83	98	67
Pork	100	59	82	123	110	113	85	100	68
Other meats	100	51	89	126	128	98	75	83	65
Poultry	100	79	100	123	118	99	70	77	62
Fish and seafood	100	57	85	115	103	126	85	92	78
Eggs	100	76	90	118	110	100	90	98	82
Dairy products	100	60	93	118	117	97	88	95	80
Fresh milk and cream	100	65	96	125	115	91	84	88	80
Other dairy products	100	58	91	114	118	100	91	100	81
Fruits and vegetables	100	59	88	118	112	103	93	100	85
Fresh fruits	100	53	85	118	111	106	96	103	88
Fresh vegetables	100	58	87	113	115	107	92	98	84
Processed fruits	100	69	92	123	110	92	91	96	85
Processed vegetables	100	65	90	120	113	98	90	100	78
Other food at home	100	63	91	120	116	101	85	93	75
Sugar and other sweets	100	54	78	124	113	106	94	100	89
Fats and oils	100	55	86	115	114	101	96	102	90
Miscellaneous foods	100	66	97	121	113	98	84	91	76
Nonalcoholic beverages	100	65	88	120	122	102	79	86	70
Food prepared by consumer unit on trips	100	42	69	100	121	133	90	129	44
Food away from home	100	75	105	121	115	100	71	84	55
ALCOHOLIC BEVERAGES	100	92	113	109	108	103	74	93	53
HOUSING	100	61	101	119	112	102	82	90	72
Shelter	100	69	107	123	113	99	73	81	63
Owned dwellings	100	21	78	128	126	114	81	94	64
Mortgage interest and charges	100	23	101	153	133	102	45	63	22
Property taxes	100	17	58	105	125	125	110	122	96
Maintenance, repair, insurance, other expenses	100	21	49	93	111	130	135	138	130
Rented dwellings	100	169	176	123	85	59	49	41	59
Other lodging	100	53	49	79	117	150	115	143	81
Utilities, fuels, and public services	100	51	88	109	116	109	94	101	84
Natural gas	100	41	81	109	115	110	102	103	101
Electricity	100	53	88	109	113	109	96	105	84
Fuel oil and other fuels	100	12	49	73	111	125	157	146	170
Telephone services	100	63	99	114	123	104	75	86	62
Water and other public services	100	39	80	109	112	113	105	112	96
Household services	100	45	121	133	86	85	97	85	112
Personal services	100	44	202	197	47	17	75	28	132
Other household services	100	46	77	98	108	123	110	116	102
Housekeeping supplies	100	44	68	114	112	117	103	113	92
Laundry and cleaning supplies	100	57	81	117	115	104	97	102	90
Other household products	100	41	68	120	108	118	102	111	92
Postage and stationery	100	35	55	96	121	130	114	129	97
Household furnishings and equipment	100	57	97	109	112	111	87	113	56
Household textiles	100	34	88	119	98	97	118	168	61
Furniture	100	73	127	113	98	117	64	88	35
Floor coverings	100	25	55	120	105	140	100	155	40

	total consumer units	under 25	25 to 34	35 to 44	45 to 54	55 to 64	65 or older total	65 to 74	75 or older
Major appliances	100	42	82	113	108	127	90	110	66
Small appliances and miscellaneous housewares	100	87	87	104	110	100	103	139	62
Miscellaneous household equipment	100	53	91	105	122	107	90	113	62
APPAREL AND RELATED SERVICES	**100**	**83**	**104**	**128**	**114**	**99**	**65**	**69**	**60**
Men and boys	**100**	**83**	**108**	**138**	**107**	**108**	**52**	**60**	**43**
Men, aged 16 or older	100	95	103	116	109	121	58	66	48
Boys, aged 2 to 15	100	31	125	230	98	54	29	36	20
Women and girls	**100**	**69**	**96**	**117**	**122**	**101**	**76**	**76**	**76**
Women, aged 16 or older	100	77	94	100	121	108	83	79	88
Girls, aged 2 to 15	100	25	107	203	126	63	36	58	9
Children under age 2	**100**	**190**	**215**	**151**	**66**	**43**	**19**	**25**	**12**
Footwear	**100**	**93**	**95**	**140**	**122**	**90**	**59**	**55**	**63**
Other apparel products and services	**100**	**84**	**105**	**121**	**101**	**106**	**77**	**95**	**55**
TRANSPORTATION	**100**	**66**	**107**	**117**	**115**	**108**	**69**	**84**	**52**
Vehicle purchases	**100**	**77**	**120**	**129**	**98**	**111**	**59**	**70**	**47**
Cars and trucks, new	100	48	98	129	88	132	77	94	57
Cars and trucks, used	100	107	139	128	108	91	44	46	41
Other vehicles	100	44	163	141	86	109	41	70	5
Gasoline and motor oil	**100**	**69**	**103**	**120**	**123**	**102**	**66**	**84**	**45**
Other vehicle expenses	**100**	**52**	**98**	**105**	**122**	**112**	**81**	**95**	**64**
Vehicle finance charges	100	55	130	141	115	96	43	62	21
Maintenance and repairs	100	57	89	106	121	118	81	102	56
Vehicle insurance	100	51	97	94	122	111	91	97	84
Vehicle rentals, leases, licenses, other charges	100	41	98	106	124	112	81	99	59
Public transportation	**100**	**58**	**103**	**99**	**121**	**112**	**80**	**105**	**50**
HEALTH CARE	**100**	**25**	**63**	**83**	**103**	**122**	**144**	**152**	**134**
Health insurance	100	24	64	82	94	114	160	164	155
Medical services	100	33	71	90	123	132	102	116	85
Drugs	100	19	47	77	105	141	146	162	127
Medical supplies	100	28	61	82	114	111	144	149	140
ENTERTAINMENT	**100**	**52**	**94**	**114**	**123**	**108**	**78**	**97**	**56**
Fees and admissions	100	44	84	136	136	96	67	92	38
Audio and visual equipment and services	100	62	97	113	114	108	83	92	71
Pets, toys, and playground equipment	100	53	95	102	118	120	81	99	60
Other entertainment products and services	100	38	101	101	137	104	78	113	37
PERSONAL CARE PRODUCTS AND SERVICES	**100**	**51**	**90**	**116**	**112**	**110**	**89**	**96**	**82**
READING	**100**	**39**	**64**	**87**	**98**	**130**	**137**	**142**	**129**
EDUCATION	**100**	**214**	**100**	**78**	**179**	**82**	**24**	**25**	**22**
TOBACCO PRODUCTS AND SMOKING SUPPLIES	**100**	**73**	**108**	**98**	**132**	**114**	**60**	**82**	**34**
MISCELLANEOUS	**100**	**37**	**78**	**101**	**122**	**120**	**97**	**106**	**87**
CASH CONTRIBUTIONS	**100**	**21**	**66**	**91**	**100**	**123**	**139**	**147**	**130**
PERSONAL INSURANCE AND PENSIONS	**100**	**41**	**99**	**130**	**137**	**125**	**37**	**55**	**15**
Life and other personal insurance	100	21	44	97	126	168	88	114	58
Pensions and Social Security	100	42	102	132	138	122	33	51	13
PERSONAL TAXES	**100**	**1**	**66**	**91**	**163**	**169**	**45**	**68**	**18**
Federal income taxes	100	–9	57	85	176	175	43	69	12
State and local income taxes	100	26	94	111	148	156	25	35	13
Other taxes	100	9	53	83	96	155	137	170	96
GIFTS FOR PEOPLE IN OTHER HOUSEHOLDS	**100**	**36**	**48**	**69**	**150**	**148**	**99**	**122**	**71**

Source: Calculations by New Strategist based on the Bureau of Labor Statistics' 2011 Consumer Expenditure Survey

Spending by Income, 2011

The average household spent $49,705 in 2011. Not surprisingly, households with incomes of $70,000 or more spend the most—65 percent more than the average household. The highest income group spends well above average on all product and service categories with the exceptions of rented dwellings and tobacco.

Households with incomes below $50,000 spend less than the average household on most categories, one of the few exceptions being rent. Households with incomes below $40,000 spend more money than they make. The income they report to government interviewers is less than their reported expenditures. These households make up the difference through borrowing, the use of savings, and unreported income.

Income makes a bigger difference in the purchasing of some products than others. Everyone has to buy food, but only those who can afford to do so will buy a new car. Households with incomes of $70,000 or more spend closer to the average on items such as eggs and drugs. But they spend more than twice the average on "other lodging" (a category that includes hotel and motel expenses as well as housing for children in college dorms), fees and admissions to entertainment events, new vehicles, and public transportation (which includes airfares), among other items.

Table 1.4 Average spending by household income, 2011

(average annual spending of consumer units by product and service category and before-tax income of consumer unit, 2011)

	total consumer units	under $10,000	$10,000– $19,999	$20,000– $29,999	$30,000– $39,999	$40,000– $49,999	$50,000– $69,999	$70,000 or more
Number of consumer units (in 000s)	122,287	10,427	15,915	14,460	13,328	11,347	17,376	39,434
Average number of persons per consumer unit	2.5	1.7	1.8	2.2	2.4	2.6	2.7	3.1
Average before-tax income of consumer units	$63,685	$3,545	$15,043	$24,940	$34,777	$44,698	$59,306	$130,588
Average annual spending of consumer units	49,705	21,875	22,318	30,398	36,769	40,306	50,034	81,767
FOOD	6,458	3,527	3,504	4,278	5,326	5,154	6,546	9,775
Food at home	3,838	2,341	2,476	2,804	3,476	3,184	3,995	5,307
Cereals and bakery products	531	321	354	390	488	447	544	727
Cereals and cereal products	175	111	115	133	159	143	181	239
Bakery products	356	210	240	258	329	304	363	489
Meats, poultry, fish, and eggs	832	517	533	632	791	674	849	1,142
Beef	223	138	137	169	209	189	235	303
Pork	162	106	105	138	175	128	169	206
Other meats	123	74	73	70	91	107	129	184
Poultry	154	95	104	116	155	119	148	214
Fish and seafood	121	67	74	94	110	87	121	174
Eggs	50	39	40	45	51	43	47	61
Dairy products	407	243	254	299	359	343	422	569
Fresh milk and cream	150	102	103	118	138	129	151	199
Other dairy products	257	141	151	181	221	215	271	369
Fruits and vegetables	715	439	448	516	647	572	728	1,009
Fresh fruits	247	148	148	173	223	196	245	358
Fresh vegetables	224	127	134	165	202	172	224	324
Processed fruits	116	78	74	83	103	104	123	157
Processed vegetables	128	87	92	95	118	101	135	170
Other food at home	1,353	820	886	967	1,191	1,147	1,452	1,861
Sugar and other sweets	144	86	94	100	125	116	154	203
Fats and oils	110	79	80	82	107	98	126	134
Miscellaneous foods	690	421	461	490	608	576	738	950
Nonalcoholic beverages	361	222	239	266	321	325	389	483
Food prepared by consumer unit on trips	48	13	13	28	28	31	45	90
Food away from home	2,620	1,186	1,028	1,473	1,850	1,969	2,551	4,467
ALCOHOLIC BEVERAGES	456	222	147	212	315	309	384	844
HOUSING	16,803	8,346	9,148	11,721	13,425	14,562	16,888	25,689
Shelter	9,825	5,052	5,264	6,789	7,758	8,429	9,628	15,229
Owned dwellings	6,148	1,494	1,758	2,778	3,747	4,590	6,238	11,605
Mortgage interest and charges	3,184	638	558	1,012	1,721	2,275	3,401	6,373
Property taxes	1,845	549	712	1,024	1,182	1,433	1,768	3,321
Maintenance, repair, insurance, other expenses	1,120	306	489	742	845	882	1,069	1,911
Rented dwellings	3,029	3,250	3,393	3,745	3,708	3,476	2,923	2,251
Other lodging	648	308	113	266	303	363	467	1,372
Utilities, fuels, and public services	3,727	2,077	2,499	2,989	3,338	3,666	4,000	4,958
Natural gas	420	220	271	324	371	380	427	592
Electricity	1,423	904	1,065	1,215	1,302	1,433	1,516	1,778
Fuel oil and other fuels	157	76	100	132	97	142	158	234
Telephone services	1,226	620	742	933	1,125	1,240	1,376	1,654
Water and other public services	501	256	320	384	443	472	524	699
Household services	1,122	415	461	703	760	837	934	2,018
Personal services	398	136	124	242	224	239	269	797
Other household services	724	279	336	461	537	598	665	1,220
Housekeeping supplies	615	283	373	409	465	530	626	924
Laundry and cleaning supplies	145	80	109	113	118	142	155	191
Other household products	340	131	192	206	274	274	334	534
Postage and stationery	130	71	72	90	73	114	138	200
Household furnishings and equipment	1,514	519	552	832	1,104	1,100	1,701	2,560
Household textiles	109	36	58	59	71	108	106	179
Furniture	358	162	126	182	236	260	310	658
Floor coverings	20	3	8	5	5	9	14	45

	total consumer units	under $10,000	$10,000– $19,999	$20,000– $29,999	$30,000– $39,999	$40,000– $49,999	$50,000– $69,999	$70,000 or more
Major appliances	$194	$60	$81	$98	$137	$157	$229	$324
Small appliances and miscellaneous housewares	89	44	28	66	62	58	92	150
Miscellaneous household equipment	744	213	250	422	592	509	949	1,203
APPAREL AND RELATED SERVICES	**1,740**	**1,028**	**778**	**942**	**1,468**	**1,175**	**1,767**	**2,821**
Men and boys	**404**	**241**	**162**	**171**	**385**	**276**	**425**	**658**
Men, aged 16 or older	324	210	125	129	312	208	336	535
Boys, aged 2 to 15	80	32	37	42	73	68	88	124
Women and girls	**721**	**408**	**304**	**355**	**575**	**480**	**746**	**1,198**
Women, aged 16 or older	604	357	255	281	484	375	625	1,012
Girls, aged 2 to 15	117	51	48	74	92	105	121	186
Children under age 2	**68**	**35**	**47**	**31**	**62**	**65**	**79**	**95**
Footwear	**321**	**212**	**171**	**243**	**286**	**204**	**308**	**486**
Other apparel products and services	**226**	**132**	**95**	**143**	**161**	**150**	**209**	**383**
TRANSPORTATION	**8,293**	**3,323**	**3,270**	**4,664**	**6,406**	**7,128**	**9,010**	**13,580**
Vehicle purchases	**2,669**	**1,105**	**684**	**1,035**	**1,988**	**1,957**	**2,879**	**4,824**
Cars and trucks, new	1,265	449	401	328	605	573	1,231	2,695
Cars and trucks, used	1,339	624	484	706	1,321	1,368	1,603	1,987
Other vehicles	64	32	9	1	62	16	44	143
Gasoline and motor oil	**2,655**	**1,129**	**1,325**	**1,971**	**2,247**	**2,679**	**2,961**	**3,841**
Other vehicle expenses	**2,454**	**896**	**1,085**	**1,470**	**1,889**	**2,149**	**2,762**	**3,879**
Vehicle finance charges	233	43	50	111	162	218	257	418
Maintenance and repairs	805	327	318	490	640	691	903	1,285
Vehicle insurance	983	398	567	634	773	892	1,204	1,396
Vehicle rentals, leases, licenses, other charges	433	129	150	234	314	347	398	780
Public transportation	**516**	**192**	**175**	**188**	**282**	**343**	**409**	**1,036**
HEALTH CARE	**3,313**	**1,163**	**1,795**	**2,646**	**2,751**	**3,317**	**3,722**	**4,742**
Health insurance	1,922	675	1,071	1,625	1,703	1,963	2,189	2,649
Medical services	768	190	340	510	523	733	880	1,230
Drugs	489	239	316	427	426	493	535	643
Medical supplies	134	59	68	85	99	127	117	220
ENTERTAINMENT	**2,572**	**950**	**1,008**	**1,636**	**1,695**	**1,876**	**2,830**	**4,325**
Fees and admissions	594	179	122	188	276	356	468	1,272
Audio and visual equipment and services	977	458	572	724	828	895	1,061	1,402
Pets, toys, and playground equipment	631	234	263	465	429	454	723	1,002
Other entertainment products and services	370	78	51	259	163	171	578	649
PERSONAL CARE PRODUCTS AND SERVICES	**634**	**272**	**276**	**367**	**479**	**519**	**620**	**1,053**
READING	**115**	**48**	**52**	**72**	**76**	**89**	**132**	**188**
EDUCATION	**1,051**	**1,392**	**343**	**523**	**441**	**539**	**630**	**1,976**
TOBACCO PRODUCTS AND SMOKING SUPPLIES	**351**	**302**	**330**	**361**	**379**	**416**	**392**	**321**
MISCELLANEOUS	**775**	**453**	**336**	**599**	**551**	**656**	**682**	**1,246**
CASH CONTRIBUTIONS	**1,721**	**550**	**788**	**885**	**1,104**	**1,269**	**1,561**	**3,123**
PERSONAL INSURANCE AND PENSIONS	**5,424**	**298**	**542**	**1,492**	**2,353**	**3,297**	**4,871**	**12,084**
Life and other personal insurance	317	71	93	271	163	209	289	585
Pensions and Social Security	5,106	226	449	1,221	2,190	3,088	4,582	11,499
PERSONAL TAXES	**2,012**	**–242**	**–268**	**–197**	**27**	**502**	**1,236**	**5,784**
Federal income taxes	1,370	–262	–315	–322	–198	202	757	4,239
State and local income taxes	505	–14	–6	40	127	211	358	1,296
Other taxes	136	34	52	85	98	89	121	248
GIFTS FOR PEOPLE IN OTHER HOUSEHOLDS	**1,037**	**517**	**376**	**442**	**652**	**526**	**913**	**1,980**

Note: Spending by category does not add to total spending because gift spending is also included in the preceding product and service categories and personal taxes are not included in the total.
Source: Bureau of Labor Statistics, 2011 Consumer Expenditure Survey, Internet site http://www.bls.gov/cex/; calculations by New Strategist

Table 1.5 Indexed spending by household income, 2011

(indexed average annual spending of consumer units by product and service category and before-tax income of consumer unit reference person, 2011; index definition: an index of 100 is the average for all consumer units; an index of 125 means that spending by consumer units in that group is 25 percent above the average for all consumer units; an index of 75 indicates spending that is 25 percent below the average for all consumer units)

	total consumer units	under $10,000	$10,000– $19,999	$20,000– $29,999	$30,000– $39,999	$40,000– $49,999	$50,000– $69,999	$70,000 or more
Average spending of consumer units, total	$49,705	$21,875	$22,318	$30,398	$36,769	$40,306	$50,034	$81,767
Average spending of consumer units, index	100	44	45	61	74	81	101	165
FOOD	100	55	54	66	82	80	101	151
Food at home	100	61	65	73	91	83	104	138
Cereals and bakery products	100	61	67	73	92	84	102	137
Cereals and cereal products	100	64	66	76	91	82	103	137
Bakery products	100	59	67	72	92	85	102	137
Meats, poultry, fish, and eggs	100	62	64	76	95	81	102	137
Beef	100	62	61	76	94	85	105	136
Pork	100	65	65	85	108	79	104	127
Other meats	100	60	59	57	74	87	105	150
Poultry	100	62	68	75	101	77	96	139
Fish and seafood	100	55	61	78	91	72	100	144
Eggs	100	77	80	90	102	86	94	122
Dairy products	100	60	62	73	88	84	104	140
Fresh milk and cream	100	68	69	79	92	86	101	133
Other dairy products	100	55	59	70	86	84	105	144
Fruits and vegetables	100	61	63	72	90	80	102	141
Fresh fruits	100	60	60	70	90	79	99	145
Fresh vegetables	100	57	60	74	90	77	100	145
Processed fruits	100	67	64	72	89	90	106	135
Processed vegetables	100	68	72	74	92	79	105	133
Other food at home	100	61	66	71	88	85	107	138
Sugar and other sweets	100	60	65	69	87	81	107	141
Fats and oils	100	72	72	75	97	89	115	122
Miscellaneous foods	100	61	67	71	88	83	107	138
Nonalcoholic beverages	100	61	66	74	89	90	108	134
Food prepared by consumer unit on trips	100	28	27	58	58	65	94	188
Food away from home	100	45	39	56	71	75	97	170
ALCOHOLIC BEVERAGES	100	49	32	46	69	68	84	185
HOUSING	100	50	54	70	80	87	101	153
Shelter	100	51	54	69	79	86	98	155
Owned dwellings	100	24	29	45	61	75	101	189
Mortgage interest and charges	100	20	18	32	54	71	107	200
Property taxes	100	30	39	56	64	78	96	180
Maintenance, repair, insurance, other expenses	100	27	44	66	75	79	95	171
Rented dwellings	100	107	112	124	122	115	97	74
Other lodging	100	48	17	41	47	56	72	212
Utilities, fuels, and public services	100	56	67	80	90	98	107	133
Natural gas	100	52	65	77	88	90	102	141
Electricity	100	64	75	85	91	101	107	125
Fuel oil and other fuels	100	48	63	84	62	90	101	149
Telephone services	100	51	61	76	92	101	112	135
Water and other public services	100	51	64	77	88	94	105	140
Household services	100	37	41	63	68	75	83	180
Personal services	100	34	31	61	56	60	68	200
Other household services	100	39	46	64	74	83	92	169
Housekeeping supplies	100	46	61	67	76	86	102	150
Laundry and cleaning supplies	100	55	75	78	81	98	107	132
Other household products	100	39	56	61	81	81	98	157
Postage and stationery	100	55	55	69	56	88	106	154
Household furnishings and equipment	100	34	36	55	73	73	112	169
Household textiles	100	33	53	54	65	99	97	164
Furniture	100	45	35	51	66	73	87	184
Floor coverings	100	17	42	25	25	45	70	225

	total consumer units	under $10,000	$10,000– $19,999	$20,000– $29,999	$30,000– $39,999	$40,000– $49,999	$50,000– $69,999	$70,000 or more
Major appliances	100	31	42	51	71	81	118	167
Small appliances and miscellaneous housewares	100	50	31	74	70	65	103	169
Miscellaneous household equipment	100	29	34	57	80	68	128	162
APPAREL AND RELATED SERVICES	**100**	**59**	**45**	**54**	**84**	**68**	**102**	**162**
Men and boys	**100**	**60**	**40**	**42**	**95**	**68**	**105**	**163**
Men, aged 16 or older	100	65	39	40	96	64	104	165
Boys, aged 2 to 15	100	39	47	53	91	85	110	155
Women and girls	**100**	**57**	**42**	**49**	**80**	**67**	**103**	**166**
Women, aged 16 or older	100	59	42	47	80	62	103	168
Girls, aged 2 to 15	100	44	41	63	79	90	103	159
Children under age 2	**100**	**51**	**69**	**46**	**91**	**96**	**116**	**140**
Footwear	**100**	**66**	**53**	**76**	**89**	**64**	**96**	**151**
Other apparel products and services	**100**	**58**	**42**	**63**	**71**	**66**	**92**	**169**
TRANSPORTATION	**100**	**40**	**39**	**56**	**77**	**86**	**109**	**164**
Vehicle purchases	**100**	**41**	**26**	**39**	**74**	**73**	**108**	**181**
Cars and trucks, new	100	36	32	26	48	45	97	213
Cars and trucks, used	100	47	36	53	99	102	120	148
Other vehicles	100	50	14	2	97	25	69	223
Gasoline and motor oil	**100**	**43**	**50**	**74**	**85**	**101**	**112**	**145**
Other vehicle expenses	**100**	**37**	**44**	**60**	**77**	**88**	**113**	**158**
Vehicle finance charges	100	18	22	48	70	94	110	179
Maintenance and repairs	100	41	39	61	80	86	112	160
Vehicle insurance	100	41	58	64	79	91	122	142
Vehicle rentals, leases, licenses, other charges	100	30	35	54	73	80	92	180
Public transportation	**100**	**37**	**34**	**36**	**55**	**66**	**79**	**201**
HEALTH CARE	**100**	**35**	**54**	**80**	**83**	**100**	**112**	**143**
Health insurance	100	35	56	85	89	102	114	138
Medical services	100	25	44	66	68	95	115	160
Drugs	100	49	65	87	87	101	109	131
Medical supplies	100	44	51	63	74	95	87	164
ENTERTAINMENT	**100**	**37**	**39**	**64**	**66**	**73**	**110**	**168**
Fees and admissions	100	30	20	32	46	60	79	214
Audio and visual equipment and services	100	47	59	74	85	92	109	144
Pets, toys, and playground equipment	100	37	42	74	68	72	115	159
Other entertainment products and services	100	21	14	70	44	46	156	175
PERSONAL CARE PRODUCTS AND SERVICES	**100**	**43**	**44**	**58**	**76**	**82**	**98**	**166**
READING	**100**	**42**	**45**	**63**	**66**	**77**	**115**	**163**
EDUCATION	**100**	**132**	**33**	**50**	**42**	**51**	**60**	**188**
TOBACCO PRODUCTS AND SMOKING SUPPLIES	**100**	**86**	**94**	**103**	**108**	**119**	**112**	**91**
MISCELLANEOUS	**100**	**58**	**43**	**77**	**71**	**85**	**88**	**161**
CASH CONTRIBUTIONS	**100**	**32**	**46**	**51**	**64**	**74**	**91**	**181**
PERSONAL INSURANCE AND PENSIONS	**100**	**5**	**10**	**28**	**43**	**61**	**90**	**223**
Life and other personal insurance	100	22	29	85	51	66	91	185
Pensions and Social Security	100	4	9	24	43	60	90	225
PERSONAL TAXES	**100**	**–12**	**–13**	**–10**	**1**	**25**	**61**	**287**
Federal income taxes	100	–19	–23	–24	–14	15	55	309
State and local income taxes	100	–3	–1	8	25	42	71	257
Other taxes	100	25	39	63	72	65	89	182
GIFTS FOR PEOPLE IN OTHER HOUSEHOLDS	**100**	**50**	**36**	**43**	**63**	**51**	**88**	**191**

Note: Spending by category does not add to total spending because gift spending is also included in the preceding product and service categories and personal taxes are not included in the total.
Source: Calculations by New Strategist based on the Bureau of Labor Statistics' 2011 Consumer Expenditure Survey

Spending by High-Income Consumer Units, 2011

The higher the income, the greater the spending. Households with incomes of $100,000 or more spent an average of $97,728 in 2011, nearly double the $49,705 spending of the average household. The Consumer Expenditure Survey examines the spending of households with incomes up to $150,000 or more. The highest-income households spent $123,056 on average in 2011. Spending surges as income rises, in part because affluent households have more earners—and consequently more expenses—than the average household.

On some products and services, the most-affluent households spend several times as much as the average household. On education, fees and admissions to entertainment events, and "other lodging" (motels, hotels, vacation homes, college dorms), households with incomes of $150,000 or more spend more than four times as much as the average household. On floor coverings they spend about six-and-one-half times the average. The most-affluent households spend nearly four times the average on public transportation (mostly airfares) and on gifts for people in other households, and they spend more than three times the average on household personal services (mostly day care), furniture, and vehicle rental and leases. The most-affluent households spend less than average on only two items: rent and tobacco.

(average annual spending of consumer units by product and service category and before-tax income of consumer unit, 2011)

	total consumer units	less than $70,000	$70,000–$79,999	$80,000–$99,999	$100,000 or more total	$100,000–$119,999	$120,000–$149,999	$150,000 or more
Number of consumer units (in 000s)	122,287	82,853	7,385	10,456	21,593	7,045	6,107	8,440
Average number of persons per consumer unit	2.5	2.2	2.8	3.0	3.2	3.2	3.1	3.2
Average before-tax income of consumer units	$63,685	$31,842	$74,742	$89,108	$169,776	$108,549	$133,318	$247,261
Average annual spending of consumer units	49,705	34,391	57,977	65,390	97,728	76,496	87,239	123,056
FOOD	**6,458**	**4,854**	**7,679**	**8,139**	**11,233**	**9,569**	**10,674**	**13,055**
Food at home	**3,838**	**3,126**	**4,474**	**4,627**	**5,897**	**5,184**	**5,533**	**6,768**
Cereals and bakery products	531	435	616	646	801	708	767	906
Cereals and cereal products	175	144	198	214	264	239	252	293
Bakery products	356	291	418	432	538	469	516	613
Meats, poultry, fish, and eggs	832	682	1,003	970	1,268	1,110	1,200	1,452
Beef	223	184	246	276	333	292	326	374
Pork	162	140	216	155	228	203	224	251
Other meats	123	93	169	166	197	155	205	228
Poultry	154	126	172	184	242	229	210	275
Fish and seafood	121	95	140	134	203	171	172	253
Eggs	50	45	61	54	64	59	62	71
Dairy products	407	328	464	498	635	552	598	734
Fresh milk and cream	150	126	181	183	213	183	191	254
Other dairy products	257	203	283	315	422	368	407	480
Fruits and vegetables	715	573	765	871	1,152	977	1,065	1,365
Fresh fruits	247	194	253	296	421	357	371	512
Fresh vegetables	224	176	232	277	375	325	346	440
Processed fruits	116	96	137	136	172	138	165	208
Processed vegetables	128	107	142	161	183	157	182	206
Other food at home	1,353	1,107	1,626	1,643	2,041	1,838	1,903	2,312
Sugar and other sweets	144	116	172	190	219	191	206	253
Fats and oils	110	98	121	125	143	133	141	154
Miscellaneous foods	690	565	824	839	1,043	941	998	1,164
Nonalcoholic beverages	361	302	458	427	518	485	453	593
Food prepared by consumer unit on trips	48	27	51	62	116	88	105	149
Food away from home	**2,620**	**1,728**	**3,205**	**3,512**	**5,336**	**4,385**	**5,141**	**6,286**
ALCOHOLIC BEVERAGES	**456**	**269**	**563**	**670**	**1,018**	**745**	**934**	**1,311**
HOUSING	**16,803**	**12,568**	**19,178**	**20,926**	**30,212**	**23,660**	**27,420**	**37,700**
Shelter	**9,825**	**7,253**	**10,887**	**12,247**	**18,158**	**13,546**	**16,546**	**23,175**
Owned dwellings	6,148	3,550	7,676	9,122	14,152	10,539	12,841	18,117
Mortgage interest and charges	3,184	1,666	4,339	5,119	7,676	5,993	6,948	9,609
Property taxes	1,845	1,142	2,106	2,493	4,138	2,880	3,645	5,545
Maintenance, repair, insurance, other expenses	1,120	743	1,231	1,510	2,338	1,666	2,249	2,962
Rented dwellings	3,029	3,400	2,711	2,364	2,039	2,112	2,101	1,934
Other lodging	648	303	500	761	1,967	895	1,603	3,124
Utilities, fuels, and public services	**3,727**	**3,141**	**4,273**	**4,537**	**5,395**	**4,903**	**5,126**	**6,001**
Natural gas	420	338	462	522	670	603	598	779
Electricity	1,423	1,254	1,600	1,662	1,895	1,710	1,760	2,147
Fuel oil and other fuels	157	120	169	187	279	228	267	331
Telephone services	1,226	1,023	1,451	1,550	1,774	1,673	1,734	1,888
Water and other public services	501	407	591	616	777	690	766	857
Household services	**1,122**	**696**	**1,379**	**1,381**	**2,543**	**1,732**	**2,035**	**3,589**
Personal services	398	208	568	546	998	751	796	1,349
Other household services	724	488	812	835	1,546	981	1,239	2,240
Housekeeping supplies	**615**	**465**	**680**	**755**	**1,083**	**1,065**	**1,026**	**1,138**
Laundry and cleaning supplies	145	123	159	184	203	199	187	218
Other household products	340	246	391	398	643	665	639	628
Postage and stationery	130	96	129	173	236	201	200	291
Household furnishings and equipment	**1,514**	**1,013**	**1,959**	**2,005**	**3,032**	**2,414**	**2,688**	**3,797**
Household textiles	109	76	155	145	203	183	143	261
Furniture	358	215	391	433	859	663	682	1,151
Floor coverings	20	8	13	18	69	30	30	131

	total consumer units	less than $70,000	$70,000–$79,999	$80,000–$99,999	$100,000 or more total	$100,000–$119,999	$120,000–$149,999	$150,000 or more
Major appliances	$194	$132	$239	$319	$356	$261	$349	$441
Small appliances and miscellaneous housewares	89	60	81	119	187	185	165	204
Miscellaneous household equipment	744	523	1,081	970	1,358	1,092	1,318	1,610
APPAREL AND RELATED SERVICES	**1,740**	**1,218**	**1,984**	**2,220**	**3,380**	**2,833**	**2,779**	**4,272**
Men and boys	**404**	**281**	**405**	**564**	**785**	**663**	**750**	**915**
Men, aged 16 or older	324	222	328	465	635	539	599	742
Boys, aged 2 to 15	80	58	78	100	151	124	151	173
Women and girls	**721**	**491**	**864**	**971**	**1,413**	**1,176**	**1,066**	**1,861**
Women, aged 16 or older	604	406	748	790	1,201	972	917	1,601
Girls, aged 2 to 15	117	84	116	181	211	205	149	261
Children under age 2	**68**	**55**	**92**	**89**	**99**	**120**	**95**	**85**
Footwear	**321**	**241**	**362**	**375**	**578**	**538**	**470**	**689**
Other apparel products and services	**226**	**150**	**261**	**220**	**504**	**336**	**398**	**722**
TRANSPORTATION	**8,293**	**5,772**	**9,804**	**12,185**	**15,538**	**13,962**	**14,274**	**17,756**
Vehicle purchases	**2,669**	**1,642**	**3,095**	**4,455**	**5,595**	**4,966**	**4,878**	**6,639**
Cars and trucks, new	1,265	585	1,955	1,910	3,328	2,792	2,968	4,035
Cars and trucks, used	1,339	1,031	1,107	2,468	2,054	1,934	1,715	2,400
Other vehicles	64	27	33	76	213	240	195	204
Gasoline and motor oil	**2,655**	**2,090**	**3,345**	**3,612**	**4,121**	**3,921**	**4,150**	**4,267**
Other vehicle expenses	**2,454**	**1,771**	**2,937**	**3,458**	**4,397**	**4,239**	**3,973**	**4,823**
Vehicle finance charges	233	144	374	376	454	442	457	461
Maintenance and repairs	805	576	991	1,149	1,449	1,308	1,343	1,642
Vehicle insurance	983	783	1,105	1,367	1,503	1,834	1,343	1,331
Vehicle rentals, leases, licenses, other charges	433	267	467	566	992	655	830	1,389
Public transportation	**516**	**269**	**427**	**660**	**1,425**	**836**	**1,273**	**2,027**
HEALTH CARE	**3,313**	**2,632**	**4,130**	**4,106**	**5,258**	**4,590**	**5,038**	**5,976**
Health insurance	1,922	1,576	2,392	2,388	2,864	2,562	2,813	3,151
Medical services	768	547	1,060	973	1,413	1,177	1,304	1,688
Drugs	489	415	467	579	733	652	657	855
Medical supplies	134	93	211	166	249	198	263	282
ENTERTAINMENT	**2,572**	**1,733**	**3,110**	**3,373**	**5,193**	**4,092**	**4,566**	**6,564**
Fees and admissions	594	271	697	741	1,724	1,061	1,350	2,550
Audio and visual equipment and services	977	774	1,174	1,250	1,553	1,334	1,549	1,739
Pets, toys, and playground equipment	631	452	815	923	1,101	1,135	892	1,219
Other entertainment products and services	370	237	424	459	815	561	775	1,056
PERSONAL CARE PRODUCTS AND SERVICES	**634**	**433**	**829**	**828**	**1,236**	**997**	**1,054**	**1,567**
READING	**115**	**81**	**123**	**151**	**228**	**169**	**214**	**289**
EDUCATION	**1,051**	**610**	**756**	**1,117**	**2,809**	**1,729**	**1,722**	**4,497**
TOBACCO PRODUCTS AND SMOKING SUPPLIES	**351**	**365**	**402**	**401**	**255**	**356**	**249**	**173**
MISCELLANEOUS	**775**	**550**	**951**	**898**	**1,517**	**1,081**	**1,240**	**2,079**
CASH CONTRIBUTIONS	**1,721**	**1,054**	**2,019**	**2,099**	**3,996**	**2,178**	**3,242**	**6,059**
PERSONAL INSURANCE AND PENSIONS	**5,424**	**2,254**	**6,449**	**8,275**	**15,856**	**10,536**	**13,835**	**21,758**
Life and other personal insurance	317	190	350	399	755	437	677	1,078
Pensions and Social Security	5,106	2,064	6,099	7,876	15,100	10,099	13,158	20,681
PERSONAL TAXES	**2,012**	**216**	**1,847**	**2,691**	**8,628**	**3,424**	**5,584**	**15,175**
Federal income taxes	1,370	5	1,143	1,773	6,493	2,261	4,040	11,801
State and local income taxes	505	129	566	753	1,809	940	1,306	2,898
Other taxes	136	83	138	165	326	223	238	476
GIFTS FOR PEOPLE IN OTHER HOUSEHOLDS	**1,037**	**587**	**1,069**	**1,223**	**2,652**	**1,526**	**2,102**	**3,995**

Note: Spending by category does not add to total spending because gift spending is also included in the preceding product and service categories and personal taxes are not included in the total.
Source: Bureau of Labor Statistics, 2011 Consumer Expenditure Survey, Internet site http://www.bls.gov/cex/

(indexed average annual spending of consumer units by product and service category and and before-tax income of consumer unit reference person, 2011; index definition: an index of 100 is the average for all consumer units; an index of 125 means that spending by consumer units in that group is 25 percent above the average for all consumer units; an index of 75 indicates spending that is 25 percent below the average for all consumer units)

	total consumer units	less than $70,000	$70,000–$79,999	$80,000–$99,999	$100,000 or more total	$100,000–$119,999	$120,000–$149,999	$150,000 or more
Average spending of consumer units, total	$49,705	$34,391	$57,977	$65,390	$97,728	$76,496	$87,239	$123,056
Average spending of consumer units, index	100	69	117	132	197	154	176	248
FOOD	100	75	119	126	174	148	165	202
Food at home	100	81	117	121	154	135	144	176
Cereals and bakery products	100	82	116	122	151	133	144	171
Cereals and cereal products	100	82	113	122	151	137	144	167
Bakery products	100	82	117	121	151	132	145	172
Meats, poultry, fish, and eggs	100	82	121	117	152	133	144	175
Beef	100	83	110	124	149	131	146	168
Pork	100	86	133	96	141	125	138	155
Other meats	100	76	137	135	160	126	167	185
Poultry	100	82	112	119	157	149	136	179
Fish and seafood	100	79	116	111	168	141	142	209
Eggs	100	90	122	108	128	118	124	142
Dairy products	100	81	114	122	156	136	147	180
Fresh milk and cream	100	84	121	122	142	122	127	169
Other dairy products	100	79	110	123	164	143	158	187
Fruits and vegetables	100	80	107	122	161	137	149	191
Fresh fruits	100	79	102	120	170	145	150	207
Fresh vegetables	100	79	104	124	167	145	154	196
Processed fruits	100	83	118	117	148	119	142	179
Processed vegetables	100	84	111	126	143	123	142	161
Other food at home	100	82	120	121	151	136	141	171
Sugar and other sweets	100	81	119	132	152	133	143	176
Fats and oils	100	89	110	114	130	121	128	140
Miscellaneous foods	100	82	119	122	151	136	145	169
Nonalcoholic beverages	100	84	127	118	143	134	125	164
Food prepared by consumer unit on trips	100	56	106	129	242	183	219	310
Food away from home	100	66	122	134	204	167	196	240
ALCOHOLIC BEVERAGES	100	59	123	147	223	163	205	288
HOUSING	100	75	114	125	180	141	163	224
Shelter	100	74	111	125	185	138	168	236
Owned dwellings	100	58	125	148	230	171	209	295
Mortgage interest and charges	100	52	136	161	241	188	218	302
Property taxes	100	62	114	135	224	156	198	301
Maintenance, repair, insurance, other expenses	100	66	110	135	209	149	201	264
Rented dwellings	100	112	90	78	67	70	69	64
Other lodging	100	47	77	117	304	138	247	482
Utilities, fuels, and public services	100	84	115	122	145	132	138	161
Natural gas	100	80	110	124	160	144	142	185
Electricity	100	88	112	117	133	120	124	151
Fuel oil and other fuels	100	76	108	119	178	145	170	211
Telephone services	100	83	118	126	145	136	141	154
Water and other public services	100	81	118	123	155	138	153	171
Household services	100	62	123	123	227	154	181	320
Personal services	100	52	143	137	251	189	200	339
Other household services	100	67	112	115	214	135	171	309
Housekeeping supplies	100	76	111	123	176	173	167	185
Laundry and cleaning supplies	100	85	110	127	140	137	129	150
Other household products	100	72	115	117	189	196	188	185
Postage and stationery	100	74	99	133	182	155	154	224
Household furnishings and equipment	100	67	129	132	200	159	178	251
Household textiles	100	70	142	133	186	168	131	239
Furniture	100	60	109	121	240	185	191	322
Floor coverings	100	40	65	90	345	150	150	655

	total consumer units	less than $70,000	$70,000– $79,999	$80,000– $99,999	$100,000 or more total	$100,000– $119,999	$120,000– $149,999	$150,000 or more
Major appliances	100	68	123	164	184	135	180	227
Small appliances and miscellaneous housewares	100	67	91	134	210	208	185	229
Miscellaneous household equipment	100	70	145	130	183	147	177	216
APPAREL AND RELATED SERVICES	**100**	**70**	**114**	**128**	**194**	**163**	**160**	**246**
Men and boys	**100**	**70**	**100**	**140**	**194**	**164**	**186**	**226**
Men, aged 16 or older	100	69	101	144	196	166	185	229
Boys, aged 2 to 15	100	73	98	125	189	155	189	216
Women and girls	**100**	**68**	**120**	**135**	**196**	**163**	**148**	**258**
Women, aged 16 or older	100	67	124	131	199	161	152	265
Girls, aged 2 to 15	100	72	99	155	180	175	127	223
Children under age 2	**100**	**81**	**135**	**131**	**146**	**176**	**140**	**125**
Footwear	**100**	**75**	**113**	**117**	**180**	**168**	**146**	**215**
Other apparel products and services	**100**	**66**	**115**	**97**	**223**	**149**	**176**	**319**
TRANSPORTATION	**100**	**70**	**118**	**147**	**187**	**168**	**172**	**214**
Vehicle purchases	**100**	**62**	**116**	**167**	**210**	**186**	**183**	**249**
Cars and trucks, new	100	46	155	151	263	221	235	319
Cars and trucks, used	100	77	83	184	153	144	128	179
Other vehicles	100	42	52	119	333	375	305	319
Gasoline and motor oil	**100**	**79**	**126**	**136**	**155**	**148**	**156**	**161**
Other vehicle expenses	**100**	**72**	**120**	**141**	**179**	**173**	**162**	**197**
Vehicle finance charges	100	62	161	161	195	190	196	198
Maintenance and repairs	100	72	123	143	180	162	167	204
Vehicle insurance	100	80	112	139	153	187	137	135
Vehicle rentals, leases, licenses, other charges	100	62	108	131	229	151	192	321
Public transportation	**100**	**52**	**83**	**128**	**276**	**162**	**247**	**393**
HEALTH CARE	**100**	**79**	**125**	**124**	**159**	**139**	**152**	**180**
Health insurance	100	82	124	124	149	133	146	164
Medical services	100	71	138	127	184	153	170	220
Drugs	100	85	96	118	150	133	134	175
Medical supplies	100	69	157	124	186	148	196	210
ENTERTAINMENT	**100**	**67**	**121**	**131**	**202**	**159**	**178**	**255**
Fees and admissions	100	46	117	125	290	179	227	429
Audio and visual equipment and services	100	79	120	128	159	137	159	178
Pets, toys, and playground equipment	100	72	129	146	174	180	141	193
Other entertainment products and services	100	64	115	124	220	152	209	285
PERSONAL CARE PRODUCTS AND SERVICES	**100**	**68**	**131**	**131**	**195**	**157**	**166**	**247**
READING	**100**	**70**	**107**	**131**	**198**	**147**	**186**	**251**
EDUCATION	**100**	**58**	**72**	**106**	**267**	**165**	**164**	**428**
TOBACCO PRODUCTS AND SMOKING SUPPLIES	**100**	**104**	**115**	**114**	**73**	**101**	**71**	**49**
MISCELLANEOUS	**100**	**71**	**123**	**116**	**196**	**139**	**160**	**268**
CASH CONTRIBUTIONS	**100**	**61**	**117**	**122**	**232**	**127**	**188**	**352**
PERSONAL INSURANCE AND PENSIONS	**100**	**42**	**119**	**153**	**292**	**194**	**255**	**401**
Life and other personal insurance	100	60	110	126	238	138	214	340
Pensions and Social Security	100	40	119	154	296	198	258	405
PERSONAL TAXES	**100**	**11**	**92**	**134**	**429**	**170**	**278**	**754**
Federal income taxes	100	0	83	129	474	165	295	861
State and local income taxes	100	26	112	149	358	186	259	574
Other taxes	100	61	101	121	240	164	175	350
GIFTS FOR PEOPLE IN OTHER HOUSEHOLDS	**100**	**57**	**103**	**118**	**256**	**147**	**203**	**385**

Source: Calculations by New Strategist based on the Bureau of Labor Statistics' 2011 Consumer Expenditure Survey

Spending by Household Type, 2011

Married couples spent 29 percent more than the average household in 2011. Among married couples, those with school-aged or older children at home spend the most, an average of slightly over $70,000 in 2011. Behind the higher spending of married couples are their higher incomes, due primarily to the greater number of earners in the household. Married couples with children at home average 1.9 earners per household. Those with adult children at home average 2.3 earners. The more earners, the greater the spending—particularly on products and services needed by workers such as food away from home, men's and women's clothes, and transportation.

Married couples with children under age 18 have distinct spending patterns. Couples with school-aged children spend 42 percent more than the average household overall. They spend 69 percent more than the average household on cereal, more than twice the average on fees and admissions to entertainment events and well over three times the average on children's clothes. The biggest spenders on household personal services (mostly day care) are married couples with preschoolers, while couples without children at home (mostly empty-nesters) spend more than other household types on alcoholic beverages.

Single parents spend less than the average household on most items. Some of the exceptions are children's clothes, household personal services (mostly day care), and rent. Single-person households spend less than the average on every category except rent.

Table 1.8 Average spending by household type, 2011

(average annual spending of consumer units by product and service category and type of consumer unit, 2011)

	total married couples	married couples, no children	married couples with children				single parent with child under age 18	single person
			total	oldest child under age 6	oldest child aged 6 to 17	oldest child aged 18 or older		
Number of consumer units (in 000s)	60,144	25,270	29,097	5,825	14,661	8,612	6,956	36,110
Average number of persons per consumer unit	3.2	2.0	4.0	3.5	4.2	3.9	2.9	1.0
Average before-tax income of consumer units	$86,700	$78,823	$93,677	$91,014	$93,029	$96,583	$37,188	$34,540
Average annual spending of consumer units	63,972	57,658	69,724	65,948	70,709	70,412	37,553	30,613
FOOD	**8,315**	**6,895**	**9,557**	**8,028**	**9,813**	**10,042**	**5,676**	**3,638**
Food at home	**4,944**	**3,935**	**5,785**	**5,010**	**5,877**	**6,080**	**3,526**	**2,072**
Cereals and bakery products	687	535	820	673	864	832	519	285
Cereals and cereal products	225	168	275	232	295	266	194	91
Bakery products	462	367	545	441	569	566	325	194
Meats, poultry, fish, and eggs	1,084	820	1,275	921	1,276	1,480	790	397
Beef	298	225	337	219	344	393	207	92
Pork	209	162	242	175	245	276	144	79
Other meats	166	116	210	145	223	224	102	58
Poultry	197	137	243	190	226	301	167	72
Fish and seafood	153	132	171	131	166	205	126	66
Eggs	62	48	73	61	72	81	45	30
Dairy products	533	420	636	597	650	635	355	221
Fresh milk and cream	194	140	238	239	239	238	139	79
Other dairy products	339	279	398	358	411	397	216	142
Fruits and vegetables	926	761	1,067	996	1,059	1,122	600	402
Fresh fruits	325	272	374	353	369	395	208	145
Fresh vegetables	294	255	325	298	321	349	159	123
Processed fruits	144	108	175	168	177	176	113	67
Processed vegetables	164	126	192	177	191	203	121	66
Other food at home	1,714	1,400	1,987	1,824	2,030	2,011	1,262	767
Sugar and other sweets	188	152	219	183	229	223	124	82
Fats and oils	142	119	158	121	155	184	91	62
Miscellaneous foods	866	687	1,033	1,078	1,037	998	684	398
Nonalcoholic beverages	445	361	510	383	533	546	343	202
Food prepared by consumer unit on trips	72	81	68	58	76	60	19	23
Food away from home	**3,370**	**2,960**	**3,772**	**3,018**	**3,936**	**3,962**	**2,150**	**1,567**
ALCOHOLIC BEVERAGES	**515**	**610**	**459**	**424**	**459**	**479**	**246**	**370**
HOUSING	**20,664**	**18,329**	**22,788**	**25,009**	**23,158**	**20,648**	**14,563**	**11,456**
Shelter	**11,780**	**10,404**	**13,122**	**14,571**	**13,609**	**11,311**	**8,426**	**7,176**
Owned dwellings	8,620	7,622	9,646	10,295	9,974	8,649	3,405	3,438
Mortgage interest and charges	4,591	3,341	5,694	6,808	5,944	4,515	1,967	1,480
Property taxes	2,565	2,558	2,658	2,412	2,748	2,673	930	1,127
Maintenance, repair, insurance, other expenses	1,464	1,724	1,294	1,074	1,282	1,461	508	831
Rented dwellings	2,145	1,471	2,649	3,608	2,792	1,758	4,851	3,443
Other lodging	1,015	1,312	826	668	843	905	170	295
Utilities, fuels, and public services	**4,540**	**4,073**	**4,797**	**3,989**	**4,856**	**5,244**	**3,445**	**2,380**
Natural gas	505	452	542	444	558	579	371	284
Electricity	1,713	1,563	1,783	1,484	1,809	1,942	1,428	927
Fuel oil and other fuels	198	212	185	142	185	213	63	113
Telephone services	1,498	1,275	1,640	1,377	1,636	1,825	1,165	745
Water and other public services	626	571	647	543	667	685	419	311
Household services	**1,451**	**1,021**	**1,891**	**3,679**	**1,660**	**1,074**	**1,185**	**692**
Personal services	549	69	997	2,817	768	157	683	166
Other household services	902	952	893	862	892	917	502	526
Housekeeping supplies	**826**	**800**	**860**	**834**	**851**	**890**	**392**	**348**
Laundry and cleaning supplies	188	172	200	169	210	203	138	76
Other household products	460	439	495	500	468	537	196	189
Postage and stationery	178	189	165	165	174	150	58	83
Household furnishings and equipment	**2,067**	**2,029**	**2,118**	**1,935**	**2,182**	**2,129**	**1,115**	**859**
Household textiles	141	144	138	159	124	151	140	71
Furniture	472	437	512	484	537	487	347	213
Floor coverings	29	37	23	14	21	31	12	12

	total married couples	married couples, no children	married couples with children				single parent with child under 18	single person
			total	oldest child under age 6	oldest child aged 6 to 17	oldest child aged 18 or older		
Major appliances	$271	$275	$275	$267	$293	$249	$163	$91
Small appliances and miscellaneous housewares	121	138	110	109	106	118	51	55
Miscellaneous household equipment	1,031	999	1,060	902	1,101	1,092	402	417
APPAREL AND RELATED SERVICES	**2,184**	**1,715**	**2,541**	**2,157**	**2,587**	**2,687**	**1,835**	**1,021**
Men and boys	**515**	**363**	**612**	**405**	**649**	**673**	**336**	**250**
Men, aged 16 or older	405	338	433	278	393	592	138	235
Boys, aged 2 to 15	110	25	179	126	256	80	198	14
Women and girls	**889**	**737**	**1,004**	**636**	**1,045**	**1,154**	**851**	**459**
Women, aged 16 or older	726	691	733	528	634	1,018	577	427
Girls, aged 2 to 15	163	47	272	108	411	136	274	32
Children under age 2	**93**	**30**	**151**	**512**	**99**	**26**	**104**	**15**
Footwear	**407**	**297**	**490**	**337**	**522**	**525**	**380**	**161**
Other apparel products and services	**280**	**288**	**283**	**268**	**273**	**309**	**163**	**137**
TRANSPORTATION	**10,972**	**9,474**	**12,182**	**10,698**	**12,218**	**13,120**	**5,471**	**4,367**
Vehicle purchases	**3,609**	**2,793**	**4,302**	**3,562**	**4,382**	**4,666**	**1,394**	**1,235**
Cars and trucks, new	1,848	1,557	2,134	1,830	2,085	2,421	334	582
Cars and trucks, used	1,683	1,158	2,074	1,725	2,136	2,206	1,028	629
Other vehicles	78	77	94	8	160	40	33	23
Gasoline and motor oil	**3,472**	**2,923**	**3,852**	**3,205**	**3,921**	**4,173**	**2,119**	**1,399**
Other vehicle expenses	**3,204**	**3,056**	**3,319**	**3,297**	**3,168**	**3,588**	**1,636**	**1,418**
Vehicle finance charges	330	248	391	452	383	364	144	99
Maintenance and repairs	1,041	981	1,105	933	1,159	1,124	520	500
Vehicle insurance	1,243	1,244	1,203	1,248	1,084	1,377	699	574
Vehicle rentals, leases, licenses, other charges	590	583	620	663	542	723	273	245
Public transportation	**687**	**702**	**709**	**633**	**747**	**693**	**323**	**316**
HEALTH CARE	**4,479**	**5,127**	**3,910**	**3,486**	**3,753**	**4,465**	**1,892**	**2,112**
Health insurance	2,619	3,004	2,268	2,161	2,157	2,530	797	1,232
Medical services	1,026	1,089	990	883	960	1,111	821	467
Drugs	661	829	505	328	485	658	211	314
Medical supplies	173	205	148	113	151	166	63	99
ENTERTAINMENT	**3,418**	**3,286**	**3,591**	**2,956**	**4,086**	**3,161**	**1,821**	**1,522**
Fees and admissions	872	719	1,044	698	1,367	724	424	290
Audio and visual equipment and services	1,180	1,071	1,278	1,073	1,355	1,282	827	672
Pets, toys, and playground equipment	794	809	774	681	801	788	405	409
Other entertainment products and services	572	687	495	504	563	367	164	151
PERSONAL CARE PRODUCTS AND SERVICES	**819**	**761**	**884**	**707**	**915**	**938**	**548**	**388**
READING	**148**	**177**	**132**	**107**	**136**	**141**	**52**	**90**
EDUCATION	**1,340**	**716**	**1,904**	**729**	**1,739**	**2,978**	**553**	**782**
TOBACCO PRODUCTS AND SMOKING SUPPLIES	**342**	**293**	**320**	**204**	**312**	**411**	**322**	**255**
MISCELLANEOUS	**897**	**902**	**865**	**973**	**811**	**883**	**668**	**577**
CASH CONTRIBUTIONS	**2,227**	**2,824**	**1,833**	**1,589**	**1,877**	**1,924**	**665**	**1,446**
PERSONAL INSURANCE AND PENSIONS	**7,652**	**6,549**	**8,759**	**8,882**	**8,843**	**8,533**	**3,241**	**2,588**
Life and other personal insurance	463	473	473	509	443	501	135	179
Pensions and Social Security	7,189	6,077	8,286	8,373	8,400	8,032	3,107	2,409
PERSONAL TAXES	**2,940**	**3,216**	**2,976**	**3,141**	**2,233**	**4,128**	**–11**	**1,378**
Federal income taxes	2,024	2,362	1,957	2,076	1,424	2,786	–279	998
State and local income taxes	719	637	832	817	662	1,130	226	293
Other taxes	197	216	187	248	147	212	42	87
GIFTS FOR PEOPLE IN OTHER HOUSEHOLDS	**1,332**	**1,635**	**1,171**	**744**	**1,052**	**1,660**	**450**	**845**

Note: Spending by category does not add to total spending because gift spending is also included in the preceding product and service categories and personal taxes are not included in the total.
Source: Bureau of Labor Statistics, 2011 Consumer Expenditure Survey, Internet site http://www.bls.gov/cex/; calculations by New Strategist

Table 1.9 Indexed spending by household type, 2011

(indexed average annual spending of consumer units by product and service category and type of consumer unit, 2011; index definition: an index of 100 is the average for all consumer units; an index of 125 means that spending by consumer units in that group is 25 percent above the average for all consumer units; an index of 75 indicates spending that is 25 percent below the average for all consumer units)

	total married couples	married couples, no children	married couples with children total	oldest child under age 6	oldest child aged 6 to 17	oldest child aged 18 or older	single parent with child under age 18	single person
Average spending of consumer units, total	$63,972	$57,658	$69,724	$65,948	$70,709	$70,412	$37,553	$30,613
Average spending of consumer units, index	129	116	140	133	142	142	76	62
FOOD	**129**	**107**	**148**	**124**	**152**	**155**	**88**	**56**
Food at home	**129**	**103**	**151**	**131**	**153**	**158**	**92**	**54**
Cereals and bakery products	129	101	154	127	163	157	98	54
Cereals and cereal products	129	96	157	133	169	152	111	52
Bakery products	130	103	153	124	160	159	91	54
Meats, poultry, fish, and eggs	130	99	153	111	153	178	95	48
Beef	134	101	151	98	154	176	93	41
Pork	129	100	149	108	151	170	89	49
Other meats	135	94	171	118	181	182	83	47
Poultry	128	89	158	123	147	195	108	47
Fish and seafood	126	109	141	108	137	169	104	55
Eggs	124	96	146	122	144	162	90	60
Dairy products	131	103	156	147	160	156	87	54
Fresh milk and cream	129	93	159	159	159	159	93	53
Other dairy products	132	109	155	139	160	154	84	55
Fruits and vegetables	130	106	149	139	148	157	84	56
Fresh fruits	132	110	151	143	149	160	84	59
Fresh vegetables	131	114	145	133	143	156	71	55
Processed fruits	124	93	151	145	153	152	97	58
Processed vegetables	128	98	150	138	149	159	95	52
Other food at home	127	103	147	135	150	149	93	57
Sugar and other sweets	131	106	152	127	159	155	86	57
Fats and oils	129	108	144	110	141	167	83	56
Miscellaneous foods	126	100	150	156	150	145	99	58
Nonalcoholic beverages	123	100	141	106	148	151	95	56
Food prepared by consumer unit on trips	150	169	142	121	158	125	40	48
Food away from home	**129**	**113**	**144**	**115**	**150**	**151**	**82**	**60**
ALCOHOLIC BEVERAGES	**113**	**134**	**101**	**93**	**101**	**105**	**54**	**81**
HOUSING	**123**	**109**	**136**	**149**	**138**	**123**	**87**	**68**
Shelter	**120**	**106**	**134**	**148**	**139**	**115**	**86**	**73**
Owned dwellings	140	124	157	167	162	141	55	56
Mortgage interest and charges	144	105	179	214	187	142	62	46
Property taxes	139	139	144	131	149	145	50	61
Maintenance, repair, insurance, other expenses	131	154	116	96	114	130	45	74
Rented dwellings	71	49	87	119	92	58	160	114
Other lodging	157	202	127	103	130	140	26	46
Utilities, fuels, and public services	**122**	**109**	**129**	**107**	**130**	**141**	**92**	**64**
Natural gas	120	108	129	106	133	138	88	68
Electricity	120	110	125	104	127	136	100	65
Fuel oil and other fuels	126	135	118	90	118	136	40	72
Telephone services	122	104	134	112	133	149	95	61
Water and other public services	125	114	129	108	133	137	84	62
Household services	**129**	**91**	**169**	**328**	**148**	**96**	**106**	**62**
Personal services	138	17	251	708	193	39	172	42
Other household services	125	131	123	119	123	127	69	73
Housekeeping supplies	**134**	**130**	**140**	**136**	**138**	**145**	**64**	**57**
Laundry and cleaning supplies	130	119	138	117	145	140	95	52
Other household products	135	129	146	147	138	158	58	56
Postage and stationery	137	145	127	127	134	115	45	64
Household furnishings and equipment	**137**	**134**	**140**	**128**	**144**	**141**	**74**	**57**
Household textiles	129	132	127	146	114	139	128	65
Furniture	132	122	143	135	150	136	97	59
Floor coverings	145	185	115	70	105	155	60	60

	total married couples	married couples, no children	married couples with children				single parent with child under age 18	single person
			total	oldest child under age 6	oldest child aged 6 to 17	oldest child aged 18 or older		
Major appliances	140	142	142	138	151	128	84	47
Small appliances and miscellaneous housewares	136	155	124	122	119	133	57	62
Miscellaneous household equipment	139	134	142	121	148	147	54	56
APPAREL AND RELATED SERVICES	**126**	**99**	**146**	**124**	**149**	**154**	**105**	**59**
Men and boys	**127**	**90**	**151**	**100**	**161**	**167**	**83**	**62**
Men, aged 16 or older	125	104	134	86	121	183	43	73
Boys, aged 2 to 15	138	31	224	158	320	100	248	18
Women and girls	**123**	**102**	**139**	**88**	**145**	**160**	**118**	**64**
Women, aged 16 or older	120	114	121	87	105	169	96	71
Girls, aged 2 to 15	139	40	232	92	351	116	234	27
Children under age 2	**137**	**44**	**222**	**753**	**146**	**38**	**153**	**22**
Footwear	**127**	**93**	**153**	**105**	**163**	**164**	**118**	**50**
Other apparel products and services	**124**	**127**	**125**	**119**	**121**	**137**	**72**	**61**
TRANSPORTATION	**132**	**114**	**147**	**129**	**147**	**158**	**66**	**53**
Vehicle purchases	**135**	**105**	**161**	**133**	**164**	**175**	**52**	**46**
Cars and trucks, new	146	123	169	145	165	191	26	46
Cars and trucks, used	126	86	155	129	160	165	77	47
Other vehicles	122	120	147	13	250	63	52	36
Gasoline and motor oil	**131**	**110**	**145**	**121**	**148**	**157**	**80**	**53**
Other vehicle expenses	**131**	**125**	**135**	**134**	**129**	**146**	**67**	**58**
Vehicle finance charges	142	106	168	194	164	156	62	42
Maintenance and repairs	129	122	137	116	144	140	65	62
Vehicle insurance	126	127	122	127	110	140	71	58
Vehicle rentals, leases, licenses, other charges	136	135	143	153	125	167	63	57
Public transportation	**133**	**136**	**137**	**123**	**145**	**134**	**63**	**61**
HEALTH CARE	**135**	**155**	**118**	**105**	**113**	**135**	**57**	**64**
Health insurance	136	156	118	112	112	132	41	64
Medical services	134	142	129	115	125	145	107	61
Drugs	135	170	103	67	99	135	43	64
Medical supplies	129	153	110	84	113	124	47	74
ENTERTAINMENT	**133**	**128**	**140**	**115**	**159**	**123**	**71**	**59**
Fees and admissions	147	121	176	118	230	122	71	49
Audio and visual equipment and services	121	110	131	110	139	131	85	69
Pets, toys, and playground equipment	126	128	123	108	127	125	64	65
Other entertainment products and services	155	186	134	136	152	99	44	41
PERSONAL CARE PRODUCTS AND SERVICES	**129**	**120**	**139**	**112**	**144**	**148**	**86**	**61**
READING	**129**	**154**	**115**	**93**	**118**	**123**	**45**	**78**
EDUCATION	**127**	**68**	**181**	**69**	**165**	**283**	**53**	**74**
TOBACCO PRODUCTS AND SMOKING SUPPLIES	**97**	**83**	**91**	**58**	**89**	**117**	**92**	**73**
MISCELLANEOUS	**116**	**116**	**112**	**126**	**105**	**114**	**86**	**74**
CASH CONTRIBUTIONS	**129**	**164**	**107**	**92**	**109**	**112**	**39**	**84**
PERSONAL INSURANCE AND PENSIONS	**141**	**121**	**161**	**164**	**163**	**157**	**60**	**48**
Life and other personal insurance	146	149	149	161	140	158	43	56
Pensions and Social Security	141	119	162	164	165	157	61	47
PERSONAL TAXES	**146**	**160**	**148**	**156**	**111**	**205**	**–1**	**68**
Federal income taxes	148	172	143	152	104	203	–20	73
State and local income taxes	142	126	165	162	131	224	45	58
Other taxes	145	159	138	182	108	156	31	64
GIFTS FOR PEOPLE IN OTHER HOUSEHOLDS	**128**	**158**	**113**	**72**	**101**	**160**	**43**	**81**

Note: Spending index for total consumer units is 100.
Source: Calculations by New Strategist based on the Bureau of Labor Statistics' 2011 Consumer Expenditure Survey

Spending by Race and Hispanic Origin, 2011

Asians spend much more than the average household, non-Hispanic whites spend close to the average, and Hispanics and blacks spend less. The $60,136 spent by the average Asian household in 2011 was 21 percent above the overall average and surpassed the spending of other racial or ethnic groups. Non-Hispanic whites spent $53,056, only 7 percent more than average and well below the spending of Asian households. Black households spent $36,644 in 2011, or 26 percent less than average. Hispanic spending, at $42,086, was 15 percent below average.

Asian spending reflects their above-average incomes, a consequence of their high educational attainment. Asian households spend more than twice the average on education and nearly three times the average on public transportation (mostly airfares) as well as on fish and seafood.

Hispanic and black spending exceeds that of the average household in many categories. Because of their larger families, Hispanic households spend more than the average household on many food items. They spend 59 percent more than the average household on rented dwellings and 34 percent more on clothes for infants.

Blacks spend more than the average household on a number of food items, including poultry, pork, and fish and seafood. They spend 41 percent more than the average household on rent as well as on footwear, 24 percent more on clothes for boys, 13 percent more on baby clothes, and 9 percent more on clothes for girls.

(average annual spending of consumer units by product and service category and by race and Hispanic origin of consumer unit reference person, 2011)

	total consumer units	Asian	black	Hispanic	non-Hispanic white and other
Number of consumer units (in 000s)	122,287	5,048	15,118	15,222	92,163
Average number of persons per consumer unit	2.5	2.7	2.6	3.4	2.4
Average before-tax income of consumer units	$63,685	$85,415	$45,552	$49,966	$68,907
Average annual spending of consumer units	49,705	60,136	36,644	42,086	53,056
FOOD	**6,458**	**8,163**	**4,743**	**6,373**	**6,743**
Food at home	**3,838**	**4,439**	**2,989**	**3,849**	**3,970**
Cereals and bakery products	531	618	405	493	556
Cereals and cereal products	175	265	143	181	179
Bakery products	356	353	263	312	377
Meats, poultry, fish, and eggs	832	1,094	822	968	813
Beef	223	201	189	268	221
Pork	162	210	183	191	154
Other meats	123	92	86	110	130
Poultry	154	186	185	196	143
Fish and seafood	121	327	134	138	116
Eggs	50	77	46	66	48
Dairy products	407	337	246	388	435
Fresh milk and cream	150	161	98	163	156
Other dairy products	257	175	148	226	279
Fruits and vegetables	715	1,059	527	778	735
Fresh fruits	247	392	157	293	255
Fresh vegetables	224	415	145	241	234
Processed fruits	116	111	109	120	116
Processed vegetables	128	139	117	124	130
Other food at home	1,353	1,332	988	1,221	1,431
Sugar and other sweets	144	157	98	117	156
Fats and oils	110	115	94	122	110
Miscellaneous foods	690	678	502	580	737
Nonalcoholic beverages	361	324	280	370	373
Food prepared by consumer unit on trips	48	57	14	32	55
Food away from home	**2,620**	**3,724**	**1,754**	**2,524**	**2,773**
ALCOHOLIC BEVERAGES	**456**	**311**	**199**	**281**	**525**
HOUSING	**16,803**	**20,834**	**13,985**	**15,648**	**17,449**
Shelter	**9,825**	**14,269**	**8,111**	**9,766**	**10,122**
Owned dwellings	6,148	8,209	3,651	4,713	6,791
Mortgage interest and charges	3,184	4,348	2,151	2,814	3,412
Property taxes	1,845	2,523	930	1,202	2,100
Maintenance, repair, insurance, other expenses	1,120	1,338	570	697	1,278
Rented dwellings	3,029	4,843	4,268	4,806	2,543
Other lodging	648	1,217	192	248	788
Utilities, fuels, and public services	**3,727**	**3,279**	**3,701**	**3,462**	**3,773**
Natural gas	420	436	429	350	429
Electricity	1,423	1,035	1,497	1,283	1,433
Fuel oil and other fuels	157	62	67	42	190
Telephone services	1,226	1,229	1,242	1,288	1,214
Water and other public services	501	517	465	499	506
Household services	**1,122**	**1,593**	**810**	**755**	**1,233**
Personal services	398	808	307	319	426
Other household services	724	785	503	436	807
Housekeeping supplies	**615**	**393**	**426**	**536**	**656**
Laundry and cleaning supplies	145	108	155	195	136
Other household products	340	211	194	255	375
Postage and stationery	130	74	76	86	145
Household furnishings and equipment	**1,514**	**1,300**	**938**	**1,129**	**1,666**
Household textiles	109	69	52	73	124
Furniture	358	381	306	310	374
Floor coverings	20	11	10	7	24

	total consumer units	Asian	black	Hispanic	non-Hispanic white and other
Major appliances	$194	$153	$152	$128	$211
Small appliances and miscellaneous housewares	89	83	39	61	102
Miscellaneous household equipment	744	603	378	550	831
APPAREL AND RELATED SERVICES	**1,740**	**2,324**	**1,669**	**1,989**	**1,714**
Men and boys	**404**	**603**	**324**	**518**	**399**
Men, aged 16 or older	324	503	224	402	328
Boys, aged 2 to 15	80	100	99	116	71
Women and girls	**721**	**911**	**629**	**672**	**743**
Women, aged 16 or older	604	761	501	532	631
Girls, aged 2 to 15	117	150	128	140	112
Children under age 2	**68**	**109**	**77**	**91**	**63**
Footwear	**321**	**342**	**454**	**452**	**281**
Other apparel products and services	**226**	**359**	**185**	**256**	**227**
TRANSPORTATION	**8,293**	**10,281**	**5,944**	**7,520**	**8,798**
Vehicle purchases	**2,669**	**3,450**	**1,608**	**2,208**	**2,919**
Cars and trucks, new	1,265	2,342	634	691	1,464
Cars and trucks, used	1,339	1,100	959	1,511	1,373
Other vehicles	64	8	14	6	82
Gasoline and motor oil	**2,655**	**2,283**	**2,221**	**2,721**	**2,714**
Other vehicle expenses	**2,454**	**3,075**	**1,833**	**2,174**	**2,596**
Vehicle finance charges	233	168	194	215	242
Maintenance and repairs	805	717	587	638	867
Vehicle insurance	983	1,608	767	934	1,023
Vehicle rentals, leases, licenses, other charges	433	582	285	386	464
Public transportation	**516**	**1,473**	**283**	**417**	**570**
HEALTH CARE	**3,313**	**2,919**	**1,897**	**1,774**	**3,793**
Health insurance	1,922	1,882	1,238	1,008	2,182
Medical services	768	667	300	453	896
Drugs	489	285	300	237	560
Medical supplies	134	84	59	75	155
ENTERTAINMENT	**2,572**	**2,301**	**1,432**	**1,738**	**2,888**
Fees and admissions	594	768	201	339	699
Audio and visual equipment and services	977	868	909	839	1,009
Pets, toys, and playground equipment	631	269	212	392	734
Other entertainment products and services	370	396	110	167	445
PERSONAL CARE PRODUCTS AND SERVICES	**634**	**602**	**533**	**611**	**654**
READING	**115**	**111**	**48**	**46**	**138**
EDUCATION	**1,051**	**2,267**	**479**	**624**	**1,212**
TOBACCO PRODUCTS AND SMOKING SUPPLIES	**351**	**152**	**260**	**164**	**396**
MISCELLANEOUS	**775**	**696**	**521**	**476**	**864**
CASH CONTRIBUTIONS	**1,721**	**1,405**	**1,341**	**812**	**1,930**
PERSONAL INSURANCE AND PENSIONS	**5,424**	**7,771**	**3,593**	**4,030**	**5,951**
Life and other personal insurance	317	337	250	115	361
Pensions and Social Security	5,106	7,434	3,344	3,915	5,590
PERSONAL TAXES	**2,012**	**3,894**	**500**	**465**	**2,511**
Federal income taxes	1,370	3,032	198	236	1,747
State and local income taxes	505	728	240	186	601
Other taxes	136	134	63	43	163
GIFTS FOR PEOPLE IN OTHER HOUSEHOLDS	**1,037**	**1,120**	**495**	**585**	**1,198**

Note: "Asian" and "black" include Hispanics and non-Hispanics who identify themselves as being of the respective race alone. "Hispanic" includes people of any race who identify themselves as Hispanic. "Other" includes people who identify themselves as non-Hispanic and as Alaska Native, American Indian, Asian (who are also included in the "Asian" column), or Native Hawaiian or other Pacific Islander, as well as non-Hispanics reporting more than one race. Spending by category does not add to total spending because gift spending is also included in the preceding product and service categories and personal taxes are not included in the total.
Source: Bureau of Labor Statistics, 2011 Consumer Expenditure Survey, Internet site http://www.bls.gov/cex/

(indexed average annual spending of consumer units by product and service category and by race and Hispanic origin of consumer unit reference person, 2011; index definition: an index of 100 is the average for all consumer units; an index of 125 means that spending by consumer units in that group is 25 percent above the average for all consumer units; an index of 75 indicates spending that is 25 percent below the average for all consumer units)

	total consumer units	Asian	black	Hispanic	non-Hispanic white and other
Average spending of consumer units, total	$49,705	$60,136	$36,644	$42,086	$53,056
Average spending of consumer units, index	100	121	74	85	107
FOOD	100	126	73	99	104
Food at home	100	116	78	100	103
Cereals and bakery products	100	116	76	93	105
Cereals and cereal products	100	151	82	103	102
Bakery products	100	99	74	88	106
Meats, poultry, fish, and eggs	100	131	99	116	98
Beef	100	90	85	120	99
Pork	100	130	113	118	95
Other meats	100	75	70	89	106
Poultry	100	121	120	127	93
Fish and seafood	100	270	111	114	96
Eggs	100	154	92	132	96
Dairy products	100	83	60	95	107
Fresh milk and cream	100	107	65	109	104
Other dairy products	100	68	58	88	109
Fruits and vegetables	100	148	74	109	103
Fresh fruits	100	159	64	119	103
Fresh vegetables	100	185	65	108	104
Processed fruits	100	96	94	103	100
Processed vegetables	100	109	91	97	102
Other food at home	100	98	73	90	106
Sugar and other sweets	100	109	68	81	108
Fats and oils	100	105	85	111	100
Miscellaneous foods	100	98	73	84	107
Nonalcoholic beverages	100	90	78	102	103
Food prepared by consumer unit on trips	100	119	29	67	115
Food away from home	100	142	67	96	106
ALCOHOLIC BEVERAGES	100	68	44	62	115
HOUSING	100	124	83	93	104
Shelter	100	145	83	99	103
Owned dwellings	100	134	59	77	110
Mortgage interest and charges	100	137	68	88	107
Property taxes	100	137	50	65	114
Maintenance, repair, insurance, other expenses	100	119	51	62	114
Rented dwellings	100	160	141	159	84
Other lodging	100	188	30	38	122
Utilities, fuels, and public services	100	88	99	93	101
Natural gas	100	104	102	83	102
Electricity	100	73	105	90	101
Fuel oil and other fuels	100	39	43	27	121
Telephone services	100	100	101	105	99
Water and other public services	100	103	93	100	101
Household services	100	142	72	67	110
Personal services	100	203	77	80	107
Other household services	100	108	69	60	111
Housekeeping supplies	100	64	69	87	107
Laundry and cleaning supplies	100	74	107	134	94
Other household products	100	62	57	75	110
Postage and stationery	100	57	58	66	112
Household furnishings and equipment	100	86	62	75	110
Household textiles	100	63	48	67	114
Furniture	100	106	85	87	104
Floor coverings	100	55	50	35	120

	total consumer units	Asian	black	Hispanic	non-Hispanic white and other
Major appliances	100	79	78	66	109
Small appliances and miscellaneous housewares	100	93	44	69	115
Miscellaneous household equipment	100	81	51	74	112
APPAREL AND RELATED SERVICES	**100**	**134**	**96**	**114**	**99**
Men and boys	**100**	**149**	**80**	**128**	**99**
Men, aged 16 or older	100	155	69	124	101
Boys, aged 2 to 15	100	125	124	145	89
Women and girls	**100**	**126**	**87**	**93**	**103**
Women, aged 16 or older	100	126	83	88	104
Girls, aged 2 to 15	100	128	109	120	96
Children under age 2	**100**	**160**	**113**	**134**	**93**
Footwear	**100**	**107**	**141**	**141**	**88**
Other apparel products and services	**100**	**159**	**82**	**113**	**100**
TRANSPORTATION	**100**	**124**	**72**	**91**	**106**
Vehicle purchases	**100**	**129**	**60**	**83**	**109**
Cars and trucks, new	100	185	50	55	116
Cars and trucks, used	100	82	72	113	103
Other vehicles	100	13	22	9	128
Gasoline and motor oil	**100**	**86**	**84**	**102**	**102**
Other vehicle expenses	**100**	**125**	**75**	**89**	**106**
Vehicle finance charges	100	72	83	92	104
Maintenance and repairs	100	89	73	79	108
Vehicle insurance	100	164	78	95	104
Vehicle rentals, leases, licenses, other charges	100	134	66	89	107
Public transportation	**100**	**285**	**55**	**81**	**110**
HEALTH CARE	**100**	**88**	**57**	**54**	**114**
Health insurance	100	98	64	52	114
Medical services	100	87	39	59	117
Drugs	100	58	61	48	115
Medical supplies	100	63	44	56	116
ENTERTAINMENT	**100**	**89**	**56**	**68**	**112**
Fees and admissions	100	129	34	57	118
Audio and visual equipment and services	100	89	93	86	103
Pets, toys, and playground equipment	100	43	34	62	116
Other entertainment products and services	100	107	30	45	120
PERSONAL CARE PRODUCTS AND SERVICES	**100**	**95**	**84**	**96**	**103**
READING	**100**	**97**	**42**	**40**	**120**
EDUCATION	**100**	**216**	**46**	**59**	**115**
TOBACCO PRODUCTS AND SMOKING SUPPLIES	**100**	**43**	**74**	**47**	**113**
MISCELLANEOUS	**100**	**90**	**67**	**61**	**111**
CASH CONTRIBUTIONS	**100**	**82**	**78**	**47**	**112**
PERSONAL INSURANCE AND PENSIONS	**100**	**143**	**66**	**74**	**110**
Life and other personal insurance	100	106	79	36	114
Pensions and Social Security	100	146	65	77	109
PERSONAL TAXES	**100**	**194**	**25**	**23**	**125**
Federal income taxes	100	221	14	17	128
State and local income taxes	100	144	48	37	119
Other taxes	100	99	46	32	120
GIFTS FOR PEOPLE IN OTHER HOUSEHOLDS	**100**	**108**	**48**	**56**	**116**

Note: "Asian" and "black" include Hispanics and non-Hispanics who identify themselves as being of the respective race alone. "Hispanic" includes people of any race who identify themselves as Hispanic. "Other" includes people who identify themselves as non-Hispanic and as Alaska Native, American Indian, Asian (who are also included in the "Asian" column), or Native Hawaiian or other Pacific Islander, as well as non-Hispanics reporting more than one race.
Source: Calculations by New Strategist based on the Bureau of Labor Statistics' 2011 Consumer Expenditure Survey

Spending by Region, 2011

Households in the West and Northeast spent nearly $55,000 on average in 2011, 10 percent more than the average household. Households in the Midwest and the South spent, respectively, 5 and 8 percent less than average in 2011.

Households in the Northeast and West spend more than the average household on most products and services, whereas those in the Midwest and the South spend less than average on most items. Households in the Northeast spend the most by far on property taxes—63 percent more than average. Those in the West spend the most on mortgage interest and rent. Households in the Midwest spend the most on laundry and cleaning supplies. Households in the Midwest and the South spend 15 percent less than average on alcoholic beverages. Southern households spend more than households in other regions on pork, vehicle finance charges, and tobacco and smoking supplies.

Households in the Northeast spend three times the average on fuel oil. The biggest consumers of natural gas, households in the Northeast and Midwest, spend, respectively, 42 and 43 percent more than the average household on this item. Households in the South spend the most on electricity. Western households spend 23 percent more than the average household on water and other public services. Average household spending on public transportation is highest in the Northeast.

Table 1.12 Average spending by region, 2011

(average annual spending of consumer units by product and service category and region of residence, 2011)

	total consumder units	Northeast	Midwest	South	West
Number of consumer units (in 000s)	122,287	22,538	27,107	44,901	27,741
Average number of persons per consumer unit	2.5	2.4	2.4	2.5	2.6
Average before-tax income of consumer units	$63,685	$71,733	$60,897	$58,780	$67,810
Average annual spending of consumer units	49,705	54,547	47,192	45,699	54,745
FOOD	**6,458**	**6,799**	**6,236**	**5,980**	**7,188**
Food at home	3,838	4,099	3,841	3,505	4,169
Cereals and bakery products	531	610	545	478	538
Cereals and cereal products	175	205	171	154	189
Bakery products	356	405	375	324	348
Meats, poultry, fish, and eggs	832	882	791	811	868
Beef	223	215	219	218	241
Pork	162	152	161	174	151
Other meats	123	149	141	107	107
Poultry	154	168	132	154	167
Fish and seafood	121	146	91	111	146
Eggs	50	52	47	48	56
Dairy products	407	444	409	356	458
Fresh milk and cream	150	149	143	142	169
Other dairy products	257	295	267	213	289
Fruits and vegetables	715	811	696	612	825
Fresh fruits	247	278	243	201	302
Fresh vegetables	224	261	203	189	273
Processed fruits	116	131	119	98	128
Processed vegetables	128	140	130	123	121
Other food at home	1,353	1,351	1,401	1,248	1,481
Sugar and other sweets	144	149	153	123	167
Fats and oils	110	113	111	102	117
Miscellaneous foods	690	666	735	637	755
Nonalcoholic beverages	361	374	359	347	374
Food prepared by consumer unit on trips	48	49	42	38	67
Food away from home	**2,620**	**2,700**	**2,395**	**2,474**	**3,019**
ALCOHOLIC BEVERAGES	**456**	**491**	**387**	**386**	**614**
HOUSING	**16,803**	**19,557**	**14,926**	**14,968**	**19,373**
Shelter	9,825	12,033	8,409	8,110	12,193
Owned dwellings	6,148	7,642	5,691	5,110	7,060
Mortgage interest and charges	3,184	3,305	2,632	2,741	4,341
Property taxes	1,845	3,000	1,936	1,340	1,634
Maintenance, repair, insurance, other expenses	1,120	1,338	1,124	1,029	1,085
Rented dwellings	3,029	3,567	2,153	2,505	4,297
Other lodging	648	823	565	494	835
Utilities, fuels, and public services	**3,727**	**4,096**	**3,486**	**3,898**	**3,385**
Natural gas	420	596	600	243	387
Electricity	1,423	1,338	1,225	1,763	1,135
Fuel oil and other fuels	157	487	121	70	64
Telephone services	1,226	1,291	1,136	1,276	1,182
Water and other public services	501	384	406	545	617
Household services	**1,122**	**1,267**	**934**	**967**	**1,439**
Personal services	398	499	334	282	568
Other household services	724	768	601	686	870
Housekeeping supplies	**615**	**641**	**645**	**567**	**642**
Laundry and cleaning supplies	145	134	156	142	149
Other household products	340	385	365	311	324
Postage and stationery	130	122	124	114	169
Household furnishings and equipment	**1,514**	**1,520**	**1,451**	**1,427**	**1,714**
Household textiles	109	102	99	95	149
Furniture	358	356	370	360	345
Floor coverings	20	41	24	12	12

	total consumer units	Northeast	Midwest	South	West
Major appliances	$194	$184	$183	$199	$204
Small appliances and miscellaneous housewares	89	93	87	70	120
Miscellaneous household equipment	744	745	689	691	883
APPAREL AND RELATED SERVICES	**1,740**	**1,905**	**1,624**	**1,615**	**1,926**
Men and boys	**404**	**445**	**354**	**392**	**438**
Men, aged 16 or older	324	355	283	324	341
Boys, aged 2 to 15	80	90	71	69	98
Women and girls	**721**	**776**	**738**	**648**	**780**
Women, aged 16 or older	604	638	643	541	640
Girls, aged 2 to 15	117	137	96	107	140
Children under age 2	**68**	**74**	**60**	**71**	**67**
Footwear	**321**	**331**	**292**	**308**	**363**
Other apparel products and services	**226**	**279**	**179**	**195**	**277**
TRANSPORTATION	**8,293**	**8,435**	**8,114**	**8,264**	**8,399**
Vehicle purchases	**2,669**	**2,675**	**2,805**	**2,736**	**2,420**
Cars and trucks, new	1,265	1,417	1,255	1,290	1,113
Cars and trucks, used	1,339	1,161	1,464	1,403	1,257
Other vehicles	64	97	86	43	50
Gasoline and motor oil	**2,655**	**2,510**	**2,632**	**2,794**	**2,569**
Other vehicle expenses	**2,454**	**2,519**	**2,223**	**2,400**	**2,713**
Vehicle finance charges	233	198	220	267	216
Maintenance and repairs	805	823	759	719	975
Vehicle insurance	983	870	848	1,098	1,023
Vehicle rentals, leases, licenses, other charges	433	628	395	316	499
Public transportation	**516**	**730**	**453**	**334**	**698**
HEALTH CARE	**3,313**	**3,368**	**3,620**	**3,160**	**3,216**
Health insurance	1,922	2,023	2,029	1,846	1,859
Medical services	768	788	928	677	742
Drugs	489	425	508	507	495
Medical supplies	134	132	155	131	120
ENTERTAINMENT	**2,572**	**2,632**	**2,505**	**2,350**	**2,950**
Fees and admissions	594	710	583	443	757
Audio and visual equipment and services	977	1,033	936	984	959
Pets, toys, and playground equipment	631	541	613	661	671
Other entertainment products and services	370	349	374	261	563
PERSONAL CARE PRODUCTS AND SERVICES	**634**	**627**	**582**	**606**	**739**
READING	**115**	**130**	**123**	**88**	**140**
EDUCATION	**1,051**	**1,620**	**1,095**	**680**	**1,145**
TOBACCO PRODUCTS AND SMOKING SUPPLIES	**351**	**356**	**364**	**391**	**268**
MISCELLANEOUS	**775**	**858**	**764**	**661**	**903**
CASH CONTRIBUTIONS	**1,721**	**1,809**	**1,675**	**1,613**	**1,869**
PERSONAL INSURANCE AND PENSIONS	**5,424**	**5,961**	**5,178**	**4,936**	**6,016**
Life and other personal insurance	317	406	296	307	282
Pensions and Social Security	5,106	5,554	4,882	4,629	5,734
PERSONAL TAXES	**2,012**	**2,398**	**1,502**	**1,575**	**2,901**
Federal income taxes	1,370	1,539	946	1,111	2,068
State and local income taxes	505	653	476	299	748
Other taxes	136	206	80	165	86
GIFTS FOR PEOPLE IN OTHER HOUSEHOLDS	**1,037**	**1,332**	**1,014**	**823**	**1,171**

Note: Spending by category does not add to total spending because gift spending is also included in the preceding product and service categories and personal taxes are not included in the total.
Source: Bureau of Labor Statistics, 2011 Consumer Expenditure Survey, Internet site http://www.bls.gov/cex/

Table 1.13 Indexed spending by region, 2011

(indexed average annual spending of consumer units by product and service category and region of residence, 2011; index definition: an index of 100 is the average for all consumer units; an index of 125 means that spending by consumer units in that group is 25 percent above the average for all consumer units; an index of 75 indicates spending that is 25 percent below the average for all consumer units)

	total consumder units	Northeast	Midwest	South	West
Average spending of consumer units, total	$49,705	$54,547	$47,192	$45,699	$54,745
Average spending of consumer units, index	100	110	95	92	110
FOOD	100	105	97	93	111
Food at home	100	107	100	91	109
Cereals and bakery products	100	115	103	90	101
Cereals and cereal products	100	117	98	88	108
Bakery products	100	114	105	91	98
Meats, poultry, fish, and eggs	100	106	95	97	104
Beef	100	96	98	98	108
Pork	100	94	99	107	93
Other meats	100	121	115	87	87
Poultry	100	109	86	100	108
Fish and seafood	100	121	75	92	121
Eggs	100	104	94	96	112
Dairy products	100	109	100	87	113
Fresh milk and cream	100	99	95	95	113
Other dairy products	100	115	104	83	112
Fruits and vegetables	100	113	97	86	115
Fresh fruits	100	113	98	81	122
Fresh vegetables	100	117	91	84	122
Processed fruits	100	113	103	84	110
Processed vegetables	100	109	102	96	95
Other food at home	100	100	104	92	109
Sugar and other sweets	100	103	106	85	116
Fats and oils	100	103	101	93	106
Miscellaneous foods	100	97	107	92	109
Nonalcoholic beverages	100	104	99	96	104
Food prepared by consumer unit on trips	100	102	88	79	140
Food away from home	100	103	91	94	115
ALCOHOLIC BEVERAGES	100	108	85	85	135
HOUSING	100	116	89	89	115
Shelter	100	122	86	83	124
Owned dwellings	100	124	93	83	115
Mortgage interest and charges	100	104	83	86	136
Property taxes	100	163	105	73	89
Maintenance, repair, insurance, other expenses	100	119	100	92	97
Rented dwellings	100	118	71	83	142
Other lodging	100	127	87	76	129
Utilities, fuels, and public services	100	110	94	105	91
Natural gas	100	142	143	58	92
Electricity	100	94	86	124	80
Fuel oil and other fuels	100	310	77	45	41
Telephone services	100	105	93	104	96
Water and other public services	100	77	81	109	123
Household services	100	113	83	86	128
Personal services	100	125	84	71	143
Other household services	100	106	83	95	120
Housekeeping supplies	100	104	105	92	104
Laundry and cleaning supplies	100	92	108	98	103
Other household products	100	113	107	91	95
Postage and stationery	100	94	95	88	130
Household furnishings and equipment	100	100	96	94	113
Household textiles	100	94	91	87	137
Furniture	100	99	103	101	96
Floor coverings	100	205	120	60	60

	total consumer units	Northeast	Midwest	South	West
Major appliances	100	95	94	103	105
Small appliances and miscellaneous housewares	100	104	98	79	135
Miscellaneous household equipment	100	100	93	93	119
APPAREL AND RELATED SERVICES	**100**	**109**	**93**	**93**	**111**
Men and boys	**100**	**110**	**88**	**97**	**108**
Men, aged 16 or older	100	110	87	100	105
Boys, aged 2 to 15	100	113	89	86	123
Women and girls	**100**	**108**	**102**	**90**	**108**
Women, aged 16 or older	100	106	106	90	106
Girls, aged 2 to 15	100	117	82	91	120
Children under age 2	**100**	**109**	**88**	**104**	**99**
Footwear	**100**	**103**	**91**	**96**	**113**
Other apparel products and services	**100**	**123**	**79**	**86**	**123**
TRANSPORTATION	**100**	**102**	**98**	**100**	**101**
Vehicle purchases	**100**	**100**	**105**	**103**	**91**
Cars and trucks, new	100	112	99	102	88
Cars and trucks, used	100	87	109	105	94
Other vehicles	100	152	134	67	78
Gasoline and motor oil	**100**	**95**	**99**	**105**	**97**
Other vehicle expenses	**100**	**103**	**91**	**98**	**111**
Vehicle finance charges	100	85	94	115	93
Maintenance and repairs	100	102	94	89	121
Vehicle insurance	100	89	86	112	104
Vehicle rentals, leases, licenses, other charges	100	145	91	73	115
Public transportation	**100**	**141**	**88**	**65**	**135**
HEALTH CARE	**100**	**102**	**109**	**95**	**97**
Health insurance	100	105	106	96	97
Medical services	100	103	121	88	97
Drugs	100	87	104	104	101
Medical supplies	100	99	116	98	90
ENTERTAINMENT	**100**	**102**	**97**	**91**	**115**
Fees and admissions	100	120	98	75	127
Audio and visual equipment and services	100	106	96	101	98
Pets, toys, and playground equipment	100	86	97	105	106
Other entertainment products and services	100	94	101	71	152
PERSONAL CARE PRODUCTS AND SERVICES	**100**	**99**	**92**	**96**	**117**
READING	**100**	**113**	**107**	**77**	**122**
EDUCATION	**100**	**154**	**104**	**65**	**109**
TOBACCO PRODUCTS AND SMOKING SUPPLIES	**100**	**101**	**104**	**111**	**76**
MISCELLANEOUS	**100**	**111**	**99**	**85**	**117**
CASH CONTRIBUTIONS	**100**	**105**	**97**	**94**	**109**
PERSONAL INSURANCE AND PENSIONS	**100**	**110**	**95**	**91**	**111**
Life and other personal insurance	100	128	93	97	89
Pensions and Social Security	100	109	96	91	112
PERSONAL TAXES	**100**	**119**	**75**	**78**	**144**
Federal income taxes	100	112	69	81	151
State and local income taxes	100	129	94	59	148
Other taxes	100	151	59	121	63
GIFTS FOR PEOPLE IN OTHER HOUSEHOLDS	**100**	**128**	**98**	**79**	**113**

Source: Calculations by New Strategist based on the Bureau of Labor Statistics' 2011 Consumer Expenditure Survey

Spending by Education, 2011

Because college graduates have the highest incomes, their spending is well above average. Households headed by college graduates spent $68,903 on average in 2011, or 39 percent more than the average household. In contrast, households headed by people who did not graduate from high school spent only $29,951 on average, 40 percent less than the average household.

Households headed by the least educated—those without a high school diploma—spend more than average on only a few items. These include pork, beef, poultry, eggs, infants' apparel, tobacco, and rent.

Households headed by high school graduates spent $39,704 on average in 2011, or 20 percent less than the average household. Their spending is below average in most categories, tobacco products being the sole substantial exception. Householders with some college experience or an associate's degree make up the largest share of households (31 percent). Their spending is close to the average on most items.

College graduates, who account for 30 percent of households, far outspend the average on most items—particularly those favored by the affluent. These include public transportation (which includes airfares), "other lodging" (which includes college dorms, vacation homes, and hotels and motels), and fees and admissions to entertainment events. They also spend close to twice the average on education.

Table 1.14 Average spending by education of householder, 2011   OVERVIEW

(average annual spending of consumer units by product and service category and educational attainment of consumer unit reference person, 2011)

	total consumer units	not a high school graduate	high school graduate	some college or associate's degree	bachelor's degree or more
Number of consumer units (in 000s)	122,287	16,146	30,810	38,273	37,058
Average number of persons per consumer unit	2.5	2.8	2.5	2.4	2.5
Average before-tax income of consumer units	$63,685	$32,564	$46,370	$56,574	$98,983
Average annual spending of consumer units	49,705	29,951	39,704	47,198	68,903
FOOD	**6,458**	**4,971**	**5,648**	**6,102**	**8,026**
Food at home	**3,838**	**3,564**	**3,595**	**3,599**	**4,365**
Cereals and bakery products	531	486	495	498	606
Cereals and cereal products	175	176	154	163	202
Bakery products	356	310	341	335	404
Meats, poultry, fish, and eggs	832	883	812	799	862
Beef	223	248	217	221	219
Pork	162	182	170	163	147
Other meats	123	117	128	111	132
Poultry	154	175	149	143	163
Fish and seafood	121	106	98	112	152
Eggs	50	55	50	48	50
Dairy products	407	359	357	386	484
Fresh milk and cream	150	150	140	146	162
Other dairy products	257	209	218	241	322
Fruits and vegetables	715	651	642	627	881
Fresh fruits	247	217	212	207	325
Fresh vegetables	224	202	198	189	287
Processed fruits	116	102	104	113	133
Processed vegetables	128	130	128	117	137
Other food at home	1,353	1,186	1,288	1,289	1,532
Sugar and other sweets	144	118	135	141	165
Fats and oils	110	114	114	105	110
Miscellaneous foods	690	569	651	656	800
Nonalcoholic beverages	361	357	363	347	374
Food prepared by consumer unit on trips	48	28	26	40	82
Food away from home	**2,620**	**1,407**	**2,053**	**2,503**	**3,661**
ALCOHOLIC BEVERAGES	**456**	**155**	**287**	**440**	**722**
HOUSING	**16,803**	**10,843**	**13,571**	**15,760**	**23,123**
Shelter	**9,825**	**6,238**	**7,585**	**8,954**	**14,152**
Owned dwellings	6,148	2,651	4,443	5,310	9,954
Mortgage interest and charges	3,184	1,238	2,230	2,786	5,234
Property taxes	1,845	845	1,373	1,531	2,995
Maintenance, repair, insurance, other expenses	1,120	567	839	992	1,725
Rented dwellings	3,029	3,441	2,845	3,166	2,862
Other lodging	648	146	297	477	1,335
Utilities, fuels, and public services	**3,727**	**3,074**	**3,622**	**3,647**	**4,180**
Natural gas	420	318	375	379	543
Electricity	1,423	1,285	1,458	1,392	1,486
Fuel oil and other fuels	157	122	168	131	189
Telephone services	1,226	947	1,167	1,251	1,372
Water and other public services	501	402	453	494	590
Household services	**1,122**	**432**	**714**	**1,027**	**1,859**
Personal services	398	141	201	344	731
Other household services	724	291	513	684	1,128
Housekeeping supplies	**615**	**429**	**536**	**599**	**762**
Laundry and cleaning supplies	145	142	144	145	147
Other household products	340	211	294	337	427
Postage and stationery	130	76	98	117	189
Household furnishings and equipment	**1,514**	**669**	**1,114**	**1,533**	**2,169**
Household textiles	109	67	78	97	163
Furniture	358	167	270	345	527
Floor coverings	20	5	11	9	45

	total consumer units	not a high school graduate	high school graduate	some college or associate's degree	bachelor's degree or more
Major appliances	$194	$102	$145	$225	$243
Small appliances and miscellaneous housewares	89	37	67	85	132
Miscellaneous household equipment	744	292	542	774	1,059
APPAREL AND RELATED SERVICES	**1,740**	**1,274**	**1,385**	**1,597**	**2,343**
Men and boys	**404**	**262**	**342**	**398**	**513**
Men, aged 16 or older	324	193	272	316	424
Boys, aged 2 to 15	80	69	70	82	90
Women and girls	**721**	**471**	**550**	**635**	**1,033**
Women, aged 16 or older	604	370	451	517	896
Girls, aged 2 to 15	117	101	99	118	137
Children under age 2	**68**	**76**	**57**	**62**	**79**
Footwear	**321**	**297**	**278**	**305**	**380**
Other apparel products and services	**226**	**168**	**157**	**197**	**337**
TRANSPORTATION	**8,293**	**4,859**	**7,120**	**8,366**	**10,662**
Vehicle purchases	**2,669**	**1,231**	**2,258**	**2,753**	**3,549**
Cars and trucks, new	1,265	206	887	1,195	2,114
Cars and trucks, used	1,339	984	1,326	1,480	1,358
Other vehicles	64	42	46	77	76
Gasoline and motor oil	**2,655**	**2,006**	**2,552**	**2,751**	**2,924**
Other vehicle expenses	**2,454**	**1,388**	**2,061**	**2,510**	**3,158**
Vehicle finance charges	233	110	206	272	268
Maintenance and repairs	805	427	634	811	1,099
Vehicle insurance	983	647	930	1,046	1,088
Vehicle rentals, leases, licenses, other charges	433	203	291	381	704
Public transportation	**516**	**233**	**249**	**352**	**1,031**
HEALTH CARE	**3,313**	**2,257**	**2,986**	**3,165**	**4,192**
Health insurance	1,922	1,325	1,803	1,787	2,421
Medical services	768	444	612	761	1,045
Drugs	489	403	458	496	541
Medical supplies	134	85	113	121	185
ENTERTAINMENT	**2,572**	**1,223**	**1,967**	**2,585**	**3,616**
Fees and admissions	594	127	289	478	1,163
Audio and visual equipment and services	977	645	926	995	1,140
Pets, toys, and playground equipment	631	330	529	631	829
Other entertainment products and services	370	122	223	482	484
PERSONAL CARE PRODUCTS AND SERVICES	**634**	**367**	**479**	**603**	**901**
READING	**115**	**40**	**70**	**102**	**200**
EDUCATION	**1,051**	**252**	**380**	**1,061**	**1,943**
TOBACCO PRODUCTS AND SMOKING SUPPLIES	**351**	**400**	**521**	**385**	**152**
MISCELLANEOUS	**775**	**392**	**615**	**807**	**1,040**
CASH CONTRIBUTIONS	**1,721**	**769**	**1,144**	**1,468**	**2,878**
PERSONAL INSURANCE AND PENSIONS	**5,424**	**2,150**	**3,533**	**4,759**	**9,108**
Life and other personal insurance	317	136	264	281	477
Pensions and Social Security	5,106	2,014	3,269	4,477	8,631
PERSONAL TAXES	**2,012**	**62**	**707**	**1,309**	**4,672**
Federal income taxes	1,370	−79	351	807	3,432
State and local income taxes	505	92	256	376	1,027
Other taxes	136	50	100	126	214
GIFTS FOR PEOPLE IN OTHER HOUSEHOLDS	**1,037**	**408**	**653**	**891**	**1,769**

Note: Spending by category does not add to total spending because gift spending is also included in the preceding product and service categories and personal taxes are not included in the total.
Source: Bureau of Labor Statistics, 2011 Consumer Expenditure Survey, Internet site http://www.bls.gov/cex/

Table 1.15 Indexed spending by education of householder, 2011

OVERVIEW

(indexed average annual spending of consumer units by product and service category and educational attainment of consumer unit reference person, 2011; index definition: an index of 100 is the average for all consumer units; an index of 125 means that spending by consumer units in that group is 25 percent above the average for all consumer units; an index of 75 indicates spending that is 25 percent below the average for all consumer units)

	total consumer units	not a high school graduate	high school graduate	some college or associate's degree	bachelor's degree or more
Average spending of consumer units, total	$49,705	$29,951	$39,704	$47,198	$68,903
Average spending of consumer units, index	100	60	80	95	139
FOOD	100	77	87	94	124
Food at home	100	93	94	94	114
Cereals and bakery products	100	92	93	94	114
Cereals and cereal products	100	101	88	93	115
Bakery products	100	87	96	94	113
Meats, poultry, fish, and eggs	100	106	98	96	104
Beef	100	111	97	99	98
Pork	100	112	105	101	91
Other meats	100	95	104	90	107
Poultry	100	114	97	93	106
Fish and seafood	100	88	81	93	126
Eggs	100	110	100	97	100
Dairy products	100	88	88	95	119
Fresh milk and cream	100	100	93	97	108
Other dairy products	100	81	85	94	125
Fruits and vegetables	100	91	90	88	123
Fresh fruits	100	88	86	84	132
Fresh vegetables	100	90	88	85	128
Processed fruits	100	88	90	97	115
Processed vegetables	100	102	100	92	107
Other food at home	100	88	95	95	113
Sugar and other sweets	100	82	94	98	115
Fats and oils	100	104	104	95	100
Miscellaneous foods	100	82	94	95	116
Nonalcoholic beverages	100	99	101	96	104
Food prepared by consumer unit on trips	100	58	54	83	171
Food away from home	100	54	78	96	140
ALCOHOLIC BEVERAGES	100	34	63	96	158
HOUSING	100	65	81	94	138
Shelter	100	63	77	91	144
Owned dwellings	100	43	72	86	162
Mortgage interest and charges	100	39	70	88	164
Property taxes	100	46	74	83	162
Maintenance, repair, insurance, other expenses	100	51	75	89	154
Rented dwellings	100	114	94	105	94
Other lodging	100	23	46	74	206
Utilities, fuels, and public services	100	82	97	98	112
Natural gas	100	76	89	90	129
Electricity	100	90	102	98	104
Fuel oil and other fuels	100	78	107	84	120
Telephone services	100	77	95	102	112
Water and other public services	100	80	90	99	118
Household services	100	39	64	92	166
Personal services	100	35	51	86	184
Other household services	100	40	71	94	156
Housekeeping supplies	100	70	87	97	124
Laundry and cleaning supplies	100	98	99	100	101
Other household products	100	62	86	99	126
Postage and stationery	100	58	75	90	145
Household furnishings and equipment	100	44	74	101	143
Household textiles	100	61	72	89	150
Furniture	100	47	75	96	147
Floor coverings	100	25	55	43	225

	total consumer units	not a high school graduate	high school graduate	some college or associate's degree	bachelor's degree or more
Major appliances	100	53	75	116	125
Small appliances and miscellaneous housewares	100	42	75	95	148
Miscellaneous household equipment	100	39	73	104	142
APPAREL AND RELATED SERVICES	**100**	**73**	**80**	**92**	**135**
Men and boys	**100**	**65**	**85**	**98**	**127**
Men, aged 16 or older	100	60	84	97	131
Boys, aged 2 to 15	100	86	88	102	113
Women and girls	**100**	**65**	**76**	**88**	**143**
Women, aged 16 or older	100	61	75	86	148
Girls, aged 2 to 15	100	86	85	101	117
Children under age 2	**100**	**112**	**84**	**92**	**116**
Footwear	**100**	**93**	**87**	**95**	**118**
Other apparel products and services	**100**	**74**	**69**	**87**	**149**
TRANSPORTATION	**100**	**59**	**86**	**101**	**129**
Vehicle purchases	**100**	**46**	**85**	**103**	**133**
Cars and trucks, new	100	16	70	94	167
Cars and trucks, used	100	73	99	111	101
Other vehicles	100	66	72	120	119
Gasoline and motor oil	**100**	**76**	**96**	**104**	**110**
Other vehicle expenses	**100**	**57**	**84**	**102**	**129**
Vehicle finance charges	100	47	88	117	115
Maintenance and repairs	100	53	79	101	137
Vehicle insurance	100	66	95	106	111
Vehicle rentals, leases, licenses, other charges	100	47	67	88	163
Public transportation	**100**	**45**	**48**	**68**	**200**
HEALTH CARE	**100**	**68**	**90**	**96**	**127**
Health insurance	100	69	94	93	126
Medical services	100	58	80	99	136
Drugs	100	82	94	101	111
Medical supplies	100	63	84	90	138
ENTERTAINMENT	**100**	**48**	**76**	**101**	**141**
Fees and admissions	100	21	49	81	196
Audio and visual equipment and services	100	66	95	102	117
Pets, toys, and playground equipment	100	52	84	100	131
Other entertainment products and services	100	33	60	130	131
PERSONAL CARE PRODUCTS AND SERVICES	**100**	**58**	**76**	**95**	**142**
READING	**100**	**35**	**61**	**89**	**174**
EDUCATION	**100**	**24**	**36**	**101**	**185**
TOBACCO PRODUCTS AND SMOKING SUPPLIES	**100**	**114**	**148**	**110**	**43**
MISCELLANEOUS	**100**	**51**	**79**	**104**	**134**
CASH CONTRIBUTIONS	**100**	**45**	**66**	**85**	**167**
PERSONAL INSURANCE AND PENSIONS	**100**	**40**	**65**	**88**	**168**
Life and other personal insurance	100	43	83	89	150
Pensions and Social Security	100	39	64	88	169
PERSONAL TAXES	**100**	**3**	**35**	**65**	**232**
Federal income taxes	100	−6	26	59	251
State and local income taxes	100	18	51	74	203
Other taxes	100	37	74	93	157
GIFTS FOR PEOPLE IN OTHER HOUSEHOLDS	**100**	**39**	**63**	**86**	**171**

Source: Calculations by New Strategist based on the Bureau of Labor Statistics' 2011 Consumer Expenditure Survey

CHAPTER 2

Spending on Apparel, 2011

Americans are spending ever less on apparel. In 2011, the average household spent $1,740 on clothes, shoes, and related items, or 28 percent less than the inflation-adjusted $2,424 spent in 2000. Spending declined in every apparel subcategory over the period. Overall, Americans devoted 3.5 percent of their spending to clothes, shoes, and related products and services in 2011, down from 4.9 percent in 2000.

Households headed by people aged 35 to 44 spent the most on apparel, $2,227 on average in 2011. Apparel spending patterns differ sharply by age. Householders aged 35 to 44 spend the most on boys' and girls' apparel—over twice the average. Householders aged 25 to 34 spend more than twice the average on infants' apparel. Householders aged 55 to 64 spend 21 percent more than average on men's apparel—more than any other age group. Householders aged 45 to 54 are the biggest spenders on women's clothes and spent 21 percent more than the average household on these in 2011.

Spending on apparel rises with income. Households with incomes of $100,000 or more spend about twice the average on clothing. They account for 18 percent of households but for over half the market for men's suits and sports coats, 58 percent of the market for professional dry cleaning, and 50 percent of the market for jewelry. In contrast, households with incomes of $100,000 or more account for only 5 percent of the market for coin-operated apparel laundry and dry cleaning.

Married couples with adult children at home spend more on apparel than any other household type, in part because their households are larger than average. Married couples without children at home (most of them empty-nesters) spend one-and-one-half times the average or more on women's sport coats and tailored jackets, sweaters and vests, material for making clothes, apparel alteration and tailoring, and jewelry. Single parents spend over twice the average on boys' and girls' clothes and children's footwear.

Among race and Hispanic origin groups, Asian households are the biggest spenders on apparel, in part because they have the highest incomes. Asians spent 34 percent more than the average household on apparel in 2011. Hispanics spend 14 percent more than the average household on apparel, while blacks and non-Hispanic whites spend about an average amount. Hispanics and blacks are the biggest spenders on footwear. Asians, blacks, and Hispanics spend much more than average on coin-operated apparel laundry, while non-Hispanic whites spend less.

Spending on apparel is greatest in the West and Northeast, where households devoted over $1,900 to clothes and related services in 2011—10 to 11 percent more than the average household. Households in the South and Midwest spend 7 percent less than average on apparel and related services.

Educated householders spend the most on clothes because they have the highest incomes. Households headed by people with a bachelor's degree spent $2,343 on clothes in 2011—35 percent more than the average household. College graduates, who represent 30 percent of households, account for 54 percent of the market for jewelry, 61 percent of the market for men's suits, and 59 percent of the market for men's sport coats and tailored jackets. The least-educated householders spend over twice the average on coin-operated laundries and 55 percent more on material for making clothes.

Table 2.1 Apparel: Average spending by age, 2011

(average annual spending of consumer units on apparel, accessories, and related services, by age of consumer unit reference person, 2011)

	total consumer units	under 25	25 to 34	35 to 44	45 to 54	55 to 64	65 to 74	75+
Number of consumer units (in 000s)	122,287	7,743	20,463	21,699	24,821	21,688	14,079	11,794
Average number of persons per consumer unit	2.5	2.1	2.9	3.3	2.8	2.1	1.9	1.6
Average before-tax income of consumer units	$63,685.00	$27,514.00	$58,179.00	$77,376.00	$78,519.00	$75,517.00	$52,521.00	$32,144.00
Average spending of consumer units, total	49,704.88	29,911.52	48,097.39	57,271.07	58,050.42	53,615.86	44,645.56	32,688.34
Apparel, average spending	**1,739.79**	**1,448.14**	**1,817.72**	**2,226.97**	**1,977.96**	**1,718.57**	**1,194.71**	**1,051.96**
MEN'S APPAREL	**324.14**	**309.36**	**334.74**	**375.01**	**352.87**	**392.85**	**213.03**	**156.45**
Suits	18.46	17.08	16.29	19.22	25.28	19.13	13.87	11.63
Sport coats and tailored jackets	5.26	1.46	4.41	8.43	4.02	7.02	6.16	1.75
Coats and jackets	26.83	32.18	29.50	41.66	21.55	30.69	16.54	6.79
Underwear	21.14	18.32	21.84	23.94	18.87	25.19	17.75	17.52
Hosiery	14.56	11.18	14.10	17.28	18.16	14.01	13.18	7.46
Nightwear	1.63	0.92	1.11	2.11	1.97	1.67	1.90	1.00
Accessories	29.84	40.03	41.27	34.84	31.21	27.18	18.80	8.23
Sweaters and vests	17.02	12.13	19.56	14.08	15.20	24.02	8.35	21.58
Active sportswear	24.92	16.55	16.42	37.25	41.71	20.67	15.68	5.77
Shirts	85.41	67.53	89.23	103.98	85.48	112.98	55.29	37.45
Pants and shorts	76.02	87.99	76.80	66.75	85.68	108.93	45.02	36.62
Uniforms	2.54	2.63	3.41	4.71	3.12	1.36	0.26	0.63
Costumes	0.51	1.36	0.80	0.75	0.62	–	0.24	0.02
BOYS' (AGED 2 TO 15) APPAREL	**79.63**	**25.17**	**100.06**	**184.11**	**78.34**	**42.80**	**29.32**	**16.31**
Coats and jackets	5.31	1.59	6.23	12.23	5.51	3.26	1.37	1.44
Sweaters	2.07	0.98	2.82	3.91	1.68	1.00	2.49	0.41
Shirts	21.84	3.48	21.82	59.68	18.09	12.79	7.01	5.56
Underwear	6.55	2.39	7.04	16.61	5.97	4.21	1.46	1.18
Nightwear	1.54	0.25	2.16	3.20	1.49	1.00	0.75	0.33
Hosiery	4.96	2.48	7.96	9.66	4.73	2.22	2.32	1.09
Accessories	6.20	1.70	6.77	12.51	5.96	5.39	4.15	0.76
Suits, sport coats, and vests	0.91	0.26	1.19	1.65	1.67	0.23	0.13	0.08
Pants and shorts	25.22	11.27	36.59	53.75	27.64	10.17	8.43	4.78
Uniforms	2.65	0.56	4.16	5.28	3.13	1.46	0.50	0.31
Active sportswear	1.38	0.02	1.59	2.99	1.84	0.67	0.69	0.08
Costumes	1.00	0.20	1.73	2.64	0.63	0.40	0.02	0.29
WOMEN'S APPAREL	**603.77**	**468.33**	**568.65**	**603.59**	**732.89**	**652.90**	**477.01**	**533.13**
Coats and jackets	51.25	20.48	30.29	63.33	60.16	54.11	27.09	89.90
Dresses	70.93	49.13	85.88	72.88	101.35	60.60	45.46	38.50
Sport coats and tailored jackets	2.28	1.49	2.88	1.80	2.11	3.24	1.78	1.83
Sweaters and vests	50.08	54.42	45.02	37.76	52.83	68.55	22.67	69.87
Shirts, blouses, and tops	123.62	115.81	120.56	120.58	164.70	113.36	118.55	77.85
Skirts	11.91	3.40	9.50	12.94	14.40	15.19	12.96	7.04
Pants and shorts	94.85	64.91	96.00	105.31	110.96	99.11	73.02	75.30
Active sportswear	36.32	25.03	35.03	38.16	52.03	38.67	19.65	23.83
Nightwear	28.82	39.89	18.08	21.17	34.60	32.55	32.18	32.17
Undergarments	34.22	25.28	39.21	28.58	39.68	41.18	20.08	32.76
Hosiery	22.46	22.43	13.16	18.86	22.59	31.18	20.97	30.87
Suits	7.69	1.99	5.69	7.82	10.66	10.04	6.80	5.13
Accessories	64.67	39.52	60.90	68.86	60.92	80.52	74.34	46.44
Uniforms	3.33	2.69	4.87	3.73	3.85	3.62	1.20	1.30
Costumes	1.35	1.85	1.57	1.82	2.04	0.99	0.26	0.34

	total consumer units	under 25	25 to 34	35 to 44	45 to 54	55 to 64	65 to 74	75+
GIRLS' (AGED 2 TO 15) APPAREL	**$117.43**	**$29.20**	**$125.09**	**$238.35**	**$148.20**	**$73.86**	**$68.29**	**$11.39**
Coats and jackets	5.26	2.61	8.15	10.36	4.82	2.77	2.99	0.79
Dresses and suits	13.78	7.15	17.42	20.16	14.24	13.33	13.33	–
Shirts, blouses, and sweaters	33.03	2.46	27.47	69.46	41.58	23.37	24.77	4.74
Skirts, pants, and shorts	25.07	8.66	36.25	57.67	26.06	9.19	9.27	2.42
Active sportswear	15.27	2.60	9.50	32.10	24.56	13.21	3.80	–
Underwear and nightwear	9.59	2.26	9.09	17.86	14.29	5.65	6.14	1.34
Hosiery	6.08	1.56	7.94	10.23	9.42	3.06	2.44	0.71
Accessories	5.15	0.56	4.13	12.95	6.65	1.33	4.15	0.66
Uniforms	2.85	0.71	3.21	3.99	5.63	1.60	0.78	0.47
Costumes	1.35	0.62	1.92	3.58	0.95	0.35	0.62	0.26
CHILDREN'S (UNDER AGE 2) APPAREL	**68.13**	**129.46**	**146.25**	**102.55**	**44.75**	**28.74**	**16.97**	**7.71**
Coats, jackets, and snowsuits	0.93	1.79	1.98	1.74	0.49	0.26	0.08	0.26
Outerwear including dresses	9.47	13.80	19.94	11.81	5.69	6.01	6.31	2.24
Underwear	45.58	93.30	103.23	74.39	26.01	15.47	4.31	3.42
Nightwear and loungewear	1.65	2.33	3.43	1.63	0.91	1.35	1.51	0.46
Accessories	10.50	18.24	17.67	12.97	11.66	5.65	4.76	1.32
FOOTWEAR	**321.14**	**297.52**	**306.02**	**449.20**	**393.03**	**288.06**	**175.96**	**203.11**
Men's	96.84	124.72	96.71	112.37	124.75	102.00	50.62	34.48
Boys'	36.67	15.65	44.78	85.08	46.92	14.60	1.90	5.79
Women's	151.99	142.48	120.57	153.59	188.88	159.98	119.48	155.90
Girls'	35.63	14.67	43.95	98.17	32.48	11.48	3.96	6.94
OTHER APPAREL PRODUCTS AND SERVICES	**225.54**	**189.09**	**236.90**	**274.16**	**227.89**	**239.35**	**214.14**	**123.87**
Material for making clothes	9.65	6.22	3.28	5.91	15.90	10.97	17.32	5.76
Sewing patterns and notions	7.88	3.09	3.82	9.02	7.12	11.48	10.45	8.00
Watches	30.27	46.96	34.82	55.30	14.41	26.44	18.62	19.25
Jewelry	71.95	46.06	76.49	83.15	67.38	84.50	80.05	37.35
Shoe repair and other shoe services	1.50	0.73	1.16	1.73	1.52	1.93	2.15	0.61
Coin-operated apparel laundry and dry cleaning	39.63	67.11	68.79	47.58	33.98	25.08	20.86	17.45
Apparel alteration, repair, and tailoring services	6.37	3.63	7.77	4.96	6.38	7.84	7.80	3.95
Clothing rental	1.68	1.79	2.35	2.28	2.26	1.41	0.52	–
Watch and jewelry repair	5.43	0.20	1.58	5.31	3.98	7.71	10.18	8.96
Professional laundry, dry cleaning	50.10	12.99	36.08	58.00	72.51	61.06	45.49	22.48
Clothing storage	1.06	0.32	0.76	0.92	2.43	0.94	0.70	0.07

Note: Subcategories may not add to total because some are not shown. "–" means sample is too small to make a reliable estimate.
Source: Bureau of Labor Statistics, unpublished data from the 2011 Consumer Expenditure Survey

Table 2.2 Apparel: Indexed spending by age, 2011

(indexed average annual spending of consumer units on apparel, accessories, and related services, by age of consumer unit reference person, 2011; index definition: an index of 100 is the average for all consumer units; an index of 125 means that spending by consumer units in that group is 25 percent above the average for all consumer units; an index of 75 indicates spending that is 25 percent below the average for all consumer units)

	total consumer units	under 25	25 to 34	35 to 44	45 to 54	55 to 64	65 to 74	75+
Average spending of consumer units, total	$49,705	$29,912	$48,097	$57,271	$58,050	$53,616	$44,646	$32,688
Average spending of consumer units, index	100	60	97	115	117	108	90	66
Apparel, average spending	100	83	104	128	114	99	69	60
MEN'S APPAREL	100	95	103	116	109	121	66	48
Suits	100	93	88	104	137	104	75	63
Sport coats and tailored jackets	100	28	84	160	76	133	117	33
Coats and jackets	100	120	110	155	80	114	62	25
Underwear	100	87	103	113	89	119	84	83
Hosiery	100	77	97	119	125	96	91	51
Nightwear	100	56	68	129	121	102	117	61
Accessories	100	134	138	117	105	91	63	28
Sweaters and vests	100	71	115	83	89	141	49	127
Active sportswear	100	66	66	149	167	83	63	23
Shirts	100	79	104	122	100	132	65	44
Pants and shorts	100	116	101	88	113	143	59	48
Uniforms	100	104	134	185	123	54	10	25
Costumes	100	267	157	147	122	–	47	4
BOYS' (AGED 2 TO 15) APPAREL	100	32	126	231	98	54	37	20
Coats and jackets	100	30	117	230	104	61	26	27
Sweaters	100	47	136	189	81	48	120	20
Shirts	100	16	100	273	83	59	32	25
Underwear	100	36	107	254	91	64	22	18
Nightwear	100	16	140	208	97	65	49	21
Hosiery	100	50	160	195	95	45	47	22
Accessories	100	27	109	202	96	87	67	12
Suits, sport coats, and vests	100	29	131	181	184	25	14	9
Pants and shorts	100	45	145	213	110	40	33	19
Uniforms	100	21	157	199	118	55	19	12
Active sportswear	100	1	115	217	133	49	50	6
Costumes	100	20	173	264	63	40	2	29
WOMEN'S APPAREL	100	78	94	100	121	108	79	88
Coats and jackets	100	40	59	124	117	106	53	175
Dresses	100	69	121	103	143	85	64	54
Sport coats and tailored jackets	100	65	126	79	93	142	78	80
Sweaters and vests	100	109	90	75	105	137	45	140
Shirts, blouses, and tops	100	94	98	98	133	92	96	63
Skirts	100	29	80	109	121	128	109	59
Pants and shorts	100	68	101	111	117	104	77	79
Active sportswear	100	69	96	105	143	106	54	66
Nightwear	100	138	63	73	120	113	112	112
Undergarments	100	74	115	84	116	120	59	96
Hosiery	100	100	59	84	101	139	93	137
Suits	100	26	74	102	139	131	88	67
Accessories	100	61	94	106	94	125	115	72
Uniforms	100	81	146	112	116	109	36	39
Costumes	100	137	116	135	151	73	19	25

	total consumer units	under 25	25 to 34	35 to 44	45 to 54	55 to 64	65 to 74	75+
GIRLS' (AGED 2 TO 15) APPAREL	**100**	**25**	**107**	**203**	**126**	**63**	**58**	**10**
Coats and jackets	100	50	155	197	92	53	57	15
Dresses and suits	100	52	126	146	103	97	97	–
Shirts, blouses, and sweaters	100	7	83	210	126	71	75	14
Skirts, pants, and shorts	100	35	145	230	104	37	37	10
Active sportswear	100	17	62	210	161	87	25	–
Underwear and nightwear	100	24	95	186	149	59	64	14
Hosiery	100	26	131	168	155	50	40	12
Accessories	100	11	80	251	129	26	81	13
Uniforms	100	25	113	140	198	56	27	16
Costumes	100	46	142	265	70	26	46	19
CHILDREN'S (UNDER AGE 2) APPAREL	**100**	**190**	**215**	**151**	**66**	**42**	**25**	**11**
Coats, jackets, and snowsuits	100	192	213	187	53	28	9	28
Outerwear including dresses	100	146	211	125	60	63	67	24
Underwear	100	205	226	163	57	34	9	8
Nightwear and loungewear	100	141	208	99	55	82	92	28
Accessories	100	174	168	124	111	54	45	13
FOOTWEAR	**100**	**93**	**95**	**140**	**122**	**90**	**55**	**63**
Men's	100	129	100	116	129	105	52	36
Boys'	100	43	122	232	128	40	5	16
Women's	100	94	79	101	124	105	79	103
Girls'	100	41	123	276	91	32	11	19
OTHER APPAREL PRODUCTS AND SERVICES	**100**	**84**	**105**	**122**	**101**	**106**	**95**	**55**
Material for making clothes	100	64	34	61	165	114	179	60
Sewing patterns and notions	100	39	48	114	90	146	133	102
Watches	100	155	115	183	48	87	62	64
Jewelry	100	64	106	116	94	117	111	52
Shoe repair and other shoe services	100	49	77	115	101	129	143	41
Coin-operated apparel laundry and dry cleaning	100	169	174	120	86	63	53	44
Apparel alteration, repair, and tailoring services	100	57	122	78	100	123	122	62
Clothing rental	100	107	140	136	135	84	31	–
Watch and jewelry repair	100	4	29	98	73	142	187	165
Professional laundry, dry cleaning	100	26	72	116	145	122	91	45
Clothing storage	100	30	72	87	229	89	66	7

Note: "–" means sample is too small to make a reliable estimate.
Source: Calculations by New Strategist based on the Bureau of Labor Statistics' 2011 Consumer Expenditure Survey

Table 2.3 Apparel: Total spending by age, 2011

(total annual spending on apparel, accessories, and related services, by consumer unit age group, 2011; consumer units and dollars in thousands)

	total consumer units	under 25	25 to 34	35 to 44	45 to 54	55 to 64	65 to 74	75+
Number of consumer units	122,287	7,743	20,463	21,699	24,821	21,688	14,079	11,794
Total spending of all consumer units	$6,078,260,661	$231,604,899	$984,216,892	$1,242,724,948	$1,440,869,475	$1,162,820,772	$628,564,839	$385,526,282
Apparel, total spending	**212,753,700**	**11,212,948**	**37,196,004**	**48,323,022**	**49,094,945**	**37,272,346**	**16,820,322**	**12,406,816**
MEN'S APPAREL	**39,638,108**	**2,395,374**	**6,849,785**	**8,137,342**	**8,758,586**	**8,520,131**	**2,999,249**	**1,845,171**
Suits	2,257,418	132,250	333,342	417,055	627,475	414,891	195,276	137,164
Sport coats and tailored jackets	643,230	11,305	90,242	182,923	99,780	152,250	86,727	20,640
Coats and jackets	3,280,960	249,170	603,659	903,980	534,893	665,605	232,867	80,081
Underwear	2,585,147	141,852	446,912	519,474	468,372	546,321	249,902	206,631
Hosiery	1,780,499	86,567	288,528	374,959	450,749	303,849	185,561	87,983
Nightwear	199,328	7,124	22,714	45,785	48,897	36,219	26,750	11,794
Accessories	3,649,044	309,952	844,508	755,993	774,663	589,480	264,685	97,065
Sweaters and vests	2,081,325	93,923	400,256	305,522	377,279	520,946	117,560	254,515
Active sportswear	3,047,392	128,147	336,002	808,288	1,035,284	448,291	220,759	68,051
Shirts	10,444,533	522,885	1,825,913	2,256,262	2,121,699	2,450,310	778,428	441,685
Pants and shorts	9,296,258	681,307	1,571,558	1,448,408	2,126,663	2,362,474	633,837	431,896
Uniforms	310,609	20,364	69,779	102,202	77,442	29,496	3,661	7,430
Costumes	62,366	10,530	16,370	16,274	15,389	–	3,379	236
BOYS' (AGED 2 TO 15) APPAREL	**9,737,714**	**194,891**	**2,047,528**	**3,995,003**	**1,944,477**	**928,246**	**412,796**	**192,360**
Coats and jackets	649,344	12,311	127,484	265,379	136,764	70,703	19,288	16,983
Sweaters	253,134	7,588	57,706	84,843	41,699	21,688	35,057	4,836
Shirts	2,670,748	26,946	446,503	1,294,996	449,012	277,390	98,694	65,575
Underwear	800,980	18,506	144,060	360,420	148,181	91,306	20,555	13,917
Nightwear	188,322	1,936	44,200	69,437	36,983	21,688	10,559	3,892
Hosiery	606,544	19,203	162,885	209,612	117,403	48,147	32,663	12,855
Accessories	758,179	13,163	138,535	271,454	147,933	116,898	58,428	8,963
Suits, sport coats, and vests	111,281	2,013	24,351	35,803	41,451	4,988	1,830	944
Pants and shorts	3,084,078	87,264	748,741	1,166,321	686,052	220,567	118,686	56,375
Uniforms	324,061	4,336	85,126	114,571	77,690	31,664	7,040	3,656
Active sportswear	168,756	155	32,536	64,880	45,671	14,531	9,715	944
Costumes	122,287	1,549	35,401	57,285	15,637	8,675	282	3,420
WOMEN'S APPAREL	**73,833,222**	**3,626,279**	**11,636,285**	**13,097,299**	**18,191,063**	**14,160,095**	**6,715,824**	**6,287,735**
Coats and jackets	6,267,209	158,577	619,824	1,374,198	1,493,231	1,173,538	381,400	1,060,281
Dresses	8,673,817	380,414	1,757,362	1,581,423	2,515,608	1,314,293	640,031	454,069
Sport coats and tailored jackets	278,814	11,537	58,933	39,058	52,372	70,269	25,061	21,583
Sweaters and vests	6,124,133	421,374	921,244	819,354	1,311,293	1,486,712	319,171	824,047
Shirts, blouses, and tops	15,117,119	896,717	2,467,019	2,616,465	4,088,019	2,458,552	1,669,065	918,163
Skirts	1,456,438	26,326	194,399	280,785	357,422	329,441	182,464	83,030
Pants and shorts	11,598,922	502,598	1,964,448	2,285,122	2,754,138	2,149,498	1,028,049	888,088
Active sportswear	4,441,464	193,807	716,819	828,034	1,291,437	838,675	276,652	281,051
Nightwear	3,524,311	308,868	369,971	459,368	858,807	705,944	453,062	379,413
Undergarments	4,184,661	195,743	802,354	620,157	984,897	893,112	282,706	386,371
Hosiery	2,746,566	173,675	269,293	409,243	560,706	676,232	295,237	364,081
Suits	940,387	15,409	116,434	169,686	264,592	217,748	95,737	60,503
Accessories	7,908,300	306,003	1,246,197	1,494,193	1,512,095	1,746,318	1,046,633	547,713
Uniforms	407,216	20,829	99,655	80,937	95,561	78,511	16,895	15,332
Costumes	165,087	14,325	32,127	39,492	50,635	21,471	3,661	4,010

	total consumer units	under 25	25 to 34	35 to 44	45 to 54	55 to 64	65 to 74	75+
GIRLS' (AGED 2 TO 15) APPAREL	$14,360,162	$226,096	$2,559,717	$5,171,957	$3,678,472	$1,601,876	$961,455	$134,334
Coats and jackets	643,230	20,209	166,773	224,802	119,637	60,076	42,096	9,317
Dresses and suits	1,685,115	55,362	356,465	437,452	353,451	289,101	187,673	–
Shirts, blouses, and sweaters	4,039,140	19,048	562,119	1,507,213	1,032,057	506,849	348,737	55,904
Skirts, pants, and shorts	3,065,735	67,054	741,784	1,251,381	646,835	199,313	130,512	28,541
Active sportswear	$1,867,322	$20,132	$194,399	$696,538	$609,604	$286,498	$53,500	–
Underwear and nightwear	1,172,732	17,499	186,009	387,544	354,692	122,537	86,445	15,804
Hosiery	743,505	12,079	162,476	221,981	233,814	66,365	34,353	8,374
Accessories	629,778	4,336	84,512	281,002	165,060	28,845	58,428	7,784
Uniforms	348,518	5,498	65,686	86,579	139,742	34,701	10,982	5,543
Costumes	165,087	4,801	39,289	77,682	23,580	7,591	8,729	3,066
CHILDREN'S (UNDER AGE 2) APPAREL	8,331,413	1,002,409	2,992,714	2,225,232	1,110,740	623,313	238,921	90,932
Coats, jackets, and snowsuits	113,727	13,860	40,517	37,756	12,162	5,639	1,126	3,066
Outerwear including dresses	1,158,058	106,853	408,032	256,265	141,231	130,345	88,838	26,419
Underwear	5,573,841	722,422	2,112,395	1,614,189	645,594	335,513	60,680	40,335
Nightwear and loungewear	201,774	18,041	70,188	35,369	22,587	29,279	21,259	5,425
Accessories	1,284,014	141,232	361,581	281,436	289,413	122,537	67,016	15,568
FOOTWEAR	39,271,247	2,303,697	6,262,087	9,747,191	9,755,398	6,247,445	2,477,341	2,395,479
Men's	11,842,273	965,707	1,978,977	2,438,317	3,096,420	2,212,176	712,679	406,657
Boys'	4,484,264	121,178	916,333	1,846,151	1,164,601	316,645	26,750	68,287
Women's	18,586,401	1,103,223	2,467,224	3,332,749	4,688,190	3,469,646	1,682,159	1,838,685
Girls'	4,357,086	113,590	899,349	2,130,191	806,186	248,978	55,753	81,850
OTHER APPAREL PRODUCTS AND SERVICES	27,580,610	1,464,124	4,847,685	5,948,998	5,656,458	5,191,023	3,014,877	1,460,923
Material for making clothes	1,180,070	48,161	67,119	128,241	394,654	237,917	243,848	67,933
Sewing patterns and notions	963,622	23,926	78,169	195,725	176,726	248,978	147,126	94,352
Watches	3,701,627	363,611	712,522	1,199,955	357,671	573,431	262,151	227,035
Jewelry	8,798,550	356,643	1,565,215	1,804,272	1,672,439	1,832,636	1,127,024	440,506
Shoe repair and other shoe services	183,431	5,652	23,737	37,539	37,728	41,858	30,270	7,194
Coin-operated apparel laundry and dry cleaning	4,846,234	519,633	1,407,650	1,032,438	843,418	543,935	293,688	205,805
Apparel alteration, repair, and tailoring services	778,968	28,107	158,998	107,627	158,358	170,034	109,816	46,586
Clothing rental	205,442	13,860	48,088	49,474	56,095	30,580	7,321	–
Watch and jewelry repair	664,018	1,549	32,332	115,222	98,788	167,214	143,324	105,674
Professional laundry, dry cleaning	6,126,579	100,582	738,305	1,258,542	1,799,771	1,324,269	640,454	265,129
Clothing storage	129,624	2,478	15,552	19,963	60,315	20,387	9,855	826

Note: Numbers may not add to total because of rounding and missing subcategories. "–" means sample is too small to make a reliable estimate.
Source: Calculations by New Strategist based on the Bureau of Labor Statistics' 2011 Consumer Expenditure Survey

Table 2.4 Apparel: Market shares by age, 2011

(percentage of total annual spending on apparel, accessories, and related services accounted for by consumer unit age groups, 2011)

	total consumer units	under 25	25 to 34	35 to 44	45 to 54	55 to 64	65 to 74	75+
Share of total consumer units	100.0%	6.3%	16.7%	17.7%	20.3%	17.7%	11.5%	9.6%
Share of total before-tax income	100.0	2.7	15.3	21.6	25.0	21.0	9.5	4.9
Share of total spending	100.0	3.8	16.2	20.4	23.7	19.1	10.3	6.3
Share of apparel spending	100.0	5.3	17.5	22.7	23.1	17.5	7.9	5.8
MEN'S APPAREL	100.0	6.0	17.3	20.5	22.1	21.5	7.6	4.7
Suits	100.0	5.9	14.8	18.5	27.8	18.4	8.7	6.1
Sport coats and tailored jackets	100.0	1.8	14.0	28.4	15.5	23.7	13.5	3.2
Coats and jackets	100.0	7.6	18.4	27.6	16.3	20.3	7.1	2.4
Underwear	100.0	5.5	17.3	20.1	18.1	21.1	9.7	8.0
Hosiery	100.0	4.9	16.2	21.1	25.3	17.1	10.4	4.9
Nightwear	100.0	3.6	11.4	23.0	24.5	18.2	13.4	5.9
Accessories	100.0	8.5	23.1	20.7	21.2	16.2	7.3	2.7
Sweaters and vests	100.0	4.5	19.2	14.7	18.1	25.0	5.6	12.2
Active sportswear	100.0	4.2	11.0	26.5	34.0	14.7	7.2	2.2
Shirts	100.0	5.0	17.5	21.6	20.3	23.5	7.5	4.2
Pants and shorts	100.0	7.3	16.9	15.6	22.9	25.4	6.8	4.6
Uniforms	100.0	6.6	22.5	32.9	24.9	9.5	1.2	2.4
Costumes	100.0	16.9	26.2	26.1	24.7	–	5.4	0.4
BOYS' (AGED 2 TO 15) APPAREL	100.0	2.0	21.0	41.0	20.0	9.5	4.2	2.0
Coats and jackets	100.0	1.9	19.6	40.9	21.1	10.9	3.0	2.6
Sweaters	100.0	3.0	22.8	33.5	16.5	8.6	13.8	1.9
Shirts	100.0	1.0	16.7	48.5	16.8	10.4	3.7	2.5
Underwear	100.0	2.3	18.0	45.0	18.5	11.4	2.6	1.7
Nightwear	100.0	1.0	23.5	36.9	19.6	11.5	5.6	2.1
Hosiery	100.0	3.2	26.9	34.6	19.4	7.9	5.4	2.1
Accessories	100.0	1.7	18.3	35.8	19.5	15.4	7.7	1.2
Suits, sport coats, and vests	100.0	1.8	21.9	32.2	37.2	4.5	1.6	0.8
Pants and shorts	100.0	2.8	24.3	37.8	22.2	7.2	3.8	1.8
Uniforms	100.0	1.3	26.3	35.4	24.0	9.8	2.2	1.1
Active sportswear	100.0	0.1	19.3	38.4	27.1	8.6	5.8	0.6
Costumes	100.0	1.3	28.9	46.8	12.8	7.1	0.2	2.8
WOMEN'S APPAREL	100.0	4.9	15.8	17.7	24.6	19.2	9.1	8.5
Coats and jackets	100.0	2.5	9.9	21.9	23.8	18.7	6.1	16.9
Dresses	100.0	4.4	20.3	18.2	29.0	15.2	7.4	5.2
Sport coats and tailored jackets	100.0	4.1	21.1	14.0	18.8	25.2	9.0	7.7
Sweaters and vests	100.0	6.9	15.0	13.4	21.4	24.3	5.2	13.5
Shirts, blouses, and tops	100.0	5.9	16.3	17.3	27.0	16.3	11.0	6.1
Skirts	100.0	1.8	13.3	19.3	24.5	22.6	12.5	5.7
Pants and shorts	100.0	4.3	16.9	19.7	23.7	18.5	8.9	7.7
Active sportswear	100.0	4.4	16.1	18.6	29.1	18.9	6.2	6.3
Nightwear	100.0	8.8	10.5	13.0	24.4	20.0	12.9	10.8
Undergarments	100.0	4.7	19.2	14.8	23.5	21.3	6.8	9.2
Hosiery	100.0	6.3	9.8	14.9	20.4	24.6	10.7	13.3
Suits	100.0	1.6	12.4	18.0	28.1	23.2	10.2	6.4
Accessories	100.0	3.9	15.8	18.9	19.1	22.1	13.2	6.9
Uniforms	100.0	5.1	24.5	19.9	23.5	19.3	4.1	3.8
Costumes	100.0	8.7	19.5	23.9	30.7	13.0	2.2	2.4

	total consumer units	under 25	25 to 34	35 to 44	45 to 54	55 to 64	65 to 74	75+
GIRLS' (AGED 2 TO 15) APPAREL	**100.0%**	**1.6%**	**17.8%**	**36.0%**	**25.6%**	**11.2%**	**6.7%**	**0.9%**
Coats and jackets	100.0	3.1	25.9	34.9	18.6	9.3	6.5	1.4
Dresses and suits	100.0	3.3	21.2	26.0	21.0	17.2	11.1	–
Shirts, blouses, and sweaters	100.0	0.5	13.9	37.3	25.6	12.5	8.6	1.4
Skirts, pants, and shorts	100.0	2.2	24.2	40.8	21.1	6.5	4.3	0.9
Active sportswear	100.0	1.1	10.4	37.3	32.6	15.3	2.9	–
Underwear and nightwear	100.0	1.5	15.9	33.0	30.2	10.4	7.4	1.3
Hosiery	100.0	1.6	21.9	29.9	31.4	8.9	4.6	1.1
Accessories	100.0	0.7	13.4	44.6	26.2	4.6	9.3	1.2
Uniforms	100.0	1.6	18.8	24.8	40.1	10.0	3.2	1.6
Costumes	100.0	2.9	23.8	47.1	14.3	4.6	5.3	1.9
CHILDREN'S (UNDER AGE 2) APPAREL	**100.0**	**12.0**	**35.9**	**26.7**	**13.3**	**7.5**	**2.9**	**1.1**
Coats, jackets, and snowsuits	100.0	12.2	35.6	33.2	10.7	5.0	1.0	2.7
Outerwear including dresses	100.0	9.2	35.2	22.1	12.2	11.3	7.7	2.3
Underwear	100.0	13.0	37.9	29.0	11.6	6.0	1.1	0.7
Nightwear and loungewear	100.0	8.9	34.8	17.5	11.2	14.5	10.5	2.7
Accessories	100.0	11.0	28.2	21.9	22.5	9.5	5.2	1.2
FOOTWEAR	**100.0**	**5.9**	**15.9**	**24.8**	**24.8**	**15.9**	**6.3**	**6.1**
Men's	100.0	8.2	16.7	20.6	26.1	18.7	6.0	3.4
Boys'	100.0	2.7	20.4	41.2	26.0	7.1	0.6	1.5
Women's	100.0	5.9	13.3	17.9	25.2	18.7	9.1	9.9
Girls'	100.0	2.6	20.6	48.9	18.5	5.7	1.3	1.9
OTHER APPAREL PRODUCTS AND SERVICES	**100.0**	**5.3**	**17.6**	**21.6**	**20.5**	**18.8**	**10.9**	**5.3**
Material for making clothes	100.0	4.1	5.7	10.9	33.4	20.2	20.7	5.8
Sewing patterns and notions	100.0	2.5	8.1	20.3	18.3	25.8	15.3	9.8
Watches	100.0	9.8	19.2	32.4	9.7	15.5	7.1	6.1
Jewelry	100.0	4.1	17.8	20.5	19.0	20.8	12.8	5.0
Shoe repair and other shoe services	100.0	3.1	12.9	20.5	20.6	22.8	16.5	3.9
Coin-operated apparel laundry and dry cleaning	100.0	10.7	29.0	21.3	17.4	11.2	6.1	4.2
Apparel alteration, repair, and tailoring services	100.0	3.6	20.4	13.8	20.3	21.8	14.1	6.0
Clothing rental	100.0	6.7	23.4	24.1	27.3	14.9	3.6	–
Watch and jewelry repair	100.0	0.2	4.9	17.4	14.9	25.2	21.6	15.9
Professional laundry, dry cleaning	100.0	1.6	12.1	20.5	29.4	21.6	10.5	4.3
Clothing storage	100.0	1.9	12.0	15.4	46.5	15.7	7.6	0.6

Note: Numbers may not add to total because of rounding. "–" means sample is too small to make a reliable estimate.
Source: Calculations by New Strategist based on the Bureau of Labor Statistics' 2011 Consumer Expenditure Survey

Table 2.5 Apparel: Average spending by income, 2011

(average annual spending on apparel, accessories, and related services, by before-tax income of consumer units, 2011)

	total consumer units	under $20,000	$20,000– $39,999	$40,000– $49,999	$50,000– $69,999	$70,000– $79,999	$80,000– $99,999	$100,000 or more
Number of consumer units (in 000s)	122,287	26,342	27,788	11,347	17,376	7,385	10,456	21,593
Average number of persons per consumer unit	2.5	1.8	2.3	2.6	2.7	2.8	3.0	3.2
Average before-tax income of consumer units	$63,685.00	$10,491.66	$29,658.14	$44,698.00	$59,306.00	$74,742.00	$89,108.00	$169,776.00
Average spending of consumer units, total	49,704.88	22,142.36	33,453.66	40,306.19	50,034.03	57,976.69	65,389.80	97,728.22
Apparel, average spending	**1,739.79**	**877.18**	**1,194.36**	**1,174.55**	**1,767.23**	**1,983.57**	**2,220.49**	**3,379.68**
MEN'S APPAREL	**324.14**	**158.35**	**216.86**	**208.36**	**336.47**	**327.64**	**464.79**	**634.75**
Suits	18.46	5.44	8.97	10.68	11.68	18.93	23.33	53.57
Sport coats and tailored jackets	5.26	2.10	2.62	0.71	3.34	4.66	5.00	16.81
Coats and jackets	26.83	10.44	22.94	33.03	37.76	19.62	44.03	32.69
Underwear	21.14	10.19	18.81	8.76	14.99	24.76	28.17	43.75
Hosiery	14.56	8.32	11.02	8.59	14.15	21.37	19.11	24.82
Nightwear	1.63	0.39	0.65	2.52	1.41	1.78	1.63	4.07
Accessories	29.84	18.78	17.80	18.88	35.17	15.58	40.65	57.99
Sweaters and vests	17.02	11.68	18.01	2.16	8.79	11.34	22.13	35.82
Active sportswear	24.92	7.95	10.98	16.15	16.82	17.95	33.46	71.12
Shirts	85.41	46.42	55.40	49.20	101.23	103.19	130.54	147.93
Pants and shorts	76.02	35.90	46.25	54.13	86.80	86.61	111.85	142.56
Uniforms	2.54	0.72	3.07	2.87	3.87	1.01	4.58	2.62
Costumes	0.51	0.25	0.33	0.68	0.44	0.84	0.31	1.00
BOYS' (AGED 2 TO 15) APPAREL	**79.63**	**34.97**	**56.56**	**67.65**	**88.12**	**77.71**	**99.51**	**150.51**
Coats and jackets	5.31	1.56	2.93	4.76	5.01	8.76	5.94	11.97
Sweaters	2.07	0.94	1.77	1.22	2.22	3.37	2.88	3.33
Shirts	21.84	11.10	16.63	18.90	24.94	13.31	26.69	39.18
Underwear	6.55	2.47	5.77	4.24	6.84	6.07	5.62	13.32
Nightwear	1.54	0.64	1.15	1.17	1.96	1.79	2.51	2.46
Hosiery	4.96	2.41	4.86	3.92	6.90	1.88	4.72	8.02
Accessories	6.20	1.55	2.81	4.91	9.53	9.27	10.69	10.44
Suits, sport coats, and vests	0.91	0.14	0.44	0.46	0.82	0.23	1.45	2.74
Pants and shorts	25.22	12.05	17.18	25.69	25.62	29.19	33.35	45.77
Uniforms	2.65	1.36	2.09	1.01	2.24	1.37	2.34	6.71
Active sportswear	1.38	0.33	0.36	0.70	1.03	1.16	2.25	4.27
Costumes	1.00	0.44	0.55	0.67	0.99	1.30	1.07	2.30
WOMEN'S APPAREL	**603.77**	**295.40**	**378.15**	**374.93**	**625.13**	**747.68**	**790.41**	**1,201.45**
Coats and jackets	51.25	35.06	44.94	15.26	43.51	46.15	37.12	110.30
Dresses	70.93	24.18	38.61	53.82	66.47	40.89	69.22	187.75
Sport coats and tailored jackets	2.28	0.62	1.21	0.64	2.94	2.17	2.91	5.74
Sweaters and vests	50.08	22.02	27.76	39.32	53.40	55.76	64.88	103.90
Shirts, blouses, and tops	123.62	65.23	71.93	82.99	138.95	193.51	171.75	216.25
Skirts	11.91	3.84	8.20	8.90	7.45	3.86	23.12	28.71
Pants and shorts	94.85	49.28	60.14	72.23	112.91	140.12	141.97	150.61
Active sportswear	36.32	14.54	19.61	7.45	38.76	39.96	83.29	71.78
Nightwear	28.82	17.37	19.45	18.47	31.09	43.31	24.71	53.28
Undergarments	34.22	14.00	27.43	22.05	30.19	45.35	48.64	63.67
Hosiery	22.46	11.28	17.33	12.71	23.29	33.57	28.85	39.32
Suits	7.69	2.19	2.27	2.34	8.35	9.27	11.92	21.04
Accessories	64.67	34.90	36.28	32.84	62.06	88.10	75.51	141.24
Uniforms	3.33	1.21	2.43	4.50	4.70	4.07	4.16	4.72
Costumes	1.35	0.45	0.54	1.41	1.06	1.59	2.36	3.14

	total consumer units	under $20,000	$20,000–$39,999	$40,000–$49,999	$50,000–$69,999	$70,000–$79,999	$80,000–$99,999	$100,000 or more
GIRLS' (AGED 2 TO 15) APPAREL	**$117.43**	**$49.37**	**$82.25**	**$104.75**	**$121.28**	**$115.88**	**$181.07**	**$211.31**
Coats and jackets	5.26	2.19	3.25	4.83	4.99	7.42	6.61	10.63
Dresses and suits	13.78	7.90	8.98	16.96	8.76	20.07	21.89	22.76
Shirts, blouses, and sweaters	33.03	12.15	29.13	34.56	30.04	32.29	57.75	50.32
Skirts, pants, and shorts	25.07	12.60	15.89	21.95	26.29	25.75	31.19	49.53
Active sportswear	15.27	2.29	9.81	8.31	21.55	6.60	27.16	32.91
Underwear and nightwear	9.59	6.61	6.18	8.50	13.18	7.07	13.93	13.68
Hosiery	6.08	2.88	3.34	3.27	7.79	9.28	11.64	9.41
Accessories	5.15	1.43	3.09	4.01	6.38	2.94	5.76	12.03
Uniforms	2.85	1.96	1.94	1.27	1.35	2.76	3.66	6.80
Costumes	1.35	0.77	0.63	1.09	0.95	1.70	1.47	3.25
CHILDREN'S (UNDER AGE 2) APPAREL	**68.13**	**42.48**	**45.47**	**65.06**	**79.17**	**91.58**	**89.44**	**99.49**
Coats, jackets, and snowsuits	0.93	0.55	0.79	1.25	1.14	1.64	0.71	1.11
Outerwear including dresses	9.47	4.26	6.24	8.11	11.86	15.61	14.67	14.15
Underwear	45.58	30.89	28.44	41.01	53.08	56.70	60.81	68.05
Nightwear and loungewear	1.65	0.96	1.73	1.33	2.37	1.10	1.73	2.15
Accessories	10.50	7.18	8.27	13.36	10.72	16.54	11.52	14.03
FOOTWEAR	**321.14**	**187.00**	**263.23**	**203.85**	**307.86**	**362.34**	**374.77**	**578.13**
Men's	96.84	59.64	76.59	66.70	92.63	78.18	105.47	187.81
Boys'	36.67	19.35	26.95	19.88	51.54	28.55	49.37	59.76
Women's	151.99	90.56	127.07	85.27	128.88	222.21	163.55	278.10
Girls'	35.63	17.44	32.62	32.00	34.81	33.40	56.39	52.46
OTHER APPAREL PRODUCTS AND SERVICES	**225.54**	**109.62**	**151.84**	**149.96**	**209.20**	**260.74**	**220.49**	**504.04**
Material for making clothes	9.65	1.86	11.14	6.82	6.27	16.79	10.55	17.76
Sewing patterns and notions	7.88	3.24	4.05	7.28	12.85	9.82	13.20	11.40
Watches	30.27	17.75	20.51	5.82	59.18	40.52	21.02	49.04
Jewelry	71.95	16.28	31.82	46.48	58.66	99.06	76.66	204.05
Shoe repair and other shoe services	1.50	0.45	0.99	1.26	0.79	2.50	1.20	3.96
Coin-operated apparel laundry and dry cleaning	39.63	56.34	57.59	47.27	31.12	23.50	24.81	11.68
Apparel alteration, repair, and tailoring services	6.37	1.80	3.33	3.76	5.87	8.69	5.96	17.06
Clothing rental	1.68	1.07	0.52	2.04	0.55	0.35	2.26	5.22
Watch and jewelry repair	5.43	1.16	3.77	3.61	2.97	5.63	5.25	15.73
Professional laundry, dry cleaning	50.10	10.20	17.61	25.40	30.79	51.15	56.34	165.74
Clothing storage	1.06	0.24	0.53	0.21	0.14	2.73	3.25	2.40

Note: Subcategories may not add to total because some are not shown.
Source: Bureau of Labor Statistics, unpublished data from the 2011 Consumer Expenditure Survey; calculations by New Strategist

Table 2.6 Apparel: Indexed spending by income, 2011

(indexed average annual spending of consumer units on apparel, accessories, and related services, by before-tax income of consumer unit, 2011; index definition: an index of 100 is the average for all consumer units; an index of 125 means that spending by consumer units in that group is 25 percent above the average for all consumer units; an index of 75 indicates spending that is 25 percent below the average for all consumer units)

	total consumer units	under $20,000	$20,000–$39,999	$40,000–$49,999	$50,000–$69,999	$70,000–$79,999	$80,000–$99,999	$100,000 or more
Average spending of consumer units, total	$49,705	$22,142	$33,454	$40,306	$50,034	$57,977	$65,390	$97,728
Average spending of consumer units, index	100	45	67	81	101	117	132	197
Apparel, spending index	**100**	**50**	**69**	**68**	**102**	**114**	**128**	**194**
MEN'S APPAREL	**100**	**49**	**67**	**64**	**104**	**101**	**143**	**196**
Suits	100	29	49	58	63	103	126	290
Sport coats and tailored jackets	100	40	50	13	63	89	95	320
Coats and jackets	100	39	85	123	141	73	164	122
Underwear	100	48	89	41	71	117	133	207
Hosiery	100	57	76	59	97	147	131	170
Nightwear	100	24	40	155	87	109	100	250
Accessories	100	63	60	63	118	52	136	194
Sweaters and vests	100	69	106	13	52	67	130	210
Active sportswear	100	32	44	65	67	72	134	285
Shirts	100	54	65	58	119	121	153	173
Pants and shorts	100	47	61	71	114	114	147	188
Uniforms	100	28	121	113	152	40	180	103
Costumes	100	50	65	133	86	165	61	196
BOYS' (AGED 2 TO 15) APPAREL	**100**	**44**	**71**	**85**	**111**	**98**	**125**	**189**
Coats and jackets	100	29	55	90	94	165	112	225
Sweaters	100	45	86	59	107	163	139	161
Shirts	100	51	76	87	114	61	122	179
Underwear	100	38	88	65	104	93	86	203
Nightwear	100	41	75	76	127	116	163	160
Hosiery	100	49	98	79	139	38	95	162
Accessories	100	25	45	79	154	150	172	168
Suits, sport coats, and vests	100	15	49	51	90	25	159	301
Pants and shorts	100	48	68	102	102	116	132	181
Uniforms	100	51	79	38	85	52	88	253
Active sportswear	100	24	26	51	75	84	163	309
Costumes	100	44	55	67	99	130	107	230
WOMEN'S APPAREL	**100**	**49**	**63**	**62**	**104**	**124**	**131**	**199**
Coats and jackets	100	68	88	30	85	90	72	215
Dresses	100	34	54	76	94	58	98	265
Sport coats and tailored jackets	100	27	53	28	129	95	128	252
Sweaters and vests	100	44	55	79	107	111	130	207
Shirts, blouses, and tops	100	53	58	67	112	157	139	175
Skirts	100	32	69	75	63	32	194	241
Pants and shorts	100	52	63	76	119	148	150	159
Active sportswear	100	40	54	21	107	110	229	198
Nightwear	100	60	67	64	108	150	86	185
Undergarments	100	41	80	64	88	133	142	186
Hosiery	100	50	77	57	104	149	128	175
Suits	100	29	30	30	109	121	155	274
Accessories	100	54	56	51	96	136	117	218
Uniforms	100	36	73	135	141	122	125	142
Costumes	100	34	40	104	79	118	175	233

	total consumer units	under $20,000	$20,000– $39,999	$40,000– $49,999	$50,000– $69,999	$70,000– $79,999	$80,000– $99,999	$100,000 or more
GIRLS' (AGED 2 TO 15) APPAREL	**100**	**42**	**70**	**89**	**103**	**99**	**154**	**180**
Coats and jackets	100	42	62	92	95	141	126	202
Dresses and suits	100	57	65	123	64	146	159	165
Shirts, blouses, and sweaters	100	37	88	105	91	98	175	152
Skirts, pants, and shorts	100	50	63	88	105	103	124	198
Active sportswear	100	15	64	54	141	43	178	216
Underwear and nightwear	100	69	64	89	137	74	145	143
Hosiery	100	47	55	54	128	153	191	155
Accessories	100	28	60	78	124	57	112	234
Uniforms	100	69	68	45	47	97	128	239
Costumes	100	57	47	81	70	126	109	241
CHILDREN'S (UNDER AGE 2) APPAREL	**100**	**62**	**67**	**95**	**116**	**134**	**131**	**146**
Coats, jackets, and snowsuits	100	60	85	134	123	176	76	119
Outerwear including dresses	100	45	66	86	125	165	155	149
Underwear	100	68	62	90	116	124	133	149
Nightwear and loungewear	100	58	105	81	144	67	105	130
Accessories	100	68	79	127	102	158	110	134
FOOTWEAR	**100**	**58**	**82**	**63**	**96**	**113**	**117**	**180**
Men's	100	62	79	69	96	81	109	194
Boys'	100	53	73	54	141	78	135	163
Women's	100	60	84	56	85	146	108	183
Girls'	100	49	92	90	98	94	158	147
OTHER APPAREL PRODUCTS AND SERVICES	**100**	**49**	**67**	**66**	**93**	**116**	**98**	**223**
Material for making clothes	100	19	115	71	65	174	109	184
Sewing patterns and notions	100	41	51	92	163	125	168	145
Watches	100	59	68	19	196	134	69	162
Jewelry	100	23	44	65	82	138	107	284
Shoe repair and other shoe services	100	30	66	84	53	167	80	264
Coin-operated apparel laundry and dry cleaning	100	142	145	119	79	59	63	29
Apparel alteration, repair, and tailoring services	100	28	52	59	92	136	94	268
Clothing rental	100	64	31	121	33	21	135	311
Watch and jewelry repair	100	21	69	66	55	104	97	290
Professional laundry, dry cleaning	100	20	35	51	61	102	112	331
Clothing storage	100	23	50	20	13	258	307	226

Source: Calculations by New Strategist based on the Bureau of Labor Statistics' 2011 Consumer Expenditure Survey

Table 2.7 Apparel: Total spending by income, 2011

(total annual spending on apparel, accessories, and related services, by before-tax income group of consumer units, 2011; consumer units and dollars in thousands)

	total consumer units	under $20,000	$20,000–$39,999	$40,000–$49,999	$50,000–$69,999	$70,000–$79,999	$80,000–$99,999	$100,000 or more
Number of consumer units	122,287	26,342	27,788	11,347	17,376	7,385	10,456	21,593
Total spending of all consumer units	$6,078,260,661	$583,273,961	$929,610,260	$457,354,338	$869,391,305	$428,157,856	$683,715,749	$2,110,245,454
Apparel, total spending	212,753,700	23,106,669	33,188,908	13,327,619	30,707,388	14,648,664	23,217,443	72,977,430
MEN'S APPAREL	**39,638,108**	**4,171,201**	**6,026,117**	**2,364,261**	**5,846,503**	**2,419,621**	**4,859,844**	**13,706,157**
Suits	2,257,418	143,328	249,335	121,186	202,952	139,798	243,938	1,156,737
Sport coats and tailored jackets	643,230	55,218	72,691	8,056	58,036	34,414	52,280	362,978
Coats and jackets	3,280,960	275,112	637,371	374,791	656,118	144,894	460,378	705,875
Underwear	2,585,147	268,336	522,816	99,400	260,466	182,853	294,546	944,694
Hosiery	1,780,499	219,047	306,208	97,471	245,870	157,817	199,814	535,938
Nightwear	199,328	10,168	17,958	28,594	24,500	13,145	17,043	87,884
Accessories	3,649,044	494,698	494,741	214,231	611,114	115,058	425,036	1,252,178
Sweaters and vests	2,081,325	307,799	500,521	24,510	152,735	83,746	231,391	773,461
Active sportswear	3,047,392	209,350	305,078	183,254	292,264	132,561	349,858	1,535,694
Shirts	10,444,533	1,222,793	1,539,581	558,272	1,758,972	762,058	1,364,926	3,194,252
Pants and shorts	9,296,258	945,658	1,285,250	614,213	1,508,237	639,615	1,169,504	3,078,298
Uniforms	310,609	19,001	85,400	32,566	67,245	7,459	47,888	56,574
Costumes	62,366	6,699	9,167	7,716	7,645	6,203	3,241	21,593
BOYS' (AGED 2 TO 15) APPAREL	**9,737,714**	**921,279**	**1,571,692**	**767,625**	**1,531,173**	**573,888**	**1,040,477**	**3,249,962**
Coats and jackets	649,344	41,091	81,329	54,012	87,054	64,693	62,109	258,468
Sweaters	253,134	24,703	49,268	13,843	38,575	24,887	30,113	71,905
Shirts	2,670,748	292,370	462,083	214,458	433,357	98,294	279,071	846,014
Underwear	800,980	65,097	160,472	48,111	118,852	44,827	58,763	287,619
Nightwear	188,322	16,786	32,054	13,276	34,057	13,219	26,245	53,119
Hosiery	606,544	63,483	135,055	44,480	119,894	13,884	49,352	173,176
Accessories	758,179	40,895	78,132	55,714	165,593	68,459	111,775	225,431
Suits, sport coats, and vests	111,281	3,563	12,357	5,220	14,248	1,699	15,161	59,165
Pants and shorts	3,084,078	317,326	477,262	291,504	445,173	215,568	348,708	988,312
Uniforms	324,061	35,910	58,199	11,460	38,922	10,117	24,467	144,889
Active sportswear	168,756	8,598	9,924	7,943	17,897	8,567	23,526	92,202
Costumes	122,287	11,539	15,290	7,602	17,202	9,601	11,188	49,664
WOMEN'S APPAREL	**73,833,222**	**7,781,313**	**10,508,003**	**4,254,331**	**10,862,259**	**5,521,617**	**8,264,527**	**25,942,910**
Coats and jackets	6,267,209	923,674	1,248,656	173,155	756,030	340,818	388,127	2,381,708
Dresses	8,673,817	636,877	1,072,828	610,696	1,154,983	301,973	723,764	4,054,086
Sport coats and tailored jackets	278,814	16,411	33,692	7,262	51,085	16,025	30,427	123,944
Sweaters and vests	6,124,133	580,178	771,376	446,164	927,878	411,788	678,385	2,243,513
Shirts, blouses, and tops	15,117,119	1,718,269	1,998,910	941,688	2,414,395	1,429,071	1,795,818	4,669,486
Skirts	1,456,438	101,255	227,813	100,988	129,451	28,506	241,743	619,935
Pants and shorts	11,598,922	1,298,176	1,671,286	819,594	1,961,924	1,034,786	1,484,438	3,252,122
Active sportswear	4,441,464	382,994	544,901	84,535	673,494	295,105	870,880	1,549,946
Nightwear	3,524,311	457,573	540,443	209,579	540,220	319,844	258,368	1,150,475
Undergarments	4,184,661	368,754	762,305	250,201	524,581	334,910	508,580	1,374,826
Hosiery	2,746,566	297,212	481,697	144,220	404,687	247,914	301,656	849,037
Suits	940,387	57,749	63,120	26,552	145,090	68,459	124,636	454,317
Accessories	7,908,300	919,375	1,008,159	372,635	1,078,355	650,619	789,533	3,049,795
Uniforms	407,216	31,987	67,547	51,062	81,667	30,057	43,497	101,919
Costumes	165,087	11,958	14,980	15,999	18,419	11,742	24,676	67,802

	total consumer units	under $20,000	$20,000–$39,999	$40,000–$49,999	$50,000–$69,999	$70,000–$79,999	$80,000–$99,999	$100,000 or more
GIRLS' (AGED 2 TO 15) APPAREL	**$14,360,162**	**$1,300,381**	**$2,285,503**	**$1,188,598**	**$2,107,361**	**$855,774**	**$1,893,268**	**$4,562,817**
Coats and jackets	643,230	57,699	90,227	54,806	86,706	54,797	69,114	229,534
Dresses and suits	1,685,115	208,119	249,627	192,445	152,214	148,217	228,882	491,457
Shirts, blouses, and sweaters	4,039,140	320,007	809,400	392,152	521,975	238,462	603,834	1,086,560
Skirts, pants, and shorts	3,065,735	332,024	441,665	249,067	456,815	190,164	326,123	1,069,501
Active sportswear	1,867,322	60,241	272,606	94,294	374,453	48,741	283,985	710,626
Underwear and nightwear	1,172,732	174,181	171,842	96,450	229,016	52,212	145,652	295,392
Hosiery	743,505	75,781	92,818	37,105	135,359	68,533	121,708	203,190
Accessories	629,778	37,635	85,906	45,501	110,859	21,712	60,227	259,764
Uniforms	348,518	51,654	53,948	14,411	23,458	20,383	38,269	146,832
Costumes	165,087	20,349	17,476	12,368	16,507	12,555	15,370	70,177
CHILDREN'S (UNDER AGE 2) APPAREL	**8,331,413**	**1,119,109**	**1,263,583**	**738,236**	**1,375,658**	**676,318**	**935,185**	**2,148,288**
Coats, jackets, and snowsuits	113,727	14,608	22,030	14,184	19,809	12,111	7,424	23,968
Outerwear including dresses	1,158,058	112,301	173,408	92,024	206,079	115,280	153,390	305,541
Underwear	5,573,841	813,625	790,160	465,340	922,318	418,730	635,829	1,469,404
Nightwear and loungewear	201,774	25,262	48,026	15,092	41,181	8,124	18,089	46,425
Accessories	1,284,014	189,137	229,692	151,596	186,271	122,148	120,453	302,950
FOOTWEAR	**39,271,247**	**4,925,939**	**7,314,572**	**2,313,086**	**5,349,375**	**2,675,881**	**3,918,595**	**12,483,561**
Men's	11,842,273	1,571,130	2,128,310	756,845	1,609,539	577,359	1,102,794	4,055,381
Boys'	4,484,264	509,843	748,902	225,578	895,559	210,842	516,213	1,290,398
Women's	18,586,401	2,385,579	3,530,917	967,559	2,239,419	1,641,021	1,710,079	6,005,013
Girls'	4,357,086	459,441	906,443	363,104	604,859	246,659	589,614	1,132,769
OTHER APPAREL PRODUCTS AND SERVICES	**27,580,610**	**2,887,529**	**4,219,437**	**1,701,596**	**3,635,059**	**1,925,565**	**2,305,443**	**10,883,736**
Material for making clothes	1,180,070	48,888	309,680	77,387	108,948	123,994	110,311	383,492
Sewing patterns and notions	963,622	85,397	112,536	82,606	223,282	72,521	138,019	246,160
Watches	3,701,627	467,690	569,949	66,040	1,028,312	299,240	219,785	1,058,921
Jewelry	8,798,550	428,916	884,353	527,409	1,019,276	731,558	801,557	4,406,052
Shoe repair and other shoe services	183,431	11,850	27,473	14,297	13,727	18,463	12,547	85,508
Coin-operated apparel laundry and dry cleaning	4,846,234	1,484,029	1,600,332	536,373	540,741	173,548	259,413	252,206
Apparel alteration, repair, and tailoring services	778,968	47,485	92,485	42,665	101,997	64,176	62,318	368,377
Clothing rental	205,442	28,203	14,316	23,148	9,557	2,585	23,631	112,715
Watch and jewelry repair	664,018	30,527	104,663	40,963	51,607	41,578	54,894	339,658
Professional laundry, dry cleaning	6,126,579	268,765	489,215	288,214	535,007	377,743	589,091	3,578,824
Clothing storage	129,624	6,443	14,592	2,383	2,433	20,161	33,982	51,823

Note: Numbers may not add to total because of rounding and missing subcategories.
Source: Calculations by New Strategist based on the Bureau of Labor Statistics' 2011 Consumer Expenditure Survey

Table 2.8 Apparel: Market shares by income, 2011

(percentage of total annual spending on apparel, accessories, and related services accounted for by before-tax income group of consumer units, 2011)

	total consumer units	under $20,000	$20,000–$39,999	$40,000–$49,999	$50,000–$69,999	$70,000–$79,999	$80,000–$99,999	$100,000 or more
Share of total consumer units	100.0%	21.5%	22.7%	9.3%	14.2%	6.0%	8.6%	17.7%
Share of total before-tax income	100.0	3.5	10.6	6.5	13.2	7.1	12.0	47.1
Share of total spending	100.0	9.6	15.3	7.5	14.3	7.0	11.2	34.7
Share of apparel spending	100.0	10.9	15.6	6.3	14.4	6.9	10.9	34.3
MEN'S APPAREL	**100.0**	**10.5**	**15.2**	**6.0**	**14.7**	**6.1**	**12.3**	**34.6**
Suits	100.0	6.3	11.0	5.4	9.0	6.2	10.8	51.2
Sport coats and tailored jackets	100.0	8.6	11.3	1.3	9.0	5.4	8.1	56.4
Coats and jackets	100.0	8.4	19.4	11.4	20.0	4.4	14.0	21.5
Underwear	100.0	10.4	20.2	3.8	10.1	7.1	11.4	36.5
Hosiery	100.0	12.3	17.2	5.5	13.8	8.9	11.2	30.1
Nightwear	100.0	5.1	9.0	14.3	12.3	6.6	8.6	44.1
Accessories	100.0	13.6	13.6	5.9	16.7	3.2	11.6	34.3
Sweaters and vests	100.0	14.8	24.0	1.2	7.3	4.0	11.1	37.2
Active sportswear	100.0	6.9	10.0	6.0	9.6	4.3	11.5	50.4
Shirts	100.0	11.7	14.7	5.3	16.8	7.3	13.1	30.6
Pants and shorts	100.0	10.2	13.8	6.6	16.2	6.9	12.6	33.1
Uniforms	100.0	6.1	27.5	10.5	21.6	2.4	15.4	18.2
Costumes	100.0	10.7	14.7	12.4	12.3	9.9	5.2	34.6
BOYS' (AGED 2 TO 15) APPAREL	**100.0**	**9.5**	**16.1**	**7.9**	**15.7**	**5.9**	**10.7**	**33.4**
Coats and jackets	100.0	6.3	12.5	8.3	13.4	10.0	9.6	39.8
Sweaters	100.0	9.8	19.5	5.5	15.2	9.8	11.9	28.4
Shirts	100.0	10.9	17.3	8.0	16.2	3.7	10.4	31.7
Underwear	100.0	8.1	20.0	6.0	14.8	5.6	7.3	35.9
Nightwear	100.0	8.9	17.0	7.0	18.1	7.0	13.9	28.2
Hosiery	100.0	10.5	22.3	7.3	19.8	2.3	8.1	28.6
Accessories	100.0	5.4	10.3	7.3	21.8	9.0	14.7	29.7
Suits, sport coats, and vests	100.0	3.2	11.1	4.7	12.8	1.5	13.6	53.2
Pants and shorts	100.0	10.3	15.5	9.5	14.4	7.0	11.3	32.0
Uniforms	100.0	11.1	18.0	3.5	12.0	3.1	7.6	44.7
Active sportswear	100.0	5.1	5.9	4.7	10.6	5.1	13.9	54.6
Costumes	100.0	9.4	12.5	6.2	14.1	7.9	9.1	40.6
WOMEN'S APPAREL	**100.0**	**10.5**	**14.2**	**5.8**	**14.7**	**7.5**	**11.2**	**35.1**
Coats and jackets	100.0	14.7	19.9	2.8	12.1	5.4	6.2	38.0
Dresses	100.0	7.3	12.4	7.0	13.3	3.5	8.3	46.7
Sport coats and tailored jackets	100.0	5.9	12.1	2.6	18.3	5.7	10.9	44.5
Sweaters and vests	100.0	9.5	12.6	7.3	15.2	6.7	11.1	36.6
Shirts, blouses, and tops	100.0	11.4	13.2	6.2	16.0	9.5	11.9	30.9
Skirts	100.0	7.0	15.6	6.9	8.9	2.0	16.6	42.6
Pants and shorts	100.0	11.2	14.4	7.1	16.9	8.9	12.8	28.0
Active sportswear	100.0	8.6	12.3	1.9	15.2	6.6	19.6	34.9
Nightwear	100.0	13.0	15.3	5.9	15.3	9.1	7.3	32.6
Undergarments	100.0	8.8	18.2	6.0	12.5	8.0	12.2	32.9
Hosiery	100.0	10.8	17.5	5.3	14.7	9.0	11.0	30.9
Suits	100.0	6.1	6.7	2.8	15.4	7.3	13.3	48.3
Accessories	100.0	11.6	12.7	4.7	13.6	8.2	10.0	38.6
Uniforms	100.0	7.9	16.6	12.5	20.1	7.4	10.7	25.0
Costumes	100.0	7.2	9.1	9.7	11.2	7.1	14.9	41.1

	total consumer units	under $20,000	$20,000–$39,999	$40,000–$49,999	$50,000–$69,999	$70,000–$79,999	$80,000–$99,999	$100,000 or more
GIRLS' (AGED 2 TO 15) APPAREL	**100.0%**	**9.1%**	**15.9%**	**8.3%**	**14.7%**	**6.0%**	**13.2%**	**31.8%**
Coats and jackets	100.0	9.0	14.0	8.5	13.5	8.5	10.7	35.7
Dresses and suits	100.0	12.4	14.8	11.4	9.0	8.8	13.6	29.2
Shirts, blouses, and sweaters	100.0	7.9	20.0	9.7	12.9	5.9	14.9	26.9
Skirts, pants, and shorts	100.0	10.8	14.4	8.1	14.9	6.2	10.6	34.9
Active sportswear	100.0	3.2	14.6	5.0	20.1	2.6	15.2	38.1
Underwear and nightwear	100.0	14.9	14.7	8.2	19.5	4.5	12.4	25.2
Hosiery	100.0	10.2	12.5	5.0	18.2	9.2	16.4	27.3
Accessories	100.0	6.0	13.6	7.2	17.6	3.4	9.6	41.2
Uniforms	100.0	14.8	15.5	4.1	6.7	5.8	11.0	42.1
Costumes	100.0	12.3	10.6	7.5	10.0	7.6	9.3	42.5
CHILDREN'S (UNDER AGE 2) APPAREL	**100.0**	**13.4**	**15.2**	**8.9**	**16.5**	**8.1**	**11.2**	**25.8**
Coats, jackets, and snowsuits	100.0	12.8	19.4	12.5	17.4	10.6	6.5	21.1
Outerwear including dresses	100.0	9.7	15.0	7.9	17.8	10.0	13.2	26.4
Underwear	100.0	14.6	14.2	8.3	16.5	7.5	11.4	26.4
Nightwear and loungewear	100.0	12.5	23.8	7.5	20.4	4.0	9.0	23.0
Accessories	100.0	14.7	17.9	11.8	14.5	9.5	9.4	23.6
FOOTWEAR	**100.0**	**12.5**	**18.6**	**5.9**	**13.6**	**6.8**	**10.0**	**31.8**
Men's	100.0	13.3	18.0	6.4	13.6	4.9	9.3	34.2
Boys'	100.0	11.4	16.7	5.0	20.0	4.7	11.5	28.8
Women's	100.0	12.8	19.0	5.2	12.0	8.8	9.2	32.3
Girls'	100.0	10.5	20.8	8.3	13.9	5.7	13.5	26.0
OTHER APPAREL PRODUCTS AND SERVICES	**100.0**	**10.5**	**15.3**	**6.2**	**13.2**	**7.0**	**8.4**	**39.5**
Material for making clothes	100.0	4.1	26.2	6.6	9.2	10.5	9.3	32.5
Sewing patterns and notions	100.0	8.9	11.7	8.6	23.2	7.5	14.3	25.5
Watches	100.0	12.6	15.4	1.8	27.8	8.1	5.9	28.6
Jewelry	100.0	4.9	10.1	6.0	11.6	8.3	9.1	50.1
Shoe repair and other shoe services	100.0	6.5	15.0	7.8	7.5	10.1	6.8	46.6
Coin-operated apparel laundry and dry cleaning	100.0	30.6	33.0	11.1	11.2	3.6	5.4	5.2
Apparel alteration, repair, and tailoring services	100.0	6.1	11.9	5.5	13.1	8.2	8.0	47.3
Clothing rental	100.0	13.7	7.0	11.3	4.7	1.3	11.5	54.9
Watch and jewelry repair	100.0	4.6	15.8	6.2	7.8	6.3	8.3	51.2
Professional laundry, dry cleaning	100.0	4.4	8.0	4.7	8.7	6.2	9.6	58.4
Clothing storage	100.0	5.0	11.3	1.8	1.9	15.6	26.2	40.0

Note: Numbers may not add to total because of rounding.
Source: Calculations by New Strategist based on the Bureau of Labor Statistics' 2011 Consumer Expenditure Survey

Table 2.9 Apparel: Average spending by high-income consumer units, 2011

(average annual spending on apparel, accessories, and related services, by before-tax income of high-income consumer units, 2011)

	total consumer units	$100,000 or more	$100,000–$119,999	$120,000–$149,999	$150,000 or more
Number of consumer units (in 000s)	122,287	21,593	7,045	6,107	8,440
Average number of persons per consumer unit	2.5	3.2	3.2	3.1	3.2
Average before-tax income of consumer units	$63,685.00	$169,776.00	$108,549.00	$133,318.00	$247,261.00
Average spending of consumer units, total	49,704.88	97,728.22	76,496.41	87,239.44	123,056.38
Apparel, average spending	**1,739.79**	**3,379.68**	**2,833.36**	**2,778.61**	**4,271.98**
MEN'S APPAREL	**324.14**	**634.75**	**538.75**	**598.74**	**742.10**
Suits	18.46	53.57	23.80	39.57	88.54
Sport coats and tailored jackets	5.26	16.81	4.74	13.13	29.55
Coats and jackets	26.83	32.69	34.41	25.69	36.17
Underwear	21.14	43.75	30.43	59.59	44.01
Hosiery	14.56	24.82	30.39	17.92	24.89
Nightwear	1.63	4.07	2.11	4.57	5.34
Accessories	29.84	57.99	62.13	36.67	69.51
Sweaters and vests	17.02	35.82	31.55	24.05	47.85
Active sportswear	24.92	71.12	48.62	88.54	78.18
Shirts	85.41	147.93	120.47	152.49	168.39
Pants and shorts	76.02	142.56	145.33	132.09	147.59
Uniforms	2.54	2.62	3.78	3.69	0.88
Costumes	0.51	1.00	1.00	0.73	1.21
BOYS' (AGED 2 TO 15) APPAREL	**79.63**	**150.51**	**124.31**	**151.08**	**172.59**
Coats and jackets	5.31	11.97	8.69	8.19	17.44
Sweaters	2.07	3.33	2.98	1.71	4.80
Shirts	21.84	39.18	35.18	39.78	42.21
Underwear	6.55	13.32	9.72	14.64	15.49
Nightwear	1.54	2.46	2.21	1.60	3.29
Hosiery	4.96	8.02	6.73	12.07	6.27
Accessories	6.20	10.44	4.65	19.69	8.87
Suits, sport coats, and vests	0.91	2.74	2.39	1.26	4.09
Pants and shorts	25.22	45.77	40.75	36.83	56.42
Uniforms	2.65	6.71	5.76	7.27	7.11
Active sportswear	1.38	4.27	4.10	4.97	3.91
Costumes	1.00	2.30	1.16	3.07	2.69
WOMEN'S APPAREL	**603.77**	**1,201.45**	**971.67**	**917.04**	**1,600.62**
Coats and jackets	51.25	110.30	96.90	43.04	169.47
Dresses	70.93	187.75	154.81	145.57	246.00
Sport coats and tailored jackets	2.28	5.74	4.38	3.58	8.45
Sweaters and vests	50.08	103.90	70.01	72.93	155.04
Shirts, blouses, and tops	123.62	216.25	188.18	202.35	250.30
Skirts	11.91	28.71	26.02	15.43	40.45
Pants and shorts	94.85	150.61	146.74	133.20	166.27
Active sportswear	36.32	71.78	52.43	46.99	106.01
Nightwear	28.82	53.28	53.29	36.76	64.97
Undergarments	34.22	63.67	42.28	50.06	91.73
Hosiery	22.46	39.32	30.35	39.90	46.63
Suits	7.69	21.04	10.41	14.05	34.97
Accessories	64.67	141.24	90.35	101.71	213.12
Uniforms	3.33	4.72	2.65	9.22	3.18
Costumes	1.35	3.14	2.85	2.25	4.02

	total consumer units	$100,000 or more	$100,000– $119,999	$120,000– $149,999	$150,000 or more
GIRLS' (AGED 2 TO 15) APPAREL	**$117.43**	**$211.31**	**$204.64**	**$149.02**	**$260.86**
Coats and jackets	5.26	10.63	8.80	9.66	12.86
Dresses and suits	13.78	22.76	26.01	19.87	22.00
Shirts, blouses, and sweaters	33.03	50.32	52.62	36.41	58.18
Skirts, pants, and shorts	25.07	49.53	37.07	46.51	62.10
Active sportswear	15.27	32.91	43.55	9.17	40.54
Underwear and nightwear	9.59	13.68	13.10	6.31	19.39
Hosiery	6.08	9.41	6.53	8.46	12.58
Accessories	5.15	12.03	8.43	7.43	18.37
Uniforms	2.85	6.80	3.76	2.64	12.34
Costumes	1.35	3.25	4.77	2.57	2.48
CHILDREN'S (UNDER AGE 2) APPAREL	**68.13**	**99.49**	**119.62**	**94.80**	**85.41**
Coats, jackets, and snowsuits	0.93	1.11	0.44	0.91	1.83
Outerwear including dresses	9.47	14.15	12.14	12.16	17.26
Underwear	45.58	68.05	92.39	68.61	46.66
Nightwear and loungewear	1.65	2.15	1.73	1.32	3.10
Accessories	10.50	14.03	12.92	11.81	16.57
FOOTWEAR	**321.14**	**578.13**	**538.45**	**470.22**	**688.75**
Men's	96.84	187.81	247.66	157.93	157.39
Boys'	36.67	59.76	56.30	60.78	62.01
Women's	151.99	278.10	173.81	202.16	421.78
Girls'	35.63	52.46	60.69	49.36	47.57
OTHER APPAREL PRODUCTS AND SERVICES	**225.54**	**504.04**	**335.92**	**397.70**	**721.63**
Material for making clothes	9.65	17.76	8.33	2.65	36.60
Sewing patterns and notions	7.88	11.40	4.91	7.31	19.89
Watches	30.27	49.04	47.83	58.30	43.53
Jewelry	71.95	204.05	148.98	159.94	281.93
Shoe repair and other shoe services	1.50	3.96	2.34	3.64	5.53
Coin-operated apparel laundry and dry cleaning	39.63	11.68	14.75	12.27	8.69
Apparel alteration, repair, and tailoring services	6.37	17.06	9.80	9.19	28.80
Clothing rental	1.68	5.22	7.02	5.60	3.45
Watch and jewelry repair	5.43	15.73	5.76	19.33	21.46
Professional laundry, dry cleaning	50.10	165.74	82.93	116.90	270.21
Clothing storage	1.06	2.40	3.28	2.59	1.54

Note: Subcategories may not add to total because some are not shown.
Source: Bureau of Labor Statistics, unpublished data from the 2011 Consumer Expenditure Survey

Table 2.10 Apparel: Indexed spending by high-income consumer units, 2011

(indexed average annual spending of consumer units on apparel, accessories, and related services, by before-tax income of consumer unit, 2011; index definition: an index of 100 is the average for all consumer units; an index of 125 means that spending by consumer units in that group is 25 percent above the average for all consumer units; an index of 75 indicates spending that is 25 percent below the average for all consumer units)

	total consumer units	$100,000 or more	$100,000–$119,999	$120,000–$149,999	$150,000 or more
Average spending of consumer units, total	$49,705	$97,728	$76,496	$87,239	$123,056
Average spending of consumer units, index	100	197	154	176	248
Apparel, spending index	**100**	**194**	**163**	**160**	**246**
MEN'S APPAREL	**100**	**196**	**166**	**185**	**229**
Suits	100	290	129	214	480
Sport coats and tailored jackets	100	320	90	250	562
Coats and jackets	100	122	128	96	135
Underwear	100	207	144	282	208
Hosiery	100	170	209	123	171
Nightwear	100	250	129	280	328
Accessories	100	194	208	123	233
Sweaters and vests	100	210	185	141	281
Active sportswear	100	285	195	355	314
Shirts	100	173	141	179	197
Pants and shorts	100	188	191	174	194
Uniforms	100	103	149	145	35
Costumes	100	196	196	143	237
BOYS' (AGED 2 TO 15) APPAREL	**100**	**189**	**156**	**190**	**217**
Coats and jackets	100	225	164	154	328
Sweaters	100	161	144	83	232
Shirts	100	179	161	182	193
Underwear	100	203	148	224	236
Nightwear	100	160	144	104	214
Hosiery	100	162	136	243	126
Accessories	100	168	75	318	143
Suits, sport coats, and vests	100	301	263	138	449
Pants and shorts	100	181	162	146	224
Uniforms	100	253	217	274	268
Active sportswear	100	309	297	360	283
Costumes	100	230	116	307	269
WOMEN'S APPAREL	**100**	**199**	**161**	**152**	**265**
Coats and jackets	100	215	189	84	331
Dresses	100	265	218	205	347
Sport coats and tailored jackets	100	252	192	157	371
Sweaters and vests	100	207	140	146	310
Shirts, blouses, and tops	100	175	152	164	202
Skirts	100	241	218	130	340
Pants and shorts	100	159	155	140	175
Active sportswear	100	198	144	129	292
Nightwear	100	185	185	128	225
Undergarments	100	186	124	146	268
Hosiery	100	175	135	178	208
Suits	100	274	135	183	455
Accessories	100	218	140	157	330
Uniforms	100	142	80	277	95
Costumes	100	233	211	167	298

	total consumer units	$100,000 or more	$100,000–$119,999	$120,000–$149,999	$150,000 or more
GIRLS' (AGED 2 TO 15) APPAREL	**100**	**180**	**174**	**127**	**222**
Coats and jackets	100	202	167	184	244
Dresses and suits	100	165	189	144	160
Shirts, blouses, and sweaters	100	152	159	110	176
Skirts, pants, and shorts	100	198	148	186	248
Active sportswear	100	216	285	60	265
Underwear and nightwear	100	143	137	66	202
Hosiery	100	155	107	139	207
Accessories	100	234	164	144	357
Uniforms	100	239	132	93	433
Costumes	100	241	353	190	184
CHILDREN'S (UNDER AGE 2) APPAREL	**100**	**146**	**176**	**139**	**125**
Coats, jackets, and snowsuits	100	119	47	98	197
Outerwear including dresses	100	149	128	128	182
Underwear	100	149	203	151	102
Nightwear and loungewear	100	130	105	80	188
Accessories	100	134	123	112	158
FOOTWEAR	**100**	**180**	**168**	**146**	**214**
Men's	100	194	256	163	163
Boys'	100	163	154	166	169
Women's	100	183	114	133	278
Girls'	100	147	170	139	134
OTHER APPAREL PRODUCTS AND SERVICES	**100**	**223**	**149**	**176**	**320**
Material for making clothes	100	184	86	27	379
Sewing patterns and notions	100	145	62	93	252
Watches	100	162	158	193	144
Jewelry	100	284	207	222	392
Shoe repair and other shoe services	100	264	156	243	369
Coin-operated apparel laundry and dry cleaning	100	29	37	31	22
Apparel alteration, repair, and tailoring services	100	268	154	144	452
Clothing rental	100	311	418	333	205
Watch and jewelry repair	100	290	106	356	395
Professional laundry, dry cleaning	100	331	166	233	539
Clothing storage	100	226	309	244	145

Source: Calculations by New Strategist based on the Bureau of Labor Statistics' 2011 Consumer Expenditure Survey

Table 2.11 Apparel: Total spending by high-income consumer units, 2011

(total annual spending on apparel, accessories, and related services, by before-tax income group of high-income consumer units, 2011; consumer units and dollars in thousands)

	total consumer units	$100,000 or more	$100,000–$119,999	$120,000–$149,999	$150,000 or more
Number of consumer units	122,287	21,593	7,045	6,107	8,440
Total spending of all consumer units	$6,078,260,661	$2,110,245,454	$538,917,208	$532,771,260	$1,038,595,847
Apparel, total spending	212,753,700	72,977,430	19,961,021	16,968,971	36,055,511
MEN'S APPAREL	39,638,108	13,706,157	3,795,494	3,656,505	6,263,324
Suits	2,257,418	1,156,737	167,671	241,654	747,278
Sport coats and tailored jackets	643,230	362,978	33,393	80,185	249,402
Coats and jackets	3,280,960	705,875	242,418	156,889	305,275
Underwear	2,585,147	944,694	214,379	363,916	371,444
Hosiery	1,780,499	535,938	214,098	109,437	210,072
Nightwear	199,328	87,884	14,865	27,909	45,070
Accessories	3,649,044	1,252,178	437,706	223,944	586,664
Sweaters and vests	2,081,325	773,461	222,270	146,873	403,854
Active sportswear	3,047,392	1,535,694	342,528	540,714	659,839
Shirts	10,444,533	3,194,252	848,711	931,256	1,421,212
Pants and shorts	9,296,258	3,078,298	1,023,850	806,674	1,245,660
Uniforms	310,609	56,574	26,630	22,535	7,427
Costumes	62,366	21,593	7,045	4,458	10,212
BOYS' (AGED 2 TO 15) APPAREL	9,737,714	3,249,962	875,764	922,646	1,456,660
Coats and jackets	649,344	258,468	61,221	50,016	147,194
Sweaters	253,134	71,905	20,994	10,443	40,512
Shirts	2,670,748	846,014	247,843	242,936	356,252
Underwear	800,980	287,619	68,477	89,406	130,736
Nightwear	188,322	53,119	15,569	9,771	27,768
Hosiery	606,544	173,176	47,413	73,711	52,919
Accessories	758,179	225,431	32,759	120,247	74,863
Suits, sport coats, and vests	111,281	59,165	16,838	7,695	34,520
Pants and shorts	3,084,078	988,312	287,084	224,921	476,185
Uniforms	324,061	144,889	40,579	44,398	60,008
Active sportswear	168,756	92,202	28,885	30,352	33,000
Costumes	122,287	49,664	8,172	18,748	22,704
WOMEN'S APPAREL	73,833,222	25,942,910	6,845,415	5,600,363	13,509,233
Coats and jackets	6,267,209	2,381,708	682,661	262,845	1,430,327
Dresses	8,673,817	4,054,086	1,090,636	888,996	2,076,240
Sport coats and tailored jackets	278,814	123,944	30,857	21,863	71,318
Sweaters and vests	6,124,133	2,243,513	493,220	445,384	1,308,538
Shirts, blouses, and tops	15,117,119	4,669,486	1,325,728	1,235,751	2,112,532
Skirts	1,456,438	619,935	183,311	94,231	341,398
Pants and shorts	11,598,922	3,252,122	1,033,783	813,452	1,403,319
Active sportswear	4,441,464	1,549,946	369,369	286,968	894,724
Nightwear	3,524,311	1,150,475	375,428	224,493	548,347
Undergarments	4,184,661	1,374,826	297,863	305,716	774,201
Hosiery	2,746,566	849,037	213,816	243,669	393,557
Suits	940,387	454,317	73,338	85,803	295,147
Accessories	7,908,300	3,049,795	636,516	621,143	1,798,733
Uniforms	407,216	101,919	18,669	56,307	26,839
Costumes	165,087	67,802	20,078	13,741	33,929

	total consumer units	$100,000 or more	$100,000– $119,999	$120,000– $149,999	$150,000 or more
GIRLS' (AGED 2 TO 15) APPAREL	**$14,360,162**	**$4,562,817**	**$1,441,689**	**$910,065**	**$2,201,658**
Coats and jackets	643,230	229,534	61,996	58,994	108,538
Dresses and suits	1,685,115	491,457	183,240	121,346	185,680
Shirts, blouses, and sweaters	4,039,140	1,086,560	370,708	222,356	491,039
Skirts, pants, and shorts	3,065,735	1,069,501	261,158	284,037	524,124
Active sportswear	1,867,322	710,626	306,810	56,001	342,158
Underwear and nightwear	1,172,732	295,392	92,290	38,535	163,652
Hosiery	743,505	203,190	46,004	51,665	106,175
Accessories	629,778	259,764	59,389	45,375	155,043
Uniforms	348,518	146,832	26,489	16,122	104,150
Costumes	165,087	70,177	33,605	15,695	20,931
CHILDREN'S (UNDER AGE 2) APPAREL	**8,331,413**	**2,148,288**	**842,723**	**578,944**	**720,860**
Coats, jackets, and snowsuits	113,727	23,968	3,100	5,557	15,445
Outerwear including dresses	1,158,058	305,541	85,526	74,261	145,674
Underwear	5,573,841	1,469,404	650,888	419,001	393,810
Nightwear and loungewear	201,774	46,425	12,188	8,061	26,164
Accessories	1,284,014	302,950	91,021	72,124	139,851
FOOTWEAR	**39,271,247**	**12,483,561**	**3,793,380**	**2,871,634**	**5,813,050**
Men's	11,842,273	4,055,381	1,744,765	964,479	1,328,372
Boys'	4,484,264	1,290,398	396,634	371,183	523,364
Women's	18,586,401	6,005,013	1,224,491	1,234,591	3,559,823
Girls'	4,357,086	1,132,769	427,561	301,442	401,491
OTHER APPAREL PRODUCTS AND SERVICES	**27,580,610**	**10,883,736**	**2,366,556**	**2,428,754**	**6,090,557**
Material for making clothes	1,180,070	383,492	58,685	16,184	308,904
Sewing patterns and notions	963,622	246,160	34,591	44,642	167,872
Watches	3,701,627	1,058,921	336,962	356,038	367,393
Jewelry	8,798,550	4,406,052	1,049,564	976,754	2,379,489
Shoe repair and other shoe services	183,431	85,508	16,485	22,229	46,673
Coin-operated apparel laundry and dry cleaning	4,846,234	252,206	103,914	74,933	73,344
Apparel alteration, repair, and tailoring services	778,968	368,377	69,041	56,123	243,072
Clothing rental	205,442	112,715	49,456	34,199	29,118
Watch and jewelry repair	664,018	339,658	40,579	118,048	181,122
Professional laundry, dry cleaning	6,126,579	3,578,824	584,242	713,908	2,280,572
Clothing storage	129,624	51,823	23,108	15,817	12,998

Note: Numbers may not add to total because of rounding and missing subcategories.
Source: Calculations by New Strategist based on the Bureau of Labor Statistics' 2011 Consumer Expenditure Survey

Table 2.12 Apparel: Market shares by high-income consumer units, 2011

(percentage of total annual spending on apparel, accessories, and related services accounted for by before-tax income group of high-income consumer units, 2011)

	total consumer units	$100,000 or more	$100,000–$119,999	$120,000–$149,999	$150,000 or more
Share of total consumer units	100.0%	17.7%	5.8%	5.0%	6.9%
Share of total before-tax income	100.0	47.1	9.8	10.5	26.8
Share of total spending	100.0	34.7	8.9	8.8	17.1
Share of apparel spending	100.0	34.3	9.4	8.0	16.9
MEN'S APPAREL	100.0	34.6	9.6	9.2	15.8
Suits	100.0	51.2	7.4	10.7	33.1
Sport coats and tailored jackets	100.0	56.4	5.2	12.5	38.8
Coats and jackets	100.0	21.5	7.4	4.8	9.3
Underwear	100.0	36.5	8.3	14.1	14.4
Hosiery	100.0	30.1	12.0	6.1	11.8
Nightwear	100.0	44.1	7.5	14.0	22.6
Accessories	100.0	34.3	12.0	6.1	16.1
Sweaters and vests	100.0	37.2	10.7	7.1	19.4
Active sportswear	100.0	50.4	11.2	17.7	21.7
Shirts	100.0	30.6	8.1	8.9	13.6
Pants and shorts	100.0	33.1	11.0	8.7	13.4
Uniforms	100.0	18.2	8.6	7.3	2.4
Costumes	100.0	34.6	11.3	7.1	16.4
BOYS' (AGED 2 TO 15) APPAREL	100.0	33.4	9.0	9.5	15.0
Coats and jackets	100.0	39.8	9.4	7.7	22.7
Sweaters	100.0	28.4	8.3	4.1	16.0
Shirts	100.0	31.7	9.3	9.1	13.3
Underwear	100.0	35.9	8.5	11.2	16.3
Nightwear	100.0	28.2	8.3	5.2	14.7
Hosiery	100.0	28.6	7.8	12.2	8.7
Accessories	100.0	29.7	4.3	15.9	9.9
Suits, sport coats, and vests	100.0	53.2	15.1	6.9	31.0
Pants and shorts	100.0	32.0	9.3	7.3	15.4
Uniforms	100.0	44.7	12.5	13.7	18.5
Active sportswear	100.0	54.6	17.1	18.0	19.6
Costumes	100.0	40.6	6.7	15.3	18.6
WOMEN'S APPAREL	100.0	35.1	9.3	7.6	18.3
Coats and jackets	100.0	38.0	10.9	4.2	22.8
Dresses	100.0	46.7	12.6	10.2	23.9
Sport coats and tailored jackets	100.0	44.5	11.1	7.8	25.6
Sweaters and vests	100.0	36.6	8.1	7.3	21.4
Shirts, blouses, and tops	100.0	30.9	8.8	8.2	14.0
Skirts	100.0	42.6	12.6	6.5	23.4
Pants and shorts	100.0	28.0	8.9	7.0	12.1
Active sportswear	100.0	34.9	8.3	6.5	20.1
Nightwear	100.0	32.6	10.7	6.4	15.6
Undergarments	100.0	32.9	7.1	7.3	18.5
Hosiery	100.0	30.9	7.8	8.9	14.3
Suits	100.0	48.3	7.8	9.1	31.4
Accessories	100.0	38.6	8.0	7.9	22.7
Uniforms	100.0	25.0	4.6	13.8	6.6
Costumes	100.0	41.1	12.2	8.3	20.6

	total consumer units	$100,000 or more	$100,000– $119,999	$120,000– $149,999	$150,000 or more
GIRLS' (AGED 2 TO 15) APPAREL	**100.0%**	**31.8%**	**10.0%**	**6.3%**	**15.3%**
Coats and jackets	100.0	35.7	9.6	9.2	16.9
Dresses and suits	100.0	29.2	10.9	7.2	11.0
Shirts, blouses, and sweaters	100.0	26.9	9.2	5.5	12.2
Skirts, pants, and shorts	100.0	34.9	8.5	9.3	17.1
Active sportswear	100.0	38.1	16.4	3.0	18.3
Underwear and nightwear	100.0	25.2	7.9	3.3	14.0
Hosiery	100.0	27.3	6.2	6.9	14.3
Accessories	100.0	41.2	9.4	7.2	24.6
Uniforms	100.0	42.1	7.6	4.6	29.9
Costumes	100.0	42.5	20.4	9.5	12.7
CHILDREN'S (UNDER AGE 2) APPAREL	**100.0**	**25.8**	**10.1**	**6.9**	**8.7**
Coats, jackets, and snowsuits	100.0	21.1	2.7	4.9	13.6
Outerwear including dresses	100.0	26.4	7.4	6.4	12.6
Underwear	100.0	26.4	11.7	7.5	7.1
Nightwear and loungewear	100.0	23.0	6.0	4.0	13.0
Accessories	100.0	23.6	7.1	5.6	10.9
FOOTWEAR	**100.0**	**31.8**	**9.7**	**7.3**	**14.8**
Men's	100.0	34.2	14.7	8.1	11.2
Boys'	100.0	28.8	8.8	8.3	11.7
Women's	100.0	32.3	6.6	6.6	19.2
Girls'	100.0	26.0	9.8	6.9	9.2
OTHER APPAREL PRODUCTS AND SERVICES	**100.0**	**39.5**	**8.6**	**8.8**	**22.1**
Material for making clothes	100.0	32.5	5.0	1.4	26.2
Sewing patterns and notions	100.0	25.5	3.6	4.6	17.4
Watches	100.0	28.6	9.1	9.6	9.9
Jewelry	100.0	50.1	11.9	11.1	27.0
Shoe repair and other shoe services	100.0	46.6	9.0	12.1	25.4
Coin-operated apparel laundry and dry cleaning	100.0	5.2	2.1	1.5	1.5
Apparel alteration, repair, and tailoring services	100.0	47.3	8.9	7.2	31.2
Clothing rental	100.0	54.9	24.1	16.6	14.2
Watch and jewelry repair	100.0	51.2	6.1	17.8	27.3
Professional laundry, dry cleaning	100.0	58.4	9.5	11.7	37.2
Clothing storage	100.0	40.0	17.8	12.2	10.0

Note: Numbers may not add to total because of rounding.
Source: Calculations by New Strategist based on the Bureau of Labor Statistics' 2011 Consumer Expenditure Survey

Table 2.13 Apparel: Average spending by household type, 2011

(average annual spending of consumer units on apparel, accessories, and related services, by type of consumer unit, 2011)

	total married couples	married couples, no children	married couples with children				single parent with child under age 18	single person
			total	oldest child under age 6	oldest child aged 6 to 17	oldest child aged 18 or older		
Number of consumer units (in 000s)	60,144	25,270	29,097	5,825	14,661	8,612	6,956	36,110
Average number of persons per consumer unit	3.2	2.0	4.0	3.5	4.2	3.9	2.9	1.0
Average before-tax income of consumer units	$86,700.00	$78,823.00	$93,677.00	$91,014.00	$93,029.00	$96,583.00	$37,188.00	$34,540.00
Average spending of consumer units, total	63,971.54	57,658.24	69,724.22	65,947.61	70,708.52	70,411.85	37,553.05	30,613.18
Apparel, average spending	**2,184.16**	**1,715.34**	**2,540.82**	**2,156.57**	**2,587.32**	**2,686.84**	**1,834.86**	**1,021.07**
MEN'S APPAREL	**404.82**	**337.64**	**433.44**	**278.35**	**393.35**	**592.22**	**137.92**	**235.23**
Suits	22.57	20.12	26.51	16.67	28.20	30.30	1.55	14.22
Sport coats and tailored jackets	7.57	8.44	6.46	4.82	6.00	8.35	–	3.50
Coats and jackets	29.44	24.37	33.03	56.39	29.27	25.83	27.35	20.06
Underwear	29.54	28.43	28.53	14.95	23.02	45.70	12.06	11.00
Hosiery	18.10	13.35	21.54	19.29	21.69	22.58	8.10	8.07
Nightwear	2.27	2.39	2.24	0.85	2.92	2.03	0.74	0.69
Accessories	38.26	29.73	39.25	31.60	35.15	50.60	4.32	21.53
Sweaters and vests	22.04	19.78	16.83	3.03	21.61	16.79	3.78	14.91
Active sportswear	30.12	16.63	41.45	30.90	29.73	67.32	18.52	17.83
Shirts	105.48	86.02	114.58	55.67	106.64	162.13	33.15	69.69
Pants and shorts	96.16	86.08	98.93	41.33	84.47	156.70	26.22	51.74
Uniforms	2.73	2.17	3.19	1.46	4.09	2.81	1.64	1.75
Costumes	0.53	0.14	0.88	1.38	0.57	1.09	0.49	0.23
BOYS' (AGED 2 TO 15) APPAREL	**110.34**	**25.11**	**178.66**	**126.30**	**256.01**	**80.40**	**198.18**	**14.46**
Coats and jackets	7.59	1.68	12.06	7.38	17.55	5.88	11.81	0.65
Sweaters	3.05	1.20	4.37	3.45	5.92	2.35	3.63	0.25
Shirts	29.35	7.04	49.07	22.20	72.55	25.08	59.17	4.83
Underwear	8.75	1.68	15.30	16.40	19.54	7.53	17.27	1.67
Nightwear	2.05	0.77	3.17	4.28	4.09	0.84	3.07	0.46
Hosiery	6.88	1.73	10.96	11.02	13.55	6.56	9.28	0.70
Accessories	8.53	2.83	11.59	10.34	16.68	3.72	13.03	1.77
Suits, sport coats, and vests	1.52	0.31	2.28	2.06	3.40	0.53	1.26	0.08
Pants and shorts	34.99	6.87	56.80	36.01	84.35	23.96	66.49	3.76
Uniforms	3.98	0.30	6.67	6.44	9.26	2.44	7.46	–
Active sportswear	2.12	0.55	3.58	3.07	5.43	0.79	3.50	0.17
Costumes	1.53	0.14	2.80	3.64	3.69	0.72	2.21	0.12
WOMEN'S APPAREL	**725.83**	**690.53**	**732.64**	**527.55**	**634.05**	**1,018.23**	**577.03**	**427.45**
Coats and jackets	55.89	66.22	42.79	33.81	25.35	77.38	87.01	43.55
Dresses	83.45	64.75	76.42	44.30	73.05	100.74	67.54	37.64
Sport coats and tailored jackets	2.51	3.37	1.65	1.42	1.33	2.36	0.94	2.08
Sweaters and vests	67.99	77.77	62.45	71.54	54.05	71.32	53.98	32.51
Shirts, blouses, and tops	146.55	134.68	158.26	96.92	140.14	224.37	98.96	90.55
Skirts	15.23	15.38	14.67	8.03	15.55	17.04	10.58	7.46
Pants and shorts	108.89	98.13	121.69	86.06	107.58	166.12	68.02	78.57
Active sportswear	42.12	32.94	53.18	38.19	44.64	76.25	56.78	28.54
Nightwear	40.22	38.11	33.73	20.51	26.54	53.50	15.50	15.11
Undergarments	39.65	33.38	41.85	40.13	36.26	52.28	23.54	26.68
Hosiery	25.62	20.76	28.65	14.19	21.28	49.46	15.34	21.22
Suits	9.94	9.91	9.06	7.13	7.95	12.23	3.93	5.63
Accessories	83.25	92.38	82.27	62.57	74.58	106.66	66.66	35.37
Uniforms	3.08	2.29	3.56	1.75	3.18	5.42	7.47	1.82
Costumes	1.44	0.46	2.41	1.00	2.56	3.10	0.80	0.72

	total married couples	married couples, no children	married couples with children				single parent with child under age 18	single person
			total	oldest child under age 6	oldest child aged 6 to 17	oldest child aged 18 or older		
GIRLS' (AGED 2 TO 15) APPAREL	**$163.24**	**$46.62**	**$271.79**	**$108.09**	**$410.57**	**$136.00**	**$273.63**	**$31.51**
Coats and jackets	7.25	1.24	12.26	5.87	20.07	3.28	12.99	0.84
Dresses and suits	19.46	12.78	27.61	24.79	37.13	13.21	22.38	5.42
Shirts, blouses, and sweaters	43.18	13.11	71.74	24.14	109.20	36.23	84.04	11.26
Skirts, pants, and shorts	34.93	5.39	59.38	26.89	96.02	18.97	79.96	3.03
Active sportswear	21.75	3.71	40.74	2.81	57.85	33.90	26.66	7.16
Underwear and nightwear	13.99	5.87	20.46	7.26	32.54	7.74	18.77	1.90
Hosiery	8.59	2.14	15.21	5.70	22.10	9.14	12.14	1.08
Accessories	7.83	1.67	13.79	2.70	18.96	11.51	9.24	0.51
Uniforms	4.18	0.51	6.82	4.51	11.05	1.20	5.40	0.02
Costumes	2.08	0.20	3.77	3.41	5.64	0.83	2.05	0.29
CHILDREN'S (UNDER AGE 2) APPAREL	**92.57**	**30.00**	**151.29**	**511.69**	**98.54**	**26.26**	**104.49**	**14.70**
Coats, jackets, and snowsuits	1.16	0.16	1.75	5.60	1.12	0.20	1.77	0.41
Outerwear including dresses	13.85	7.93	18.09	61.64	9.19	3.79	10.06	1.96
Underwear	62.97	15.73	109.93	380.60	72.36	16.28	77.61	7.35
Nightwear and loungewear	2.01	1.13	2.78	8.36	1.67	0.91	3.24	0.67
Accessories	12.58	5.04	18.74	55.50	14.19	5.09	11.81	4.31
FOOTWEAR	**407.47**	**297.43**	**490.07**	**336.60**	**522.23**	**524.88**	**380.13**	**160.57**
Men's	120.27	105.03	115.73	107.38	89.15	165.35	60.33	56.34
Boys'	52.18	5.61	92.63	44.10	142.48	36.79	80.99	4.37
Women's	187.01	180.21	194.33	137.92	156.71	290.42	155.06	89.99
Girls'	48.02	6.58	87.39	47.20	133.89	32.33	83.75	9.87
OTHER APPAREL PRODUCTS AND SERVICES	**279.90**	**288.02**	**282.93**	**267.99**	**272.56**	**308.85**	**163.48**	**137.15**
Material for making clothes	15.75	15.07	13.79	7.03	14.44	16.62	2.87	4.44
Sewing patterns and notions	11.03	10.72	12.07	27.24	4.75	15.61	2.01	2.86
Watches	42.81	31.13	53.40	28.37	46.05	80.30	33.45	11.73
Jewelry	92.80	121.83	76.14	79.70	75.03	75.62	25.92	36.14
Shoe repair and other shoe services	1.66	1.56	1.83	1.59	1.74	2.15	1.06	1.57
Coin-operated apparel laundry and dry cleaning	27.29	17.85	32.75	40.88	35.79	22.06	72.67	40.66
Apparel alteration, repair, and tailoring services	7.93	10.48	6.58	5.79	5.92	8.23	2.59	4.80
Clothing rental	2.60	1.30	3.53	3.88	2.33	5.33	1.72	0.34
Watch and jewelry repair	8.12	12.21	5.26	6.29	4.07	6.59	0.30	2.35
Professional laundry, dry cleaning	68.66	64.06	76.67	66.74	82.13	74.09	19.78	32.06
Clothing storage	1.25	1.80	0.91	0.47	0.30	2.24	1.10	0.20

Note: Average spending figures for total consumer units can be found on Average Spending by Age and Average Spending by Region tables. Subcategories do not add to total because some are not shown.
"–" means sample is too small to make a reliable estimate.
Source: Bureau of Labor Statistics, unpublished data from the 2011 Consumer Expenditure Survey

Table 2.14 Apparel: Indexed spending by household type, 2011

(indexed average annual spending of consumer units on apparel, accessories, and related services, by type of consumer unit, 2011; index definition: an index of 100 is the average for all consumer units; an index of 125 means that spending by consumer units in that group is 25 percent above the average for all consumer units; an index of 75 indicates spending that is 25 percent below the average for all consumer units)

	total married couples	married couples, no children	married couples with children				single parent with child under age 18	single person
			total	oldest child under age 6	oldest child aged 6 to 17	oldest child aged 18 or older		
Average spending of consumer units, total	$63,972	$57,658	$69,724	$65,948	$70,709	$70,412	$37,553	$30,613
Average spending of consumer units, index	129	116	140	133	142	142	76	62
Apparel, spending index	**126**	**99**	**146**	**124**	**149**	**154**	**105**	**59**
MEN'S APPAREL	**125**	**104**	**134**	**86**	**121**	**183**	**43**	**73**
Suits	122	109	144	90	153	164	8	77
Sport coats and tailored jackets	144	160	123	92	114	159	–	67
Coats and jackets	110	91	123	210	109	96	102	75
Underwear	140	134	135	71	109	216	57	52
Hosiery	124	92	148	132	149	155	56	55
Nightwear	139	147	137	52	179	125	45	42
Accessories	128	100	132	106	118	170	14	72
Sweaters and vests	129	116	99	18	127	99	22	88
Active sportswear	121	67	166	124	119	270	74	72
Shirts	123	101	134	65	125	190	39	82
Pants and shorts	126	113	130	54	111	206	34	68
Uniforms	107	85	126	57	161	111	65	69
Costumes	104	27	173	271	112	214	96	45
BOYS' (AGED 2 TO 15) APPAREL	**139**	**32**	**224**	**159**	**321**	**101**	**249**	**18**
Coats and jackets	143	32	227	139	331	111	222	12
Sweaters	147	58	211	167	286	114	175	12
Shirts	134	32	225	102	332	115	271	22
Underwear	134	26	234	250	298	115	264	25
Nightwear	133	50	206	278	266	55	199	30
Hosiery	139	35	221	222	273	132	187	14
Accessories	138	46	187	167	269	60	210	29
Suits, sport coats, and vests	167	34	251	226	374	58	138	9
Pants and shorts	139	27	225	143	334	95	264	15
Uniforms	150	11	252	243	349	92	282	–
Active sportswear	154	40	259	222	393	57	254	12
Costumes	153	14	280	364	369	72	221	12
WOMEN'S APPAREL	**120**	**114**	**121**	**87**	**105**	**169**	**96**	**71**
Coats and jackets	109	129	83	66	49	151	170	85
Dresses	118	91	108	62	103	142	95	53
Sport coats and tailored jackets	110	148	72	62	58	104	41	91
Sweaters and vests	136	155	125	143	108	142	108	65
Shirts, blouses, and tops	119	109	128	78	113	181	80	73
Skirts	128	129	123	67	131	143	89	63
Pants and shorts	115	103	128	91	113	175	72	83
Active sportswear	116	91	146	105	123	210	156	79
Nightwear	140	132	117	71	92	186	54	52
Undergarments	116	98	122	117	106	153	69	78
Hosiery	114	92	128	63	95	220	68	94
Suits	129	129	118	93	103	159	51	73
Accessories	129	143	127	97	115	165	103	55
Uniforms	92	69	107	53	95	163	224	55
Costumes	107	34	179	74	190	230	59	53

	total married couples	married couples, no children	married couples with children				single parent with child under age 18	single person
			total	oldest child under age 6	oldest child aged 6 to 17	oldest child aged 18 or older		
GIRLS' (AGED 2 TO 15) APPAREL	**139**	**40**	**231**	**92**	**350**	**116**	**233**	**27**
Coats and jackets	138	24	233	112	382	62	247	16
Dresses and suits	141	93	200	180	269	96	162	39
Shirts, blouses, and sweaters	131	40	217	73	331	110	254	34
Skirts, pants, and shorts	139	21	237	107	383	76	319	12
Active sportswear	142	24	267	18	379	222	175	47
Underwear and nightwear	146	61	213	76	339	81	196	20
Hosiery	141	35	250	94	363	150	200	18
Accessories	152	32	268	52	368	223	179	10
Uniforms	147	18	239	158	388	42	189	1
Costumes	154	15	279	253	418	61	152	21
CHILDREN'S (UNDER AGE 2) APPAREL	**136**	**44**	**222**	**751**	**145**	**39**	**153**	**22**
Coats, jackets, and snowsuits	125	17	188	602	120	22	190	44
Outerwear including dresses	146	84	191	651	97	40	106	21
Underwear	138	35	241	835	159	36	170	16
Nightwear and loungewear	122	68	168	507	101	55	196	41
Accessories	120	48	178	529	135	48	112	41
FOOTWEAR	**127**	**93**	**153**	**105**	**163**	**163**	**118**	**50**
Men's	124	108	120	111	92	171	62	58
Boys'	142	15	253	120	389	100	221	12
Women's	123	119	128	91	103	191	102	59
Girls'	135	18	245	132	376	91	235	28
OTHER APPAREL PRODUCTS AND SERVICES	**124**	**128**	**125**	**119**	**121**	**137**	**72**	**61**
Material for making clothes	163	156	143	73	150	172	30	46
Sewing patterns and notions	140	136	153	346	60	198	26	36
Watches	141	103	176	94	152	265	111	39
Jewelry	129	169	106	111	104	105	36	50
Shoe repair and other shoe services	111	104	122	106	116	143	71	105
Coin-operated apparel laundry and dry cleaning	69	45	83	103	90	56	183	103
Apparel alteration, repair, and tailoring services	124	165	103	91	93	129	41	75
Clothing rental	155	77	210	231	139	317	102	20
Watch and jewelry repair	150	225	97	116	75	121	6	43
Professional laundry, dry cleaning	137	128	153	133	164	148	39	64
Clothing storage	118	170	86	44	28	211	104	19

Note: Spending index for total consumer units is 100. "–" means sample is too small to make a reliable estimate.
Source: Calculations by New Strategist based on the Bureau of Labor Statistics' 2011 Consumer Expenditure Survey

Table 2.15 Apparel: Total spending by household type, 2011

(total annual spending on apparel, accessories, and related services, by consumer unit type, 2011; consumer units and dollars in thousands)

	total married couples	married couples, no children	married couples with children				single parent with child under age 18	single person
			total	oldest child under age 6	oldest child aged 6 to 17	oldest child aged 18 or older		
Number of consumer units	60,144	25,270	29,097	5,825	14,661	8,612	6,956	36,110
Total spending of all consumer units	$3,847,504,302	$1,457,023,725	$2,028,765,629	$384,144,828	$1,036,657,612	$606,386,852	$261,219,016	$1,105,441,930
Apparel, total spending	131,364,119	43,346,642	73,930,240	12,562,020	37,932,699	23,139,066	12,763,286	36,870,838
MEN'S APPAREL	**24,347,494**	**8,532,163**	**12,611,804**	**1,621,389**	**5,766,904**	**5,100,199**	**959,372**	**8,494,155**
Suits	1,357,450	508,432	771,361	97,103	413,440	260,944	10,782	513,484
Sport coats and tailored jackets	455,290	213,279	187,967	28,077	87,966	71,910	–	126,385
Coats and jackets	1,770,639	615,830	961,074	328,472	429,127	222,448	190,247	724,367
Underwear	1,776,654	718,426	830,137	87,084	337,496	393,568	83,889	397,210
Hosiery	1,088,606	337,355	626,749	112,364	317,997	194,459	56,344	291,408
Nightwear	136,527	60,395	65,177	4,951	42,810	17,482	5,147	24,916
Accessories	2,301,109	751,277	1,142,057	184,070	515,334	435,767	30,050	777,448
Sweaters and vests	1,325,574	499,841	489,703	17,650	316,824	144,595	26,294	538,400
Active sportswear	1,811,537	420,240	1,206,071	179,993	435,872	579,760	128,825	643,841
Shirts	6,343,989	2,173,725	3,333,934	324,278	1,563,449	1,396,264	230,591	2,516,506
Pants and shorts	5,783,447	2,175,242	2,878,566	240,747	1,238,415	1,349,500	182,386	1,868,331
Uniforms	164,193	54,836	92,819	8,505	59,963	24,200	11,408	63,193
Costumes	31,876	3,538	25,605	8,039	8,357	9,387	3,408	8,305
BOYS' (AGED 2 TO 15) APPAREL	**6,636,289**	**634,530**	**5,198,470**	**735,698**	**3,753,363**	**692,405**	**1,378,540**	**522,151**
Coats and jackets	456,493	42,454	350,910	42,989	257,301	50,639	82,150	23,472
Sweaters	183,439	30,324	127,154	20,096	86,793	20,238	25,250	9,028
Shirts	1,765,226	177,901	1,427,790	129,315	1,063,656	215,989	411,587	174,411
Underwear	526,260	42,454	445,184	95,530	286,476	64,848	120,130	60,304
Nightwear	123,295	19,458	92,237	24,931	59,963	7,234	21,355	16,611
Hosiery	413,791	43,717	318,903	64,192	198,657	56,495	64,552	25,277
Accessories	513,028	71,514	337,234	60,231	244,545	32,037	90,637	63,915
Suits, sport coats, and vests	91,419	7,834	66,341	12,000	49,847	4,564	8,765	2,889
Pants and shorts	2,104,439	173,605	1,652,710	209,758	1,236,655	206,344	462,504	135,774
Uniforms	239,373	7,581	194,077	37,513	135,761	21,013	51,892	–
Active sportswear	127,505	13,899	104,167	17,883	79,609	6,803	24,346	6,139
Costumes	92,020	3,538	81,472	21,203	54,099	6,201	15,373	4,333
WOMEN'S APPAREL	**43,654,320**	**17,449,693**	**21,317,626**	**3,072,979**	**9,295,807**	**8,768,997**	**4,013,821**	**15,435,220**
Coats and jackets	3,361,448	1,673,379	1,245,061	196,943	371,656	666,397	605,242	1,572,591
Dresses	5,019,017	1,636,233	2,223,593	258,048	1,070,986	867,573	469,808	1,359,180
Sport coats and tailored jackets	150,961	85,160	48,010	8,272	19,499	20,324	6,539	75,109
Sweaters and vests	4,089,191	1,965,248	1,817,108	416,721	792,427	614,208	375,485	1,173,936
Shirts, blouses, and tops	8,814,103	3,403,364	4,604,891	564,559	2,054,593	1,932,274	688,366	3,269,761
Skirts	915,993	388,653	426,853	46,775	227,979	146,748	73,594	269,381
Pants and shorts	6,549,080	2,479,745	3,540,814	501,300	1,577,230	1,430,625	473,147	2,837,163
Active sportswear	2,533,265	832,394	1,547,378	222,457	654,467	656,665	394,962	1,030,579
Nightwear	2,418,992	963,040	981,442	119,471	389,103	460,742	107,818	545,622
Undergarments	2,384,710	843,513	1,217,709	233,757	531,608	450,235	163,744	963,415
Hosiery	1,540,889	524,605	833,629	82,657	311,986	425,950	106,705	766,254
Suits	597,831	250,426	263,619	41,532	116,555	105,325	27,337	203,299
Accessories	5,006,988	2,334,443	2,393,810	364,470	1,093,417	918,556	463,687	1,277,211
Uniforms	185,244	57,868	103,585	10,194	46,622	46,677	51,961	65,720
Costumes	86,607	11,624	70,124	5,825	37,532	26,697	5,565	25,999

	total married couples	married couples, no children	married couples with children				single parent with child under age 18	single person
			total	oldest child under age 6	oldest child aged 6 to 17	oldest child aged 18 or older		
GIRLS' (AGED 2 TO 15) APPAREL	**$9,817,907**	**$1,178,087**	**$7,908,274**	**$629,624**	**$6,019,367**	**$1,171,232**	**$1,903,370**	**$1,137,826**
Coats and jackets	436,044	31,335	356,729	34,193	294,246	28,247	90,358	30,332
Dresses and suits	1,170,402	322,951	803,368	144,402	544,363	113,765	155,675	195,716
Shirts, blouses, and sweaters	2,597,018	331,290	2,087,419	140,616	1,600,981	312,013	584,582	406,599
Skirts, pants, and shorts	2,100,830	136,205	1,727,780	156,634	1,407,749	163,370	556,202	109,413
Active sportswear	1,308,132	93,752	1,185,412	16,368	848,139	291,947	185,447	258,548
Underwear and nightwear	841,415	148,335	595,325	42,290	477,069	66,657	130,564	68,609
Hosiery	516,637	54,078	442,565	33,203	324,008	78,714	84,446	38,999
Accessories	470,928	42,201	401,248	15,728	277,973	99,124	64,273	18,416
Uniforms	251,402	12,888	198,442	26,271	162,004	10,334	37,562	722
Costumes	125,100	5,054	109,696	19,863	82,688	7,148	14,260	10,472
CHILDREN'S (UNDER AGE 2) APPAREL	**5,567,530**	**758,100**	**4,402,085**	**2,980,594**	**1,444,695**	**226,151**	**726,832**	**530,817**
Coats, jackets, and snowsuits	69,767	4,043	50,920	32,620	16,420	1,722	12,312	14,805
Outerwear including dresses	832,994	200,391	526,365	359,053	134,735	32,639	69,977	70,776
Underwear	3,787,268	397,497	3,198,633	2,216,995	1,060,870	140,203	539,855	265,409
Nightwear and loungewear	120,889	28,555	80,890	48,697	24,484	7,837	22,537	24,194
Accessories	756,612	127,361	545,278	323,288	208,040	43,835	82,150	155,634
FOOTWEAR	**24,506,876**	**7,516,056**	**14,259,567**	**1,960,695**	**7,656,414**	**4,520,267**	**2,644,184**	**5,798,183**
Men's	7,233,519	2,654,108	3,367,396	625,489	1,307,028	1,423,994	419,655	2,034,437
Boys'	3,138,314	141,765	2,695,255	256,883	2,088,899	316,835	563,366	157,801
Women's	11,247,529	4,553,907	5,654,420	803,384	2,297,525	2,501,097	1,078,597	3,249,539
Girls'	2,888,115	166,277	2,542,787	274,940	1,962,961	278,426	582,565	356,406
OTHER APPAREL PRODUCTS AND SERVICES	**16,834,306**	**7,278,265**	**8,232,414**	**1,561,042**	**3,996,002**	**2,659,816**	**1,137,167**	**4,952,487**
Material for making clothes	947,268	380,819	401,248	40,950	211,705	143,131	19,964	160,328
Sewing patterns and notions	663,388	270,894	351,201	158,673	69,640	134,433	13,982	103,275
Watches	2,574,765	786,655	1,553,780	165,255	675,139	691,544	232,678	423,570
Jewelry	5,581,363	3,078,644	2,215,446	464,253	1,100,015	651,239	180,300	1,305,015
Shoe repair and other shoe services	99,839	39,421	53,248	9,262	25,510	18,516	7,373	56,693
Coin-operated apparel laundry and dry cleaning	1,641,330	451,070	952,927	238,126	524,717	189,981	505,493	1,468,233
Apparel alteration, repair, and tailoring services	476,942	264,830	191,458	33,727	86,793	70,877	18,016	173,328
Clothing rental	156,374	32,851	102,712	22,601	34,160	45,902	11,964	12,277
Watch and jewelry repair	488,369	308,547	153,050	36,639	59,670	56,753	2,087	84,859
Professional laundry, dry cleaning	4,129,487	1,618,796	2,230,867	388,761	1,204,108	638,063	137,590	1,157,687
Clothing storage	75,180	45,486	26,478	2,738	4,398	19,291	7,652	7,222

Note: Total spending figures for total consumer units can be found on Total Spending by Age and Total Spending by Region tables. Spending by type of consumer unit does not add to total because not all types of consumer units are shown. Numbers may not add to category total because of rounding and missing subcategories. "–" means sample is too small to make a reliable estimate.
Source: Calculations by New Strategist based on the Bureau of Labor Statistics' 2011 Consumer Expenditure Survey

Table 2.16 Apparel: Market shares by household type, 2011

(percentage of total annual spending on apparel, accessories, and related services accounted for by types of consumer units, 2011)

	total married couples	married couples, no children	married couples with children				single parent with child under age 18	single person
			total	oldest child under age 6	oldest child aged 6 to 17	oldest child aged 18 or older		
Share of total consumer units	49.2%	20.7%	23.8%	4.8%	12.0%	7.0%	5.7%	29.5%
Share of total before-tax income	67.0	25.6	35.0	6.8	17.5	10.7	3.3	16.0
Share of total spending	63.3	24.0	33.4	6.3	17.1	10.0	4.3	18.2
Share of apparel spending	61.7	20.4	34.7	5.9	17.8	10.9	6.0	17.3
MEN'S APPAREL	**61.4**	**21.5**	**31.8**	**4.1**	**14.5**	**12.9**	**2.4**	**21.4**
Suits	60.1	22.5	34.2	4.3	18.3	11.6	0.5	22.7
Sport coats and tailored jackets	70.8	33.2	29.2	4.4	13.7	11.2	–	19.6
Coats and jackets	54.0	18.8	29.3	10.0	13.1	6.8	5.8	22.1
Underwear	68.7	27.8	32.1	3.4	13.1	15.2	3.2	15.4
Hosiery	61.1	18.9	35.2	6.3	17.9	10.9	3.2	16.4
Nightwear	68.5	30.3	32.7	2.5	21.5	8.8	2.6	12.5
Accessories	63.1	20.6	31.3	5.0	14.1	11.9	0.8	21.3
Sweaters and vests	63.7	24.0	23.5	0.8	15.2	6.9	1.3	25.9
Active sportswear	59.4	13.8	39.6	5.9	14.3	19.0	4.2	21.1
Shirts	60.7	20.8	31.9	3.1	15.0	13.4	2.2	24.1
Pants and shorts	62.2	23.4	31.0	2.6	13.3	14.5	2.0	20.1
Uniforms	52.9	17.7	29.9	2.7	19.3	7.8	3.7	20.3
Costumes	51.1	5.7	41.1	12.9	13.4	15.1	5.5	13.3
BOYS' (AGED 2 TO 15) APPAREL	**68.2**	**6.5**	**53.4**	**7.6**	**38.5**	**7.1**	**14.2**	**5.4**
Coats and jackets	70.3	6.5	54.0	6.6	39.6	7.8	12.7	3.6
Sweaters	72.5	12.0	50.2	7.9	34.3	8.0	10.0	3.6
Shirts	66.1	6.7	53.5	4.8	39.8	8.1	15.4	6.5
Underwear	65.7	5.3	55.6	11.9	35.8	8.1	15.0	7.5
Nightwear	65.5	10.3	49.0	13.2	31.8	3.8	11.3	8.8
Hosiery	68.2	7.2	52.6	10.6	32.8	9.3	10.6	4.2
Accessories	67.7	9.4	44.5	7.9	32.3	4.2	12.0	8.4
Suits, sport coats, and vests	82.2	7.0	59.6	10.8	44.8	4.1	7.9	2.6
Pants and shorts	68.2	5.6	53.6	6.8	40.1	6.7	15.0	4.4
Uniforms	73.9	2.3	59.9	11.6	41.9	6.5	16.0	–
Active sportswear	75.6	8.2	61.7	10.6	47.2	4.0	14.4	3.6
Costumes	75.2	2.9	66.6	17.3	44.2	5.1	12.6	3.5
WOMEN'S APPAREL	**59.1**	**23.6**	**28.9**	**4.2**	**12.6**	**11.9**	**5.4**	**20.9**
Coats and jackets	53.6	26.7	19.9	3.1	5.9	10.6	9.7	25.1
Dresses	57.9	18.9	25.6	3.0	12.3	10.0	5.4	15.7
Sport coats and tailored jackets	54.1	30.5	17.2	3.0	7.0	7.3	2.3	26.9
Sweaters and vests	66.8	32.1	29.7	6.8	12.9	10.0	6.1	19.2
Shirts, blouses, and tops	58.3	22.5	30.5	3.7	13.6	12.8	4.6	21.6
Skirts	62.9	26.7	29.3	3.2	15.7	10.1	5.1	18.5
Pants and shorts	56.5	21.4	30.5	4.3	13.6	12.3	4.1	24.5
Active sportswear	57.0	18.7	34.8	5.0	14.7	14.8	8.9	23.2
Nightwear	68.6	27.3	27.8	3.4	11.0	13.1	3.1	15.5
Undergarments	57.0	20.2	29.1	5.6	12.7	10.8	3.9	23.0
Hosiery	56.1	19.1	30.4	3.0	11.4	15.5	3.9	27.9
Suits	63.6	26.6	28.0	4.4	12.4	11.2	2.9	21.6
Accessories	63.3	29.5	30.3	4.6	13.8	11.6	5.9	16.2
Uniforms	45.5	14.2	25.4	2.5	11.4	11.5	12.8	16.1
Costumes	52.5	7.0	42.5	3.5	22.7	16.2	3.4	15.7

	total married couples	married couples, no children	married couples with children				single parent with child under age 18	single person
			total	oldest child under age 6	oldest child aged 6 to 17	oldest child aged 18 or older		
GIRLS' (AGED 2 TO 15) APPAREL	**68.4%**	**8.2%**	**55.1%**	**4.4%**	**41.9%**	**8.2%**	**13.3%**	**7.9%**
Coats and jackets	67.8	4.9	55.5	5.3	45.7	4.4	14.0	4.7
Dresses and suits	69.5	19.2	47.7	8.6	32.3	6.8	9.2	11.6
Shirts, blouses, and sweaters	64.3	8.2	51.7	3.5	39.6	7.7	14.5	10.1
Skirts, pants, and shorts	68.5	4.4	56.4	5.1	45.9	5.3	18.1	3.6
Active sportswear	70.1	5.0	63.5	0.9	45.4	15.6	9.9	13.8
Underwear and nightwear	71.7	12.6	50.8	3.6	40.7	5.7	11.1	5.9
Hosiery	69.5	7.3	59.5	4.5	43.6	10.6	11.4	5.2
Accessories	74.8	6.7	63.7	2.5	44.1	15.7	10.2	2.9
Uniforms	72.1	3.7	56.9	7.5	46.5	3.0	10.8	0.2
Costumes	75.8	3.1	66.4	12.0	50.1	4.3	8.6	6.3
CHILDREN'S (UNDER AGE 2) APPAREL	**66.8**	**9.1**	**52.8**	**35.8**	**17.3**	**2.7**	**8.7**	**6.4**
Coats, jackets, and snowsuits	61.3	3.6	44.8	28.7	14.4	1.5	10.8	13.0
Outerwear including dresses	71.9	17.3	45.5	31.0	11.6	2.8	6.0	6.1
Underwear	67.9	7.1	57.4	39.8	19.0	2.5	9.7	4.8
Nightwear and loungewear	59.9	14.2	40.1	24.1	12.1	3.9	11.2	12.0
Accessories	58.9	9.9	42.5	25.2	16.2	3.4	6.4	12.1
FOOTWEAR	**62.4**	**19.1**	**36.3**	**5.0**	**19.5**	**11.5**	**6.7**	**14.8**
Men's	61.1	22.4	28.4	5.3	11.0	12.0	3.5	17.2
Boys'	70.0	3.2	60.1	5.7	46.6	7.1	12.6	3.5
Women's	60.5	24.5	30.4	4.3	12.4	13.5	5.8	17.5
Girls'	66.3	3.8	58.4	6.3	45.1	6.4	13.4	8.2
OTHER APPAREL PRODUCTS AND SERVICES	**61.0**	**26.4**	**29.8**	**5.7**	**14.5**	**9.6**	**4.1**	**18.0**
Material for making clothes	80.3	32.3	34.0	3.5	17.9	12.1	1.7	13.6
Sewing patterns and notions	68.8	28.1	36.4	16.5	7.2	14.0	1.5	10.7
Watches	69.6	21.3	42.0	4.5	18.2	18.7	6.3	11.4
Jewelry	63.4	35.0	25.2	5.3	12.5	7.4	2.0	14.8
Shoe repair and other shoe services	54.4	21.5	29.0	5.0	13.9	10.1	4.0	30.9
Coin-operated apparel laundry and dry cleaning	33.9	9.3	19.7	4.9	10.8	3.9	10.4	30.3
Apparel alteration, repair, and tailoring services	61.2	34.0	24.6	4.3	11.1	9.1	2.3	22.3
Clothing rental	76.1	16.0	50.0	11.0	16.6	22.3	5.8	6.0
Watch and jewelry repair	73.5	46.5	23.0	5.5	9.0	8.5	0.3	12.8
Professional laundry, dry cleaning	67.4	26.4	36.4	6.3	19.7	10.4	2.2	18.9
Clothing storage	58.0	35.1	20.4	2.1	3.4	14.9	5.9	5.6

Note: Market share for total consumer units is 100.0%. Market shares by type of consumer unit do not add to total because not all types of consumer units are shown. "–" means sample is too small to make a reliable estimate.
Source: Calculations by New Strategist based on the Bureau of Labor Statistics' 2011 Consumer Expenditure Survey

Table 2.17 Apparel: Average spending by race and Hispanic origin, 2011

(average annual spending of consumer units on apparel, accessories, and related services, by race and Hispanic origin of consumer unit reference person, 2011)

	total consumer units	Asian	black	Hispanic	non-Hispanic white and other
Number of consumer units (in 000s)	122,287	5,048	15,118	15,222	92,163
Average number of persons per consumer unit	2.5	2.7	2.6	3.4	2.4
Average before-tax income of consumer units	$63,685.00	$85,415.00	$45,552.00	$49,966.00	$68,907.00
Average spending of consumer units, total	49,704.88	60,136.04	36,643.75	42,085.98	53,055.68
Apparel, average spending	**1,739.79**	**2,323.82**	**1,669.20**	**1,988.93**	**1,713.52**
MEN'S APPAREL	**324.14**	**503.49**	**224.32**	**402.44**	**327.68**
Suits	18.46	45.23	23.83	16.30	17.89
Sport coats and tailored jackets	5.26	11.50	3.42	2.80	5.96
Coats and jackets	26.83	54.36	19.17	32.09	27.14
Underwear	21.14	41.88	17.82	14.82	22.55
Hosiery	14.56	21.02	9.36	13.38	15.62
Nightwear	1.63	1.44	0.54	1.50	1.83
Accessories	29.84	37.25	13.88	44.79	29.97
Sweaters and vests	17.02	27.31	15.74	14.56	17.54
Active sportswear	24.92	29.80	18.44	36.11	24.17
Shirts	85.41	123.28	53.71	110.63	86.51
Pants and shorts	76.02	107.79	45.15	110.41	75.77
Uniforms	2.54	2.34	2.88	4.07	2.24
Costumes	0.51	0.29	0.38	0.99	0.49
BOYS' (AGED 2 TO 15) APPAREL	**79.63**	**99.71**	**99.47**	**115.76**	**71.02**
Coats and jackets	5.31	12.88	5.33	6.58	5.10
Sweaters	2.07	2.63	2.67	5.00	1.49
Shirts	21.84	23.46	30.32	32.24	19.06
Underwear	6.55	12.46	8.40	9.01	5.85
Nightwear	1.54	1.00	1.47	1.75	1.52
Hosiery	4.96	6.29	7.01	8.22	4.32
Accessories	6.20	12.01	7.48	8.59	5.61
Suits, sport coats, and vests	0.91	0.20	1.57	1.47	0.73
Pants and shorts	25.22	23.53	30.66	35.68	22.59
Uniforms	2.65	2.02	3.13	5.29	2.13
Active sportswear	1.38	2.05	0.81	0.90	1.57
Costumes	1.00	1.19	0.62	1.03	1.05
WOMEN'S APPAREL	**603.77**	**761.38**	**501.48**	**532.18**	**630.61**
Coats and jackets	51.25	34.37	48.76	45.52	52.31
Dresses	70.93	124.32	81.62	67.25	69.50
Sport coats and tailored jackets	2.28	7.70	0.76	1.74	2.62
Sweaters and vests	50.08	65.82	17.63	44.84	55.82
Shirts, blouses, and tops	123.62	151.24	83.81	112.26	131.64
Skirts	11.91	23.92	8.26	11.38	12.52
Pants and shorts	94.85	94.93	82.94	93.65	97.03
Active sportswear	36.32	47.88	35.54	13.96	39.72
Nightwear	28.82	32.23	22.27	38.74	28.30
Undergarments	34.22	49.10	31.11	28.81	35.40
Hosiery	22.46	25.37	17.65	16.41	24.09
Suits	7.69	13.87	15.74	3.99	6.96
Accessories	64.67	86.66	50.22	49.75	69.94
Uniforms	3.33	1.79	4.40	3.01	3.24
Costumes	1.35	2.18	0.76	0.87	1.53

	total consumer units	Asian	black	Hispanic	non-Hispanic white and other
GIRLS' (AGED 2 TO 15) APPAREL	**$117.43**	**$149.65**	**$127.77**	**$140.28**	**$112.46**
Coats and jackets	5.26	8.52	8.08	8.02	4.35
Dresses and suits	13.78	14.48	9.37	16.25	14.05
Shirts, blouses, and sweaters	33.03	29.89	39.51	38.65	31.54
Skirts, pants, and shorts	25.07	19.12	32.85	32.45	22.70
Active sportswear	15.27	58.24	9.84	10.70	16.77
Underwear and nightwear	9.59	4.98	9.10	16.36	8.64
Hosiery	6.08	5.35	4.09	7.43	6.18
Accessories	5.15	4.11	7.74	3.54	4.96
Uniforms	2.85	1.98	5.93	5.73	1.87
Costumes	1.35	2.97	1.27	1.15	1.39
CHILDREN'S (UNDER AGE 2) APPAREL	**68.13**	**109.23**	**77.34**	**90.99**	**63.03**
Coats, jackets, and snowsuits	0.93	0.34	1.03	2.14	0.77
Outerwear including dresses	9.47	14.98	7.98	15.76	8.68
Underwear	45.58	84.73	46.71	56.70	43.64
Nightwear and loungewear	1.65	1.33	1.11	2.58	1.58
Accessories	10.50	7.85	20.50	13.81	8.36
FOOTWEAR	**321.14**	**341.81**	**453.61**	**451.61**	**281.49**
Men's	96.84	120.20	121.72	145.54	85.67
Boys'	36.67	49.95	65.98	79.55	25.83
Women's	151.99	143.25	210.13	171.78	140.63
Girls'	35.63	28.41	55.78	54.74	29.37
OTHER APPAREL PRODUCTS AND SERVICES	**225.54**	**358.55**	**185.22**	**255.68**	**227.23**
Material for making clothes	9.65	2.12	5.99	1.22	11.49
Sewing patterns and notions	7.88	2.03	0.95	4.27	9.52
Watches	30.27	85.08	17.03	41.14	30.59
Jewelry	71.95	141.67	29.13	49.24	82.99
Shoe repair and other shoe services	1.50	1.77	0.89	1.22	1.65
Coin-operated apparel laundry and dry cleaning	39.63	54.34	64.04	116.68	23.05
Apparel alteration, repair, and tailoring services	6.37	10.99	4.09	3.47	7.21
Clothing rental	1.68	3.35	0.54	1.09	1.96
Watch and jewelry repair	5.43	1.75	2.12	2.66	6.42
Professional laundry, dry cleaning	50.10	53.88	58.79	34.52	51.26
Clothing storage	1.06	1.58	1.67	0.18	1.10

Note: "Asian" and "black" include Hispanics and non-Hispanics who identify themselves as being of the respective race alone. "Hispanic" includes people of any race who identify themselves as Hispanic.
"Other" includes people who identify themselves as non-Hispanic and as Alaska Native, American Indian, Asian (who are also included in the "Asian" column), or Native Hawaiian or other Pacific Islander, as well as non-Hispanics reporting more than one race. Subcategories may not add to total because some are not shown.
Source: Bureau of Labor Statistics, unpublished data from the 2011 Consumer Expenditure Survey

Table 2.18 Apparel: Indexed spending by race and Hispanic origin, 2011

(indexed average annual spending of consumer units on apparel, accessories, and related services, by race and Hispanic origin of consumer unit reference person, 2011; index definition: an index of 100 is the average for all consumer units; an index of 125 means that spending by consumer units in that group is 25 percent above the average for all consumer units; an index of 75 indicates spending that is 25 percent below the average for all consumer units)

	total consumer units	Asian	black	Hispanic	non-Hispanic white and other
Average spending of consumer units, total	$49,705	$60,136	$36,644	$42,086	$53,056
Average spending of consumer units, index	100	121	74	85	107
Apparel, spending index	**100**	**134**	**96**	**114**	**98**
MEN'S APPAREL	**100**	**155**	**69**	**124**	**101**
Suits	100	245	129	88	97
Sport coats and tailored jackets	100	219	65	53	113
Coats and jackets	100	203	71	120	101
Underwear	100	198	84	70	107
Hosiery	100	144	64	92	107
Nightwear	100	88	33	92	112
Accessories	100	125	47	150	100
Sweaters and vests	100	160	92	86	103
Active sportswear	100	120	74	145	97
Shirts	100	144	63	130	101
Pants and shorts	100	142	59	145	100
Uniforms	100	92	113	160	88
Costumes	100	57	75	194	96
BOYS' (AGED 2 TO 15) APPAREL	**100**	**125**	**125**	**145**	**89**
Coats and jackets	100	243	100	124	96
Sweaters	100	127	129	242	72
Shirts	100	107	139	148	87
Underwear	100	190	128	138	89
Nightwear	100	65	95	114	99
Hosiery	100	127	141	166	87
Accessories	100	194	121	139	90
Suits, sport coats, and vests	100	22	173	162	80
Pants and shorts	100	93	122	141	90
Uniforms	100	76	118	200	80
Active sportswear	100	149	59	65	114
Costumes	100	119	62	103	105
WOMEN'S APPAREL	**100**	**126**	**83**	**88**	**104**
Coats and jackets	100	67	95	89	102
Dresses	100	175	115	95	98
Sport coats and tailored jackets	100	338	33	76	115
Sweaters and vests	100	131	35	90	111
Shirts, blouses, and tops	100	122	68	91	106
Skirts	100	201	69	96	105
Pants and shorts	100	100	87	99	102
Active sportswear	100	132	98	38	109
Nightwear	100	112	77	134	98
Undergarments	100	143	91	84	103
Hosiery	100	113	79	73	107
Suits	100	180	205	52	91
Accessories	100	134	78	77	108
Uniforms	100	54	132	90	97
Costumes	100	161	56	64	113

	total consumer units	Asian	black	Hispanic	non-Hispanic white and other
GIRLS' (AGED 2 TO 15) APPAREL	100	127	109	119	96
Coats and jackets	100	162	154	152	83
Dresses and suits	100	105	68	118	102
Shirts, blouses, and sweaters	100	90	120	117	95
Skirts, pants, and shorts	100	76	131	129	91
Active sportswear	100	381	64	70	110
Underwear and nightwear	100	52	95	171	90
Hosiery	100	88	67	122	102
Accessories	100	80	150	69	96
Uniforms	100	69	208	201	66
Costumes	100	220	94	85	103
CHILDREN'S (UNDER AGE 2) APPAREL	100	160	114	134	93
Coats, jackets, and snowsuits	100	37	111	230	83
Outerwear including dresses	100	158	84	166	92
Underwear	100	186	102	124	96
Nightwear and loungewear	100	81	67	156	96
Accessories	100	75	195	132	80
FOOTWEAR	100	106	141	141	88
Men's	100	124	126	150	88
Boys'	100	136	180	217	70
Women's	100	94	138	113	93
Girls'	100	80	157	154	82
OTHER APPAREL PRODUCTS AND SERVICES	100	159	82	113	101
Material for making clothes	100	22	62	13	119
Sewing patterns and notions	100	26	12	54	121
Watches	100	281	56	136	101
Jewelry	100	197	40	68	115
Shoe repair and other shoe services	100	118	59	81	110
Coin-operated apparel laundry and dry cleaning	100	137	162	294	58
Apparel alteration, repair, and tailoring services	100	173	64	54	113
Clothing rental	100	199	32	65	117
Watch and jewelry repair	100	32	39	49	118
Professional laundry, dry cleaning	100	108	117	69	102
Clothing storage	100	149	158	17	104

Note: "Asian" and "black" include Hispanics and non-Hispanics who identify themselves as being of the respective race alone. "Hispanic" includes people of any race who identify themselves as Hispanic. "Other" includes people who identify themselves as non-Hispanic and as Alaska Native, American Indian, Asian (who are also included in the "Asian" column), or Native Hawaiian or other Pacific Islander, as well as non-Hispanics reporting more than one race.
Source: Calculations by New Strategist based on the Bureau of Labor Statistics' 2011 Consumer Expenditure Survey

Table 2.19 Apparel: Total spending by race and Hispanic origin, 2011

(total annual spending on apparel, accessories, and related services, by race and Hispanic origin groups, 2011; consumer units and dollars in thousands)

	total consumer units	Asian	black	Hispanic	non-Hispanic white and other
Number of consumer units	122,287	5,048	15,118	15,222	92,163
Total spending of all consumer units	$6,078,260,661	$303,566,730	$553,980,213	$640,632,788	$4,889,770,636
Apparel, total spending	212,753,700	11,730,643	25,234,966	30,275,492	157,923,144
MEN'S APPAREL	**39,638,108**	**2,541,618**	**3,391,270**	**6,125,942**	**30,199,972**
Suits	2,257,418	228,321	360,262	248,119	1,648,796
Sport coats and tailored jackets	643,230	58,052	51,704	42,622	549,291
Coats and jackets	3,280,960	274,409	289,812	488,474	2,501,304
Underwear	2,585,147	211,410	269,403	225,590	2,078,276
Hosiery	1,780,499	106,109	141,504	203,670	1,439,586
Nightwear	199,328	7,269	8,164	22,833	168,658
Accessories	3,649,044	188,038	209,838	681,793	2,762,125
Sweaters and vests	2,081,325	137,861	237,957	221,632	1,616,539
Active sportswear	3,047,392	150,430	278,776	549,666	2,227,580
Shirts	10,444,533	622,317	811,988	1,684,010	7,973,021
Pants and shorts	9,296,258	544,124	682,578	1,680,661	6,983,191
Uniforms	310,609	11,812	43,540	61,954	206,445
Costumes	62,366	1,464	5,745	15,070	45,160
BOYS' (AGED 2 TO 15) APPAREL	**9,737,714**	**503,336**	**1,503,787**	**1,762,099**	**6,545,416**
Coats and jackets	649,344	65,018	80,579	100,161	470,031
Sweaters	253,134	13,276	40,365	76,110	137,323
Shirts	2,670,748	118,426	458,378	490,757	1,756,627
Underwear	800,980	62,898	126,991	137,150	539,154
Nightwear	188,322	5,048	22,223	26,639	140,088
Hosiery	606,544	31,752	105,977	125,125	398,144
Accessories	758,179	60,626	113,083	130,757	517,034
Suits, sport coats, and vests	111,281	1,010	23,735	22,376	67,279
Pants and shorts	3,084,078	118,779	463,518	543,121	2,081,962
Uniforms	324,061	10,197	47,319	80,524	196,307
Active sportswear	168,756	10,348	12,246	13,700	144,696
Costumes	122,287	6,007	9,373	15,679	96,771
WOMEN'S APPAREL	**73,833,222**	**3,843,446**	**7,581,375**	**8,100,844**	**58,118,909**
Coats and jackets	6,267,209	173,500	737,154	692,905	4,821,047
Dresses	8,673,817	627,567	1,233,931	1,023,680	6,405,329
Sport coats and tailored jackets	278,814	38,870	11,490	26,486	241,467
Sweaters and vests	6,124,133	332,259	266,530	682,554	5,144,539
Shirts, blouses, and tops	15,117,119	763,460	1,267,040	1,708,822	12,132,337
Skirts	1,456,438	120,748	124,875	173,226	1,153,881
Pants and shorts	11,598,922	479,207	1,253,887	1,425,540	8,942,576
Active sportswear	4,441,464	241,698	537,294	212,499	3,660,714
Nightwear	3,524,311	162,697	336,678	589,700	2,608,213
Undergarments	4,184,661	247,857	470,321	438,546	3,262,570
Hosiery	2,746,566	128,068	266,833	249,793	2,220,207
Suits	940,387	70,016	237,957	60,736	641,454
Accessories	7,908,300	437,460	759,226	757,295	6,445,880
Uniforms	407,216	9,036	66,519	45,818	298,608
Costumes	165,087	11,005	11,490	13,243	141,009

	total consumer units	Asian	black	Hispanic	non-Hispanic white and other
GIRLS' (AGED 2 TO 15) APPAREL	**$14,360,162**	**$755,433**	**$1,931,627**	**$2,135,342**	**$10,364,651**
Coats and jackets	643,230	43,009	122,153	122,080	400,909
Dresses and suits	1,685,115	73,095	141,656	247,358	1,294,890
Shirts, blouses, and sweaters	4,039,140	150,885	597,312	588,330	2,906,821
Skirts, pants, and shorts	3,065,735	96,518	496,626	493,954	2,092,100
Active sportswear	1,867,322	293,996	148,761	162,875	1,545,574
Underwear and nightwear	1,172,732	25,139	137,574	249,032	796,288
Hosiery	743,505	27,007	61,833	113,099	569,567
Accessories	629,778	20,747	117,013	53,886	457,128
Uniforms	348,518	9,995	89,650	87,222	172,345
Costumes	165,087	14,993	19,200	17,505	128,107
CHILDREN'S (UNDER AGE 2) APPAREL	**8,331,413**	**551,393**	**1,169,226**	**1,385,050**	**5,809,034**
Coats, jackets, and snowsuits	113,727	1,716	15,572	32,575	70,966
Outerwear including dresses	1,158,058	75,619	120,642	239,899	799,975
Underwear	5,573,841	427,717	706,162	863,087	4,021,993
Nightwear and loungewear	201,774	6,714	16,781	39,273	145,618
Accessories	1,284,014	39,627	309,919	210,216	770,483
FOOTWEAR	**39,271,247**	**1,725,457**	**6,857,676**	**6,874,407**	**25,942,963**
Men's	11,842,273	606,770	1,840,163	2,215,410	7,895,604
Boys'	4,484,264	252,148	997,486	1,210,910	2,380,570
Women's	18,586,401	723,126	3,176,745	2,614,835	12,960,883
Girls'	4,357,086	143,414	843,282	833,252	2,706,827
OTHER APPAREL PRODUCTS AND SERVICES	**27,580,610**	**1,809,960**	**2,800,156**	**3,891,961**	**20,942,198**
Material for making clothes	1,180,070	10,702	90,557	18,571	1,058,953
Sewing patterns and notions	963,622	10,247	14,362	64,998	877,392
Watches	3,701,627	429,484	257,460	626,233	2,819,266
Jewelry	8,798,550	715,150	440,387	749,531	7,648,607
Shoe repair and other shoe services	183,431	8,935	13,455	18,571	152,069
Coin-operated apparel laundry and dry cleaning	4,846,234	274,308	968,157	1,776,103	2,124,357
Apparel alteration, repair, and tailoring services	778,968	55,478	61,833	52,820	664,495
Clothing rental	205,442	16,911	8,164	16,592	180,639
Watch and jewelry repair	664,018	8,834	32,050	40,491	591,686
Professional laundry, dry cleaning	6,126,579	271,986	888,787	525,463	4,724,275
Clothing storage	129,624	7,976	25,247	2,740	101,379

Note: "Asian" and "black" include Hispanics and non-Hispanics who identify themselves as being of the respective race alone. "Hispanic" includes people of any race who identify themselves as Hispanic. "Other" includes people who identify themselves as non-Hispanic and as Alaska Native, American Indian, Asian (who are also included in the "Asian" column), or Native Hawaiian or other Pacific Islander, as well as non-Hispanics reporting more than one race. Subcategories may not add to total because some are not shown.
Source: Calculations by New Strategist based on the Bureau of Labor Statistics' 2011 Consumer Expenditure Survey

Table 2.20 Apparel: Market shares by race and Hispanic origin, 2011

(percentage of total annual spending on apparel, accessories, and related services accounted for by race and Hispanic origin groups, 2011)

	total consumer units	Asian	black	Hispanic	non-Hispanic white and other
Share of total consumer units	100.0%	4.1%	12.4%	12.4%	75.4%
Share of total before-tax income	100.0	5.5	8.8	9.8	81.5
Share of total spending	100.0	5.0	9.1	10.5	80.4
Share of apparel spending	100.0	5.5	11.9	14.2	74.2
MEN'S APPAREL	**100.0**	**6.4**	**8.6**	**15.5**	**76.2**
Suits	100.0	10.1	16.0	11.0	73.0
Sport coats and tailored jackets	100.0	9.0	8.0	6.6	85.4
Coats and jackets	100.0	8.4	8.8	14.9	76.2
Underwear	100.0	8.2	10.4	8.7	80.4
Hosiery	100.0	6.0	7.9	11.4	80.9
Nightwear	100.0	3.6	4.1	11.5	84.6
Accessories	100.0	5.2	5.8	18.7	75.7
Sweaters and vests	100.0	6.6	11.4	10.6	77.7
Active sportswear	100.0	4.9	9.1	18.0	73.1
Shirts	100.0	6.0	7.8	16.1	76.3
Pants and shorts	100.0	5.9	7.3	18.1	75.1
Uniforms	100.0	3.8	14.0	19.9	66.5
Costumes	100.0	2.3	9.2	24.2	72.4
BOYS' (AGED 2 TO 15) APPAREL	**100.0**	**5.2**	**15.4**	**18.1**	**67.2**
Coats and jackets	100.0	10.0	12.4	15.4	72.4
Sweaters	100.0	5.2	15.9	30.1	54.2
Shirts	100.0	4.4	17.2	18.4	65.8
Underwear	100.0	7.9	15.9	17.1	67.3
Nightwear	100.0	2.7	11.8	14.1	74.4
Hosiery	100.0	5.2	17.5	20.6	65.6
Accessories	100.0	8.0	14.9	17.2	68.2
Suits, sport coats, and vests	100.0	0.9	21.3	20.1	60.5
Pants and shorts	100.0	3.9	15.0	17.6	67.5
Uniforms	100.0	3.1	14.6	24.8	60.6
Active sportswear	100.0	6.1	7.3	8.1	85.7
Costumes	100.0	4.9	7.7	12.8	79.1
WOMEN'S APPAREL	**100.0**	**5.2**	**10.3**	**11.0**	**78.7**
Coats and jackets	100.0	2.8	11.8	11.1	76.9
Dresses	100.0	7.2	14.2	11.8	73.8
Sport coats and tailored jackets	100.0	13.9	4.1	9.5	86.6
Sweaters and vests	100.0	5.4	4.4	11.1	84.0
Shirts, blouses, and tops	100.0	5.1	8.4	11.3	80.3
Skirts	100.0	8.3	8.6	11.9	79.2
Pants and shorts	100.0	4.1	10.8	12.3	77.1
Active sportswear	100.0	5.4	12.1	4.8	82.4
Nightwear	100.0	4.6	9.6	16.7	74.0
Undergarments	100.0	5.9	11.2	10.5	78.0
Hosiery	100.0	4.7	9.7	9.1	80.8
Suits	100.0	7.4	25.3	6.5	68.2
Accessories	100.0	5.5	9.6	9.6	81.5
Uniforms	100.0	2.2	16.3	11.3	73.3
Costumes	100.0	6.7	7.0	8.0	85.4

	total consumer units	Asian	black	Hispanic	non-Hispanic white and other
GIRLS' (AGED 2 TO 15) APPAREL	**100.0%**	**5.3%**	**13.5%**	**14.9%**	**72.2%**
Coats and jackets	100.0	6.7	19.0	19.0	62.3
Dresses and suits	100.0	4.3	8.4	14.7	76.8
Shirts, blouses, and sweaters	100.0	3.7	14.8	14.6	72.0
Skirts, pants, and shorts	100.0	3.1	16.2	16.1	68.2
Active sportswear	100.0	15.7	8.0	8.7	82.8
Underwear and nightwear	100.0	2.1	11.7	21.2	67.9
Hosiery	100.0	3.6	8.3	15.2	76.6
Accessories	100.0	3.3	18.6	8.6	72.6
Uniforms	100.0	2.9	25.7	25.0	49.5
Costumes	100.0	9.1	11.6	10.6	77.6
CHILDREN'S (UNDER AGE 2) APPAREL	**100.0**	**6.6**	**14.0**	**16.6**	**69.7**
Coats, jackets, and snowsuits	100.0	1.5	13.7	28.6	62.4
Outerwear including dresses	100.0	6.5	10.4	20.7	69.1
Underwear	100.0	7.7	12.7	15.5	72.2
Nightwear and loungewear	100.0	3.3	8.3	19.5	72.2
Accessories	100.0	3.1	24.1	16.4	60.0
FOOTWEAR	**100.0**	**4.4**	**17.5**	**17.5**	**66.1**
Men's	100.0	5.1	15.5	18.7	66.7
Boys'	100.0	5.6	22.2	27.0	53.1
Women's	100.0	3.9	17.1	14.1	69.7
Girls'	100.0	3.3	19.4	19.1	62.1
OTHER APPAREL PRODUCTS AND SERVICES	**100.0**	**6.6**	**10.2**	**14.1**	**75.9**
Material for making clothes	100.0	0.9	7.7	1.6	89.7
Sewing patterns and notions	100.0	1.1	1.5	6.7	91.1
Watches	100.0	11.6	7.0	16.9	76.2
Jewelry	100.0	8.1	5.0	8.5	86.9
Shoe repair and other shoe services	100.0	4.9	7.3	10.1	82.9
Coin-operated apparel laundry and dry cleaning	100.0	5.7	20.0	36.6	43.8
Apparel alteration, repair, and tailoring services	100.0	7.1	7.9	6.8	85.3
Clothing rental	100.0	8.2	4.0	8.1	87.9
Watch and jewelry repair	100.0	1.3	4.8	6.1	89.1
Professional laundry, dry cleaning	100.0	4.4	14.5	8.6	77.1
Clothing storage	100.0	6.2	19.5	2.1	78.2

Note: "Asian" and "black" include Hispanics and non-Hispanics who identify themselves as being of the respective race alone. "Hispanic" includes people of any race who identify themselves as Hispanic. "Other" includes people who identify themselves as non-Hispanic and as Alaska Native, American Indian, Asian (who are also included in the "Asian" column), or Native Hawaiian or other Pacific Islander, as well as non-Hispanics reporting more than one race.
Source: Calculations by New Strategist based on the Bureau of Labor Statistics' 2011 Consumer Expenditure Survey

Table 2.21 Apparel: Average spending by region, 2011

(average annual spending of consumer units on apparel, accessories, and related services, by region in which consumer unit lives, 2011)

	total consumer units	Northeast	Midwest	South	West
Number of consumer units (in 000s)	122,287	22,538	27,107	44,901	27,741
Average number of persons per consumer unit	2.5	2.4	2.4	2.5	2.6
Average before-tax income of consumer units	$63,685.00	$71,733.00	$60,897.00	$58,780.00	$67,810.00
Average spending of consumer units, total	49,704.88	54,547.45	47,191.54	45,698.60	54,745.43
Apparel, average spending	**1,739.79**	**1,905.37**	**1,623.83**	**1,614.62**	**1,925.73**
MEN'S APPAREL	**324.14**	**354.95**	**283.34**	**323.54**	**340.57**
Suits	18.46	28.51	15.02	16.47	16.88
Sport coats and tailored jackets	5.26	7.98	2.98	5.40	5.07
Coats and jackets	26.83	30.99	26.78	22.85	30.07
Underwear	21.14	25.04	21.99	17.19	23.63
Hosiery	14.56	15.79	14.33	12.66	16.92
Nightwear	1.63	3.14	1.43	1.21	1.28
Accessories	29.84	30.31	22.02	27.55	41.10
Sweaters and vests	17.02	24.16	12.40	17.44	15.11
Active sportswear	24.92	34.85	24.02	23.38	20.19
Shirts	85.41	76.12	76.69	95.82	84.54
Pants and shorts	76.02	75.41	64.57	79.84	81.65
Uniforms	2.54	2.19	0.81	3.44	3.05
Costumes	0.51	0.46	0.31	0.30	1.08
BOYS' (AGED 2 TO 15) APPAREL	**79.63**	**90.38**	**70.96**	**68.61**	**97.56**
Coats and jackets	5.31	6.98	4.32	3.92	7.15
Sweaters	2.07	2.69	1.63	1.97	2.17
Shirts	21.84	23.81	20.44	16.07	31.15
Underwear	6.55	7.16	6.34	4.53	9.60
Nightwear	1.54	1.61	1.80	1.39	1.48
Hosiery	4.96	4.34	4.50	4.46	6.74
Accessories	6.20	7.04	6.82	4.16	8.28
Suits, sport coats, and vests	0.91	1.09	1.06	0.71	0.95
Pants and shorts	25.22	28.24	20.58	26.58	25.09
Uniforms	2.65	3.47	0.75	3.41	2.61
Active sportswear	1.38	2.68	1.79	0.71	1.00
Costumes	1.00	1.28	0.94	0.69	1.33
WOMEN'S APPAREL	**603.77**	**638.18**	**642.72**	**541.06**	**640.17**
Coats and jackets	51.25	76.00	45.68	35.52	62.51
Dresses	70.93	64.27	60.89	72.55	83.77
Sport coats and tailored jackets	2.28	2.77	1.18	1.94	3.51
Sweaters and vests	50.08	65.65	78.05	31.66	39.73
Shirts, blouses, and tops	123.62	119.81	122.51	114.28	143.29
Skirts	11.91	9.81	9.48	13.77	12.98
Pants and shorts	94.85	90.63	123.74	88.18	80.44
Active sportswear	36.32	45.24	36.60	31.51	36.67
Nightwear	28.82	27.40	22.85	22.47	46.48
Undergarments	34.22	39.07	36.10	31.24	33.27
Hosiery	22.46	22.59	26.00	23.16	17.66
Suits	7.69	8.43	4.99	8.75	8.01
Accessories	64.67	61.64	69.92	61.74	66.73
Uniforms	3.33	2.66	3.52	3.80	2.95
Costumes	1.35	2.22	1.22	0.50	2.16

	total consumer units	Northeast	Midwest	South	West
GIRLS' (AGED 2 TO 15) APPAREL	**$117.43**	**$137.33**	**$95.66**	**$107.01**	**$140.16**
Coats and jackets	5.26	8.91	5.25	4.20	4.00
Dresses and suits	13.78	21.61	7.53	10.42	19.18
Shirts, blouses, and sweaters	33.03	38.81	26.20	26.39	46.12
Skirts, pants, and shorts	25.07	25.22	25.09	25.87	23.62
Active sportswear	15.27	14.23	12.80	13.12	22.18
Underwear and nightwear	9.59	9.80	5.89	11.30	10.32
Hosiery	6.08	5.47	5.64	6.46	6.39
Accessories	5.15	9.17	5.11	3.42	4.75
Uniforms	2.85	3.08	0.98	4.55	1.76
Costumes	1.35	1.03	1.19	1.29	1.85
CHILDREN'S (UNDER AGE 2) APPAREL	**68.13**	**73.82**	**59.96**	**70.86**	**67.10**
Coats, jackets, and snowsuits	0.93	1.19	0.79	0.83	1.03
Outerwear including dresses	9.47	8.34	10.42	9.39	9.58
Underwear	45.58	52.71	39.53	46.76	43.82
Nightwear and loungewear	1.65	2.52	1.00	1.46	1.90
Accessories	10.50	9.06	8.21	12.43	10.77
FOOTWEAR	**321.14**	**331.38**	**292.21**	**308.07**	**363.33**
Men's	96.84	85.21	84.15	98.48	116.39
Boys'	36.67	41.44	42.20	23.64	48.80
Women's	151.99	174.71	137.89	147.82	154.37
Girls'	35.63	30.03	27.97	38.13	43.78
OTHER APPAREL PRODUCTS AND SERVICES	**225.54**	**279.32**	**178.97**	**195.45**	**276.85**
Material for making clothes	9.65	7.25	10.30	6.39	16.39
Sewing patterns and notions	7.88	5.89	5.72	6.55	13.88
Watches	30.27	49.84	17.58	18.19	46.89
Jewelry	71.95	73.53	67.61	70.48	77.30
Shoe repair and other shoe services	1.50	1.40	1.33	1.31	2.06
Coin-operated apparel laundry and dry cleaning	39.63	65.86	29.02	27.84	47.78
Apparel alteration, repair, and tailoring services	6.37	6.43	5.94	6.31	6.84
Clothing rental	1.68	1.31	2.11	1.35	2.09
Watch and jewelry repair	5.43	6.48	5.04	4.55	6.38
Professional laundry, dry cleaning	50.10	60.71	33.83	50.49	56.76
Clothing storage	1.06	0.62	0.48	1.99	0.48

Note: Subcategories may not add to total because some are not shown.
Source: Bureau of Labor Statistics, unpublished data from the 2011 Consumer Expenditure Survey

Table 2.22 Apparel: Indexed spending by region, 2011

(indexed average annual spending of consumer units on apparel, accessories, and related services, by region in which consumer unit lives, 2011; index definition: an index of 100 is the average for all consumer units; an index of 125 means that spending by consumer units in that group is 25 percent above the average for all consumer units; an index of 75 indicates spending that is 25 percent below the average for all consumer units)

	total consumer units	Northeast	Midwest	South	West
Average spending of consumer units, total	$49,705	$54,547	$47,192	$45,699	$54,745
Average spending of consumer units, index	100	110	95	92	110
Apparel, spending index	100	110	93	93	111
MEN'S APPAREL	100	110	87	100	105
Suits	100	154	81	89	91
Sport coats and tailored jackets	100	152	57	103	96
Coats and jackets	100	116	100	85	112
Underwear	100	118	104	81	112
Hosiery	100	108	98	87	116
Nightwear	100	193	88	74	79
Accessories	100	102	74	92	138
Sweaters and vests	100	142	73	102	89
Active sportswear	100	140	96	94	81
Shirts	100	89	90	112	99
Pants and shorts	100	99	85	105	107
Uniforms	100	86	32	135	120
Costumes	100	90	61	59	212
BOYS' (AGED 2 TO 15) APPAREL	100	113	89	86	123
Coats and jackets	100	131	81	74	135
Sweaters	100	130	79	95	105
Shirts	100	109	94	74	143
Underwear	100	109	97	69	147
Nightwear	100	105	117	90	96
Hosiery	100	88	91	90	136
Accessories	100	114	110	67	134
Suits, sport coats, and vests	100	120	116	78	104
Pants and shorts	100	112	82	105	99
Uniforms	100	131	28	129	98
Active sportswear	100	194	130	51	72
Costumes	100	128	94	69	133
WOMEN'S APPAREL	100	106	106	90	106
Coats and jackets	100	148	89	69	122
Dresses	100	91	86	102	118
Sport coats and tailored jackets	100	121	52	85	154
Sweaters and vests	100	131	156	63	79
Shirts, blouses, and tops	100	97	99	92	116
Skirts	100	82	80	116	109
Pants and shorts	100	96	130	93	85
Active sportswear	100	125	101	87	101
Nightwear	100	95	79	78	161
Undergarments	100	114	105	91	97
Hosiery	100	101	116	103	79
Suits	100	110	65	114	104
Accessories	100	95	108	95	103
Uniforms	100	80	106	114	89
Costumes	100	164	90	37	160

	total consumer units	Northeast	Midwest	South	West
GIRLS' (AGED 2 TO 15) APPAREL	**100**	**117**	**81**	**91**	**119**
Coats and jackets	100	169	100	80	76
Dresses and suits	100	157	55	76	139
Shirts, blouses, and sweaters	100	117	79	80	140
Skirts, pants, and shorts	100	101	100	103	94
Active sportswear	100	93	84	86	145
Underwear and nightwear	100	102	61	118	108
Hosiery	100	90	93	106	105
Accessories	100	178	99	66	92
Uniforms	100	108	34	160	62
Costumes	100	76	88	96	137
CHILDREN'S (UNDER AGE 2) APPAREL	**100**	**108**	**88**	**104**	**98**
Coats, jackets, and snowsuits	100	128	85	89	111
Outerwear including dresses	100	88	110	99	101
Underwear	100	116	87	103	96
Nightwear and loungewear	100	153	61	88	115
Accessories	100	86	78	118	103
FOOTWEAR	**100**	**103**	**91**	**96**	**113**
Men's	100	88	87	102	120
Boys'	100	113	115	64	133
Women's	100	115	91	97	102
Girls'	100	84	79	107	123
OTHER APPAREL PRODUCTS AND SERVICES	**100**	**124**	**79**	**87**	**123**
Material for making clothes	100	75	107	66	170
Sewing patterns and notions	100	75	73	83	176
Watches	100	165	58	60	155
Jewelry	100	102	94	98	107
Shoe repair and other shoe services	100	93	89	87	137
Coin-operated apparel laundry and dry cleaning	100	166	73	70	121
Apparel alteration, repair, and tailoring services	100	101	93	99	107
Clothing rental	100	78	126	80	124
Watch and jewelry repair	100	119	93	84	117
Professional laundry, dry cleaning	100	121	68	101	113
Clothing storage	100	58	45	188	45

Source: Calculations by New Strategist based on the Bureau of Labor Statistics' 2011 Consumer Expenditure Survey

Table 2.23 Apparel: Total spending by region, 2011

(total annual spending on apparel, accessories, and related services, by region in which consumer units live, 2011; consumer units and dollars in thousands)

	total consumer units	Northeast	Midwest	South	West
Number of consumer units	122,287	22,538	27,107	44,901	27,741
Total spending of all consumer units	$6,078,260,661	$1,229,390,428	$1,279,221,075	$2,051,912,839	$1,518,692,974
Apparel, total spending	212,753,700	42,943,229	44,017,160	72,498,053	53,421,676
MEN'S APPAREL	**39,638,108**	**7,999,863**	**7,680,497**	**14,527,270**	**9,447,752**
Suits	2,257,418	642,558	407,147	739,519	468,268
Sport coats and tailored jackets	643,230	179,853	80,779	242,465	140,647
Coats and jackets	3,280,960	698,453	725,925	1,025,988	834,172
Underwear	2,585,147	564,352	596,083	771,848	655,520
Hosiery	1,780,499	355,875	388,443	568,447	469,378
Nightwear	199,328	70,769	38,763	54,330	35,508
Accessories	3,649,044	683,127	596,896	1,237,023	1,140,155
Sweaters and vests	2,081,325	544,518	336,127	783,073	419,167
Active sportswear	3,047,392	785,449	651,110	1,049,785	560,091
Shirts	10,444,533	1,715,593	2,078,836	4,302,414	2,345,224
Pants and shorts	9,296,258	1,699,591	1,750,299	3,584,896	2,265,053
Uniforms	310,609	49,358	21,957	154,459	84,610
Costumes	62,366	10,367	8,403	13,470	29,960
BOYS' (AGED 2 TO 15) APPAREL	**9,737,714**	**2,036,984**	**1,923,513**	**3,080,658**	**2,706,412**
Coats and jackets	649,344	157,315	117,102	176,012	198,348
Sweaters	253,134	60,627	44,184	88,455	60,198
Shirts	2,670,748	536,630	554,067	721,559	864,132
Underwear	800,980	161,372	171,858	203,402	266,314
Nightwear	188,322	36,286	48,793	62,412	41,057
Hosiery	606,544	97,815	121,982	200,258	186,974
Accessories	758,179	158,668	184,870	186,788	229,695
Suits, sport coats, and vests	111,281	24,566	28,733	31,880	26,354
Pants and shorts	3,084,078	636,473	557,862	1,193,469	696,022
Uniforms	324,061	78,207	20,330	153,112	72,404
Active sportswear	168,756	60,402	48,522	31,880	27,741
Costumes	122,287	28,849	25,481	30,982	36,896
WOMEN'S APPAREL	**73,833,222**	**14,383,301**	**17,422,211**	**24,294,135**	**17,758,956**
Coats and jackets	6,267,209	1,712,888	1,238,248	1,594,884	1,734,090
Dresses	8,673,817	1,448,517	1,650,545	3,257,568	2,323,864
Sport coats and tailored jackets	278,814	62,430	31,986	87,108	97,371
Sweaters and vests	6,124,133	1,479,620	2,115,701	1,421,566	1,102,150
Shirts, blouses, and tops	15,117,119	2,700,278	3,320,879	5,131,286	3,975,008
Skirts	1,456,438	221,098	256,974	618,287	360,078
Pants and shorts	11,598,922	2,042,619	3,354,220	3,959,370	2,231,486
Active sportswear	4,441,464	1,019,619	992,116	1,414,831	1,017,262
Nightwear	3,524,311	617,541	619,395	1,008,925	1,289,402
Undergarments	4,184,661	880,560	978,563	1,402,707	922,943
Hosiery	2,746,566	509,133	704,782	1,039,907	489,906
Suits	940,387	189,995	135,264	392,884	222,205
Accessories	7,908,300	1,389,242	1,895,321	2,772,188	1,851,157
Uniforms	407,216	59,951	95,417	170,624	81,836
Costumes	165,087	50,034	33,071	22,451	59,921

	total consumer units	Northeast	Midwest	South	West
GIRLS' (AGED 2 TO 15) APPAREL	**$14,360,162**	**$3,095,144**	**$2,593,056**	**$4,804,856**	**$3,888,179**
Coats and jackets	643,230	200,814	142,312	188,584	110,964
Dresses and suits	1,685,115	487,046	204,116	467,868	532,072
Shirts, blouses, and sweaters	4,039,140	874,700	710,203	1,184,937	1,279,415
Skirts, pants, and shorts	3,065,735	568,408	680,115	1,161,589	655,242
Active sportswear	1,867,322	320,716	346,970	589,101	615,295
Underwear and nightwear	1,172,732	220,872	159,660	507,381	286,287
Hosiery	743,505	123,283	152,883	290,060	177,265
Accessories	629,778	206,673	138,517	153,561	131,770
Uniforms	348,518	69,417	26,565	204,300	48,824
Costumes	165,087	23,214	32,257	57,922	51,321
CHILDREN'S (UNDER AGE 2) APPAREL	**8,331,413**	**1,663,755**	**1,625,336**	**3,181,685**	**1,861,421**
Coats, jackets, and snowsuits	113,727	26,820	21,415	37,268	28,573
Outerwear including dresses	1,158,058	187,967	282,455	421,620	265,759
Underwear	5,573,841	1,187,978	1,071,540	2,099,571	1,215,611
Nightwear and loungewear	201,774	56,796	27,107	65,555	52,708
Accessories	1,284,014	204,194	222,548	558,119	298,771
FOOTWEAR	**39,271,247**	**7,468,642**	**7,920,936**	**13,832,651**	**10,079,138**
Men's	11,842,273	1,920,463	2,281,054	4,421,850	3,228,775
Boys'	4,484,264	933,975	1,143,915	1,061,460	1,353,761
Women's	18,586,401	3,937,614	3,737,784	6,637,266	4,282,378
Girls'	4,357,086	676,816	758,183	1,712,075	1,214,501
OTHER APPAREL PRODUCTS AND SERVICES	**27,580,610**	**6,295,314**	**4,851,340**	**8,775,900**	**7,680,096**
Material for making clothes	1,180,070	163,401	279,202	286,917	454,675
Sewing patterns and notions	963,622	132,749	155,052	294,102	385,045
Watches	3,701,627	1,123,294	476,541	816,749	1,300,775
Jewelry	8,798,550	1,657,219	1,832,704	3,164,622	2,144,379
Shoe repair and other shoe services	183,431	31,553	36,052	58,820	57,146
Coin-operated apparel laundry and dry cleaning	4,846,234	1,484,353	786,645	1,250,044	1,325,465
Apparel alteration, repair, and tailoring services	778,968	144,919	161,016	283,325	189,748
Clothing rental	205,442	29,525	57,196	60,616	57,979
Watch and jewelry repair	664,018	146,046	136,619	204,300	176,988
Professional laundry, dry cleaning	6,126,579	1,368,282	917,030	2,267,051	1,574,579
Clothing storage	129,624	13,974	13,011	89,353	13,316

Note: Numbers may not add to total because of rounding and missing subcategories.
Source: Calculations by New Strategist based on the Bureau of Labor Statistics' 2011 Consumer Expenditure Survey

Table 2.24 Apparel: Market shares by region, 2011

(percentage of total annual spending on apparel, accessories, and related services accounted for by consumer units by region of residence, 2011)

	total consumer units	Northeast	Midwest	South	West
Share of total consumer units	100.0%	18.4%	22.2%	36.7%	22.7%
Share of total before-tax income	100.0	20.8	21.2	33.9	24.2
Share of total spending	100.0	20.2	21.0	33.8	25.0
Share of apparel spending	100.0	20.2	20.7	34.1	25.1
MEN'S APPAREL	**100.0**	**20.2**	**19.4**	**36.6**	**23.8**
Suits	100.0	28.5	18.0	32.8	20.7
Sport coats and tailored jackets	100.0	28.0	12.6	37.7	21.9
Coats and jackets	100.0	21.3	22.1	31.3	25.4
Underwear	100.0	21.8	23.1	29.9	25.4
Hosiery	100.0	20.0	21.8	31.9	26.4
Nightwear	100.0	35.5	19.4	27.3	17.8
Accessories	100.0	18.7	16.4	33.9	31.2
Sweaters and vests	100.0	26.2	16.1	37.6	20.1
Active sportswear	100.0	25.8	21.4	34.4	18.4
Shirts	100.0	16.4	19.9	41.2	22.5
Pants and shorts	100.0	18.3	18.8	38.6	24.4
Uniforms	100.0	15.9	7.1	49.7	27.2
Costumes	100.0	16.6	13.5	21.6	48.0
BOYS' (AGED 2 TO 15) APPAREL	**100.0**	**20.9**	**19.8**	**31.6**	**27.8**
Coats and jackets	100.0	24.2	18.0	27.1	30.5
Sweaters	100.0	24.0	17.5	34.9	23.8
Shirts	100.0	20.1	20.7	27.0	32.4
Underwear	100.0	20.1	21.5	25.4	33.2
Nightwear	100.0	19.3	25.9	33.1	21.8
Hosiery	100.0	16.1	20.1	33.0	30.8
Accessories	100.0	20.9	24.4	24.6	30.3
Suits, sport coats, and vests	100.0	22.1	25.8	28.6	23.7
Pants and shorts	100.0	20.6	18.1	38.7	22.6
Uniforms	100.0	24.1	6.3	47.2	22.3
Active sportswear	100.0	35.8	28.8	18.9	16.4
Costumes	100.0	23.6	20.8	25.3	30.2
WOMEN'S APPAREL	**100.0**	**19.5**	**23.6**	**32.9**	**24.1**
Coats and jackets	100.0	27.3	19.8	25.4	27.7
Dresses	100.0	16.7	19.0	37.6	26.8
Sport coats and tailored jackets	100.0	22.4	11.5	31.2	34.9
Sweaters and vests	100.0	24.2	34.5	23.2	18.0
Shirts, blouses, and tops	100.0	17.9	22.0	33.9	26.3
Skirts	100.0	15.2	17.6	42.5	24.7
Pants and shorts	100.0	17.6	28.9	34.1	19.2
Active sportswear	100.0	23.0	22.3	31.9	22.9
Nightwear	100.0	17.5	17.6	28.6	36.6
Undergarments	100.0	21.0	23.4	33.5	22.1
Hosiery	100.0	18.5	25.7	37.9	17.8
Suits	100.0	20.2	14.4	41.8	23.6
Accessories	100.0	17.6	24.0	35.1	23.4
Uniforms	100.0	14.7	23.4	41.9	20.1
Costumes	100.0	30.3	20.0	13.6	36.3

	total consumer units	Northeast	Midwest	South	West
GIRLS' (AGED 2 TO 15) APPAREL	**100.0%**	**21.6%**	**18.1%**	**33.5%**	**27.1%**
Coats and jackets	100.0	31.2	22.1	29.3	17.3
Dresses and suits	100.0	28.9	12.1	27.8	31.6
Shirts, blouses, and sweaters	100.0	21.7	17.6	29.3	31.7
Skirts, pants, and shorts	100.0	18.5	22.2	37.9	21.4
Active sportswear	100.0	17.2	18.6	31.5	33.0
Underwear and nightwear	100.0	18.8	13.6	43.3	24.4
Hosiery	100.0	16.6	20.6	39.0	23.8
Accessories	100.0	32.8	22.0	24.4	20.9
Uniforms	100.0	19.9	7.6	58.6	14.0
Costumes	100.0	14.1	19.5	35.1	31.1
CHILDREN'S (UNDER AGE 2) APPAREL	**100.0**	**20.0**	**19.5**	**38.2**	**22.3**
Coats, jackets, and snowsuits	100.0	23.6	18.8	32.8	25.1
Outerwear including dresses	100.0	16.2	24.4	36.4	22.9
Underwear	100.0	21.3	19.2	37.7	21.8
Nightwear and loungewear	100.0	28.1	13.4	32.5	26.1
Accessories	100.0	15.9	17.3	43.5	23.3
FOOTWEAR	**100.0**	**19.0**	**20.2**	**35.2**	**25.7**
Men's	100.0	16.2	19.3	37.3	27.3
Boys'	100.0	20.8	25.5	23.7	30.2
Women's	100.0	21.2	20.1	35.7	23.0
Girls'	100.0	15.5	17.4	39.3	27.9
OTHER APPAREL PRODUCTS AND SERVICES	**100.0**	**22.8**	**17.6**	**31.8**	**27.8**
Material for making clothes	100.0	13.8	23.7	24.3	38.5
Sewing patterns and notions	100.0	13.8	16.1	30.5	40.0
Watches	100.0	30.3	12.9	22.1	35.1
Jewelry	100.0	18.8	20.8	36.0	24.4
Shoe repair and other shoe services	100.0	17.2	19.7	32.1	31.2
Coin-operated apparel laundry and dry cleaning	100.0	30.6	16.2	25.8	27.4
Apparel alteration, repair, and tailoring services	100.0	18.6	20.7	36.4	24.4
Clothing rental	100.0	14.4	27.8	29.5	28.2
Watch and jewelry repair	100.0	22.0	20.6	30.8	26.7
Professional laundry, dry cleaning	100.0	22.3	15.0	37.0	25.7
Clothing storage	100.0	10.8	10.0	68.9	10.3

Note: Numbers may not add to total because of rounding.
Source: Calculations by New Strategist based on the Bureau of Labor Statistics' 2011 Consumer Expenditure Survey

Table 2.25 Apparel: Average spending by education, 2011

(average annual spending of consumer units on apparel, accessories, and related services, by education of consumer unit reference person, 2011)

	total consumer units	less than high school graduate	high school graduate	some college	associate's degree	bachelor's degree or more total	bachelor's degree	graduate degree
Number of consumer units (in 000s)	122,287	16,146	30,810	25,361	12,912	37,058	23,578	13,480
Average number of persons per consumer unit	2.5	2.8	2.5	2.3	2.6	2.5	2.5	2.4
Average before-tax income of consumer units	$63,685.00	$32,564.00	$46,370.00	$52,965.00	$63,664.00	$98,983.00	$90,962.00	$113,013.00
Average spending of consumer units, total	49,704.88	29,950.97	39,704.28	45,355.33	50,819.44	68,902.95	65,051.01	75,731.40
Apparel, average spending	**1,739.79**	**1,273.89**	**1,384.98**	**1,552.41**	**1,686.27**	**2,342.52**	**2,231.93**	**2,553.84**
MEN'S APPAREL	**324.14**	**192.74**	**271.83**	**329.50**	**289.68**	**423.56**	**393.33**	**481.73**
Suits	18.46	9.33	8.28	13.43	10.51	37.11	33.76	42.96
Sport coats and tailored jackets	5.26	2.00	1.93	3.72	6.16	10.20	8.00	14.06
Coats and jackets	26.83	19.30	27.63	22.05	22.44	33.49	36.36	27.88
Underwear	21.14	14.01	18.97	22.69	24.78	23.33	20.19	29.47
Hosiery	14.56	9.03	12.33	13.21	16.26	18.69	17.31	21.39
Nightwear	1.63	0.88	1.40	1.35	1.48	2.40	2.32	2.53
Accessories	29.84	29.69	22.79	37.30	29.26	30.82	33.65	25.30
Sweaters and vests	17.02	3.14	16.50	12.80	10.51	27.39	24.95	32.18
Active sportswear	24.92	6.91	16.50	28.35	17.79	38.27	30.21	54.07
Shirts	85.41	45.45	74.82	93.11	63.00	110.75	104.67	122.64
Pants and shorts	76.02	50.46	68.89	77.87	83.14	87.63	77.74	106.98
Uniforms	2.54	2.18	1.59	2.98	3.71	2.78	3.29	1.87
Costumes	0.51	0.34	0.20	0.64	0.65	0.70	0.87	0.40
BOYS' (AGED 2 TO 15) APPAREL	**79.63**	**69.02**	**70.24**	**73.61**	**97.42**	**89.83**	**86.00**	**97.39**
Coats and jackets	5.31	3.54	4.65	5.26	6.21	6.34	6.78	5.57
Sweaters	2.07	1.26	1.96	2.11	1.81	2.59	2.59	2.58
Shirts	21.84	19.31	20.70	16.22	29.13	24.97	22.49	29.82
Underwear	6.55	6.87	6.88	5.14	6.87	6.98	6.01	8.88
Nightwear	1.54	0.72	1.36	1.62	1.87	1.88	1.94	1.77
Hosiery	4.96	5.50	4.90	6.08	3.60	4.51	4.60	4.34
Accessories	6.20	4.36	3.54	10.07	11.23	4.87	4.12	6.36
Suits, sport coats, and vests	0.91	0.35	0.79	0.64	0.94	1.42	1.41	1.45
Pants and shorts	25.22	21.95	22.30	22.16	27.96	30.21	30.05	30.48
Uniforms	2.65	4.16	1.47	2.57	4.55	2.37	2.64	1.88
Active sportswear	1.38	0.52	0.93	0.99	1.98	2.18	1.82	2.82
Costumes	1.00	0.48	0.76	0.74	1.25	1.51	1.56	1.43
WOMEN'S APPAREL	**603.77**	**369.72**	**450.80**	**496.98**	**556.78**	**895.93**	**863.23**	**959.87**
Coats and jackets	51.25	32.17	29.54	43.76	55.13	79.01	89.28	58.90
Dresses	70.93	41.65	71.79	58.82	42.46	98.03	86.92	119.80
Sport coats and tailored jackets	2.28	1.10	1.11	1.67	2.31	4.17	4.80	3.07
Sweaters and vests	50.08	16.74	24.53	41.96	37.97	91.66	83.34	107.94
Shirts, blouses, and tops	123.62	76.71	91.56	107.83	143.82	169.98	163.71	182.27
Skirts	11.91	11.39	7.44	6.33	10.32	19.73	21.33	16.59
Pants and shorts	94.85	61.77	75.92	85.00	94.86	128.38	114.66	155.25
Active sportswear	36.32	18.12	25.14	24.93	20.49	64.29	62.87	67.08
Nightwear	28.82	15.62	26.88	29.12	16.41	39.02	35.30	46.30
Undergarments	34.22	19.61	21.26	29.22	41.68	50.67	53.16	45.79
Hosiery	22.46	16.52	17.10	15.38	34.17	29.72	28.23	32.65
Suits	7.69	2.15	5.04	3.30	6.02	15.88	13.52	20.01
Accessories	64.67	54.14	50.65	44.07	42.91	99.86	99.31	100.92
Uniforms	3.33	1.59	2.35	3.30	7.26	3.57	4.55	1.84
Costumes	1.35	0.44	0.49	2.29	0.97	1.96	2.25	1.47

	total consumer units	less than high school graduate	high school graduate	some college	associate's degree	bachelor's degree or more		
						total	bachelor's degree	graduate degree
GIRLS' (AGED 2 TO 15) APPAREL	**$117.43**	**$101.23**	**$99.39**	**$109.35**	**$136.37**	**$137.44**	**$125.96**	**$158.74**
Coats and jackets	5.26	4.38	4.64	5.27	5.16	6.17	4.83	8.52
Dresses and suits	13.78	12.51	14.88	17.98	16.39	9.84	8.08	13.29
Shirts, blouses, and sweaters	33.03	34.29	28.88	33.97	34.15	34.88	32.32	39.88
Skirts, pants, and shorts	25.07	20.66	21.07	21.08	32.11	30.59	27.80	35.49
Active sportswear	15.27	8.43	7.52	7.68	20.92	27.01	25.14	30.68
Underwear and nightwear	9.59	10.06	9.12	9.89	9.86	9.52	10.13	8.32
Hosiery	6.08	3.52	6.97	4.52	7.18	6.98	6.86	7.21
Accessories	5.15	4.04	4.43	4.11	6.11	6.49	6.31	6.84
Uniforms	2.85	2.86	1.38	3.08	2.91	3.91	2.70	6.02
Costumes	1.35	0.48	0.49	1.80	1.58	2.04	1.78	2.50
CHILDREN'S (UNDER AGE 2) APPAREL	**68.13**	**76.42**	**57.27**	**56.94**	**73.29**	**79.25**	**72.45**	**92.19**
Coats, jackets, and snowsuits	0.93	1.11	0.69	0.66	1.02	1.22	1.44	0.83
Outerwear including dresses	9.47	8.73	7.07	7.80	14.08	11.32	9.75	14.05
Underwear	45.58	51.81	41.55	36.00	48.87	51.57	48.77	57.04
Nightwear and loungewear	1.65	2.71	1.47	0.98	1.33	1.91	1.45	2.73
Accessories	10.50	12.05	6.48	11.50	7.98	13.24	11.05	17.53
FOOTWEAR	**321.14**	**297.02**	**278.36**	**288.62**	**336.28**	**379.93**	**366.43**	**406.38**
Men's	96.84	90.17	87.53	91.54	80.07	115.44	110.75	124.61
Boys'	36.67	50.67	36.91	34.09	31.33	34.68	31.26	41.37
Women's	151.99	115.92	116.27	128.64	180.92	199.33	201.51	195.05
Girls'	35.63	40.26	37.65	34.34	43.97	30.49	22.90	45.36
OTHER APPAREL PRODUCTS AND SERVICES	**225.54**	**167.74**	**157.09**	**197.42**	**196.45**	**336.59**	**324.52**	**357.54**
Material for making clothes	9.65	14.95	6.39	7.28	14.74	10.17	9.54	11.40
Sewing patterns and notions	7.88	5.82	5.71	6.64	7.49	11.28	9.37	15.03
Watches	30.27	18.05	31.66	35.42	35.01	28.86	32.08	22.56
Jewelry	71.95	22.41	43.69	60.50	62.79	128.07	130.02	124.67
Shoe repair and other shoe services	1.50	0.31	0.51	1.29	1.05	3.16	3.01	3.40
Coin-operated apparel laundry and dry cleaning	39.63	87.72	41.55	33.19	29.38	25.07	25.06	25.08
Apparel alteration, repair, and tailoring services	6.37	1.24	3.30	5.70	4.97	12.11	10.15	15.55
Clothing rental	1.68	0.06	0.84	1.48	3.54	2.58	1.47	4.51
Watch and jewelry repair	5.43	1.50	3.44	5.14	4.09	9.46	8.19	11.69
Professional laundry, dry cleaning	50.10	13.83	19.78	39.97	32.68	104.12	93.04	123.50
Clothing storage	1.06	1.84	0.22	0.81	0.73	1.70	2.60	0.13

Note: Subcategories may not add to total because some are not shown.
Source: Bureau of Labor Statistics, unpublished data from the 2011 Consumer Expenditure Survey

Table 2.26 Apparel: Indexed spending by education, 2011

(indexed average annual spending of consumer units on apparel, accessories, and related services, by education of consumer unit reference person, 2011; index definition: an index of 100 is the average for all consumer units; an index of 125 means that spending by consumer units in that group is 25 percent above the average for all consumer units; an index of 75 indicates spending that is 25 percent below the average for all consumer units)

	total consumer units	less than high school graduate	high school graduate	some college	associate's degree	bachelor's degree or more total	bachelor's degree	graduate degree
Average spending of consumer units, total	$49,705	$29,951	$39,704	$45,355	$50,819	$68,903	$65,051	$75,731
Average spending of consumer units, index	100	60	80	91	102	139	131	152
Apparel, spending index	100	73	80	89	97	135	128	147
MEN'S APPAREL	**100**	**59**	**84**	**102**	**89**	**131**	**121**	**149**
Suits	100	51	45	73	57	201	183	233
Sport coats and tailored jackets	100	38	37	71	117	194	152	267
Coats and jackets	100	72	103	82	84	125	136	104
Underwear	100	66	90	107	117	110	96	139
Hosiery	100	62	85	91	112	128	119	147
Nightwear	100	54	86	83	91	147	142	155
Accessories	100	99	76	125	98	103	113	85
Sweaters and vests	100	18	97	75	62	161	147	189
Active sportswear	100	28	66	114	71	154	121	217
Shirts	100	53	88	109	74	130	123	144
Pants and shorts	100	66	91	102	109	115	102	141
Uniforms	100	86	63	117	146	109	130	74
Costumes	100	67	39	125	127	137	171	78
BOYS' (AGED 2 TO 15) APPAREL	**100**	**87**	**88**	**92**	**122**	**113**	**108**	**122**
Coats and jackets	100	67	88	99	117	119	128	105
Sweaters	100	61	95	102	87	125	125	125
Shirts	100	88	95	74	133	114	103	137
Underwear	100	105	105	78	105	107	92	136
Nightwear	100	47	88	105	121	122	126	115
Hosiery	100	111	99	123	73	91	93	88
Accessories	100	70	57	162	181	79	66	103
Suits, sport coats, and vests	100	38	87	70	103	156	155	159
Pants and shorts	100	87	88	88	111	120	119	121
Uniforms	100	157	55	97	172	89	100	71
Active sportswear	100	38	67	72	143	158	132	204
Costumes	100	48	76	74	125	151	156	143
WOMEN'S APPAREL	**100**	**61**	**75**	**82**	**92**	**148**	**143**	**159**
Coats and jackets	100	63	58	85	108	154	174	115
Dresses	100	59	101	83	60	138	123	169
Sport coats and tailored jackets	100	48	49	73	101	183	211	135
Sweaters and vests	100	33	49	84	76	183	166	216
Shirts, blouses, and tops	100	62	74	87	116	138	132	147
Skirts	100	96	62	53	87	166	179	139
Pants and shorts	100	65	80	90	100	135	121	164
Active sportswear	100	50	69	69	56	177	173	185
Nightwear	100	54	93	101	57	135	122	161
Undergarments	100	57	62	85	122	148	155	134
Hosiery	100	74	76	68	152	132	126	145
Suits	100	28	66	43	78	207	176	260
Accessories	100	84	78	68	66	154	154	156
Uniforms	100	48	71	99	218	107	137	55
Costumes	100	33	36	170	72	145	167	109

	total consumer units	less than high school graduate	high school graduate	some college	associate's degree	bachelor's degree or more		
						total	bachelor's degree	graduate degree
GIRLS' (AGED 2 TO 15) APPAREL	**100**	**86**	**85**	**93**	**116**	**117**	**107**	**135**
Coats and jackets	100	83	88	100	98	117	92	162
Dresses and suits	100	91	108	130	119	71	59	96
Shirts, blouses, and sweaters	100	104	87	103	103	106	98	121
Skirts, pants, and shorts	100	82	84	84	128	122	111	142
Active sportswear	100	55	49	50	137	177	165	201
Underwear and nightwear	100	105	95	103	103	99	106	87
Hosiery	100	58	115	74	118	115	113	119
Accessories	100	78	86	80	119	126	123	133
Uniforms	100	100	48	108	102	137	95	211
Costumes	100	36	36	133	117	151	132	185
CHILDREN'S (UNDER AGE 2) APPAREL	**100**	**112**	**84**	**84**	**108**	**116**	**106**	**135**
Coats, jackets, and snowsuits	100	119	74	71	110	131	155	89
Outerwear including dresses	100	92	75	82	149	120	103	148
Underwear	100	114	91	79	107	113	107	125
Nightwear and loungewear	100	164	89	59	81	116	88	165
Accessories	100	115	62	110	76	126	105	167
FOOTWEAR	**100**	**92**	**87**	**90**	**105**	**118**	**114**	**127**
Men's	100	93	90	95	83	119	114	129
Boys'	100	138	101	93	85	95	85	113
Women's	100	76	76	85	119	131	133	128
Girls'	100	113	106	96	123	86	64	127
OTHER APPAREL PRODUCTS AND SERVICES	**100**	**74**	**70**	**88**	**87**	**149**	**144**	**159**
Material for making clothes	100	155	66	75	153	105	99	118
Sewing patterns and notions	100	74	72	84	95	143	119	191
Watches	100	60	105	117	116	95	106	75
Jewelry	100	31	61	84	87	178	181	173
Shoe repair and other shoe services	100	21	34	86	70	211	201	227
Coin-operated apparel laundry and dry cleaning	100	221	105	84	74	63	63	63
Apparel alteration, repair, and tailoring services	100	19	52	89	78	190	159	244
Clothing rental	100	4	50	88	211	154	88	268
Watch and jewelry repair	100	28	63	95	75	174	151	215
Professional laundry, dry cleaning	100	28	39	80	65	208	186	247
Clothing storage	100	174	21	76	69	160	245	12

Source: Calculations by New Strategist based on the Bureau of Labor Statistics' 2011 Consumer Expenditure Survey

Table 2.27 Apparel: Total spending by education, 2011

(total annual spending on apparel, accessories, and related services, by consumer unit educational attainment group, 2011; consumer units and dollars in thousands)

	total consumer units	less than high school graduate	high school graduate	some college	associate's degree	bachelor's degree or more total	bachelor's degree	graduate degree
Number of consumer units	122,287	16,146	30,810	25,361	12,912	37,058	23,578	13,480
Total spending of all consumer units	$6,078,260,661	$483,588,362	$1,223,288,867	$1,150,256,524	$656,180,609	$2,553,405,521	$1,533,772,714	$1,020,859,272
Apparel, total spending	212,753,700	20,568,228	42,671,234	39,370,670	21,773,118	86,809,106	52,624,446	34,425,763
MEN'S APPAREL	**39,638,108**	**3,111,980**	**8,375,082**	**8,356,450**	**3,740,348**	**15,696,286**	**9,273,935**	**6,493,720**
Suits	2,257,418	150,642	255,107	340,598	135,705	1,375,222	795,993	579,101
Sport coats and tailored jackets	643,230	32,292	59,463	94,343	79,538	377,992	188,624	189,529
Coats and jackets	3,280,960	311,618	851,280	559,210	289,745	1,241,072	857,296	375,822
Underwear	2,585,147	226,205	584,466	575,441	319,959	864,563	476,040	397,256
Hosiery	1,780,499	145,798	379,887	335,019	209,949	692,614	408,135	288,337
Nightwear	199,328	14,208	43,134	34,237	19,110	88,939	54,701	34,104
Accessories	3,649,044	479,375	702,160	945,965	377,805	1,142,128	793,400	341,044
Sweaters and vests	2,081,325	50,698	508,365	324,621	135,705	1,015,019	588,271	433,786
Active sportswear	3,047,392	111,569	508,365	718,984	229,704	1,418,210	712,291	728,864
Shirts	10,444,533	733,836	2,305,204	2,361,363	813,456	4,104,174	2,467,909	1,653,187
Pants and shorts	9,296,258	814,727	2,122,501	1,974,861	1,073,504	3,247,393	1,832,954	1,442,090
Uniforms	310,609	35,198	48,988	75,576	47,904	103,021	77,572	25,208
Costumes	62,366	5,490	6,162	16,231	8,393	25,941	20,513	5,392
BOYS' (AGED 2 TO 15) APPAREL	**9,737,714**	**1,114,397**	**2,164,094**	**1,866,823**	**1,257,887**	**3,328,920**	**2,027,708**	**1,312,817**
Coats and jackets	649,344	57,157	143,267	133,399	80,184	234,948	159,859	75,084
Sweaters	253,134	20,344	60,388	53,512	23,371	95,980	61,067	34,778
Shirts	2,670,748	311,779	637,767	411,355	376,127	925,338	530,269	401,974
Underwear	800,980	110,923	211,973	130,356	88,705	258,665	141,704	119,702
Nightwear	188,322	11,625	41,902	41,085	24,145	69,669	45,741	23,860
Hosiery	606,544	88,803	150,969	154,195	46,483	167,132	108,459	58,503
Accessories	758,179	70,397	109,067	255,385	145,002	180,472	97,141	85,733
Suits, sport coats, and vests	111,281	5,651	24,340	16,231	12,137	52,622	33,245	19,546
Pants and shorts	3,084,078	354,405	687,063	562,000	361,020	1,119,522	708,519	410,870
Uniforms	324,061	67,167	45,291	65,178	58,750	87,827	62,246	25,342
Active sportswear	168,756	8,396	28,653	25,107	25,566	80,786	42,912	38,014
Costumes	122,287	7,750	23,416	18,767	16,140	55,958	36,782	19,276
WOMEN'S APPAREL	**73,833,222**	**5,969,499**	**13,889,148**	**12,603,910**	**7,189,143**	**33,201,374**	**20,353,237**	**12,939,048**
Coats and jackets	6,267,209	519,417	910,127	1,109,797	711,839	2,927,953	2,105,044	793,972
Dresses	8,673,817	672,481	2,211,850	1,491,734	548,244	3,632,796	2,049,400	1,614,904
Sport coats and tailored jackets	278,814	17,761	34,199	42,353	29,827	154,532	113,174	41,384
Sweaters and vests	6,124,133	270,284	755,769	1,064,148	490,269	3,396,736	1,964,991	1,455,031
Shirts, blouses, and tops	15,117,119	1,238,560	2,820,964	2,734,677	1,857,004	6,299,119	3,859,954	2,457,000
Skirts	1,456,438	183,903	229,226	160,535	133,252	731,154	502,919	223,633
Pants and shorts	11,598,922	997,338	2,339,095	2,155,685	1,224,832	4,757,506	2,703,453	2,092,770
Active sportswear	4,441,464	292,566	774,563	632,250	264,567	2,382,459	1,482,349	904,238
Nightwear	3,524,311	252,201	828,173	738,512	211,886	1,446,003	832,303	624,124
Undergarments	4,184,661	316,623	655,021	741,048	538,172	1,877,729	1,253,406	617,249
Hosiery	2,746,566	266,732	526,851	390,052	441,203	1,101,364	665,607	440,122
Suits	940,387	34,714	155,282	83,691	77,730	588,481	318,775	269,735
Accessories	7,908,300	874,144	1,560,527	1,117,659	554,054	3,700,612	2,341,531	1,360,402
Uniforms	407,216	25,672	72,404	83,691	93,741	132,297	107,280	24,803
Costumes	165,087	7,104	15,097	58,077	12,525	72,634	53,051	19,816

	total consumer units	less than high school graduate	high school graduate	some college	associate's degree	bachelor's degree or more		
						total	bachelor's degree	graduate degree
GIRLS' (AGED 2 TO 15) APPAREL	**$14,360,162**	**$1,634,460**	**$3,062,206**	**$2,773,225**	**$1,760,809**	**$5,093,252**	**$2,969,885**	**$2,139,815**
Coats and jackets	643,230	70,719	142,958	133,652	66,626	228,648	113,882	114,850
Dresses and suits	1,685,115	201,986	458,453	455,991	211,628	364,651	190,510	179,149
Shirts, blouses, and sweaters	4,039,140	553,646	889,793	861,513	440,945	1,292,583	762,041	537,582
Skirts, pants, and shorts	3,065,735	333,576	649,167	534,610	414,604	1,133,604	655,468	478,405
Active sportswear	1,867,322	136,111	231,691	194,772	270,119	1,000,937	592,751	413,566
Underwear and nightwear	1,172,732	162,429	280,987	250,820	127,312	352,792	238,845	112,154
Hosiery	743,505	56,834	214,746	114,632	92,708	258,665	161,745	97,191
Accessories	629,778	65,230	136,488	104,234	78,892	240,506	148,777	92,203
Uniforms	348,518	46,178	42,518	78,112	37,574	144,897	63,661	81,150
Costumes	165,087	7,750	15,097	45,650	20,401	75,598	41,969	33,700
CHILDREN'S (UNDER AGE 2) APPAREL	**8,331,413**	**1,233,877**	**1,764,489**	**1,444,055**	**946,320**	**2,936,847**	**1,708,226**	**1,242,721**
Coats, jackets, and snowsuits	113,727	17,922	21,259	16,738	13,170	45,211	33,952	11,188
Outerwear including dresses	1,158,058	140,955	217,827	197,816	181,801	419,497	229,886	189,394
Underwear	5,573,841	836,524	1,280,156	912,996	631,009	1,911,081	1,149,899	768,899
Nightwear and loungewear	201,774	43,756	45,291	24,854	17,173	70,781	34,188	36,800
Accessories	1,284,014	194,559	199,649	291,652	103,038	490,648	260,537	236,304
FOOTWEAR	**39,271,247**	**4,795,685**	**8,576,272**	**7,319,692**	**4,342,047**	**14,079,446**	**8,639,687**	**5,478,002**
Men's	11,842,273	1,455,885	2,696,799	2,321,546	1,033,864	4,277,976	2,611,264	1,679,743
Boys'	4,484,264	818,118	1,137,197	864,556	404,533	1,285,171	737,048	557,668
Women's	18,586,401	1,871,644	3,582,279	3,262,439	2,336,039	7,386,771	4,751,203	2,629,274
Girls'	4,357,086	650,038	1,159,997	870,897	567,741	1,129,898	539,936	611,453
OTHER APPAREL PRODUCTS AND SERVICES	**27,580,610**	**2,708,330**	**4,839,943**	**5,006,769**	**2,536,562**	**12,473,352**	**7,651,533**	**4,819,639**
Material for making clothes	1,180,070	241,383	196,876	184,628	190,323	376,880	224,934	153,672
Sewing patterns and notions	963,622	93,970	175,925	168,397	96,711	418,014	220,926	202,604
Watches	3,701,627	291,435	975,445	898,287	452,049	1,069,494	756,382	304,109
Jewelry	8,798,550	361,832	1,346,089	1,534,341	810,744	4,746,018	3,065,612	1,680,552
Shoe repair and other shoe services	183,431	5,005	15,713	32,716	13,558	117,103	70,970	45,832
Coin-operated apparel laundry and dry cleaning	4,846,234	1,416,327	1,280,156	841,732	379,355	929,044	590,865	338,078
Apparel alteration, repair, and tailoring services	778,968	20,021	101,673	144,558	64,173	448,772	239,317	209,614
Clothing rental	205,442	969	25,880	37,534	45,708	95,610	34,660	60,795
Watch and jewelry repair	664,018	24,219	105,986	130,356	52,810	350,569	193,104	157,581
Professional laundry, dry cleaning	6,126,579	223,299	609,422	1,013,679	421,964	3,858,479	2,193,697	1,664,780
Clothing storage	129,624	29,709	6,778	20,542	9,426	62,999	61,303	1,752

Note: Numbers may not add to total because of rounding and missing subcategories.
Source: Calculations by New Strategist based on the Bureau of Labor Statistics' 2011 Consumer Expenditure Survey

Table 2.28 Apparel: Market shares by education, 2011

(percentage of total annual spending on apparel, accessories, and related services accounted for by consumer unit educational attainment groups, 2011)

	total consumer units	less than high school graduate	high school graduate	some college	associate's degree	bachelor's degree or more total	bachelor's degree	graduate degree
Share of total consumer units	100.0%	13.2%	25.2%	20.7%	10.6%	30.3%	19.3%	11.0%
Share of total before-tax income	100.0	6.8	18.3	17.2	10.6	47.1	27.5	19.6
Share of total spending	100.0	8.0	20.1	18.9	10.8	42.0	25.2	16.8
Share of apparel spending	100.0	9.7	20.1	18.5	10.2	40.8	24.7	16.2
MEN'S APPAREL	100.0	7.9	21.1	21.1	9.4	39.6	23.4	16.4
Suits	100.0	6.7	11.3	15.1	6.0	60.9	35.3	25.7
Sport coats and tailored jackets	100.0	5.0	9.2	14.7	12.4	58.8	29.3	29.5
Coats and jackets	100.0	9.5	25.9	17.0	8.8	37.8	26.1	11.5
Underwear	100.0	8.8	22.6	22.3	12.4	33.4	18.4	15.4
Hosiery	100.0	8.2	21.3	18.8	11.8	38.9	22.9	16.2
Nightwear	100.0	7.1	21.6	17.2	9.6	44.6	27.4	17.1
Accessories	100.0	13.1	19.2	25.9	10.4	31.3	21.7	9.3
Sweaters and vests	100.0	2.4	24.4	15.6	6.5	48.8	28.3	20.8
Active sportswear	100.0	3.7	16.7	23.6	7.5	46.5	23.4	23.9
Shirts	100.0	7.0	22.1	22.6	7.8	39.3	23.6	15.8
Pants and shorts	100.0	8.8	22.8	21.2	11.5	34.9	19.7	15.5
Uniforms	100.0	11.3	15.8	24.3	15.4	33.2	25.0	8.1
Costumes	100.0	8.8	9.9	26.0	13.5	41.6	32.9	8.6
BOYS' (AGED 2 TO 15) APPAREL	100.0	11.4	22.2	19.2	12.9	34.2	20.8	13.5
Coats and jackets	100.0	8.8	22.1	20.5	12.3	36.2	24.6	11.6
Sweaters	100.0	8.0	23.9	21.1	9.2	37.9	24.1	13.7
Shirts	100.0	11.7	23.9	15.4	14.1	34.6	19.9	15.1
Underwear	100.0	13.8	26.5	16.3	11.1	32.3	17.7	14.9
Nightwear	100.0	6.2	22.2	21.8	12.8	37.0	24.3	12.7
Hosiery	100.0	14.6	24.9	25.4	7.7	27.6	17.9	9.6
Accessories	100.0	9.3	14.4	33.7	19.1	23.8	12.8	11.3
Suits, sport coats, and vests	100.0	5.1	21.9	14.6	10.9	47.3	29.9	17.6
Pants and shorts	100.0	11.5	22.3	18.2	11.7	36.3	23.0	13.3
Uniforms	100.0	20.7	14.0	20.1	18.1	27.1	19.2	7.8
Active sportswear	100.0	5.0	17.0	14.9	15.1	47.9	25.4	22.5
Costumes	100.0	6.3	19.1	15.3	13.2	45.8	30.1	15.8
WOMEN'S APPAREL	100.0	8.1	18.8	17.1	9.7	45.0	27.6	17.5
Coats and jackets	100.0	8.3	14.5	17.7	11.4	46.7	33.6	12.7
Dresses	100.0	7.8	25.5	17.2	6.3	41.9	23.6	18.6
Sport coats and tailored jackets	100.0	6.4	12.3	15.2	10.7	55.4	40.6	14.8
Sweaters and vests	100.0	4.4	12.3	17.4	8.0	55.5	32.1	23.8
Shirts, blouses, and tops	100.0	8.2	18.7	18.1	12.3	41.7	25.5	16.3
Skirts	100.0	12.6	15.7	11.0	9.1	50.2	34.5	15.4
Pants and shorts	100.0	8.6	20.2	18.6	10.6	41.0	23.3	18.0
Active sportswear	100.0	6.6	17.4	14.2	6.0	53.6	33.4	20.4
Nightwear	100.0	7.2	23.5	21.0	6.0	41.0	23.6	17.7
Undergarments	100.0	7.6	15.7	17.7	12.9	44.9	30.0	14.8
Hosiery	100.0	9.7	19.2	14.2	16.1	40.1	24.2	16.0
Suits	100.0	3.7	16.5	8.9	8.3	62.6	33.9	28.7
Accessories	100.0	11.1	19.7	14.1	7.0	46.8	29.6	17.2
Uniforms	100.0	6.3	17.8	20.6	23.0	32.5	26.3	6.1
Costumes	100.0	4.3	9.1	35.2	7.6	44.0	32.1	12.0

	total consumer units	less than high school graduate	high school graduate	some college	associate's degree	bachelor's degree or more		
						total	bachelor's degree	graduate degree
GIRLS' (AGED 2 TO 15) APPAREL	**100.0%**	**11.4%**	**21.3%**	**19.3%**	**12.3%**	**35.5%**	**20.7%**	**14.9%**
Coats and jackets	100.0	11.0	22.2	20.8	10.4	35.5	17.7	17.9
Dresses and suits	100.0	12.0	27.2	27.1	12.6	21.6	11.3	10.6
Shirts, blouses, and sweaters	100.0	13.7	22.0	21.3	10.9	32.0	18.9	13.3
Skirts, pants, and shorts	100.0	10.9	21.2	17.4	13.5	37.0	21.4	15.6
Active sportswear	100.0	7.3	12.4	10.4	14.5	53.6	31.7	22.1
Underwear and nightwear	100.0	13.9	24.0	21.4	10.9	30.1	20.4	9.6
Hosiery	100.0	7.6	28.9	15.4	12.5	34.8	21.8	13.1
Accessories	100.0	10.4	21.7	16.6	12.5	38.2	23.6	14.6
Uniforms	100.0	13.2	12.2	22.4	10.8	41.6	18.3	23.3
Costumes	100.0	4.7	9.1	27.7	12.4	45.8	25.4	20.4
CHILDREN'S (UNDER AGE 2) APPAREL	**100.0**	**14.8**	**21.2**	**17.3**	**11.4**	**35.3**	**20.5**	**14.9**
Coats, jackets, and snowsuits	100.0	15.8	18.7	14.7	11.6	39.8	29.9	9.8
Outerwear including dresses	100.0	12.2	18.8	17.1	15.7	36.2	19.9	16.4
Underwear	100.0	15.0	23.0	16.4	11.3	34.3	20.6	13.8
Nightwear and loungewear	100.0	21.7	22.4	12.3	8.5	35.1	16.9	18.2
Accessories	100.0	15.2	15.5	22.7	8.0	38.2	20.3	18.4
FOOTWEAR	**100.0**	**12.2**	**21.8**	**18.6**	**11.1**	**35.9**	**22.0**	**13.9**
Men's	100.0	12.3	22.8	19.6	8.7	36.1	22.1	14.2
Boys'	100.0	18.2	25.4	19.3	9.0	28.7	16.4	12.4
Women's	100.0	10.1	19.3	17.6	12.6	39.7	25.6	14.1
Girls'	100.0	14.9	26.6	20.0	13.0	25.9	12.4	14.0
OTHER APPAREL PRODUCTS AND SERVICES	**100.0**	**9.8**	**17.5**	**18.2**	**9.2**	**45.2**	**27.7**	**17.5**
Material for making clothes	100.0	20.5	16.7	15.6	16.1	31.9	19.1	13.0
Sewing patterns and notions	100.0	9.8	18.3	17.5	10.0	43.4	22.9	21.0
Watches	100.0	7.9	26.4	24.3	12.2	28.9	20.4	8.2
Jewelry	100.0	4.1	15.3	17.4	9.2	53.9	34.8	19.1
Shoe repair and other shoe services	100.0	2.7	8.6	17.8	7.4	63.8	38.7	25.0
Coin-operated apparel laundry and dry cleaning	100.0	29.2	26.4	17.4	7.8	19.2	12.2	7.0
Apparel alteration, repair, and tailoring services	100.0	2.6	13.1	18.6	8.2	57.6	30.7	26.9
Clothing rental	100.0	0.5	12.6	18.3	22.2	46.5	16.9	29.6
Watch and jewelry repair	100.0	3.6	16.0	19.6	8.0	52.8	29.1	23.7
Professional laundry, dry cleaning	100.0	3.6	9.9	16.5	6.9	63.0	35.8	27.2
Clothing storage	100.0	22.9	5.2	15.8	7.3	48.6	47.3	1.4

Note: Numbers may not add to total because of rounding.
Source: Calculations by New Strategist based on the Bureau of Labor Statistics' 2011 Consumer Expenditure Survey

CHAPTER 3

Spending on Entertainment, 2011

Until recently, entertainment spending seemed to be immune from the ups and downs of the economy. Average household spending on entertainment grew even as the Great Recession set in, peaking in 2009 at $2,824 (in 2011 dollars). But in the past few years, economic reality finally caught up with entertainment. The average household spent $2,572 on entertainment in 2011, 9 percent below the 2009 peak and 3 percent less than in 2006, after adjusting for inflation. Still, entertainment spending in 2011 was 6 percent greater than in 2000. Overall, Americans devoted 5.2 percent of their spending to entertainment in 2011, less than the 5.5 percent of 2009 but more than the 4.9 percent of 2000. Behind the growth in entertainment spending are bigger cable bills and much more spending on pets—in particular, pet medicines.

Household spending on entertainment peaks in the 45-to-54 age group at 23 percent above average. This age group spends the most on a variety of entertainment categories including health club memberships. Householders aged 35 to 44 spend more than twice the average on fees for recreational lessons, much of it for their children. Entertainment spending by householders aged 65 or older exceeds that of householders under age 25. Householders aged 65 to 74 spend 97 percent as much as the average household on entertainment, while householders under age 25 spend only 52 percent as much. Even householders aged 75 or older spend slightly more on entertainment than the youngest householders.

Households with incomes of $100,000 or more spent an average of $5,193 on entertainment in 2011, twice what the average household spent. High-income households spend far more than average on almost every entertainment category. Households with incomes of $100,000 or more account for 18 percent of households, but they control 36 percent of entertainment spending. They account for 57 percent of all spending on social, recreation, and health club memberships, for 57 percent of spending on fees for recreational lessons, and for 57 percent of spending on admission to sports events.

Married couples with children aged 6 to 17 at home spend much more on entertainment than other household types—59 percent more than the average household. They are especially big spenders on fees for recreational lessons, to which they devote four-and-one-half times the average amount. They spend three-and-one-half times the average on video game software, over two-and-one-half times the average on video game hardware, and also over two-and-one-half times the average on personal digital audio players. Married couples without children at home, many of them empty-nesters, spend nearly three-and-one-half times the average on motorized recreational vehicles, over twice the average on docking and landing fees, and more than one-and-one-half times the average on rental of recreational vehicles.

Asians, Hispanics, and blacks spend less than the average household on entertainment. In some categories, however, they spend more. Asians spend twice the average on fees for recreational lessons and nearly three times the average on musical instruments and accessories as well as athletic gear, game tables, and exercise equipment. Hispanics spend over twice the average on the rental of television sets. Black households spend more than twice the average on fireworks. Non-Hispanic whites spend more than average on nearly all entertainment categories.

Households in the West spend the most on entertainment, 15 percent more than the average household, whereas Southern households spend the least, 9 percent less than average. Spending on fees and admissions, online gaming services, streamed and downloaded video, and personal digital audio players, among others, is highest in the West. Spending on playground equipment, live entertainment at catered affairs, and rental of party supplies for catered affairs is highest in the Northeast. Southern households lead the nation in spending on pet purchase, supply, and medicines and on stamp and coin collecting. Households in the Midwest spend more than those in other regions on fireworks, photo processing, hunting and fishing equipment, and admission to sports events, among others.

College graduates spend 41 percent more than the average household on entertainment. They account for only 30 percent of all households but control 67 percent of spending on social, recreation, and health club memberships; 65 percent of spending on fees for recreational lessons; 64 percent of spending on participant sports on trips; 64 percent of spending on docking and landing fees; and 61 percent of spending on rental of recreational vehicles. Householders with no more than a high school diploma are a mix of young and old, which accounts for the fact that they spend more than average on video game software and on stamp and coin collecting.

Table 3.1 Entertainment: Average spending by age, 2011

(average annual spending of consumer units on entertainment, by age of consumer unit reference person, 2011)

	total consumer units	under 25	25 to 34	35 to 44	45 to 54	55 to 64	65 to 74	75+
Number of consumer units (in 000s)	122,287	7,743	20,463	21,699	24,821	21,688	14,079	11,794
Average number of persons per consumer unit	2.5	2.1	2.9	3.3	2.8	2.1	1.9	1.6
Average before-tax income of consumer units	$63,685.00	$27,514.00	$58,179.00	$77,376.00	$78,519.00	$75,517.00	$52,521.00	$32,144.00
Average spending of consumer units, total	49,704.88	29,911.52	48,097.39	57,271.07	58,050.42	53,615.86	44,645.56	32,688.34
Entertainment, average spending	**2,571.95**	**1,344.92**	**2,422.63**	**2,926.07**	**3,169.21**	**2,769.20**	**2,493.33**	**1,437.07**
FEES AND ADMISSIONS	**594.27**	**263.93**	**500.90**	**809.65**	**808.01**	**570.82**	**547.84**	**223.97**
Recreation expenses on trips	21.42	7.79	17.32	22.65	28.85	23.32	29.13	6.91
Social, recreation, health club membership	121.90	49.70	89.96	150.08	158.53	134.02	126.84	67.55
Fees for participant sports	99.72	27.16	76.70	142.50	149.88	93.63	82.13	33.63
Participant sports on trips	24.07	8.24	19.43	24.79	30.11	26.81	35.80	9.40
Movie, theater, amusement park, and other admissions	115.88	87.50	114.35	144.35	135.46	118.42	105.20	51.65
Movie and other admissions on trips	43.77	22.07	44.98	50.69	49.91	47.66	49.38	16.44
Admission to sports events	45.91	20.50	46.03	51.51	67.21	44.94	43.55	11.90
Admission to sports events on trips	14.58	7.35	14.99	16.89	16.63	15.83	16.45	5.48
Fees for recreational lessons	85.60	25.84	59.80	183.55	142.58	42.86	30.25	14.11
Other entertainment services on trips	21.42	7.79	17.32	22.65	28.85	23.32	29.13	6.91
AUDIO AND VISUAL EQUIPMENT AND SERVICES	**976.58**	**607.87**	**947.99**	**1,100.90**	**1,110.67**	**1,055.06**	**901.53**	**697.16**
Sound components, equipment, and accessories	26.88	25.90	31.95	27.36	26.07	43.47	11.11	6.28
Television sets	112.69	97.42	121.03	133.11	122.10	129.88	84.86	52.46
Cable and satellite television services	640.40	334.09	561.56	652.08	709.50	715.63	712.82	586.59
Miscellaneous video equipment	7.67	10.37	6.68	11.71	8.96	7.56	5.19	0.49
Satellite radio service	13.48	2.62	9.43	18.10	16.31	16.80	15.26	4.96
Online gaming services	3.09	5.01	5.14	4.14	3.62	1.60	1.26	0.17
VCRs and video disc players	8.66	4.91	10.88	12.82	10.15	8.80	3.80	2.01
Video cassettes, tapes, and discs	33.29	24.63	31.06	46.38	47.71	25.22	23.40	14.65
Video game software	1.99	–	3.65	4.89	1.78	0.71	–	–
Video game hardware and accessories	40.41	32.93	62.97	63.79	46.97	28.72	4.39	10.64
Streamed and downloaded video	3.92	3.24	6.46	6.28	3.94	2.84	1.50	0.45
Applications, games, ringtones for handheld devices	3.66	4.55	6.01	3.88	5.57	2.25	0.94	0.38
Repair of television, radio, and sound equipment	3.39	1.04	1.05	4.12	3.23	6.54	3.51	2.06
Rental of television sets	0.32	–	1.11	0.29	0.29	–	0.23	–
Personal digital audio players	10.29	5.52	8.73	19.43	17.42	5.65	3.16	1.29
Satellite dishes	1.05	–	2.66	0.69	0.46	1.02	1.54	0.34
Compact discs, records, and audio tapes	11.57	14.82	10.26	11.88	14.02	10.92	12.91	5.57
Streamed and downloaded audio	9.62	8.22	13.60	14.54	12.82	7.66	1.97	0.55
Rental of VCR, radio, and sound equipment	0.18	0.03	0.20	0.64	–	0.09	0.16	–
Musical instruments and accessories	22.60	12.58	23.53	34.92	35.24	22.12	3.35	2.19
Rental and repair of musical instruments	1.60	0.28	0.94	2.13	3.13	1.11	0.48	1.67
Rental of video cassettes, tapes, discs, films	18.54	19.59	27.83	25.62	19.70	15.61	8.62	3.55
Installation of television sets	0.85	–	0.20	1.78	1.51	0.58	0.54	0.31
PETS, TOYS, HOBBIES, AND PLAYGROUND EQUIPMENT	**630.67**	**332.77**	**599.21**	**643.14**	**744.25**	**758.60**	**626.27**	**379.53**
Pets	**502.05**	**279.43**	**426.67**	**464.78**	**625.02**	**636.39**	**546.60**	**286.27**
Pet food	182.75	111.51	147.43	170.48	225.71	234.60	190.93	115.77
Pet purchase, supplies, and medicines	140.90	62.03	111.48	178.35	187.92	159.08	118.35	69.33
Pet services	35.72	9.86	31.42	36.55	47.74	50.10	32.45	10.83
Veterinarian services	142.67	96.03	136.33	79.40	163.65	192.61	204.87	90.34
Toys, games, hobbies, and tricycles	**115.02**	**52.13**	**162.57**	**167.45**	**113.99**	**107.82**	**70.44**	**38.89**
Stamp and coin collecting	**9.97**	**0.07**	**3.11**	**1.49**	**3.47**	**13.44**	**7.62**	**54.09**
Playground equipment	**3.63**	**1.15**	**6.85**	**9.41**	**1.76**	**0.95**	**1.61**	**0.29**

	total consumer units	under 25	25 to 34	35 to 44	45 to 54	55 to 64	65 to 74	75+
OTHER ENTERTAINMENT SUPPLIES, EQUIPMENT, AND SERVICES	**$370.43**	**$140.35**	**$374.54**	**$372.38**	**$506.27**	**$384.73**	**$417.69**	**$136.40**
Unmotored recreational vehicles	54.49	–	68.95	19.63	33.99	71.14	166.24	8.46
Motorized recreational vehicles	80.37	–	26.57	41.25	202.88	59.32	110.31	43.55
Rental of recreational vehicles	5.48	0.34	5.49	4.25	5.82	6.65	9.78	3.05
Docking and landing fees	7.14	0.10	0.38	6.88	11.55	11.64	12.47	0.02
Sports, recreation, exercise equipment	145.28	93.53	158.37	208.19	166.93	155.67	76.68	52.59
Athletic gear, game tables, exercise equipment	52.52	21.42	42.04	106.21	61.74	42.85	18.52	29.56
Bicycles	21.92	19.38	27.12	30.12	33.62	14.94	10.97	0.73
Camping equipment	14.09	31.63	8.26	12.54	15.02	23.87	9.98	0.51
Hunting and fishing equipment	33.06	14.03	59.21	24.75	25.57	56.64	12.60	7.86
Winter sports equipment	4.52	1.39	4.51	5.63	7.34	5.08	2.56	–
Water sports equipment	5.31	1.45	6.05	7.35	9.91	2.33	2.82	1.55
Other sports equipment	6.34	3.49	9.66	10.06	6.25	5.30	3.17	1.44
Global positioning system devices	4.91	–	–	7.14	3.78	3.10	13.69	8.50
Rental and repair of miscellaneous sports equipment	2.62	0.75	1.51	4.38	3.70	1.56	2.38	2.46
Photographic equipment, supplies, and services	54.54	39.24	79.49	71.55	57.17	54.59	30.37	13.15
Photo processing	8.92	6.14	9.73	10.76	8.87	9.31	10.08	3.98
Repair and rental of photographic equipment	0.43	0.85	0.55	0.63	0.41	0.33	0.18	0.11
Photographic equipment	26.84	24.98	31.96	37.44	32.34	28.20	8.74	7.21
Photographer fees	17.09	6.91	36.09	20.13	14.40	15.90	10.48	0.92
Fireworks	1.95	–	2.20	5.71	2.49	0.31	–	–
Pinball, electronic video games	2.67	–	7.28	3.00	2.59	0.01	0.97	2.60
Live entertainment for catered affairs	6.58	1.36	10.55	2.76	8.57	10.73	4.92	0.28
Rental of party supplies for catered affairs	8.78	3.48	13.30	6.30	13.07	10.12	2.54	4.94

Note: Subcategories may not add to total because some are not shown. "–" means sample is too small to make a reliable estimate.
Source: Bureau of Labor Statistics, unpublished data from the 2011 Consumer Expenditure Survey

Table 3.2 Entertainment: Indexed spending by age, 2011

(indexed average annual spending of consumer units on entertainment by age of consumer unit reference person, 2011; index definition: an index of 100 is the average for all consumer units; an index of 125 means that spending by consumer units in that group is 25 percent above the average for all consumer units; an index of 75 indicates spending that is 25 percent below the average for all consumer units)

	total consumer units	under 25	25 to 34	35 to 44	45 to 54	55 to 64	65 to 74	75+
Average spending of consumer units, total	$49,705	$29,912	$48,097	$57,271	$58,050	$53,616	$44,646	$32,688
Average spending of consumer units, index	100	60	97	115	117	108	90	66
Entertainment, spending index	**100**	**52**	**94**	**114**	**123**	**108**	**97**	**56**
FEES AND ADMISSIONS	**100**	**44**	**84**	**136**	**136**	**96**	**92**	**38**
Recreation expenses on trips	100	36	81	106	135	109	136	32
Social, recreation, health club membership	100	41	74	123	130	110	104	55
Fees for participant sports	100	27	77	143	150	94	82	34
Participant sports on trips	100	34	81	103	125	111	149	39
Movie, theater, amusement park, and other admissions	100	76	99	125	117	102	91	45
Movie and other admissions on trips	100	50	103	116	114	109	113	38
Admission to sports events	100	45	100	112	146	98	95	26
Admission to sports events on trips	100	50	103	116	114	109	113	38
Fees for recreational lessons	100	30	70	214	167	50	35	16
Other entertainment services on trips	100	36	81	106	135	109	136	32
AUDIO AND VISUAL EQUIPMENT AND SERVICES	**100**	**62**	**97**	**113**	**114**	**108**	**92**	**71**
Sound components, equipment, and accessories	100	96	119	102	97	162	41	23
Television sets	100	86	107	118	108	115	75	47
Cable and satellite television services	100	52	88	102	111	112	111	92
Miscellaneous video equipment	100	135	87	153	117	99	68	6
Satellite radio service	100	19	70	134	121	125	113	37
Online gaming services	100	162	166	134	117	52	41	6
VCRs and video disc players	100	57	126	148	117	102	44	23
Video cassettes, tapes, and discs	100	74	93	139	143	76	70	44
Video game software	100	–	183	246	89	36	–	–
Video game hardware and accessories	100	81	156	158	116	71	11	26
Streamed and downloaded video	100	83	165	160	101	72	38	11
Applications, games, ringtones for handheld devices	100	124	164	106	152	61	26	10
Repair of television, radio, and sound equipment	100	31	31	122	95	193	104	61
Rental of television sets	100	–	347	91	91	–	72	–
Personal digital audio players	100	54	85	189	169	55	31	13
Satellite dishes	100	–	253	66	44	97	147	32
Compact discs, records, and audio tapes	100	128	89	103	121	94	112	48
Streamed and downloaded audio	100	85	141	151	133	80	20	6
Rental of VCR, radio, and sound equipment	100	17	111	356	–	50	89	–
Musical instruments and accessories	100	56	104	155	156	98	15	10
Rental and repair of musical instruments	100	18	59	133	196	69	30	104
Rental of video cassettes, tapes, discs, films	100	106	150	138	106	84	46	19
Installation of television sets	100	–	24	209	178	68	64	36
PETS, TOYS, HOBBIES, AND PLAYGROUND EQUIPMENT	**100**	**53**	**95**	**102**	**118**	**120**	**99**	**60**
Pets	**100**	**56**	**85**	**93**	**124**	**127**	**109**	**57**
Pet food	100	61	81	93	124	128	104	63
Pet purchase, supplies, and medicines	100	44	79	127	133	113	84	49
Pet services	100	28	88	102	134	140	91	30
Veterinarian services	100	67	96	56	115	135	144	63
Toys, games, hobbies, and tricycles	**100**	**45**	**141**	**146**	**99**	**94**	**61**	**34**
Stamp and coin collecting	**100**	**1**	**31**	**15**	**35**	**135**	**76**	**543**
Playground equipment	**100**	**32**	**189**	**259**	**48**	**26**	**44**	**8**

	total consumer units	under 25	25 to 34	35 to 44	45 to 54	55 to 64	65 to 74	75+
OTHER ENTERTAINMENT SUPPLIES, EQUIPMENT, AND SERVICES	100	38	101	101	137	104	113	37
Unmotored recreational vehicles	100	–	127	36	62	131	305	16
Motorized recreational vehicles	100	–	33	51		74	137	54
Rental of recreational vehicles	100	6	100	78	106	121	178	56
Docking and landing fees	100	1	5	96	162	163	175	0
Sports, recreation, exercise equipment	100	64	109	143	252	107	53	36
Athletic gear, game tables, exercise equipment	100	41	80	202	118	82	35	56
Bicycles	100	88	124	137	153	68	50	3
Camping equipment	100	224	59	89	107	169	71	4
Hunting and fishing equipment	100	42	179	75	77	171	38	24
Winter sports equipment	100	31	100	125	162	112	57	–
Water sports equipment	100	27	114	138	187	44	53	29
Other sports equipment	100	55	152	159	99	84	50	23
Global positioning system devices	100	–	–	145	77	63	279	173
Rental and repair of miscellaneous sports equipment	100	29	58	167	141	60	91	94
Photographic equipment, supplies, and services	100	72	146	131	105	100	56	24
Photo processing	100	69	109	121	99	104	113	45
Repair and rental of photographic equipment	100	198	128	147	95	77	42	26
Photographic equipment	100	93	119	139	120	105	33	27
Photographer fees	100	40	211	118	84	93	61	5
Fireworks	100	–	113	293	128	16	–	–
Pinball, electronic video games	100	–	273	112	97	0	36	97
Live entertainment for catered affairs	100	21	160	42	130	163	75	4
Rental of party supplies for catered affairs	100	40	151	72	149	115	29	56

Note: "–" means sample is too small to make a reliable estimate.
Source: Calculations by New Strategist based on the Bureau of Labor Statistics' 2011 Consumer Expenditure Survey

Table 3.3 Entertainment: Total spending by age, 2011

(total annual spending on entertainment, by consumer unit age groups, 2011; consumer units and dollars in thousands)

	total consumer units	under 25	25 to 34	35 to 44	45 to 54	55 to 64	65 to 74	75+
Number of consumer units	122,287	7,743	20,463	21,699	24,821	21,688	14,079	11,794
Total spending of all consumer units	$6,078,260,661	$231,604,899	$984,216,892	$1,242,724,948	$1,440,869,475	$1,162,820,772	$628,564,839	$385,526,282
Entertainment, total spending	314,516,050	10,413,716	49,574,278	63,492,793	78,662,961	60,058,410	35,103,593	16,948,804
FEES AND ADMISSIONS	**72,671,495**	**2,043,610**	**10,249,917**	**17,568,595**	**20,055,616**	**12,379,944**	**7,713,039**	**2,641,502**
Recreation expenses on trips	2,619,388	60,318	354,419	491,482	716,086	505,764	410,121	81,497
Social, recreation, health club membership	14,906,785	384,827	1,840,851	3,256,586	3,934,873	2,906,626	1,785,780	796,685
Fees for participant sports	12,194,460	210,300	1,569,512	3,092,108	3,720,171	2,030,647	1,156,308	396,632
Participant sports on trips	2,943,448	63,802	397,596	537,918	747,360	581,455	504,028	110,864
Movie, theater, amusement park, and other admissions	14,170,618	677,513	2,339,944	3,132,251	3,362,253	2,568,293	1,481,111	609,160
Movie and other admissions on trips	5,352,502	170,888	920,426	1,099,922	1,238,816	1,033,650	695,221	193,893
Admission to sports events	5,614,196	158,732	941,912	1,117,715	1,668,219	974,659	613,140	140,349
Admission to sports events on trips	1,782,944	56,911	306,740	366,496	412,773	343,321	231,600	64,631
Fees for recreational lessons	10,467,767	200,079	1,223,687	3,982,851	3,538,978	929,548	425,890	166,413
Other entertainment services on trips	2,619,388	60,318	354,419	491,482	716,086	505,764	410,121	81,497
AUDIO AND VISUAL EQUIPMENT AND SERVICES	**119,423,038**	**4,706,737**	**19,398,719**	**23,888,429**	**27,567,940**	**22,882,141**	**12,692,641**	**8,222,305**
Sound components, equipment, and accessories	3,287,075	200,544	653,793	593,685	647,083	942,777	156,418	74,066
Television sets	13,780,522	754,323	2,476,637	2,888,354	3,030,644	2,816,837	1,194,744	618,713
Cable and satellite television services	78,312,595	2,586,859	11,491,202	14,149,484	17,610,500	15,520,583	10,035,793	6,918,242
Miscellaneous video equipment	937,941	80,295	136,693	254,095	222,396	163,961	73,070	5,779
Satellite radio service	1,648,429	20,287	192,966	392,752	404,831	364,358	214,846	58,498
Online gaming services	377,867	38,792	105,180	89,834	89,852	34,701	17,740	2,005
VCRs and video disc players	1,059,005	38,018	222,637	278,181	251,933	190,854	53,500	23,706
Video cassettes, tapes, and discs	4,070,934	190,710	635,581	1,006,400	1,184,210	546,971	329,449	172,782
Video game software	243,351	–	74,690	106,108	44,181	15,398	–	–
Video game hardware and accessories	4,941,618	254,977	1,288,555	1,384,179	1,165,842	622,879	61,807	125,488
Streamed and downloaded video	479,365	25,087	132,191	136,270	97,795	61,594	21,119	5,307
Applications, games, ringtones for handheld devices	447,570	35,231	122,983	84,192	138,253	48,798	13,234	4,482
Repair of television, radio, and sound equipment	414,553	8,053	21,486	89,400	80,172	141,840	49,417	24,296
Rental of television sets	39,132	–	22,714	6,293	7,198	–	3,238	–
Personal digital audio players	1,258,333	42,741	178,642	421,612	432,382	122,537	44,490	15,214
Satellite dishes	128,401	–	54,432	14,972	11,418	22,122	21,682	4,010
Compact discs, records, and audio tapes	1,414,861	114,751	209,950	257,784	347,990	236,833	181,760	65,693
Streamed and downloaded audio	1,176,401	63,647	278,297	315,503	318,205	166,130	27,736	6,487
Rental of VCR, radio, and sound equipment	22,012	232	4,093	13,887	–	1,952	2,253	–
Musical instruments and accessories	2,763,686	97,407	481,494	757,729	874,692	479,739	47,165	25,829
Rental and repair of musical instruments	195,659	2,168	19,235	46,219	77,690	24,074	6,758	19,696
Rental of video cassettes, tapes, discs, films	2,267,201	151,685	569,485	555,928	488,974	338,550	121,361	41,869
Installation of television sets	103,944	–	4,093	38,624	37,480	12,579	7,603	3,656
PETS, TOYS, HOBBIES, AND PLAYGROUND EQUIPMENT	**77,122,742**	**2,576,638**	**12,261,634**	**13,955,495**	**18,473,029**	**16,452,517**	**8,817,255**	**4,476,177**
Pets	**61,394,188**	**2,163,626**	**8,730,948**	**10,085,261**	**15,513,621**	**13,802,026**	**7,695,581**	**3,376,268**
Pet food	22,347,949	863,422	3,016,860	3,699,246	5,602,348	5,088,005	2,688,103	1,365,391
Pet purchase, supplies, and medicines	17,230,238	480,298	2,281,215	3,870,017	4,664,362	3,450,127	1,666,250	817,678
Pet services	4,368,092	76,346	642,947	793,098	1,184,955	1,086,569	456,864	127,729
Veterinarian services	17,446,686	743,560	2,789,721	1,722,901	4,061,957	4,177,326	2,884,365	1,065,470
Toys, games, hobbies, and tricycles	**14,065,451**	**403,643**	**3,326,670**	**3,633,498**	**2,829,346**	**2,338,400**	**991,725**	**458,669**
Stamp and coin collecting	**1,219,201**	**542**	**63,640**	**32,332**	**86,129**	**291,487**	**107,282**	**637,937**
Playground equipment	**443,902**	**8,904**	**140,172**	**204,188**	**43,685**	**20,604**	**22,667**	**3,420**

	total consumer units	under 25	25 to 34	35 to 44	45 to 54	55 to 64	65 to 74	75+
OTHER ENTERTAINMENT SUPPLIES, EQUIPMENT, AND SERVICES	$45,298,773	$1,086,730	$7,664,212	$8,080,274	$12,566,128	$8,344,024	$5,880,658	$1,608,702
Unmotored recreational vehicles	6,663,419	–	1,410,924	425,951	843,666	1,542,884	2,340,493	99,777
Motorized recreational vehicles	9,828,206	–	543,702	895,084	5,035,684	1,286,532	1,553,054	513,629
Rental of recreational vehicles	670,133	2,633	112,342	92,221	144,458	144,225	137,693	35,972
Docking and landing fees	873,129	774	7,776	149,289	286,683	252,448	175,565	236
Sports, recreation, exercise equipment	17,765,855	724,203	3,240,725	4,517,515	4,143,370	3,376,171	1,079,578	620,246
Athletic gear, game tables, exercise equipment	6,422,513	165,855	860,265	2,304,651	1,532,449	929,331	260,743	348,631
Bicycles	2,680,531	150,059	554,957	653,574	834,482	324,019	154,447	8,610
Camping equipment	1,723,024	244,911	169,024	272,105	372,811	517,693	140,508	6,015
Hunting and fishing equipment	4,042,808	108,634	1,211,614	537,050	634,673	1,228,408	177,395	92,701
Winter sports equipment	552,737	10,763	92,288	122,165	182,186	110,175	36,042	–
Water sports equipment	649,344	11,227	123,801	159,488	245,976	50,533	39,703	18,281
Other sports equipment	775,300	27,023	197,673	218,292	155,131	114,946	44,630	16,983
Global positioning system devices	600,429	–	–	154,931	93,823	67,233	192,742	100,249
Rental and repair of miscellaneous sports equipment	320,392	5,807	30,899	95,042	91,838	33,833	33,508	29,013
Photographic equipment, supplies, and services	6,669,533	303,835	1,626,604	1,552,563	1,419,017	1,183,948	427,579	155,091
Photo processing	1,090,800	47,542	199,105	233,481	220,162	201,915	141,916	46,940
Repair and rental of photographic equipment	52,583	6,582	11,255	13,670	10,177	7,157	2,534	1,297
Photographic equipment	3,282,183	193,420	653,997	812,411	802,711	611,602	123,050	85,035
Photographer fees	2,089,885	53,504	738,510	436,801	357,422	344,839	147,548	10,850
Fireworks	238,460	–	45,019	123,901	61,804	6,723	–	–
Pinball, electronic video games	326,506	–	148,971	65,097	64,286	217	13,657	30,664
Live entertainment for catered affairs	804,648	10,530	215,885	59,889	212,716	232,712	69,269	3,302
Rental of party supplies for catered affairs	1,073,680	26,946	272,158	136,704	324,410	219,483	35,761	58,262

Note: Numbers may not add to total because of rounding and missing subcategories. "–" means sample is too small to make a reliable estimate.
Source: Calculations by New Strategist based on the Bureau of Labor Statistics' 2011 Consumer Expenditure Survey

Table 3.4 Entertainment: Market shares by age, 2011

(percentage of total annual spending on entertainment accounted for by consumer unit age groups, 2011)

	total consumer units	under 25	25 to 34	35 to 44	45 to 54	55 to 64	65 to 74	75+
Share of total consumer units	100.0%	6.3%	16.7%	17.7%	20.3%	17.7%	11.5%	9.6%
Share of total before-tax income	100.0	2.7	15.3	21.6	25.0	21.0	9.5	4.9
Share of total spending	100.0	3.8	16.2	20.4	23.7	19.1	10.3	6.3
Share of entertainment spending	100.0	3.3	15.8	20.2	25.0	19.1	11.2	5.4
FEES AND ADMISSIONS	100.0	2.8	14.1	24.2	27.6	17.0	10.6	3.6
Recreation expenses on trips	100.0	2.3	13.5	18.8	27.3	19.3	15.7	3.1
Social, recreation, health club membership	100.0	2.6	12.3	21.8	26.4	19.5	12.0	5.3
Fees for participant sports	100.0	1.7	12.9	25.4	30.5	16.7	9.5	3.3
Participant sports on trips	100.0	2.2	13.5	18.3	25.4	19.8	17.1	3.8
Movie, theater, amusement park, and other admissions	100.0	4.8	16.5	22.1	23.7	18.1	10.5	4.3
Movie and other admissions on trips	100.0	3.2	17.2	20.5	23.1	19.3	13.0	3.6
Admission to sports events	100.0	2.8	16.8	19.9	29.7	17.4	10.9	2.5
Admission to sports events on trips	100.0	3.2	17.2	20.6	23.2	19.3	13.0	3.6
Fees for recreational lessons	100.0	1.9	11.7	38.0	33.8	8.9	4.1	1.6
Other entertainment services on trips	100.0	2.3	13.5	18.8	27.3	19.3	15.7	3.1
AUDIO AND VISUAL EQUIPMENT AND SERVICES	100.0	3.9	16.2	20.0	23.1	19.2	10.6	6.9
Sound components, equipment, and accessories	100.0	6.1	19.9	18.1	19.7	28.7	4.8	2.3
Television sets	100.0	5.5	18.0	21.0	22.0	20.4	8.7	4.5
Cable and satellite television services	100.0	3.3	14.7	18.1	22.5	19.8	12.8	8.8
Miscellaneous video equipment	100.0	8.6	14.6	27.1	23.7	17.5	7.8	0.6
Satellite radio service	100.0	1.2	11.7	23.8	24.6	22.1	13.0	3.5
Online gaming services	100.0	10.3	27.8	23.8	23.8	9.2	4.7	0.5
VCRs and video disc players	100.0	3.6	21.0	26.3	23.8	18.0	5.1	2.2
Video cassettes, tapes, and discs	100.0	4.7	15.6	24.7	29.1	13.4	8.1	4.2
Video game software	100.0	–	30.7	43.6	18.2	6.3	–	–
Video game hardware and accessories	100.0	5.2	26.1	28.0	23.6	12.6	1.3	2.5
Streamed and downloaded video	100.0	5.2	27.6	28.4	20.4	12.8	4.4	1.1
Applications, games, ringtones for handheld devices	100.0	7.9	27.5	18.8	30.9	10.9	3.0	1.0
Repair of television, radio, and sound equipment	100.0	1.9	5.2	21.6	19.3	34.2	11.9	5.9
Rental of television sets	100.0	–	58.0	16.1	18.4	–	8.3	–
Personal digital audio players	100.0	3.4	14.2	33.5	34.4	9.7	3.5	1.2
Satellite dishes	100.0	–	42.4	11.7	8.9	17.2	16.9	3.1
Compact discs, records, and audio tapes	100.0	8.1	14.8	18.2	24.6	16.7	12.8	4.6
Streamed and downloaded audio	100.0	5.4	23.7	26.8	27.0	14.1	2.4	0.6
Rental of VCR, radio, and sound equipment	100.0	1.1	18.6	63.1	–	8.9	10.2	–
Musical instruments and accessories	100.0	3.5	17.4	27.4	31.6	17.4	1.7	0.9
Rental and repair of musical instruments	100.0	1.1	9.8	23.6	39.7	12.3	3.5	10.1
Rental of video cassettes, tapes, discs, films	100.0	6.7	25.1	24.5	21.6	14.9	5.4	1.8
Installation of television sets	100.0	–	3.9	37.2	36.1	12.1	7.3	3.5
PETS, TOYS, HOBBIES, AND PLAYGROUND EQUIPMENT	100.0	3.3	15.9	18.1	24.0	21.3	11.4	5.8
Pets	100.0	3.5	14.2	16.4	25.3	22.5	12.5	5.5
Pet food	100.0	3.9	13.5	16.6	25.1	22.8	12.0	6.1
Pet purchase, supplies, and medicines	100.0	2.8	13.2	22.5	27.1	20.0	9.7	4.7
Pet services	100.0	1.7	14.7	18.2	27.1	24.9	10.5	2.9
Veterinarian services	100.0	4.3	16.0	9.9	23.3	23.9	16.5	6.1
Toys, games, hobbies, and tricycles	100.0	2.9	23.7	25.8	20.1	16.6	7.1	3.3
Stamp and coin collecting	100.0	0.0	5.2	2.7	7.1	23.9	8.8	52.3
Playground equipment	100.0	2.0	31.6	46.0	9.8	4.6	5.1	0.8

	total consumer units	under 25	25 to 34	35 to 44	45 to 54	55 to 64	65 to 74	75+
OTHER ENTERTAINMENT SUPPLIES, EQUIPMENT, AND SERVICES	100.0%	2.4%	16.9%	17.8%	27.7%	18.4%	13.0%	3.6%
Unmotored recreational vehicles	100.0	–	21.2	6.4	12.7	23.2	35.1	1.5
Motorized recreational vehicles	100.0	–	5.5	9.1	51.2	13.1	15.8	5.2
Rental of recreational vehicles	100.0	0.4	16.8	13.8	21.6	21.5	20.5	5.4
Docking and landing fees	100.0	0.1	0.9	17.1	32.8	28.9	20.1	0.0
Sports, recreation, exercise equipment	100.0	4.1	18.2	25.4	23.3	19.0	6.1	3.5
Athletic gear, game tables, exercise equipment	100.0	2.6	13.4	35.9	23.9	14.5	4.1	5.4
Bicycles	100.0	5.6	20.7	24.4	31.1	12.1	5.8	0.3
Camping equipment	100.0	14.2	9.8	15.8	21.6	30.0	8.2	0.3
Hunting and fishing equipment	100.0	2.7	30.0	13.3	15.7	30.4	4.4	2.3
Winter sports equipment	100.0	1.9	16.7	22.1	33.0	19.9	6.5	–
Water sports equipment	100.0	1.7	19.1	24.6	37.9	7.8	6.1	2.8
Other sports equipment	100.0	3.5	25.5	28.2	20.0	14.8	5.8	2.2
Global positioning system devices	100.0	–	–	25.8	15.6	11.2	32.1	16.7
Rental and repair of miscellaneous sports equipment	100.0	1.8	9.6	29.7	28.7	10.6	10.5	9.1
Photographic equipment, supplies, and services	100.0	4.6	24.4	23.3	21.3	17.8	6.4	2.3
Photo processing	100.0	4.4	18.3	21.4	20.2	18.5	13.0	4.3
Repair and rental of photographic equipment	100.0	12.5	21.4	26.0	19.4	13.6	4.8	2.5
Photographic equipment	100.0	5.9	19.9	24.8	24.5	18.6	3.7	2.6
Photographer fees	100.0	2.6	35.3	20.9	17.1	16.5	7.1	0.5
Fireworks	100.0	–	18.9	52.0	25.9	2.8	–	–
Pinball, electronic video games	100.0	–	45.6	19.9	19.7	0.1	4.2	9.4
Live entertainment for catered affairs	100.0	1.3	26.8	7.4	26.4	28.9	8.6	0.4
Rental of party supplies for catered affairs	100.0	2.5	25.3	12.7	30.2	20.4	3.3	5.4

Note: Numbers may not add to total because of rounding. "–" means sample is too small to make a reliable estimate.
Source: Calculations by New Strategist based on the Bureau of Labor Statistics' 2011 Consumer Expenditure Survey

Table 3.5 Entertainment: Average spending by income, 2011

(average annual spending on entertainment, by before-tax income of consumer units, 2011)

	total consumer units	under $20,000	$20,000– $39,999	$40,000– $49,999	$50,000– $69,999	$70,000– $79,999	$80,000– $99,999	$100,000 or more
Number of consumer units (in 000s)	122,287	26,342	27,788	11,347	17,376	7,385	10,456	21,593
Average number of persons per consumer unit	2.5	1.8	2.3	2.6	2.7	2.8	3.0	3.2
Average before-tax income of consumer units	$63,685.00	$10,491.66	$29,658.14	$44,698.00	$59,306.00	$74,742.00	$89,108.00	$169,776.00
Average spending of consumer units, total	49,704.88	22,142.36	33,453.66	40,306.19	50,034.03	57,976.69	65,389.80	97,728.22
Entertainment, average spending	**2,571.95**	**984.71**	**1,664.34**	**1,876.37**	**2,830.18**	**3,109.76**	**3,373.47**	**5,193.37**
FEES AND ADMISSIONS	**594.27**	**144.37**	**230.12**	**356.49**	**468.10**	**696.89**	**741.33**	**1,724.35**
Recreation expenses on trips	21.42	4.70	9.78	16.34	18.14	22.15	30.20	57.62
Social, recreation, health club membership	121.90	28.72	44.15	66.10	91.73	108.91	126.99	391.19
Fees for participant sports	99.72	25.88	27.41	58.15	58.15	196.70	129.48	283.01
Participant sports on trips	24.07	2.13	7.50	12.70	27.98	24.39	27.54	73.17
Movie, theater, amusement park, and other admissions	115.88	37.06	65.53	83.95	110.12	116.32	160.72	276.37
Movie and other admissions on trips	43.77	11.14	17.20	30.49	40.16	52.11	54.27	119.73
Admission to sports events	45.91	9.65	15.67	16.56	36.34	50.63	50.83	148.22
Admission to sports events on trips	14.58	3.71	5.73	10.16	13.38	17.36	18.09	39.84
Fees for recreational lessons	85.60	16.68	27.35	45.70	53.96	86.18	113.00	277.58
Other entertainment services on trips	21.42	4.70	9.78	16.34	18.14	22.15	30.20	57.62
AUDIO AND VISUAL EQUIPMENT AND SERVICES	**976.58**	**526.65**	**773.75**	**895.16**	**1,060.89**	**1,174.18**	**1,249.77**	**1,552.58**
Sound components, equipment, and accessories	26.88	9.41	11.39	22.49	35.69	34.01	29.50	58.57
Television sets	112.69	37.98	79.47	102.07	144.41	130.29	144.70	205.11
Cable and satellite television services	640.40	417.71	549.63	646.17	688.57	767.19	781.51	875.39
Miscellaneous video equipment	7.67	1.44	4.17	1.31	8.03	17.90	9.88	18.08
Satellite radio service	13.48	4.55	8.47	12.58	12.28	17.49	21.44	27.03
Online gaming services	3.09	1.29	2.81	2.46	2.90	3.30	5.16	5.05
VCRs and video disc players	8.66	3.23	5.60	6.83	11.06	7.70	10.99	17.44
Video cassettes, tapes, and discs	33.29	11.03	27.07	13.77	48.37	32.70	52.00	54.29
Video game software	1.99	–	–	0.75	0.05	9.06	6.49	1.32
Video game hardware and accessories	40.41	14.85	35.29	29.21	25.93	65.12	65.33	74.77
Streamed and downloaded video	3.92	0.98	2.11	2.97	3.54	3.62	5.92	9.79
Applications, games, ringtones for handheld devices	3.66	1.90	1.84	3.52	3.26	3.48	6.92	7.01
Repair of television, radio, and sound equipment	3.39	1.15	1.67	2.38	3.85	4.36	1.49	9.09
Rental of television sets	0.32	0.53	0.80	–	0.30	0.16	–	0.18
Personal digital audio players	10.29	2.09	5.01	6.95	11.01	12.49	16.88	24.31
Satellite dishes	1.05	0.85	1.43	1.08	0.94	0.80	0.55	1.42
Compact discs, records, and audio tapes	11.57	5.70	8.65	9.72	14.42	15.17	17.18	17.24
Streamed and downloaded audio	9.62	3.09	3.91	4.79	7.96	9.86	13.68	26.75
Rental of VCR, radio, and sound equipment	0.18	0.05	0.28	0.02	0.66	0.18	0.23	0.13
Musical instruments and accessories	22.60	2.78	6.48	8.04	15.35	14.00	31.98	79.43
Rental and repair of musical instruments	1.60	0.51	1.31	0.31	0.60	2.95	1.61	4.50
Rental of video cassettes, tapes, discs, films	18.54	8.19	13.05	17.17	20.81	21.94	26.14	32.30
Installation of television sets	0.85	0.11	0.89	0.30	0.55	0.34	0.15	2.85
PETS, TOYS, HOBBIES, AND PLAYGROUND EQUIPMENT	**630.67**	**251.75**	**447.47**	**453.91**	**722.78**	**814.74**	**923.43**	**1,101.26**
Pets	**502.05**	**215.15**	**338.35**	**370.68**	**607.53**	**627.87**	**719.81**	**868.18**
Pet food	182.75	98.36	134.24	139.67	208.89	248.96	261.15	275.69
Pet purchase, supplies, and medicines	140.90	66.12	102.43	129.02	165.59	171.81	217.28	220.45
Pet services	35.72	9.84	15.61	26.53	28.11	39.23	57.20	92.55
Veterinarian services	142.67	40.83	86.07	75.47	204.94	167.87	184.19	279.49
Toys, games, hobbies, and tricycles	**115.02**	**34.50**	**80.87**	**79.72**	**107.72**	**171.68**	**197.63**	**210.96**
Stamp and coin collecting	**9.97**	**1.48**	**24.29**	**1.74**	**4.98**	**9.40**	**2.20**	**14.21**
Playground equipment	**3.63**	**0.61**	**3.96**	**1.77**	**2.55**	**5.79**	**3.79**	**7.92**

	total consumer units	under $20,000	$20,000–$39,999	$40,000–$49,999	$50,000–$69,999	$70,000–$79,999	$80,000–$99,999	$100,000 or more
OTHER ENTERTAINMENT SUPPLIES, EQUIPMENT, AND SERVICES	**$370.43**	**$61.96**	**$213.00**	**$170.81**	**$578.41**	**$423.95**	**$458.95**	**$815.18**
Unmotored recreational vehicles	**54.49**	–	**124.06**	**26.36**	**33.78**	**43.46**	**133.62**	**104.92**
Motorized recreational vehicles	**80.37**	**8.14**	**29.94**	**7.49**	**319.33**	**72.21**	**43.46**	**104.99**
Rental of recreational vehicles	**5.48**	**1.05**	**2.34**	**3.57**	**5.22**	**5.95**	**5.66**	**16.11**
Docking and landing fees	**7.14**	**3.15**	**2.72**	**5.78**	**1.03**	**5.13**	**7.33**	**25.09**
Sports, recreation, exercise equipment	**145.28**	**30.94**	**72.80**	**91.31**	**135.90**	**197.11**	**170.28**	**373.72**
Athletic gear, game tables, exercise equipment	52.52	5.95	18.37	21.51	48.04	88.10	35.07	164.22
Bicycles	21.92	9.09	9.53	13.57	15.80	13.84	34.98	59.26
Camping equipment	14.09	5.84	6.57	17.71	16.45	5.68	9.05	34.31
Hunting and fishing equipment	33.06	5.23	25.81	22.69	19.96	67.53	61.76	63.31
Winter sports equipment	4.52	1.70	0.31	0.63	5.42	11.76	8.70	10.23
Water sports equipment	5.31	0.75	2.74	1.38	8.99	2.14	2.44	15.75
Other sports equipment	6.34	1.19	6.99	5.78	11.23	4.02	9.64	7.31
Global positioning system devices	4.91	–	1.71	7.95	7.52	–	6.02	12.82
Rental and repair of miscellaneous sports equipment	2.62	1.51	1.66	0.09	2.50	4.04	2.62	6.52
Photographic equipment, supplies, and services	**54.54**	**11.75**	**28.45**	**28.55**	**63.25**	**65.12**	**67.92**	**136.80**
Photo processing	8.92	2.68	5.33	5.84	8.91	8.91	11.47	21.57
Repair and rental of photographic equipment	0.43	0.30	0.28	0.29	0.30	1.85	0.69	0.55
Photographic equipment	26.84	5.81	14.18	14.44	36.64	32.12	28.33	64.91
Photographer fees	17.09	2.6	7.3	7.1	15.7	20.0	26.2	48.3
Fireworks	**1.95**	**3.14**	**0.47**	**1.04**	**1.75**	**4.25**	**1.92**	**3.57**
Pinball, electronic video games	**2.67**	**17.47**	**0.66**	–	**3.34**	**0.48**	**0.15**	**4.82**
Live entertainment for catered affairs	**6.58**	**0.73**	**3.67**	**1.84**	**4.00**	**17.61**	**12.36**	**15.80**
Rental of party supplies for catered affairs	**8.78**	**1.77**	**4.57**	**2.97**	**9.94**	**3.34**	**10.48**	**25.91**

Note: Subcategories may not add to total because some are not shown. "–" means sample is too small to make a reliable estimate.
Source: Bureau of Labor Statistics, unpublished data from the 2011 Consumer Expenditure Survey; calculations by New Strategist

Table 3.6 Entertainment: Indexed spending by income, 2011

(indexed average annual spending of consumer units on entertainment by before-tax income of consumer unit, 2011; index definition: an index of 100 is the average for all consumer units; an index of 125 means that spending by consumer units in that group is 25 percent above the average for all consumer units; an index of 75 indicates spending that is 25 percent below the average for all consumer units)

	total consumer units	under $20,000	$20,000–$39,999	$40,000–$49,999	$50,000–$69,999	$70,000–$79,999	$80,000–$99,999	$100,000 or more
Average spending of consumer units, total	$49,705	$22,142	$33,454	$40,306	$50,034	$57,977	$65,390	$97,728
Average spending of consumer units, index	100	45	67	81	101	117	132	197
Entertainment, spending index	**100**	**38**	**65**	**73**	**110**	**121**	**131**	**202**
FEES AND ADMISSIONS	**100**	**24**	**39**	**60**	**79**	**117**	**125**	**290**
Recreation expenses on trips	100	22	46	76	85	103	141	269
Social, recreation, health club membership	100	24	36	54	75	89	104	321
Fees for participant sports	100	26	27	58	58	197	130	284
Participant sports on trips	100	9	31	53	116	101	114	304
Movie, theater, amusement park, and other admissions	100	32	57	72	95	100	139	238
Movie and other admissions on trips	100	25	39	70	92	119	124	274
Admission to sports events	100	21	34	36	79	110	111	323
Admission to sports events on trips	100	25	39	70	92	119	124	273
Fees for recreational lessons	100	19	32	53	63	101	132	324
Other entertainment services on trips	100	22	46	76	85	103	141	269
AUDIO AND VISUAL EQUIPMENT AND SERVICES	**100**	**54**	**79**	**92**	**109**	**120**	**128**	**159**
Sound components, equipment, and accessories	100	35	42	84	133	127	110	218
Television sets	100	34	71	91	128	116	128	182
Cable and satellite television services	100	65	86	101	108	120	122	137
Miscellaneous video equipment	100	19	54	17	105	233	129	236
Satellite radio service	100	34	63	93	91	130	159	201
Online gaming services	100	42	91	80	94	107	167	163
VCRs and video disc players	100	37	65	79	128	89	127	201
Video cassettes, tapes, and discs	100	33	81	41	145	98	156	163
Video game software	100	–	–	38	3	455	326	66
Video game hardware and accessories	100	37	87	72	64	161	162	185
Streamed and downloaded video	100	25	54	76	90	92	151	250
Applications, games, ringtones for handheld devices	100	52	50	96	89	95	189	192
Repair of television, radio, and sound equipment	100	34	49	70	114	129	44	268
Rental of television sets	100	165	249	–	94	50	–	56
Personal digital audio players	100	20	49	68	107	121	164	236
Satellite dishes	100	81	137	103	90	76	52	135
Compact discs, records, and audio tapes	100	49	75	84	125	131	148	149
Streamed and downloaded audio	100	32	41	50	83	102	142	278
Rental of VCR, radio, and sound equipment	100	28	156	11	367	100	128	72
Musical instruments and accessories	100	12	29	36	68	62	142	351
Rental and repair of musical instruments	100	32	82	19	38	184	101	281
Rental of video cassettes, tapes, discs, films	100	44	70	93	112	118	141	174
Installation of television sets	100	13	105	35	65	40	18	335
PETS, TOYS, HOBBIES, AND PLAYGROUND EQUIPMENT	**100**	**40**	**71**	**72**	**115**	**129**	**146**	**175**
Pets	**100**	**43**	**67**	**74**	**121**	**125**	**143**	**173**
Pet food	100	54	73	76	114	136	143	151
Pet purchase, supplies, and medicines	100	47	73	92	118	122	154	156
Pet services	100	28	44	74	79	110	160	259
Veterinarian services	100	29	60	53	144	118	129	196
Toys, games, hobbies, and tricycles	**100**	**30**	**70**	**69**	**94**	**149**	**172**	**183**
Stamp and coin collecting	**100**	**15**	**244**	**17**	**50**	**94**	**22**	**143**
Playground equipment	**100**	**17**	**109**	**49**	**70**	**160**	**104**	**218**

	total consumer units	under $20,000	$20,000–$39,999	$40,000–$49,999	$50,000–$69,999	$70,000–$79,999	$80,000–$99,999	$100,000 or more
OTHER ENTERTAINMENT SUPPLIES, EQUIPMENT, AND SERVICES	100	17	57	46	156	114	124	220
Unmotored recreational vehicles	100	–	228	48	62	80	245	193
Motorized recreational vehicles	100	10	37	9	397	90	54	131
Rental of recreational vehicles	100	19	43	65	95	109	103	294
Docking and landing fees	100	44	38	81	14	72	103	351
Sports, recreation, exercise equipment	100	21	50	63	94	136	117	257
Athletic gear, game tables, exercise equipment	100	11	35	41	91	168	67	313
Bicycles	100	41	43	62	72	63	160	270
Camping equipment	100	41	47	126	117	40	64	244
Hunting and fishing equipment	100	16	78	69	60	204	187	192
Winter sports equipment	100	38	7	14	120	260	192	226
Water sports equipment	100	14	52	26	169	40	46	297
Other sports equipment	100	19	110	91	177	63	152	115
Global positioning system devices	100	–	35	162	153	–	123	261
Rental and repair of miscellaneous sports equipment	100	58	63	3	95	154	100	249
Photographic equipment, supplies, and services	100	22	52	52	116	119	125	251
Photo processing	100	30	60	65	100	100	129	242
Repair and rental of photographic equipment	100	69	64	67	70	430	160	128
Photographic equipment	100	22	53	54	137	120	106	242
Photographer fees	100	15	43	41	92	117	153	283
Fireworks	100	161	24	53	90	218	98	183
Pinball, electronic video games	100	654	25	–	125	18	6	181
Live entertainment for catered affairs	100	11	56	28	61	268	188	240
Rental of party supplies for catered affairs	100	20	52	34	113	38	119	295

Note: "–" means sample is too small to make a reliable estimate.
Source: Calculations by New Strategist based on the Bureau of Labor Statistics' 2011 Consumer Expenditure Survey

Table 3.7 Entertainment: Total spending by income, 2011

(total annual spending on entertainment, by before-tax income group of consumer units, 2011; consumer units and dollars in thousands)

	total consumer units	under $20,000	$20,000– $39,999	$40,000– $49,999	$50,000– $69,999	$70,000– $79,999	$80,000– $99,999	$100,000 or more
Number of consumer units	122,287	26,342	27,788	11,347	17,376	7,385	10,456	21,593
Total spending of all consumer units	$6,078,260,661	$583,273,961	$929,610,260	$457,354,338	$869,391,305	$428,157,856	$683,715,749	$2,110,245,454
Entertainment, total spending	314,516,050	25,939,333	46,248,791	21,291,170	49,177,208	22,965,578	35,273,002	112,140,438
FEES AND ADMISSIONS	72,671,495	3,802,924	6,394,666	4,045,092	8,133,706	5,146,533	7,751,346	37,233,890
Recreation expenses on trips	2,619,388	123,814	271,811	185,410	315,201	163,578	315,771	1,244,189
Social, recreation, health club membership	14,906,785	756,460	1,226,957	750,037	1,593,900	804,300	1,327,807	8,446,966
Fees for participant sports	12,194,460	681,704	761,605	659,828	1,010,414	1,452,630	1,353,843	6,111,035
Participant sports on trips	2,943,448	56,066	208,503	144,107	486,180	180,120	287,958	1,579,960
Movie, theater, amusement park, and other admissions	14,170,618	976,337	1,821,050	952,581	1,913,445	859,023	1,680,488	5,967,657
Movie and other admissions on trips	5,352,502	293,421	477,913	345,970	697,820	384,832	567,447	2,585,330
Admission to sports events	5,614,196	254,099	435,453	187,906	631,444	373,903	531,478	3,200,514
Admission to sports events on trips	1,782,944	97,772	159,127	115,286	232,491	128,204	189,149	860,265
Fees for recreational lessons	10,467,767	439,468	760,035	518,558	937,609	636,439	1,181,528	5,993,785
Other entertainment services on trips	2,619,388	123,814	271,811	185,410	315,201	163,578	315,771	1,244,189
AUDIO AND VISUAL EQUIPMENT AND SERVICES	119,423,038	13,872,970	21,501,096	10,157,381	18,434,025	8,671,319	13,067,595	33,524,860
Sound components, equipment, and accessories	3,287,075	247,793	316,624	255,194	620,149	251,164	308,452	1,264,702
Television sets	13,780,522	1,000,434	2,208,181	1,158,188	2,509,268	962,192	1,512,983	4,428,940
Cable and satellite television services	78,312,595	11,003,358	15,273,194	7,332,091	11,964,592	5,665,698	8,171,469	18,902,296
Miscellaneous video equipment	937,941	37,853	115,830	14,865	139,529	132,192	103,305	390,401
Satellite radio service	1,648,429	119,987	235,321	142,745	213,377	129,164	224,177	583,659
Online gaming services	377,867	34,018	78,214	27,914	50,390	24,371	53,953	109,045
VCRs and video disc players	1,059,005	85,002	155,489	77,500	192,179	56,865	114,911	376,582
Video cassettes, tapes, and discs	4,070,934	290,471	752,213	156,248	840,477	241,490	543,712	1,172,284
Video game software	243,351	–	–	8,510	869	66,908	67,859	28,503
Video game hardware and accessories	4,941,618	391,168	980,588	331,446	450,560	480,911	683,090	1,614,509
Streamed and downloaded video	479,365	25,833	58,514	33,701	61,511	26,734	61,900	211,395
Applications, games, ringtones for handheld devices	447,570	50,055	51,268	39,941	56,646	25,700	72,356	151,367
Repair of television, radio, and sound equipment	414,553	30,266	46,369	27,006	66,898	32,199	15,579	196,280
Rental of television sets	39,132	13,931	22,139	–	5,213	1,182	–	3,887
Personal digital audio players	1,258,333	54,932	139,206	78,862	191,310	92,239	176,497	524,926
Satellite dishes	128,401	22,316	39,835	12,255	16,333	5,908	5,751	30,662
Compact discs, records, and audio tapes	1,414,861	150,173	240,286	110,293	250,562	112,030	179,634	372,263
Streamed and downloaded audio	1,176,401	81,335	108,545	54,352	138,313	72,816	143,038	577,613
Rental of VCR, radio, and sound equipment	22,012	1,317	7,781	227	11,468	1,329	2,405	2,807
Musical instruments and accessories	2,763,686	73,137	180,199	91,230	266,722	103,390	334,383	1,715,132
Rental and repair of musical instruments	195,659	13,413	36,513	3,518	10,426	21,786	16,834	97,169
Rental of video cassettes, tapes, discs, films	2,267,201	215,814	362,751	194,828	361,595	162,027	273,320	697,454
Installation of television sets	103,944	2,898	24,707	3,404	9,557	2,511	1,568	61,540
PETS, TOYS, HOBBIES, AND PLAYGROUND EQUIPMENT	77,122,742	6,631,492	12,434,319	5,150,517	12,559,025	6,016,855	9,655,384	23,779,507
Pets	61,394,188	5,667,360	9,402,208	4,206,106	10,556,441	4,636,820	7,526,333	18,746,611
Pet food	22,347,949	2,590,889	3,730,224	1,584,835	3,629,673	1,838,570	2,730,584	5,952,974
Pet purchase, supplies, and medicines	17,230,238	1,741,847	2,846,327	1,463,990	2,877,292	1,268,817	2,271,880	4,760,177
Pet services	4,368,092	259,110	433,807	301,036	488,439	289,714	598,083	1,998,432
Veterinarian services	17,446,686	1,075,432	2,391,716	856,358	3,561,037	1,239,720	1,925,891	6,035,028
Toys, games, hobbies, and tricycles	14,065,451	908,888	2,247,324	904,583	1,871,743	1,267,857	2,066,419	4,555,259
Stamp and coin collecting	1,219,201	39,080	674,836	19,744	86,532	69,419	23,003	306,837
Playground equipment	443,902	15,976	109,952	20,084	44,309	42,759	39,628	171,017

	total consumer units	under $20,000	$20,000–$39,999	$40,000–$49,999	$50,000–$69,999	$70,000–$79,999	$80,000–$99,999	$100,000 or more
OTHER ENTERTAINMENT SUPPLIES, EQUIPMENT, AND SERVICES	$45,298,773	$1,632,129	$5,918,710	$1,938,181	$10,050,452	$3,130,871	$4,798,781	$17,602,182
Unmotored recreational vehicles	6,663,419	–	3,447,379	299,107	586,961	320,952	1,397,131	2,265,538
Motorized recreational vehicles	9,828,206	214,395	831,942	84,989	5,548,678	533,271	454,418	2,267,049
Rental of recreational vehicles	670,133	27,620	65,026	40,509	90,703	43,941	59,181	347,863
Docking and landing fees	873,129	83,047	75,586	65,586	17,897	37,885	76,642	541,768
Sports, recreation, exercise equipment	17,765,855	815,033	2,023,099	1,036,095	2,361,398	1,455,657	1,780,448	8,069,736
Athletic gear, game tables, exercise equipment	6,422,513	156,660	510,514	244,074	834,743	650,619	366,692	3,546,002
Bicycles	2,680,531	239,469	264,793	153,979	274,541	102,208	365,751	1,279,601
Camping equipment	1,723,024	153,885	182,550	200,955	285,835	41,947	94,627	740,856
Hunting and fishing equipment	4,042,808	137,787	717,243	257,463	346,825	498,709	645,763	1,367,053
Winter sports equipment	552,737	44,721	8,708	7,149	94,178	86,848	90,967	220,896
Water sports equipment	649,344	19,716	76,072	15,659	156,210	15,804	25,513	340,090
Other sports equipment	775,300	31,426	194,248	65,586	195,132	29,688	100,796	157,845
Global positioning system devices	600,429	–	47,517	90,209	130,668	–	62,945	276,822
Rental and repair of miscellaneous sports equipment	320,392	39,773	46,035	1,021	43,440	29,835	27,395	140,786
Photographic equipment, supplies, and services	6,669,533	309,440	790,679	323,957	1,099,032	480,911	710,172	2,953,922
Photo processing	1,090,800	70,582	148,138	66,266	154,820	65,800	119,930	465,761
Repair and rental of photographic equipment	52,583	7,788	7,647	3,291	5,213	13,662	7,215	11,876
Photographic equipment	3,282,183	153,027	393,923	163,851	636,657	237,206	296,218	1,401,602
Photographer fees	2,089,885	69,063	201,889	80,110	273,324	147,848	274,261	1,042,942
Fireworks	238,460	82,743	13,190	11,801	30,408	31,386	20,076	77,087
Pinball, electronic video games	326,506	460,195	18,380	–	58,036	3,545	1,568	104,078
Live entertainment for catered affairs	804,648	19,114	101,886	20,878	69,504	130,050	129,236	341,169
Rental of party supplies for catered affairs	1,073,680	46,513	127,088	33,701	172,717	24,666	109,579	559,475

Note: Numbers may not add to total because of rounding and missing subcategories. "–" means sample is too small to make a reliable estimate.
Source: Calculations by New Strategist based on the Bureau of Labor Statistics' 2011 Consumer Expenditure Survey

Table 3.8 Entertainment: Market shares by income, 2011

(percentage of total annual spending on entertainment accounted for by before-tax income group of consumer units, 2011)

	total consumer units	under $20,000	$20,000– $39,999	$40,000– $49,999	$50,000– $69,999	$70,000– $79,999	$80,000– $99,999	$100,000 or more
Share of total consumer units	100.0%	21.5%	22.7%	9.3%	14.2%	6.0%	8.6%	17.7%
Share of total before-tax income	100.0	3.5	10.6	6.5	13.2	7.1	12.0	47.1
Share of total spending	100.0	9.6	15.3	7.5	14.3	7.0	11.2	34.7
Share of entertainment spending	100.0	8.2	14.7	6.8	15.6	7.3	11.2	35.7
FEES AND ADMISSIONS	100.0	5.2	8.8	5.6	11.2	7.1	10.7	51.2
Recreation expenses on trips	100.0	4.7	10.4	7.1	12.0	6.2	12.1	47.5
Social, recreation, health club membership	100.0	5.1	8.2	5.0	10.7	5.4	8.9	56.7
Fees for participant sports	100.0	5.6	6.2	5.4	8.3	11.9	11.1	50.1
Participant sports on trips	100.0	1.9	7.1	4.9	16.5	6.1	9.8	53.7
Movie, theater, amusement park, and other admissions	100.0	6.9	12.9	6.7	13.5	6.1	11.9	42.1
Movie and other admissions on trips	100.0	5.5	8.9	6.5	13.0	7.2	10.6	48.3
Admission to sports events	100.0	4.5	7.8	3.3	11.2	6.7	9.5	57.0
Admission to sports events on trips	100.0	5.5	8.9	6.5	13.0	7.2	10.6	48.2
Fees for recreational lessons	100.0	4.2	7.3	5.0	9.0	6.1	11.3	57.3
Other entertainment services on trips	100.0	4.7	10.4	7.1	12.0	6.2	12.1	47.5
AUDIO AND VISUAL EQUIPMENT AND SERVICES	100.0	11.6	18.0	8.5	15.4	7.3	10.9	28.1
Sound components, equipment, and accessories	100.0	7.5	9.6	7.8	18.9	7.6	9.4	38.5
Television sets	100.0	7.3	16.0	8.4	18.2	7.0	11.0	32.1
Cable and satellite television services	100.0	14.1	19.5	9.4	15.3	7.2	10.4	24.1
Miscellaneous video equipment	100.0	4.0	12.3	1.6	14.9	14.1	11.0	41.6
Satellite radio service	100.0	7.3	14.3	8.7	12.9	7.8	13.6	35.4
Online gaming services	100.0	9.0	20.7	7.4	13.3	6.4	14.3	28.9
VCRs and video disc players	100.0	8.0	14.7	7.3	18.1	5.4	10.9	35.6
Video cassettes, tapes, and discs	100.0	7.1	18.5	3.8	20.6	5.9	13.4	28.8
Video game software	100.0	–	–	3.5	0.4	27.5	27.9	11.7
Video game hardware and accessories	100.0	7.9	19.8	6.7	9.1	9.7	13.8	32.7
Streamed and downloaded video	100.0	5.4	12.2	7.0	12.8	5.6	12.9	44.1
Applications, games, ringtones for handheld devices	100.0	11.2	11.5	8.9	12.7	5.7	16.2	33.8
Repair of television, radio, and sound equipment	100.0	7.3	11.2	6.5	16.1	7.8	3.8	47.3
Rental of television sets	100.0	35.6	56.6	–	13.3	3.0	–	9.9
Personal digital audio players	100.0	4.4	11.1	6.3	15.2	7.3	14.0	41.7
Satellite dishes	100.0	17.4	31.0	9.5	12.7	4.6	4.5	23.9
Compact discs, records, and audio tapes	100.0	10.6	17.0	7.8	17.7	7.9	12.7	26.3
Streamed and downloaded audio	100.0	6.9	9.2	4.6	11.8	6.2	12.2	49.1
Rental of VCR, radio, and sound equipment	100.0	6.0	35.3	1.0	52.1	6.0	10.9	12.8
Musical instruments and accessories	100.0	2.6	6.5	3.3	9.7	3.7	12.1	62.1
Rental and repair of musical instruments	100.0	6.9	18.7	1.8	5.3	11.1	8.6	49.7
Rental of video cassettes, tapes, discs, films	100.0	9.5	16.0	8.6	15.9	7.1	12.1	30.8
Installation of television sets	100.0	2.8	23.8	3.3	9.2	2.4	1.5	59.2
PETS, TOYS, HOBBIES, AND PLAYGROUND EQUIPMENT	100.0	8.6	16.1	6.7	16.3	7.8	12.5	30.8
Pets	100.0	9.2	15.3	6.9	17.2	7.6	12.3	30.5
Pet food	100.0	11.6	16.7	7.1	16.2	8.2	12.2	26.6
Pet purchase, supplies, and medicines	100.0	10.1	16.5	8.5	16.7	7.4	13.2	27.6
Pet services	100.0	5.9	9.9	6.9	11.2	6.6	13.7	45.8
Veterinarian services	100.0	6.2	13.7	4.9	20.4	7.1	11.0	34.6
Toys, games, hobbies, and tricycles	100.0	6.5	16.0	6.4	13.3	9.0	14.7	32.4
Stamp and coin collecting	100.0	3.2	55.4	1.6	7.1	5.7	1.9	25.2
Playground equipment	100.0	3.6	24.8	4.5	10.0	9.6	8.9	38.5

	total consumer units	under $20,000	$20,000–$39,999	$40,000–$49,999	$50,000–$69,999	$70,000–$79,999	$80,000–$99,999	$100,000 or more
OTHER ENTERTAINMENT SUPPLIES, EQUIPMENT, AND SERVICES	100.0%	3.6%	13.1%	4.3%	22.2%	6.9%	10.6%	38.9%
Unmotored recreational vehicles	100.0	–	51.7	4.5	8.8	4.8	21.0	34.0
Motorized recreational vehicles	100.0	2.2	8.5	0.9	56.5	5.4	4.6	23.1
Rental of recreational vehicles	100.0	4.1	9.7	6.0	13.5	6.6	8.8	51.9
Docking and landing fees	100.0	9.5	8.7	7.5	2.0	4.3	8.8	62.0
Sports, recreation, exercise equipment	100.0	4.6	11.4	5.8	13.3	8.2	10.0	45.4
Athletic gear, game tables, exercise equipment	100.0	2.4	7.9	3.8	13.0	10.1	5.7	55.2
Bicycles	100.0	8.9	9.9	5.7	10.2	3.8	13.6	47.7
Camping equipment	100.0	8.9	10.6	11.7	16.6	2.4	5.5	43.0
Hunting and fishing equipment	100.0	3.4	17.7	6.4	8.6	12.3	16.0	33.8
Winter sports equipment	100.0	8.1	1.6	1.3	17.0	15.7	16.5	40.0
Water sports equipment	100.0	3.0	11.7	2.4	24.1	2.4	3.9	52.4
Other sports equipment	100.0	4.1	25.1	8.5	25.2	3.8	13.0	20.4
Global positioning system devices	100.0	–	7.9	15.0	21.8	–	10.5	46.1
Rental and repair of miscellaneous sports equipment	100.0	12.4	14.4	0.3	13.6	9.3	8.6	43.9
Photographic equipment, supplies, and services	100.0	4.6	11.9	4.9	16.5	7.2	10.6	44.3
Photo processing	100.0	6.5	13.6	6.1	14.2	6.0	11.0	42.7
Repair and rental of photographic equipment	100.0	14.8	14.5	6.3	9.9	26.0	13.7	22.6
Photographic equipment	100.0	4.7	12.0	5.0	19.4	7.2	9.0	42.7
Photographer fees	100.0	3.3	9.7	3.8	13.1	7.1	13.1	49.9
Fireworks	100.0	34.7	5.5	4.9	12.8	13.2	8.4	32.3
Pinball, electronic video games	100.0	140.9	5.6	–	17.8	1.1	0.5	31.9
Live entertainment for catered affairs	100.0	2.4	12.7	2.6	8.6	16.2	16.1	42.4
Rental of party supplies for catered affairs	100.0	4.3	11.8	3.1	16.1	2.3	10.2	52.1

Note: Numbers may not add to total because of rounding. "–" means sample is too small to make a reliable estimate.
Source: Calculations by New Strategist based on the Bureau of Labor Statistics' 2011 Consumer Expenditure Survey

Table 3.9 Entertainment: Average spending by high-income consumer units, 2011

(average annual spending on entertainment, by before-tax income of high-income consumer units, 2011)

	total consumer units	$100,000 or more	$100,000– $119,999	$120,000– $149,999	$150,000 or more
Number of consumer units (in 000s)	122,287	21,593	7,045	6,107	8,440
Average number of persons per consumer unit	2.5	3.2	3.2	3.1	3.2
Average before-tax income of consumer units	$63,685.00	$169,776.00	$108,549.00	$133,318.00	$247,261.00
Average spending of consumer units, total	49,704.88	97,728.22	76,496.41	87,239.44	123,056.38
Entertainment, average spending	**2,571.95**	**5,193.37**	**4,091.68**	**4,566.03**	**6,564.39**
FEES AND ADMISSIONS	**594.27**	**1,724.35**	**1,060.77**	**1,349.53**	**2,549.82**
Recreation expenses on trips	21.42	57.62	34.59	48.80	83.21
Social, recreation, health club membership	121.90	391.19	208.97	253.09	643.21
Fees for participant sports	99.72	283.01	217.29	191.93	404.16
Participant sports on trips	24.07	73.17	40.95	52.90	114.74
Movie, theater, amusement park, and other admissions	115.88	276.37	182.94	271.52	357.85
Movie and other admissions on trips	43.77	119.73	77.16	113.23	159.97
Admission to sports events	45.91	148.22	88.93	102.19	231.01
Admission to sports events on trips	14.58	39.84	25.71	37.73	53.17
Fees for recreational lessons	85.60	277.58	149.66	229.33	419.27
Other entertainment services on trips	21.42	57.62	34.59	48.80	83.21
AUDIO AND VISUAL EQUIPMENT AND SERVICES	**976.58**	**1,552.58**	**1,334.40**	**1,549.40**	**1,738.96**
Sound components, equipment, and accessories	26.88	58.57	48.07	53.63	70.87
Television sets	112.69	205.11	162.52	223.29	227.49
Cable and satellite television services	640.40	875.39	835.63	885.43	901.32
Miscellaneous video equipment	7.67	18.08	11.62	13.68	26.77
Satellite radio service	13.48	27.03	18.95	22.60	36.98
Online gaming services	3.09	5.05	4.19	4.99	5.82
VCRs and video disc players	8.66	17.44	16.26	14.36	20.66
Video cassettes, tapes, and discs	33.29	54.29	47.47	64.95	52.63
Video game software	1.99	1.32	–	1.24	2.52
Video game hardware and accessories	40.41	74.77	34.54	102.31	89.95
Streamed and downloaded video	3.92	9.79	7.43	10.48	11.25
Applications, games, ringtones for handheld devices	3.66	7.01	6.49	7.05	7.41
Repair of television, radio, and sound equipment	3.39	9.09	14.06	6.02	7.15
Rental of television sets	0.32	0.18	0.22	0.38	–
Personal digital audio players	10.29	24.31	20.32	26.10	26.33
Satellite dishes	1.05	1.42	0.64	0.75	2.56
Compact discs, records, and audio tapes	11.57	17.24	15.71	14.44	20.54
Streamed and downloaded audio	9.62	26.75	20.34	24.70	33.59
Rental of VCR, radio, and sound equipment	0.18	0.13	0.07	0.37	–
Musical instruments and accessories	22.60	79.43	36.39	36.32	146.54
Rental and repair of musical instruments	1.60	4.50	2.47	2.90	7.36
Rental of video cassettes, tapes, discs, films	18.54	32.30	30.19	31.90	34.34
Installation of television sets	0.85	2.85	0.44	0.41	6.62
PETS, TOYS, HOBBIES, AND PLAYGROUND EQUIPMENT	**630.67**	**1,101.26**	**1,135.27**	**891.75**	**1,219.19**
Pets	**502.05**	**868.18**	**958.13**	**703.13**	**906.64**
Pet food	182.75	275.69	302.54	226.98	287.04
Pet purchase, supplies, and medicines	140.90	220.45	206.61	222.54	230.48
Pet services	35.72	92.55	66.97	77.05	125.12
Veterinarian services	142.67	279.49	382.01	176.57	263.99
Toys, games, hobbies, and tricycles	**115.02**	**210.96**	**166.43**	**170.76**	**277.81**
Stamp and coin collecting	**9.97**	**14.21**	**9.04**	**5.27**	**24.99**
Playground equipment	**3.63**	**7.92**	**1.66**	**12.59**	**9.75**

	total consumer units	$100,000 or more	$100,000–$119,999	$120,000–$149,999	$150,000 or more
OTHER ENTERTAINMENT SUPPLIES, EQUIPMENT, AND SERVICES	**$370.43**	**$815.18**	**$561.24**	**$775.36**	**$1,056.42**
Unmotored recreational vehicles	**54.49**	**104.92**	**68.25**	**125.66**	**120.52**
Motorized recreational vehicles	**80.37**	**104.99**	**38.02**	**17.40**	**224.27**
Rental of recreational vehicles	**5.48**	**16.11**	**15.21**	**11.14**	**20.47**
Docking and landing fees	**7.14**	**25.09**	**2.05**	**19.66**	**48.25**
Sports, recreation, exercise equipment	**145.28**	**373.72**	**329.30**	**395.39**	**395.53**
Athletic gear, game tables, exercise equipment	52.52	164.22	163.77	199.06	139.93
Bicycles	21.92	59.26	35.13	61.92	77.47
Camping equipment	14.09	34.31	16.68	7.84	68.26
Hunting and fishing equipment	33.06	63.31	78.31	52.80	57.82
Winter sports equipment	4.52	10.23	5.71	12.00	12.72
Water sports equipment	5.31	15.75	7.40	12.48	25.08
Other sports equipment	6.34	7.31	8.17	6.02	7.54
Global positioning system devices	4.91	12.82	11.12	32.97	–
Rental and repair of miscellaneous sports equipment	2.62	6.52	3.01	10.29	6.72
Photographic equipment, supplies, and services	**54.54**	**136.80**	**79.44**	**128.98**	**190.34**
Photo processing	8.92	21.57	16.93	16.47	29.13
Repair and rental of photographic equipment	0.43	0.55	0.38	0.43	0.79
Photographic equipment	26.84	64.91	35.14	69.90	86.14
Photographer fees	17.09	48.30	26.07	40.08	72.81
Fireworks	**1.95**	**3.57**	**2.84**	**9.49**	**–**
Pinball, electronic video games	**2.67**	**4.82**	**6.06**	**7.50**	**1.87**
Live entertainment for catered affairs	**6.58**	**15.80**	**2.85**	**26.39**	**18.94**
Rental of party supplies for catered affairs	**8.78**	**25.91**	**13.43**	**33.77**	**30.64**

Note: Subcategories may not add to total because some are not shown. "–" means sample is too small to make a reliable estimate.
Source: Bureau of Labor Statistics, unpublished data from the 2011 Consumer Expenditure Survey

Table 3.10 Entertainment: Indexed spending by high-income consumer units, 2011

(indexed average annual spending of consumer units on entertainment by before-tax income of consumer unit, 2011; index definition: an index of 100 is the average for all consumer units; an index of 125 means that spending by consumer units in that group is 25 percent above the average for all consumer units; an index of 75 indicates spending that is 25 percent below the average for all consumer units)

	total consumer units	$100,000 or more	$100,000–$119,999	$120,000–$149,999	$150,000 or more
Average spending of consumer units, total	$49,705	$97,728	$76,496	$87,239	$123,056
Average spending of consumer units, index	100	197	154	176	248
Entertainment, spending index	**100**	**202**	**159**	**178**	**255**
FEES AND ADMISSIONS	**100**	**290**	**178**	**227**	**429**
Recreation expenses on trips	100	269	161	228	388
Social, recreation, health club membership	100	321	171	208	528
Fees for participant sports	100	284	218	192	405
Participant sports on trips	100	304	170	220	477
Movie, theater, amusement park, and other admissions	100	238	158	234	309
Movie and other admissions on trips	100	274	176	259	365
Admission to sports events	100	323	194	223	503
Admission to sports events on trips	100	273	176	259	365
Fees for recreational lessons	100	324	175	268	490
Other entertainment services on trips	100	269	161	228	388
AUDIO AND VISUAL EQUIPMENT AND SERVICES	**100**	**159**	**137**	**159**	**178**
Sound components, equipment, and accessories	100	218	179	200	264
Television sets	100	182	144	198	202
Cable and satellite television services	100	137	130	138	141
Miscellaneous video equipment	100	236	151	178	349
Satellite radio service	100	201	141	168	274
Online gaming services	100	163	136	161	188
VCRs and video disc players	100	201	188	166	239
Video cassettes, tapes, and discs	100	163	143	195	158
Video game software	100	66	–	62	127
Video game hardware and accessories	100	185	85	253	223
Streamed and downloaded video	100	250	190	267	287
Applications, games, ringtones for handheld devices	100	192	177	193	202
Repair of television, radio, and sound equipment	100	268	415	178	211
Rental of television sets	100	56	69	119	–
Personal digital audio players	100	236	197	254	256
Satellite dishes	100	135	61	71	244
Compact discs, records, and audio tapes	100	149	136	125	178
Streamed and downloaded audio	100	278	211	257	349
Rental of VCR, radio, and sound equipment	100	72	39	206	–
Musical instruments and accessories	100	351	161	161	648
Rental and repair of musical instruments	100	281	154	181	460
Rental of video cassettes, tapes, discs, films	100	174	163	172	185
Installation of television sets	100	335	52	48	779
PETS, TOYS, HOBBIES, AND PLAYGROUND EQUIPMENT	**100**	**175**	**180**	**141**	**193**
Pets	**100**	**173**	**191**	**140**	**181**
Pet food	100	151	166	124	157
Pet purchase, supplies, and medicines	100	156	147	158	164
Pet services	100	259	187	216	350
Veterinarian services	100	196	268	124	185
Toys, games, hobbies, and tricycles	**100**	**183**	**145**	**148**	**242**
Stamp and coin collecting	**100**	**143**	**91**	**53**	**251**
Playground equipment	**100**	**218**	**46**	**347**	**269**

	total consumer units	$100,000 or more	$100,000– $119,999	$120,000– $149,999	$150,000 or more
OTHER ENTERTAINMENT SUPPLIES, EQUIPMENT, AND SERVICES	100	220	152	209	285
Unmotored recreational vehicles	100	193	125	231	221
Motorized recreational vehicles	100	131	47	22	279
Rental of recreational vehicles	100	294	278	203	374
Docking and landing fees	100	351	29	275	676
Sports, recreation, exercise equipment	100	257	227	272	272
Athletic gear, game tables, exercise equipment	100	313	312	379	266
Bicycles	100	270	160	282	353
Camping equipment	100	244	118	56	484
Hunting and fishing equipment	100	192	237	160	175
Winter sports equipment	100	226	126	265	281
Water sports equipment	100	297	139	235	472
Other sports equipment	100	115	129	95	119
Global positioning system devices	100	261	226	671	–
Rental and repair of miscellaneous sports equipment	100	249	115	393	256
Photographic equipment, supplies, and services	100	251	146	236	349
Photo processing	100	242	190	185	327
Repair and rental of photographic equipment	100	128	88	100	184
Photographic equipment	100	242	131	260	321
Photographer fees	100	283	153	235	426
Fireworks	100	183	146	487	–
Pinball, electronic video games	100	181	227	281	70
Live entertainment for catered affairs	100	240	43	401	288
Rental of party supplies for catered affairs	100	295	153	385	349

Note: "–" means sample is too small to make a reliable estimate.
Source: Calculations by New Strategist based on the Bureau of Labor Statistics' 2011 Consumer Expenditure Survey

Table 3.11 Entertainment: Total spending by high-income consumer units, 2011

(total annual spending on entertainment, by before-tax income group of high-income consumer units, 2011; consumer units and dollars in thousands)

	total consumer units	$100,000 or more	$100,000–$119,999	$120,000–$149,999	$150,000 or more
Number of consumer units	122,287	21,593	7,045	6,107	8,440
Total spending of all consumer units	$6,078,260,661	$2,110,245,454	$538,917,208	$532,771,260	$1,038,595,847
Entertainment, total spending	**314,516,050**	**112,140,438**	**28,825,886**	**27,884,745**	**55,403,452**
FEES AND ADMISSIONS	**72,671,495**	**37,233,890**	**7,473,125**	**8,241,580**	**21,520,481**
Recreation expenses on trips	2,619,388	1,244,189	243,687	298,022	702,292
Social, recreation, health club membership	14,906,785	8,446,966	1,472,194	1,545,621	5,428,692
Fees for participant sports	12,194,460	6,111,035	1,530,808	1,172,117	3,411,110
Participant sports on trips	2,943,448	1,579,960	288,493	323,060	968,406
Movie, theater, amusement park, and other admissions	14,170,618	5,967,657	1,288,812	1,658,173	3,020,254
Movie and other admissions on trips	5,352,502	2,585,330	543,592	691,496	1,350,147
Admission to sports events	5,614,196	3,200,514	626,512	624,074	1,949,724
Admission to sports events on trips	1,782,944	860,265	181,127	230,417	448,755
Fees for recreational lessons	10,467,767	5,993,785	1,054,355	1,400,518	3,538,639
Other entertainment services on trips	2,619,388	1,244,189	243,687	298,022	702,292
AUDIO AND VISUAL EQUIPMENT AND SERVICES	**119,423,038**	**33,524,860**	**9,400,848**	**9,462,186**	**14,676,822**
Sound components, equipment, and accessories	3,287,075	1,264,702	338,653	327,518	598,143
Television sets	13,780,522	4,428,940	1,144,953	1,363,632	1,920,016
Cable and satellite television services	78,312,595	18,902,296	5,887,013	5,407,321	7,607,141
Miscellaneous video equipment	937,941	390,401	81,863	83,544	225,939
Satellite radio service	1,648,429	583,659	133,503	138,018	312,111
Online gaming services	377,867	109,045	29,519	30,474	49,121
VCRs and video disc players	1,059,005	376,582	114,552	87,697	174,370
Video cassettes, tapes, and discs	4,070,934	1,172,284	334,426	396,650	444,197
Video game software	243,351	28,503	–	7,573	21,269
Video game hardware and accessories	4,941,618	1,614,509	243,334	624,807	759,178
Streamed and downloaded video	479,365	211,395	52,344	64,001	94,950
Applications, games, ringtones for handheld devices	447,570	151,367	45,722	43,054	62,540
Repair of television, radio, and sound equipment	414,553	196,280	99,053	36,764	60,346
Rental of television sets	39,132	3,887	1,550	2,321	–
Personal digital audio players	1,258,333	524,926	143,154	159,393	222,225
Satellite dishes	128,401	30,662	4,509	4,580	21,606
Compact discs, records, and audio tapes	1,414,861	372,263	110,677	88,185	173,358
Streamed and downloaded audio	1,176,401	577,613	143,295	150,843	283,500
Rental of VCR, radio, and sound equipment	22,012	2,807	493	2,260	–
Musical instruments and accessories	2,763,686	1,715,132	256,368	221,806	1,236,798
Rental and repair of musical instruments	195,659	97,169	17,401	17,710	62,118
Rental of video cassettes, tapes, discs, films	2,267,201	697,454	212,689	194,813	289,830
Installation of television sets	103,944	61,540	3,100	2,504	55,873
PETS, TOYS, HOBBIES, AND PLAYGROUND EQUIPMENT	**77,122,742**	**23,779,507**	**7,997,977**	**5,445,917**	**10,289,964**
Pets	**61,394,188**	**18,746,611**	**6,750,026**	**4,294,015**	**7,652,042**
Pet food	22,347,949	5,952,974	2,131,394	1,386,167	2,422,618
Pet purchase, supplies, and medicines	17,230,238	4,760,177	1,455,567	1,359,052	1,945,251
Pet services	4,368,092	1,998,432	471,804	470,544	1,056,013
Veterinarian services	17,446,686	6,035,028	2,691,260	1,078,313	2,228,076
Toys, games, hobbies, and tricycles	**14,065,451**	**4,555,259**	**1,172,499**	**1,042,831**	**2,344,716**
Stamp and coin collecting	**1,219,201**	**306,837**	**63,687**	**32,184**	**210,916**
Playground equipment	**443,902**	**171,017**	**11,695**	**76,887**	**82,290**

	total consumer units	$100,000 or more	$100,000– $119,999	$120,000– $149,999	$150,000 or more
OTHER ENTERTAINMENT SUPPLIES, EQUIPMENT, AND SERVICES	**$45,298,773**	**$17,602,182**	**$3,953,936**	**$4,735,124**	**$8,916,185**
Unmotored recreational vehicles	**6,663,419**	**2,265,538**	**480,821**	**767,406**	**1,017,189**
Motorized recreational vehicles	**9,828,206**	**2,267,049**	**267,851**	**106,262**	**1,892,839**
Rental of recreational vehicles	**670,133**	**347,863**	**107,154**	**68,032**	**172,767**
Docking and landing fees	**873,129**	**541,768**	**14,442**	**120,064**	**407,230**
Sports, recreation, exercise equipment	**17,765,855**	**8,069,736**	**2,319,919**	**2,414,647**	**3,338,273**
Athletic gear, game tables, exercise equipment	6,422,513	3,546,002	1,153,760	1,215,659	1,181,009
Bicycles	2,680,531	1,279,601	247,491	378,145	653,847
Camping equipment	1,723,024	740,856	117,511	47,879	576,114
Hunting and fishing equipment	4,042,808	1,367,053	551,694	322,450	488,001
Winter sports equipment	552,737	220,896	40,227	73,284	107,357
Water sports equipment	649,344	340,090	52,133	76,215	211,675
Other sports equipment	775,300	157,845	57,558	36,764	63,638
Global positioning system devices	600,429	276,822	78,340	201,348	–
Rental and repair of miscellaneous sports equipment	320,392	140,786	21,205	62,841	56,717
Photographic equipment, supplies, and services	**6,669,533**	**2,953,922**	**559,655**	**787,681**	**1,606,470**
Photo processing	1,090,800	465,761	119,272	100,582	245,857
Repair and rental of photographic equipment	52,583	11,876	2,677	2,626	6,668
Photographic equipment	3,282,183	1,401,602	247,561	426,879	727,022
Photographer fees	2,089,885	1,042,942	183,663	244,769	614,516
Fireworks	**238,460**	**77,087**	**20,008**	**57,955**	**–**
Pinball, electronic video games	**326,506**	**104,078**	**42,693**	**45,803**	**15,783**
Live entertainment for catered affairs	**804,648**	**341,169**	**20,078**	**161,164**	**159,854**
Rental of party supplies for catered affairs	**1,073,680**	**559,475**	**94,614**	**206,233**	**258,602**

Note: Numbers may not add to total because of rounding and missing subcategories. "–" means sample is too small to make a reliable estimate.
Source: Calculations by New Strategist based on the Bureau of Labor Statistics' 2011 Consumer Expenditure Survey

Table 3.12 Entertainment: Market shares by high-income consumer units, 2011

(percentage of total annual spending on entertainment accounted for by before-tax income group of high-income consumer units, 2011)

	total consumer units	$100,000 or more	$100,000– $119,999	$120,000– $149,999	$150,000 or more
Share of total consumer units	100.0%	17.7%	5.8%	5.0%	6.9%
Share of total before-tax income	100.0	47.1	9.8	10.5	26.8
Share of total spending	100.0	34.7	8.9	8.8	17.1
Share of entertainment spending	100.0	35.7	9.2	8.9	17.6
FEES AND ADMISSIONS	100.0	51.2	10.3	11.3	29.6
Recreation expenses on trips	100.0	47.5	9.3	11.4	26.8
Social, recreation, health club membership	100.0	56.7	9.9	10.4	36.4
Fees for participant sports	100.0	50.1	12.6	9.6	28.0
Participant sports on trips	100.0	53.7	9.8	11.0	32.9
Movie, theater, amusement park, and other admissions	100.0	42.1	9.1	11.7	21.3
Movie and other admissions on trips	100.0	48.3	10.2	12.9	25.2
Admission to sports events	100.0	57.0	11.2	11.1	34.7
Admission to sports events on trips	100.0	48.2	10.2	12.9	25.2
Fees for recreational lessons	100.0	57.3	10.1	13.4	33.8
Other entertainment services on trips	100.0	47.5	9.3	11.4	26.8
AUDIO AND VISUAL EQUIPMENT AND SERVICES	100.0	28.1	7.9	7.9	12.3
Sound components, equipment, and accessories	100.0	38.5	10.3	10.0	18.2
Television sets	100.0	32.1	8.3	9.9	13.9
Cable and satellite television services	100.0	24.1	7.5	6.9	9.7
Miscellaneous video equipment	100.0	41.6	8.7	8.9	24.1
Satellite radio service	100.0	35.4	8.1	8.4	18.9
Online gaming services	100.0	28.9	7.8	8.1	13.0
VCRs and video disc players	100.0	35.6	10.8	8.3	16.5
Video cassettes, tapes, and discs	100.0	28.8	8.2	9.7	10.9
Video game software	100.0	11.7	–	3.1	8.7
Video game hardware and accessories	100.0	32.7	4.9	12.6	15.4
Streamed and downloaded video	100.0	44.1	10.9	13.4	19.8
Applications, games, ringtones for handheld devices	100.0	33.8	10.2	9.6	14.0
Repair of television, radio, and sound equipment	100.0	47.3	23.9	8.9	14.6
Rental of television sets	100.0	9.9	4.0	5.9	–
Personal digital audio players	100.0	41.7	11.4	12.7	17.7
Satellite dishes	100.0	23.9	3.5	3.6	16.8
Compact discs, records, and audio tapes	100.0	26.3	7.8	6.2	12.3
Streamed and downloaded audio	100.0	49.1	12.2	12.8	24.1
Rental of VCR, radio, and sound equipment	100.0	12.8	2.2	10.3	–
Musical instruments and accessories	100.0	62.1	9.3	8.0	44.8
Rental and repair of musical instruments	100.0	49.7	8.9	9.1	31.7
Rental of video cassettes, tapes, discs, films	100.0	30.8	9.4	8.6	12.8
Installation of television sets	100.0	59.2	3.0	2.4	53.8
PETS, TOYS, HOBBIES, AND PLAYGROUND EQUIPMENT	100.0	30.8	10.4	7.1	13.3
Pets	100.0	30.5	11.0	7.0	12.5
Pet food	100.0	26.6	9.5	6.2	10.8
Pet purchase, supplies, and medicines	100.0	27.6	8.4	7.9	11.3
Pet services	100.0	45.8	10.8	10.8	24.2
Veterinarian services	100.0	34.6	15.4	6.2	12.8
Toys, games, hobbies, and tricycles	100.0	32.4	8.3	7.4	16.7
Stamp and coin collecting	100.0	25.2	5.2	2.6	17.3
Playground equipment	100.0	38.5	2.6	17.3	18.5

	total consumer units	$100,000 or more	$100,000– $119,999	$120,000– $149,999	$150,000 or more
OTHER ENTERTAINMENT SUPPLIES, EQUIPMENT, AND SERVICES	**100.0%**	**38.9%**	**8.7%**	**10.5%**	**19.7%**
Unmotored recreational vehicles	**100.0**	**34.0**	**7.2**	**11.5**	**15.3**
Motorized recreational vehicles	**100.0**	**23.1**	**2.7**	**1.1**	**19.3**
Rental of recreational vehicles	**100.0**	**51.9**	**16.0**	**10.2**	**25.8**
Docking and landing fees	**100.0**	**62.0**	**1.7**	**13.8**	**46.6**
Sports, recreation, exercise equipment	**100.0**	**45.4**	**13.1**	**13.6**	**18.8**
Athletic gear, game tables, exercise equipment	100.0	55.2	18.0	18.9	18.4
Bicycles	100.0	47.7	9.2	14.1	24.4
Camping equipment	100.0	43.0	6.8	2.8	33.4
Hunting and fishing equipment	100.0	33.8	13.6	8.0	12.1
Winter sports equipment	100.0	40.0	7.3	13.3	19.4
Water sports equipment	100.0	52.4	8.0	11.7	32.6
Other sports equipment	100.0	20.4	7.4	4.7	8.2
Global positioning system devices	100.0	46.1	13.0	33.5	–
Rental and repair of miscellaneous sports equipment	100.0	43.9	6.6	19.6	17.7
Photographic equipment, supplies, and services	**100.0**	**44.3**	**8.4**	**11.8**	**24.1**
Photo processing	100.0	42.7	10.9	9.2	22.5
Repair and rental of photographic equipment	100.0	22.6	5.1	5.0	12.7
Photographic equipment	100.0	42.7	7.5	13.0	22.2
Photographer fees	100.0	49.9	8.8	11.7	29.4
Fireworks	**100.0**	**32.3**	**8.4**	**24.3**	**–**
Pinball, electronic video games	**100.0**	**31.9**	**13.1**	**14.0**	**4.8**
Live entertainment for catered affairs	**100.0**	**42.4**	**2.5**	**20.0**	**19.9**
Rental of party supplies for catered affairs	**100.0**	**52.1**	**8.8**	**19.2**	**24.1**

Note: Numbers may not add to total because of rounding. "–" means sample is too small to make a reliable estimate.
Source: Calculations by New Strategist based on the Bureau of Labor Statistics' 2011 Consumer Expenditure Survey

Table 3.13 Entertainment: Average spending by household type, 2011

(average annual spending of consumer units on entertainment, by type of consumer unit, 2011)

	total married couples	married couples, no children	married couples with children				single parent with child under age 18	single person
			total	oldest child under age 6	oldest child aged 6 to 17	oldest child aged 18 or older		
Number of consumer units (in 000s)	60,144	25,270	29,097	5,825	14,661	8,612	6,956	36,110
Average number of persons per consumer unit	3.2	2.0	4.0	3.5	4.2	3.9	2.9	1.0
Average before-tax income of consumer units	$86,700.00	$78,823.00	$93,677.00	$91,014.00	$93,029.00	$96,583.00	$37,188.00	$34,540.00
Average spending of consumer units, total	63,971.54	57,658.24	69,724.22	65,947.61	70,708.52	70,411.85	37,553.05	30,613.18
Entertainment, average spending	**3,418.05**	**3,285.54**	**3,591.10**	**2,956.03**	**4,086.28**	**3,160.89**	**1,820.91**	**1,522.34**
FEES AND ADMISSIONS	**871.64**	**719.23**	**1,044.37**	**697.67**	**1,367.31**	**724.49**	**424.08**	**290.45**
Recreation expenses on trips	31.31	29.48	32.58	19.19	38.32	31.88	13.78	11.36
Social, recreation, health club membership	184.92	188.73	202.67	176.62	246.91	144.99	51.80	57.94
Fees for participant sports	154.37	109.93	182.78	127.13	226.46	141.46	60.71	45.74
Participant sports on trips	35.77	43.61	31.65	16.92	42.06	23.90	15.30	10.11
Movie, theater, amusement park, and other admissions	151.62	137.19	171.22	142.14	193.06	153.70	106.04	69.55
Movie and other admissions on trips	63.38	64.23	63.97	37.92	80.08	54.15	28.86	20.79
Admission to sports events	61.59	57.36	72.18	47.89	92.71	53.65	15.74	33.65
Admission to sports events on trips	21.10	21.40	21.32	12.64	26.69	18.04	9.61	6.93
Fees for recreational lessons	136.28	37.80	233.42	98.04	382.70	70.85	108.46	23.01
Other entertainment services on trips	31.31	29.48	32.58	19.19	38.32	31.88	13.78	11.36
AUDIO AND VISUAL EQUIPMENT AND SERVICES	**1,180.40**	**1,070.85**	**1,278.13**	**1,073.46**	**1,354.78**	**1,281.73**	**827.42**	**672.09**
Sound components, equipment, and accessories	31.99	23.99	38.53	39.23	36.55	42.21	17.38	25.92
Television sets	151.91	143.04	154.29	106.00	173.11	154.91	100.25	62.44
Cable and satellite television services	736.46	736.40	733.27	656.55	725.47	798.45	537.81	493.15
Miscellaneous video equipment	11.80	8.29	14.72	5.12	16.86	16.70	1.57	3.67
Satellite radio service	19.03	23.06	17.12	15.36	17.53	17.62	10.68	6.09
Online gaming services	3.32	2.26	4.10	2.88	5.57	2.43	2.48	2.56
VCRs and video disc players	10.97	6.74	14.10	24.79	14.66	5.92	6.21	5.09
Video cassettes, tapes, and discs	38.50	26.87	48.96	33.32	52.92	51.35	31.23	16.58
Video game software	2.12	–	4.50	0.62	6.90	2.71	6.69	0.42
Video game hardware and accessories	52.90	23.68	82.23	51.24	110.61	52.36	43.05	11.78
Streamed and downloaded video	4.94	4.27	5.79	6.90	7.03	2.92	2.65	2.27
Applications, games, ringtones for handheld devices	4.49	3.35	5.19	4.69	6.40	3.46	4.43	1.72
Repair of television, radio, and sound equipment	4.38	6.23	3.00	0.60	3.46	3.85	4.15	2.23
Rental of television sets	0.29	0.49	0.17	–	–	0.56	0.06	0.18
Personal digital audio players	14.45	5.74	21.68	9.19	27.51	20.20	15.17	3.47
Satellite dishes	0.89	0.78	1.07	1.13	0.51	1.97	0.52	1.38
Compact discs, records, and audio tapes	13.14	12.78	14.04	10.08	13.45	17.74	7.75	9.73
Streamed and downloaded audio	12.55	6.65	18.24	14.19	20.00	18.00	7.34	5.93
Rental of VCR, radio, and sound equipment	0.16	0.25	0.11	–	0.17	0.08	0.09	0.26
Musical instruments and accessories	38.73	16.74	61.70	59.09	75.95	39.20	7.71	6.72
Rental and repair of musical instruments	2.65	1.88	3.46	–	4.15	4.62	0.35	0.30
Rental of video cassettes, tapes, discs, films	23.01	16.29	29.34	32.35	31.97	22.84	17.83	9.87
Installation of television sets	1.41	0.74	2.18	0.14	3.35	1.59	1.29	0.16
PETS, TOYS, HOBBIES, AND PLAYGROUND EQUIPMENT	**794.46**	**808.76**	**774.08**	**680.94**	**801.28**	**788.00**	**404.99**	**409.25**
Pets	**619.96**	**698.06**	**544.79**	**412.00**	**535.58**	**644.14**	**267.39**	**348.88**
Pet food	238.42	250.59	222.47	173.71	213.68	265.56	104.78	122.32
Pet purchase, supplies, and medicines	175.72	175.16	170.59	104.65	174.98	207.74	87.27	87.29
Pet services	49.32	60.82	39.90	33.70	43.44	38.06	11.85	26.10
Veterinarian services	156.50	211.49	111.83	99.94	103.48	132.79	63.49	113.17
Toys, games, hobbies, and tricycles	**163.49**	**102.17**	**215.90**	**244.07**	**253.98**	**135.42**	**135.35**	**40.25**
Stamp and coin collecting	**4.64**	**6.92**	**3.48**	**4.81**	**2.19**	**4.75**	**0.25**	**19.62**
Playground equipment	**6.37**	**1.61**	**9.91**	**20.06**	**9.52**	**3.69**	**2.00**	**0.50**

	total married couples	married couples, no children	married couples with children				single parent with child under age 18	single person
			total	oldest child under age 6	oldest child aged 6 to 17	oldest child aged 18 or older		
OTHER ENTERTAINMENT SUPPLIES, EQUIPMENT, AND SERVICES	**$571.55**	**$686.71**	**$494.53**	**$503.95**	**$562.91**	**$366.66**	**$164.41**	**$150.55**
Unmotored recreational vehicles	**85.67**	**114.59**	**63.54**	**136.29**	**68.18**	**6.43**	**2.92**	**30.68**
Motorized recreational vehicles	**136.68**	**272.99**	**27.73**	**10.71**	**42.22**	**14.57**	**13.34**	**23.16**
Rental of recreational vehicles	**6.81**	**9.20**	**5.37**	**3.85**	**5.83**	**5.64**	**1.82**	**3.50**
Docking and landing fees	**11.65**	**15.52**	**9.72**	**8.63**	**13.79**	**3.54**	–	**3.06**
Sports, recreation, exercise equipment	**223.12**	**175.85**	**263.60**	**199.08**	**303.80**	**234.55**	**90.28**	**59.27**
Athletic gear, game tables, exercise equipment	82.90	62.20	108.88	24.69	139.35	106.34	52.41	12.69
Bicycles	31.91	26.18	38.53	39.98	35.47	42.77	14.87	9.37
Camping equipment	25.84	14.16	30.72	7.88	37.72	32.19	1.76	3.84
Hunting and fishing equipment	48.21	48.15	42.14	95.05	37.39	19.45	10.54	19.04
Winter sports equipment	7.01	6.80	8.27	3.94	13.58	2.15	2.45	1.23
Water sports equipment	8.01	3.93	11.90	2.10	17.07	9.73	2.56	1.84
Other sports equipment	6.35	4.17	8.74	6.97	8.18	10.87	3.50	7.86
Global positioning system devices	8.66	7.34	8.38	12.72	7.12	7.98	–	2.33
Rental and repair of miscellaneous sports equipment	4.22	2.91	6.04	5.75	7.91	3.07	2.19	1.08
Photographic equipment, supplies, and services	**77.40**	**62.00**	**97.34**	**131.26**	**98.10**	**73.16**	**40.81**	**22.48**
Photo processing	13.55	11.91	16.50	23.34	14.97	14.50	5.79	3.64
Repair and rental of photographic equipment	0.66	0.41	0.86	2.38	0.51	0.41	0.98	0.03
Photographic equipment	37.86	26.59	50.04	55.46	55.06	37.85	23.08	13.06
Photographer fees	23.45	22.36	26.85	46.09	24.14	18.43	10.49	5.12
Fireworks	**2.63**	–	**5.59**	–	**8.90**	**3.27**	**0.54**	**1.49**
Pinball, electronic video games	**2.33**	**0.50**	**3.30**	–	**6.38**	**0.02**	–	**1.00**
Live entertainment for catered affairs	**8.21**	**12.70**	**5.53**	**1.91**	**4.37**	**9.93**	**1.49**	**1.81**
Rental of party supplies for catered affairs	**12.51**	**17.47**	**9.52**	**11.25**	**8.98**	**9.26**	**13.13**	**1.28**

Note: Average spending figures for total consumer units can be found in Average Spending by Age and Average Spending by Region tables. Subcategories may not add to total because some are not shown.
"–" means sample is too small to make a reliable estimate.
Source: Bureau of Labor Statistics, unpublished data from the 2011 Consumer Expenditure Survey

Table 3.14 Entertainment: Indexed spending by household type, 2011

(indexed average annual spending of consumer units on entertainment by type of consumer unit, 2011; index definition: an index of 100 is the average for all consumer units; an index of 125 means that spending by consumer units in that group is 25 percent above the average for all consumer units; an index of 75 indicates spending that is 25 percent below the average for all consumer units)

| | total married couples | married couples, no children | married couples with children | | | | single parent with child under age 18 | single person |
			total	oldest child under age 6	oldest child aged 6 to 17	oldest child aged 18 or older		
Average spending of consumer units, total	$63,972	$57,658	$69,724	$65,948	$70,709	$70,412	$37,553	$30,613
Average spending of consumer units, index	129	116	140	133	142	142	76	62
Entertainment, spending index	**133**	**128**	**140**	**115**	**159**	**123**	**71**	**59**
FEES AND ADMISSIONS	**147**	**121**	**176**	**117**	**230**	**122**	**71**	**49**
Recreation expenses on trips	146	138	152	90	179	149	64	53
Social, recreation, health club membership	152	155	166	145	203	119	42	48
Fees for participant sports	155	110	183	127	227	142	61	46
Participant sports on trips	149	181	131	70	175	99	64	42
Movie, theater, amusement park, and other admissions	131	118	148	123	167	133	92	60
Movie and other admissions on trips	145	147	146	87	183	124	66	47
Admission to sports events	134	125	157	104	202	117	34	73
Admission to sports events on trips	145	147	146	87	183	124	66	48
Fees for recreational lessons	159	44	273	115	447	83	127	27
Other entertainment services on trips	146	138	152	90	179	149	64	53
AUDIO AND VISUAL EQUIPMENT AND SERVICES	**121**	**110**	**131**	**110**	**139**	**131**	**85**	**69**
Sound components, equipment, and accessories	119	89	143	146	136	157	65	96
Television sets	135	127	137	94	154	137	89	55
Cable and satellite television services	115	115	115	103	113	125	84	77
Miscellaneous video equipment	154	108	192	67	220	218	20	48
Satellite radio service	141	171	127	114	130	131	79	45
Online gaming services	107	73	133	93	180	79	80	83
VCRs and video disc players	127	78	163	286	169	68	72	59
Video cassettes, tapes, and discs	116	81	147	100	159	154	94	50
Video game software	107	–	226	31	347	136	336	21
Video game hardware and accessories	131	59	203	127	274	130	107	29
Streamed and downloaded video	126	109	148	176	179	74	68	58
Applications, games, ringtones for handheld devices	123	92	142	128	175	95	121	47
Repair of television, radio, and sound equipment	129	184	88	18	102	114	122	66
Rental of television sets	91	153	53	–	–	175	19	56
Personal digital audio players	140	56	211	89	267	196	147	34
Satellite dishes	85	74	102	108	49	188	50	131
Compact discs, records, and audio tapes	114	110	121	87	116	153	67	84
Streamed and downloaded audio	130	69	190	148	208	187	76	62
Rental of VCR, radio, and sound equipment	89	139	61	–	94	44	50	144
Musical instruments and accessories	171	74	273	261	336	173	34	30
Rental and repair of musical instruments	166	118	216	–	259	289	22	19
Rental of video cassettes, tapes, discs, films	124	88	158	174	172	123	96	53
Installation of television sets	166	87	256	16	394	187	152	19
PETS, TOYS, HOBBIES, AND PLAYGROUND EQUIPMENT	**126**	**128**	**123**	**108**	**127**	**125**	**64**	**65**
Pets	**123**	**139**	**109**	**82**	**107**	**128**	**53**	**69**
Pet food	130	137	122	95	117	145	57	67
Pet purchase, supplies, and medicines	125	124	121	74	124	147	62	62
Pet services	138	170	112	94	122	107	33	73
Veterinarian services	110	148	78	70	73	93	45	79
Toys, games, hobbies, and tricycles	**142**	**89**	**188**	**212**	**221**	**118**	**118**	**35**
Stamp and coin collecting	**47**	**69**	**35**	**48**	**22**	**48**	**3**	**197**
Playground equipment	**175**	**44**	**273**	**553**	**262**	**102**	**55**	**14**

	total married couples	married couples, no children	married couples with children				single parent with child under age 18	single person
			total	oldest child under age 6	oldest child aged 6 to 17	oldest child aged 18 or older		
OTHER ENTERTAINMENT SUPPLIES, EQUIPMENT, AND SERVICES	154	185	134	136	152	99	44	41
Unmotored recreational vehicles	157	210	117	250	125	12	5	56
Motorized recreational vehicles	170	340	35	13	53	18	17	29
Rental of recreational vehicles	124	168	98	70	106	103	33	64
Docking and landing fees	163	217	136	121	193	50	–	43
Sports, recreation, exercise equipment	154	121	181	137	209	161	62	41
Athletic gear, game tables, exercise equipment	158	118	207	47	265	202	100	24
Bicycles	146	119	176	182	162	195	68	43
Camping equipment	183	100	218	56	268	228	12	27
Hunting and fishing equipment	146	146	127	288	113	59	32	58
Winter sports equipment	155	150	183	87	300	48	54	27
Water sports equipment	151	74	224	40	321	183	48	35
Other sports equipment	100	66	138	110	129	171	55	124
Global positioning system devices	176	149	171	259	145	163	–	47
Rental and repair of miscellaneous sports equipment	161	111	231	219	302	117	84	41
Photographic equipment, supplies, and services	142	114	178	241	180	134	75	41
Photo processing	152	134	185	262	168	163	65	41
Repair and rental of photographic equipment	153	95	200	553	119	95	228	7
Photographic equipment	141	99	186	207	205	141	86	49
Photographer fees	137	131	157	270	141	108	61	30
Fireworks	135	–	287	–	456	168	28	76
Pinball, electronic video games	87	19	124	–	239	1	–	37
Live entertainment for catered affairs	125	193	84	29	66	151	23	28
Rental of party supplies for catered affairs	142	199	108	128	102	105	150	15

Note: Spending index for total consumer units is 100. "–" means sample is too small to make a reliable estimate.
Source: Calculations by New Strategist based on the Bureau of Labor Statistics' 2011 Consumer Expenditure Survey

Table 3.15 Entertainment: Total spending by household type, 2011

(total annual spending on entertainment, by consumer unit type, 2011; consumer units and dollars in thousands)

	total married couples	married couples, no children	married couples with children				single parent with child under age 18	single person
			total	oldest child under age 6	oldest child aged 6 to 17	oldest child aged 18 or older		
Number of consumer units	60,144	25,270	29,097	5,825	14,661	8,612	6,956	36,110
Total spending of all consumer units	$3,847,504,302	$1,457,023,725	$2,028,765,629	$384,144,828	$1,036,657,612	$606,386,852	$261,219,016	$1,105,441,930
Entertainment, total spending	**205,575,199**	**83,025,596**	**104,490,237**	**17,218,875**	**59,908,951**	**27,221,585**	**12,666,250**	**54,971,697**
FEES AND ADMISSIONS	**52,423,916**	**18,174,942**	**30,388,034**	**4,063,928**	**20,046,132**	**6,239,308**	**2,949,900**	**10,488,150**
Recreation expenses on trips	1,883,109	744,960	947,980	111,782	561,810	274,551	95,854	410,210
Social, recreation, health club membership	11,121,828	4,769,207	5,897,089	1,028,812	3,619,948	1,248,654	360,321	2,092,213
Fees for participant sports	9,284,429	2,777,931	5,318,350	740,532	3,320,130	1,218,254	422,299	1,651,671
Participant sports on trips	2,151,351	1,102,025	920,920	98,559	616,642	205,827	106,427	365,072
Movie, theater, amusement park, and other admissions	9,119,033	3,466,791	4,981,988	827,966	2,830,453	1,323,664	737,614	2,511,451
Movie and other admissions on trips	3,811,927	1,623,092	1,861,335	220,884	1,174,053	466,340	200,750	750,727
Admission to sports events	3,704,269	1,449,487	2,100,221	278,959	1,359,221	462,034	109,487	1,215,102
Admission to sports events on trips	1,269,038	540,778	620,348	73,628	391,302	155,360	66,847	250,242
Fees for recreational lessons	8,196,424	955,206	6,791,822	571,083	5,610,765	610,160	754,448	830,891
Other entertainment services on trips	1,883,109	744,960	947,980	111,782	561,810	274,551	95,854	410,210
AUDIO AND VISUAL EQUIPMENT AND SERVICES	**70,993,978**	**27,060,380**	**37,189,749**	**6,252,905**	**19,862,430**	**11,038,259**	**5,755,534**	**24,269,170**
Sound components, equipment, and accessories	1,924,007	606,227	1,121,107	228,515	535,860	363,513	120,895	935,971
Television sets	9,136,475	3,614,621	4,489,376	617,450	2,537,966	1,334,085	697,339	2,254,708
Cable and satellite television services	44,293,650	18,608,828	21,335,957	3,824,404	10,636,116	6,876,251	3,741,006	17,807,647
Miscellaneous video equipment	709,699	209,488	428,308	29,824	247,184	143,820	10,921	132,524
Satellite radio service	1,144,540	582,726	498,141	89,472	257,007	151,743	74,290	219,910
Online gaming services	199,678	57,110	119,298	16,776	81,662	20,927	17,251	92,442
VCRs and video disc players	659,780	170,320	410,268	144,402	214,930	50,983	43,197	183,800
Video cassettes, tapes, and discs	2,315,544	679,005	1,424,589	194,089	775,860	442,226	217,236	598,704
Video game software	127,505	–	130,937	3,612	101,161	23,339	46,536	15,166
Video game hardware and accessories	3,181,618	598,394	2,392,646	298,473	1,621,653	450,924	299,456	425,376
Streamed and downloaded video	297,111	107,903	168,472	40,193	103,067	25,147	18,433	81,970
Applications, games, ringtones for handheld devices	270,047	84,655	151,013	27,319	93,830	29,798	30,815	62,109
Repair of television, radio, and sound equipment	263,431	157,432	87,291	3,495	50,727	33,156	28,867	80,525
Rental of television sets	17,442	12,382	4,946	–	–	4,823	417	6,500
Personal digital audio players	869,081	145,050	630,823	53,532	403,324	173,962	105,523	125,302
Satellite dishes	53,528	19,711	31,134	6,582	7,477	16,966	3,617	49,832
Compact discs, records, and audio tapes	790,292	322,951	408,522	58,716	197,190	152,777	53,909	351,350
Streamed and downloaded audio	754,807	168,046	530,729	82,657	293,220	155,016	51,057	214,132
Rental of VCR, radio, and sound equipment	9,623	6,318	3,201	–	2,492	689	626	9,389
Musical instruments and accessories	2,329,377	423,020	1,795,285	344,199	1,113,503	337,590	53,631	242,659
Rental and repair of musical instruments	159,382	47,508	100,676	–	60,843	39,787	2,435	10,833
Rental of video cassettes, tapes, discs, films	1,383,913	411,648	853,706	188,439	468,712	196,698	124,025	356,406
Installation of television sets	84,803	18,700	63,431	816	49,114	13,693	8,973	5,778
PETS, TOYS, HOBBIES, AND PLAYGROUND EQUIPMENT	**47,782,002**	**20,437,365**	**22,523,406**	**3,966,476**	**11,747,566**	**6,786,256**	**2,817,110**	**14,778,018**
Pets	**37,286,874**	**17,639,976**	**15,851,755**	**2,399,900**	**7,852,138**	**5,547,334**	**1,859,965**	**12,598,057**
Pet food	14,339,532	6,332,409	6,473,210	1,011,861	3,132,762	2,287,003	728,850	4,416,975
Pet purchase, supplies, and medicines	10,568,504	4,426,293	4,963,657	609,586	2,565,382	1,789,057	607,050	3,152,042
Pet services	2,966,302	1,536,921	1,160,970	196,303	636,874	327,773	82,429	942,471
Veterinarian services	9,412,536	5,344,352	3,253,918	582,151	1,517,120	1,143,587	441,636	4,086,569
Toys, games, hobbies, and tricycles	**9,832,943**	**2,581,836**	**6,282,042**	**1,421,708**	**3,723,601**	**1,166,237**	**941,495**	**1,453,428**
Stamp and coin collecting	**279,068**	**174,868**	**101,258**	**28,018**	**32,108**	**40,907**	**1,739**	**708,478**
Playground equipment	**383,117**	**40,685**	**288,351**	**116,850**	**139,573**	**31,778**	**13,912**	**18,055**

	total married couples	married couples, no children	married couples with children				single parent with child under age 18	single person
			total	oldest child under age 6	oldest child aged 6 to 17	oldest child aged 18 or older		
OTHER ENTERTAINMENT SUPPLIES, EQUIPMENT, AND SERVICES	**$34,375,303**	**$17,353,162**	**$14,389,339**	**$2,935,509**	**$8,252,824**	**$3,157,676**	**$1,143,636**	**$5,436,361**
Unmotored recreational vehicles	5,152,536	2,895,689	1,848,823	793,889	999,587	55,375	20,312	1,107,855
Motorized recreational vehicles	8,220,482	6,898,457	806,860	62,386	618,987	125,477	92,793	836,308
Rental of recreational vehicles	409,581	232,484	156,251	22,426	85,474	48,572	12,660	126,385
Docking and landing fees	700,678	392,190	282,823	50,270	202,175	30,486	–	110,497
Sports, recreation, exercise equipment	13,419,329	4,443,730	7,669,969	1,159,641	4,454,012	2,019,945	627,988	2,140,240
Athletic gear, game tables, exercise equipment	4,985,938	1,571,794	3,168,081	143,819	2,043,010	915,800	364,564	458,236
Bicycles	1,919,195	661,569	1,121,107	232,884	520,026	368,335	103,436	338,351
Camping equipment	1,554,121	357,823	893,860	45,901	553,013	277,220	12,243	138,662
Hunting and fishing equipment	2,899,542	1,216,751	1,226,148	553,666	548,175	167,503	73,316	687,534
Winter sports equipment	421,609	171,836	240,632	22,951	199,096	18,516	17,042	44,415
Water sports equipment	481,753	99,311	346,254	12,233	250,263	83,795	17,807	66,442
Other sports equipment	381,914	105,376	254,308	40,600	119,927	93,612	24,346	283,825
Global positioning system devices	520,847	185,482	243,833	74,094	104,386	68,724	–	84,136
Rental and repair of miscellaneous sports equipment	253,808	73,536	175,746	33,494	115,969	26,439	15,234	38,999
Photographic equipment, supplies, and services	4,655,146	1,566,740	2,832,302	764,590	1,438,244	630,054	283,874	811,753
Photo processing	814,951	300,966	480,101	135,956	219,475	124,874	40,275	131,440
Repair and rental of photographic equipment	39,695	10,361	25,023	13,864	7,477	3,531	6,817	1,083
Photographic equipment	2,277,052	671,929	1,456,014	323,055	807,235	325,964	160,544	471,597
Photographer fees	1,410,377	565,037	781,254	268,474	353,917	158,719	72,968	184,883
Fireworks	158,179	–	162,652	–	130,483	28,161	3,756	53,804
Pinball, electronic video games	140,136	12,635	96,020	–	93,537	172	–	36,110
Live entertainment for catered affairs	493,782	320,929	160,906	11,126	64,069	85,517	10,364	65,359
Rental of party supplies for catered affairs	752,401	441,467	277,003	65,531	131,656	79,747	91,332	46,221

Note: Total spending figures for total consumer units can be found in Total Spending by Age and Total Spending by Region tables. Spending by type of consumer unit does not add to total because not all types of consumer units are shown. Numbers may not add to category total because of rounding and missing subcategories. "–" means sample is too small to make a reliable estimate.
Source: Calculations by New Strategist based on the Bureau of Labor Statistics' 2011 Consumer Expenditure Survey

Table 3.16 Entertainment: Market shares by household type, 2011

(percentage of total annual spending on entertainment accounted for by types of consumer units, 2011)

	total married couples	married couples, no children	married couples with children				single parent with child under age 18	single person
			total	oldest child under age 6	oldest child aged 6 to 17	oldest child aged 18 or older		
Share of total consumer units	49.2%	20.7%	23.8%	4.8%	12.0%	7.0%	5.7%	29.5%
Share of total before-tax income	67.0	25.6	35.0	6.8	17.5	10.7	3.3	16.0
Share of total spending	63.3	24.0	33.4	6.3	17.1	10.0	4.3	18.2
Share of entertainment spending	65.4	26.4	33.2	5.5	19.0	8.7	4.0	17.5
FEES AND ADMISSIONS	**72.1**	**25.0**	**41.8**	**5.6**	**27.6**	**8.6**	**4.1**	**14.4**
Recreation expenses on trips	71.9	28.4	36.2	4.3	21.4	10.5	3.7	15.7
Social, recreation, health club membership	74.6	32.0	39.6	6.9	24.3	8.4	2.4	14.0
Fees for participant sports	76.1	22.8	43.6	6.1	27.2	10.0	3.5	13.5
Participant sports on trips	73.1	37.4	31.3	3.3	20.9	7.0	3.6	12.4
Movie, theater, amusement park, and other admissions	64.4	24.5	35.2	5.8	20.0	9.3	5.2	17.7
Movie and other admissions on trips	71.2	30.3	34.8	4.1	21.9	8.7	3.8	14.0
Admission to sports events	66.0	25.8	37.4	5.0	24.2	8.2	2.0	21.6
Admission to sports events on trips	71.2	30.3	34.8	4.1	21.9	8.7	3.7	14.0
Fees for recreational lessons	78.3	9.1	64.9	5.5	53.6	5.8	7.2	7.9
Other entertainment services on trips	71.9	28.4	36.2	4.3	21.4	10.5	3.7	15.7
AUDIO AND VISUAL EQUIPMENT AND SERVICES	**59.4**	**22.7**	**31.1**	**5.2**	**16.6**	**9.2**	**4.8**	**20.3**
Sound components, equipment, and accessories	58.5	18.4	34.1	7.0	16.3	11.1	3.7	28.5
Television sets	66.3	26.2	32.6	4.5	18.4	9.7	5.1	16.4
Cable and satellite television services	56.6	23.8	27.2	4.9	13.6	8.8	4.8	22.7
Miscellaneous video equipment	75.7	22.3	45.7	3.2	26.4	15.3	1.2	14.1
Satellite radio service	69.4	35.4	30.2	5.4	15.6	9.2	4.5	13.3
Online gaming services	52.8	15.1	31.6	4.4	21.6	5.5	4.6	24.5
VCRs and video disc players	62.3	16.1	38.7	13.6	20.3	4.8	4.1	17.4
Video cassettes, tapes, and discs	56.9	16.7	35.0	4.8	19.1	10.9	5.3	14.7
Video game software	52.4	–	53.8	1.5	41.6	9.6	19.1	6.2
Video game hardware and accessories	64.4	12.1	48.4	6.0	32.8	9.1	6.1	8.6
Streamed and downloaded video	62.0	22.5	35.1	8.4	21.5	5.2	3.8	17.1
Applications, games, ringtones for handheld devices	60.3	18.9	33.7	6.1	21.0	6.7	6.9	13.9
Repair of television, radio, and sound equipment	63.5	38.0	21.1	0.8	12.2	8.0	7.0	19.4
Rental of television sets	44.6	31.6	12.6	–	–	12.3	1.1	16.6
Personal digital audio players	69.1	11.5	50.1	4.3	32.1	13.8	8.4	10.0
Satellite dishes	41.7	15.4	24.2	5.1	5.8	13.2	2.8	38.8
Compact discs, records, and audio tapes	55.9	22.8	28.9	4.1	13.9	10.8	3.8	24.8
Streamed and downloaded audio	64.2	14.3	45.1	7.0	24.9	13.2	4.3	18.2
Rental of VCR, radio, and sound equipment	43.7	28.7	14.5	–	11.3	3.1	2.8	42.7
Musical instruments and accessories	84.3	15.3	65.0	12.5	40.3	12.2	1.9	8.8
Rental and repair of musical instruments	81.5	24.3	51.5	–	31.1	20.3	1.2	5.5
Rental of video cassettes, tapes, discs, films	61.0	18.2	37.7	8.3	20.7	8.7	5.5	15.7
Installation of television sets	81.6	18.0	61.0	0.8	47.3	13.2	8.6	5.6
PETS, TOYS, HOBBIES, AND PLAYGROUND EQUIPMENT	**62.0**	**26.5**	**29.2**	**5.1**	**15.2**	**8.8**	**3.7**	**19.2**
Pets	**60.7**	**28.7**	**25.8**	**3.9**	**12.8**	**9.0**	**3.0**	**20.5**
Pet food	64.2	28.3	29.0	4.5	14.0	10.2	3.3	19.8
Pet purchase, supplies, and medicines	61.3	25.7	28.8	3.5	14.9	10.4	3.5	18.3
Pet services	67.9	35.2	26.6	4.5	14.6	7.5	1.9	21.6
Veterinarian services	54.0	30.6	18.7	3.3	8.7	6.6	2.5	23.4
Toys, games, hobbies, and tricycles	**69.9**	**18.4**	**44.7**	**10.1**	**26.5**	**8.3**	**6.7**	**10.3**
Stamp and coin collecting	**22.9**	**14.3**	**8.3**	**2.3**	**2.6**	**3.4**	**0.1**	**58.1**
Playground equipment	**86.3**	**9.2**	**65.0**	**26.3**	**31.4**	**7.2**	**3.1**	**4.1**

	total married couples	married couples, no children	married couples with children				single parent with child under age 18	single person
			total	oldest child under age 6	oldest child aged 6 to 17	oldest child aged 18 or older		
OTHER ENTERTAINMENT SUPPLIES, EQUIPMENT, AND SERVICES	75.9%	38.3%	31.8%	6.5%	18.2%	7.0%	2.5%	12.0%
Unmotored recreational vehicles	77.3	43.5	27.7	11.9	15.0	0.8	0.3	16.6
Motorized recreational vehicles	83.6	70.2	8.2	0.6	6.3	1.3	0.9	8.5
Rental of recreational vehicles	61.1	34.7	23.3	3.3	12.8	7.2	1.9	18.9
Docking and landing fees	80.2	44.9	32.4	5.8	23.2	3.5	–	12.7
Sports, recreation, exercise equipment	75.5	25.0	43.2	6.5	25.1	11.4	3.5	12.0
Athletic gear, game tables, exercise equipment	77.6	24.5	49.3	2.2	31.8	14.3	5.7	7.1
Bicycles	71.6	24.7	41.8	8.7	19.4	13.7	3.9	12.6
Camping equipment	90.2	20.8	51.9	2.7	32.1	16.1	0.7	8.0
Hunting and fishing equipment	71.7	30.1	30.3	13.7	13.6	4.1	1.8	17.0
Winter sports equipment	76.3	31.1	43.5	4.2	36.0	3.3	3.1	8.0
Water sports equipment	74.2	15.3	53.3	1.9	38.5	12.9	2.7	10.2
Other sports equipment	49.3	13.6	32.8	5.2	15.5	12.1	3.1	36.6
Global positioning system devices	86.7	30.9	40.6	12.3	17.4	11.4	–	14.0
Rental and repair of miscellaneous sports equipment	79.2	23.0	54.9	10.5	36.2	8.3	4.8	12.2
Photographic equipment, supplies, and services	69.8	23.5	42.5	11.5	21.6	9.4	4.3	12.2
Photo processing	74.7	27.6	44.0	12.5	20.1	11.4	3.7	12.0
Repair and rental of photographic equipment	75.5	19.7	47.6	26.4	14.2	6.7	13.0	2.1
Photographic equipment	69.4	20.5	44.4	9.8	24.6	9.9	4.9	14.4
Photographer fees	67.5	27.0	37.4	12.8	16.9	7.6	3.5	8.8
Fireworks	66.3	–	68.2	–	54.7	11.8	1.6	22.6
Pinball, electronic video games	42.9	3.9	29.4	–	28.6	0.1	–	11.1
Live entertainment for catered affairs	61.4	39.9	20.0	1.4	8.0	10.6	1.3	8.1
Rental of party supplies for catered affairs	70.1	41.1	25.8	6.1	12.3	7.4	8.5	4.3

Note: Market share for total consumer units is 100.0%. Market shares by type of consumer unit do not add to total because not all types of consumer units are shown. "–" means sample is too small to make a reliable estimate.
Source: Calculations by New Strategist based on the Bureau of Labor Statistics' 2011 Consumer Expenditure Survey

Table 3.17 Entertainment: Average spending by race and Hispanic origin, 2011

(average annual spending of consumer units on entertainment, by race and Hispanic origin of consumer unit reference person, 2011)

	total consumer units	Asian	black	Hispanic	non-Hispanic white and other
Number of consumer units (in 000s)	122,287	5,048	15,118	15,222	92,163
Average number of persons per consumer unit	2.5	2.7	2.6	3.4	2.4
Average before-tax income of consumer units	$63,685.00	$85,415.00	$45,552.00	$49,966.00	$68,907.00
Average spending of consumer units, total	49,704.88	60,136.04	36,643.75	42,085.98	53,055.68
Entertainment, average spending	**2,571.95**	**2,301.11**	**1,431.61**	**1,737.64**	**2,887.60**
FEES AND ADMISSIONS	**594.27**	**767.65**	**201.33**	**339.17**	**699.09**
Recreation expenses on trips	21.42	39.61	6.22	14.16	25.09
Social, recreation, health club membership	121.90	94.37	30.10	50.65	148.52
Fees for participant sports	99.72	137.84	24.87	44.51	119.91
Participant sports on trips	24.07	39.41	4.03	8.29	29.91
Movie, theater, amusement park, and other admissions	115.88	130.74	61.29	101.17	127.27
Movie and other admissions on trips	43.77	67.16	15.09	27.35	51.11
Admission to sports events	45.91	18.69	11.55	23.50	55.15
Admission to sports events on trips	14.58	22.37	5.03	9.11	17.02
Fees for recreational lessons	85.60	177.85	36.93	46.27	100.03
Other entertainment services on trips	21.42	39.61	6.22	14.16	25.09
AUDIO AND VISUAL EQUIPMENT AND SERVICES	**976.58**	**867.87**	**908.70**	**839.25**	**1,009.43**
Sound components, equipment, and accessories	26.88	43.30	19.88	18.64	29.15
Television sets	112.69	138.05	94.92	132.71	112.47
Cable and satellite television services	640.40	440.71	660.03	527.62	655.57
Miscellaneous video equipment	7.67	1.04	2.64	10.63	7.98
Satellite radio service	13.48	11.45	8.25	11.05	14.71
Online gaming services	3.09	2.33	1.39	2.19	3.52
VCRs and video disc players	8.66	13.23	9.70	5.94	8.92
Video cassettes, tapes, and discs	33.29	43.97	18.70	23.66	36.97
Video game software	1.99	0.38	0.78	1.04	2.32
Video game hardware and accessories	40.41	53.13	17.04	42.26	43.67
Streamed and downloaded video	3.92	5.16	1.19	2.62	4.58
Applications, games, ringtones for handheld devices	3.66	2.66	3.72	2.83	3.79
Repair of television, radio, and sound equipment	3.39	1.54	2.97	3.48	3.49
Rental of television sets	0.32	–	0.08	0.69	0.30
Personal digital audio players	10.29	12.98	7.73	9.79	10.76
Satellite dishes	1.05	0.19	0.17	0.31	1.31
Compact discs, records, and audio tapes	11.57	7.56	12.00	9.05	11.92
Streamed and downloaded audio	9.62	6.65	3.99	6.40	11.07
Rental of VCR, radio, and sound equipment	0.18	0.31	0.04	0.16	0.21
Musical instruments and accessories	22.60	65.38	31.32	9.82	23.25
Rental and repair of musical instruments	1.60	0.39	0.89	0.94	1.82
Rental of video cassettes, tapes, discs, films	18.54	17.29	10.50	16.54	20.18
Installation of television sets	0.85	0.16	0.69	0.44	0.94
PETS, TOYS, HOBBIES, AND PLAYGROUND EQUIPMENT	**630.67**	**269.30**	**212.07**	**391.97**	**734.04**
Pets	**502.05**	**170.19**	**145.73**	**290.11**	**591.25**
Pet food	182.75	77.07	54.57	130.04	210.79
Pet purchase, supplies, and medicines	140.90	48.59	54.60	90.56	163.14
Pet services	35.72	11.62	7.01	15.97	43.63
Veterinarian services	142.67	32.91	29.55	53.54	173.68
Toys, games, hobbies, and tricycles	**115.02**	**97.69**	**62.16**	**99.62**	**125.80**
Stamp and coin collecting	**9.97**	**1.35**	**0.54**	**0.36**	**13.08**
Playground equipment	**3.63**	**0.07**	**3.64**	**1.88**	**3.90**

	total consumer units	Asian	black	Hispanic	non-Hispanic white and other
OTHER ENTERTAINMENT SUPPLIES, EQUIPMENT, AND SERVICES	**$370.43**	**$396.29**	**$109.51**	**$167.25**	**$445.04**
Unmotored recreational vehicles	**54.49**	–	–	**9.03**	**70.81**
Motorized recreational vehicles	**80.37**	**85.76**	**0.12**	**2.71**	**106.17**
Rental of recreational vehicles	**5.48**	**9.52**	**2.60**	**4.33**	**6.13**
Docking and landing fees	**7.14**	–	**1.58**	**0.43**	**9.14**
Sports, recreation, exercise equipment	**145.28**	**200.35**	**59.40**	**93.29**	**166.70**
Athletic gear, game tables, exercise equipment	52.52	148.53	23.64	27.45	60.72
Bicycles	21.92	22.22	7.01	16.22	25.25
Camping equipment	14.09	6.99	5.19	31.89	12.73
Hunting and fishing equipment	33.06	0.33	18.51	10.67	38.66
Winter sports equipment	4.52	1.07	0.01	3.26	5.47
Water sports equipment	5.31	3.89	0.18	0.77	6.88
Other sports equipment	6.34	4.18	4.50	2.49	7.26
Global positioning system devices	4.91	12.61	–	–	6.42
Rental and repair of miscellaneous sports equipment	2.62	0.54	0.36	0.54	3.32
Photographic equipment, supplies, and services	**54.54**	**84.89**	**31.82**	**35.81**	**61.31**
Photo processing	8.92	9.85	3.12	5.14	10.48
Repair and rental of photographic equipment	0.43	1.37	0.44	0.56	0.41
Photographic equipment	26.84	58.67	15.16	18.16	30.19
Photographer fees	17.09	13.59	11.27	11.20	18.99
Fireworks	**1.95**	–	**4.89**	–	**1.78**
Pinball, electronic video games	**2.67**	**2.41**	**3.30**	**1.98**	**2.66**
Live entertainment for catered affairs	**6.58**	**1.18**	**1.84**	**7.83**	**7.13**
Rental of party supplies for catered affairs	**8.78**	**11.24**	**3.26**	**11.12**	**9.28**

Note: "Asian" and "black" include Hispanics and non-Hispanics who identify themselves as being of the respective race alone. "Hispanic" includes people of any race who identify themselves as Hispanic. "Other" includes people who identify themselves as non-Hispanic and as Alaska Native, American Indian, Asian (who are also included in the "Asian" column), or Native Hawaiian or other Pacific Islander, as well as non-Hispanics reporting more than one race. Subcategories may not add to total because some are not shown. "–" means sample is too small to make a reliable estimate.
Source: Bureau of Labor Statistics, unpublished data from the 2011 Consumer Expenditure Survey

Table 3.18 Entertainment: Indexed spending by race and Hispanic origin, 2011

(indexed average annual spending of consumer units on entertainment, by race and Hispanic origin of consumer unit reference person, 2011; index definition: an index of 100 is the average for all consumer units; an index of 125 means that spending by consumer units in that group is 25 percent above the average for all consumer units; an index of 75 indicates spending that is 25 percent below the average for all consumer units)

	total consumer units	Asian	black	Hispanic	non-Hispanic white and other
Average spending of consumer units, total	$49,705	$60,136	$36,644	$42,086	$53,056
Average spending of consumer units, index	100	121	74	85	107
Entertainment, spending index	**100**	**89**	**56**	**68**	**112**
FEES AND ADMISSIONS	**100**	**129**	**34**	**57**	**118**
Recreation expenses on trips	100	185	29	66	117
Social, recreation, health club membership	100	77	25	42	122
Fees for participant sports	100	138	25	45	120
Participant sports on trips	100	164	17	34	124
Movie, theater, amusement park, and other admissions	100	113	53	87	110
Movie and other admissions on trips	100	153	34	62	117
Admission to sports events	100	41	25	51	120
Admission to sports events on trips	100	153	34	62	117
Fees for recreational lessons	100	208	43	54	117
Other entertainment services on trips	100	185	29	66	117
AUDIO AND VISUAL EQUIPMENT AND SERVICES	**100**	**89**	**93**	**86**	**103**
Sound components, equipment, and accessories	100	161	74	69	108
Television sets	100	123	84	118	100
Cable and satellite television services	100	69	103	82	102
Miscellaneous video equipment	100	14	34	139	104
Satellite radio service	100	85	61	82	109
Online gaming services	100	75	45	71	114
VCRs and video disc players	100	153	112	69	103
Video cassettes, tapes, and discs	100	132	56	71	111
Video game software	100	19	39	52	117
Video game hardware and accessories	100	131	42	105	108
Streamed and downloaded video	100	132	30	67	117
Applications, games, ringtones for handheld devices	100	73	102	77	104
Repair of television, radio, and sound equipment	100	45	88	103	103
Rental of television sets	100	–	25	216	94
Personal digital audio players	100	126	75	95	105
Satellite dishes	100	18	16	30	125
Compact discs, records, and audio tapes	100	65	104	78	103
Streamed and downloaded audio	100	69	41	67	115
Rental of VCR, radio, and sound equipment	100	172	22	89	117
Musical instruments and accessories	100	289	139	43	103
Rental and repair of musical instruments	100	24	56	59	114
Rental of video cassettes, tapes, discs, films	100	93	57	89	109
Installation of television sets	100	19	81	52	111
PETS, TOYS, HOBBIES, AND PLAYGROUND EQUIPMENT	**100**	**43**	**34**	**62**	**116**
Pets	**100**	**34**	**29**	**58**	**118**
Pet food	100	42	30	71	115
Pet purchase, supplies, and medicines	100	34	39	64	116
Pet services	100	33	20	45	122
Veterinarian services	100	23	21	38	122
Toys, games, hobbies, and tricycles	**100**	**85**	**54**	**87**	**109**
Stamp and coin collecting	**100**	**14**	**5**	**4**	**131**
Playground equipment	**100**	**2**	**100**	**52**	**107**

	total consumer units	Asian	black	Hispanic	non-Hispanic white and other
OTHER ENTERTAINMENT SUPPLIES, EQUIPMENT, AND SERVICES	100	107	30	45	120
Unmotored recreational vehicles	100	–	–	17	130
Motorized recreational vehicles	100	107	0	3	132
Rental of recreational vehicles	100	174	47	79	112
Docking and landing fees	100	–	22	6	128
Sports, recreation, exercise equipment	100	138	41	64	115
Athletic gear, game tables, exercise equipment	100	283	45	52	116
Bicycles	100	101	32	74	115
Camping equipment	100	50	37	226	90
Hunting and fishing equipment	100	1	56	32	117
Winter sports equipment	100	24	0	72	121
Water sports equipment	100	73	3	15	130
Other sports equipment	100	66	71	39	115
Global positioning system devices	100	257	–	–	131
Rental and repair of miscellaneous sports equipment	100	21	14	21	127
Photographic equipment, supplies, and services	100	156	58	66	112
Photo processing	100	110	35	58	117
Repair and rental of photographic equipment	100	319	102	130	95
Photographic equipment	100	219	56	68	112
Photographer fees	100	80	66	66	111
Fireworks	100	–	251	–	91
Pinball, electronic video games	100	90	124	74	100
Live entertainment for catered affairs	100	18	28	119	108
Rental of party supplies for catered affairs	100	128	37	127	106

Table 3.19 Entertainment: Total spending by race and Hispanic origin, 2011

(total annual spending on entertainment, by consumer unit race and Hispanic origin groups, 2011; consumer units and dollars in thousands)

	total consumer units	Asian	black	Hispanic	non-Hispanic white and other
Number of consumer units	122,287	5,048	15,118	15,222	92,163
Total spending of all consumer units	$6,078,260,661	$303,566,730	$553,980,213	$640,632,788	$4,889,770,636
Entertainment, total spending	**314,516,050**	**11,616,003**	**21,643,080**	**26,450,356**	**266,129,879**
FEES AND ADMISSIONS	**72,671,495**	**3,875,097**	**3,043,707**	**5,162,846**	**64,430,232**
Recreation expenses on trips	2,619,388	199,951	94,034	215,544	2,312,370
Social, recreation, health club membership	14,906,785	476,380	455,052	770,994	13,688,049
Fees for participant sports	12,194,460	695,816	375,985	677,531	11,051,265
Participant sports on trips	2,943,448	198,942	60,926	126,190	2,756,595
Movie, theater, amusement park, and other admissions	14,170,618	659,976	926,582	1,540,010	11,729,585
Movie and other admissions on trips	5,352,502	339,024	228,131	416,322	4,710,451
Admission to sports events	5,614,196	94,347	174,613	357,717	5,082,789
Admission to sports events on trips	1,782,944	112,924	76,044	138,672	1,568,614
Fees for recreational lessons	10,467,767	897,787	558,308	704,322	9,219,065
Other entertainment services on trips	2,619,388	199,951	94,034	215,544	2,312,370
AUDIO AND VISUAL EQUIPMENT AND SERVICES	**119,423,038**	**4,381,008**	**13,737,727**	**12,775,064**	**93,032,097**
Sound components, equipment, and accessories	3,287,075	218,578	300,546	283,738	2,686,551
Television sets	13,780,522	696,876	1,435,001	2,020,112	10,365,573
Cable and satellite television services	78,312,595	2,224,704	9,978,334	8,031,432	60,419,298
Miscellaneous video equipment	937,941	5,250	39,912	161,810	735,461
Satellite radio service	1,648,429	57,800	124,724	168,203	1,355,718
Online gaming services	377,867	11,762	21,014	33,336	324,414
VCRs and video disc players	1,059,005	66,785	146,645	90,419	822,094
Video cassettes, tapes, and discs	4,070,934	221,961	282,707	360,153	3,407,266
Video game software	243,351	1,918	11,792	15,831	213,818
Video game hardware and accessories	4,941,618	268,200	257,611	643,282	4,024,758
Streamed and downloaded video	479,365	26,048	17,990	39,882	422,107
Applications, games, ringtones for handheld devices	447,570	13,428	56,239	43,078	349,298
Repair of television, radio, and sound equipment	414,553	7,774	44,900	52,973	321,649
Rental of television sets	39,132	–	1,209	10,503	27,649
Personal digital audio players	1,258,333	65,523	116,862	149,023	991,674
Satellite dishes	128,401	959	2,570	4,719	120,734
Compact discs, records, and audio tapes	1,414,861	38,163	181,416	137,759	1,098,583
Streamed and downloaded audio	1,176,401	33,569	60,321	97,421	1,020,244
Rental of VCR, radio, and sound equipment	22,012	1,565	605	2,436	19,354
Musical instruments and accessories	2,763,686	330,038	473,496	149,480	2,142,790
Rental and repair of musical instruments	195,659	1,969	13,455	14,309	167,737
Rental of video cassettes, tapes, discs, films	2,267,201	87,280	158,739	251,772	1,859,849
Installation of television sets	103,944	808	10,431	6,698	86,633
PETS, TOYS, HOBBIES, AND PLAYGROUND EQUIPMENT	**77,122,742**	**1,359,426**	**3,206,074**	**5,966,567**	**67,651,329**
Pets	**61,394,188**	**859,119**	**2,203,146**	**4,416,054**	**54,491,374**
Pet food	22,347,949	389,049	824,989	1,979,469	19,427,039
Pet purchase, supplies, and medicines	17,230,238	245,282	825,443	1,378,504	15,035,472
Pet services	4,368,092	58,658	105,977	243,095	4,021,072
Veterinarian services	17,446,686	166,130	446,737	814,986	16,006,870
Toys, games, hobbies, and tricycles	**14,065,451**	**493,139**	**939,735**	**1,516,416**	**11,594,105**
Stamp and coin collecting	**1,219,201**	**6,815**	**8,164**	**5,480**	**1,205,492**
Playground equipment	**443,902**	**353**	**55,030**	**28,617**	**359,436**

	total consumer units	Asian	black	Hispanic	non-Hispanic white and other
OTHER ENTERTAINMENT SUPPLIES, EQUIPMENT, AND SERVICES	$45,298,773	$2,000,472	$1,655,572	$2,545,880	$41,016,222
Unmotored recreational vehicles	6,663,419	–	–	137,455	6,526,062
Motorized recreational vehicles	9,828,206	432,916	1,814	41,252	9,784,946
Rental of recreational vehicles	670,133	48,057	39,307	65,911	564,959
Docking and landing fees	873,129	–	23,886	6,545	842,370
Sports, recreation, exercise equipment	17,765,855	1,011,367	898,009	1,420,060	15,363,572
Athletic gear, game tables, exercise equipment	6,422,513	749,779	357,390	417,844	5,596,137
Bicycles	2,680,531	112,167	105,977	246,901	2,327,116
Camping equipment	1,723,024	35,286	78,462	485,430	1,173,235
Hunting and fishing equipment	4,042,808	1,666	279,834	162,419	3,563,022
Winter sports equipment	552,737	5,401	151	49,624	504,132
Water sports equipment	649,344	19,637	2,721	11,721	634,081
Other sports equipment	775,300	21,101	68,031	37,903	669,103
Global positioning system devices	600,429	63,655	–	–	591,686
Rental and repair of miscellaneous sports equipment	320,392	2,726	5,442	8,220	305,981
Photographic equipment, supplies, and services	6,669,533	428,525	481,055	545,100	5,650,514
Photo processing	1,090,800	49,723	47,168	78,241	965,868
Repair and rental of photographic equipment	52,583	6,916	6,652	8,524	37,787
Photographic equipment	3,282,183	296,166	229,189	276,432	2,782,401
Photographer fees	2,089,885	68,602	170,380	170,486	1,750,175
Fireworks	238,460	–	73,927	–	164,050
Pinball, electronic video games	326,506	12,166	49,889	30,140	245,154
Live entertainment for catered affairs	804,648	5,957	27,817	119,188	657,122
Rental of party supplies for catered affairs	1,073,680	56,740	49,285	169,269	855,273

Note: "Asian" and "black" include Hispanics and non-Hispanics who identify themselves as being of the respective race alone. "Hispanic" includes people of any race who identify themselves as Hispanic. "Other" includes people who identify themselves as non-Hispanic and as Alaska Native, American Indian, Asian (who are also included in the "Asian" column), or Native Hawaiian or other Pacific Islander, as well as non-Hispanics reporting more than one race. Numbers may not add to total because of rounding and missing subcategories. "–" means sample is too small to make a reliable estimate.
Source: Calculations by New Strategist based on the Bureau of Labor Statistics' 2011 Consumer Expenditure Survey

Table 3.20 Entertainment: Market shares by race and Hispanic origin, 2011

(percentage of total annual spending on entertainment accounted for by consumer unit race and Hispanic origin groups, 2011)

	total consumer units	Asian	black	Hispanic	non-Hispanic white and other
Share of total consumer units	100.0%	4.1%	12.4%	12.4%	75.4%
Share of total before-tax income	100.0	5.5	8.8	9.8	81.5
Share of total spending	100.0	5.0	9.1	10.5	80.4
Share of entertainment spending	**100.0**	**3.7**	**6.9**	**8.4**	**84.6**
FEES AND ADMISSIONS	**100.0**	**5.3**	**4.2**	**7.1**	**88.7**
Recreation expenses on trips	100.0	7.6	3.6	8.2	88.3
Social, recreation, health club membership	100.0	3.2	3.1	5.2	91.8
Fees for participant sports	100.0	5.7	3.1	5.6	90.6
Participant sports on trips	100.0	6.8	2.1	4.3	93.7
Movie, theater, amusement park, and other admissions	100.0	4.7	6.5	10.9	82.8
Movie and other admissions on trips	100.0	6.3	4.3	7.8	88.0
Admission to sports events	100.0	1.7	3.1	6.4	90.5
Admission to sports events on trips	100.0	6.3	4.3	7.8	88.0
Fees for recreational lessons	100.0	8.6	5.3	6.7	88.1
Other entertainment services on trips	100.0	7.6	3.6	8.2	88.3
AUDIO AND VISUAL EQUIPMENT AND SERVICES	**100.0**	**3.7**	**11.5**	**10.7**	**77.9**
Sound components, equipment, and accessories	100.0	6.6	9.1	8.6	81.7
Television sets	100.0	5.1	10.4	14.7	75.2
Cable and satellite television services	100.0	2.8	12.7	10.3	77.2
Miscellaneous video equipment	100.0	0.6	4.3	17.3	78.4
Satellite radio service	100.0	3.5	7.6	10.2	82.2
Online gaming services	100.0	3.1	5.6	8.8	85.9
VCRs and video disc players	100.0	6.3	13.8	8.5	77.6
Video cassettes, tapes, and discs	100.0	5.5	6.9	8.8	83.7
Video game software	100.0	0.8	4.8	6.5	87.9
Video game hardware and accessories	100.0	5.4	5.2	13.0	81.4
Streamed and downloaded video	100.0	5.4	3.8	8.3	88.1
Applications, games, ringtones for handheld devices	100.0	3.0	12.6	9.6	78.0
Repair of television, radio, and sound equipment	100.0	1.9	10.8	12.8	77.6
Rental of television sets	100.0	–	3.1	26.8	70.7
Personal digital audio players	100.0	5.2	9.3	11.8	78.8
Satellite dishes	100.0	0.7	2.0	3.7	94.0
Compact discs, records, and audio tapes	100.0	2.7	12.8	9.7	77.6
Streamed and downloaded audio	100.0	2.9	5.1	8.3	86.7
Rental of VCR, radio, and sound equipment	100.0	7.1	2.7	11.1	87.9
Musical instruments and accessories	100.0	11.9	17.1	5.4	77.5
Rental and repair of musical instruments	100.0	1.0	6.9	7.3	85.7
Rental of video cassettes, tapes, discs, films	100.0	3.8	7.0	11.1	82.0
Installation of television sets	100.0	0.8	10.0	6.4	83.3
PETS, TOYS, HOBBIES, AND PLAYGROUND EQUIPMENT	**100.0**	**1.8**	**4.2**	**7.7**	**87.7**
Pets	**100.0**	**1.4**	**3.6**	**7.2**	**88.8**
Pet food	100.0	1.7	3.7	8.9	86.9
Pet purchase, supplies, and medicines	100.0	1.4	4.8	8.0	87.3
Pet services	100.0	1.3	2.4	5.6	92.1
Veterinarian services	100.0	1.0	2.6	4.7	91.7
Toys, games, hobbies, and tricycles	**100.0**	**3.5**	**6.7**	**10.8**	**82.4**
Stamp and coin collecting	**100.0**	**0.6**	**0.7**	**0.4**	**98.9**
Playground equipment	**100.0**	**0.1**	**12.4**	**6.4**	**81.0**

	total consumer units	Asian	black	Hispanic	non-Hispanic white and other
OTHER ENTERTAINMENT SUPPLIES, EQUIPMENT, AND SERVICES	**100.0%**	**4.4%**	**3.7%**	**5.6%**	**90.5%**
Unmotored recreational vehicles	**100.0**	–	–	2.1	97.9
Motorized recreational vehicles	**100.0**	4.4	0.0	0.4	99.6
Rental of recreational vehicles	**100.0**	7.2	5.9	9.8	84.3
Docking and landing fees	**100.0**	–	2.7	0.7	96.5
Sports, recreation, exercise equipment	**100.0**	5.7	5.1	8.0	86.5
Athletic gear, game tables, exercise equipment	100.0	11.7	5.6	6.5	87.1
Bicycles	100.0	4.2	4.0	9.2	86.8
Camping equipment	100.0	2.0	4.6	28.2	68.1
Hunting and fishing equipment	100.0	0.0	6.9	4.0	88.1
Winter sports equipment	100.0	1.0	0.0	9.0	91.2
Water sports equipment	100.0	3.0	0.4	1.8	97.6
Other sports equipment	100.0	2.7	8.8	4.9	86.3
Global positioning system devices	100.0	10.6	–	–	98.5
Rental and repair of miscellaneous sports equipment	100.0	0.9	1.7	2.6	95.5
Photographic equipment, supplies, and services	**100.0**	6.4	7.2	8.2	84.7
Photo processing	100.0	4.6	4.3	7.2	88.5
Repair and rental of photographic equipment	100.0	13.2	12.7	16.2	71.9
Photographic equipment	100.0	9.0	7.0	8.4	84.8
Photographer fees	100.0	3.3	8.2	8.2	83.7
Fireworks	**100.0**	–	31.0	–	68.8
Pinball, electronic video games	**100.0**	3.7	15.3	9.2	75.1
Live entertainment for catered affairs	**100.0**	0.7	3.5	14.8	81.7
Rental of party supplies for catered affairs	**100.0**	5.3	4.6	15.8	79.7

Note: "Asian" and "black" include Hispanics and non-Hispanics who identify themselves as being of the respective race alone. "Hispanic" includes people of any race who identify themselves as Hispanic. "Other" includes people who identify themselves as non-Hispanic and as Alaska Native, American Indian, Asian (who are also included in the "Asian" column), or Native Hawaiian or other Pacific Islander, as well as non-Hispanics reporting more than one race. "–" means sample is too small to make a reliable estimate.
Source: Calculations by New Strategist based on the Bureau of Labor Statistics' 2011 Consumer Expenditure Survey

Table 3.21 Entertainment: Average spending by region, 2011

(average annual spending of consumer units on entertainment, by region in which consumer unit lives, 2011)

	total consumer units	Northeast	Midwest	South	West
Number of consumer units (in 000s)	122,287	22,538	27,107	44,901	27,741
Average number of persons per consumer unit	2.5	2.4	2.4	2.5	2.6
Average before-tax income of consumer units	$63,685.00	$71,733.00	$60,897.00	$58,780.00	$67,810.00
Average spending of consumer units, total	49,704.88	54,547.45	47,191.54	45,698.60	54,745.43
Entertainment, average spending	**2,571.95**	**2,631.98**	**2,505.12**	**2,349.79**	**2,950.33**
FEES AND ADMISSIONS	**594.27**	**709.66**	**583.11**	**443.21**	**756.99**
Recreation expenses on trips	21.42	25.24	20.30	15.50	29.00
Social, recreation, health club membership	121.90	152.23	110.02	100.43	143.60
Fees for participant sports	99.72	97.10	99.81	70.26	150.51
Participant sports on trips	24.07	26.69	20.58	15.19	39.70
Movie, theater, amusement park, and other admissions	115.88	141.47	98.81	91.24	151.65
Movie and other admissions on trips	43.77	45.50	48.95	32.99	54.76
Admission to sports events	45.91	46.76	59.79	38.03	44.43
Admission to sports events on trips	14.58	15.16	16.31	10.97	18.24
Fees for recreational lessons	85.60	134.27	88.25	53.09	96.09
Other entertainment services on trips	21.42	25.24	20.30	15.50	29.00
AUDIO AND VISUAL EQUIPMENT AND SERVICES	**976.58**	**1,032.54**	**935.72**	**984.03**	**959.35**
Sound components, equipment, and accessories	26.88	29.73	22.82	28.44	26.00
Television sets	112.69	112.99	116.83	106.96	117.67
Cable and satellite television services	640.40	695.45	611.69	674.81	568.04
Miscellaneous video equipment	7.67	2.40	10.81	9.12	6.44
Satellite radio service	13.48	15.77	11.49	14.66	11.66
Online gaming services	3.09	2.86	4.03	1.90	4.29
VCRs and video disc players	8.66	6.37	10.49	8.30	9.30
Video cassettes, tapes, and discs	33.29	23.63	35.10	30.33	44.30
Video game software	1.99	1.68	1.28	2.84	1.54
Video game hardware and accessories	40.41	43.94	34.30	35.12	52.37
Streamed and downloaded video	3.92	3.91	3.44	2.46	6.77
Applications, games, ringtones for handheld devices	3.66	3.88	3.34	3.67	3.78
Repair of television, radio, and sound equipment	3.39	3.14	2.11	2.79	5.81
Rental of television sets	0.32	0.43	–	0.37	0.48
Personal digital audio players	10.29	10.97	11.03	8.10	12.54
Satellite dishes	1.05	0.59	1.59	0.71	1.45
Compact discs, records, and audio tapes	11.57	12.25	10.61	9.96	14.56
Streamed and downloaded audio	9.62	9.15	10.52	7.82	12.02
Rental of VCR, radio, and sound equipment	0.18	–	–	–	–
Musical instruments and accessories	22.60	34.70	12.88	17.73	30.16
Rental and repair of musical instruments	1.60	3.22	1.74	0.90	1.28
Rental of video cassettes, tapes, discs, films	18.54	14.14	18.04	16.01	26.71
Installation of television sets	0.85	1.13	1.14	0.37	1.13
PETS, TOYS, HOBBIES, AND PLAYGROUND EQUIPMENT	**630.67**	**541.09**	**612.61**	**661.48**	**671.41**
Pets	**502.05**	**428.70**	**472.21**	**542.87**	**524.60**
Pet food	182.75	127.40	193.48	195.08	197.10
Pet purchase, supplies, and medicines	140.90	128.26	130.24	154.43	139.68
Pet services	35.72	39.35	33.26	31.56	41.94
Veterinarian services	142.67	133.69	115.24	161.80	145.88
Toys, games, hobbies, and tricycles	**115.02**	**99.91**	**128.55**	**100.23**	**138.34**
Stamp and coin collecting	**9.97**	**4.85**	**9.35**	**15.58**	**5.67**
Playground equipment	**3.63**	**7.63**	**2.50**	**2.81**	**2.80**

	total consumer units	Northeast	Midwest	South	West
OTHER ENTERTAINMENT SUPPLIES, EQUIPMENT, AND SERVICES	$370.43	$348.69	$373.67	$261.07	$562.58
Unmotored recreational vehicles	54.49	37.48	72.76	50.92	56.24
Motorized recreational vehicles	80.37	65.50	58.30	26.66	200.93
Rental of recreational vehicles	5.48	6.62	4.56	4.13	7.62
Docking and landing fees	7.14	6.45	11.38	3.92	8.76
Sports, recreation, exercise equipment	145.28	142.33	141.23	119.30	194.30
Athletic gear, game tables, exercise equipment	52.52	46.34	35.71	50.92	77.07
Bicycles	21.92	28.41	20.87	12.40	33.07
Camping equipment	14.09	16.78	10.49	6.17	28.61
Hunting and fishing equipment	33.06	23.55	49.23	33.80	23.45
Winter sports equipment	4.52	4.46	5.45	1.63	8.37
Water sports equipment	5.31	7.54	4.19	3.91	6.85
Other sports equipment	6.34	9.66	6.91	5.56	4.33
Global positioning system devices	4.91	4.61	3.92	3.06	9.19
Rental and repair of miscellaneous sports equipment	2.62	0.99	4.45	1.86	3.37
Photographic equipment, supplies, and services	54.54	57.40	58.87	42.72	67.11
Photo processing	8.92	7.96	13.31	6.35	9.58
Repair and rental of photographic equipment	0.43	0.75	0.31	0.11	0.80
Photographic equipment	26.84	29.78	27.62	19.46	35.63
Photographer fees	17.09	17.83	16.75	15.27	19.75
Fireworks	1.95	0.67	4.68	0.84	2.13
Pinball, electronic video games	2.67	0.47	4.20	0.68	6.23
Live entertainment for catered affairs	6.58	10.75	7.83	2.94	7.83
Rental of party supplies for catered affairs	8.78	19.94	7.01	4.12	8.99

Note: Subcategories may not add to total because some are not shown. "–" means sample is too small to make a reliable estimate.
Source: Bureau of Labor Statistics, unpublished data from the 2011 Consumer Expenditure Survey

Table 3.22 Entertainment: Indexed spending by region, 2011

(indexed average annual spending of consumer units on entertainment, by region in which consumer unit lives, 2011; index definition: an index of 100 is the average for all consumer units; an index of 125 means that spending by consumer units in that group is 25 percent above the average for all consumer units; an index of 75 indicates spending that is 25 percent below the average for all consumer units)

	total consumer units	Northeast	Midwest	South	West
Average spending of consumer units, total	$49,705	$54,547	$47,192	$45,699	$54,745
Average spending of consumer units, index	100	110	95	92	110
Entertainment, spending index	100	102	97	91	115
FEES AND ADMISSIONS	100	119	98	75	127
Recreation expenses on trips	100	118	95	72	135
Social, recreation, health club membership	100	125	90	82	118
Fees for participant sports	100	97	100	70	151
Participant sports on trips	100	111	86	63	165
Movie, theater, amusement park, and other admissions	100	122	85	79	131
Movie and other admissions on trips	100	104	112	75	125
Admission to sports events	100	102	130	83	97
Admission to sports events on trips	100	104	112	75	125
Fees for recreational lessons	100	157	103	62	112
Other entertainment services on trips	100	118	95	72	135
AUDIO AND VISUAL EQUIPMENT AND SERVICES	100	106	96	101	98
Sound components, equipment, and accessories	100	111	85	106	97
Television sets	100	100	104	95	104
Cable and satellite television services	100	109	96	105	89
Miscellaneous video equipment	100	31	141	119	84
Satellite radio service	100	117	85	109	86
Online gaming services	100	93	130	61	139
VCRs and video disc players	100	74	121	96	107
Video cassettes, tapes, and discs	100	71	105	91	133
Video game software	100	84	64	143	77
Video game hardware and accessories	100	109	85	87	130
Streamed and downloaded video	100	100	88	63	173
Applications, games, ringtones for handheld devices	100	106	91	100	103
Repair of television, radio, and sound equipment	100	93	62	82	171
Rental of television sets	100	134	–	116	150
Personal digital audio players	100	107	107	79	122
Satellite dishes	100	56	151	68	138
Compact discs, records, and audio tapes	100	106	92	86	126
Streamed and downloaded audio	100	95	109	81	125
Rental of VCR, radio, and sound equipment	100	–	–	–	–
Musical instruments and accessories	100	154	57	78	133
Rental and repair of musical instruments	100	201	109	56	80
Rental of video cassettes, tapes, discs, films	100	76	97	86	144
Installation of television sets	100	133	134	44	133
PETS, TOYS, HOBBIES, AND PLAYGROUND EQUIPMENT	100	86	97	105	106
Pets	100	85	94	108	104
Pet food	100	70	106	107	108
Pet purchase, supplies, and medicines	100	91	92	110	99
Pet services	100	110	93	88	117
Veterinarian services	100	94	81	113	102
Toys, games, hobbies, and tricycles	100	87	112	87	120
Stamp and coin collecting	100	49	94	156	57
Playground equipment	100	210	69	77	77

	total consumer units	Northeast	Midwest	South	West
OTHER ENTERTAINMENT SUPPLIES, EQUIPMENT, AND SERVICES	100	94	101	70	152
Unmotored recreational vehicles	100	69	134	93	103
Motorized recreational vehicles	100	81	73	33	250
Rental of recreational vehicles	100	121	83	75	139
Docking and landing fees	100	90	159	55	123
Sports, recreation, exercise equipment	100	98	97	82	134
Athletic gear, game tables, exercise equipment	100	88	68	97	147
Bicycles	100	130	95	57	151
Camping equipment	100	119	74	44	203
Hunting and fishing equipment	100	71	149	102	71
Winter sports equipment	100	99	121	36	185
Water sports equipment	100	142	79	74	129
Other sports equipment	100	152	109	88	68
Global positioning system devices	100	94	80	62	187
Rental and repair of miscellaneous sports equipment	100	38	170	71	129
Photographic equipment, supplies, and services	100	105	108	78	123
Photo processing	100	89	149	71	107
Repair and rental of photographic equipment	100	174	72	26	186
Photographic equipment	100	111	103	73	133
Photographer fees	100	104	98	89	116
Fireworks	100	34	240	43	109
Pinball, electronic video games	100	18	157	25	233
Live entertainment for catered affairs	100	163	119	45	119
Rental of party supplies for catered affairs	100	227	80	47	102

Note: "–" means sample is too small to make a reliable estimate.
Source: Calculations by New Strategist based on the Bureau of Labor Statistics' 2011 Consumer Expenditure Survey

Table 3.23 Entertainment: Total spending by region, 2011

(total annual spending on entertainment, by region in which consumer unit lives, 2011; consumer units and dollars in thousands)

	total consumer units	Northeast	Midwest	South	West
Number of consumer units	122,287	22,538	27,107	44,901	27,741
Total spending of all consumer units	$6,078,260,661	$1,229,390,428	$1,279,221,075	$2,051,912,839	$1,518,692,974
Entertainment, total spending	314,516,050	59,319,565	67,906,288	105,507,921	81,845,105
FEES AND ADMISSIONS	72,671,495	15,994,317	15,806,363	19,900,572	20,999,660
Recreation expenses on trips	2,619,388	568,859	550,272	695,966	804,489
Social, recreation, health club membership	14,906,785	3,430,960	2,982,312	4,509,407	3,983,608
Fees for participant sports	12,194,460	2,188,440	2,705,550	3,154,744	4,175,298
Participant sports on trips	2,943,448	601,539	557,862	682,046	1,101,318
Movie, theater, amusement park, and other admissions	14,170,618	3,188,451	2,678,443	4,096,767	4,206,923
Movie and other admissions on trips	5,352,502	1,025,479	1,326,888	1,481,284	1,519,097
Admission to sports events	5,614,196	1,053,877	1,620,728	1,707,585	1,232,533
Admission to sports events on trips	1,782,944	341,676	442,115	492,564	505,996
Fees for recreational lessons	10,467,767	3,026,177	2,392,193	2,383,794	2,665,633
Other entertainment services on trips	2,619,388	568,859	550,272	695,966	804,489
AUDIO AND VISUAL EQUIPMENT AND SERVICES	119,423,038	23,271,387	25,364,562	44,183,931	26,613,328
Sound components, equipment, and accessories	3,287,075	670,055	618,582	1,276,984	721,266
Television sets	13,780,522	2,546,569	3,166,911	4,802,611	3,264,283
Cable and satellite television services	78,312,595	15,674,052	16,581,081	30,299,644	15,757,998
Miscellaneous video equipment	937,941	54,091	293,027	409,497	178,652
Satellite radio service	1,648,429	355,424	311,459	658,249	323,460
Online gaming services	377,867	64,459	109,241	85,312	119,009
VCRs and video disc players	1,059,005	143,567	284,352	372,678	257,991
Video cassettes, tapes, and discs	4,070,934	532,573	951,456	1,361,847	1,228,926
Video game software	243,351	37,864	34,697	127,519	42,721
Video game hardware and accessories	4,941,618	990,320	929,770	1,576,923	1,452,796
Streamed and downloaded video	479,365	88,124	93,248	110,456	187,807
Applications, games, ringtones for handheld devices	447,570	87,447	90,537	164,787	104,861
Repair of television, radio, and sound equipment	414,553	70,769	57,196	125,274	161,175
Rental of television sets	39,132	9,691	–	16,613	13,316
Personal digital audio players	1,258,333	247,242	298,990	363,698	347,872
Satellite dishes	128,401	13,297	43,100	31,880	40,224
Compact discs, records, and audio tapes	1,414,861	276,091	287,605	447,214	403,909
Streamed and downloaded audio	1,176,401	206,223	285,166	351,126	333,447
Rental of VCR, radio, and sound equipment	22,012	–	–	–	–
Musical instruments and accessories	2,763,686	782,069	349,138	796,095	836,669
Rental and repair of musical instruments	195,659	72,572	47,166	40,411	35,508
Rental of video cassettes, tapes, discs, films	2,267,201	318,687	489,010	718,865	740,962
Installation of television sets	103,944	25,468	30,902	16,613	31,347
PETS, TOYS, HOBBIES, AND PLAYGROUND EQUIPMENT	77,122,742	12,195,086	16,606,019	29,701,113	18,625,585
Pets	61,394,188	9,662,041	12,800,196	24,375,406	14,552,929
Pet food	22,347,949	2,871,341	5,244,662	8,759,287	5,467,751
Pet purchase, supplies, and medicines	17,230,238	2,890,724	3,530,416	6,934,061	3,874,863
Pet services	4,368,092	886,870	901,579	1,417,076	1,163,458
Veterinarian services	17,446,686	3,013,105	3,123,811	7,264,982	4,046,857
Toys, games, hobbies, and tricycles	14,065,451	2,251,772	3,484,605	4,500,427	3,837,690
Stamp and coin collecting	1,219,201	109,309	253,450	699,558	157,291
Playground equipment	443,902	171,965	67,768	126,172	77,675

	total consumer units	Northeast	Midwest	South	West
OTHER ENTERTAINMENT SUPPLIES, EQUIPMENT, AND SERVICES	**$45,298,773**	**$7,858,775**	**$10,129,073**	**$11,722,304**	**$15,606,532**
Unmotored recreational vehicles	**6,663,419**	**844,724**	**1,972,305**	**2,286,359**	**1,560,154**
Motorized recreational vehicles	**9,828,206**	**1,476,239**	**1,580,338**	**1,197,061**	**5,573,999**
Rental of recreational vehicles	**670,133**	**149,202**	**123,608**	**185,441**	**211,386**
Docking and landing fees	**873,129**	**145,370**	**308,478**	**176,012**	**243,011**
Sports, recreation, exercise equipment	**17,765,855**	**3,207,834**	**3,828,322**	**5,356,689**	**5,390,076**
Athletic gear, game tables, exercise equipment	6,422,513	1,044,411	967,991	2,286,359	2,137,999
Bicycles	2,680,531	640,305	565,723	556,772	917,395
Camping equipment	1,723,024	378,188	284,352	277,039	793,670
Hunting and fishing equipment	4,042,808	530,770	1,334,478	1,517,654	650,526
Winter sports equipment	552,737	100,519	147,733	73,189	232,192
Water sports equipment	649,344	169,937	113,578	175,563	190,026
Other sports equipment	775,300	217,717	187,309	249,650	120,119
Global positioning system devices	600,429	103,900	106,259	137,397	254,940
Rental and repair of miscellaneous sports equipment	320,392	22,313	120,626	83,516	93,487
Photographic equipment, supplies, and services	**6,669,533**	**1,293,681**	**1,595,789**	**1,918,171**	**1,861,699**
Photo processing	1,090,800	179,402	360,794	285,121	265,759
Repair and rental of photographic equipment	52,583	16,904	8,403	4,939	22,193
Photographic equipment	3,282,183	671,182	748,695	873,773	988,412
Photographer fees	2,089,885	401,853	454,042	685,638	547,885
Fireworks	**238,460**	**15,100**	**126,861**	**37,717**	**59,088**
Pinball, electronic video games	**326,506**	**10,593**	**113,849**	**30,533**	**172,826**
Live entertainment for catered affairs	**804,648**	**242,284**	**212,248**	**132,009**	**217,212**
Rental of party supplies for catered affairs	**1,073,680**	**449,408**	**190,020**	**184,992**	**249,392**

Note: Numbers may not add to total because of rounding and missing subcategories. "–" means sample is too small to make a reliable estimate.
Source: Calculations by New Strategist based on the Bureau of Labor Statistics' 2011 Consumer Expenditure Survey

Table 3.24 Entertainment: Market shares by region, 2011

(percentage of total annual spending on entertainment accounted for by consumer units by region of residence, 2011)

	total consumer units	Northeast	Midwest	South	West
Share of total consumer units	100.0%	18.4%	22.2%	36.7%	22.7%
Share of total before-tax income	100.0	20.8	21.2	33.9	24.2
Share of total spending	100.0	20.2	21.0	33.8	25.0
Share of entertainment spending	100.0	18.9	21.6	33.5	26.0
FEES AND ADMISSIONS	100.0	22.0	21.8	27.4	28.9
Recreation expenses on trips	100.0	21.7	21.0	26.6	30.7
Social, recreation, health club membership	100.0	23.0	20.0	30.3	26.7
Fees for participant sports	100.0	17.9	22.2	25.9	34.2
Participant sports on trips	100.0	20.4	19.0	23.2	37.4
Movie, theater, amusement park, and other admissions	100.0	22.5	18.9	28.9	29.7
Movie and other admissions on trips	100.0	19.2	24.8	27.7	28.4
Admission to sports events	100.0	18.8	28.9	30.4	22.0
Admission to sports events on trips	100.0	19.2	24.8	27.6	28.4
Fees for recreational lessons	100.0	28.9	22.9	22.8	25.5
Other entertainment services on trips	100.0	21.7	21.0	26.6	30.7
AUDIO AND VISUAL EQUIPMENT AND SERVICES	100.0	19.5	21.2	37.0	22.3
Sound components, equipment, and accessories	100.0	20.4	18.8	38.8	21.9
Television sets	100.0	18.5	23.0	34.9	23.7
Cable and satellite television services	100.0	20.0	21.2	38.7	20.1
Miscellaneous video equipment	100.0	5.8	31.2	43.7	19.0
Satellite radio service	100.0	21.6	18.9	39.9	19.6
Online gaming services	100.0	17.1	28.9	22.6	31.5
VCRs and video disc players	100.0	13.6	26.9	35.2	24.4
Video cassettes, tapes, and discs	100.0	13.1	23.4	33.5	30.2
Video game software	100.0	15.6	14.3	52.4	17.6
Video game hardware and accessories	100.0	20.0	18.8	31.9	29.4
Streamed and downloaded video	100.0	18.4	19.5	23.0	39.2
Applications, games, ringtones for handheld devices	100.0	19.5	20.2	36.8	23.4
Repair of television, radio, and sound equipment	100.0	17.1	13.8	30.2	38.9
Rental of television sets	100.0	24.8	–	42.5	34.0
Personal digital audio players	100.0	19.6	23.8	28.9	27.6
Satellite dishes	100.0	10.4	33.6	24.8	31.3
Compact discs, records, and audio tapes	100.0	19.5	20.3	31.6	28.5
Streamed and downloaded audio	100.0	17.5	24.2	29.8	28.3
Rental of VCR, radio, and sound equipment	100.0	–	–	–	–
Musical instruments and accessories	100.0	28.3	12.6	28.8	30.3
Rental and repair of musical instruments	100.0	37.1	24.1	20.7	18.1
Rental of video cassettes, tapes, discs, films	100.0	14.1	21.6	31.7	32.7
Installation of television sets	100.0	24.5	29.7	16.0	30.2
PETS, TOYS, HOBBIES, AND PLAYGROUND EQUIPMENT	100.0	15.8	21.5	38.5	24.2
Pets	100.0	15.7	20.8	39.7	23.7
Pet food	100.0	12.8	23.5	39.2	24.5
Pet purchase, supplies, and medicines	100.0	16.8	20.5	40.2	22.5
Pet services	100.0	20.3	20.6	32.4	26.6
Veterinarian services	100.0	17.3	17.9	41.6	23.2
Toys, games, hobbies, and tricycles	100.0	16.0	24.8	32.0	27.3
Stamp and coin collecting	100.0	9.0	20.8	57.4	12.9
Playground equipment	100.0	38.7	15.3	28.4	17.5

	total consumer units	Northeast	Midwest	South	West
OTHER ENTERTAINMENT SUPPLIES, EQUIPMENT, AND SERVICES	**100.0%**	**17.3%**	**22.4%**	**25.9%**	**34.5%**
Unmotored recreational vehicles	**100.0**	**12.7**	**29.6**	**34.3**	**23.4**
Motorized recreational vehicles	**100.0**	**15.0**	**16.1**	**12.2**	**56.7**
Rental of recreational vehicles	**100.0**	**22.3**	**18.4**	**27.7**	**31.5**
Docking and landing fees	**100.0**	**16.6**	**35.3**	**20.2**	**27.8**
Sports, recreation, exercise equipment	**100.0**	**18.1**	**21.5**	**30.2**	**30.3**
Athletic gear, game tables, exercise equipment	100.0	16.3	15.1	35.6	33.3
Bicycles	100.0	23.9	21.1	20.8	34.2
Camping equipment	100.0	21.9	16.5	16.1	46.1
Hunting and fishing equipment	100.0	13.1	33.0	37.5	16.1
Winter sports equipment	100.0	18.2	26.7	13.2	42.0
Water sports equipment	100.0	26.2	17.5	27.0	29.3
Other sports equipment	100.0	28.1	24.2	32.2	15.5
Global positioning system devices	100.0	17.3	17.7	22.9	42.5
Rental and repair of miscellaneous sports equipment	100.0	7.0	37.6	26.1	29.2
Photographic equipment, supplies, and services	**100.0**	**19.4**	**23.9**	**28.8**	**27.9**
Photo processing	100.0	16.4	33.1	26.1	24.4
Repair and rental of photographic equipment	100.0	32.1	16.0	9.4	42.2
Photographic equipment	100.0	20.4	22.8	26.6	30.1
Photographer fees	100.0	19.2	21.7	32.8	26.2
Fireworks	**100.0**	**6.3**	**53.2**	**15.8**	**24.8**
Pinball, electronic video games	**100.0**	**3.2**	**34.9**	**9.4**	**52.9**
Live entertainment for catered affairs	**100.0**	**30.1**	**26.4**	**16.4**	**27.0**
Rental of party supplies for catered affairs	**100.0**	**41.9**	**17.7**	**17.2**	**23.2**

Note: Numbers may not add to total because of rounding. "–" means sample is too small to make a reliable estimate.
Source: Calculations by New Strategist based on the Bureau of Labor Statistics' 2011 Consumer Expenditure Survey

Table 3.25 Entertainment: Average spending by education, 2011

(average annual spending of consumer units on entertainment, by education of consumer unit reference person, 2011)

	total consumer units	less than high school graduate	high school graduate	some college	associate's degree	bachelor's degree or more total	bachelor's degree	graduate degree
Number of consumer units (in 000s)	122,287	16,146	30,810	25,361	12,912	37,058	23,578	13,480
Average number of persons per consumer unit	2.5	2.8	2.5	2.3	2.6	2.5	2.5	2.4
Average before-tax income of consumer units	$63,685.00	$32,564.00	$46,370.00	$52,965.00	$63,664.00	$98,983.00	$90,962.00	$113,013.00
Average spending of consumer units, total	49,704.88	29,950.97	39,704.28	45,355.33	50,819.44	68,902.95	65,051.01	75,731.40
Entertainment, average spending	**2,571.95**	**1,222.98**	**1,966.55**	**2,465.06**	**2,822.08**	**3,615.82**	**3,499.02**	**3,822.45**
FEES AND ADMISSIONS	**594.27**	**126.53**	**288.97**	**461.85**	**510.13**	**1,163.23**	**1,027.24**	**1,402.74**
Recreation expenses on trips	21.42	9.99	12.37	17.30	19.37	37.47	31.45	47.99
Social, recreation, health club membership	121.90	14.03	44.13	76.56	107.54	269.57	241.77	318.21
Fees for participant sports	99.72	18.51	74.99	65.23	68.69	181.50	173.73	196.70
Participant sports on trips	24.07	3.66	8.34	16.62	23.84	51.20	46.91	58.71
Movie, theater, amusement park, and other admissions	115.88	33.36	59.33	110.54	110.34	204.43	180.62	246.08
Movie and other admissions on trips	43.77	12.47	21.12	37.51	39.97	81.85	68.87	104.55
Admission to sports events	45.91	5.77	18.56	47.44	38.58	87.66	84.58	93.05
Admission to sports events on trips	14.58	4.16	7.04	12.49	13.31	27.25	22.90	34.85
Fees for recreational lessons	85.60	14.60	30.73	60.85	69.11	184.83	144.94	254.61
Other entertainment services on trips	21.42	9.99	12.37	17.30	19.37	37.47	31.45	47.99
AUDIO AND VISUAL EQUIPMENT AND SERVICES	**976.58**	**645.13**	**926.29**	**995.46**	**994.02**	**1,139.75**	**1,141.81**	**1,138.54**
Sound components, equipment, and accessories	26.88	8.72	12.79	24.35	28.29	46.37	34.28	70.60
Television sets	112.69	58.40	116.24	119.11	98.47	133.94	146.56	111.87
Cable and satellite television services	640.40	503.65	643.56	620.34	677.15	698.28	702.67	690.60
Miscellaneous video equipment	7.67	0.06	4.93	8.83	4.11	13.02	10.19	18.56
Satellite radio service	13.48	6.81	12.57	10.08	12.76	19.73	19.32	20.46
Online gaming services	3.09	1.20	1.89	4.15	5.14	3.47	3.80	2.89
VCRs and video disc players	8.66	3.04	6.01	11.33	9.72	11.11	13.12	7.59
Video cassettes, tapes, and discs	33.29	18.91	38.27	32.76	43.71	31.71	30.28	34.51
Video game software	1.99	0.37	3.18	2.90	0.51	1.53	2.01	0.60
Video game hardware and accessories	40.41	13.44	34.92	60.34	29.28	45.41	52.53	31.46
Streamed and downloaded video	3.92	0.84	1.23	4.37	5.74	6.56	5.54	8.34
Applications, games, ringtones for handheld devices	3.66	1.05	2.02	4.36	5.44	5.05	5.48	4.30
Repair of television, radio, and sound equipment	3.39	2.05	2.27	3.08	1.88	5.65	4.11	8.34
Rental of television sets	0.32	0.42	0.83	0.29	–	–	–	–
Personal digital audio players	10.29	3.42	7.73	14.94	10.99	11.97	11.85	12.18
Satellite dishes	1.05	0.39	0.89	0.85	0.53	1.78	1.44	2.39
Compact discs, records, and audio tapes	11.57	7.22	8.14	12.55	10.27	16.10	14.89	18.23
Streamed and downloaded audio	9.62	1.62	3.97	9.87	11.22	17.07	16.27	18.45
Rental of VCR, radio, and sound equipment	0.18	0.03	0.13	0.22	0.70	0.09	0.05	0.18
Musical instruments and accessories	22.60	4.56	7.97	27.00	17.45	41.42	40.41	43.18
Rental and repair of musical instruments	1.60	0.12	0.48	2.06	1.37	2.94	1.06	6.24
Rental of video cassettes, tapes, discs, films	18.54	7.99	15.12	19.75	18.72	25.10	24.72	25.78
Installation of television sets	0.85	0.70	0.46	1.26	0.38	1.12	0.90	1.51
PETS, TOYS, HOBBIES, AND PLAYGROUND EQUIPMENT	**630.67**	**329.73**	**528.55**	**597.66**	**696.16**	**829.32**	**839.00**	**810.62**
Pets	**502.05**	**254.65**	**404.94**	**480.14**	**574.02**	**667.22**	**683.35**	**635.54**
Pet food	182.75	128.94	164.56	186.47	198.64	209.54	211.95	204.82
Pet purchase, supplies, and medicines	140.90	84.82	114.12	142.15	190.54	169.44	172.17	164.68
Pet services	35.72	9.63	21.48	26.99	41.23	62.99	59.90	68.39
Veterinarian services	142.67	31.26	104.76	124.53	143.60	225.24	239.33	197.65
Toys, games, hobbies, and tricycles	**115.02**	**69.14**	**99.33**	**112.89**	**111.82**	**146.78**	**138.77**	**162.45**
Stamp and coin collecting	**9.97**	**0.95**	**21.98**	**3.15**	**6.19**	**9.91**	**12.04**	**6.18**
Playground equipment	**3.63**	**5.00**	**2.30**	**1.49**	**4.14**	**5.42**	**4.83**	**6.43**

	total consumer units	less than high school graduate	high school graduate	some college	associate's degree	bachelor's degree or more		
						total	bachelor's degree	graduate degree
OTHER ENTERTAINMENT SUPPLIES, EQUIPMENT, AND SERVICES	**$370.43**	**$121.59**	**$222.74**	**$410.08**	**$621.77**	**$483.52**	**$490.98**	**$470.56**
Unmotored recreational vehicles	**54.49**	**8.21**	**33.78**	**44.63**	**76.29**	**91.03**	**104.12**	**68.14**
Motorized recreational vehicles	**80.37**	**8.09**	**30.53**	**126.94**	**295.88**	**46.33**	**48.97**	**41.70**
Rental of recreational vehicles	**5.48**	**0.51**	**1.65**	**5.48**	**4.89**	**11.02**	**10.01**	**12.79**
Docking and landing fees	**7.14**	**0.62**	**4.77**	**4.09**	**3.93**	**15.14**	**15.18**	**15.07**
Sports, recreation, exercise equipment	**145.28**	**83.22**	**92.15**	**162.60**	**146.21**	**201.06**	**204.59**	**194.63**
Athletic gear, game tables, exercise equipment	52.52	17.78	35.22	71.83	31.74	73.18	74.48	70.62
Bicycles	21.92	9.46	16.96	17.99	18.52	35.34	34.17	37.39
Camping equipment	14.09	32.24	6.73	16.40	14.93	11.41	11.79	10.69
Hunting and fishing equipment	33.06	18.76	17.16	27.51	66.51	43.75	45.81	39.72
Winter sports equipment	4.52	0.09	1.65	4.62	3.76	9.05	10.55	6.42
Water sports equipment	5.31	1.33	5.15	4.32	2.54	8.81	11.53	4.05
Other sports equipment	6.34	2.50	6.86	7.43	4.91	7.32	6.62	8.54
Global positioning system devices	4.91	–	0.76	9.95	–	8.31	5.75	13.31
Rental and repair of miscellaneous sports equipment	2.62	1.05	1.67	2.57	3.31	3.88	3.87	3.90
Photographic equipment, supplies, and services	**54.54**	**14.07**	**36.07**	**51.30**	**58.76**	**88.22**	**79.34**	**103.67**
Photo processing	8.92	2.49	6.14	7.54	8.71	15.06	13.24	18.24
Repair and rental of photographic equipment	0.43	0.76	0.56	0.11	0.09	0.51	0.46	0.60
Photographic equipment	26.84	7.84	18.96	27.16	31.47	39.84	38.79	41.68
Photographer fees	17.09	2.51	9.76	14.79	17.81	30.85	24.48	42.00
Fireworks	**1.95**	**0.87**	**2.18**	**0.52**	**4.46**	**2.30**	**2.38**	**2.13**
Pinball, electronic video games	**2.67**	**1.77**	**0.77**	**6.16**	**3.79**	**1.89**	**0.38**	**4.84**
Live entertainment for catered affairs	**6.58**	**0.21**	**7.28**	**1.69**	**13.84**	**9.57**	**10.90**	**7.25**
Rental of party supplies for catered affairs	**8.78**	**3.95**	**10.48**	**3.20**	**7.51**	**13.74**	**12.20**	**16.42**

Note: Subcategories may not add to total because some are not shown. "–" means sample is too small to make a reliable estimate.
Source: Bureau of Labor Statistics, unpublished data from the 2011 Consumer Expenditure Survey

Table 3.26 Entertainment: Indexed spending by education, 2011

(indexed average annual spending of consumer units on entertainment by education of consumer unit reference person, 2011; index definition: an index of 100 is the average for all consumer units; an index of 125 means that spending by consumer units in that group is 25 percent above the average for all consumer units; an index of 75 indicates spending that is 25 percent below the average for all consumer units)

	total consumer units	less than high school graduate	high school graduate	some college	associate's degree	bachelor's degree or more		
						total	bachelor's degree	graduate degree
Average spending of consumer units, total	$49,705	$29,951	$39,704	$45,355	$50,819	$68,903	$65,051	$75,731
Average spending of consumer units, index	100	60	80	91	102	139	131	15
Entertainment, spending index	100	48	76	96	110	141	136	149
FEES AND ADMISSIONS	100	21	49	78	86	196	173	236
Recreation expenses on trips	100	47	58	81	90	175	147	224
Social, recreation, health club membership	100	12	36	63	88	221	198	261
Fees for participant sports	100	19	75	65	69	182	174	197
Participant sports on trips	100	15	35	69	99	213	195	244
Movie, theater, amusement park, and other admissions	100	29	51	95	95	176	156	212
Movie and other admissions on trips	100	28	48	86	91	187	157	239
Admission to sports events	100	13	40	103	84	191	184	203
Admission to sports events on trips	100	29	48	86	91	187	157	239
Fees for recreational lessons	100	17	36	71	81	216	169	297
Other entertainment services on trips	100	47	58	81	90	175	147	224
AUDIO AND VISUAL EQUIPMENT AND SERVICES	100	66	95	102	102	117	117	117
Sound components, equipment, and accessories	100	32	48	91	105	173	128	263
Television sets	100	52	103	106	87	119	130	99
Cable and satellite television services	100	79	100	97	106	109	110	108
Miscellaneous video equipment	100	1	64	115	54	170	133	242
Satellite radio service	100	51	93	75	95	146	143	152
Online gaming services	100	39	61	134	166	112	123	94
VCRs and video disc players	100	35	69	131	112	128	152	88
Video cassettes, tapes, and discs	100	57	115	98	131	95	91	104
Video game software	100	19	160	146	26	77	101	30
Video game hardware and accessories	100	33	86	149	72	112	130	78
Streamed and downloaded video	100	21	31	111	146	167	141	213
Applications, games, ringtones for handheld devices	100	29	55	119	149	138	150	117
Repair of television, radio, and sound equipment	100	60	67	91	55	167	121	246
Rental of television sets	100	131	259	91	–	–	–	–
Personal digital audio players	100	33	75	145	107	116	115	118
Satellite dishes	100	37	85	81	50	170	137	228
Compact discs, records, and audio tapes	100	62	70	108	89	139	129	158
Streamed and downloaded audio	100	17	41	103	117	177	169	192
Rental of VCR, radio, and sound equipment	100	17	72	122	389	50	28	100
Musical instruments and accessories	100	20	35	119	77	183	179	191
Rental and repair of musical instruments	100	8	30	129	86	184	66	390
Rental of video cassettes, tapes, discs, films	100	43	82	107	101	135	133	139
Installation of television sets	100	82	54	148	45	132	106	178
PETS, TOYS, HOBBIES, AND PLAYGROUND EQUIPMENT	100	52	84	95	110	131	133	129
Pets	100	51	81	96	114	133	136	127
Pet food	100	71	90	102	109	115	116	112
Pet purchase, supplies, and medicines	100	60	81	101	135	120	122	117
Pet services	100	27	60	76	115	176	168	191
Veterinarian services	100	22	73	87	101	158	168	139
Toys, games, hobbies, and tricycles	100	60	86	98	97	128	121	141
Stamp and coin collecting	100	10	220	32	62	99	121	62
Playground equipment	100	138	63	41	114	149	133	177

	total consumer units	less than high school graduate	high school graduate	some college	associate's degree	bachelor's degree or more		
						total	bachelor's degree	graduate degree
OTHER ENTERTAINMENT SUPPLIES, EQUIPMENT, AND SERVICES	**100**	**33**	**60**	**111**	**168**	**131**	**133**	**127**
Unmotored recreational vehicles	**100**	**15**	**62**	**82**	**140**	**167**	**191**	**125**
Motorized recreational vehicles	**100**	**10**	**38**	**158**	**368**	**58**	**61**	**52**
Rental of recreational vehicles	**100**	**9**	**30**	**100**	**89**	**201**	**183**	**233**
Docking and landing fees	**100**	**9**	**67**	**57**	**55**	**212**	**213**	**211**
Sports, recreation, exercise equipment	**100**	**57**	**63**	**112**	**101**	**138**	**141**	**134**
Athletic gear, game tables, exercise equipment	100	34	67	137	60	139	142	134
Bicycles	100	43	77	82	84	161	156	171
Camping equipment	100	229	48	116	106	81	84	76
Hunting and fishing equipment	100	57	52	83	201	132	139	120
Winter sports equipment	100	2	37	102	83	200	233	142
Water sports equipment	100	25	97	81	48	166	217	76
Other sports equipment	100	39	108	117	77	115	104	135
Global positioning system devices	100	–	15	203	–	169	117	271
Rental and repair of miscellaneous sports equipment	100	40	64	98	126	148	148	149
Photographic equipment, supplies, and services	**100**	**26**	**66**	**94**	**108**	**162**	**145**	**190**
Photo processing	100	28	69	85	98	169	148	204
Repair and rental of photographic equipment	100	177	130	26	21	119	107	140
Photographic equipment	100	29	71	101	117	148	145	155
Photographer fees	100	15	57	87	104	181	143	246
Fireworks	**100**	**45**	**112**	**27**	**229**	**118**	**122**	**109**
Pinball, electronic video games	**100**	**66**	**29**	**231**	**142**	**71**	**14**	**181**
Live entertainment for catered affairs	**100**	**3**	**111**	**26**	**210**	**145**	**166**	**110**
Rental of party supplies for catered affairs	**100**	**45**	**119**	**36**	**86**	**156**	**139**	**187**

Note: "–" means sample is too small to make a reliable estimate
Source: Calculations by New Strategist based on the Bureau of Labor Statistics' 2011 Consumer Expenditure Survey

Table 3.27 Entertainment: Total spending by education, 2011

(total annual spending on entertainment, by consumer unit educational attainment group, 2011; consumer units and dollars in thousands)

	total consumer units	less than high school graduate	high school graduate	some college	associate's degree	bachelor's degree or more total	bachelor's degree	graduate degree
Number of consumer units	122,287	16,146	30,810	25,361	12,912	37,058	23,578	13,480
Total spending of all consumer units	$6,078,260,661	$483,588,362	$1,223,288,867	$1,150,256,524	$656,180,609	$2,553,405,521	$1,533,772,714	$1,020,859,272
Entertainment, total spending	314,516,050	19,746,235	60,589,406	62,516,387	36,438,697	133,995,058	82,499,894	51,526,626
FEES AND ADMISSIONS	72,671,495	2,042,953	8,903,166	11,712,978	6,586,799	43,106,977	24,220,265	18,908,935
Recreation expenses on trips	2,619,388	161,299	381,120	438,745	250,105	1,388,563	741,528	646,905
Social, recreation, health club membership	14,906,785	226,528	1,359,645	1,941,638	1,388,556	9,989,725	5,700,453	4,289,471
Fees for participant sports	12,194,460	298,862	2,310,442	1,654,298	886,925	6,726,027	4,096,206	2,651,516
Participant sports on trips	2,943,448	59,094	256,955	421,500	307,822	1,897,370	1,106,044	791,411
Movie, theater, amusement park, and other admissions	14,170,618	538,631	1,827,957	2,803,405	1,424,710	7,575,767	4,258,658	3,317,158
Movie and other admissions on trips	5,352,502	201,341	650,707	951,291	516,093	3,033,197	1,623,817	1,409,334
Admission to sports events	5,614,196	93,162	571,834	1,203,126	498,145	3,248,504	1,994,227	1,254,314
Admission to sports events on trips	1,782,944	67,167	216,902	316,759	171,859	1,009,831	539,936	469,778
Fees for recreational lessons	10,467,767	235,732	946,791	1,543,217	892,348	6,849,430	3,417,395	3,432,143
Other entertainment services on trips	2,619,388	161,299	381,120	438,745	250,105	1,388,563	741,528	646,905
AUDIO AND VISUAL EQUIPMENT AND SERVICES	119,423,038	10,416,269	28,538,995	25,245,861	12,834,786	42,236,856	26,921,596	15,347,519
Sound components, equipment, and accessories	3,287,075	140,793	394,060	617,540	365,280	1,718,379	808,254	951,688
Television sets	13,780,522	942,926	3,581,354	3,020,749	1,271,445	4,963,549	3,455,592	1,508,008
Cable and satellite television services	78,312,595	8,131,933	19,828,084	15,732,443	8,743,361	25,876,860	16,567,553	9,309,288
Miscellaneous video equipment	937,941	969	151,893	223,938	53,068	482,495	240,260	250,189
Satellite radio service	1,648,429	109,954	387,282	255,639	164,757	731,154	455,527	275,801
Online gaming services	377,867	19,375	58,231	105,248	66,368	128,591	89,596	38,957
VCRs and video disc players	1,059,005	49,084	185,168	287,340	125,505	411,714	309,343	102,313
Video cassettes, tapes, and discs	4,070,934	305,321	1,179,099	830,826	564,384	1,175,109	713,942	465,195
Video game software	243,351	5,974	97,976	73,547	6,585	56,699	47,392	8,088
Video game hardware and accessories	4,941,618	217,002	1,075,885	1,530,283	378,063	1,682,804	1,238,552	424,081
Streamed and downloaded video	479,365	13,563	37,896	110,828	74,115	243,100	130,622	112,423
Applications, games, ringtones for handheld devices	447,570	16,953	62,236	110,574	70,241	187,143	129,207	57,964
Repair of television, radio, and sound equipment	414,553	33,099	69,939	78,112	24,275	209,378	96,906	112,423
Rental of television sets	39,132	6,781	25,572	7,355	–	–	–	–
Personal digital audio players	1,258,333	55,219	238,161	378,893	141,903	443,584	279,399	164,186
Satellite dishes	128,401	6,297	27,421	21,557	6,843	65,963	33,952	32,217
Compact discs, records, and audio tapes	1,414,861	116,574	250,793	318,281	132,606	596,634	351,076	245,740
Streamed and downloaded audio	1,176,401	26,157	122,316	250,313	144,873	632,580	383,614	248,706
Rental of VCR, radio, and sound equipment	22,012	484	4,005	5,579	9,038	3,335	1,179	2,426
Musical instruments and accessories	2,763,686	73,626	245,556	684,747	225,314	1,534,942	952,787	582,066
Rental and repair of musical instruments	195,659	1,938	14,789	52,244	17,689	108,951	24,993	84,115
Rental of video cassettes, tapes, discs, films	2,267,201	129,007	465,847	500,880	241,713	930,156	582,848	347,514
Installation of television sets	103,944	11,302	14,173	31,955	4,907	41,505	21,220	20,355
PETS, TOYS, HOBBIES, AND PLAYGROUND EQUIPMENT	77,122,742	5,323,821	16,284,626	15,157,255	8,988,818	30,732,941	19,781,942	10,927,158
Pets	61,394,188	4,111,579	12,476,201	12,176,831	7,411,746	24,725,839	16,112,026	8,567,079
Pet food	22,347,949	2,081,865	5,070,094	4,729,066	2,564,840	7,765,133	4,997,357	2,760,974
Pet purchase, supplies, and medicines	17,230,238	1,369,504	3,516,037	3,605,066	2,460,252	6,279,108	4,059,424	2,219,886
Pet services	4,368,092	155,486	661,799	684,493	532,362	2,334,283	1,412,322	921,897
Veterinarian services	17,446,686	504,724	3,227,656	3,158,205	1,854,163	8,346,944	5,642,923	2,664,322
Toys, games, hobbies, and tricycles	14,065,451	1,116,334	3,060,357	2,863,003	1,443,820	5,439,373	3,271,919	2,189,826
Stamp and coin collecting	1,219,201	15,339	677,204	79,887	79,925	367,245	283,879	83,306
Playground equipment	443,902	80,730	70,863	37,788	53,456	200,854	113,882	86,676

	total consumer units	less than high school graduate	high school graduate	some college	associate's degree	bachelor's degree or more		
						total	bachelor's degree	graduate degree
OTHER ENTERTAINMENT SUPPLIES, EQUIPMENT, AND SERVICES	$45,298,773	$1,963,192	$6,862,619	$10,400,039	$8,028,294	$17,918,284	$11,576,326	$6,343,149
Unmotored recreational vehicles	6,663,419	132,559	1,040,762	1,131,861	985,056	3,373,390	2,454,941	918,527
Motorized recreational vehicles	9,828,206	130,621	940,629	3,219,325	3,820,403	1,716,897	1,154,615	562,116
Rental of recreational vehicles	670,133	8,234	50,837	138,978	63,140	408,379	236,016	172,409
Docking and landing fees	873,129	10,011	146,964	103,726	50,744	561,058	357,914	203,144
Sports, recreation, exercise equipment	17,765,855	1,343,670	2,839,142	4,123,699	1,887,864	7,450,881	4,823,823	2,623,612
Athletic gear, game tables, exercise equipment	6,422,513	287,076	1,085,128	1,821,681	409,827	2,711,904	1,756,089	951,958
Bicycles	2,680,531	152,741	522,538	456,244	239,130	1,309,630	805,660	504,017
Camping equipment	1,723,024	520,547	207,351	415,920	192,776	422,832	277,985	144,101
Hunting and fishing equipment	4,042,808	302,899	528,700	697,681	858,777	1,621,288	1,080,108	535,426
Winter sports equipment	552,737	1,453	50,837	117,168	48,549	335,375	248,748	86,542
Water sports equipment	649,344	21,474	158,672	109,560	32,796	326,481	271,854	54,594
Other sports equipment	775,300	40,365	211,357	188,432	63,398	271,265	156,086	115,119
Global positioning system devices	600,429	–	23,416	252,342	–	307,952	135,574	179,419
Rental and repair of miscellaneous sports equipment	320,392	16,953	51,453	65,178	42,739	143,785	91,247	52,572
Photographic equipment, supplies, and services	6,669,533	227,174	1,111,317	1,301,019	758,709	3,269,257	1,870,679	1,397,472
Photo processing	1,090,800	40,204	189,173	191,222	112,464	558,093	312,173	245,875
Repair and rental of photographic equipment	52,583	12,271	17,254	2,790	1,162	18,900	10,846	8,088
Photographic equipment	3,282,183	126,585	584,158	688,805	406,341	1,476,391	914,591	561,846
Photographer fees	2,089,885	40,526	300,706	375,089	229,963	1,143,239	577,189	566,160
Fireworks	238,460	14,047	67,166	13,188	57,588	85,233	56,116	28,712
Pinball, electronic video games	326,506	28,578	23,724	156,224	48,936	70,040	8,960	65,243
Live entertainment for catered affairs	804,648	3,391	224,297	42,860	178,702	354,645	257,000	97,730
Rental of party supplies for catered affairs	1,073,680	63,777	322,889	81,155	96,969	509,177	287,652	221,342

Note: Numbers may not add to total because of rounding and missing subcategories. "–" means sample is too small to make a reliable estimate.
Source: Calculations by New Strategist based on the Bureau of Labor Statistics' 2011 Consumer Expenditure Survey

Table 3.28 Entertainment: Market shares by education, 2011

(percentage of total annual spending on entertainment accounted for by consumer unit educational attainment groups, 2011)

	total consumer units	less than high school graduate	high school graduate	some college	associate's degree	bachelor's degree or more total	bachelor's degree	graduate degree
Share of total consumer units	100.0%	13.2%	25.2%	20.7%	10.6%	30.3%	19.3%	11.0%
Share of total before-tax income	100.0	6.8	18.3	17.2	10.6	47.1	27.5	19.6
Share of total spending	100.0	8.0	20.1	18.9	10.8	42.0	25.2	16.8
Share of entertainment spending	100.0	6.3	19.3	19.9	11.6	42.6	26.2	16.4
FEES AND ADMISSIONS	100.0	2.8	12.3	16.1	9.1	59.3	33.3	26.0
Recreation expenses on trips	100.0	6.2	14.5	16.7	9.5	53.0	28.3	24.7
Social, recreation, health club membership	100.0	1.5	9.1	13.0	9.3	67.0	38.2	28.8
Fees for participant sports	100.0	2.5	18.9	13.6	7.3	55.2	33.6	21.7
Participant sports on trips	100.0	2.0	8.7	14.3	10.5	64.5	37.6	26.9
Movie, theater, amusement park, and other admissions	100.0	3.8	12.9	19.8	10.1	53.5	30.1	23.4
Movie and other admissions on trips	100.0	3.8	12.2	17.8	9.6	56.7	30.3	26.3
Admission to sports events	100.0	1.7	10.2	21.4	8.9	57.9	35.5	22.3
Admission to sports events on trips	100.0	3.8	12.2	17.8	9.6	56.6	30.3	26.3
Fees for recreational lessons	100.0	2.3	9.0	14.7	8.5	65.4	32.6	32.8
Other entertainment services on trips	100.0	6.2	14.5	16.7	9.5	53.0	28.3	24.7
AUDIO AND VISUAL EQUIPMENT AND SERVICES	100.0	8.7	23.9	21.1	10.7	35.4	22.5	12.9
Sound components, equipment, and accessories	100.0	4.3	12.0	18.8	11.1	52.3	24.6	29.0
Television sets	100.0	6.8	26.0	21.9	9.2	36.0	25.1	10.9
Cable and satellite television services	100.0	10.4	25.3	20.1	11.2	33.0	21.2	11.9
Miscellaneous video equipment	100.0	0.1	16.2	23.9	5.7	51.4	25.6	26.7
Satellite radio service	100.0	6.7	23.5	15.5	10.0	44.4	27.6	16.7
Online gaming services	100.0	5.1	15.4	27.9	17.6	34.0	23.7	10.3
VCRs and video disc players	100.0	4.6	17.5	27.1	11.9	38.9	29.2	9.7
Video cassettes, tapes, and discs	100.0	7.5	29.0	20.4	13.9	28.9	17.5	11.4
Video game software	100.0	2.5	40.3	30.2	2.7	23.3	19.5	3.3
Video game hardware and accessories	100.0	4.4	21.8	31.0	7.7	34.1	25.1	8.6
Streamed and downloaded video	100.0	2.8	7.9	23.1	15.5	50.7	27.2	23.5
Applications, games, ringtones for handheld devices	100.0	3.8	13.9	24.7	15.7	41.8	28.9	13.0
Repair of television, radio, and sound equipment	100.0	8.0	16.9	18.8	5.9	50.5	23.4	27.1
Rental of television sets	100.0	17.3	65.3	18.8	–	–	–	–
Personal digital audio players	100.0	4.4	18.9	30.1	11.3	35.3	22.2	13.0
Satellite dishes	100.0	4.9	21.4	16.8	5.3	51.4	26.4	25.1
Compact discs, records, and audio tapes	100.0	8.2	17.7	22.5	9.4	42.2	24.8	17.4
Streamed and downloaded audio	100.0	2.2	10.4	21.3	12.3	53.8	32.6	21.1
Rental of VCR, radio, and sound equipment	100.0	2.2	18.2	25.3	41.1	15.2	5.4	11.0
Musical instruments and accessories	100.0	2.7	8.9	24.8	8.2	55.5	34.5	21.1
Rental and repair of musical instruments	100.0	1.0	7.6	26.7	9.0	55.7	12.8	43.0
Rental of video cassettes, tapes, discs, films	100.0	5.7	20.5	22.1	10.7	41.0	25.7	15.3
Installation of television sets	100.0	10.9	13.6	30.7	4.7	39.9	20.4	19.6
PETS, TOYS, HOBBIES, AND PLAYGROUND EQUIPMENT	100.0	6.9	21.1	19.7	11.7	39.8	25.6	14.2
Pets	100.0	6.7	20.3	19.8	12.1	40.3	26.2	14.0
Pet food	100.0	9.3	22.7	21.2	11.5	34.7	22.4	12.4
Pet purchase, supplies, and medicines	100.0	7.9	20.4	20.9	14.3	36.4	23.6	12.9
Pet services	100.0	3.6	15.2	15.7	12.2	53.4	32.3	21.1
Veterinarian services	100.0	2.9	18.5	18.1	10.6	47.8	32.3	15.3
Toys, games, hobbies, and tricycles	100.0	7.9	21.8	20.4	10.3	38.7	23.3	15.6
Stamp and coin collecting	100.0	1.3	55.5	6.6	6.6	30.1	23.3	6.8
Playground equipment	100.0	18.2	16.0	8.5	12.0	45.2	25.7	19.5

	total consumer units	less than high school graduate	high school graduate	some college	associate's degree	bachelor's degree or more		
						total	bachelor's degree	graduate degree
OTHER ENTERTAINMENT SUPPLIES, EQUIPMENT, AND SERVICES	**100.0%**	**4.3%**	**15.1%**	**23.0%**	**17.7%**	**39.6%**	**25.6%**	**14.0%**
Unmotored recreational vehicles	**100.0**	**2.0**	**15.6**	**17.0**	**14.8**	**50.6**	**36.8**	**13.8**
Motorized recreational vehicles	**100.0**	**1.3**	**9.6**	**32.8**	**38.9**	**17.5**	**11.7**	**5.7**
Rental of recreational vehicles	**100.0**	**1.2**	**7.6**	**20.7**	**9.4**	**60.9**	**35.2**	**25.7**
Docking and landing fees	**100.0**	**1.1**	**16.8**	**11.9**	**5.8**	**64.3**	**41.0**	**23.3**
Sports, recreation, exercise equipment	**100.0**	**7.6**	**16.0**	**23.2**	**10.6**	**41.9**	**27.2**	**14.8**
Athletic gear, game tables, exercise equipment	100.0	4.5	16.9	28.4	6.4	42.2	27.3	14.8
Bicycles	100.0	5.7	19.5	17.0	8.9	48.9	30.1	18.8
Camping equipment	100.0	30.2	12.0	24.1	11.2	24.5	16.1	8.4
Hunting and fishing equipment	100.0	7.5	13.1	17.3	21.2	40.1	26.7	13.2
Winter sports equipment	100.0	0.3	9.2	21.2	8.8	60.7	45.0	15.7
Water sports equipment	100.0	3.3	24.4	16.9	5.1	50.3	41.9	8.4
Other sports equipment	100.0	5.2	27.3	24.3	8.2	35.0	20.1	14.8
Global positioning system devices	100.0	–	3.9	42.0	–	51.3	22.6	29.9
Rental and repair of miscellaneous sports equipment	100.0	5.3	16.1	20.3	13.3	44.9	28.5	16.4
Photographic equipment, supplies, and services	**100.0**	**3.4**	**16.7**	**19.5**	**11.4**	**49.0**	**28.0**	**21.0**
Photo processing	100.0	3.7	17.3	17.5	10.3	51.2	28.6	22.5
Repair and rental of photographic equipment	100.0	23.3	32.8	5.3	2.2	35.9	20.6	15.4
Photographic equipment	100.0	3.9	17.8	21.0	12.4	45.0	27.9	17.1
Photographer fees	100.0	1.9	14.4	17.9	11.0	54.7	27.6	27.1
Fireworks	**100.0**	**5.9**	**28.2**	**5.5**	**24.1**	**35.7**	**23.5**	**12.0**
Pinball, electronic video games	**100.0**	**8.8**	**7.3**	**47.8**	**15.0**	**21.5**	**2.7**	**20.0**
Live entertainment for catered affairs	**100.0**	**0.4**	**27.9**	**5.3**	**22.2**	**44.1**	**31.9**	**12.1**
Rental of party supplies for catered affairs	**100.0**	**5.9**	**30.1**	**7.6**	**9.0**	**47.4**	**26.8**	**20.6**

Note: Numbers may not add to total because of rounding. "–" means sample is too small to make a reliable estimate.
Source: Calculations by New Strategist based on the Bureau of Labor Statistics' 2011 Consumer Expenditure Survey

CHAPTER 4

Spending on Financial Products and Services, 2011

Trends in spending on financial products and services have been mixed over the past decade. Spending on cash contributions (a category that includes child support as well as gifts to churches and charities) rose by an inflation-adjusted 34 percent between 2000 and 2006, then fell 17 percent between 2006 and 2011 as households reacted to the economic downturn. Spending on life and other personal insurance fell 31 percent between 2000 and 2006, and decreased another 12 percent between 2006 and 2011. The average household spent much less on taxes in 2011 than in 2000. Because of changes in survey methodology in mid-decade, it is impossible to compare spending on pensions and Social Security.

Households headed by 45-to-54-year-olds spend more than other age groups on financial products and services—$947 in 2011. Households in that age group spend more than others on occupational expenses and credit card memberships. Householders aged 65 or older spend the most on cash contributions overall, but householders aged 45 to 54 spend the most on support for college students and those aged 35 to 44 spend the most on child support. Householders under age 25 spend far less than average on most of the items covered in this section. One of the exceptions is dating services.

Households with incomes of $100,000 or more represent just 18 percent of consumer units but account for 27 percent of spending on legal fees, 39 percent of spending on accounting fees, 64 percent of spending on support for college students, and 77 percent of alimony payments. These affluent households account for 59 percent of contributions to charities, for 61 percent of contributions to educational institutions, and for 60 percent of contributions to political organizations.

Married couples without children at home spend more than other household types on cash contributions overall. In particular, they are the biggest spenders on contributions to charities as well as religious and political organizations, and on gifts of cash, stocks, bonds, and mutual funds to members of other households (primarily their children and grandchildren). Representing 21 percent of all households, these empty-nesters account for 31 percent of spending to support college students. Single parents spend more than average on legal fees. Single-person households spend more than average on dating services.

Blacks and Hispanics spend less than average on nearly every financial product and service. Non-Hispanic white households spend more than average on most items, and Asians spend more on many—including cash gifts to members of other households.

Households in the West spend 17 percent more than the average household on financial products and services, including 45 percent more on dating services. Northeastern householders pay more than others on legal fees, accounting fees, and contributions to charities, among other things. Households in the South spend 19 percent more than average on contributions to religious organization. Households in the Midwest spend the most on vacation clubs.

Households headed by college graduates account for 30 percent of households, but they provide 65 percent of cash gifts to political organizations and 77 percent of cash contributions to educational institutions. Households headed by college graduates spend nearly twice the average on support for college students.

Table 4.1 Financial: Average spending by age, 2011

(average annual spending of consumer units on financial products and services, cash contributions, and miscellaneous items, by age of consumer unit reference person, 2011)

	total consumer units	under 25	25 to 34	35 to 44	45 to 54	55 to 64	65 to 74	75+
Number of consumer units (in 000s)	122,287	7,743	20,463	21,699	24,821	21,688	14,079	11,794
Average number of persons per consumer unit	2.5	2.1	2.9	3.3	2.8	2.1	1.9	1.6
Average before-tax income of consumer units	$63,685.00	$27,514.00	$58,179.00	$77,376.00	$78,519.00	$75,517.00	$52,521.00	$32,144.00
Average spending of consumer units, total	49,704.88	29,911.52	48,097.39	57,271.07	58,050.42	53,615.86	44,645.56	32,688.34
FINANCIAL PRODUCTS AND SERVICES	**774.92**	**285.30**	**606.47**	**780.80**	**947.01**	**930.63**	**820.59**	**674.09**
Miscellaneous fees	1.44	–	0.77	1.47	2.71	1.93	0.08	1.44
Lottery and gambling losses	56.00	8.91	65.72	23.40	50.96	85.29	101.10	32.12
Legal fees	158.75	47.92	103.07	145.53	229.25	162.82	231.40	109.82
Funeral expenses	67.67	0.07	12.54	33.50	57.65	104.88	80.74	207.59
Safe deposit box rental	3.27	0.03	0.60	1.65	2.32	4.98	6.63	7.84
Checking accounts, other bank service charges	22.58	18.17	24.29	29.16	26.54	21.44	19.27	8.09
Cemetery lots, vaults, and maintenance fees	8.54	0.47	–	2.91	3.46	16.86	10.56	32.05
Accounting fees	62.95	17.83	30.93	65.72	70.84	72.47	92.16	74.03
Miscellaneous personal services	51.94	81.14	41.80	77.18	60.71	39.60	22.78	43.15
Dating services	0.44	0.87	0.63	0.21	0.89	0.34	–	–
Finance charges, except mortgage and vehicles	154.94	86.86	177.54	241.60	196.76	149.53	64.76	30.59
Occupational expenses	47.22	11.68	49.81	52.55	70.72	61.62	23.64	8.50
Expenses for other properties	122.10	6.75	87.39	89.01	152.98	182.46	150.59	108.96
Credit card memberships	2.35	0.25	1.65	2.31	3.75	2.69	2.46	1.36
Shopping club membership fees	9.27	3.75	7.14	9.19	10.95	10.87	12.06	6.97
Vacation clubs	4.86	0.60	2.14	4.73	4.55	12.81	2.34	1.61
CASH CONTRIBUTIONS	**1,720.87**	**366.52**	**1,129.84**	**1,569.64**	**1,721.94**	**2,111.56**	**2,526.32**	**2,231.47**
Support for college students	117.18	4.67	18.64	64.65	225.78	202.18	121.15	69.06
Alimony expenditures	47.29	34.83	60.61	31.58	25.34	43.59	135.58	8.90
Child support expenditures	224.93	66.90	300.30	487.89	287.20	99.96	54.68	16.16
Gifts of stocks, bonds, and mutual funds to members of other households	46.27	–	0.78	15.48	12.20	103.26	8.89	223.73
Cash contributions to charities	215.69	27.10	74.34	166.70	165.45	363.17	427.59	256.51
Cash contributions to church, religious organizations	649.17	147.21	465.17	588.41	670.80	769.87	963.72	766.72
Cash contributions to educational institutions	25.37	0.97	5.64	18.61	22.99	48.20	39.53	34.23
Cash contributions to political organizations	10.14	3.68	1.57	5.28	5.03	23.00	19.08	14.59
Cash gifts to members of other households	384.82	81.15	202.78	191.06	307.15	458.35	756.09	841.57
PERSONAL INSURANCE AND PENSIONS	**5,423.57**	**2,220.36**	**5,345.60**	**7,067.53**	**7,452.86**	**6,775.22**	**2,956.89**	**825.50**
Life and other personal insurance	**317.12**	**66.63**	**138.31**	**307.71**	**400.73**	**533.64**	**360.99**	**182.65**
Life, endowment, annuity, other personal insurance	298.52	61.75	127.18	294.00	378.43	508.99	333.78	162.24
Other nonhealth insurance	18.60	4.88	11.13	13.71	22.30	24.64	27.22	20.41
Pensions and Social Security	**5,106.45**	**2,153.73**	**5,207.30**	**6,759.82**	**7,052.13**	**6,241.59**	**2,595.90**	**642.85**
Deductions for government retirement	90.65	18.37	105.17	99.11	123.48	144.03	27.22	5.82
Deductions for railroad retirement	3.79	–	12.75	1.37	4.00	3.42	–	–
Deductions for private pensions	556.40	82.53	544.34	747.92	796.64	752.63	260.65	22.68
Nonpayroll deposit to retirement plans	500.06	121.33	253.49	477.16	730.86	814.35	543.73	102.86
Deductions for Social Security	3,955.54	1,931.49	4,291.55	5,434.27	5,397.16	4,527.16	1,764.30	511.49
PERSONAL TAXES	**2,011.61**	**18.57**	**1,328.06**	**1,839.40**	**3,284.38**	**3,401.95**	**1,360.24**	**365.12**
Federal income taxes	**1,370.41**	**−123.02**	**779.16**	**1,166.40**	**2,406.66**	**2,404.45**	**952.37**	**168.71**
Federal income tax deducted	1,899.25	668.76	2,277.76	2,295.97	2,871.39	2,179.11	737.50	146.70
Additional federal income tax paid	531.19	13.92	126.08	350.71	751.29	1,095.04	655.29	257.52
Federal income tax refunds	−1,060.03	−805.70	−1,624.69	−1,480.28	−1,216.01	−869.70	−440.42	−235.51
State and local income taxes	**505.23**	**129.78**	**477.40**	**560.00**	**747.28**	**786.17**	**176.94**	**65.12**
State and local income tax deducted	531.84	197.89	606.68	653.45	800.51	669.88	146.25	38.51
Additional state and local income tax paid	105.11	3.62	36.31	67.22	107.40	264.07	102.75	66.51
State and local income tax refunds	−131.72	−71.73	−165.59	−160.68	−160.63	−147.78	−72.06	−39.90
Other taxes	**135.97**	**11.81**	**71.51**	**113.00**	**130.44**	**211.33**	**230.93**	**131.29**

Note: Subcategories may not add to total because some are not shown. "–" means sample is too small to make a reliable estimate.
Source: Bureau of Labor Statistics, unpublished tables from the 2011 Consumer Expenditure Survey

Table 4.2 Financial: Indexed spending by age, 2011

(indexed average annual spending of consumer units on financial products and services, cash contributions, and miscellaneous items, by age of consumer unit reference person, 2011; index definition: an index of 100 is the average for all consumer units; an index of 125 means that spending by consumer units in that group is 25 percent above the average for all consumer units; an index of 75 indicates spending that is 25 percent below the average for all consumer units)

	total consumer units	under 25	25 to 34	35 to 44	45 to 54	55 to 64	65 to 74	75+
Average spending of consumer units, total	$49,705	$29,912	$48,097	$57,271	$58,050	$53,616	$44,646	$32,688
Average spending of consumer units, index	100	60	97	115	117	108	90	66
FINANCIAL PRODUCTS AND SERVICES	100	37	78	101	122	120	106	87
Miscellaneous fees	100	–	53	102	188	134	6	100
Lottery and gambling losses	100	16	117	42	91	152	181	57
Legal fees	100	30	65	92	144	103	146	69
Funeral expenses	100	0	19	50	85	155	119	307
Safe deposit box rental	100	1	18	50	71	152	203	240
Checking accounts, other bank service charges	100	80	108	129	118	95	85	36
Cemetery lots, vaults, and maintenance fees	100	6	–	34	41	197	124	375
Accounting fees	100	28	49	104	113	115	146	118
Miscellaneous personal services	100	156	80	149	117	76	44	83
Dating services	100	198	143	48	202	77	–	–
Finance charges, except mortgage and vehicles	100	56	115	156	127	97	42	20
Occupational expenses	100	25	105	111	150	130	50	18
Expenses for other properties	100	6	72	73	125	149	123	89
Credit card memberships	100	11	70	98	160	114	105	58
Shopping club membership fees	100	40	77	99	118	117	130	75
Vacation clubs	100	12	44	97	94	264	48	33
CASH CONTRIBUTIONS	100	21	66	91	100	123	147	130
Support for college students	100	4	16	55	193	173	103	59
Alimony expenditures	100	74	128	67	54	92	287	19
Child support expenditures	100	30	134	217	128	44	24	7
Gifts of stocks, bonds, and mutual funds to members of other households	100	–	2	33	26	223	19	484
Cash contributions to charities	100	13	34	77	77	168	198	119
Cash contributions to church, religious organizations	100	23	72	91	103	119	148	118
Cash contributions to educational institutions	100	4	22	73	91	190	156	135
Cash contributions to political organizations	100	36	15	52	50	227	188	144
Cash gifts to members of other households	100	21	53	50	80	119	196	219
PERSONAL INSURANCE AND PENSIONS	100	41	99	130	137	125	55	15
Life and other personal insurance	100	21	44	97	126	168	114	58
Life, endowment, annuity, other personal insurance	100	21	43	98	127	171	112	54
Other nonhealth insurance	100	26	60	74	120	132	146	110
Pensions and Social Security	100	42	102	132	138	122	51	13
Deductions for government retirement	100	20	116	109	136	159	30	6
Deductions for railroad retirement	100	–	336	36	106	90	–	–
Deductions for private pensions	100	15	98	134	143	135	47	4
Nonpayroll deposit to retirement plans	100	24	51	95	146	163	109	21
Deductions for Social Security	100	49	108	137	136	114	45	13
PERSONAL TAXES	100	1	66	91	163	169	68	18
Federal income taxes	100	–9	57	85	176	175	69	12
Federal income tax deducted	100	35	120	121	151	115	39	8
Additional federal income tax paid	100	3	24	66	141	206	123	48
Federal income tax refunds	100	76	153	140	115	82	42	22
State and local income taxes	100	26	94	111	148	156	35	13
State and local income tax deducted	100	37	114	123	151	126	27	7
Additional state and local income tax paid	100	3	35	64	102	251	98	63
State and local income tax refunds	100	54	126	122	122	112	55	30
Other taxes	100	9	53	83	96	155	170	97

Note: "–" means sample is too small to make a reliable estimate.
Source: Calculations by New Strategist based on the Bureau of Labor Statistics' 2011 Consumer Expenditure Survey

Table 4.3 Financial: Total spending by age, 2011

(total annual spending on financial products and services, cash contributions, and miscellaneous items, by consumer unit age groups, 2011; consumer units and dollars in thousands)

	total consumer units	under 25	25 to 34	35 to 44	45 to 54	55 to 64	65 to 74	75+
Number of consumer units	122,287	7,743	20,463	21,699	24,821	21,688	14,079	11,794
Total spending of all consumer units	$6,078,260,661	$231,604,899	$984,216,892	$1,242,724,948	$1,440,869,475	$1,162,820,772	$628,564,839	$385,526,282
FINANCIAL PRODUCTS AND SERVICES	**94,762,642**	**2,209,078**	**12,410,196**	**16,942,579**	**23,505,735**	**20,183,503**	**11,553,087**	**7,950,217**
Miscellaneous fees	176,093	–	15,757	31,898	67,265	41,858	1,126	16,983
Lottery and gambling losses	6,848,072	68,990	1,344,828	507,757	1,264,878	1,849,770	1,423,387	378,823
Legal fees	19,413,061	371,045	2,109,121	3,157,855	5,690,214	3,531,240	3,257,881	1,295,217
Funeral expenses	8,275,161	542	256,606	726,917	1,430,931	2,274,637	1,136,738	2,448,316
Safe deposit box rental	399,878	232	12,278	35,803	57,585	108,006	93,344	92,465
Checking accounts, other bank service charges	2,761,240	140,690	497,046	632,743	658,749	464,991	271,302	95,413
Cemetery lots, vaults, and maintenance fees	1,044,331	3,639	–	63,144	85,881	365,660	148,674	377,998
Accounting fees	7,697,967	138,058	632,921	1,426,058	1,758,320	1,571,729	1,297,521	873,110
Miscellaneous personal services	6,351,587	628,267	855,353	1,674,729	1,506,883	858,845	320,720	508,911
Dating services	53,806	6,736	12,892	4,557	22,091	7,374	–	–
Finance charges, except mortgage and vehicles	18,947,148	672,557	3,633,001	5,242,478	4,883,780	3,243,007	911,756	360,778
Occupational expenses	5,774,392	90,438	1,019,262	1,140,282	1,755,341	1,336,415	332,828	100,249
Expenses for other properties	14,931,243	52,265	1,788,262	1,931,428	3,797,117	3,957,192	2,120,157	1,285,074
Credit card memberships	287,374	1,936	33,764	50,125	93,079	58,341	34,634	16,040
Shopping club membership fees	1,133,600	29,036	146,106	199,414	271,790	235,749	169,793	82,204
Vacation clubs	594,315	4,646	43,791	102,636	112,936	277,823	32,945	18,988
CASH CONTRIBUTIONS	**210,440,030**	**2,837,964**	**23,119,916**	**34,059,618**	**42,740,273**	**45,795,513**	**35,568,059**	**26,317,957**
Support for college students	14,329,591	36,160	381,430	1,402,840	5,604,085	4,384,880	1,705,671	814,494
Alimony expenditures	5,782,952	269,689	1,240,262	685,254	628,964	945,380	1,908,831	104,967
Child support expenditures	27,506,015	518,007	6,145,039	10,586,725	7,128,591	2,167,932	769,840	190,591
Gifts of stocks, bonds, and mutual funds to members of other households	5,658,219	–	15,961	335,901	302,816	2,239,503	125,162	2,638,672
Cash contributions to charities	26,376,083	209,835	1,521,219	3,617,223	4,106,634	7,876,431	6,020,040	3,025,279
Cash contributions to church, religious organizations	79,385,052	1,139,847	9,518,774	12,767,909	16,649,927	16,696,941	13,568,214	9,042,696
Cash contributions to educational institutions	3,102,421	7,511	115,411	403,818	570,635	1,045,362	556,543	403,709
Cash contributions to political organizations	1,239,990	28,494	32,127	114,571	124,850	498,824	268,627	172,074
Cash gifts to members of other households	47,058,483	628,344	4,149,487	4,145,811	7,623,770	9,940,695	10,644,991	9,925,477
PERSONAL INSURANCE AND PENSIONS	**663,232,105**	**17,192,247**	**109,387,013**	**153,358,333**	**184,987,438**	**146,940,971**	**41,630,054**	**9,735,947.00**
Life and other personal insurance	**38,779,653**	**515,916**	**2,830,238**	**6,676,999**	**9,946,519**	**11,573,584**	**5,082,378**	**2,154,174**
Life, endowment, annuity, other personal insurance	36,505,115	478,130	2,602,484	6,379,506	9,393,011	11,038,975	4,699,289	1,913,459
Other nonhealth insurance	2,274,538	37,786	227,753	297,493	553,508	534,392	383,230	240,716
Pensions and Social Security	**624,452,451**	**16,676,331**	**106,556,980**	**146,681,334**	**175,040,919**	**135,367,604**	**36,547,676**	**7,581,773**
Deductions for government retirement	11,085,317	142,239	2,152,094	2,150,588	3,064,897	3,123,723	383,230	68,641
Deductions for railroad retirement	463,468	–	260,903	29,728	99,284	74,173	–	–
Deductions for private pensions	68,040,487	639,030	11,138,829	16,229,116	19,773,401	16,323,039	3,669,691	267,488
Nonpayroll deposit to retirement plans	61,150,837	939,458	5,187,166	10,353,895	18,140,676	17,661,623	7,655,175	1,213,131
Deductions for Social Security	483,711,120	14,955,527	87,817,988	117,918,225	133,962,908	98,185,046	24,839,580	6,032,513
PERSONAL TAXES	**245,993,752**	**143,788**	**27,176,092**	**39,913,141**	**81,521,596**	**73,781,492**	**19,150,819**	**4,306,225**
Federal income taxes	**167,583,328**	**–952,544**	**15,943,951**	**25,309,714**	**59,735,708**	**52,147,712**	**13,408,417**	**1,989,766**
Federal income tax deducted	232,253,585	5,178,209	46,609,803	49,820,253	71,270,771	47,260,538	10,383,263	1,730,180
Additional federal income tax paid	64,957,632	107,783	2,579,975	7,610,056	18,647,769	23,749,228	9,225,828	3,037,191
Federal income tax refunds	–129,627,889	–6,238,535	–33,246,031	–32,120,596	–30,182,584	–18,862,054	–6,200,673	–2,777,605
State and local income taxes	**61,783,061**	**1,004,887**	**9,769,036**	**12,151,440**	**18,548,237**	**17,050,455**	**2,491,138**	**768,025**
State and local income tax deducted	65,037,118	1,532,262	12,414,493	14,179,212	19,869,459	14,528,357	2,059,054	454,187
Additional state and local income tax paid	12,853,587	28,030	743,012	1,458,607	2,665,775	5,727,150	1,446,617	784,419
State and local income tax refunds	–16,107,644	–555,405	–3,388,468	–3,486,595	–3,986,997	–3,205,053	–1,014,533	–470,581
Other taxes	**16,627,363**	**91,445**	**1,463,309**	**2,451,987**	**3,237,651**	**4,583,325**	**3,251,263**	**1,548,434**

Note: Numbers may not add to total because of rounding and missing subcategories. "–" means sample is too small to make a reliable estimate.
Source: Calculations by New Strategist based on the Bureau of Labor Statistics' 2011 Consumer Expenditure Survey

Table 4.4 Financial: Market shares by age, 2011

(percentage of total annual spending on financial products and services, cash contributions, and miscellaneous items accounted for by consumer unit age groups, 2011)

	total consumer units	under 25	25 to 34	35 to 44	45 to 54	55 to 64	65 to 74	75+
Share of total consumer units	100.0%	6.3%	16.7%	17.7%	20.3%	17.7%	11.5%	9.6%
Share of total before-tax income	100.0	2.7	15.3	21.6	25.0	21.0	9.5	4.9
Share of total spending	100.0	3.8	16.2	20.4	23.7	19.1	10.3	6.3
FINANCIAL PRODUCTS AND SERVICES	100.0	2.3	13.1	17.9	24.8	21.3	12.2	8.4
Miscellaneous fees	100.0	–	8.9	18.1	38.2	23.8	0.6	9.6
Lottery and gambling losses	100.0	1.0	19.6	7.4	18.5	27.0	20.8	5.5
Legal fees	100.0	1.9	10.9	16.3	29.3	18.2	16.8	6.7
Funeral expenses	100.0	0.0	3.1	8.8	17.3	27.5	13.7	29.6
Safe deposit box rental	100.0	0.1	3.1	9.0	14.4	27.0	23.3	23.1
Checking accounts, other bank service charges	100.0	5.1	18.0	22.9	23.9	16.8	9.8	3.5
Cemetery lots, vaults, and maintenance fees	100.0	0.3	–	6.0	8.2	35.0	14.2	36.2
Accounting fees	100.0	1.8	8.2	18.5	22.8	20.4	16.9	11.3
Miscellaneous personal services	100.0	9.9	13.5	26.4	23.7	13.5	5.0	8.0
Dating services	100.0	12.5	24.0	8.5	41.1	13.7	–	–
Finance charges, except mortgage and vehicles	100.0	3.5	19.2	27.7	25.8	17.1	4.8	1.9
Occupational expenses	100.0	1.6	17.7	19.7	30.4	23.1	5.8	1.7
Expenses for other properties	100.0	0.4	12.0	12.9	25.4	26.5	14.2	8.6
Credit card memberships	100.0	0.7	11.7	17.4	32.4	20.3	12.1	5.6
Shopping club membership fees	100.0	2.6	12.9	17.6	24.0	20.8	15.0	7.3
Vacation clubs	100.0	0.8	7.4	17.3	19.0	46.7	5.5	3.2
CASH CONTRIBUTIONS	100.0	1.3	11.0	16.2	20.3	21.8	16.9	12.5
Support for college students	100.0	0.3	2.7	9.8	39.1	30.6	11.9	5.7
Alimony expenditures	100.0	4.7	21.4	11.8	10.9	16.3	33.0	1.8
Child support expenditures	100.0	1.9	22.3	38.5	25.9	7.9	2.8	0.7
Gifts of stocks, bonds, and mutual funds to members of other households	100.0	–	0.3	5.9	5.4	39.6	2.2	46.6
Cash contributions to charities	100.0	0.8	5.8	13.7	15.6	29.9	22.8	11.5
Cash contributions to church, religious organizations	100.0	1.4	12.0	16.1	21.0	21.0	17.1	11.4
Cash contributions to educational institutions	100.0	0.2	3.7	13.0	18.4	33.7	17.9	13.0
Cash contributions to political organizations	100.0	2.3	2.6	9.2	10.1	40.2	21.7	13.9
Cash gifts to members of other households	100.0	1.3	8.8	8.8	16.2	21.1	22.6	21.1
PERSONAL INSURANCE AND PENSIONS	100.0	2.6	16.5	23.1	27.9	22.2	6.3	1.5
Life and other personal insurance	100.0	1.3	7.3	17.2	25.6	29.8	13.1	5.6
Life, endowment, annuity, other personal insurance	100.0	1.3	7.1	17.5	25.7	30.2	12.9	5.2
Other nonhealth insurance	100.0	1.7	10.0	13.1	24.3	23.5	16.8	10.6
Pensions and Social Security	100.0	2.7	17.1	23.5	28.0	21.7	5.9	1.2
Deductions for government retirement	100.0	1.3	19.4	19.4	27.6	28.2	3.5	0.6
Deductions for railroad retirement	100.0	–	56.3	6.4	21.4	16.0	–	–
Deductions for private pensions	100.0	0.9	16.4	23.9	29.1	24.0	5.4	0.4
Nonpayroll deposit to retirement plans	100.0	1.5	8.5	16.9	29.7	28.9	12.5	2.0
Deductions for Social Security	100.0	3.1	18.2	24.4	27.7	20.3	5.1	1.2
PERSONAL TAXES	100.0	0.1	11.0	16.2	33.1	30.0	7.8	1.8
Federal income taxes	100.0	−0.6	9.5	15.1	35.6	31.1	8.0	1.2
Federal income tax deducted	100.0	2.2	20.1	21.5	30.7	20.3	4.5	0.7
Additional federal income tax paid	100.0	0.2	4.0	11.7	28.7	36.6	14.2	4.7
Federal income tax refunds	100.0	4.8	25.6	24.8	23.3	14.6	4.8	2.1
State and local income taxes	100.0	1.6	15.8	19.7	30.0	27.6	4.0	1.2
State and local income tax deducted	100.0	2.4	19.1	21.8	30.6	22.3	3.2	0.7
Additional state and local income tax paid	100.0	0.2	5.8	11.3	20.7	44.6	11.3	6.1
State and local income tax refunds	100.0	3.4	21.0	21.6	24.8	19.9	6.3	2.9
Other taxes	100.0	0.5	8.8	14.7	19.5	27.6	19.6	9.3

Note: Numbers may not add to total because of rounding. "–" means sample is too small to make a reliable estimate.
Source: Calculations by New Strategist based on the Bureau of Labor Statistics' 2011 Consumer Expenditure Survey

Table 4.5 Financial: Average spending by income, 2011

(average annual spending on financial products and services, cash contributions, and miscellaneous items, by before-tax income of consumer units, 2011)

	total consumer units	under $20,000	$20,000–$39,999	$40,000–$49,999	$50,000–$69,999	$70,000–$79,999	$80,000–$99,999	$100,000 or more
Number of consumer units (in 000s)	122,287	26,342	27,788	11,347	17,376	7,385	10,456	21,593
Average number of persons per consumer unit	2.5	1.8	2.3	2.6	2.7	2.8	3.0	3.2
Average before-tax income of consumer units	$63,685.00	$10,491.66	$29,658.14	$44,698.00	$59,306.00	$74,742.00	$89,108.00	$169,776.00
Average spending of consumer units, total	49,704.88	22,142.36	33,453.66	40,306.19	50,034.03	57,976.69	65,389.80	97,728.22
FINANCIAL PRODUCTS AND SERVICES	**774.92**	**382.31**	**576.16**	**656.13**	**681.67**	**950.53**	**898.13**	**1,517.08**
Miscellaneous fees	1.44	–	–	0.64	1.74	3.25	0.64	4.04
Lottery and gambling losses	56.00	11.55	48.80	63.68	32.63	175.66	65.37	84.53
Legal fees	158.75	142.41	115.82	162.52	161.70	119.14	158.90	243.04
Funeral expenses	67.67	55.67	87.61	63.77	63.52	114.18	73.15	43.45
Safe deposit box rental	3.27	1.74	2.87	2.12	3.00	3.55	2.85	6.57
Checking accounts, other bank service charges	22.58	16.27	17.70	30.38	24.00	26.31	28.74	27.05
Cemetery lots, vaults, and maintenance fees	8.54	4.92	11.04	0.79	14.99	7.61	12.96	6.83
Accounting fees	62.95	22.39	44.72	49.16	63.94	77.84	62.34	137.53
Miscellaneous personal services	51.94	12.69	43.34	20.01	61.42	76.50	37.20	112.87
Dating services	0.44	–	–	0.89	0.64	0.28	0.61	0.15
Finance charges, except mortgage and vehicles	154.94	60.99	100.03	141.70	117.96	182.41	229.43	331.48
Occupational expenses	47.22	6.65	13.89	36.12	48.22	54.95	97.28	117.76
Expenses for other properties	122.10	42.83	79.68	71.63	71.31	94.83	107.18	357.37
Credit card memberships	2.35	0.59	1.46	1.68	1.95	1.62	2.98	6.28
Shopping club membership fees	9.27	3.11	6.98	6.03	9.79	11.35	12.09	18.96
Vacation clubs	4.86	0.24	1.09	5.03	4.85	1.05	5.57	16.21
CASH CONTRIBUTIONS	**1,720.87**	**693.59**	**990.02**	**1,269.26**	**1,560.87**	**2,018.85**	**2,098.51**	**3,995.95**
Support for college students	117.18	30.73	31.16	33.31	75.09	77.06	122.19	422.60
Alimony expenditures	47.29	4.62	7.83	2.79	37.36	37.49	9.33	204.91
Child support expenditures	224.93	79.71	159.29	254.42	276.44	302.86	348.67	343.07
Gifts of stocks, bonds, and mutual funds to members of other households	46.27	98.57	0.83	19.47	2.39	3.99	21.49	116.77
Cash contributions to charities	215.69	49.91	75.79	94.84	132.60	240.68	214.36	720.46
Cash contributions to church, religious organizations	649.17	262.38	412.62	504.12	619.16	803.27	956.43	1,324.31
Cash contributions to educational institutions	25.37	5.67	5.01	16.03	27.80	8.78	18.70	87.48
Cash contributions to political organizations	10.14	2.81	2.34	5.43	10.61	7.28	5.74	34.32
Cash gifts to members of other households	384.82	160.54	295.14	338.86	379.41	537.44	401.61	742.04
PERSONAL INSURANCE AND PENSIONS	**5,423.57**	**445.44**	**1,904.64**	**3,296.98**	**4,871.28**	**6,448.95**	**8,275.18**	**15,855.65**
Life and other personal insurance	**317.12**	**84.47**	**219.23**	**208.76**	**289.12**	**349.86**	**399.45**	**755.34**
Life, endowment, annuity, other personal insurance	298.52	79.16	211.03	191.55	267.36	332.15	378.60	709.72
Other nonhealth insurance	18.60	5.31	8.20	17.21	21.75	17.70	20.85	45.62
Pensions and Social Security	**5,106.45**	**360.97**	**1,685.40**	**3,088.21**	**4,582.17**	**6,099.10**	**7,875.73**	**15,100.31**
Deductions for government retirement	90.65	1.00	19.34	63.55	81.80	168.79	130.58	267.09
Deductions for railroad retirement	3.79	–	0.99	–	1.89	0.28	25.58	6.86
Deductions for private pensions	556.40	8.88	58.39	201.05	375.89	432.47	837.26	2,103.64
Nonpayroll deposit to retirement plans	500.06	35.22	96.86	161.33	262.23	375.10	653.47	1,923.90
Deductions for Social Security	3,955.54	315.88	1,510.34	2,662.28	3,860.34	5,122.46	6,228.83	10,798.82
PERSONAL TAXES	**2,011.61**	**–257.56**	**–89.52**	**502.40**	**1,236.29**	**1,846.52**	**2,691.00**	**8,628.38**
Federal income taxes	**1,370.41**	**–293.89**	**–262.67**	**201.86**	**757.03**	**1,142.68**	**1,773.07**	**6,493.03**
Federal income tax deducted	1,899.25	95.12	487.49	1,100.47	1,654.81	2,187.10	2,876.66	5,961.71
Additional federal income tax paid	531.19	53.09	143.70	196.51	330.27	382.93	297.61	2,114.52
Federal income tax refunds	–1,060.03	–442.10	–893.86	–1,095.12	–1,228.06	–1,427.35	–1,401.20	–1,583.21
State and local income taxes	**505.23**	**–8.91**	**81.95**	**211.24**	**358.07**	**565.93**	**753.33**	**1,809.19**
State and local income tax deducted	531.84	20.98	135.79	299.62	460.92	686.31	856.72	1,633.70
Additional state and local income tax paid	105.11	10.51	32.33	39.46	57.80	58.50	69.08	420.16
State and local income tax refunds	–131.72	–40.39	–86.16	–127.84	–160.64	–178.88	–172.46	–244.67
Other taxes	**135.97**	**45.25**	**91.19**	**89.30**	**121.18**	**137.91**	**164.60**	**326.16**

Note: Subcategories may not add to total because some are not shown. "–" means sample is too small to make a reliable estimate.
Source: Bureau of Labor Statistics, unpublished tables from the 2011 Consumer Expenditure Survey; calculations by New Strategist

Table 4.6 Financial: Indexed spending by income, 2011

(indexed average annual spending of consumer units on financial products and services, cash contributions, and miscellaneous items, by before-tax income of consumer unit, 2011; index definition: an index of 100 is the average for all consumer units; an index of 125 means that spending by consumer units in that group is 25 percent above the average for all consumer units; an index of 75 indicates spending that is 25 percent below the average for all consumer units)

	total consumer units	under $20,000	$20,000–$39,999	$40,000–$49,999	$50,000–$69,999	$70,000–$79,999	$80,000–$99,999	$100,000 or more
Average spending of consumer units, total	$49,705	$22,142	$33,454	$40,306	$50,034	$57,977	$65,390	$97,728
Average spending of consumer units, index	100	45	67	81	101	117	132	197
FINANCIAL PRODUCTS AND SERVICES	**100**	**49**	**74**	**85**	**88**	**123**	**116**	**196**
Miscellaneous fees	100	–	–	44	121	226	44	281
Lottery and gambling losses	100	21	87	114	58	314	117	151
Legal fees	100	90	73	102	102	75	100	153
Funeral expenses	100	82	129	94	94	169	108	64
Safe deposit box rental	100	53	88	65	92	109	87	201
Checking accounts, other bank service charges	100	72	78	135	106	117	127	120
Cemetery lots, vaults, and maintenance fees	100	58	129	9	176	89	152	80
Accounting fees	100	36	71	78	102	124	99	218
Miscellaneous personal services	100	24	83	39	118	147	72	217
Dating services	100	–	–	202	145	64	139	34
Finance charges, except mortgage and vehicles	100	39	65	91	76	118	148	214
Occupational expenses	100	14	29	76	102	116	206	249
Expenses for other properties	100	35	65	59	58	78	88	293
Credit card memberships	100	25	62	71	83	69	127	267
Shopping club membership fees	100	34	75	65	106	122	130	205
Vacation clubs	100	5	22	103	100	22	115	334
CASH CONTRIBUTIONS	**100**	**40**	**58**	**74**	**91**	**117**	**122**	**232**
Support for college students	100	26	27	28	64	66	104	361
Alimony expenditures	100	10	17	6	79	79	20	433
Child support expenditures	100	35	71	113	123	135	155	153
Gifts of stocks, bonds, and mutual funds to members of other households	100	213	2	42	5	9	46	252
Cash contributions to charities	100	23	35	44	61	112	99	334
Cash contributions to church, religious organizations	100	40	64	78	95	124	147	204
Cash contributions to educational institutions	100	22	20	63	110	35	74	345
Cash contributions to political organizations	100	28	23	54	105	72	57	338
Cash gifts to members of other households	100	42	77	88	99	140	104	193
PERSONAL INSURANCE AND PENSIONS	**100**	**8**	**35**	**61**	**90**	**119**	**153**	**292**
Life and other personal insurance	**100**	**27**	**69**	**66**	**91**	**110**	**126**	**238**
Life, endowment, annuity, other personal insurance	100	27	71	64	90	111	127	238
Other nonhealth insurance	100	29	44	93	117	95	112	245
Pensions and Social Security	**100**	**7**	**33**	**60**	**90**	**119**	**154**	**296**
Deductions for government retirement	100	1	21	70	90	186	144	295
Deductions for railroad retirement	100	–	26	–	50	7	675	181
Deductions for private pensions	100	2	10	36	68	78	150	378
Nonpayroll deposit to retirement plans	100	7	19	32	52	75	131	385
Deductions for Social Security	100	8	38	67	98	130	157	273
PERSONAL TAXES	**100**	**−13**	**−4**	**25**	**61**	**92**	**134**	**429**
Federal income taxes	**100**	**−21**	**−19**	**15**	**55**	**83**	**129**	**474**
Federal income tax deducted	100	5	26	58	87	115	151	314
Additional federal income tax paid	100	10	27	37	62	72	56	398
Federal income tax refunds	100	42	84	103	116	135	132	149
State and local income taxes	**100**	**−2**	**16**	**42**	**71**	**112**	**149**	**358**
State and local income tax deducted	100	4	26	56	87	129	161	307
Additional state and local income tax paid	100	10	31	38	55	56	66	400
State and local income tax refunds	100	31	65	97	122	136	131	186
Other taxes	**100**	**33**	**67**	**66**	**89**	**101**	**121**	**240**

Note: "−" means sample is too small to make a reliable estimate.
Source: Calculations by New Strategist based on the Bureau of Labor Statistics' 2011 Consumer Expenditure Survey

Table 4.7 Financial: Total spending by income, 2011

(total annual spending on financial products and services, cash contributions, and miscellaneous items, by before-tax income group of consumer units, 2011; consumer units and dollars in thousands)

	total consumer units	under $20,000	$20,000–$39,999	$40,000–$49,999	$50,000–$69,999	$70,000–$79,999	$80,000–$99,999	$100,000 or more
Number of consumer units	122,287	26,342	27,788	11,347	17,376	7,385	10,456	21,593
Total spending of all consumer units	$6,078,260,661	$583,273,961	$929,610,260	$457,354,338	$869,391,305	$428,157,856	$683,715,749	$2,110,245,454
FINANCIAL PRODUCTS AND SERVICES	94,762,642	10,070,710	16,010,252	7,445,107	11,844,698	7,019,664	9,390,847	32,758,308
Miscellaneous fees	176,093	–	–	7,262	30,234	24,001	6,692	87,236
Lottery and gambling losses	6,848,072	304,120	1,356,037	722,577	566,979	1,297,249	683,509	1,825,256
Legal fees	19,413,061	3,751,478	3,218,535	1,844,114	2,809,699	879,849	1,661,458	5,247,963
Funeral expenses	8,275,161	1,466,582	2,434,581	723,598	1,103,724	843,219	764,856	938,216
Safe deposit box rental	399,878	45,765	79,675	24,056	52,128	26,217	29,800	141,866
Checking accounts, other bank service charges	2,761,240	428,471	491,775	344,722	417,024	194,299	300,505	584,091
Cemetery lots, vaults, and maintenance fees	1,044,331	129,664	306,649	8,964	260,466	56,200	135,510	147,480
Accounting fees	7,697,967	589,871	1,242,675	557,819	1,111,021	574,848	651,827	2,969,685
Miscellaneous personal services	6,351,587	334,344	1,204,384	227,053	1,067,234	564,953	388,963	2,437,202
Dating services	53,806	–	–	10,099	11,121	2,068	6,378	3,239
Finance charges, except mortgage and vehicles	18,947,148	1,606,600	2,779,727	1,607,870	2,049,673	1,347,098	2,398,920	7,157,648
Occupational expenses	5,774,392	175,182	385,918	409,854	837,871	405,806	1,017,160	2,542,792
Expenses for other properties	14,931,243	1,128,158	2,214,226	812,786	1,239,083	700,320	1,120,674	7,716,690
Credit card memberships	287,374	15,471	40,451	19,063	33,883	11,964	31,159	135,604
Shopping club membership fees	1,133,600	81,985	193,884	68,422	170,111	83,820	126,413	409,403
Vacation clubs	594,315	6,305	30,379	57,075	84,274	7,754	58,240	350,023
CASH CONTRIBUTIONS	210,440,030	18,270,643	27,510,637	14,402,293	27,121,677	14,909,207	21,942,021	86,284,548
Support for college students	14,329,591	809,484	865,827	377,969	1,304,764	569,088	1,277,619	9,125,202
Alimony expenditures	5,782,952	121,737	217,557	31,658	649,167	276,864	97,554	4,424,622
Child support expenditures	27,506,015	2,099,765	4,426,390	2,886,904	4,803,421	2,236,621	3,645,694	7,407,911
Gifts of stocks, bonds, and mutual funds to members of other households	5,658,219	2,596,657	23,042	220,926	41,529	29,466	224,699	2,521,415
Cash contributions to charities	26,376,083	1,314,812	2,106,068	1,076,149	2,304,058	1,777,422	2,241,348	15,556,893
Cash contributions to church, religious organizations	79,385,052	6,911,714	11,465,833	5,720,250	10,758,524	5,932,149	10,000,432	28,595,826
Cash contributions to educational institutions	3,102,421	149,381	139,302	181,892	483,053	64,840	195,527	1,888,956
Cash contributions to political organizations	1,239,990	73,945	65,151	61,614	184,359	53,763	60,017	741,072
Cash gifts to members of other households	47,058,483	4,228,813	8,201,323	3,845,044	6,592,628	3,968,994	4,199,234	16,022,870
PERSONAL INSURANCE AND PENSIONS	663,232,105	11,733,754	52,926,031	37,410,832	84,643,361	47,625,496	86,525,282	342,371,050
Life and other personal insurance	38,779,653	2,225,096	6,092,100	2,368,800	5,023,749	2,583,716	4,176,649	16,310,057
Life, endowment, annuity, other personal insurance	36,505,115	2,085,110	5,864,179	2,173,518	4,645,647	2,452,928	3,958,642	15,324,984
Other nonhealth insurance	2,274,538	139,937	227,920	195,282	377,928	130,715	218,008	985,073
Pensions and Social Security	624,452,451	9,508,658	46,833,931	35,041,919	79,619,786	45,041,854	82,348,633	326,060,994
Deductions for government retirement	11,085,317	26,237	537,473	721,102	1,421,357	1,246,514	1,365,344	5,767,274
Deductions for railroad retirement	463,468	–	27,510	–	32,841	2,068	267,464	148,128
Deductions for private pensions	68,040,487	233,893	1,622,607	2,281,314	6,531,465	3,193,791	8,754,391	45,423,899
Nonpayroll deposit to retirement plans	61,150,837	927,656	2,691,496	1,830,612	4,556,508	2,770,114	6,832,682	41,542,773
Deductions for Social Security	483,711,120	8,321,005	41,969,305	30,208,891	67,077,268	37,829,367	65,128,646	233,178,920
PERSONAL TAXES	245,993,752	–6,784,632	–2,487,568	5,700,733	21,481,775	13,636,550	28,137,096	186,312,609
Federal income taxes	167,583,328	–7,741,761	–7,298,954	2,290,505	13,154,153	8,438,692	18,539,220	140,203,997
Federal income tax deducted	232,253,585	2,505,560	13,546,441	12,487,033	28,753,979	16,151,734	30,078,357	128,731,204
Additional federal income tax paid	64,957,632	1,398,524	3,993,150	2,229,799	5,738,772	2,827,938	3,111,810	45,658,830
Federal income tax refunds	–129,627,889	–11,645,845	–24,838,546	–12,426,327	–21,338,771	–10,540,980	–14,650,947	–34,186,254
State and local income taxes	61,783,061	–234,815	2,277,294	2,396,940	6,221,824	4,179,393	7,876,818	39,065,840
State and local income tax deducted	65,037,118	552,538	3,773,201	3,399,788	8,008,946	5,068,399	8,957,864	35,276,484
Additional state and local income tax paid	12,853,587	276,801	898,415	447,753	1,004,333	432,023	722,300	9,072,515
State and local income tax refunds	–16,107,644	–1,063,945	–2,394,322	–1,450,600	–2,791,281	–1,321,029	–1,803,242	–5,283,159
Other taxes	16,627,363	1,191,944	2,534,092	1,013,287	2,105,624	1,018,465	1,721,058	7,042,773

Note: Numbers may not add to total because of rounding and missing subcategories. "–" means sample is too small to make a reliable estimate.
Source: Calculations by New Strategist based on the Bureau of Labor Statistics' 2011 Consumer Expenditure Survey

Table 4.8 Financial: Market shares by income, 2011

(percentage of total annual spending on financial products and services, cash contributions, and miscellaneous items accounted for by before-tax income group of consumer units, 2011)

	total consumer units	under $20,000	$20,000– $39,999	$40,000– $49,999	$50,000– $69,999	$70,000– $79,999	$80,000– $99,999	$100,000 or more
Share of total consumer units	100.0%	21.5%	22.7%	9.3%	14.2%	6.0%	8.6%	17.7%
Share of total before-tax income	100.0	3.5	10.6	6.5	13.2	7.1	12.0	47.1
Share of total spending	100.0	9.6	15.3	7.5	14.3	7.0	11.2	34.7
FINANCIAL PRODUCTS AND SERVICES	**100.0**	**10.6**	**16.9**	**7.9**	**12.5**	**7.4**	**9.9**	**34.6**
Miscellaneous fees	100.0	–	–	4.1	17.2	13.6	3.8	49.5
Lottery and gambling losses	100.0	4.4	19.8	10.6	8.3	18.9	10.0	26.7
Legal fees	100.0	19.3	16.6	9.5	14.5	4.5	8.6	27.0
Funeral expenses	100.0	17.7	29.4	8.7	13.3	10.2	9.2	11.3
Safe deposit box rental	100.0	11.4	19.9	6.0	13.0	6.6	7.5	35.5
Checking accounts, other bank service charges	100.0	15.5	17.8	12.5	15.1	7.0	10.9	21.2
Cemetery lots, vaults, and maintenance fees	100.0	12.4	29.4	0.9	24.9	5.4	13.0	14.1
Accounting fees	100.0	7.7	16.1	7.2	14.4	7.5	8.5	38.6
Miscellaneous personal services	100.0	5.3	19.0	3.6	16.8	8.9	6.1	38.4
Dating services	100.0	–	–	18.8	20.7	3.8	11.9	6.0
Finance charges, except mortgage and vehicles	100.0	8.5	14.7	8.5	10.8	7.1	12.7	37.8
Occupational expenses	100.0	3.0	6.7	7.1	14.5	7.0	17.6	44.0
Expenses for other properties	100.0	7.6	14.8	5.4	8.3	4.7	7.5	51.7
Credit card memberships	100.0	5.4	14.1	6.6	11.8	4.2	10.8	47.2
Shopping club membership fees	100.0	7.2	17.1	6.0	15.0	7.4	11.2	36.1
Vacation clubs	100.0	1.1	5.1	9.6	14.2	1.3	9.8	58.9
CASH CONTRIBUTIONS	**100.0**	**8.7**	**13.1**	**6.8**	**12.9**	**7.1**	**10.4**	**41.0**
Support for college students	100.0	5.6	6.0	2.6	9.1	4.0	8.9	63.7
Alimony expenditures	100.0	2.1	3.8	0.5	11.2	4.8	1.7	76.5
Child support expenditures	100.0	7.6	16.1	10.5	17.5	8.1	13.3	26.9
Gifts of stocks, bonds, and mutual funds to members of other households	100.0	45.9	0.4	3.9	0.7	0.5	4.0	44.6
Cash contributions to charities	100.0	5.0	8.0	4.1	8.7	6.7	8.5	59.0
Cash contributions to church, religious organizations	100.0	8.7	14.4	7.2	13.6	7.5	12.6	36.0
Cash contributions to educational institutions	100.0	4.8	4.5	5.9	15.6	2.1	6.3	60.9
Cash contributions to political organizations	100.0	6.0	5.3	5.0	14.9	4.3	4.8	59.8
Cash gifts to members of other households	100.0	9.0	17.4	8.2	14.0	8.4	8.9	34.0
PERSONAL INSURANCE AND PENSIONS	**100.0**	**1.8**	**8.0**	**5.6**	**12.8**	**7.2**	**13.0**	**51.6**
Life and other personal insurance	**100.0**	**5.7**	**15.7**	**6.1**	**13.0**	**6.7**	**10.8**	**42.1**
Life, endowment, annuity, other personal insurance	100.0	5.7	16.1	6.0	12.7	6.7	10.8	42.0
Other nonhealth insurance	100.0	6.2	10.0	8.6	16.6	5.7	9.6	43.3
Pensions and Social Security	**100.0**	**1.5**	**7.5**	**5.6**	**12.8**	**7.2**	**13.2**	**52.2**
Deductions for government retirement	100.0	0.2	4.8	6.5	12.8	11.2	12.3	52.0
Deductions for railroad retirement	100.0	–	5.9	–	7.1	0.4	57.7	32.0
Deductions for private pensions	100.0	0.3	2.4	3.4	9.6	4.7	12.9	66.8
Nonpayroll deposit to retirement plans	100.0	1.5	4.4	3.0	7.5	4.5	11.2	67.9
Deductions for Social Security	100.0	1.7	8.7	6.2	13.9	7.8	13.5	48.2
PERSONAL TAXES	**100.0**	**–2.8**	**–1.0**	**2.3**	**8.7**	**5.5**	**11.4**	**75.7**
Federal income taxes	**100.0**	**–4.6**	**–4.4**	**1.4**	**7.8**	**5.0**	**11.1**	**83.7**
Federal income tax deducted	100.0	1.1	5.8	5.4	12.4	7.0	13.0	55.4
Additional federal income tax paid	100.0	2.2	6.1	3.4	8.8	4.4	4.8	70.3
Federal income tax refunds	100.0	9.0	19.2	9.6	16.5	8.1	11.3	26.4
State and local income taxes	**100.0**	**–0.4**	**3.7**	**3.9**	**10.1**	**6.8**	**12.7**	**63.2**
State and local income tax deducted	100.0	0.8	5.8	5.2	12.3	7.8	13.8	54.2
Additional state and local income tax paid	100.0	2.2	7.0	3.5	7.8	3.4	5.6	70.6
State and local income tax refunds	100.0	6.6	14.9	9.0	17.3	8.2	11.2	32.8
Other taxes	**100.0**	**7.2**	**15.2**	**6.1**	**12.7**	**6.1**	**10.4**	**42.4**

Note: Numbers may not add to total because of rounding. "–" means sample is too small to make a reliable estimate.
Source: Calculations by New Strategist based on the Bureau of Labor Statistics' 2011 Consumer Expenditure Survey

Table 4.9 Financial: Average spending by high-income consumer units, 2011

(average annual spending on financial products and services, cash contributions, and miscellaneous items, by before-tax income of high-income consumer units, 2011)

	total consumer units	$100,000 or more	$100,000– $119,999	$120,000– $149,999	$150,000 or more
Number of consumer units (in 000s)	122,287	21,593	7,045	6,107	8,440
Average number of persons per consumer unit	2.5	3.2	3.2	3.1	3.2
Average before-tax income of consumer units	$63,685.00	$169,776.00	$108,549.00	$133,318.00	$247,261.00
Average spending of consumer units, total	49,704.88	97,728.22	76,496.41	87,239.44	123,056.38
FINANCIAL PRODUCTS AND SERVICES	**774.92**	**1,517.08**	**1,081.00**	**1,239.71**	**2,079.24**
Miscellaneous fees	1.44	4.04	1.33	11.02	1.44
Lottery and gambling losses	56.00	84.53	142.03	48.76	60.28
Legal fees	158.75	243.04	116.61	208.01	373.93
Funeral expenses	67.67	43.45	47.44	48.84	36.22
Safe deposit box rental	3.27	6.57	5.86	6.18	7.44
Checking accounts, other bank service charges	22.58	27.05	20.14	30.66	30.21
Cemetery lots, vaults, and maintenance fees	8.54	6.83	2.49	14.58	4.85
Accounting fees	62.95	137.53	69.26	98.85	222.51
Miscellaneous personal services	51.94	112.87	116.22	81.66	132.08
Dating services	0.44	0.15	–	0.50	0.02
Finance charges, except mortgage and vehicles	154.94	331.48	257.70	383.67	355.30
Occupational expenses	47.22	117.76	101.39	133.18	120.27
Expenses for other properties	122.10	357.37	156.26	132.47	687.96
Credit card memberships	2.35	6.28	2.44	3.37	11.60
Shopping club membership fees	9.27	18.96	13.20	21.98	21.58
Vacation clubs	4.86	16.21	21.72	15.99	11.76
CASH CONTRIBUTIONS	**1,720.87**	**3,995.95**	**2,178.04**	**3,242.24**	**6,058.69**
Support for college students	117.18	422.60	176.75	299.13	717.15
Alimony expenditures	47.29	204.91	6.38	9.23	512.21
Child support expenditures	224.93	343.07	351.56	235.99	413.45
Gifts of stocks, bonds, and mutual funds to members of other households	46.27	116.77	0.91	37.27	270.99
Cash contributions to charities	215.69	720.46	222.43	428.39	1,347.48
Cash contributions to church, religious organizations	649.17	1,324.31	983.98	1,236.16	1,672.17
Cash contributions to educational institutions	25.37	87.48	49.22	44.20	150.72
Cash contributions to political organizations	10.14	34.32	11.52	15.66	66.84
Cash gifts to members of other households	384.82	742.04	375.29	936.19	907.68
PERSONAL INSURANCE AND PENSIONS	**5,423.57**	**15,855.65**	**10,535.53**	**13,835.13**	**21,758.26**
Life and other personal insurance	**317.12**	**755.34**	**436.89**	**677.12**	**1,077.75**
Life, endowment, annuity, other personal insurance	298.52	709.72	409.39	626.38	1,020.71
Other nonhealth insurance	18.60	45.62	27.50	50.74	57.05
Pensions and Social Security	**5,106.45**	**15,100.31**	**10,098.64**	**13,158.02**	**20,680.51**
Deductions for government retirement	90.65	267.09	210.42	311.54	282.22
Deductions for railroad retirement	3.79	6.86	14.08	–	5.79
Deductions for private pensions	556.40	2,103.64	1,151.93	1,942.22	3,014.81
Nonpayroll deposit to retirement plans	500.06	1,923.90	835.39	1,452.55	3,173.52
Deductions for Social Security	3,955.54	10,798.82	7,886.81	9,451.70	14,204.16
PERSONAL TAXES	**2,011.61**	**8,628.38**	**3,423.93**	**5,584.29**	**15,175.04**
Federal income taxes	**1,370.41**	**6,493.03**	**2,260.91**	**4,039.69**	**11,800.65**
Federal income tax deducted	1,899.25	5,961.71	3,525.24	4,812.46	8,826.96
Additional federal income tax paid	531.19	2,114.52	396.26	728.14	4,551.86
Federal income tax refunds	–1,060.03	–1,583.21	–1,660.58	–1,500.91	–1,578.17
State and local income taxes	**505.23**	**1,809.19**	**940.44**	**1,306.38**	**2,898.14**
State and local income tax deducted	531.84	1,633.70	1,082.26	1,376.52	2,280.06
Additional state and local income tax paid	105.11	420.16	84.16	160.28	888.65
State and local income tax refunds	–131.72	–244.67	–225.98	–230.43	–270.57
Other taxes	**135.97**	**326.16**	**222.58**	**238.22**	**476.25**

Note: Subcategories may not add to total because some are not shown. "–" means sample is too small to make a reliable estimate.
Source: Bureau of Labor Statistics, unpublished tables from the 2011 Consumer Expenditure Survey

Table 4.10 Financial: Indexed spending by high-income consumer units, 2011

(indexed average annual spending of consumer units on financial products and services, cash contributions, and miscellaneous items, by before-tax income of consumer unit, 2011; index definition: an index of 100 is the average for all consumer units; an index of 125 means that spending by consumer units in that group is 25 percent above the average for all consumer units; an index of 75 indicates spending that is 25 percent below the average for all consumer units)

	total consumer units	$100,000 or more	$100,000– $119,999	$120,000– $149,999	$150,000 or more
Average spending of consumer units, total	$49,705	$97,728	$76,496	$87,239	$123,056
Average spending of consumer units, index	100	197	154	176	248
FINANCIAL PRODUCTS AND SERVICES	**100**	**196**	**139**	**160**	**268**
Miscellaneous fees	100	281	92	765	100
Lottery and gambling losses	100	151	254	87	108
Legal fees	100	153	73	131	236
Funeral expenses	100	64	70	72	54
Safe deposit box rental	100	201	179	189	228
Checking accounts, other bank service charges	100	120	89	136	134
Cemetery lots, vaults, and maintenance fees	100	80	29	171	57
Accounting fees	100	218	110	157	353
Miscellaneous personal services	100	217	224	157	254
Dating services	100	34	–	114	5
Finance charges, except mortgage and vehicles	100	214	166	248	229
Occupational expenses	100	249	215	282	255
Expenses for other properties	100	293	128	108	563
Credit card memberships	100	267	104	143	494
Shopping club membership fees	100	205	142	237	233
Vacation clubs	100	334	447	329	242
CASH CONTRIBUTIONS	**100**	**232**	**127**	**188**	**352**
Support for college students	100	361	151	255	612
Alimony expenditures	100	433	13	20	1083
Child support expenditures	100	153	156	105	184
Gifts of stocks, bonds, and mutual funds to members of other households	100	252	2	81	586
Cash contributions to charities	100	334	103	199	625
Cash contributions to church, religious organizations	100	204	152	190	258
Cash contributions to educational institutions	100	345	194	174	594
Cash contributions to political organizations	100	338	114	154	659
Cash gifts to members of other households	100	193	98	243	236
PERSONAL INSURANCE AND PENSIONS	**100**	**292**	**194**	**255**	**401**
Life and other personal insurance	**100**	**238**	**138**	**214**	**340**
Life, endowment, annuity, other personal insurance	100	238	137	210	342
Other nonhealth insurance	100	245	148	273	307
Pensions and Social Security	**100**	**296**	**198**	**258**	**405**
Deductions for government retirement	100	295	232	344	311
Deductions for railroad retirement	100	181	372	–	153
Deductions for private pensions	100	378	207	349	542
Nonpayroll deposit to retirement plans	100	385	167	290	635
Deductions for Social Security	100	273	199	239	359
PERSONAL TAXES	**100**	**429**	**170**	**278**	**754**
Federal income taxes	**100**	**474**	**165**	**295**	**861**
Federal income tax deducted	100	314	186	253	465
Additional federal income tax paid	100	398	75	137	857
Federal income tax refunds	100	149	157	142	149
State and local income taxes	**100**	**358**	**186**	**259**	**574**
State and local income tax deducted	100	307	203	259	429
Additional state and local income tax paid	100	400	80	152	845
State and local income tax refunds	100	186	172	175	205
Other taxes	**100**	**240**	**164**	**175**	**350**

Note: "–" means sample is too small to make a reliable estimate.
Source: Calculations by New Strategist based on the Bureau of Labor Statistics' 2011 Consumer Expenditure Survey

Table 4.11 Financial: Total spending by high-income consumer units, 2011

(total annual spending on financial products and services, cash contributions, and miscellaneous items, by before-tax income group of high-income consumer units, 2011; consumer units and dollars in thousands)

	total consumer units	$100,000 or more	$100,000– $119,999	$120,000– $149,999	$150,000 or more
Number of consumer units	122,287	21,593	7,045	6,107	8,440
Total spending of all consumer units	$6,078,260,661	$2,110,245,454	$538,917,208	$532,771,260	$1,038,595,847
FINANCIAL PRODUCTS AND SERVICES	94,762,642	32,758,308	7,615,645	7,570,909	17,548,786
Miscellaneous fees	176,093	87,236	9,370	67,299	12,154
Lottery and gambling losses	6,848,072	1,825,256	1,000,601	297,777	508,763
Legal fees	19,413,061	5,247,963	821,517	1,270,317	3,155,969
Funeral expenses	8,275,161	938,216	334,215	298,266	305,697
Safe deposit box rental	399,878	141,866	41,284	37,741	62,794
Checking accounts, other bank service charges	2,761,240	584,091	141,886	187,241	254,972
Cemetery lots, vaults, and maintenance fees	1,044,331	147,480	17,542	89,040	40,934
Accounting fees	7,697,967	2,969,685	487,937	603,677	1,877,984
Miscellaneous personal services	6,351,587	2,437,202	818,770	498,698	1,114,755
Dating services	53,806	3,239	–	3,054	169
Finance charges, except mortgage and vehicles	18,947,148	7,157,648	1,815,497	2,343,073	2,998,732
Occupational expenses	5,774,392	2,542,792	714,293	813,330	1,015,079
Expenses for other properties	14,931,243	7,716,690	1,100,852	808,994	5,806,382
Credit card memberships	287,374	135,604	17,190	20,581	97,904
Shopping club membership fees	1,133,600	409,403	92,994	134,232	182,135
Vacation clubs	594,315	350,023	153,017	97,651	99,254
CASH CONTRIBUTIONS	210,440,030	86,284,548	15,344,292	19,800,360	51,135,344
Support for college students	14,329,591	9,125,202	1,245,204	1,826,787	6,052,746
Alimony expenditures	5,782,952	4,424,622	44,947	56,368	4,323,052
Child support expenditures	27,506,015	7,407,911	2,476,740	1,441,191	3,489,518
Gifts of stocks, bonds, and mutual funds to members of other households	5,658,219	2,521,415	6,411	227,608	2,287,156
Cash contributions to charities	26,376,083	15,556,893	1,567,019	2,616,178	11,372,731
Cash contributions to church, religious organizations	79,385,052	28,595,826	6,932,139	7,549,229	14,113,115
Cash contributions to educational institutions	3,102,421	1,888,956	346,755	269,929	1,272,077
Cash contributions to political organizations	1,239,990	741,072	81,158	95,636	564,130
Cash gifts to members of other households	47,058,483	16,022,870	2,643,918	5,717,312	7,660,819
PERSONAL INSURANCE AND PENSIONS	663,232,105	342,371,050	74,222,809	84,491,139	183,639,714
Life and other personal insurance	38,779,653	16,310,057	3,077,890	4,135,172	9,096,210
Life, endowment, annuity, other personal insurance	36,505,115	15,324,984	2,884,153	3,825,303	8,614,792
Other nonhealth insurance	2,274,538	985,073	193,738	309,869	481,502
Pensions and Social Security	624,452,451	326,060,994	71,144,919	80,356,028	174,543,504
Deductions for government retirement	11,085,317	5,767,274	1,482,409	1,902,575	2,381,937
Deductions for railroad retirement	463,468	148,128	99,194	–	48,868
Deductions for private pensions	68,040,487	45,423,899	8,115,347	11,861,138	25,444,996
Nonpayroll deposit to retirement plans	61,150,837	41,542,773	5,885,323	8,870,723	26,784,509
Deductions for Social Security	483,711,120	233,178,920	55,562,576	57,721,532	119,883,110
PERSONAL TAXES	245,993,752	186,312,609	24,121,587	34,103,259	128,077,338
Federal income taxes	167,583,328	140,203,997	15,928,111	24,670,387	99,597,486
Federal income tax deducted	232,253,585	128,731,204	24,835,316	29,389,693	74,499,542
Additional federal income tax paid	64,957,632	45,658,830	2,791,652	4,446,751	38,417,698
Federal income tax refunds	−129,627,889	−34,186,254	−11,698,786	−9,166,057	−13,319,755
State and local income taxes	61,783,061	39,065,840	6,625,400	7,978,063	24,460,302
State and local income tax deducted	65,037,118	35,276,484	7,624,522	8,406,408	19,243,706
Additional state and local income tax paid	12,853,587	9,072,515	592,907	978,830	7,500,206
State and local income tax refunds	−16,107,644	−5,283,159	−1,592,029	−1,407,236	−2,283,611
Other taxes	16,627,363	7,042,773	1,568,076	1,454,810	4,019,550

Note: Numbers may not add to total because of rounding and missing subcategories. "–" means sample is too small to make a reliable estimate.
Source: Calculations by New Strategist based on the Bureau of Labor Statistics' 2011 Consumer Expenditure Survey

Table 4.12 Financial: Market shares by high-income consumer units, 2011

(percentage of total annual spending on financial products and services, cash contributions, and miscellaneous items accounted for by before-tax income group of high-income consumer units, 2011)

	total consumer units	$100,000 or more	$100,000– $119,999	$120,000– $149,999	$150,000 or more
Share of total consumer units	100.0%	17.7%	5.8%	5.0%	6.9%
Share of total before-tax income	100.0	47.1	9.8	10.5	26.8
Share of total spending	100.0	34.7	8.9	8.8	17.1
FINANCIAL PRODUCTS AND SERVICES	**100.0**	**34.6**	**8.0**	**8.0**	**18.5**
Miscellaneous fees	100.0	49.5	5.3	38.2	6.9
Lottery and gambling losses	100.0	26.7	14.6	4.3	7.4
Legal fees	100.0	27.0	4.2	6.5	16.3
Funeral expenses	100.0	11.3	4.0	3.6	3.7
Safe deposit box rental	100.0	35.5	10.3	9.4	15.7
Checking accounts, other bank service charges	100.0	21.2	5.1	6.8	9.2
Cemetery lots, vaults, and maintenance fees	100.0	14.1	1.7	8.5	3.9
Accounting fees	100.0	38.6	6.3	7.8	24.4
Miscellaneous personal services	100.0	38.4	12.9	7.9	17.6
Dating services	100.0	6.0	–	5.7	0.3
Finance charges, except mortgage and vehicles	100.0	37.8	9.6	12.4	15.8
Occupational expenses	100.0	44.0	12.4	14.1	17.6
Expenses for other properties	100.0	51.7	7.4	5.4	38.9
Credit card memberships	100.0	47.2	6.0	7.2	34.1
Shopping club membership fees	100.0	36.1	8.2	11.8	16.1
Vacation clubs	100.0	58.9	25.7	16.4	16.7
CASH CONTRIBUTIONS	**100.0**	**41.0**	**7.3**	**9.4**	**24.3**
Support for college students	100.0	63.7	8.7	12.7	42.2
Alimony expenditures	100.0	76.5	0.8	1.0	74.8
Child support expenditures	100.0	26.9	9.0	5.2	12.7
Gifts of stocks, bonds, and mutual funds to members of other households	100.0	44.6	0.1	4.0	40.4
Cash contributions to charities	100.0	59.0	5.9	9.9	43.1
Cash contributions to church, religious organizations	100.0	36.0	8.7	9.5	17.8
Cash contributions to educational institutions	100.0	60.9	11.2	8.7	41.0
Cash contributions to political organizations	100.0	59.8	6.5	7.7	45.5
Cash gifts to members of other households	100.0	34.0	5.6	12.1	16.3
PERSONAL INSURANCE AND PENSIONS	**100.0**	**51.6**	**11.2**	**12.7**	**27.7**
Life and other personal insurance	**100.0**	**42.1**	**7.9**	**10.7**	**23.5**
Life, endowment, annuity, other personal insurance	100.0	42.0	7.9	10.5	23.6
Other nonhealth insurance	100.0	43.3	8.5	13.6	21.2
Pensions and Social Security	**100.0**	**52.2**	**11.4**	**12.9**	**28.0**
Deductions for government retirement	100.0	52.0	13.4	17.2	21.5
Deductions for railroad retirement	100.0	32.0	21.4	–	10.5
Deductions for private pensions	100.0	66.8	11.9	17.4	37.4
Nonpayroll deposit to retirement plans	100.0	67.9	9.6	14.5	43.8
Deductions for Social Security	100.0	48.2	11.5	11.9	24.8
PERSONAL TAXES	**100.0**	**75.7**	**9.8**	**13.9**	**52.1**
Federal income taxes	**100.0**	**83.7**	**9.5**	**14.7**	**59.4**
Federal income tax deducted	100.0	55.4	10.7	12.7	32.1
Additional federal income tax paid	100.0	70.3	4.3	6.8	59.1
Federal income tax refunds	100.0	26.4	9.0	7.1	10.3
State and local income taxes	**100.0**	**63.2**	**10.7**	**12.9**	**39.6**
State and local income tax deducted	100.0	54.2	11.7	12.9	29.6
Additional state and local income tax paid	100.0	70.6	4.6	7.6	58.4
State and local income tax refunds	100.0	32.8	9.9	8.7	14.2
Other taxes	**100.0**	**42.4**	**9.4**	**8.7**	**24.2**

Note: Numbers may not add to total because of rounding. "–" means sample is too small to make a reliable estimate.
Source: Calculations by New Strategist based on the Bureau of Labor Statistics' 2011 Consumer Expenditure Survey

Table 4.13 Financial: Average spending by household type, 2011

(average annual spending of consumer units on financial products and services, cash contributions, and miscellaneous items, by type of consumer unit, 2011)

	total married couples	married couples, no children	married couples with children total	married couples with children oldest child under age 6	married couples with children oldest child aged 6 to 17	married couples with children oldest child aged 18 or older	single parent with child under age 18	single person
Number of consumer units (in 000s)	60,144	25,270	29,097	5,825	14,661	8,612	6,956	36,110
Average number of persons per consumer unit	3.2	2.0	4.0	3.5	4.2	3.9	2.9	1.0
Average before-tax income of consumer units	$86,700.00	$78,823.00	$93,677.00	$91,014.00	$93,029.00	$96,583.00	$37,188.00	$34,540.00
Average spending of consumer units, total	63,971.54	57,658.24	69,724.22	65,947.61	70,708.52	70,411.85	37,553.05	30,613.18
FINANCIAL PRODUCTS AND SERVICES	**896.85**	**902.08**	**864.53**	**972.82**	**811.00**	**883.13**	**667.69**	**576.91**
Miscellaneous fees	2.07	1.46	2.77	1.98	3.76	1.57	4.24	0.57
Lottery and gambling losses	70.06	81.62	34.81	11.35	29.49	57.38	4.47	29.90
Legal fees	135.61	134.49	124.10	106.30	106.07	166.83	260.60	162.79
Funeral expenses	51.49	50.60	41.92	19.50	34.34	70.00	83.82	85.56
Safe deposit box rental	4.20	6.69	2.65	2.58	1.92	3.92	0.69	3.04
Checking accounts, other bank service charges	21.27	17.12	23.95	17.12	27.43	22.65	21.78	21.43
Cemetery lots, vaults, and maintenance fees	7.44	12.10	1.85	1.89	1.10	3.11	1.87	9.72
Accounting fees	87.25	105.15	77.06	101.29	76.82	61.06	26.11	39.61
Miscellaneous personal services	58.90	33.77	85.74	113.22	114.18	21.89	87.75	29.04
Dating services	0.10	0.21	0.02	–	–	0.06	0.36	1.04
Finance charges, except mortgage and vehicles	182.58	109.57	240.26	239.71	235.92	248.02	107.64	93.90
Occupational expenses	62.72	55.16	73.92	99.58	57.06	85.26	28.85	24.10
Expenses for other properties	187.43	263.78	132.29	242.24	97.97	116.34	33.06	68.65
Credit card memberships	3.21	3.67	3.14	2.05	4.06	2.31	0.85	1.61
Shopping club membership fees	13.42	14.80	12.57	11.70	12.83	12.71	3.33	4.83
Vacation clubs	8.67	11.54	6.97	2.30	7.03	10.03	2.29	0.87
CASH CONTRIBUTIONS	**2,226.52**	**2,823.96**	**1,833.13**	**1,589.04**	**1,876.76**	**1,923.95**	**665.04**	**1,445.64**
Support for college students	160.57	177.96	159.84	113.59	122.50	254.70	44.40	94.53
Alimony expenditures	19.34	9.86	25.37	96.69	11.51	0.71	49.67	83.28
Child support expenditures	177.00	132.28	215.19	203.23	264.44	139.44	212.82	274.06
Gifts of stocks, bonds, and mutual funds to members of other households	42.93	93.30	7.41	0.14	14.03	1.07	11.97	79.81
Cash contributions to charities	319.26	505.25	199.22	128.87	224.15	204.36	49.88	140.96
Cash contributions to church, religious organizations	984.86	1,073.66	936.71	821.51	930.45	1,025.30	201.12	384.29
Cash contributions to educational institutions	33.71	38.62	33.10	33.48	42.21	17.35	9.58	24.95
Cash contributions to political organizations	12.41	22.75	5.01	1.41	5.94	5.88	4.92	9.92
Cash gifts to members of other households	476.45	770.27	251.26	190.11	261.54	275.14	80.69	353.85
PERSONAL INSURANCE AND PENSIONS	**7,652.07**	**6,549.45**	**8,759.14**	**8,881.51**	**8,843.48**	**8,532.78**	**3,241.47**	**2,588.15**
Life and other personal insurance	**462.96**	**472.83**	**473.19**	**508.72**	**443.01**	**500.52**	**134.51**	**179.20**
Life, endowment, annuity, other personal insurance	437.52	443.73	448.68	486.64	418.41	474.55	126.85	165.74
Other nonhealth insurance	25.45	29.10	24.50	22.08	24.60	25.97	7.66	13.46
Pensions and Social Security	**7,189.11**	**6,076.62**	**8,285.96**	**8,372.80**	**8,400.47**	**8,032.26**	**3,106.95**	**2,408.94**
Deductions for government retirement	124.78	98.29	159.10	151.93	167.13	150.27	51.79	61.22
Deductions for railroad retirement	5.91	8.95	4.45	–	2.07	11.52	13.66	–
Deductions for private pensions	803.82	719.55	925.39	999.52	914.40	893.96	299.82	292.75
Nonpayroll deposit to retirement plans	712.06	882.03	645.99	736.88	725.94	448.42	394.56	278.36
Deductions for Social Security	5,542.53	4,367.80	6,551.03	6,484.46	6,590.94	6,528.10	2,347.13	1,776.62
PERSONAL TAXES	**2,939.56**	**3,216.40**	**2,975.85**	**3,141.27**	**2,233.30**	**4,128.10**	**–10.97**	**1,377.74**
Federal income taxes	**2,023.73**	**2,362.49**	**1,957.41**	**2,076.08**	**1,423.81**	**2,785.54**	**–279.04**	**997.55**
Federal income tax deducted	2,539.14	2,189.40	2,912.77	3,664.98	2,594.50	2,945.78	1,178.50	1,224.24
Additional federal income tax paid	820.50	990.52	808.56	315.65	801.26	1,154.41	225.47	283.71
Federal income tax refunds	–1,335.90	–817.43	–1,763.92	–1,904.55	–1,971.95	–1,314.64	–1,683.01	–510.40
State and local income taxes	**719.18**	**637.46**	**831.89**	**817.47**	**662.45**	**1,130.12**	**226.18**	**293.23**
State and local income tax deducted	726.44	589.59	863.05	990.36	768.67	937.61	347.11	315.42
Additional state and local income tax paid	162.44	174.45	176.98	59.78	122.81	348.47	22.92	58.23
State and local income tax refunds	–169.70	–126.58	–208.13	–232.67	–229.03	–155.95	–143.84	–80.42
Other taxes	**196.65**	**216.45**	**186.55**	**247.72**	**147.04**	**212.44**	**41.89**	**86.95**

Note: Average spending figures for total consumer units can be found in Average Spending by Age and Average Spending by Region tables. Subcategories may not add to total because some are not shown.
"–" means sample is too small to make a reliable estimate.
Source: Bureau of Labor Statistics, unpublished tables from the 2011 Consumer Expenditure Survey

Table 4.14 Financial: Indexed spending by household type, 2011

(indexed average annual spending of consumer units on financial products and services, cash contributions, and miscellaneous items, by type of consumer unit, 2011; index definition: an index of 100 is the average for all consumer units; an index of 125 means that spending by consumer units in that group is 25 percent above the average for all consumer units; an index of 75 indicates spending that is 25 percent below the average for all consumer units)

	total married couples	married couples, no children	married couples with children				single parent with child under age 18	single person
			total	oldest child under age 6	oldest child aged 6 to 17	oldest child aged 18 or older		
Average spending of consumer units, total	$63,972	$57,658	$69,724	$65,948	$70,709	$70,412	$37,553	$30,613
Average spending of consumer units, index	129	116	140	133	142	142	76	62
FINANCIAL PRODUCTS AND SERVICES	**116**	**116**	**112**	**126**	**105**	**114**	**86**	**74**
Miscellaneous fees	144	101	192	138	261	109	294	40
Lottery and gambling losses	125	146	62	20	53	102	8	53
Legal fees	85	85	78	67	67	105	164	103
Funeral expenses	76	75	62	29	51	103	124	126
Safe deposit box rental	128	205	81	79	59	120	21	93
Checking accounts, other bank service charges	94	76	106	76	121	100	96	95
Cemetery lots, vaults, and maintenance fees	87	142	22	22	13	36	22	114
Accounting fees	139	167	122	161	122	97	41	63
Miscellaneous personal services	113	65	165	218	220	42	169	56
Dating services	23	48	5	–	–	14	82	236
Finance charges, except mortgage and vehicles	118	71	155	155	152	160	69	61
Occupational expenses	133	117	157	211	121	181	61	51
Expenses for other properties	154	216	108	198	80	95	27	56
Credit card memberships	137	156	134	87	173	98	36	69
Shopping club membership fees	145	160	136	126	138	137	36	52
Vacation clubs	178	237	143	47	145	206	47	18
CASH CONTRIBUTIONS	**129**	**164**	**107**	**92**	**109**	**112**	**39**	**84**
Support for college students	137	152	136	97	105	217	38	81
Alimony expenditures	41	21	54	204	24	2	105	176
Child support expenditures	79	59	96	90	118	62	95	122
Gifts of stocks, bonds, and mutual funds to members of other households	93	202	16	0	30	2	26	172
Cash contributions to charities	148	234	92	60	104	95	23	65
Cash contributions to church, religious organizations	152	165	144	127	143	158	31	59
Cash contributions to educational institutions	133	152	130	132	166	68	38	98
Cash contributions to political organizations	122	224	49	14	59	58	49	98
Cash gifts to members of other households	124	200	65	49	68	71	21	92
PERSONAL INSURANCE AND PENSIONS	**141**	**121**	**162**	**164**	**163**	**157**	**60**	**48**
Life and other personal insurance	**146**	**149**	**149**	**160**	**140**	**158**	**42**	**57**
Life, endowment, annuity, other personal insurance	147	149	150	163	140	159	42	56
Other nonhealth insurance	137	156	132	119	132	140	41	72
Pensions and Social Security	**141**	**119**	**162**	**164**	**165**	**157**	**61**	**47**
Deductions for government retirement	138	108	176	168	184	166	57	68
Deductions for railroad retirement	156	236	117	–	55	304	360	–
Deductions for private pensions	144	129	166	180	164	161	54	53
Nonpayroll deposit to retirement plans	142	176	129	147	145	90	79	56
Deductions for Social Security	140	110	166	164	167	165	59	45
PERSONAL TAXES	**146**	**160**	**148**	**156**	**111**	**205**	**–1**	**68**
Federal income taxes	**148**	**172**	**143**	**151**	**104**	**203**	**–20**	**73**
Federal income tax deducted	134	115	153	193	137	155	62	64
Additional federal income tax paid	154	186	152	59	151	217	42	53
Federal income tax refunds	126	77	166	180	186	124	159	48
State and local income taxes	**142**	**126**	**165**	**162**	**131**	**224**	**45**	**58**
State and local income tax deducted	137	111	162	186	145	176	65	59
Additional state and local income tax paid	155	166	168	57	117	332	22	55
State and local income tax refunds	129	96	158	177	174	118	109	61
Other taxes	**145**	**159**	**137**	**182**	**108**	**156**	**31**	**64**

Note: Spending index for total consumer units is 100. "–" means sample is too small to make a reliable estimate.
Source: Calculations by New Strategist based on the Bureau of Labor Statistics' 2011 Consumer Expenditure Survey

Table 4.15 Financial: Total spending by household type, 2011

(total annual spending on financial products and services, cash contributions, and miscellaneous items, by consumer unit type, 2011; consumer units and dollars in thousands)

	total married couples	married couples, no children	married couples with children				single parent with child under age 18	single person
			total	oldest child under age 6	oldest child aged 6 to 17	oldest child aged 18 or older		
Number of consumer units	60,144	25,270	29,097	5,825	14,661	8,612	6,956	36,110
Total spending of all consumer units	$3,847,504,302	$1,457,023,725	$2,028,765,629	$384,144,828	$1,036,657,612	$606,386,852	$261,219,016	$1,105,441,930
FINANCIAL PRODUCTS AND SERVICES	53,940,146	22,795,562	25,155,229	5,666,677	11,890,071	7,605,516	4,644,452	20,832,220
Miscellaneous fees	124,498	36,894	80,599	11,534	55,125	13,521	29,493	20,583
Lottery and gambling losses	4,213,689	2,062,537	1,012,867	66,114	432,353	494,157	31,093	1,079,689
Legal fees	8,156,128	3,398,562	3,610,938	619,198	1,555,092	1,436,740	1,812,734	5,878,347
Funeral expenses	3,096,815	1,278,662	1,219,746	113,588	503,459	602,840	583,052	3,089,572
Safe deposit box rental	252,605	169,056	77,107	15,029	28,149	33,759	4,800	109,774
Checking accounts, other bank service charges	1,279,263	432,622	696,873	99,724	402,151	195,062	151,502	773,837
Cemetery lots, vaults, and maintenance fees	447,471	305,767	53,829	11,009	16,127	26,783	13,008	350,989
Accounting fees	5,247,564	2,657,141	2,242,215	590,014	1,126,258	525,849	181,621	1,430,317
Miscellaneous personal services	3,542,482	853,368	2,494,777	659,507	1,673,993	188,517	610,389	1,048,634
Dating services	6,014	5,307	582	–	–	517	2,504	37,554
Finance charges, except mortgage and vehicles	10,981,092	2,768,834	6,990,845	1,396,311	3,458,823	2,135,948	748,744	3,390,729
Occupational expenses	3,772,232	1,393,893	2,150,850	580,054	836,557	734,259	200,681	870,251
Expenses for other properties	11,272,790	6,665,721	3,849,242	1,411,048	1,436,338	1,001,920	229,965	2,478,952
Credit card memberships	193,062	92,741	91,365	11,941	59,524	19,894	5,913	58,137
Shopping club membership fees	807,132	373,996	365,749	68,153	188,101	109,459	23,163	174,411
Vacation clubs	521,448	291,616	202,806	13,398	103,067	86,378	15,929	31,416
CASH CONTRIBUTIONS	133,911,819	71,361,469	53,338,584	9,256,158	27,515,178	16,569,057	4,626,018	52,202,060
Support for college students	9,657,322	4,497,049	4,650,864	661,662	1,795,973	2,193,476	308,846	3,413,478
Alimony expenditures	1,163,185	249,162	738,191	563,219	168,748	6,115	345,505	3,007,241
Child support expenditures	10,645,488	3,342,716	6,261,383	1,183,815	3,876,955	1,200,857	1,480,376	9,896,307
Gifts of stocks, bonds, and mutual funds to members of other households	2,581,982	2,357,691	215,609	816	205,694	9,215	83,263	2,881,939
Cash contributions to charities	19,201,573	12,767,668	5,796,704	750,668	3,286,263	1,759,948	346,965	5,090,066
Cash contributions to church, religious organizations	59,233,420	27,131,388	27,255,451	4,785,296	13,641,327	8,829,884	1,398,991	13,876,712
Cash contributions to educational institutions	2,027,454	975,927	963,111	195,021	618,841	149,418	66,638	900,945
Cash contributions to political organizations	746,387	574,893	145,776	8,213	87,086	50,639	34,224	358,211
Cash gifts to members of other households	28,655,609	19,464,723	7,310,912	1,107,391	3,834,438	2,369,506	561,280	12,777,524
PERSONAL INSURANCE AND PENSIONS	460,226,098	165,504,602	254,864,697	51,734,796	129,654,260	73,484,301	22,547,665	93,458,097
Life and other personal insurance	27,844,266	11,948,414	13,768,409	2,963,294	6,494,970	4,310,478	935,652	6,470,912
Life, endowment, annuity, other personal insurance	26,314,203	11,213,057	13,055,242	2,834,678	6,134,309	4,086,825	882,369	5,984,871
Other nonhealth insurance	1,530,665	735,357	712,877	128,616	360,661	223,654	53,283	486,041
Pensions and Social Security	432,381,832	153,556,187	241,096,578	48,771,560	123,159,291	69,173,823	21,611,944	86,986,823
Deductions for government retirement	7,504,768	2,483,788	4,629,333	884,992	2,450,293	1,294,125	360,251	2,210,654
Deductions for railroad retirement	355,451	226,167	129,482	–	30,348	99,210	95,019	–
Deductions for private pensions	48,344,950	18,183,029	26,926,073	5,822,204	13,406,018	7,698,784	2,085,548	10,571,203
Nonpayroll deposit to retirement plans	42,826,137	22,288,898	18,796,371	4,292,326	10,643,006	3,861,793	2,744,559	10,051,580
Deductions for Social Security	333,349,924	110,374,306	190,615,320	37,771,980	96,629,771	56,219,997	16,326,636	64,153,748
PERSONAL TAXES	176,796,897	81,278,428	86,588,307	18,297,898	32,742,411	35,551,197	−76,307	49,750,191
Federal income taxes	121,715,217	59,700,122	56,954,759	12,093,166	20,874,478	23,989,070	−1,941,002	36,021,531
Federal income tax deducted	152,714,036	55,326,138	84,752,869	21,348,509	38,037,965	25,369,057	8,197,646	44,207,306
Additional federal income tax paid	49,348,152	25,030,440	23,526,670	1,838,661	11,747,273	9,941,779	1,568,369	10,244,768
Federal income tax refunds	−80,346,370	−20,656,456	−51,324,780	−11,094,004	−28,910,759	−11,321,680	−11,707,018	−18,430,544
State and local income taxes	43,254,362	16,108,614	24,205,503	4,761,763	9,712,179	9,732,593	1,573,308	10,588,535
State and local income tax deducted	43,691,007	14,898,939	25,112,166	5,768,847	11,269,471	8,074,697	2,414,497	11,389,816
Additional state and local income tax paid	9,769,791	4,408,352	5,149,587	348,219	1,800,517	3,001,024	159,432	2,102,685
State and local income tax refunds	−10,206,437	−3,198,677	−6,055,959	−1,355,303	−3,357,809	−1,343,041	−1,000,551	−2,903,966
Other taxes	11,827,318	5,469,692	5,428,045	1,442,969	2,155,753	1,829,533	291,387	3,139,765

Note: Total spending figures for total consumer units can be found in Total Spending by Age and Total Spending by Region tables. Spending by type of consumer unit does not add to total because not all types of consumer units are shown. Numbers may not add to category total because of rounding and missing subcategories. "–" means sample is too small to make a reliable estimate.
Source: Calculations by New Strategist based on the Bureau of Labor Statistics' 2011 Consumer Expenditure Survey

Table 4.16 Financial: Market shares by household type, 2011

(percentage of total annual spending on financial products and services, cash contributions, and miscellaneous items accounted for by types of consumer units, 2011)

	total married couples	married couples, no children	married couples with children				single parent with child under age 18	single person
			total	oldest child under age 6	oldest child aged 6 to 17	oldest child aged 18 or older		
Share of total consumer units	49.2%	20.7%	23.8%	4.8%	12.0%	7.0%	5.7%	29.5%
Share of total before-tax income	67.0	25.6	35.0	6.8	17.5	10.7	3.3	16.0
Share of total spending	63.3	24.0	33.4	6.3	17.1	10.0	4.3	18.2
FINANCIAL PRODUCTS AND SERVICES	**56.9**	**24.1**	**26.5**	**6.0**	**12.5**	**8.0**	**4.9**	**22.0**
Miscellaneous fees	70.7	21.0	45.8	6.5	31.3	7.7	16.7	11.7
Lottery and gambling losses	61.5	30.1	14.8	1.0	6.3	7.2	0.5	15.8
Legal fees	42.0	17.5	18.6	3.2	8.0	7.4	9.3	30.3
Funeral expenses	37.4	15.5	14.7	1.4	6.1	7.3	7.0	37.3
Safe deposit box rental	63.2	42.3	19.3	3.8	7.0	8.4	1.2	27.5
Checking accounts, other bank service charges	46.3	15.7	25.2	3.6	14.6	7.1	5.5	28.0
Cemetery lots, vaults, and maintenance fees	42.8	29.3	5.2	1.1	1.5	2.6	1.2	33.6
Accounting fees	68.2	34.5	29.1	7.7	14.6	6.8	2.4	18.6
Miscellaneous personal services	55.8	13.4	39.3	10.4	26.4	3.0	9.6	16.5
Dating services	11.2	9.9	1.1	–	–	1.0	4.7	69.8
Finance charges, except mortgage and vehicles	58.0	14.6	36.9	7.4	18.3	11.3	4.0	17.9
Occupational expenses	65.3	24.1	37.2	10.0	14.5	12.7	3.5	15.1
Expenses for other properties	75.5	44.6	25.8	9.5	9.6	6.7	1.5	16.6
Credit card memberships	67.2	32.3	31.8	4.2	20.7	6.9	2.1	20.2
Shopping club membership fees	71.2	33.0	32.3	6.0	16.6	9.7	2.0	15.4
Vacation clubs	87.7	49.1	34.1	2.3	17.3	14.5	2.7	5.3
CASH CONTRIBUTIONS	**63.6**	**33.9**	**25.3**	**4.4**	**13.1**	**7.9**	**2.2**	**24.8**
Support for college students	67.4	31.4	32.5	4.6	12.5	15.3	2.2	23.8
Alimony expenditures	20.1	4.3	12.8	9.7	2.9	0.1	6.0	52.0
Child support expenditures	38.7	12.2	22.8	4.3	14.1	4.4	5.4	36.0
Gifts of stocks, bonds, and mutual funds to members of other households	45.6	41.7	3.8	0.0	3.6	0.2	1.5	50.9
Cash contributions to charities	72.8	48.4	22.0	2.8	12.5	6.7	1.3	19.3
Cash contributions to church, religious organizations	74.6	34.2	34.3	6.0	17.2	11.1	1.8	17.5
Cash contributions to educational institutions	65.4	31.5	31.0	6.3	19.9	4.8	2.1	29.0
Cash contributions to political organizations	60.2	46.4	11.8	0.7	7.0	4.1	2.8	28.9
Cash gifts to members of other households	60.9	41.4	15.5	2.4	8.1	5.0	1.2	27.2
PERSONAL INSURANCE AND PENSIONS	**69.4**	**25.0**	**38.4**	**7.8**	**19.5**	**11.1**	**3.4**	**14.1**
Life and other personal insurance	**71.8**	**30.8**	**35.5**	**7.6**	**16.7**	**11.1**	**2.4**	**16.7**
Life, endowment, annuity, other personal insurance	72.1	30.7	35.8	7.8	16.8	11.2	2.4	16.4
Other nonhealth insurance	67.3	32.3	31.3	5.7	15.9	9.8	2.3	21.4
Pensions and Social Security	**69.2**	**24.6**	**38.6**	**7.8**	**19.7**	**11.1**	**3.5**	**13.9**
Deductions for government retirement	67.7	22.4	41.8	8.0	22.1	11.7	3.2	19.9
Deductions for railroad retirement	76.7	48.8	27.9	–	6.5	21.4	20.5	–
Deductions for private pensions	71.1	26.7	39.6	8.6	19.7	11.3	3.1	15.5
Nonpayroll deposit to retirement plans	70.0	36.4	30.7	7.0	17.4	6.3	4.5	16.4
Deductions for Social Security	68.9	22.8	39.4	7.8	20.0	11.6	3.4	13.3
PERSONAL TAXES	**71.9**	**33.0**	**35.2**	**7.4**	**13.3**	**14.5**	**0.0**	**20.2**
Federal income taxes	**72.6**	**35.6**	**34.0**	**7.2**	**12.5**	**14.3**	**−1.2**	**21.5**
Federal income tax deducted	65.8	23.8	36.5	9.2	16.4	10.9	3.5	19.0
Additional federal income tax paid	76.0	38.5	36.2	2.8	18.1	15.3	2.4	15.8
Federal income tax refunds	62.0	15.9	39.6	8.6	22.3	8.7	9.0	14.2
State and local income taxes	**70.0**	**26.1**	**39.2**	**7.7**	**15.7**	**15.8**	**2.5**	**17.1**
State and local income tax deducted	67.2	22.9	38.6	8.9	17.3	12.4	3.7	17.5
Additional state and local income tax paid	76.0	34.3	40.1	2.7	14.0	23.3	1.2	16.4
State and local income tax refunds	63.4	19.9	37.6	8.4	20.8	8.3	6.2	18.0
Other taxes	**71.1**	**32.9**	**32.6**	**8.7**	**13.0**	**11.0**	**1.8**	**18.9**

Note: Market share for total consumer units is 100.0%. Market shares by type of consumer unit do not add to total because not all types of consumer units are shown. "–" means sample is too small to make a reliable estimate.

Source: Calculations by New Strategist based on the Bureau of Labor Statistics' 2011 Consumer Expenditure Survey

Table 4.17 Financial: Average spending by race and Hispanic origin, 2011

(average annual spending of consumer units on financial products and services, cash contributions, and miscellaneous items, by race and Hispanic origin of consumer unit reference person, 2011)

	total consumer units	Asian	black	Hispanic	non-Hispanic white and other
Number of consumer units (in 000s)	122,287	5,048	15,118	15,222	92,163
Average number of persons per consumer unit	2.5	2.7	2.6	3.4	2.4
Average before-tax income of consumer units	$63,685.00	$85,415.00	$45,552.00	$49,966.00	$68,907.00
Average spending of consumer units, total	49,704.88	60,136.04	36,643.75	42,085.98	53,055.68
FINANCIAL PRODUCTS AND SERVICES	774.92	696.02	520.87	476.49	863.87
Miscellaneous fees	1.44	–	0.42	–	1.81
Lottery and gambling losses	56.00	26.70	98.20	34.09	52.50
Legal fees	158.75	74.85	58.65	65.41	190.21
Funeral expenses	67.67	100.37	59.82	83.34	66.20
Safe deposit box rental	3.27	7.40	0.94	0.37	4.12
Checking accounts, other bank service charges	22.58	13.31	26.43	20.91	22.26
Cemetery lots, vaults, and maintenance fees	8.54	21.95	5.21	6.29	9.44
Accounting fees	62.95	50.30	23.44	36.33	73.74
Miscellaneous personal services	51.94	142.89	36.31	15.39	59.80
Dating services	0.44	0.05	0.05	0.37	0.52
Finance charges, except mortgage and vehicles	154.94	62.39	106.40	102.84	171.27
Occupational expenses	47.22	48.63	28.85	43.94	50.86
Expenses for other properties	122.10	126.56	67.62	54.30	141.95
Credit card memberships	2.35	4.07	1.21	1.95	2.61
Shopping club membership fees	9.27	13.36	6.68	9.43	9.68
Vacation clubs	4.86	0.20	0.62	1.53	6.09
CASH CONTRIBUTIONS	1,720.87	1,405.15	1,341.01	812.13	1,930.50
Support for college students	117.18	90.73	81.80	50.20	133.88
Alimony expenditures	47.29	5.56	–	5.81	61.79
Child support expenditures	224.93	29.70	252.83	217.66	221.40
Gifts of stocks, bonds, and mutual funds to members of other households	46.27	1.76	0.05	0.80	61.25
Cash contributions to charities	215.69	227.11	71.10	47.74	266.72
Cash contributions to church, religious organizations	649.17	522.32	739.86	286.05	692.95
Cash contributions to educational institutions	25.37	29.98	3.91	5.06	32.19
Cash contributions to political organizations	10.14	4.83	4.96	0.44	12.56
Cash gifts to members of other households	384.82	493.15	186.50	198.37	447.74
PERSONAL INSURANCE AND PENSIONS	5,423.57	7,770.60	3,593.09	4,029.81	5,951.39
Life and other personal insurance	317.12	337.05	249.51	115.14	361.16
Life, endowment, annuity, other personal insurance	298.52	324.73	241.42	108.95	338.83
Other nonhealth insurance	18.60	12.32	8.09	6.19	22.33
Pensions and Social Security	5,106.45	7,433.55	3,343.58	3,914.66	5,590.23
Deductions for government retirement	90.65	138.11	55.50	69.51	99.69
Deductions for railroad retirement	3.79	–	–	0.09	5.02
Deductions for private pensions	556.40	846.24	253.67	189.98	665.41
Nonpayroll deposit to retirement plans	500.06	987.12	178.33	104.19	617.05
Deductions for Social Security	3,955.54	5,462.08	2,856.07	3,550.89	4,203.07
PERSONAL TAXES	2,011.61	3,894.16	500.37	464.80	2,511.38
Federal income taxes	1,370.41	3,032.32	198.00	235.74	1,747.19
Federal income tax deducted	1,899.25	3,209.65	1,053.85	1,371.80	2,124.87
Additional federal income tax paid	531.19	606.14	87.01	83.89	676.69
Federal income tax refunds	–1,060.03	–783.47	–942.86	–1,219.95	–1,054.37
State and local income taxes	505.23	727.66	239.82	185.98	601.16
State and local income tax deducted	531.84	859.65	323.06	257.03	611.19
Additional state and local income tax paid	105.11	40.67	17.69	24.49	132.52
State and local income tax refunds	–131.72	–172.66	–100.94	–95.54	–142.55
Other taxes	135.97	134.18	62.55	43.09	163.03

Note: "Asian" and "black" include Hispanics and non-Hispanics who identify themselves as being of the respective race alone. "Hispanic" includes people of any race who identify themselves as Hispanic. "Other" includes people who identify themselves as non-Hispanic and as Alaska Native, American Indian, Asian (who are also included in the "Asian" column), or Native Hawaiian or other Pacific Islander, as well as non-Hispanics reporting more than one race. Subcategories may not add to total because some are not shown. "–" means sample is too small to make a reliable estimate.
Source: Bureau of Labor Statistics, unpublished tables from the 2011 Consumer Expenditure Survey

Table 4.18 Financial: Indexed spending by race and Hispanic origin, 2011

(indexed average annual spending of consumer units on financial products and services, cash contributions, and miscellaneous items, by race and Hispanic origin of consumer unit reference person, 2011; index definition: an index of 100 is the average for all consumer units; an index of 125 means that spending by consumer units in that group is 25 percent above the average for all consumer units; an index of 75 indicates spending that is 25 percent below the average for all consumer units)

	total consumer units	Asian	black	Hispanic	non-Hispanic white and other
Average spending of consumer units, total	$49,705	$60,136	$36,644	$42,086	$53,056
Average spending of consumer units, index	100	121	74	85	107
FINANCIAL PRODUCTS AND SERVICES	**100**	**90**	**67**	**61**	**111**
Miscellaneous fees	100	–	29	–	126
Lottery and gambling losses	100	48	175	61	94
Legal fees	100	47	37	41	120
Funeral expenses	100	148	88	123	98
Safe deposit box rental	100	226	29	11	126
Checking accounts, other bank service charges	100	59	117	93	99
Cemetery lots, vaults, and maintenance fees	100	257	61	74	111
Accounting fees	100	80	37	58	117
Miscellaneous personal services	100	275	70	30	115
Dating services	100	11	11	84	118
Finance charges, except mortgage and vehicles	100	40	69	66	111
Occupational expenses	100	103	61	93	108
Expenses for other properties	100	104	55	44	116
Credit card memberships	100	173	51	83	111
Shopping club membership fees	100	144	72	102	104
Vacation clubs	100	4	13	31	125
CASH CONTRIBUTIONS	**100**	**82**	**78**	**47**	**112**
Support for college students	100	77	70	43	114
Alimony expenditures	100	12	–	12	131
Child support expenditures	100	13	112	97	98
Gifts of stocks, bonds, and mutual funds to members of other households	100	4	0	2	132
Cash contributions to charities	100	105	33	22	124
Cash contributions to church, religious organizations	100	80	114	44	107
Cash contributions to educational institutions	100	118	15	20	127
Cash contributions to political organizations	100	48	49	4	124
Cash gifts to members of other households	100	128	48	52	116
PERSONAL INSURANCE AND PENSIONS	**100**	**143**	**66**	**74**	**110**
Life and other personal insurance	**100**	**106**	**79**	**36**	**114**
Life, endowment, annuity, other personal insurance	100	109	81	36	114
Other nonhealth insurance	100	66	43	33	120
Pensions and Social Security	**100**	**146**	**65**	**77**	**109**
Deductions for government retirement	100	152	61	77	110
Deductions for railroad retirement	100	–	–	2	132
Deductions for private pensions	100	152	46	34	120
Nonpayroll deposit to retirement plans	100	197	36	21	123
Deductions for Social Security	100	138	72	90	106
PERSONAL TAXES	**100**	**194**	**25**	**23**	**125**
Federal income taxes	**100**	**221**	**14**	**17**	**127**
Federal income tax deducted	100	169	55	72	112
Additional federal income tax paid	100	114	16	16	127
Federal income tax refunds	100	74	89	115	99
State and local income taxes	**100**	**144**	**47**	**37**	**119**
State and local income tax deducted	100	162	61	48	115
Additional state and local income tax paid	100	39	17	23	126
State and local income tax refunds	100	131	77	73	108
Other taxes	**100**	**99**	**46**	**32**	**120**

Note: "Asian" and "black" include Hispanics and non-Hispanics who identify themselves as being of the respective race alone. "Hispanic" includes people of any race who identify themselves as Hispanic. "Other" includes people who identify themselves as non-Hispanic and as Alaska Native, American Indian, Asian (who are also included in the "Asian" column), or Native Hawaiian or other Pacific Islander, as well as non-Hispanics reporting more than one race. "–" means sample is too small to make a reliable estimate.
Source: Calculations by New Strategist based on the Bureau of Labor Statistics' 2011 Consumer Expenditure Survey

Table 4.19 Financial: Total spending by race and Hispanic origin, 2011

(total annual spending on financial products and services, cash contributions, and miscellaneous items, by consumer unit race and Hispanic origin groups, 2011; consumer units and dollars in thousands)

	total consumer units	Asian	black	Hispanic	non-Hispanic white and other
Number of consumer units	122,287	5,048	15,118	15,222	92,163
Total spending of all consumer units	$6,078,260,661	$303,566,730	$553,980,213	$640,632,788	$4,889,770,636
FINANCIAL PRODUCTS AND SERVICES	94,762,642	3,513,509	7,874,513	7,253,131	79,616,851
Miscellaneous fees	176,093	–	6,350	–	166,815
Lottery and gambling losses	6,848,072	134,782	1,484,588	518,918	4,838,558
Legal fees	19,413,061	377,843	886,671	995,671	17,530,324
Funeral expenses	8,275,161	506,668	904,359	1,268,601	6,101,191
Safe deposit box rental	399,878	37,355	14,211	5,632	379,712
Checking accounts, other bank service charges	2,761,240	67,189	399,569	318,292	2,051,548
Cemetery lots, vaults, and maintenance fees	1,044,331	110,804	78,765	95,746	870,019
Accounting fees	7,697,967	253,914	354,366	553,015	6,796,100
Miscellaneous personal services	6,351,587	721,309	548,935	234,267	5,511,347
Dating services	53,806	252	756	5,632	47,925
Finance charges, except mortgage and vehicles	18,947,148	314,945	1,608,555	1,565,430	15,784,757
Occupational expenses	5,774,392	245,484	436,154	668,855	4,687,410
Expenses for other properties	14,931,243	638,875	1,022,279	826,555	13,082,538
Credit card memberships	287,374	20,545	18,293	29,683	240,545
Shopping club membership fees	1,133,600	67,441	100,988	143,543	892,138
Vacation clubs	594,315	1,010	9,373	23,290	561,273
CASH CONTRIBUTIONS	210,440,030	7,093,197	20,273,389	12,362,243	177,920,672
Support for college students	14,329,591	458,005	1,236,652	764,144	12,338,782
Alimony expenditures	5,782,952	28,067	–	88,440	5,694,752
Child support expenditures	27,506,015	149,926	3,822,284	3,313,221	20,404,888
Gifts of stocks, bonds, and mutual funds to members of other households	5,658,219	8,884	756	12,178	5,644,984
Cash contributions to charities	26,376,083	1,146,451	1,074,890	726,698	24,581,715
Cash contributions to church, religious organizations	79,385,052	2,636,671	11,185,203	4,354,253	63,864,351
Cash contributions to educational institutions	3,102,421	151,339	59,111	77,023	2,966,727
Cash contributions to political organizations	1,239,990	24,382	74,985	6,698	1,157,567
Cash gifts to members of other households	47,058,483	2,489,421	2,819,507	3,019,588	41,265,062
PERSONAL INSURANCE AND PENSIONS	663,232,105	39,225,989	54,320,335	61,341,768	548,497,957
Life and other personal insurance	38,779,653	1,701,428	3,772,092	1,752,661	33,285,589
Life, endowment, annuity, other personal insurance	36,505,115	1,639,237	3,649,788	1,658,437	31,227,589
Other nonhealth insurance	2,274,538	62,191	122,305	94,224	2,058,000
Pensions and Social Security	624,452,451	37,524,560	50,548,242	59,588,955	515,212,367
Deductions for government retirement	11,085,317	697,179	839,049	1,058,081	9,187,729
Deductions for railroad retirement	463,468	–	–	1,370	462,658
Deductions for private pensions	68,040,487	4,271,820	3,834,983	2,891,876	61,326,182
Nonpayroll deposit to retirement plans	61,150,837	4,982,982	2,695,993	1,585,980	56,869,179
Deductions for Social Security	483,711,120	27,572,580	43,178,066	54,051,648	387,367,540
PERSONAL TAXES	245,993,752	19,657,720	7,564,594	7,075,186	231,456,315
Federal income taxes	167,583,328	15,307,151	2,993,364	3,588,434	161,026,272
Federal income tax deducted	232,253,585	16,202,313	15,932,104	20,881,540	195,834,394
Additional federal income tax paid	64,957,632	3,059,795	1,315,417	1,276,974	62,365,780
Federal income tax refunds	−129,627,889	−3,954,957	−14,254,157	−18,570,079	−97,173,902
State and local income taxes	61,783,061	3,673,228	3,625,599	2,830,988	55,404,709
State and local income tax deducted	65,037,118	4,339,513	4,884,021	3,912,511	56,329,104
Additional state and local income tax paid	12,853,587	205,302	267,437	372,787	12,213,441
State and local income tax refunds	−16,107,644	−871,588	−1,526,011	−1,454,310	−13,137,836
Other taxes	16,627,363	677,341	945,631	655,916	15,025,334

Note: "Asian" and "black" include Hispanics and non-Hispanics who identify themselves as being of the respective race alone. "Hispanic" includes people of any race who identify themselves as Hispanic. "Other" includes people who identify themselves as non-Hispanic and as Alaska Native, American Indian, Asian (who are also included in the "Asian" column), or Native Hawaiian or other Pacific Islander, as well as non-Hispanics reporting more than one race. Numbers may not add to total because of rounding and missing subcategories. "–" means sample is too small to make a reliable estimate.
Source: Calculations by New Strategist based on the Bureau of Labor Statistics' 2011 Consumer Expenditure Survey

Table 4.20 Financial: Market shares by race and Hispanic origin, 2011

(percentage of total annual spending on financial products and services, cash contributions, and miscellaneous items accounted for by consumer unit race and Hispanic origin groups, 2011)

	total consumer units	Asian	black	Hispanic	non-Hispanic white and other
Share of total consumer units	100.0%	4.1%	12.4%	12.4%	75.4%
Share of total before-tax income	100.0	5.5	8.8	9.8	81.5
Share of total spending	100.0	5.0	9.1	10.5	80.4
FINANCIAL PRODUCTS AND SERVICES	**100.0**	**3.7**	**8.3**	**7.7**	**84.0**
Miscellaneous fees	100.0	–	3.6	–	94.7
Lottery and gambling losses	100.0	2.0	21.7	7.6	70.7
Legal fees	100.0	1.9	4.6	5.1	90.3
Funeral expenses	100.0	6.1	10.9	15.3	73.7
Safe deposit box rental	100.0	9.3	3.6	1.4	95.0
Checking accounts, other bank service charges	100.0	2.4	14.5	11.5	74.3
Cemetery lots, vaults, and maintenance fees	100.0	10.6	7.5	9.2	83.3
Accounting fees	100.0	3.3	4.6	7.2	88.3
Miscellaneous personal services	100.0	11.4	8.6	3.7	86.8
Dating services	100.0	0.5	1.4	10.5	89.1
Finance charges, except mortgage and vehicles	100.0	1.7	8.5	8.3	83.3
Occupational expenses	100.0	4.3	7.6	11.6	81.2
Expenses for other properties	100.0	4.3	6.8	5.5	87.6
Credit card memberships	100.0	7.1	6.4	10.3	83.7
Shopping club membership fees	100.0	5.9	8.9	12.7	78.7
Vacation clubs	100.0	0.2	1.6	3.9	94.4
CASH CONTRIBUTIONS	**100.0**	**3.4**	**9.6**	**5.9**	**84.5**
Support for college students	100.0	3.2	8.6	5.3	86.1
Alimony expenditures	100.0	0.5	–	1.5	98.5
Child support expenditures	100.0	0.5	13.9	12.0	74.2
Gifts of stocks, bonds, and mutual funds to members of other households	100.0	0.2	0.0	0.2	99.8
Cash contributions to charities	100.0	4.3	4.1	2.8	93.2
Cash contributions to church, religious organizations	100.0	3.3	14.1	5.5	80.4
Cash contributions to educational institutions	100.0	4.9	1.9	2.5	95.6
Cash contributions to political organizations	100.0	2.0	6.0	0.5	93.4
Cash gifts to members of other households	100.0	5.3	6.0	6.4	87.7
PERSONAL INSURANCE AND PENSIONS	**100.0**	**5.9**	**8.2**	**9.2**	**82.7**
Life and other personal insurance	**100.0**	**4.4**	**9.7**	**4.5**	**85.8**
Life, endowment, annuity, other personal insurance	100.0	4.5	10.0	4.5	85.5
Other nonhealth insurance	100.0	2.7	5.4	4.1	90.5
Pensions and Social Security	**100.0**	**6.0**	**8.1**	**9.5**	**82.5**
Deductions for government retirement	100.0	6.3	7.6	9.5	82.9
Deductions for railroad retirement	100.0	–	–	0.3	99.8
Deductions for private pensions	100.0	6.3	5.6	4.3	90.1
Nonpayroll deposit to retirement plans	100.0	8.1	4.4	2.6	93.0
Deductions for Social Security	100.0	5.7	8.9	11.2	80.1
PERSONAL TAXES	**100.0**	**8.0**	**3.1**	**2.9**	**94.1**
Federal income taxes	**100.0**	**9.1**	**1.8**	**2.1**	**96.1**
Federal income tax deducted	100.0	7.0	6.9	9.0	84.3
Additional federal income tax paid	100.0	4.7	2.0	2.0	96.0
Federal income tax refunds	100.0	3.1	11.0	14.3	75.0
State and local income taxes	**100.0**	**5.9**	**5.9**	**4.6**	**89.7**
State and local income tax deducted	100.0	6.7	7.5	6.0	86.6
Additional state and local income tax paid	100.0	1.6	2.1	2.9	95.0
State and local income tax refunds	100.0	5.4	9.5	9.0	81.6
Other taxes	**100.0**	**4.1**	**5.7**	**3.9**	**90.4**

Note: "Asian" and "black" include Hispanics and non-Hispanics who identify themselves as being of the respective race alone. "Hispanic" includes people of any race who identify themselves as Hispanic. "Other" includes people who identify themselves as non-Hispanic and as Alaska Native, American Indian, Asian (who are also included in the "Asian" column), or Native Hawaiian or other Pacific Islander, as well as non-Hispanics reporting more than one race. "–" means sample is too small to make a reliable estimate.
Source: Calculations by New Strategist based on the Bureau of Labor Statistics' 2011 Consumer Expenditure Survey

Table 4.21 Financial: Average spending by region, 2011

(average annual spending of consumer units on financial products and services, cash contributions, and miscellaneous items, by region in which consumer unit lives, 2011)

	total consumer units	Northeast	Midwest	South	West
Number of consumer units (in 000s)	122,287	22,538	27,107	44,901	27,741
Average number of persons per consumer unit	2.5	2.4	2.4	2.5	2.6
Average before-tax income of consumer units	$63,685.00	$71,733.00	$60,897.00	$58,780.00	$67,810.00
Average spending of consumer units, total	49,704.88	54,547.45	47,191.54	45,698.60	54,745.43
FINANCIAL PRODUCTS AND SERVICES	**774.92**	**858.21**	**764.43**	**660.58**	**903.10**
Miscellaneous fees	1.44	2.41	1.47	0.22	2.62
Lottery and gambling losses	56.00	46.94	44.23	60.82	67.26
Legal fees	158.75	204.45	131.13	130.62	194.13
Funeral expenses	67.67	72.92	81.24	59.16	63.90
Safe deposit box rental	3.27	3.41	3.77	2.76	3.48
Checking accounts, other bank service charges	22.58	23.12	21.53	18.84	29.22
Cemetery lots, vaults, and maintenance fees	8.54	8.48	13.41	6.79	6.68
Accounting fees	62.95	93.08	47.02	42.07	87.82
Miscellaneous personal services	51.94	38.21	51.44	47.55	70.98
Dating services	0.44	0.32	0.57	0.30	0.64
Finance charges, except mortgage and vehicles	154.94	153.33	163.47	120.30	204.00
Occupational expenses	47.22	64.17	49.88	25.35	66.26
Expenses for other properties	122.10	132.06	138.07	131.66	82.94
Credit card memberships	2.35	2.09	1.81	2.48	2.89
Shopping club membership fees	9.27	7.18	6.29	8.11	15.78
Vacation clubs	4.86	5.38	8.76	3.55	2.73
CASH CONTRIBUTIONS	**1,720.87**	**1,808.51**	**1,674.52**	**1,613.46**	**1,868.82**
Support for college students	117.18	117.50	106.35	102.16	151.82
Alimony expenditures	47.29	136.43	14.97	14.45	59.61
Child support expenditures	224.93	219.04	228.81	242.87	196.90
Gifts of stocks, bonds, and mutual funds to members of other households	46.27	2.85	107.66	10.97	78.69
Cash contributions to charities	215.69	388.84	195.19	133.66	227.82
Cash contributions to church, religious organizations	649.17	351.64	657.25	770.66	686.35
Cash contributions to educational institutions	25.37	23.38	20.80	17.80	43.73
Cash contributions to political organizations	10.14	8.03	9.46	9.32	13.83
Cash gifts to members of other households	384.82	560.79	334.03	311.57	410.06
PERSONAL INSURANCE AND PENSIONS	**5,423.57**	**5,960.59**	**5,178.40**	**4,935.82**	**6,016.29**
Life and other personal insurance	**317.12**	**406.24**	**296.47**	**306.68**	**281.80**
Life, endowment, annuity, other personal insurance	298.52	390.21	279.92	291.47	253.60
Other nonhealth insurance	18.60	16.03	16.56	15.20	28.19
Pensions and Social Security	**5,106.45**	**5,554.35**	**4,881.93**	**4,629.15**	**5,734.50**
Deductions for government retirement	90.65	57.60	84.14	85.60	132.04
Deductions for railroad retirement	3.79	–	5.46	1.45	9.03
Deductions for private pensions	556.40	637.10	615.81	390.72	700.96
Nonpayroll deposit to retirement plans	500.06	479.57	373.99	457.93	708.10
Deductions for Social Security	3,955.54	4,380.07	3,802.53	3,693.45	4,184.37
PERSONAL TAXES	**2,011.61**	**2,398.14**	**1,502.22**	**1,575.33**	**2,901.46**
Federal income taxes	**1,370.41**	**1,538.77**	**945.93**	**1,111.37**	**2,067.66**
Federal income tax deducted	1,899.25	2,016.17	1,593.58	1,831.90	2,211.93
Additional federal income tax paid	531.19	606.54	393.93	357.06	885.95
Federal income tax refunds	−1,060.03	−1,083.94	−1,041.58	−1,077.58	−1,030.22
State and local income taxes	**505.23**	**652.95**	**476.24**	**298.81**	**747.64**
State and local income tax deducted	531.84	663.41	555.72	369.03	665.12
Additional state and local income tax paid	105.11	124.33	76.10	29.47	240.28
State and local income tax refunds	−131.72	−134.78	−155.58	−99.69	−157.76
Other taxes	**135.97**	**206.41**	**80.04**	**165.14**	**86.17**

Note: Subcategories may not add to total because some are not shown. "–" means sample is too small to make a reliable estimate.
Source: Bureau of Labor Statistics, unpublished tables from the 2011 Consumer Expenditure Survey

Table 4.22 Financial: Indexed spending by region, 2011

(indexed average annual spending of consumer units on financial products and services, cash contributions, and miscellaneous items, by region in which consumer unit lives, 2011; index definition: an index of 100 is the average for all consumer units; an index of 125 means that spending by consumer units in that group is 25 percent above the average for all consumer units; an index of 75 indicates spending that is 25 percent below the average for all consumer units)

	total consumer units	Northeast	Midwest	South	West
Average spending of consumer units, total	$49,705	$54,547	$47,192	$45,699	$54,745
Average spending of consumer units, index	100	110	95	92	110
FINANCIAL PRODUCTS AND SERVICES	**100**	**111**	**99**	**85**	**117**
Miscellaneous fees	100	167	102	15	182
Lottery and gambling losses	100	84	79	109	120
Legal fees	100	129	83	82	122
Funeral expenses	100	108	120	87	94
Safe deposit box rental	100	104	115	84	106
Checking accounts, other bank service charges	100	102	95	83	129
Cemetery lots, vaults, and maintenance fees	100	99	157	80	78
Accounting fees	100	148	75	67	140
Miscellaneous personal services	100	74	99	92	137
Dating services	100	73	130	68	145
Finance charges, except mortgage and vehicles	100	99	106	78	132
Occupational expenses	100	136	106	54	140
Expenses for other properties	100	108	113	108	68
Credit card memberships	100	89	77	106	123
Shopping club membership fees	100	77	68	87	170
Vacation clubs	100	111	180	73	56
CASH CONTRIBUTIONS	**100**	**105**	**97**	**94**	**109**
Support for college students	100	100	91	87	130
Alimony expenditures	100	288	32	31	126
Child support expenditures	100	97	102	108	88
Gifts of stocks, bonds, and mutual funds to members of other households	100	6	233	24	170
Cash contributions to charities	100	180	90	62	106
Cash contributions to church, religious organizations	100	54	101	119	106
Cash contributions to educational institutions	100	92	82	70	172
Cash contributions to political organizations	100	79	93	92	136
Cash gifts to members of other households	100	146	87	81	107
PERSONAL INSURANCE AND PENSIONS	**100**	**110**	**95**	**91**	**111**
Life and other personal insurance	**100**	**128**	**93**	**97**	**89**
Life, endowment, annuity, other personal insurance	100	131	94	98	85
Other nonhealth insurance	100	86	89	82	152
Pensions and Social Security	**100**	**109**	**96**	**91**	**112**
Deductions for government retirement	100	64	93	94	146
Deductions for railroad retirement	100	–	144	38	238
Deductions for private pensions	100	115	111	70	126
Nonpayroll deposit to retirement plans	100	96	75	92	142
Deductions for Social Security	100	111	96	93	106
PERSONAL TAXES	**100**	**119**	**75**	**78**	**144**
Federal income taxes	**100**	**112**	**69**	**81**	**151**
Federal income tax deducted	100	106	84	96	116
Additional federal income tax paid	100	114	74	67	167
Federal income tax refunds	100	102	98	102	97
State and local income taxes	**100**	**129**	**94**	**59**	**148**
State and local income tax deducted	100	125	104	69	125
Additional state and local income tax paid	100	118	72	28	229
State and local income tax refunds	100	102	118	76	120
Other taxes	**100**	**152**	**59**	**121**	**63**

Note: "–" means sample is too small to make a reliable estimate.
Source: Calculations by New Strategist based on the Bureau of Labor Statistics' 2011 Consumer Expenditure Survey

Table 4.23 Financial: Total spending by region, 2011

(total annual spending on financial products and services, cash contributions, and miscellaneous items, by region in which consumer units live, 2011; consumer units and dollars in thousands)

	total consumer units	Northeast	Midwest	South	West
Number of consumer units	122,287	22,538	27,107	44,901	27,741
Total spending of all consumer units	$6,078,260,661	$1,229,390,428	$1,279,221,075	$2,051,912,839	$1,518,692,974
FINANCIAL PRODUCTS AND SERVICES	94,762,642	19,342,337	20,721,404	29,660,703	25,052,897
Miscellaneous fees	176,093	54,317	39,847	9,878	72,681
Lottery and gambling losses	6,848,072	1,057,934	1,198,943	2,730,879	1,865,860
Legal fees	19,413,061	4,607,894	3,554,541	5,864,969	5,385,360
Funeral expenses	8,275,161	1,643,471	2,202,173	2,656,343	1,772,650
Safe deposit box rental	399,878	76,855	102,193	123,927	96,539
Checking accounts, other bank service charges	2,761,240	521,079	583,614	845,935	810,592
Cemetery lots, vaults, and maintenance fees	1,044,331	191,122	363,505	304,878	185,310
Accounting fees	7,697,967	2,097,837	1,274,571	1,888,985	2,436,215
Miscellaneous personal services	6,351,587	861,177	1,394,384	2,135,043	1,969,056
Dating services	53,806	7,212	15,451	13,470	17,754
Finance charges, except mortgage and vehicles	18,947,148	3,455,752	4,431,181	5,401,590	5,659,164
Occupational expenses	5,774,392	1,446,263	1,352,097	1,138,240	1,838,119
Expenses for other properties	14,931,243	2,976,368	3,742,663	5,911,666	2,300,839
Credit card memberships	287,374	47,104	49,064	111,354	80,171
Shopping club membership fees	1,133,600	161,823	170,503	364,147	437,753
Vacation clubs	594,315	121,254	237,457	159,399	75,733
CASH CONTRIBUTIONS	210,440,030	40,760,198	45,391,214	72,445,967	51,842,936
Support for college students	14,329,591	2,648,215	2,882,829	4,587,086	4,211,639
Alimony expenditures	5,782,952	3,074,859	405,792	648,819	1,653,641
Child support expenditures	27,506,015	4,936,724	6,202,353	10,905,106	5,462,203
Gifts of stocks, bonds, and mutual funds to members of other households	5,658,219	64,233	2,918,340	492,564	2,182,939
Cash contributions to charities	26,376,083	8,763,676	5,291,015	6,001,468	6,319,955
Cash contributions to church, religious organizations	79,385,052	7,925,262	17,816,076	34,603,405	19,040,035
Cash contributions to educational institutions	3,102,421	526,938	563,826	799,238	1,213,114
Cash contributions to political organizations	1,239,990	180,980	256,432	418,477	383,658
Cash gifts to members of other households	47,058,483	12,639,085	9,054,551	13,989,805	11,375,474
PERSONAL INSURANCE AND PENSIONS	663,232,105	134,339,777	140,370,889	221,623,254	166,897,901
Life and other personal insurance	38,779,653	9,155,837	8,036,412	13,770,239	7,817,414
Life, endowment, annuity, other personal insurance	36,505,115	8,794,553	7,587,791	13,087,294	7,035,118
Other nonhealth insurance	2,274,538	361,284	448,892	682,495	782,019
Pensions and Social Security	624,452,451	125,183,940	132,334,477	207,853,464	159,080,765
Deductions for government retirement	11,085,317	1,298,189	2,280,783	3,843,526	3,662,922
Deductions for railroad retirement	463,468	–	148,004	65,106	250,501
Deductions for private pensions	68,040,487	14,358,960	16,692,762	17,543,719	19,445,331
Nonpayroll deposit to retirement plans	61,150,837	10,808,549	10,137,747	20,561,515	19,643,402
Deductions for Social Security	483,711,120	98,718,018	103,075,181	165,839,598	116,078,608
PERSONAL TAXES	245,993,752	54,049,279	40,720,678	70,733,892	80,489,402
Federal income taxes	167,583,328	34,680,798	25,641,325	49,901,624	57,358,956
Federal income tax deducted	232,253,585	45,440,439	43,197,173	82,254,142	61,361,150
Additional federal income tax paid	64,957,632	13,670,199	10,678,261	16,032,351	24,577,139
Federal income tax refunds	−129,627,889	−24,429,840	−28,234,109	−48,384,420	−28,579,333
State and local income taxes	61,783,061	14,716,187	12,909,438	13,416,868	20,740,281
State and local income tax deducted	65,037,118	14,951,935	15,063,902	16,569,816	18,451,094
Additional state and local income tax paid	12,853,587	2,802,150	2,062,843	1,323,232	6,665,607
State and local income tax refunds	−16,107,644	−3,037,672	−4,217,307	−4,476,181	−4,376,420
Other taxes	16,627,363	4,652,069	2,169,644	7,414,951	2,390,442

Note: Numbers may not add to total because of rounding and missing subcategories. "–" means sample is too small to make a reliable estimate.
Source: Calculations by New Strategist based on the Bureau of Labor Statistics' 2011 Consumer Expenditure Survey

Table 4.24 Financial: Market shares by region, 2011

(percentage of total annual spending on financial products and services, cash contributions, and miscellaneous items accounted for by consumer units by region of residence, 2011)

	total consumer units	Northeast	Midwest	South	West
Share of total consumer units	100.0%	18.4%	22.2%	36.7%	22.7%
Share of total before-tax income	100.0	20.8	21.2	33.9	24.2
Share of total spending	100.0	20.2	21.0	33.8	25.0
FINANCIAL PRODUCTS AND SERVICES	100.0	20.4	21.9	31.3	26.4
Miscellaneous fees	100.0	30.8	22.6	5.6	41.3
Lottery and gambling losses	100.0	15.4	17.5	39.9	27.2
Legal fees	100.0	23.7	18.3	30.2	27.7
Funeral expenses	100.0	19.9	26.6	32.1	21.4
Safe deposit box rental	100.0	19.2	25.6	31.0	24.1
Checking accounts, other bank service charges	100.0	18.9	21.1	30.6	29.4
Cemetery lots, vaults, and maintenance fees	100.0	18.3	34.8	29.2	17.7
Accounting fees	100.0	27.3	16.6	24.5	31.6
Miscellaneous personal services	100.0	13.6	22.0	33.6	31.0
Dating services	100.0	13.4	28.7	25.0	33.0
Finance charges, except mortgage and vehicles	100.0	18.2	23.4	28.5	29.9
Occupational expenses	100.0	25.0	23.4	19.7	31.8
Expenses for other properties	100.0	19.9	25.1	39.6	15.4
Credit card memberships	100.0	16.4	17.1	38.7	27.9
Shopping club membership fees	100.0	14.3	15.0	32.1	38.6
Vacation clubs	100.0	20.4	40.0	26.8	12.7
CASH CONTRIBUTIONS	100.0	19.4	21.6	34.4	24.6
Support for college students	100.0	18.5	20.1	32.0	29.4
Alimony expenditures	100.0	53.2	7.0	11.2	28.6
Child support expenditures	100.0	17.9	22.5	39.6	19.9
Gifts of stocks, bonds, and mutual funds to members of other households	100.0	1.1	51.6	8.7	38.6
Cash contributions to charities	100.0	33.2	20.1	22.8	24.0
Cash contributions to church, religious organizations	100.0	10.0	22.4	43.6	24.0
Cash contributions to educational institutions	100.0	17.0	18.2	25.8	39.1
Cash contributions to political organizations	100.0	14.6	20.7	33.7	30.9
Cash gifts to members of other households	100.0	26.9	19.2	29.7	24.2
PERSONAL INSURANCE AND PENSIONS	100.0	20.3	21.2	33.4	25.2
Life and other personal insurance	100.0	23.6	20.7	35.5	20.2
Life, endowment, annuity, other personal insurance	100.0	24.1	20.8	35.9	19.3
Other nonhealth insurance	100.0	15.9	19.7	30.0	34.4
Pensions and Social Security	100.0	20.0	21.2	33.3	25.5
Deductions for government retirement	100.0	11.7	20.6	34.7	33.0
Deductions for railroad retirement	100.0	–	31.9	14.0	54.0
Deductions for private pensions	100.0	21.1	24.5	25.8	28.6
Nonpayroll deposit to retirement plans	100.0	17.7	16.6	33.6	32.1
Deductions for Social Security	100.0	20.4	21.3	34.3	24.0
PERSONAL TAXES	100.0	22.0	16.6	28.8	32.7
Federal income taxes	100.0	20.7	15.3	29.8	34.2
Federal income tax deducted	100.0	19.6	18.6	35.4	26.4
Additional federal income tax paid	100.0	21.0	16.4	24.7	37.8
Federal income tax refunds	100.0	18.8	21.8	37.3	22.0
State and local income taxes	100.0	23.8	20.9	21.7	33.6
State and local income tax deducted	100.0	23.0	23.2	25.5	28.4
Additional state and local income tax paid	100.0	21.8	16.0	10.3	51.9
State and local income tax refunds	100.0	18.9	26.2	27.8	27.2
Other taxes	100.0	28.0	13.0	44.6	14.4

Note: Numbers may not add to total because of rounding. "–" means sample is too small to make a reliable estimate.
Source: Calculations by New Strategist based on the Bureau of Labor Statistics' 2011 Consumer Expenditure Survey

Table 4.25 Financial: Average spending by education, 2011

(average annual spending of consumer units on financial products and services, cash contributions, and miscellaneous items, by education of consumer unit reference person, 2011)

	total consumer units	less than high school graduate	high school graduate	some college	associate's degree	bachelor's degree or more		
						total	bachelor's degree	graduate degree
Number of consumer units (in 000s)	122,287	16,146	30,810	25,361	12,912	37,058	23,578	13,480
Average number of persons per consumer unit	2.5	2.8	2.5	2.3	2.6	2.5	2.5	2.4
Average before-tax income of consumer units	$63,685.00	$32,564.00	$46,370.00	$52,965.00	$63,664.00	$98,983.00	$90,962.00	$113,013.00
Average spending of consumer units, total	49,704.88	29,950.97	39,704.28	45,355.33	50,819.44	68,902.95	65,051.01	75,731.40
FINANCIAL PRODUCTS AND SERVICES	**774.92**	**391.58**	**614.54**	**714.53**	**986.53**	**1,039.92**	**906.57**	**1,269.29**
Miscellaneous fees	1.44	1.33	2.40	1.69	–	1.02	1.54	–
Lottery and gambling losses	56.00	25.25	52.22	39.85	131.89	56.55	66.12	37.78
Legal fees	158.75	102.72	121.67	177.63	177.80	194.42	135.59	297.32
Funeral expenses	67.67	79.00	82.26	57.73	77.21	54.06	34.02	89.13
Safe deposit box rental	3.27	1.48	2.35	2.53	3.00	5.40	4.78	6.49
Checking accounts, other bank service charges	22.58	12.03	19.92	25.39	28.18	25.50	24.54	27.19
Cemetery lots, vaults, and maintenance fees	8.54	5.10	8.49	5.99	12.62	10.42	8.90	13.09
Accounting fees	62.95	25.03	44.87	59.61	47.07	102.32	77.34	146.03
Miscellaneous personal services	51.94	18.08	51.42	46.93	54.02	67.47	76.02	50.73
Dating services	0.44	–	0.08	0.63	0.73	0.70	0.83	0.47
Finance charges, except mortgage and vehicles	154.94	47.70	105.00	163.12	169.77	232.42	232.31	232.62
Occupational expenses	47.22	17.03	34.24	40.78	55.29	72.77	56.16	101.82
Expenses for other properties	122.10	50.55	79.60	72.50	213.19	190.82	164.64	236.63
Credit card memberships	2.35	0.58	0.99	1.92	1.56	4.83	4.94	4.64
Shopping club membership fees	9.27	4.73	6.85	8.56	10.88	13.20	12.61	14.22
Vacation clubs	4.86	0.98	0.90	9.29	3.32	7.34	5.81	10.01
CASH CONTRIBUTIONS	**1,720.87**	**768.57**	**1,143.50**	**1,375.69**	**1,647.56**	**2,877.58**	**2,580.10**	**3,397.94**
Support for college students	117.18	19.35	69.04	93.38	92.50	224.72	163.75	331.37
Alimony expenditures	47.29	10.37	5.82	29.42	63.25	104.53	61.06	180.58
Child support expenditures	224.93	164.55	282.85	231.43	229.74	196.97	192.36	205.05
Gifts of stocks, bonds, and mutual funds to members of other households	46.27	0.89	1.29	7.58	0.90	145.72	122.37	186.55
Cash contributions to charities	215.69	40.46	70.95	143.73	127.22	492.45	403.62	647.84
Cash contributions to church, religious organizations	649.17	304.65	422.64	532.77	654.72	1,065.33	1,006.23	1,168.70
Cash contributions to educational institutions	25.37	1.46	4.93	9.23	24.34	64.20	37.07	111.65
Cash contributions to political organizations	10.14	1.83	5.03	5.66	8.03	21.80	20.08	24.79
Cash gifts to members of other households	384.82	225.02	280.95	322.48	446.86	561.86	573.56	541.40
PERSONAL INSURANCE AND PENSIONS	**5,423.57**	**2,150.05**	**3,533.28**	**4,413.32**	**5,438.15**	**9,107.73**	**8,133.51**	**10,811.81**
Life and other personal insurance	**317.12**	**136.03**	**264.23**	**218.27**	**406.15**	**476.63**	**414.46**	**585.37**
Life, endowment, annuity, other personal insurance	298.52	129.65	246.44	207.25	386.07	447.34	393.12	542.19
Other nonhealth insurance	18.60	6.38	17.79	11.01	20.08	29.28	21.34	43.17
Pensions and Social Security	**5,106.45**	**2,014.02**	**3,269.05**	**4,195.05**	**5,031.99**	**8,631.10**	**7,719.05**	**10,226.44**
Deductions for government retirement	90.65	9.41	35.74	59.78	87.19	194.03	156.95	258.90
Deductions for railroad retirement	3.79	–	6.54	1.66	7.68	3.27	–	8.99
Deductions for private pensions	556.40	81.18	250.49	354.53	538.55	1,162.17	932.28	1,564.29
Nonpayroll deposit to retirement plans	500.06	66.31	125.65	492.44	237.26	1,097.12	823.89	1,575.06
Deductions for Social Security	3,955.54	1,857.11	2,850.64	3,286.65	4,161.30	6,174.51	5,805.94	6,819.20
PERSONAL TAXES	**2,011.61**	**61.74**	**706.71**	**1,231.07**	**1,461.18**	**4,672.02**	**3,841.52**	**6,124.70**
Federal income taxes	**1,370.41**	**−79.40**	**350.56**	**760.14**	**899.12**	**3,431.85**	**2,768.70**	**4,591.82**
Federal income tax deducted	1,899.25	594.20	1,082.98	1,519.94	1,819.79	3,433.76	2,896.15	4,374.13
Additional federal income tax paid	531.19	61.82	247.46	252.00	300.33	1,243.10	1,072.63	1,541.29
Federal income tax refunds	−1,060.03	−735.42	−979.88	−1,011.81	−1,221.00	−1,245.00	−1,200.07	−1,323.59
State and local income taxes	**505.23**	**91.58**	**255.86**	**347.23**	**431.58**	**1,026.57**	**890.36**	**1,264.83**
State and local income tax deducted	531.84	130.61	331.65	413.68	495.02	966.78	834.66	1,197.88
Additional state and local income tax paid	105.11	25.08	33.21	43.40	76.92	251.81	232.42	285.73
State and local income tax refunds	−131.72	−64.12	−109.00	−109.84	−140.36	−192.02	−176.73	−218.78
Other taxes	**135.97**	**49.56**	**100.28**	**123.70**	**130.47**	**213.60**	**182.46**	**268.05**

Note: Subcategories may not add to total because some are not shown. "–" means sample is too small to make a reliable estimate.
Source: Bureau of Labor Statistics, unpublished tables from the 2011 Consumer Expenditure Survey

Table 4.26 Financial: Indexed spending by education, 2011

(indexed average annual spending of consumer units on financial products and services, cash contributions, and miscellaneous items, by education of consumer unit reference person, 2011; index definition: an index of 100 is the average for all consumer units; an index of 125 means that spending by consumer units in that group is 25 percent above the average for all consumer units; an index of 75 indicates spending that is 25 percent below the average for all consumer units)

	total consumer units	less than high school graduate	high school graduate	some college	associate's degree	bachelor's degree or more total	bachelor's degree	graduate degree
Average spending of consumer units, total	$49,705	$29,951	$39,704	$45,355	$50,819	$68,903	$65,051	$75,731
Average spending of consumer units, index	100	60	80	91	102	139	131	152
FINANCIAL PRODUCTS AND SERVICES	100	51	79	92	127	134	117	164
Miscellaneous fees	100	92	167	117	–	71	107	–
Lottery and gambling losses	100	45	93	71	236	101	118	67
Legal fees	100	65	77	112	112	122	85	187
Funeral expenses	100	117	122	85	114	80	50	132
Safe deposit box rental	100	45	72	77	92	165	146	198
Checking accounts, other bank service charges	100	53	88	112	125	113	109	120
Cemetery lots, vaults, and maintenance fees	100	60	99	70	148	122	104	153
Accounting fees	100	40	71	95	75	163	123	232
Miscellaneous personal services	100	35	99	90	104	130	146	98
Dating services	100	–	18	143	166	159	189	107
Finance charges, except mortgage and vehicles	100	31	68	105	110	150	150	150
Occupational expenses	100	36	73	86	117	154	119	216
Expenses for other properties	100	41	65	59	175	156	135	194
Credit card memberships	100	25	42	82	66	206	210	197
Shopping club membership fees	100	51	74	92	117	142	136	153
Vacation clubs	100	20	19	191	68	151	120	206
CASH CONTRIBUTIONS	100	45	66	80	96	167	150	197
Support for college students	100	17	59	80	79	192	140	283
Alimony expenditures	100	22	12	62	134	221	129	382
Child support expenditures	100	73	126	103	102	88	86	91
Gifts of stocks, bonds, and mutual funds to members of other households	100	2	3	16	2	315	264	403
Cash contributions to charities	100	19	33	67	59	228	187	300
Cash contributions to church, religious organizations	100	47	65	82	101	164	155	180
Cash contributions to educational institutions	100	6	19	36	96	253	146	440
Cash contributions to political organizations	100	18	50	56	79	215	198	244
Cash gifts to members of other households	100	58	73	84	116	146	149	141
PERSONAL INSURANCE AND PENSIONS	100	40	65	81	100	168	150	199
Life and other personal insurance	100	43	83	69	128	150	131	185
Life, endowment, annuity, other personal insurance	100	43	83	69	129	150	132	182
Other nonhealth insurance	100	34	96	59	108	157	115	232
Pensions and Social Security	100	39	64	82	99	169	151	200
Deductions for government retirement	100	10	39	66	96	214	173	286
Deductions for railroad retirement	100	–	173	44	203	86	–	237
Deductions for private pensions	100	15	45	64	97	209	168	281
Nonpayroll deposit to retirement plans	100	13	25	98	47	219	165	315
Deductions for Social Security	100	47	72	83	105	156	147	172
PERSONAL TAXES	100	3	35	61	73	232	191	304
Federal income taxes	100	–6	26	55	66	250	202	335
Federal income tax deducted	100	31	57	80	96	181	152	230
Additional federal income tax paid	100	12	47	47	57	234	202	290
Federal income tax refunds	100	69	92	95	115	117	113	125
State and local income taxes	100	18	51	69	85	203	176	250
State and local income tax deducted	100	25	62	78	93	182	157	225
Additional state and local income tax paid	100	24	32	41	73	240	221	272
State and local income tax refunds	100	49	83	83	107	146	134	166
Other taxes	100	36	74	91	96	157	134	197

Note: "–" means sample is too small to make a reliable estimate.
Source: Calculations by New Strategist based on the Bureau of Labor Statistics' 2011 Consumer Expenditure Survey

Table 4.27 Financial: Total spending by education, 2011

(total annual spending on financial products and services, cash contributions, and miscellaneous items, by consumer unit educational attainment group, 2011; consumer units and dollars in thousands)

	total consumer units	less than high school graduate	high school graduate	some college	associate's degree	bachelor's degree or more total	bachelor's degree	graduate degree
Number of consumer units	122,287	16,146	30,810	25,361	12,912	37,058	23,578	13,480
Total spending of all consumer units	$6,078,260,661	$483,588,362	$1,223,288,867	$1,150,256,524	$656,180,609	$2,553,405,521	$1,533,772,714	$1,020,859,272
FINANCIAL PRODUCTS AND SERVICES	94,762,642	6,322,451	18,933,977	18,121,195	12,738,075	38,537,355	21,375,107	17,110,029
Miscellaneous fees	176,093	21,474	73,944	42,860	–	37,799	36,310	–
Lottery and gambling losses	6,848,072	407,687	1,608,898	1,010,636	1,702,964	2,095,630	1,558,977	509,274
Legal fees	19,413,061	1,658,517	3,748,653	4,504,874	2,295,754	7,204,816	3,196,941	4,007,874
Funeral expenses	8,275,161	1,275,534	2,534,431	1,464,091	996,936	2,003,355	802,124	1,201,472
Safe deposit box rental	399,878	23,896	72,404	64,163	38,736	200,113	112,703	87,485
Checking accounts, other bank service charges	2,761,240	194,236	613,735	643,916	363,860	944,979	578,604	366,521
Cemetery lots, vaults, and maintenance fees	1,044,331	82,345	261,577	151,912	162,949	386,144	209,844	176,453
Accounting fees	7,697,967	404,134	1,382,445	1,511,769	607,768	3,791,775	1,823,523	1,968,484
Miscellaneous personal services	6,351,587	291,920	1,584,250	1,190,192	697,506	2,500,303	1,792,400	683,840
Dating services	53,806	–	2,465	15,977	9,426	25,941	19,570	6,336
Finance charges, except mortgage and vehicles	18,947,148	770,164	3,235,050	4,136,886	2,192,070	8,613,020	5,477,405	3,135,718
Occupational expenses	5,774,392	274,966	1,054,934	1,034,222	713,904	2,696,711	1,324,140	1,372,534
Expenses for other properties	14,931,243	816,180	2,452,476	1,838,673	2,752,709	7,071,408	3,881,882	3,189,772
Credit card memberships	287,374	9,365	30,502	48,693	20,143	178,990	116,475	62,547
Shopping club membership fees	1,133,600	76,371	211,049	217,090	140,483	489,166	297,319	191,686
Vacation clubs	594,315	15,823	27,729	235,604	42,868	272,006	136,988	134,935
CASH CONTRIBUTIONS	210,440,030	12,409,331	35,231,235	34,888,874	21,273,295	106,637,360	60,833,598	45,804,231
Support for college students	14,329,591	312,425	2,127,122	2,368,210	1,194,360	8,327,674	3,860,898	4,466,868
Alimony expenditures	5,782,952	167,434	179,314	746,121	816,684	3,873,673	1,439,673	2,434,218
Child support expenditures	27,506,015	2,656,824	8,714,609	5,869,296	2,966,403	7,299,314	4,535,464	2,764,074
Gifts of stocks, bonds, and mutual funds to members of other households	5,658,219	14,370	39,745	192,236	11,621	5,400,092	2,885,240	2,514,694
Cash contributions to charities	26,376,083	653,267	2,185,970	3,645,137	1,642,665	18,249,212	9,516,552	8,732,883
Cash contributions to church, religious organizations	79,385,052	4,918,879	13,021,538	13,511,580	8,453,745	39,478,999	23,724,891	15,754,076
Cash contributions to educational institutions	3,102,421	23,573	151,893	234,082	314,278	2,379,124	874,036	1,505,042
Cash contributions to political organizations	1,239,990	29,547	154,974	143,543	103,683	807,864	473,446	334,169
Cash gifts to members of other households	47,058,483	3,633,173	8,656,070	8,178,415	5,769,856	20,821,408	13,523,398	7,298,072
PERSONAL INSURANCE AND PENSIONS	663,232,105	34,714,707	108,860,357	111,926,209	70,217,393	337,514,258	191,771,899	145,743,199
Life and other personal insurance	38,779,653	2,196,340	8,140,926	5,535,545	5,244,209	17,662,955	9,772,138	7,890,788
Life, endowment, annuity, other personal insurance	36,505,115	2,093,329	7,592,816	5,256,067	4,984,936	16,577,526	9,268,983	7,308,721
Other nonhealth insurance	2,274,538	103,011	548,110	279,225	259,273	1,085,058	503,155	581,932
Pensions and Social Security	624,452,451	32,518,367	100,719,431	106,390,663	64,973,055	319,851,304	181,999,761	137,852,411
Deductions for government retirement	11,085,317	151,934	1,101,149	1,516,081	1,125,797	7,190,364	3,700,567	3,489,972
Deductions for railroad retirement	463,468	–	201,497	42,099	99,164	121,180	–	121,185
Deductions for private pensions	68,040,487	1,310,732	7,717,597	8,991,235	6,953,758	43,067,696	21,981,298	21,086,629
Nonpayroll deposit to retirement plans	61,150,837	1,070,641	3,871,277	12,488,771	3,063,501	40,657,073	19,425,678	21,231,809
Deductions for Social Security	483,711,120	29,984,898	87,828,218	83,352,731	53,730,706	228,814,992	136,892,453	91,922,816
PERSONAL TAXES	245,993,752	996,854	21,773,735	31,221,166	18,866,756	173,135,717	90,575,359	82,560,956
Federal income taxes	167,583,328	–1,281,992	10,800,754	19,277,911	11,609,437	127,177,497	65,280,409	61,897,734
Federal income tax deducted	232,253,585	9,593,953	33,366,614	38,547,198	23,497,128	127,248,278	68,285,425	58,963,272
Additional federal income tax paid	64,957,632	998,146	7,624,243	6,390,972	3,877,861	46,066,800	25,290,470	20,776,589
Federal income tax refunds	–129,627,889	–11,874,091	–30,190,103	–25,660,513	–15,765,552	–46,137,210	–28,295,250	–17,841,993
State and local income taxes	61,783,061	1,478,651	7,883,047	8,806,100	5,572,561	38,042,631	20,992,908	17,049,908
State and local income tax deducted	65,037,118	2,108,829	10,218,137	10,491,338	6,391,698	35,826,933	19,679,613	16,147,422
Additional state and local income tax paid	12,853,587	404,942	1,023,200	1,100,667	993,191	9,331,575	5,479,999	3,851,640
State and local income tax refunds	–16,107,644	–1,035,282	–3,358,290	–2,785,652	–1,812,328	–7,115,877	–4,166,940	–2,949,154
Other taxes	16,627,363	800,196	3,089,627	3,137,156	1,684,629	7,915,589	4,302,042	3,613,314

Note: Numbers may not add to total because of rounding and missing subcategories. "–" means sample is too small to make a reliable estimate.
Source: Calculations by New Strategist based on the Bureau of Labor Statistics' 2011 Consumer Expenditure Survey

Table 4.28 Financial: Market shares by education, 2011

(percentage of total annual spending on financial products and services, cash contributions, and miscellaneous items accounted for by consumer unit educational attainment groups, 2011)

	total consumer units	less than high school graduate	high school graduate	some college	associate's degree	bachelor's degree or more total	bachelor's degree	graduate degree
Share of total consumer units	100.0%	13.2%	25.2%	20.7%	10.6%	30.3%	19.3%	11.0%
Share of total before-tax income	100.0	6.8	18.3	17.2	10.6	47.1	27.5	19.6
Share of total spending	100.0	8.0	20.1	18.9	10.8	42.0	25.2	16.8
FINANCIAL PRODUCTS AND SERVICES	100.0	6.7	20.0	19.1	13.4	40.7	22.6	18.1
Miscellaneous fees	100.0	12.2	42.0	24.3	–	21.5	20.6	–
Lottery and gambling losses	100.0	6.0	23.5	14.8	24.9	30.6	22.8	7.4
Legal fees	100.0	8.5	19.3	23.2	11.8	37.1	16.5	20.6
Funeral expenses	100.0	15.4	30.6	17.7	12.0	24.2	9.7	14.5
Safe deposit box rental	100.0	6.0	18.1	16.0	9.7	50.0	28.2	21.9
Checking accounts, other bank service charges	100.0	7.0	22.2	23.3	13.2	34.2	21.0	13.3
Cemetery lots, vaults, and maintenance fees	100.0	7.9	25.0	14.5	15.6	37.0	20.1	16.9
Accounting fees	100.0	5.2	18.0	19.6	7.9	49.3	23.7	25.6
Miscellaneous personal services	100.0	4.6	24.9	18.7	11.0	39.4	28.2	10.8
Dating services	100.0	–	4.6	29.7	17.5	48.2	36.4	11.8
Finance charges, except mortgage and vehicles	100.0	4.1	17.1	21.8	11.6	45.5	28.9	16.5
Occupational expenses	100.0	4.8	18.3	17.9	12.4	46.7	22.9	23.8
Expenses for other properties	100.0	5.5	16.4	12.3	18.4	47.4	26.0	21.4
Credit card memberships	100.0	3.3	10.6	16.9	7.0	62.3	40.5	21.8
Shopping club membership fees	100.0	6.7	18.6	19.2	12.4	43.2	26.2	16.9
Vacation clubs	100.0	2.7	4.7	39.6	7.2	45.8	23.0	22.7
CASH CONTRIBUTIONS	100.0	5.9	16.7	16.6	10.1	50.7	28.9	21.8
Support for college students	100.0	2.2	14.8	16.5	8.3	58.1	26.9	31.2
Alimony expenditures	100.0	2.9	3.1	12.9	14.1	67.0	24.9	42.1
Child support expenditures	100.0	9.7	31.7	21.3	10.8	26.5	16.5	10.0
Gifts of stocks, bonds, and mutual funds to members of other households	100.0	0.3	0.7	3.4	0.2	95.4	51.0	44.4
Cash contributions to charities	100.0	2.5	8.3	13.8	6.2	69.2	36.1	33.1
Cash contributions to church, religious organizations	100.0	6.2	16.4	17.0	10.6	49.7	29.9	19.8
Cash contributions to educational institutions	100.0	0.8	4.9	7.5	10.1	76.7	28.2	48.5
Cash contributions to political organizations	100.0	2.4	12.5	11.6	8.4	65.2	38.2	26.9
Cash gifts to members of other households	100.0	7.7	18.4	17.4	12.3	44.2	28.7	15.5
PERSONAL INSURANCE AND PENSIONS	100.0	5.2	16.4	16.9	10.6	50.9	28.9	22.0
Life and other personal insurance	100.0	5.7	21.0	14.3	13.5	45.5	25.2	20.3
Life, endowment, annuity, other personal insurance	100.0	5.7	20.8	14.4	13.7	45.4	25.4	20.0
Other nonhealth insurance	100.0	4.5	24.1	12.3	11.4	47.7	22.1	25.6
Pensions and Social Security	100.0	5.2	16.1	17.0	10.4	51.2	29.1	22.1
Deductions for government retirement	100.0	1.4	9.9	13.7	10.2	64.9	33.4	31.5
Deductions for railroad retirement	100.0	–	43.5	9.1	21.4	26.1	–	26.1
Deductions for private pensions	100.0	1.9	11.3	13.2	10.2	63.3	32.3	31.0
Nonpayroll deposit to retirement plans	100.0	1.8	6.3	20.4	5.0	66.5	31.8	34.7
Deductions for Social Security	100.0	6.2	18.2	17.2	11.1	47.3	28.3	19.0
PERSONAL TAXES	100.0	0.4	8.9	12.7	7.7	70.4	36.8	33.6
Federal income taxes	100.0	−0.8	6.4	11.5	6.9	75.9	39.0	36.9
Federal income tax deducted	100.0	4.1	14.4	16.6	10.1	54.8	29.4	25.4
Additional federal income tax paid	100.0	1.5	11.7	9.8	6.0	70.9	38.9	32.0
Federal income tax refunds	100.0	9.2	23.3	19.8	12.2	35.6	21.8	13.8
State and local income taxes	100.0	2.4	12.8	14.3	9.0	61.6	34.0	27.6
State and local income tax deducted	100.0	3.2	15.7	16.1	9.8	55.1	30.3	24.8
Additional state and local income tax paid	100.0	3.2	8.0	8.6	7.7	72.6	42.6	30.0
State and local income tax refunds	100.0	6.4	20.8	17.3	11.3	44.2	25.9	18.3
Other taxes	100.0	4.8	18.6	18.9	10.1	47.6	25.9	21.7

Note: Numbers may not add to total because of rounding. "–" means sample is too small to make a reliable estimate.
Source: Calculations by New Strategist based on the Bureau of Labor Statistics' 2011 Consumer Expenditure Survey

CHAPTER 5

Spending on Food and Alcoholic Beverages, 2011

Average household spending on groceries (food at home) in 2011 was 3 percent less than in 2000, after adjusting for inflation, while spending on food away from home (primarily sit-down meals and take-outs from restaurants) fell 6 percent during those years. These relatively small variations mask substantial change in spending on food over the 11-year period. Between 2000 and 2006 (the year overall household spending peaked), the average household cut spending on food at home by 3 percent and boosted spending on food away from home by 8 percent. Between 2006 and 2011, however, the average household reduced its spending on restaurant meals by 13 percent. Overall, the average household devoted $6,458 to food in 2011—or 13.0 percent of its expenditures. The figure was a higher 13.6 percent in 2000.

Spending on alcoholic beverages followed a similar pattern as spending on restaurant meals, but the ups and downs were even more dramatic. Between 2000 and 2006, the average household boosted its spending on alcoholic beverages by 14 percent, after adjusting for inflation. Between 2006 and 2011, the average household cut its spending on alcohol by 18 percent. In 2011, households spent an average of $456 on alcoholic beverages, down 6 percent from the inflation-adjusted $486 of 2000.

Householders aged 35 to 54 spend the most on food—15 to 20 percent more than average—in part because of their relatively large households. Householders aged 35 to 44 spend the most on foods demanded by children such as cereal, white bread, milk, sugar, and potato chips. Householders aged 45 to 54 spend the most on cheese and coffee, among other items. Householders aged 25 to 34 spend less than average on most food items, but they spend two-and-one-half times the average on baby food. Those aged 55 to 64 spend the most on breakfast at full-service restaurants. Householders aged 45 to 54 spend the most on alcoholic beverages consumed at home, whereas those aged 25 to 34 spend the most on alcohol consumed in bars and restaurants.

Households with incomes of $100,000 or more spend more than twice as much as the average household on food away from home and alcoholic beverages. Only 18 percent of households have incomes of $100,000 or more, but they control 27 percent of all food-at-home spending and 36 percent of all spending on food away from home. The high-income group accounts for 40 percent of spending on dinners in full-service restaurants and 43 percent of spending on wine consumed at home.

Married couples with school-aged or older children at home spend more on food than other household types. These households are not only the largest, but also have the highest incomes. Married couples with school-aged or older children at home also spend more than other household types on food away from home. They spend 51 percent more than average on dinner at fast-food restaurants. Couples without children at home (most of them empty-nesters) spend the most on alcoholic beverages.

Asian households spend the most on food—26 percent more than the average household—driven in part by their disproportionate spending on restaurant food. Hispanic households are the largest (an average of 3.4 persons vs. 2.5 in the average household), but they spend only an average amount on food at home, whereas Asian householders outspend the average by 16 percent. Black households spend less than average on food overall but exceed the average on pork, poultry, fish and seafood, and canned and bottled fruit juice, among other items. Black households spend only 67 percent of the average on food away from home, while Asians spend 42 percent more than average on this item. Non-Hispanic whites spend 15 percent more than average on alcoholic beverages.

Households in the West and Northeast spend, respectively, 9 and 7 percent more than the average household on food at home, while those in the South spend 9 percent less than average. Households in the West spend 15 percent more than the average household on food away from home, while households in the Midwest spend 9 percent less than average on this category. Households in the West also spend the most on alcoholic beverages (34 percent more than average), while households in the South and Midwest spend 15 percent less than average.

Because college graduates dominate the affluent, they account for a large share of the food-away-from-home market. College graduates control 47 percent of household spending on dinners at full-service restaurants, for example, a much greater portion than their 30 percent share of all households. They account for 55 percent of household spending on wine consumed at home and 60 percent of spending on wine consumed in bars and restaurants. They also account for 62 percent of spending on alcoholic beverages purchased on trips.

Table 5.1 Food and Alcohol: Average spending by age, 2011

(average annual spending of consumer units on food and alcoholic beverages, by age of consumer unit reference person, 2011)

	total consumer units	under 25	25 to 34	35 to 44	45 to 54	55 to 64	65 to 74	75+
Number of consumer units (in 000s)	122,287	7,743	20,463	21,699	24,821	21,688	14,079	11,794
Average number of persons per consumer unit	2.5	2.1	2.9	3.3	2.8	2.1	1.9	1.6
Average before-tax income of consumer units	$63,685.00	$27,514.00	$58,179.00	$77,376.00	$78,519.00	$75,517.00	$52,521.00	$32,144.00
Average spending of consumer units, total	49,704.88	29,911.52	48,097.39	57,271.07	58,050.42	53,615.86	44,645.56	32,688.34
Food, average spending	**6,458.00**	**4,354.00**	**6,211.00**	**7,765.00**	**7,424.00**	**6,520.00**	**5,804.00**	**4,408.00**
Alcoholic beverages, average spending	**456.43**	**417.75**	**512.63**	**497.49**	**494.29**	**468.34**	**421.65**	**240.69**
FOOD AT HOME	**3,837.76**	**2,381.73**	**3,447.12**	**4,594.19**	**4,420.63**	**3,908.42**	**3,593.90**	**2,979.82**
Cereals and bakery products	**530.68**	**336.26**	**478.68**	**644.00**	**610.20**	**515.38**	**479.42**	**457.91**
Cereals and cereal products	174.86	114.10	175.28	217.69	201.06	161.19	144.20	139.09
Flour	7.67	3.77	7.47	10.67	7.66	6.57	7.34	7.46
Prepared flour mixes	14.88	10.20	14.78	17.57	15.68	13.66	16.04	12.38
Ready-to-eat and cooked cereals	91.39	56.25	95.02	109.48	105.20	82.34	77.35	77.75
Rice	25.66	21.33	23.83	34.13	27.98	26.41	18.42	17.97
Pasta, cornmeal, and other cereal products	35.26	22.56	34.18	45.84	44.55	32.21	25.06	23.53
Bakery products	355.81	222.16	303.40	426.31	409.14	354.19	335.21	318.83
Bread	106.53	75.60	87.00	123.60	120.35	111.21	100.51	98.62
White bread	44.93	33.17	36.37	55.42	51.66	45.82	40.88	37.14
Bread, other than white	61.60	42.43	50.63	68.18	68.69	65.39	59.63	61.49
Cookies and crackers	83.59	51.68	68.78	97.65	94.32	85.53	80.05	82.34
Cookies	46.96	27.17	38.86	52.17	51.55	51.37	44.64	49.20
Crackers	36.63	24.52	29.92	45.48	42.78	34.17	35.41	33.13
Frozen and refrigerated bakery products	28.60	17.99	28.33	40.01	30.15	27.41	22.21	21.00
Other bakery products	137.09	76.88	119.29	165.04	164.31	130.04	132.43	116.87
Biscuits and rolls	52.93	26.90	45.13	62.19	66.82	50.89	53.82	39.88
Cakes and cupcakes	37.81	21.22	36.81	49.10	48.25	30.56	31.10	28.63
Bread and cracker products	7.13	4.86	6.06	8.52	7.39	7.37	7.42	6.62
Sweetrolls, coffee cakes, doughnuts	23.86	13.60	19.90	27.91	25.06	23.44	24.23	27.88
Pies, tarts, turnovers	15.36	10.30	11.40	17.32	16.80	17.78	15.86	13.86
Meats, poultry, fish, and eggs	**832.41**	**526.85**	**733.20**	**1,006.29**	**965.18**	**894.03**	**759.48**	**569.21**
Beef	222.60	137.15	188.12	264.03	267.44	235.21	217.68	149.14
Ground beef	90.50	48.07	88.04	105.31	110.85	94.37	83.35	52.25
Roast	30.59	10.58	24.04	36.01	34.81	33.23	35.89	25.06
Chuck roast	7.65	2.83	6.66	9.65	7.68	6.55	8.77	9.59
Round roast	6.11	1.65	3.11	7.99	6.25	5.82	9.66	7.03
Other roast	16.82	6.10	14.26	18.37	20.88	20.86	17.46	8.45
Steak	82.49	65.12	64.33	99.56	97.07	85.63	78.34	62.62
Round steak	15.90	12.51	14.53	19.25	16.50	16.85	16.35	10.75
Sirloin steak	21.86	15.20	20.98	25.02	27.30	24.22	16.78	11.67
Other steak	44.73	37.42	28.82	55.29	53.28	44.56	45.21	40.20
Other beef	19.02	13.37	11.72	23.15	24.70	21.97	20.10	9.21
Pork	161.95	96.14	133.39	200.07	177.88	183.41	162.26	109.89
Bacon	33.87	18.82	28.32	41.84	36.45	37.48	36.60	23.25
Pork chops	27.24	17.51	25.95	36.89	28.55	29.66	24.84	13.27
Ham	34.29	21.66	27.78	40.53	34.77	39.83	34.72	30.50
Ham, not canned	33.51	20.21	27.03	39.44	34.13	38.86	34.70	29.87
Canned ham	0.78	1.45	0.75	1.09	0.64	0.97	0.02	0.63
Sausage	28.55	14.42	21.52	35.64	32.60	35.38	27.51	16.76
Other pork	37.99	23.74	29.81	45.17	45.50	41.06	38.58	26.11
Other meats	122.54	63.35	109.68	154.53	156.74	120.34	101.74	79.83
Frankfurters	23.67	15.74	22.45	31.10	27.38	23.43	19.95	14.02
Lunch meats (cold cuts)	87.67	42.05	79.55	103.85	113.74	87.72	75.93	59.59
Bologna, liverwurst, salami	26.83	14.56	24.67	31.66	32.86	26.75	26.79	17.06
Other lunch meats	60.84	27.49	54.88	72.19	80.89	60.97	49.14	42.53
Lamb, organ meats, and others	11.20	5.55	7.68	19.58	15.61	9.18	5.86	6.22

	total consumer units	under 25	25 to 34	35 to 44	45 to 54	55 to 64	65 to 74	75+
Poultry	$154.49	$122.48	$154.15	$190.31	$182.48	$152.32	$118.51	$95.10
Fresh and frozen chicken	124.44	91.29	126.07	157.03	146.82	123.51	89.12	77.06
Fresh and frozen whole chicken	35.97	28.90	31.89	50.91	41.15	34.50	27.81	21.27
Fresh and frozen chicken parts	88.48	62.39	94.18	106.13	105.66	89.00	61.32	55.79
Other poultry	30.05	31.19	28.08	33.28	35.67	28.81	29.39	18.04
Fish and seafood	120.76	69.35	103.18	138.58	125.30	152.42	110.65	94.17
Canned fish and seafood	19.90	11.71	15.66	24.43	19.45	22.10	22.15	18.62
Fresh fish and shellfish	59.51	27.52	54.59	65.65	61.54	77.18	50.00	50.48
Frozen fish and shellfish	41.35	30.13	32.92	48.50	44.30	53.14	38.50	25.07
Eggs	50.07	38.38	44.68	58.78	55.34	50.33	48.64	41.08
Dairy products	**406.84**	**244.45**	**378.70**	**481.16**	**475.01**	**393.53**	**387.44**	**326.45**
Fresh milk and cream	149.73	96.74	144.50	188.13	171.67	137.15	131.73	119.87
Fresh milk, all types	127.38	85.82	124.42	160.75	144.68	116.17	113.37	97.99
Cream	22.36	10.92	20.08	27.37	26.99	20.98	18.36	21.88
Other dairy products	257.10	147.71	234.20	293.04	303.34	256.38	255.71	206.58
Butter	24.64	11.51	17.71	27.64	29.04	28.22	23.95	24.71
Cheese	124.74	70.83	115.97	139.97	155.13	124.71	119.71	88.13
Ice cream and related products	57.28	37.08	50.14	65.22	62.29	55.81	62.07	55.03
Miscellaneous dairy products	50.43	28.29	50.38	60.21	56.87	47.63	49.98	38.72
Fruits and vegetables	**714.89**	**424.33**	**626.75**	**841.09**	**802.94**	**733.93**	**712.74**	**605.22**
Fresh fruits	247.28	131.59	210.13	290.65	273.31	262.16	253.77	217.00
Apples	38.17	28.06	36.04	49.05	41.00	35.90	37.52	27.33
Bananas	41.08	24.57	35.48	46.93	45.30	41.91	39.37	42.30
Oranges	26.99	13.70	20.81	34.41	29.41	28.69	29.45	21.70
Citrus fruits, excluding oranges	37.63	17.91	32.59	45.33	41.84	41.11	36.95	30.35
Other fresh fruits	103.42	47.36	85.22	114.93	115.76	114.55	110.48	95.33
Fresh vegetables	224.21	129.74	194.51	253.60	257.58	239.37	219.94	189.04
Potatoes	38.78	27.41	33.16	45.06	44.69	39.42	36.51	33.38
Lettuce	32.17	17.70	27.15	37.59	35.70	36.83	30.46	26.03
Tomatoes	41.03	27.42	39.23	47.02	44.71	41.32	39.22	35.56
Other fresh vegetables	112.24	57.21	94.98	123.93	132.48	121.79	113.74	94.07
Processed fruits	115.73	80.07	107.00	143.19	128.05	107.17	110.57	99.46
Frozen fruits and fruit juices	13.31	6.23	12.12	16.41	18.03	10.42	13.80	9.17
Frozen orange juice	3.73	1.09	3.00	4.76	5.30	2.82	3.22	3.81
Frozen fruits	6.92	4.06	6.08	7.31	9.64	5.64	9.08	3.66
Frozen fruit juices, excluding orange	2.67	1.08	3.04	4.34	3.08	1.96	1.51	1.70
Canned fruits	21.24	11.60	18.15	23.35	21.32	22.97	24.92	21.34
Dried fruits	8.13	3.85	5.48	9.11	10.71	7.80	9.37	7.53
Fresh fruit juice	17.28	11.20	16.74	22.06	18.88	14.70	18.36	13.51
Canned and bottled fruit juice	55.78	47.17	54.51	72.25	59.12	51.29	44.12	47.91
Processed vegetables	127.66	82.94	115.11	153.66	144.01	125.23	128.45	99.72
Frozen vegetables	34.98	22.18	30.05	41.99	41.76	32.92	34.20	29.48
Canned and dried vegetables and juices	92.68	60.76	85.05	111.66	102.25	92.31	94.25	70.25
Canned beans	19.08	13.03	18.22	21.85	20.71	19.75	19.62	14.01
Canned corn	9.73	6.53	9.06	11.34	11.07	11.24	8.20	6.05
Canned miscellaneous vegetables	25.50	12.67	21.04	28.07	26.89	26.22	32.74	24.31
Dried peas	0.84	1.13	0.90	0.58	0.62	1.19	0.93	0.77
Dried beans	4.99	6.10	4.43	7.01	6.53	3.31	5.04	1.43
Dried miscellaneous vegetables	11.55	7.62	9.64	15.97	14.84	10.25	10.44	6.07
Dried processed vegetables	2.05	1.44	0.93	1.93	2.61	1.31	3.06	3.69
Fresh and canned vegetable juices	18.59	12.24	20.58	23.78	18.70	18.86	14.12	13.86
Sugar and other sweets	**144.39**	**77.81**	**111.92**	**178.99**	**162.96**	**152.36**	**143.74**	**127.65**
Candy and chewing gum	86.75	43.38	61.98	102.86	106.92	92.91	85.00	76.91
Sugar	23.89	17.12	21.02	34.30	22.39	25.14	22.08	16.92
Artificial sweeteners	5.61	2.82	4.62	6.21	5.96	4.96	8.66	5.07
Jams, preserves, other sweets	28.14	14.49	24.31	35.62	27.69	29.35	28.00	28.75

	total consumer units	under 25	25 to 34	35 to 44	45 to 54	55 to 64	65 to 74	75+
Fats and oils	**$109.61**	**$61.29**	**$94.78**	**$126.43**	**$124.94**	**$110.58**	**$112.07**	**$98.93**
Margarine	9.77	5.91	6.46	10.15	10.51	11.00	12.09	10.96
Fats and oils	34.84	20.99	30.18	43.49	39.56	33.17	34.04	30.13
Salad dressings	31.16	13.62	28.11	32.47	33.63	34.38	34.51	30.22
Nondairy cream and imitation milk	18.59	10.40	15.53	23.52	22.19	17.60	18.69	14.34
Peanut butter	15.25	10.38	14.51	16.80	19.05	14.42	12.74	13.28
Miscellaneous foods	**690.48**	**454.15**	**670.82**	**834.35**	**779.23**	**677.25**	**626.21**	**520.64**
Frozen prepared foods	136.23	92.48	138.28	173.58	156.80	122.77	102.97	111.34
Frozen meals	62.14	31.41	54.84	69.87	70.43	64.58	56.99	64.30
Other frozen prepared foods	74.09	61.07	83.43	103.70	86.37	58.19	45.98	47.05
Canned and packaged soups	46.90	31.36	36.05	49.49	51.54	51.49	53.58	45.43
Potato chips, nuts, and other snacks	145.02	86.26	122.63	183.03	174.55	147.01	128.46	105.08
Potato chips and other snacks	108.01	69.13	101.21	146.89	132.36	101.93	81.69	63.08
Nuts	37.01	17.14	21.42	36.14	42.19	45.09	46.77	42.00
Condiments and seasonings	133.90	77.13	126.78	157.05	154.69	132.42	131.73	101.29
Salt, spices, and other seasonings	35.41	22.12	35.02	42.19	42.93	32.42	34.80	22.39
Olives, pickles, relishes	16.13	10.89	12.08	17.04	18.59	18.62	16.04	15.28
Sauces and gravies	58.43	32.70	58.10	72.49	66.47	56.00	55.49	40.36
Baking needs and miscellaneous products	23.93	11.42	21.58	25.34	26.70	25.38	25.40	23.26
Other canned or packaged prepared foods	228.42	166.91	247.09	271.19	241.65	223.55	209.48	157.49
Prepared salads	36.22	16.82	32.95	39.74	36.38	42.85	36.98	34.18
Prepared desserts	15.03	6.02	13.35	18.65	16.31	14.27	15.99	14.68
Baby food	27.80	32.47	70.55	41.48	17.51	8.64	6.91	4.30
Miscellaneous prepared foods	147.11	110.59	128.50	169.04	169.75	156.62	142.37	102.73
Nonalcoholic beverages	**360.97**	**236.46**	**319.48**	**433.82**	**442.34**	**367.65**	**310.49**	**253.02**
Cola	78.77	53.54	67.10	98.84	98.24	80.79	71.45	41.97
Other carbonated drinks	66.72	48.06	67.68	78.67	87.73	63.85	46.06	39.28
Tea	31.16	23.87	22.14	35.67	37.15	37.44	29.85	20.63
Coffee	75.03	31.58	52.51	78.99	89.41	86.21	78.78	80.10
Noncarbonated fruit-flavored drinks	24.76	20.04	24.15	35.41	26.02	19.52	23.15	18.23
Other noncarbonated beverages and ice	14.93	13.42	15.92	20.79	16.45	13.51	9.44	9.03
Bottled water	53.48	32.76	52.74	64.00	69.28	50.80	39.18	36.53
Sports drinks	15.73	13.19	17.23	21.44	17.78	14.78	10.81	7.10
Food prepared by consumer unit on trips	**47.50**	**20.13**	**32.78**	**48.06**	**57.82**	**63.71**	**62.32**	**20.78**
FOOD AWAY FROM HOME	**2,619.89**	**1,972.76**	**2,764.38**	**3,170.57**	**3,002.91**	**2,611.42**	**2,210.48**	**1,428.65**
Meals at restaurants, carry-outs, etc.	**2,195.89**	**1,698.28**	**2,396.39**	**2,689.31**	**2,423.82**	**2,149.71**	**1,811.66**	**1,280.38**
Lunch	752.89	553.17	831.15	941.19	822.60	721.53	617.53	456.49
At fast-food restaurants*	368.78	325.60	464.51	489.29	403.30	328.41	233.96	157.84
At full-service restaurants	302.01	180.45	280.22	287.10	313.89	339.74	355.74	288.07
At vending machines, mobile vendors	7.16	8.20	7.27	9.30	9.44	7.99	2.80	0.88
At employer and school cafeterias	74.94	38.92	79.15	155.50	95.97	45.39	25.04	9.70
Dinner	1,051.05	831.92	1,127.58	1,260.94	1,175.73	1,030.58	896.75	614.43
At fast-food restaurants*	365.13	423.67	446.15	513.23	390.04	313.47	221.47	116.47
At full-service restaurants	676.06	387.29	666.33	736.86	780.67	711.02	664.70	489.82
At vending machines, mobile vendors	3.02	1.93	9.95	2.13	1.52	0.73	2.63	0.77
At employer and school cafeterias	6.85	19.03	5.14	8.73	3.50	5.36	7.95	7.38
Snacks and nonalcoholic beverages	166.09	149.87	208.47	225.38	187.52	146.40	97.76	60.12
At fast-food restaurants*	109.65	85.47	130.79	155.55	123.68	93.53	73.98	43.49
At full-service restaurants	32.72	28.25	45.36	36.46	38.57	34.61	14.74	10.38
At vending machines, mobile vendors	17.28	25.98	25.35	22.90	17.87	13.59	6.62	4.72
At employer and school cafeterias	6.43	10.16	6.96	10.47	7.39	4.67	2.42	1.53
Breakfast and brunch	225.86	163.33	229.19	261.79	237.97	251.20	199.62	149.34
At fast-food restaurants*	123.77	100.45	151.38	158.33	137.60	112.58	86.50	59.28
At full-service restaurants	89.39	43.30	62.92	90.28	84.75	122.80	109.84	87.95
At vending machines, mobile vendors	3.03	2.18	2.87	4.49	3.55	4.28	0.84	0.23
At employer and school cafeterias	9.66	17.40	12.03	8.69	12.07	11.53	2.43	1.88

	total consumer units	under 25	25 to 34	35 to 44	45 to 54	55 to 64	65 to 74	75+
Board (including at school)	$43.87	$61.26	$3.69	$27.27	$121.53	$52.33	$1.06	$4.83
Catered affairs	52.63	19.80	64.30	41.91	63.59	79.60	41.96	13.72
Food on trips	236.49	100.79	194.85	231.71	265.80	287.83	340.47	126.40
School lunches	62.16	13.02	51.13	147.59	108.96	20.41	5.38	2.49
Meals as pay	28.85	79.61	54.03	32.79	19.21	21.55	9.96	0.83
ALCOHOLIC BEVERAGES	456.43	417.75	512.63	497.49	494.29	468.34	421.65	240.69
At home	242.35	149.20	212.59	275.48	292.06	247.82	257.07	161.33
Beer and ale	109.76	88.03	121.83	146.97	138.69	97.20	68.46	42.60
Whiskey	9.60	9.82	8.60	7.77	9.95	8.55	12.00	13.12
Wine	104.03	36.82	62.62	104.33	117.32	123.25	159.44	92.87
Other alcoholic beverages	18.97	14.52	19.54	16.41	26.10	18.82	17.17	12.74
Away from home	214.08	268.55	300.05	222.01	202.23	220.52	164.58	79.36
Beer and ale	76.98	114.09	126.57	91.57	71.84	68.28	33.27	14.08
At fast-food restaurants*	12.47	22.55	16.43	18.63	15.92	7.31	3.02	0.73
At full-service restaurants	63.32	82.81	108.08	72.29	55.81	60.81	29.16	13.18
At vending machines, mobile vendors	0.65	0.19	2.06	0.60	0.11	0.13	1.09	0.17
Wine	41.96	39.95	41.34	35.17	43.92	49.71	47.75	31.44
At fast-food restaurants*	2.96	3.91	3.64	3.40	3.66	2.52	2.15	0.54
At full-service restaurants	38.20	24.65	37.71	31.21	40.17	47.19	45.60	30.90
Other alcoholic beverages	50.30	85.35	80.47	52.96	40.23	51.19	27.01	14.79
At fast-food restaurants*	4.25	14.57	8.09	5.54	1.47	3.23	0.56	0.41
At full-service restaurants	45.99	69.79	72.39	47.42	38.77	47.95	26.45	14.38
Alcoholic beverages purchased on trips	44.84	29.17	51.66	42.31	46.24	51.34	56.55	19.05

* The category fast-food restaurants also includes take-out, delivery, concession stands, buffets, and cafeterias other than employer and school.
Note: Subcategories may not add to total because some are not shown.
Source: Bureau of Labor Statistics, unpublished tables from the 2011 Consumer Expenditure Survey

Table 5.2 Food and Alcohol: Indexed spending by age, 2011

(indexed average annual spending of consumer units on food and alcoholic beverages, by age of consumer unit reference person, 2011; index definition: an index of 100 is the average for all consumer units; an index of 125 means that spending by consumer units in that group is 25 percent above the average for all consumer units; an index of 75 indicates spending that is 25 percent below the average for all consumer units)

	total consumer units	under 25	25 to 34	35 to 44	45 to 54	55 to 64	65 to 74	75+
Average spending of consumer units, total	$49,705	$29,912	$48,097	$57,271	$58,050	$53,616	$44,646	$32,688
Average spending of consumer units, index	100	60	97	115	117	108	90	66
Food, spending index	100	67	96	120	115	101	90	68
Alcoholic beverages, spending index	100	92	112	109	108	103	92	53
FOOD AT HOME	100	62	90	120	115	102	94	78
Cereals and bakery products	100	63	90	121	115	97	90	86
Cereals and cereal products	100	65	100	124	115	92	82	80
Flour	100	49	97	139	100	86	96	97
Prepared flour mixes	100	69	99	118	105	92	108	83
Ready-to-eat and cooked cereals	100	62	104	120	115	90	85	85
Rice	100	83	93	133	109	103	72	70
Pasta, cornmeal, and other cereal products	100	64	97	130	126	91	71	67
Bakery products	100	62	85	120	115	100	94	90
Bread	100	71	82	116	113	104	94	93
White bread	100	74	81	123	115	102	91	83
Bread, other than white	100	69	82	111	112	106	97	100
Cookies and crackers	100	62	82	117	113	102	96	99
Cookies	100	58	83	111	110	109	95	105
Crackers	100	67	82	124	117	93	97	90
Frozen and refrigerated bakery products	100	63	99	140	105	96	78	73
Other bakery products	100	56	87	120	120	95	97	85
Biscuits and rolls	100	51	85	117	126	96	102	75
Cakes and cupcakes	100	56	97	130	128	81	82	76
Bread and cracker products	100	68	85	119	104	103	104	93
Sweetrolls, coffee cakes, doughnuts	100	57	83	117	105	98	102	117
Pies, tarts, turnovers	100	67	74	113	109	116	103	90
Meats, poultry, fish, and eggs	100	63	88	121	116	107	91	68
Beef	100	62	85	119	120	106	98	67
Ground beef	100	53	97	116	122	104	92	58
Roast	100	35	79	118	114	109	117	82
Chuck roast	100	37	87	126	100	86	115	125
Round roast	100	27	51	131	102	95	158	115
Other roast	100	36	85	109	124	124	104	50
Steak	100	79	78	121	118	104	95	76
Round steak	100	79	91	121	104	106	103	68
Sirloin steak	100	70	96	114	125	111	77	53
Other steak	100	84	64	124	119	100	101	90
Other beef	100	70	62	122	130	116	106	48
Pork	100	59	82	124	110	113	100	68
Bacon	100	56	84	124	108	111	108	69
Pork chops	100	64	95	135	105	109	91	49
Ham	100	63	81	118	101	116	101	89
Ham, not canned	100	60	81	118	102	116	104	89
Canned ham	100	186	96	140	82	124	3	81
Sausage	100	51	75	125	114	124	96	59
Other pork	100	62	78	119	120	108	102	69
Other meats	100	52	90	126	128	98	83	65
Frankfurters	100	66	95	131	116	99	84	59
Lunch meats (cold cuts)	100	48	91	118	130	100	87	68
Bologna, liverwurst, salami	100	54	92	118	122	100	100	64
Other lunch meats	100	45	90	119	133	100	81	70
Lamb, organ meats, and others	100	50	69	175	139	82	52	56

	total consumer units	under 25	25 to 34	35 to 44	45 to 54	55 to 64	65 to 74	75+
Poultry	100	79	100	123	118	99	77	62
Fresh and frozen chicken	100	73	101	126	118	99	72	62
Fresh and frozen whole chicken	100	80	89	142	114	96	77	59
Fresh and frozen chicken parts	100	71	106	120	119	101	69	63
Other poultry	100	104	93	111	119	96	98	60
Fish and seafood	100	57	85	115	104	126	92	78
Canned fish and seafood	100	59	79	123	98	111	111	94
Fresh fish and shellfish	100	46	92	110	103	130	84	85
Frozen fish and shellfish	100	73	80	117	107	129	93	61
Eggs	100	77	89	117	111	101	97	82
Dairy products	**100**	**60**	**93**	**118**	**117**	**97**	**95**	**80**
Fresh milk and cream	100	65	97	126	115	92	88	80
Fresh milk, all types	100	67	98	126	114	91	89	77
Cream	100	49	90	122	121	94	82	98
Other dairy products	100	57	91	114	118	100	99	80
Butter	100	47	72	112	118	115	97	100
Cheese	100	57	93	112	124	100	96	71
Ice cream and related products	100	65	88	114	109	97	108	96
Miscellaneous dairy products	100	56	100	119	113	94	99	77
Fruits and vegetables	**100**	**59**	**88**	**118**	**112**	**103**	**100**	**85**
Fresh fruits	100	53	85	118	111	106	103	88
Apples	100	74	94	129	107	94	98	72
Bananas	100	60	86	114	110	102	96	103
Oranges	100	51	77	127	109	106	109	80
Citrus fruits, excluding oranges	100	48	87	120	111	109	98	81
Other fresh fruits	100	46	82	111	112	111	107	92
Fresh vegetables	100	58	87	113	115	107	98	84
Potatoes	100	71	86	116	115	102	94	86
Lettuce	100	55	84	117	111	114	95	81
Tomatoes	100	67	96	115	109	101	96	87
Other fresh vegetables	100	51	85	110	118	109	101	84
Processed fruits	100	69	92	124	111	93	96	86
Frozen fruits and fruit juices	100	47	91	123	135	78	104	69
Frozen orange juice	100	29	80	128	142	76	86	102
Frozen fruits	100	59	88	106	139	82	131	53
Frozen fruit juices, excluding orange	100	40	114	163	115	73	57	64
Canned fruits	100	55	85	110	100	108	117	100
Dried fruits	100	47	67	112	132	96	115	93
Fresh fruit juice	100	65	97	128	109	85	106	78
Canned and bottled fruit juice	100	85	98	130	106	92	79	86
Processed vegetables	100	65	90	120	113	98	101	78
Frozen vegetables	100	63	86	120	119	94	98	84
Canned and dried vegetables and juices	100	66	92	120	110	100	102	76
Canned beans	100	68	95	115	109	104	103	73
Canned corn	100	67	93	117	114	116	84	62
Canned miscellaneous vegetables	100	50	83	110	105	103	128	95
Dried peas	100	135	107	69	74	142	111	92
Dried beans	100	122	89	140	131	66	101	29
Dried miscellaneous vegetables	100	66	83	138	128	89	90	53
Dried processed vegetables	100	70	45	94	127	64	149	180
Fresh and canned vegetable juices	100	66	111	128	101	101	76	75
Sugar and other sweets	**100**	**54**	**78**	**124**	**113**	**106**	**100**	**88**
Candy and chewing gum	100	50	71	119	123	107	98	89
Sugar	100	72	88	144	94	105	92	71
Artificial sweeteners	100	50	82	111	106	88	154	90
Jams, preserves, other sweets	100	51	86	127	98	104	100	102

	total consumer units	under 25	25 to 34	35 to 44	45 to 54	55 to 64	65 to 74	75+
Fats and oils	**100**	**56**	**86**	**115**	**114**	**101**	**102**	**90**
Margarine	100	60	66	104	108	113	124	112
Fats and oils	100	60	87	125	114	95	98	86
Salad dressings	100	44	90	104	108	110	111	97
Nondairy cream and imitation milk	100	56	84	127	119	95	101	77
Peanut butter	100	68	95	110	125	95	84	87
Miscellaneous foods	**100**	**66**	**97**	**121**	**113**	**98**	**91**	**75**
Frozen prepared foods	100	68	102	127	115	90	76	82
Frozen meals	100	51	88	112	113	104	92	103
Other frozen prepared foods	100	82	113	140	117	79	62	64
Canned and packaged soups	100	67	77	106	110	110	114	97
Potato chips, nuts, and other snacks	100	59	85	126	120	101	89	72
Potato chips and other snacks	100	64	94	136	123	94	76	58
Nuts	100	46	58	98	114	122	126	113
Condiments and seasonings	100	58	95	117	116	99	98	76
Salt, spices, and other seasonings	100	62	99	119	121	92	98	63
Olives, pickles, relishes	100	68	75	106	115	115	99	95
Sauces and gravies	100	56	99	124	114	96	95	69
Baking needs and miscellaneous products	100	48	90	106	112	106	106	97
Other canned or packaged prepared foods	100	73	108	119	106	98	92	69
Prepared salads	100	46	91	110	100	118	102	94
Prepared desserts	100	40	89	124	109	95	106	98
Baby food	100	117	254	149	63	31	25	15
Miscellaneous prepared foods	100	75	87	115	115	106	97	70
Nonalcoholic beverages	**100**	**66**	**89**	**120**	**123**	**102**	**86**	**70**
Cola	100	68	85	125	125	103	91	53
Other carbonated drinks	100	72	101	118	131	96	69	59
Tea	100	77	71	114	119	120	96	66
Coffee	100	42	70	105	119	115	105	107
Noncarbonated fruit-flavored drinks	100	81	98	143	105	79	93	74
Other noncarbonated beverages and ice	100	90	107	139	110	90	63	60
Bottled water	100	61	99	120	130	95	73	68
Sports drinks	100	84	110	136	113	94	69	45
Food prepared by consumer unit on trips	**100**	**42**	**69**	**101**	**122**	**134**	**131**	**44**
FOOD AWAY FROM HOME	**100**	**75**	**106**	**121**	**115**	**100**	**84**	**55**
Meals at restaurants, carry-outs, etc.	**100**	**77**	**109**	**122**	**110**	**98**	**83**	**58**
Lunch	100	73	110	125	109	96	82	61
At fast-food restaurants*	100	88	126	133	109	89	63	43
At full-service restaurants	100	60	93	95	104	112	118	95
At vending machines, mobile vendors	100	115	102	130	132	112	39	12
At employer and school cafeterias	100	52	106	207	128	61	33	13
Dinner	100	79	107	120	112	98	85	58
At fast-food restaurants*	100	116	122	141	107	86	61	32
At full-service restaurants	100	57	99	109	115	105	98	72
At vending machines, mobile vendors	100	64	329	71	50	24	87	25
At employer and school cafeterias	100	278	75	127	51	78	116	108
Snacks and nonalcoholic beverages	100	90	126	136	113	88	59	36
At fast-food restaurants*	100	78	119	142	113	85	67	40
At full-service restaurants	100	86	139	111	118	106	45	32
At vending machines, mobile vendors	100	150	147	133	103	79	38	27
At employer and school cafeterias	100	158	108	163	115	73	38	24
Breakfast and brunch	100	72	101	116	105	111	88	66
At fast-food restaurants*	100	81	122	128	111	91	70	48
At full-service restaurants	100	48	70	101	95	137	123	98
At vending machines, mobile vendors	100	72	95	148	117	141	28	8
At employer and school cafeterias	100	180	125	90	125	119	25	19

	total consumer units	under 25	25 to 34	35 to 44	45 to 54	55 to 64	65 to 74	75+
Board (including at school)	**100**	**140**	**8**	**62**	**277**	**119**	**2**	**11**
Catered affairs	**100**	**38**	**122**	**80**	**121**	**151**	**80**	**26**
Food on trips	**100**	**43**	**82**	**98**	**112**	**122**	**144**	**53**
School lunches	**100**	**21**	**82**	**237**	**175**	**33**	**9**	**4**
Meals as pay	**100**	**276**	**187**	**114**	**67**	**75**	**35**	**3**
ALCOHOLIC BEVERAGES	**100**	**92**	**112**	**109**	**108**	**103**	**92**	**53**
At home	**100**	**62**	**88**	**114**	**121**	**102**	**106**	**67**
Beer and ale	100	80	111	134	126	89	62	39
Whiskey	100	102	90	81	104	89	125	137
Wine	100	35	60	100	113	118	153	89
Other alcoholic beverages	100	77	103	87	138	99	91	67
Away from home	**100**	**125**	**140**	**104**	**94**	**103**	**77**	**37**
Beer and ale	100	148	164	119	93	89	43	18
At fast-food restaurants*	100	181	132	149	128	59	24	6
At full-service restaurants	100	131	171	114	88	96	46	21
At vending machines, mobile vendors	100	29	317	92	17	20	168	26
Wine	100	95	99	84	105	118	114	75
At fast-food restaurants*	100	132	123	115	124	85	73	18
At full-service restaurants	100	65	99	82	105	124	119	81
Other alcoholic beverages	100	170	160	105	80	102	54	29
At fast-food restaurants*	100	343	190	130	35	76	13	10
At full-service restaurants	100	152	157	103	84	104	58	31
Alcoholic beverages purchased on trips	100	65	115	94	103	114	126	42

The category fast-food restaurants also includes take-out, delivery, concession stands, buffets, and cafeterias other than employer and school.
Source: Calculations by New Strategist based on the Bureau of Labor Statistics' 2011 Consumer Expenditure Survey

Table 5.3 Food and Alcohol: Total spending by age, 2011

(total annual spending on food and alcoholic beverages, by consumer unit age groups, 2011; consumer units and dollars in thousands)

	total consumer units	under 25	25 to 34	35 to 44	45 to 54	55 to 64	65 to 74	75+
Number of consumer units	122,287	7,743	20,463	21,699	24,821	21,688	14,079	11,794
Total spending of all consumer units	$6,078,260,661	$231,604,899	$984,216,892	$1,242,724,948	$1,440,869,475	$1,162,820,772	$628,564,839	$385,526,282
Food, total spending	789,729,446	33,713,022	127,095,693	168,492,735	184,271,104	141,405,760	81,714,516	51,987,952
Alcoholic beverages, total spending	55,815,455	3,234,638	10,489,948	10,795,036	12,268,772	10,157,358	5,936,410	2,838,698
FOOD AT HOME	469,308,157	18,441,735	70,538,417	99,689,329	109,724,457	84,765,813	50,598,518	35,143,997
Cereals and bakery products	64,895,265	2,603,661	9,795,229	13,974,156	15,145,774	11,177,561	6,749,754	5,400,591
Cereals and cereal products	21,383,105	883,476	3,586,755	4,723,655	4,990,510	3,495,889	2,030,192	1,640,427
Flour	937,941	29,191	152,859	231,528	190,129	142,490	103,340	87,983
Prepared flour mixes	1,819,631	78,979	302,443	381,251	389,193	296,258	225,827	146,010
Ready-to-eat and cooked cereals	11,175,809	435,544	1,944,394	2,375,607	2,611,169	1,785,790	1,089,011	916,984
Rice	3,137,884	165,158	487,633	740,587	694,492	572,780	259,335	211,938
Pasta, cornmeal, and other cereal products	4,311,840	174,682	699,425	994,682	1,105,776	698,570	352,820	277,513
Bakery products	43,510,937	1,720,185	6,208,474	9,250,501	10,155,264	7,681,673	4,719,422	3,760,281
Bread	13,027,234	585,371	1,780,281	2,681,996	2,987,207	2,411,922	1,415,080	1,163,124
White bread	5,494,355	256,835	744,239	1,202,559	1,282,253	993,744	575,550	438,029
Bread, other than white	7,532,879	328,535	1,036,042	1,479,438	1,704,954	1,418,178	839,531	725,213
Cookies and crackers	10,221,970	400,158	1,407,445	2,118,907	2,341,117	1,854,975	1,127,024	971,118
Cookies	5,742,598	210,377	795,192	1,132,037	1,279,523	1,114,113	628,487	580,265
Crackers	4,479,373	189,858	612,253	986,871	1,061,842	741,079	498,537	390,735
Frozen and refrigerated bakery products	3,497,408	139,297	579,717	868,177	748,353	594,468	312,695	247,674
Other bakery products	16,764,325	595,282	2,441,031	3,581,203	4,078,339	2,820,308	1,864,482	1,378,365
Biscuits and rolls	6,472,651	208,287	923,495	1,349,461	1,658,539	1,103,702	757,732	470,345
Cakes and cupcakes	4,623,671	164,306	753,243	1,065,421	1,197,613	662,785	437,857	337,662
Bread and cracker products	871,906	37,631	124,006	184,875	183,427	159,841	104,466	78,076
Sweetrolls, coffee cakes, doughnuts	2,917,768	105,305	407,214	605,619	622,014	508,367	341,134	328,817
Pies, tarts, turnovers	1,878,328	79,753	233,278	375,827	416,993	385,613	223,293	163,465
Meats, poultry, fish, and eggs	101,792,922	4,079,400	15,003,472	21,835,487	23,956,733	19,389,723	10,692,719	6,713,263
Beef	27,221,086	1,061,952	3,849,500	5,729,187	6,638,128	5,101,234	3,064,717	1,758,957
Ground beef	11,066,974	372,206	1,801,563	2,285,122	2,751,408	2,046,697	1,173,485	616,237
Roast	3,740,759	81,921	491,931	781,381	864,019	720,692	505,295	295,558
Chuck roast	935,496	21,913	136,284	209,395	190,625	142,056	123,473	113,104
Round roast	747,174	12,776	63,640	173,375	155,131	126,224	136,003	82,912
Other roast	2,056,867	47,232	291,802	398,611	518,262	452,412	245,819	99,659
Steak	10,087,455	504,224	1,316,385	2,160,352	2,409,374	1,857,143	1,102,949	738,540
Round steak	1,944,363	96,865	297,327	417,706	409,547	365,443	230,192	126,786
Sirloin steak	2,673,194	117,694	429,314	542,909	677,613	525,283	236,246	137,636
Other steak	5,469,898	289,743	589,744	1,199,738	1,322,463	966,417	636,512	474,119
Other beef	2,325,899	103,524	239,826	502,332	613,079	476,485	282,988	108,623
Pork	19,804,380	744,412	2,729,560	4,341,319	4,415,159	3,977,796	2,284,459	1,296,043
Bacon	4,141,861	145,723	579,512	907,886	904,725	812,866	515,291	274,211
Pork chops	3,331,098	135,580	531,015	800,476	708,640	643,266	349,722	156,506
Ham	4,193,221	167,713	568,462	879,460	863,026	863,833	488,823	359,717
Ham, not canned	4,097,837	156,486	553,115	855,809	847,141	842,796	488,541	352,287
Canned ham	95,384	11,227	15,347	23,652	15,885	21,037	282	7,430
Sausage	3,491,294	111,654	440,364	773,352	809,165	767,321	387,313	197,667
Other pork	4,645,683	183,819	610,002	980,144	1,129,356	890,509	543,168	307,941
Other meats	14,985,049	490,519	2,244,382	3,353,146	3,890,444	2,609,934	1,432,397	941,515
Frankfurters	2,894,533	121,875	459,394	674,839	679,599	508,150	280,876	165,352
Lunch meats (cold cuts)	10,720,901	325,593	1,627,832	2,253,441	2,823,141	1,902,471	1,069,018	702,804
Bologna, liverwurst, salami	3,280,960	112,738	504,822	686,990	815,618	580,154	377,176	201,206
Other lunch meats	7,439,941	212,855	1,123,009	1,566,451	2,007,771	1,322,317	691,842	501,599
Lamb, organ meats, and others	1,369,614	42,974	157,156	424,866	387,456	199,096	82,503	73,359

	total consumer units	under 25	25 to 34	35 to 44	45 to 54	55 to 64	65 to 74	75+
Poultry	$18,892,119	$948,363	$3,154,371	$4,129,537	$4,529,336	$3,303,516	$1,668,502	$1,121,609
Fresh and frozen chicken	15,217,394	706,858	2,579,770	3,407,394	3,644,219	2,678,685	1,254,720	908,846
Fresh and frozen whole chicken	4,398,663	223,773	652,565	1,104,696	1,021,384	748,236	391,537	250,858
Fresh and frozen chicken parts	10,819,954	483,086	1,927,205	2,302,915	2,622,587	1,930,232	863,324	657,987
Other poultry	3,674,724	241,504	574,601	722,143	885,365	624,831	413,782	212,764
Fish and seafood	14,767,378	536,977	2,111,372	3,007,047	3,110,071	3,305,685	1,557,841	1,110,641
Canned fish and seafood	2,433,511	90,671	320,451	530,107	482,768	479,305	311,850	219,604
Fresh fish and shellfish	7,277,299	213,087	1,117,075	1,424,539	1,527,484	1,673,880	703,950	595,361
Frozen fish and shellfish	5,056,567	233,297	673,642	1,052,402	1,099,570	1,152,500	542,042	295,676
Eggs	6,122,910	297,176	914,287	1,275,467	1,373,594	1,091,557	684,803	484,498
Dairy products	**49,751,243**	**1,892,776**	**7,749,338**	**10,440,691**	**11,790,223**	**8,534,879**	**5,454,768**	**3,850,151**
Fresh milk and cream	18,310,033	749,058	2,956,904	4,082,233	4,261,021	2,974,509	1,854,627	1,413,747
Fresh milk, all types	15,576,918	664,504	2,546,006	3,488,114	3,591,102	2,519,495	1,596,136	1,155,694
Cream	2,734,337	84,554	410,897	593,902	669,919	455,014	258,490	258,053
Other dairy products	31,439,988	1,143,719	4,792,435	6,358,675	7,529,202	5,560,369	3,600,141	2,436,405
Butter	3,013,152	89,122	362,400	599,760	720,802	612,035	337,192	291,430
Cheese	15,254,080	548,437	2,373,094	3,037,209	3,850,482	2,704,710	1,685,397	1,039,405
Ice cream and related products	7,004,599	287,110	1,026,015	1,415,209	1,546,100	1,210,407	873,884	649,024
Miscellaneous dairy products	6,166,933	219,049	1,030,926	1,306,497	1,411,570	1,032,999	703,668	456,664
Fruits and vegetables	**87,421,753**	**3,285,587**	**12,825,185**	**18,250,812**	**19,929,774**	**15,917,474**	**10,034,666**	**7,137,965**
Fresh fruits	30,239,129	1,018,901	4,299,890	6,306,814	6,783,828	5,685,726	3,572,828	2,559,298
Apples	4,667,695	217,269	737,487	1,064,336	1,017,661	778,599	528,244	322,330
Bananas	5,023,550	190,246	726,027	1,018,334	1,124,391	908,944	554,290	498,886
Oranges	3,300,526	106,079	425,835	746,663	729,986	622,229	414,627	255,930
Citrus fruits, excluding oranges	4,601,660	138,677	666,889	983,616	1,038,511	891,594	520,219	357,948
Other fresh fruits	12,646,922	366,708	1,743,857	2,493,866	2,873,279	2,484,360	1,555,448	1,124,322
Fresh vegetables	27,417,968	1,004,577	3,980,258	5,502,866	6,393,393	5,191,457	3,096,535	2,229,538
Potatoes	4,742,290	212,236	678,553	977,757	1,109,250	854,941	514,024	393,684
Lettuce	3,933,973	137,051	555,570	815,665	886,110	798,769	428,846	306,998
Tomatoes	5,017,436	212,313	802,763	1,020,287	1,109,747	896,148	552,178	419,395
Other fresh vegetables	13,725,493	442,977	1,943,576	2,689,157	3,288,286	2,641,382	1,601,345	1,109,462
Processed fruits	14,152,275	619,982	2,189,541	3,107,080	3,178,329	2,324,303	1,556,715	1,173,031
Frozen fruits and fruit juices	1,627,640	48,239	248,012	356,081	447,523	225,989	194,290	108,151
Frozen orange juice	456,131	8,440	61,389	103,287	131,551	61,160	45,334	44,935
Frozen fruits	846,226	31,437	124,415	158,620	239,274	122,320	127,837	43,166
Frozen fruit juices, excluding orange	326,506	8,362	62,208	94,174	76,449	42,508	21,259	20,050
Canned fruits	2,597,376	89,819	371,403	506,672	529,184	498,173	350,849	251,684
Dried fruits	994,193	29,811	112,137	197,678	265,833	169,166	131,920	88,809
Fresh fruit juice	2,113,119	86,722	342,551	478,680	468,620	318,814	258,490	159,337
Canned and bottled fruit juice	6,821,169	365,237	1,115,438	1,567,753	1,467,418	1,112,378	621,165	565,051
Processed vegetables	15,611,158	642,204	2,355,496	3,334,268	3,574,472	2,715,988	1,808,448	1,176,098
Frozen vegetables	4,277,599	171,740	614,913	911,141	1,036,525	713,969	481,502	347,687
Canned and dried vegetables and juices	11,333,559	470,465	1,740,378	2,422,910	2,537,947	2,002,019	1,326,946	828,529
Canned beans	2,333,236	100,891	372,836	474,123	514,043	428,338	276,230	165,234
Canned corn	1,189,853	50,562	185,395	246,067	274,768	243,773	115,448	71,354
Canned miscellaneous vegetables	3,118,319	98,104	430,542	609,091	667,437	568,659	460,946	286,712
Dried peas	102,721	8,750	18,417	12,585	15,389	25,809	13,093	9,081
Dried beans	610,212	47,232	90,651	152,110	162,081	71,787	70,958	16,865
Dried miscellaneous vegetables	1,412,415	59,002	197,263	346,533	368,344	222,302	146,985	71,590
Dried processed vegetables	250,688	11,150	19,031	41,879	64,783	28,411	43,082	43,520
Fresh and canned vegetable juices	2,273,315	94,774	421,129	516,002	464,153	409,036	198,795	163,465
Sugar and other sweets	**17,657,020**	**602,483**	**2,290,219**	**3,883,904**	**4,044,830**	**3,304,384**	**2,023,715**	**1,505,504**
Candy and chewing gum	10,608,397	335,891	1,268,297	2,231,959	2,653,861	2,015,032	1,196,715	907,077
Sugar	2,921,436	132,560	430,132	744,276	555,742	545,236	310,864	199,554
Artificial sweeteners	686,030	21,835	94,539	134,751	147,933	107,572	121,924	59,796
Jams, preserves, other sweets	3,441,156	112,196	497,456	772,918	687,293	636,543	394,212	339,078

	total consumer units	under 25	25 to 34	35 to 44	45 to 54	55 to 64	65 to 74	75+
Fats and oils	**$13,403,878**	**$474,568**	**$1,939,483**	**$2,743,405**	**$3,101,136**	**$2,398,259**	**$1,577,834**	**$1,166,780**
Margarine	1,194,744	45,761	132,191	220,245	260,869	238,568	170,215	129,262
Fats and oils	4,260,479	162,526	617,573	943,690	981,919	719,391	479,249	355,353
Salad dressings	3,810,463	105,460	575,215	704,567	834,730	745,633	485,866	356,415
Nondairy cream and imitation milk	2,273,315	80,527	317,790	510,360	550,778	381,709	263,137	169,126
Peanut butter	1,864,877	80,372	296,918	364,543	472,840	312,741	179,366	156,624
Miscellaneous foods	**84,436,728**	**3,516,483**	**13,726,990**	**18,104,561**	**19,341,268**	**14,688,198**	**8,816,411**	**6,140,428**
Frozen prepared foods	16,659,158	716,073	2,829,624	3,766,512	3,891,933	2,662,636	1,449,715	1,313,144
Frozen meals	7,598,914	243,208	1,122,191	1,516,109	1,748,143	1,400,611	802,362	758,354
Other frozen prepared foods	9,060,244	472,865	1,707,228	2,250,186	2,143,790	1,262,025	647,352	554,908
Canned and packaged soups	5,735,260	242,820	737,691	1,073,884	1,279,274	1,116,715	754,353	535,801
Potato chips, nuts, and other snacks	17,734,061	667,911	2,509,378	3,971,568	4,332,506	3,188,353	1,808,588	1,239,314
Potato chips and other snacks	13,208,219	535,274	2,071,060	3,187,366	3,285,308	2,210,658	1,150,114	743,966
Nuts	4,525,842	132,715	438,317	784,202	1,047,198	977,912	658,475	495,348
Condiments and seasonings	16,374,229	597,218	2,594,299	3,407,828	3,839,560	2,871,925	1,854,627	1,194,614
Salt, spices, and other seasonings	4,330,183	171,275	716,614	915,481	1,065,566	703,125	489,949	264,068
Olives, pickles, relishes	1,972,489	84,321	247,193	369,751	461,422	403,831	225,827	180,212
Sauces and gravies	7,145,229	253,196	1,188,900	1,572,961	1,649,852	1,214,528	781,244	476,006
Baking needs and miscellaneous products	2,926,328	88,425	441,592	549,853	662,721	550,441	357,607	274,328
Other canned or packaged prepared foods	27,932,797	1,292,384	5,056,203	5,884,552	5,997,995	4,848,352	2,949,269	1,857,437
Prepared salads	4,429,235	130,237	674,256	862,318	902,988	929,331	520,641	403,119
Prepared desserts	1,837,974	46,613	273,181	404,686	404,831	309,488	225,123	173,136
Baby food	3,399,579	251,415	1,443,665	900,075	434,616	187,384	97,286	50,714
Miscellaneous prepared foods	17,989,641	856,298	2,629,496	3,667,999	4,213,365	3,396,775	2,004,427	1,211,598
Nonalcoholic beverages	**44,141,938**	**1,830,910**	**6,537,519**	**9,413,460**	**10,979,321**	**7,973,593**	**4,371,389**	**2,984,118**
Cola	9,632,547	414,560	1,373,067	2,144,729	2,438,415	1,752,174	1,005,945	494,994
Other carbonated drinks	8,158,989	372,129	1,384,936	1,707,060	2,177,546	1,384,779	648,479	463,268
Tea	3,810,463	184,825	453,051	774,003	922,100	811,999	420,258	243,310
Coffee	9,175,194	244,524	1,074,512	1,714,004	2,219,246	1,869,722	1,109,144	944,699
Noncarbonated fruit-flavored drinks	3,027,826	155,170	494,181	768,362	645,842	423,350	325,929	215,005
Other noncarbonated beverages and ice	1,825,745	103,911	325,771	451,122	408,305	293,005	132,906	106,500
Bottled water	6,539,909	253,661	1,079,219	1,388,736	1,719,599	1,101,750	551,615	430,835
Sports drinks	1,923,575	102,130	352,577	465,227	441,317	320,549	152,194	83,737
Food prepared by consumer unit on trips	**5,808,633**	**155,867**	**670,777**	**1,042,854**	**1,435,150**	**1,381,742**	**877,403**	**245,079**
FOOD AWAY FROM HOME	**320,378,488**	**15,275,081**	**56,567,508**	**68,798,198**	**74,535,229**	**56,636,477**	**31,121,348**	**16,849,498**
Meals at restaurants, carry-outs, etc.	**268,528,800**	**13,149,782**	**49,037,329**	**58,355,338**	**60,161,636**	**46,622,910**	**25,506,361**	**15,100,802**
Lunch	92,068,659	4,283,195	17,007,822	20,422,882	20,417,755	15,648,543	8,694,205	5,383,843
At fast-food restaurants*	45,097,000	2,521,121	9,505,268	10,617,104	10,010,309	7,122,556	3,293,923	1,861,565
At full-service restaurants	36,931,897	1,397,224	5,734,142	6,229,783	7,791,064	7,368,281	5,008,463	3,397,498
At vending machines, mobile vendors	875,575	63,493	148,766	201,801	234,310	173,287	39,421	10,379
At employer and school cafeterias	9,164,188	301,358	1,619,646	3,374,195	2,382,071	984,418	352,538	114,402
Dinner	128,529,751	6,441,557	23,073,670	27,361,137	29,182,794	22,351,219	12,625,343	7,246,587
At fast-food restaurants*	44,650,652	3,280,477	9,129,567	11,136,578	9,681,183	6,798,537	3,118,076	1,373,647
At full-service restaurants	82,673,349	2,998,786	13,635,111	15,989,125	19,377,010	15,420,602	9,358,311	5,776,937
At vending machines, mobile vendors	369,307	14,944	203,607	46,219	37,728	15,832	37,028	9,081
At employer and school cafeterias	837,666	147,349	105,180	189,432	86,874	116,248	111,928	87,040
Snacks and nonalcoholic beverages	20,310,648	1,160,443	4,265,922	4,890,521	4,654,434	3,175,123	1,376,363	709,055
At fast-food restaurants*	13,408,770	661,794	2,676,356	3,375,279	3,069,861	2,028,479	1,041,564	512,921
At full-service restaurants	4,001,231	218,740	928,202	791,146	957,346	750,622	207,524	122,422
At vending machines, mobile vendors	2,113,119	201,163	518,737	496,907	443,551	294,740	93,203	55,668
At employer and school cafeterias	786,305	78,669	142,422	227,189	183,427	101,283	34,071	18,045
Breakfast and brunch	27,619,742	1,264,664	4,689,915	5,680,581	5,906,653	5,448,026	2,810,450	1,761,316
At fast-food restaurants*	15,135,462	777,784	3,097,689	3,435,603	3,415,370	2,441,635	1,217,834	699,148
At full-service restaurants	10,931,235	335,272	1,287,532	1,958,986	2,103,580	2,663,286	1,546,437	1,037,282
At vending machines, mobile vendors	370,530	16,880	58,729	97,429	88,115	92,825	11,826	2,713
At employer and school cafeterias	1,181,292	134,728	246,170	188,564	299,589	250,063	34,212	22,173

	total consumer units	under 25	25 to 34	35 to 44	45 to 54	55 to 64	65 to 74	75+
Board (including at school)	$5,364,731	$474,336	$75,508	$591,732	$3,016,496	$1,134,933	$14,924	$56,965
Catered affairs	6,435,965	153,311	1,315,771	909,405	1,578,367	1,726,365	590,755	161,814
Food on trips	28,919,653	780,417	3,987,216	5,027,875	6,597,422	6,242,457	4,793,477	1,490,762
School lunches	7,601,360	100,814	1,046,273	3,202,555	2,704,496	442,652	75,745	29,367
Meals as pay	3,527,980	616,420	1,105,616	711,510	476,811	467,376	140,227	9,789
ALCOHOLIC BEVERAGES	55,815,455	3,234,638	10,489,948	10,795,036	12,268,772	10,157,358	5,936,410	2,838,698
At home	29,636,254	1,155,256	4,350,229	5,977,641	7,249,221	5,374,720	3,619,289	1,902,726
Beer and ale	13,422,221	681,616	2,493,007	3,189,102	3,442,424	2,108,074	963,848	502,424
Whiskey	1,173,955	76,036	175,982	168,601	246,969	185,432	168,948	154,737
Wine	12,721,517	285,097	1,281,393	2,263,857	2,912,000	2,673,046	2,244,756	1,095,309
Other alcoholic beverages	2,319,784	112,428	399,847	356,081	647,828	408,168	241,736	150,256
Away from home	26,179,201	2,079,383	6,139,923	4,817,395	5,019,551	4,782,638	2,317,122	935,972
Beer and ale	9,413,653	883,399	2,590,002	1,986,977	1,783,141	1,480,857	468,408	166,060
At fast-food restaurants*	1,524,919	174,605	336,207	404,252	395,150	158,539	42,519	8,610
At full-service restaurants	7,743,213	641,198	2,211,641	1,568,621	1,385,260	1,318,847	410,544	155,445
At vending machines, mobile vendors	79,487	1,471	42,154	13,019	2,730	2,819	15,346	2,005
Wine	5,131,163	309,333	845,940	763,154	1,090,138	1,078,110	672,272	370,803
At fast-food restaurants*	361,970	30,275	74,485	73,777	90,845	54,654	30,270	6,369
At full-service restaurants	4,671,363	190,865	771,660	677,226	997,060	1,023,457	642,002	364,435
Other alcoholic beverages	6,151,036	660,865	1,646,658	1,149,179	998,549	1,110,209	380,274	174,433
At fast-food restaurants*	519,720	112,816	165,546	120,212	36,487	70,052	7,884	4,836
At full-service restaurants	5,623,979	540,384	1,481,317	1,028,967	962,310	1,039,940	372,390	169,598
Alcoholic beverages purchased on trips	5,483,349	225,863	1,057,119	918,085	1,147,723	1,113,462	796,167	224,676

* The category fast-food restaurants also includes take-out, delivery, concession stands, buffets, and cafeterias other than employer and school.
Note: Numbers may not add to total because of rounding and missing subcategories.
Source: Calculations by New Strategist based on the Bureau of Labor Statistics' 2011 Consumer Expenditure Survey

Table 5.4 Food and Alcohol: Market shares by age, 2011

(percentage of total annual spending on food and alcoholic beverages accounted for by consumer unit age groups, 2011)

	total consumer units	under 25	25 to 34	35 to 44	45 to 54	55 to 64	65 to 74	75+
Share of total consumer units	100.0%	6.3%	16.7%	17.7%	20.3%	17.7%	11.5%	9.6%
Share of total before-tax income	100.0	2.7	15.3	21.6	25.0	21.0	9.5	4.9
Share of total spending	100.0	3.8	16.2	20.4	23.7	19.1	10.3	6.3
Share of food spending	100.0	4.3	16.1	21.3	23.3	17.9	10.3	6.6
Share of alcoholic beverages spending	100.0	5.8	18.8	19.3	22.0	18.2	10.6	5.1
FOOD AT HOME	100.0	3.9	15.0	21.2	23.4	18.1	10.8	7.5
Cereals and bakery products	100.0	4.0	15.1	21.5	23.3	17.2	10.4	8.3
Cereals and cereal products	100.0	4.1	16.8	22.1	23.3	16.3	9.5	7.7
Flour	100.0	3.1	16.3	24.7	20.3	15.2	11.0	9.4
Prepared flour mixes	100.0	4.3	16.6	21.0	21.4	16.3	12.4	8.0
Ready-to-eat and cooked cereals	100.0	3.9	17.4	21.3	23.4	16.0	9.7	8.2
Rice	100.0	5.3	15.5	23.6	22.1	18.3	8.3	6.8
Pasta, cornmeal, and other cereal products	100.0	4.1	16.2	23.1	25.6	16.2	8.2	6.4
Bakery products	100.0	4.0	14.3	21.3	23.3	17.7	10.8	8.6
Bread	100.0	4.5	13.7	20.6	22.9	18.5	10.9	8.9
White bread	100.0	4.7	13.5	21.9	23.3	18.1	10.5	8.0
Bread, other than white	100.0	4.4	13.8	19.6	22.6	18.8	11.1	9.6
Cookies and crackers	100.0	3.9	13.8	20.7	22.9	18.1	11.0	9.5
Cookies	100.0	3.7	13.8	19.7	22.3	19.4	10.9	10.1
Crackers	100.0	4.2	13.7	22.0	23.7	16.5	11.1	8.7
Frozen and refrigerated bakery products	100.0	4.0	16.6	24.8	21.4	17.0	8.9	7.1
Other bakery products	100.0	3.6	14.6	21.4	24.3	16.8	11.1	8.2
Biscuits and rolls	100.0	3.2	14.3	20.8	25.6	17.1	11.7	7.3
Cakes and cupcakes	100.0	3.6	16.3	23.0	25.9	14.3	9.5	7.3
Bread and cracker products	100.0	4.3	14.2	21.2	21.0	18.3	12.0	9.0
Sweetrolls, coffee cakes, doughnuts	100.0	3.6	14.0	20.8	21.3	17.4	11.7	11.3
Pies, tarts, turnovers	100.0	4.2	12.4	20.0	22.2	20.5	11.9	8.7
Meats, poultry, fish, and eggs	100.0	4.0	14.7	21.5	23.5	19.0	10.5	6.6
Beef	100.0	3.9	14.1	21.0	24.4	18.7	11.3	6.5
Ground beef	100.0	3.4	16.3	20.6	24.9	18.5	10.6	5.6
Roast	100.0	2.2	13.2	20.9	23.1	19.3	13.5	7.9
Chuck roast	100.0	2.3	14.6	22.4	20.4	15.2	13.2	12.1
Round roast	100.0	1.7	8.5	23.2	20.8	16.9	18.2	11.1
Other roast	100.0	2.3	14.2	19.4	25.2	22.0	12.0	4.8
Steak	100.0	5.0	13.0	21.4	23.9	18.4	10.9	7.3
Round steak	100.0	5.0	15.3	21.5	21.1	18.8	11.8	6.5
Sirloin steak	100.0	4.4	16.1	20.3	25.3	19.7	8.8	5.1
Other steak	100.0	5.3	10.8	21.9	24.2	17.7	11.6	8.7
Other beef	100.0	4.5	10.3	21.6	26.4	20.5	12.2	4.7
Pork	100.0	3.8	13.8	21.9	22.3	20.1	11.5	6.5
Bacon	100.0	3.5	14.0	21.9	21.8	19.6	12.4	6.6
Pork chops	100.0	4.1	15.9	24.0	21.3	19.3	10.5	4.7
Ham	100.0	4.0	13.6	21.0	20.6	20.6	11.7	8.6
Ham, not canned	100.0	3.8	13.5	20.9	20.7	20.6	11.9	8.6
Canned ham	100.0	11.8	16.1	24.8	16.7	22.1	0.3	7.8
Sausage	100.0	3.2	12.6	22.2	23.2	22.0	11.1	5.7
Other pork	100.0	4.0	13.1	21.1	24.3	19.2	11.7	6.6
Other meats	100.0	3.3	15.0	22.4	26.0	17.4	9.6	6.3
Frankfurters	100.0	4.2	15.9	23.3	23.5	17.6	9.7	5.7
Lunch meats (cold cuts)	100.0	3.0	15.2	21.0	26.3	17.7	10.0	6.6
Bologna, liverwurst, salami	100.0	3.4	15.4	20.9	24.9	17.7	11.5	6.1
Other lunch meats	100.0	2.9	15.1	21.1	27.0	17.8	9.3	6.7
Lamb, organ meats, and others	100.0	3.1	11.5	31.0	28.3	14.5	6.0	5.4

	total consumer units	under 25	25 to 34	35 to 44	45 to 54	55 to 64	65 to 74	75+
Poultry	100.0%	5.0%	16.7%	21.9%	24.0%	17.5%	8.8%	5.9%
Fresh and frozen chicken	100.0	4.6	17.0	22.4	23.9	17.6	8.2	6.0
Fresh and frozen whole chicken	100.0	5.1	14.8	25.1	23.2	17.0	8.9	5.7
Fresh and frozen chicken parts	100.0	4.5	17.8	21.3	24.2	17.8	8.0	6.1
Other poultry	100.0	6.6	15.6	19.7	24.1	17.0	11.3	5.8
Fish and seafood	100.0	3.6	14.3	20.4	21.1	22.4	10.5	7.5
Canned fish and seafood	100.0	3.7	13.2	21.8	19.8	19.7	12.8	9.0
Fresh fish and shellfish	100.0	2.9	15.4	19.6	21.0	23.0	9.7	8.2
Frozen fish and shellfish	100.0	4.6	13.3	20.8	21.7	22.8	10.7	5.8
Eggs	100.0	4.9	14.9	20.8	22.4	17.8	11.2	7.9
Dairy products	**100.0**	**3.8**	**15.6**	**21.0**	**23.7**	**17.2**	**11.0**	**7.7**
Fresh milk and cream	100.0	4.1	16.1	22.3	23.3	16.2	10.1	7.7
Fresh milk, all types	100.0	4.3	16.3	22.4	23.1	16.2	10.2	7.4
Cream	100.0	3.1	15.0	21.7	24.5	16.6	9.5	9.4
Other dairy products	100.0	3.6	15.2	20.2	23.9	17.7	11.5	7.7
Butter	100.0	3.0	12.0	19.9	23.9	20.3	11.2	9.7
Cheese	100.0	3.6	15.6	19.9	25.2	17.7	11.0	6.8
Ice cream and related products	100.0	4.1	14.6	20.2	22.1	17.3	12.5	9.3
Miscellaneous dairy products	100.0	3.6	16.7	21.2	22.9	16.8	11.4	7.4
Fruits and vegetables	**100.0**	**3.8**	**14.7**	**20.9**	**22.8**	**18.2**	**11.5**	**8.2**
Fresh fruits	100.0	3.4	14.2	20.9	22.4	18.8	11.8	8.5
Apples	100.0	4.7	15.8	22.8	21.8	16.7	11.3	6.9
Bananas	100.0	3.8	14.5	20.3	22.4	18.1	11.0	9.9
Oranges	100.0	3.2	12.9	22.6	22.1	18.9	12.6	7.8
Citrus fruits, excluding oranges	100.0	3.0	14.5	21.4	22.6	19.4	11.3	7.8
Other fresh fruits	100.0	2.9	13.8	19.7	22.7	19.6	12.3	8.9
Fresh vegetables	100.0	3.7	14.5	20.1	23.3	18.9	11.3	8.1
Potatoes	100.0	4.5	14.3	20.6	23.4	18.0	10.8	8.3
Lettuce	100.0	3.5	14.1	20.7	22.5	20.3	10.9	7.8
Tomatoes	100.0	4.2	16.0	20.3	22.1	17.9	11.0	8.4
Other fresh vegetables	100.0	3.2	14.2	19.6	24.0	19.2	11.7	8.1
Processed fruits	100.0	4.4	15.5	22.0	22.5	16.4	11.0	8.3
Frozen fruits and fruit juices	100.0	3.0	15.2	21.9	27.5	13.9	11.9	6.6
Frozen orange juice	100.0	1.9	13.5	22.6	28.8	13.4	9.9	9.9
Frozen fruits	100.0	3.7	14.7	18.7	28.3	14.5	15.1	5.1
Frozen fruit juices, excluding orange	100.0	2.6	19.1	28.8	23.4	13.0	6.5	6.1
Canned fruits	100.0	3.5	14.3	19.5	20.4	19.2	13.5	9.7
Dried fruits	100.0	3.0	11.3	19.9	26.7	17.0	13.3	8.9
Fresh fruit juice	100.0	4.1	16.2	22.7	22.2	15.1	12.2	7.5
Canned and bottled fruit juice	100.0	5.4	16.4	23.0	21.5	16.3	9.1	8.3
Processed vegetables	100.0	4.1	15.1	21.4	22.9	17.4	11.6	7.5
Frozen vegetables	100.0	4.0	14.4	21.3	24.2	16.7	11.3	8.1
Canned and dried vegetables and juices	100.0	4.2	15.4	21.4	22.4	17.7	11.7	7.3
Canned beans	100.0	4.3	16.0	20.3	22.0	18.4	11.8	7.1
Canned corn	100.0	4.2	15.6	20.7	23.1	20.5	9.7	6.0
Canned miscellaneous vegetables	100.0	3.1	13.8	19.5	21.4	18.2	14.8	9.2
Dried peas	100.0	8.5	17.9	12.3	15.0	25.1	12.7	8.8
Dried beans	100.0	7.7	14.9	24.9	26.6	11.8	11.6	2.8
Dried miscellaneous vegetables	100.0	4.2	14.0	24.5	26.1	15.7	10.4	5.1
Dried processed vegetables	100.0	4.4	7.6	16.7	25.8	11.3	17.2	17.4
Fresh and canned vegetable juices	100.0	4.2	18.5	22.7	20.4	18.0	8.7	7.2
Sugar and other sweets	**100.0**	**3.4**	**13.0**	**22.0**	**22.9**	**18.7**	**11.5**	**8.5**
Candy and chewing gum	100.0	3.2	12.0	21.0	25.0	19.0	11.3	8.6
Sugar	100.0	4.5	14.7	25.5	19.0	18.7	10.6	6.8
Artificial sweeteners	100.0	3.2	13.8	19.6	21.6	15.7	17.8	8.7
Jams, preserves, other sweets	100.0	3.3	14.5	22.5	20.0	18.5	11.5	9.9

	total consumer units	under 25	25 to 34	35 to 44	45 to 54	55 to 64	65 to 74	75+
Fats and oils	**100.0%**	**3.5%**	**14.5%**	**20.5%**	**23.1%**	**17.9%**	**11.8%**	**8.7%**
Margarine	100.0	3.8	11.1	18.4	21.8	20.0	14.2	10.8
Fats and oils	100.0	3.8	14.5	22.1	23.0	16.9	11.2	8.3
Salad dressings	100.0	2.8	15.1	18.5	21.9	19.6	12.8	9.4
Nondairy cream and imitation milk	100.0	3.5	14.0	22.5	24.2	16.8	11.6	7.4
Peanut butter	100.0	4.3	15.9	19.5	25.4	16.8	9.6	8.4
Miscellaneous foods	**100.0**	**4.2**	**16.3**	**21.4**	**22.9**	**17.4**	**10.4**	**7.3**
Frozen prepared foods	100.0	4.3	17.0	22.6	23.4	16.0	8.7	7.9
Frozen meals	100.0	3.2	14.8	20.0	23.0	18.4	10.6	10.0
Other frozen prepared foods	100.0	5.2	18.8	24.8	23.7	13.9	7.1	6.1
Canned and packaged soups	100.0	4.2	12.9	18.7	22.3	19.5	13.2	9.3
Potato chips, nuts, and other snacks	100.0	3.8	14.2	22.4	24.4	18.0	10.2	7.0
Potato chips and other snacks	100.0	4.1	15.7	24.1	24.9	16.7	8.7	5.6
Nuts	100.0	2.9	9.7	17.3	23.1	21.6	14.5	10.9
Condiments and seasonings	100.0	3.6	15.8	20.8	23.4	17.5	11.3	7.3
Salt, spices, and other seasonings	100.0	4.0	16.5	21.1	24.6	16.2	11.3	6.1
Olives, pickles, relishes	100.0	4.3	12.5	18.7	23.4	20.5	11.4	9.1
Sauces and gravies	100.0	3.5	16.6	22.0	23.1	17.0	10.9	6.7
Baking needs and miscellaneous products	100.0	3.0	15.1	18.8	22.6	18.8	12.2	9.4
Other canned or packaged prepared foods	100.0	4.6	18.1	21.1	21.5	17.4	10.6	6.6
Prepared salads	100.0	2.9	15.2	19.5	20.4	21.0	11.8	9.1
Prepared desserts	100.0	2.5	14.9	22.0	22.0	16.8	12.2	9.4
Baby food	100.0	7.4	42.5	26.5	12.8	5.5	2.9	1.5
Miscellaneous prepared foods	100.0	4.8	14.6	20.4	23.4	18.9	11.1	6.7
Nonalcoholic beverages	**100.0**	**4.1**	**14.8**	**21.3**	**24.9**	**18.1**	**9.9**	**6.8**
Cola	100.0	4.3	14.3	22.3	25.3	18.2	10.4	5.1
Other carbonated drinks	100.0	4.6	17.0	20.9	26.7	17.0	7.9	5.7
Tea	100.0	4.9	11.9	20.3	24.2	21.3	11.0	6.4
Coffee	100.0	2.7	11.7	18.7	24.2	20.4	12.1	10.3
Noncarbonated fruit-flavored drinks	100.0	5.1	16.3	25.4	21.3	14.0	10.8	7.1
Other noncarbonated beverages and ice	100.0	5.7	17.8	24.7	22.4	16.0	7.3	5.8
Bottled water	100.0	3.9	16.5	21.2	26.3	16.8	8.4	6.6
Sports drinks	100.0	5.3	18.3	24.2	22.9	16.7	7.9	4.4
Food prepared by consumer unit on trips	**100.0**	**2.7**	**11.5**	**18.0**	**24.7**	**23.8**	**15.1**	**4.2**
FOOD AWAY FROM HOME	**100.0**	**4.8**	**17.7**	**21.5**	**23.3**	**17.7**	**9.7**	**5.3**
Meals at restaurants, carry-outs, etc.	**100.0**	**4.9**	**18.3**	**21.7**	**22.4**	**17.4**	**9.5**	**5.6**
Lunch	100.0	4.7	18.5	22.2	22.2	17.0	9.4	5.8
At fast-food restaurants*	100.0	5.6	21.1	23.5	22.2	15.8	7.3	4.1
At full-service restaurants	100.0	3.8	15.5	16.9	21.1	20.0	13.6	9.2
At vending machines, mobile vendors	100.0	7.3	17.0	23.0	26.8	19.8	4.5	1.2
At employer and school cafeterias	100.0	3.3	17.7	36.8	26.0	10.7	3.8	1.2
Dinner	100.0	5.0	18.0	21.3	22.7	17.4	9.8	5.6
At fast-food restaurants*	100.0	7.3	20.4	24.9	21.7	15.2	7.0	3.1
At full-service restaurants	100.0	3.6	16.5	19.3	23.4	18.7	11.3	7.0
At vending machines, mobile vendors	100.0	4.0	55.1	12.5	10.2	4.3	10.0	2.5
At employer and school cafeterias	100.0	17.6	12.6	22.6	10.4	13.9	13.4	10.4
Snacks and nonalcoholic beverages	100.0	5.7	21.0	24.1	22.9	15.6	6.8	3.5
At fast-food restaurants*	100.0	4.9	20.0	25.2	22.9	15.1	7.8	3.8
At full-service restaurants	100.0	5.5	23.2	19.8	23.9	18.8	5.2	3.1
At vending machines, mobile vendors	100.0	9.5	24.5	23.5	21.0	13.9	4.4	2.6
At employer and school cafeterias	100.0	10.0	18.1	28.9	23.3	12.9	4.3	2.3
Breakfast and brunch	100.0	4.6	17.0	20.6	21.4	19.7	10.2	6.4
At fast-food restaurants*	100.0	5.1	20.5	22.7	22.6	16.1	8.0	4.6
At full-service restaurants	100.0	3.1	11.8	17.9	19.2	24.4	14.1	9.5
At vending machines, mobile vendors	100.0	4.6	15.8	26.3	23.8	25.1	3.2	0.7
At employer and school cafeterias	100.0	11.4	20.8	16.0	25.4	21.2	2.9	1.9

	total consumer units	under 25	25 to 34	35 to 44	45 to 54	55 to 64	65 to 74	75+
Board (including at school)	100.0%	8.8%	1.4%	11.0%	56.2%	21.2%	0.3%	1.1%
Catered affairs	100.0	2.4	20.4	14.1	24.5	26.8	9.2	2.5
Food on trips	100.0	2.7	13.8	17.4	22.8	21.6	16.6	5.2
School lunches	100.0	1.3	13.8	42.1	35.6	5.8	1.0	0.4
Meals as pay	100.0	17.5	31.3	20.2	13.5	13.2	4.0	0.3
ALCOHOLIC BEVERAGES	100.0	5.8	18.8	19.3	22.0	18.2	10.6	5.1
At home	100.0	3.9	14.7	20.2	24.5	18.1	12.2	6.4
Beer and ale	100.0	5.1	18.6	23.8	25.6	15.7	7.2	3.7
Whiskey	100.0	6.5	15.0	14.4	21.0	15.8	14.4	13.2
Wine	100.0	2.2	10.1	17.8	22.9	21.0	17.6	8.6
Other alcoholic beverages	100.0	4.8	17.2	15.3	27.9	17.6	10.4	6.5
Away from home	100.0	7.9	23.5	18.4	19.2	18.3	8.9	3.6
Beer and ale	100.0	9.4	27.5	21.1	18.9	15.7	5.0	1.8
At fast-food restaurants*	100.0	11.5	22.0	26.5	25.9	10.4	2.8	0.6
At full-service restaurants	100.0	8.3	28.6	20.3	17.9	17.0	5.3	2.0
At vending machines, mobile vendors	100.0	1.9	53.0	16.4	3.4	3.5	19.3	2.5
Wine	100.0	6.0	16.5	14.9	21.2	21.0	13.1	7.2
At fast-food restaurants*	100.0	8.4	20.6	20.4	25.1	15.1	8.4	1.8
At full-service restaurants	100.0	4.1	16.5	14.5	21.3	21.9	13.7	7.8
Other alcoholic beverages	100.0	10.7	26.8	18.7	16.2	18.0	6.2	2.8
At fast-food restaurants*	100.0	21.7	31.9	23.1	7.0	13.5	1.5	0.9
At full-service restaurants	100.0	9.6	26.3	18.3	17.1	18.5	6.6	3.0
Alcoholic beverages purchased on trips	100.0	4.1	19.3	16.7	20.9	20.3	14.5	4.1

The category fast-food restaurants also includes take-out, delivery, concession stands, buffets, and cafeterias other than employer and school.
Note: Numbers may not add to total because of rounding.
Source: Calculations by New Strategist based on the Bureau of Labor Statistics' 2011 Consumer Expenditure Survey

Table 5.5 Food and Alcohol: Average spending by income, 2011

(average annual spending on food and alcoholic beverages, by before-tax income of consumer units, 2011)

	total consumer units	under $20,000	$20,000–$39,999	$40,000–$49,999	$50,000–$69,999	$70,000–$79,999	$80,000–$99,999	$100,000 or more
Number of consumer units (in 000s)	122,287	26,342	27,788	11,347	17,376	7,385	10,456	21,593
Average number of persons per consumer unit	2.5	1.8	2.3	2.6	2.7	2.8	3.0	3.2
Average before-tax income of consumer units	$63,685.00	$10,491.66	$29,658.14	$44,698.00	$59,306.00	$74,742.00	$89,108.00	$169,776.00
Average spending of consumer units, total	49,704.88	22,142.36	33,453.66	40,306.19	50,034.03	57,976.69	65,389.80	97,728.22
Food, average spending	**6,458.00**	**3,512.78**	**4,780.65**	**5,154.00**	**6,546.00**	**7,679.00**	**8,139.00**	**11,233.00**
Alcoholic beverages, average spending	**456.43**	**177.17**	**261.47**	**308.62**	**383.83**	**563.06**	**670.19**	**1,018.04**
FOOD AT HOME	**3,837.76**	**2,422.39**	**3,126.23**	**3,184.38**	**3,995.00**	**4,474.34**	**4,627.47**	**5,896.88**
Cereals and bakery products	**530.68**	**341.36**	**437.11**	**447.34**	**544.09**	**616.32**	**646.34**	**801.45**
Cereals and cereal products	174.86	113.61	145.40	143.24	180.74	197.87	214.18	263.54
Flour	7.67	4.86	6.74	4.95	8.16	8.69	7.43	12.62
Prepared flour mixes	14.88	10.17	12.19	10.54	16.48	18.23	17.40	22.05
Ready-to-eat and cooked cereals	91.39	57.93	75.63	76.27	95.31	105.57	116.47	134.98
Rice	25.66	19.12	23.92	22.59	27.58	22.28	30.61	33.72
Pasta, cornmeal, and other cereal products	35.26	21.52	26.93	28.89	33.21	43.10	42.27	60.18
Bakery products	355.81	227.75	291.71	304.10	363.35	418.44	432.16	537.91
Bread	106.53	75.11	91.97	89.01	107.98	115.92	120.69	156.52
White bread	44.93	34.80	40.80	35.66	45.25	51.25	50.54	60.59
Bread, other than white	61.60	40.30	51.17	53.35	62.73	64.67	70.15	95.93
Cookies and crackers	83.59	47.75	67.20	69.63	85.68	113.73	107.00	127.60
Cookies	46.96	29.12	38.02	42.43	48.19	68.14	56.74	67.53
Crackers	36.63	18.64	29.18	27.20	37.49	45.59	50.26	60.07
Frozen and refrigerated bakery products	28.60	16.61	25.02	21.82	29.18	35.15	33.84	44.26
Other bakery products	137.09	88.29	107.50	123.65	140.51	153.65	170.63	209.52
Biscuits and rolls	52.93	29.73	40.21	42.77	55.24	58.52	75.02	85.42
Cakes and cupcakes	37.81	26.34	28.23	39.73	38.36	35.62	48.00	56.56
Bread and cracker products	7.13	5.27	5.68	5.30	7.99	10.15	7.37	10.16
Sweetrolls, coffee cakes, doughnuts	23.86	17.43	20.01	23.75	22.62	29.83	24.01	34.39
Pies, tarts, turnovers	15.36	9.52	13.38	12.10	16.29	19.53	16.24	22.99
Meats, poultry, fish, and eggs	**832.41**	**526.77**	**708.46**	**674.23**	**849.21**	**1,003.34**	**969.53**	**1,267.61**
Beef	222.60	137.11	188.23	189.02	235.19	245.96	276.04	333.25
Ground beef	90.50	65.88	79.18	80.90	95.12	105.36	111.59	117.81
Roast	30.59	16.46	24.09	25.35	37.74	43.39	41.86	41.49
Chuck roast	7.65	3.92	7.31	5.60	9.45	8.82	11.08	9.64
Round roast	6.11	3.07	4.40	7.05	7.11	9.87	8.52	7.92
Other roast	16.82	9.47	12.38	12.71	21.17	24.71	22.26	23.93
Steak	82.49	45.52	70.83	67.41	87.63	76.44	98.05	136.04
Round steak	15.90	10.19	14.16	14.07	15.46	14.57	19.38	24.37
Sirloin steak	21.86	13.31	19.03	18.38	20.52	18.56	20.24	39.76
Other steak	44.73	22.03	37.64	34.95	51.64	43.31	58.44	71.90
Other beef	19.02	9.25	14.13	15.36	14.70	20.77	24.54	37.91
Pork	161.95	105.44	156.00	128.28	169.24	215.97	154.66	227.65
Bacon	33.87	21.54	31.59	25.93	35.17	47.12	36.68	47.52
Pork chops	27.24	17.42	28.51	26.48	29.30	34.56	21.65	35.23
Ham	34.29	24.51	30.07	27.91	37.94	51.44	33.05	45.78
Ham, not canned	33.51	23.99	29.67	27.27	37.05	51.44	31.78	44.22
Canned ham	0.78	0.52	0.40	0.64	0.89	–	1.27	1.57
Sausage	28.55	19.58	26.19	23.65	29.37	36.02	35.50	37.24
Other pork	37.99	22.37	39.64	24.31	37.47	46.82	27.78	61.88
Other meats	122.54	73.57	80.13	106.90	129.04	169.14	166.47	197.32
Frankfurters	23.67	16.86	19.85	20.06	26.37	24.26	31.24	31.65
Lunch meats (cold cuts)	87.67	53.66	55.69	81.59	89.94	107.47	118.54	146.37
Bologna, liverwurst, salami	26.83	17.31	18.90	28.36	26.32	34.08	30.88	42.86
Other lunch meats	60.84	36.34	36.78	53.23	63.61	73.39	87.67	103.51
Lamb, organ meats, and others	11.20	3.05	4.60	5.25	12.74	37.41	16.68	19.29

	total consumer units	under $20,000	$20,000—$39,999	$40,000—$49,999	$50,000—$69,999	$70,000—$79,999	$80,000—$99,999	$100,000 or more
Poultry	$154.49	$100.25	$134.66	$119.34	$147.64	$172.02	$184.46	$241.67
Fresh and frozen chicken	124.44	82.21	112.29	96.55	122.17	141.22	127.26	194.74
Fresh and frozen whole chicken	35.97	24.11	32.76	30.09	34.46	40.03	42.60	52.69
Fresh and frozen chicken parts	88.48	58.11	79.53	66.46	87.71	101.18	84.66	142.05
Other poultry	30.05	18.03	22.38	22.79	25.47	30.81	57.20	46.93
Fish and seafood	120.76	71.14	101.49	87.39	120.71	139.53	133.62	203.33
Canned fish and seafood	19.90	14.18	16.98	21.16	22.31	26.99	20.14	25.02
Fresh fish and shellfish	59.51	31.13	50.34	32.83	55.52	65.17	66.15	113.27
Frozen fish and shellfish	41.35	25.83	34.17	33.40	42.89	47.37	47.34	65.04
Eggs	50.07	39.26	47.94	43.29	47.39	60.72	54.27	64.39
Dairy products	**406.84**	**249.89**	**327.80**	**343.49**	**421.67**	**463.98**	**497.86**	**635.44**
Fresh milk and cream	149.73	102.34	127.78	128.85	150.85	181.05	182.85	213.10
Fresh milk, all types	127.38	89.91	109.78	113.54	125.45	154.05	154.21	177.92
Cream	22.36	12.43	17.99	15.31	25.39	27.00	28.64	35.18
Other dairy products	257.10	147.55	200.02	214.63	270.82	282.93	315.00	422.34
Butter	24.64	14.66	19.22	20.18	29.62	23.06	28.52	39.26
Cheese	124.74	69.85	98.27	96.59	132.02	141.06	153.48	207.12
Ice cream and related products	57.28	36.46	45.81	54.73	56.23	70.78	69.57	86.09
Miscellaneous dairy products	50.43	26.58	36.71	43.13	52.94	48.03	63.44	89.87
Fruits and vegetables	**714.89**	**444.14**	**578.88**	**572.42**	**727.74**	**764.91**	**870.88**	**1,151.85**
Fresh fruits	247.28	147.56	197.06	196.15	245.17	253.40	296.33	421.00
Apples	38.17	22.83	31.94	26.76	39.49	44.17	44.29	62.25
Bananas	41.08	26.57	36.72	38.14	39.82	48.29	46.18	59.41
Oranges	26.99	16.95	21.78	23.86	26.80	22.93	34.05	44.07
Citrus fruits, excluding oranges	37.63	23.73	29.76	29.59	37.56	35.74	42.89	65.17
Other fresh fruits	103.42	57.48	76.86	77.79	101.49	102.27	128.91	190.09
Fresh vegetables	224.21	131.30	182.99	172.08	224.49	232.16	277.03	375.40
Potatoes	38.78	25.61	32.25	32.04	41.06	42.23	45.13	58.64
Lettuce	32.17	18.12	24.95	26.03	34.58	36.30	40.98	52.14
Tomatoes	41.03	26.01	34.94	31.22	38.08	40.93	52.86	66.79
Other fresh vegetables	112.24	61.56	90.84	82.79	110.78	112.70	138.05	197.83
Processed fruits	115.73	75.28	92.82	103.69	122.62	137.44	136.47	172.49
Frozen fruits and fruit juices	13.31	6.50	11.17	12.55	15.27	16.39	17.42	19.14
Frozen orange juice	3.73	2.11	3.33	3.76	4.17	5.46	3.58	5.07
Frozen fruits	6.92	2.36	5.61	5.37	8.07	8.49	11.52	10.57
Frozen fruit juices, excluding orange	2.67	2.03	2.23	3.42	3.03	2.44	2.32	3.49
Canned fruits	21.24	14.81	17.47	17.13	22.14	28.70	26.25	29.51
Dried fruits	8.13	4.95	6.44	6.31	8.60	6.34	11.18	13.39
Fresh fruit juice	17.28	11.77	12.12	17.83	16.67	19.58	17.93	29.20
Canned and bottled fruit juice	55.78	37.27	45.62	49.87	59.95	66.43	63.70	81.25
Processed vegetables	127.66	90.00	106.02	100.51	135.46	141.92	161.04	182.96
Frozen vegetables	34.98	19.77	27.23	25.63	37.83	39.75	52.77	53.36
Canned and dried vegetables and juices	92.68	70.22	78.78	74.88	97.63	102.17	108.27	129.60
Canned beans	19.08	14.66	16.73	15.57	20.58	24.90	19.98	25.20
Canned corn	9.73	8.81	9.40	7.17	10.52	9.37	11.11	11.39
Canned miscellaneous vegetables	25.50	19.70	19.78	18.32	29.15	26.96	30.70	36.43
Dried peas	0.84	0.66	0.63	1.02	0.70	0.35	1.03	1.39
Dried beans	4.99	4.35	5.56	4.73	4.07	3.99	5.94	5.79
Dried miscellaneous vegetables	11.55	7.57	11.35	8.99	11.05	11.53	14.56	16.72
Dried processed vegetables	2.05	1.69	1.47	1.45	4.02	2.56	1.88	2.39
Fresh and canned vegetable juices	18.59	12.94	13.69	17.24	17.18	22.42	22.47	29.80
Sugar and other sweets	**144.39**	**90.39**	**112.18**	**116.17**	**153.64**	**171.83**	**189.73**	**219.31**
Candy and chewing gum	86.75	49.21	60.41	70.30	90.99	108.96	121.01	142.31
Sugar	23.89	20.72	23.76	22.67	24.26	25.16	25.71	26.17
Artificial sweeteners	5.61	2.69	4.87	2.83	8.20	3.02	6.29	9.22
Jams, preserves, other sweets	28.14	17.78	23.14	20.37	30.19	34.68	36.72	41.61

	total consumer units	under $20,000	$20,000–$39,999	$40,000–$49,999	$50,000–$69,999	$70,000–$79,999	$80,000–$99,999	$100,000 or more
Fats and oils	**$109.61**	**$79.14**	**$94.13**	**$98.45**	**$126.20**	**$121.00**	**$124.67**	**$143.26**
Margarine	9.77	7.66	7.07	11.51	11.00	15.85	9.95	11.52
Fats and oils	34.84	27.91	34.98	30.50	36.44	33.97	36.11	42.96
Salad dressings	31.16	19.06	25.62	29.02	39.30	30.73	34.19	44.46
Nondairy cream and imitation milk	18.59	12.10	14.26	17.80	22.93	21.64	24.85	23.75
Peanut butter	15.25	12.41	12.20	9.61	16.54	18.80	19.55	20.57
Miscellaneous foods	**690.48**	**445.27**	**546.74**	**576.26**	**737.89**	**823.65**	**839.47**	**1,043.46**
Frozen prepared foods	136.23	93.95	110.88	120.82	139.07	154.98	180.61	192.55
Frozen meals	62.14	45.55	48.80	49.27	62.15	65.41	88.60	89.49
Other frozen prepared foods	74.09	48.40	62.08	71.55	76.92	89.57	92.01	103.06
Canned and packaged soups	46.90	31.63	39.80	38.46	50.60	57.50	52.78	67.80
Potato chips, nuts, and other snacks	145.02	80.00	109.99	121.92	158.59	176.89	178.33	233.74
Potato chips and other snacks	108.01	63.90	83.91	93.74	117.70	135.50	136.23	162.77
Nuts	37.01	16.10	26.08	28.18	40.89	41.39	42.10	70.97
Condiments and seasonings	133.90	82.32	107.44	107.66	144.66	155.93	165.89	206.12
Salt, spices, and other seasonings	35.41	24.01	28.28	25.98	38.84	38.53	40.02	55.70
Olives, pickles, relishes	16.13	10.35	11.74	11.72	18.67	16.82	20.35	26.46
Sauces and gravies	58.43	34.07	48.44	49.25	60.78	69.25	74.11	89.07
Baking needs and miscellaneous products	23.93	13.88	18.97	20.71	26.37	31.32	31.41	34.89
Other canned or packaged prepared foods	228.42	157.37	178.64	187.42	244.97	278.35	261.86	343.25
Prepared salads	36.22	21.04	28.57	29.33	39.91	42.44	37.74	59.70
Prepared desserts	15.03	8.97	12.95	13.09	17.32	19.34	16.11	21.24
Baby food	27.80	22.31	23.85	20.20	39.99	33.97	32.21	28.69
Miscellaneous prepared foods	147.11	104.74	112.97	121.17	145.32	179.27	168.17	230.49
Nonalcoholic beverages	**360.97**	**232.56**	**292.75**	**324.63**	**389.35**	**458.07**	**426.51**	**518.14**
Cola	78.77	48.87	67.55	71.90	86.01	109.58	95.52	104.10
Other carbonated drinks	66.72	41.05	51.36	60.95	82.87	91.35	70.00	94.18
Tea	31.16	22.82	26.39	26.09	33.94	32.46	32.35	45.94
Coffee	75.03	42.73	60.04	67.51	76.80	83.32	103.48	114.88
Noncarbonated fruit-flavored drinks	24.76	23.08	20.33	19.93	25.11	24.10	31.40	31.51
Other noncarbonated beverages and ice	14.93	10.41	13.56	11.16	17.21	16.88	21.87	18.13
Bottled water	53.48	36.13	42.67	51.81	53.27	74.30	51.97	80.15
Sports drinks	15.73	6.42	10.84	15.13	13.78	26.07	19.92	28.48
Food prepared by consumer unit on trips	**47.50**	**12.86**	**28.19**	**31.40**	**45.22**	**51.25**	**62.49**	**116.37**
FOOD AWAY FROM HOME	**2,619.89**	**1,090.54**	**1,653.97**	**1,969.21**	**2,550.88**	**3,204.58**	**3,511.57**	**5,336.29**
Meals at restaurants, carry-outs, etc.	**2,195.89**	**962.55**	**1,467.60**	**1,682.87**	**2,167.09**	**2,795.48**	**2,957.77**	**4,198.41**
Lunch	752.89	341.64	511.52	584.69	719.82	963.45	984.04	1,441.55
At fast-food restaurants*	368.78	186.17	272.18	302.29	375.78	499.09	506.68	609.42
At full-service restaurants	302.01	131.44	195.50	215.42	272.56	353.10	360.53	646.93
At vending machines, mobile vendors	7.16	3.66	6.78	6.53	9.29	9.51	5.90	9.52
At employer and school cafeterias	74.94	20.38	37.05	60.45	62.19	101.75	110.93	175.68
Dinner	1,051.05	431.53	669.50	746.99	1,035.34	1,303.28	1,458.59	2,111.63
At fast-food restaurants*	365.13	201.78	273.84	299.70	403.11	482.87	493.57	564.72
At full-service restaurants	676.06	222.28	385.85	441.33	625.47	802.55	947.86	1,535.49
At vending machines, mobile vendors	3.02	0.38	4.31	2.51	3.92	3.39	7.69	1.45
At employer and school cafeterias	6.85	7.16	5.50	3.45	2.84	14.48	9.46	9.96
Snacks and nonalcoholic beverages	166.09	84.99	110.70	156.69	170.69	200.17	219.24	288.54
At fast-food restaurants*	109.65	51.38	67.86	101.19	118.23	127.40	143.73	201.67
At full-service restaurants	32.72	19.02	19.56	34.47	28.05	43.45	44.93	56.85
At vending machines, mobile vendors	17.28	10.92	18.07	13.58	17.44	20.46	22.07	21.77
At employer and school cafeterias	6.43	3.68	5.21	7.45	6.97	8.86	8.51	8.24
Breakfast and brunch	225.86	104.39	175.88	194.51	241.25	328.59	295.90	356.69
At fast-food restaurants*	123.77	56.73	97.21	107.43	130.82	170.40	154.86	203.17
At full-service restaurants	89.39	41.24	67.58	74.84	98.87	145.70	121.49	134.50
At vending machines, mobile vendors	3.03	1.28	2.45	5.22	3.05	1.49	6.64	3.29
At employer and school cafeterias	9.66	5.14	8.66	7.01	8.52	11.00	12.92	15.73

	total consumer units	under $20,000	$20,000– $39,999	$40,000– $49,999	$50,000– $69,999	$70,000– $79,999	$80,000– $99,999	$100,000 or more
Board (including at school)	$43.87	$19.92	$13.83	$13.68	$11.85	$8.40	$42.43	$166.22
Catered affairs	52.63	5.50	19.55	14.16	53.53	28.60	70.32	171.82
Food on trips	236.49	65.18	106.24	172.30	217.12	243.77	306.44	626.06
School lunches	62.16	13.94	25.11	55.09	72.02	70.55	102.07	142.27
Meals as pay	28.85	23.44	21.63	31.11	29.27	57.78	32.55	31.51
ALCOHOLIC BEVERAGES	456.43	177.17	261.47	308.62	383.83	563.06	670.19	1,018.04
At home	242.35	106.45	159.32	173.38	215.94	290.42	375.78	478.69
Beer and ale	109.76	63.72	89.57	86.34	98.43	152.79	161.98	171.45
Whiskey	9.60	5.45	3.50	11.54	8.84	12.55	20.46	16.46
Wine	104.03	29.71	51.62	62.00	88.55	106.13	167.49	255.39
Other alcoholic beverages	18.97	7.58	14.62	13.49	20.11	18.93	25.85	35.39
Away from home	214.08	70.72	102.15	135.25	167.90	272.64	294.41	539.36
Beer and ale	76.98	24.91	42.52	48.62	63.17	126.65	110.51	171.89
At fast-food restaurants*	12.47	6.36	9.10	7.72	14.92	21.65	9.27	21.94
At full-service restaurants	63.32	17.99	32.99	40.65	47.02	95.01	99.90	149.34
At vending machines, mobile vendors	0.65	–	0.40	0.25	1.23	1.02	1.34	0.55
Wine	41.96	7.59	17.93	22.10	25.42	48.14	54.19	125.99
At fast-food restaurants*	2.96	0.35	1.23	1.68	1.64	4.59	4.77	8.48
At full-service restaurants	38.20	7.38	16.70	20.42	23.78	31.59	49.42	116.87
Other alcoholic beverages	50.30	25.07	24.60	36.73	36.24	51.91	72.90	118.10
At fast-food restaurants*	4.25	–	2.40	6.08	2.21	5.50	6.59	4.73
At full-service restaurants	45.99	20.17	22.09	30.65	34.03	46.40	66.32	113.17
Alcoholic beverages purchased on trips	44.84	13.14	17.11	27.79	43.06	45.95	56.80	123.39

* The category fast-food restaurants also includes take-out, delivery, concession stands, buffets, and cafeterias other than employer and school.
Note: Subcategories may not add to total because some are not shown. "–" means sample is too small to make a reliable estimate.
Source: Bureau of Labor Statistics, unpublished tables from the 2011 Consumer Expenditure Survey; calculations by New Strategist

Table 5.6 Food and Alcohol: Indexed spending by income, 2011

(indexed average annual spending of consumer units on food and beverages, by before-tax income of consumer unit, 2011; index definition: an index of 100 is the average for all consumer units; an index of 125 means that spending by consumer units in that group is 25 percent above the average for all consumer units; an index of 75 indicates spending that is 25 percent below the average for all consumer units)

	total consumer units	under $20,000	$20,000–$39,999	$40,000–$49,999	$50,000–$69,999	$70,000–$79,999	$80,000–$99,999	$100,000 or more
Average spending of consumer units, total	$49,705	$22,142	$33,454	$40,306	$50,034	$57,977	$65,390	$97,728
Average spending of consumer units, index	100	45	67	81	101	117	132	197
Food, spending index	100	54	74	80	101	119	126	174
Alcoholic beverages, spending index	100	39	57	68	84	123	147	223
FOOD AT HOME	100	63	81	83	104	117	121	154
Cereals and bakery products	100	64	82	84	103	116	122	151
Cereals and cereal products	100	65	83	82	103	113	122	151
Flour	100	63	88	65	106	113	97	165
Prepared flour mixes	100	68	82	71	111	123	117	148
Ready-to-eat and cooked cereals	100	63	83	83	104	116	127	148
Rice	100	74	93	88	107	87	119	131
Pasta, cornmeal, and other cereal products	100	61	76	82	94	122	120	171
Bakery products	100	64	82	85	102	118	121	151
Bread	100	71	86	84	101	109	113	147
White bread	100	77	91	79	101	114	112	135
Bread, other than white	100	65	83	87	102	105	114	156
Cookies and crackers	100	57	80	83	103	136	128	153
Cookies	100	62	81	90	103	145	121	144
Crackers	100	51	80	74	102	124	137	164
Frozen and refrigerated bakery products	100	58	87	76	102	123	118	155
Other bakery products	100	64	78	90	102	112	124	153
Biscuits and rolls	100	56	76	81	104	111	142	161
Cakes and cupcakes	100	70	75	105	101	94	127	150
Bread and cracker products	100	74	80	74	112	142	103	142
Sweetrolls, coffee cakes, doughnuts	100	73	84	100	95	125	101	144
Pies, tarts, turnovers	100	62	87	79	106	127	106	150
Meats, poultry, fish, and eggs	100	63	85	81	102	121	116	152
Beef	100	62	85	85	106	110	124	150
Ground beef	100	73	87	89	105	116	123	130
Roast	100	54	79	83	123	142	137	136
Chuck roast	100	51	96	73	124	115	145	126
Round roast	100	50	72	115	116	162	139	130
Other roast	100	56	74	76	126	147	132	142
Steak	100	55	86	82	106	93	119	165
Round steak	100	64	89	88	97	92	122	153
Sirloin steak	100	61	87	84	94	85	93	182
Other steak	100	49	84	78	115	97	131	161
Other beef	100	49	74	81	77	109	129	199
Pork	100	65	96	79	105	133	95	141
Bacon	100	64	93	77	104	139	108	140
Pork chops	100	64	105	97	108	127	79	129
Ham	100	71	88	81	111	150	96	134
Ham, not canned	100	72	89	81	111	154	95	132
Canned ham	100	67	52	82	114	–	163	201
Sausage	100	69	92	83	103	126	124	130
Other pork	100	59	104	64	99	123	73	163
Other meats	100	60	65	87	105	138	136	161
Frankfurters	100	71	84	85	111	102	132	134
Lunch meats (cold cuts)	100	61	64	93	103	123	135	167
Bologna, liverwurst, salami	100	65	70	106	98	127	115	160
Other lunch meats	100	60	60	87	105	121	144	170
Lamb, organ meats, and others	100	27	41	47	114	334	149	172

	total consumer units	under $20,000	$20,000– $39,999	$40,000– $49,999	$50,000– $69,999	$70,000– $79,999	$80,000– $99,999	$100,000 or more
Poultry	100	65	87	77	96	111	119	156
Fresh and frozen chicken	100	66	90	78	98	113	102	156
Fresh and frozen whole chicken	100	67	91	84	96	111	118	146
Fresh and frozen chicken parts	100	66	90	75	99	114	96	161
Other poultry	100	60	74	76	85	103	190	156
Fish and seafood	100	59	84	72	100	116	111	168
Canned fish and seafood	100	71	85	106	112	136	101	126
Fresh fish and shellfish	100	52	85	55	93	110	111	190
Frozen fish and shellfish	100	62	83	81	104	115	114	157
Eggs	100	78	96	86	95	121	108	129
Dairy products	**100**	**61**	**81**	**84**	**104**	**114**	**122**	**156**
Fresh milk and cream	100	68	85	86	101	121	122	142
Fresh milk, all types	100	71	86	89	98	121	121	140
Cream	100	56	80	68	114	121	128	157
Other dairy products	100	57	78	83	105	110	123	164
Butter	100	60	78	82	120	94	116	159
Cheese	100	56	79	77	106	113	123	166
Ice cream and related products	100	64	80	96	98	124	121	150
Miscellaneous dairy products	100	53	73	86	105	95	126	178
Fruits and vegetables	**100**	**62**	**81**	**80**	**102**	**107**	**122**	**161**
Fresh fruits	100	60	80	79	99	102	120	170
Apples	100	60	84	70	103	116	116	163
Bananas	100	65	89	93	97	118	112	145
Oranges	100	63	81	88	99	85	126	163
Citrus fruits, excluding oranges	100	63	79	79	100	95	114	173
Other fresh fruits	100	56	74	75	98	99	125	184
Fresh vegetables	100	59	82	77	100	104	124	167
Potatoes	100	66	83	83	106	109	116	151
Lettuce	100	56	78	81	107	113	127	162
Tomatoes	100	63	85	76	93	100	129	163
Other fresh vegetables	100	55	81	74	99	100	123	176
Processed fruits	100	65	80	90	106	119	118	149
Frozen fruits and fruit juices	100	49	84	94	115	123	131	144
Frozen orange juice	100	57	89	101	112	146	96	136
Frozen fruits	100	34	81	78	117	123	166	153
Frozen fruit juices, excluding orange	100	76	84	128	113	91	87	131
Canned fruits	100	70	82	81	104	135	124	139
Dried fruits	100	61	79	78	106	78	138	165
Fresh fruit juice	100	68	70	103	96	113	104	169
Canned and bottled fruit juice	100	67	82	89	107	119	114	146
Processed vegetables	100	70	83	79	106	111	126	143
Frozen vegetables	100	57	78	73	108	114	151	153
Canned and dried vegetables and juices	100	76	85	81	105	110	117	140
Canned beans	100	77	88	82	108	131	105	132
Canned corn	100	91	97	74	108	96	114	117
Canned miscellaneous vegetables	100	77	78	72	114	106	120	143
Dried peas	100	78	75	121	83	42	123	165
Dried beans	100	87	112	95	82	80	119	116
Dried miscellaneous vegetables	100	66	98	78	96	100	126	145
Dried processed vegetables	100	83	72	71	196	125	92	117
Fresh and canned vegetable juices	100	70	74	93	92	121	121	160
Sugar and other sweets	**100**	**63**	**78**	**80**	**106**	**119**	**131**	**152**
Candy and chewing gum	100	57	70	81	105	126	139	164
Sugar	100	87	99	95	102	105	108	110
Artificial sweeteners	100	48	87	50	146	54	112	164
Jams, preserves, other sweets	100	63	82	72	107	123	130	148

	total consumer units	under $20,000	$20,000–$39,999	$40,000–$49,999	$50,000–$69,999	$70,000–$79,999	$80,000–$99,999	$100,000 or more
Fats and oils	**100**	**72**	**86**	**90**	**115**	**110**	**114**	**131**
Margarine	100	78	72	118	113	162	102	118
Fats and oils	100	80	100	88	105	98	104	123
Salad dressings	100	61	82	93	126	99	110	143
Nondairy cream and imitation milk	100	65	77	96	123	116	134	128
Peanut butter	100	81	80	63	108	123	128	135
Miscellaneous foods	**100**	**64**	**79**	**83**	**107**	**119**	**122**	**151**
Frozen prepared foods	100	69	81	89	102	114	133	141
Frozen meals	100	73	79	79	100	105	143	144
Other frozen prepared foods	100	65	84	97	104	121	124	139
Canned and packaged soups	100	67	85	82	108	123	113	145
Potato chips, nuts, and other snacks	100	55	76	84	109	122	123	161
Potato chips and other snacks	100	59	78	87	109	125	126	151
Nuts	100	44	70	76	110	112	114	192
Condiments and seasonings	100	61	80	80	108	116	124	154
Salt, spices, and other seasonings	100	68	80	73	110	109	113	157
Olives, pickles, relishes	100	64	73	73	116	104	126	164
Sauces and gravies	100	58	83	84	104	119	127	152
Baking needs and miscellaneous products	100	58	79	87	110	131	131	146
Other canned or packaged prepared foods	100	69	78	82	107	122	115	150
Prepared salads	100	58	79	81	110	117	104	165
Prepared desserts	100	60	86	87	115	129	107	141
Baby food	100	80	86	73	144	122	116	103
Miscellaneous prepared foods	100	71	77	82	99	122	114	157
Nonalcoholic beverages	**100**	**64**	**81**	**90**	**108**	**127**	**118**	**144**
Cola	100	62	86	91	109	139	121	132
Other carbonated drinks	100	62	77	91	124	137	105	141
Tea	100	73	85	84	109	104	104	147
Coffee	100	57	80	90	102	111	138	153
Noncarbonated fruit-flavored drinks	100	93	82	80	101	97	127	127
Other noncarbonated beverages and ice	100	70	91	75	115	113	146	121
Bottled water	100	68	80	97	100	139	97	150
Sports drinks	100	41	69	96	88	166	127	181
Food prepared by consumer unit on trips	**100**	**27**	**59**	**66**	**95**	**108**	**132**	**245**
FOOD AWAY FROM HOME	**100**	**42**	**63**	**75**	**97**	**122**	**134**	**204**
Meals at restaurants, carry-outs, etc.	**100**	**44**	**67**	**77**	**99**	**127**	**135**	**191**
Lunch	100	45	68	78	96	128	131	191
At fast-food restaurants*	100	50	74	82	102	135	137	165
At full-service restaurants	100	44	65	71	90	117	119	214
At vending machines, mobile vendors	100	51	95	91	130	133	82	133
At employer and school cafeterias	100	27	49	81	83	136	148	234
Dinner	100	41	64	71	99	124	139	201
At fast-food restaurants*	100	55	75	82	110	132	135	155
At full-service restaurants	100	33	57	65	93	119	140	227
At vending machines, mobile vendors	100	13	143	83	130	112	255	48
At employer and school cafeterias	100	104	80	50	41	211	138	145
Snacks and nonalcoholic beverages	100	51	67	94	103	121	132	174
At fast-food restaurants*	100	47	62	92	108	116	131	184
At full-service restaurants	100	58	60	105	86	133	137	174
At vending machines, mobile vendors	100	63	105	79	101	118	128	126
At employer and school cafeterias	100	57	81	116	108	138	132	128
Breakfast and brunch	100	46	78	86	107	145	131	158
At fast-food restaurants*	100	46	79	87	106	138	125	164
At full-service restaurants	100	46	76	84	111	163	136	150
At vending machines, mobile vendors	100	42	81	172	101	49	219	109
At employer and school cafeterias	100	53	90	73	88	114	134	163

	total consumer units	under $20,000	$20,000– $39,999	$40,000– $49,999	$50,000– $69,999	$70,000– $79,999	$80,000– $99,999	$100,000 or more
Board (including at school)	100	45	32	31	27	19	97	379
Catered affairs	100	10	37	27	102	54	134	326
Food on trips	100	28	45	73	92	103	130	265
School lunches	100	22	40	89	116	113	164	229
Meals as pay	100	81	75	108	101	200	113	109
ALCOHOLIC BEVERAGES	100	39	57	68	84	123	147	223
At home	100	44	66	72	89	120	155	198
Beer and ale	100	58	82	79	90	139	148	156
Whiskey	100	57	36	120	92	131	213	171
Wine	100	29	50	60	85	102	161	245
Other alcoholic beverages	100	40	77	71	106	100	136	187
Away from home	100	33	48	63	78	127	138	252
Beer and ale	100	32	55	63	82	165	144	223
At fast-food restaurants*	100	51	73	62	120	174	74	176
At full-service restaurants	100	28	52	64	74	150	158	236
At vending machines, mobile vendors	100	–	61	38	189	157	206	85
Wine	100	18	43	53	61	115	129	300
At fast-food restaurants*	100	12	41	57	55	155	161	286
At full-service restaurants	100	19	44	53	62	83	129	306
Other alcoholic beverages	100	50	49	73	72	103	145	235
At fast-food restaurants*	100	–	56	143	52	129	155	111
At full-service restaurants	100	44	48	67	74	101	144	246
Alcoholic beverages purchased on trips	100	29	38	62	96	102	127	275

* The category fast-food restaurants also includes take-out, delivery, concession stands, buffets, and cafeterias other than employer and school.
Note: "–" means sample is too small to make a reliable estimate.
Source: Calculations by New Strategist based on the Bureau of Labor Statistics' 2011 Consumer Expenditure Survey

Table 5.7 Food and Alcohol: Total spending by income, 2011

(total annual spending on food and alcoholic beverages, by before-tax income group of consumer units, 2011; consumer units and dollars in thousands)

	total consumer units	under $20,000	$20,000–$39,999	$40,000–$49,999	$50,000–$69,999	$70,000–$79,999	$80,000–$99,999	$100,000 or more
Number of consumer units	122,287	26,342	27,788	11,347	17,376	7,385	10,456	21,593
Total spending of all consumer units	$6,078,260,661	$583,273,961	$929,610,260	$457,354,338	$869,391,305	$428,157,856	$683,715,749	$2,110,245,454
Food, total spending	789,729,446	92,533,711	132,844,808	58,482,438	113,743,296	56,709,415	85,101,384	242,554,169
Alcoholic beverages, total spending	55,815,455	4,667,000	7,265,705	3,501,911	6,669,430	4,158,198	7,007,507	21,982,538
FOOD AT HOME	469,308,157	63,810,547	86,871,563	36,133,160	69,417,120	33,043,001	48,384,826	127,331,330
Cereals and bakery products	64,895,265	8,992,086	12,146,338	5,075,967	9,454,108	4,551,523	6,758,131	17,305,710
Cereals and cereal products	21,383,105	2,992,675	4,040,382	1,625,344	3,140,538	1,461,270	2,239,466	5,690,619
Flour	937,941	128,013	187,180	56,168	141,788	64,176	77,688	272,504
Prepared flour mixes	1,819,631	268,024	338,857	119,597	286,356	134,629	181,934	476,126
Ready-to-eat and cooked cereals	11,175,809	1,526,021	2,101,551	865,436	1,656,107	779,634	1,217,810	2,914,623
Rice	3,137,884	503,544	664,569	256,329	479,230	164,538	320,058	728,116
Pasta, cornmeal, and other cereal products	4,311,840	566,986	748,358	327,815	577,057	318,294	441,975	1,299,467
Bakery products	43,510,937	5,999,362	8,106,101	3,450,623	6,313,570	3,090,179	4,518,665	11,615,091
Bread	13,027,234	1,978,417	2,555,761	1,009,996	1,876,260	856,069	1,261,935	3,379,736
White bread	5,494,355	916,833	1,133,749	404,634	786,264	378,481	528,446	1,308,320
Bread, other than white	7,532,879	1,061,584	1,422,012	605,362	1,089,996	477,588	733,488	2,071,416
Cookies and crackers	10,221,970	1,257,887	1,867,488	790,092	1,488,776	839,896	1,118,792	2,755,267
Cookies	5,742,598	766,951	1,056,591	481,453	837,349	503,214	593,273	1,458,175
Crackers	4,479,373	491,014	810,764	308,638	651,426	336,682	525,519	1,297,092
Frozen and refrigerated bakery products	3,497,408	437,551	695,394	247,592	507,032	259,583	353,831	955,706
Other bakery products	16,764,325	2,325,612	2,987,314	1,403,057	2,441,502	1,134,705	1,784,107	4,524,165
Biscuits and rolls	6,472,651	783,078	1,117,380	485,311	959,850	432,170	784,409	1,844,474
Cakes and cupcakes	4,623,671	693,963	784,496	450,816	666,543	263,054	501,888	1,221,300
Bread and cracker products	871,906	138,788	157,762	60,139	138,834	74,958	77,061	219,385
Sweetrolls, coffee cakes, doughnuts	2,917,768	459,148	556,171	269,491	393,045	220,295	251,049	742,583
Pies, tarts, turnovers	1,878,328	250,745	371,784	137,299	283,055	144,229	169,805	496,423
Meats, poultry, fish, and eggs	101,792,922	13,876,112	19,686,576	7,650,488	14,755,873	7,409,666	10,137,406	27,371,503
Beef	27,221,086	3,611,812	5,230,658	2,144,810	4,086,661	1,816,415	2,886,274	7,195,867
Ground beef	11,066,974	1,735,327	2,200,227	917,972	1,652,805	778,084	1,166,785	2,543,871
Roast	3,740,759	433,639	669,282	287,646	655,770	320,435	437,688	895,894
Chuck roast	935,496	103,164	203,147	63,543	164,203	65,136	115,852	208,157
Round roast	747,174	80,978	122,276	79,996	123,543	72,890	89,085	171,017
Other roast	2,056,867	249,365	344,005	144,220	367,850	182,483	232,751	516,720
Steak	10,087,455	1,199,158	1,968,339	764,901	1,522,659	564,509	1,025,211	2,937,512
Round steak	1,944,363	268,313	393,587	159,652	268,633	107,599	202,637	526,221
Sirloin steak	2,673,194	350,583	528,844	208,558	356,556	137,066	211,629	858,538
Other steak	5,469,898	580,258	1,045,909	396,578	897,297	319,844	611,049	1,552,537
Other beef	2,325,899	243,688	392,532	174,290	255,427	153,386	256,590	818,591
Pork	19,804,380	2,777,395	4,334,813	1,455,593	2,940,714	1,594,938	1,617,125	4,915,646
Bacon	4,141,861	567,404	877,797	294,228	611,114	347,981	383,526	1,026,099
Pork chops	3,331,098	458,946	792,109	300,469	509,117	255,226	226,372	760,721
Ham	4,193,221	645,688	835,502	316,695	659,245	379,884	345,571	988,528
Ham, not canned	4,097,837	631,826	824,335	309,433	643,781	379,884	332,292	954,842
Canned ham	95,384	13,807	11,167	7,262	15,465	–	13,279	33,901
Sausage	3,491,294	515,852	727,832	268,357	510,333	266,008	371,188	804,123
Other pork	4,645,683	589,369	1,101,429	275,846	651,079	345,766	290,468	1,336,175
Other meats	14,985,049	1,937,905	2,226,744	1,212,994	2,242,199	1,249,099	1,740,610	4,260,731
Frankfurters	2,894,533	444,171	551,456	227,621	458,205	179,160	326,645	683,418
Lunch meats (cold cuts)	10,720,901	1,413,543	1,547,489	925,802	1,562,797	793,666	1,239,454	3,160,567
Bologna, liverwurst, salami	3,280,960	456,079	525,171	321,801	457,336	251,681	322,881	925,476
Other lunch meats	7,439,941	957,382	1,022,174	604,001	1,105,287	541,985	916,678	2,235,091
Lamb, organ meats, and others	1,369,614	80,218	127,933	59,572	221,370	276,273	174,406	416,529

	total consumer units	under $20,000	$20,000– $39,999	$40,000– $49,999	$50,000– $69,999	$70,000– $79,999	$80,000– $99,999	$100,000 or more
Poultry	$18,892,119	$2,640,822	$3,742,024	$1,354,151	$2,565,393	$1,270,368	$1,928,714	$5,218,380
Fresh and frozen chicken	15,217,394	2,165,692	3,120,210	1,095,553	2,122,826	1,042,910	1,330,631	4,205,021
Fresh and frozen whole chicken	4,398,663	634,988	910,289	341,431	598,777	295,622	445,426	1,137,735
Fresh and frozen chicken parts	10,819,954	1,530,786	2,209,921	754,122	1,524,049	747,214	885,205	3,067,286
Other poultry	3,674,724	475,020	621,815	258,598	442,567	227,532	598,083	1,013,359
Fish and seafood	14,767,378	1,874,099	2,820,194	991,614	2,097,457	1,030,429	1,397,131	4,390,505
Canned fish and seafood	2,433,511	373,630	471,814	240,103	387,659	199,321	210,584	540,257
Fresh fish and shellfish	7,277,299	820,119	1,398,976	372,522	964,716	481,280	691,664	2,445,839
Frozen fish and shellfish	5,056,567	680,355	949,404	378,990	745,257	349,827	494,987	1,404,409
Eggs	6,122,910	1,034,292	1,332,143	491,212	823,449	448,417	567,447	1,390,373
Dairy products	**49,751,243**	**6,582,635**	**9,108,780**	**3,897,581**	**7,326,938**	**3,426,492**	**5,205,624**	**13,721,056**
Fresh milk and cream	18,310,033	2,695,714	3,550,863	1,462,061	2,621,170	1,337,054	1,911,880	4,601,468
Fresh milk, all types	15,576,918	2,368,349	3,050,596	1,288,338	2,179,819	1,137,659	1,612,420	3,841,827
Cream	2,734,337	327,365	499,989	173,723	441,177	199,395	299,460	759,642
Other dairy products	31,439,988	3,886,843	5,558,062	2,435,407	4,705,768	2,089,438	3,293,640	9,119,588
Butter	3,013,152	386,294	533,951	228,982	514,677	170,298	298,205	847,741
Cheese	15,254,080	1,839,950	2,730,678	1,096,007	2,293,980	1,041,728	1,604,787	4,472,342
Ice cream and related products	7,004,599	960,372	1,272,941	621,021	977,052	522,710	727,424	1,858,941
Miscellaneous dairy products	6,166,933	700,222	1,020,214	489,396	919,885	354,702	663,329	1,940,563
Fruits and vegetables	**87,421,753**	**11,699,415**	**16,085,939**	**6,495,250**	**12,645,210**	**5,648,860**	**9,105,921**	**24,871,897**
Fresh fruits	30,239,129	3,886,953	5,475,802	2,225,714	4,260,074	1,871,359	3,098,426	9,090,653
Apples	4,667,695	601,425	887,476	303,646	686,178	326,195	463,096	1,344,164
Bananas	5,023,550	699,858	1,020,378	432,775	691,912	356,622	482,858	1,282,840
Oranges	3,300,526	446,396	605,130	270,739	465,677	169,338	356,027	951,604
Citrus fruits, excluding oranges	4,601,660	625,186	827,043	335,758	652,643	263,940	448,458	1,407,216
Other fresh fruits	12,646,922	1,514,166	2,135,921	882,683	1,763,490	755,264	1,347,883	4,104,613
Fresh vegetables	27,417,968	3,458,618	5,084,802	1,952,592	3,900,738	1,714,502	2,896,626	8,106,012
Potatoes	4,742,290	674,563	896,254	363,558	713,459	311,869	471,879	1,266,214
Lettuce	3,933,973	477,275	693,445	295,362	600,862	268,076	428,487	1,125,859
Tomatoes	5,017,436	685,266	970,822	354,253	661,678	302,268	552,704	1,442,196
Other fresh vegetables	13,725,493	1,621,514	2,524,293	939,418	1,924,913	832,290	1,443,451	4,271,743
Processed fruits	14,152,275	1,983,154	2,579,217	1,176,570	2,130,645	1,014,994	1,426,930	3,724,577
Frozen fruits and fruit juices	1,627,640	171,125	310,318	142,405	265,332	121,040	182,144	413,290
Frozen orange juice	456,131	55,593	92,562	42,665	72,458	40,322	37,432	109,477
Frozen fruits	846,226	62,085	155,783	60,933	140,224	62,699	120,453	228,238
Frozen fruit juices, excluding orange	326,506	53,529	61,972	38,807	52,649	18,019	24,258	75,360
Canned fruits	2,597,376	390,022	485,542	194,374	384,705	211,950	274,470	637,209
Dried fruits	994,193	130,296	179,015	71,600	149,434	46,821	116,898	289,130
Fresh fruit juice	2,113,119	310,027	336,911	202,317	289,658	144,598	187,476	630,516
Canned and bottled fruit juice	6,821,169	981,738	1,267,697	565,875	1,041,691	490,586	666,047	1,754,431
Processed vegetables	15,611,158	2,370,690	2,946,117	1,140,487	2,353,753	1,048,079	1,683,834	3,950,655
Frozen vegetables	4,277,599	520,906	756,769	290,824	657,334	293,554	551,763	1,152,202
Canned and dried vegetables and juices	11,333,559	1,849,784	2,189,204	849,663	1,696,419	754,525	1,132,071	2,798,453
Canned beans	2,333,236	386,282	464,946	176,673	357,598	183,887	208,911	544,144
Canned corn	1,189,853	232,177	261,138	81,358	182,796	69,197	116,166	245,944
Canned miscellaneous vegetables	3,118,319	518,906	549,756	207,877	506,510	199,100	320,999	786,633
Dried peas	102,721	17,267	17,609	11,574	12,163	2,585	10,770	30,014
Dried beans	610,212	114,630	154,637	53,671	70,720	29,466	62,109	125,023
Dried miscellaneous vegetables	1,412,415	199,368	315,287	102,010	192,005	85,149	152,239	361,035
Dried processed vegetables	250,688	44,561	40,733	16,453	69,852	18,906	19,657	51,607
Fresh and canned vegetable juices	2,273,315	340,911	380,526	195,622	298,520	165,572	234,946	643,471
Sugar and other sweets	**17,657,020**	**2,381,139**	**3,117,155**	**1,318,181**	**2,669,649**	**1,268,965**	**1,983,817**	**4,735,561**
Candy and chewing gum	10,608,397	1,296,188	1,678,653	797,694	1,581,042	804,670	1,265,281	3,072,900
Sugar	2,921,436	545,719	660,171	257,236	421,542	185,807	268,824	565,089
Artificial sweeteners	686,030	70,853	135,255	32,112	142,483	22,303	65,768	199,087
Jams, preserves, other sweets	3,441,156	468,402	643,088	231,138	524,581	256,112	383,944	898,485

	total consumer units	under $20,000	$20,000– $39,999	$40,000– $49,999	$50,000– $69,999	$70,000– $79,999	$80,000– $99,999	$100,000 or more
Fats and oils	**$13,403,878**	**$2,084,667**	**$2,615,760**	**$1,117,112**	**$2,192,851**	**$893,585**	**$1,303,550**	**$3,093,413**
Margarine	1,194,744	201,784	196,386	130,604	191,136	117,052	104,037	248,751
Fats and oils	4,260,479	735,139	971,986	346,084	633,181	250,868	377,566	927,635
Salad dressings	3,810,463	502,174	712,035	329,290	682,877	226,941	357,491	960,025
Nondairy cream and imitation milk	2,273,315	318,688	396,262	201,977	398,432	159,811	259,832	512,834
Peanut butter	1,864,877	326,987	339,091	109,045	287,399	138,838	204,415	444,168
Miscellaneous foods	**84,436,728**	**11,729,365**	**15,192,876**	**6,538,822**	**12,821,577**	**6,082,655**	**8,777,498**	**22,531,432**
Frozen prepared foods	16,659,158	2,474,803	3,081,095	1,370,945	2,416,480	1,144,527	1,888,458	4,157,732
Frozen meals	7,598,914	1,199,826	1,356,154	559,067	1,079,918	483,053	926,402	1,932,358
Other frozen prepared foods	9,060,244	1,274,976	1,724,941	811,878	1,336,562	661,474	962,057	2,225,375
Canned and packaged soups	5,735,260	833,204	1,105,928	436,406	879,226	424,638	551,868	1,464,005
Potato chips, nuts, and other snacks	17,734,061	2,107,413	3,056,380	1,383,426	2,755,660	1,306,333	1,864,618	5,047,148
Potato chips and other snacks	13,208,219	1,683,265	2,331,602	1,063,668	2,045,155	1,000,668	1,424,421	3,514,693
Nuts	4,525,842	424,148	724,778	319,758	710,505	305,665	440,198	1,532,455
Condiments and seasonings	16,374,229	2,168,485	2,985,503	1,221,618	2,513,612	1,151,543	1,734,546	4,450,749
Salt, spices, and other seasonings	4,330,183	632,441	785,713	294,795	674,884	284,544	418,449	1,202,730
Olives, pickles, relishes	1,972,489	272,733	326,115	132,987	324,410	124,216	212,780	571,351
Sauces and gravies	7,145,229	897,583	1,346,159	558,840	1,056,113	511,411	774,894	1,923,289
Baking needs and miscellaneous products	2,926,328	365,701	527,237	234,996	458,205	231,298	328,423	753,380
Other canned or packaged prepared foods	27,932,797	4,145,411	4,964,115	2,126,655	4,256,599	2,055,615	2,738,008	7,411,797
Prepared salads	4,429,235	554,141	794,010	332,808	693,476	313,419	394,609	1,289,102
Prepared desserts	1,837,974	236,159	359,725	148,532	300,952	142,826	168,446	458,635
Baby food	3,399,579	587,640	662,827	229,209	694,866	250,868	336,788	619,503
Miscellaneous prepared foods	17,989,641	2,759,110	3,139,167	1,374,916	2,525,080	1,323,909	1,758,386	4,976,971
Nonalcoholic beverages	**44,141,938**	**6,126,139**	**8,134,805**	**3,683,577**	**6,765,346**	**3,382,847**	**4,459,589**	**11,188,197**
Cola	9,632,547	1,287,224	1,877,179	815,849	1,494,510	809,248	998,757	2,247,831
Other carbonated drinks	8,158,989	1,081,448	1,427,168	691,600	1,439,949	674,620	731,920	2,033,629
Tea	3,810,463	601,148	733,423	296,043	589,741	239,717	338,252	991,982
Coffee	9,175,194	1,125,605	1,668,271	766,036	1,334,477	615,318	1,081,987	2,480,604
Noncarbonated fruit-flavored drinks	3,027,826	607,864	564,825	226,146	436,311	177,979	328,318	680,395
Other noncarbonated beverages and ice	1,825,745	274,304	376,694	126,633	299,041	124,659	228,673	391,481
Bottled water	6,539,909	951,853	1,185,701	587,888	925,620	548,706	543,398	1,730,679
Sports drinks	1,923,575	169,038	301,266	171,680	239,441	192,527	208,284	614,969
Food prepared by consumer unit on trips	**5,808,633**	**338,675**	**783,466**	**356,296**	**785,743**	**378,481**	**653,395**	**2,512,777**
FOOD AWAY FROM HOME	**320,378,488**	**28,726,961**	**45,960,440**	**22,344,626**	**44,324,091**	**23,665,823**	**36,716,976**	**115,226,510**
Meals at restaurants, carry-outs, etc.	**268,528,800**	**25,355,611**	**40,781,655**	**19,095,526**	**37,655,356**	**20,644,620**	**30,926,443**	**90,656,267**
Lunch	92,068,659	8,999,512	14,214,029	6,634,477	12,507,592	7,115,078	10,289,122	31,127,389
At fast-food restaurants*	45,097,000	4,904,151	7,563,254	3,430,085	6,529,553	3,685,780	5,297,846	13,159,206
At full-service restaurants	36,931,897	3,462,283	5,432,583	2,444,371	4,736,003	2,607,644	3,769,702	13,969,159
At vending machines, mobile vendors	875,575	96,355	188,523	74,096	161,423	70,231	61,690	205,565
At employer and school cafeterias	9,164,188	536,854	1,029,536	685,926	1,080,613	751,424	1,159,884	3,793,458
Dinner	128,529,751	11,367,310	18,604,051	8,476,096	17,990,068	9,624,723	15,251,017	45,596,427
At fast-food restaurants*	44,650,652	5,315,280	7,609,565	3,400,696	7,004,439	3,565,995	5,160,768	12,193,999
At full-service restaurants	82,673,349	5,855,378	10,721,978	5,007,772	10,868,167	5,926,832	9,910,824	33,155,836
At vending machines, mobile vendors	369,307	10,134	119,773	28,481	68,114	25,035	80,407	31,310
At employer and school cafeterias	837,666	188,511	152,735	39,147	49,348	106,935	98,914	215,066
Snacks and nonalcoholic beverages	20,310,648	2,238,856	3,076,217	1,777,961	2,965,909	1,478,255	2,292,373	6,230,444
At fast-food restaurants*	13,408,770	1,353,387	1,885,650	1,148,203	2,054,364	940,849	1,502,841	4,354,660
At full-service restaurants	4,001,231	500,931	543,579	391,131	487,397	320,878	469,788	1,227,562
At vending machines, mobile vendors	2,113,119	287,718	502,176	154,092	303,037	151,097	230,764	470,080
At employer and school cafeterias	786,305	96,879	144,812	84,535	121,111	65,431	88,981	177,926
Breakfast and brunch	27,619,742	2,749,856	4,887,492	2,207,105	4,191,960	2,426,637	3,093,930	7,702,007
At fast-food restaurants*	15,135,462	1,494,385	2,701,270	1,219,008	2,273,128	1,258,404	1,619,216	4,387,050
At full-service restaurants	10,931,235	1,086,312	1,877,830	849,209	1,717,965	1,075,995	1,270,299	2,904,259
At vending machines, mobile vendors	370,530	33,632	67,957	59,231	52,997	11,004	69,428	71,041
At employer and school cafeterias	1,181,292	135,527	240,568	79,542	148,044	81,235	135,092	339,658

	total consumer units	under $20,000	$20,000–$39,999	$40,000–$49,999	$50,000–$69,999	$70,000–$79,999	$80,000–$99,999	$100,000 or more
Board (including at school)	$5,364,731	$524,733	$384,409	$155,227	$205,906	$62,034	$443,648	$3,589,188
Catered affairs	6,435,965	144,911	543,338	160,674	930,137	211,211	735,266	3,710,109
Food on trips	28,919,653	1,716,899	2,952,142	1,955,088	3,772,677	1,800,241	3,204,137	13,518,514
School lunches	7,601,360	367,289	697,704	625,106	1,251,420	521,012	1,067,244	3,072,036
Meals as pay	3,527,980	617,469	601,181	353,005	508,596	426,705	340,343	680,395
ALCOHOLIC BEVERAGES	55,815,455	4,667,000	7,265,705	3,501,911	6,669,430	4,158,198	7,007,507	21,982,538
At home	29,636,254	2,804,179	4,427,045	1,967,343	3,752,173	2,144,752	3,929,156	10,336,353
Beer and ale	13,422,221	1,678,408	2,488,931	979,700	1,710,320	1,128,354	1,693,663	3,702,120
Whiskey	1,173,955	143,456	97,305	130,944	153,604	92,682	213,930	355,421
Wine	12,721,517	782,525	1,434,325	703,514	1,538,645	783,770	1,751,275	5,514,636
Other alcoholic beverages	2,319,784	199,658	406,340	153,071	349,431	139,798	270,288	764,176
Away from home	26,179,201	1,862,899	2,838,660	1,534,682	2,917,430	2,013,446	3,078,351	11,646,400
Beer and ale	9,413,653	656,125	1,181,534	551,691	1,097,642	935,310	1,155,493	3,711,621
At fast-food restaurants*	1,524,919	167,576	252,921	87,599	259,250	159,885	96,927	473,750
At full-service restaurants	7,743,213	473,963	916,669	461,256	817,020	701,649	1,044,554	3,224,699
At vending machines, mobile vendors	79,487	–	11,076	2,837	21,372	7,533	14,011	11,876
Wine	5,131,163	199,918	498,125	250,769	441,698	355,514	566,611	2,720,502
At fast-food restaurants*	361,970	9,227	34,093	19,063	28,497	33,897	49,875	183,109
At full-service restaurants	4,671,363	194,343	464,032	231,706	413,201	233,292	516,736	2,523,574
Other alcoholic beverages	6,151,036	660,471	683,480	416,775	629,706	383,355	762,242	2,550,133
At fast-food restaurants*	519,720	–	66,618	68,990	38,401	40,618	68,905	102,135
At full-service restaurants	5,623,979	531,296	613,797	347,786	591,305	342,664	693,442	2,443,680
Alcoholic beverages purchased on trips	5,483,349	346,230	475,520	315,333	748,211	339,341	593,901	2,664,360

* The category fast-food restaurants also includes take-out, delivery, concession stands, buffets, and cafeterias other than employer and school.
Note: Numbers may not add to total because of rounding and missing subcategories. "–" means sample is too small to make a reliable estimate.
Source: Calculations by New Strategist based on the Bureau of Labor Statistics' 2011 Consumer Expenditure Survey

Table 5.8 Food and Alcohol: Market shares by income, 2011

(percentage of total annual spending on food and alcoholic beverages accounted for by before-tax income group of consumer units, 2011)

	total consumer units	under $20,000	$20,000– $39,999	$40,000– $49,999	$50,000– $69,999	$70,000– $79,999	$80,000– $99,999	$100,000 or more
Share of total consumer units	100.0%	21.5%	22.7%	9.3%	14.2%	6.0%	8.6%	17.7%
Share of total before-tax income	100.0	3.5	10.6	6.5	13.2	7.1	12.0	47.1
Share of total spending	100.0	9.6	15.3	7.5	14.3	7.0	11.2	34.7
Share of food spending	100.0	11.7	16.8	7.4	14.4	7.2	10.8	30.7
Share of alcoholic beverages spending	100.0	8.4	13.0	6.3	11.9	7.4	12.6	39.4
FOOD AT HOME	100.0	13.6	18.5	7.7	14.8	7.0	10.3	27.1
Cereals and bakery products	100.0	13.9	18.7	7.8	14.6	7.0	10.4	26.7
Cereals and cereal products	100.0	14.0	18.9	7.6	14.7	6.8	10.5	26.6
Flour	100.0	13.6	20.0	6.0	15.1	6.8	8.3	29.1
Prepared flour mixes	100.0	14.7	18.6	6.6	15.7	7.4	10.0	26.2
Ready-to-eat and cooked cereals	100.0	13.7	18.8	7.7	14.8	7.0	10.9	26.1
Rice	100.0	16.0	21.2	8.2	15.3	5.2	10.2	23.2
Pasta, cornmeal, and other cereal products	100.0	13.1	17.4	7.6	13.4	7.4	10.3	30.1
Bakery products	100.0	13.8	18.6	7.9	14.5	7.1	10.4	26.7
Bread	100.0	15.2	19.6	7.8	14.4	6.6	9.7	25.9
White bread	100.0	16.7	20.6	7.4	14.3	6.9	9.6	23.8
Bread, other than white	100.0	14.1	18.9	8.0	14.5	6.3	9.7	27.5
Cookies and crackers	100.0	12.3	18.3	7.7	14.6	8.2	10.9	27.0
Cookies	100.0	13.4	18.4	8.4	14.6	8.8	10.3	25.4
Crackers	100.0	11.0	18.1	6.9	14.5	7.5	11.7	29.0
Frozen and refrigerated bakery products	100.0	12.5	19.9	7.1	14.5	7.4	10.1	27.3
Other bakery products	100.0	13.9	17.8	8.4	14.6	6.8	10.6	27.0
Biscuits and rolls	100.0	12.1	17.3	7.5	14.8	6.7	12.1	28.5
Cakes and cupcakes	100.0	15.0	17.0	9.8	14.4	5.7	10.9	26.4
Bread and cracker products	100.0	15.9	18.1	6.9	15.9	8.6	8.8	25.2
Sweetrolls, coffee cakes, doughnuts	100.0	15.7	19.1	9.2	13.5	7.6	8.6	25.5
Pies, tarts, turnovers	100.0	13.3	19.8	7.3	15.1	7.7	9.0	26.4
Meats, poultry, fish, and eggs	100.0	13.6	19.3	7.5	14.5	7.3	10.0	26.9
Beef	100.0	13.3	19.2	7.9	15.0	6.7	10.6	26.4
Ground beef	100.0	15.7	19.9	8.3	14.9	7.0	10.5	23.0
Roast	100.0	11.6	17.9	7.7	17.5	8.6	11.7	23.9
Chuck roast	100.0	11.0	21.7	6.8	17.6	7.0	12.4	22.3
Round roast	100.0	10.8	16.4	10.7	16.5	9.8	11.9	22.9
Other roast	100.0	12.1	16.7	7.0	17.9	8.9	11.3	25.1
Steak	100.0	11.9	19.5	7.6	15.1	5.6	10.2	29.1
Round steak	100.0	13.8	20.2	8.2	13.8	5.5	10.4	27.1
Sirloin steak	100.0	13.1	19.8	7.8	13.3	5.1	7.9	32.1
Other steak	100.0	10.6	19.1	7.3	16.4	5.8	11.2	28.4
Other beef	100.0	10.5	16.9	7.5	11.0	6.6	11.0	35.2
Pork	100.0	14.0	21.9	7.3	14.8	8.1	8.2	24.8
Bacon	100.0	13.7	21.2	7.1	14.8	8.4	9.3	24.8
Pork chops	100.0	13.8	23.8	9.0	15.3	7.7	6.8	22.8
Ham	100.0	15.4	19.9	7.6	15.7	9.1	8.2	23.6
Ham, not canned	100.0	15.4	20.1	7.6	15.7	9.3	8.1	23.3
Canned ham	100.0	14.5	11.7	7.6	16.2	–	13.9	35.5
Sausage	100.0	14.8	20.8	7.7	14.6	7.6	10.6	23.0
Other pork	100.0	12.7	23.7	5.9	14.0	7.4	6.3	28.8
Other meats	100.0	12.9	14.9	8.1	15.0	8.3	11.6	28.4
Frankfurters	100.0	15.3	19.1	7.9	15.8	6.2	11.3	23.6
Lunch meats (cold cuts)	100.0	13.2	14.4	8.6	14.6	7.4	11.6	29.5
Bologna, liverwurst, salami	100.0	13.9	16.0	9.8	13.9	7.7	9.8	28.2
Other lunch meats	100.0	12.9	13.7	8.1	14.9	7.3	12.3	30.0
Lamb, organ meats, and others	100.0	5.9	9.3	4.3	16.2	20.2	12.7	30.4

	total consumer units	under $20,000	$20,000– $39,999	$40,000– $49,999	$50,000– $69,999	$70,000– $79,999	$80,000– $99,999	$100,000 or more
Poultry	100.0%	14.0%	19.8%	7.2%	13.6%	6.7%	10.2%	27.6%
Fresh and frozen chicken	100.0	14.2	20.5	7.2	13.9	6.9	8.7	27.6
Fresh and frozen whole chicken	100.0	14.4	20.7	7.8	13.6	6.7	10.1	25.9
Fresh and frozen chicken parts	100.0	14.1	20.4	7.0	14.1	6.9	8.2	28.3
Other poultry	100.0	12.9	16.9	7.0	12.0	6.2	16.3	27.6
Fish and seafood	100.0	12.7	19.1	6.7	14.2	7.0	9.5	29.7
Canned fish and seafood	100.0	15.4	19.4	9.9	15.9	8.2	8.7	22.2
Fresh fish and shellfish	100.0	11.3	19.2	5.1	13.3	6.6	9.5	33.6
Frozen fish and shellfish	100.0	13.5	18.8	7.5	14.7	6.9	9.8	27.8
Eggs	100.0	16.9	21.8	8.0	13.4	7.3	9.3	22.7
Dairy products	**100.0**	**13.2**	**18.3**	**7.8**	**14.7**	**6.9**	**10.5**	**27.6**
Fresh milk and cream	100.0	14.7	19.4	8.0	14.3	7.3	10.4	25.1
Fresh milk, all types	100.0	15.2	19.6	8.3	14.0	7.3	10.4	24.7
Cream	100.0	12.0	18.3	6.4	16.1	7.3	11.0	27.8
Other dairy products	100.0	12.4	17.7	7.7	15.0	6.6	10.5	29.0
Butter	100.0	12.8	17.7	7.6	17.1	5.7	9.9	28.1
Cheese	100.0	12.1	17.9	7.2	15.0	6.8	10.5	29.3
Ice cream and related products	100.0	13.7	18.2	8.9	13.9	7.5	10.4	26.5
Miscellaneous dairy products	100.0	11.4	16.5	7.9	14.9	5.8	10.8	31.5
Fruits and vegetables	**100.0**	**13.4**	**18.4**	**7.4**	**14.5**	**6.5**	**10.4**	**28.5**
Fresh fruits	100.0	12.9	18.1	7.4	14.1	6.2	10.2	30.1
Apples	100.0	12.9	19.0	6.5	14.7	7.0	9.9	28.8
Bananas	100.0	13.9	20.3	8.6	13.8	7.1	9.6	25.5
Oranges	100.0	13.5	18.3	8.2	14.1	5.1	10.8	28.8
Citrus fruits, excluding oranges	100.0	13.6	18.0	7.3	14.2	5.7	9.7	30.6
Other fresh fruits	100.0	12.0	16.9	7.0	13.9	6.0	10.7	32.5
Fresh vegetables	100.0	12.6	18.5	7.1	14.2	6.3	10.6	29.6
Potatoes	100.0	14.2	18.9	7.7	15.0	6.6	10.0	26.7
Lettuce	100.0	12.1	17.6	7.5	15.3	6.8	10.9	28.6
Tomatoes	100.0	13.7	19.3	7.1	13.2	6.0	11.0	28.7
Other fresh vegetables	100.0	11.8	18.4	6.8	14.0	6.1	10.5	31.1
Processed fruits	100.0	14.0	18.2	8.3	15.1	7.2	10.1	26.3
Frozen fruits and fruit juices	100.0	10.5	19.1	8.7	16.3	7.4	11.2	25.4
Frozen orange juice	100.0	12.2	20.3	9.4	15.9	8.8	8.2	24.0
Frozen fruits	100.0	7.3	18.4	7.2	16.6	7.4	14.2	27.0
Frozen fruit juices, excluding orange	100.0	16.4	19.0	11.9	16.1	5.5	7.4	23.1
Canned fruits	100.0	15.0	18.7	7.5	14.8	8.2	10.6	24.5
Dried fruits	100.0	13.1	18.0	7.2	15.0	4.7	11.8	29.1
Fresh fruit juice	100.0	14.7	15.9	9.6	13.7	6.8	8.9	29.8
Canned and bottled fruit juice	100.0	14.4	18.6	8.3	15.3	7.2	9.8	25.7
Processed vegetables	100.0	15.2	18.9	7.3	15.1	6.7	10.8	25.3
Frozen vegetables	100.0	12.2	17.7	6.8	15.4	6.9	12.9	26.9
Canned and dried vegetables and juices	100.0	16.3	19.3	7.5	15.0	6.7	10.0	24.7
Canned beans	100.0	16.6	19.9	7.6	15.3	7.9	9.0	23.3
Canned corn	100.0	19.5	21.9	6.8	15.4	5.8	9.8	20.7
Canned miscellaneous vegetables	100.0	16.6	17.6	6.7	16.2	6.4	10.3	25.2
Dried peas	100.0	16.8	17.1	11.3	11.8	2.5	10.5	29.2
Dried beans	100.0	18.8	25.3	8.8	11.6	4.8	10.2	20.5
Dried miscellaneous vegetables	100.0	14.1	22.3	7.2	13.6	6.0	10.8	25.6
Dried processed vegetables	100.0	17.8	16.2	6.6	27.9	7.5	7.8	20.6
Fresh and canned vegetable juices	100.0	15.0	16.7	8.6	13.1	7.3	10.3	28.3
Sugar and other sweets	**100.0**	**13.5**	**17.7**	**7.5**	**15.1**	**7.2**	**11.2**	**26.8**
Candy and chewing gum	100.0	12.2	15.8	7.5	14.9	7.6	11.9	29.0
Sugar	100.0	18.7	22.6	8.8	14.4	6.4	9.2	19.3
Artificial sweeteners	100.0	10.3	19.7	4.7	20.8	3.3	9.6	29.0
Jams, preserves, other sweets	100.0	13.6	18.7	6.7	15.2	7.4	11.2	26.1

	total consumer units	under $20,000	$20,000–$39,999	$40,000–$49,999	$50,000–$69,999	$70,000–$79,999	$80,000–$99,999	$100,000 or more
Fats and oils	100.0%	15.6%	19.5%	8.3%	16.4%	6.7%	9.7%	23.1%
Margarine	100.0	16.9	16.4	10.9	16.0	9.8	8.7	20.8
Fats and oils	100.0	17.3	22.8	8.1	14.9	5.9	8.9	21.8
Salad dressings	100.0	13.2	18.7	8.6	17.9	6.0	9.4	25.2
Nondairy cream and imitation milk	100.0	14.0	17.4	8.9	17.5	7.0	11.4	22.6
Peanut butter	100.0	17.5	18.2	5.8	15.4	7.4	11.0	23.8
Miscellaneous foods	100.0	13.9	18.0	7.7	15.2	7.2	10.4	26.7
Frozen prepared foods	100.0	14.9	18.5	8.2	14.5	6.9	11.3	25.0
Frozen meals	100.0	15.8	17.8	7.4	14.2	6.4	12.2	25.4
Other frozen prepared foods	100.0	14.1	19.0	9.0	14.8	7.3	10.6	24.6
Canned and packaged soups	100.0	14.5	19.3	7.6	15.3	7.4	9.6	25.5
Potato chips, nuts, and other snacks	100.0	11.9	17.2	7.8	15.5	7.4	10.5	28.5
Potato chips and other snacks	100.0	12.7	17.7	8.1	15.5	7.6	10.8	26.6
Nuts	100.0	9.4	16.0	7.1	15.7	6.8	9.7	33.9
Condiments and seasonings	100.0	13.2	18.2	7.5	15.4	7.0	10.6	27.2
Salt, spices, and other seasonings	100.0	14.6	18.1	6.8	15.6	6.6	9.7	27.8
Olives, pickles, relishes	100.0	13.8	16.5	6.7	16.4	6.3	10.8	29.0
Sauces and gravies	100.0	12.6	18.8	7.8	14.8	7.2	10.8	26.9
Baking needs and miscellaneous products	100.0	12.5	18.0	8.0	15.7	7.9	11.2	25.7
Other canned or packaged prepared foods	100.0	14.8	17.8	7.6	15.2	7.4	9.8	26.5
Prepared salads	100.0	12.5	17.9	7.5	15.7	7.1	8.9	29.1
Prepared desserts	100.0	12.8	19.6	8.1	16.4	7.8	9.2	25.0
Baby food	100.0	17.3	19.5	6.7	20.4	7.4	9.9	18.2
Miscellaneous prepared foods	100.0	15.3	17.4	7.6	14.0	7.4	9.8	27.7
Nonalcoholic beverages	100.0	13.9	18.4	8.3	15.3	7.7	10.1	25.3
Cola	100.0	13.4	19.5	8.5	15.5	8.4	10.4	23.3
Other carbonated drinks	100.0	13.3	17.5	8.5	17.6	8.3	9.0	24.9
Tea	100.0	15.8	19.2	7.8	15.5	6.3	8.9	26.0
Coffee	100.0	12.3	18.2	8.3	14.5	6.7	11.8	27.0
Noncarbonated fruit-flavored drinks	100.0	20.1	18.7	7.5	14.4	5.9	10.8	22.5
Other noncarbonated beverages and ice	100.0	15.0	20.6	6.9	16.4	6.8	12.5	21.4
Bottled water	100.0	14.6	18.1	9.0	14.2	8.4	8.3	26.5
Sports drinks	100.0	8.8	15.7	8.9	12.4	10.0	10.8	32.0
Food prepared by consumer unit on trips	100.0	5.8	13.5	6.1	13.5	6.5	11.2	43.3
FOOD AWAY FROM HOME	100.0	9.0	14.3	7.0	13.8	7.4	11.5	36.0
Meals at restaurants, carry-outs, etc.	100.0	9.4	15.2	7.1	14.0	7.7	11.5	33.8
Lunch	100.0	9.8	15.4	7.2	13.6	7.7	11.2	33.8
At fast-food restaurants*	100.0	10.9	16.8	7.6	14.5	8.2	11.7	29.2
At full-service restaurants	100.0	9.4	14.7	6.6	12.8	7.1	10.2	37.8
At vending machines, mobile vendors	100.0	11.0	21.5	8.5	18.4	8.0	7.0	23.5
At employer and school cafeterias	100.0	5.9	11.2	7.5	11.8	8.2	12.7	41.4
Dinner	100.0	8.8	14.5	6.6	14.0	7.5	11.9	35.5
At fast-food restaurants*	100.0	11.9	17.0	7.6	15.7	8.0	11.6	27.3
At full-service restaurants	100.0	7.1	13.0	6.1	13.1	7.2	12.0	40.1
At vending machines, mobile vendors	100.0	2.7	32.4	7.7	18.4	6.8	21.8	8.5
At employer and school cafeterias	100.0	22.5	18.2	4.7	5.9	12.8	11.8	25.7
Snacks and nonalcoholic beverages	100.0	11.0	15.1	8.8	14.6	7.3	11.3	30.7
At fast-food restaurants*	100.0	10.1	14.1	8.6	15.3	7.0	11.2	32.5
At full-service restaurants	100.0	12.5	13.6	9.8	12.2	8.0	11.7	30.7
At vending machines, mobile vendors	100.0	13.6	23.8	7.3	14.3	7.2	10.9	22.2
At employer and school cafeterias	100.0	12.3	18.4	10.8	15.4	8.3	11.3	22.6
Breakfast and brunch	100.0	10.0	17.7	8.0	15.2	8.8	11.2	27.9
At fast-food restaurants*	100.0	9.9	17.8	8.1	15.0	8.3	10.7	29.0
At full-service restaurants	100.0	9.9	17.2	7.8	15.7	9.8	11.6	26.6
At vending machines, mobile vendors	100.0	9.1	18.3	16.0	14.3	3.0	18.7	19.2
At employer and school cafeterias	100.0	11.5	20.4	6.7	12.5	6.9	11.4	28.8

	total consumer units	under $20,000	$20,000–$39,999	$40,000–$49,999	$50,000–$69,999	$70,000–$79,999	$80,000–$99,999	$100,000 or more
Board (including at school)	100.0%	9.8%	7.2%	2.9%	3.8%	1.2%	8.3%	66.9%
Catered affairs	100.0	2.3	8.4	2.5	14.5	3.3	11.4	57.6
Food on trips	100.0	5.9	10.2	6.8	13.0	6.2	11.1	46.7
School lunches	100.0	4.8	9.2	8.2	16.5	6.9	14.0	40.4
Meals as pay	100.0	17.5	17.0	10.0	14.4	12.1	9.6	19.3
ALCOHOLIC BEVERAGES	100.0	8.4	13.0	6.3	11.9	7.4	12.6	39.4
At home	100.0	9.5	14.9	6.6	12.7	7.2	13.3	34.9
Beer and ale	100.0	12.5	18.5	7.3	12.7	8.4	12.6	27.6
Whiskey	100.0	12.2	8.3	11.2	13.1	7.9	18.2	30.3
Wine	100.0	6.2	11.3	5.5	12.1	6.2	13.8	43.3
Other alcoholic beverages	100.0	8.6	17.5	6.6	15.1	6.0	11.7	32.9
Away from home	100.0	7.1	10.8	5.9	11.1	7.7	11.8	44.5
Beer and ale	100.0	7.0	12.6	5.9	11.7	9.9	12.3	39.4
At fast-food restaurants*	100.0	11.0	16.6	5.7	17.0	10.5	6.4	31.1
At full-service restaurants	100.0	6.1	11.8	6.0	10.6	9.1	13.5	41.6
At vending machines, mobile vendors	100.0	–	13.9	3.6	26.9	9.5	17.6	14.9
Wine	100.0	3.9	9.7	4.9	8.6	6.9	11.0	53.0
At fast-food restaurants*	100.0	2.5	9.4	5.3	7.9	9.4	13.8	50.6
At full-service restaurants	100.0	4.2	9.9	5.0	8.8	5.0	11.1	54.0
Other alcoholic beverages	100.0	10.7	11.1	6.8	10.2	6.2	12.4	41.5
At fast-food restaurants*	100.0	–	12.8	13.3	7.4	7.8	13.3	19.7
At full-service restaurants	100.0	9.4	10.9	6.2	10.5	6.1	12.3	43.5
Alcoholic beverages purchased on trips	100.0	6.3	8.7	5.8	13.6	6.2	10.8	48.6

* The category fast-food restaurants also includes take-out, delivery, concession stands, buffets, and cafeterias other than employer and school.
Note: Numbers may not add to total because of rounding. "–" means sample is too small to make a reliable estimate.
Source: Calculations by New Strategist based on the Bureau of Labor Statistics' 2011 Consumer Expenditure Survey

Table 5.9 Food and Alcohol: Average spending by high-income consumer units, 2011

(average annual spending on food and alcoholic beverages, by before-tax income of high-income consumer units, 2011)

	total consumer units	$100,000 or more	$100,000– $119,999	$120,000– $149,999	$150,000 or more
Number of consumer units (in 000s)	122,287	21,593	7,045	6,107	8,440
Average number of persons per consumer unit	2.5	3.2	3.2	3.1	3.2
Average before-tax income of consumer units	$63,685.00	$169,776.00	$108,549.00	$133,318.00	$247,261.00
Average spending of consumer units, total	49,704.88	97,728.22	76,496.41	87,239.44	123,056.38
Food, average spending	**6,458.00**	**11,233.00**	**9,569.00**	**10,674.00**	**13,055.00**
Alcoholic beverages, average spending	**456.43**	**1,018.04**	**745.30**	**934.25**	**1,311.43**
FOOD AT HOME	**3,837.76**	**5,896.88**	**5,184.28**	**5,533.10**	**6,768.19**
Cereals and bakery products	**530.68**	**801.45**	**708.32**	**767.37**	**905.87**
Cereals and cereal products	174.86	263.54	239.31	251.63	292.88
Flour	7.67	12.62	7.83	13.37	16.23
Prepared flour mixes	14.88	22.05	17.52	22.94	25.32
Ready-to-eat and cooked cereals	91.39	134.98	124.34	139.78	140.75
Rice	25.66	33.72	37.88	25.24	36.13
Pasta, cornmeal, and other cereal products	35.26	60.18	51.75	50.29	74.44
Bakery products	355.81	537.91	469.01	515.74	613.00
Bread	106.53	156.52	137.98	142.75	182.26
White bread	44.93	60.59	53.06	53.43	72.15
Bread, other than white	61.60	95.93	84.92	89.32	110.11
Cookies and crackers	83.59	127.60	107.22	122.24	148.97
Cookies	46.96	67.53	56.77	64.48	78.97
Crackers	36.63	60.07	50.46	57.76	70.00
Frozen and refrigerated bakery products	28.60	44.26	35.34	48.19	49.17
Other bakery products	137.09	209.52	188.47	202.56	232.60
Biscuits and rolls	52.93	85.42	70.76	83.15	99.68
Cakes and cupcakes	37.81	56.56	55.40	49.94	62.25
Bread and cracker products	7.13	10.16	7.33	10.49	12.37
Sweetrolls, coffee cakes, doughnuts	23.86	34.39	35.64	29.38	36.86
Pies, tarts, turnovers	15.36	22.99	19.35	29.61	21.44
Meats, poultry, fish, and eggs	**832.41**	**1,267.61**	**1,109.81**	**1,199.67**	**1,451.75**
Beef	222.60	333.25	292.30	326.21	373.54
Ground beef	90.50	117.81	114.53	94.37	137.24
Roast	30.59	41.49	36.68	45.16	43.03
Chuck roast	7.65	9.64	5.47	12.41	11.26
Round roast	6.11	7.92	7.21	7.22	9.04
Other roast	16.82	23.93	24.00	25.53	22.73
Steak	82.49	136.04	120.88	150.93	138.56
Round steak	15.90	24.37	25.63	25.31	22.62
Sirloin steak	21.86	39.76	39.75	39.41	40.03
Other steak	44.73	71.90	55.50	86.21	75.92
Other beef	19.02	37.91	20.20	35.74	54.70
Pork	161.95	227.65	203.48	224.22	250.91
Bacon	33.87	47.52	41.42	49.12	51.65
Pork chops	27.24	35.23	40.64	29.24	34.80
Ham	34.29	45.78	43.48	47.14	46.81
Ham, not canned	33.51	44.22	40.68	46.75	45.47
Canned ham	0.78	1.57	2.80	0.39	1.34
Sausage	28.55	37.24	30.00	35.78	44.50
Other pork	37.99	61.88	47.94	62.94	73.13
Other meats	122.54	197.32	155.10	204.80	228.42
Frankfurters	23.67	31.65	25.99	35.91	33.53
Lunch meats (cold cuts)	87.67	146.37	117.21	135.99	178.86
Bologna, liverwurst, salami	26.83	42.86	32.00	41.43	53.24
Other lunch meats	60.84	103.51	85.21	94.56	125.62
Lamb, organ meats, and others	11.20	19.29	11.90	32.90	16.03

	total consumer units	$100,000 or more	$100,000–$119,999	$120,000–$149,999	$150,000 or more
Poultry	$154.49	$241.67	$229.01	$209.76	$275.18
Fresh and frozen chicken	124.44	194.74	187.69	168.77	219.21
Fresh and frozen whole chicken	35.97	52.69	42.33	44.39	67.50
Fresh and frozen chicken parts	88.48	142.05	145.36	124.38	151.70
Other poultry	30.05	46.93	41.32	40.98	55.98
Fish and seafood	120.76	203.33	171.04	172.44	253.05
Canned fish and seafood	19.90	25.02	21.37	23.33	29.37
Fresh fish and shellfish	59.51	113.27	99.03	88.80	142.87
Frozen fish and shellfish	41.35	65.04	50.64	60.30	80.80
Eggs	50.07	64.39	58.89	62.24	70.65
Dairy products	**406.84**	**635.44**	**551.54**	**598.30**	**734.06**
Fresh milk and cream	149.73	213.10	183.18	191.48	254.18
Fresh milk, all types	127.38	177.92	155.32	158.74	210.98
Cream	22.36	35.18	27.86	32.74	43.21
Other dairy products	257.10	422.34	368.36	406.82	479.87
Butter	24.64	39.26	32.86	40.39	43.98
Cheese	124.74	207.12	183.59	191.62	238.39
Ice cream and related products	57.28	86.09	80.19	87.04	90.49
Miscellaneous dairy products	50.43	89.87	71.71	87.77	107.02
Fruits and vegetables	**714.89**	**1,151.85**	**976.59**	**1,064.63**	**1,364.70**
Fresh fruits	247.28	421.00	356.95	371.16	511.50
Apples	38.17	62.25	57.18	62.27	66.62
Bananas	41.08	59.41	56.65	51.56	67.36
Oranges	26.99	44.07	34.09	39.06	56.21
Citrus fruits, excluding oranges	37.63	65.17	56.97	56.17	78.62
Other fresh fruits	103.42	190.09	152.07	162.10	242.69
Fresh vegetables	224.21	375.40	324.64	345.87	440.07
Potatoes	38.78	58.64	54.00	64.71	58.35
Lettuce	32.17	52.14	45.10	48.10	61.06
Tomatoes	41.03	66.79	59.19	64.32	75.09
Other fresh vegetables	112.24	197.83	166.34	168.73	245.57
Processed fruits	115.73	172.49	137.60	165.34	207.62
Frozen fruits and fruit juices	13.31	19.14	13.35	21.44	22.49
Frozen orange juice	3.73	5.07	5.23	6.09	4.22
Frozen fruits	6.92	10.57	5.46	11.56	14.27
Frozen fruit juices, excluding orange	2.67	3.49	2.66	3.79	4.00
Canned fruits	21.24	29.51	25.39	25.05	36.21
Dried fruits	8.13	13.39	8.84	11.44	18.69
Fresh fruit juice	17.28	29.20	21.97	30.49	34.53
Canned and bottled fruit juice	55.78	81.25	68.04	76.92	95.70
Processed vegetables	127.66	182.96	157.40	182.25	205.50
Frozen vegetables	34.98	53.36	52.75	47.25	58.21
Canned and dried vegetables and juices	92.68	129.60	104.65	135.00	147.30
Canned beans	19.08	25.20	25.64	27.91	22.89
Canned corn	9.73	11.39	6.77	11.36	15.41
Canned miscellaneous vegetables	25.50	36.43	26.43	38.33	43.72
Dried peas	0.84	1.39	1.27	0.90	1.85
Dried beans	4.99	5.79	6.67	6.06	4.84
Dried miscellaneous vegetables	11.55	16.72	13.95	17.38	18.64
Dried processed vegetables	2.05	2.39	0.09	2.79	4.09
Fresh and canned vegetable juices	18.59	29.80	23.16	29.84	35.48
Sugar and other sweets	**144.39**	**219.31**	**190.76**	**206.04**	**253.32**
Candy and chewing gum	86.75	142.31	121.69	126.87	171.01
Sugar	23.89	26.17	23.52	27.68	27.38
Artificial sweeteners	5.61	9.22	10.97	8.40	8.30
Jams, preserves, other sweets	28.14	41.61	34.57	43.09	46.63

	total consumer units	$100,000 or more	$100,000– $119,999	$120,000– $149,999	$150,000 or more
Fats and oils	**$109.61**	**$143.26**	**$133.29**	**$140.54**	**$153.79**
Margarine	9.77	11.52	11.30	12.56	10.98
Fats and oils	34.84	42.96	44.21	37.73	45.58
Salad dressings	31.16	44.46	36.21	47.19	49.64
Nondairy cream and imitation milk	18.59	23.75	24.17	21.66	24.88
Peanut butter	15.25	20.57	17.39	21.40	22.71
Miscellaneous foods	**690.48**	**1,043.46**	**941.35**	**998.20**	**1,163.53**
Frozen prepared foods	136.23	192.55	174.06	180.33	217.13
Frozen meals	62.14	89.49	89.76	84.98	92.46
Other frozen prepared foods	74.09	103.06	84.30	95.35	124.68
Canned and packaged soups	46.90	67.80	57.78	69.82	75.01
Potato chips, nuts, and other snacks	145.02	233.74	210.78	215.97	266.11
Potato chips and other snacks	108.01	162.77	149.25	160.04	176.36
Nuts	37.01	70.97	61.53	55.94	89.76
Condiments and seasonings	133.90	206.12	181.40	197.65	233.42
Salt, spices, and other seasonings	35.41	55.70	51.06	48.45	64.83
Olives, pickles, relishes	16.13	26.46	21.62	28.18	29.40
Sauces and gravies	58.43	89.07	74.67	95.02	97.28
Baking needs and miscellaneous products	23.93	34.89	34.05	26.00	41.90
Other canned or packaged prepared foods	228.42	343.25	317.32	334.43	371.85
Prepared salads	36.22	59.70	54.15	58.54	65.31
Prepared desserts	15.03	21.24	15.89	23.49	24.25
Baby food	27.80	28.69	40.46	20.02	24.69
Miscellaneous prepared foods	147.11	230.49	204.48	231.23	252.38
Nonalcoholic beverages	**360.97**	**518.14**	**484.98**	**453.27**	**592.65**
Cola	78.77	104.10	104.45	90.27	113.59
Other carbonated drinks	66.72	94.18	92.82	78.54	106.43
Tea	31.16	45.94	48.42	42.84	46.01
Coffee	75.03	114.88	96.28	91.94	147.15
Noncarbonated fruit-flavored drinks	24.76	31.51	32.98	34.15	28.37
Other noncarbonated beverages and ice	14.93	18.13	13.65	15.38	23.94
Bottled water	53.48	80.15	73.84	69.20	93.36
Sports drinks	15.73	28.48	22.54	29.29	33.03
Food prepared by consumer unit on trips	**47.50**	**116.37**	**87.63**	**105.06**	**148.54**
FOOD AWAY FROM HOME	**2,619.89**	**5,336.29**	**4,384.65**	**5,140.74**	**6,286.44**
Meals at restaurants, carry-outs, etc.	**2,195.89**	**4,198.41**	**3,617.21**	**4,094.20**	**4,773.26**
Lunch	752.89	1,441.55	1,235.75	1,423.57	1,631.71
At fast-food restaurants*	368.78	609.42	581.50	621.92	624.64
At full-service restaurants	302.01	646.93	491.26	627.39	794.98
At vending machines, mobile vendors	7.16	9.52	10.35	12.44	6.72
At employer and school cafeterias	74.94	175.68	152.65	161.82	205.36
Dinner	1,051.05	2,111.63	1,755.99	2,075.57	2,443.75
At fast-food restaurants*	365.13	564.72	555.99	581.67	560.24
At full-service restaurants	676.06	1,535.49	1,197.41	1,474.52	1,870.13
At vending machines, mobile vendors	3.02	1.45	0.48	3.22	1.04
At employer and school cafeterias	6.85	9.96	2.11	16.16	12.33
Snacks and nonalcoholic beverages	166.09	288.54	284.23	247.46	321.34
At fast-food restaurants*	109.65	201.67	201.89	159.34	231.47
At full-service restaurants	32.72	56.85	50.97	56.33	62.29
At vending machines, mobile vendors	17.28	21.77	23.28	27.60	16.35
At employer and school cafeterias	6.43	8.24	8.10	4.20	11.23
Breakfast and brunch	225.86	356.69	341.24	347.59	376.47
At fast-food restaurants*	123.77	203.17	204.90	206.57	199.28
At full-service restaurants	89.39	134.50	122.82	119.16	155.43
At vending machines, mobile vendors	3.03	3.29	3.54	3.98	2.59
At employer and school cafeterias	9.66	15.73	9.97	17.88	19.16

	total consumer units	$100,000 or more	$100,000–$119,999	$120,000–$149,999	$150,000 or more
Board (including at school)	$43.87	$166.22	$86.05	$114.98	$270.22
Catered affairs	52.63	171.82	91.93	173.71	237.13
Food on trips	236.49	626.06	419.29	587.65	826.43
School lunches	62.16	142.27	144.29	138.79	143.11
Meals as pay	28.85	31.51	25.89	31.41	36.27
ALCOHOLIC BEVERAGES	456.43	1,018.04	745.30	934.25	1,311.43
At home	242.35	478.69	351.26	511.50	565.30
Beer and ale	109.76	171.45	151.39	170.29	189.57
Whiskey	9.60	16.46	10.93	21.61	17.57
Wine	104.03	255.39	165.75	275.50	318.43
Other alcoholic beverages	18.97	35.39	23.19	44.10	39.72
Away from home	214.08	539.36	394.04	422.75	746.13
Beer and ale	76.98	171.89	155.48	125.78	218.68
At fast-food restaurants*	12.47	21.94	26.72	12.50	24.51
At full-service restaurants	63.32	149.34	128.23	113.28	193.08
At vending machines, mobile vendors	0.65	0.55	0.38	–	1.09
Wine	41.96	125.99	84.76	85.44	190.23
At fast-food restaurants*	2.96	8.48	3.00	4.57	15.98
At full-service restaurants	38.20	116.87	79.85	80.88	174.26
Other alcoholic beverages	50.30	118.10	75.06	97.79	169.58
At fast-food restaurants*	4.25	4.73	6.21	4.39	3.70
At full-service restaurants	45.99	113.17	68.85	92.71	165.88
Alcoholic beverages purchased on trips	44.84	123.39	78.74	113.74	167.64

* The category fast-food restaurants also includes take-out, delivery, concession stands, buffets, and cafeterias other than employer and school.
Note: Subcategories may not add to total because some are not shown. "–" means sample is too small to make a reliable estimate.
Source: Bureau of Labor Statistics, unpublished tables from the 2011 Consumer Expenditure Survey; calculations by New Strategist

Table 5.10 Food and Alcohol: Indexed spending by high-income consumer units, 2011

(indexed average annual spending of high-income consumer units on food and beverages, by before-tax income of consumer unit, 2011; index definition: an index of 100 is the average for all consumer units; an index of 125 means that spending by consumer units in that group is 25 percent above the average for all consumer units; an index of 75 indicates spending that is 25 percent below the average for all consumer units)

	total consumer units	$100,000 or more	$100,000– $119,999	$120,000– $149,999	$150,000 or more
Average spending of consumer units, total	$49,705	$97,728	$76,496	$87,239	$123,056
Average spending of consumer units, index	100	197	154	176	248
Food, spending index	100	174	148	165	202
Alcoholic beverages, spending index	100	223	163	205	287
FOOD AT HOME	**100**	**154**	**135**	**144**	**176**
Cereals and bakery products	**100**	**151**	**133**	**145**	**171**
Cereals and cereal products	100	151	137	144	167
Flour	100	165	102	174	212
Prepared flour mixes	100	148	118	154	170
Ready-to-eat and cooked cereals	100	148	136	153	154
Rice	100	131	148	98	141
Pasta, cornmeal, and other cereal products	100	171	147	143	211
Bakery products	100	151	132	145	172
Bread	100	147	130	134	171
White bread	100	135	118	119	161
Bread, other than white	100	156	138	145	179
Cookies and crackers	100	153	128	146	178
Cookies	100	144	121	137	168
Crackers	100	164	138	158	191
Frozen and refrigerated bakery products	100	155	124	168	172
Other bakery products	100	153	137	148	170
Biscuits and rolls	100	161	134	157	188
Cakes and cupcakes	100	150	147	132	165
Bread and cracker products	100	142	103	147	173
Sweetrolls, coffee cakes, doughnuts	100	144	149	123	154
Pies, tarts, turnovers	100	150	126	193	140
Meats, poultry, fish, and eggs	**100**	**152**	**133**	**144**	**174**
Beef	100	150	131	147	168
Ground beef	100	130	127	104	152
Roast	100	136	120	148	141
Chuck roast	100	126	72	162	147
Round roast	100	130	118	118	148
Other roast	100	142	143	152	135
Steak	100	165	147	183	168
Round steak	100	153	161	159	142
Sirloin steak	100	182	182	180	183
Other steak	100	161	124	193	170
Other beef	100	199	106	188	288
Pork	100	141	126	138	155
Bacon	100	140	122	145	152
Pork chops	100	129	149	107	128
Ham	100	134	127	137	137
Ham, not canned	100	132	121	140	136
Canned ham	100	201	359	50	172
Sausage	100	130	105	125	156
Other pork	100	163	126	166	192
Other meats	100	161	127	167	186
Frankfurters	100	134	110	152	142
Lunch meats (cold cuts)	100	167	134	155	204
Bologna, liverwurst, salami	100	160	119	154	198
Other lunch meats	100	170	140	155	206
Lamb, organ meats, and others	100	172	106	294	143

	total consumer units	$100,000 or more	$100,000– $119,999	$120,000– $149,999	$150,000 or more
Poultry	100	156	148	136	178
Fresh and frozen chicken	100	156	151	136	176
Fresh and frozen whole chicken	100	146	118	123	188
Fresh and frozen chicken parts	100	161	164	141	171
Other poultry	100	156	138	136	186
Fish and seafood	100	168	142	143	210
Canned fish and seafood	100	126	107	117	148
Fresh fish and shellfish	100	190	166	149	240
Frozen fish and shellfish	100	157	122	146	195
Eggs	100	129	118	124	141
Dairy products	**100**	**156**	**136**	**147**	**180**
Fresh milk and cream	100	142	122	128	170
Fresh milk, all types	100	140	122	125	166
Cream	100	157	125	146	193
Other dairy products	100	164	143	158	187
Butter	100	159	133	164	178
Cheese	100	166	147	154	191
Ice cream and related products	100	150	140	152	158
Miscellaneous dairy products	100	178	142	174	212
Fruits and vegetables	**100**	**161**	**137**	**149**	**191**
Fresh fruits	100	170	144	150	207
Apples	100	163	150	163	175
Bananas	100	145	138	126	164
Oranges	100	163	126	145	208
Citrus fruits, excluding oranges	100	173	151	149	209
Other fresh fruits	100	184	147	157	235
Fresh vegetables	100	167	145	154	196
Potatoes	100	151	139	167	150
Lettuce	100	162	140	150	190
Tomatoes	100	163	144	157	183
Other fresh vegetables	100	176	148	150	219
Processed fruits	100	149	119	143	179
Frozen fruits and fruit juices	100	144	100	161	169
Frozen orange juice	100	136	140	163	113
Frozen fruits	100	153	79	167	206
Frozen fruit juices, excluding orange	100	131	100	142	150
Canned fruits	100	139	120	118	170
Dried fruits	100	165	109	141	230
Fresh fruit juice	100	169	127	176	200
Canned and bottled fruit juice	100	146	122	138	172
Processed vegetables	100	143	123	143	161
Frozen vegetables	100	153	151	135	166
Canned and dried vegetables and juices	100	140	113	146	159
Canned beans	100	132	134	146	120
Canned corn	100	117	70	117	158
Canned miscellaneous vegetables	100	143	104	150	171
Dried peas	100	165	151	107	220
Dried beans	100	116	134	121	97
Dried miscellaneous vegetables	100	145	121	150	161
Dried processed vegetables	100	117	4	136	200
Fresh and canned vegetable juices	100	160	125	161	191
Sugar and other sweets	**100**	**152**	**132**	**143**	**175**
Candy and chewing gum	100	164	140	146	197
Sugar	100	110	98	116	115
Artificial sweeteners	100	164	196	150	148
Jams, preserves, other sweets	100	148	123	153	166

	total consumer units	$100,000 or more	$100,000– $119,999	$120,000– $149,999	$150,000 or more
Fats and oils	100	131	122	128	140
Margarine	100	118	116	129	112
Fats and oils	100	123	127	108	131
Salad dressings	100	143	116	151	159
Nondairy cream and imitation milk	100	128	130	117	134
Peanut butter	100	135	114	140	149
Miscellaneous foods	100	151	136	145	169
Frozen prepared foods	100	141	128	132	159
Frozen meals	100	144	144	137	149
Other frozen prepared foods	100	139	114	129	168
Canned and packaged soups	100	145	123	149	160
Potato chips, nuts, and other snacks	100	161	145	149	183
Potato chips and other snacks	100	151	138	148	163
Nuts	100	192	166	151	243
Condiments and seasonings	100	154	135	148	174
Salt, spices, and other seasonings	100	157	144	137	183
Olives, pickles, relishes	100	164	134	175	182
Sauces and gravies	100	152	128	163	166
Baking needs and miscellaneous products	100	146	142	109	175
Other canned or packaged prepared foods	100	150	139	146	163
Prepared salads	100	165	150	162	180
Prepared desserts	100	141	106	156	161
Baby food	100	103	146	72	89
Miscellaneous prepared foods	100	157	139	157	172
Nonalcoholic beverages	100	144	134	126	164
Cola	100	132	133	115	144
Other carbonated drinks	100	141	139	118	160
Tea	100	147	155	137	148
Coffee	100	153	128	123	196
Noncarbonated fruit-flavored drinks	100	127	133	138	115
Other noncarbonated beverages and ice	100	121	91	103	160
Bottled water	100	150	138	129	175
Sports drinks	100	181	143	186	210
Food prepared by consumer unit on trips	100	245	184	221	313
FOOD AWAY FROM HOME	100	204	167	196	240
Meals at restaurants, carry-outs, etc.	100	191	165	186	217
Lunch	100	191	164	189	217
At fast-food restaurants*	100	165	158	169	169
At full-service restaurants	100	214	163	208	263
At vending machines, mobile vendors	100	133	145	174	94
At employer and school cafeterias	100	234	204	216	274
Dinner	100	201	167	197	233
At fast-food restaurants*	100	155	152	159	153
At full-service restaurants	100	227	177	218	277
At vending machines, mobile vendors	100	48	16	107	34
At employer and school cafeterias	100	145	31	236	180
Snacks and nonalcoholic beverages	100	174	171	149	193
At fast-food restaurants*	100	184	184	145	211
At full-service restaurants	100	174	156	172	190
At vending machines, mobile vendors	100	126	135	160	95
At employer and school cafeterias	100	128	126	65	175
Breakfast and brunch	100	158	151	154	167
At fast-food restaurants*	100	164	166	167	161
At full-service restaurants	100	150	137	133	174
At vending machines, mobile vendors	100	109	117	131	85
At employer and school cafeterias	100	163	103	185	198

	total consumer units	$100,000 or more	$100,000–$119,999	$120,000–$149,999	$150,000 or more
Board (including at school)	100	379	196	262	616
Catered affairs	100	326	175	330	451
Food on trips	100	265	177	248	349
School lunches	100	229	232	223	230
Meals as pay	100	109	90	109	126
ALCOHOLIC BEVERAGES	100	223	163	205	287
At home	100	198	145	211	233
Beer and ale	100	156	138	155	173
Whiskey	100	171	114	225	183
Wine	100	245	159	265	306
Other alcoholic beverages	100	187	122	232	209
Away from home	100	252	184	197	349
Beer and ale	100	223	202	163	284
At fast-food restaurants*	100	176	214	100	197
At full-service restaurants	100	236	203	179	305
At vending machines, mobile vendors	100	85	58	–	168
Wine	100	300	202	204	453
At fast-food restaurants*	100	286	101	154	540
At full-service restaurants	100	306	209	212	456
Other alcoholic beverages	100	235	149	194	337
At fast-food restaurants*	100	111	146	103	87
At full-service restaurants	100	246	150	202	361
Alcoholic beverages purchased on trips	100	275	176	254	374

The category fast-food restaurants also includes take-out, delivery, concession stands, buffets, and cafeterias other than employer and school.
Note: "–" means sample is too small to make a reliable estimate.
Source: Calculations by New Strategist based on the Bureau of Labor Statistics' 2011 Consumer Expenditure Survey

Table 5.11 Food and Alcohol: Total spending by high-income consumer units, 2011

(total annual spending on food and alcoholic beverages, by before-tax income group of high-income consumer units, 2011; consumer units and dollars in thousands)

	total consumer units	$100,000 or more	$100,000–$119,999	$120,000–$149,999	$150,000 or more
Number of consumer units	122,287	21,593	7,045	6,107	8,440
Total spending of all consumer units	$6,078,260,661	$2,110,245,454	$538,917,208	$532,771,260	$1,038,595,847
Food, total spending	789,729,446	242,554,169	67,413,605	65,186,118	110,184,200
Alcoholic beverages, total spending	55,815,455	21,982,538	5,250,639	5,705,465	11,068,469
FOOD AT HOME	469,308,157	127,331,330	36,523,253	33,790,642	57,123,524
Cereals and bakery products	64,895,265	17,305,710	4,990,114	4,686,329	7,645,543
Cereals and cereal products	21,383,105	5,690,619	1,685,939	1,536,704	2,471,907
Flour	937,941	272,504	55,162	81,651	136,981
Prepared flour mixes	1,819,631	476,126	123,428	140,095	213,701
Ready-to-eat and cooked cereals	11,175,809	2,914,623	875,975	853,636	1,187,930
Rice	3,137,884	728,116	266,865	154,141	304,937
Pasta, cornmeal, and other cereal products	4,311,840	1,299,467	364,579	307,121	628,274
Bakery products	43,510,937	11,615,091	3,304,175	3,149,624	5,173,720
Bread	13,027,234	3,379,736	972,069	871,774	1,538,274
White bread	5,494,355	1,308,320	373,808	326,297	608,946
Bread, other than white	7,532,879	2,071,416	598,261	545,477	929,328
Cookies and crackers	10,221,970	2,755,267	755,365	746,520	1,257,307
Cookies	5,742,598	1,458,175	399,945	393,779	666,507
Crackers	4,479,373	1,297,092	355,491	352,740	590,800
Frozen and refrigerated bakery products	3,497,408	955,706	248,970	294,296	414,995
Other bakery products	16,764,325	4,524,165	1,327,771	1,237,034	1,963,144
Biscuits and rolls	6,472,651	1,844,474	498,504	507,797	841,299
Cakes and cupcakes	4,623,671	1,221,300	390,293	304,984	525,390
Bread and cracker products	871,906	219,385	51,640	64,062	104,403
Sweetrolls, coffee cakes, doughnuts	2,917,768	742,583	251,084	179,424	311,098
Pies, tarts, turnovers	1,878,328	496,423	136,321	180,828	180,954
Meats, poultry, fish, and eggs	101,792,922	27,371,503	7,818,611	7,326,385	12,252,770
Beef	27,221,086	7,195,867	2,059,254	1,992,164	3,152,678
Ground beef	11,066,974	2,543,871	806,864	576,318	1,158,306
Roast	3,740,759	895,894	258,411	275,792	363,173
Chuck roast	935,496	208,157	38,536	75,788	95,034
Round roast	747,174	171,017	50,794	44,093	76,298
Other roast	2,056,867	516,720	169,080	155,912	191,841
Steak	10,087,455	2,937,512	851,600	921,730	1,169,446
Round steak	1,944,363	526,221	180,563	154,568	190,913
Sirloin steak	2,673,194	858,538	280,039	240,677	337,853
Other steak	5,469,898	1,552,537	390,998	526,484	640,765
Other beef	2,325,899	818,591	142,309	218,264	461,668
Pork	19,804,380	4,915,646	1,433,517	1,369,312	2,117,680
Bacon	4,141,861	1,026,099	291,804	299,976	435,926
Pork chops	3,331,098	760,721	286,309	178,569	293,712
Ham	4,193,221	988,528	306,317	287,884	395,076
Ham, not canned	4,097,837	954,842	286,591	285,502	383,767
Canned ham	95,384	33,901	19,726	2,382	11,310
Sausage	3,491,294	804,123	211,350	218,508	375,580
Other pork	4,645,683	1,336,175	337,737	384,375	617,217
Other meats	14,985,049	4,260,731	1,092,680	1,250,714	1,927,865
Frankfurters	2,894,533	683,418	183,100	219,302	282,993
Lunch meats (cold cuts)	10,720,901	3,160,567	825,744	830,491	1,509,578
Bologna, liverwurst, salami	3,280,960	925,476	225,440	253,013	449,346
Other lunch meats	7,439,941	2,235,091	600,304	577,478	1,060,233
Lamb, organ meats, and others	1,369,614	416,529	83,836	200,920	135,293

	total consumer units	$100,000 or more	$100,000– $119,999	$120,000– $149,999	$150,000 or more
Poultry	$18,892,119	$5,218,380	$1,613,375	$1,281,004	$2,322,519
Fresh and frozen chicken	15,217,394	4,205,021	1,322,276	1,030,678	1,850,132
Fresh and frozen whole chicken	4,398,663	1,137,735	298,215	271,090	569,700
Fresh and frozen chicken parts	10,819,954	3,067,286	1,024,061	759,589	1,280,348
Other poultry	3,674,724	1,013,359	291,099	250,265	472,471
Fish and seafood	14,767,378	4,390,505	1,204,977	1,053,091	2,135,742
Canned fish and seafood	2,433,511	540,257	150,552	142,476	247,883
Fresh fish and shellfish	7,277,299	2,445,839	697,666	542,302	1,205,823
Frozen fish and shellfish	5,056,567	1,404,409	356,759	368,252	681,952
Eggs	6,122,910	1,390,373	414,880	380,100	596,286
Dairy products	**49,751,243**	**13,721,056**	**3,885,599**	**3,653,818**	**6,195,466**
Fresh milk and cream	18,310,033	4,601,468	1,290,503	1,169,368	2,145,279
Fresh milk, all types	15,576,918	3,841,827	1,094,229	969,425	1,780,671
Cream	2,734,337	759,642	196,274	199,943	364,692
Other dairy productsa	31,439,988	9,119,588	2,595,096	2,484,450	4,050,103
Butter	3,013,152	847,741	231,499	246,662	371,191
Cheese	15,254,080	4,472,342	1,293,392	1,170,223	2,012,012
Ice cream and related products	7,004,599	1,858,941	564,939	531,553	763,736
Miscellaneous dairy products	6,166,933	1,940,563	505,197	536,011	903,249
Fruits and vegetables	**87,421,753**	**24,871,897**	**6,880,077**	**6,501,695**	**11,518,068**
Fresh fruits	30,239,129	9,090,653	2,514,713	2,266,674	4,317,060
Apples	4,667,695	1,344,164	402,833	380,283	562,273
Bananas	5,023,550	1,282,840	399,099	314,877	568,518
Oranges	3,300,526	951,604	240,164	238,539	474,412
Citrus fruits, excluding oranges	4,601,660	1,407,216	401,354	343,030	663,553
Other fresh fruits	12,646,922	4,104,613	1,071,333	989,945	2,048,304
Fresh vegetables	27,417,968	8,106,012	2,287,089	2,112,228	3,714,191
Potatoes	4,742,290	1,266,214	380,430	395,184	492,474
Lettuce	3,933,973	1,125,859	317,730	293,747	515,346
Tomatoes	5,017,436	1,442,196	416,994	392,802	633,760
Other fresh vegetables	13,725,493	4,271,743	1,171,865	1,030,434	2,072,611
Processed fruits	14,152,275	3,724,577	969,392	1,009,731	1,752,313
Frozen fruits and fruit juices	1,627,640	413,290	94,051	130,934	189,816
Frozen orange juice	456,131	109,477	36,845	37,192	35,617
Frozen fruits	846,226	228,238	38,466	70,597	120,439
Frozen fruit juices, excluding orange	326,506	75,360	18,740	23,146	33,760
Canned fruits	2,597,376	637,209	178,873	152,980	305,612
Dried fruits	994,193	289,130	62,278	69,864	157,744
Fresh fruit juice	2,113,119	630,516	154,779	186,202	291,433
Canned and bottled fruit juice	6,821,169	1,754,431	479,342	469,750	807,708
Processed vegetables	15,611,158	3,950,655	1,108,883	1,113,001	1,734,420
Frozen vegetables	4,277,599	1,152,202	371,624	288,556	491,292
Canned and dried vegetables and juices	11,333,559	2,798,453	737,259	824,445	1,243,212
Canned beans	2,333,236	544,144	180,634	170,446	193,192
Canned corn	1,189,853	245,944	47,695	69,376	130,060
Canned miscellaneous vegetables	3,118,319	786,633	186,199	234,081	368,997
Dried peas	102,721	30,014	8,947	5,496	15,614
Dried beans	610,212	125,023	46,990	37,008	40,850
Dried miscellaneous vegetables	1,412,415	361,035	98,278	106,140	157,322
Dried processed vegetables	250,688	51,607	634	17,039	34,520
Fresh and canned vegetable juices	2,273,315	643,471	163,162	182,233	299,451
Sugar and other sweets	**17,657,020**	**4,735,561**	**1,343,904**	**1,258,286**	**2,138,021**
Candy and chewing gum	10,608,397	3,072,900	857,306	774,795	1,443,324
Sugar	2,921,436	565,089	165,698	169,042	231,087
Artificial sweeteners	686,030	199,087	77,284	51,299	70,052
Jams, preserves, other sweets	3,441,156	898,485	243,546	263,151	393,557

	total consumer units	$100,000 or more	$100,000– $119,999	$120,000– $149,999	$150,000 or more
Fats and oils	$13,403,878	$3,093,413	$939,028	$858,278	$1,297,988
Margarine	1,194,744	248,751	79,609	76,704	92,671
Fats and oils	4,260,479	927,635	311,459	230,417	384,695
Salad dressings	3,810,463	960,025	255,099	288,189	418,962
Nondairy cream and imitation milk	2,273,315	512,834	170,278	132,278	209,987
Peanut butter	1,864,877	444,168	122,513	130,690	191,672
Miscellaneous foods	84,436,728	22,531,432	6,631,811	6,096,007	9,820,193
Frozen prepared foods	16,659,158	4,157,732	1,226,253	1,101,275	1,832,577
Frozen meals	7,598,914	1,932,358	632,359	518,973	780,362
Other frozen prepared foods	9,060,244	2,225,375	593,894	582,302	1,052,299
Canned and packaged soups	5,735,260	1,464,005	407,060	426,391	633,084
Potato chips, nuts, and other snacks	17,734,061	5,047,148	1,484,945	1,318,929	2,245,968
Potato chips and other snacks	13,208,219	3,514,693	1,051,466	977,364	1,488,478
Nuts	4,525,842	1,532,455	433,479	341,626	757,574
Condiments and seasonings	16,374,229	4,450,749	1,277,963	1,207,049	1,970,065
Salt, spices, and other seasonings	4,330,183	1,202,730	359,718	295,884	547,165
Olives, pickles, relishes	1,972,489	571,351	152,313	172,095	248,136
Sauces and gravies	7,145,229	1,923,289	526,050	580,287	821,043
Baking needs and miscellaneous products	2,926,328	753,380	239,882	158,782	353,636
Other canned or packaged prepared foods	27,932,797	7,411,797	2,235,519	2,042,364	3,138,414
Prepared salads	4,429,235	1,289,102	381,487	357,504	551,216
Prepared desserts	1,837,974	458,635	111,945	143,453	204,670
Baby food	3,399,579	619,503	285,041	122,262	208,384
Miscellaneous prepared foods	17,989,641	4,976,971	1,440,562	1,412,122	2,130,087
Nonalcoholic beverages	44,141,938	11,188,197	3,416,684	2,768,120	5,001,966
Cola	9,632,547	2,247,831	735,850	551,279	958,700
Other carbonated drinks	8,158,989	2,033,629	653,917	479,644	898,269
Tea	3,810,463	991,982	341,119	261,624	388,324
Coffee	9,175,194	2,480,604	678,293	561,478	1,241,946
Noncarbonated fruit-flavored drinks	3,027,826	680,395	232,344	208,554	239,443
Other noncarbonated beverages and ice	1,825,745	391,481	96,164	93,926	202,054
Bottled water	6,539,909	1,730,679	520,203	422,604	787,958
Sports drinks	1,923,575	614,969	158,794	178,874	278,773
Food prepared by consumer unit on trips	5,808,633	2,512,777	617,353	641,601	1,253,678
FOOD AWAY FROM HOME	320,378,488	115,226,510	30,889,859	31,394,499	53,057,554
Meals at restaurants, carry-outs, etc.	268,528,800	90,656,267	25,483,244	25,003,279	40,286,314
Lunch	92,068,659	31,127,389	8,705,859	8,693,742	13,771,632
At fast-food restaurants*	45,097,000	13,159,206	4,096,668	3,798,065	5,271,962
At full-service restaurants	36,931,897	13,969,159	3,460,927	3,831,471	6,709,631
At vending machines, mobile vendors	875,575	205,565	72,916	75,971	56,717
At employer and school cafeterias	9,164,188	3,793,458	1,075,419	988,235	1,733,238
Dinner	128,529,751	45,596,427	12,370,950	12,675,506	20,625,250
At fast-food restaurants*	44,650,652	12,193,999	3,916,950	3,552,259	4,728,426
At full-service restaurants	82,673,349	33,155,836	8,435,753	9,004,894	15,783,897
At vending machines, mobile vendors	369,307	31,310	3,382	19,665	8,778
At employer and school cafeterias	837,666	215,066	14,865	98,689	104,065
Snacks and nonalcoholic beverages	20,310,648	6,230,444	2,002,400	1,511,238	2,712,110
At fast-food restaurants*	13,408,770	4,354,660	1,422,315	973,089	1,953,607
At full-service restaurants	4,001,231	1,227,562	359,084	344,007	525,728
At vending machines, mobile vendors	2,113,119	470,080	164,008	168,553	137,994
At employer and school cafeterias	786,305	177,926	57,065	25,649	94,781
Breakfast and brunch	27,619,742	7,702,007	2,404,036	2,122,732	3,177,407
At fast-food restaurants*	15,135,462	4,387,050	1,443,521	1,261,523	1,681,923
At full-service restaurants	10,931,235	2,904,259	865,267	727,710	1,311,829
At vending machines, mobile vendors	370,530	71,041	24,939	24,306	21,860
At employer and school cafeterias	1,181,292	339,658	70,239	109,193	161,710

	total consumer units	$100,000 or more	$100,000– $119,999	$120,000– $149,999	$150,000 or more
Board (including at school)	$5,364,731	$3,589,188	$606,222	$702,183	$2,280,657
Catered affairs	6,435,965	3,710,109	647,647	1,060,847	2,001,377
Food on trips	28,919,653	13,518,514	2,953,898	3,588,779	6,975,069
School lunches	7,601,360	3,072,036	1,016,523	847,591	1,207,848
Meals as pay	3,527,980	680,395	182,395	191,821	306,119
ALCOHOLIC BEVERAGES	55,815,455	21,982,538	5,250,639	5,705,465	11,068,469
At home	29,636,254	10,336,353	2,474,627	3,123,731	4,771,132
Beer and ale	13,422,221	3,702,120	1,066,543	1,039,961	1,599,971
Whiskey	1,173,955	355,421	77,002	131,972	148,291
Wine	12,721,517	5,514,636	1,167,709	1,682,479	2,687,549
Other alcoholic beverages	2,319,784	764,176	163,374	269,319	335,237
Away from home	26,179,201	11,646,400	2,776,012	2,581,734	6,297,337
Beer and ale	9,413,653	3,711,621	1,095,357	768,138	1,845,659
At fast-food restaurants*	1,524,919	473,750	188,242	76,338	206,864
At full-service restaurants	7,743,213	3,224,699	903,380	691,801	1,629,595
At vending machines, mobile vendors	79,487	11,876	2,677	–	9,200
Wine	5,131,163	2,720,502	597,134	521,782	1,605,541
At fast-food restaurants*	361,970	183,109	21,135	27,909	134,871
At full-service restaurants	4,671,363	2,523,574	562,543	493,934	1,470,754
Other alcoholic beverages	6,151,036	2,550,133	528,798	597,204	1,431,255
At fast-food restaurants*	519,720	102,135	43,749	26,810	31,228
At full-service restaurants	5,623,979	2,443,680	485,048	566,180	1,400,027
Alcoholic beverages purchased on trips	5,483,349	2,664,360	554,723	694,610	1,414,882

* The category fast-food restaurants also includes take-out, delivery, concession stands, buffets, and cafeterias other than employer and school.
Note: Numbers may not add to total because of rounding and missing subcategories. "–" means sample is too small to make a reliable estimate.
Source: Calculations by New Strategist based on the Bureau of Labor Statistics' 2011 Consumer Expenditure Survey

Table 5.12 Food and Alcohol: Market shares by high-income consumer units, 2011

(percentage of total annual spending on food and alcoholic beverages accounted for by before-tax income group of high-income consumer units, 2011)

	total consumer units	$100,000 or more	$100,000–$119,999	$120,000–$149,999	$150,000 or more
Share of total consumer units	100.0%	17.7%	5.8%	5.0%	6.9%
Share of total before-tax income	100.0	47.1	9.8	10.5	26.8
Share of total spending	100.0	34.7	8.9	8.8	17.1
Share of food spending	100.0	30.7	8.5	8.3	14.0
Share of alcoholic beverages spending	100.0	39.4	9.4	10.2	19.8
FOOD AT HOME	100.0	27.1	7.8	7.2	12.2
Cereals and bakery products	100.0	26.7	7.7	7.2	11.8
Cereals and cereal products	100.0	26.6	7.9	7.2	11.6
Flour	100.0	29.1	5.9	8.7	14.6
Prepared flour mixes	100.0	26.2	6.8	7.7	11.7
Ready-to-eat and cooked cereals	100.0	26.1	7.8	7.6	10.6
Rice	100.0	23.2	8.5	4.9	9.7
Pasta, cornmeal, and other cereal products	100.0	30.1	8.5	7.1	14.6
Bakery products	100.0	26.7	7.6	7.2	11.9
Bread	100.0	25.9	7.5	6.7	11.8
White bread	100.0	23.8	6.8	5.9	11.1
Bread, other than white	100.0	27.5	7.9	7.2	12.3
Cookies and crackers	100.0	27.0	7.4	7.3	12.3
Cookies	100.0	25.4	7.0	6.9	11.6
Crackers	100.0	29.0	7.9	7.9	13.2
Frozen and refrigerated bakery products	100.0	27.3	7.1	8.4	11.9
Other bakery products	100.0	27.0	7.9	7.4	11.7
Biscuits and rolls	100.0	28.5	7.7	7.8	13.0
Cakes and cupcakes	100.0	26.4	8.4	6.6	11.4
Bread and cracker products	100.0	25.2	5.9	7.3	12.0
Sweetrolls, coffee cakes, doughnuts	100.0	25.5	8.6	6.1	10.7
Pies, tarts, turnovers	100.0	26.4	7.3	9.6	9.6
Meats, poultry, fish, and eggs	100.0	26.9	7.7	7.2	12.0
Beef	100.0	26.4	7.6	7.3	11.6
Ground beef	100.0	23.0	7.3	5.2	10.5
Roast	100.0	23.9	6.9	7.4	9.7
Chuck roast	100.0	22.3	4.1	8.1	10.2
Round roast	100.0	22.9	6.8	5.9	10.2
Other roast	100.0	25.1	8.2	7.6	9.3
Steak	100.0	29.1	8.4	9.1	11.6
Round steak	100.0	27.1	9.3	7.9	9.8
Sirloin steak	100.0	32.1	10.5	9.0	12.6
Other steak	100.0	28.4	7.1	9.6	11.7
Other beef	100.0	35.2	6.1	9.4	19.8
Pork	100.0	24.8	7.2	6.9	10.7
Bacon	100.0	24.8	7.0	7.2	10.5
Pork chops	100.0	22.8	8.6	5.4	8.8
Ham	100.0	23.6	7.3	6.9	9.4
Ham, not canned	100.0	23.3	7.0	7.0	9.4
Canned ham	100.0	35.5	20.7	2.5	11.9
Sausage	100.0	23.0	6.1	6.3	10.8
Other pork	100.0	28.8	7.3	8.3	13.3
Other meats	100.0	28.4	7.3	8.3	12.9
Frankfurters	100.0	23.6	6.3	7.6	9.8
Lunch meats (cold cuts)	100.0	29.5	7.7	7.7	14.1
Bologna, liverwurst, salami	100.0	28.2	6.9	7.7	13.7
Other lunch meats	100.0	30.0	8.1	7.8	14.3
Lamb, organ meats, and others	100.0	30.4	6.1	14.7	9.9

	total consumer units	$100,000 or more	$100,000–$119,999	$120,000–$149,999	$150,000 or more
Poultry	100.0%	27.6%	8.5%	6.8%	12.3%
Fresh and frozen chicken	100.0	27.6	8.7	6.8	12.2
Fresh and frozen whole chicken	100.0	25.9	6.8	6.2	13.0
Fresh and frozen chicken parts	100.0	28.3	9.5	7.0	11.8
Other poultry	100.0	27.6	7.9	6.8	12.9
Fish and seafood	100.0	29.7	8.2	7.1	14.5
Canned fish and seafood	100.0	22.2	6.2	5.9	10.2
Fresh fish and shellfish	100.0	33.6	9.6	7.5	16.6
Frozen fish and shellfish	100.0	27.8	7.1	7.3	13.5
Eggs	100.0	22.7	6.8	6.2	9.7
Dairy products	**100.0**	**27.6**	**7.8**	**7.3**	**12.5**
Fresh milk and cream	100.0	25.1	7.0	6.4	11.7
Fresh milk, all types	100.0	24.7	7.0	6.2	11.4
Cream	100.0	27.8	7.2	7.3	13.3
Other dairy products	100.0	29.0	8.3	7.9	12.9
Butter	100.0	28.1	7.7	8.2	12.3
Cheese	100.0	29.3	8.5	7.7	13.2
Ice cream and related products	100.0	26.5	8.1	7.6	10.9
Miscellaneous dairy products	100.0	31.5	8.2	8.7	14.6
Fruits and vegetables	**100.0**	**28.5**	**7.9**	**7.4**	**13.2**
Fresh fruits	100.0	30.1	8.3	7.5	14.3
Apples	100.0	28.8	8.6	8.1	12.0
Bananas	100.0	25.5	7.9	6.3	11.3
Oranges	100.0	28.8	7.3	7.2	14.4
Citrus fruits, excluding oranges	100.0	30.6	8.7	7.5	14.4
Other fresh fruits	100.0	32.5	8.5	7.8	16.2
Fresh vegetables	100.0	29.6	8.3	7.7	13.5
Potatoes	100.0	26.7	8.0	8.3	10.4
Lettuce	100.0	28.6	8.1	7.5	13.1
Tomatoes	100.0	28.7	8.3	7.8	12.6
Other fresh vegetables	100.0	31.1	8.5	7.5	15.1
Processed fruits	100.0	26.3	6.8	7.1	12.4
Frozen fruits and fruit juices	100.0	25.4	5.8	8.0	11.7
Frozen orange juice	100.0	24.0	8.1	8.2	7.8
Frozen fruits	100.0	27.0	4.5	8.3	14.2
Frozen fruit juices, excluding orange	100.0	23.1	5.7	7.1	10.3
Canned fruits	100.0	24.5	6.9	5.9	11.8
Dried fruits	100.0	29.1	6.3	7.0	15.9
Fresh fruit juice	100.0	29.8	7.3	8.8	13.8
Canned and bottled fruit juice	100.0	25.7	7.0	6.9	11.8
Processed vegetables	100.0	25.3	7.1	7.1	11.1
Frozen vegetables	100.0	26.9	8.7	6.7	11.5
Canned and dried vegetables and juices	100.0	24.7	6.5	7.3	11.0
Canned beans	100.0	23.3	7.7	7.3	8.3
Canned corn	100.0	20.7	4.0	5.8	10.9
Canned miscellaneous vegetables	100.0	25.2	6.0	7.5	11.8
Dried peas	100.0	29.2	8.7	5.4	15.2
Dried beans	100.0	20.5	7.7	6.1	6.7
Dried miscellaneous vegetables	100.0	25.6	7.0	7.5	11.1
Dried processed vegetables	100.0	20.6	0.3	6.8	13.8
Fresh and canned vegetable juices	100.0	28.3	7.2	8.0	13.2
Sugar and other sweets	**100.0**	**26.8**	**7.6**	**7.1**	**12.1**
Candy and chewing gum	100.0	29.0	8.1	7.3	13.6
Sugar	100.0	19.3	5.7	5.8	7.9
Artificial sweeteners	100.0	29.0	11.3	7.5	10.2
Jams, preserves, other sweets	100.0	26.1	7.1	7.6	11.4

	total consumer units	$100,000 or more	$100,000– $119,999	$120,000– $149,999	$150,000 or more
Fats and oils	100.0%	23.1%	7.0%	6.4%	9.7%
Margarine	100.0	20.8	6.7	6.4	7.8
Fats and oils	100.0	21.8	7.3	5.4	9.0
Salad dressings	100.0	25.2	6.7	7.6	11.0
Nondairy cream and imitation milk	100.0	22.6	7.5	5.8	9.2
Peanut butter	100.0	23.8	6.6	7.0	10.3
Miscellaneous foods	100.0	26.7	7.9	7.2	11.6
Frozen prepared foods	100.0	25.0	7.4	6.6	11.0
Frozen meals	100.0	25.4	8.3	6.8	10.3
Other frozen prepared foods	100.0	24.6	6.6	6.4	11.6
Canned and packaged soups	100.0	25.5	7.1	7.4	11.0
Potato chips, nuts, and other snacks	100.0	28.5	8.4	7.4	12.7
Potato chips and other snacks	100.0	26.6	8.0	7.4	11.3
Nuts	100.0	33.9	9.6	7.5	16.7
Condiments and seasonings	100.0	27.2	7.8	7.4	12.0
Salt, spices, and other seasonings	100.0	27.8	8.3	6.8	12.6
Olives, pickles, relishes	100.0	29.0	7.7	8.7	12.6
Sauces and gravies	100.0	26.9	7.4	8.1	11.5
Baking needs and miscellaneous products	100.0	25.7	8.2	5.4	12.1
Other canned or packaged prepared foods	100.0	26.5	8.0	7.3	11.2
Prepared salads	100.0	29.1	8.6	8.1	12.4
Prepared desserts	100.0	25.0	6.1	7.8	11.1
Baby food	100.0	18.2	8.4	3.6	6.1
Miscellaneous prepared foods	100.0	27.7	8.0	7.8	11.8
Nonalcoholic beverages	100.0	25.3	7.7	6.3	11.3
Cola	100.0	23.3	7.6	5.7	10.0
Other carbonated drinks	100.0	24.9	8.0	5.9	11.0
Tea	100.0	26.0	9.0	6.9	10.2
Coffee	100.0	27.0	7.4	6.1	13.5
Noncarbonated fruit-flavored drinks	100.0	22.5	7.7	6.9	7.9
Other noncarbonated beverages and ice	100.0	21.4	5.3	5.1	11.1
Bottled water	100.0	26.5	8.0	6.5	12.0
Sports drinks	100.0	32.0	8.3	9.3	14.5
Food prepared by consumer unit on trips	100.0	43.3	10.6	11.0	21.6
FOOD AWAY FROM HOME	100.0	36.0	9.6	9.8	16.6
Meals at restaurants, carry-outs, etc.	100.0	33.8	9.5	9.3	15.0
Lunch	100.0	33.8	9.5	9.4	15.0
At fast-food restaurants*	100.0	29.2	9.1	8.4	11.7
At full-service restaurants	100.0	37.8	9.4	10.4	18.2
At vending machines, mobile vendors	100.0	23.5	8.3	8.7	6.5
At employer and school cafeterias	100.0	41.4	11.7	10.8	18.9
Dinner	100.0	35.5	9.6	9.9	16.0
At fast-food restaurants*	100.0	27.3	8.8	8.0	10.6
At full-service restaurants	100.0	40.1	10.2	10.9	19.1
At vending machines, mobile vendors	100.0	8.5	0.9	5.3	2.4
At employer and school cafeterias	100.0	25.7	1.8	11.8	12.4
Snacks and nonalcoholic beverages	100.0	30.7	9.9	7.4	13.4
At fast-food restaurants*	100.0	32.5	10.6	7.3	14.6
At full-service restaurants	100.0	30.7	9.0	8.6	13.1
At vending machines, mobile vendors	100.0	22.2	7.8	8.0	6.5
At employer and school cafeterias	100.0	22.6	7.3	3.3	12.1
Breakfast and brunch	100.0	27.9	8.7	7.7	11.5
At fast-food restaurants*	100.0	29.0	9.5	8.3	11.1
At full-service restaurants	100.0	26.6	7.9	6.7	12.0
At vending machines, mobile vendors	100.0	19.2	6.7	6.6	5.9
At employer and school cafeterias	100.0	28.8	5.9	9.2	13.7

	total consumer units	$100,000 or more	$100,000– $119,999	$120,000– $149,999	$150,000 or more
Board (including at school)	100.0%	66.9%	11.3%	13.1%	42.5%
Catered affairs	100.0	57.6	10.1	16.5	31.1
Food on trips	100.0	46.7	10.2	12.4	24.1
School lunches	100.0	40.4	13.4	11.2	15.9
Meals as pay	100.0	19.3	5.2	5.4	8.7
ALCOHOLIC BEVERAGES	100.0	39.4	9.4	10.2	19.8
At home	100.0	34.9	8.3	10.5	16.1
Beer and ale	100.0	27.6	7.9	7.7	11.9
Whiskey	100.0	30.3	6.6	11.2	12.6
Wine	100.0	43.3	9.2	13.2	21.1
Other alcoholic beverages	100.0	32.9	7.0	11.6	14.5
Away from home	100.0	44.5	10.6	9.9	24.1
Beer and ale	100.0	39.4	11.6	8.2	19.6
At fast-food restaurants*	100.0	31.1	12.3	5.0	13.6
At full-service restaurants	100.0	41.6	11.7	8.9	21.0
At vending machines, mobile vendors	100.0	14.9	3.4	–	11.6
Wine	100.0	53.0	11.6	10.2	31.3
At fast-food restaurants*	100.0	50.6	5.8	7.7	37.3
At full-service restaurants	100.0	54.0	12.0	10.6	31.5
Other alcoholic beverages	100.0	41.5	8.6	9.7	23.3
At fast-food restaurants*	100.0	19.7	8.4	5.2	6.0
At full-service restaurants	100.0	43.5	8.6	10.1	24.9
Alcoholic beverages purchased on trips	100.0	48.6	10.1	12.7	25.8

* The category fast-food restaurants also includes take-out, delivery, concession stands, buffets, and cafeterias other than employer and school.
Note: Numbers may not add to total because of rounding. "–" means sample is too small to make a reliable estimate.
Source: Calculations by New Strategist based on the Bureau of Labor Statistics' 2011 Consumer Expenditure

Table 5.13 Food and Alcohol: Average spending by household type, 2011

(average annual spending of consumer units on food and alcoholic beverages, by type of consumer unit, 2011)

	total married couples	married couples, no children	married couples with children				single parent with child under age 18	single person
			total	oldest child under age 6	oldest child aged 6 to 17	oldest child aged 18 or older		
Number of consumer units (in 000s)	60,144	25,270	29,097	5,825	14,661	8,612	6,956	36,110
Average number of persons per consumer unit	3.2	2.0	4.0	3.5	4.2	3.9	2.9	1.0
Average before-tax income of consumer units	$86,700.00	$78,823.00	$93,677.00	$91,014.00	$93,029.00	$96,583.00	$37,188.00	$34,540.00
Average spending of consumer units, total	63,971.54	57,658.24	69,724.22	65,947.61	70,708.52	70,411.85	37,553.05	30,613.18
Food, average spending	**8,315.00**	**6,895.00**	**9,557.00**	**8,028.00**	**9,813.00**	**10,042.00**	**5,676.00**	**3,638.00**
Alcoholic beverages, average spending	**514.95**	**610.23**	**458.71**	**423.96**	**458.65**	**479.45**	**245.71**	**369.87**
FOOD AT HOME	**4,944.39**	**3,935.46**	**5,785.25**	**5,009.91**	**5,877.30**	**6,080.49**	**3,526.18**	**2,071.50**
Cereals and bakery products	**686.89**	**535.11**	**820.11**	**672.91**	**863.65**	**832.11**	**519.48**	**284.55**
Cereals and cereal products	224.69	167.80	274.99	231.95	294.95	266.31	194.40	90.94
Flour	9.97	6.94	12.36	10.23	13.91	10.97	4.04	5.46
Prepared flour mixes	19.85	17.05	22.66	19.45	23.60	22.93	17.87	6.76
Ready-to-eat and cooked cereals	117.68	86.88	147.54	122.82	161.60	138.20	102.74	48.01
Rice	30.67	22.17	36.21	26.66	38.35	38.14	36.24	12.50
Pasta, cornmeal, and other cereal products	46.51	34.77	56.22	52.79	57.48	56.08	33.51	18.19
Bakery products	462.20	367.30	545.13	440.96	568.70	565.80	325.08	193.61
Bread	133.93	111.37	152.59	121.76	155.00	166.41	85.11	63.72
White bread	55.50	43.34	65.37	46.39	66.60	74.31	43.98	24.81
Bread, other than white	78.44	68.03	87.22	75.37	88.40	92.10	41.13	38.91
Cookies and crackers	111.45	91.94	130.41	105.90	138.13	131.59	72.47	45.81
Cookies	61.16	51.06	69.11	51.47	74.57	70.14	42.03	27.10
Crackers	50.29	40.88	61.30	54.43	63.57	61.45	30.44	18.70
Frozen and refrigerated bakery products	37.67	25.75	49.63	53.47	54.36	39.43	28.16	14.78
Other bakery products	179.15	138.24	212.50	159.84	221.21	228.36	139.35	69.31
Biscuits and rolls	72.99	58.62	86.63	63.39	91.36	92.15	49.30	25.99
Cakes and cupcakes	47.14	31.44	57.47	46.40	63.04	54.49	45.10	17.50
Bread and cracker products	9.09	7.51	10.46	8.30	8.67	14.73	6.41	3.40
Sweetrolls, coffee cakes, doughnuts	30.84	25.93	35.27	28.09	34.50	40.72	21.35	14.08
Pies, tarts, turnovers	19.09	14.75	22.68	13.66	23.65	26.27	17.20	8.33
Meats, poultry, fish, and eggs	**1,084.45**	**819.51**	**1,275.22**	**920.59**	**1,275.68**	**1,480.06**	**789.91**	**397.10**
Beef	297.66	224.54	336.84	219.09	344.21	392.71	206.83	92.35
Ground beef	113.64	78.16	135.34	99.73	133.61	158.89	113.29	38.61
Roast	44.88	37.68	49.31	28.42	57.12	48.25	21.92	10.23
Chuck roast	11.25	9.78	11.10	4.25	12.50	12.72	5.58	3.10
Round roast	8.32	6.77	8.80	3.13	12.05	6.62	3.89	2.65
Other roast	25.31	21.13	29.40	21.04	32.58	28.91	12.45	4.48
Steak	111.22	89.57	120.28	71.73	122.35	144.95	59.12	36.21
Round steak	20.51	15.55	20.77	10.73	21.17	25.92	17.24	7.24
Sirloin steak	28.82	25.67	30.24	23.20	28.21	37.75	19.59	11.01
Other steak	61.89	48.35	69.27	37.80	72.97	81.27	22.30	17.96
Other beef	27.92	19.13	31.92	19.21	31.13	40.62	12.50	7.30
Pork	209.41	161.67	241.95	174.58	245.03	275.84	144.02	79.21
Bacon	43.75	35.20	50.47	36.73	54.37	51.87	29.13	18.57
Pork chops	34.75	23.61	40.55	28.15	42.45	44.55	28.43	11.95
Ham	45.44	33.60	55.32	37.91	57.06	62.47	25.82	18.16
Ham, not canned	44.34	32.79	54.12	36.11	55.78	61.75	25.19	17.97
Canned ham	1.10	0.81	1.20	1.80	1.28	0.72	0.63	0.19
Sausage	35.69	31.00	39.03	38.16	38.14	41.05	27.92	13.89
Other pork	49.78	38.26	56.58	33.62	53.01	75.91	32.72	16.63
Other meats	165.62	116.14	209.54	144.91	222.91	224.49	101.92	57.90
Frankfurters	31.27	21.41	37.72	32.17	38.32	39.92	27.57	11.10
Lunch meats (cold cuts)	117.05	86.69	143.89	101.16	152.40	154.33	71.21	42.55
Bologna, liverwurst, salami	34.78	26.18	40.52	23.52	44.30	43.99	21.18	14.23
Other lunch meats	82.27	60.51	103.37	77.63	108.10	110.33	50.04	28.31
Lamb, organ meats, and others	17.30	8.05	27.94	11.58	32.20	30.24	3.14	4.25

	total married couples	married couples, no children	married couples with children				single parent with child under age 18	single person
			total	oldest child under age 6	oldest child aged 6 to 17	oldest child aged 18 or older		
Poultry	$197.06	$137.33	$242.79	$189.98	$226.27	$301.25	$166.99	$72.24
Fresh and frozen chicken	156.34	108.62	191.77	143.49	182.26	235.78	135.02	59.36
Fresh and frozen whole chicken	45.53	30.36	55.70	43.35	55.52	63.15	42.73	17.65
Fresh and frozen chicken parts	110.82	78.27	136.07	100.14	126.74	172.63	92.28	41.71
Other poultry	40.72	28.71	51.02	46.49	44.02	65.47	31.97	12.88
Fish and seafood	152.88	131.94	171.47	130.76	165.52	205.11	125.55	65.56
Canned fish and seafood	24.85	21.35	27.85	19.91	26.95	33.97	16.69	13.81
Fresh fish and shellfish	75.32	65.43	84.44	53.91	85.19	100.87	62.79	30.21
Frozen fish and shellfish	52.72	45.16	59.18	56.93	53.38	70.27	46.07	21.54
Eggs	61.81	47.88	72.61	61.28	71.74	80.66	44.61	29.84
Dairy products	**533.16**	**419.67**	**635.98**	**596.65**	**649.81**	**635.46**	**355.04**	**221.09**
Fresh milk and cream	193.80	140.23	238.46	238.52	238.74	237.97	138.81	78.84
Fresh milk, all types	164.08	114.03	205.80	214.82	204.70	202.44	122.27	66.60
Cream	29.73	26.20	32.66	23.70	34.04	35.54	16.54	12.24
Other dairy products	339.36	279.44	397.51	358.13	411.08	397.49	216.24	142.25
Butter	32.96	30.96	35.77	24.13	38.32	38.22	16.52	12.95
Cheese	165.28	134.34	195.61	176.94	197.74	202.82	98.85	69.06
Ice cream and related products	74.98	64.89	84.61	59.45	90.49	89.29	59.75	30.91
Miscellaneous dairy products	66.13	49.25	81.52	97.61	84.52	67.15	41.13	29.33
Fruits and vegetables	**926.20**	**761.47**	**1,066.98**	**996.06**	**1,058.59**	**1,122.23**	**600.21**	**401.74**
Fresh fruits	324.69	272.42	374.21	353.01	369.40	394.60	207.79	145.27
Apples	50.25	38.99	61.26	55.56	65.95	56.66	33.51	21.99
Bananas	52.37	42.22	59.12	55.81	55.09	67.83	37.36	24.88
Oranges	34.88	28.57	40.58	32.83	44.38	38.68	22.91	15.54
Citrus fruits, excluding oranges	49.25	41.11	56.49	50.72	54.92	62.49	30.88	22.91
Other fresh fruits	137.94	121.54	156.75	158.09	149.06	168.94	83.13	59.95
Fresh vegetables	293.53	254.63	325.42	297.91	321.15	348.58	158.71	123.34
Potatoes	50.50	44.13	54.32	44.42	52.80	62.63	36.52	19.75
Lettuce	42.42	36.54	48.57	36.37	48.90	55.11	21.01	17.58
Tomatoes	53.48	45.00	60.24	60.15	53.62	71.46	27.75	23.37
Other fresh vegetables	147.13	128.95	162.28	156.97	165.83	159.38	73.43	62.64
Processed fruits	143.83	108.05	174.98	168.17	176.80	175.86	112.56	67.13
Frozen fruits and fruit juices	17.10	13.57	21.48	21.59	20.44	23.17	10.45	9.32
Frozen orange juice	5.30	3.87	6.72	4.73	7.88	5.90	2.75	1.96
Frozen fruits	8.33	7.82	9.64	11.44	8.18	11.04	4.45	5.90
Frozen fruit juices, excluding orange	3.47	1.87	5.13	5.41	4.38	6.23	3.25	1.46
Canned fruits	28.10	21.90	33.48	32.05	33.82	33.73	22.52	11.26
Dried fruits	10.34	8.12	12.70	8.03	14.92	11.66	5.18	5.22
Fresh fruit juice	20.78	15.67	24.78	28.95	23.49	24.55	16.70	11.18
Canned and bottled fruit juice	67.50	48.80	82.54	77.55	84.13	82.75	57.71	30.15
Processed vegetables	164.15	126.38	192.37	176.97	191.25	203.19	121.15	66.01
Frozen vegetables	46.49	37.63	53.48	52.87	52.08	56.18	26.81	18.89
Canned and dried vegetables and juices	117.66	88.75	138.89	124.10	139.16	147.02	94.33	47.11
Canned beans	23.24	18.38	25.81	24.30	26.71	25.18	20.19	10.46
Canned corn	12.38	8.35	15.19	12.92	15.45	16.07	9.69	4.61
Canned miscellaneous vegetables	32.94	29.00	35.94	33.29	33.72	41.22	23.41	13.59
Dried peas	1.13	0.86	1.33	0.41	1.08	2.30	1.64	0.24
Dried beans	6.30	4.19	8.04	5.25	7.09	11.24	3.72	2.18
Dried miscellaneous vegetables	15.72	10.70	19.72	18.46	20.69	18.81	12.31	4.58
Dried processed vegetables	2.77	3.15	1.84	1.64	1.16	3.11	1.11	0.95
Fresh and canned vegetable juices	22.69	13.88	30.27	27.60	31.91	29.06	21.63	10.43
Sugar and other sweets	**188.49**	**151.99**	**218.95**	**183.50**	**228.71**	**223.05**	**124.26**	**81.74**
Candy and chewing gum	114.55	96.18	129.07	98.66	136.66	133.92	72.99	50.74
Sugar	29.01	20.76	35.45	32.71	35.14	37.57	23.80	13.30
Artificial sweeteners	8.19	7.52	8.58	9.23	8.12	8.98	2.42	1.93
Jams, preserves, other sweets	36.74	27.53	45.84	42.90	48.79	42.59	25.05	15.77

	total married couples	married couples, no children	married couples with children				single parent with child under age 18	single person
			total	oldest child under age 6	oldest child aged 6 to 17	oldest child aged 18 or older		
Fats and oils	**$142.42**	**$119.07**	**$157.64**	**$121.03**	**$154.83**	**$183.58**	**$91.30**	**$62.49**
Margarine	12.04	11.14	11.86	8.68	10.90	15.31	8.53	6.54
Fats and oils	44.35	36.73	48.86	37.61	47.62	57.47	33.70	19.19
Salad dressings	42.73	36.79	46.93	35.98	44.41	57.52	25.33	16.56
Nondairy cream and imitation milk	24.58	21.80	26.26	21.80	26.11	29.11	13.86	9.89
Peanut butter	18.73	12.61	23.73	16.96	25.79	24.18	9.89	10.31
Miscellaneous foods	**865.68**	**687.24**	**1,032.53**	**1,077.84**	**1,037.26**	**998.30**	**683.79**	**397.51**
Frozen prepared foods	162.33	121.29	202.85	174.57	223.20	184.96	158.95	88.84
Frozen meals	71.31	60.71	83.33	81.62	82.97	84.93	54.43	49.26
Other frozen prepared foods	91.01	60.58	119.52	92.96	140.23	100.02	104.51	39.59
Canned and packaged soups	59.45	53.51	65.02	59.32	64.06	69.94	32.28	28.93
Potato chips, nuts, and other snacks	189.38	159.83	219.82	173.97	233.07	224.09	138.41	81.72
Potato chips and other snacks	140.45	104.47	175.57	146.24	186.88	173.52	116.74	57.09
Nuts	48.93	55.37	44.26	27.74	46.20	50.57	21.68	24.63
Condiments and seasonings	173.37	144.76	198.56	184.28	193.48	215.41	126.29	70.12
Salt, spices, and other seasonings	45.25	38.09	50.44	46.02	51.50	51.23	32.86	17.62
Olives, pickles, relishes	20.34	20.13	20.78	18.10	18.90	25.51	12.23	9.78
Sauces and gravies	75.96	57.38	93.09	84.87	89.39	104.08	63.43	28.46
Baking needs and miscellaneous products	31.82	29.16	34.25	35.30	33.69	34.58	17.78	14.26
Other canned or packaged prepared foods	281.15	207.85	346.28	485.70	323.45	303.91	227.85	127.89
Prepared salads	43.76	38.67	47.95	46.61	47.65	49.23	27.96	26.95
Prepared desserts	19.15	14.59	22.81	13.61	23.68	26.66	14.71	7.98
Baby food	34.46	6.36	59.37	205.45	33.80	17.76	43.56	6.89
Miscellaneous prepared foods	181.09	145.46	213.74	216.80	216.15	207.89	140.48	84.04
Nonalcoholic beverages	**445.42**	**360.63**	**510.24**	**382.89**	**533.03**	**545.67**	**342.71**	**202.31**
Cola	97.41	81.39	105.37	79.77	104.56	121.56	74.96	41.06
Other carbonated drinks	80.56	60.41	96.84	78.27	97.10	107.18	61.02	34.14
Tea	38.11	30.85	43.59	32.55	44.22	48.94	32.97	18.40
Coffee	98.25	97.56	99.26	85.17	103.18	100.83	49.75	45.63
Noncarbonated fruit-flavored drinks	29.33	20.92	37.39	28.31	41.16	36.31	36.43	13.07
Other noncarbonated beverages and ice	17.74	12.65	22.47	18.73	27.35	16.42	16.56	9.69
Bottled water	63.79	44.71	78.35	44.90	84.42	87.53	52.89	32.88
Sports drinks	20.01	12.04	26.59	15.19	30.80	26.12	18.12	6.52
Food prepared by consumer unit on trips	**71.68**	**80.79**	**67.62**	**58.43**	**75.73**	**60.02**	**19.46**	**22.99**
FOOD AWAY FROM HOME	**3,370.30**	**2,959.87**	**3,772.07**	**3,018.48**	**3,935.61**	**3,961.63**	**2,150.06**	**1,566.86**
Meals at restaurants, carry-outs, etc.	**2,762.39**	**2,400.28**	**3,082.28**	**2,643.11**	**3,118.91**	**3,275.22**	**1,796.16**	**1,367.36**
Lunch	951.00	756.94	1,109.94	1,012.25	1,136.21	1,122.32	602.13	468.12
At fast-food restaurants*	440.68	312.69	552.55	519.79	547.87	579.43	321.80	226.27
At full-service restaurants	396.92	403.02	384.21	404.93	348.51	432.36	161.46	202.38
At vending machines, mobile vendors	7.77	3.98	9.93	9.09	7.11	15.15	7.59	4.91
At employer and school cafeterias	105.62	37.25	163.25	78.43	232.72	95.38	111.28	34.56
Dinner	1,336.51	1,257.56	1,436.48	1,246.27	1,410.57	1,590.41	858.83	635.51
At fast-food restaurants*	430.13	289.33	540.99	493.99	550.80	551.70	489.40	198.97
At full-service restaurants	897.60	959.18	886.30	742.22	850.22	1,030.65	367.12	425.22
At vending machines, mobile vendors	2.83	3.47	2.46	2.76	2.05	2.99	0.67	3.56
At employer and school cafeterias	5.95	5.58	6.72	7.31	7.51	5.07	1.64	7.76
Snacks and nonalcoholic beverages	197.40	144.60	244.37	204.52	280.39	206.79	146.86	106.38
At fast-food restaurants*	136.71	99.20	170.20	132.32	203.94	135.33	93.75	63.71
At full-service restaurants	34.00	30.37	36.83	45.49	34.71	35.37	27.52	25.92
At vending machines, mobile vendors	19.26	10.81	27.36	21.21	29.24	27.75	19.48	12.30
At employer and school cafeterias	7.43	4.21	9.99	5.50	12.52	8.34	6.12	4.45
Breakfast and brunch	277.49	241.18	291.49	180.07	291.73	355.70	188.34	157.35
At fast-food restaurants*	149.16	106.31	174.47	138.22	174.59	195.29	111.15	84.93
At full-service restaurants	115.44	126.12	101.38	30.22	103.71	138.72	57.78	62.24
At vending machines, mobile vendors	2.62	1.84	2.90	3.03	1.55	5.11	5.18	2.70
At employer and school cafeterias	10.27	6.91	12.74	8.60	11.88	16.58	14.23	7.48

	total married couples	married couples, no children	married couples with children				single parent with child under age 18	single person
			total	oldest child under age 6	oldest child aged 6 to 17	oldest child aged 18 or older		
Board (including at school)	$75.00	$64.12	$95.78	$2.28	$97.98	$155.27	$13.52	$12.39
Catered affairs	80.18	89.50	82.90	71.49	62.16	125.94	18.64	21.29
Food on trips	336.28	393.81	308.48	244.19	352.15	277.64	121.49	135.12
School lunches	96.99	0.08	177.97	24.37	281.12	106.27	164.39	0.95
Meals as pay	19.47	12.09	24.66	33.04	23.30	21.29	35.86	29.75
ALCOHOLIC BEVERAGES	514.95	610.23	458.71	423.96	458.65	479.45	245.71	369.87
At home	298.70	341.78	274.60	238.10	258.81	322.35	181.66	163.76
Beer and ale	128.50	121.46	141.35	138.60	128.09	165.30	76.90	74.28
Whiskey	12.58	18.84	6.18	7.93	8.45	1.36	–	8.32
Wine	135.30	176.35	106.07	80.21	95.53	138.85	95.88	65.69
Other alcoholic beverages	22.32	25.13	20.99	11.37	26.75	16.85	8.88	15.47
Away from home	216.26	268.45	184.12	185.86	199.83	157.09	64.06	206.11
Beer and ale	72.02	75.15	71.93	85.48	79.08	52.02	17.20	78.50
At fast-food restaurants*	12.70	11.41	12.97	14.09	14.08	10.47	2.47	14.44
At full-service restaurants	58.52	62.54	58.39	71.39	64.09	41.25	14.58	61.40
At vending machines, mobile vendors	0.81	1.20	0.57	–	0.92	0.31	–	0.81
Wine	45.58	65.55	31.63	23.14	35.86	29.43	7.82	38.66
At fast-food restaurants*	3.21	5.57	1.44	–	1.59	2.02	0.88	2.84
At full-service restaurants	42.17	59.97	29.76	23.14	33.44	27.42	6.94	33.40
Other alcoholic beverages	42.68	54.71	34.65	36.69	35.99	31.21	17.31	55.19
At fast-food restaurants*	2.35	2.94	1.86	0.45	2.58	1.44	2.58	7.34
At full-service restaurants	40.33	51.77	32.79	36.24	33.40	29.76	14.73	47.75
Alcoholic beverages purchased on trips	55.97	73.05	45.91	40.55	48.90	44.44	21.73	33.76

* The category fast-food restaurants also includes take-out, delivery, concession stands, buffets, and cafeterias other than employer and school.
Note: Average spending figures for total consumer units can be found on Average Spending by Age and Average Spending by Region tables. Subcategories may not add to total because some are not shown. "–" means sample is too small to make a reliable estimate.
Source: Bureau of Labor Statistics, unpublished tables from the 2011 Consumer Expenditure Survey

Table 5.14 Food and Alcohol: Indexed spending by household type, 2011

(indexed average annual spending of consumer units on food and alcoholic beverages, by type of consumer unit, 2011; index definition: an index of 100 is the average for all consumer units; an index of 125 means that spending by consumer units in that group is 25 percent above the average for all consumer units; an index of 75 indicates spending that is 25 percent below the average for all consumer units)

	total married couples	married couples, no children	married couples with children				single parent with child under age 18	single person
			total	oldest child under age 6	oldest child aged 6 to 17	oldest child aged 18 or older		
Average spending of consumer units, total	$63,972	$57,658	$69,724	$65,948	$70,709	$70,412	$37,553	$30,613
Average spending of consumer units, index	129	116	140	133	142	142	76	62
Food, spending index	129	107	148	124	152	155	88	56
Alcoholic beverages, spending index	113	134	100	93	100	105	54	81
FOOD AT HOME	129	103	151	131	153	158	92	54
Cereals and bakery products	129	101	155	127	163	157	98	54
Cereals and cereal products	128	96	157	133	169	152	111	52
Flour	130	90	161	133	181	143	53	71
Prepared flour mixes	133	115	152	131	159	154	120	45
Ready-to-eat and cooked cereals	129	95	161	134	177	151	112	53
Rice	120	86	141	104	149	149	141	49
Pasta, cornmeal, and other cereal products	132	99	159	150	163	159	95	52
Bakery products	130	103	153	124	160	159	91	54
Bread	126	105	143	114	145	156	80	60
White bread	124	96	145	103	148	165	98	55
Bread, other than white	127	110	142	122	144	150	67	63
Cookies and crackers	133	110	156	127	165	157	87	55
Cookies	130	109	147	110	159	149	90	58
Crackers	137	112	167	149	174	168	83	51
Frozen and refrigerated bakery products	132	90	174	187	190	138	98	52
Other bakery products	131	101	155	117	161	167	102	51
Biscuits and rolls	138	111	164	120	173	174	93	49
Cakes and cupcakes	125	83	152	123	167	144	119	46
Bread and cracker products	127	105	147	116	122	207	90	48
Sweetrolls, coffee cakes, doughnuts	129	109	148	118	145	171	89	59
Pies, tarts, turnovers	124	96	148	89	154	171	112	54
Meats, poultry, fish, and eggs	130	98	153	111	153	178	95	48
Beef	134	101	151	98	155	176	93	41
Ground beef	126	86	150	110	148	176	125	43
Roast	147	123	161	93	187	158	72	33
Chuck roast	147	128	145	56	163	166	73	41
Round roast	136	111	144	51	197	108	64	43
Other roast	150	126	175	125	194	172	74	27
Steak	135	109	146	87	148	176	72	44
Round steak	129	98	131	67	133	163	108	46
Sirloin steak	132	117	138	106	129	173	90	50
Other steak	138	108	155	85	163	182	50	40
Other beef	147	101	168	101	164	214	66	38
Pork	129	100	149	108	151	170	89	49
Bacon	129	104	149	108	161	153	86	55
Pork chops	128	87	149	103	156	164	104	44
Ham	133	98	161	111	166	182	75	53
Ham, not canned	132	98	162	108	166	184	75	54
Canned ham	141	104	154	231	164	92	81	24
Sausage	125	109	137	134	134	144	98	49
Other pork	131	101	149	88	140	200	86	44
Other meats	135	95	171	118	182	183	83	47
Frankfurters	132	90	159	136	162	169	116	47
Lunch meats (cold cuts)	134	99	164	115	174	176	81	49
Bologna, liverwurst, salami	130	98	151	88	165	164	79	53
Other lunch meats	135	99	170	128	178	181	82	47
Lamb, organ meats, and others	154	72	249	103	288	270	28	38

	total married couples	married couples, no children	married couples with children				single parent with child under age 18	single person
			total	oldest child under age 6	oldest child aged 6 to 17	oldest child aged 18 or older		
Poultry	128	89	157	123	146	195	108	47
Fresh and frozen chicken	126	87	154	115	146	189	109	48
Fresh and frozen whole chicken	127	84	155	121	154	176	119	49
Fresh and frozen chicken parts	125	88	154	113	143	195	104	47
Other poultry	136	96	170	155	146	218	106	43
Fish and seafood	127	109	142	108	137	170	104	54
Canned fish and seafood	125	107	140	100	135	171	84	69
Fresh fish and shellfish	127	110	142	91	143	170	106	51
Frozen fish and shellfish	127	109	143	138	129	170	111	52
Eggs	123	96	145	122	143	161	89	60
Dairy products	**131**	**103**	**156**	**147**	**160**	**156**	**87**	**54**
Fresh milk and cream	129	94	159	159	159	159	93	53
Fresh milk, all types	129	90	162	169	161	159	96	52
Cream	133	117	146	106	152	159	74	55
Other dairy products	132	109	155	139	160	155	84	55
Butter	134	126	145	98	156	155	67	53
Cheese	132	108	157	142	159	163	79	55
Ice cream and related products	131	113	148	104	158	156	104	54
Miscellaneous dairy products	131	98	162	194	168	133	82	58
Fruits and vegetables	**130**	**107**	**149**	**139**	**148**	**157**	**84**	**56**
Fresh fruits	131	110	151	143	149	160	84	59
Apples	132	102	160	146	173	148	88	58
Bananas	127	103	144	136	134	165	91	61
Oranges	129	106	150	122	164	143	85	58
Citrus fruits, excluding oranges	131	109	150	135	146	166	82	61
Other fresh fruits	133	118	152	153	144	163	80	58
Fresh vegetables	131	114	145	133	143	155	71	55
Potatoes	130	114	140	115	136	162	94	51
Lettuce	132	114	151	113	152	171	65	55
Tomatoes	130	110	147	147	131	174	68	57
Other fresh vegetables	131	115	145	140	148	142	65	56
Processed fruits	124	93	151	145	153	152	97	58
Frozen fruits and fruit juices	128	102	161	162	154	174	79	70
Frozen orange juice	142	104	180	127	211	158	74	53
Frozen fruits	120	113	139	165	118	160	64	85
Frozen fruit juices, excluding orange	130	70	192	203	164	233	122	55
Canned fruits	132	103	158	151	159	159	106	53
Dried fruits	127	100	156	99	184	143	64	64
Fresh fruit juice	120	91	143	168	136	142	97	65
Canned and bottled fruit juice	121	87	148	139	151	148	103	54
Processed vegetables	129	99	151	139	150	159	95	52
Frozen vegetables	133	108	153	151	149	161	77	54
Canned and dried vegetables and juices	127	96	150	134	150	159	102	51
Canned beans	122	96	135	127	140	132	106	55
Canned corn	127	86	156	133	159	165	100	47
Canned miscellaneous vegetables	129	114	141	131	132	162	92	53
Dried peas	135	102	158	49	129	274	195	29
Dried beans	126	84	161	105	142	225	75	44
Dried miscellaneous vegetables	136	93	171	160	179	163	107	40
Dried processed vegetables	135	154	90	80	57	152	54	46
Fresh and canned vegetable juices	122	75	163	148	172	156	116	56
Sugar and other sweets	**131**	**105**	**152**	**127**	**158**	**154**	**86**	**57**
Candy and chewing gum	132	111	149	114	158	154	84	58
Sugar	121	87	148	137	147	157	100	56
Artificial sweeteners	146	134	153	165	145	160	43	34
Jams, preserves, other sweets	131	98	163	152	173	151	89	56

| | total married couples | married couples, no children | married couples with children | | | | single parent with child under age 18 | single person |
			total	oldest child under age 6	oldest child aged 6 to 17	oldest child aged 18 or older		
Fats and oils	**130**	**109**	**144**	**110**	**141**	**167**	**83**	**57**
Margarine	123	114	121	89	112	157	87	67
Fats and oils	127	105	140	108	137	165	97	55
Salad dressings	137	118	151	115	143	185	81	53
Nondairy cream and imitation milk	132	117	141	117	140	157	75	53
Peanut butter	123	83	156	111	169	159	65	68
Miscellaneous foods	**125**	**100**	**150**	**156**	**150**	**145**	**99**	**58**
Frozen prepared foods	119	89	149	128	164	136	117	65
Frozen meals	115	98	134	131	134	137	88	79
Other frozen prepared foods	123	82	161	125	189	135	141	53
Canned and packaged soups	127	114	139	126	137	149	69	62
Potato chips, nuts, and other snacks	131	110	152	120	161	155	95	56
Potato chips and other snacks	130	97	163	135	173	161	108	53
Nuts	132	150	120	75	125	137	59	67
Condiments and seasonings	129	108	148	138	144	161	94	52
Salt, spices, and other seasonings	128	108	142	130	145	145	93	50
Olives, pickles, relishes	126	125	129	112	117	158	76	61
Sauces and gravies	130	98	159	145	153	178	109	49
Baking needs and miscellaneous products	133	122	143	148	141	145	74	60
Other canned or packaged prepared foods	123	91	152	213	142	133	100	56
Prepared salads	121	107	132	129	132	136	77	74
Prepared desserts	127	97	152	91	158	177	98	53
Baby food	124	23	214	739	122	64	157	25
Miscellaneous prepared foods	123	99	145	147	147	141	95	57
Nonalcoholic beverages	**123**	**100**	**141**	**106**	**148**	**151**	**95**	**56**
Cola	124	103	134	101	133	154	95	52
Other carbonated drinks	121	91	145	117	146	161	91	51
Tea	122	99	140	104	142	157	106	59
Coffee	131	130	132	114	138	134	66	61
Noncarbonated fruit-flavored drinks	118	84	151	114	166	147	147	53
Other noncarbonated beverages and ice	119	85	151	125	183	110	111	65
Bottled water	119	84	147	84	158	164	99	61
Sports drinks	127	77	169	97	196	166	115	41
Food prepared by consumer unit on trips	**151**	**170**	**142**	**123**	**159**	**126**	**41**	**48**
FOOD AWAY FROM HOME	**129**	**113**	**144**	**115**	**150**	**151**	**82**	**60**
Meals at restaurants, carry-outs, etc.	**126**	**109**	**140**	**120**	**142**	**149**	**82**	**62**
Lunch	126	101	147	134	151	149	80	62
At fast-food restaurants*	119	85	150	141	149	157	87	61
At full-service restaurants	131	133	127	134	115	143	53	67
At vending machines, mobile vendors	109	56	139	127	99	212	106	69
At employer and school cafeterias	141	50	218	105	311	127	148	46
Dinner	127	120	137	119	134	151	82	60
At fast-food restaurants*	118	79	148	135	151	151	134	54
At full-service restaurants	133	142	131	110	126	152	54	63
At vending machines, mobile vendors	94	115	81	91	68	99	22	118
At employer and school cafeterias	87	81	98	107	110	74	24	113
Snacks and nonalcoholic beverages	119	87	147	123	169	125	88	64
At fast-food restaurants*	125	90	155	121	186	123	85	58
At full-service restaurants	104	93	113	139	106	108	84	79
At vending machines, mobile vendors	111	63	158	123	169	161	113	71
At employer and school cafeterias	116	65	155	86	195	130	95	69
Breakfast and brunch	123	107	129	80	129	157	83	70
At fast-food restaurants*	121	86	141	112	141	158	90	69
At full-service restaurants	129	141	113	34	116	155	65	70
At vending machines, mobile vendors	86	61	96	100	51	169	171	89
At employer and school cafeterias	106	72	132	89	123	172	147	77

	total married couples	married couples, no children	married couples with children				single parent with child under 18	single person
			total	oldest child under age 6	oldest child aged 6 to 17	oldest child aged 18 or older		
Board (including at school)	171	146	218	5	223	354	31	28
Catered affairs	152	170	158	136	118	239	35	40
Food on trips	142	167	130	103	149	117	51	57
School lunches	156	0	286	39	452	171	264	2
Meals as pay	67	42	85	115	81	74	124	103
ALCOHOLIC BEVERAGES	113	134	100	93	100	105	54	81
At home	123	141	113	98	107	133	75	68
Beer and ale	117	111	129	126	117	151	70	68
Whiskey	131	196	64	83	88	14	–	87
Wine	130	170	102	77	92	133	92	63
Other alcoholic beverages	118	132	111	60	141	89	47	82
Away from home	101	125	86	87	93	73	30	96
Beer and ale	94	98	93	111	103	68	22	102
At fast-food restaurants*	102	91	104	113	113	84	20	116
At full-service restaurants	92	99	92	113	101	65	23	97
At vending machines, mobile vendors	125	185	88	–	142	48	–	125
Wine	109	156	75	55	85	70	19	92
At fast-food restaurants*	108	188	49	–	54	68	30	96
At full-service restaurants	110	157	78	61	88	72	18	87
Other alcoholic beverages	85	109	69	73	72	62	34	110
At fast-food restaurants*	55	69	44	11	61	34	61	173
At full-service restaurants	88	113	71	79	73	65	32	104
Alcoholic beverages purchased on trips	125	163	102	90	109	99	48	75

The category fast-food restaurants also includes take-out, delivery, concession stands, buffets, and cafeterias other than employer and school.
Note: Spending index for total consumer units is 100. "–" means sample is too small to make a reliable estimate.
Source: Calculations by New Strategist based on the Bureau of Labor Statistics' 2011 Consumer Expenditure Survey

Table 5.15 Food and Alcohol: Total spending by household type, 2011

(total annual spending on food and alcoholic beverages, by consumer unit type, 2011; consumer units and dollars in thousands)

	total married couples	married couples, no children	married couples with children				single parent with child under age 18	single person
			total	oldest child under age 6	oldest child aged 6 to 17	oldest child aged 18 or older		
Number of consumer units	60,144	25,270	29,097	5,825	14,661	8,612	6,956	36,110
Total spending of all consumer units	$3,847,504,302	$1,457,023,725	$2,028,765,629	$384,144,828	$1,036,657,612	$606,386,852	$261,219,016	$1,105,441,930
Food, total spending	500,097,360	174,236,650	278,080,029	46,763,100	143,868,393	86,481,704	39,482,256	131,368,180
Alcoholic beverages, total spending	30,971,153	15,420,512	13,347,085	2,469,567	6,724,268	4,129,023	1,709,159	13,356,006
FOOD AT HOME	297,375,392	99,449,074	168,333,419	29,182,726	86,167,095	52,365,180	24,528,108	74,801,865
Cereals and bakery products	41,312,312	13,522,230	23,862,741	3,919,701	12,661,973	7,166,131	3,613,503	10,275,101
Cereals and cereal products	13,513,755	4,240,306	8,001,384	1,351,109	4,324,262	2,293,462	1,352,246	3,283,843
Flour	599,636	175,374	359,639	59,590	203,935	94,474	28,102	197,161
Prepared flour mixes	1,193,858	430,854	659,338	113,296	346,000	197,473	124,304	244,104
Ready-to-eat and cooked cereals	7,077,746	2,195,458	4,292,971	715,427	2,369,218	1,190,178	714,659	1,733,641
Rice	1,844,616	560,236	1,053,602	155,295	562,249	328,462	252,085	451,375
Pasta, cornmeal, and other cereal products	2,797,297	878,638	1,635,833	307,502	842,714	482,961	233,096	656,841
Bakery products	27,798,557	9,281,671	15,861,648	2,568,592	8,337,711	4,872,670	2,261,256	6,991,257
Bread	8,055,086	2,814,320	4,439,911	709,252	2,272,455	1,433,123	592,025	2,300,929
White bread	3,337,992	1,095,202	1,902,071	270,222	976,423	639,958	305,925	895,889
Bread, other than white	4,717,695	1,719,118	2,537,840	439,030	1,296,032	793,165	286,100	1,405,040
Cookies and crackers	6,703,049	2,323,324	3,794,540	616,868	2,025,124	1,133,253	504,101	1,654,199
Cookies	3,678,407	1,290,286	2,010,894	299,813	1,093,271	604,046	292,361	978,581
Crackers	3,024,642	1,033,038	1,783,646	317,055	932,000	529,207	211,741	675,257
Frozen and refrigerated bakery products	2,265,624	650,703	1,444,084	311,463	796,972	339,571	195,881	533,706
Other bakery products	10,774,798	3,493,325	6,183,113	931,068	3,243,160	1,966,636	969,319	2,502,784
Biscuits and rolls	4,389,911	1,481,327	2,520,673	369,247	1,339,429	793,596	342,931	938,499
Cakes and cupcakes	2,835,188	794,489	1,672,205	270,280	924,229	469,268	313,716	631,925
Bread and cracker products	546,709	189,778	304,355	48,348	127,111	126,855	44,588	122,774
Sweetrolls, coffee cakes, doughnuts	1,854,841	655,251	1,026,251	163,624	505,805	350,681	148,511	508,429
Pies, tarts, turnovers	1,148,149	372,733	659,920	79,570	346,733	226,237	119,643	300,796
Meats, poultry, fish, and eggs	65,223,161	20,709,018	37,105,076	5,362,437	18,702,744	12,746,277	5,494,614	14,339,281
Beef	17,902,463	5,674,126	9,801,033	1,276,199	5,046,463	3,382,019	1,438,709	3,334,759
Ground beef	6,834,764	1,975,103	3,937,988	580,927	1,958,856	1,368,361	788,045	1,394,207
Roast	2,699,263	952,174	1,434,773	165,547	837,436	415,529	152,476	369,405
Chuck roast	676,620	247,141	322,977	24,756	183,263	109,545	38,814	111,941
Round roast	500,398	171,078	256,054	18,232	176,665	57,011	27,059	95,692
Other roast	1,522,245	533,955	855,452	122,558	477,655	248,973	86,602	161,773
Steak	6,689,216	2,263,434	3,499,787	417,827	1,793,773	1,248,309	411,239	1,307,543
Round steak	1,233,553	392,949	604,345	62,502	310,373	223,223	119,921	261,436
Sirloin steak	1,733,350	648,681	879,893	135,140	413,587	325,103	136,268	397,571
Other steak	3,722,312	1,221,805	2,015,549	220,185	1,069,813	699,897	155,119	648,536
Other beef	1,679,220	483,415	928,776	111,898	456,397	349,819	86,950	263,603
Pork	12,594,755	4,085,401	7,040,019	1,016,929	3,592,385	2,375,534	1,001,803	2,860,273
Bacon	2,631,300	889,504	1,468,526	213,952	797,119	446,704	202,628	670,563
Pork chops	2,090,004	596,625	1,179,883	163,974	622,359	383,665	197,759	431,515
Ham	2,732,943	849,072	1,609,646	220,826	836,557	537,992	179,604	655,758
Ham, not canned	2,666,785	828,603	1,574,730	210,341	817,791	531,791	175,222	648,897
Canned ham	66,158	20,469	34,916	10,485	18,766	6,201	4,382	6,861
Sausage	2,146,539	783,370	1,135,656	222,282	559,171	353,523	194,212	501,568
Other pork	2,993,968	966,830	1,646,308	195,837	777,180	653,737	227,600	600,509
Other meats	9,961,049	2,934,858	6,096,985	844,101	3,268,084	1,933,308	708,956	2,090,769
Frankfurters	1,880,703	541,031	1,097,539	187,390	561,810	343,791	191,777	400,821
Lunch meats (cold cuts)	7,039,855	2,190,656	4,186,767	589,257	2,234,336	1,329,090	495,337	1,536,481
Bologna, liverwurst, salami	2,091,808	661,569	1,179,010	137,004	649,482	378,842	147,328	513,845
Other lunch meats	4,948,047	1,529,088	3,007,757	452,195	1,584,854	950,162	348,078	1,022,274
Lamb, organ meats, and others	1,040,491	203,424	812,970	67,454	472,084	260,427	21,842	153,468

	total married couples	married couples, no children	married couples with children				single parent with child under age 18	single person
			total	oldest child under age 6	oldest child aged 6 to 17	oldest child aged 18 or older		
Poultry	$11,851,977	$3,470,329	$7,064,461	$1,106,634	$3,317,344	$2,594,365	$1,161,582	$2,608,586
Fresh and frozen chicken	9,402,913	2,744,827	5,579,932	835,829	2,672,114	2,030,537	939,199	2,143,490
Fresh and frozen whole chicken	2,738,356	767,197	1,620,703	252,514	813,979	543,848	297,230	637,342
Fresh and frozen chicken parts	6,665,158	1,977,883	3,959,229	583,316	1,858,135	1,486,690	641,900	1,506,148
Other poultry	2,449,064	725,502	1,484,529	270,804	645,377	563,828	222,383	465,097
Fish and seafood	9,194,815	3,334,124	4,989,263	761,677	2,426,689	1,766,407	873,326	2,367,372
Canned fish and seafood	1,494,578	539,515	810,351	115,976	395,114	292,550	116,096	498,679
Fresh fish and shellfish	4,530,046	1,653,416	2,456,951	314,026	1,248,971	868,692	436,767	1,090,883
Frozen fish and shellfish	3,170,792	1,141,193	1,721,960	331,617	782,604	605,165	320,463	777,809
Eggs	3,717,501	1,209,928	2,112,733	356,956	1,051,780	694,644	310,307	1,077,522
Dairy products	**32,066,375**	**10,605,061**	**18,505,110**	**3,475,486**	**9,526,864**	**5,472,582**	**2,469,658**	**7,983,560**
Fresh milk and cream	11,655,907	3,543,612	6,938,471	1,389,379	3,500,167	2,049,398	965,562	2,846,912
Fresh milk, all types	9,868,428	2,881,538	5,988,163	1,251,327	3,001,107	1,743,413	850,510	2,404,926
Cream	1,788,081	662,074	950,308	138,053	499,060	306,070	115,052	441,986
Other dairy products	20,410,468	7,061,449	11,566,348	2,086,107	6,026,844	3,423,184	1,504,165	5,136,648
Butter	1,982,346	782,359	1,040,800	140,557	561,810	329,151	114,913	467,625
Cheese	9,940,600	3,394,772	5,691,664	1,030,676	2,899,066	1,746,686	687,601	2,493,757
Ice cream and related products	4,509,597	1,639,770	2,461,897	346,296	1,326,674	768,965	415,621	1,116,160
Miscellaneous dairy products	3,977,323	1,244,548	2,371,987	568,578	1,239,148	578,296	286,100	1,059,106
Fruits and vegetables	**55,705,373**	**19,242,347**	**31,045,917**	**5,802,050**	**15,519,988**	**9,664,645**	**4,175,061**	**14,506,831**
Fresh fruits	19,528,155	6,884,053	10,888,388	2,056,283	5,415,773	3,398,295	1,445,387	5,245,700
Apples	3,022,236	985,277	1,782,482	323,637	966,893	487,956	233,096	794,059
Bananas	3,149,741	1,066,899	1,720,215	325,093	807,674	584,152	259,876	898,417
Oranges	2,097,823	721,964	1,180,756	191,235	650,655	333,112	159,362	561,149
Citrus fruits, excluding oranges	2,962,092	1,038,850	1,643,690	295,444	805,182	538,164	214,801	827,280
Other fresh fruits	8,296,263	3,071,316	4,560,955	920,874	2,185,369	1,454,911	578,252	2,164,795
Fresh vegetables	17,654,068	6,434,500	9,468,746	1,735,326	4,708,380	3,001,971	1,103,987	4,453,807
Potatoes	3,037,272	1,115,165	1,580,549	258,747	774,101	539,370	254,033	713,173
Lettuce	2,551,308	923,366	1,413,241	211,855	716,923	474,607	146,146	634,814
Tomatoes	3,216,501	1,137,150	1,752,803	350,374	786,123	615,414	193,029	843,891
Other fresh vegetables	8,848,987	3,258,567	4,721,861	914,350	2,431,234	1,372,581	510,779	2,261,930
Processed fruits	8,650,512	2,730,424	5,091,393	979,590	2,592,065	1,514,506	782,967	2,424,064
Frozen fruits and fruit juices	1,028,462	342,914	625,004	125,762	299,671	199,540	72,690	336,545
Frozen orange juice	318,763	97,795	195,532	27,552	115,529	50,811	19,129	70,776
Frozen fruits	501,000	197,611	280,495	66,638	119,927	95,076	30,954	213,049
Frozen fruit juices, excluding orange	208,700	47,255	149,268	31,513	64,215	53,653	22,607	52,721
Canned fruits	1,690,046	553,413	974,168	186,691	495,835	290,483	156,649	406,599
Dried fruits	621,889	205,192	369,532	46,775	218,742	100,416	36,032	188,494
Fresh fruit juice	1,249,792	395,981	721,024	168,634	344,387	211,425	116,165	403,710
Canned and bottled fruit juice	4,059,720	1,233,176	2,401,666	451,729	1,233,430	712,643	401,431	1,088,717
Processed vegetables	9,872,638	3,193,623	5,597,390	1,030,850	2,803,916	1,749,872	842,719	2,383,621
Frozen vegetables	2,796,095	950,910	1,556,108	307,968	763,545	483,822	186,490	682,118
Canned and dried vegetables and juices	7,076,543	2,242,713	4,041,282	722,883	2,040,225	1,266,136	656,159	1,701,142
Canned beans	1,397,747	464,463	750,994	141,548	391,595	216,850	140,442	377,711
Canned corn	744,583	211,005	441,983	75,259	226,512	138,395	67,404	166,467
Canned miscellaneous vegetables	1,981,143	732,830	1,045,746	193,914	494,369	354,987	162,840	490,735
Dried peas	67,963	21,732	38,699	2,388	15,834	19,808	11,408	8,666
Dried beans	378,907	105,881	233,940	30,581	103,946	96,799	25,876	78,720
Dried miscellaneous vegetables	945,464	270,389	573,793	107,530	303,336	161,992	85,628	165,384
Dried processed vegetables	166,599	79,601	53,538	9,553	17,007	26,783	7,721	34,305
Fresh and canned vegetable juices	1,364,667	350,748	880,766	160,770	467,833	250,265	150,458	376,627
Sugar and other sweets	**11,336,543**	**3,840,787**	**6,370,788**	**1,068,888**	**3,353,117**	**1,920,907**	**864,353**	**2,951,631**
Candy and chewing gum	6,889,495	2,430,469	3,755,550	574,695	2,003,572	1,153,319	507,718	1,832,221
Sugar	1,744,777	524,605	1,031,489	190,536	515,188	323,553	165,553	480,263
Artificial sweeteners	492,579	190,030	249,652	53,765	119,047	77,336	16,834	69,692
Jams, preserves, other sweets	2,209,691	695,683	1,333,806	249,893	715,310	366,785	174,248	569,455

	total married couples	married couples, no children	married couples with children				single parent with child under age 18	single person
			total	oldest child under age 6	oldest child aged 6 to 17	oldest child aged 18 or older		
Fats and oils	**$8,565,708**	**$3,008,899**	**$4,586,851**	**$705,000**	**$2,269,963**	**$1,580,991**	**$635,083**	**$2,256,514**
Margarine	724,134	281,508	345,090	50,561	159,805	131,850	59,335	236,159
Fats and oils	2,667,386	928,167	1,421,679	219,078	698,157	494,932	234,417	692,951
Salad dressings	2,569,953	929,683	1,365,522	209,584	651,095	495,362	176,195	597,982
Nondairy cream and imitation milk	1,478,340	550,886	764,087	126,985	382,799	250,695	96,410	357,128
Peanut butter	1,126,497	318,655	690,472	98,792	378,107	208,238	68,795	372,294
Miscellaneous foods	**52,065,458**	**17,366,555**	**30,043,525**	**6,278,418**	**15,207,269**	**8,597,360**	**4,756,443**	**14,354,086**
Frozen prepared foods	9,763,176	3,064,998	5,902,326	1,016,870	3,272,335	1,592,876	1,105,656	3,208,012
Frozen meals	4,288,869	1,534,142	2,424,653	475,437	1,216,423	731,417	378,615	1,778,779
Other frozen prepared foods	5,473,705	1,530,857	3,477,673	541,492	2,055,912	861,372	726,972	1,429,595
Canned and packaged soups	3,575,561	1,352,198	1,891,887	345,539	939,184	602,323	224,540	1,044,662
Potato chips, nuts, and other snacks	11,390,071	4,038,904	6,396,103	1,013,375	3,417,039	1,929,863	962,780	2,950,909
Potato chips and other snacks	8,447,225	2,639,957	5,108,560	851,848	2,739,848	1,494,354	812,043	2,061,520
Nuts	2,942,846	1,399,200	1,287,833	161,586	677,338	435,509	150,806	889,389
Condiments and seasonings	10,427,165	3,658,085	5,777,500	1,073,431	2,836,610	1,855,111	878,473	2,532,033
Salt, spices, and other seasonings	2,721,516	962,534	1,467,653	268,067	755,042	441,193	228,574	636,258
Olives, pickles, relishes	1,223,329	508,685	604,636	105,433	277,093	219,692	85,072	353,156
Sauces and gravies	4,568,538	1,449,993	2,708,640	494,368	1,310,547	896,337	441,219	1,027,691
Baking needs and miscellaneous products	1,913,782	736,873	996,572	205,623	493,929	297,803	123,678	514,929
Other canned or packaged prepared foods	16,909,486	5,252,370	10,075,709	2,829,203	4,742,100	2,617,273	1,584,925	4,618,108
Prepared salads	2,631,901	977,191	1,395,201	271,503	698,597	423,969	194,490	973,165
Prepared desserts	1,151,758	368,689	663,703	79,278	347,172	229,596	102,323	288,158
Baby food	2,072,562	160,717	1,727,489	1,196,746	495,542	152,949	303,003	248,798
Miscellaneous prepared foods	10,891,477	3,675,774	6,219,193	1,262,860	3,168,975	1,790,349	977,179	3,034,684
Nonalcoholic beverages	**26,789,340**	**9,113,120**	**14,846,453**	**2,230,334**	**7,814,753**	**4,699,310**	**2,383,891**	**7,305,414**
Cola	5,858,627	2,056,725	3,065,951	464,660	1,532,954	1,046,875	521,422	1,482,677
Other carbonated drinks	4,845,201	1,526,561	2,817,753	455,923	1,423,583	923,034	424,455	1,232,795
Tea	2,292,088	779,580	1,268,338	189,604	648,309	421,471	229,339	664,424
Coffee	5,909,148	2,465,341	2,888,168	496,115	1,512,722	868,348	346,061	1,647,699
Noncarbonated fruit-flavored drinks	1,764,024	528,648	1,087,937	164,906	603,447	312,702	253,407	471,958
Other noncarbonated beverages and ice	1,066,955	319,666	653,810	109,102	400,978	141,409	115,191	349,906
Bottled water	3,836,586	1,129,822	2,279,750	261,543	1,237,682	753,808	367,903	1,187,297
Sports drinks	1,203,481	304,251	773,689	88,482	451,559	224,945	126,043	235,437
Food prepared by consumer unit on trips	**4,311,122**	**2,041,563**	**1,967,539**	**340,355**	**1,110,278**	**516,892**	**135,364**	**830,169**
FOOD AWAY FROM HOME	**202,703,323**	**74,795,915**	**109,755,921**	**17,582,646**	**57,699,978**	**34,117,558**	**14,955,817**	**56,579,315**
Meals at restaurants, carry-outs, etc.	**166,141,184**	**60,655,076**	**89,685,101**	**15,396,116**	**45,726,340**	**28,206,195**	**12,494,089**	**49,375,370**
Lunch	57,196,944	19,127,874	32,295,924	5,896,356	16,657,975	9,665,420	4,188,416	16,903,813
At fast-food restaurants*	26,504,258	7,901,676	16,077,547	3,027,777	8,032,322	4,990,051	2,238,441	8,170,610
At full-service restaurants	23,872,356	10,184,315	11,179,358	2,358,717	5,109,505	3,723,484	1,123,116	7,307,942
At vending machines, mobile vendors	467,319	100,575	288,933	52,949	104,240	130,472	52,796	177,300
At employer and school cafeterias	6,352,409	941,308	4,750,085	456,855	3,411,908	821,413	774,064	1,247,962
Dinner	80,383,057	31,778,541	41,797,259	7,259,523	20,680,367	13,696,611	5,974,021	22,948,266
At fast-food restaurants*	25,869,739	7,311,369	15,741,186	2,877,492	8,075,279	4,751,240	3,404,266	7,184,807
At full-service restaurants	53,985,254	24,238,479	25,788,671	4,323,432	12,465,075	8,875,958	2,553,687	15,354,694
At vending machines, mobile vendors	170,208	87,687	71,579	16,077	30,055	25,750	4,661	128,552
At employer and school cafeterias	357,857	141,007	195,532	42,581	110,104	43,663	11,408	280,214
Snacks and nonalcoholic beverages	11,872,426	3,654,042	7,110,434	1,191,329	4,110,798	1,780,875	1,021,558	3,841,382
At fast-food restaurants*	8,222,286	2,506,784	4,952,309	770,764	2,989,964	1,165,462	652,125	2,300,568
At full-service restaurants	2,044,896	767,450	1,071,643	264,979	508,883	304,606	191,429	935,971
At vending machines, mobile vendors	1,158,373	273,169	796,094	123,548	428,688	238,983	135,503	444,153
At employer and school cafeterias	446,870	106,387	290,679	32,038	183,556	71,824	42,571	160,690
Breakfast and brunch	16,689,359	6,094,619	8,481,485	1,048,908	4,277,054	3,063,288	1,310,093	5,681,909
At fast-food restaurants*	8,971,079	2,686,454	5,076,554	805,132	2,559,664	1,681,837	773,159	3,066,822
At full-service restaurants	6,943,023	3,187,052	2,949,854	176,032	1,520,492	1,194,657	401,918	2,247,486
At vending machines, mobile vendors	157,577	46,497	84,381	17,650	22,725	44,007	36,032	97,497
At employer and school cafeterias	617,679	174,616	370,696	50,095	174,173	142,787	98,984	270,103

	total married couples	married couples, no children	married couples with children				single parent with child under age 18	single person
			total	oldest child under age 6	oldest child aged 6 to 17	oldest child aged 18 or older		
Board (including at school)	$4,510,800	$1,620,312	$2,786,911	$13,281	$1,436,485	$1,337,185	$94,045	$447,403
Catered affairs	4,822,346	2,261,665	2,412,141	416,429	911,328	1,084,595	129,660	768,782
Food on trips	20,225,224	9,951,579	8,975,843	1,422,407	5,162,871	2,391,036	845,084	4,879,183
School lunches	5,833,367	2,022	5,178,393	141,955	4,121,500	915,197	1,143,497	34,305
Meals as pay	1,171,004	305,514	717,532	192,458	341,601	183,349	249,442	1,074,273
ALCOHOLIC BEVERAGES	30,971,153	15,420,512	13,347,085	2,469,567	6,724,268	4,129,023	1,709,159	13,356,006
At home	17,965,013	8,636,781	7,990,036	1,386,933	3,794,413	2,776,078	1,263,627	5,913,374
Beer and ale	7,728,504	3,069,294	4,112,861	807,345	1,877,927	1,423,564	534,916	2,682,251
Whiskey	756,612	476,087	179,819	46,192	123,885	11,712	–	300,435
Wine	8,137,483	4,456,365	3,086,319	467,223	1,400,565	1,195,776	666,941	2,372,066
Other alcoholic beverages	1,342,414	635,035	610,746	66,230	392,182	145,112	61,769	558,622
Away from home	13,006,741	6,783,732	5,357,340	1,082,635	2,929,708	1,352,859	445,601	7,442,632
Beer and ale	4,331,571	1,899,041	2,092,947	497,921	1,159,392	447,996	119,643	2,834,635
At fast-food restaurants*	763,829	288,331	377,388	82,074	206,427	90,168	17,181	521,428
At full-service restaurants	3,519,627	1,580,386	1,698,974	415,847	939,623	355,245	101,418	2,217,154
At vending machines, mobile vendors	48,717	30,324	16,585	–	13,488	2,670	–	29,249
Wine	2,741,364	1,656,449	920,338	134,791	525,743	253,451	54,396	1,396,013
At fast-food restaurants*	193,062	140,754	41,900	–	23,311	17,396	6,121	102,552
At full-service restaurants	2,536,272	1,515,442	865,927	134,791	490,264	236,141	48,275	1,206,074
Other alcoholic beverages	2,566,946	1,382,522	1,008,211	213,719	527,649	268,781	120,408	1,992,911
At fast-food restaurants*	141,338	74,294	54,120	2,621	37,825	12,401	17,946	265,047
At full-service restaurants	2,425,608	1,308,228	954,091	211,098	489,677	256,293	102,462	1,724,253
Alcoholic beverages purchased on trips	3,366,260	1,845,974	1,335,843	236,204	716,923	382,717	151,154	1,219,074

* The category fast-food restaurants also includes take-out, delivery, concession stands, buffets, and cafeterias other than employer and school.
Note: Total spending figures for total consumer units can be found on Total Spending by Age and Total Spending by Region tables. Spending by type of consumer unit does not add to total because not all types of consumer units are shown. Numbers may not add to category total because of rounding and missing subcategories. "–" means sample is too small to make a reliable estimate.
Source: Calculations by New Strategist based on the Bureau of Labor Statistics' 2011 Consumer Expenditure Survey

Table 5.16 Food and Alcohol: Market shares by household type, 2011

(percentage of total annual spending on food and alcoholic beverages accounted for by types of consumer units, 2011)

	total married couples	married couples, no children	married couples with children				single parent with child under age 18	single person
			total	oldest child under age 6	oldest child aged 6 to 17	oldest child aged 18 or older		
Share of total consumer units	49.2%	20.7%	23.8%	4.8%	12.0%	7.0%	5.7%	29.5%
Share of total before-tax income	67.0	25.6	35.0	6.8	17.5	10.7	3.3	16.0
Share of total spending	63.3	24.0	33.4	6.3	17.1	10.0	4.3	18.2
Share of food spending	63.3	22.1	35.2	5.9	18.2	11.0	5.0	16.6
Share of alcoholic beverages spending	55.5	27.6	23.9	4.4	12.0	7.4	3.1	23.9
FOOD AT HOME	**63.4**	**21.2**	**35.9**	**6.2**	**18.4**	**11.2**	**5.2**	**15.9**
Cereals and bakery products	**63.7**	**20.8**	**36.8**	**6.0**	**19.5**	**11.0**	**5.6**	**15.8**
Cereals and cereal products	63.2	19.8	37.4	6.3	20.2	10.7	6.3	15.4
Flour	63.9	18.7	38.3	6.4	21.7	10.1	3.0	21.0
Prepared flour mixes	65.6	23.7	36.2	6.2	19.0	10.9	6.8	13.4
Ready-to-eat and cooked cereals	63.3	19.6	38.4	6.4	21.2	10.6	6.4	15.5
Rice	58.8	17.9	33.6	4.9	17.9	10.5	8.0	14.4
Pasta, cornmeal, and other cereal products	64.9	20.4	37.9	7.1	19.5	11.2	5.4	15.2
Bakery products	63.9	21.3	36.5	5.9	19.2	11.2	5.2	16.1
Bread	61.8	21.6	34.1	5.4	17.4	11.0	4.5	17.7
White bread	60.8	19.9	34.6	4.9	17.8	11.6	5.6	16.3
Bread, other than white	62.6	22.8	33.7	5.8	17.2	10.5	3.8	18.7
Cookies and crackers	65.6	22.7	37.1	6.0	19.8	11.1	4.9	16.2
Cookies	64.1	22.5	35.0	5.2	19.0	10.5	5.1	17.0
Crackers	67.5	23.1	39.8	7.1	20.8	11.8	4.7	15.1
Frozen and refrigerated bakery products	64.8	18.6	41.3	8.9	22.8	9.7	5.6	15.3
Other bakery products	64.3	20.8	36.9	5.6	19.3	11.7	5.8	14.9
Biscuits and rolls	67.8	22.9	38.9	5.7	20.7	12.3	5.3	14.5
Cakes and cupcakes	61.3	17.2	36.2	5.8	20.0	10.1	6.8	13.7
Bread and cracker products	62.7	21.8	34.9	5.5	14.6	14.5	5.1	14.1
Sweetrolls, coffee cakes, doughnuts	63.6	22.5	35.2	5.6	17.3	12.0	5.1	17.4
Pies, tarts, turnovers	61.1	19.8	35.1	4.2	18.5	12.0	6.4	16.0
Meats, poultry, fish, and eggs	**64.1**	**20.3**	**36.5**	**5.3**	**18.4**	**12.5**	**5.4**	**14.1**
Beef	65.8	20.8	36.0	4.7	18.5	12.4	5.3	12.3
Ground beef	61.8	17.8	35.6	5.2	17.7	12.4	7.1	12.6
Roast	72.2	25.5	38.4	4.4	22.4	11.1	4.1	9.9
Chuck roast	72.3	26.4	34.5	2.6	19.6	11.7	4.1	12.0
Round roast	67.0	22.9	34.3	2.4	23.6	7.6	3.6	12.8
Other roast	74.0	26.0	41.6	6.0	23.2	12.1	4.2	7.9
Steak	66.3	22.4	34.7	4.1	17.8	12.4	4.1	13.0
Round steak	63.4	20.2	31.1	3.2	16.0	11.5	6.2	13.4
Sirloin steak	64.8	24.3	32.9	5.1	15.5	12.2	5.1	14.9
Other steak	68.1	22.3	36.8	4.0	19.6	12.8	2.8	11.9
Other beef	72.2	20.8	39.9	4.8	19.6	15.0	3.7	11.3
Pork	63.6	20.6	35.5	5.1	18.1	12.0	5.1	14.4
Bacon	63.5	21.5	35.5	5.2	19.2	10.8	4.9	16.2
Pork chops	62.7	17.9	35.4	4.9	18.7	11.5	5.9	13.0
Ham	65.2	20.2	38.4	5.3	20.0	12.8	4.3	15.6
Ham, not canned	65.1	20.2	38.4	5.1	20.0	13.0	4.3	15.8
Canned ham	69.4	21.5	36.6	11.0	19.7	6.5	4.6	7.2
Sausage	61.5	22.4	32.5	6.4	16.0	10.1	5.6	14.4
Other pork	64.4	20.8	35.4	4.2	16.7	14.1	4.9	12.9
Other meats	66.5	19.6	40.7	5.6	21.8	12.9	4.7	14.0
Frankfurters	65.0	18.7	37.9	6.5	19.4	11.9	6.6	13.8
Lunch meats (cold cuts)	65.7	20.4	39.1	5.5	20.8	12.4	4.6	14.3
Bologna, liverwurst, salami	63.8	20.2	35.9	4.2	19.8	11.5	4.5	15.7
Other lunch meats	66.5	20.6	40.4	6.1	21.3	12.8	4.7	13.7
Lamb, organ meats, and others	76.0	14.9	59.4	4.9	34.5	19.0	1.6	11.2

	total married couples	married couples, no children	married couples with children				single parent with child under age 18	single person
			total	oldest child under age 6	oldest child aged 6 to 17	oldest child aged 18 or older		
Poultry	62.7%	18.4%	37.4%	5.9%	17.6%	13.7%	6.1%	13.8%
Fresh and frozen chicken	61.8	18.0	36.7	5.5	17.6	13.3	6.2	14.1
Fresh and frozen whole chicken	62.3	17.4	36.8	5.7	18.5	12.4	6.8	14.5
Fresh and frozen chicken parts	61.6	18.3	36.6	5.4	17.2	13.7	5.9	13.9
Other poultry	66.6	19.7	40.4	7.4	17.6	15.3	6.1	12.7
Fish and seafood	62.3	22.6	33.8	5.2	16.4	12.0	5.9	16.0
Canned fish and seafood	61.4	22.2	33.3	4.8	16.2	12.0	4.8	20.5
Fresh fish and shellfish	62.2	22.7	33.8	4.3	17.2	11.9	6.0	15.0
Frozen fish and shellfish	62.7	22.6	34.1	6.6	15.5	12.0	6.3	15.4
Eggs	60.7	19.8	34.5	5.8	17.2	11.3	5.1	17.6
Dairy products	**64.5**	**21.3**	**37.2**	**7.0**	**19.1**	**11.0**	**5.0**	**16.0**
Fresh milk and cream	63.7	19.4	37.9	7.6	19.1	11.2	5.3	15.5
Fresh milk, all types	63.4	18.5	38.4	8.0	19.3	11.2	5.5	15.4
Cream	65.4	24.2	34.8	5.0	18.3	11.2	4.2	16.2
Other dairy products	64.9	22.5	36.8	6.6	19.2	10.9	4.8	16.3
Butter	65.8	26.0	34.5	4.7	18.6	10.9	3.8	15.5
Cheese	65.2	22.3	37.3	6.8	19.0	11.5	4.5	16.3
Ice cream and related products	64.4	23.4	35.1	4.9	18.9	11.0	5.9	15.9
Miscellaneous dairy products	64.5	20.2	38.5	9.2	20.1	9.4	4.6	17.2
Fruits and vegetables	**63.7**	**22.0**	**35.5**	**6.6**	**17.8**	**11.1**	**4.8**	**16.6**
Fresh fruits	64.6	22.8	36.0	6.8	17.9	11.2	4.8	17.3
Apples	64.7	21.1	38.2	6.9	20.7	10.5	5.0	17.0
Bananas	62.7	21.2	34.2	6.5	16.1	11.6	5.2	17.9
Oranges	63.6	21.9	35.8	5.8	19.7	10.1	4.8	17.0
Citrus fruits, excluding oranges	64.4	22.6	35.7	6.4	17.5	11.7	4.7	18.0
Other fresh fruits	65.6	24.3	36.1	7.3	17.3	11.5	4.6	17.1
Fresh vegetables	64.4	23.5	34.5	6.3	17.2	10.9	4.0	16.2
Potatoes	64.0	23.5	33.3	5.5	16.3	11.4	5.4	15.0
Lettuce	64.9	23.5	35.9	5.4	18.2	12.1	3.7	16.1
Tomatoes	64.1	22.7	34.9	7.0	15.7	12.3	3.8	16.8
Other fresh vegetables	64.5	23.7	34.4	6.7	17.7	10.0	3.7	16.5
Processed fruits	61.1	19.3	36.0	6.9	18.3	10.7	5.5	17.1
Frozen fruits and fruit juices	63.2	21.1	38.4	7.7	18.4	12.3	4.5	20.7
Frozen orange juice	69.9	21.4	42.9	6.0	25.3	11.1	4.2	15.5
Frozen fruits	59.2	23.4	33.1	7.9	14.2	11.2	3.7	25.2
Frozen fruit juices, excluding orange	63.9	14.5	45.7	9.7	19.7	16.4	6.9	16.1
Canned fruits	65.1	21.3	37.5	7.2	19.1	11.2	6.0	15.7
Dried fruits	62.6	20.6	37.2	4.7	22.0	10.1	3.6	19.0
Fresh fruit juice	59.1	18.7	34.1	8.0	16.3	10.0	5.5	19.1
Canned and bottled fruit juice	59.5	18.1	35.2	6.6	18.1	10.4	5.9	16.0
Processed vegetables	63.2	20.5	35.9	6.6	18.0	11.2	5.4	15.3
Frozen vegetables	65.4	22.2	36.4	7.2	17.8	11.3	4.4	15.9
Canned and dried vegetables and juices	62.4	19.8	35.7	6.4	18.0	11.2	5.8	15.0
Canned beans	59.9	19.9	32.2	6.1	16.8	9.3	6.0	16.2
Canned corn	62.6	17.7	37.1	6.3	19.0	11.6	5.7	14.0
Canned miscellaneous vegetables	63.5	23.5	33.5	6.2	15.9	11.4	5.2	15.7
Dried peas	66.2	21.2	37.7	2.3	15.4	19.3	11.1	8.4
Dried beans	62.1	17.4	38.3	5.0	17.0	15.9	4.2	12.9
Dried miscellaneous vegetables	66.9	19.1	40.6	7.6	21.5	11.5	6.1	11.7
Dried processed vegetables	66.5	31.8	21.4	3.8	6.8	10.7	3.1	13.7
Fresh and canned vegetable juices	60.0	15.4	38.7	7.1	20.6	11.0	6.6	16.6
Sugar and other sweets	**64.2**	**21.8**	**36.1**	**6.1**	**19.0**	**10.9**	**4.9**	**16.7**
Candy and chewing gum	64.9	22.9	35.4	5.4	18.9	10.9	4.8	17.3
Sugar	59.7	18.0	35.3	6.5	17.6	11.1	5.7	16.4
Artificial sweeteners	71.8	27.7	36.4	7.8	17.4	11.3	2.5	10.2
Jams, preserves, other sweets	64.2	20.2	38.8	7.3	20.8	10.7	5.1	16.5

	total married couples	married couples, no children	married couples with children				single parent with child under age 18	single person
			total	oldest child under age 6	oldest child aged 6 to 17	oldest child aged 18 or older		
Fats and oils	**63.9%**	**22.4%**	**34.2%**	**5.3%**	**16.9%**	**11.8%**	**4.7%**	**16.8%**
Margarine	60.6	23.6	28.9	4.2	13.4	11.0	5.0	19.8
Fats and oils	62.6	21.8	33.4	5.1	16.4	11.6	5.5	16.3
Salad dressings	67.4	24.4	35.8	5.5	17.1	13.0	4.6	15.7
Nondairy cream and imitation milk	65.0	24.2	33.6	5.6	16.8	11.0	4.2	15.7
Peanut butter	60.4	17.1	37.0	5.3	20.3	11.2	3.7	20.0
Miscellaneous foods	**61.7**	**20.6**	**35.6**	**7.4**	**18.0**	**10.2**	**5.6**	**17.0**
Frozen prepared foods	58.6	18.4	35.4	6.1	19.6	9.6	6.6	19.3
Frozen meals	56.4	20.2	31.9	6.3	16.0	9.6	5.0	23.4
Other frozen prepared foods	60.4	16.9	38.4	6.0	22.7	9.5	8.0	15.8
Canned and packaged soups	62.3	23.6	33.0	6.0	16.4	10.5	3.9	18.2
Potato chips, nuts, and other snacks	64.2	22.8	36.1	5.7	19.3	10.9	5.4	16.6
Potato chips and other snacks	64.0	20.0	38.7	6.4	20.7	11.3	6.1	15.6
Nuts	65.0	30.9	28.5	3.6	15.0	9.6	3.3	19.7
Condiments and seasonings	63.7	22.3	35.3	6.6	17.3	11.3	5.4	15.5
Salt, spices, and other seasonings	62.8	22.2	33.9	6.2	17.4	10.2	5.3	14.7
Olives, pickles, relishes	62.0	25.8	30.7	5.3	14.0	11.1	4.3	17.9
Sauces and gravies	63.9	20.3	37.9	6.9	18.3	12.5	6.2	14.4
Baking needs and miscellaneous products	65.4	25.2	34.1	7.0	16.9	10.2	4.2	17.6
Other canned or packaged prepared foods	60.5	18.8	36.1	10.1	17.0	9.4	5.7	16.5
Prepared salads	59.4	22.1	31.5	6.1	15.8	9.6	4.4	22.0
Prepared desserts	62.7	20.1	36.1	4.3	18.9	12.5	5.6	15.7
Baby food	61.0	4.7	50.8	35.2	14.6	4.5	8.9	7.3
Miscellaneous prepared foods	60.5	20.4	34.6	7.0	17.6	10.0	5.4	16.9
Nonalcoholic beverages	**60.7**	**20.6**	**33.6**	**5.1**	**17.7**	**10.6**	**5.4**	**16.5**
Cola	60.8	21.4	31.8	4.8	15.9	10.9	5.4	15.4
Other carbonated drinks	59.4	18.7	34.5	5.6	17.4	11.3	5.2	15.1
Tea	60.2	20.5	33.3	5.0	17.0	11.1	6.0	17.4
Coffee	64.4	26.9	31.5	5.4	16.5	9.5	3.8	18.0
Noncarbonated fruit-flavored drinks	58.3	17.5	35.9	5.4	19.9	10.3	8.4	15.6
Other noncarbonated beverages and ice	58.4	17.5	35.8	6.0	22.0	7.7	6.3	19.2
Bottled water	58.7	17.3	34.9	4.0	18.9	11.5	5.6	18.2
Sports drinks	62.6	15.8	40.2	4.6	23.5	11.7	6.6	12.2
Food prepared by consumer unit on trips	**74.2**	**35.1**	**33.9**	**5.9**	**19.1**	**8.9**	**2.3**	**14.3**
FOOD AWAY FROM HOME	**63.3**	**23.3**	**34.3**	**5.5**	**18.0**	**10.6**	**4.7**	**17.7**
Meals at restaurants, carry-outs, etc.	**61.9**	**22.6**	**33.4**	**5.7**	**17.0**	**10.5**	**4.7**	**18.4**
Lunch	62.1	20.8	35.1	6.4	18.1	10.5	4.5	18.4
At fast-food restaurants*	58.8	17.5	35.7	6.7	17.8	11.1	5.0	18.1
At full-service restaurants	64.6	27.6	30.3	6.4	13.8	10.1	3.0	19.8
At vending machines, mobile vendors	53.4	11.5	33.0	6.0	11.9	14.9	6.0	20.2
At employer and school cafeterias	69.3	10.3	51.8	5.0	37.2	9.0	8.4	13.6
Dinner	62.5	24.7	32.5	5.6	16.1	10.7	4.6	17.9
At fast-food restaurants*	57.9	16.4	35.3	6.4	18.1	10.6	7.6	16.1
At full-service restaurants	65.3	29.3	31.2	5.2	15.1	10.7	3.1	18.6
At vending machines, mobile vendors	46.1	23.7	19.4	4.4	8.1	7.0	1.3	34.8
At employer and school cafeterias	42.7	16.8	23.3	5.1	13.1	5.2	1.4	33.5
Snacks and nonalcoholic beverages	58.5	18.0	35.0	5.9	20.2	8.8	5.0	18.9
At fast-food restaurants*	61.3	18.7	36.9	5.7	22.3	8.7	4.9	17.2
At full-service restaurants	51.1	19.2	26.8	6.6	12.7	7.6	4.8	23.4
At vending machines, mobile vendors	54.8	12.9	37.7	5.8	20.3	11.3	6.4	21.0
At employer and school cafeterias	56.8	13.5	37.0	4.1	23.3	9.1	5.4	20.4
Breakfast and brunch	60.4	22.1	30.7	3.8	15.5	11.1	4.7	20.6
At fast-food restaurants*	59.3	17.7	33.5	5.3	16.9	11.1	5.1	20.3
At full-service restaurants	63.5	29.2	27.0	1.6	13.9	10.9	3.7	20.6
At vending machines, mobile vendors	42.5	12.5	22.8	4.8	6.1	11.9	9.7	26.3
At employer and school cafeterias	52.3	14.8	31.4	4.2	14.7	12.1	8.4	22.9

	total married couples	married couples, no children	married couples with children				single parent with child under age 18	single person
			total	oldest child under age 6	oldest child aged 6 to 17	oldest child aged 18 or older		
Board (including at school)	84.1%	30.2%	51.9%	0.2%	26.8%	24.9%	1.8%	8.3%
Catered affairs	74.9	35.1	37.5	6.5	14.2	16.9	2.0	11.9
Food on trips	69.9	34.4	31.0	4.9	17.9	8.3	2.9	16.9
School lunches	76.7	0.0	68.1	1.9	54.2	12.0	15.0	0.5
Meals as pay	33.2	8.7	20.3	5.5	9.7	5.2	7.1	30.5
ALCOHOLIC BEVERAGES	55.5	27.6	23.9	4.4	12.0	7.4	3.1	23.9
At home	60.6	29.1	27.0	4.7	12.8	9.4	4.3	20.0
Beer and ale	57.6	22.9	30.6	6.0	14.0	10.6	4.0	20.0
Whiskey	64.4	40.6	15.3	3.9	10.6	1.0	–	25.6
Wine	64.0	35.0	24.3	3.7	11.0	9.4	5.2	18.6
Other alcoholic beverages	57.9	27.4	26.3	2.9	16.9	6.3	2.7	24.1
Away from home	49.7	25.9	20.5	4.1	11.2	5.2	1.7	28.4
Beer and ale	46.0	20.2	22.2	5.3	12.3	4.8	1.3	30.1
At fast-food restaurants*	50.1	18.9	24.7	5.4	13.5	5.9	1.1	34.2
At full-service restaurants	45.5	20.4	21.9	5.4	12.1	4.6	1.3	28.6
At vending machines, mobile vendors	61.3	38.1	20.9	–	17.0	3.4	–	36.8
Wine	53.4	32.3	17.9	2.6	10.2	4.9	1.1	27.2
At fast-food restaurants*	53.3	38.9	11.6	–	6.4	4.8	1.7	28.3
At full-service restaurants	54.3	32.4	18.5	2.9	10.5	5.1	1.0	25.8
Other alcoholic beverages	41.7	22.5	16.4	3.5	8.6	4.4	2.0	32.4
At fast-food restaurants*	27.2	14.3	10.4	0.5	7.3	2.4	3.5	51.0
At full-service restaurants	43.1	23.3	17.0	3.8	8.7	4.6	1.8	30.7
Alcoholic beverages purchased on trips	61.4	33.7	24.4	4.3	13.1	7.0	2.8	22.2

*The category fast-food restaurants also includes take-out, delivery, concession stands, buffets, and cafeterias other than employer and school.
Note: Market share for total consumer units is 100.0%. Market shares by type of consumer unit do not add to total because not all types of consumer units are shown. "–" means sample is too small to make a reliable estimate.
Source: Calculations by New Strategist based on the Bureau of Labor Statistics' 2011 Consumer Expenditure Survey

(average annual spending of consumer units on food and alcoholic beverages, by race and Hispanic origin of consumer unit reference person, 2011)

	total consumer units	Asian	black	Hispanic	non-Hispanic white and other
Number of consumer units (in 000s)	122,287	5,048	15,118	15,222	92,163
Average number of persons per consumer unit	2.5	2.7	2.6	3.4	2.4
Average before-tax income of consumer units	$63,685.00	$85,415.00	$45,552.00	$49,966.00	$68,907.00
Average spending of consumer units, total	49,704.88	60,136.04	36,643.75	42,085.98	53,055.68
Food, average spending	**6,458.00**	**8,163.00**	**4,743.00**	**6,373.00**	**6,743.00**
Alcoholic beverages, average spending	**456.43**	**311.31**	**199.36**	**281.07**	**524.59**
FOOD AT HOME	**3,837.76**	**4,438.98**	**2,988.62**	**3,849.31**	**3,970.49**
Cereals and bakery products	**530.68**	**618.21**	**405.49**	**493.34**	**556.26**
Cereals and cereal products	174.86	264.71	142.77	181.43	178.99
Flour	7.67	14.72	6.45	7.73	7.88
Prepared flour mixes	14.88	7.02	13.72	11.82	15.61
Ready-to-eat and cooked cereals	91.39	69.00	73.54	86.34	94.89
Rice	25.66	111.48	26.94	47.11	22.29
Pasta, cornmeal, and other cereal products	35.26	62.51	22.11	28.44	38.32
Bakery products	355.81	353.49	262.72	311.91	377.27
Bread	106.53	102.72	79.94	107.87	110.51
White bread	44.93	45.21	39.51	49.67	45.07
Bread, other than white	61.60	57.52	40.43	58.20	65.44
Cookies and crackers	83.59	92.83	56.08	65.40	90.76
Cookies	46.96	59.95	36.05	38.76	49.97
Crackers	36.63	32.88	20.03	26.64	40.79
Frozen and refrigerated bakery products	28.60	31.12	23.12	21.77	30.53
Other bakery products	137.09	126.81	103.59	116.88	145.47
Biscuits and rolls	52.93	42.77	33.73	36.89	58.37
Cakes and cupcakes	37.81	37.17	37.09	38.83	37.80
Bread and cracker products	7.13	7.41	5.98	3.84	7.79
Sweetrolls, coffee cakes, doughnuts	23.86	23.00	16.01	26.31	24.76
Pies, tarts, turnovers	15.36	16.46	10.76	11.00	16.75
Meats, poultry, fish, and eggs	**832.41**	**1,093.95**	**822.26**	**968.42**	**812.70**
Beef	222.60	201.32	189.10	268.01	220.71
Ground beef	90.50	60.52	89.69	93.50	89.96
Roast	30.59	31.16	18.61	38.66	31.26
Chuck roast	7.65	4.52	6.27	14.61	6.85
Round roast	6.11	10.80	3.08	5.38	6.67
Other roast	16.82	15.84	9.26	18.68	17.74
Steak	82.49	68.54	64.65	106.42	81.62
Round steak	15.90	12.38	10.90	24.11	15.51
Sirloin steak	21.86	20.87	14.34	29.09	21.86
Other steak	44.73	35.29	39.41	53.21	44.25
Other beef	19.02	41.11	16.15	29.43	17.87
Pork	161.95	209.88	183.38	190.93	154.21
Bacon	33.87	35.98	34.98	33.95	33.65
Pork chops	27.24	24.40	41.17	37.35	23.62
Ham	34.29	29.78	25.12	41.32	34.65
Ham, not canned	33.51	28.36	24.59	39.98	33.92
Canned ham	0.78	1.42	0.53	1.34	0.73
Sausage	28.55	33.83	39.19	26.35	27.22
Other pork	37.99	85.89	42.92	51.96	35.07
Other meats	122.54	92.23	85.69	109.52	130.30
Frankfurters	23.67	16.18	23.00	28.66	23.05
Lunch meats (cold cuts)	87.67	51.16	56.53	70.11	95.22
Bologna, liverwurst, salami	26.83	16.02	17.39	25.12	28.55
Other lunch meats	60.84	35.13	39.14	44.99	66.67
Lamb, organ meats, and others	11.20	24.89	6.16	10.76	12.02

	total consumer units	Asian	black	Hispanic	non-Hispanic white and other
Poultry	$154.49	$186.41	$184.74	$195.77	$143.22
Fresh and frozen chicken	124.44	161.70	148.33	167.76	113.87
Fresh and frozen whole chicken	35.97	52.73	33.32	57.33	33.06
Fresh and frozen chicken parts	88.48	108.97	115.01	110.44	80.80
Other poultry	30.05	24.72	36.41	28.00	29.35
Fish and seafood	120.76	326.65	133.57	137.89	116.04
Canned fish and seafood	19.90	22.49	18.33	21.52	19.90
Fresh fish and shellfish	59.51	196.89	70.48	74.36	55.46
Frozen fish and shellfish	41.35	107.28	44.75	42.01	40.68
Eggs	50.07	77.45	45.77	66.31	48.22
Dairy products	**406.84**	**336.59**	**245.80**	**388.41**	**434.93**
Fresh milk and cream	149.73	161.37	98.28	162.90	155.69
Fresh milk, all types	127.38	149.31	86.63	143.99	131.09
Cream	22.36	12.07	11.65	18.91	24.60
Other dairy products	257.10	175.22	147.52	225.51	279.24
Butter	24.64	15.81	15.17	15.40	27.55
Cheese	124.74	58.07	63.23	111.17	136.43
Ice cream and related products	57.28	54.29	41.89	47.10	61.25
Miscellaneous dairy products	50.43	47.04	27.23	51.83	54.00
Fruits and vegetables	**714.89**	**1,058.65**	**526.95**	**778.18**	**735.14**
Fresh fruits	247.28	392.35	156.69	293.34	254.81
Apples	38.17	51.38	24.82	40.33	40.01
Bananas	41.08	55.99	28.64	60.50	40.19
Oranges	26.99	50.14	20.95	33.07	27.08
Citrus fruits, excluding oranges	37.63	68.78	18.19	54.54	38.09
Other fresh fruits	103.42	166.07	64.09	104.90	109.43
Fresh vegetables	224.21	415.34	144.90	241.04	234.06
Potatoes	38.78	64.87	31.88	43.78	39.09
Lettuce	32.17	41.74	20.27	29.73	34.46
Tomatoes	41.03	65.16	23.92	50.03	42.38
Other fresh vegetables	112.24	243.57	68.83	117.49	118.12
Processed fruits	115.73	111.49	108.51	119.87	116.31
Frozen fruits and fruit juices	13.31	9.21	7.54	12.96	14.24
Frozen orange juice	3.73	1.85	1.71	3.96	4.00
Frozen fruits	6.92	4.37	3.49	6.27	7.54
Frozen fruit juices, excluding orange	2.67	2.98	2.34	2.74	2.70
Canned fruits	21.24	19.62	17.32	17.42	22.39
Dried fruits	8.13	8.78	3.98	5.93	9.11
Fresh fruit juice	17.28	15.00	17.08	16.60	17.47
Canned and bottled fruit juice	55.78	58.88	62.60	66.96	53.10
Processed vegetables	127.66	139.48	116.85	123.94	129.96
Frozen vegetables	34.98	37.17	31.45	23.74	37.24
Canned and dried vegetables and juices	92.68	102.31	85.40	100.20	92.72
Canned beans	19.08	12.90	17.48	23.55	18.73
Canned corn	9.73	8.42	10.58	10.87	9.43
Canned miscellaneous vegetables	25.50	22.36	20.24	21.11	26.92
Dried peas	0.84	1.05	0.93	1.04	0.80
Dried beans	4.99	7.66	4.38	11.18	4.19
Dried miscellaneous vegetables	11.55	20.68	10.73	10.83	11.84
Dried processed vegetables	2.05	1.61	2.35	1.22	2.14
Fresh and canned vegetable juices	18.59	27.62	18.68	19.91	18.30
Sugar and other sweets	**144.39**	**156.89**	**97.90**	**116.69**	**155.92**
Candy and chewing gum	86.75	93.69	47.97	59.05	97.02
Sugar	23.89	31.30	26.29	28.12	22.84
Artificial sweeteners	5.61	5.87	3.56	5.08	6.02
Jams, preserves, other sweets	28.14	26.03	20.08	24.44	30.04

	total consumer units	Asian	black	Hispanic	non-Hispanic white and other
Fats and oils	**$109.61**	**$115.44**	**$94.01**	**$121.96**	**$110.34**
Margarine	9.77	4.91	10.36	8.46	9.95
Fats and oils	34.84	62.66	38.56	57.88	30.87
Salad dressings	31.16	22.58	24.69	27.36	32.76
Nondairy cream and imitation milk	18.59	14.11	10.33	16.35	20.20
Peanut butter	15.25	11.17	10.07	11.92	16.55
Miscellaneous foods	**690.48**	**678.45**	**502.04**	**579.86**	**737.28**
Frozen prepared foods	136.23	95.57	102.89	85.58	149.56
Frozen meals	62.14	37.54	48.23	33.84	68.77
Other frozen prepared foods	74.09	58.04	54.66	51.74	80.79
Canned and packaged soups	46.90	54.77	33.94	32.32	51.19
Potato chips, nuts, and other snacks	145.02	126.54	91.56	110.00	158.80
Potato chips and other snacks	108.01	82.02	69.46	86.61	117.32
Nuts	37.01	44.51	22.10	23.40	41.48
Condiments and seasonings	133.90	137.74	105.60	116.93	141.01
Salt, spices, and other seasonings	35.41	44.76	31.12	40.20	35.37
Olives, pickles, relishes	16.13	13.99	9.52	10.17	18.08
Sauces and gravies	58.43	64.57	49.23	49.30	61.26
Baking needs and miscellaneous products	23.93	14.42	15.71	17.27	26.30
Other canned or packaged prepared foods	228.42	263.83	168.06	235.03	236.72
Prepared salads	36.22	28.98	26.71	22.68	39.86
Prepared desserts	15.03	13.62	10.35	16.43	15.61
Baby food	27.80	66.11	19.71	31.73	28.37
Miscellaneous prepared foods	147.11	155.12	110.67	164.19	150.01
Nonalcoholic beverages	**360.97**	**323.92**	**280.30**	**369.98**	**372.54**
Cola	78.77	50.50	61.02	79.87	81.29
Other carbonated drinks	66.72	49.75	50.77	67.75	69.01
Tea	31.16	46.77	23.44	25.19	33.31
Coffee	75.03	64.20	39.33	62.42	82.64
Noncarbonated fruit-flavored drinks	24.76	27.50	31.95	33.65	22.59
Other noncarbonated beverages and ice	14.93	11.61	12.14	15.04	15.36
Bottled water	53.48	63.93	50.96	71.96	50.96
Sports drinks	15.73	9.67	10.69	14.12	16.85
Food prepared by consumer unit on trips	**47.50**	**56.88**	**13.88**	**32.45**	**55.39**
FOOD AWAY FROM HOME	**2,619.89**	**3,724.02**	**1,753.98**	**2,524.15**	**2,772.60**
Meals at restaurants, carry-outs, etc.	**2,195.89**	**3,032.89**	**1,571.19**	**2,204.98**	**2,292.48**
Lunch	752.89	1,184.59	536.48	783.22	782.34
At fast-food restaurants*	368.78	555.08	330.57	427.45	366.54
At full-service restaurants	302.01	466.69	120.79	287.14	332.17
At vending machines, mobile vendors	7.16	4.68	6.31	16.11	5.92
At employer and school cafeterias	74.94	158.15	78.81	52.52	77.70
Dinner	1,051.05	1,370.59	754.12	959.91	1,110.44
At fast-food restaurants*	365.13	444.14	367.83	438.23	353.04
At full-service restaurants	676.06	912.44	381.96	516.47	745.99
At vending machines, mobile vendors	3.02	2.08	1.45	2.57	3.32
At employer and school cafeterias	6.85	11.92	2.88	2.64	8.10
Snacks and nonalcoholic beverages	166.09	208.34	114.44	164.09	174.76
At fast-food restaurants*	109.65	141.69	69.87	99.98	117.78
At full-service restaurants	32.72	27.84	22.40	37.07	33.57
At vending machines, mobile vendors	17.28	27.29	19.33	22.13	16.20
At employer and school cafeterias	6.43	11.53	2.84	4.92	7.21
Breakfast and brunch	225.86	269.37	166.15	297.76	224.93
At fast-food restaurants*	123.77	166.69	94.66	171.09	121.25
At full-service restaurants	89.39	83.61	49.85	110.17	93.03
At vending machines, mobile vendors	3.03	7.29	3.22	7.39	2.32
At employer and school cafeterias	9.66	11.78	18.41	9.11	8.33

	total consumer units	Asian	black	Hispanic	non-Hispanic white and other
Board (including at school)	$43.87	$119.58	$10.08	$22.36	$52.87
Catered affairs	52.63	124.57	29.53	46.34	57.33
Food on trips	236.49	344.11	77.72	146.24	277.04
School lunches	62.16	72.27	47.34	51.40	66.26
Meals as pay	28.85	30.59	18.13	52.83	26.64
ALCOHOLIC BEVERAGES	456.43	311.31	199.36	281.07	524.59
At home	242.35	167.34	130.60	152.68	274.03
Beer and ale	109.76	71.05	82.93	94.92	116.52
Whiskey	9.60	10.01	6.49	5.05	10.74
Wine	104.03	72.77	28.36	39.02	125.66
Other alcoholic beverages	18.97	13.51	12.83	13.69	21.11
Away from home	214.08	143.97	68.76	128.39	250.56
Beer and ale	76.98	24.16	22.48	59.14	88.32
At fast-food restaurants*	12.47	0.38	7.24	15.13	13.05
At full-service restaurants	63.32	23.78	14.60	43.83	73.84
At vending machines, mobile vendors	0.65	–	0.65	0.18	0.72
Wine	41.96	27.88	13.15	16.91	50.42
At fast-food restaurants*	2.96	2.55	2.23	0.96	3.36
At full-service restaurants	38.20	25.33	10.92	15.95	46.00
Other alcoholic beverages	50.30	47.25	20.24	30.64	57.97
At fast-food restaurants*	4.25	–	4.71	1.86	4.53
At full-service restaurants	45.99	47.25	15.53	28.78	53.36
Alcoholic beverages purchased on trips	44.84	44.68	12.88	21.69	53.85

* The category fast-food restaurants also includes take-out, delivery, concession stands, buffets, and cafeterias other than employer and school.
Note: "Asian" and "black" include Hispanics and non-Hispanics who identify themselves as being of the respective race alone. "Hispanic" includes people of any race who identify themselves as Hispanic.
"Other" includes people who identify themselves as non-Hispanic and as Alaska Native, American Indian, Asian (who are also included in the "Asian" column), or Native Hawaiian or other Pacific Islander, as well as non-Hispanics reporting more than one race. Subcategories may not add to total because some are not shown. "–" means sample is too small to make a reliable estimate.
Source: Bureau of Labor Statistics, unpublished tables from the 2011 Consumer Expenditure Survey

Table 5.18 Food and Alcohol: Indexed spending by race and Hispanic origin, 2011

(indexed average annual spending of consumer units on food and alcoholic beverages, by race and Hispanic origin of consumer unit reference person, 2011; index definition: an index of 100 is the average for all consumer units; an index of 125 means that spending by consumer units in that group is 25 percent above the average for all consumer units; an index of 75 indicates spending that is 25 percent below the average for all consumer units)

	total consumer units	Asian	black	Hispanic	non-Hispanic white and other
Average spending of consumer units, total	$49,705	$60,136	$36,644	$42,086	$53,056
Average spending of consumer units, index	100	121	74	85	107
Food, spending index	100	126	73	99	104
Alcoholic beverages, spending index	100	68	44	62	115
FOOD AT HOME	100	116	78	100	103
Cereals and bakery products	100	116	76	93	105
Cereals and cereal products	100	151	82	104	102
Flour	100	192	84	101	103
Prepared flour mixes	100	47	92	79	105
Ready-to-eat and cooked cereals	100	76	80	94	104
Rice	100	434	105	184	87
Pasta, cornmeal, and other cereal products	100	177	63	81	109
Bakery products	100	99	74	88	106
Bread	100	96	75	101	104
White bread	100	101	88	111	100
Bread, other than white	100	93	66	94	106
Cookies and crackers	100	111	67	78	109
Cookies	100	128	77	83	106
Crackers	100	90	55	73	111
Frozen and refrigerated bakery products	100	109	81	76	107
Other bakery products	100	93	76	85	106
Biscuits and rolls	100	81	64	70	110
Cakes and cupcakes	100	98	98	103	100
Bread and cracker products	100	104	84	54	109
Sweetrolls, coffee cakes, doughnuts	100	96	67	110	104
Pies, tarts, turnovers	100	107	70	72	109
Meats, poultry, fish, and eggs	100	131	99	116	98
Beef	100	90	85	120	99
Ground beef	100	67	99	103	99
Roast	100	102	61	126	102
Chuck roast	100	59	82	191	90
Round roast	100	177	50	88	109
Other roast	100	94	55	111	105
Steak	100	83	78	129	99
Round steak	100	78	69	152	98
Sirloin steak	100	95	66	133	100
Other steak	100	79	88	119	99
Other beef	100	216	85	155	94
Pork	100	130	113	118	95
Bacon	100	106	103	100	99
Pork chops	100	90	151	137	87
Ham	100	87	73	121	101
Ham, not canned	100	85	73	119	101
Canned ham	100	182	68	172	94
Sausage	100	118	137	92	95
Other pork	100	226	113	137	92
Other meats	100	75	70	89	106
Frankfurters	100	68	97	121	97
Lunch meats (cold cuts)	100	58	64	80	109
Bologna, liverwurst, salami	100	60	65	94	106
Other lunch meats	100	58	64	74	110
Lamb, organ meats, and others	100	222	55	96	107

	total consumer units	Asian	black	Hispanic	non-Hispanic white and other
Poultry	100	121	120	127	93
Fresh and frozen chicken	100	130	119	135	92
Fresh and frozen whole chicken	100	147	93	159	92
Fresh and frozen chicken parts	100	123	130	125	91
Other poultry	100	82	121	93	98
Fish and seafood	100	270	111	114	96
Canned fish and seafood	100	113	92	108	100
Fresh fish and shellfish	100	331	118	125	93
Frozen fish and shellfish	100	259	108	102	98
Eggs	100	155	91	132	96
Dairy products	**100**	**83**	**60**	**95**	**107**
Fresh milk and cream	100	108	66	109	104
Fresh milk, all types	100	117	68	113	103
Cream	100	54	52	85	110
Other dairy products	100	68	57	88	109
Butter	100	64	62	63	112
Cheese	100	47	51	89	109
Ice cream and related products	100	95	73	82	107
Miscellaneous dairy products	100	93	54	103	107
Fruits and vegetables	**100**	**148**	**74**	**109**	**103**
Fresh fruits	100	159	63	119	103
Apples	100	135	65	106	105
Bananas	100	136	70	147	98
Oranges	100	186	78	123	100
Citrus fruits, excluding oranges	100	183	48	145	101
Other fresh fruits	100	161	62	101	106
Fresh vegetables	100	185	65	108	104
Potatoes	100	167	82	113	101
Lettuce	100	130	63	92	107
Tomatoes	100	159	58	122	103
Other fresh vegetables	100	217	61	105	105
Processed fruits	100	96	94	104	101
Frozen fruits and fruit juices	100	69	57	97	107
Frozen orange juice	100	50	46	106	107
Frozen fruits	100	63	50	91	109
Frozen fruit juices, excluding orange	100	112	88	103	101
Canned fruits	100	92	82	82	105
Dried fruits	100	108	49	73	112
Fresh fruit juice	100	87	99	96	101
Canned and bottled fruit juice	100	106	112	120	95
Processed vegetables	100	109	92	97	102
Frozen vegetables	100	106	90	68	106
Canned and dried vegetables and juices	100	110	92	108	100
Canned beans	100	68	92	123	98
Canned corn	100	87	109	112	97
Canned miscellaneous vegetables	100	88	79	83	106
Dried peas	100	125	111	124	95
Dried beans	100	154	88	224	84
Dried miscellaneous vegetables	100	179	93	94	103
Dried processed vegetables	100	79	115	60	104
Fresh and canned vegetable juices	100	149	100	107	98
Sugar and other sweets	**100**	**109**	**68**	**81**	**108**
Candy and chewing gum	100	108	55	68	112
Sugar	100	131	110	118	96
Artificial sweeteners	100	105	63	91	107
Jams, preserves, other sweets	100	93	71	87	107

	total consumer units	Asian	black	Hispanic	non-Hispanic white and other
Fats and oils	**100**	**105**	**86**	**111**	**101**
Margarine	100	50	106	87	102
Fats and oils	100	180	111	166	89
Salad dressings	100	72	79	88	105
Nondairy cream and imitation milk	100	76	56	88	109
Peanut butter	100	73	66	78	109
Miscellaneous foods	**100**	**98**	**73**	**84**	**107**
Frozen prepared foods	100	70	76	63	110
Frozen meals	100	60	78	54	111
Other frozen prepared foods	100	78	74	70	109
Canned and packaged soups	100	117	72	69	109
Potato chips, nuts, and other snacks	100	87	63	76	110
Potato chips and other snacks	100	76	64	80	109
Nuts	100	120	60	63	112
Condiments and seasonings	100	103	79	87	105
Salt, spices, and other seasonings	100	126	88	114	100
Olives, pickles, relishes	100	87	59	63	112
Sauces and gravies	100	111	84	84	105
Baking needs and miscellaneous products	100	60	66	72	110
Other canned or packaged prepared foods	100	116	74	103	104
Prepared salads	100	80	74	63	110
Prepared desserts	100	91	69	109	104
Baby food	100	238	71	114	102
Miscellaneous prepared foods	100	105	75	112	102
Nonalcoholic beverages	**100**	**90**	**78**	**102**	**103**
Cola	100	64	77	101	103
Other carbonated drinks	100	75	76	102	103
Tea	100	150	75	81	107
Coffee	100	86	52	83	110
Noncarbonated fruit-flavored drinks	100	111	129	136	91
Other noncarbonated beverages and ice	100	78	81	101	103
Bottled water	100	120	95	135	95
Sports drinks	100	61	68	90	107
Food prepared by consumer unit on trips	**100**	**120**	**29**	**68**	**117**
FOOD AWAY FROM HOME	**100**	**142**	**67**	**96**	**106**
Meals at restaurants, carry-outs, etc.	**100**	**138**	**72**	**100**	**104**
Lunch	100	157	71	104	104
At fast-food restaurants*	100	151	90	116	99
At full-service restaurants	100	155	40	95	110
At vending machines, mobile vendors	100	65	88	225	83
At employer and school cafeterias	100	211	105	70	104
Dinner	100	130	72	91	106
At fast-food restaurants*	100	122	101	120	97
At full-service restaurants	100	135	56	76	110
At vending machines, mobile vendors	100	69	48	85	110
At employer and school cafeterias	100	174	42	39	118
Snacks and nonalcoholic beverages	100	125	69	99	105
At fast-food restaurants*	100	129	64	91	107
At full-service restaurants	100	85	68	113	103
At vending machines, mobile vendors	100	158	112	128	94
At employer and school cafeterias	100	179	44	77	112
Breakfast and brunch	100	119	74	132	100
At fast-food restaurants*	100	135	76	138	98
At full-service restaurants	100	94	56	123	104
At vending machines, mobile vendors	100	241	106	244	77
At employer and school cafeterias	100	122	191	94	86

	total consumer units	Asian	black	Hispanic	non-Hispanic white and other
Board (including at school)	100	273	23	51	121
Catered affairs	100	237	56	88	109
Food on trips	100	146	33	62	117
School lunches	100	116	76	83	107
Meals as pay	100	106	63	183	92
ALCOHOLIC BEVERAGES	100	68	44	62	115
At home	100	69	54	63	113
Beer and ale	100	65	76	86	106
Whiskey	100	104	68	53	112
Wine	100	70	27	38	121
Other alcoholic beverages	100	71	68	72	111
Away from home	100	67	32	60	117
Beer and ale	100	31	29	77	115
At fast-food restaurants*	100	3	58	121	105
At full-service restaurants	100	38	23	69	117
At vending machines, mobile vendors	100	–	100	28	111
Wine	100	66	31	40	120
At fast-food restaurants*	100	86	75	32	114
At full-service restaurants	100	66	29	42	120
Other alcoholic beverages	100	94	40	61	115
At fast-food restaurants*	100	–	111	44	107
At full-service restaurants	100	103	34	63	116
Alcoholic beverages purchased on trips	100	100	29	48	120

* The category fast-food restaurants also includes take-out, delivery, concession stands, buffets, and cafeterias other than employer and school.
Note: "Asian" and "black" include Hispanics and non-Hispanics who identify themselves as being of the respective race alone. "Hispanic" includes people of any race who identify themselves as Hispanic. "Other" includes people who identify themselves as non-Hispanic and as Alaska Native, American Indian, Asian (who are also included in the "Asian" column), or Native Hawaiian or other Pacific Islander, as well as non-Hispanics reporting more than one race. "–" means sample is too small to make a reliable estimate.
Source: Calculations by New Strategist based on the Bureau of Labor Statistics' 2011 Consumer Expenditure Survey

Table 5.19 Food and Alcohol: Total spending by race and Hispanic origin, 2011

(total annual spending on food and alcoholic beverages, by consumer unit race and Hispanic origin groups, 2011; consumer units and dollars in thousands)

	total consumer units	Asian	black	Hispanic	non-Hispanic white and other
Number of consumer units	122,287	5,048	15,118	15,222	92,163
Total spending of all consumer units	$6,078,260,661	$303,566,730	$553,980,213	$640,632,788	$4,889,770,636
Food, total spending	789,729,446	41,206,824	71,704,674	97,009,806	621,455,109
Alcoholic beverages, total spending	55,815,455	1,571,493	3,013,924	4,278,448	48,347,788
FOOD AT HOME	**469,308,157**	**22,407,971**	**45,181,957**	**58,594,197**	**365,932,270**
Cereals and bakery products	**64,895,265**	**3,120,724**	**6,130,198**	**7,509,621**	**51,266,590**
Cereals and cereal products	21,383,105	1,336,256	2,158,397	2,761,727	16,496,255
Flour	937,941	74,307	97,511	117,666	726,244
Prepared flour mixes	1,819,631	35,437	207,419	179,924	1,438,664
Ready-to-eat and cooked cereals	11,175,809	348,312	1,111,778	1,314,267	8,745,347
Rice	3,137,884	562,751	407,279	717,108	2,054,313
Pasta, cornmeal, and other cereal products	4,311,840	315,550	334,259	432,914	3,531,686
Bakery products	43,510,937	1,784,418	3,971,801	4,747,894	34,770,335
Bread	13,027,234	518,531	1,208,533	1,641,997	10,184,933
White bread	5,494,355	228,220	597,312	756,077	4,153,786
Bread, other than white	7,532,879	290,361	611,221	885,920	6,031,147
Cookies and crackers	10,221,970	468,606	847,817	995,519	8,364,714
Cookies	5,742,598	302,628	545,004	590,005	4,605,385
Crackers	4,479,373	165,978	302,814	405,514	3,759,329
Frozen and refrigerated bakery products	3,497,408	157,094	349,528	331,383	2,813,736
Other bakery products	16,764,325	640,137	1,566,074	1,779,147	13,406,952
Biscuits and rolls	6,472,651	215,903	509,930	561,540	5,379,554
Cakes and cupcakes	4,623,671	187,634	560,727	591,070	3,483,761
Bread and cracker products	871,906	37,406	90,406	58,452	717,950
Sweetrolls, coffee cakes, doughnuts	2,917,768	116,104	242,039	400,491	2,281,956
Pies, tarts, turnovers	1,878,328	83,090	162,670	167,442	1,543,730
Meats, poultry, fish, and eggs	**101,792,922**	**5,522,260**	**12,430,927**	**14,741,289**	**74,900,870**
Beef	27,221,086	1,016,263	2,858,814	4,079,648	20,341,296
Ground beef	11,066,974	305,505	1,355,933	1,423,257	8,290,983
Roast	3,740,759	157,296	281,346	588,483	2,881,015
Chuck roast	935,496	22,817	94,790	222,393	631,317
Round roast	747,174	54,518	46,563	81,894	614,727
Other roast	2,056,867	79,960	139,993	284,347	1,634,972
Steak	10,087,455	345,990	977,379	1,619,925	7,522,344
Round steak	1,944,363	62,494	164,786	367,002	1,429,448
Sirloin steak	2,673,194	105,352	216,792	442,808	2,014,683
Other steak	5,469,898	178,144	595,800	809,963	4,078,213
Other beef	2,325,899	207,523	244,156	447,983	1,646,953
Pork	19,804,380	1,059,474	2,772,339	2,906,336	14,212,456
Bacon	4,141,861	181,627	528,828	516,787	3,101,285
Pork chops	3,331,098	123,171	622,408	568,542	2,176,890
Ham	4,193,221	150,329	379,764	628,973	3,193,448
Ham, not canned	4,097,837	143,161	371,752	608,576	3,126,169
Canned ham	95,384	7,168	8,013	20,397	67,279
Sausage	3,491,294	170,774	592,474	401,100	2,508,677
Other pork	4,645,683	433,573	648,865	790,935	3,232,156
Other meats	14,985,049	465,577	1,295,461	1,667,113	12,008,839
Frankfurters	2,894,533	81,677	347,714	436,263	2,124,357
Lunch meats (cold cuts)	10,720,901	258,256	854,621	1,067,214	8,775,761
Bologna, liverwurst, salami	3,280,960	80,869	262,902	382,377	2,631,254
Other lunch meats	7,439,941	177,336	591,719	684,838	6,144,507
Lamb, organ meats, and others	1,369,614	125,645	93,127	163,789	1,107,799

	total consumer units	Asian	black	Hispanic	non-Hispanic white and other
Poultry	$18,892,119	$940,998	$2,792,899	$2,980,011	$13,199,585
Fresh and frozen chicken	15,217,394	816,262	2,242,453	2,553,643	10,494,601
Fresh and frozen whole chicken	4,398,663	266,181	503,732	872,677	3,046,909
Fresh and frozen chicken parts	10,819,954	550,081	1,738,721	1,681,118	7,446,770
Other poultry	3,674,724	124,787	550,446	426,216	2,704,984
Fish and seafood	14,767,378	1,648,929	2,019,311	2,098,962	10,694,595
Canned fish and seafood	2,433,511	113,530	277,113	327,577	1,834,044
Fresh fish and shellfish	7,277,299	993,901	1,065,517	1,131,908	5,111,360
Frozen fish and shellfish	5,056,567	541,549	676,531	639,476	3,749,191
Eggs	6,122,910	390,968	691,951	1,009,371	4,444,100
Dairy products	**49,751,243**	**1,699,106**	**3,716,004**	**5,912,377**	**40,084,454**
Fresh milk and cream	18,310,033	814,596	1,485,797	2,479,664	14,348,857
Fresh milk, all types	15,576,918	753,717	1,309,672	2,191,816	12,081,648
Cream	2,734,337	60,929	176,125	287,848	2,267,210
Other dairy products	31,439,988	884,511	2,230,207	3,432,713	25,735,596
Butter	3,013,152	79,809	229,340	234,419	2,539,091
Cheese	15,254,080	293,137	955,911	1,692,230	12,573,798
Ice cream and related products	7,004,599	274,056	633,293	716,956	5,644,984
Miscellaneous dairy products	6,166,933	237,458	411,663	788,956	4,976,802
Fruits and vegetables	**87,421,753**	**5,344,065**	**7,966,430**	**11,845,456**	**67,752,708**
Fresh fruits	30,239,129	1,980,583	2,368,839	4,465,221	23,484,054
Apples	4,667,695	259,366	375,229	613,903	3,687,442
Bananas	5,023,550	282,638	432,980	920,931	3,704,031
Oranges	3,300,526	253,107	316,722	503,392	2,495,774
Citrus fruits, excluding oranges	4,601,660	347,201	274,996	830,208	3,510,489
Other fresh fruits	12,646,922	838,321	968,913	1,596,788	10,085,397
Fresh vegetables	27,417,968	2,096,636	2,190,598	3,669,111	21,571,672
Potatoes	4,742,290	327,464	481,962	666,419	3,602,652
Lettuce	3,933,973	210,704	306,442	452,550	3,175,937
Tomatoes	5,017,436	328,928	361,623	761,557	3,905,868
Other fresh vegetables	13,725,493	1,229,541	1,040,572	1,788,433	10,886,294
Processed fruits	14,152,275	562,802	1,640,454	1,824,661	10,719,479
Frozen fruits and fruit juices	1,627,640	46,492	113,990	197,277	1,312,401
Frozen orange juice	456,131	9,339	25,852	60,279	368,652
Frozen fruits	846,226	22,060	52,762	95,442	694,909
Frozen fruit juices, excluding orange	326,506	15,043	35,376	41,708	248,840
Canned fruits	2,597,376	99,042	261,844	265,167	2,063,530
Dried fruits	994,193	44,321	60,170	90,266	839,605
Fresh fruit juice	2,113,119	75,720	258,215	252,685	1,610,088
Canned and bottled fruit juice	6,821,169	297,226	946,387	1,019,265	4,893,855
Processed vegetables	15,611,158	704,095	1,766,538	1,886,615	11,977,503
Frozen vegetables	4,277,599	187,634	475,461	361,370	3,432,150
Canned and dried vegetables and juices	11,333,559	516,461	1,291,077	1,525,244	8,545,353
Canned beans	2,333,236	65,119	264,263	358,478	1,726,213
Canned corn	1,189,853	42,504	159,948	165,463	869,097
Canned miscellaneous vegetables	3,118,319	112,873	305,988	321,336	2,481,028
Dried peas	102,721	5,300	14,060	15,831	73,730
Dried beans	610,212	38,668	66,217	170,182	386,163
Dried miscellaneous vegetables	1,412,415	104,393	162,216	164,854	1,091,210
Dried processed vegetables	250,688	8,127	35,527	18,571	197,229
Fresh and canned vegetable juices	2,273,315	139,426	282,404	303,070	1,686,583
Sugar and other sweets	**17,657,020**	**791,981**	**1,480,052**	**1,776,255**	**14,370,055**
Candy and chewing gum	10,608,397	472,947	725,210	898,859	8,941,654
Sugar	2,921,436	158,002	397,452	428,043	2,105,003
Artificial sweeteners	686,030	29,632	53,820	77,328	554,821
Jams, preserves, other sweets	3,441,156	131,399	303,569	372,026	2,768,577

	total consumer units	Asian	black	Hispanic	non-Hispanic white and other
Fats and oils	$13,403,878	$582,741	$1,421,243	$1,856,475	$10,169,265
Margarine	1,194,744	24,786	156,622	128,778	917,022
Fats and oils	4,260,479	316,308	582,950	881,049	2,845,072
Salad dressings	3,810,463	113,984	373,263	416,474	3,019,260
Nondairy cream and imitation milk	2,273,315	71,227	156,169	248,880	1,861,693
Peanut butter	1,864,877	56,386	152,238	181,446	1,525,298
Miscellaneous foods	84,436,728	3,424,816	7,589,841	8,826,629	67,949,937
Frozen prepared foods	16,659,158	482,437	1,555,491	1,302,699	13,783,898
Frozen meals	7,598,914	189,502	729,141	515,112	6,338,050
Other frozen prepared foods	9,060,244	292,986	826,350	787,586	7,445,849
Canned and packaged soups	5,735,260	276,479	513,105	491,975	4,717,824
Potato chips, nuts, and other snacks	17,734,061	638,774	1,384,204	1,674,420	14,635,484
Potato chips and other snacks	13,208,219	414,037	1,050,096	1,318,377	10,812,563
Nuts	4,525,842	224,686	334,108	356,195	3,822,921
Condiments and seasonings	16,374,229	695,312	1,596,461	1,779,908	12,995,905
Salt, spices, and other seasonings	4,330,183	225,948	470,472	611,924	3,259,805
Olives, pickles, relishes	1,972,489	70,622	143,923	154,808	1,666,307
Sauces and gravies	7,145,229	325,949	744,259	750,445	5,645,905
Baking needs and miscellaneous products	2,926,328	72,792	237,504	262,884	2,423,887
Other canned or packaged prepared foods	27,932,797	1,331,814	2,540,731	3,577,627	21,816,825
Prepared salads	4,429,235	146,291	403,802	345,235	3,673,617
Prepared desserts	1,837,974	68,754	156,471	250,097	1,438,664
Baby food	3,399,579	333,723	297,976	482,994	2,614,664
Miscellaneous prepared foods	17,989,641	783,046	1,673,109	2,499,300	13,825,372
Nonalcoholic beverages	44,141,938	1,635,148	4,237,575	5,631,836	34,334,404
Cola	9,632,547	254,924	922,500	1,215,781	7,491,930
Other carbonated drinks	8,158,989	251,138	767,541	1,031,291	6,360,169
Tea	3,810,463	236,095	354,366	383,442	3,069,950
Coffee	9,175,194	324,082	594,591	950,157	7,616,350
Noncarbonated fruit-flavored drinks	3,027,826	138,820	483,020	512,220	2,081,962
Other noncarbonated beverages and ice	1,825,745	58,607	183,533	228,939	1,415,624
Bottled water	6,539,909	322,719	770,413	1,095,375	4,696,626
Sports drinks	1,923,575	48,814	161,611	214,935	1,552,947
Food prepared by consumer unit on trips	5,808,633	287,130	209,838	493,954	5,104,909
FOOD AWAY FROM HOME	320,378,488	18,798,853	26,516,670	38,422,611	255,531,134
Meals at restaurants, carry-outs, etc.	268,528,800	15,310,029	23,753,250	33,564,206	211,281,834
Lunch	92,068,659	5,979,810	8,110,505	11,922,175	72,102,801
At fast-food restaurants*	45,097,000	2,802,044	4,997,557	6,506,644	33,781,426
At full-service restaurants	36,931,897	2,355,851	1,826,103	4,370,845	30,613,784
At vending machines, mobile vendors	875,575	23,625	95,395	245,226	545,605
At employer and school cafeterias	9,164,188	798,341	1,191,450	799,459	7,161,065
Dinner	128,529,751	6,918,738	11,400,786	14,611,750	102,341,482
At fast-food restaurants*	44,650,652	2,242,019	5,560,854	6,670,737	32,537,226
At full-service restaurants	82,673,349	4,605,997	5,774,471	7,861,706	68,752,676
At vending machines, mobile vendors	369,307	10,500	21,921	39,121	305,981
At employer and school cafeterias	837,666	60,172	43,540	40,186	746,520
Snacks and nonalcoholic beverages	20,310,648	1,051,700	1,730,104	2,497,778	16,106,406
At fast-food restaurants*	13,408,770	715,251	1,056,295	1,521,896	10,854,958
At full-service restaurants	4,001,231	140,536	338,643	564,280	3,093,912
At vending machines, mobile vendors	2,113,119	137,760	292,231	336,863	1,493,041
At employer and school cafeterias	786,305	58,203	42,935	74,892	664,495
Breakfast and brunch	27,619,742	1,359,780	2,511,856	4,532,503	20,730,224
At fast-food restaurants*	15,135,462	841,451	1,431,070	2,604,332	11,174,764
At full-service restaurants	10,931,235	422,063	753,632	1,677,008	8,573,924
At vending machines, mobile vendors	370,530	36,800	48,680	112,491	213,818
At employer and school cafeterias	1,181,292	59,465	278,322	138,672	767,718

	total consumer units	Asian	black	Hispanic	non-Hispanic white and other
Board (including at school)	$5,364,731	$603,640	$152,389	$340,364	$4,872,658
Catered affairs	6,435,965	628,829	446,435	705,387	5,283,705
Food on trips	28,919,653	1,737,067	1,174,971	2,226,065	25,532,838
School lunches	7,601,360	364,819	715,686	782,411	6,106,720
Meals as pay	3,527,980	154,418	274,089	804,178	2,455,222
ALCOHOLIC BEVERAGES	55,815,455	1,571,493	3,013,924	4,278,448	48,347,788
At home	29,636,254	844,732	1,974,411	2,324,095	25,255,427
Beer and ale	13,422,221	358,660	1,253,736	1,444,872	10,738,833
Whiskey	1,173,955	50,530	98,116	76,871	989,831
Wine	12,721,517	367,343	428,746	593,962	11,581,203
Other alcoholic beverages	2,319,784	68,198	193,964	208,389	1,945,561
Away from home	26,179,201	726,761	1,039,514	1,954,353	23,092,361
Beer and ale	9,413,653	121,960	339,853	900,229	8,139,836
At fast-food restaurants*	1,524,919	1,918	109,454	230,309	1,202,727
At full-service restaurants	7,743,213	120,041	220,723	667,180	6,805,316
At vending machines, mobile vendors	79,487	–	9,827	2,740	66,357
Wine	5,131,163	140,738	198,802	257,404	4,646,858
At fast-food restaurants*	361,970	12,872	33,713	14,613	309,668
At full-service restaurants	4,671,363	127,866	165,089	242,791	4,239,498
Other alcoholic beverages	6,151,036	238,518	305,988	466,402	5,342,689
At fast-food restaurants*	519,720	–	71,206	28,313	417,498
At full-service restaurants	5,623,979	238,518	234,783	438,089	4,917,818
Alcoholic beverages purchased on trips	5,483,349	225,545	194,720	330,165	4,962,978

* The category fast-food restaurants also includes take-out, delivery, concession stands, buffets, and cafeterias other than employer and school.
Note: "Asian" and "black" include Hispanics and non-Hispanics who identify themselves as being of the respective race alone. "Hispanic" includes people of any race who identify themselves as Hispanic. "Other" includes people who identify themselves as non-Hispanic and as Alaska Native, American Indian, Asian (who are also included in the "Asian" column), or Native Hawaiian or other Pacific Islander, as well as non-Hispanics reporting more than one race. Numbers may not add to total because of rounding and missing subcategories. "–" means sample is too small to make a reliable estimate.
Source: Calculations by New Strategist based on the Bureau of Labor Statistics' 2011 Consumer Expenditure Survey

Table 5.20 Food and Alcohol: Market shares by race and Hispanic origin, 2011

(percentage of total annual spending on food and alcoholic beverages accounted for by consumer unit race and Hispanic origin groups, 2011)

	total consumer units	Asian	black	Hispanic	non-Hispanic white and other
Share of total consumer units	100.0%	4.1%	12.4%	12.4%	75.4%
Share of total before-tax income	100.0	5.5	8.8	9.8	81.5
Share of total spending	100.0	5.0	9.1	10.5	80.4
Share of food spending	100.0	5.2	9.1	12.3	78.7
Share of alcoholic beverages spending	100.0	2.8	5.4	7.7	86.6
FOOD AT HOME	100.0	4.8	9.6	12.5	78.0
Cereals and bakery products	100.0	4.8	9.4	11.6	79.0
Cereals and cereal products	100.0	6.2	10.1	12.9	77.1
Flour	100.0	7.9	10.4	12.5	77.4
Prepared flour mixes	100.0	1.9	11.4	9.9	79.1
Ready-to-eat and cooked cereals	100.0	3.1	9.9	11.8	78.3
Rice	100.0	17.9	13.0	22.9	65.5
Pasta, cornmeal, and other cereal products	100.0	7.3	7.8	10.0	81.9
Bakery products	100.0	4.1	9.1	10.9	79.9
Bread	100.0	4.0	9.3	12.6	78.2
White bread	100.0	4.2	10.9	13.8	75.6
Bread, other than white	100.0	3.9	8.1	11.8	80.1
Cookies and crackers	100.0	4.6	8.3	9.7	81.8
Cookies	100.0	5.3	9.5	10.3	80.2
Crackers	100.0	3.7	6.8	9.1	83.9
Frozen and refrigerated bakery products	100.0	4.5	10.0	9.5	80.5
Other bakery products	100.0	3.8	9.3	10.6	80.0
Biscuits and rolls	100.0	3.3	7.9	8.7	83.1
Cakes and cupcakes	100.0	4.1	12.1	12.8	75.3
Bread and cracker products	100.0	4.3	10.4	6.7	82.3
Sweetrolls, coffee cakes, doughnuts	100.0	4.0	8.3	13.7	78.2
Pies, tarts, turnovers	100.0	4.4	8.7	8.9	82.2
Meats, poultry, fish, and eggs	100.0	5.4	12.2	14.5	73.6
Beef	100.0	3.7	10.5	15.0	74.7
Ground beef	100.0	2.8	12.3	12.9	74.9
Roast	100.0	4.2	7.5	15.7	77.0
Chuck roast	100.0	2.4	10.1	23.8	67.5
Round roast	100.0	7.3	6.2	11.0	82.3
Other roast	100.0	3.9	6.8	13.8	79.5
Steak	100.0	3.4	9.7	16.1	74.6
Round steak	100.0	3.2	8.5	18.9	73.5
Sirloin steak	100.0	3.9	8.1	16.6	75.4
Other steak	100.0	3.3	10.9	14.8	74.6
Other beef	100.0	8.9	10.5	19.3	70.8
Pork	100.0	5.3	14.0	14.7	71.8
Bacon	100.0	4.4	12.8	12.5	74.9
Pork chops	100.0	3.7	18.7	17.1	65.4
Ham	100.0	3.6	9.1	15.0	76.2
Ham, not canned	100.0	3.5	9.1	14.9	76.3
Canned ham	100.0	7.5	8.4	21.4	70.5
Sausage	100.0	4.9	17.0	11.5	71.9
Other pork	100.0	9.3	14.0	17.0	69.6
Other meats	100.0	3.1	8.6	11.1	80.1
Frankfurters	100.0	2.8	12.0	15.1	73.4
Lunch meats (cold cuts)	100.0	2.4	8.0	10.0	81.9
Bologna, liverwurst, salami	100.0	2.5	8.0	11.7	80.2
Other lunch meats	100.0	2.4	8.0	9.2	82.6
Lamb, organ meats, and others	100.0	9.2	6.8	12.0	80.9

	total consumer units	Asian	black	Hispanic	non-Hispanic white and other
Poultry	100.0%	5.0%	14.8%	15.8%	69.9%
Fresh and frozen chicken	100.0	5.4	14.7	16.8	69.0
Fresh and frozen whole chicken	100.0	6.1	11.5	19.8	69.3
Fresh and frozen chicken parts	100.0	5.1	16.1	15.5	68.8
Other poultry	100.0	3.4	15.0	11.6	73.6
Fish and seafood	100.0	11.2	13.7	14.2	72.4
Canned fish and seafood	100.0	4.7	11.4	13.5	75.4
Fresh fish and shellfish	100.0	13.7	14.6	15.6	70.2
Frozen fish and shellfish	100.0	10.7	13.4	12.6	74.1
Eggs	100.0	6.4	11.3	16.5	72.6
Dairy products	**100.0**	**3.4**	**7.5**	**11.9**	**80.6**
Fresh milk and cream	100.0	4.4	8.1	13.5	78.4
Fresh milk, all types	100.0	4.8	8.4	14.1	77.6
Cream	100.0	2.2	6.4	10.5	82.9
Other dairy products	100.0	2.8	7.1	10.9	81.9
Butter	100.0	2.6	7.6	7.8	84.3
Cheese	100.0	1.9	6.3	11.1	82.4
Ice cream and related products	100.0	3.9	9.0	10.2	80.6
Miscellaneous dairy products	100.0	3.9	6.7	12.8	80.7
Fruits and vegetables	**100.0**	**6.1**	**9.1**	**13.5**	**77.5**
Fresh fruits	100.0	6.5	7.8	14.8	77.7
Apples	100.0	5.6	8.0	13.2	79.0
Bananas	100.0	5.6	8.6	18.3	73.7
Oranges	100.0	7.7	9.6	15.3	75.6
Citrus fruits, excluding oranges	100.0	7.5	6.0	18.0	76.3
Other fresh fruits	100.0	6.6	7.7	12.6	79.7
Fresh vegetables	100.0	7.6	8.0	13.4	78.7
Potatoes	100.0	6.9	10.2	14.1	76.0
Lettuce	100.0	5.4	7.8	11.5	80.7
Tomatoes	100.0	6.6	7.2	15.2	77.8
Other fresh vegetables	100.0	9.0	7.6	13.0	79.3
Processed fruits	100.0	4.0	11.6	12.9	75.7
Frozen fruits and fruit juices	100.0	2.9	7.0	12.1	80.6
Frozen orange juice	100.0	2.0	5.7	13.2	80.8
Frozen fruits	100.0	2.6	6.2	11.3	82.1
Frozen fruit juices, excluding orange	100.0	4.6	10.8	12.8	76.2
Canned fruits	100.0	3.8	10.1	10.2	79.4
Dried fruits	100.0	4.5	6.1	9.1	84.5
Fresh fruit juice	100.0	3.6	12.2	12.0	76.2
Canned and bottled fruit juice	100.0	4.4	13.9	14.9	71.7
Processed vegetables	100.0	4.5	11.3	12.1	76.7
Frozen vegetables	100.0	4.4	11.1	8.4	80.2
Canned and dried vegetables and juices	100.0	4.6	11.4	13.5	75.4
Canned beans	100.0	2.8	11.3	15.4	74.0
Canned corn	100.0	3.6	13.4	13.9	73.0
Canned miscellaneous vegetables	100.0	3.6	9.8	10.3	79.6
Dried peas	100.0	5.2	13.7	15.4	71.8
Dried beans	100.0	6.3	10.9	27.9	63.3
Dried miscellaneous vegetables	100.0	7.4	11.5	11.7	77.3
Dried processed vegetables	100.0	3.2	14.2	7.4	78.7
Fresh and canned vegetable juices	100.0	6.1	12.4	13.3	74.2
Sugar and other sweets	**100.0**	**4.5**	**8.4**	**10.1**	**81.4**
Candy and chewing gum	100.0	4.5	6.8	8.5	84.3
Sugar	100.0	5.4	13.6	14.7	72.1
Artificial sweeteners	100.0	4.3	7.8	11.3	80.9
Jams, preserves, other sweets	100.0	3.8	8.8	10.8	80.5

	total consumer units	Asian	black	Hispanic	non-Hispanic white and other
Fats and oils	**100.0%**	**4.3%**	**10.6%**	**13.9%**	**75.9%**
Margarine	100.0	2.1	13.1	10.8	76.8
Fats and oils	100.0	7.4	13.7	20.7	66.8
Salad dressings	100.0	3.0	9.8	10.9	79.2
Nondairy cream and imitation milk	100.0	3.1	6.9	10.9	81.9
Peanut butter	100.0	3.0	8.2	9.7	81.8
Miscellaneous foods	**100.0**	**4.1**	**9.0**	**10.5**	**80.5**
Frozen prepared foods	100.0	2.9	9.3	7.8	82.7
Frozen meals	100.0	2.5	9.6	6.8	83.4
Other frozen prepared foods	100.0	3.2	9.1	8.7	82.2
Canned and packaged soups	100.0	4.8	8.9	8.6	82.3
Potato chips, nuts, and other snacks	100.0	3.6	7.8	9.4	82.5
Potato chips and other snacks	100.0	3.1	8.0	10.0	81.9
Nuts	100.0	5.0	7.4	7.9	84.5
Condiments and seasonings	100.0	4.2	9.7	10.9	79.4
Salt, spices, and other seasonings	100.0	5.2	10.9	14.1	75.3
Olives, pickles, relishes	100.0	3.6	7.3	7.8	84.5
Sauces and gravies	100.0	4.6	10.4	10.5	79.0
Baking needs and miscellaneous products	100.0	2.5	8.1	9.0	82.8
Other canned or packaged prepared foods	100.0	4.8	9.1	12.8	78.1
Prepared salads	100.0	3.3	9.1	7.8	82.9
Prepared desserts	100.0	3.7	8.5	13.6	78.3
Baby food	100.0	9.8	8.8	14.2	76.9
Miscellaneous prepared foods	100.0	4.4	9.3	13.9	76.9
Nonalcoholic beverages	**100.0**	**3.7**	**9.6**	**12.8**	**77.8**
Cola	100.0	2.6	9.6	12.6	77.8
Other carbonated drinks	100.0	3.1	9.4	12.6	78.0
Tea	100.0	6.2	9.3	10.1	80.6
Coffee	100.0	3.5	6.5	10.4	83.0
Noncarbonated fruit-flavored drinks	100.0	4.6	16.0	16.9	68.8
Other noncarbonated beverages and ice	100.0	3.2	10.1	12.5	77.5
Bottled water	100.0	4.9	11.8	16.7	71.8
Sports drinks	100.0	2.5	8.4	11.2	80.7
Food prepared by consumer unit on trips	**100.0**	**4.9**	**3.6**	**8.5**	**87.9**
FOOD AWAY FROM HOME	**100.0**	**5.9**	**8.3**	**12.0**	**79.8**
Meals at restaurants, carry-outs, etc.	**100.0**	**5.7**	**8.8**	**12.5**	**78.7**
Lunch	100.0	6.5	8.8	12.9	78.3
At fast-food restaurants*	100.0	6.2	11.1	14.4	74.9
At full-service restaurants	100.0	6.4	4.9	11.8	82.9
At vending machines, mobile vendors	100.0	2.7	10.9	28.0	62.3
At employer and school cafeterias	100.0	8.7	13.0	8.7	78.1
Dinner	100.0	5.4	8.9	11.4	79.6
At fast-food restaurants*	100.0	5.0	12.5	14.9	72.9
At full-service restaurants	100.0	5.6	7.0	9.5	83.2
At vending machines, mobile vendors	100.0	2.8	5.9	10.6	82.9
At employer and school cafeterias	100.0	7.2	5.2	4.8	89.1
Snacks and nonalcoholic beverages	100.0	5.2	8.5	12.3	79.3
At fast-food restaurants*	100.0	5.3	7.9	11.4	81.0
At full-service restaurants	100.0	3.5	8.5	14.1	77.3
At vending machines, mobile vendors	100.0	6.5	13.8	15.9	70.7
At employer and school cafeterias	100.0	7.4	5.5	9.5	84.5
Breakfast and brunch	100.0	4.9	9.1	16.4	75.1
At fast-food restaurants*	100.0	5.6	9.5	17.2	73.8
At full-service restaurants	100.0	3.9	6.9	15.3	78.4
At vending machines, mobile vendors	100.0	9.9	13.1	30.4	57.7
At employer and school cafeterias	100.0	5.0	23.6	11.7	65.0

	total consumer units	Asian	black	Hispanic	non-Hispanic white and other
Board (including at school)	100.0%	11.3%	2.8%	6.3%	90.8%
Catered affairs	100.0	9.8	6.9	11.0	82.1
Food on trips	100.0	6.0	4.1	7.7	88.3
School lunches	100.0	4.8	9.4	10.3	80.3
Meals as pay	100.0	4.4	7.8	22.8	69.6
ALCOHOLIC BEVERAGES	100.0	2.8	5.4	7.7	86.6
At home	100.0	2.9	6.7	7.8	85.2
Beer and ale	100.0	2.7	9.3	10.8	80.0
Whiskey	100.0	4.3	8.4	6.5	84.3
Wine	100.0	2.9	3.4	4.7	91.0
Other alcoholic beverages	100.0	2.9	8.4	9.0	83.9
Away from home	100.0	2.8	4.0	7.5	88.2
Beer and ale	100.0	1.3	3.6	9.6	86.5
At fast-food restaurants*	100.0	0.1	7.2	15.1	78.9
At full-service restaurants	100.0	1.6	2.9	8.6	87.9
At vending machines, mobile vendors	100.0	–	12.4	3.4	83.5
Wine	100.0	2.7	3.9	5.0	90.6
At fast-food restaurants*	100.0	3.6	9.3	4.0	85.6
At full-service restaurants	100.0	2.7	3.5	5.2	90.8
Other alcoholic beverages	100.0	3.9	5.0	7.6	86.9
At fast-food restaurants*	100.0	–	13.7	5.4	80.3
At full-service restaurants	100.0	4.2	4.2	7.8	87.4
Alcoholic beverages purchased on trips	100.0	4.1	3.6	6.0	90.5

The category fast-food restaurants also includes take-out, delivery, concession stands, buffets, and cafeterias other than employer and school.

Note: "Asian" and "black" include Hispanics and non-Hispanics who identify themselves as being of the respective race alone. "Hispanic" includes people of any race who identify themselves as Hispanic. "Other" includes people who identify themselves as non-Hispanic and as Alaska Native, American Indian, Asian (who are also included in the "Asian" column), or Native Hawaiian or other Pacific Islander, as well as non-Hispanics reporting more than one race. "–" means sample is too small to make a reliable estimate.

Source: Calculations by New Strategist based on the Bureau of Labor Statistics' 2011 Consumer Expenditure Survey

Table 5.21 Food and Alcohol: Average spending by region, 2011

(average annual spending of consumer units on food and alcoholic beverages, by region in which consumer unit lives, 2011)

	total consumer units	Northeast	Midwest	South	West
Number of consumer units (in 000s)	122,287	22,538	27,107	44,901	27,741
Average number of persons per consumer unit	2.5	2.4	2.4	2.5	2.6
Average before-tax income of consumer units	$63,685.00	$71,733.00	$60,897.00	$58,780.00	$67,810.00
Average spending of consumer units, total	49,704.88	54,547.45	47,191.54	45,698.60	54,745.43
Food, average spending	**6,458.00**	**6,799.00**	**6,236.00**	**5,980.00**	**7,188.00**
Alcoholic beverages, average spending	**456.43**	**490.73**	**386.75**	**386.21**	**613.84**
FOOD AT HOME	**3,837.76**	**4,098.90**	**3,841.00**	**3,505.46**	**4,169.23**
Cereals and bakery products	**530.68**	**610.11**	**545.06**	**478.39**	**537.50**
Cereals and cereal products	174.86	204.64	170.52	153.90	189.44
Flour	7.67	8.47	7.83	6.52	8.76
Prepared flour mixes	14.88	16.65	16.67	13.07	14.63
Ready-to-eat and cooked cereals	91.39	104.22	89.91	83.78	94.92
Rice	25.66	34.40	19.40	22.40	30.13
Pasta, cornmeal, and other cereal products	35.26	40.91	36.71	28.12	40.99
Bakery products	355.81	405.47	374.54	324.50	348.07
Bread	106.53	119.35	101.81	98.46	114.07
White bread	44.93	49.52	43.21	43.81	44.73
Bread, other than white	61.60	69.83	58.59	54.65	69.34
Cookies and crackers	83.59	92.35	92.12	74.49	82.93
Cookies	46.96	51.09	49.31	43.58	46.82
Crackers	36.63	41.26	42.81	30.91	36.10
Frozen and refrigerated bakery products	28.60	28.37	31.31	28.58	26.11
Other bakery products	137.09	165.41	149.30	122.97	124.96
Biscuits and rolls	52.93	69.04	57.46	45.52	47.42
Cakes and cupcakes	37.81	43.37	38.35	36.90	34.22
Bread and cracker products	7.13	10.22	8.88	5.79	5.08
Sweetrolls, coffee cakes, doughnuts	23.86	25.33	26.22	20.80	25.34
Pies, tarts, turnovers	15.36	17.45	18.39	13.96	12.91
Meats, poultry, fish, and eggs	**832.41**	**882.38**	**790.53**	**811.40**	**868.03**
Beef	222.60	215.46	218.50	217.71	240.66
Ground beef	90.50	81.39	96.66	94.75	84.80
Roast	30.59	30.86	26.68	27.53	39.33
Chuck roast	7.65	7.46	6.93	6.39	10.63
Round roast	6.11	5.88	4.41	6.70	7.01
Other roast	16.82	17.52	15.34	14.44	21.68
Steak	82.49	85.53	73.16	79.19	94.80
Round steak	15.90	13.79	17.02	14.41	18.98
Sirloin steak	21.86	24.63	17.51	20.21	26.67
Other steak	44.73	47.11	38.62	44.56	49.16
Other beef	19.02	17.68	22.00	16.23	21.73
Pork	161.95	151.66	161.24	174.03	151.12
Bacon	33.87	28.09	35.35	34.84	35.53
Pork chops	27.24	27.94	26.35	30.89	21.54
Ham	34.29	33.83	37.66	35.17	29.83
Ham, not canned	33.51	33.30	36.66	34.45	28.96
Canned ham	0.78	0.52	1.00	0.72	0.86
Sausage	28.55	25.54	26.72	32.26	26.73
Other pork	37.99	36.27	35.15	40.86	37.50
Other meats	122.54	149.42	141.36	106.99	107.36
Frankfurters	23.67	28.26	24.30	23.06	20.29
Lunch meats (cold cuts)	87.67	109.23	99.04	75.83	78.18
Bologna, liverwurst, salami	26.83	34.33	31.10	22.38	23.77
Other lunch meats	60.84	74.90	67.93	53.45	54.42
Lamb, organ meats, and others	11.20	11.93	18.03	8.10	8.88

	total consumer units	Northeast	Midwest	South	West
Poultry	$154.49	$168.16	$132.18	$153.57	$167.12
Fresh and frozen chicken	124.44	137.34	102.86	123.84	136.46
Fresh and frozen whole chicken	35.97	42.74	28.92	30.85	45.93
Fresh and frozen chicken parts	88.48	94.60	73.95	92.99	90.53
Other poultry	30.05	30.82	29.32	29.73	30.66
Fish and seafood	120.76	145.69	90.76	111.32	145.95
Canned fish and seafood	19.90	21.18	18.30	19.50	21.13
Fresh fish and shellfish	59.51	84.45	37.34	51.66	74.20
Frozen fish and shellfish	41.35	40.06	35.12	40.16	50.62
Eggs	50.07	52.00	46.50	47.78	55.84
Dairy products	**406.84**	**444.33**	**409.16**	**355.69**	**458.31**
Fresh milk and cream	149.73	149.39	142.66	142.27	169.43
Fresh milk, all types	127.38	125.05	119.60	124.48	141.88
Cream	22.36	24.35	23.06	17.80	27.56
Other dairy products	257.10	294.93	266.50	213.41	288.88
Butter	24.64	27.43	28.11	19.34	27.66
Cheese	124.74	135.28	136.84	101.43	142.54
Ice cream and related products	57.28	67.69	52.64	53.59	59.48
Miscellaneous dairy products	50.43	64.53	48.91	39.05	59.21
Fruits and vegetables	**714.89**	**811.13**	**695.65**	**612.39**	**824.66**
Fresh fruits	247.28	278.34	243.30	201.34	301.75
Apples	38.17	43.49	38.43	32.00	43.73
Bananas	41.08	48.47	39.60	33.99	48.21
Oranges	26.99	28.43	27.33	22.79	32.41
Citrus fruits, excluding oranges	37.63	40.90	35.79	28.93	51.19
Other fresh fruits	103.42	117.06	102.14	83.63	126.21
Fresh vegetables	224.21	260.96	203.05	189.18	273.15
Potatoes	38.78	45.49	34.88	37.60	39.10
Lettuce	32.17	38.28	34.16	26.27	34.91
Tomatoes	41.03	48.97	38.13	35.37	46.76
Other fresh vegetables	112.24	128.21	95.88	89.93	152.39
Processed fruits	115.73	131.44	119.04	98.37	128.25
Frozen fruits and fruit juices	13.31	11.72	15.20	9.17	19.58
Frozen orange juice	3.73	2.77	5.14	2.35	5.39
Frozen fruits	6.92	7.33	6.50	4.20	11.49
Frozen fruit juices, excluding orange	2.67	1.62	3.57	2.62	2.71
Canned fruits	21.24	20.33	25.81	19.34	20.54
Dried fruits	8.13	9.22	9.75	6.21	8.76
Fresh fruit juice	17.28	23.45	17.51	15.17	15.47
Canned and bottled fruit juice	55.78	66.73	50.76	48.48	63.90
Processed vegetables	127.66	140.38	130.26	123.50	121.50
Frozen vegetables	34.98	40.51	36.43	32.74	32.70
Canned and dried vegetables and juices	92.68	99.87	93.83	90.76	88.80
Canned beans	19.08	21.28	18.85	20.61	14.97
Canned corn	9.73	11.09	11.51	9.34	7.47
Canned miscellaneous vegetables	25.50	26.84	27.45	25.48	22.47
Dried peas	0.84	1.62	1.06	0.51	0.54
Dried beans	4.99	4.78	4.03	4.91	6.26
Dried miscellaneous vegetables	11.55	11.90	11.58	11.73	10.94
Dried processed vegetables	2.05	1.71	1.29	2.08	3.03
Fresh and canned vegetable juices	18.59	20.30	17.62	15.89	22.65
Sugar and other sweets	**144.39**	**149.37**	**152.72**	**123.02**	**167.29**
Candy and chewing gum	86.75	86.39	95.17	69.60	106.98
Sugar	23.89	26.10	21.50	23.85	24.51
Artificial sweeteners	5.61	5.44	6.57	4.61	6.44
Jams, preserves, other sweets	28.14	31.43	29.48	24.96	29.37

	total consumer units	Northeast	Midwest	South	West
Fats and oils	$109.61	$112.64	$111.39	$102.33	$117.40
Margarine	9.77	11.64	10.52	9.69	7.62
Fats and oils	34.84	40.37	30.10	32.37	39.12
Salad dressings	31.16	29.44	33.18	30.31	31.96
Nondairy cream and imitation milk	18.59	16.28	20.65	16.50	21.88
Peanut butter	15.25	14.91	16.95	13.46	16.81
Miscellaneous foods	690.48	665.75	735.09	636.56	755.31
Frozen prepared foods	136.23	124.59	162.48	129.08	131.33
Frozen meals	62.14	59.81	71.02	59.62	59.31
Other frozen prepared foods	74.09	64.79	91.46	69.46	72.02
Canned and packaged soups	46.90	48.56	51.92	41.12	50.09
Potato chips, nuts, and other snacks	145.02	139.24	163.93	124.99	163.96
Potato chips and other snacks	108.01	102.40	123.84	96.47	115.83
Nuts	37.01	36.83	40.08	28.52	48.13
Condiments and seasonings	133.90	140.78	146.21	118.10	142.08
Salt, spices, and other seasonings	35.41	36.57	39.49	32.07	35.87
Olives, pickles, relishes	16.13	19.64	18.88	12.33	16.79
Sauces and gravies	58.43	60.27	59.39	54.25	62.89
Baking needs and miscellaneous products	23.93	24.31	28.45	19.44	26.53
Other canned or packaged prepared foods	228.42	212.58	210.56	223.27	267.85
Prepared salads	36.22	38.87	38.77	33.22	36.45
Prepared desserts	15.03	15.63	17.15	14.11	13.91
Baby food	27.80	34.12	18.10	35.86	18.97
Miscellaneous prepared foods	147.11	123.18	135.31	137.49	194.52
Nonalcoholic beverages	360.97	374.24	359.42	347.43	374.03
Cola	78.77	66.13	83.96	85.95	72.07
Other carbonated drinks	66.72	67.54	67.66	66.08	66.15
Tea	31.16	38.64	30.01	27.89	31.59
Coffee	75.03	81.21	72.18	66.29	87.25
Noncarbonated fruit-flavored drinks	24.76	26.60	25.09	24.12	23.97
Other noncarbonated beverages and ice	14.93	12.50	14.56	14.30	18.34
Bottled water	53.48	63.16	48.94	48.05	59.05
Sports drinks	15.73	18.38	16.78	14.43	14.62
Food prepared by consumer unit on trips	47.50	48.95	41.98	38.26	66.68
FOOD AWAY FROM HOME	2,619.89	2,700.13	2,394.60	2,474.07	3,018.82
Meals at restaurants, carry-outs, etc.	2,195.89	2,201.53	1,962.11	2,130.71	2,533.20
Lunch	752.89	688.49	655.54	767.75	878.71
At fast-food restaurants*	368.78	317.78	336.36	377.67	428.46
At full-service restaurants	302.01	261.19	227.08	321.86	377.73
At vending machines, mobile vendors	7.16	7.86	6.97	5.98	8.72
At employer and school cafeterias	74.94	101.65	85.13	62.24	63.80
Dinner	1,051.05	1,090.02	975.28	1,012.66	1,158.45
At fast-food restaurants*	365.13	349.71	350.23	356.60	406.81
At full-service restaurants	676.06	727.17	609.23	649.56	744.84
At vending machines, mobile vendors	3.02	4.83	4.83	1.56	2.12
At employer and school cafeterias	6.85	8.31	10.99	4.93	4.68
Snacks and nonalcoholic beverages	166.09	167.76	143.45	140.48	229.76
At fast-food restaurants*	109.65	110.52	88.06	93.25	157.69
At full-service restaurants	32.72	35.05	29.01	24.23	48.56
At vending machines, mobile vendors	17.28	14.21	18.14	18.76	16.51
At employer and school cafeterias	6.43	7.98	8.23	4.24	7.00
Breakfast and brunch	225.86	255.28	187.85	209.82	266.29
At fast-food restaurants*	123.77	156.77	86.45	121.82	137.27
At full-service restaurants	89.39	82.62	88.92	77.17	115.65
At vending machines, mobile vendors	3.03	4.40	2.39	1.92	4.40
At employer and school cafeterias	9.66	11.49	10.08	8.92	8.98

	total consumer units	Northeast	Midwest	South	West
Board (including at school)	$43.87	$67.21	$46.74	$35.37	$35.87
Catered affairs	52.63	90.84	58.30	31.55	50.15
Food on trips	236.49	248.00	229.05	195.86	300.17
School lunches	62.16	58.52	75.01	63.07	51.11
Meals as pay	28.85	34.03	23.39	17.51	48.32
ALCOHOLIC BEVERAGES	456.43	490.73	386.75	386.21	613.84
At home	242.35	244.48	196.12	227.55	311.38
Beer and ale	109.76	105.06	94.62	117.32	116.26
Whiskey	9.60	12.42	9.86	9.86	6.57
Wine	104.03	104.95	71.50	86.35	165.08
Other alcoholic beverages	18.97	22.05	20.15	14.01	23.46
Away from home	214.08	246.25	190.63	158.66	302.46
Beer and ale	76.98	84.96	75.98	60.89	98.05
At fast-food restaurants*	12.47	9.65	15.93	12.17	11.80
At full-service restaurants	63.32	72.06	58.46	48.17	86.10
At vending machines, mobile vendors	0.65	0.42	1.55	0.53	0.16
Wine	41.96	58.73	25.44	29.73	64.97
At fast-food restaurants*	2.96	4.39	1.36	2.81	3.62
At full-service restaurants	38.20	50.55	23.64	26.88	61.35
Other alcoholic beverages	50.30	57.95	46.37	32.11	78.05
At fast-food restaurants*	4.25	4.93	5.75	3.22	3.89
At full-service restaurants	45.99	52.83	40.62	28.89	74.04
Alcoholic beverages purchased on trips	44.84	44.61	42.84	35.93	61.39

The category fast-food restaurants also includes take-out, delivery, concession stands, buffets, and cafeterias other than employer and school.
Note: Subcategories may not add to total because some are not shown.
Source: Bureau of Labor Statistics, unpublished tables from the 2011 Consumer Expenditure Survey

Table 5.22 Food and Alcohol: Indexed spending by region, 2011

(indexed average annual spending of consumer units on food and alcoholic beverages, by region in which consumer unit lives, 2011; index definition: an index of 100 is the average for all consumer units; an index of 125 means that spending by consumer units in that group is 25 percent above the average for all consumer units; an index of 75 indicates spending that is 25 percent below the average for all consumer units)

	total consumer units	Northeast	Midwest	South	West
Average spending of consumer units, total	$49,705	$54,547	$47,192	$45,699	$54,745
Average spending of consumer units, index	100	110	95	92	110
Food, spending index	100	105	97	93	111
Alcoholic beverages, spending index	100	108	85	85	134
FOOD AT HOME	100	107	100	91	109
Cereals and bakery products	100	115	103	90	101
Cereals and cereal products	100	117	98	88	108
Flour	100	110	102	85	114
Prepared flour mixes	100	112	112	88	98
Ready-to-eat and cooked cereals	100	114	98	92	104
Rice	100	134	76	87	117
Pasta, cornmeal, and other cereal products	100	116	104	80	116
Bakery products	100	114	105	91	98
Bread	100	112	96	92	107
White bread	100	110	96	98	100
Bread, other than white	100	113	95	89	113
Cookies and crackers	100	110	110	89	99
Cookies	100	109	105	93	100
Crackers	100	113	117	84	99
Frozen and refrigerated bakery products	100	99	109	100	91
Other bakery products	100	121	109	90	91
Biscuits and rolls	100	130	109	86	90
Cakes and cupcakes	100	115	101	98	91
Bread and cracker products	100	143	125	81	71
Sweetrolls, coffee cakes, doughnuts	100	106	110	87	106
Pies, tarts, turnovers	100	114	120	91	84
Meats, poultry, fish, and eggs	100	106	95	97	104
Beef	100	97	98	98	108
Ground beef	100	90	107	105	94
Roast	100	101	87	90	129
Chuck roast	100	98	91	84	139
Round roast	100	96	72	110	115
Other roast	100	104	91	86	129
Steak	100	104	89	96	115
Round steak	100	87	107	91	119
Sirloin steak	100	113	80	92	122
Other steak	100	105	86	100	110
Other beef	100	93	116	85	114
Pork	100	94	100	107	93
Bacon	100	83	104	103	105
Pork chops	100	103	97	113	79
Ham	100	99	110	103	87
Ham, not canned	100	99	109	103	86
Canned ham	100	67	128	92	110
Sausage	100	89	94	113	94
Other pork	100	95	93	108	99
Other meats	100	122	115	87	88
Frankfurters	100	119	103	97	86
Lunch meats (cold cuts)	100	125	113	86	89
Bologna, liverwurst, salami	100	128	116	83	89
Other lunch meats	100	123	112	88	89
Lamb, organ meats, and others	100	107	161	72	79

	total consumer units	Northeast	Midwest	South	West
Poultry	100	109	86	99	108
Fresh and frozen chicken	100	110	83	100	110
Fresh and frozen whole chicken	100	119	80	86	128
Fresh and frozen chicken parts	100	107	84	105	102
Other poultry	100	103	98	99	102
Fish and seafood	100	121	75	92	121
Canned fish and seafood	100	106	92	98	106
Fresh fish and shellfish	100	142	63	87	125
Frozen fish and shellfish	100	97	85	97	122
Eggs	100	104	93	95	112
Dairy products	**100**	**109**	**101**	**87**	**113**
Fresh milk and cream	100	100	95	95	113
Fresh milk, all types	100	98	94	98	111
Cream	100	109	103	80	123
Other dairy products	100	115	104	83	112
Butter	100	111	114	78	112
Cheese	100	108	110	81	114
Ice cream and related products	100	118	92	94	104
Miscellaneous dairy products	100	128	97	77	117
Fruits and vegetables	**100**	**113**	**97**	**86**	**115**
Fresh fruits	100	113	98	81	122
Apples	100	114	101	84	115
Bananas	100	118	96	83	117
Oranges	100	105	101	84	120
Citrus fruits, excluding oranges	100	109	95	77	136
Other fresh fruits	100	113	99	81	122
Fresh vegetables	100	116	91	84	122
Potatoes	100	117	90	97	101
Lettuce	100	119	106	82	109
Tomatoes	100	119	93	86	114
Other fresh vegetables	100	114	85	80	136
Processed fruits	100	114	103	85	111
Frozen fruits and fruit juices	100	88	114	69	147
Frozen orange juice	100	74	138	63	145
Frozen fruits	100	106	94	61	166
Frozen fruit juices, excluding orange	100	61	134	98	101
Canned fruits	100	96	122	91	97
Dried fruits	100	113	120	76	108
Fresh fruit juice	100	136	101	88	90
Canned and bottled fruit juice	100	120	91	87	115
Processed vegetables	100	110	102	97	95
Frozen vegetables	100	116	104	94	93
Canned and dried vegetables and juices	100	108	101	98	96
Canned beans	100	112	99	108	78
Canned corn	100	114	118	96	77
Canned miscellaneous vegetables	100	105	108	100	88
Dried peas	100	193	126	61	64
Dried beans	100	96	81	98	125
Dried miscellaneous vegetables	100	103	100	102	95
Dried processed vegetables	100	83	63	101	148
Fresh and canned vegetable juices	100	109	95	85	122
Sugar and other sweets	**100**	**103**	**106**	**85**	**116**
Candy and chewing gum	100	100	110	80	123
Sugar	100	109	90	100	103
Artificial sweeteners	100	97	117	82	115
Jams, preserves, other sweets	100	112	105	89	104

	total consumer units	Northeast	Midwest	South	West
Fats and oils	**100**	**103**	**102**	**93**	**107**
Margarine	100	119	108	99	78
Fats and oils	100	116	86	93	112
Salad dressings	100	94	106	97	103
Nondairy cream and imitation milk	100	88	111	89	118
Peanut butter	100	98	111	88	110
Miscellaneous foods	**100**	**96**	**106**	**92**	**109**
Frozen prepared foods	100	91	119	95	96
Frozen meals	100	96	114	96	95
Other frozen prepared foods	100	87	123	94	97
Canned and packaged soups	100	104	111	88	107
Potato chips, nuts, and other snacks	100	96	113	86	113
Potato chips and other snacks	100	95	115	89	107
Nuts	100	100	108	77	130
Condiments and seasonings	100	105	109	88	106
Salt, spices, and other seasonings	100	103	112	91	101
Olives, pickles, relishes	100	122	117	76	104
Sauces and gravies	100	103	102	93	108
Baking needs and miscellaneous products	100	102	119	81	111
Other canned or packaged prepared foods	100	93	92	98	117
Prepared salads	100	107	107	92	101
Prepared desserts	100	104	114	94	93
Baby food	100	123	65	129	68
Miscellaneous prepared foods	100	84	92	93	132
Nonalcoholic beverages	**100**	**104**	**100**	**96**	**104**
Cola	100	84	107	109	91
Other carbonated drinks	100	101	101	99	99
Tea	100	124	96	90	101
Coffee	100	108	96	88	116
Noncarbonated fruit-flavored drinks	100	107	101	97	97
Other noncarbonated beverages and ice	100	84	98	96	123
Bottled water	100	118	92	90	110
Sports drinks	100	117	107	92	93
Food prepared by consumer unit on trips	**100**	**103**	**88**	**81**	**140**
FOOD AWAY FROM HOME	**100**	**103**	**91**	**94**	**115**
Meals at restaurants, carry-outs, etc.	**100**	**100**	**89**	**97**	**115**
Lunch	100	91	87	102	117
At fast-food restaurants*	100	86	91	102	116
At full-service restaurants	100	86	75	107	125
At vending machines, mobile vendors	100	110	97	84	122
At employer and school cafeterias	100	136	114	83	85
Dinner	100	104	93	96	110
At fast-food restaurants*	100	96	96	98	111
At full-service restaurants	100	108	90	96	110
At vending machines, mobile vendors	100	160	160	52	70
At employer and school cafeterias	100	121	160	72	68
Snacks and nonalcoholic beverages	100	101	86	85	138
At fast-food restaurants*	100	101	80	85	144
At full-service restaurants	100	107	89	74	148
At vending machines, mobile vendors	100	82	105	109	96
At employer and school cafeterias	100	124	128	66	109
Breakfast and brunch	100	113	83	93	118
At fast-food restaurants*	100	127	70	98	111
At full-service restaurants	100	92	99	86	129
At vending machines, mobile vendors	100	145	79	63	145
At employer and school cafeterias	100	119	104	92	93

	total consumer units	Northeast	Midwest	South	West
Board (including at school)	100	153	107	81	82
Catered affairs	100	173	111	60	95
Food on trips	100	105	97	83	127
School lunches	100	94	121	101	82
Meals as pay	100	118	81	61	167
ALCOHOLIC BEVERAGES	100	108	85	85	134
At home	100	101	81	94	128
Beer and ale	100	96	86	107	106
Whiskey	100	129	103	103	68
Wine	100	101	69	83	159
Other alcoholic beverages	100	116	106	74	124
Away from home	100	115	89	74	141
Beer and ale	100	110	99	79	127
At fast-food restaurants*	100	77	128	98	95
At full-service restaurants	100	114	92	76	136
At vending machines, mobile vendors	100	65	238	82	25
Wine	100	140	61	71	155
At fast-food restaurants*	100	148	46	95	122
At full-service restaurants	100	132	62	70	161
Other alcoholic beverages	100	115	92	64	155
At fast-food restaurants*	100	116	135	76	92
At full-service restaurants	100	115	88	63	161
Alcoholic beverages purchased on trips	100	99	96	80	137

The category fast-food restaurants also includes take-out, delivery, concession stands, buffets, and cafeterias other than employer and school.
Source: Calculations by New Strategist based on the Bureau of Labor Statistics' 2011 Consumer Expenditure Survey

Table 5.23 Food and Alcohol: Total spending by region, 2011

(total annual spending on food and alcoholic beverages, by region in which consumer units live, 2011; consumer units and dollars in thousands)

	total consumer units	Northeast	Midwest	South	West
Number of consumer units	122,287	22,538	27,107	44,901	27,741
Total spending of all consumer units	$6,078,260,661	$1,229,390,428	$1,279,221,075	$2,051,912,839	$1,518,692,974
Food, total spending	789,729,446	153,235,862	169,039,252	268,507,980	199,402,308
Alcoholic beverages, total spending	55,815,455	11,060,073	10,483,632	17,341,215	17028535.44
FOOD AT HOME	**469,308,157**	**92,381,008**	**104,117,987**	**157,398,659**	**115,658,609**
Cereals and bakery products	**64,895,265**	**13,750,659**	**14,774,941**	**21,480,189**	**14,910,788**
Cereals and cereal products	21,383,105	4,612,176	4,622,286	6,910,264	5,255,255
Flour	937,941	190,897	212,248	292,755	243,011
Prepared flour mixes	1,819,631	375,258	451,874	586,856	405,851
Ready-to-eat and cooked cereals	11,175,809	2,348,910	2,437,190	3,761,806	2,633,176
Rice	3,137,884	775,307	525,876	1,005,782	835,836
Pasta, cornmeal, and other cereal products	4,311,840	922,030	995,098	1,262,616	1,137,104
Bakery products	43,510,937	9,138,483	10,152,656	14,570,375	9,655,810
Bread	13,027,234	2,689,910	2,759,764	4,420,952	3,164,416
White bread	5,494,355	1,116,082	1,171,293	1,967,113	1,240,855
Bread, other than white	7,532,879	1,573,829	1,588,199	2,453,840	1,923,561
Cookies and crackers	10,221,970	2,081,384	2,497,097	3,344,675	2,300,561
Cookies	5,742,598	1,151,466	1,336,646	1,956,786	1,298,834
Crackers	4,479,373	929,918	1,160,451	1,387,890	1,001,450
Frozen and refrigerated bakery products	3,497,408	639,403	848,720	1,283,271	724,318
Other bakery products	16,764,325	3,728,011	4,047,075	5,521,476	3,466,515
Biscuits and rolls	6,472,651	1,556,024	1,557,568	2,043,894	1,315,478
Cakes and cupcakes	4,623,671	977,473	1,039,553	1,656,847	949,297
Bread and cracker products	871,906	230,338	240,710	259,977	140,924
Sweetrolls, coffee cakes, doughnuts	2,917,768	570,888	710,746	933,941	702,957
Pies, tarts, turnovers	1,878,328	393,288	498,498	626,818	358,136
Meats, poultry, fish, and eggs	**101,792,922**	**19,887,080**	**21,428,897**	**36,432,671**	**24,080,020**
Beef	27,221,086	4,856,037	5,922,880	9,775,397	6,676,149
Ground beef	11,066,974	1,834,368	2,620,163	4,254,370	2,352,437
Roast	3,740,759	695,523	723,215	1,236,125	1,091,054
Chuck roast	935,496	168,133	187,852	286,917	294,887
Round roast	747,174	132,523	119,542	300,837	194,464
Other roast	2,056,867	394,866	415,821	648,370	601,425
Steak	10,087,455	1,927,675	1,983,148	3,555,710	2,629,847
Round steak	1,944,363	310,799	461,361	647,023	526,524
Sirloin steak	2,673,194	555,111	474,644	907,449	739,852
Other steak	5,469,898	1,061,765	1,046,872	2,000,789	1,363,748
Other beef	2,325,899	398,472	596,354	728,743	602,812
Pork	19,804,380	3,418,113	4,370,733	7,814,121	4,192,220
Bacon	4,141,861	633,092	958,232	1,564,351	985,638
Pork chops	3,331,098	629,712	714,269	1,386,992	597,541
Ham	4,193,221	762,461	1,020,850	1,579,168	827,514
Ham, not canned	4,097,837	750,515	993,743	1,546,839	803,379
Canned ham	95,384	11,720	27,107	32,329	23,857
Sausage	3,491,294	575,621	724,299	1,448,506	741,517
Other pork	4,645,683	817,453	952,811	1,834,655	1,040,288
Other meats	14,985,049	3,367,628	3,831,846	4,803,958	2,978,274
Frankfurters	2,894,533	636,924	658,700	1,035,417	562,865
Lunch meats (cold cuts)	10,720,901	2,461,826	2,684,677	3,404,843	2,168,791
Bologna, liverwurst, salami	3,280,960	773,730	843,028	1,004,884	659,404
Other lunch meats	7,439,941	1,688,096	1,841,379	2,399,958	1,509,665
Lamb, organ meats, and others	1,369,614	268,878	488,739	363,698	246,340

	total consumer units	Northeast	Midwest	South	West
Poultry	$18,892,119	$3,789,990	$3,583,003	$6,895,447	$4,636,076
Fresh and frozen chicken	15,217,394	3,095,369	2,788,226	5,560,540	3,785,537
Fresh and frozen whole chicken	4,398,663	963,274	783,934	1,385,196	1,274,144
Fresh and frozen chicken parts	10,819,954	2,132,095	2,004,563	4,175,344	2,511,393
Other poultry	3,674,724	694,621	794,777	1,334,907	850,539
Fish and seafood	14,767,378	3,283,561	2,460,231	4,998,379	4,048,799
Canned fish and seafood	2,433,511	477,355	496,058	875,570	586,167
Fresh fish and shellfish	7,277,299	1,903,334	1,012,175	2,319,586	2,058,382
Frozen fish and shellfish	5,056,567	902,872	951,998	1,803,224	1,404,249
Eggs	6,122,910	1,171,976	1,260,476	2,145,370	1,549,057
Dairy products	**49,751,243**	**10,014,310**	**11,091,100**	**15,970,837**	**12,713,978**
Fresh milk and cream	18,310,033	3,366,952	3,867,085	6,388,065	4,700,158
Fresh milk, all types	15,576,918	2,818,377	3,241,997	5,589,276	3,935,893
Cream	2,734,337	548,800	625,087	799,238	764,542
Other dairy products	31,439,988	6,647,132	7,224,016	9,582,322	8,013,820
Butter	3,013,152	618,217	761,978	868,385	767,316
Cheese	15,254,080	3,048,941	3,709,322	4,554,308	3,954,202
Ice cream and related products	7,004,599	1,525,597	1,426,912	2,406,245	1,650,035
Miscellaneous dairy products	6,166,933	1,454,377	1,325,803	1,753,384	1,642,545
Fruits and vegetables	**87,421,753**	**18,281,248**	**18,856,985**	**27,496,923**	**22,876,893**
Fresh fruits	30,239,129	6,273,227	6,595,133	9,040,367	8,370,847
Apples	4,667,695	980,178	1,041,722	1,436,832	1,213,114
Bananas	5,023,550	1,092,417	1,073,437	1,526,185	1,337,394
Oranges	3,300,526	640,755	740,834	1,023,294	899,086
Citrus fruits, excluding oranges	4,601,660	921,804	970,160	1,298,986	1,420,062
Other fresh fruits	12,646,922	2,638,298	2,768,709	3,755,071	3,501,192
Fresh vegetables	27,417,968	5,881,516	5,504,076	8,494,371	7,577,454
Potatoes	4,742,290	1,025,254	945,492	1,688,278	1,084,673
Lettuce	3,933,973	862,755	925,975	1,179,549	968,438
Tomatoes	5,017,436	1,103,686	1,033,590	1,588,148	1,297,169
Other fresh vegetables	13,725,493	2,889,597	2,599,019	4,037,947	4,227,451
Processed fruits	14,152,275	2,962,395	3,226,817	4,416,911	3,557,783
Frozen fruits and fruit juices	1,627,640	264,145	412,026	411,742	543,169
Frozen orange juice	456,131	62,430	139,330	105,517	149,524
Frozen fruits	846,226	165,204	176,196	188,584	318,744
Frozen fruit juices, excluding orange	326,506	36,512	96,772	117,641	75,178
Canned fruits	2,597,376	458,198	699,632	868,385	569,800
Dried fruits	994,193	207,800	264,293	278,835	243,011
Fresh fruit juice	2,113,119	528,516	474,644	681,148	429,153
Canned and bottled fruit juice	6,821,169	1,503,961	1,375,951	2,176,800	1,772,650
Processed vegetables	15,611,158	3,163,884	3,530,958	5,545,274	3,370,532
Frozen vegetables	4,277,599	913,014	987,508	1,470,059	907,131
Canned and dried vegetables and juices	11,333,559	2,250,870	2,543,450	4,075,215	2,463,401
Canned beans	2,333,236	479,609	510,967	925,410	415,283
Canned corn	1,189,853	249,946	312,002	419,375	207,225
Canned miscellaneous vegetables	3,118,319	604,920	744,087	1,144,077	623,340
Dried peas	102,721	36,512	28,733	22,900	14,980
Dried beans	610,212	107,732	109,241	220,464	173,659
Dried miscellaneous vegetables	1,412,415	268,202	313,899	526,689	303,487
Dried processed vegetables	250,688	38,540	34,968	93,394	84,055
Fresh and canned vegetable juices	2,273,315	457,521	477,625	713,477	628,334
Sugar and other sweets	**17,657,020**	**3,366,501**	**4,139,781**	**5,523,721**	**4,640,792**
Candy and chewing gum	10,608,397	1,947,058	2,579,773	3,125,110	2,967,732
Sugar	2,921,436	588,242	582,801	1,070,889	679,932
Artificial sweeteners	686,030	122,607	178,093	206,994	178,652
Jams, preserves, other sweets	3,441,156	708,369	799,114	1,120,729	814,753

	total consumer units	Northeast	Midwest	South	West
Fats and oils	$13,403,878	$2,538,680	$3,019,449	$4,594,719	$3,256,793
Margarine	1,194,744	262,342	285,166	435,091	211,386
Fats and oils	4,260,479	909,859	815,921	1,453,445	1,085,228
Salad dressings	3,810,463	663,519	899,410	1,360,949	886,602
Nondairy cream and imitation milk	2,273,315	366,919	559,760	740,867	606,973
Peanut butter	1,864,877	336,042	459,464	604,367	466,326
Miscellaneous foods	84,436,728	15,004,674	19,926,085	28,582,181	20,953,055
Frozen prepared foods	16,659,158	2,808,009	4,404,345	5,795,821	3,643,226
Frozen meals	7,598,914	1,347,998	1,925,139	2,676,998	1,645,319
Other frozen prepared foods	9,060,244	1,460,237	2,479,206	3,118,823	1,997,907
Canned and packaged soups	5,735,260	1,094,445	1,407,395	1,846,329	1,389,547
Potato chips, nuts, and other snacks	17,734,061	3,138,191	4,443,651	5,612,176	4,548,414
Potato chips and other snacks	13,208,219	2,307,891	3,356,931	4,331,599	3,213,240
Nuts	4,525,842	830,075	1,086,449	1,280,577	1,335,174
Condiments and seasonings	16,374,229	3,172,900	3,963,314	5,302,808	3,941,441
Salt, spices, and other seasonings	4,330,183	824,215	1,070,455	1,439,975	995,070
Olives, pickles, relishes	1,972,489	442,646	511,780	553,629	465,771
Sauces and gravies	7,145,229	1,358,365	1,609,885	2,435,879	1,744,631
Baking needs and miscellaneous products	2,926,328	547,899	771,194	872,875	735,969
Other canned or packaged prepared foods	27,932,797	4,791,128	5,707,650	10,025,046	7,430,427
Prepared salads	4,429,235	876,052	1,050,938	1,491,611	1,011,159
Prepared desserts	1,837,974	352,269	464,885	633,553	385,877
Baby food	3,399,579	768,997	490,637	1,610,150	526,247
Miscellaneous prepared foods	17,989,641	2,776,231	3,667,848	6,173,438	5,396,179
Nonalcoholic beverages	44,141,938	8,434,621	9,742,798	15,599,954	10,375,966
Cola	9,632,547	1,490,438	2,275,904	3,859,241	1,999,294
Other carbonated drinks	8,158,989	1,522,217	1,834,060	2,967,058	1,835,067
Tea	3,810,463	870,868	813,481	1,252,289	876,338
Coffee	9,175,194	1,830,311	1,956,583	2,976,487	2,420,402
Noncarbonated fruit-flavored drinks	3,027,826	599,511	680,115	1,083,012	664,952
Other noncarbonated beverages and ice	1,825,745	281,725	394,678	642,084	508,770
Bottled water	6,539,909	1,423,500	1,326,617	2,157,493	1,638,106
Sports drinks	1,923,575	414,248	454,855	647,921	405,573
Food prepared by consumer unit on trips	5,808,633	1,103,235	1,137,952	1,717,912	1,849,770
FOOD AWAY FROM HOME	320,378,488	60,855,530	64,910,422	111,088,217	83,745,086
Meals at restaurants, carry-outs, etc.	268,528,800	49,618,083	53,186,916	95,671,010	70,273,501
Lunch	92,068,659	15,517,188	17,769,723	34,472,743	24,376,294
At fast-food restaurants*	45,097,000	7,162,126	9,117,711	16,957,761	11,885,909
At full-service restaurants	36,931,897	5,886,700	6,155,458	14,451,836	10,478,608
At vending machines, mobile vendors	875,575	177,149	188,936	268,508	241,902
At employer and school cafeterias	9,164,188	2,290,988	2,307,619	2,794,638	1,769,876
Dinner	128,529,751	24,566,871	26,436,915	45,469,447	32,136,561
At fast-food restaurants*	44,650,652	7,881,764	9,493,685	16,011,697	11,285,316
At full-service restaurants	82,673,349	16,388,957	16,514,398	29,165,894	20,662,606
At vending machines, mobile vendors	369,307	108,859	130,927	70,046	58,811
At employer and school cafeterias	837,666	187,291	297,906	221,362	129,828
Snacks and nonalcoholic beverages	20,310,648	3,780,975	3,888,499	6,307,692	6,373,772
At fast-food restaurants*	13,408,770	2,490,900	2,387,042	4,187,018	4,374,478
At full-service restaurants	4,001,231	789,957	786,374	1,087,951	1,347,103
At vending machines, mobile vendors	2,113,119	320,265	491,721	842,343	458,004
At employer and school cafeterias	786,305	179,853	223,091	190,380	194,187
Breakfast and brunch	27,619,742	5,753,501	5,092,050	9,421,128	7,387,151
At fast-food restaurants*	15,135,462	3,533,282	2,343,400	5,469,840	3,808,007
At full-service restaurants	10,931,235	1,862,090	2,410,354	3,465,010	3,208,247
At vending machines, mobile vendors	370,530	99,167	64,786	86,210	122,060
At employer and school cafeterias	1,181,292	258,962	273,239	400,517	249,114

	total consumer units	Northeast	Midwest	South	West
Board (including at school)	$5,364,731	$1,514,779	$1,266,981	$1,588,148	$995,070
Catered affairs	6,435,965	2,047,352	1,580,338	1,416,627	1,391,211
Food on trips	28,919,653	5,589,424	6,208,858	8,794,310	8,327,016
School lunches	7,601,360	1,318,924	2,033,296	2,831,906	1,417,843
Meals as pay	3,527,980	766,968	634,033	786,217	1,340,445
ALCOHOLIC BEVERAGES	55,815,455	11,060,073	10,483,632	17,341,215	17,028,535
At home	29,636,254	5,510,090	5,316,225	10,217,223	8,637,993
Beer and ale	13,422,221	2,367,842	2,564,864	5,267,785	3,225,169
Whiskey	1,173,955	279,922	267,275	442,724	182,258
Wine	12,721,517	2,365,363	1,938,151	3,877,201	4,579,484
Other alcoholic beverages	2,319,784	496,963	546,206	629,063	650,804
Away from home	26,179,201	5,549,983	5,167,407	7,123,993	8,390,543
Beer and ale	9,413,653	1,914,828	2,059,590	2,734,022	2,720,005
At fast-food restaurants*	1,524,919	217,492	431,815	546,445	327,344
At full-service restaurants	7,743,213	1,624,088	1,584,675	2,162,881	2,388,500
At vending machines, mobile vendors	79,487	9,466	42,016	23,798	4,439
Wine	5,131,163	1,323,657	689,602	1,334,907	1,802,333
At fast-food restaurants*	361,970	98,942	36,866	126,172	100,422
At full-service restaurants	4,671,363	1,139,296	640,809	1,206,939	1,701,910
Other alcoholic beverages	6,151,036	1,306,077	1,256,952	1,441,771	2,165,185
At fast-food restaurants*	519,720	111,112	155,865	144,581	107,912
At full-service restaurants	5,623,979	1,190,683	1,101,086	1,297,190	2,053,944
Alcoholic beverages purchased on trips	5,483,349	1,005,420	1,161,264	1,613,293	1,703,020

*The category fast-food restaurants also includes take-out, delivery, concession stands, buffets, and cafeterias other than employer and school.
Note: Numbers may not add to total because of rounding and missing subcategories.
Source: Calculations by New Strategist based on the Bureau of Labor Statistics' 2011 Consumer Expenditure Survey

Table 5.24 Food and Alcohol: Market shares by region, 2011

(percentage of total annual spending on food and alcoholic beverages accounted for by consumer units by region of residence, 2011)

	total consumer units	Northeast	Midwest	South	West
Share of total consumer units	100.0%	18.4%	22.2%	36.7%	22.7%
Share of total before-tax income	100.0	20.8	21.2	33.9	24.2
Share of total spending	100.0	20.2	21.0	33.8	25.0
Share of food spending	100.0	19.4	21.4	34.0	25.2
Share of alcoholic beverages spending	100.0	19.8	18.8	31.1	30.5
FOOD AT HOME	100.0	19.7	22.2	33.5	24.6
Cereals and bakery products	100.0	21.2	22.8	33.1	23.0
Cereals and cereal products	100.0	21.6	21.6	32.3	24.6
Flour	100.0	20.4	22.6	31.2	25.9
Prepared flour mixes	100.0	20.6	24.8	32.3	22.3
Ready-to-eat and cooked cereals	100.0	21.0	21.8	33.7	23.6
Rice	100.0	24.7	16.8	32.1	26.6
Pasta, cornmeal, and other cereal products	100.0	21.4	23.1	29.3	26.4
Bakery products	100.0	21.0	23.3	33.5	22.2
Bread	100.0	20.6	21.2	33.9	24.3
White bread	100.0	20.3	21.3	35.8	22.6
Bread, other than white	100.0	20.9	21.1	32.6	25.5
Cookies and crackers	100.0	20.4	24.4	32.7	22.5
Cookies	100.0	20.1	23.3	34.1	22.6
Crackers	100.0	20.8	25.9	31.0	22.4
Frozen and refrigerated bakery products	100.0	18.3	24.3	36.7	20.7
Other bakery products	100.0	22.2	24.1	32.9	20.7
Biscuits and rolls	100.0	24.0	24.1	31.6	20.3
Cakes and cupcakes	100.0	21.1	22.5	35.8	20.5
Bread and cracker products	100.0	26.4	27.6	29.8	16.2
Sweetrolls, coffee cakes, doughnuts	100.0	19.6	24.4	32.0	24.1
Pies, tarts, turnovers	100.0	20.9	26.5	33.4	19.1
Meats, poultry, fish, and eggs	100.0	19.5	21.1	35.8	23.7
Beef	100.0	17.8	21.8	35.9	24.5
Ground beef	100.0	16.6	23.7	38.4	21.3
Roast	100.0	18.6	19.3	33.0	29.2
Chuck roast	100.0	18.0	20.1	30.7	31.5
Round roast	100.0	17.7	16.0	40.3	26.0
Other roast	100.0	19.2	20.2	31.5	29.2
Steak	100.0	19.1	19.7	35.2	26.1
Round steak	100.0	16.0	23.7	33.3	27.1
Sirloin steak	100.0	20.8	17.8	33.9	27.7
Other steak	100.0	19.4	19.1	36.6	24.9
Other beef	100.0	17.1	25.6	31.3	25.9
Pork	100.0	17.3	22.1	39.5	21.2
Bacon	100.0	15.3	23.1	37.8	23.8
Pork chops	100.0	18.9	21.4	41.6	17.9
Ham	100.0	18.2	24.3	37.7	19.7
Ham, not canned	100.0	18.3	24.3	37.7	19.6
Canned ham	100.0	12.3	28.4	33.9	25.0
Sausage	100.0	16.5	20.7	41.5	21.2
Other pork	100.0	17.6	20.5	39.5	22.4
Other meats	100.0	22.5	25.6	32.1	19.9
Frankfurters	100.0	22.0	22.8	35.8	19.4
Lunch meats (cold cuts)	100.0	23.0	25.0	31.8	20.2
Bologna, liverwurst, salami	100.0	23.6	25.7	30.6	20.1
Other lunch meats	100.0	22.7	24.7	32.3	20.3
Lamb, organ meats, and others	100.0	19.6	35.7	26.6	18.0

	total consumer units	Northeast	Midwest	South	West
Poultry	100.0%	20.1%	19.0%	36.5%	24.5%
Fresh and frozen chicken	100.0	20.3	18.3	36.5	24.9
Fresh and frozen whole chicken	100.0	21.9	17.8	31.5	29.0
Fresh and frozen chicken parts	100.0	19.7	18.5	38.6	23.2
Other poultry	100.0	18.9	21.6	36.3	23.1
Fish and seafood	100.0	22.2	16.7	33.8	27.4
Canned fish and seafood	100.0	19.6	20.4	36.0	24.1
Fresh fish and shellfish	100.0	26.2	13.9	31.9	28.3
Frozen fish and shellfish	100.0	17.9	18.8	35.7	27.8
Eggs	100.0	19.1	20.6	35.0	25.3
Dairy products	**100.0**	**20.1**	**22.3**	**32.1**	**25.6**
Fresh milk and cream	100.0	18.4	21.1	34.9	25.7
Fresh milk, all types	100.0	18.1	20.8	35.9	25.3
Cream	100.0	20.1	22.9	29.2	28.0
Other dairy products	100.0	21.1	23.0	30.5	25.5
Butter	100.0	20.5	25.3	28.8	25.5
Cheese	100.0	20.0	24.3	29.9	25.9
Ice cream and related products	100.0	21.8	20.4	34.4	23.6
Miscellaneous dairy products	100.0	23.6	21.5	28.4	26.6
Fruits and vegetables	**100.0**	**20.9**	**21.6**	**31.5**	**26.2**
Fresh fruits	100.0	20.7	21.8	29.9	27.7
Apples	100.0	21.0	22.3	30.8	26.0
Bananas	100.0	21.7	21.4	30.4	26.6
Oranges	100.0	19.4	22.4	31.0	27.2
Citrus fruits, excluding oranges	100.0	20.0	21.1	28.2	30.9
Other fresh fruits	100.0	20.9	21.9	29.7	27.7
Fresh vegetables	100.0	21.5	20.1	31.0	27.6
Potatoes	100.0	21.6	19.9	35.6	22.9
Lettuce	100.0	21.9	23.5	30.0	24.6
Tomatoes	100.0	22.0	20.6	31.7	25.9
Other fresh vegetables	100.0	21.1	18.9	29.4	30.8
Processed fruits	100.0	20.9	22.8	31.2	25.1
Frozen fruits and fruit juices	100.0	16.2	25.3	25.3	33.4
Frozen orange juice	100.0	13.7	30.5	23.1	32.8
Frozen fruits	100.0	19.5	20.8	22.3	37.7
Frozen fruit juices, excluding orange	100.0	11.2	29.6	36.0	23.0
Canned fruits	100.0	17.6	26.9	33.4	21.9
Dried fruits	100.0	20.9	26.6	28.0	24.4
Fresh fruit juice	100.0	25.0	22.5	32.2	20.3
Canned and bottled fruit juice	100.0	22.0	20.2	31.9	26.0
Processed vegetables	100.0	20.3	22.6	35.5	21.6
Frozen vegetables	100.0	21.3	23.1	34.4	21.2
Canned and dried vegetables and juices	100.0	19.9	22.4	36.0	21.7
Canned beans	100.0	20.6	21.9	39.7	17.8
Canned corn	100.0	21.0	26.2	35.2	17.4
Canned miscellaneous vegetables	100.0	19.4	23.9	36.7	20.0
Dried peas	100.0	35.5	28.0	22.3	14.6
Dried beans	100.0	17.7	17.9	36.1	28.5
Dried miscellaneous vegetables	100.0	19.0	22.2	37.3	21.5
Dried processed vegetables	100.0	15.4	13.9	37.3	33.5
Fresh and canned vegetable juices	100.0	20.1	21.0	31.4	27.6
Sugar and other sweets	**100.0**	**19.1**	**23.4**	**31.3**	**26.3**
Candy and chewing gum	100.0	18.4	24.3	29.5	28.0
Sugar	100.0	20.1	19.9	36.7	23.3
Artificial sweeteners	100.0	17.9	26.0	30.2	26.0
Jams, preserves, other sweets	100.0	20.6	23.2	32.6	23.7

	total consumer units	Northeast	Midwest	South	West
Fats and oils	**100.0%**	**18.9%**	**22.5%**	**34.3%**	**24.3%**
Margarine	100.0	22.0	23.9	36.4	17.7
Fats and oils	100.0	21.4	19.2	34.1	25.5
Salad dressings	100.0	17.4	23.6	35.7	23.3
Nondairy cream and imitation milk	100.0	16.1	24.6	32.6	26.7
Peanut butter	100.0	18.0	24.6	32.4	25.0
Miscellaneous foods	**100.0**	**17.8**	**23.6**	**33.9**	**24.8**
Frozen prepared foods	100.0	16.9	26.4	34.8	21.9
Frozen meals	100.0	17.7	25.3	35.2	21.7
Other frozen prepared foods	100.0	16.1	27.4	34.4	22.1
Canned and packaged soups	100.0	19.1	24.5	32.2	24.2
Potato chips, nuts, and other snacks	100.0	17.7	25.1	31.6	25.6
Potato chips and other snacks	100.0	17.5	25.4	32.8	24.3
Nuts	100.0	18.3	24.0	28.3	29.5
Condiments and seasonings	100.0	19.4	24.2	32.4	24.1
Salt, spices, and other seasonings	100.0	19.0	24.7	33.3	23.0
Olives, pickles, relishes	100.0	22.4	25.9	28.1	23.6
Sauces and gravies	100.0	19.0	22.5	34.1	24.4
Baking needs and miscellaneous products	100.0	18.7	26.4	29.8	25.1
Other canned or packaged prepared foods	100.0	17.2	20.4	35.9	26.6
Prepared salads	100.0	19.8	23.7	33.7	22.8
Prepared desserts	100.0	19.2	25.3	34.5	21.0
Baby food	100.0	22.6	14.4	47.4	15.5
Miscellaneous prepared foods	100.0	15.4	20.4	34.3	30.0
Nonalcoholic beverages	**100.0**	**19.1**	**22.1**	**35.3**	**23.5**
Cola	100.0	15.5	23.6	40.1	20.8
Other carbonated drinks	100.0	18.7	22.5	36.4	22.5
Tea	100.0	22.9	21.3	32.9	23.0
Coffee	100.0	19.9	21.3	32.4	26.4
Noncarbonated fruit-flavored drinks	100.0	19.8	22.5	35.8	22.0
Other noncarbonated beverages and ice	100.0	15.4	21.6	35.2	27.9
Bottled water	100.0	21.8	20.3	33.0	25.0
Sports drinks	100.0	21.5	23.6	33.7	21.1
Food prepared by consumer unit on trips	**100.0**	**19.0**	**19.6**	**29.6**	**31.8**
FOOD AWAY FROM HOME	**100.0**	**19.0**	**20.3**	**34.7**	**26.1**
Meals at restaurants, carry-outs, etc.	**100.0**	**18.5**	**19.8**	**35.6**	**26.2**
Lunch	100.0	16.9	19.3	37.4	26.5
At fast-food restaurants*	100.0	15.9	20.2	37.6	26.4
At full-service restaurants	100.0	15.9	16.7	39.1	28.4
At vending machines, mobile vendors	100.0	20.2	21.6	30.7	27.6
At employer and school cafeterias	100.0	25.0	25.2	30.5	19.3
Dinner	100.0	19.1	20.6	35.4	25.0
At fast-food restaurants*	100.0	17.7	21.3	35.9	25.3
At full-service restaurants	100.0	19.8	20.0	35.3	25.0
At vending machines, mobile vendors	100.0	29.5	35.5	19.0	15.9
At employer and school cafeterias	100.0	22.4	35.6	26.4	15.5
Snacks and nonalcoholic beverages	100.0	18.6	19.1	31.1	31.4
At fast-food restaurants*	100.0	18.6	17.8	31.2	32.6
At full-service restaurants	100.0	19.7	19.7	27.2	33.7
At vending machines, mobile vendors	100.0	15.2	23.3	39.9	21.7
At employer and school cafeterias	100.0	22.9	28.4	24.2	24.7
Breakfast and brunch	100.0	20.8	18.4	34.1	26.7
At fast-food restaurants*	100.0	23.3	15.5	36.1	25.2
At full-service restaurants	100.0	17.0	22.1	31.7	29.3
At vending machines, mobile vendors	100.0	26.8	17.5	23.3	32.9
At employer and school cafeterias	100.0	21.9	23.1	33.9	21.1

	total consumer units	Northeast	Midwest	South	West
Board (including at school)	100.0%	28.2%	23.6%	29.6%	18.5%
Catered affairs	100.0	31.8	24.6	22.0	21.6
Food on trips	100.0	19.3	21.5	30.4	28.8
School lunches	100.0	17.4	26.7	37.3	18.7
Meals as pay	100.0	21.7	18.0	22.3	38.0
ALCOHOLIC BEVERAGES	100.0	19.8	18.8	31.1	30.5
At home	100.0	18.6	17.9	34.5	29.1
Beer and ale	100.0	17.6	19.1	39.2	24.0
Whiskey	100.0	23.8	22.8	37.7	15.5
Wine	100.0	18.6	15.2	30.5	36.0
Other alcoholic beverages	100.0	21.4	23.5	27.1	28.1
Away from home	100.0	21.2	19.7	27.2	32.1
Beer and ale	100.0	20.3	21.9	29.0	28.9
At fast-food restaurants*	100.0	14.3	28.3	35.8	21.5
At full-service restaurants	100.0	21.0	20.5	27.9	30.8
At vending machines, mobile vendors	100.0	11.9	52.9	29.9	5.6
Wine	100.0	25.8	13.4	26.0	35.1
At fast-food restaurants*	100.0	27.3	10.2	34.9	27.7
At full-service restaurants	100.0	24.4	13.7	25.8	36.4
Other alcoholic beverages	100.0	21.2	20.4	23.4	35.2
At fast-food restaurants*	100.0	21.4	30.0	27.8	20.8
At full-service restaurants	100.0	21.2	19.6	23.1	36.5
Alcoholic beverages purchased on trips	100.0	18.3	21.2	29.4	31.1

* The category fast-food restaurants also includes take-out, delivery, concession stands, buffets, and cafeterias other than employer and school.
Note: Numbers may not add to total because of rounding.
Source: Calculations by New Strategist based on the Bureau of Labor Statistics' 2011 Consumer Expenditure Survey

Table 5.25 Food and Alcohol: Average spending by education, 2011

(average annual spending of consumer units on food and alcoholic beverages, by education of consumer unit reference person, 2011)

	total consumer units	less than high school graduate	high school graduate	some college	associate's degree	bachelor's degree or more total	bachelor's degree	graduate degree
Number of consumer units (in 000s)	122,287	16,146	30,810	25,361	12,912	37,058	23,578	13,480
Average number of persons per consumer unit	2.5	2.8	2.5	2.3	2.6	2.5	2.5	2.4
Average before-tax income of consumer units	$63,685.00	$32,564.00	$46,370.00	$52,965.00	$63,664.00	$98,983.00	$90,962.00	$113,013.00
Average spending of consumer units, total	49,704.88	29,950.97	39,704.28	45,355.33	50,819.44	68,902.95	65,051.01	75,731.40
Food, average spending	**6,458.00**	**4,971.00**	**5,648.00**	**5,907.00**	**6,486.00**	**8,026.00**	**7,615.00**	**8,807.00**
Alcoholic beverages, average spending	**456.43**	**155.25**	**286.86**	**426.81**	**465.13**	**721.95**	**689.15**	**785.21**
FOOD AT HOME	**3,837.76**	**3,564.23**	**3,595.14**	**3,509.76**	**3,774.22**	**4,365.10**	**4,183.94**	**4,718.35**
Cereals and bakery products	**530.68**	**485.87**	**495.42**	**483.39**	**527.88**	**606.48**	**589.82**	**639.10**
Cereals and cereal products	174.86	176.30	154.12	159.06	170.26	202.33	197.65	211.51
Flour	7.67	11.42	5.20	4.23	6.50	10.82	10.05	12.34
Prepared flour mixes	14.88	15.46	13.21	14.60	14.87	16.17	15.50	17.46
Ready-to-eat and cooked cereals	91.39	82.00	83.33	87.13	92.63	103.58	102.63	105.42
Rice	25.66	34.71	22.80	20.62	20.51	29.45	29.47	29.42
Pasta, cornmeal, and other cereal products	35.26	32.71	29.59	32.48	35.75	42.32	40.00	46.86
Bakery products	355.81	309.58	341.30	324.32	357.62	404.14	392.17	427.59
Bread	106.53	102.52	101.41	98.53	109.68	116.20	109.03	130.23
White bread	44.93	51.38	44.92	40.54	46.99	44.72	42.42	49.24
Bread, other than white	61.60	51.14	56.49	57.98	62.69	71.48	66.61	81.00
Cookies and crackers	83.59	66.95	78.94	75.33	80.94	99.61	95.32	108.02
Cookies	46.96	41.79	45.88	42.00	46.49	53.10	52.05	55.16
Crackers	36.63	25.16	33.07	33.33	34.46	46.51	43.27	52.86
Frozen and refrigerated bakery products	28.60	21.50	27.03	26.63	27.57	34.07	32.22	37.69
Other bakery products	137.09	118.60	133.91	123.84	139.43	154.26	155.59	151.65
Biscuits and rolls	52.93	38.50	46.94	51.04	54.87	63.60	61.70	67.32
Cakes and cupcakes	37.81	33.15	36.53	33.59	43.79	41.37	44.41	35.42
Bread and cracker products	7.13	8.24	8.67	5.50	5.10	7.22	6.56	8.52
Sweetrolls, coffee cakes, doughnuts	23.86	25.17	26.20	21.05	22.19	23.87	22.73	26.11
Pies, tarts, turnovers	15.36	13.53	15.58	12.66	13.48	18.20	20.20	14.29
Meats, poultry, fish, and eggs	**832.41**	**882.94**	**812.28**	**778.86**	**839.07**	**861.97**	**837.68**	**909.54**
Beef	222.60	248.47	217.02	218.01	228.06	218.61	216.72	222.32
Ground beef	90.50	102.57	96.52	89.94	97.11	79.55	80.10	78.48
Roast	30.59	42.11	25.86	29.11	45.28	26.29	25.96	26.93
Chuck roast	7.65	13.11	6.72	5.78	12.82	5.93	5.92	5.94
Round roast	6.11	9.08	5.04	6.47	7.24	5.25	4.98	5.78
Other roast	16.82	19.91	14.10	16.87	25.23	15.11	15.06	15.20
Steak	82.49	89.08	76.35	81.26	68.30	90.21	85.91	98.64
Round steak	15.90	18.40	15.43	14.59	14.02	16.80	15.86	18.64
Sirloin steak	21.86	23.21	18.74	21.82	15.41	25.92	22.51	32.59
Other steak	44.73	47.47	42.19	44.86	38.87	47.50	47.54	47.41
Other beef	19.02	14.71	18.30	17.70	17.36	22.56	24.75	18.27
Pork	161.95	182.37	170.17	164.76	160.13	146.66	149.76	140.58
Bacon	33.87	41.68	33.05	33.77	34.82	31.38	32.95	28.31
Pork chops	27.24	29.86	31.28	29.21	28.83	21.32	22.17	19.65
Ham	34.29	33.37	34.94	38.03	34.84	31.52	31.56	31.45
Ham, not canned	33.51	32.55	34.02	36.94	34.37	30.97	30.89	31.14
Canned ham	0.78	0.82	0.92	1.09	0.48	0.55	0.67	0.30
Sausage	28.55	28.96	31.15	28.68	30.49	25.65	26.10	24.76
Other pork	37.99	48.49	39.75	35.07	31.15	36.79	36.98	36.42
Other meats	122.54	116.62	128.06	107.03	118.57	131.70	130.98	133.11
Frankfurters	23.67	26.78	26.58	20.99	21.43	22.67	22.46	23.10
Lunch meats (cold cuts)	87.67	69.43	90.31	78.25	91.01	97.38	98.64	94.93
Bologna, liverwurst, salami	26.83	23.95	30.45	25.37	27.11	25.91	27.73	22.36
Other lunch meats	60.84	45.48	59.87	52.88	63.89	71.47	70.91	72.58
Lamb, organ meats, and others	11.20	20.40	11.16	7.79	6.13	11.64	9.88	15.08

	total consumer units	less than high school graduate	high school graduate	some college	associate's degree	bachelor's degree or more		
						total	bachelor's degree	graduate degree
Poultry	$154.49	$174.95	$148.60	$135.98	$156.45	$162.86	$156.39	$175.53
Fresh and frozen chicken	124.44	149.07	123.29	108.03	118.79	128.64	125.69	134.41
Fresh and frozen whole chicken	35.97	47.39	35.11	32.12	30.93	36.50	35.82	37.82
Fresh and frozen chicken parts	88.48	101.68	88.17	75.90	87.86	92.14	89.87	96.58
Other poultry	30.05	25.89	25.32	27.96	37.65	34.22	30.70	41.13
Fish and seafood	120.76	105.92	98.30	104.88	126.63	152.32	136.13	184.03
Canned fish and seafood	19.90	15.38	17.82	21.55	23.13	21.13	19.69	23.96
Fresh fish and shellfish	59.51	53.44	47.13	48.32	57.98	79.22	72.51	92.35
Frozen fish and shellfish	41.35	37.11	33.35	35.02	45.52	51.97	43.93	67.72
Eggs	50.07	54.60	50.13	48.19	49.23	49.83	47.71	53.97
Dairy products	**406.84**	**358.82**	**357.37**	**367.05**	**423.76**	**483.86**	**464.91**	**520.99**
Fresh milk and cream	149.73	149.78	139.74	136.52	162.55	162.02	158.01	169.88
Fresh milk, all types	127.38	130.09	119.96	115.33	135.97	137.24	134.47	142.66
Cream	22.36	19.68	19.78	21.19	26.58	24.78	23.54	27.22
Other dairy products	257.10	209.04	217.63	230.53	261.20	321.84	306.90	351.11
Butter	24.64	24.48	21.20	22.77	25.73	28.28	26.27	32.22
Cheese	124.74	102.47	102.12	110.11	137.03	156.33	151.19	166.40
Ice cream and related products	57.28	47.72	53.16	53.10	53.90	67.85	64.83	73.77
Miscellaneous dairy products	50.43	34.37	41.15	44.54	44.54	69.38	64.62	78.72
Fruits and vegetables	**714.89**	**650.64**	**642.06**	**626.61**	**627.01**	**881.16**	**816.02**	**1,008.75**
Fresh fruits	247.28	216.90	212.12	207.05	206.94	325.11	292.94	388.13
Apples	38.17	32.02	34.13	33.74	30.12	49.07	45.27	56.51
Bananas	41.08	42.21	39.96	35.81	37.37	46.12	44.23	49.82
Oranges	26.99	25.04	23.46	26.05	22.23	32.62	30.87	36.02
Citrus fruits, excluding oranges	37.63	39.56	32.04	29.96	27.08	49.66	42.75	63.18
Other fresh fruits	103.42	78.07	82.53	81.49	90.14	147.66	129.82	182.59
Fresh vegetables	224.21	202.06	197.63	192.21	184.23	286.80	260.63	338.04
Potatoes	38.78	42.12	39.73	33.41	36.42	41.00	37.83	47.19
Lettuce	32.17	27.08	29.68	28.84	27.34	39.71	37.24	44.55
Tomatoes	41.03	42.16	39.49	33.67	31.23	49.71	44.74	59.44
Other fresh vegetables	112.24	90.70	88.73	96.29	89.24	156.38	140.82	186.86
Processed fruits	115.73	102.13	104.07	110.47	118.18	132.57	130.51	136.62
Frozen fruits and fruit juices	13.31	10.88	11.21	11.53	16.73	15.93	16.38	15.05
Frozen orange juice	3.73	3.93	3.62	2.80	5.01	3.93	4.19	3.43
Frozen fruits	6.92	3.10	4.97	6.50	7.68	9.88	10.04	9.57
Frozen fruit juices, excluding orange	2.67	3.85	2.62	2.23	4.04	2.11	2.15	2.04
Canned fruits	21.24	19.40	20.01	20.77	19.11	23.86	23.62	24.35
Dried fruits	8.13	4.97	6.54	7.49	9.36	10.57	10.48	10.73
Fresh fruit juice	17.28	15.35	14.55	15.36	17.52	21.29	20.38	23.08
Canned and bottled fruit juice	55.78	51.54	51.76	55.33	55.46	60.92	59.65	63.40
Processed vegetables	127.66	129.54	128.23	116.88	117.66	136.68	131.94	145.96
Frozen vegetables	34.98	24.81	33.14	31.44	37.53	41.67	37.64	49.58
Canned and dried vegetables and juices	92.68	104.74	95.10	85.43	80.13	95.01	94.30	96.38
Canned beans	19.08	22.62	20.57	16.24	18.65	18.57	17.28	21.10
Canned corn	9.73	10.21	11.17	10.01	8.73	8.56	8.87	7.97
Canned miscellaneous vegetables	25.50	27.25	26.20	22.92	21.61	27.20	26.98	27.64
Dried peas	0.84	1.77	0.56	1.12	0.29	0.72	0.41	1.33
Dried beans	4.99	9.74	4.84	4.21	3.26	4.41	4.54	4.16
Dried miscellaneous vegetables	11.55	14.01	11.43	9.16	9.91	12.80	12.76	12.87
Dried processed vegetables	2.05	1.97	1.97	2.43	1.86	1.95	2.05	1.75
Fresh and canned vegetable juices	18.59	16.95	17.78	19.08	15.52	20.52	21.13	19.32
Sugar and other sweets	**144.39**	**117.73**	**135.32**	**133.83**	**154.39**	**165.03**	**160.05**	**174.77**
Candy and chewing gum	86.75	57.65	79.47	79.64	98.08	104.24	102.58	107.50
Sugar	23.89	29.03	26.67	23.44	20.63	21.11	20.39	22.53
Artificial sweeteners	5.61	3.50	4.86	6.32	6.10	6.37	5.56	7.94
Jams, preserves, other sweets	28.14	27.55	24.32	24.43	29.58	33.31	31.53	36.80

	total consumer units	less than high school graduate	high school graduate	some college	associate's degree	bachelor's degree or more		
						total	bachelor's degree	graduate degree
Fats and oils	$109.61	$114.12	$113.61	$104.74	$104.28	$109.65	$109.54	$109.87
Margarine	9.77	9.72	11.61	8.97	8.85	9.16	8.89	9.69
Fats and oils	34.84	45.38	34.43	32.40	30.52	34.20	33.41	35.75
Salad dressings	31.16	27.92	32.83	28.32	32.54	32.44	32.63	32.06
Nondairy cream and imitation milk	18.59	18.62	19.42	17.77	18.40	18.52	19.33	16.93
Peanut butter	15.25	12.48	15.32	17.27	13.98	15.33	15.28	15.45
Miscellaneous foods	690.48	569.04	650.87	630.22	707.35	800.21	763.67	871.78
Frozen prepared foods	136.23	97.21	134.06	121.63	148.79	157.82	155.66	162.06
Frozen meals	62.14	39.42	62.62	54.11	64.69	74.55	70.21	83.03
Other frozen prepared foods	74.09	57.79	71.43	67.53	84.09	83.28	85.45	79.03
Canned and packaged soups	46.90	38.42	45.29	46.47	41.57	53.30	51.01	57.78
Potato chips, nuts, and other snacks	145.02	96.23	133.37	138.44	150.00	174.93	166.10	192.24
Potato chips and other snacks	108.01	77.21	106.30	107.60	114.52	118.95	114.73	127.22
Nuts	37.01	19.02	27.07	30.84	35.48	55.98	51.37	65.02
Condiments and seasonings	133.90	121.90	124.15	121.55	138.20	152.64	149.27	159.24
Salt, spices, and other seasonings	35.41	34.87	32.27	33.22	32.59	40.38	40.50	40.16
Olives, pickles, relishes	16.13	12.20	15.02	14.32	15.73	19.77	18.56	22.13
Sauces and gravies	58.43	55.76	54.59	51.67	64.75	64.81	64.84	64.74
Baking needs and miscellaneous products	23.93	19.06	22.28	22.34	25.13	27.68	25.36	32.22
Other canned or packaged prepared foods	228.42	215.28	214.00	202.13	228.80	261.51	241.63	300.46
Prepared salads	36.22	23.20	31.82	31.17	35.74	47.92	46.29	51.12
Prepared desserts	15.03	15.38	15.86	14.57	15.02	14.54	13.53	16.51
Baby food	27.80	23.31	34.57	30.35	18.98	25.30	24.02	27.80
Miscellaneous prepared foods	147.11	152.98	130.38	124.77	158.85	168.79	153.08	199.54
Nonalcoholic beverages	360.97	357.29	362.58	347.21	347.41	374.30	367.27	388.08
Cola	78.77	90.57	80.82	78.42	80.01	72.60	74.13	69.62
Other carbonated drinks	66.72	69.25	70.50	60.68	72.46	64.87	62.57	69.36
Tea	31.16	27.38	30.83	29.39	27.67	35.09	34.53	36.19
Coffee	75.03	57.24	73.89	70.02	69.24	87.61	84.23	94.23
Noncarbonated fruit-flavored drinks	24.76	29.56	23.94	25.13	26.76	22.75	22.62	22.99
Other noncarbonated beverages and ice	14.93	14.21	13.05	15.48	14.83	16.36	16.53	16.03
Bottled water	53.48	55.65	51.44	52.59	47.53	56.76	53.17	63.78
Sports drinks	15.73	13.30	17.92	15.40	8.93	17.29	18.17	15.56
Food prepared by consumer unit on trips	47.50	27.78	25.62	37.85	43.07	82.43	74.98	95.46
FOOD AWAY FROM HOME	2,619.89	1,406.93	2,053.14	2,396.84	2,711.77	3,660.66	3,431.06	4,088.93
Meals at restaurants, carry-outs, etc.	2,195.89	1,283.38	1,783.40	2,056.39	2,312.25	2,911.81	2,784.55	3,161.04
Lunch	752.89	450.28	571.26	724.03	830.05	1,002.02	936.51	1,130.31
At fast-food restaurants*	368.78	247.08	310.27	375.27	450.93	429.51	413.05	461.76
At full-service restaurants	302.01	166.31	194.96	269.89	277.86	465.05	427.73	538.13
At vending machines, mobile vendors	7.16	6.72	7.67	7.76	11.23	5.22	5.54	4.59
At employer and school cafeterias	74.94	30.18	58.36	71.10	90.03	102.24	90.19	125.83
Dinner	1,051.05	553.60	862.38	948.55	1,053.07	1,449.58	1,388.40	1,569.39
At fast-food restaurants*	365.13	270.87	356.24	349.58	458.15	387.37	398.18	366.19
At full-service restaurants	676.06	273.82	499.09	590.12	587.33	1,048.38	978.98	1,184.31
At vending machines, mobile vendors	3.02	6.33	2.25	1.30	4.39	3.06	2.11	4.91
At employer and school cafeterias	6.85	2.58	4.80	7.55	3.20	10.77	9.13	13.98
Snacks and nonalcoholic beverages	166.09	107.01	141.87	160.47	186.14	204.27	209.04	194.92
At fast-food restaurants*	109.65	62.64	95.89	99.75	126.92	138.79	137.33	141.65
At full-service restaurants	32.72	24.60	22.54	31.54	36.97	43.14	47.14	35.30
At vending machines, mobile vendors	17.28	15.85	16.57	21.71	14.97	16.26	17.42	13.99
At employer and school cafeterias	6.43	3.92	6.87	7.47	7.28	6.08	7.14	3.99
Breakfast and brunch	225.86	172.49	207.89	223.34	242.99	255.94	250.59	266.42
At fast-food restaurants*	123.77	102.91	113.94	122.56	137.16	135.75	130.46	146.11
At full-service restaurants	89.39	59.16	81.28	89.74	91.37	106.13	108.43	101.62
At vending machines, mobile vendors	3.03	3.81	2.87	2.72	4.40	2.63	2.38	3.12
At employer and school cafeterias	9.66	6.61	9.79	8.32	10.06	11.43	9.32	15.57

	total consumer units	less than high school graduate	high school graduate	some college	associate's degree	bachelor's degree or more		
						total	bachelor's degree	graduate degree
Board (including at school)	$43.87	$3.73	$21.20	$50.08	$36.74	$78.44	$69.18	$94.65
Catered affairs	52.63	8.56	39.38	22.90	43.74	106.28	70.19	169.41
Food on trips	236.49	76.47	119.79	180.15	222.07	446.81	389.52	547.03
School lunches	62.16	22.41	53.30	59.64	75.76	83.84	84.20	83.22
Meals as pay	28.85	12.39	36.07	27.68	21.21	33.48	33.43	33.57
ALCOHOLIC BEVERAGES	456.43	155.25	286.86	426.81	465.13	721.95	689.15	785.21
At home	242.35	106.79	176.08	229.28	266.16	345.60	298.54	437.76
Beer and ale	109.76	76.30	118.94	116.83	115.42	108.55	102.57	120.27
Whiskey	9.60	3.56	6.02	7.33	6.74	17.02	12.50	25.87
Wine	104.03	22.69	38.24	90.84	121.31	188.96	154.37	256.68
Other alcoholic beverages	18.97	4.23	12.88	14.28	22.68	31.07	29.10	34.93
Away from home	214.08	48.46	110.78	197.52	198.97	376.35	390.61	347.45
Beer and ale	76.98	23.15	52.36	73.54	86.37	115.54	122.24	102.40
At fast-food restaurants*	12.47	5.08	11.23	13.57	11.27	15.85	17.03	13.55
At full-service restaurants	63.32	18.06	40.42	59.71	73.27	97.29	102.06	87.94
At vending machines, mobile vendors	0.65	–	0.69	0.23	1.83	0.77	0.69	0.91
Wine	41.96	8.21	16.92	34.31	31.43	82.50	88.00	71.71
At fast-food restaurants*	2.96	0.73	1.92	1.52	2.26	5.75	6.01	5.24
At full-service restaurants	38.20	7.49	14.61	32.79	29.00	74.58	78.72	66.47
Other alcoholic beverages	50.30	7.48	23.54	54.10	42.77	87.19	93.90	74.04
At fast-food restaurants*	4.25	0.33	4.29	4.46	4.22	5.55	7.24	2.24
At full-service restaurants	45.99	7.16	19.26	49.64	38.55	81.45	86.37	71.80
Alcoholic beverages purchased on trips	44.84	9.61	17.95	35.57	38.39	91.13	86.46	99.29

The category fast-food restaurants also includes take-out, delivery, concession stands, buffets, and cafeterias other than employer and school.
Note: Subcategories may not add to total because some are not shown. "–" means sample is too small to make a reliable estimate.
Source: Bureau of Labor Statistics, unpublished tables from the 2011 Consumer Expenditure Survey

Table 5.26 Food and Alcohol: Indexed spending by education, 2011

(indexed average annual spending of consumer units on food and alcoholic beverages, by education of consumer unit reference person, 2011; index definition: an index of 100 is the average for all consumer units; an index of 125 means that spending by consumer units in that group is 25 percent above the average for all consumer units; an index of 75 indicates spending that is 25 percent below the average for all consumer units)

	total consumer units	less than high school graduate	high school graduate	some college	associate's degree	bachelor's degree or more — total	bachelor's degree	graduate degree
Average spending of consumer units, total	$49,705	$29,951	$39,704	$45,355	$50,819	$68,903	$65,051	$75,731
Average spending of consumer units, index	100	60	80	91	102	139	131	152
Food, spending index	100	77	87	91	100	124	118	136
Alcoholic beverages, spending index	100	34	63	94	102	158	151	172
FOOD AT HOME	100	93	94	91	98	114	109	123
Cereals and bakery products	100	92	93	91	99	114	111	120
Cereals and cereal products	100	101	88	91	97	116	113	121
Flour	100	149	68	55	85	141	131	161
Prepared flour mixes	100	104	89	98	100	109	104	117
Ready-to-eat and cooked cereals	100	90	91	95	101	113	112	115
Rice	100	135	89	80	80	115	115	115
Pasta, cornmeal, and other cereal products	100	93	84	92	101	120	113	133
Bakery products	100	87	96	91	101	114	110	120
Bread	100	96	95	92	103	109	102	122
White bread	100	114	100	90	105	100	94	110
Bread, other than white	100	83	92	94	102	116	108	131
Cookies and crackers	100	80	94	90	97	119	114	129
Cookies	100	89	98	89	99	113	111	117
Crackers	100	69	90	91	94	127	118	144
Frozen and refrigerated bakery products	100	75	95	93	96	119	113	132
Other bakery products	100	87	98	90	102	113	113	111
Biscuits and rolls	100	73	89	96	104	120	117	127
Cakes and cupcakes	100	88	97	89	116	109	117	94
Bread and cracker products	100	116	122	77	72	101	92	119
Sweetrolls, coffee cakes, doughnuts	100	105	110	88	93	100	95	109
Pies, tarts, turnovers	100	88	101	82	88	118	132	93
Meats, poultry, fish, and eggs	100	106	98	94	101	104	101	109
Beef	100	112	97	98	102	98	97	100
Ground beef	100	113	107	99	107	88	89	87
Roast	100	138	85	95	148	86	85	88
Chuck roast	100	171	88	76	168	78	77	78
Round roast	100	149	82	106	118	86	82	95
Other roast	100	118	84	100	150	90	90	90
Steak	100	108	93	99	83	109	104	120
Round steak	100	116	97	92	88	106	100	117
Sirloin steak	100	106	86	100	70	119	103	149
Other steak	100	106	94	100	87	106	106	106
Other beef	100	77	96	93	91	119	130	96
Pork	100	113	105	102	99	91	92	87
Bacon	100	123	98	100	103	93	97	84
Pork chops	100	110	115	107	106	78	81	72
Ham	100	97	102	111	102	92	92	92
Ham, not canned	100	97	102	110	103	92	92	93
Canned ham	100	105	118	140	62	71	86	38
Sausage	100	101	109	100	107	90	91	87
Other pork	100	128	105	92	82	97	97	96
Other meats	100	95	105	87	97	107	107	109
Frankfurters	100	113	112	89	91	96	95	98
Lunch meats (cold cuts)	100	79	103	89	104	111	113	108
Bologna, liverwurst, salami	100	89	113	95	101	97	103	83
Other lunch meats	100	75	98	87	105	117	117	119
Lamb, organ meats, and others	100	182	100	70	55	104	88	135

	total consumer units	less than high school graduate	high school graduate	some college	associate's degree	bachelor's degree or more		
						total	bachelor's degree	graduate degree
Poultry	100	113	96	88	101	105	101	114
Fresh and frozen chicken	100	120	99	87	95	103	101	108
Fresh and frozen whole chicken	100	132	98	89	86	101	100	105
Fresh and frozen chicken parts	100	115	100	86	99	104	102	109
Other poultry	100	86	84	93	125	114	102	137
Fish and seafood	100	88	81	87	105	126	113	152
Canned fish and seafood	100	77	90	108	116	106	99	120
Fresh fish and shellfish	100	90	79	81	97	133	122	155
Frozen fish and shellfish	100	90	81	85	110	126	106	164
Eggs	100	109	100	96	98	100	95	108
Dairy products	**100**	**88**	**88**	**90**	**104**	**119**	**114**	**128**
Fresh milk and cream	100	100	93	91	109	108	106	113
Fresh milk, all types	100	102	94	91	107	108	106	112
Cream	100	88	88	95	119	111	105	122
Other dairy products	100	81	85	90	102	125	119	137
Butter	100	99	86	92	104	115	107	131
Cheese	100	82	82	88	110	125	121	133
Ice cream and related products	100	83	93	93	94	118	113	129
Miscellaneous dairy products	100	68	82	88	88	138	128	156
Fruits and vegetables	**100**	**91**	**90**	**88**	**88**	**123**	**114**	**141**
Fresh fruits	100	88	86	84	84	131	118	157
Apples	100	84	89	88	79	129	119	148
Bananas	100	103	97	87	91	112	108	121
Oranges	100	93	87	97	82	121	114	133
Citrus fruits, excluding oranges	100	105	85	80	72	132	114	168
Other fresh fruits	100	75	80	79	87	143	126	177
Fresh vegetables	100	90	88	86	82	128	116	151
Potatoes	100	109	102	86	94	106	98	122
Lettuce	100	84	92	90	85	123	116	138
Tomatoes	100	103	96	82	76	121	109	145
Other fresh vegetables	100	81	79	86	80	139	125	166
Processed fruits	100	88	90	95	102	115	113	118
Frozen fruits and fruit juices	100	82	84	87	126	120	123	113
Frozen orange juice	100	105	97	75	134	105	112	92
Frozen fruits	100	45	72	94	111	143	145	138
Frozen fruit juices, excluding orange	100	144	98	84	151	79	81	76
Canned fruits	100	91	94	98	90	112	111	115
Dried fruits	100	61	80	92	115	130	129	132
Fresh fruit juice	100	89	84	89	101	123	118	134
Canned and bottled fruit juice	100	92	93	99	99	109	107	114
Processed vegetables	100	101	100	92	92	107	103	114
Frozen vegetables	100	71	95	90	107	119	108	142
Canned and dried vegetables and juices	100	113	103	92	86	103	102	104
Canned beans	100	119	108	85	98	97	91	111
Canned corn	100	105	115	103	90	88	91	82
Canned miscellaneous vegetables	100	107	103	90	85	107	106	108
Dried peas	100	211	67	133	35	86	49	158
Dried beans	100	195	97	84	65	88	91	83
Dried miscellaneous vegetables	100	121	99	79	86	111	110	111
Dried processed vegetables	100	96	96	119	91	95	100	85
Fresh and canned vegetable juices	100	91	96	103	83	110	114	104
Sugar and other sweets	**100**	**82**	**94**	**93**	**107**	**114**	**111**	**121**
Candy and chewing gum	100	66	92	92	113	120	118	124
Sugar	100	122	112	98	86	88	85	94
Artificial sweeteners	100	62	87	113	109	114	99	142
Jams, preserves, other sweets	100	98	86	87	105	118	112	131

	total consumer units	less than high school graduate	high school graduate	some college	associate's degree	bachelor's degree or more		
						total	bachelor's degree	graduate degree
Fats and oils	100	104	104	96	95	100	100	100
Margarine	100	99	119	92	91	94	91	99
Fats and oils	100	130	99	93	88	98	96	103
Salad dressings	100	90	105	91	104	104	105	103
Nondairy cream and imitation milk	100	100	104	96	99	100	104	91
Peanut butter	100	82	100	113	92	101	100	101
Miscellaneous foods	100	82	94	91	102	116	111	126
Frozen prepared foods	100	71	98	89	109	116	114	119
Frozen meals	100	63	101	87	104	120	113	134
Other frozen prepared foods	100	78	96	91	113	112	115	107
Canned and packaged soups	100	82	97	99	89	114	109	123
Potato chips, nuts, and other snacks	100	66	92	95	103	121	115	133
Potato chips and other snacks	100	71	98	100	106	110	106	118
Nuts	100	51	73	83	96	151	139	176
Condiments and seasonings	100	91	93	91	103	114	111	119
Salt, spices, and other seasonings	100	98	91	94	92	114	114	113
Olives, pickles, relishes	100	76	93	89	98	123	115	137
Sauces and gravies	100	95	93	88	111	111	111	111
Baking needs and miscellaneous products	100	80	93	93	105	116	106	135
Other canned or packaged prepared foods	100	94	94	88	100	114	106	132
Prepared salads	100	64	88	86	99	132	128	141
Prepared desserts	100	102	106	97	100	97	90	110
Baby food	100	84	124	109	68	91	86	100
Miscellaneous prepared foods	100	104	89	85	108	115	104	136
Nonalcoholic beverages	100	99	100	96	96	104	102	108
Cola	100	115	103	100	102	92	94	88
Other carbonated drinks	100	104	106	91	109	97	94	104
Tea	100	88	99	94	89	113	111	116
Coffee	100	76	98	93	92	117	112	126
Noncarbonated fruit-flavored drinks	100	119	97	101	108	92	91	93
Other noncarbonated beverages and ice	100	95	87	104	99	110	111	107
Bottled water	100	104	96	98	89	106	99	119
Sports drinks	100	85	114	98	57	110	116	99
Food prepared by consumer unit on trips	100	58	54	80	91	174	158	201
FOOD AWAY FROM HOME	100	54	78	91	104	140	131	156
Meals at restaurants, carry-outs, etc.	100	58	81	94	105	133	127	144
Lunch	100	60	76	96	110	133	124	150
At fast-food restaurants*	100	67	84	102	122	116	112	125
At full-service restaurants	100	55	65	89	92	154	142	178
At vending machines, mobile vendors	100	94	107	108	157	73	77	64
At employer and school cafeterias	100	40	78	95	120	136	120	168
Dinner	100	53	82	90	100	138	132	149
At fast-food restaurants*	100	74	98	96	125	106	109	100
At full-service restaurants	100	41	74	87	87	155	145	175
At vending machines, mobile vendors	100	210	75	43	145	101	70	163
At employer and school cafeterias	100	38	70	110	47	157	133	204
Snacks and nonalcoholic beverages	100	64	85	97	112	123	126	117
At fast-food restaurants*	100	57	87	91	116	127	125	129
At full-service restaurants	100	75	69	96	113	132	144	108
At vending machines, mobile vendors	100	92	96	126	87	94	101	81
At employer and school cafeterias	100	61	107	116	113	95	111	62
Breakfast and brunch	100	76	92	99	108	113	111	118
At fast-food restaurants*	100	83	92	99	111	110	105	118
At full-service restaurants	100	66	91	100	102	119	121	114
At vending machines, mobile vendors	100	126	95	90	145	87	79	103
At employer and school cafeterias	100	68	101	86	104	118	96	161

	total consumer units	less than high school graduate	high school graduate	some college	associate's degree	bachelor's degree or more		
						total	bachelor's degree	graduate degree
Board (including at school)	100	9	48	114	84	179	158	216
Catered affairs	100	16	75	44	83	202	133	322
Food on trips	100	32	51	76	94	189	165	231
School lunches	100	36	86	96	122	135	135	134
Meals as pay	100	43	125	96	74	116	116	116
ALCOHOLIC BEVERAGES	100	34	63	94	102	158	151	172
At home	100	44	73	95	110	143	123	181
Beer and ale	100	70	108	106	105	99	93	110
Whiskey	100	37	63	76	70	177	130	269
Wine	100	22	37	87	117	182	148	247
Other alcoholic beverages	100	22	68	75	120	164	153	184
Away from home	100	23	52	92	93	176	182	162
Beer and ale	100	30	68	96	112	150	159	133
At fast-food restaurants*	100	41	90	109	90	127	137	109
At full-service restaurants	100	29	64	94	116	154	161	139
At vending machines, mobile vendors	100	–	106	35	282	118	106	140
Wine	100	20	40	82	75	197	210	171
At fast-food restaurants*	100	25	65	51	76	194	203	177
At full-service restaurants	100	20	38	86	76	195	206	174
Other alcoholic beverages	100	15	47	108	85	173	187	147
At fast-food restaurants*	100	8	101	105	99	131	170	53
At full-service restaurants	100	16	42	108	84	177	188	156
Alcoholic beverages purchased on trips	100	21	40	79	86	203	193	221

* The category fast-food restaurants also includes take-out, delivery, concession stands, buffets, and cafeterias other than employer and school.
Note: "–" means sample is too small to make a reliable estimate.
Source: Calculations by New Strategist based on the Bureau of Labor Statistics' 2011 Consumer Expenditure Survey

Table 5.27 Food and Alcohol: Total spending by education, 2011

(total annual spending on food and alcoholic beverages, by consumer unit educational attainment group, 2011; consumer units and dollars in thousands)

	total consumer units	less than high school graduate	high school graduate	some college	associate's degree	bachelor's degree or more total	bachelor's degree	graduate degree
Number of consumer units	122,287	16,146	30,810	25,361	12,912	37,058	23,578	13,480
Total spending of all consumer units	$6,078,260,661	$483,588,362	$1,223,288,867	$1,150,256,524	$656,180,609	$2,553,405,521	$1,533,772,714	$1,020,859,272
Food, total spending	789,729,446	80,261,766	174,014,880	149,807,427	83,747,232	297,427,508	179,546,470	118,718,360
Alcoholic beverages, total spending	55,815,455	2,506,667	8,838,157	10,824,328	6,005,759	26,754,023	16,248,779	10,584,631
FOOD AT HOME	469,308,157	57,548,058	110,766,263	89,011,023	48,732,729	161,761,876	98,648,937	63,603,358
Cereals and bakery products	64,895,265	7,844,857	15,263,890	12,259,254	6,815,987	22,474,936	13,906,776	8,615,068
Cereals and cereal products	21,383,105	2,846,540	4,748,437	4,033,921	2,198,397	7,497,945	4,660,192	2,851,155
Flour	937,941	184,387	160,212	107,277	83,928	400,968	236,959	166,343
Prepared flour mixes	1,819,631	249,617	407,000	370,271	192,001	599,228	365,459	235,361
Ready-to-eat and cooked cereals	11,175,809	1,323,972	2,567,397	2,209,704	1,196,039	3,838,468	2,419,810	1,421,062
Rice	3,137,884	560,428	702,468	522,944	264,825	1,091,358	694,844	396,582
Pasta, cornmeal, and other cereal products	4,311,840	528,136	911,668	823,725	461,604	1,568,295	943,120	631,673
Bakery products	43,510,937	4,998,479	10,515,453	8,225,080	4,617,589	14,976,620	9,246,584	5,763,913
Bread	13,027,234	1,655,288	3,124,442	2,498,819	1,416,188	4,306,140	2,570,709	1,755,500
White bread	5,494,355	829,581	1,383,985	1,028,135	606,735	1,657,234	1,000,179	663,755
Bread, other than white	7,532,879	825,706	1,740,457	1,470,431	809,453	2,648,906	1,570,531	1,091,880
Cookies and crackers	10,221,970	1,080,975	2,432,141	1,910,444	1,045,097	3,691,347	2,247,455	1,456,110
Cookies	5,742,598	674,741	1,413,563	1,065,162	600,279	1,967,780	1,227,235	743,557
Crackers	4,479,373	406,233	1,018,887	845,282	444,948	1,723,568	1,020,220	712,553
Frozen and refrigerated bakery products	3,497,408	347,139	832,794	675,363	355,984	1,262,566	759,683	508,061
Other bakery products	16,764,325	1,914,916	4,125,767	3,140,706	1,800,320	5,716,567	3,668,501	2,044,242
Biscuits and rolls	6,472,651	621,621	1,446,221	1,294,425	708,481	2,356,889	1,454,763	907,474
Cakes and cupcakes	4,623,671	535,240	1,125,489	851,876	565,416	1,533,089	1,047,099	477,462
Bread and cracker products	871,906	133,043	267,123	139,486	65,851	267,559	154,672	114,850
Sweetrolls, coffee cakes, doughnuts	2,917,768	406,395	807,222	533,849	286,517	884,574	535,928	351,963
Pies, tarts, turnovers	1,878,328	218,455	480,020	321,070	174,054	674,456	476,276	192,629
Meats, poultry, fish, and eggs	101,792,922	14,255,949	25,026,347	19,752,668	10,834,072	31,942,884	19,750,819	12,260,599
Beef	27,221,086	4,011,797	6,686,386	5,528,952	2,944,711	8,101,249	5,109,824	2,996,874
Ground beef	11,066,974	1,656,095	2,973,781	2,280,968	1,253,884	2,947,964	1,888,598	1,057,910
Roast	3,740,759	679,908	796,747	738,259	584,655	974,255	612,085	363,016
Chuck roast	935,496	211,674	207,043	146,587	165,532	219,754	139,582	80,071
Round roast	747,174	146,606	155,282	164,086	93,483	194,555	117,418	77,914
Other roast	2,056,867	321,467	434,421	427,840	325,770	559,946	355,085	204,896
Steak	10,087,455	1,438,286	2,352,344	2,060,835	881,890	3,343,002	2,025,586	1,329,667
Round steak	1,944,363	297,086	475,398	370,017	181,026	622,574	373,947	251,267
Sirloin steak	2,673,194	374,749	577,379	553,377	198,974	960,543	530,741	439,313
Other steak	5,469,898	766,451	1,299,874	1,137,694	501,889	1,760,255	1,120,898	639,087
Other beef	2,325,899	237,508	563,823	448,890	224,152	836,028	583,556	246,280
Pork	19,804,380	2,944,546	5,242,938	4,178,478	2,067,599	5,434,926	3,531,041	1,895,018
Bacon	4,141,861	672,965	1,018,271	856,441	449,596	1,162,880	776,895	381,619
Pork chops	3,331,098	482,120	963,737	740,795	372,253	790,077	522,724	264,882
Ham	4,193,221	538,792	1,076,501	964,479	449,854	1,168,068	744,122	423,946
Ham, not canned	4,097,837	525,552	1,048,156	936,835	443,785	1,147,686	728,324	419,767
Canned ham	95,384	13,240	28,345	27,643	6,198	20,382	15,797	4,044
Sausage	3,491,294	467,588	959,732	727,353	393,687	950,538	615,386	333,765
Other pork	4,645,683	782,920	1,224,698	889,410	402,209	1,363,364	871,914	490,942
Other meats	14,985,049	1,882,947	3,945,529	2,714,388	1,530,976	4,880,539	3,088,246	1,794,323
Frankfurters	2,894,533	432,390	818,930	532,327	276,704	840,105	529,562	311,388
Lunch meats (cold cuts)	10,720,901	1,121,017	2,782,451	1,984,498	1,175,121	3,608,708	2,325,734	1,279,656
Bologna, liverwurst, salami	3,280,960	386,697	938,165	643,409	350,044	960,173	653,818	301,413
Other lunch meats	7,439,941	734,320	1,844,595	1,341,090	824,948	2,648,535	1,671,916	978,378
Lamb, organ meats, and others	1,369,614	329,378	343,840	197,562	79,151	431,355	232,951	203,278

	total consumer units	less than high school graduate	high school graduate	some college	associate's degree	bachelor's degree or more		
						total	bachelor's degree	graduate degree
Poultry	$18,892,119	$2,824,743	$4,578,366	$3,448,589	$2,020,082	$6,035,266	$3,687,363	$2,366,144
Fresh and frozen chicken	15,217,394	2,406,884	3,798,565	2,739,749	1,533,816	4,767,141	2,963,519	1,811,847
Fresh and frozen whole chicken	4,398,663	765,159	1,081,739	814,595	399,368	1,352,617	844,564	509,814
Fresh and frozen chicken parts	10,819,954	1,641,725	2,716,518	1,924,900	1,134,448	3,414,524	2,118,955	1,301,898
Other poultry	3,674,724	418,020	780,109	709,094	486,137	1,268,125	723,845	554,432
Fish and seafood	14,767,378	1,710,184	3,028,623	2,659,862	1,635,047	5,644,675	3,209,673	2,480,724
Canned fish and seafood	2,433,511	248,325	549,034	546,530	298,655	783,036	464,251	322,981
Fresh fish and shellfish	7,277,299	862,842	1,452,075	1,225,444	748,638	2,935,735	1,709,641	1,244,878
Frozen fish and shellfish	5,056,567	599,178	1,027,514	888,142	587,754	1,925,904	1,035,782	912,866
Eggs	6,122,910	881,572	1,544,505	1,222,147	635,658	1,846,600	1,124,906	727,516
Dairy products	**49,751,243**	**5,793,508**	**11,010,570**	**9,308,755**	**5,471,589**	**17,930,884**	**10,961,648**	**7,022,945**
Fresh milk and cream	18,310,033	2,418,348	4,305,389	3,462,284	2,098,846	6,004,137	3,725,560	2,289,982
Fresh milk, all types	15,576,918	2,100,433	3,695,968	2,924,884	1,755,645	5,085,840	3,170,534	1,923,057
Cream	2,734,337	317,753	609,422	537,400	343,201	918,297	555,026	366,926
Other dairy products	31,439,988	3,375,160	6,705,180	5,846,471	3,372,614	11,926,747	7,236,088	4,732,963
Butter	3,013,152	395,254	653,172	577,470	332,226	1,048,000	619,394	434,326
Cheese	15,254,080	1,654,481	3,146,317	2,792,500	1,769,331	5,793,277	3,564,758	2,243,072
Ice cream and related products	7,004,599	770,487	1,637,860	1,346,669	695,957	2,514,385	1,528,562	994,420
Miscellaneous dairy products	6,166,933	554,938	1,267,832	1,129,579	575,100	2,571,084	1,523,610	1,061,146
Fruits and vegetables	**87,421,753**	**10,505,233**	**19,781,869**	**15,891,456**	**8,095,953**	**32,654,027**	**19,240,120**	**13,597,950**
Fresh fruits	30,239,129	3,502,067	6,535,417	5,250,995	2,672,009	12,047,926	6,906,939	5,231,992
Apples	4,667,695	516,995	1,051,545	855,680	388,909	1,818,436	1,067,376	761,755
Bananas	5,023,550	681,523	1,231,168	908,177	482,521	1,709,115	1,042,855	671,574
Oranges	3,300,526	404,296	722,803	660,654	287,034	1,208,832	727,853	485,550
Citrus fruits, excluding oranges	4,601,660	638,736	987,152	759,816	349,657	1,840,300	1,007,960	851,666
Other fresh fruits	12,646,922	1,260,518	2,542,749	2,066,668	1,163,888	5,471,984	3,060,896	2,461,313
Fresh vegetables	27,417,968	3,262,461	6,088,980	4,874,638	2,378,778	10,628,234	6,145,134	4,556,779
Potatoes	4,742,290	680,070	1,224,081	847,311	470,255	1,519,378	891,956	636,121
Lettuce	3,933,973	437,234	914,441	731,411	353,014	1,471,573	878,045	600,534
Tomatoes	5,017,436	680,715	1,216,687	853,905	403,242	1,842,153	1,054,880	801,251
Other fresh vegetables	13,725,493	1,464,442	2,733,771	2,442,011	1,152,267	5,795,130	3,320,254	2,518,873
Processed fruits	14,152,275	1,648,991	3,206,397	2,801,630	1,525,940	4,912,779	3,077,165	1,841,638
Frozen fruits and fruit juices	1,627,640	175,668	345,380	292,412	216,018	590,334	386,208	202,874
Frozen orange juice	456,131	63,454	111,532	71,011	64,689	145,638	98,792	46,236
Frozen fruits	846,226	50,053	153,126	164,847	99,164	366,133	236,723	129,004
Frozen fruit juices, excluding orange	326,506	62,162	80,722	56,555	52,164	78,192	50,693	27,499
Canned fruits	2,597,376	313,232	616,508	526,748	246,748	884,204	556,912	328,238
Dried fruits	994,193	80,246	201,497	189,954	120,856	391,703	247,097	144,640
Fresh fruit juice	2,113,119	247,841	448,286	389,545	226,218	788,965	480,520	311,118
Canned and bottled fruit juice	6,821,169	832,165	1,594,726	1,403,224	716,100	2,257,573	1,406,428	854,632
Processed vegetables	15,611,158	2,091,553	3,950,766	2,964,194	1,519,226	5,065,087	3,110,881	1,967,541
Frozen vegetables	4,277,599	400,582	1,021,043	797,350	484,587	1,544,207	887,476	668,338
Canned and dried vegetables and juices	11,333,559	1,691,132	2,930,031	2,166,590	1,034,639	3,520,881	2,223,405	1,299,202
Canned beans	2,333,236	365,223	633,762	411,863	240,809	688,167	407,428	284,428
Canned corn	1,189,853	164,851	344,148	253,864	112,722	317,216	209,137	107,436
Canned miscellaneous vegetables	3,118,319	439,979	807,222	581,274	279,028	1,007,978	636,134	372,587
Dried peas	102,721	28,578	17,254	28,404	3,744	26,682	9,667	17,928
Dried beans	610,212	157,262	149,120	106,770	42,093	163,426	107,044	56,077
Dried miscellaneous vegetables	1,412,415	226,205	352,158	232,307	127,958	474,342	300,855	173,488
Dried processed vegetables	250,688	31,808	60,696	61,627	24,016	72,263	48,335	23,590
Fresh and canned vegetable juices	2,273,315	273,675	547,802	483,888	200,394	760,430	498,203	260,434
Sugar and other sweets	**17,657,020**	**1,900,869**	**4,169,209**	**3,394,063**	**1,993,484**	**6,115,682**	**3,773,659**	**2,355,900**
Candy and chewing gum	10,608,397	930,817	2,448,471	2,019,750	1,266,409	3,862,926	2,418,631	1,449,100
Sugar	2,921,436	468,718	821,703	594,462	266,375	782,294	480,755	303,704
Artificial sweeteners	686,030	56,511	149,737	160,282	78,763	236,059	131,094	107,031
Jams, preserves, other sweets	3,441,156	444,822	749,299	619,569	381,937	1,234,402	743,414	496,064

	total consumer units	less than high school graduate	high school graduate	some college	associate's degree	bachelor's degree or more total	bachelor's degree	graduate degree
Fats and oils	**$13,403,878**	**$1,842,582**	**$3,500,324**	**$2,656,311**	**$1,346,463**	**$4,063,410**	**$2,582,734**	**$1,481,048**
Margarine	1,194,744	156,939	357,704	227,488	114,271	339,451	209,608	130,621
Fats and oils	4,260,479	732,705	1,060,788	821,696	394,074	1,267,384	787,741	481,910
Salad dressings	3,810,463	450,796	1,011,492	718,224	420,156	1,202,162	769,350	432,169
Nondairy cream and imitation milk	2,273,315	300,639	598,330	450,665	237,581	686,314	455,763	228,216
Peanut butter	1,864,877	201,502	472,009	437,984	180,510	568,099	360,272	208,266
Miscellaneous foods	**84,436,728**	**9,187,720**	**20,053,305**	**15,983,009**	**9,133,303**	**29,654,182**	**18,005,811**	**11,751,594**
Frozen prepared foods	16,659,158	1,569,553	4,130,389	3,084,658	1,921,176	5,848,494	3,670,151	2,184,569
Frozen meals	7,598,914	636,475	1,929,322	1,372,284	835,277	2,762,674	1,655,411	1,119,244
Other frozen prepared foods	9,060,244	933,077	2,200,758	1,712,628	1,085,770	3,086,190	2,014,740	1,065,324
Canned and packaged soups	5,735,260	620,329	1,395,385	1,178,526	536,752	1,975,191	1,202,714	778,874
Potato chips, nuts, and other snacks	17,734,061	1,553,730	4,109,130	3,510,977	1,936,800	6,482,556	3,916,306	2,591,395
Potato chips and other snacks	13,208,219	1,246,633	3,275,103	2,728,844	1,478,682	4,408,049	2,705,104	1,714,926
Nuts	4,525,842	307,097	834,027	782,133	458,118	2,074,507	1,211,202	876,470
Condiments and seasonings	16,374,229	1,968,197	3,825,062	3,082,630	1,784,438	5,656,533	3,519,488	2,146,555
Salt, spices, and other seasonings	4,330,183	563,011	994,239	842,492	420,802	1,496,402	954,909	541,357
Olives, pickles, relishes	1,972,489	196,981	462,766	363,170	203,106	732,637	437,608	298,312
Sauces and gravies	7,145,229	900,301	1,681,918	1,310,403	836,052	2,401,729	1,528,798	872,695
Baking needs and miscellaneous products	2,926,328	307,743	686,447	566,565	324,479	1,025,765	597,938	434,326
Other canned or packaged prepared foods	27,932,797	3,475,911	6,593,340	5,126,219	2,954,266	9,691,038	5,697,152	4,050,201
Prepared salads	4,429,235	374,587	980,374	790,502	461,475	1,775,819	1,091,426	689,098
Prepared desserts	1,837,974	248,325	488,647	369,510	193,938	538,823	319,010	222,555
Baby food	3,399,579	376,363	1,065,102	769,706	245,070	937,567	566,344	374,744
Miscellaneous prepared foods	17,989,641	2,470,015	4,017,008	3,164,292	2,051,071	6,255,020	3,609,320	2,689,799
Nonalcoholic beverages	**44,141,938**	**5,768,804**	**11,171,090**	**8,805,593**	**4,485,758**	**13,870,809**	**8,659,492**	**5,231,318**
Cola	9,632,547	1,462,343	2,490,064	1,988,810	1,033,089	2,690,411	1,747,837	938,478
Other carbonated drinks	8,158,989	1,118,111	2,172,105	1,538,905	935,604	2,403,952	1,475,275	934,973
Tea	3,810,463	442,077	949,872	745,360	357,275	1,300,365	814,148	487,841
Coffee	9,175,194	924,197	2,276,551	1,775,777	894,027	3,246,651	1,985,975	1,270,220
Noncarbonated fruit-flavored drinks	3,027,826	477,276	737,591	637,322	345,525	843,070	533,334	309,905
Other noncarbonated beverages and ice	1,825,745	229,435	402,071	392,588	191,485	606,269	389,744	216,084
Bottled water	6,539,909	898,525	1,584,866	1,333,735	613,707	2,103,412	1,253,642	859,754
Sports drinks	1,923,575	214,742	552,115	390,559	115,304	640,733	428,412	209,749
Food prepared by consumer unit on trips	**5,808,633**	**448,536**	**789,352**	**959,914**	**556,120**	**3,054,691**	**1,767,878**	**1,286,801**
FOOD AWAY FROM HOME	**320,378,488**	**22,716,292**	**63,257,243**	**60,786,259**	**35,014,374**	**135,656,738**	**80,897,533**	**55,118,776**
Meals at restaurants, carry-outs, etc.	**268,528,800**	**20,721,453**	**54,946,554**	**52,152,107**	**29,855,772**	**107,905,855**	**65,654,120**	**42,610,819**
Lunch	92,068,659	7,270,221	17,600,521	18,362,125	10,717,606	37,132,857	22,081,033	15,236,579
At fast-food restaurants*	45,097,000	3,989,354	9,559,419	9,517,222	5,822,408	15,916,782	9,738,893	6,224,525
At full-service restaurants	36,931,897	2,685,241	6,006,718	6,844,680	3,587,728	17,233,823	10,085,018	7,253,992
At vending machines, mobile vendors	875,575	108,501	236,313	196,801	145,002	193,443	130,622	61,873
At employer and school cafeterias	9,164,188	487,286	1,798,072	1,803,167	1,162,467	3,788,810	2,126,500	1,696,188
Dinner	128,529,751	8,938,426	26,569,928	24,056,177	13,597,240	53,718,536	32,735,695	21,155,377
At fast-food restaurants*	44,650,652	4,373,467	10,975,754	8,865,698	5,915,633	14,355,157	9,388,288	4,936,241
At full-service restaurants	82,673,349	4,421,098	15,376,963	14,966,033	7,583,605	38,850,866	23,082,390	15,964,499
At vending machines, mobile vendors	369,307	102,204	69,323	32,969	56,684	113,397	49,750	66,187
At employer and school cafeterias	837,666	41,657	147,888	191,476	41,318	399,115	215,267	188,450
Snacks and nonalcoholic beverages	20,310,648	1,727,783	4,371,015	4,069,680	2,403,440	7,569,838	4,928,745	2,627,522
At fast-food restaurants*	13,408,770	1,011,385	2,954,371	2,529,760	1,638,791	5,143,280	3,237,967	1,909,442
At full-service restaurants	4,001,231	397,192	694,457	799,886	477,357	1,598,682	1,111,467	475,844
At vending machines, mobile vendors	2,113,119	255,914	510,522	550,587	193,293	602,563	410,729	188,585
At employer and school cafeterias	786,305	63,292	211,665	189,447	93,999	225,313	168,347	53,785
Breakfast and brunch	27,619,742	2,785,024	6,405,091	5,664,126	3,137,487	9,484,625	5,908,411	3,591,342
At fast-food restaurants*	15,135,462	1,661,585	3,510,491	3,108,244	1,771,010	5,030,624	3,075,986	1,969,563
At full-service restaurants	10,931,235	955,197	2,504,237	2,275,896	1,179,769	3,932,966	2,556,563	1,369,838
At vending machines, mobile vendors	370,530	61,516	88,425	68,982	56,813	97,463	56,116	42,058
At employer and school cafeterias	1,181,292	106,725	301,630	211,004	129,895	423,573	219,747	209,884

	total consumer units	less than high school graduate	high school graduate	some college	associate's degree	bachelor's degree or more		
						total	bachelor's degree	graduate degree
Board (including at school)	$5,364,731	$60,225	$653,172	$1,270,079	$474,387	$2,906,830	$1,631,126	$1,275,882
Catered affairs	6,435,965	138,210	1,213,298	580,767	564,771	3,938,524	1,654,940	2,283,647
Food on trips	28,919,653	1,234,685	3,690,730	4,568,784	2,867,368	16,557,885	9,184,103	7,373,964
School lunches	7,601,360	361,832	1,642,173	1,512,530	978,213	3,106,943	1,985,268	1,121,806
Meals as pay	3,527,980	200,049	1,111,317	701,992	273,864	1,240,702	788,213	452,524
ALCOHOLIC BEVERAGES	55,815,455	2,506,667	8,838,157	10,824,328	6,005,759	26,754,023	16,248,779	10,584,631
At home	29,636,254	1,724,231	5,425,025	5,814,770	3,436,658	12,807,245	7,038,976	5,901,005
Beer and ale	13,422,221	1,231,940	3,664,541	2,962,926	1,490,303	4,022,646	2,418,395	1,621,240
Whiskey	1,173,955	57,480	185,476	185,896	87,027	630,727	294,725	348,728
Wine	12,721,517	366,353	1,178,174	2,303,793	1,566,355	7,002,480	3,639,736	3,460,046
Other alcoholic beverages	2,319,784	68,298	396,833	362,155	292,844	1,151,392	686,120	470,856
Away from home	26,179,201	782,435	3,413,132	5,009,305	2,569,101	13,946,778	9,209,803	4,683,626
Beer and ale	9,413,653	373,780	1,613,212	1,865,048	1,115,209	4,281,681	2,882,175	1,380,352
At fast-food restaurants*	1,524,919	82,022	345,996	344,149	145,518	587,369	401,533	182,654
At full-service restaurants	7,743,213	291,597	1,245,340	1,514,305	946,062	3,605,373	2,406,371	1,185,431
At vending machines, mobile vendors	79,487	–	21,259	5,833	23,629	28,535	16,269	12,267
Wine	5,131,163	132,559	521,305	870,136	405,824	3,057,285	2,074,864	966,651
At fast-food restaurants*	361,970	11,787	59,155	38,549	29,181	213,084	141,704	70,635
At full-service restaurants	4,671,363	120,934	450,134	831,587	374,448	2,763,786	1,856,060	896,016
Other alcoholic beverages	6,151,036	120,772	725,267	1,372,030	552,246	3,231,087	2,213,974	998,059
At fast-food restaurants*	519,720	5,328	132,175	113,110	54,489	205,672	170,705	30,195
At full-service restaurants	5,623,979	115,605	593,401	1,258,920	497,758	3,018,374	2,036,432	967,864
Alcoholic beverages purchased on trips	5,483,349	155,163	553,040	902,091	495,692	3,377,096	2,038,554	1,338,429

*The category fast-food restaurants also includes take-out, delivery, concession stands, buffets, and cafeterias other than employer and school.
Note: Numbers may not add to total because of rounding and missing subcategories. "–" means sample is too small to make a reliable estimate.
Source: Calculations by New Strategist based on the Bureau of Labor Statistics' 2011 Consumer Expenditure Survey

Table 5.28 Food and Alcohol: Market shares by education, 2011

(percentage of total annual spending on food and alcoholic beverages accounted for by consumer unit educational attainment groups, 2011)

	total consumer units	less than high school graduate	high school graduate	some college	associate's degree	bachelor's degree or more total	bachelor's degree	graduate degree
Share of total consumer units	100.0%	13.2%	25.2%	20.7%	10.6%	30.3%	19.3%	11.0%
Share of total before-tax income	100.0	6.8	18.3	17.2	10.6	47.1	27.5	19.6
Share of total spending	100.0	8.0	20.1	18.9	10.8	42.0	25.2	16.8
Share of food spending	100.0	10.2	22.0	19.0	10.6	37.7	22.7	15.0
Share of alcoholic beverages spending	100.0	4.5	15.8	19.4	10.8	47.9	29.1	19.0
FOOD AT HOME	100.0	12.3	23.6	19.0	10.4	34.5	21.0	13.6
Cereals and bakery products	100.0	12.1	23.5	18.9	10.5	34.6	21.4	13.3
Cereals and cereal products	100.0	13.3	22.2	18.9	10.3	35.1	21.8	13.3
Flour	100.0	19.7	17.1	11.4	8.9	42.7	25.3	17.7
Prepared flour mixes	100.0	13.7	22.4	20.3	10.6	32.9	20.1	12.9
Ready-to-eat and cooked cereals	100.0	11.8	23.0	19.8	10.7	34.3	21.7	12.7
Rice	100.0	17.9	22.4	16.7	8.4	34.8	22.1	12.6
Pasta, cornmeal, and other cereal products	100.0	12.2	21.1	19.1	10.7	36.4	21.9	14.6
Bakery products	100.0	11.5	24.2	18.9	10.6	34.4	21.3	13.2
Bread	100.0	12.7	24.0	19.2	10.9	33.1	19.7	13.5
White bread	100.0	15.1	25.2	18.7	11.0	30.2	18.2	12.1
Bread, other than white	100.0	11.0	23.1	19.5	10.7	35.2	20.8	14.5
Cookies and crackers	100.0	10.6	23.8	18.7	10.2	36.1	22.0	14.2
Cookies	100.0	11.7	24.6	18.5	10.5	34.3	21.4	12.9
Crackers	100.0	9.1	22.7	18.9	9.9	38.5	22.8	15.9
Frozen and refrigerated bakery products	100.0	9.9	23.8	19.3	10.2	36.1	21.7	14.5
Other bakery products	100.0	11.4	24.6	18.7	10.7	34.1	21.9	12.2
Biscuits and rolls	100.0	9.6	22.3	20.0	10.9	36.4	22.5	14.0
Cakes and cupcakes	100.0	11.6	24.3	18.4	12.2	33.2	22.6	10.3
Bread and cracker products	100.0	15.3	30.6	16.0	7.6	30.7	17.7	13.2
Sweetrolls, coffee cakes, doughnuts	100.0	13.9	27.7	18.3	9.8	30.3	18.4	12.1
Pies, tarts, turnovers	100.0	11.6	25.6	17.1	9.3	35.9	25.4	10.3
Meats, poultry, fish, and eggs	100.0	14.0	24.6	19.4	10.6	31.4	19.4	12.0
Beef	100.0	14.7	24.6	20.3	10.8	29.8	18.8	11.0
Ground beef	100.0	15.0	26.9	20.6	11.3	26.6	17.1	9.6
Roast	100.0	18.2	21.3	19.7	15.6	26.0	16.4	9.7
Chuck roast	100.0	22.6	22.1	15.7	17.7	23.5	14.9	8.6
Round roast	100.0	19.6	20.8	22.0	12.5	26.0	15.7	10.4
Other roast	100.0	15.6	21.1	20.8	15.8	27.2	17.3	10.0
Steak	100.0	14.3	23.3	20.4	8.7	33.1	20.1	13.2
Round steak	100.0	15.3	24.5	19.0	9.3	32.0	19.2	12.9
Sirloin steak	100.0	14.0	21.6	20.7	7.4	35.9	19.9	16.4
Other steak	100.0	14.0	23.8	20.8	9.2	32.2	20.5	11.7
Other beef	100.0	10.2	24.2	19.3	9.6	35.9	25.1	10.6
Pork	100.0	14.9	26.5	21.1	10.4	27.4	17.8	9.6
Bacon	100.0	16.2	24.6	20.7	10.9	28.1	18.8	9.2
Pork chops	100.0	14.5	28.9	22.2	11.2	23.7	15.7	8.0
Ham	100.0	12.8	25.7	23.0	10.7	27.9	17.7	10.1
Ham, not canned	100.0	12.8	25.6	22.9	10.8	28.0	17.8	10.2
Canned ham	100.0	13.9	29.7	29.0	6.5	21.4	16.6	4.2
Sausage	100.0	13.4	27.5	20.8	11.3	27.2	17.6	9.6
Other pork	100.0	16.9	26.4	19.1	8.7	29.3	18.8	10.6
Other meats	100.0	12.6	26.3	18.1	10.2	32.6	20.6	12.0
Frankfurters	100.0	14.9	28.3	18.4	9.6	29.0	18.3	10.8
Lunch meats (cold cuts)	100.0	10.5	26.0	18.5	11.0	33.7	21.7	11.9
Bologna, liverwurst, salami	100.0	11.8	28.6	19.6	10.7	29.3	19.9	9.2
Other lunch meats	100.0	9.9	24.8	18.0	11.1	35.6	22.5	13.2
Lamb, organ meats, and others	100.0	24.0	25.1	14.4	5.8	31.5	17.0	14.8

	total consumer units	less than high school graduate	high school graduate	some college	associate's degree	bachelor's degree or more		
						total	bachelor's degree	graduate degree
Poultry	100.0%	15.0%	24.2%	18.3%	10.7%	31.9%	19.5%	12.5%
Fresh and frozen chicken	100.0	15.8	25.0	18.0	10.1	31.3	19.5	11.9
Fresh and frozen whole chicken	100.0	17.4	24.6	18.5	9.1	30.8	19.2	11.6
Fresh and frozen chicken parts	100.0	15.2	25.1	17.8	10.5	31.6	19.6	12.0
Other poultry	100.0	11.4	21.2	19.3	13.2	34.5	19.7	15.1
Fish and seafood	100.0	11.6	20.5	18.0	11.1	38.2	21.7	16.8
Canned fish and seafood	100.0	10.2	22.6	22.5	12.3	32.2	19.1	13.3
Fresh fish and shellfish	100.0	11.9	20.0	16.8	10.3	40.3	23.5	17.1
Frozen fish and shellfish	100.0	11.8	20.3	17.6	11.6	38.1	20.5	18.1
Eggs	100.0	14.4	25.2	20.0	10.4	30.2	18.4	11.9
Dairy products	**100.0**	**11.6**	**22.1**	**18.7**	**11.0**	**36.0**	**22.0**	**14.1**
Fresh milk and cream	100.0	13.2	23.5	18.9	11.5	32.8	20.3	12.5
Fresh milk, all types	100.0	13.5	23.7	18.8	11.3	32.6	20.4	12.3
Cream	100.0	11.6	22.3	19.7	12.6	33.6	20.3	13.4
Other dairy products	100.0	10.7	21.3	18.6	10.7	37.9	23.0	15.1
Butter	100.0	13.1	21.7	19.2	11.0	34.8	20.6	14.4
Cheese	100.0	10.8	20.6	18.3	11.6	38.0	23.4	14.7
Ice cream and related products	100.0	11.0	23.4	19.2	9.9	35.9	21.8	14.2
Miscellaneous dairy products	100.0	9.0	20.6	18.3	9.3	41.7	24.7	17.2
Fruits and vegetables	**100.0**	**12.0**	**22.6**	**18.2**	**9.3**	**37.4**	**22.0**	**15.6**
Fresh fruits	100.0	11.6	21.6	17.4	8.8	39.8	22.8	17.3
Apples	100.0	11.1	22.5	18.3	8.3	39.0	22.9	16.3
Bananas	100.0	13.6	24.5	18.1	9.6	34.0	20.8	13.4
Oranges	100.0	12.2	21.9	20.0	8.7	36.6	22.1	14.7
Citrus fruits, excluding oranges	100.0	13.9	21.5	16.5	7.6	40.0	21.9	18.5
Other fresh fruits	100.0	10.0	20.1	16.3	9.2	43.3	24.2	19.5
Fresh vegetables	100.0	11.9	22.2	17.8	8.7	38.8	22.4	16.6
Potatoes	100.0	14.3	25.8	17.9	9.9	32.0	18.8	13.4
Lettuce	100.0	11.1	23.2	18.6	9.0	37.4	22.3	15.3
Tomatoes	100.0	13.6	24.2	17.0	8.0	36.7	21.0	16.0
Other fresh vegetables	100.0	10.7	19.9	17.8	8.4	42.2	24.2	18.4
Processed fruits	100.0	11.7	22.7	19.8	10.8	34.7	21.7	13.0
Frozen fruits and fruit juices	100.0	10.8	21.2	18.0	13.3	36.3	23.7	12.5
Frozen orange juice	100.0	13.9	24.5	15.6	14.2	31.9	21.7	10.1
Frozen fruits	100.0	5.9	18.1	19.5	11.7	43.3	28.0	15.2
Frozen fruit juices, excluding orange	100.0	19.0	24.7	17.3	16.0	23.9	15.5	8.4
Canned fruits	100.0	12.1	23.7	20.3	9.5	34.0	21.4	12.6
Dried fruits	100.0	8.1	20.3	19.1	12.2	39.4	24.9	14.5
Fresh fruit juice	100.0	11.7	21.2	18.4	10.7	37.3	22.7	14.7
Canned and bottled fruit juice	100.0	12.2	23.4	20.6	10.5	33.1	20.6	12.5
Processed vegetables	100.0	13.4	25.3	19.0	9.7	32.4	19.9	12.6
Frozen vegetables	100.0	9.4	23.9	18.6	11.3	36.1	20.7	15.6
Canned and dried vegetables and juices	100.0	14.9	25.9	19.1	9.1	31.1	19.6	11.5
Canned beans	100.0	15.7	27.2	17.7	10.3	29.5	17.5	12.2
Canned corn	100.0	13.9	28.9	21.3	9.5	26.7	17.6	9.0
Canned miscellaneous vegetables	100.0	14.1	25.9	18.6	8.9	32.3	20.4	11.9
Dried peas	100.0	27.8	16.8	27.7	3.6	26.0	9.4	17.5
Dried beans	100.0	25.8	24.4	17.5	6.9	26.8	17.5	9.2
Dried miscellaneous vegetables	100.0	16.0	24.9	16.4	9.1	33.6	21.3	12.3
Dried processed vegetables	100.0	12.7	24.2	24.6	9.6	28.8	19.3	9.4
Fresh and canned vegetable juices	100.0	12.0	24.1	21.3	8.8	33.5	21.9	11.5
Sugar and other sweets	**100.0**	**10.8**	**23.6**	**19.2**	**11.3**	**34.6**	**21.4**	**13.3**
Candy and chewing gum	100.0	8.8	23.1	19.0	11.9	36.4	22.8	13.7
Sugar	100.0	16.0	28.1	20.3	9.1	26.8	16.5	10.4
Artificial sweeteners	100.0	8.2	21.8	23.4	11.5	34.4	19.1	15.6
Jams, preserves, other sweets	100.0	12.9	21.8	18.0	11.1	35.9	21.6	14.4

	total consumer units	less than high school graduate	high school graduate	some college	associate's degree	bachelor's degree or more		
						total	bachelor's degree	graduate degree
Fats and oils	**100.0%**	**13.7%**	**26.1%**	**19.8%**	**10.0%**	**30.3%**	**19.3%**	**11.0%**
Margarine	100.0	13.1	29.9	19.0	9.6	28.4	17.5	10.9
Fats and oils	100.0	17.2	24.9	19.3	9.2	29.7	18.5	11.3
Salad dressings	100.0	11.8	26.5	18.8	11.0	31.5	20.2	11.3
Nondairy cream and imitation milk	100.0	13.2	26.3	19.8	10.5	30.2	20.0	10.0
Peanut butter	100.0	10.8	25.3	23.5	9.7	30.5	19.3	11.2
Miscellaneous foods	**100.0**	**10.9**	**23.7**	**18.9**	**10.8**	**35.1**	**21.3**	**13.9**
Frozen prepared foods	100.0	9.4	24.8	18.5	11.5	35.1	22.0	13.1
Frozen meals	100.0	8.4	25.4	18.1	11.0	36.4	21.8	14.7
Other frozen prepared foods	100.0	10.3	24.3	18.9	12.0	34.1	22.2	11.8
Canned and packaged soups	100.0	10.8	24.3	20.5	9.4	34.4	21.0	13.6
Potato chips, nuts, and other snacks	100.0	8.8	23.2	19.8	10.9	36.6	22.1	14.6
Potato chips and other snacks	100.0	9.4	24.8	20.7	11.2	33.4	20.5	13.0
Nuts	100.0	6.8	18.4	17.3	10.1	45.8	26.8	19.4
Condiments and seasonings	100.0	12.0	23.4	18.8	10.9	34.5	21.5	13.1
Salt, spices, and other seasonings	100.0	13.0	23.0	19.5	9.7	34.6	22.1	12.5
Olives, pickles, relishes	100.0	10.0	23.5	18.4	10.3	37.1	22.2	15.1
Sauces and gravies	100.0	12.6	23.5	18.3	11.7	33.6	21.4	12.2
Baking needs and miscellaneous products	100.0	10.5	23.5	19.4	11.1	35.1	20.4	14.8
Other canned or packaged prepared foods	100.0	12.4	23.6	18.4	10.6	34.7	20.4	14.5
Prepared salads	100.0	8.5	22.1	17.8	10.4	40.1	24.6	15.6
Prepared desserts	100.0	13.5	26.6	20.1	10.6	29.3	17.4	12.1
Baby food	100.0	11.1	31.3	22.6	7.2	27.6	16.7	11.0
Miscellaneous prepared foods	100.0	13.7	22.3	17.6	11.4	34.8	20.1	15.0
Nonalcoholic beverages	**100.0**	**13.1**	**25.3**	**19.9**	**10.2**	**31.4**	**19.6**	**11.9**
Cola	100.0	15.2	25.9	20.6	10.7	27.9	18.1	9.7
Other carbonated drinks	100.0	13.7	26.6	18.9	11.5	29.5	18.1	11.5
Tea	100.0	11.6	24.9	19.6	9.4	34.1	21.4	12.8
Coffee	100.0	10.1	24.8	19.4	9.7	35.4	21.6	13.8
Noncarbonated fruit-flavored drinks	100.0	15.8	24.4	21.0	11.4	27.8	17.6	10.2
Other noncarbonated beverages and ice	100.0	12.6	22.0	21.5	10.5	33.2	21.3	11.8
Bottled water	100.0	13.7	24.2	20.4	9.4	32.2	19.2	13.1
Sports drinks	100.0	11.2	28.7	20.3	6.0	33.3	22.3	10.9
Food prepared by consumer unit on trips	**100.0**	**7.7**	**13.6**	**16.5**	**9.6**	**52.6**	**30.4**	**22.2**
FOOD AWAY FROM HOME	**100.0**	**7.1**	**19.7**	**19.0**	**10.9**	**42.3**	**25.3**	**17.2**
Meals at restaurants, carry-outs, etc.	**100.0**	**7.7**	**20.5**	**19.4**	**11.1**	**40.2**	**24.4**	**15.9**
Lunch	100.0	7.9	19.1	19.9	11.6	40.3	24.0	16.5
At fast-food restaurants*	100.0	8.8	21.2	21.1	12.9	35.3	21.6	13.8
At full-service restaurants	100.0	7.3	16.3	18.5	9.7	46.7	27.3	19.6
At vending machines, mobile vendors	100.0	12.4	27.0	22.5	16.6	22.1	14.9	7.1
At employer and school cafeterias	100.0	5.3	19.6	19.7	12.7	41.3	23.2	18.5
Dinner	100.0	7.0	20.7	18.7	10.6	41.8	25.5	16.5
At fast-food restaurants*	100.0	9.8	24.6	19.9	13.2	32.1	21.0	11.1
At full-service restaurants	100.0	5.3	18.6	18.1	9.2	47.0	27.9	19.3
At vending machines, mobile vendors	100.0	27.7	18.8	8.9	15.3	30.7	13.5	17.9
At employer and school cafeterias	100.0	5.0	17.7	22.9	4.9	47.6	25.7	22.5
Snacks and nonalcoholic beverages	100.0	8.5	21.5	20.0	11.8	37.3	24.3	12.9
At fast-food restaurants*	100.0	7.5	22.0	18.9	12.2	38.4	24.1	14.2
At full-service restaurants	100.0	9.9	17.4	20.0	11.9	40.0	27.8	11.9
At vending machines, mobile vendors	100.0	12.1	24.2	26.1	9.1	28.5	19.4	8.9
At employer and school cafeterias	100.0	8.0	26.9	24.1	12.0	28.7	21.4	6.8
Breakfast and brunch	100.0	10.1	23.2	20.5	11.4	34.3	21.4	13.0
At fast-food restaurants*	100.0	11.0	23.2	20.5	11.7	33.2	20.3	13.0
At full-service restaurants	100.0	8.7	22.9	20.8	10.8	36.0	23.4	12.5
At vending machines, mobile vendors	100.0	16.6	23.9	18.6	15.3	26.3	15.1	11.4
At employer and school cafeterias	100.0	9.0	25.5	17.9	11.0	35.9	18.6	17.8

	total consumer units	less than high school graduate	high school graduate	some college	associate's degree	bachelor's degree or more		
						total	bachelor's degree	graduate degree
Board (including at school)	100.0%	1.1%	12.2%	23.7%	8.8%	54.2%	30.4%	23.8%
Catered affairs	100.0	2.1	18.9	9.0	8.8	61.2	25.7	35.5
Food on trips	100.0	4.3	12.8	15.8	9.9	57.3	31.8	25.5
School lunches	100.0	4.8	21.6	19.9	12.9	40.9	26.1	14.8
Meals as pay	100.0	5.7	31.5	19.9	7.8	35.2	22.3	12.8
ALCOHOLIC BEVERAGES	100.0	4.5	15.8	19.4	10.8	47.9	29.1	19.0
At home	100.0	5.8	18.3	19.6	11.6	43.2	23.8	19.9
Beer and ale	100.0	9.2	27.3	22.1	11.1	30.0	18.0	12.1
Whiskey	100.0	4.9	15.8	15.8	7.4	53.7	25.1	29.7
Wine	100.0	2.9	9.3	18.1	12.3	55.0	28.6	27.2
Other alcoholic beverages	100.0	2.9	17.1	15.6	12.6	49.6	29.6	20.3
Away from home	100.0	3.0	13.0	19.1	9.8	53.3	35.2	17.9
Beer and ale	100.0	4.0	17.1	19.8	11.8	45.5	30.6	14.7
At fast-food restaurants*	100.0	5.4	22.7	22.6	9.5	38.5	26.3	12.0
At full-service restaurants	100.0	3.8	16.1	19.6	12.2	46.6	31.1	15.3
At vending machines, mobile vendors	100.0	–	26.7	7.3	29.7	35.9	20.5	15.4
Wine	100.0	2.6	10.2	17.0	7.9	59.6	40.4	18.8
At fast-food restaurants*	100.0	3.3	16.3	10.6	8.1	58.9	39.1	19.5
At full-service restaurants	100.0	2.6	9.6	17.8	8.0	59.2	39.7	19.2
Other alcoholic beverages	100.0	2.0	11.8	22.3	9.0	52.5	36.0	16.2
At fast-food restaurants*	100.0	1.0	25.4	21.8	10.5	39.6	32.8	5.8
At full-service restaurants	100.0	2.1	10.6	22.4	8.9	53.7	36.2	17.2
Alcoholic beverages purchased on trips	100.0	2.8	10.1	16.5	9.0	61.6	37.2	24.4

The category fast-food restaurants also includes take-out, delivery, concession stands, buffets, and cafeterias other than employer and school.
Note: Numbers may not add to total because of rounding. "–" means sample is too small to make a reliable estimate.
Source: Calculations by New Strategist based on the Bureau of Labor Statistics' 2011 Consumer Expenditure Survey

CHAPTER 6

Spending on Gifts for People in Other Households, 2011

Average household spending on gifts for people in other households stood at $1,037 in 2011, a substantial 27 percent less than in 2000 after adjusting for inflation.

Households headed by 45-to-64-year-olds spend the most on gifts for people in other households, a total of over $1,500 in 2011 and 48 to 50 percent more than the average household. Only one other age group spends more than average on gifts for people in other households: 65-to-74-year-olds, 22 percent more than average. Behind the above-average spending by older householders is their family status; many buy gifts for adult children who are establishing their own households and for grandchildren.

Households with incomes of $100,000 or more spent an average of $2,652 on gifts for people in other households in 2011, more than two-and-one-half times as much as the average household. While overall spending on gifts is less in lower-income households, gift spending by category varies by household income. The lowest-income households spend more than average on practical gifts such as buying electricity for people living in other households (in other words, helping relatives and friends pay their utility bills).

Among household types, married couples without children at home (most of them empty-nesters) and those with adult children at home spend the most on gifts for people in other households—58 and 60 percent, respectively, more than the average household in 2011. Spending on gifts for people in other households is 28 percent less than average among married couples with preschoolers and less than one-half the average among single parents.

Asian and non-Hispanic white households spend far more than their black and Hispanic counterparts on gifts for people in other households. In 2011, the average non-Hispanic white household devoted $1,198 to gift giving (15 percent more than average), while Asians spent $1,121 (8 percent more than average). Black and Hispanic households spend only about half as much as the average household on gifts for people living elsewhere. Hispanics far exceed the average on gifts of footwear, clothes for boys and men, natural gas for a renter, babysitting, and major appliances, however. Blacks far exceed the average on gifts of electricity for a renter, day care center fees, footwear, postage, and natural gas for a renter.

Households in the Northeast spend the most on gifts for people in other households—28 percent more than the average household. Western households spend 13 percent more than average, whereas Midwestern households spend about an average amount on gifts for people in other households. Spending on gifts is 21 percent below average in the South.

Because college graduates dominate the nation's affluent households, they spend the most on gifts for people in other households. In 2011, the 30 percent of households headed by college graduates accounted for 52 percent of all gift spending outside the household. They spent an average of $1,769 on gifts for people living elsewhere—70 percent more than average. College graduates spend two-and-one-half times the average on gifts of college tuition.

Table 6.1 Gifts for People in Other Households: Average spending by age, 2011

(average annual spending of consumer units on selected gifts of products and services for people in other households by age of consumer unit reference person, 2011)

	total consumer units	under 25	25 to 34	35 to 44	45 to 54	55 to 64	65 to 74	75+
Number of consumer units (in 000s)	122,287	7,743	20,463	21,699	24,821	21,688	14,079	11,794
Average number of persons per consumer unit	2.5	2.1	2.9	3.3	2.8	2.1	1.9	1.6
Average before-tax income of consumer units	$63,685.00	$27,514.00	$58,179.00	$77,376.00	$78,519.00	$75,517.00	$52,521.00	$32,144.00
Average spending of consumer units, total	49,704.88	29,911.52	48,097.39	57,271.07	58,050.42	53,615.86	44,645.56	32,688.34
Gifts, average spending	**1,037.47**	**377.77**	**496.49**	**710.70**	**1,552.72**	**1,534.96**	**1,269.40**	**735.62**
Food	**84.17**	**13.64**	**32.20**	**60.83**	**132.33**	**155.22**	**71.83**	**45.98**
Cakes and cupcakes	2.25	1.21	3.01	2.86	2.42	2.41	0.95	1.25
Candy and chewing gum	8.01	1.96	7.12	8.01	7.71	12.08	7.48	7.00
Food or board at school	22.64	–	0.20	17.27	62.31	35.68	0.93	4.83
Catered affairs	15.55	0.99	0.52	6.34	18.84	52.18	9.68	0.82
Food on trips	2.48	0.39	1.73	3.45	2.57	1.90	5.41	0.71
Alcoholic beverages	**16.63**	**7.26**	**14.37**	**8.83**	**30.23**	**9.05**	**35.72**	**4.73**
Housing	**194.31**	**57.60**	**107.28**	**151.57**	**251.57**	**272.60**	**309.91**	**113.96**
Housekeeping supplies	24.81	7.25	14.41	27.33	28.33	32.93	30.98	20.18
Stationery, stationery supplies, giftwrap	12.30	2.84	8.93	13.67	12.31	18.52	11.34	11.18
Postage	2.45	1.18	1.05	2.36	3.16	4.49	2.40	0.67
Household textiles	10.63	1.11	9.09	5.04	11.52	15.57	22.47	4.94
Major appliances	6.94	–	0.91	4.12	8.12	17.44	11.36	0.11
Small appliances and miscellaneous housewares	10.98	2.97	6.21	5.78	11.14	14.11	30.13	6.02
Infants' equipment	3.53	–	1.73	9.62	4.61	2.55	1.23	–
Household decorative items	10.88	8.59	8.26	7.46	4.25	20.31	20.85	8.13
Indoor plants, fresh flowers	7.17	2.09	4.31	4.38	7.38	12.10	11.16	6.33
Computers and computer hardware for nonbusiness use	7.53	1.43	4.54	4.39	16.32	8.60	6.37	3.42
Housing while attending school	33.13	–	0.49	9.42	103.15	48.26	10.42	7.04
Lodging on trips	4.18	0.67	2.60	3.97	3.28	2.03	16.35	0.99
Natural gas (renter)	1.80	2.05	1.46	2.36	0.96	2.06	0.59	3.92
Electricity (renter)	10.60	12.91	12.68	17.02	9.96	8.37	6.89	3.49
Babysitting	1.49	1.10	2.68	4.38	0.60	–	0.42	0.15
Day care centers, nurseries, and preschools	8.72	0.79	20.09	4.58	5.71	13.93	7.48	–
Apparel and services	**204.98**	**168.82**	**147.60**	**208.60**	**205.38**	**263.07**	**223.77**	**191.55**
Men and boys, aged 2 or older	53.06	39.23	47.99	44.04	48.48	67.53	63.25	58.14
Women and girls, aged 2 or older	77.38	43.45	34.51	62.29	82.57	119.35	110.06	76.15
Children under age 2	22.22	35.00	24.06	21.11	27.30	23.64	16.32	5.99
Watches	6.37	–	5.00	16.06	1.22	8.27	1.37	7.99
Jewelry	11.66	17.10	6.98	11.39	13.44	13.77	15.94	3.98
Footwear	32.51	32.74	28.68	52.92	27.22	29.36	14.73	38.97
Transportation	**90.43**	**17.28**	**57.16**	**56.01**	**141.54**	**117.48**	**144.10**	**38.13**
Vehicle purchases	40.42	4.05	21.32	10.94	81.92	51.34	67.30	12.05
Gasoline on trips	20.05	4.09	14.83	14.79	20.73	32.21	29.10	14.68
Airline fares	13.06	2.53	10.65	13.52	15.47	14.70	22.30	4.25
Intercity train fares	1.27	0.32	0.88	1.33	1.54	1.37	2.38	0.43
Ship fares	7.46	2.22	3.72	8.80	10.56	8.73	11.19	1.60
Health care	**30.20**	**0.37**	**4.73**	**14.63**	**38.62**	**39.04**	**52.41**	**62.13**
Entertainment	**92.88**	**48.30**	**68.38**	**80.25**	**95.48**	**162.41**	**102.73**	**41.08**
Toys, games, hobbies, and tricycles	26.07	6.10	27.65	31.94	19.56	40.77	27.97	8.76
Personal care products and services	**14.51**	**9.81**	**9.26**	**10.62**	**13.38**	**26.35**	**22.19**	**5.29**
Cosmetics, perfume, bath preparations	8.31	6.25	3.16	6.92	8.35	13.18	15.81	3.56
Education	**215.93**	**46.24**	**11.50**	**75.42**	**547.79**	**333.02**	**101.18**	**163.48**
College tuition	181.45	43.00	3.12	57.39	509.51	296.86	80.54	27.79
All other gifts	**91.31**	**7.23**	**42.32**	**42.45**	**93.62**	**153.63**	**203.08**	**68.32**
Gifts of out-of-town trip expenses	52.34	6.17	29.86	24.39	44.94	82.44	138.42	30.56

Note: Numbers may not add to total because not all categories are shown. "–" means sample is too small to make a reliable estimate. Spending on gifts is also included in the product and service categories in other chapters.
Source: Bureau of Labor Statistics, unpublished tables from the 2011 Consumer Expenditure Survey

Table 6.2 Gifts for People in Other Households: Indexed spending by age, 2011

(indexed average annual spending of consumer units on selected gifts of products and services for people in other households by age of consumer unit reference person, 2011; index definition: an index of 100 is the average for all consumer units; an index of 125 means that spending by consumer units in that group is 25 percent above the average for all consumer units; an index of 75 indicates spending that is 25 percent below the average for all consumer units)

	total consumer units	under 25	25 to 34	35 to 44	45 to 54	55 to 64	65 to 74	75+
Average spending of consumer units, total	$49,705	$29,912	$48,097	$57,271	$58,050	$53,616	$44,646	$32,688
Average spending of consumer units, index	100	60	97	115	117	108	90	66
Gifts, spending index	**100**	**36**	**48**	**69**	**150**	**148**	**122**	**71**
Food	**100**	**16**	**38**	**72**	**157**	**184**	**85**	**55**
Cakes and cupcakes	100	54	134	127	108	107	42	56
Candy and chewing gum	100	24	89	100	96	151	93	87
Food or board at school	100	–	1	76	275	158	4	21
Catered affairs	100	6	3	41	121	336	62	5
Food on trips	100	16	70	139	104	77	218	29
Alcoholic beverages	**100**	**44**	**86**	**53**	**182**	**54**	**215**	**28**
Housing	**100**	**30**	**55**	**78**	**129**	**140**	**159**	**59**
Housekeeping supplies	100	29	58	110	114	133	125	81
Stationery, stationery supplies, giftwrap	100	23	73	111	100	151	92	91
Postage	100	48	43	96	129	183	98	27
Household textiles	100	10	86	47	108	146	211	46
Major appliances	100	–	13	59	117	251	164	2
Small appliances and miscellaneous housewares	100	27	57	53	101	129	274	55
Infants' equipment	100	–	49	273	131	72	35	–
Household decorative items	100	79	76	69	39	187	192	75
Indoor plants, fresh flowers	100	29	60	61	103	169	156	88
Computers and computer hardware for nonbusiness use	100	19	60	58	217	114	85	45
Housing while attending school	100	–	1	28	311	146	31	21
Lodging on trips	100	16	62	95	78	49	391	24
Natural gas (renter)	100	114	81	131	53	114	33	218
Electricity (renter)	100	122	120	161	94	79	65	33
Babysitting	100	74	180	294	40	–	28	10
Day care centers, nurseries, and preschools	100	9	230	53	65	160	86	–
Apparel and services	**100**	**82**	**72**	**102**	**100**	**128**	**109**	**93**
Men and boys, aged 2 or older	100	74	90	83	91	127	119	110
Women and girls, aged 2 or older	100	56	45	80	107	154	142	98
Children under age 2	100	158	108	95	123	106	73	27
Watches	100	–	78	252	19	130	22	125
Jewelry	100	147	60	98	115	118	137	34
Footwear	100	101	88	163	84	90	45	120
Transportation	**100**	**19**	**63**	**62**	**157**	**130**	**159**	**42**
Vehicle purchases	100	10	53	27	203	127	167	30
Gasoline on trips	100	20	74	74	103	161	145	73
Airline fares	100	19	82	104	118	113	171	33
Intercity train fares	100	25	69	105	121	108	187	34
Ship fares	100	30	50	118	142	117	150	21
Health care	**100**	**1**	**16**	**48**	**128**	**129**	**174**	**206**
Entertainment	**100**	**52**	**74**	**86**	**103**	**175**	**111**	**44**
Toys, games, hobbies, and tricycles	100	23	106	123	75	156	107	34
Personal care products and services	**100**	**68**	**64**	**73**	**92**	**182**	**153**	**36**
Cosmetics, perfume, bath preparations	100	75	38	83	100	159	190	43
Education	**100**	**21**	**5**	**35**	**254**	**154**	**47**	**76**
College tuition	100	24	2	32	281	164	44	15
All other gifts	**100**	**8**	**46**	**46**	**103**	**168**	**222**	**75**
Gifts of out-of-town trip expenses	100	12	57	47	86	158	264	58

Note: "–" means sample is too small to make a reliable estimate. Spending on gifts is also included in the product and service categories in other chapters.
Source: Calculations by New Strategist based on the Bureau of Labor Statistics' 2011 Consumer Expenditure Survey

Table 6.3 Gifts for People in Other Households: Total spending by age, 2011

(total annual spending on selected gifts of products and services for people in other households by consumer unit age groups, 2011; consumer units and dollars in thousands)

	total consumer units	under 25	25 to 34	35 to 44	45 to 54	55 to 64	65 to 74	75+
Number of consumer units	122,287	7,743	20,463	21,699	24,821	21,688	14,079	11,794
Total spending of all consumer units	$6,078,260,661	$231,604,899	$984,216,892	$1,242,724,948	$1,440,869,475	$1,162,820,772	$628,564,839	$385,526,282
Gifts, total spending	126,869,094	2,925,073	10,159,675	15,421,479	38,540,063	33,290,212	17,871,883	8,675,902
Food	10,292,897	105,615	658,909	1,319,950	3,284,563	3,366,411	1,011,295	542,288
Cakes and cupcakes	275,146	9,369	61,594	62,059	60,067	52,268	13,375	14,743
Candy and chewing gum	979,519	15,176	145,697	173,809	191,370	261,991	105,311	82,558
Food or board at school	2,768,578	–	4,093	374,742	1,546,597	773,828	13,093	56,965
Catered affairs	1,901,563	7,666	10,641	137,572	467,628	1,131,680	136,285	9,671
Food on trips	303,272	3,020	35,401	74,862	63,790	41,207	76,167	8,374
Alcoholic beverages	2,033,633	56,214	294,053	191,602	750,339	196,276	502,902	55,786
Housing	23,761,587	445,997	2,195,271	3,288,917	6,244,219	5,912,149	4,363,223	1,344,044
Housekeeping supplies	3,033,940	56,137	294,872	593,034	703,179	714,186	436,167	238,003
Stationery, stationery supplies, giftwrap	1,504,130	21,990	182,735	296,625	305,547	401,662	159,656	131,857
Postage	299,603	9,137	21,486	51,210	78,434	97,379	33,790	7,902
Household textiles	1,299,911	8,595	186,009	109,363	285,938	337,682	316,355	58,262
Major appliances	848,672	–	18,621	89,400	201,547	378,239	159,937	1,297
Small appliances and miscellaneous housewares	1,342,711	22,997	127,075	125,420	276,506	306,018	424,200	71,000
Infants' equipment	431,673	–	35,401	208,744	114,425	55,304	17,317	–
Household decorative items	1,330,483	66,512	169,024	161,875	105,489	440,483	293,547	95,885
Indoor plants, fresh flowers	876,798	16,183	88,196	95,042	183,179	262,425	157,122	74,656
Computers and computer hardware for nonbusiness use	920,821	11,072	92,902	95,259	405,079	186,517	89,683	40,335
Housing while attending school	4,051,368	–	10,027	204,405	2,560,286	1,046,663	146,703	83,030
Lodging on trips	511,160	5,188	53,204	86,145	81,413	44,027	230,192	11,676
Natural gas (renter)	220,117	15,873	29,876	51,210	23,828	44,677	8,307	46,232
Electricity (renter)	1,296,242	99,962	259,471	369,317	247,217	181,529	97,004	41,161
Babysitting	182,208	8,517	54,841	95,042	14,893	–	5,913	1,769
Day care centers, nurseries, and preschools	1,066,343	6,117	411,102	99,381	141,728	302,114	105,311	–
Apparel and services	25,066,389	1,307,173	3,020,339	4,526,411	5,097,737	5,705,462	3,150,458	2,259,141
Men and boys, aged 2 or older	6,488,548	303,758	982,019	955,624	1,203,322	1,464,591	890,497	685,703
Women and girls, aged 2 or older	9,462,568	336,433	706,178	1,351,631	2,049,470	2,588,463	1,549,535	898,113
Children under age 2	2,717,217	271,005	492,340	458,066	677,613	512,704	229,769	70,646
Watches	778,968	–	102,315	348,486	30,282	179,360	19,288	94,234
Jewelry	1,425,866	132,405	142,832	247,152	333,594	298,644	224,419	46,940
Footwear	3,975,550	253,506	586,879	1,148,311	675,628	636,760	207,384	459,612
Transportation	11,058,413	133,799	1,169,665	1,215,361	3,513,164	2,547,906	2,028,784	449,705
Vehicle purchases	4,942,841	31,359	436,271	237,387	2,033,336	1,113,462	947,517	142,118
Gasoline on trips	2,451,854	31,669	303,466	320,928	514,539	698,570	409,699	173,136
Airline fares	1,597,068	19,590	217,931	293,370	383,981	318,814	313,962	50,125
Intercity train fares	155,304	2,478	18,007	28,860	38,224	29,713	33,508	5,071
Ship fares	912,261	17,189	76,122	190,951	262,110	189,336	157,544	18,870
Health care	3,693,067	2,865	96,790	317,456	958,587	846,700	737,880	732,761
Entertainment	11,358,017	373,987	1,399,260	1,741,345	2,369,909	3,522,348	1,446,336	484,498
Toys, games, hobbies, and tricycles	3,188,022	47,232	565,802	693,066	485,499	884,220	393,790	103,315
Personal care products and services	1,774,384	75,959	189,487	230,443	332,105	571,479	312,413	62,390
Cosmetics, perfume, bath preparations	1,016,205	48,394	64,663	150,157	207,255	285,848	222,589	41,987
Education	26,405,432	358,036	235,325	1,636,539	13,596,696	7,222,538	1,424,513	1,928,083
College tuition	22,188,976	332,949	63,845	1,245,306	12,646,548	6,438,300	1,133,923	327,755
All other gifts	11,166,026	55,982	865,994	921,123	2,323,742	3,331,927	2,859,163	805,766
Gifts of out-of-town trip expenses	6,400,502	47,774	611,025	529,239	1,115,456	1,787,959	1,948,815	360,425

Note: Numbers may not add to total because of rounding and because not all categories are shown. "–" means sample is too small to make a reliable estimate. Spending on gifts is also included in the product and service categories in other chapters.
Source: Calculations by New Strategist based on the Bureau of Labor Statistics' 2011 Consumer Expenditure Survey

Table 6.4 Gifts for People in Other Households: Market shares by age, 2011

(percentage of total annual spending on selected gifts of products and services for people in other households accounted for by consumer unit age groups, 2011)

	total consumer units	under 25	25 to 34	35 to 44	45 to 54	55 to 64	65 to 74	75+
Share of total consumer units	100.0%	6.3%	16.7%	17.7%	20.3%	17.7%	11.5%	9.6%
Share of total before-tax income	100.0	2.7	15.3	21.6	25.0	21.0	9.5	4.9
Share of total spending	100.0	3.8	16.2	20.4	23.7	19.1	10.3	6.3
Share of gifts spending	100.0	2.3	8.0	12.2	30.4	26.2	14.1	6.8
Food	100.0	1.0	6.4	12.8	31.9	32.7	9.8	5.3
Cakes and cupcakes	100.0	3.4	22.4	22.6	21.8	19.0	4.9	5.4
Candy and chewing gum	100.0	1.5	14.9	17.7	19.5	26.7	10.8	8.4
Food or board at school	100.0	–	0.1	13.5	55.9	28.0	0.5	2.1
Catered affairs	100.0	0.4	0.6	7.2	24.6	59.5	7.2	0.5
Food on trips	100.0	1.0	11.7	24.7	21.0	13.6	25.1	2.8
Alcoholic beverages	100.0	2.8	14.5	9.4	36.9	9.7	24.7	2.7
Housing	100.0	1.9	9.2	13.8	26.3	24.9	18.4	5.7
Housekeeping supplies	100.0	1.9	9.7	19.5	23.2	23.5	14.4	7.8
Stationery, stationery supplies, giftwrap	100.0	1.5	12.1	19.7	20.3	26.7	10.6	8.8
Postage	100.0	3.0	7.2	17.1	26.2	32.5	11.3	2.6
Household textiles	100.0	0.7	14.3	8.4	22.0	26.0	24.3	4.5
Major appliances	100.0	–	2.2	10.5	23.7	44.6	18.8	0.2
Small appliances and miscellaneous housewares	100.0	1.7	9.5	9.3	20.6	22.8	31.6	5.3
Infants' equipment	100.0	–	8.2	48.4	26.5	12.8	4.0	–
Household decorative items	100.0	5.0	12.7	12.2	7.9	33.1	22.1	7.2
Indoor plants, fresh flowers	100.0	1.8	10.1	10.8	20.9	29.9	17.9	8.5
Computers and computer hardware for nonbusiness use	100.0	1.2	10.1	10.3	44.0	20.3	9.7	4.4
Housing while attending school	100.0	–	0.2	5.0	63.2	25.8	3.6	2.0
Lodging on trips	100.0	1.0	10.4	16.9	15.9	8.6	45.0	2.3
Natural gas (renter)	100.0	7.2	13.6	23.3	10.8	20.3	3.8	21.0
Electricity (renter)	100.0	7.7	20.0	28.5	19.1	14.0	7.5	3.2
Babysitting	100.0	4.7	30.1	52.2	8.2	–	3.2	1.0
Day care centers, nurseries, and preschools	100.0	0.6	38.6	9.3	13.3	28.3	9.9	–
Apparel and services	100.0	5.2	12.0	18.1	20.3	22.8	12.6	9.0
Men and boys, aged 2 or older	100.0	4.7	15.1	14.7	18.5	22.6	13.7	10.6
Women and girls, aged 2 or older	100.0	3.6	7.5	14.3	21.7	27.4	16.4	9.5
Children under age 2	100.0	10.0	18.1	16.9	24.9	18.9	8.5	2.6
Watches	100.0	–	13.1	44.7	3.9	23.0	2.5	12.1
Jewelry	100.0	9.3	10.0	17.3	23.4	20.9	15.7	3.3
Footwear	100.0	6.4	14.8	28.9	17.0	16.0	5.2	11.6
Transportation	100.0	1.2	10.6	11.0	31.8	23.0	18.3	4.1
Vehicle purchases	100.0	0.6	8.8	4.8	41.1	22.5	19.2	2.9
Gasoline on trips	100.0	1.3	12.4	13.1	21.0	28.5	16.7	7.1
Airline fares	100.0	1.2	13.6	18.4	24.0	20.0	19.7	3.1
Intercity train fares	100.0	1.6	11.6	18.6	24.6	19.1	21.6	3.3
Ship fares	100.0	1.9	8.3	20.9	28.7	20.8	17.3	2.1
Health care	100.0	0.1	2.6	8.6	26.0	22.9	20.0	19.8
Entertainment	100.0	3.3	12.3	15.3	20.9	31.0	12.7	4.3
Toys, games, hobbies, and tricycles	100.0	1.5	17.7	21.7	15.2	27.7	12.4	3.2
Personal care products and services	100.0	4.3	10.7	13.0	18.7	32.2	17.6	3.5
Cosmetics, perfume, bath preparations	100.0	4.8	6.4	14.8	20.4	28.1	21.9	4.1
Education	100.0	1.4	0.9	6.2	51.5	27.4	5.4	7.3
College tuition	100.0	1.5	0.3	5.6	57.0	29.0	5.1	1.5
All other gifts	100.0	0.5	7.8	8.2	20.8	29.8	25.6	7.2
Gifts of out-of-town trip expenses	100.0	0.7	9.5	8.3	17.4	27.9	30.4	5.6

Note: Numbers may not add to total because of rounding. "–" means sample is too small to make a reliable estimate. Spending on gifts is also included in the product and service categories in other chapters.
Source: Calculations by New Strategist based on the Bureau of Labor Statistics' 2011 Consumer Expenditure Survey

Table 6.5 Gifts for People in Other Households: Average spending by income, 2011

(average annual spending on selected gifts of products and services for people in other households by before-tax income of consumer units, 2011)

	total consumer units	under $20,000	$20,000– $39,999	$40,000– $49,999	$50,000– $69,999	$70,000– $79,999	$80,000– $99,999	$100,000 or more
Number of consumer units (in 000s)	122,287	26,342	27,788	11,347	17,376	7,385	10,456	21,593
Average number of persons per consumer unit	2.5	1.8	2.3	2.6	2.7	2.8	3.0	3.2
Average before-tax income of consumer units	$63,685.00	$10,491.66	$29,658.14	$44,698.00	$59,306.00	$74,742.00	$89,108.00	$169,776.00
Average spending of consumer units, total	49,704.88	22,142.36	33,453.66	40,306.19	50,034.03	57,976.69	65,389.80	97,728.22
Gifts, average spending	**1,037.47**	**431.77**	**542.71**	**526.47**	**913.26**	**1,069.43**	**1,223.48**	**2,652.36**
Food	**84.17**	**23.43**	**48.35**	**48.51**	**74.92**	**46.10**	**79.15**	**241.96**
Cakes and cupcakes	2.25	0.96	1.24	0.41	3.05	1.26	1.95	6.06
Candy and chewing gum	8.01	2.17	7.84	7.77	10.14	10.70	7.74	11.99
Food or board at school	22.64	–	7.13	10.63	7.12	1.44	10.15	98.23
Catered affairs	15.55	0.76	7.37	3.10	12.84	3.02	13.68	58.00
Food on trips	2.48	0.33	0.90	0.13	2.80	1.04	4.30	7.70
Alcoholic beverages	**16.63**	**3.45**	**3.40**	**8.77**	**23.37**	**10.00**	**21.22**	**46.41**
Housing	**194.31**	**85.89**	**126.86**	**99.91**	**175.81**	**234.58**	**226.44**	**440.53**
Housekeeping supplies	24.81	6.59	14.06	16.89	24.80	31.32	37.43	53.88
Stationery, stationery supplies, giftwrap	12.30	2.04	9.30	9.17	12.21	17.91	18.90	23.68
Postage	2.45	0.97	1.23	2.95	1.37	1.78	4.92	5.63
Household textiles	10.63	3.20	3.36	2.42	11.57	7.41	14.96	30.23
Major appliances	6.94	1.95	2.04	2.96	3.61	20.00	16.16	15.20
Small appliances and miscellaneous housewares	10.98	2.30	4.98	3.48	11.76	7.44	17.89	29.35
Infants' equipment	3.53	1.38	1.28	1.96	2.47	9.87	0.59	10.81
Household decorative items	10.88	6.66	8.54	6.52	15.64	13.92	4.85	19.63
Indoor plants, fresh flowers	7.17	3.11	4.71	7.72	8.57	7.23	11.04	11.98
Computers and computer hardware for nonbusiness use	7.53	1.78	3.13	0.66	5.57	2.23	18.81	23.06
Housing while attending school	33.13	–	10.56	7.19	9.41	23.97	14.88	134.79
Lodging on trips	4.18	1.51	1.94	1.36	4.20	3.39	2.53	12.88
Natural gas (renter)	1.80	2.21	3.01	0.90	1.01	0.78	2.24	0.99
Electricity (renter)	10.60	17.19	11.64	10.80	10.54	5.30	9.45	3.50
Babysitting	1.49	0.27	2.15	2.34	1.40	0.33	0.10	2.92
Day care centers, nurseries, and preschools	8.72	2.07	5.17	6.09	9.34	7.14	17.70	18.97
Apparel and services	**204.98**	**137.24**	**155.10**	**149.30**	**206.82**	**229.81**	**247.16**	**345.66**
Men and boys, aged 2 or older	53.06	39.79	37.74	39.99	61.16	49.13	48.29	92.64
Women and girls, aged 2 or older	77.38	46.37	59.23	61.60	81.97	80.50	103.25	124.91
Children under age 2	22.22	12.98	18.16	14.95	19.97	38.10	31.28	34.15
Watches	6.37	–	3.09	–	1.09	18.67	10.84	14.55
Jewelry	11.66	5.40	8.84	8.66	8.99	13.43	14.59	24.62
Footwear	32.51	28.24	25.95	23.26	32.32	23.90	37.87	52.13
Transportation	**90.43**	**18.19**	**38.78**	**37.77**	**102.68**	**102.95**	**83.45**	**261.83**
Vehicle purchases	40.42	6.87	31.33	11.37	54.59	60.06	14.28	125.52
Gasoline on trips	20.05	5.66	10.57	17.36	21.94	26.29	28.90	43.30
Airline fares	13.06	3.00	5.19	2.30	10.94	8.68	19.10	41.42
Intercity train fares	1.27	0.35	0.64	0.31	1.21	0.98	1.85	3.60
Ship fares	7.46	1.22	2.67	1.46	5.73	1.57	6.41	28.30
Health care	**30.20**	**28.38**	**17.14**	**4.92**	**21.54**	**32.55**	**13.34**	**76.62**
Entertainment	**92.88**	**22.43**	**50.87**	**59.86**	**75.10**	**112.05**	**140.32**	**228.16**
Toys, games, hobbies, and tricycles	26.07	7.62	18.10	21.78	18.79	33.40	53.14	50.24
Personal care products and services	**14.51**	**4.38**	**7.23**	**10.18**	**15.37**	**25.00**	**22.76**	**29.09**
Cosmetics, perfume, bath preparations	8.31	2.70	3.62	6.07	6.84	16.08	11.64	19.36
Education	**215.93**	**65.71**	**42.29**	**39.54**	**80.80**	**116.78**	**302.39**	**815.49**
College tuition	181.45	59.75	25.53	29.04	59.62	97.31	270.29	694.46
All other gifts	**91.31**	**41.92**	**51.71**	**65.39**	**133.73**	**156.70**	**84.91**	**162.67**
Gifts of out-of-town trip expenses	52.34	13.26	17.26	45.71	76.65	59.09	43.30	131.17

Note: Numbers may not add to total because not all categories are shown. "–" means sample is too small to make a reliable estimate. Spending on gifts is also included in the product and service categories in other chapters.
Source: Bureau of Labor Statistics, unpublished tables from the 2011 Consumer Expenditure Survey; calculations by New Strategist

Table 6.6 Gifts for People in Other Households: Indexed spending by income, 2011

(indexed average annual spending of consumer units on selected gifts of products and services for people in other households by before-tax income of consumer unit, 2011; index definition: an index of 100 is the average for all consumer units; an index of 125 means that spending by consumer units in that group is 25 percent above the average for all consumer units; an index of 75 indicates spending that is 25 percent below the average for all consumer units)

	total consumer units	under $20,000	$20,000–$39,999	$40,000–$49,999	$50,000–$69,999	$70,000–$79,999	$80,000–$99,999	$100,000 or more
Average spending of consumer units, total	$49,705	$22,142	$33,454	$40,306	$50,034	$57,977	$65,390	$97,728
Average spending of consumer units, index	100	45	67	81	101	117	132	197
Gifts, spending index	**100**	**42**	**52**	**51**	**88**	**103**	**118**	**256**
Food	**100**	**28**	**57**	**58**	**89**	**55**	**94**	**287**
Cakes and cupcakes	100	43	55	18	136	56	87	269
Candy and chewing gum	100	27	98	97	127	134	97	150
Food or board at school	100	–	32	47	31	6	45	434
Catered affairs	100	5	47	20	83	19	88	373
Food on trips	100	13	36	5	113	42	173	310
Alcoholic beverages	**100**	**21**	**20**	**53**	**141**	**60**	**128**	**279**
Housing	**100**	**44**	**65**	**51**	**90**	**121**	**117**	**227**
Housekeeping supplies	100	27	57	68	100	126	151	217
Stationery, stationery supplies, giftwrap	100	17	76	75	99	146	154	193
Postage	100	40	50	120	56	73	201	230
Household textiles	100	30	32	23	109	70	141	284
Major appliances	100	28	29	43	52	288	233	219
Small appliances and miscellaneous housewares	100	21	45	32	107	68	163	267
Infants' equipment	100	39	36	56	70	280	17	306
Household decorative items	100	61	79	60	144	128	45	180
Indoor plants, fresh flowers	100	43	66	108	120	101	154	167
Computers and computer hardware for nonbusiness use	100	24	42	9	74	30	250	306
Housing while attending school	100	–	32	22	28	72	45	407
Lodging on trips	100	36	46	33	100	81	61	308
Natural gas (renter)	100	123	167	50	56	43	124	55
Electricity (renter)	100	162	110	102	99	50	89	33
Babysitting	100	18	144	157	94	22	7	196
Day care centers, nurseries, and preschools	100	24	59	70	107	82	203	218
Apparel and services	**100**	**67**	**76**	**73**	**101**	**112**	**121**	**169**
Men and boys, aged 2 or older	100	75	71	75	115	93	91	175
Women and girls, aged 2 or older	100	60	77	80	106	104	133	161
Children under age 2	100	58	82	67	90	171	141	154
Watches	100	–	49	–	17	293	170	228
Jewelry	100	46	76	74	77	115	125	211
Footwear	100	87	80	72	99	74	116	160
Transportation	**100**	**20**	**43**	**42**	**114**	**114**	**92**	**290**
Vehicle purchases	100	17	78	28	135	149	35	311
Gasoline on trips	100	28	53	87	109	131	144	216
Airline fares	100	23	40	18	84	66	146	317
Intercity train fares	100	27	51	24	95	77	146	283
Ship fares	100	16	36	20	77	21	86	379
Health care	**100**	**94**	**57**	**16**	**71**	**108**	**44**	**254**
Entertainment	**100**	**24**	**55**	**64**	**81**	**121**	**151**	**246**
Toys, games, hobbies, and tricycles	100	29	69	84	72	128	204	193
Personal care products and services	**100**	**30**	**50**	**70**	**106**	**172**	**157**	**200**
Cosmetics, perfume, bath preparations	100	32	44	73	82	194	140	233
Education	**100**	**30**	**20**	**18**	**37**	**54**	**140**	**378**
College tuition	100	33	14	16	33	54	149	383
All other gifts	**100**	**46**	**57**	**72**	**146**	**172**	**93**	**178**
Gifts of out-of-town trip expenses	100	25	33	87	146	113	83	251

Note: "–" means sample is too small to make a reliable estimate. Spending on gifts is also included in the product and service categories in other chapters.
Source: Calculations by New Strategist based on the Bureau of Labor Statistics' 2011 Consumer Expenditure Survey

Table 6.7 Gifts for People in Other Households: Total spending by income, 2011

(total annual spending on selected gifts of products and services for people in other households by before-tax income group of consumer units, 2011; consumer units and dollars in thousands)

	total consumer units	under $20,000	$20,000–$39,999	$40,000–$49,999	$50,000–$69,999	$70,000–$79,999	$80,000–$99,999	$100,000 or more
Number of consumer units	122,287	26,342	27,788	11,347	17,376	7,385	10,456	21,593
Total spending of all consumer units	$6,078,260,661	$583,273,961	$929,610,260	$457,354,338	$869,391,305	$428,157,856	$683,715,749	$2,110,245,454
Gifts, total spending	**126,869,094**	**11,373,695**	**15,080,707**	**5,973,855**	**15,868,806**	**7,897,741**	**12,792,707**	**57,272,409**
Food	**10,292,897**	**617,115**	**1,343,436**	**550,443**	**1,301,810**	**340,449**	**827,592**	**5,224,642**
Cakes and cupcakes	275,146	25,342	34,323	4,652	52,997	9,305	20,389	130,854
Candy and chewing gum	979,519	57,225	217,960	88,166	176,193	79,020	80,929	258,900
Food or board at school	2,768,578	–	198,193	120,619	123,717	10,634	106,128	2,121,080
Catered affairs	1,901,563	20,103	204,773	35,176	223,108	22,303	143,038	1,252,394
Food on trips	303,272	8,802	25,131	1,475	48,653	7,680	44,961	166,266
Alcoholic beverages	**2,033,633**	**90,990**	**94,346**	**99,513**	**406,077**	**73,850**	**221,876**	**1,002,131**
Housing	**23,761,587**	**2,262,623**	**3,525,065**	**1,133,679**	**3,054,875**	**1,732,373**	**2,367,657**	**9,512,364**
Housekeeping supplies	3,033,940	173,504	390,569	191,651	430,925	231,298	391,368	1,163,431
Stationery, stationery supplies, giftwrap	1,504,130	53,847	258,377	104,052	212,161	132,265	197,618	511,322
Postage	299,603	25,529	34,063	33,474	23,805	13,145	51,444	121,569
Household textiles	1,299,911	84,335	93,245	27,460	201,040	54,723	156,422	652,756
Major appliances	848,672	51,257	56,593	33,587	62,727	147,700	168,969	328,214
Small appliances and miscellaneous housewares	1,342,711	60,503	138,503	39,488	204,342	54,944	187,058	633,755
Infants' equipment	431,673	36,352	35,464	22,240	42,919	72,890	6,169	233,420
Household decorative items	1,330,483	175,504	237,433	73,982	271,761	102,799	50,712	423,871
Indoor plants, fresh flowers	876,798	81,804	130,860	87,599	148,912	53,394	115,434	258,684
Computers and computer hardware for nonbusiness use	920,821	46,948	87,101	7,489	96,784	16,469	196,677	497,935
Housing while attending school	4,051,368	–	293,440	81,585	163,508	177,018	155,585	2,910,520
Lodging on trips	511,160	39,666	53,788	15,432	72,979	25,035	26,454	278,118
Natural gas (renter)	220,117	58,226	83,544	10,212	17,550	5,760	23,421	21,377
Electricity (renter)	1,296,242	452,698	323,569	122,548	183,143	39,141	98,809	75,576
Babysitting	182,208	7,235	59,621	26,552	24,326	2,437	1,046	63,052
Day care centers, nurseries, and preschools	1,066,343	54,419	143,800	69,103	162,292	52,729	185,071	409,619
Apparel and services	**25,066,389**	**3,615,283**	**4,309,894**	**1,694,107**	**3,593,704**	**1,697,147**	**2,584,305**	**7,463,836**
Men and boys, aged 2 or older	6,488,548	1,048,071	1,048,704	453,767	1,062,716	362,825	504,920	2,000,376
Women and girls, aged 2 or older	9,462,568	1,221,485	1,645,886	698,975	1,424,311	594,493	1,079,582	2,697,182
Children under age 2	2,717,217	341,844	504,496	169,638	346,999	281,369	327,064	737,401
Watches	778,968	–	85,965	–	18,940	137,878	113,343	314,178
Jewelry	1,425,866	142,355	245,780	98,265	156,210	99,181	152,553	531,620
Footwear	3,975,550	744,001	720,997	263,931	561,592	176,502	395,969	1,125,643
Transportation	**11,058,413**	**479,067**	**1,077,582**	**428,576**	**1,784,168**	**760,286**	**872,553**	**5,653,695**
Vehicle purchases	4,942,841	180,858	870,598	129,015	948,556	443,543	149,312	2,710,353
Gasoline on trips	2,451,854	149,035	293,725	196,984	381,229	194,152	302,178	934,977
Airline fares	1,597,068	78,974	144,182	26,098	190,093	64,102	199,710	894,382
Intercity train fares	155,304	9,152	17,881	3,518	21,025	7,237	19,344	77,735
Ship fares	912,261	32,092	74,182	16,567	99,564	11,594	67,023	611,082
Health care	**3,693,067**	**747,593**	**476,383**	**55,827**	**374,279**	**240,382**	**139,483**	**1,654,456**
Entertainment	**11,358,017**	**590,789**	**1,413,664**	**679,231**	**1,304,938**	**827,489**	**1,467,186**	**4,926,659**
Toys, games, hobbies, and tricycles	3,188,022	200,628	502,890	247,138	326,495	246,659	555,632	1,084,832
Personal care products and services	**1,774,384**	**115,271**	**200,932**	**115,512**	**267,069**	**184,625**	**237,979**	**628,140**
Cosmetics, perfume, bath preparations	1,016,205	71,030	100,712	68,876	118,852	118,751	121,708	418,040
Education	**26,405,432**	**1,730,937**	**1,175,163**	**448,660**	**1,403,981**	**862,420**	**3,161,790**	**17,608,876**
College tuition	22,188,976	1,573,989	709,407	329,517	1,035,957	718,634	2,826,152	14,995,475
All other gifts	**11,6**	**1,104,310**	**1,436,821**	**741,980**	**2,323,692**	**1,157,230**	**887,819**	**3,512,533**
Gifts of out-of-town trip expenses	6,400,502	349,377	479,696	518,671	1,331,870	436,380	452,745	2,832,354

Note: Numbers may not add to total because of rounding and because not all categories are shown. "–" means sample is too small to make a reliable estimate. Spending on gifts is also included in the product and service categories in other chapters.
Source: Calculations by New Strategist based on the Bureau of Labor Statistics' 2011 Consumer Expenditure Survey

Table 6.8 Gifts for People in Other Households: Market shares by income, 2011

(percentage of total annual spending on selected gifts of products and services for people in other households accounted for by before-tax income group of consumer units, 2011)

	total consumer units	under $20,000	$20,000–$39,999	$40,000–$49,999	$50,000–$69,999	$70,000–$79,999	$80,000–$99,999	$100,000 or more
Share of total consumer units	100.0%	21.5%	22.7%	9.3%	14.2%	6.0%	8.6%	17.7%
Share of total before-tax income	100.0	3.5	10.6	6.5	13.2	7.1	12.0	47.1
Share of total spending	100.0	9.6	15.3	7.5	14.3	7.0	11.2	34.7
Share of gifts spending	100.0	9.0	11.9	4.7	12.5	6.2	10.1	45.1
Food	100.0	6.0	13.1	5.3	12.6	3.3	8.0	50.8
Cakes and cupcakes	100.0	9.2	12.5	1.7	19.3	3.4	7.4	47.6
Candy and chewing gum	100.0	5.8	22.3	9.0	18.0	8.1	8.3	26.4
Food or board at school	100.0	–	7.2	4.4	4.5	0.4	3.8	76.6
Catered affairs	100.0	1.1	10.8	1.8	11.7	1.2	7.5	65.9
Food on trips	100.0	2.9	8.3	0.5	16.0	2.5	14.8	54.8
Alcoholic beverages	100.0	4.5	4.6	4.9	20.0	3.6	10.9	49.3
Housing	100.0	9.5	14.8	4.8	12.9	7.3	10.0	40.0
Housekeeping supplies	100.0	5.7	12.9	6.3	14.2	7.6	12.9	38.3
Stationery, stationery supplies, giftwrap	100.0	3.6	17.2	6.9	14.1	8.8	13.1	34.0
Postage	100.0	8.5	11.4	11.2	7.9	4.4	17.2	40.6
Household textiles	100.0	6.5	7.2	2.1	15.5	4.2	12.0	50.2
Major appliances	100.0	6.0	6.7	4.0	7.4	17.4	19.9	38.7
Small appliances and miscellaneous housewares	100.0	4.5	10.3	2.9	15.2	4.1	13.9	47.2
Infants' equipment	100.0	8.4	8.2	5.2	9.9	16.9	1.4	54.1
Household decorative items	100.0	13.2	17.8	5.6	20.4	7.7	3.8	31.9
Indoor plants, fresh flowers	100.0	9.3	14.9	10.0	17.0	6.1	13.2	29.5
Computers and computer hardware for nonbusiness use	100.0	5.1	9.5	0.8	10.5	1.8	21.4	54.1
Housing while attending school	100.0	–	7.2	2.0	4.0	4.4	3.8	71.8
Lodging on trips	100.0	7.8	10.5	3.0	14.3	4.9	5.2	54.4
Natural gas (renter)	100.0	26.5	38.0	4.6	8.0	2.6	10.6	9.7
Electricity (renter)	100.0	34.9	25.0	9.5	14.1	3.0	7.6	5.8
Babysitting	100.0	4.0	32.7	14.6	13.4	1.3	0.6	34.6
Day care centers, nurseries, and preschools	100.0	5.1	13.5	6.5	15.2	4.9	17.4	38.4
Apparel and services	100.0	14.4	17.2	6.8	14.3	6.8	10.3	29.8
Men and boys, aged 2 or older	100.0	16.2	16.2	7.0	16.4	5.6	7.8	30.8
Women and girls, aged 2 or older	100.0	12.9	17.4	7.4	15.1	6.3	11.4	28.5
Children under age 2	100.0	12.6	18.6	6.2	12.8	10.4	12.0	27.1
Watches	100.0	–	11.0	–	2.4	17.7	14.6	40.3
Jewelry	100.0	10.0	17.2	6.9	11.0	7.0	10.7	37.3
Footwear	100.0	18.7	18.1	6.6	14.1	4.4	10.0	28.3
Transportation	100.0	4.3	9.7	3.9	16.1	6.9	7.9	51.1
Vehicle purchases	100.0	3.7	17.6	2.6	19.2	9.0	3.0	54.8
Gasoline on trips	100.0	6.1	12.0	8.0	15.5	7.9	12.3	38.1
Airline fares	100.0	4.9	9.0	1.6	11.9	4.0	12.5	56.0
Intercity train fares	100.0	5.9	11.5	2.3	13.5	4.7	12.5	50.1
Ship fares	100.0	3.5	8.1	1.8	10.9	1.3	7.3	67.0
Health care	100.0	20.2	12.9	1.5	10.1	6.5	3.8	44.8
Entertainment	100.0	5.2	12.4	6.0	11.5	7.3	12.9	43.4
Toys, games, hobbies, and tricycles	100.0	6.3	15.8	7.8	10.2	7.7	17.4	34.0
Personal care products and services	100.0	6.5	11.3	6.5	15.1	10.4	13.4	35.4
Cosmetics, perfume, bath preparations	100.0	7.0	9.9	6.8	11.7	11.7	12.0	41.1
Education	100.0	6.6	4.5	1.7	5.3	3.3	12.0	66.7
College tuition	100.0	7.1	3.2	1.5	4.7	3.2	12.7	67.6
All other gifts	100.0	9.9	12.9	6.6	20.8	10.4	8.0	31.5
Gifts of out-of-town trip expenses	100.0	5.5	7.5	8.1	20.8	6.8	7.1	44.3

Note: Numbers may not add to total because of rounding. "–" means sample is too small to make a reliable estimate. Spending on gifts is also included in the product and service categories in other chapters.
Source: Calculations by New Strategist based on the Bureau of Labor Statistics' 2011 Consumer Expenditure Survey

Table 6.9 Gifts for People in Other Households: Average spending by high-income consumer units, 2011

(average annual spending on selected gifts of products and services for people in other households by before-tax income of high-income consumer units, 2011)

	total consumer units	$100,000 or more	$100,000– $119,999	$120,000– $149,999	$150,000 or more
Number of consumer units (in 000s)	122,287	21,593	7,045	6,107	8,440
Average number of persons per consumer unit	2.5	3.2	3.2	3.1	3.2
Average before-tax income of consumer units	$63,685.00	$169,776.00	$108,549.00	$133,318.00	$247,261.00
Average spending of consumer units, total	49,704.88	97,728.22	76,496.41	87,239.44	123,056.38
Gifts, average spending	**1,037.47**	**2,652.36**	**1,525.98**	**2,102.01**	**3,994.82**
Food	**84.17**	**241.96**	**164.47**	**213.72**	**327.16**
Cakes and cupcakes	2.25	6.06	7.59	7.63	3.62
Candy and chewing gum	8.01	11.99	9.42	9.32	16.10
Food or board at school	22.64	98.23	50.75	69.73	158.49
Catered affairs	15.55	58.00	47.61	67.95	59.49
Food on trips	2.48	7.70	1.55	15.71	7.02
Alcoholic beverages	**16.63**	**46.41**	**11.37**	**69.85**	**59.94**
Housing	**194.31**	**440.53**	**263.58**	**409.90**	**611.13**
Housekeeping supplies	24.81	53.88	41.68	53.76	64.48
Stationery, stationery supplies, giftwrap	12.30	23.68	16.47	26.89	27.63
Postage	2.45	5.63	7.37	4.72	4.78
Household textiles	10.63	30.23	22.93	27.22	38.63
Major appliances	6.94	15.20	14.70	9.08	20.04
Small appliances and miscellaneous housewares	10.98	29.35	25.93	22.20	37.31
Infants' equipment	3.53	10.81	6.14	8.57	16.42
Household decorative items	10.88	19.63	15.94	38.83	9.22
Indoor plants, fresh flowers	7.17	11.98	8.86	12.07	14.53
Computers and computer hardware for nonbusiness use	7.53	23.06	11.06	22.95	33.17
Housing while attending school	33.13	134.79	34.26	89.90	251.19
Lodging on trips	4.18	12.88	2.42	28.48	10.33
Natural gas (renter)	1.80	0.99	1.02	0.74	1.14
Electricity (renter)	10.60	3.50	2.81	2.04	5.14
Babysitting	1.49	2.92	2.13	2.36	3.97
Day care centers, nurseries, and preschools	8.72	18.97	8.26	1.86	40.28
Apparel and services	**204.98**	**345.66**	**292.76**	**347.41**	**389.66**
Men and boys, aged 2 or older	53.06	92.64	67.26	100.54	108.91
Women and girls, aged 2 or older	77.38	124.91	100.73	109.76	156.52
Children under age 2	22.22	34.15	54.74	23.06	24.22
Watches	6.37	14.55	9.21	28.20	9.50
Jewelry	11.66	24.62	15.85	37.99	22.26
Footwear	32.51	52.13	39.82	47.00	66.37
Transportation	**90.43**	**261.83**	**128.75**	**284.58**	**356.38**
Vehicle purchases	40.42	125.52	60.56	116.44	186.32
Gasoline on trips	20.05	43.30	30.87	44.10	53.09
Airline fares	13.06	41.42	13.60	57.67	52.89
Intercity train fares	1.27	3.60	1.24	4.80	4.69
Ship fares	7.46	28.30	7.97	38.27	38.05
Health care	**30.20**	**76.62**	**62.52**	**39.67**	**115.24**
Entertainment	**92.88**	**228.16**	**163.35**	**191.80**	**309.01**
Toys, games, hobbies, and tricycles	26.07	50.24	42.51	67.83	44.46
Personal care products and services	**14.51**	**29.09**	**23.39**	**26.99**	**35.50**
Cosmetics, perfume, bath preparations	8.31	19.36	14.84	14.82	26.47
Education	**215.93**	**815.49**	**302.61**	**382.80**	**1,556.75**
College tuition	181.45	694.46	257.87	346.45	1,310.67
All other gifts	**91.31**	**162.67**	**111.78**	**128.78**	**229.86**
Gifts of out-of-town trip expenses	52.34	131.17	101.49	80.84	192.36

Note: Numbers may not add to total because not all categories are shown. Spending on gifts is also included in the product and service categories in other chapters.
Source: Bureau of Labor Statistics, unpublished tables from the 2011 Consumer Expenditure Survey

Table 6.10 Gifts for People in Other Households: Indexed spending by high-income consumer units, 2011

(indexed average annual spending of high-income consumer units on selected gifts of products and services for people in other households by before-tax income of consumer unit, 2011; index definition: an index of 100 is the average for all consumer units; an index of 125 means that spending by consumer units in that group is 25 percent above the average for all consumer units; an index of 75 indicates spending that is 25 percent below the average for all consumer units)

	total consumer units	$100,000 or more	$100,000– $119,999	$120,000– $149,999	$150,000 or more
Average spending of consumer units, total	$49,705	$97,728	$76,496	$87,239	$123,056
Average spending of consumer units, index	100	197	154	176	248
Gifts, spending index	100	256	147	203	385
Food	100	287	195	254	389
Cakes and cupcakes	100	269	337	339	161
Candy and chewing gum	100	150	118	116	201
Food or board at school	100	434	224	308	700
Catered affairs	100	373	306	437	383
Food on trips	100	310	63	633	283
Alcoholic beverages	100	279	68	420	360
Housing	100	227	136	211	315
Housekeeping supplies	100	217	168	217	260
Stationery, stationery supplies, giftwrap	100	193	134	219	225
Postage	100	230	301	193	195
Household textiles	100	284	216	256	363
Major appliances	100	219	212	131	289
Small appliances and miscellaneous housewares	100	267	236	202	340
Infants' equipment	100	306	174	243	465
Household decorative items	100	180	147	357	85
Indoor plants, fresh flowers	100	167	124	168	203
Computers and computer hardware for nonbusiness use	100	306	147	305	441
Housing while attending school	100	407	103	271	758
Lodging on trips	100	308	58	681	247
Natural gas (renter)	100	55	57	41	63
Electricity (renter)	100	33	27	19	48
Babysitting	100	196	143	158	266
Day care centers, nurseries, and preschools	100	218	95	21	462
Apparel and services	100	169	143	169	190
Men and boys, aged 2 or older	100	175	127	189	205
Women and girls, aged 2 or older	100	161	130	142	202
Children under age 2	100	154	246	104	109
Watches	100	228	145	443	149
Jewelry	100	211	136	326	191
Footwear	100	160	122	145	204
Transportation	100	290	142	315	394
Vehicle purchases	100	311	150	288	461
Gasoline on trips	100	216	154	220	265
Airline fares	100	317	104	442	405
Intercity train fares	100	283	98	378	369
Ship fares	100	379	107	513	510
Health care	100	254	207	131	382
Entertainment	100	246	176	207	333
Toys, games, hobbies, and tricycles	100	193	163	260	171
Personal care products and services	100	200	161	186	245
Cosmetics, perfume, bath preparations	100	233	179	178	319
Education	100	378	140	177	721
College tuition	100	383	142	191	722
All other gifts	100	178	122	141	252
Gifts of out-of-town trip expenses	100	251	194	154	368

Note: Spending on gifts is also included in the product and service categories in other chapters.
Source: Calculations by New Strategist based on the Bureau of Labor Statistics' 2011 Consumer Expenditure Survey

Table 6.11 Gifts for People in Other Households: Total spending by high-income consumer units, 2011

(total annual spending on selected gifts of products and services for people in other households by before-tax income group of high-income consumer units, 2011; consumer units and dollars in thousands)

	total consumer units	$100,000 or more	$100,000–$119,999	$120,000–$149,999	$150,000 or more
Number of consumer units	122,287	21,593	7,045	6,107	8,440
Total spending of all consumer units	$6,078,260,661	$2,110,245,454	$538,917,208	$532,771,260	$1,038,595,847
Gifts, total spending	**126,869,094**	**57,272,409**	**10,750,529**	**12,836,975**	**33,716,281**
Food	**10,292,897**	**5,224,642**	**1,158,691**	**1,305,188**	**2,761,230**
Cakes and cupcakes	275,146	130,854	53,472	46,596	30,553
Candy and chewing gum	979,519	258,900	66,364	56,917	135,884
Food or board at school	2,768,578	2,121,080	357,534	425,841	1,337,656
Catered affairs	1,901,563	1,252,394	335,412	414,971	502,096
Food on trips	303,272	166,266	10,920	95,941	59,249
Alcoholic beverages	**2,033,633**	**1,002,131**	**80,102**	**426,574**	**505,894**
Housing	**23,761,587**	**9,512,364**	**1,856,921**	**2,503,259**	**5,157,937**
Housekeeping supplies	3,033,940	1,163,431	293,636	328,312	544,211
Stationery, stationery supplies, giftwrap	1,504,130	511,322	116,031	164,217	233,197
Postage	299,603	121,569	51,922	28,825	40,343
Household textiles	1,299,911	652,756	161,542	166,233	326,037
Major appliances	848,672	328,214	103,562	55,452	169,138
Small appliances and miscellaneous housewares	1,342,711	633,755	182,677	135,575	314,896
Infants' equipment	431,673	233,420	43,256	52,337	138,585
Household decorative items	1,330,483	423,871	112,297	237,135	77,817
Indoor plants, fresh flowers	876,798	258,684	62,419	73,711	122,633
Computers and computer hardware for nonbusiness use	920,821	497,935	77,918	140,156	279,955
Housing while attending school	4,051,368	2,910,520	241,362	549,019	2,120,044
Lodging on trips	511,160	278,118	17,049	173,927	87,185
Natural gas (renter)	220,117	21,377	7,186	4,519	9,622
Electricity (renter)	1,296,242	75,576	19,796	12,458	43,382
Babysitting	182,208	63,052	15,006	14,413	33,507
Day care centers, nurseries, and preschools	1,066,343	409,619	58,192	11,359	339,963
Apparel and services	**25,066,389**	**7,463,836**	**2,062,494**	**2,121,633**	**3,288,730**
Men and boys, aged 2 or older	6,488,548	2,000,376	473,847	613,998	919,200
Women and girls, aged 2 or older	9,462,568	2,697,182	709,643	670,304	1,321,029
Children under age 2	2,717,217	737,401	385,643	140,827	204,417
Watches	778,968	314,178	64,884	172,217	80,180
Jewelry	1,425,866	531,620	111,663	232,005	187,874
Footwear	3,975,550	1,125,643	280,532	287,029	560,163
Transportation	**11,058,413**	**5,653,695**	**907,044**	**1,737,930**	**3,007,847**
Vehicle purchases	4,942,841	2,710,353	426,645	711,099	1,572,541
Gasoline on trips	2,451,854	934,977	217,479	269,319	448,080
Airline fares	1,597,068	894,382	95,812	352,191	446,392
Intercity train fares	155,304	77,735	8,736	29,314	39,584
Ship fares	912,261	611,082	56,149	233,715	321,142
Health care	**3,693,067**	**1,654,456**	**440,453**	**242,265**	**972,626**
Entertainment	**11,358,017**	**4,926,659**	**1,150,801**	**1,171,323**	**2,608,044**
Toys, games, hobbies, and tricycles	3,188,022	1,084,832	299,483	414,238	375,242
Personal care products and services	**1,774,384**	**628,140**	**164,783**	**164,828**	**299,620**
Cosmetics, perfume, bath preparations	1,016,205	418,040	104,548	90,506	223,407
Education	**26,405,432**	**17,608,876**	**2,131,887**	**2,337,760**	**13,138,970**
College tuition	22,188,976	14,995,475	1,816,694	2,115,770	11,062,055
All other gifts	**11,166,026**	**3,512,533**	**787,490**	**786,459**	**1,940,018**
Gifts of out-of-town trip expenses	6,400,502	2,832,354	714,997	493,690	1,623,518

Note: Numbers may not add to total because of rounding and because not all categories are shown. Spending on gifts is also included in the product and service categories in other chapters.
Source: Calculations by New Strategist based on the Bureau of Labor Statistics' 2011 Consumer Expenditure Survey

Table 6.12 Gifts for People in Other Households: Market shares by high-income consumer units, 2011

(percentage of total annual spending on selected gifts of products and services for people in other households accounted for by before-tax income group of high-income consumer units, 2011)

	total consumer units	$100,000 or more	$100,000– $119,999	$120,000– $149,999	$150,000 or more
Share of total consumer units	100.0%	17.7%	5.8%	5.0%	6.9%
Share of total before-tax income	100.0	47.1	9.8	10.5	26.8
Share of total spending	100.0	34.7	8.9	8.8	17.1
Share of gifts spending	100.0	45.1	8.5	10.1	26.6
Food	100.0	50.8	11.3	12.7	26.8
Cakes and cupcakes	100.0	47.6	19.4	16.9	11.1
Candy and chewing gum	100.0	26.4	6.8	5.8	13.9
Food or board at school	100.0	76.6	12.9	15.4	48.3
Catered affairs	100.0	65.9	17.6	21.8	26.4
Food on trips	100.0	54.8	3.6	31.6	19.5
Alcoholic beverages	100.0	49.3	3.9	21.0	24.9
Housing	100.0	40.0	7.8	10.5	21.7
Housekeeping supplies	100.0	38.3	9.7	10.8	17.9
Stationery, stationery supplies, giftwrap	100.0	34.0	7.7	10.9	15.5
Postage	100.0	40.6	17.3	9.6	13.5
Household textiles	100.0	50.2	12.4	12.8	25.1
Major appliances	100.0	38.7	12.2	6.5	19.9
Small appliances and miscellaneous housewares	100.0	47.2	13.6	10.1	23.5
Infants' equipment	100.0	54.1	10.0	12.1	32.1
Household decorative items	100.0	31.9	8.4	17.8	5.8
Indoor plants, fresh flowers	100.0	29.5	7.1	8.4	14.0
Computers and computer hardware for nonbusiness use	100.0	54.1	8.5	15.2	30.4
Housing while attending school	100.0	71.8	6.0	13.6	52.3
Lodging on trips	100.0	54.4	3.3	34.0	17.1
Natural gas (renter)	100.0	9.7	3.3	2.1	4.4
Electricity (renter)	100.0	5.8	1.5	1.0	3.3
Babysitting	100.0	34.6	8.2	7.9	18.4
Day care centers, nurseries, and preschools	100.0	38.4	5.5	1.1	31.9
Apparel and services	100.0	29.8	8.2	8.5	13.1
Men and boys, aged 2 or older	100.0	30.8	7.3	9.5	14.2
Women and girls, aged 2 or older	100.0	28.5	7.5	7.1	14.0
Children under age 2	100.0	27.1	14.2	5.2	7.5
Watches	100.0	40.3	8.3	22.1	10.3
Jewelry	100.0	37.3	7.8	16.3	13.2
Footwear	100.0	28.3	7.1	7.2	14.1
Transportation	100.0	51.1	8.2	15.7	27.2
Vehicle purchases	100.0	54.8	8.6	14.4	31.8
Gasoline on trips	100.0	38.1	8.9	11.0	18.3
Airline fares	100.0	56.0	6.0	22.1	28.0
Intercity train fares	100.0	50.1	5.6	18.9	25.5
Ship fares	100.0	67.0	6.2	25.6	35.2
Health care	100.0	44.8	11.9	6.6	26.3
Entertainment	100.0	43.4	10.1	10.3	23.0
Toys, games, hobbies, and tricycles	100.0	34.0	9.4	13.0	11.8
Personal care products and services	100.0	35.4	9.3	9.3	16.9
Cosmetics, perfume, bath preparations	100.0	41.1	10.3	8.9	22.0
Education	100.0	66.7	8.1	8.9	49.8
College tuition	100.0	67.6	8.2	9.5	49.9
All other gifts	100.0	31.5	7.1	7.0	17.4
Gifts of out-of-town trip expenses	100.0	44.3	11.2	7.7	25.4

Note: Numbers may not add to total because of rounding. "–" means sample is too small to make a reliable estimate. Spending on gifts is also included in the product and service categories in other chapters.
Source: Calculations by New Strategist based on the Bureau of Labor Statistics' 2011 Consumer Expenditure Survey

Table 6.13 Gifts for People in Other Households: Average spending by household type, 2011

(average annual spending of consumer units on selected gifts of products and services for people in other households by type of consumer unit, 2011)

	total married couples	married couples, no children	married couples with children				single parent with child under age 18	single person
			total	oldest child under age 6	oldest child aged 6 to 17	oldest child aged 18 or older		
Number of consumer units (in 000s)	60,144	25,270	29,097	5,825	14,661	8,612	6,956	36,110
Average number of persons per consumer unit	3.2	2.0	4.0	3.5	4.2	3.9	2.9	1.0
Average before-tax income of consumer units	$86,700.00	$78,823.00	$93,677.00	$91,014.00	$93,029.00	$96,583.00	$37,188.00	$34,540.00
Average spending of consumer units, total	63,971.54	57,658.24	69,724.22	65,947.61	70,708.52	70,411.85	37,553.05	30,613.18
Gifts, average spending	**1,332.08**	**1,634.81**	**1,171.27**	**743.71**	**1,051.92**	**1,660.28**	**449.52**	**845.32**
Food	**121.92**	**161.24**	**100.42**	**51.38**	**101.42**	**132.10**	**29.45**	**59.97**
Cakes and cupcakes	3.05	3.12	2.97	8.22	1.32	2.71	1.02	1.27
Candy and chewing gum	10.13	11.94	9.14	12.91	10.05	5.44	0.90	7.03
Food or board at school	42.05	51.83	40.34	0.27	43.71	61.72	1.58	3.99
Catered affairs	23.96	41.37	12.68	–	2.86	37.96	10.14	9.13
Food on trips	2.80	4.40	1.71	4.84	0.52	1.63	2.00	1.89
Alcoholic beverages	**23.45**	**25.65**	**23.94**	**15.59**	**16.08**	**41.96**	**15.46**	**6.64**
Housing	**251.09**	**300.78**	**229.81**	**156.63**	**189.14**	**349.16**	**87.15**	**154.87**
Housekeeping supplies	33.26	37.36	32.03	28.67	39.00	22.23	5.12	20.39
Stationery, stationery supplies, giftwrap	16.20	16.20	16.70	16.86	19.48	11.94	4.09	10.57
Postage	2.83	2.74	3.37	0.41	4.83	2.63	–	2.43
Household textiles	17.30	20.82	15.32	10.76	11.59	24.32	–	6.59
Major appliances	9.46	9.07	10.52	0.58	6.98	23.27	7.95	4.12
Small appliances and miscellaneous housewares	17.35	27.51	9.27	9.44	10.15	7.80	2.20	6.19
Infants' equipment	6.29	3.52	9.96	38.58	3.52	4.22	1.63	–
Household decorative items	11.71	15.76	7.16	4.73	4.95	12.29	5.13	11.57
Indoor plants, fresh flowers	7.46	10.71	4.95	3.74	4.09	7.22	3.01	8.30
Computers and computer hardware for nonbusiness use	10.65	11.90	10.28	4.94	9.05	15.97	3.27	4.51
Housing while attending school	57.06	56.97	65.16	–	47.88	138.64	3.45	12.05
Lodging on trips	5.25	8.62	2.99	9.07	0.61	2.94	2.66	3.51
Natural gas (renter)	1.58	1.33	1.24	1.46	0.57	2.24	2.02	1.51
Electricity (renter)	8.08	7.46	7.93	9.15	6.10	10.23	33.81	11.06
Babysitting	1.25	0.26	2.29	5.67	2.29	–	0.56	1.42
Day care centers, nurseries, and preschools	4.93	6.30	4.72	1.04	3.09	10.00	2.59	10.13
Apparel and services	**223.86**	**254.12**	**201.62**	**179.39**	**185.04**	**243.52**	**173.63**	**209.28**
Men and boys, aged 2 or older	60.57	74.46	46.81	42.83	40.84	59.56	31.70	56.65
Women and girls, aged 2 or older	84.09	101.27	71.61	23.58	56.97	124.35	72.51	75.91
Children under age 2	26.90	30.00	25.37	57.39	20.92	14.39	21.12	14.70
Watches	9.36	5.05	14.02	15.42	14.59	12.24	–	6.26
Jewelry	7.62	11.17	4.65	2.32	3.96	7.41	7.12	20.26
Footwear	33.18	30.44	36.29	37.86	45.76	19.40	40.24	33.94
Transportation	**117.27**	**170.38**	**77.40**	**76.61**	**71.78**	**87.42**	**45.28**	**64.70**
Vehicle purchases	49.32	84.84	19.26	–	23.60	24.90	16.17	29.06
Gasoline on trips	27.23	36.40	20.51	15.28	21.45	22.45	11.01	13.13
Airline fares	17.77	21.26	16.02	29.21	11.25	15.22	7.58	9.36
Intercity train fares	1.71	2.15	1.46	2.85	1.10	1.13	0.87	1.11
Ship fares	11.05	13.09	11.01	20.82	7.31	10.65	4.36	4.79
Health care	**25.95**	**29.61**	**23.74**	**9.77**	**12.98**	**51.27**	**7.87**	**44.38**
Entertainment	**127.00**	**163.69**	**98.89**	**60.10**	**93.72**	**131.20**	**22.03**	**49.76**
Toys, games, hobbies, and tricycles	37.50	39.07	37.13	27.91	39.38	38.69	5.67	11.44
Personal care products and services	**22.25**	**30.09**	**16.75**	**28.08**	**14.48**	**14.01**	**3.02**	**7.53**
Cosmetics, perfume, bath preparations	13.56	17.61	11.26	24.95	10.26	5.01	–	3.63
Education	**305.89**	**316.48**	**329.60**	**104.57**	**312.22**	**512.02**	**8.67**	**183.29**
College tuition	267.22	272.44	295.13	85.12	292.51	441.64	6.36	136.16
All other gifts	**111.17**	**180.13**	**66.96**	**60.15**	**53.72**	**93.68**	**56.93**	**62.45**
Gifts of out-of-town trip expenses	72.35	128.63	33.89	40.89	28.34	38.60	22.62	35.00

Note: Average spending figures for total consumer units can be found on Average Spending by Age and Average Spending by Region tables. "–" means sample is too small to make a reliable estimate.
Subcategories may not add to total because some are not shown. Spending on gifts is also included in the product and service categories in other chapters.
Source: Bureau of Labor Statistics, unpublished tables from the 2011 Consumer Expenditure Survey

Table 6.14 Gifts for People in Other Households: Indexed spending by household type, 2011

(indexed average annual spending of consumer units on selected gifts of products and services for people in other households by type of consumer unit, 2011; index definition: an index of 100 is the average for all consumer units; an index of 125 means that spending by consumer units in that group is 25 percent above the average for all consumer units; an index of 75 indicates spending that is 25 percent below the average for all consumer units)

	total married couples	married couples, no children	married couples with children				single parent with child under age 18	single person
			total	oldest child under age 6	oldest child aged 6 to 17	oldest child aged 18 or older		
Average spending of consumer units, total	$63,972	$57,658	$69,724	$65,948	$70,709	$70,412	$37,553	$30,613
Average spending of consumer units, index	129	116	140	133	142	142	76	62
Gifts, spending index	**128**	**158**	**113**	**72**	**101**	**160**	**43**	**81**
Food	**145**	**192**	**119**	**61**	**120**	**157**	**35**	**71**
Cakes and cupcakes	136	139	132	365	59	120	45	56
Candy and chewing gum	126	149	114	161	125	68	11	88
Food or board at school	186	229	178	1	193	273	7	18
Catered affairs	154	266	82	–	18	244	65	59
Food on trips	113	177	69	195	21	66	81	76
Alcoholic beverages	**141**	**154**	**144**	**94**	**97**	**252**	**93**	**40**
Housing	**129**	**155**	**118**	**81**	**97**	**180**	**45**	**80**
Housekeeping supplies	134	151	129	116	157	90	21	82
Stationery, stationery supplies, giftwrap	132	132	136	137	158	97	33	86
Postage	116	112	138	17	197	107	–	99
Household textiles	163	196	144	101	109	229	–	62
Major appliances	136	131	152	8	101	335	115	59
Small appliances and miscellaneous housewares	158	251	84	86	92	71	20	56
Infants' equipment	178	100	282	1093	100	120	46	–
Household decorative items	108	145	66	43	45	113	47	106
Indoor plants, fresh flowers	104	149	69	52	57	101	42	116
Computers and computer hardware for nonbusiness use	141	158	137	66	120	212	43	60
Housing while attending school	172	172	197	–	145	418	10	36
Lodging on trips	126	206	72	217	15	70	64	84
Natural gas (renter)	88	74	69	81	32	124	112	84
Electricity (renter)	76	70	75	86	58	97	319	104
Babysitting	84	17	154	381	154	–	38	95
Day care centers, nurseries, and preschools	57	72	54	12	35	115	30	116
Apparel and services	**109**	**124**	**98**	**88**	**90**	**119**	**85**	**102**
Men and boys, aged 2 or older	114	140	88	81	77	112	60	107
Women and girls, aged 2 or older	109	131	93	30	74	161	94	98
Children under age 2	121	135	114	258	94	65	95	66
Watches	147	79	220	242	229	192	–	98
Jewelry	65	96	40	20	34	64	61	174
Footwear	102	94	112	116	141	60	124	104
Transportation	**130**	**188**	**86**	**85**	**79**	**97**	**50**	**72**
Vehicle purchases	122	210	48	–	58	62	40	72
Gasoline on trips	136	182	102	76	107	112	55	65
Airline fares	136	163	123	224	86	117	58	72
Intercity train fares	135	169	115	224	87	89	69	87
Ship fares	148	175	148	279	98	143	58	64
Health care	**86**	**98**	**79**	**32**	**43**	**170**	**26**	**147**
Entertainment	**137**	**176**	**106**	**65**	**101**	**141**	**24**	**54**
Toys, games, hobbies, and tricycles	144	150	142	107	151	148	22	44
Personal care products and services	**153**	**207**	**115**	**194**	**100**	**97**	**21**	**52**
Cosmetics, perfume, bath preparations	163	212	135	300	123	60	–	44
Education	**142**	**147**	**153**	**48**	**145**	**237**	**4**	**85**
College tuition	147	150	163	47	161	243	4	75
All other gifts	**122**	**197**	**73**	**66**	**59**	**103**	**62**	**68**
Gifts of out-of-town trip expenses	138	246	65	78	54	74	43	67

Note: Spending index for total consumer units is 100. "–" means sample is too small to make a reliable estimate. Spending on gifts is also included in the product and service categories in other chapters.
Source: Calculations by New Strategist based on the Bureau of Labor Statistics' 2011 Consumer Expenditure Survey

Table 6.15 Gifts for People in Other Households: Total spending by household type, 2011

(total annual spending on selected gifts of products and services for people in other households by consumer unit type, 2011; consumer units and dollars in thousands)

	total married couples	married couples, no children	married couples with children				single parent with child under age 18	single person
			total	oldest child under age 6	oldest child aged 6 to 17	oldest child aged 18 or older		
Number of consumer units	60,144	25,270	29,097	5,825	14,661	8,612	6,956	36,110
Total spending of all consumer units	$3,847,504,302	$1,457,023,725	$2,028,765,629	$384,144,828	$1,036,657,612	$606,386,852	$261,219,016	$1,105,441,930
Gifts, total spending	**80,116,620**	**41,311,649**	**34,080,443**	**4,332,111**	**15,422,199**	**14,298,331**	**3,126,861**	**30,524,505**
Food	**7,332,756**	**4,074,535**	**2,921,921**	**299,289**	**1,486,919**	**1,137,645**	**204,854**	**2,165,517**
Cakes and cupcakes	183,439	78,842	86,418	47,882	19,353	23,339	7,095	45,860
Candy and chewing gum	609,259	301,724	265,947	75,201	147,343	46,849	6,260	253,853
Food or board at school	2,529,055	1,309,744	1,173,773	1,573	640,832	531,533	10,990	144,079
Catered affairs	1,441,050	1,045,420	368,950	–	41,930	326,912	70,534	329,684
Food on trips	168,403	111,188	49,756	28,193	7,624	14,038	13,912	68,248
Alcoholic beverages	**1,410,377**	**648,176**	**696,582**	**90,812**	**235,749**	**361,360**	**107,540**	**239,770**
Housing	**15,101,557**	**7,600,711**	**6,686,782**	**912,370**	**2,772,982**	**3,006,966**	**606,215**	**5,592,356**
Housekeeping supplies	2,000,389	944,087	931,977	167,003	571,779	191,445	35,615	736,283
Stationery, stationery supplies, giftwrap	974,333	409,374	485,920	98,210	285,596	102,827	28,450	381,683
Postage	170,208	69,240	98,057	2,388	70,813	22,650	–	87,747
Household textiles	1,040,491	526,121	445,766	62,677	169,921	209,444	–	237,965
Major appliances	568,962	229,199	306,100	3,379	102,334	200,401	55,300	148,773
Small appliances and miscellaneous housewares	1,043,498	695,178	269,729	54,988	148,809	67,174	15,303	223,521
Infants' equipment	378,306	88,950	289,806	224,729	51,607	36,343	11,338	–
Household decorative items	704,286	398,255	208,335	27,552	72,572	105,841	35,684	417,793
Indoor plants, fresh flowers	448,674	270,642	144,030	21,786	59,963	62,179	20,938	299,713
Computers and computer hardware for nonbusiness use	640,534	300,713	299,117	28,776	132,682	137,534	22,746	162,856
Housing while attending school	3,431,817	1,439,632	1,895,961	–	701,969	1,193,968	23,998	435,126
Lodging on trips	315,756	217,827	87,000	52,833	8,943	25,319	18,503	126,746
Natural gas (renter)	95,028	33,609	36,080	8,505	8,357	19,291	14,051	54,526
Electricity (renter)	485,964	188,514	230,739	53,299	89,432	88,101	235,182	399,377
Babysitting	75,180	6,570	66,632	33,028	33,574	–	3,895	51,276
Day care centers, nurseries, and preschools	296,510	159,201	137,338	6,058	45,302	86,120	18,016	365,794
Apparel and services	**13,463,836**	**6,421,612**	**5,866,537**	**1,044,947**	**2,712,871**	**2,097,194**	**1,207,770**	**7,557,101**
Men and boys, aged 2 or older	3,642,922	1,881,604	1,362,031	249,485	598,755	512,931	220,505	2,045,632
Women and girls, aged 2 or older	5,057,509	2,559,093	2,083,636	137,354	835,237	1,070,902	504,380	2,741,110
Children under age 2	1,617,874	758,100	738,191	334,297	306,708	123,927	146,911	530,817
Watches	562,948	127,614	407,940	89,822	213,904	105,411	–	226,049
Jewelry	458,297	282,266	135,301	13,514	58,058	63,815	49,527	731,589
Footwear	1,995,578	769,219	1,055,930	220,535	670,887	167,073	279,909	1,225,573
Transportation	**7,053,087**	**4,305,503**	**2,252,108**	**446,253**	**1,052,367**	**752,861**	**314,968**	**2,336,317**
Vehicle purchases	2,966,302	2,143,907	560,408	–	346,000	214,439	112,479	1,049,357
Gasoline on trips	1,637,721	919,828	596,779	89,006	314,478	193,339	76,586	474,124
Airline fares	1,068,759	537,240	466,134	170,148	164,936	131,075	52,726	337,990
Intercity train fares	102,846	54,331	42,482	16,601	16,127	9,732	6,052	40,082
Ship fares	664,591	330,784	320,358	121,277	107,172	91,718	30,328	172,967
Health care	**1,560,737**	**748,245**	**690,763**	**56,910**	**190,300**	**441,537**	**54,744**	**1,602,562**
Entertainment	**7,638,288**	**4,136,446**	**2,877,402**	**350,083**	**1,374,029**	**1,129,894**	**153,241**	**1,796,834**
Toys, games, hobbies, and tricycles	2,255,400	987,299	1,080,372	162,576	577,350	333,198	39,441	413,098
Personal care products and services	**1,338,204**	**760,374**	**487,375**	**163,566**	**212,291**	**120,654**	**21,007**	**271,908**
Cosmetics, perfume, bath preparations	815,553	445,005	327,632	145,334	150,422	43,146	–	131,079
Education	**18,397,448**	**7,997,450**	**9,590,371**	**609,120**	**4,577,457**	**4,409,516**	**60,309**	**6,618,602**
College tuition	16,071,680	6,884,559	8,587,398	495,824	4,288,489	3,803,404	44,240	4,916,738
All other gifts	**6,686,208**	**4,551,885**	**1,948,335**	**350,374**	**787,589**	**806,772**	**396,005**	**2,255,070**
Gifts of out-of-town trip expenses	4,351,418	3,250,480	986,097	238,184	415,493	332,423	157,345	1,263,850

Note: Total spending figures for total consumer units can be found on Total Spending by Age and Total Spending by Region tables. Spending by type of consumer unit does not add to total because not all types of consumer units are shown. "–" means sample is too small to make a reliable estimate.
Source: Calculations by New Strategist based on the Bureau of Labor Statistics' 2011 Consumer Expenditure Survey

Table 6.16 Gifts for People in Other Households: Market shares by household type, 2011

(percentage of total annual spending on selected gifts of products and services for people in other households accounted for by types of consumer units, 2011)

	total married couples	married couples, no children	married couples with children				single parent with child under age 18	single person
			total	oldest child under age 6	oldest child aged 6 to 17	oldest child aged 18 or older		
Share of total consumer units	49.2%	20.7%	23.8%	4.8%	12.0%	7.0%	5.7%	29.5%
Share of total before-tax income	67.0	25.6	35.0	6.8	17.5	10.7	3.3	16.0
Share of total spending	63.3	24.0	33.4	6.3	17.1	10.0	4.3	18.2
Share of gifts spending	63.1	32.6	26.9	3.4	12.2	11.3	2.5	24.1
Food	71.2	39.6	28.4	2.9	14.4	11.1	2.0	21.0
Cakes and cupcakes	66.7	28.7	31.4	17.4	7.0	8.5	2.6	16.7
Candy and chewing gum	62.2	30.8	27.2	7.7	15.0	4.8	0.6	25.9
Food or board at school	91.3	47.3	42.4	0.1	23.1	19.2	0.4	5.2
Catered affairs	75.8	55.0	19.4	–	2.2	17.2	3.7	17.3
Food on trips	55.5	36.7	16.4	9.3	2.5	4.6	4.6	22.5
Alcoholic beverages	69.4	31.9	34.3	4.5	11.6	17.8	5.3	11.8
Housing	63.6	32.0	28.1	3.8	11.7	12.7	2.6	23.5
Housekeeping supplies	65.9	31.1	30.7	5.5	18.8	6.3	1.2	24.3
Stationery, stationery supplies, giftwrap	64.8	27.2	32.3	6.5	19.0	6.8	1.9	25.4
Postage	56.8	23.1	32.7	0.8	23.6	7.6	–	29.3
Household textiles	80.0	40.5	34.3	4.8	13.1	16.1	–	18.3
Major appliances	67.0	27.0	36.1	0.4	12.1	23.6	6.5	17.5
Small appliances and miscellaneous housewares	77.7	51.8	20.1	4.1	11.1	5.0	1.1	16.6
Infants' equipment	87.6	20.6	67.1	52.1	12.0	8.4	2.6	–
Household decorative items	52.9	29.9	15.7	2.1	5.5	8.0	2.7	31.4
Indoor plants, fresh flowers	51.2	30.9	16.4	2.5	6.8	7.1	2.4	34.2
Computers and computer hardware for nonbusiness use	69.6	32.7	32.5	3.1	14.4	14.9	2.5	17.7
Housing while attending school	84.7	35.5	46.8	–	17.3	29.5	0.6	10.7
Lodging on trips	61.8	42.6	17.0	10.3	1.7	5.0	3.6	24.8
Natural gas (renter)	43.2	15.3	16.4	3.9	3.8	8.8	6.4	24.8
Electricity (renter)	37.5	14.5	17.8	4.1	6.9	6.8	18.1	30.8
Babysitting	41.3	3.6	36.6	18.1	18.4	–	2.1	28.1
Day care centers, nurseries, and preschools	27.8	14.9	12.9	0.6	4.2	8.1	1.7	34.3
Apparel and services	53.7	25.6	23.4	4.2	10.8	8.4	4.8	30.1
Men and boys, aged 2 or older	56.1	29.0	21.0	3.8	9.2	7.9	3.4	31.5
Women and girls, aged 2 or older	53.4	27.0	22.0	1.5	8.8	11.3	5.3	29.0
Children under age 2	59.5	27.9	27.2	12.3	11.3	4.6	5.4	19.5
Watches	72.3	16.4	52.4	11.5	27.5	13.5	–	29.0
Jewelry	32.1	19.8	9.5	0.9	4.1	4.5	3.5	51.3
Footwear	50.2	19.3	26.6	5.5	16.9	4.2	7.0	30.8
Transportation	63.8	38.9	20.4	4.0	9.5	6.8	2.8	21.1
Vehicle purchases	60.0	43.4	11.3	–	7.0	4.3	2.3	21.2
Gasoline on trips	66.8	37.5	24.3	3.6	12.8	7.9	3.1	19.3
Airline fares	66.9	33.6	29.2	10.7	10.3	8.2	3.3	21.2
Intercity train fares	66.2	35.0	27.4	10.7	10.4	6.3	3.9	25.8
Ship fares	72.9	36.3	35.1	13.3	11.7	10.1	3.3	19.0
Health care	42.3	20.3	18.7	1.5	5.2	12.0	1.5	43.4
Entertainment	67.3	36.4	25.3	3.1	12.1	9.9	1.3	15.8
Toys, games, hobbies, and tricycles	70.7	31.0	33.9	5.1	18.1	10.5	1.2	13.0
Personal care products and services	75.4	42.9	27.5	9.2	12.0	6.8	1.2	15.3
Cosmetics, perfume, bath preparations	80.3	43.8	32.2	14.3	14.8	4.2	–	12.9
Education	69.7	30.3	36.3	2.3	17.3	16.7	0.2	25.1
College tuition	72.4	31.0	38.7	2.2	19.3	17.1	0.2	22.2
All other gifts	59.9	40.8	17.4	3.1	7.1	7.2	3.5	20.2
Gifts of out-of-town trip expenses	68.0	50.8	15.4	3.7	6.5	5.2	2.5	19.7

Note: Market share for total consumer units is 100.0%. Market shares by type of consumer unit do not add to total because not all types of consumer units are shown. "–" means sample is too small to make a reliable estimate.

Source: Calculations by New Strategist based on the Bureau of Labor Statistics' 2011 Consumer Expenditure Survey

Table 6.17 Gifts for People in Other Households: Average spending by race and Hispanic origin, 2011

(average annual spending of consumer units on selected gifts of products and services for people in other households by race and Hispanic origin of consumer unit reference person, 2011)

	total consumer units	Asian	black	Hispanic	non-Hispanic white and other
Number of consumer units (in 000s)	122,287	5,048	15,118	15,222	92,163
Average number of persons per consumer unit	2.5	2.7	2.6	3.4	2.4
Average before-tax income of consumer units	$63,685.00	$85,415.00	$45,552.00	$49,966.00	$68,907.00
Average spending of consumer units, total	49,704.88	60,136.04	36,643.75	42,085.98	53,055.68
Gifts, average spending	**1,037.47**	**1,120.50**	**494.89**	**584.61**	**1,197.92**
Food	**84.17**	**124.04**	**21.33**	**36.25**	**101.68**
Cakes and cupcakes	2.25	2.03	1.06	1.72	2.51
Candy and chewing gum	8.01	9.83	4.22	4.93	9.06
Food or board at school	22.64	25.79	2.69	12.96	27.46
Catered affairs	15.55	56.72	4.90	1.49	19.58
Food on trips	2.48	4.52	0.38	2.17	2.86
Alcoholic beverages	**16.63**	**14.63**	**0.12**	**14.78**	**19.47**
Housing	**194.31**	**246.48**	**100.37**	**91.59**	**225.24**
Housekeeping supplies	24.81	10.88	9.28	7.28	29.88
Stationery, stationery supplies, giftwrap	12.30	6.19	3.35	3.28	15.07
Postage	2.45	2.08	3.49	1.16	2.48
Household textiles	10.63	3.43	1.31	4.46	13.02
Major appliances	6.94	0.25	2.68	9.89	7.14
Small appliances and miscellaneous housewares	10.98	12.86	1.40	1.93	13.88
Infants' equipment	3.53	–	2.62	1.86	3.92
Household decorative items	10.88	0.53	3.50	3.41	13.15
Indoor plants, fresh flowers	7.17	7.07	4.44	4.47	8.05
Computers and computer hardware for nonbusiness use	7.53	4.69	3.71	4.16	8.70
Housing while attending school	33.13	41.38	3.11	5.67	42.51
Lodging on trips	4.18	4.91	0.91	2.68	4.96
Natural gas (renter)	1.80	3.64	2.33	2.78	1.54
Electricity (renter)	10.60	6.43	24.64	9.23	8.49
Babysitting	1.49	5.98	1.73	2.20	1.32
Day care centers, nurseries, and preschools	8.72	6.73	14.31	2.75	8.76
Apparel and services	**204.98**	**174.52**	**188.93**	**202.69**	**208.20**
Men and boys, aged 2 or older	53.06	55.75	45.67	71.73	51.45
Women and girls, aged 2 or older	77.38	66.86	50.85	47.65	86.34
Children under age 2	22.22	6.66	28.20	26.01	20.76
Watches	6.37	12.67	7.80	1.72	6.83
Jewelry	11.66	9.11	3.52	2.30	14.51
Footwear	32.51	23.46	52.62	53.00	26.04
Transportation	**90.43**	**90.06**	**43.40**	**44.70**	**105.47**
Vehicle purchases	40.42	10.15	17.54	11.87	48.78
Gasoline on trips	20.05	11.43	6.50	9.59	23.96
Airline fares	13.06	37.00	9.39	12.45	13.74
Intercity train fares	1.27	2.59	0.86	1.20	1.35
Ship fares	7.46	20.06	3.93	5.82	8.29
Health care	**30.20**	**20.66**	**3.53**	**17.70**	**36.55**
Entertainment	**92.88**	**54.82**	**16.66**	**56.91**	**111.07**
Toys, games, hobbies, and tricycles	26.07	6.59	8.87	30.47	28.53
Personal care products and services	**14.51**	**20.13**	**5.37**	**9.34**	**17.04**
Cosmetics, perfume, bath preparations	8.31	15.87	1.44	2.89	10.19
Education	**215.93**	**191.08**	**81.72**	**46.14**	**265.43**
College tuition	181.45	173.38	69.70	39.80	222.75
All other gifts	**91.31**	**184.08**	**31.55**	**64.06**	**105.36**
Gifts of out-of-town trip expenses	52.34	97.16	11.70	16.75	64.78

Note: "Asian" and "black" include Hispanics and non-Hispanics who identify themselves as being of the respective race alone. "Hispanic" includes people of any race who identify themselves as Hispanic. "Other" includes people who identify themselves as non-Hispanic and as Alaska Native, American Indian, Asian (who are also included in the "Asian" column), or Native Hawaiian or other Pacific Islander, as well as non-Hispanics reporting more than one race. "–" means sample is too small to make a reliable estimate. Numbers may not add to total because not all categories are shown. Spending on gifts is also included in the product and service categories in other chapters.
Source: Bureau of Labor Statistics, unpublished tables from the 2011 Consumer Expenditure Survey

Table 6.18 Gifts for People in Other Households: Indexed spending by race and Hispanic origin, 2011

(indexed average annual spending of consumer units on selected gifts of products and services for people in other households by race and Hispanic origin of consumer unit reference person, 2011; index definition: an index of 100 is the average for all consumer units; an index of 125 means that spending by consumer units in that group is 25 percent above the average for all consumer units; an index of 75 indicates spending that is 25 percent below the average for all consumer units)

	total consumer units	Asian	black	Hispanic	non-Hispanic white and other
Average spending of consumer units, total	$49,705	$60,136	$36,644	$42,086	$53,056
Average spending of consumer units, index	100	121	74	85	107
Gifts, spending index	**100**	**108**	**48**	**56**	**115**
Food	**100**	**147**	**25**	**43**	**121**
Cakes and cupcakes	100	90	47	76	112
Candy and chewing gum	100	123	53	62	113
Food or board at school	100	114	12	57	121
Catered affairs	100	365	32	10	126
Food on trips	100	182	15	88	115
Alcoholic beverages	**100**	**88**	**1**	**89**	**117**
Housing	**100**	**127**	**52**	**47**	**116**
Housekeeping supplies	100	44	37	29	120
Stationery, stationery supplies, giftwrap	100	50	27	27	123
Postage	100	85	142	47	101
Household textiles	100	32	12	42	122
Major appliances	100	4	39	143	103
Small appliances and miscellaneous housewares	100	117	13	18	126
Infants' equipment	100	–	74	53	111
Household decorative items	100	5	32	31	121
Indoor plants, fresh flowers	100	99	62	62	112
Computers and computer hardware for nonbusiness use	100	62	49	55	116
Housing while attending school	100	125	9	17	128
Lodging on trips	100	117	22	64	119
Natural gas (renter)	100	202	129	154	86
Electricity (renter)	100	61	232	87	80
Babysitting	100	401	116	148	89
Day care centers, nurseries, and preschools	100	77	164	32	100
Apparel and services	**100**	**85**	**92**	**99**	**102**
Men and boys, aged 2 or older	100	105	86	135	97
Women and girls, aged 2 or older	100	86	66	62	112
Children under age 2	100	30	127	117	93
Watches	100	199	122	27	107
Jewelry	100	78	30	20	124
Footwear	100	72	162	163	80
Transportation	**100**	**100**	**48**	**49**	**117**
Vehicle purchases	100	25	43	29	121
Gasoline on trips	100	57	32	48	120
Airline fares	100	283	72	95	105
Intercity train fares	100	204	68	94	106
Ship fares	100	269	53	78	111
Health care	**100**	**68**	**12**	**59**	**121**
Entertainment	**100**	**59**	**18**	**61**	**120**
Toys, games, hobbies, and tricycles	100	25	34	117	109
Personal care products and services	**100**	**139**	**37**	**64**	**117**
Cosmetics, perfume, bath preparations	100	191	17	35	123
Education	**100**	**88**	**38**	**21**	**123**
College tuition	100	96	38	22	123
All other gifts	**100**	**202**	**35**	**70**	**115**
Gifts of out-of-town trip expenses	100	186	22	32	124

Note: "Asian" and "black" include Hispanics and non-Hispanics who identify themselves as being of the respective race alone. "Hispanic" includes people of any race who identify themselves as Hispanic. "Other" includes people who identify themselves as non-Hispanic and as Alaska Native, American Indian, Asian (who are also included in the "Asian" column), or Native Hawaiian or other Pacific Islander, as well as non-Hispanics reporting more than one race. "–" means sample is too small to make a reliable estimate. Spending on gifts is also included in the product and service categories in other chapters.
Source: Calculations by New Strategist based on the Bureau of Labor Statistics' 2011 Consumer Expenditure Survey

Table 6.19 Gifts for People in Other Households: Total spending by race and Hispanic origin, 2011

(total annual spending on selected gifts of products and services for people in other households by consumer unit race and Hispanic origin groups, 2011; consumer units and dollars in thousands)

	total consumer units	Asian	black	Hispanic	non-Hispanic white and other
Number of consumer units	122,287	5,048	15,118	15,222	92,163
Total spending of all consumer units	$6,078,260,661	$303,566,730	$553,980,213	$640,632,788	$4,889,770,636
Gifts, total spending	**126,869,094**	**5,656,284**	**7,481,747**	**8,898,933**	**110,403,901**
Food	**10,292,897**	**626,154**	**322,467**	**551,798**	**9,371,134**
Cakes and cupcakes	275,146	10,247	16,025	26,182	231,329
Candy and chewing gum	979,519	49,622	63,798	75,044	834,997
Food or board at school	2,768,578	130,188	40,667	197,277	2,530,796
Catered affairs	1,901,563	286,323	74,078	22,681	1,804,552
Food on trips	303,272	22,817	5,745	33,032	263,586
Alcoholic beverages	**2,033,633**	**73,852**	**1,814**	**224,981**	**1,794,414**
Housing	**23,761,587**	**1,244,231**	**1,517,394**	**1,394,183**	**20,758,794**
Housekeeping supplies	3,033,940	54,922	140,295	110,816	2,753,830
Stationery, stationery supplies, giftwrap	1,504,130	31,247	50,645	49,928	1,388,896
Postage	299,603	10,500	52,762	17,658	228,564
Household textiles	1,299,911	17,315	19,805	67,890	1,199,962
Major appliances	848,672	1,262	40,516	150,546	658,044
Small appliances and miscellaneous housewares	1,342,711	64,917	21,165	29,378	1,279,222
Infants' equipment	431,673	–	39,609	28,313	361,279
Household decorative items	1,330,483	2,675	52,913	51,907	1,211,943
Indoor plants, fresh flowers	876,798	35,689	67,124	68,042	741,912
Computers and computer hardware for nonbusiness use	920,821	23,675	56,088	63,324	801,818
Housing while attending school	4,051,368	208,886	47,017	86,309	3,917,849
Lodging on trips	511,160	24,786	13,757	40,795	457,128
Natural gas (renter)	220,117	18,375	35,225	42,317	141,931
Electricity (renter)	1,296,242	32,459	372,508	140,499	782,464
Babysitting	182,208	30,187	26,154	33,488	121,655
Day care centers, nurseries, and preschools	1,066,343	33,973	216,339	41,861	807,348
Apparel and services	**25,066,389**	**880,977**	**2,856,244**	**3,085,347**	**19,188,337**
Men and boys, aged 2 or older	6,488,548	281,426	690,439	1,091,874	4,741,786
Women and girls, aged 2 or older	9,462,568	337,509	768,750	725,328	7,957,353
Children under age 2	2,717,217	33,620	426,328	395,924	1,913,304
Watches	778,968	63,958	117,920	26,182	629,473
Jewelry	1,425,866	45,987	53,215	35,011	1,337,285
Footwear	3,975,550	118,426	795,509	806,766	2,399,925
Transportation	**11,058,413**	**454,623**	**656,121**	**680,423**	**9,720,432**
Vehicle purchases	4,942,841	51,237	265,170	180,685	4,495,711
Gasoline on trips	2,451,854	57,699	98,267	145,979	2,208,225
Airline fares	1,597,068	186,776	141,958	189,514	1,266,320
Intercity train fares	155,304	13,074	13,001	18,266	124,420
Ship fares	912,261	101,263	59,414	88,592	764,031
Health care	**3,693,067**	**104,292**	**53,367**	**269,429**	**3,368,558**
Entertainment	**11,358,017**	**276,731**	**251,866**	**866,284**	**10,236,544**
Toys, games, hobbies, and tricycles	3,188,022	33,266	134,097	463,814	2,629,410
Personal care products and services	**1,774,384**	**101,616**	**81,184**	**142,173**	**1,570,458**
Cosmetics, perfume, bath preparations	1,016,205	80,112	21,770	43,992	939,141
Education	**26,405,432**	**964,572**	**1,235,443**	**702,343**	**24,462,825**
College tuition	22,188,976	875,222	1,053,725	605,836	20,529,308
All other gifts	**11,166,026**	**929,236**	**476,973**	**975,121**	**9,710,294**
Gifts of out-of-town trip expenses	6,400,502	490,464	176,881	254,969	5,970,319

Note: "Asian" and "black" include Hispanics and non-Hispanics who identify themselves as being of the respective race alone. "Hispanic" includes people of any race who identify themselves as Hispanic. "Other" includes people who identify themselves as non-Hispanic and as Alaska Native, American Indian, Asian (who are also included in the "Asian" column), or Native Hawaiian or other Pacific Islander, as well as non-Hispanics reporting more than one race. "–" means sample is too small to make a reliable estimate. Spending on gifts is also included in the product and service categories in other chapters.
Source: Calculations by New Strategist based on the Bureau of Labor Statistics' 2011 Consumer Expenditure Survey

Table 6.20 Gifts for People in Other Households: Market shares by race and Hispanic origin, 2011

(percentage of total annual spending on selected gifts of products and services for people in other households accounted for by before-tax income group of high-income consumer units, 2011)

	total consumer units	Asian	black	Hispanic	non-Hispanic white and other
Share of total consumer units	100.0%	4.1%	12.4%	12.4%	75.4%
Share of total before-tax income	100.0	5.5	8.8	9.8	81.5
Share of total spending	100.0	5.0	9.1	10.5	80.4
Share of gifts spending	100.0	4.5	5.9	7.0	87.0
Food	100.0	6.1	3.1	5.4	91.0
Cakes and cupcakes	100.0	3.7	5.8	9.5	84.1
Candy and chewing gum	100.0	5.1	6.5	7.7	85.2
Food or board at school	100.0	4.7	1.5	7.1	91.4
Catered affairs	100.0	15.1	3.9	1.2	94.9
Food on trips	100.0	7.5	1.9	10.9	86.9
Alcoholic beverages	100.0	3.6	0.1	11.1	88.2
Housing	100.0	5.2	6.4	5.9	87.4
Housekeeping supplies	100.0	1.8	4.6	3.7	90.8
Stationery, stationery supplies, giftwrap	100.0	2.1	3.4	3.3	92.3
Postage	100.0	3.5	17.6	5.9	76.3
Household textiles	100.0	1.3	1.5	5.2	92.3
Major appliances	100.0	0.1	4.8	17.7	77.5
Small appliances and miscellaneous housewares	100.0	4.8	1.6	2.2	95.3
Infants' equipment	100.0	–	9.2	6.6	83.7
Household decorative items	100.0	0.2	4.0	3.9	91.1
Indoor plants, fresh flowers	100.0	4.1	7.7	7.8	84.6
Computers and computer hardware for nonbusiness use	100.0	2.6	6.1	6.9	87.1
Housing while attending school	100.0	5.2	1.2	2.1	96.7
Lodging on trips	100.0	4.8	2.7	8.0	89.4
Natural gas (renter)	100.0	8.3	16.0	19.2	64.5
Electricity (renter)	100.0	2.5	28.7	10.8	60.4
Babysitting	100.0	16.6	14.4	18.4	66.8
Day care centers, nurseries, and preschools	100.0	3.2	20.3	3.9	75.7
Apparel and services	100.0	3.5	11.4	12.3	76.6
Men and boys, aged 2 or older	100.0	4.3	10.6	16.8	73.1
Women and girls, aged 2 or older	100.0	3.6	8.1	7.7	84.1
Children under age 2	100.0	1.2	15.7	14.6	70.4
Watches	100.0	8.2	15.1	3.4	80.8
Jewelry	100.0	3.2	3.7	2.5	93.8
Footwear	100.0	3.0	20.0	20.3	60.4
Transportation	100.0	4.1	5.9	6.2	87.9
Vehicle purchases	100.0	1.0	5.4	3.7	91.0
Gasoline on trips	100.0	2.4	4.0	6.0	90.1
Airline fares	100.0	11.7	8.9	11.9	79.3
Intercity train fares	100.0	8.4	8.4	11.8	80.1
Ship fares	100.0	11.1	6.5	9.7	83.8
Health care	100.0	2.8	1.4	7.3	91.2
Entertainment	100.0	2.4	2.2	7.6	90.1
Toys, games, hobbies, and tricycles	100.0	1.0	4.2	14.5	82.5
Personal care products and services	100.0	5.7	4.6	8.0	88.5
Cosmetics, perfume, bath preparations	100.0	7.9	2.1	4.3	92.4
Education	100.0	3.7	4.7	2.7	92.6
College tuition	100.0	3.9	4.7	2.7	92.5
All other gifts	100.0	8.3	4.3	8.7	87.0
Gifts of out-of-town trip expenses	100.0	7.7	2.8	4.0	93.3

Note: "Asian" and "black" include Hispanics and non-Hispanics who identify themselves as being of the respective race alone. "Hispanic" includes people of any race who identify themselves as Hispanic. "Other" includes people who identify themselves as non-Hispanic and as Alaska Native, American Indian, Asian (who are also included in the "Asian" column), or Native Hawaiian or other Pacific Islander, as well as non-Hispanics reporting more than one race. "–" means sample is too small to make a reliable estimate. Spending on gifts is also included in the product and service categories in other chapters.
Source: Calculations by New Strategist based on the Bureau of Labor Statistics' 2011 Consumer Expenditure Survey

Table 6.21 Gifts for People in Other Households: Average spending by region, 2011

(average annual spending of consumer units on selected gifts of products and services for people in other households by region in which consumer unit lives, 2011)

	total consumer units	Northeast	Midwest	South	West
Number of consumer units (in 000s)	122,287	22,538	27,107	44,901	27,741
Average number of persons per consumer unit	2.5	2.4	2.4	2.5	2.6
Average before-tax income of consumer units	$63,685.00	$71,733.00	$60,897.00	$58,780.00	$67,810.00
Average spending of consumer units, total	49,704.88	54,547.45	47,191.54	45,698.60	54,745.43
Gifts, average spending	**1,037.47**	**1,331.70**	**1,014.44**	**822.56**	**1,171.47**
Food	**84.17**	**113.16**	**94.55**	**60.29**	**89.34**
Cakes and cupcakes	2.25	1.65	2.67	2.79	1.43
Candy and chewing gum	8.01	9.67	8.30	4.50	12.15
Food or board at school	22.64	25.23	29.16	20.87	17.04
Catered affairs	15.55	40.68	11.10	6.07	14.81
Food on trips	2.48	0.97	3.86	2.02	3.09
Alcoholic beverages	**16.63**	**19.54**	**12.78**	**18.24**	**15.45**
Housing	**194.31**	**201.24**	**204.21**	**147.90**	**254.63**
Housekeeping supplies	24.81	29.58	24.09	18.11	32.71
Stationery, stationery supplies, giftwrap	12.30	13.80	12.37	8.58	17.15
Postage	2.45	2.90	1.43	1.90	4.03
Household textiles	10.63	9.27	13.18	8.87	12.12
Major appliances	6.94	4.25	6.70	7.45	8.53
Small appliances and miscellaneous housewares	10.98	8.99	17.94	6.14	13.65
Infants' equipment	3.53	2.82	8.28	1.92	2.04
Household decorative items	10.88	8.86	10.88	9.54	14.76
Indoor plants, fresh flowers	7.17	9.19	6.05	6.28	8.06
Computers and computer hardware for nonbusiness use	7.53	10.04	6.91	7.02	6.94
Housing while attending school	33.13	30.00	38.67	17.80	55.06
Lodging on trips	4.18	2.59	6.68	4.39	2.71
Natural gas (renter)	1.80	2.96	2.09	1.12	1.68
Electricity (renter)	10.60	10.76	8.23	13.02	8.84
Babysitting	1.49	0.17	2.14	1.54	1.82
Day care centers, nurseries, and preschools	8.72	14.67	3.38	9.70	7.49
Apparel and services	**204.98**	**239.24**	**179.95**	**185.24**	**234.68**
Men and boys, aged 2 or older	53.06	66.73	36.92	60.80	45.18
Women and girls, aged 2 or older	77.38	94.00	69.31	59.30	101.74
Children under age 2	22.22	25.21	25.14	21.67	17.78
Watches	6.37	19.27	0.83	3.71	5.71
Jewelry	11.66	10.33	10.80	15.09	8.03
Footwear	32.51	20.79	35.41	23.96	53.35
Transportation	**90.43**	**76.63**	**101.54**	**87.61**	**95.37**
Vehicle purchases	40.42	36.81	44.02	44.00	33.99
Gasoline on trips	20.05	12.63	20.79	19.63	26.05
Airline fares	13.06	9.91	17.08	11.23	14.67
Intercity train fares	1.27	0.91	1.68	1.06	1.51
Ship fares	7.46	7.03	9.03	6.41	7.96
Health care	**30.20**	**37.03**	**37.90**	**18.33**	**36.34**
Entertainment	**92.88**	**134.88**	**85.63**	**73.32**	**97.87**
Toys, games, hobbies, and tricycles	26.07	23.00	32.02	20.47	31.90
Personal care products and services	**14.51**	**21.52**	**9.32**	**12.77**	**16.84**
Cosmetics, perfume, bath preparations	8.31	11.64	7.08	6.43	9.91
Education	**215.93**	**393.20**	**213.62**	**125.82**	**220.02**
College tuition	181.45	324.16	178.66	101.31	197.94
All other gifts	**91.31**	**92.22**	**73.21**	**90.91**	**109.20**
Gifts of out-of-town trip expenses	52.34	65.94	54.63	44.79	51.29

Note: Numbers may not add to total because not all categories are shown. Spending on gifts is also included in the product and service categories in other chapters.
Source: Bureau of Labor Statistics, unpublished tables from the 2011 Consumer Expenditure Survey

Table 6.22 Gifts for People in Other Households: Indexed spending by region, 2011

(indexed average annual spending of consumer units on selected gifts of products and services for people in other households by region in which consumer unit lives, 2011; index definition: an index of 100 is the average for all consumer units; an index of 125 means that spending by consumer units in that group is 25 percent above the average for all consumer units; an index of 75 indicates spending that is 25 percent below the average for all consumer units)

	total consumer units	Northeast	Midwest	South	West
Average spending of consumer units, total	$49,705	$54,547	$47,192	$45,699	$54,745
Average spending of consumer units, index	100	110	95	92	110
Gifts, spending index	**100**	**128**	**98**	**79**	**113**
Food	**100**	**134**	**112**	**72**	**106**
Cakes and cupcakes	100	73	119	124	64
Candy and chewing gum	100	121	104	56	152
Food or board at school	100	111	129	92	75
Catered affairs	100	262	71	39	95
Food on trips	100	39	156	81	125
Alcoholic beverages	**100**	**117**	**77**	**110**	**93**
Housing	**100**	**104**	**105**	**76**	**131**
Housekeeping supplies	100	119	97	73	132
Stationery, stationery supplies, giftwrap	100	112	101	70	139
Postage	100	118	58	78	164
Household textiles	100	87	124	83	114
Major appliances	100	61	97	107	123
Small appliances and miscellaneous housewares	100	82	163	56	124
Infants' equipment	100	80	235	54	58
Household decorative items	100	81	100	88	136
Indoor plants, fresh flowers	100	128	84	88	112
Computers and computer hardware for nonbusiness use	100	133	92	93	92
Housing while attending school	100	91	117	54	166
Lodging on trips	100	62	160	105	65
Natural gas (renter)	100	164	116	62	93
Electricity (renter)	100	102	78	123	83
Babysitting	100	11	144	103	122
Day care centers, nurseries, and preschools	100	168	39	111	86
Apparel and services	**100**	**117**	**88**	**90**	**114**
Men and boys, aged 2 or older	100	126	70	115	85
Women and girls, aged 2 or older	100	121	90	77	131
Children under age 2	100	113	113	98	80
Watches	100	303	13	58	90
Jewelry	100	89	93	129	69
Footwear	100	64	109	74	164
Transportation	**100**	**85**	**112**	**97**	**105**
Vehicle purchases	100	91	109	109	84
Gasoline on trips	100	63	104	98	130
Airline fares	100	76	131	86	112
Intercity train fares	100	72	132	83	119
Ship fares	100	94	121	86	107
Health care	**100**	**123**	**125**	**61**	**120**
Entertainment	**100**	**145**	**92**	**79**	**105**
Toys, games, hobbies, and tricycles	100	88	123	79	122
Personal care products and services	**100**	**148**	**64**	**88**	**116**
Cosmetics, perfume, bath preparations	100	140	85	77	119
Education	**100**	**182**	**99**	**58**	**102**
College tuition	100	179	98	56	109
All other gifts	**100**	**101**	**80**	**100**	**120**
Gifts of out-of-town trip expenses	100	126	104	86	98

Note: Spending on gifts is also included in the product and service categories in other chapters.
Source: Calculations by New Strategist based on the Bureau of Labor Statistics' 2011 Consumer Expenditure Survey

Table 6.23 Gifts for People in Other Households: Total spending by region, 2011

(total annual spending on selected gifts of products and services for people in other households by region in which consumer units live, 2011; consumer units and dollars in thousands)

	total consumer units	Northeast	Midwest	South	West
Number of consumer units	122,287	22,538	27,107	44,901	27,741
Total spending of all consumer units	$6,078,260,661	$1,229,390,428	$1,279,221,075	$2,051,912,839	$1,518,692,974
Gifts, total spending	126,869,094	30,013,855	27,498,425	36,933,767	32,497,749
Food	10,292,897	2,550,400	2,562,967	2,707,081	2,478,381
Cakes and cupcakes	275,146	37,188	72,376	125,274	39,670
Candy and chewing gum	979,519	217,942	224,988	202,055	337,053
Food or board at school	2,768,578	568,634	790,440	937,084	472,707
Catered affairs	1,901,563	916,846	300,888	272,549	410,844
Food on trips	303,272	21,862	104,633	90,700	85,720
Alcoholic beverages	2,033,633	440,393	346,427	818,994	428,598
Housing	23,761,587	4,535,547	5,535,520	6,640,858	7,063,691
Housekeeping supplies	3,033,940	666,674	653,008	813,157	907,408
Stationery, stationery supplies, giftwrap	1,504,130	311,024	335,314	385,251	475,758
Postage	299,603	65,360	38,763	85,312	111,796
Household textiles	1,299,911	208,927	357,270	398,272	336,221
Major appliances	848,672	95,787	181,617	334,512	236,631
Small appliances and miscellaneous housewares	1,342,711	202,617	486,300	275,692	378,665
Infants' equipment	431,673	63,557	224,446	86,210	56,592
Household decorative items	1,330,483	199,687	294,924	428,356	409,457
Indoor plants, fresh flowers	876,798	207,124	163,997	281,978	223,592
Computers and computer hardware for nonbusiness use	920,821	226,282	187,309	315,205	192,523
Housing while attending school	4,051,368	676,140	1,048,228	799,238	1,527,419
Lodging on trips	511,160	58,373	181,075	197,115	75,178
Natural gas (renter)	220,117	66,712	56,654	50,289	46,605
Electricity (renter)	1,296,242	242,509	223,091	584,611	245,230
Babysitting	182,208	3,831	58,009	69,148	50,489
Day care centers, nurseries, and preschools	1,066,343	330,632	91,622	435,540	207,780
Apparel and services	25,066,389	5,391,991	4,877,905	8,317,461	6,510,258
Men and boys, aged 2 or older	6,488,548	1,503,961	1,000,790	2,729,981	1,253,338
Women and girls, aged 2 or older	9,462,568	2,118,572	1,878,786	2,662,629	2,822,369
Children under age 2	2,717,217	568,183	681,470	973,005	493,235
Watches	778,968	434,307	22,499	166,583	158,401
Jewelry	1,425,866	232,818	292,756	677,556	222,760
Footwear	3,975,550	468,565	959,859	1,075,828	1,479,982
Transportation	11,058,413	1,727,087	2,752,445	3,933,777	2,645,659
Vehicle purchases	4,942,841	829,624	1,193,250	1,975,644	942,917
Gasoline on trips	2,451,854	284,655	563,555	881,407	722,653
Airline fares	1,597,068	223,352	462,988	504,238	406,960
Intercity train fares	155,304	20,510	45,540	47,595	41,889
Ship fares	912,261	158,442	244,776	287,815	220,818
Health care	3,693,067	834,582	1,027,355	823,035	1,008,108
Entertainment	11,358,017	3,039,925	2,321,172	3,292,141	2,715,012
Toys, games, hobbies, and tricycles	3,188,022	518,374	867,966	919,123	884,938
Personal care products and services	1,774,384	485,018	252,637	573,386	467,158
Cosmetics, perfume, bath preparations	1,016,205	262,342	191,918	288,713	274,913
Education	26,405,432	8,861,942	5,790,597	5,649,444	6,103,575
College tuition	22,188,976	7,305,918	4,842,937	4,548,920	5,491,054
All other gifts	11,166,026	2,078,454	1,984,503	4,081,950	3,029,317
Gifts of out-of-town trip expenses	6,400,502	1,486,156	1,480,855	2,011,116	1,422,836

Note: Numbers may not add to total because of rounding and because not all categories are shown. Spending on gifts is also included in the product and service categories in other chapters.
Source: Calculations by New Strategist based on the Bureau of Labor Statistics' 2011 Consumer Expenditure Survey

Table 6.24 Gifts for People in Other Households: Market shares by region, 2011

(percentage of total annual spending on selected gifts of products and services for people in other households accounted for by consumer units by region of residence, 2011)

	total consumer units	Northeast	Midwest	South	West
Share of total consumer units	100.0%	18.4%	22.2%	36.7%	22.7%
Share of total before-tax income	100.0	20.8	21.2	33.9	24.2
Share of total spending	100.0	20.2	21.0	33.8	25.0
Share of gifts spending	100.0	23.7	21.7	29.1	25.6
Food	100.0	24.8	24.9	26.3	24.1
Cakes and cupcakes	100.0	13.5	26.3	45.5	14.4
Candy and chewing gum	100.0	22.2	23.0	20.6	34.4
Food or board at school	100.0	20.5	28.6	33.8	17.1
Catered affairs	100.0	48.2	15.8	14.3	21.6
Food on trips	100.0	7.2	34.5	29.9	28.3
Alcoholic beverages	100.0	21.7	17.0	40.3	21.1
Housing	100.0	19.1	23.3	27.9	29.7
Housekeeping supplies	100.0	22.0	21.5	26.8	29.9
Stationery, stationery supplies, giftwrap	100.0	20.7	22.3	25.6	31.6
Postage	100.0	21.8	12.9	28.5	37.3
Household textiles	100.0	16.1	27.5	30.6	25.9
Major appliances	100.0	11.3	21.4	39.4	27.9
Small appliances and miscellaneous housewares	100.0	15.1	36.2	20.5	28.2
Infants' equipment	100.0	14.7	52.0	20.0	13.1
Household decorative items	100.0	15.0	22.2	32.2	30.8
Indoor plants, fresh flowers	100.0	23.6	18.7	32.2	25.5
Computers and computer hardware for nonbusiness use	100.0	24.6	20.3	34.2	20.9
Housing while attending school	100.0	16.7	25.9	19.7	37.7
Lodging on trips	100.0	11.4	35.4	38.6	14.7
Natural gas (renter)	100.0	30.3	25.7	22.8	21.2
Electricity (renter)	100.0	18.7	17.2	45.1	18.9
Babysitting	100.0	2.1	31.8	37.9	27.7
Day care centers, nurseries, and preschools	100.0	31.0	8.6	40.8	19.5
Apparel and services	100.0	21.5	19.5	33.2	26.0
Men and boys, aged 2 or older	100.0	23.2	15.4	42.1	19.3
Women and girls, aged 2 or older	100.0	22.4	19.9	28.1	29.8
Children under age 2	100.0	20.9	25.1	35.8	18.2
Watches	100.0	55.8	2.9	21.4	20.3
Jewelry	100.0	16.3	20.5	47.5	15.6
Footwear	100.0	11.8	24.1	27.1	37.2
Transportation	100.0	15.6	24.9	35.6	23.9
Vehicle purchases	100.0	16.8	24.1	40.0	19.1
Gasoline on trips	100.0	11.6	23.0	35.9	29.5
Airline fares	100.0	14.0	29.0	31.6	25.5
Intercity train fares	100.0	13.2	29.3	30.6	27.0
Ship fares	100.0	17.4	26.8	31.5	24.2
Health care	100.0	22.6	27.8	22.3	27.3
Entertainment	100.0	26.8	20.4	29.0	23.9
Toys, games, hobbies, and tricycles	100.0	16.3	27.2	28.8	27.8
Personal care products and services	100.0	27.3	14.2	32.3	26.3
Cosmetics, perfume, bath preparations	100.0	25.8	18.9	28.4	27.1
Education	100.0	33.6	21.9	21.4	23.1
College tuition	100.0	32.9	21.8	20.5	24.7
All other gifts	100.0	18.6	17.8	36.6	27.1
Gifts of out-of-town trip expenses	100.0	23.2	23.1	31.4	22.2

Note: Numbers may not add to total because of rounding and because not all categories are shown. Spending on gifts is also included in the product and service categories in other chapters.
Source: Calculations by New Strategist based on the Bureau of Labor Statistics' 2011 Consumer Expenditure Survey

Table 6.25 Gifts for People in Other Households: Average spending by education, 2011

(average annual spending of consumer units on selected gifts of products and services for people in other households by education of consumer unit reference person, 2011)

	total consumer units	less than high school graduate	high school graduate	some college	associate's degree	bachelor's degree or more		
						total	bachelor's degree	graduate degree
Number of consumer units (in 000s)	122,287	16,146	30,810	25,361	12,912	37,058	23,578	13,480
Average number of persons per consumer unit	2.5	2.8	2.5	2.3	2.6	2.5	2.5	2.4
Average before-tax income of consumer units	$63,685.00	$32,564.00	$46,370.00	$52,965.00	$63,664.00	$98,983.00	$90,962.00	$113,013.00
Average spending of consumer units, total	49,704.88	29,950.97	39,704.28	45,355.33	50,819.44	68,902.95	65,051.01	75,731.40
Gifts, average spending	**1,037.47**	**407.59**	**652.56**	**869.65**	**930.62**	**1,768.52**	**1,592.96**	**2,081.37**
Food	**84.17**	**23.21**	**55.00**	**75.05**	**80.63**	**140.06**	**126.61**	**163.28**
Cakes and cupcakes	2.25	0.19	0.88	2.13	2.55	4.07	4.15	3.92
Candy and chewing gum	8.01	2.58	2.78	7.95	11.31	13.12	13.12	13.12
Food or board at school	22.64	0.24	10.01	24.08	16.79	43.97	38.42	53.67
Catered affairs	15.55	1.20	22.14	9.08	10.05	22.66	15.79	34.68
Food on trips	2.48	1.09	0.65	1.96	4.24	4.34	1.84	8.71
Alcoholic beverages	**16.63**	**1.78**	**5.32**	**12.08**	**33.96**	**28.48**	**24.97**	**35.21**
Housing	**194.31**	**86.27**	**101.61**	**185.01**	**205.69**	**316.78**	**300.68**	**345.79**
Housekeeping supplies	24.81	4.61	16.22	20.56	29.62	40.27	39.73	41.34
Stationery, stationery supplies, giftwrap	12.30	1.93	6.05	11.13	16.53	20.47	20.10	21.20
Postage	2.45	0.30	1.83	3.14	1.17	3.71	3.71	3.71
Household textiles	10.63	3.00	10.30	11.07	5.97	14.96	10.48	23.76
Major appliances	6.94	2.59	1.15	7.49	8.38	12.78	9.88	17.85
Small appliances and miscellaneous housewares	10.98	2.95	4.96	9.39	7.76	21.00	19.79	23.16
Infants' equipment	3.53	1.92	3.32	1.35	10.66	3.43	3.89	2.52
Household decorative items	10.88	2.37	5.83	10.89	19.91	15.12	14.71	15.93
Indoor plants, fresh flowers	7.17	2.53	6.90	6.29	9.40	9.25	7.75	11.86
Computers and computer hardware for nonbusiness use	7.53	1.29	3.92	5.47	5.86	15.25	15.37	15.03
Housing while attending school	33.13	4.67	5.22	25.58	9.74	82.05	72.87	98.11
Lodging on trips	4.18	2.18	0.63	3.33	2.05	9.34	3.83	18.99
Natural gas (renter)	1.80	5.98	0.94	1.94	0.73	0.97	1.03	0.86
Electricity (renter)	10.60	22.29	9.27	13.42	6.77	6.00	7.96	2.57
Babysitting	1.49	1.50	0.86	0.66	2.90	2.06	1.86	2.40
Day care centers, nurseries, and preschools	8.72	7.27	4.10	3.52	9.68	16.40	20.24	9.69
Apparel and services	**204.98**	**160.82**	**183.85**	**186.95**	**196.88**	**253.47**	**225.27**	**308.56**
Men and boys, aged 2 or older	53.06	33.33	48.03	50.44	54.71	65.71	54.47	87.49
Women and girls, aged 2 or older	77.38	61.15	62.14	76.24	52.27	104.26	101.07	110.41
Children under age 2	22.22	25.19	21.07	16.92	29.74	23.12	15.74	37.31
Watches	6.37	0.91	4.32	8.32	5.49	9.03	7.28	12.44
Jewelry	11.66	1.84	10.22	10.10	11.18	18.38	21.49	12.93
Footwear	32.51	38.40	36.82	23.83	36.15	31.35	24.13	45.46
Transportation	**90.43**	**38.44**	**32.96**	**86.37**	**76.86**	**168.26**	**168.68**	**167.51**
Vehicle purchases	40.42	23.04	8.12	40.93	25.71	79.60	103.20	38.29
Gasoline on trips	20.05	4.56	12.33	21.07	25.49	30.63	27.92	35.37
Airline fares	13.06	5.05	5.07	8.11	14.38	26.13	15.78	44.23
Intercity train fares	1.27	0.45	0.45	1.00	1.16	2.54	1.63	4.14
Ship fares	7.46	2.92	2.39	7.07	4.48	14.94	9.40	24.64
Health care	**30.20**	**13.50**	**28.60**	**28.79**	**36.71**	**37.43**	**18.40**	**70.83**
Entertainment	**92.88**	**29.52**	**73.69**	**101.50**	**88.81**	**129.07**	**137.62**	**111.64**
Toys, games, hobbies, and tricycles	26.07	13.09	25.64	25.24	27.52	31.29	26.93	39.82
Personal care products and services	**14.51**	**8.69**	**6.75**	**9.56**	**21.41**	**23.77**	**16.30**	**38.41**
Cosmetics, perfume, bath preparations	8.31	4.52	2.81	6.28	8.66	15.24	8.89	27.70
Education	**215.93**	**15.80**	**66.01**	**104.46**	**116.57**	**538.09**	**463.51**	**668.31**
College tuition	181.45	12.04	55.88	89.41	92.17	453.76	371.37	597.87
All other gifts	**91.31**	**29.53**	**97.54**	**78.28**	**70.11**	**129.31**	**108.65**	**165.37**
Gifts of out-of-town trip expenses	52.34	10.67	41.98	28.49	36.69	100.89	89.10	121.52

Note: Numbers may not add to total because not all categories are shown. Spending on gifts is also included in the product and service categories in other chapters.
Source: Bureau of Labor Statistics, unpublished tables from the 2011 Consumer Expenditure Survey

Table 6.26 Gifts for People in Other Households: Indexed spending by education, 2011

(indexed average annual spending of consumer units on selected gifts of products and services for people in other households by education of consumer unit reference person, 2011; index definition: an index of 100 is the average for all consumer units; an index of 125 means that spending by consumer units in that group is 25 percent above the average for all consumer units; an index of 75 indicates spending that is 25 percent below the average for all consumer units)

	total consumer units	less than high school graduate	high school graduate	some college	associate's degree	bachelor's degree or more		
						total	bachelor's degree	graduate degree
Average spending of consumer units, total	$49,705	$29,951	$39,704	$45,355	$50,819	$68,903	$65,051	$75,731
Average spending of consumer units, index	100	60	80	91	102	139	131	152
Gifts, spending index	**100**	**39**	**63**	**84**	**90**	**170**	**154**	**201**
Food	**100**	**28**	**65**	**89**	**96**	**166**	**150**	**194**
Cakes and cupcakes	100	8	39	95	113	181	184	174
Candy and chewing gum	100	32	35	99	141	164	164	164
Food or board at school	100	1	44	106	74	194	170	237
Catered affairs	100	8	142	58	65	146	102	223
Food on trips	100	44	26	79	171	175	74	351
Alcoholic beverages	**100**	**11**	**32**	**73**	**204**	**171**	**150**	**212**
Housing	**100**	**44**	**52**	**95**	**106**	**163**	**155**	**178**
Housekeeping supplies	100	19	65	83	119	162	160	167
Stationery, stationery supplies, giftwrap	100	16	49	90	134	166	163	172
Postage	100	12	75	128	48	151	151	151
Household textiles	100	28	97	104	56	141	99	224
Major appliances	100	37	17	108	121	184	142	257
Small appliances and miscellaneous housewares	100	27	45	86	71	191	180	211
Infants' equipment	100	54	94	38	302	97	110	71
Household decorative items	100	22	54	100	183	139	135	146
Indoor plants, fresh flowers	100	35	96	88	131	129	108	165
Computers and computer hardware for nonbusiness use	100	17	52	73	78	203	204	200
Housing while attending school	100	14	16	77	29	248	220	296
Lodging on trips	100	52	15	80	49	223	92	454
Natural gas (renter)	100	332	52	108	41	54	57	48
Electricity (renter)	100	210	87	127	64	57	75	24
Babysitting	100	101	58	44	195	138	125	161
Day care centers, nurseries, and preschools	100	83	47	40	111	188	232	111
Apparel and services	**100**	**78**	**90**	**91**	**96**	**124**	**110**	**151**
Men and boys, aged 2 or older	100	63	91	95	103	124	103	165
Women and girls, aged 2 or older	100	79	80	99	68	135	131	143
Children under age 2	100	113	95	76	134	104	71	168
Watches	100	14	68	131	86	142	114	195
Jewelry	100	16	88	87	96	158	184	111
Footwear	100	118	113	73	111	96	74	140
Transportation	**100**	**43**	**36**	**96**	**85**	**186**	**187**	**185**
Vehicle purchases	100	57	20	101	64	197	255	95
Gasoline on trips	100	23	61	105	127	153	139	176
Airline fares	100	39	39	62	110	200	121	339
Intercity train fares	100	35	35	79	91	200	128	326
Ship fares	100	39	32	95	60	200	126	330
Health care	**100**	**45**	**95**	**95**	**122**	**124**	**61**	**235**
Entertainment	**100**	**32**	**79**	**109**	**96**	**139**	**148**	**120**
Toys, games, hobbies, and tricycles	100	50	98	97	106	120	103	153
Personal care products and services	**100**	**60**	**47**	**66**	**148**	**164**	**112**	**265**
Cosmetics, perfume, bath preparations	100	54	34	76	104	183	107	333
Education	**100**	**7**	**31**	**48**	**54**	**249**	**215**	**310**
College tuition	100	7	31	49	51	250	205	329
All other gifts	**100**	**32**	**107**	**86**	**77**	**142**	**119**	**181**
Gifts of out-of-town trip expenses	100	20	80	54	70	193	170	232

Note: Spending on gifts is also included in the product and service categories in other chapters.
Source: Calculations by New Strategist based on the Bureau of Labor Statistics' 2011 Consumer Expenditure Survey

Table 6.27 Gifts for People in Other Households: Total spending by education, 2011

(total annual spending on selected gifts of products and services for people in other households by consumer unit educational attainment group, 2011; consumer units and dollars in thousands)

	total consumer units	less than high school graduate	high school graduate	some college	associate's degree	bachelor's degree or more — total	bachelor's degree	graduate degree
Number of consumer units	122,287	16,146	30,810	25,361	12,912	37,058	23,578	13,480
Total spending of all consumer units	$6,078,260,661	$483,588,362	$1,223,288,867	$1,150,256,524	$656,180,609	$2,553,405,521	$1,533,772,714	$1,020,859,272
Gifts, total spending	126,869,094	6,580,948	20,105,374	22,055,194	12,016,165	65,537,814	37,558,811	28,056,868
Food	**10,292,897**	**374,749**	**1,694,550**	**1,903,343**	**1,041,095**	**5,190,343**	**2,985,211**	**2,201,014**
Cakes and cupcakes	275,146	3,068	27,113	54,019	32,926	150,826	97,849	52,842
Candy and chewing gum	979,519	41,657	85,652	201,620	146,035	486,201	309,343	176,858
Food or board at school	2,768,578	3,875	308,408	610,693	216,792	1,629,440	905,867	723,472
Catered affairs	1,901,563	19,375	682,133	230,278	129,766	839,734	372,297	467,486
Food on trips	303,272	17,599	20,027	49,708	54,747	160,832	43,384	117,411
Alcoholic beverages	**2,033,633**	**28,740**	**163,909**	**306,361**	**438,492**	**1,055,412**	**588,743**	**474,631**
Housing	**23,761,587**	**1,392,915**	**3,130,604**	**4,692,039**	**2,655,869**	**11,739,233**	**7,089,433**	**4,661,249**
Housekeeping supplies	3,033,940	74,433	499,738	521,422	382,453	1,492,326	936,754	557,263
Stationery, stationery supplies, giftwrap	1,504,130	31,162	186,401	282,268	213,435	758,577	473,918	285,776
Postage	299,603	4,844	56,382	79,634	15,107	137,485	87,474	50,011
Household textiles	1,299,911	48,438	317,343	280,746	77,085	554,388	247,097	320,285
Major appliances	848,672	41,818	35,432	189,954	108,203	473,601	232,951	240,618
Small appliances and miscellaneous housewares	1,342,711	47,631	152,818	238,140	100,197	778,218	466,609	312,197
Infants' equipment	431,673	31,000	102,289	34,237	137,642	127,109	91,718	33,970
Household decorative items	1,330,483	38,266	179,622	276,181	257,078	560,317	346,832	214,736
Indoor plants, fresh flowers	876,798	40,849	212,589	159,521	121,373	342,787	182,730	159,873
Computers and computer hardware for nonbusiness use	920,821	20,828	120,775	138,725	75,664	565,135	362,394	202,604
Housing while attending school	4,051,368	75,402	160,828	648,734	125,763	3,040,609	1,718,129	1,322,523
Lodging on trips	511,160	35,198	19,410	84,452	26,470	346,122	90,304	255,985
Natural gas (renter)	220,117	96,553	28,961	49,200	9,426	35,946	24,285	11,593
Electricity (renter)	1,296,242	359,894	285,609	340,345	87,414	222,348	187,681	34,644
Babysitting	182,208	24,219	26,497	16,738	37,445	76,339	43,855	32,352
Day care centers, nurseries, and preschools	1,066,343	117,381	126,321	89,271	124,988	607,751	477,219	130,621
Apparel and services	**25,066,389**	**2,596,600**	**5,664,419**	**4,741,239**	**2,542,115**	**9,393,091**	**5,311,416**	**4,159,389**
Men and boys, aged 2 or older	6,488,548	538,146	1,479,804	1,279,209	706,416	2,435,081	1,284,294	1,179,365
Women and girls, aged 2 or older	9,462,568	987,328	1,914,533	1,933,523	674,910	3,863,667	2,383,028	1,488,327
Children under age 2	2,717,217	406,718	649,167	429,108	384,003	856,781	371,118	502,939
Watches	778,968	14,693	133,099	211,004	70,887	334,634	171,648	167,691
Jewelry	1,425,866	29,709	314,878	256,146	144,356	681,126	506,691	174,296
Footwear	3,975,550	620,006	1,134,424	604,353	466,769	1,161,768	568,937	612,801
Transportation	**11,058,413**	**620,652**	**1,015,498**	**2,190,430**	**992,416**	**6,235,379**	**3,977,137**	**2,258,035**
Vehicle purchases	4,942,841	372,004	250,177	1,038,026	331,968	2,949,817	2,433,250	516,149
Gasoline on trips	2,451,854	73,626	379,887	534,356	329,127	1,135,087	658,298	476,788
Airline fares	1,597,068	81,537	156,207	205,678	185,675	968,326	372,061	596,220
Intercity train fares	155,304	7,266	13,865	25,361	14,978	94,127	38,432	55,807
Ship fares	912,261	47,146	73,636	179,302	57,846	553,647	221,633	332,147
Health care	**3,693,067**	**217,971**	**881,166**	**730,143**	**474,000**	**1,387,081**	**433,835**	**954,788**
Entertainment	**11,358,017**	**476,630**	**2,270,389**	**2,574,142**	**1,146,715**	**4,783,076**	**3,244,804**	**1,504,907**
Toys, games, hobbies, and tricycles	3,188,022	211,351	789,968	640,112	355,338	1,159,545	634,956	536,774
Personal care products and services	**1,774,384**	**140,309**	**207,968**	**242,451**	**276,446**	**880,869**	**384,321**	**517,767**
Cosmetics, perfume, bath preparations	1,016,205	72,980	86,576	159,267	111,818	564,764	209,608	373,396
Education	**26,405,432**	**255,107**	**2,033,768**	**2,649,210**	**1,505,152**	**19,940,539**	**10,928,639**	**9,008,819**
College tuition	22,188,976	194,398	1,721,663	2,267,527	1,190,099	16,815,438	8,756,162	8,059,288
All other gifts	**11,166,026**	**476,791**	**3,005,207**	**1,985,259**	**905,260**	**4,791,970**	**2,561,750**	**2,229,188**
Gifts of out-of-town trip expenses	6,400,502	172,278	1,293,404	722,535	473,741	3,738,782	2,100,800	1,638,090

Note: Numbers may not add to total because of rounding and because not all categories are shown. Spending on gifts is also included in the product and service categories in other chapters.
Source: Calculations by New Strategist based on the Bureau of Labor Statistics' 2011 Consumer Expenditure Survey

Table 6.28 Gifts for People in Other Households: Market shares by education, 2011

(percentage of total annual spending on selected gifts of products and services for people in other households accounted for by consumer unit educational attainment groups, 2011)

	total consumer units	less than high school graduate	high school graduate	some college	associate's degree	bachelor's degree or more total	bachelor's degree	graduate degree
Share of total consumer units	100.0%	13.2%	25.2%	20.7%	10.6%	30.3%	19.3%	11.0%
Share of total before-tax income	100.0	6.8	18.3	17.2	10.6	47.1	27.5	19.6
Share of total spending	100.0	8.0	20.1	18.9	10.8	42.0	25.2	16.8
Share of gifts spending	100.0	5.2	15.8	17.4	9.5	51.7	29.6	22.1
Food	100.0	3.6	16.5	18.5	10.1	50.4	29.0	21.4
Cakes and cupcakes	100.0	1.1	9.9	19.6	12.0	54.8	35.6	19.2
Candy and chewing gum	100.0	4.3	8.7	20.6	14.9	49.6	31.6	18.1
Food or board at school	100.0	0.1	11.1	22.1	7.8	58.9	32.7	26.1
Catered affairs	100.0	1.0	35.9	12.1	6.8	44.2	19.6	24.6
Food on trips	100.0	5.8	6.6	16.4	18.1	53.0	14.3	38.7
Alcoholic beverages	100.0	1.4	8.1	15.1	21.6	51.9	29.0	23.3
Housing	100.0	5.9	13.2	19.7	11.2	49.4	29.8	19.6
Housekeeping supplies	100.0	2.5	16.5	17.2	12.6	49.2	30.9	18.4
Stationery, stationery supplies, giftwrap	100.0	2.1	12.4	18.8	14.2	50.4	31.5	19.0
Postage	100.0	1.6	18.8	26.6	5.0	45.9	29.2	16.7
Household textiles	100.0	3.7	24.4	21.6	5.9	42.6	19.0	24.6
Major appliances	100.0	4.9	4.2	22.4	12.7	55.8	27.4	28.4
Small appliances and miscellaneous housewares	100.0	3.5	11.4	17.7	7.5	58.0	34.8	23.3
Infants' equipment	100.0	7.2	23.7	7.9	31.9	29.4	21.2	7.9
Household decorative items	100.0	2.9	13.5	20.8	19.3	42.1	26.1	16.1
Indoor plants, fresh flowers	100.0	4.7	24.2	18.2	13.8	39.1	20.8	18.2
Computers and computer hardware for nonbusiness use	100.0	2.3	13.1	15.1	8.2	61.4	39.4	22.0
Housing while attending school	100.0	1.9	4.0	16.0	3.1	75.1	42.4	32.6
Lodging on trips	100.0	6.9	3.8	16.5	5.2	67.7	17.7	50.1
Natural gas (renter)	100.0	43.9	13.2	22.4	4.3	16.3	11.0	5.3
Electricity (renter)	100.0	27.8	22.0	26.3	6.7	17.2	14.5	2.7
Babysitting	100.0	13.3	14.5	9.2	20.6	41.9	24.1	17.8
Day care centers, nurseries, and preschools	100.0	11.0	11.8	8.4	11.7	57.0	44.8	12.2
Apparel and services	100.0	10.4	22.6	18.9	10.1	37.5	21.2	16.6
Men and boys, aged 2 or older	100.0	8.3	22.8	19.7	10.9	37.5	19.8	18.2
Women and girls, aged 2 or older	100.0	10.4	20.2	20.4	7.1	40.8	25.2	15.7
Children under age 2	100.0	15.0	23.9	15.8	14.1	31.5	13.7	18.5
Watches	100.0	1.9	17.1	27.1	9.1	43.0	22.0	21.5
Jewelry	100.0	2.1	22.1	18.0	10.1	47.8	35.5	12.2
Footwear	100.0	15.6	28.5	15.2	11.7	29.2	14.3	15.4
Transportation	100.0	5.6	9.2	19.8	9.0	56.4	36.0	20.4
Vehicle purchases	100.0	7.5	5.1	21.0	6.7	59.7	49.2	10.4
Gasoline on trips	100.0	3.0	15.5	21.8	13.4	46.3	26.8	19.4
Airline fares	100.0	5.1	9.8	12.9	11.6	60.6	23.3	37.3
Intercity train fares	100.0	4.7	8.9	16.3	9.6	60.6	24.7	35.9
Ship fares	100.0	5.2	8.1	19.7	6.3	60.7	24.3	36.4
Health care	100.0	5.9	23.9	19.8	12.8	37.6	11.7	25.9
Entertainment	100.0	4.2	20.0	22.7	10.1	42.1	28.6	13.2
Toys, games, hobbies, and tricycles	100.0	6.6	24.8	20.1	11.1	36.4	19.9	16.8
Personal care products and services	100.0	7.9	11.7	13.7	15.6	49.6	21.7	29.2
Cosmetics, perfume, bath preparations	100.0	7.2	8.5	15.7	11.0	55.6	20.6	36.7
Education	100.0	1.0	7.7	10.0	5.7	75.5	41.4	34.1
College tuition	100.0	0.9	7.8	10.2	5.4	75.8	39.5	36.3
All other gifts	100.0	4.3	26.9	17.8	8.1	42.9	22.9	20.0
Gifts of out-of-town trip expenses	100.0	2.7	20.2	11.3	7.4	58.4	32.8	25.6

Note: Numbers may not add to total because of rounding. Spending on gifts is also included in the product and service categories in other chapters.
Source: Calculations by New Strategist based on the Bureau of Labor Statistics' 2011 Consumer Expenditure Survey

CHAPTER 7

Spending on Health Care, 2011

American households spent 23 percent more on out-of-pocket health care costs in 2011 than in 2000, after adjusting for inflation. Out-of-pocket spending on health insurance rose by a budget-busting 50 percent during those years. Out-of-pocket health care costs absorbed 6.7 percent of the household budget in 2010, up from 5.4 percent in 2000.

Not surprisingly, out-of-pocket health care spending rises with age. It peaks among householders aged 65 to 74 at $5,038 in 2011. This age group spends more than any other on out-of-pocket health insurance costs ($3,154 on average) and prescription drugs ($602). Out-of-pocket spending on medical services is highest among 55-to-64-year-old householders at $1,013.

Out-of-pocket spending on health care rises with income, largely because household size also grows with income. In 2011, households with incomes of $100,000 or more spent on average $5,258 out-of-pocket on health care, 59 percent more than the average household. Spending on health care is below average only for households with incomes below $40,000.

Among household types, married couples without children at home, most of them older empty-nesters, spend the most on out-of-pocket health care costs, $5,127 in 2011—55 percent more than the average household. Married couples with children at home spend 18 percent more than the average household on health care overall, but they spend 44 percent more than average on physician services.

Asians, blacks, and Hispanics spend far less than the average household on out-of-pocket health care costs, while non-Hispanic whites spend more. One factor behind these differences is the older age of the non-Hispanic white population.

There is relatively little difference in households' average spending on health care by region of residence, the gap between highest (Midwest) and lowest (South) spending being $460. Household out-of-pocket spending on dental services is 27 percent above average in the Northeast, whereas Midwestern households pay 55 percent more than average for lab tests and X-rays and 56 percent more than average on hospital room and services.

College graduates spend the most on out-of-pocket health care costs, an average of $4,192 in 2011—27 percent more than the average household. They spend 36 percent more than average out-of-pocket on medical services and 49 percent more on eyeglasses and contact lenses. College graduates spend only 4 percent more than average on prescription drugs.

Table 7.1 Health Care: Average spending by age, 2011

(average annual out-of-pocket spending of consumer units on health care, by age of consumer unit reference person, 2011)

	total consumer units	under 25	25 to 34	35 to 44	45 to 54	55 to 64	65 to 74	75+
Number of consumer units (in 000s)	122,287	7,743	20,463	21,699	24,821	21,688	14,079	11,794
Average number of persons per consumer unit	2.5	2.1	2.9	3.3	2.8	2.1	1.9	1.6
Average before-tax income of consumer units	$63,685.00	$27,514.00	$58,179.00	$77,376.00	$78,519.00	$75,517.00	$52,521.00	$32,144.00
Average spending of consumer units, total	49,704.88	29,911.52	48,097.39	57,271.07	58,050.42	53,615.86	44,645.56	32,688.34
Health care, average spending	**3,312.92**	**840.77**	**2,093.82**	**2,761.77**	**3,411.06**	**4,047.60**	**5,038.32**	**4,449.34**
HEALTH INSURANCE	**1,922.19**	**455.93**	**1,236.64**	**1,580.98**	**1,801.13**	**2,196.13**	**3,154.13**	**2,982.31**
Commercial health insurance	**338.85**	**104.74**	**296.64**	**394.25**	**433.66**	**463.20**	**236.36**	**158.02**
Traditional fee-for-service health plan (not BCBS)	92.61	37.14	57.19	88.87	105.02	143.33	83.74	88.59
Preferred-provider health plan (not BCBS)	246.24	67.60	239.46	305.38	328.64	319.88	152.62	69.43
Blue Cross, Blue Shield	**608.29**	**189.57**	**493.81**	**652.37**	**718.54**	**822.08**	**516.15**	**485.53**
Traditional fee-for-service health plan	108.55	42.71	79.66	91.97	118.11	176.70	97.34	100.40
Preferred-provider health plan	246.31	60.45	201.08	293.81	345.57	355.41	136.89	80.54
Health maintenance organization	190.30	69.60	189.85	244.95	205.59	241.62	145.77	96.42
Commercial Medicare supplement	54.22	11.70	19.93	16.32	32.76	36.52	129.39	199.29
Other BCBS health insurance	8.91	5.12	3.29	5.33	16.51	11.83	6.75	8.89
Health maintenance plans (HMOs)	**319.41**	**87.09**	**319.87**	**360.66**	**377.84**	**394.59**	**276.98**	**184.70**
Medicare payments	**368.66**	**36.96**	**35.40**	**64.57**	**124.98**	**229.66**	**1,358.32**	**1,311.15**
Medicare prescription drug premium	**62.70**	**2.39**	**4.24**	**8.57**	**19.83**	**44.79**	**210.71**	**249.76**
Commercial Medicare supplements and other health insurance	**156.97**	**34.70**	**73.33**	**85.42**	**100.70**	**131.03**	**374.95**	**419.94**
Commercial Medicare supplement (not BCBS)	100.35	28.33	35.28	32.17	34.11	55.96	306.30	361.15
Other health insurance (not BCBS)	56.62	6.36	38.05	53.25	66.60	75.07	68.65	58.79
Long-term care insurance	**67.29**	**0.49**	**13.35**	**15.13**	**25.58**	**110.77**	**180.66**	**173.21**
MEDICAL SERVICES	**767.64**	**254.20**	**546.12**	**693.54**	**942.28**	**1,012.74**	**894.20**	**656.35**
Physician's services	179.40	64.44	147.34	184.59	233.28	231.03	154.66	122.13
Dental services	285.67	85.04	136.22	242.44	294.08	401.28	461.32	316.17
Eye care services	37.11	12.54	30.04	35.29	35.87	37.86	51.01	53.51
Service by professionals other than physician	56.63	19.59	49.33	55.92	88.11	78.59	23.42	27.93
Lab tests, X-rays	47.97	14.91	31.34	27.24	84.07	76.31	40.20	17.83
Hospital room and services	129.10	49.31	130.52	131.00	184.30	157.05	87.64	57.49
Care in convalescent or nursing home	10.32	–	4.84	0.42	3.98	0.48	49.77	29.11
Other medical services	17.68	8.37	16.49	16.18	18.58	21.92	15.78	21.16
DRUGS	**489.06**	**92.57**	**229.34**	**376.78**	**514.52**	**689.87**	**791.36**	**622.89**
Nonprescription drugs	92.57	24.90	75.09	92.02	90.08	112.47	120.86	103.43
Nonprescription vitamins	51.94	10.69	30.64	45.75	48.04	83.46	68.66	57.46
Prescription drugs	344.56	56.99	123.61	239.01	376.40	493.95	601.84	462.00
MEDICAL SUPPLIES	**134.03**	**38.07**	**81.73**	**110.48**	**153.12**	**148.85**	**198.62**	**187.79**
Eyeglasses and contact lenses	63.53	25.53	39.85	62.44	91.86	73.17	72.07	44.09
Hearing aids	16.89	0.48	0.38	2.75	9.73	15.03	36.20	77.74
Topicals and dressings	40.69	10.27	32.35	36.40	37.35	47.33	74.81	38.43
Adult diapers	2.87	1.55	4.87	3.82	1.56	1.56	2.32	4.27
Medical equipment for general use	3.81	0.14	1.90	2.00	4.19	5.15	3.76	9.63
Supportive and convalescent medical equipment	4.04	0.02	1.30	2.11	5.68	4.32	6.36	8.22
Rental of medical equipment	1.04	–	0.30	0.51	1.41	1.21	1.51	2.28
Rental of supportive and convalescent medical equipment	1.17	0.08	0.78	0.44	1.35	1.08	1.60	3.13

Note: Subcategories may not add to total because some are not shown. "–" means sample is too small to make a reliable estimate.
Source: Bureau of Labor Statistics, unpublished tables from the 2011 Consumer Expenditure Survey

Table 7.2 Health Care: Indexed spending by age, 2011

(indexed average annual out-of-pocket spending of consumer units on health care, by age of consumer unit reference person, 2011; index definition: an index of 100 is the average for all consumer units; an index of 125 means that spending by consumer units in that group is 25 percent above the average for all consumer units; an index of 75 indicates spending that is 25 percent below the average for all consumer units)

	total consumer units	under 25	25 to 34	35 to 44	45 to 54	55 to 64	65 to 74	75+
Average spending of consumer units, total	$49,705	$29,912	$48,097	$57,271	$58,050	$53,616	$44,646	$32,688
Average spending of consumer units, index	100	60	97	115	117	108	90	66
Health care, spending index	**100**	**25**	**63**	**83**	**103**	**122**	**152**	**134**
HEALTH INSURANCE	**100**	**24**	**64**	**82**	**94**	**114**	**164**	**155**
Commercial health insurance	**100**	**31**	**88**	**116**	**128**	**137**	**70**	**47**
Traditional fee-for-service health plan (not BCBS)	100	40	62	96	113	155	90	96
Preferred-provider health plan (not BCBS)	100	27	97	124	133	130	62	28
Blue Cross, Blue Shield	**100**	**31**	**81**	**107**	**118**	**135**	**85**	**80**
Traditional fee-for-service health plan	100	39	73	85	109	163	90	92
Preferred-provider health plan	100	25	82	119	140	144	56	33
Health maintenance organization	100	37	100	129	108	127	77	51
Commercial Medicare supplement	100	22	37	30	60	67	239	368
Other BCBS health insurance	100	57	37	60	185	133	76	100
Health maintenance plans (HMOs)	**100**	**27**	**100**	**113**	**118**	**124**	**87**	**58**
Medicare payments	**100**	**10**	**10**	**18**	**34**	**62**	**368**	**356**
Medicare prescription drug premium	**100**	**4**	**7**	**14**	**32**	**71**	**336**	**398**
Commercial Medicare supplements and other health insurance	**100**	**22**	**47**	**54**	**64**	**83**	**239**	**268**
Commercial Medicare supplement (not BCBS)	100	28	35	32	34	56	305	360
Other health insurance (not BCBS)	100	11	67	94	118	133	121	104
Long-term care insurance	**100**	**1**	**20**	**22**	**38**	**165**	**268**	**257**
MEDICAL SERVICES	**100**	**33**	**71**	**90**	**123**	**132**	**116**	**86**
Physician's services	100	36	82	103	130	129	86	68
Dental services	100	30	48	85	103	140	161	111
Eye care services	100	34	81	95	97	102	137	144
Service by professionals other than physician	100	35	87	99	156	139	41	49
Lab tests, X-rays	100	31	65	57	175	159	84	37
Hospital room and services	100	38	101	101	143	122	68	45
Care in convalescent or nursing home	100	–	47	4	39	5	482	282
Other medical services	100	47	93	92	105	124	89	120
DRUGS	**100**	**19**	**47**	**77**	**105**	**141**	**162**	**127**
Nonprescription drugs	100	27	81	99	97	121	131	112
Nonprescription vitamins	100	21	59	88	92	161	132	111
Prescription drugs	100	17	36	69	109	143	175	134
MEDICAL SUPPLIES	**100**	**28**	**61**	**82**	**114**	**111**	**148**	**140**
Eyeglasses and contact lenses	100	40	63	98	145	115	113	69
Hearing aids	100	3	2	16	58	89	214	460
Topicals and dressings	100	25	80	89	92	116	184	94
Adult diapers	100	54	170	133	54	54	81	149
Medical equipment for general use	100	4	50	52	110	135	99	253
Supportive and convalescent medical equipment	100	0	32	52	141	107	157	203
Rental of medical equipment	100	–	29	49	136	116	145	219
Rental of supportive and convalescent medical equipment	100	7	67	38	115	92	137	268

Note: "–" means sample is too small to make a reliable estimate.
Source: Calculations by New Strategist based on the Bureau of Labor Statistics' 2011 Consumer Expenditure Survey

Table 7.3 Health Care: Total spending by age, 2011

(total annual out-of-pocket spending on health care, by consumer unit age groups, 2011; consumer units and dollars in thousands)

	total consumer units	under 25	25 to 34	35 to 44	45 to 54	55 to 64	65 to 74	75+
Number of consumer units	122,287	7,743	20,463	21,699	24,821	21,688	14,079	11,794
Total spending of all consumer units	$6,078,260,661	$231,604,899	$984,216,892	$1,242,724,948	$1,440,869,475	$1,162,820,772	$628,564,839	$385,526,282
Health care, total spending	**405,127,048**	**6,510,082**	**42,845,839**	**59,927,647**	**84,665,920**	**87,784,349**	**70,934,507**	**52,475,516**
HEALTH INSURANCE	**235,058,849**	**3,530,266**	**25,305,364**	**34,305,685**	**44,705,848**	**47,629,667**	**44,406,996**	**35,173,364**
Commercial health insurance	41,436,950	811,002	6,070,144	8,554,831	10,763,875	10,045,882	3,327,712	1,863,688
Traditional fee-for-service health plan (not BCBS)	11,324,999	287,575	1,170,279	1,928,390	2,606,701	3,108,541	1,178,975	1,044,830
Preferred-provider health plan (not BCBS)	30,111,951	523,427	4,900,070	6,626,441	8,157,173	6,937,557	2,148,737	818,857
Blue Cross, Blue Shield	**74,385,959**	**1,467,841**	**10,104,834**	**14,155,777**	**17,834,881**	**17,829,271**	**7,266,876**	**5,726,341**
Traditional fee-for-service health plan	13,274,254	330,704	1,630,083	1,995,657	2,931,608	3,832,270	1,370,450	1,184,118
Preferred-provider health plan	30,120,511	468,064	4,114,700	6,375,383	8,577,393	7,708,132	1,927,274	949,889
Health maintenance organization	23,271,216	538,913	3,884,901	5,315,170	5,102,949	5,240,255	2,052,296	1,137,177
Commercial Medicare supplement	6,630,401	90,593	407,828	354,128	813,136	792,046	1,821,682	2,350,426
Other BCBS health insurance	1,089,577	39,644	67,323	115,656	409,795	256,569	95,033	104,849
Health maintenance plans (HMOs)	**39,059,691**	**674,338**	**6,545,500**	**7,825,961**	**9,378,367**	**8,557,868**	**3,899,601**	**2,178,352**
Medicare payments	**45,082,325**	**286,181**	**724,390**	**1,401,104**	**3,102,129**	**4,980,866**	**19,123,787**	**15,463,703**
Medicare prescription drug premium	**7,667,395**	**18,506**	**86,763**	**185,960**	**492,200**	**971,406**	**2,966,586**	**2,945,669**
Commercial Medicare supplements and other health insurance	**19,195,390**	**268,682**	**1,500,552**	**1,853,529**	**2,499,475**	**2,841,779**	**5,278,921**	**4,952,772**
Commercial Medicare supplement (not BCBS)	12,271,500	219,359	721,935	698,057	846,644	1,213,660	4,312,398	4,259,403
Other health insurance (not BCBS)	6,923,890	49,245	778,617	1,155,472	1,653,079	1,628,118	966,523	693,369
Long-term care insurance	**8,228,692**	**3,794**	**273,181**	**328,306**	**634,921**	**2,402,380**	**2,543,512**	**2,042,839**
MEDICAL SERVICES	**93,872,393**	**1,968,271**	**11,175,254**	**15,049,124**	**23,388,332**	**21,964,305**	**12,589,442**	**7,740,992**
Physician's services	21,938,288	498,959	3,015,018	4,005,418	5,790,243	5,010,579	2,177,458	1,440,401
Dental services	34,933,727	658,465	2,787,470	5,260,706	7,299,360	8,702,961	6,494,924	3,728,909
Eye care services	4,538,071	97,097	614,709	765,758	890,329	821,108	718,170	631,097
Service by professionals other than physician	6,925,113	151,685	1,009,440	1,213,408	2,186,978	1,704,460	329,730	329,406
Lab tests, X-rays	5,866,107	115,448	641,310	591,081	2,086,701	1,655,011	565,976	210,287
Hospital room and services	15,787,252	381,807	2,670,831	2,842,569	4,574,510	3,406,100	1,233,884	678,037
Care in convalescent or nursing home	1,262,002	–	99,041	9,114	98,788	10,410	700,712	343,323
Other medical services	2,162,034	64,809	337,435	351,090	461,174	475,401	222,167	249,561
DRUGS	**59,805,680**	**716,770**	**4,692,984**	**8,175,749**	**12,770,901**	**14,961,901**	**11,141,557**	**7,346,365**
Nonprescription drugs	11,320,108	192,801	1,536,567	1,996,742	2,235,876	2,439,249	1,701,588	1,219,853
Nonprescription vitamins	6,351,587	82,773	626,986	992,729	1,192,401	1,810,080	966,664	677,683
Prescription drugs	42,135,209	441,274	2,529,431	5,186,278	9,342,624	10,712,788	8,473,305	5,448,828
MEDICAL SUPPLIES	**16,390,127**	**294,776**	**1,672,441**	**2,397,306**	**3,800,592**	**3,228,259**	**2,796,371**	**2,214,795**
Eyeglasses and contact lenses	7,768,893	197,679	815,451	1,354,886	2,280,057	1,586,911	1,014,674	519,997
Hearing aids	2,065,427	3,717	7,776	59,672	241,508	325,971	509,660	916,866
Topicals and dressings	4,975,858	79,521	661,978	789,844	927,064	1,026,493	1,053,250	453,243
Adult diapers	350,964	12,002	99,655	82,890	38,721	33,833	32,663	50,360
Medical equipment for general use	465,913	1,084	38,880	43,398	104,000	111,693	52,937	113,576
Supportive and convalescent medical equipment	494,039	155	26,602	45,785	140,983	93,692	89,542	96,947
Rental of medical equipment	127,178	–	6,139	11,066	34,998	26,242	21,259	26,890
Rental of supportive and convalescent medical equipment	143,076	619	15,961	9,548	33,508	23,423	22,526	36,915

Note: Numbers may not add to total because of rounding and missing subcategories. "–" means sample is too small to make a reliable estimate
Source: Calculations by New Strategist based on the Bureau of Labor Statistics' 2011 Consumer Expenditure Survey

Table 7.4 Health Care: Market shares by age, 2011

(percentage of total annual out-of-pocket spending on health care accounted for by consumer unit age groups, 2011)

	total consumer units	under 25	25 to 34	35 to 44	45 to 54	55 to 64	65 to 74	75+
Share of total consumer units	100.0%	6.3%	16.7%	17.7%	20.3%	17.7%	11.5%	9.6%
Share of total before-tax income	100.0	2.7	15.3	21.6	25.0	21.0	9.5	4.9
Share of total spending	100.0	3.8	16.2	20.4	23.7	19.1	10.3	6.3
Share of health care spending	100.0	1.6	10.6	14.8	20.9	21.7	17.5	13.0
HEALTH INSURANCE	100.0	1.5	10.8	14.6	19.0	20.3	18.9	15.0
Commercial health insurance	100.0	2.0	14.6	20.6	26.0	24.2	8.0	4.5
Traditional fee-for-service health plan (not BCBS)	100.0	2.5	10.3	17.0	23.0	27.4	10.4	9.2
Preferred-provider health plan (not BCBS)	100.0	1.7	16.3	22.0	27.1	23.0	7.1	2.7
Blue Cross, Blue Shield	100.0	2.0	13.6	19.0	24.0	24.0	9.8	7.7
Traditional fee-for-service health plan	100.0	2.5	12.3	15.0	22.1	28.9	10.3	8.9
Preferred-provider health plan	100.0	1.6	13.7	21.2	28.5	25.6	6.4	3.2
Health maintenance organization	100.0	2.3	16.7	22.8	21.9	22.5	8.8	4.9
Commercial Medicare supplement	100.0	1.4	6.2	5.3	12.3	11.9	27.5	35.4
Other BCBS health insurance	100.0	3.6	6.2	10.6	37.6	23.5	8.7	9.6
Health maintenance plans (HMOs)	100.0	1.7	16.8	20.0	24.0	21.9	10.0	5.6
Medicare payments	100.0	0.6	1.6	3.1	6.9	11.0	42.4	34.3
Medicare prescription drug premium	100.0	0.2	1.1	2.4	6.4	12.7	38.7	38.4
Commercial Medicare supplements and other health insurance	100.0	1.4	7.8	9.7	13.0	14.8	27.5	25.8
Commercial Medicare supplement (not BCBS)	100.0	1.8	5.9	5.7	6.9	9.9	35.1	34.7
Other health insurance (not BCBS)	100.0	0.7	11.2	16.7	23.9	23.5	14.0	10.0
Long-term care insurance	100.0	0.0	3.3	4.0	7.7	29.2	30.9	24.8
MEDICAL SERVICES	100.0	2.1	11.9	16.0	24.9	23.4	13.4	8.2
Physician's services	100.0	2.3	13.7	18.3	26.4	22.8	9.9	6.6
Dental services	100.0	1.9	8.0	15.1	20.9	24.9	18.6	10.7
Eye care services	100.0	2.1	13.5	16.9	19.6	18.1	15.8	13.9
Service by professionals other than physician	100.0	2.2	14.6	17.5	31.6	24.6	4.8	4.8
Lab tests, X-rays	100.0	2.0	10.9	10.1	35.6	28.2	9.6	3.6
Hospital room and services	100.0	2.4	16.9	18.0	29.0	21.6	7.8	4.3
Care in convalescent or nursing home	100.0	–	7.8	0.7	7.8	0.8	55.5	27.2
Other medical services	100.0	3.0	15.6	16.2	21.3	22.0	10.3	11.5
DRUGS	100.0	1.2	7.8	13.7	21.4	25.0	18.6	12.3
Nonprescription drugs	100.0	1.7	13.6	17.6	19.8	21.5	15.0	10.8
Nonprescription vitamins	100.0	1.3	9.9	15.6	18.8	28.5	15.2	10.7
Prescription drugs	100.0	1.0	6.0	12.3	22.2	25.4	20.1	12.9
MEDICAL SUPPLIES	100.0	1.8	10.2	14.6	23.2	19.7	17.1	13.5
Eyeglasses and contact lenses	100.0	2.5	10.5	17.4	29.3	20.4	13.1	6.7
Hearing aids	100.0	0.2	0.4	2.9	11.7	15.8	24.7	44.4
Topicals and dressings	100.0	1.6	13.3	15.9	18.6	20.6	21.2	9.1
Adult diapers	100.0	3.4	28.4	23.6	11.0	9.6	9.3	14.3
Medical equipment for general use	100.0	0.2	8.3	9.3	22.3	24.0	11.4	24.4
Supportive and convalescent medical equipment	100.0	0.0	5.4	9.3	28.5	19.0	18.1	19.6
Rental of medical equipment	100.0	–	4.8	8.7	27.5	20.6	16.7	21.1
Rental of supportive and convalescent medical equipment	100.0	0.4	11.2	6.7	23.4	16.4	15.7	25.8

Note: Numbers may not add to total because of rounding. "–" means sample is too small to make a reliable estimate.
Source: Calculations by New Strategist based on the Bureau of Labor Statistics' 2011 Consumer Expenditure Survey

Table 7.5 Health Care: Average spending by income, 2011

(average annual out-of-pocket spending on health care, by before-tax income of consumer units, 2011)

	total consumer units	under $20,000	$20,000–$39,999	$40,000–$49,999	$50,000–$69,999	$70,000–$79,999	$80,000–$99,999	$100,000 or more
Number of consumer units (in 000s)	122,287	26,342	27,788	11,347	17,376	7,385	10,456	21,593
Average number of persons per consumer unit	2.5	1.8	2.3	2.6	2.7	2.8	3.0	3.2
Average before-tax income of consumer units	$63,685.00	$10,491.66	$29,658.14	$44,698.00	$59,306.00	$74,742.00	$89,108.00	$169,776.00
Average spending of consumer units, total	49,704.88	22,142.36	33,453.66	40,306.19	50,034.03	57,976.69	65,389.80	97,728.22
Health care, average spending	**3,312.92**	**1,545.00**	**2,696.68**	**3,316.61**	**3,721.62**	**4,130.33**	**4,105.72**	**5,258.16**
HEALTH INSURANCE	**1,922.19**	**914.28**	**1,662.21**	**1,963.16**	**2,189.19**	**2,392.02**	**2,388.27**	**2,863.55**
Commercial health insurance	**338.85**	**88.68**	**216.34**	**275.60**	**379.57**	**426.92**	**530.92**	**679.06**
Traditional fee-for-service health plan (not BCBS)	92.61	40.20	89.72	83.75	105.19	116.44	121.82	132.51
Preferred-provider health plan (not BCBS)	246.24	48.48	126.62	191.84	274.38	310.48	409.10	546.54
Blue Cross, Blue Shield	**608.29**	**152.80**	**387.92**	**614.11**	**745.90**	**966.95**	**876.36**	**1,081.28**
Traditional fee-for-service health plan	108.55	37.85	81.64	92.86	124.71	188.71	154.10	175.22
Preferred-provider health plan	246.31	36.38	123.85	241.55	305.26	373.74	356.01	518.38
Health maintenance organization	190.30	36.28	104.49	220.98	236.00	327.30	299.73	335.90
Commercial Medicare supplement	54.22	33.76	70.21	53.93	73.10	55.08	56.64	42.07
Other BCBS health insurance	8.91	8.53	7.73	4.79	6.84	22.13	9.89	9.71
Health maintenance plans (HMOs)	**319.41**	**84.55**	**198.53**	**317.98**	**399.73**	**440.90**	**488.40**	**574.24**
Medicare payments	**368.66**	**412.35**	**517.62**	**404.80**	**353.73**	**273.24**	**248.46**	**207.56**
Medicare prescription drug premium	**62.70**	**73.75**	**90.98**	**68.08**	**59.77**	**43.68**	**32.05**	**33.69**
Commercial Medicare supplements and other health insurance	**156.97**	**83.46**	**181.98**	**203.62**	**170.19**	**155.33**	**167.31**	**174.89**
Commercial Medicare supplement (not BCBS)	100.35	71.22	142.84	146.03	100.10	95.45	86.91	65.58
Other health insurance (not BCBS)	56.62	12.24	39.13	57.59	70.09	59.88	80.39	109.31
Long-term care insurance	**67.29**	**18.70**	**68.85**	**78.99**	**80.29**	**85.00**	**44.77**	**112.83**
MEDICAL SERVICES	**767.64**	**280.48**	**516.21**	**733.48**	**880.34**	**1,060.36**	**972.97**	**1,412.68**
Physician's services	179.40	57.79	122.68	174.88	201.68	236.80	220.96	345.43
Dental services	285.67	117.81	177.64	252.23	247.70	437.31	368.79	585.47
Eye care services	37.11	21.05	30.66	28.33	32.91	19.76	86.18	55.17
Service by professionals other than physician	56.63	0.28	33.01	36.42	93.58	64.55	58.66	132.98
Lab tests, X-rays	47.97	14.21	27.08	37.34	60.74	59.09	65.50	99.04
Hospital room and services	129.10	38.50	92.94	160.78	218.51	206.31	156.00	158.16
Care in convalescent or nursing home	10.32	–	9.28	7.48	2.52	15.81	4.37	1.94
Other medical services	17.68	5.39	22.62	23.82	22.14	20.72	12.52	20.94
DRUGS	**489.06**	**285.74**	**426.38**	**493.33**	**535.17**	**467.15**	**578.55**	**732.87**
Nonprescription drugs	92.57	45.93	73.93	86.18	92.23	127.73	120.01	144.55
Nonprescription vitamins	51.94	27.30	32.28	43.45	48.34	57.80	68.12	102.29
Prescription drugs	344.56	212.50	320.17	363.70	394.60	281.62	390.42	486.03
MEDICAL SUPPLIES	**134.03**	**64.51**	**91.87**	**126.64**	**116.92**	**210.80**	**165.93**	**249.06**
Eyeglasses and contact lenses	63.53	20.04	48.77	53.05	63.48	92.44	90.16	118.36
Hearing aids	16.89	11.84	9.94	29.17	10.91	15.77	11.37	33.40
Topicals and dressings	40.69	22.79	21.27	32.97	31.16	90.33	50.31	77.02
Adult diapers	2.87	–	3.37	1.44	1.69	4.82	5.49	3.98
Medical equipment for general use	3.81	2.10	3.40	5.09	6.23	1.28	1.74	5.65
Supportive and convalescent medical equipment	4.04	2.44	3.32	3.70	2.00	4.43	5.98	7.66
Rental of medical equipment	1.04	0.73	1.19	0.48	0.62	1.54	0.55	1.90
Rental of supportive and convalescent medical equipment	1.17	0.98	2.37	0.74	0.83	0.19	0.33	1.09

Note: Subcategories may not add to total because some are not shown. "–" means sample is too small to make a reliable estimate.
Source: Bureau of Labor Statistics, unpublished tables from the 2011 Consumer Expenditure Survey; calculations by New Strategist

Table 7.6 Health Care: Indexed spending by income, 2011

(indexed average annual out-of-pocket spending of consumer units on health care, by before-tax income of consumer unit, 2011; index definition: an index of 100 is the average for all consumer units; an index of 125 means that spending by consumer units in that group is 25 percent above the average for all consumer units; an index of 75 indicates spending that is 25 percent below the average for all consumer units)

	total consumer units	under $20,000	$20,000–$39,999	$40,000–$49,999	$50,000–$69,999	$70,000–$79,999	$80,000–$99,999	$100,000 or more
Average spending of consumer units, total	$49,705	$22,142	$33,454	$40,306	$50,034	$57,977	$65,390	$97,728
Average spending of consumer units, index	100	45	67	81	101	117	132	197
Health care, spending index	100	47	81	100	112	125	124	159
HEALTH INSURANCE	100	48	86	102	114	124	124	149
Commercial health insurance	100	26	64	81	112	126	157	200
Traditional fee-for-service health plan (not BCBS)	100	43	97	90	114	126	132	143
Preferred-provider health plan (not BCBS)	100	20	51	78	111	126	166	222
Blue Cross, Blue Shield	100	25	64	101	123	159	144	178
Traditional fee-for-service health plan	100	35	75	86	115	174	142	161
Preferred-provider health plan	100	15	50	98	124	152	145	210
Health maintenance organization	100	19	55	116	124	172	158	177
Commercial Medicare supplement	100	62	129	99	135	102	104	78
Other BCBS health insurance	100	96	87	54	77	248	111	109
Health maintenance plans (HMOs)	100	26	62	100	125	138	153	180
Medicare payments	100	112	140	110	96	74	67	56
Medicare prescription drug premium	100	118	145	109	95	70	51	54
Commercial Medicare supplements and other health insurance	100	53	116	130	108	99	107	111
Commercial Medicare supplement (not BCBS)	100	71	142	146	100	95	87	65
Other health insurance (not BCBS)	100	22	69	102	124	106	142	193
Long-term care insurance	100	28	102	117	119	126	67	168
MEDICAL SERVICES	100	37	67	96	115	138	127	184
Physician's services	100	32	68	97	112	132	123	193
Dental services	100	41	62	88	87	153	129	205
Eye care services	100	57	83	76	89	53	232	149
Service by professionals other than physician	100	0	58	64	165	114	104	235
Lab tests, X-rays	100	30	56	78	127	123	137	206
Hospital room and services	100	30	72	125	169	160	121	123
Care in convalescent or nursing home	100	–	90	72	24	153	42	19
Other medical services	100	30	128	135	125	117	71	118
DRUGS	100	58	87	101	109	96	118	150
Nonprescription drugs	100	50	80	93	100	138	130	156
Nonprescription vitamins	100	53	62	84	93	111	131	197
Prescription drugs	100	62	93	106	115	82	113	141
MEDICAL SUPPLIES	100	48	69	94	87	157	124	186
Eyeglasses and contact lenses	100	32	77	84	100	146	142	186
Hearing aids	100	70	59	173	65	93	67	198
Topicals and dressings	100	56	52	81	77	222	124	189
Adult diapers	100	–	117	50	59	168	191	139
Medical equipment for general use	100	55	89	134	164	34	46	148
Supportive and convalescent medical equipment	100	60	82	92	50	110	148	190
Rental of medical equipment	100	70	115	46	60	148	53	183
Rental of supportive and convalescent medical equipment	100	83	202	63	71	16	28	93

Note: "–" means sample is too small to make a reliable estimate.
Source: Calculations by New Strategist based on the Bureau of Labor Statistics' 2011 Consumer Expenditure Survey

Table 7.7 Health Care: Total spending by income, 2011

(total annual out-of-pocket spending on health care, by before-tax income group of consumer units, 2011; consumer units and dollars in thousands)

	total consumer units	under $20,000	$20,000–$39,999	$40,000–$49,999	$50,000–$69,999	$70,000–$79,999	$80,000–$99,999	$100,000 or more
Number of consumer units	122,287	26,342	27,788	11,347	17,376	7,385	10,456	21,593
Total spending of all consumer units	$6,078,260,661	$583,273,961	$929,610,260	$457,354,338	$869,391,305	$428,157,856	$683,715,749	$2,110,245,454
Health care, total spending	405,127,048	40,698,469	74,935,283	37,633,574	64,666,869	30,502,487	42,929,408	113,539,449
HEALTH INSURANCE	**235,058,849**	**24,083,941**	**46,189,524**	**22,275,977**	**38,039,365**	**17,665,068**	**24,971,751**	**61,832,635**
Commercial health insurance	41,436,950	2,335,923	6,011,736	3,127,233	6,595,408	3,152,804	5,551,300	14,662,943
Traditional fee-for-service health plan (not BCBS)	11,324,999	1,058,934	2,493,084	950,311	1,827,781	859,909	1,273,750	2,861,288
Preferred-provider health plan (not BCBS)	30,111,951	1,277,039	3,518,652	2,176,808	4,767,627	2,292,895	4,277,550	11,801,438
Blue Cross, Blue Shield	**74,385,959**	**4,025,081**	**10,779,597**	**6,968,306**	**12,960,758**	**7,140,926**	**9,163,220**	**23,348,079**
Traditional fee-for-service health plan	13,274,254	996,983	2,268,564	1,053,682	2,166,961	1,393,623	1,611,270	3,783,525
Preferred-provider health plan	30,120,511	958,428	3,441,656	2,740,868	5,304,198	2,760,070	3,722,441	11,193,379
Health maintenance organization	23,271,216	955,582	2,903,626	2,507,460	4,100,736	2,417,111	3,133,977	7,253,089
Commercial Medicare supplement	6,630,401	889,286	1,951,078	611,944	1,270,186	406,766	592,228	908,418
Other BCBS health insurance	1,089,577	224,747	214,672	54,352	118,852	163,430	103,410	209,668
Health maintenance plans (HMOs)	**39,059,691**	**2,227,176**	**5,516,696**	**3,608,119**	**6,945,708**	**3,256,047**	**5,106,710**	**12,399,564**
Medicare payments	**45,082,325**	**10,862,050**	**14,383,525**	**4,593,266**	**6,146,412**	**2,017,877**	**2,597,898**	**4,481,843**
Medicare prescription drug premium	**7,667,395**	**1,942,682**	**2,528,192**	**772,504**	**1,038,564**	**322,577**	**335,115**	**727,468**
Commercial Medicare supplements and other health insurance	**19,195,390**	**2,198,484**	**5,056,835**	**2,310,476**	**2,957,221**	**1,147,112**	**1,749,393**	**3,776,400**
Commercial Medicare supplement (not BCBS)	12,271,500	1,876,084	3,969,230	1,657,002	1,739,338	704,898	908,731	1,416,069
Other health insurance (not BCBS)	6,923,890	322,482	1,087,460	653,474	1,217,884	442,214	840,558	2,360,331
Long-term care insurance	**8,228,692**	**492,523**	**1,913,087**	**896,300**	**1,395,119**	**627,725**	**468,115**	**2,436,338**
MEDICAL SERVICES	**93,872,393**	**7,388,278**	**14,344,559**	**8,322,798**	**15,296,788**	**7,830,759**	**10,173,374**	**30,503,999**
Physician's services	21,938,288	1,522,259	3,409,001	1,984,363	3,504,392	1,748,768	2,310,358	7,458,870
Dental services	34,933,727	3,103,391	4,936,331	2,862,054	4,304,035	3,229,534	3,856,068	12,642,054
Eye care services	4,538,071	554,544	852,084	321,461	571,844	145,928	901,098	1,191,286
Service by professionals other than physician	6,925,113	7,315	917,162	413,258	1,626,046	476,702	613,349	2,871,437
Lab tests, X-rays	5,866,107	374,356	752,494	423,697	1,055,418	436,380	684,868	2,138,571
Hospital room and services	15,787,252	1,014,072	2,582,547	1,824,371	3,796,830	1,523,599	1,631,136	3,415,149
Care in convalescent or nursing home	1,262,002	–	257,940	84,876	43,788	116,757	45,693	41,890
Other medical services	2,162,034	142,008	628,470	270,286	384,705	153,017	130,909	452,157
DRUGS	**59,805,680**	**7,526,996**	**11,848,354**	**5,597,816**	**9,299,114**	**3,449,903**	**6,049,319**	**15,824,862**
Nonprescription drugs	11,320,108	1,210,011	2,054,269	977,884	1,602,588	943,286	1,254,825	3,121,268
Nonprescription vitamins	6,351,587	719,252	897,133	493,027	839,956	426,853	712,263	2,208,748
Prescription drugs	42,135,209	5,597,733	8,896,820	4,126,904	6,856,570	2,079,764	4,082,232	10,494,846
MEDICAL SUPPLIES	**16,390,127**	**1,699,281**	**2,552,834**	**1,436,984**	**2,031,602**	**1,556,758**	**1,734,964**	**5,377,953**
Eyeglasses and contact lenses	7,768,893	527,951	1,355,254	601,958	1,103,028	682,669	942,713	2,555,747
Hearing aids	2,065,427	311,904	276,121	330,992	189,572	116,461	118,885	721,206
Topicals and dressings	4,975,858	600,234	591,016	374,111	541,436	667,087	526,041	1,663,093
Adult diapers	350,964	–	93,646	16,340	29,365	35,596	57,403	85,940
Medical equipment for general use	465,913	55,357	94,600	57,756	108,252	9,453	18,193	122,000
Supportive and convalescent medical equipment	494,039	64,188	92,217	41,984	34,752	32,716	62,527	165,402
Rental of medical equipment	127,178	19,244	33,101	5,447	10,773	11,373	5,751	41,027
Rental of supportive and convalescent medical equipment	143,076	25,691	65,755	8,397	14,422	1,403	3,450	23,536

Note: Numbers may not add to total because of rounding and missing subcategories. "–" means sample is too small to make a reliable estimate.
Source: Calculations by New Strategist based on the Bureau of Labor Statistics' 2011 Consumer Expenditure Survey

Table 7.8 Health Care: Market shares by income, 2011

(percentage of total annual out-of-pocket spending on health care accounted for by before-tax income group of consumer units, 2011)

	total consumer units	under $20,000	$20,000– $39,999	$40,000– $49,999	$50,000– $69,999	$70,000– $79,999	$80,000– $99,999	$100,000 or more
Share of total consumer units	100.0%	21.5%	22.7%	9.3%	14.2%	6.0%	8.6%	17.7%
Share of total before-tax income	100.0	3.5	10.6	6.5	13.2	7.1	12.0	47.1
Share of total spending	100.0	9.6	15.3	7.5	14.3	7.0	11.2	34.7
Share of health care spending	100.0	10.0	18.5	9.3	16.0	7.5	10.6	28.0
HEALTH INSURANCE	100.0	10.2	19.7	9.5	16.2	7.5	10.6	26.3
Commercial health insurance	100.0	5.6	14.5	7.5	15.9	7.6	13.4	35.4
Traditional fee-for-service health plan (not BCBS)	100.0	9.4	22.0	8.4	16.1	7.6	11.2	25.3
Preferred-provider health plan (not BCBS)	100.0	4.2	11.7	7.2	15.8	7.6	14.2	39.2
Blue Cross, Blue Shield	100.0	5.4	14.5	9.4	17.4	9.6	12.3	31.4
Traditional fee-for-service health plan	100.0	7.5	17.1	7.9	16.3	10.5	12.1	28.5
Preferred-provider health plan	100.0	3.2	11.4	9.1	17.6	9.2	12.4	37.2
Health maintenance organization	100.0	4.1	12.5	10.8	17.6	10.4	13.5	31.2
Commercial Medicare supplement	100.0	13.4	29.4	9.2	19.2	6.1	8.9	13.7
Other BCBS health insurance	100.0	20.6	19.7	5.0	10.9	15.0	9.5	19.2
Health maintenance plans (HMOs)	100.0	5.7	14.1	9.2	17.8	8.3	13.1	31.7
Medicare payments	100.0	24.1	31.9	10.2	13.6	4.5	5.8	9.9
Medicare prescription drug premium	100.0	25.3	33.0	10.1	13.5	4.2	4.4	9.5
Commercial Medicare supplements and other health insurance	100.0	11.5	26.3	12.0	15.4	6.0	9.1	19.7
Commercial Medicare supplement (not BCBS)	100.0	15.3	32.3	13.5	14.2	5.7	7.4	11.5
Other health insurance (not BCBS)	100.0	4.7	15.7	9.4	17.6	6.4	12.1	34.1
Long-term care insurance	100.0	6.0	23.2	10.9	17.0	7.6	5.7	29.6
MEDICAL SERVICES	100.0	7.9	15.3	8.9	16.3	8.3	10.8	32.5
Physician's services	100.0	6.9	15.5	9.0	16.0	8.0	10.5	34.0
Dental services	100.0	8.9	14.1	8.2	12.3	9.2	11.0	36.2
Eye care services	100.0	12.2	18.8	7.1	12.6	3.2	19.9	26.3
Service by professionals other than physician	100.0	0.1	13.2	6.0	23.5	6.9	8.9	41.5
Lab tests, X-rays	100.0	6.4	12.8	7.2	18.0	7.4	11.7	36.5
Hospital room and services	100.0	6.4	16.4	11.6	24.0	9.7	10.3	21.6
Care in convalescent or nursing home	100.0	–	20.4	6.7	3.5	9.3	3.6	3.3
Other medical services	100.0	6.6	29.1	12.5	17.8	7.1	6.1	20.9
DRUGS	100.0	12.6	19.8	9.4	15.5	5.8	10.1	26.5
Nonprescription drugs	100.0	10.7	18.1	8.6	14.2	8.3	11.1	27.6
Nonprescription vitamins	100.0	11.3	14.1	7.8	13.2	6.7	11.2	34.8
Prescription drugs	100.0	13.3	21.1	9.8	16.3	4.9	9.7	24.9
MEDICAL SUPPLIES	100.0	10.4	15.6	8.8	12.4	9.5	10.6	32.8
Eyeglasses and contact lenses	100.0	6.8	17.4	7.7	14.2	8.8	12.1	32.9
Hearing aids	100.0	15.1	13.4	16.0	9.2	5.6	5.8	34.9
Topicals and dressings	100.0	12.1	11.9	7.5	10.9	13.4	10.6	33.4
Adult diapers	100.0	–	26.7	4.7	8.4	10.1	16.4	24.5
Medical equipment for general use	100.0	11.9	20.3	12.4	23.2	2.0	3.9	26.2
Supportive and convalescent medical equipment	100.0	13.0	18.7	8.5	7.0	6.6	12.7	33.5
Rental of medical equipment	100.0	15.1	26.0	4.3	8.5	8.9	4.5	32.3
Rental of supportive and convalescent medical equipment	100.0	18.0	46.0	5.9	10.1	1.0	2.4	16.5

Note: Numbers may not add to total because of rounding. "–" means sample is too small to make a reliable estimate.
Source: Calculations by New Strategist based on the Bureau of Labor Statistics' 2011 Consumer Expenditure Survey

Table 7.9 Health Care: Average spending by high-income consumer units, 2011

(average annual out-of-pocket spending on health care, by before-tax income of high-income consumer units, 2011)

	total consumer units	$100,000 or more	$100,000– $119,999	$120,000– $149,999	$150,000 or more
Number of consumer units (in 000s)	122,287	21,593	7,045	6,107	8,440
Average number of persons per consumer unit	2.5	3.2	3.2	3.1	3.2
Average before-tax income of consumer units	$63,685.00	$169,776.00	$108,549.00	$133,318.00	$247,261.00
Average spending of consumer units, total	49,704.88	97,728.22	76,496.41	87,239.44	123,056.38
Health care, average spending	**3,312.92**	**5,258.16**	**4,589.51**	**5,037.77**	**5,975.86**
HEALTH INSURANCE	**1,922.19**	**2,863.55**	**2,562.33**	**2,813.30**	**3,151.33**
Commercial health insurance	**338.85**	**679.06**	**574.87**	**671.54**	**771.46**
Traditional fee-for-service health plan (not BCBS)	92.61	132.51	120.59	112.74	156.76
Preferred-provider health plan (not BCBS)	246.24	546.54	454.27	558.79	614.70
Blue Cross, Blue Shield	**608.29**	**1,081.28**	**953.68**	**1,093.12**	**1,179.22**
Traditional fee-for-service health plan	108.55	175.22	147.03	172.49	200.74
Preferred-provider health plan	246.31	518.38	432.28	528.73	582.74
Health maintenance organization	190.30	335.90	310.59	343.98	351.18
Commercial Medicare supplement	54.22	42.07	55.81	37.03	34.24
Other BCBS health insurance	8.91	9.71	7.97	10.89	10.31
Health maintenance plans (HMOs)	**319.41**	**574.24**	**541.54**	**543.33**	**623.91**
Medicare payments	**368.66**	**207.56**	**205.13**	**223.44**	**198.09**
Medicare prescription drug premium	**62.70**	**33.69**	**26.32**	**39.22**	**35.86**
Commercial Medicare supplements and other health insurance	**156.97**	**174.89**	**190.07**	**130.04**	**194.67**
Commercial Medicare supplement (not BCBS)	100.35	65.58	83.28	45.12	65.61
Other health insurance (not BCBS)	56.62	109.31	106.79	84.92	129.06
Long-term care insurance	**67.29**	**112.83**	**70.73**	**112.62**	**148.11**
MEDICAL SERVICES	**767.64**	**1,412.68**	**1,176.81**	**1,304.44**	**1,687.61**
Physician's services	179.40	345.43	222.86	341.36	450.68
Dental services	285.67	585.47	514.72	536.20	680.17
Eye care services	37.11	55.17	57.07	44.11	61.59
Service by professionals other than physician	56.63	132.98	141.25	141.12	120.18
Lab tests, X-rays	47.97	99.04	70.59	79.34	137.05
Hospital room and services	129.10	158.16	138.62	153.71	177.69
Care in convalescent or nursing home	10.32	1.94	9.94	−11.35	4.88
Other medical services	17.68	20.94	5.76	19.95	34.33
DRUGS	**489.06**	**732.87**	**652.04**	**657.11**	**854.74**
Nonprescription drugs	92.57	144.55	153.04	123.20	152.36
Nonprescription vitamins	51.94	102.29	77.31	68.45	147.78
Prescription drugs	344.56	486.03	421.69	465.47	554.60
MEDICAL SUPPLIES	**134.03**	**249.06**	**198.32**	**262.91**	**282.18**
Eyeglasses and contact lenses	63.53	118.36	92.23	123.55	136.42
Hearing aids	16.89	33.40	30.24	23.47	43.22
Topicals and dressings	40.69	77.02	59.72	95.94	78.54
Adult diapers	2.87	3.98	2.50	2.45	6.35
Medical equipment for general use	3.81	5.65	6.32	7.34	3.87
Supportive and convalescent medical equipment	4.04	7.66	3.94	9.04	9.78
Rental of medical equipment	1.04	1.90	0.76	0.94	3.54
Rental of supportive and convalescent medical equipment	1.17	1.09	2.62	0.18	0.46

Note: Subcategories may not add to total because some are not shown.
Source: Bureau of Labor Statistics, unpublished tables from the 2011 Consumer Expenditure Survey; calculations by New Strategist

Table 7.10 Health Care: Indexed spending by high-income consumer units, 2011

(indexed average annual out-of-pocket spending of high-income consumer units on health care, by before-tax income of consumer unit, 2011; index definition: an index of 100 is the average for all consumer units; an index of 125 means that spending by consumer units in that group is 25 percent above the average for all consumer units; an index of 75 indicates spending that is 25 percent below the average for all consumer units)

	total consumer units	$100,000 or more	$100,000– $119,999	$120,000– $149,999	$150,000 or more
Average spending of consumer units, total	$49,705	$97,728	$76,496	$87,239	$123,056
Average spending of consumer units, index	100	197	154	176	248
Health care, spending index	100	159	139	152	180
HEALTH INSURANCE	100	149	133	146	164
Commercial health insurance	100	200	170	198	228
Traditional fee-for-service health plan (not BCBS)	100	143	130	122	169
Preferred-provider health plan (not BCBS)	100	222	184	227	250
Blue Cross, Blue Shield	100	178	157	180	194
Traditional fee-for-service health plan	100	161	135	159	185
Preferred-provider health plan	100	210	176	215	237
Health maintenance organization	100	177	163	181	185
Commercial Medicare supplement	100	78	103	68	63
Other BCBS health insurance	100	109	89	122	116
Health maintenance plans (HMOs)	100	180	170	170	195
Medicare payments	100	56	56	61	54
Medicare prescription drug premium	100	54	42	63	57
Commercial Medicare supplements and other health insurance	100	111	121	83	124
Commercial Medicare supplement (not BCBS)	100	65	83	45	65
Other health insurance (not BCBS)	100	193	189	150	228
Long-term care insurance	100	168	105	167	220
MEDICAL SERVICES	100	184	153	170	220
Physician's services	100	193	124	190	251
Dental services	100	205	180	188	238
Eye care services	100	149	154	119	166
Service by professionals other than physician	100	235	249	249	212
Lab tests, X-rays	100	206	147	165	286
Hospital room and services	100	123	107	119	138
Care in convalescent or nursing home	100	19	96	–	47
Other medical services	100	118	33	113	194
DRUGS	100	150	133	134	175
Nonprescription drugs	100	156	165	133	165
Nonprescription vitamins	100	197	149	132	285
Prescription drugs	100	141	122	135	161
MEDICAL SUPPLIES	100	186	148	196	211
Eyeglasses and contact lenses	100	186	145	194	215
Hearing aids	100	198	179	139	256
Topicals and dressings	100	189	147	236	193
Adult diapers	100	139	87	85	221
Medical equipment for general use	100	148	166	193	102
Supportive and convalescent medical equipment	100	190	98	224	242
Rental of medical equipment	100	183	73	90	340
Rental of supportive and convalescent medical equipment	100	93	224	15	39

Note: "–" means refund.
Source: Calculations by New Strategist based on the Bureau of Labor Statistics' 2011 Consumer Expenditure Survey

Table 7.11 Health Care: Total spending by high-income consumer units, 2011

(total annual out-of-pocket spending on health care, by before-tax income group of high-income consumer units, 2011; consumer units and dollars in thousands)

	total consumer units	$100,000 or more	$100,000– $119,999	$120,000– $149,999	$150,000 or more
Number of consumer units	122,287	21,593	7,045	6,107	8,440
Total spending of all consumer units	$6,078,260,661	$2,110,245,454	$538,917,208	$532,771,260	$1,038,595,847
Health care, total spending	405,127,048	113,539,449	32,333,098	30,765,661	50,436,258
HEALTH INSURANCE	235,058,849	61,832,635	18,051,615	17,180,823	26,597,225
Commercial health insurance	41,436,950	14,662,943	4,049,959	4,101,095	6,511,122
Traditional fee-for-service health plan (not BCBS)	11,324,999	2,861,288	849,557	688,503	1,323,054
Preferred-provider health plan (not BCBS)	30,111,951	11,801,438	3,200,332	3,412,531	5,188,068
Blue Cross, Blue Shield	74,385,959	23,348,079	6,718,676	6,675,684	9,952,617
Traditional fee-for-service health plan	13,274,254	3,783,525	1,035,826	1,053,396	1,694,246
Preferred-provider health plan	30,120,511	11,193,379	3,045,413	3,228,954	4,918,326
Health maintenance organization	23,271,216	7,253,089	2,188,107	2,100,686	2,963,959
Commercial Medicare supplement	6,630,401	908,418	393,181	226,142	288,986
Other BCBS health insurance	1,089,577	209,668	56,149	66,505	87,016
Health maintenance plans (HMOs)	39,059,691	12,399,564	3,815,149	3,318,116	5,265,800
Medicare payments	45,082,325	4,481,843	1,445,141	1,364,548	1,671,880
Medicare prescription drug premium	7,667,395	727,468	185,424	239,517	302,658
Commercial Medicare supplements and other health insurance	19,195,390	3,776,400	1,339,043	794,154	1,643,015
Commercial Medicare supplement (not BCBS)	12,271,500	1,416,069	586,708	275,548	553,748
Other health insurance (not BCBS)	6,923,890	2,360,331	752,336	518,606	1,089,266
Long-term care insurance	8,228,692	2,436,338	498,293	687,770	1,250,048
MEDICAL SERVICES	93,872,393	30,503,999	8,290,626	7,966,215	14,243,428
Physician's services	21,938,288	7,458,870	1,570,049	2,084,686	3,803,739
Dental services	34,933,727	12,642,054	3,626,202	3,274,573	5,740,635
Eye care services	4,538,071	1,191,286	402,058	269,380	519,820
Service by professionals other than physician	6,925,113	2,871,437	995,106	861,820	1,014,319
Lab tests, X-rays	5,866,107	2,138,571	497,307	484,529	1,156,702
Hospital room and services	15,787,252	3,415,149	976,578	938,707	1,499,704
Care in convalescent or nursing home	1,262,002	41,890	70,027	−69,314	41,187
Other medical services	2,162,034	452,157	40,579	121,835	289,745
DRUGS	59,805,680	15,824,862	4,593,622	4,012,971	7,214,006
Nonprescription drugs	11,320,108	3,121,268	1,078,167	752,382	1,285,918
Nonprescription vitamins	6,351,587	2,208,748	544,649	418,024	1,247,263
Prescription drugs	42,135,209	10,494,846	2,970,806	2,842,625	4,680,824
MEDICAL SUPPLIES	16,390,127	5,377,953	1,397,164	1,605,591	2,381,599
Eyeglasses and contact lenses	7,768,893	2,555,747	649,760	754,520	1,151,385
Hearing aids	2,065,427	721,206	213,041	143,331	364,777
Topicals and dressings	4,975,858	1,663,093	420,727	585,906	662,878
Adult diapers	350,964	85,940	17,613	14,962	53,594
Medical equipment for general use	465,913	122,000	44,524	44,825	32,663
Supportive and convalescent medical equipment	494,039	165,402	27,757	55,207	82,543
Rental of medical equipment	127,178	41,027	5,354	5,741	29,878
Rental of supportive and convalescent medical equipment	143,076	23,536	18,458	1,099	3,882

Note: Numbers may not add to total because of rounding and missing subcategories.
Source: Calculations by New Strategist based on the Bureau of Labor Statistics' 2011 Consumer Expenditure Survey

Table 7.12 Health Care: Market shares by high-income consumer units, 2011

(percentage of total annual out-of-pocket spending on health care accounted for by before-tax income group of high-income consumer units, 2011)

	total consumer units	$100,000 or more	$100,000–$119,999	$120,000–$149,999	$150,000 or more
Share of total consumer units	100.0%	17.7%	5.8%	5.0%	6.9%
Share of total before-tax income	100.0	47.1	9.8	10.5	26.8
Share of total spending	100.0	34.7	8.9	8.8	17.1
Share of health care spending	100.0	28.0	8.0	7.6	12.4
HEALTH INSURANCE	100.0	26.3	7.7	7.3	11.3
Commercial health insurance	100.0	35.4	9.8	9.9	15.7
Traditional fee-for-service health plan (not BCBS)	100.0	25.3	7.5	6.1	11.7
Preferred-provider health plan (not BCBS)	100.0	39.2	10.6	11.3	17.2
Blue Cross, Blue Shield	100.0	31.4	9.0	9.0	13.4
Traditional fee-for-service health plan	100.0	28.5	7.8	7.9	12.8
Preferred-provider health plan	100.0	37.2	10.1	10.7	16.3
Health maintenance organization	100.0	31.2	9.4	9.0	12.7
Commercial Medicare supplement	100.0	13.7	5.9	3.4	4.4
Other BCBS health insurance	100.0	19.2	5.2	6.1	8.0
Health maintenance plans (HMOs)	100.0	31.7	9.8	8.5	13.5
Medicare payments	100.0	9.9	3.2	3.0	3.7
Medicare prescription drug premium	100.0	9.5	2.4	3.1	3.9
Commercial Medicare supplements and other health insurance	100.0	19.7	7.0	4.1	8.6
Commercial Medicare supplement (not BCBS)	100.0	11.5	4.8	2.2	4.5
Other health insurance (not BCBS)	100.0	34.1	10.9	7.5	15.7
Long-term care insurance	100.0	29.6	6.1	8.4	15.2
MEDICAL SERVICES	100.0	32.5	8.8	8.5	15.2
Physician's services	100.0	34.0	7.2	9.5	17.3
Dental services	100.0	36.2	10.4	9.4	16.4
Eye care services	100.0	26.3	8.9	5.9	11.5
Service by professionals other than physician	100.0	41.5	14.4	12.4	14.6
Lab tests, X-rays	100.0	36.5	8.5	8.3	19.7
Hospital room and services	100.0	21.6	6.2	5.9	9.5
Care in convalescent or nursing home	100.0	3.3	5.5	–	3.3
Other medical services	100.0	20.9	1.9	5.6	13.4
DRUGS	100.0	26.5	7.7	6.7	12.1
Nonprescription drugs	100.0	27.6	9.5	6.6	11.4
Nonprescription vitamins	100.0	34.8	8.6	6.6	19.6
Prescription drugs	100.0	24.9	7.1	6.7	11.1
MEDICAL SUPPLIES	100.0	32.8	8.5	9.8	14.5
Eyeglasses and contact lenses	100.0	32.9	8.4	9.7	14.8
Hearing aids	100.0	34.9	10.3	6.9	17.7
Topicals and dressings	100.0	33.4	8.5	11.8	13.3
Adult diapers	100.0	24.5	5.0	4.3	15.3
Medical equipment for general use	100.0	26.2	9.6	9.6	7.0
Supportive and convalescent medical equipment	100.0	33.5	5.6	11.2	16.7
Rental of medical equipment	100.0	32.3	4.2	4.5	23.5
Rental of supportive and convalescent medical equipment	100.0	16.5	12.9	0.8	2.7

Note: Numbers may not add to total because of rounding. "–" means refund.
Source: Calculations by New Strategist based on the Bureau of Labor Statistics' 2011 Consumer Expenditure Survey

Table 7.13 Health Care: Average spending by household type, 2011

(average annual out-of-pocket spending of consumer units on health care, by type of consumer unit, 2011)

	total married couples	married couples, no children	married couples with children				single parent with child under age 18	single person
			total	oldest child under age 6	oldest child aged 6 to 17	oldest child aged 18 or older		
Number of consumer units (in 000s)	60,144	25,270	29,097	5,825	14,661	8,612	6,956	36,110
Average number of persons per consumer unit	3.2	2.0	4.0	3.5	4.2	3.9	2.9	1.0
Average before-tax income of consumer units	$86,700.00	$78,823.00	$93,677.00	$91,014.00	$93,029.00	$96,583.00	$37,188.00	$34,540.00
Average spending of consumer units, total	63,971.54	57,658.24	69,724.22	65,947.61	70,708.52	70,411.85	37,553.05	30,613.18
Health care, average spending	**4,479.02**	**5,126.65**	**3,910.33**	**3,485.75**	**3,753.29**	**4,465.10**	**1,891.67**	**2,112.30**
HEALTH INSURANCE	**2,619.31**	**3,003.56**	**2,268.00**	**2,160.87**	**2,156.77**	**2,529.82**	**797.14**	**1,232.38**
Commercial health insurance	**485.45**	**404.48**	**559.69**	**601.39**	**573.16**	**508.56**	**170.30**	**187.08**
Traditional fee-for-service health plan (not BCBS)	120.07	108.87	126.10	90.38	143.62	120.42	46.64	66.09
Preferred-provider health plan (not BCBS)	365.37	295.62	433.60	511.01	429.54	388.14	123.66	120.99
Blue Cross, Blue Shield	**871.79**	**787.85**	**938.86**	**968.99**	**916.91**	**955.86**	**286.13**	**322.27**
Traditional fee-for-service health plan	148.08	145.22	153.23	151.69	149.18	161.17	39.08	70.30
Preferred-provider health plan	372.39	315.31	406.08	364.31	391.78	458.68	127.28	98.08
Health maintenance organization	274.01	212.42	333.68	422.00	331.38	277.87	110.06	99.18
Commercial Medicare supplement	64.16	104.88	29.31	28.09	24.37	38.56	6.07	49.97
Other BCBS health insurance	13.14	10.02	16.55	2.91	20.19	19.58	3.66	4.75
Health maintenance plans (HMOs)	**465.86**	**447.25**	**485.75**	**460.51**	**469.07**	**531.21**	**237.59**	**140.38**
Medicare payments	**426.59**	**767.77**	**105.00**	**9.32**	**49.13**	**264.82**	**52.16**	**339.45**
Medicare prescription drug premium	**72.68**	**132.28**	**16.38**	**0.16**	**3.68**	**48.98**	**2.84**	**60.91**
Commercial Medicare supplements and other health insurance	**205.05**	**301.07**	**125.59**	**92.55**	**118.04**	**160.80**	**41.51**	**125.30**
Commercial Medicare supplement (not BCBS)	123.61	213.79	42.27	39.46	30.19	64.74	18.15	91.34
Other health insurance (not BCBS)	81.44	87.28	83.32	53.08	87.84	96.06	23.35	33.97
Long-term care insurance	**91.91**	**162.85**	**36.73**	**27.95**	**26.78**	**59.60**	**6.61**	**56.99**
MEDICAL SERVICES	**1,025.70**	**1,089.21**	**989.63**	**883.31**	**960.45**	**1,111.22**	**821.36**	**466.81**
Physician's services	249.92	253.00	257.59	255.85	212.82	335.00	173.01	94.28
Dental services	387.31	428.37	347.69	152.63	385.29	415.62	160.39	182.81
Eye care services	47.61	55.91	40.25	40.75	32.33	53.39	16.10	30.84
Service by professionals other than physician	70.69	53.31	87.07	97.70	78.48	94.52	125.65	35.98
Lab tests, X-rays	68.25	89.24	50.79	43.95	42.96	68.74	51.31	21.77
Hospital room and services	164.82	171.83	168.20	246.63	174.94	103.68	286.17	59.53
Care in convalescent or nursing home	5.17	4.28	5.08	8.09	3.73	5.34	–	26.28
Other medical services	24.56	17.05	32.94	37.69	29.91	34.90	8.73	14.77
DRUGS	**661.34**	**829.02**	**505.02**	**328.36**	**484.85**	**658.03**	**210.64**	**313.85**
Nonprescription drugs	124.23	138.23	113.72	107.23	110.64	122.67	41.91	60.03
Nonprescription vitamins	73.79	91.41	52.67	50.76	54.33	50.99	15.24	32.54
Prescription drugs	463.32	599.37	338.63	170.37	319.88	484.37	153.49	221.28
MEDICAL SUPPLIES	**172.68**	**204.86**	**147.68**	**113.22**	**151.22**	**166.03**	**62.52**	**99.25**
Eyeglasses and contact lenses	87.21	97.08	82.67	41.93	89.66	98.33	40.62	39.76
Hearing aids	17.95	36.05	0.72	0.54	0.95	0.44	–	17.22
Topicals and dressings	51.82	53.16	51.70	59.08	49.41	51.29	16.33	30.77
Adult diapers	3.52	3.27	3.43	7.58	3.78	0.44	0.66	3.35
Medical equipment for general use	4.75	6.03	3.78	1.92	2.43	7.35	3.65	3.26
Supportive and convalescent medical equipment	5.13	6.19	3.41	0.95	2.38	6.84	0.20	3.28
Rental of medical equipment	1.26	1.82	0.94	1.21	1.18	0.35	0.12	0.63
Rental of supportive and convalescent medical equipment	1.03	1.24	1.01	–	1.43	1.00	0.95	0.97

Note: Average spending figures for total consumer units can be found on Average Spending by Age and Average Spending by Region tables. Subcategories may not add to total because some are not shown. "–" means sample is too small to make a reliable estimate.
Source: Bureau of Labor Statistics, unpublished tables from the 2011 Consumer Expenditure Survey

Table 7.14 Health Care: Indexed spending by household type, 2011

(indexed average annual out-of-pocket spending of consumer units on health care, by type of consumer unit, 2011; index definition: an index of 100 is the average for all consumer units; an index of 125 means that spending by consumer units in that group is 25 percent above the average for all consumer units; an index of 75 indicates spending that is 25 percent below the average for all consumer units)

	total married couples	married couples, no children	married couples with children				single parent with child under age 18	single person
			total	oldest child under age 6	oldest child aged 6 to 17	oldest child aged 18 or older		
Average spending of consumer units, total	$63,972	$57,658	$69,724	$65,948	$70,709	$70,412	$37,553	$30,613
Average spending of consumer units, index	129	116	140	133	142	142	76	62
Health care, spending index	135	155	118	105	113	135	57	64
HEALTH INSURANCE	136	156	118	112	112	132	41	64
Commercial health insurance	143	119	165	177	169	150	50	55
Traditional fee-for-service health plan (not BCBS)	130	118	136	98	155	130	50	71
Preferred-provider health plan (not BCBS)	148	120	176	208	174	158	50	49
Blue Cross, Blue Shield	143	130	154	159	151	157	47	53
Traditional fee-for-service health plan	136	134	141	140	137	148	36	65
Preferred-provider health plan	151	128	165	148	159	186	52	40
Health maintenance organization	144	112	175	222	174	146	58	52
Commercial Medicare supplement	118	193	54	52	45	71	11	92
Other BCBS health insurance	147	112	186	33	227	220	41	53
Health maintenance plans (HMOs)	146	140	152	144	147	166	74	44
Medicare payments	116	208	28	3	13	72	14	92
Medicare prescription drug premium	116	211	26	0	6	78	5	97
Commercial Medicare supplements and other health insurance	131	192	80	59	75	102	26	80
Commercial Medicare supplement (not BCBS)	123	213	42	39	30	65	18	91
Other health insurance (not BCBS)	144	154	147	94	155	170	41	60
Long-term care insurance	137	242	55	42	40	89	10	85
MEDICAL SERVICES	134	142	129	115	125	145	107	61
Physician's services	139	141	144	143	119	187	96	53
Dental services	136	150	122	53	135	145	56	64
Eye care services	128	151	108	110	87	144	43	83
Service by professionals other than physician	125	94	154	173	139	167	222	64
Lab tests, X-rays	142	186	106	92	90	143	107	45
Hospital room and services	128	133	130	191	136	80	222	46
Care in convalescent or nursing home	50	41	49	78	36	52	–	255
Other medical services	139	96	186	213	169	197	49	84
DRUGS	135	170	103	67	99	135	43	64
Nonprescription drugs	134	149	123	116	120	133	45	65
Nonprescription vitamins	142	176	101	98	105	98	29	63
Prescription drugs	134	174	98	49	93	141	45	64
MEDICAL SUPPLIES	129	153	110	84	113	124	47	74
Eyeglasses and contact lenses	137	153	130	66	141	155	64	63
Hearing aids	106	213	4	3	6	3	–	102
Topicals and dressings	127	131	127	145	121	126	40	76
Adult diapers	123	114	120	264	132	15	23	117
Medical equipment for general use	125	158	99	50	64	193	96	86
Supportive and convalescent medical equipment	127	153	84	24	59	169	5	81
Rental of medical equipment	121	175	90	116	113	34	12	61
Rental of supportive and convalescent medical equipment	88	106	86	–	122	85	81	83

Note: Spending index for total consumer units is 100. "–" means sample is too small to make a reliable estimate.
Source: Calculations by New Strategist based on the Bureau of Labor Statistics' 2011 Consumer Expenditure Survey

Table 7.15 Health Care: Total spending by household type, 2011

(total annual out-of-pocket spending on health care, by consumer unit type, 2011; consumer units and dollars in thousands)

	total married couples	married couples, no children	married couples with children				single parent with child under age 18	single person
			total	oldest child under age 6	oldest child aged 6 to 17	oldest child aged 18 or older		
Number of consumer units	60,144	25,270	29,097	5,825	14,661	8,612	6,956	36,110
Total spending of all consumer units	$3,847,504,302	$1,457,023,725	$2,028,765,629	$384,144,828	$1,036,657,612	$606,386,852	$261,219,016	$1,105,441,930
Health care, total spending	269,386,179	129,550,446	113,778,872	20,304,494	55,026,985	38,453,441	13,158,457	76,275,153
HEALTH INSURANCE	157,535,781	75,899,961	65,991,996	12,587,068	31,620,405	21,786,810	5,544,906	44,501,242
Commercial health insurance	29,196,905	10,221,210	16,285,300	3,503,097	8,403,099	4,379,719	1,184,607	6,755,459
Traditional fee-for-service health plan (not BCBS)	7,221,490	2,751,145	3,669,132	526,464	2,105,613	1,037,057	324,428	2,386,510
Preferred-provider health plan (not BCBS)	21,974,813	7,470,317	12,616,459	2,976,633	6,297,486	3,342,662	860,179	4,368,949
Blue Cross, Blue Shield	52,432,938	19,908,970	27,318,009	5,644,367	13,442,818	8,231,866	1,990,320	11,637,170
Traditional fee-for-service health plan	8,906,124	3,669,709	4,458,533	883,594	2,187,128	1,387,996	271,840	2,538,533
Preferred-provider health plan	22,397,024	7,967,884	11,815,710	2,122,106	5,743,887	3,950,152	885,360	3,541,669
Health maintenance organization	16,480,057	5,367,853	9,709,087	2,458,150	4,858,362	2,393,016	765,577	3,581,390
Commercial Medicare supplement	3,858,839	2,650,318	852,833	163,624	357,289	332,079	42,223	1,804,417
Other BCBS health insurance	790,292	253,205	481,555	16,951	296,006	168,623	25,459	171,523
Health maintenance plans (HMOs)	28,018,684	11,302,008	14,133,868	2,682,471	6,877,035	4,574,781	1,652,676	5,069,122
Medicare payments	25,656,829	19,401,548	3,055,185	54,289	720,295	2,280,630	362,825	12,257,540
Medicare prescription drug premium	4,371,266	3,342,716	476,609	932	53,952	421,816	19,755	2,199,460
Commercial Medicare supplements and other health insurance	12,332,527	7,608,039	3,654,292	539,104	1,730,584	1,384,810	288,744	4,524,583
Commercial Medicare supplement (not BCBS)	7,434,400	5,402,473	1,229,930	229,855	442,616	557,541	126,251	3,298,287
Other health insurance (not BCBS)	4,898,127	2,205,566	2,424,362	309,191	1,287,822	827,269	162,423	1,226,657
Long-term care insurance	5,527,835	4,115,220	1,068,733	162,809	392,622	513,275	45,979	2,057,909
MEDICAL SERVICES	61,689,701	27,524,337	28,795,264	5,145,281	14,081,157	9,569,827	5,713,380	16,856,509
Physician's services	15,031,188	6,393,310	7,495,096	1,490,326	3,120,154	2,885,020	1,203,458	3,404,451
Dental services	23,294,373	10,824,910	10,116,736	889,070	5,648,737	3,579,319	1,115,673	6,601,269
Eye care services	2,863,456	1,412,846	1,171,154	237,369	473,990	459,795	111,992	1,113,632
Service by professionals other than physician	4,251,579	1,347,144	2,533,476	569,103	1,150,595	814,006	874,021	1,299,238
Lab tests, X-rays	4,104,828	2,255,095	1,477,837	256,009	629,837	591,989	356,912	786,115
Hospital room and services	9,912,934	4,342,144	4,894,115	1,436,620	2,564,795	892,892	1,990,599	2,149,628
Care in convalescent or nursing home	310,944	108,156	147,813	47,124	54,686	45,988	–	948,971
Other medical services	1,477,137	430,854	958,455	219,544	438,511	300,559	60,726	533,345
DRUGS	39,775,633	20,949,335	14,694,567	1,912,697	7,108,386	5,666,954	1,465,212	11,333,124
Nonprescription drugs	7,471,689	3,493,072	3,308,911	624,615	1,622,093	1,056,434	291,526	2,167,683
Nonprescription vitamins	4,438,026	2,309,931	1,532,539	295,677	796,532	439,126	106,009	1,175,019
Prescription drugs	27,865,918	15,146,080	9,853,117	992,405	4,689,761	4,171,394	1,067,676	7,990,421
MEDICAL SUPPLIES	10,385,666	5,176,812	4,297,045	659,507	2,217,036	1,429,850	434,889	3,583,918
Eyeglasses and contact lenses	5,245,158	2,453,212	2,405,449	244,242	1,314,505	846,818	282,553	1,435,734
Hearing aids	1,079,585	910,984	20,950	3,146	13,928	3,789	–	621,814
Topicals and dressings	3,116,662	1,343,353	1,504,315	344,141	724,400	441,709	113,591	1,111,105
Adult diapers	211,707	82,633	99,803	44,154	55,419	3,789	4,591	120,969
Medical equipment for general use	285,684	152,378	109,987	11,184	35,626	63,298	25,389	117,719
Supportive and convalescent medical equipment	308,539	156,421	99,221	5,534	34,893	58,906	1,391	118,441
Rental of medical equipment	75,781	45,991	27,351	7,048	17,300	3,014	835	22,749
Rental of supportive and convalescent medical equipment	61,948	31,335	29,388	–	20,965	8,612	6,608	35,027

Note: Total spending figures for total consumer units can be found on Total Spending by Age and Total Spending by Region tables. Spending by type of consumer unit does not add to total because not all types of consumer units are shown. Numbers may not add to category total because of rounding and missing subcategories. "–" means sample is too small to make a reliable estimate.
Source: Calculations by New Strategist based on the Bureau of Labor Statistics' 2011 Consumer Expenditure Survey

Table 7.16 Health Care: Market shares by household type, 2011

(percentage of total annual out-of-pocket spending on health care accounted for by types of consumer units, 2011)

	total married couples	married couples, no children	married couples with children				single parent with child under age 18	single person
			total	oldest child under age 6	oldest child aged 6 to 17	oldest child aged 18 or older		
Share of total consumer units	49.2%	20.7%	23.8%	4.8%	12.0%	7.0%	5.7%	29.5%
Share of total before-tax income	67.0	25.6	35.0	6.8	17.5	10.7	3.3	16.0
Share of total spending	63.3	24.0	33.4	6.3	17.1	10.0	4.3	18.2
Share of health care spending	66.5	32.0	28.1	5.0	13.6	9.5	3.2	18.8
HEALTH INSURANCE	**67.0**	**32.3**	**28.1**	**5.4**	**13.5**	**9.3**	**2.4**	**18.9**
Commercial health insurance	**70.5**	**24.7**	**39.3**	**8.5**	**20.3**	**10.6**	**2.9**	**16.3**
Traditional fee-for-service health plan (not BCBS)	63.8	24.3	32.4	4.6	18.6	9.2	2.9	21.1
Preferred-provider health plan (not BCBS)	73.0	24.8	41.9	9.9	20.9	11.1	2.9	14.5
Blue Cross, Blue Shield	**70.5**	**26.8**	**36.7**	**7.6**	**18.1**	**11.1**	**2.7**	**15.6**
Traditional fee-for-service health plan	67.1	27.6	33.6	6.7	16.5	10.5	2.0	19.1
Preferred-provider health plan	74.4	26.5	39.2	7.0	19.1	13.1	2.9	11.8
Health maintenance organization	70.8	23.1	41.7	10.6	20.9	10.3	3.3	15.4
Commercial Medicare supplement	58.2	40.0	12.9	2.5	5.4	5.0	0.6	27.2
Other BCBS health insurance	72.5	23.2	44.2	1.6	27.2	15.5	2.3	15.7
Health maintenance plans (HMOs)	**71.7**	**28.9**	**36.2**	**6.9**	**17.6**	**11.7**	**4.2**	**13.0**
Medicare payments	**56.9**	**43.0**	**6.8**	**0.1**	**1.6**	**5.1**	**0.8**	**27.2**
Medicare prescription drug premium	**57.0**	**43.6**	**6.2**	**0.0**	**0.7**	**5.5**	**0.3**	**28.7**
Commercial Medicare supplements and other health insurance	**64.2**	**39.6**	**19.0**	**2.8**	**9.0**	**7.2**	**1.5**	**23.6**
Commercial Medicare supplement (not BCBS)	60.6	44.0	10.0	1.9	3.6	4.5	1.0	26.9
Other health insurance (not BCBS)	70.7	31.9	35.0	4.5	18.6	11.9	2.3	17.7
Long-term care insurance	**67.2**	**50.0**	**13.0**	**2.0**	**4.8**	**6.2**	**0.6**	**25.0**
MEDICAL SERVICES	**65.7**	**29.3**	**30.7**	**5.5**	**15.0**	**10.2**	**6.1**	**18.0**
Physician's services	68.5	29.1	34.2	6.8	14.2	13.2	5.5	15.5
Dental services	66.7	31.0	29.0	2.5	16.2	10.2	3.2	18.9
Eye care services	63.1	31.1	25.8	5.2	10.4	10.1	2.5	24.5
Service by professionals other than physician	61.4	19.5	36.6	8.2	16.6	11.8	12.6	18.8
Lab tests, X-rays	70.0	38.4	25.2	4.4	10.7	10.1	6.1	13.4
Hospital room and services	62.8	27.5	31.0	9.1	16.2	5.7	12.6	13.6
Care in convalescent or nursing home	24.6	8.6	11.7	3.7	4.3	3.6	–	75.2
Other medical services	68.3	19.9	44.3	10.2	20.3	13.9	2.8	24.7
DRUGS	**66.5**	**35.0**	**24.6**	**3.2**	**11.9**	**9.5**	**2.4**	**18.9**
Nonprescription drugs	66.0	30.9	29.2	5.5	14.3	9.3	2.6	19.1
Nonprescription vitamins	69.9	36.4	24.1	4.7	12.5	6.9	1.7	18.5
Prescription drugs	66.1	35.9	23.4	2.4	11.1	9.9	2.5	19.0
MEDICAL SUPPLIES	**63.4**	**31.6**	**26.2**	**4.0**	**13.5**	**8.7**	**2.7**	**21.9**
Eyeglasses and contact lenses	67.5	31.6	31.0	3.1	16.9	10.9	3.6	18.5
Hearing aids	52.3	44.1	1.0	0.2	0.7	0.2	–	30.1
Topicals and dressings	62.6	27.0	30.2	6.9	14.6	8.9	2.3	22.3
Adult diapers	60.3	23.5	28.4	12.6	15.8	1.1	1.3	34.5
Medical equipment for general use	61.3	32.7	23.6	2.4	7.6	13.6	5.4	25.3
Supportive and convalescent medical equipment	62.5	31.7	20.1	1.1	7.1	11.9	0.3	24.0
Rental of medical equipment	59.6	36.2	21.5	5.5	13.6	2.4	0.7	17.9
Rental of supportive and convalescent medical equipment	43.3	21.9	20.5	–	14.7	6.0	4.6	24.5

Note: Market share for total consumer units is 100.0%. Market shares by type of consumer unit do not add to total because not all types of consumer units are shown. "–" means sample is too small to make a reliable estimate.
Source: Calculations by New Strategist based on the Bureau of Labor Statistics' 2011 Consumer Expenditure Survey

Table 7.17 Health Care: Average spending by race and Hispanic origin, 2011

(average annual out-of-pocket spending of consumer units on health care, by race and Hispanic origin of consumer unit reference person, 2011)

	total consumer units	Asian	black	Hispanic	non-Hispanic white and other
Number of consumer units (in 000s)	122,287	5,048	15,118	15,222	92,163
Average number of persons per consumer unit	2.5	2.7	2.6	3.4	2.4
Average before-tax income of consumer units	$63,685.00	$85,415.00	$45,552.00	$49,966.00	$68,907.00
Average spending of consumer units, total	49,704.88	60,136.04	36,643.75	42,085.98	53,055.68
Health care, average spending	**3,312.92**	**2,918.59**	**1,896.55**	**1,773.71**	**3,793.10**
HEALTH INSURANCE	**1,922.19**	**1,882.33**	**1,238.33**	**1,008.49**	**2,182.28**
Commercial health insurance	**338.85**	**341.49**	**212.00**	**130.52**	**393.50**
Traditional fee-for-service health plan (not BCBS)	92.61	39.28	52.41	30.86	109.19
Preferred-provider health plan (not BCBS)	246.24	302.20	159.59	99.65	284.32
Blue Cross, Blue Shield	**608.29**	**593.15**	**370.68**	**311.40**	**695.49**
Traditional fee-for-service health plan	108.55	72.88	48.24	33.18	130.75
Preferred-provider health plan	246.31	277.37	132.34	139.50	282.18
Health maintenance organization	190.30	196.24	168.66	129.78	203.80
Commercial Medicare supplement	54.22	36.30	18.22	4.40	68.22
Other BCBS health insurance	8.91	10.37	3.22	4.54	10.54
Health maintenance plans (HMOs)	**319.41**	**490.33**	**220.54**	**284.52**	**340.78**
Medicare payments	**368.66**	**222.17**	**280.69**	**183.90**	**413.06**
Medicare prescription drug premium	**62.70**	**40.16**	**51.21**	**33.13**	**69.36**
Commercial Medicare supplements and other health insurance	**156.97**	**160.11**	**61.68**	**51.71**	**189.80**
Commercial Medicare supplement (not BCBS)	100.35	109.97	33.99	27.05	123.11
Other health insurance (not BCBS)	56.62	50.14	27.69	24.66	66.70
Long-term care insurance	**67.29**	**34.92**	**41.53**	**13.31**	**80.28**
MEDICAL SERVICES	**767.64**	**667.07**	**299.79**	**453.19**	**895.74**
Physician's services	179.40	114.46	72.44	89.32	211.40
Dental services	285.67	317.52	119.49	176.34	330.31
Eye care services	37.11	31.75	24.59	30.15	41.50
Service by professionals other than physician	56.63	38.32	15.97	28.73	67.79
Lab tests, X-rays	47.97	57.35	15.03	35.59	55.32
Hospital room and services	129.10	78.10	35.31	85.32	151.42
Care in convalescent or nursing home	10.32	4.51	2.94	3.90	12.56
Other medical services	17.68	25.06	13.34	3.85	20.63
DRUGS	**489.06**	**284.77**	**299.68**	**236.82**	**559.58**
Nonprescription drugs	92.57	53.81	53.66	77.60	100.77
Nonprescription vitamins	51.94	68.52	15.16	17.46	62.84
Prescription drugs	344.56	162.44	230.86	141.75	395.98
MEDICAL SUPPLIES	**134.03**	**84.43**	**58.74**	**75.20**	**155.49**
Eyeglasses and contact lenses	63.53	42.28	31.12	42.51	72.17
Hearing aids	16.89	3.70	0.60	0.02	22.30
Topicals and dressings	40.69	29.96	19.90	23.01	46.58
Adult diapers	2.87	–	3.37	6.70	2.20
Medical equipment for general use	3.81	0.87	0.24	0.33	4.96
Supportive and convalescent medical equipment	4.04	7.22	2.30	1.64	4.71
Rental of medical equipment	1.04	0.26	0.52	0.33	1.25
Rental of supportive and convalescent medical equipment	1.17	0.12	0.69	0.65	1.33

Note: "Asian" and "black" include Hispanics and non-Hispanics who identify themselves as being of the respective race alone. "Hispanic" includes people of any race who identify themselves as Hispanic. "Other" includes people who identify themselves as non-Hispanic and as Alaska Native, American Indian, Asian (who are also included in the "Asian" column), or Native Hawaiian or other Pacific Islander, as well as non-Hispanics reporting more than one race. Subcategories may not add to total because some are not shown. "–" means sample is too small to make a reliable estimate.
Source: Bureau of Labor Statistics, unpublished tables from the 2011 Consumer Expenditure Survey

Table 7.18 Health Care: Indexed spending by race and Hispanic origin, 2011

(indexed average annual out-of-pocket spending of consumer units on health care, by race and Hispanic origin of consumer unit reference person, 2011; index definition: an index of 100 is the average for all consumer units; an index of 125 means that spending by consumer units in that group is 25 percent above the average for all consumer units; an index of 75 indicates spending that is 25 percent below the average for all consumer units)

	total consumer units	Asian	black	Hispanic	non-Hispanic white and other
Average spending of consumer units, total	$49,705	$60,136	$36,644	$42,086	$53,056
Average spending of consumer units, index	100	121	74	85	107
Health care, spending index	100	88	57	54	114
HEALTH INSURANCE	100	98	64	52	114
Commercial health insurance	100	101	63	39	116
Traditional fee-for-service health plan (not BCBS)	100	42	57	33	118
Preferred-provider health plan (not BCBS)	100	123	65	40	115
Blue Cross, Blue Shield	100	98	61	51	114
Traditional fee-for-service health plan	100	67	44	31	120
Preferred-provider health plan	100	113	54	57	115
Health maintenance organization	100	103	89	68	107
Commercial Medicare supplement	100	67	34	8	126
Other BCBS health insurance	100	116	36	51	118
Health maintenance plans (HMOs)	100	154	69	89	107
Medicare payments	100	60	76	50	112
Medicare prescription drug premium	100	64	82	53	111
Commercial Medicare supplements and other health insurance	100	102	39	33	121
Commercial Medicare supplement (not BCBS)	100	110	34	27	123
Other health insurance (not BCBS)	100	89	49	44	118
Long-term care insurance	100	52	62	20	119
MEDICAL SERVICES	100	87	39	59	117
Physician's services	100	64	40	50	118
Dental services	100	111	42	62	116
Eye care services	100	86	66	81	112
Service by professionals other than physician	100	68	28	51	120
Lab tests, X-rays	100	120	31	74	115
Hospital room and services	100	60	27	66	117
Care in convalescent or nursing home	100	44	28	38	122
Other medical services	100	142	75	22	117
DRUGS	100	58	61	48	114
Nonprescription drugs	100	58	58	84	109
Nonprescription vitamins	100	132	29	34	121
Prescription drugs	100	47	67	41	115
MEDICAL SUPPLIES	100	63	44	56	116
Eyeglasses and contact lenses	100	67	49	67	114
Hearing aids	100	22	4	0	132
Topicals and dressings	100	74	49	57	114
Adult diapers	100	–	117	233	77
Medical equipment for general use	100	23	6	9	130
Supportive and convalescent medical equipment	100	179	57	41	117
Rental of medical equipment	100	25	50	32	120
Rental of supportive and convalescent medical equipment	100	10	59	56	114

Note: "Asian" and "black" include Hispanics and non-Hispanics who identify themselves as being of the respective race alone. "Hispanic" includes people of any race who identify themselves as Hispanic. "Other" includes people who identify themselves as non-Hispanic and as Alaska Native, American Indian, Asian (who are also included in the "Asian" column), or Native Hawaiian or other Pacific Islander, as well as non-Hispanics reporting more than one race. "–" means sample is too small to make a reliable estimate.
Source: Calculations by New Strategist based on the Bureau of Labor Statistics' 2011 Consumer Expenditure Survey

Table 7.19 Health Care: Total spending by race and Hispanic origin, 2011

(total annual out-of-pocket spending on health care, by consumer unit race and Hispanic origin groups, 2011; consumer units and dollars in thousands)

	total consumer units	Asian	black	Hispanic	non-Hispanic white and other
Number of consumer units	122,287	5,048	15,118	15,222	92,163
Total spending of all consumer units	$6,078,260,661	$303,566,730	$553,980,213	$640,632,788	$4,889,770,636
Health care, total spending	405,127,048	14,733,042	28,672,043	26,999,414	349,583,475
HEALTH INSURANCE	235,058,849	9,502,002	18,721,073	15,351,235	201,125,472
Commercial health insurance	41,436,950	1,723,842	3,205,016	1,986,775	36,266,141
Traditional fee-for-service health plan (not BCBS)	11,324,999	198,285	792,334	469,751	10,063,278
Preferred-provider health plan (not BCBS)	30,111,951	1,525,506	2,412,682	1,516,872	26,203,784
Blue Cross, Blue Shield	74,385,959	2,994,221	5,603,940	4,740,131	64,098,445
Traditional fee-for-service health plan	13,274,254	367,898	729,292	505,066	12,050,312
Preferred-provider health plan	30,120,511	1,400,164	2,000,716	2,123,469	26,006,555
Health maintenance organization	23,271,216	990,620	2,549,802	1,975,511	18,782,819
Commercial Medicare supplement	6,630,401	183,242	275,450	66,977	6,287,360
Other BCBS health insurance	1,089,577	52,348	48,680	69,108	971,398
Health maintenance plans (HMOs)	39,059,691	2,475,186	3,334,124	4,330,963	31,407,307
Medicare payments	45,082,325	1,121,514	4,243,471	2,799,326	38,068,849
Medicare prescription drug premium	7,667,395	202,728	774,193	504,305	6,392,426
Commercial Medicare supplements and other health insurance	19,195,390	808,235	932,478	787,130	17,492,537
Commercial Medicare supplement (not BCBS)	12,271,500	555,129	513,861	411,755	11,346,187
Other health insurance (not BCBS)	6,923,890	253,107	418,617	375,375	6,147,272
Long-term care insurance	8,228,692	176,276	627,851	202,605	7,398,846
MEDICAL SERVICES	93,872,393	3,367,369	4,532,225	6,898,458	82,554,086
Physician's services	21,938,288	577,794	1,095,148	1,359,629	19,483,258
Dental services	34,933,727	1,602,841	1,806,450	2,684,247	30,442,361
Eye care services	4,538,071	160,274	371,752	458,943	3,824,765
Service by professionals other than physician	6,925,113	193,439	241,434	437,328	6,247,730
Lab tests, X-rays	5,866,107	289,503	227,224	541,751	5,098,457
Hospital room and services	15,787,252	394,249	533,817	1,298,741	13,955,321
Care in convalescent or nursing home	1,262,002	22,766	44,447	59,366	1,157,567
Other medical services	2,162,034	126,503	201,674	58,605	1,901,323
DRUGS	59,805,680	1,437,519	4,530,562	3,604,874	51,572,572
Nonprescription drugs	11,320,108	271,633	811,232	1,181,227	9,287,266
Nonprescription vitamins	6,351,587	345,889	229,189	265,776	5,791,523
Prescription drugs	42,135,209	819,997	3,490,141	2,157,719	36,494,705
MEDICAL SUPPLIES	16,390,127	426,203	888,031	1,144,694	14,330,425
Eyeglasses and contact lenses	7,768,893	213,429	470,472	647,087	6,651,404
Hearing aids	2,065,427	18,678	9,071	304	2,055,235
Topicals and dressings	4,975,858	151,238	300,848	350,258	4,292,953
Adult diapers	350,964	–	50,948	101,987	202,759
Medical equipment for general use	465,913	4,392	3,628	5,023	457,128
Supportive and convalescent medical equipment	494,039	36,447	34,771	24,964	434,088
Rental of medical equipment	127,178	1,312	7,861	5,023	115,204
Rental of supportive and convalescent medical equipment	143,076	606	10,431	9,894	122,577

Note: "Asian" and "black" include Hispanics and non-Hispanics who identify themselves as being of the respective race alone. "Hispanic" includes people of any race who identify themselves as Hispanic. "Other" includes people who identify themselves as non-Hispanic and as Alaska Native, American Indian, Asian (who are also included in the "Asian" column), or Native Hawaiian or other Pacific Islander, as well as non-Hispanics reporting more than one race. Numbers may not add to total because of rounding and missing subcategories. "–" means sample is too small to make a reliable estimate.
Source: Calculations by New Strategist based on the Bureau of Labor Statistics' 2011 Consumer Expenditure Survey

Table 7.20 Health Care: Market shares by race and Hispanic origin, 2011

(percentage of total annual out-of-pocket spending on health care accounted for by consumer unit race and Hispanic origin groups, 2011)

	total consumer units	Asian	black	Hispanic	non-Hispanic white and other
Share of total consumer units	100.0%	4.1%	12.4%	12.4%	75.4%
Share of total before-tax income	100.0	5.5	8.8	9.8	81.5
Share of total spending	100.0	5.0	9.1	10.5	80.4
Share of health care spending	100.0	3.6	7.1	6.7	86.3
HEALTH INSURANCE	100.0	4.0	8.0	6.5	85.6
Commercial health insurance	100.0	4.2	7.7	4.8	87.5
Traditional fee-for-service health plan (not BCBS)	100.0	1.8	7.0	4.1	88.9
Preferred-provider health plan (not BCBS)	100.0	5.1	8.0	5.0	87.0
Blue Cross, Blue Shield	100.0	4.0	7.5	6.4	86.2
Traditional fee-for-service health plan	100.0	2.8	5.5	3.8	90.8
Preferred-provider health plan	100.0	4.6	6.6	7.0	86.3
Health maintenance organization	100.0	4.3	11.0	8.5	80.7
Commercial Medicare supplement	100.0	2.8	4.2	1.0	94.8
Other BCBS health insurance	100.0	4.8	4.5	6.3	89.2
Health maintenance plans (HMOs)	100.0	6.3	8.5	11.1	80.4
Medicare payments	100.0	2.5	9.4	6.2	84.4
Medicare prescription drug premium	100.0	2.6	10.1	6.6	83.4
Commercial Medicare supplements and other health insurance	100.0	4.2	4.9	4.1	91.1
Commercial Medicare supplement (not BCBS)	100.0	4.5	4.2	3.4	92.5
Other health insurance (not BCBS)	100.0	3.7	6.0	5.4	88.8
Long-term care insurance	100.0	2.1	7.6	2.5	89.9
MEDICAL SERVICES	100.0	3.6	4.8	7.3	87.9
Physician's services	100.0	2.6	5.0	6.2	88.8
Dental services	100.0	4.6	5.2	7.7	87.1
Eye care services	100.0	3.5	8.2	10.1	84.3
Service by professionals other than physician	100.0	2.8	3.5	6.3	90.2
Lab tests, X-rays	100.0	4.9	3.9	9.2	86.9
Hospital room and services	100.0	2.5	3.4	8.2	88.4
Care in convalescent or nursing home	100.0	1.8	3.5	4.7	91.7
Other medical services	100.0	5.9	9.3	2.7	87.9
DRUGS	100.0	2.4	7.6	6.0	86.2
Nonprescription drugs	100.0	2.4	7.2	10.4	82.0
Nonprescription vitamins	100.0	5.4	3.6	4.2	91.2
Prescription drugs	100.0	1.9	8.3	5.1	86.6
MEDICAL SUPPLIES	100.0	2.6	5.4	7.0	87.4
Eyeglasses and contact lenses	100.0	2.7	6.1	8.3	85.6
Hearing aids	100.0	0.9	0.4	0.0	99.5
Topicals and dressings	100.0	3.0	6.0	7.0	86.3
Adult diapers	100.0	–	14.5	29.1	57.8
Medical equipment for general use	100.0	0.9	0.8	1.1	98.1
Supportive and convalescent medical equipment	100.0	7.4	7.0	5.1	87.9
Rental of medical equipment	100.0	1.0	6.2	3.9	90.6
Rental of supportive and convalescent medical equipment	100.0	0.4	7.3	6.9	85.7

Note: "Asian" and "black" include Hispanics and non-Hispanics who identify themselves as being of the respective race alone. "Hispanic" includes people of any race who identify themselves as Hispanic. "Other" includes people who identify themselves as non-Hispanic and as Alaska Native, American Indian, Asian (who are also included in the "Asian" column), or Native Hawaiian or other Pacific Islander, as well as non-Hispanics reporting more than one race. "–" means sample is too small to make a reliable estimate.
Source: Calculations by New Strategist based on the Bureau of Labor Statistics' 2011 Consumer Expenditure Survey

Table 7.21 Health Care: Average spending by region, 2011

(average annual out-of-pocket spending of consumer units on health care, by region in which consumer unit lives, 2011)

	total consumer units	Northeast	Midwest	South	West
Number of consumer units (in 000s)	122,287	22,538	27,107	44,901	27,741
Average number of persons per consumer unit	2.5	2.4	2.4	2.5	2.6
Average before-tax income of consumer units	$63,685.00	$71,733.00	$60,897.00	$58,780.00	$67,810.00
Average spending of consumer units, total	49,704.88	54,547.45	47,191.54	45,698.60	54,745.43
Health care, average spending	**3,312.92**	**3,368.32**	**3,620.08**	**3,160.10**	**3,215.93**
HEALTH INSURANCE	**1,922.19**	**2,023.20**	**2,029.01**	**1,846.20**	**1,858.73**
Commercial health insurance	**338.85**	**259.93**	**385.58**	**336.83**	**360.58**
Traditional fee-for-service health plan (not BCBS)	92.61	104.54	115.79	77.40	84.89
Preferred-provider health plan (not BCBS)	246.24	155.39	269.79	259.43	275.69
Blue Cross, Blue Shield	**608.29**	**681.13**	**665.97**	**597.95**	**509.50**
Traditional fee-for-service health plan	108.55	117.20	120.22	97.01	108.81
Preferred-provider health plan	246.31	183.59	288.10	271.23	216.11
Health maintenance organization	190.30	303.13	161.55	181.07	141.68
Commercial Medicare supplement	54.22	65.94	78.89	42.63	39.34
Other BCBS health insurance	8.91	11.26	17.22	6.01	3.55
Health maintenance plans (HMOs)	**319.41**	**397.90**	**297.35**	**260.53**	**372.50**
Medicare payments	**368.66**	**371.36**	**362.13**	**387.20**	**342.85**
Medicare prescription drug premium	**62.70**	**64.86**	**60.99**	**66.85**	**55.90**
Commercial Medicare supplements and other health insurance	**156.97**	**172.47**	**187.01**	**132.43**	**154.77**
Commercial Medicare supplement (not BCBS)	100.35	120.11	106.09	85.82	102.21
Other health insurance (not BCBS)	56.62	52.36	80.92	46.61	52.56
Long-term care insurance	**67.29**	**75.55**	**69.98**	**64.41**	**62.62**
MEDICAL SERVICES	**767.64**	**788.27**	**927.55**	**676.65**	**741.93**
Physician's services	179.40	155.30	220.46	161.29	188.16
Dental services	285.67	363.59	266.77	256.98	287.24
Eye care services	37.11	33.27	38.25	40.71	33.30
Service by professionals other than physician	56.63	52.11	90.40	40.45	53.50
Lab tests, X-rays	47.97	32.82	74.24	43.42	41.96
Hospital room and services	129.10	109.04	201.82	111.62	102.65
Care in convalescent or nursing home	10.32	23.48	10.91	4.01	9.24
Other medical services	17.68	18.67	19.97	15.07	18.85
DRUGS	**489.06**	**425.08**	**508.02**	**506.62**	**494.95**
Nonprescription drugs	92.57	81.29	95.48	90.17	102.90
Nonprescription vitamins	51.94	41.58	45.53	38.43	89.21
Prescription drugs	344.56	302.21	367.01	378.02	302.84
MEDICAL SUPPLIES	**134.03**	**131.77**	**155.50**	**130.64**	**120.32**
Eyeglasses and contact lenses	63.53	74.65	78.37	53.27	56.62
Hearing aids	16.89	11.68	19.72	24.40	6.18
Topicals and dressings	40.69	32.22	43.65	42.02	42.49
Adult diapers	2.87	2.26	1.73	4.68	1.52
Medical equipment for general use	3.81	6.87	5.42	1.62	3.28
Supportive and convalescent medical equipment	4.04	2.58	4.51	2.59	7.10
Rental of medical equipment	1.04	0.32	1.26	0.81	1.77
Rental of supportive and convalescent medical equipment	1.17	1.18	0.83	1.24	1.36

Note: Subcategories may not add to total because some are not shown.
Source: Bureau of Labor Statistics, unpublished tables from the 2011 Consumer Expenditure Survey

Table 7.22 Health Care: Indexed spending by region, 2011

(indexed average annual out-of-pocket spending of consumer units on health care, by region in which consumer unit lives, 2011; index definition: an index of 100 is the average for all consumer units; an index of 125 means that spending by consumer units in that group is 25 percent above the average for all consumer units; an index of 75 indicates spending that is 25 percent below the average for all consumer units)

	total consumer units	Northeast	Midwest	South	West
Average spending of consumer units, total	$49,705	$54,547	$47,192	$45,699	$54,745
Average spending of consumer units, index	100	110	95	92	110
Health care, spending index	100	102	109	95	97
HEALTH INSURANCE	100	105	106	96	97
Commercial health insurance	100	77	114	99	106
Traditional fee-for-service health plan (not BCBS)	100	113	125	84	92
Preferred-provider health plan (not BCBS)	100	63	110	105	112
Blue Cross, Blue Shield	100	112	109	98	84
Traditional fee-for-service health plan	100	108	111	89	100
Preferred-provider health plan	100	75	117	110	88
Health maintenance organization	100	159	85	95	74
Commercial Medicare supplement	100	122	145	79	73
Other BCBS health insurance	100	126	193	67	40
Health maintenance plans (HMOs)	100	125	93	82	117
Medicare payments	100	101	98	105	93
Medicare prescription drug premium	100	103	97	107	89
Commercial Medicare supplements and other health insurance	100	110	119	84	99
Commercial Medicare supplement (not BCBS)	100	120	106	86	102
Other health insurance (not BCBS)	100	92	143	82	93
Long-term care insurance	100	112	104	96	93
MEDICAL SERVICES	100	103	121	88	97
Physician's services	100	87	123	90	105
Dental services	100	127	93	90	101
Eye care services	100	90	103	110	90
Service by professionals other than physician	100	92	160	71	94
Lab tests, X-rays	100	68	155	91	87
Hospital room and services	100	84	156	86	80
Care in convalescent or nursing home	100	228	106	39	90
Other medical services	100	106	113	85	107
DRUGS	100	87	104	104	101
Nonprescription drugs	100	88	103	97	111
Nonprescription vitamins	100	80	88	74	172
Prescription drugs	100	88	107	110	88
MEDICAL SUPPLIES	100	98	116	97	90
Eyeglasses and contact lenses	100	118	123	84	89
Hearing aids	100	69	117	144	37
Topicals and dressings	100	79	107	103	104
Adult diapers	100	79	60	163	53
Medical equipment for general use	100	180	142	43	86
Supportive and convalescent medical equipment	100	64	112	64	176
Rental of medical equipment	100	31	121	78	170
Rental of supportive and convalescent medical equipment	100	101	71	106	116

Source: Calculations by New Strategist based on the Bureau of Labor Statistics' 2011 Consumer Expenditure Survey

Table 7.23 Health Care: Total spending by region, 2011

(total annual out-of-pocket spending on health care, by region in which consumer units live, 2011; consumer units and dollars in thousands)

	total consumer units	Northeast	Midwest	South	West
Number of consumer units	122,287	22,538	27,107	44,901	27,741
Total spending of all consumer units	$6,078,260,661	$1,229,390,428	$1,279,221,075	$2,051,912,839	$1,518,692,974
Health care, total spending	405,127,048	75,915,196	98,129,509	141,891,650	89,213,114
HEALTH INSURANCE	235,058,849	45,598,882	55,000,374	82,896,226	51,563,029
Commercial health insurance	41,436,950	5,858,302	10,451,917	15,124,004	10,002,850
Traditional fee-for-service health plan (not BCBS)	11,324,999	2,356,123	3,138,720	3,475,337	2,354,933
Preferred-provider health plan (not BCBS)	30,111,951	3,502,180	7,313,198	11,648,666	7,647,916
Blue Cross, Blue Shield	74,385,959	15,351,308	18,052,449	26,848,553	14,134,040
Traditional fee-for-service health plan	13,274,254	2,641,454	3,258,804	4,355,846	3,018,498
Preferred-provider health plan	30,120,511	4,137,751	7,809,527	12,178,498	5,995,108
Health maintenance organization	23,271,216	6,831,944	4,379,136	8,130,224	3,930,345
Commercial Medicare supplement	6,630,401	1,486,156	2,138,471	1,914,130	1,091,331
Other BCBS health insurance	1,089,577	253,778	466,783	269,855	98,481
Health maintenance plans (HMOs)	39,059,691	8,967,870	8,060,266	11,698,058	10,333,523
Medicare payments	45,082,325	8,369,712	9,816,258	17,385,667	9,511,002
Medicare prescription drug premium	7,667,395	1,461,815	1,653,256	3,001,632	1,550,722
Commercial Medicare supplements and other health insurance	19,195,390	3,887,129	5,069,280	5,946,239	4,293,475
Commercial Medicare supplement (not BCBS)	12,271,500	2,707,039	2,875,782	3,853,404	2,835,408
Other health insurance (not BCBS)	6,923,890	1,180,090	2,193,498	2,092,836	1,458,067
Long-term care insurance	8,228,692	1,702,746	1,896,948	2,892,073	1,737,141
MEDICAL SERVICES	93,872,393	17,766,029	25,143,098	30,382,262	20,581,880
Physician's services	21,938,288	3,500,151	5,976,009	7,242,082	5,219,747
Dental services	34,933,727	8,194,591	7,231,334	11,538,659	7,968,325
Eye care services	4,538,071	749,839	1,036,843	1,827,920	923,775
Service by professionals other than physician	6,925,113	1,174,455	2,450,473	1,816,245	1,484,144
Lab tests, X-rays	5,866,107	739,697	2,012,424	1,949,601	1,164,012
Hospital room and services	15,787,252	2,457,544	5,470,735	5,011,850	2,847,614
Care in convalescent or nursing home	1,262,002	529,192	295,737	180,053	256,327
Other medical services	2,162,034	420,784	541,327	676,658	522,918
DRUGS	59,805,680	9,580,453	13,770,898	22,747,745	13,730,408
Nonprescription drugs	11,320,108	1,832,114	2,588,176	4,048,723	2,854,549
Nonprescription vitamins	6,351,587	937,130	1,234,182	1,725,545	2,474,775
Prescription drugs	42,135,209	6,811,209	9,948,540	16,973,476	8,401,084
MEDICAL SUPPLIES	16,390,127	2,969,832	4,215,139	5,865,867	3,337,797
Eyeglasses and contact lenses	7,768,893	1,682,462	2,124,376	2,391,876	1,570,695
Hearing aids	2,065,427	263,244	534,550	1,095,584	171,439
Topicals and dressings	4,975,858	726,174	1,183,221	1,886,740	1,178,715
Adult diapers	350,964	50,936	46,895	210,137	42,166
Medical equipment for general use	465,913	154,836	146,920	72,740	90,990
Supportive and convalescent medical equipment	494,039	58,148	122,253	116,294	196,961
Rental of medical equipment	127,178	7,212	34,155	36,370	49,102
Rental of supportive and convalescent medical equipment	143,076	26,595	22,499	55,677	37,728

Note: Numbers may not add to total because of rounding and missing subcategories.
Source: Calculations by New Strategist based on the Bureau of Labor Statistics' 2011 Consumer Expenditure Survey

Table 7.24 Health Care: Market shares by region, 2011

(percentage of total annual out-of-pocket spending on health care accounted for by consumer units by region of residence, 2011)

	total consumer units	Northeast	Midwest	South	West
Share of total consumer units	100.0%	18.4%	22.2%	36.7%	22.7%
Share of total before-tax income	100.0	20.8	21.2	33.9	24.2
Share of total spending	100.0	20.2	21.0	33.8	25.0
Share of health care spending	100.0	18.7	24.2	35.0	22.0
HEALTH INSURANCE	100.0	19.4	23.4	35.3	21.9
Commercial health insurance	100.0	14.1	25.2	36.5	24.1
Traditional fee-for-service health plan (not BCBS)	100.0	20.8	27.7	30.7	20.8
Preferred-provider health plan (not BCBS)	100.0	11.6	24.3	38.7	25.4
Blue Cross, Blue Shield	100.0	20.6	24.3	36.1	19.0
Traditional fee-for-service health plan	100.0	19.9	24.5	32.8	22.7
Preferred-provider health plan	100.0	13.7	25.9	40.4	19.9
Health maintenance organization	100.0	29.4	18.8	34.9	16.9
Commercial Medicare supplement	100.0	22.4	32.3	28.9	16.5
Other BCBS health insurance	100.0	23.3	42.8	24.8	9.0
Health maintenance plans (HMOs)	100.0	23.0	20.6	29.9	26.5
Medicare payments	100.0	18.6	21.8	38.6	21.1
Medicare prescription drug premium	100.0	19.1	21.6	39.1	20.2
Commercial Medicare supplements and other health insurance	100.0	20.3	26.4	31.0	22.4
Commercial Medicare supplement (not BCBS)	100.0	22.1	23.4	31.4	23.1
Other health insurance (not BCBS)	100.0	17.0	31.7	30.2	21.1
Long-term care insurance	100.0	20.7	23.1	35.1	21.1
MEDICAL SERVICES	100.0	18.9	26.8	32.4	21.9
Physician's services	100.0	16.0	27.2	33.0	23.8
Dental services	100.0	23.5	20.7	33.0	22.8
Eye care services	100.0	16.5	22.8	40.3	20.4
Service by professionals other than physician	100.0	17.0	35.4	26.2	21.4
Lab tests, X-rays	100.0	12.6	34.3	33.2	19.8
Hospital room and services	100.0	15.6	34.7	31.7	18.0
Care in convalescent or nursing home	100.0	41.9	23.4	14.3	20.3
Other medical services	100.0	19.5	25.0	31.3	24.2
DRUGS	100.0	16.0	23.0	38.0	23.0
Nonprescription drugs	100.0	16.2	22.9	35.8	25.2
Nonprescription vitamins	100.0	14.8	19.4	27.2	39.0
Prescription drugs	100.0	16.2	23.6	40.3	19.9
MEDICAL SUPPLIES	100.0	18.1	25.7	35.8	20.4
Eyeglasses and contact lenses	100.0	21.7	27.3	30.8	20.2
Hearing aids	100.0	12.7	25.9	53.0	8.3
Topicals and dressings	100.0	14.6	23.8	37.9	23.7
Adult diapers	100.0	14.5	13.4	59.9	12.0
Medical equipment for general use	100.0	33.2	31.5	15.6	19.5
Supportive and convalescent medical equipment	100.0	11.8	24.7	23.5	39.9
Rental of medical equipment	100.0	5.7	26.9	28.6	38.6
Rental of supportive and convalescent medical equipment	100.0	18.6	15.7	38.9	26.4

Note: Numbers may not add to total because of rounding.
Source: Calculations by New Strategist based on the Bureau of Labor Statistics' 2011 Consumer Expenditure Survey

Table 7.25 Health Care: Average spending by education, 2011

(average annual out-of-pocket spending of consumer units on health care, by education of consumer unit reference person, 2011)

	total consumer units	less than high school graduate	high school graduate	some college	associate's degree	bachelor's degree or more total	bachelor's degree	graduate degree
Number of consumer units (in 000s)	122,287	16,146	30,810	25,361	12,912	37,058	23,578	13,480
Average number of persons per consumer unit	2.5	2.8	2.5	2.3	2.6	2.5	2.5	2.4
Average before-tax income of consumer units	$63,685.00	$32,564.00	$46,370.00	$52,965.00	$63,664.00	$98,983.00	$90,962.00	$113,013.00
Average spending of consumer units, total	49,704.88	29,950.97	39,704.28	45,355.33	50,819.44	68,902.95	65,051.01	75,731.40
Health care, average spending	**3,312.92**	**2,256.98**	**2,986.38**	**3,020.26**	**3,449.33**	**4,191.58**	**4,022.09**	**4,490.33**
HEALTH INSURANCE	**1,922.19**	**1,325.28**	**1,803.25**	**1,742.90**	**1,874.13**	**2,420.57**	**2,333.69**	**2,572.54**
Commercial health insurance	338.85	116.98	256.01	321.49	409.45	491.68	462.90	542.01
Traditional fee-for-service health plan (not BCBS)	92.61	46.73	100.98	87.21	96.61	107.95	104.74	113.55
Preferred-provider health plan (not BCBS)	246.24	70.25	155.02	234.29	312.83	383.73	358.16	428.46
Blue Cross, Blue Shield	608.29	295.20	561.89	548.78	571.99	836.65	853.16	807.78
Traditional fee-for-service health plan	108.55	59.71	96.58	91.05	70.74	164.94	166.07	162.97
Preferred-provider health plan	246.31	109.21	192.31	219.82	248.35	368.37	384.79	339.64
Health maintenance organization	190.30	76.94	190.35	182.63	181.96	247.81	241.00	259.73
Commercial Medicare supplement	54.22	48.31	73.80	49.20	63.09	40.85	43.57	36.07
Other BCBS health insurance	8.91	1.03	8.85	6.07	7.85	14.69	17.74	9.36
Health maintenance plans (HMOs)	319.41	177.45	271.09	289.78	359.98	427.59	394.67	485.16
Medicare payments	368.66	486.66	441.91	341.34	285.83	303.92	271.75	360.18
Medicare prescription drug premium	62.70	91.95	66.06	65.02	42.86	52.48	47.15	61.82
Commercial Medicare supplements and other health insurance	156.97	125.17	161.03	130.63	158.56	184.93	181.97	190.11
Commercial Medicare supplement (not BCBS)	100.35	102.78	124.59	86.45	75.68	97.25	96.79	98.07
Other health insurance (not BCBS)	56.62	22.39	36.44	44.19	82.88	87.68	85.18	92.05
Long-term care insurance	67.29	31.86	45.26	45.86	45.47	123.32	122.09	125.47
MEDICAL SERVICES	**767.64**	**444.13**	**611.94**	**702.57**	**875.89**	**1,044.71**	**980.33**	**1,156.83**
Physician's services	179.40	110.58	133.95	165.31	172.12	259.34	254.81	267.27
Dental services	285.67	122.43	193.59	263.64	355.44	424.11	384.91	492.66
Eye care services	37.11	16.03	30.49	30.11	46.63	53.28	50.79	57.61
Service by professionals other than physician	56.63	34.51	42.00	42.26	49.22	90.84	67.12	132.33
Lab tests, X-rays	47.97	20.11	39.19	46.78	52.57	66.61	70.34	60.08
Hospital room and services	129.10	129.40	132.84	116.62	166.58	121.36	122.73	118.96
Care in convalescent or nursing home	10.32	2.19	25.20	11.30	2.56	3.51	3.25	3.97
Other medical services	17.68	8.89	14.66	21.07	19.61	21.01	19.33	23.94
DRUGS	**489.06**	**402.98**	**457.93**	**456.04**	**575.13**	**541.37**	**545.70**	**535.74**
Nonprescription drugs	92.57	68.12	80.19	91.78	101.01	109.20	108.15	111.25
Nonprescription vitamins	51.94	39.68	28.92	57.60	45.86	72.89	64.60	89.12
Prescription drugs	344.56	295.18	348.83	306.66	428.26	359.28	372.95	335.38
MEDICAL SUPPLIES	**134.03**	**84.59**	**113.27**	**118.74**	**124.18**	**184.93**	**162.37**	**225.21**
Eyeglasses and contact lenses	63.53	34.58	49.88	54.66	61.03	94.44	87.26	107.02
Hearing aids	16.89	13.63	19.39	18.78	8.96	17.68	10.16	30.84
Topicals and dressings	40.69	23.28	29.85	32.53	42.48	60.38	56.43	68.13
Adult diapers	2.87	4.07	3.10	2.18	3.03	2.65	2.65	2.66
Medical equipment for general use	3.81	3.37	5.32	2.98	1.90	3.96	2.00	7.40
Supportive and convalescent medical equipment	4.04	3.00	4.11	3.85	4.93	4.25	3.22	6.04
Rental of medical equipment	1.04	1.08	0.68	1.58	0.49	1.12	0.46	2.28
Rental of supportive and convalescent medical equipment	1.17	1.58	0.93	2.17	1.35	0.43	0.20	0.84

Note: Subcategories may not add to total because some are not shown.
Source: Bureau of Labor Statistics, unpublished tables from the 2011 Consumer Expenditure Survey

Table 7.26 Health Care: Indexed spending by education, 2011

(indexed average annual out-of-pocket spending of consumer units on health care, by education of consumer unit reference person, 2011; index definition: an index of 100 is the average for all consumer units; an index of 125 means that spending by consumer units in that group is 25 percent above the average for all consumer units; an index of 75 indicates spending that is 25 percent below the average for all consumer units)

	total consumer units	less than high school graduate	high school graduate	some college	associate's degree	bachelor's degree or more total	bachelor's degree	graduate degree
Average spending of consumer units, total	$49,705	$29,951	$39,704	$45,355	$50,819	$68,903	$65,051	$75,731
Average spending of consumer units, index	100	60	80	91	102	139	131	152
Health care, spending index	**100**	**68**	**90**	**91**	**104**	**127**	**121**	**136**
HEALTH INSURANCE	**100**	**69**	**94**	**91**	**97**	**126**	**121**	**134**
Commercial health insurance	**100**	**35**	**76**	**95**	**121**	**145**	**137**	**160**
Traditional fee-for-service health plan (not BCBS)	100	50	109	94	104	117	113	123
Preferred-provider health plan (not BCBS)	100	29	63	95	127	156	145	174
Blue Cross, Blue Shield	**100**	**49**	**92**	**90**	**94**	**138**	**140**	**133**
Traditional fee-for-service health plan	100	55	89	84	65	152	153	150
Preferred-provider health plan	100	44	78	89	101	150	156	138
Health maintenance organization	100	40	100	96	96	130	127	136
Commercial Medicare supplement	100	89	136	91	116	75	80	67
Other BCBS health insurance	100	12	99	68	88	165	199	105
Health maintenance plans (HMOs)	**100**	**56**	**85**	**91**	**113**	**134**	**124**	**152**
Medicare payments	**100**	**132**	**120**	**93**	**78**	**82**	**74**	**98**
Medicare prescription drug premium	**100**	**147**	**105**	**104**	**68**	**84**	**75**	**99**
Commercial Medicare supplements and other health insurance	**100**	**80**	**103**	**83**	**101**	**118**	**116**	**121**
Commercial Medicare supplement (not BCBS)	100	102	124	86	75	97	96	98
Other health insurance (not BCBS)	100	40	64	78	146	155	150	163
Long-term care insurance	**100**	**47**	**67**	**68**	**68**	**183**	**181**	**186**
MEDICAL SERVICES	**100**	**58**	**80**	**92**	**114**	**136**	**128**	**151**
Physician's services	100	62	75	92	96	145	142	149
Dental services	100	43	68	92	124	148	135	172
Eye care services	100	43	82	81	126	144	137	155
Service by professionals other than physician	100	61	74	75	87	160	119	234
Lab tests, X-rays	100	42	82	98	110	139	147	125
Hospital room and services	100	100	103	90	129	94	95	92
Care in convalescent or nursing home	100	21	244	109	25	34	31	38
Other medical services	100	50	83	119	111	119	109	135
DRUGS	**100**	**82**	**94**	**93**	**118**	**111**	**112**	**110**
Nonprescription drugs	100	74	87	99	109	118	117	120
Nonprescription vitamins	100	76	56	111	88	140	124	172
Prescription drugs	100	86	101	89	124	104	108	97
MEDICAL SUPPLIES	**100**	**63**	**85**	**89**	**93**	**138**	**121**	**168**
Eyeglasses and contact lenses	100	54	79	86	96	149	137	168
Hearing aids	100	81	115	111	53	105	60	183
Topicals and dressings	100	57	73	80	104	148	139	167
Adult diapers	100	142	108	76	106	92	92	93
Medical equipment for general use	100	88	140	78	50	104	52	194
Supportive and convalescent medical equipment	100	74	102	95	122	105	80	150
Rental of medical equipment	100	104	65	152	47	108	44	219
Rental of supportive and convalescent medical equipment	100	135	79	185	115	37	17	72

Source: Calculations by New Strategist based on the Bureau of Labor Statistics' 2011 Consumer Expenditure Survey

Table 7.27 Health Care: Total spending by education, 2011

(total annual out-of-pocket spending on health care, by consumer unit educational attainment groups, 2011; consumer units and dollars in thousands)

	total consumer units	less than high school graduate	high school graduate	some college	associate's degree	bachelor's degree or more — total	bachelor's degree	graduate degree
Number of consumer units	122,287	16,146	30,810	25,361	12,912	37,058	23,578	13,480
Total spending of all consumer units	$6,078,260,661	$483,588,362	$1,223,288,867	$1,150,256,524	$656,180,609	$2,553,405,521	$1,533,772,714	$1,020,859,272
Health care, total spending	405,127,048	36,441,199	92,010,368	76,596,814	44,537,749	155,331,572	94,832,838	60,529,648
HEALTH INSURANCE	235,058,849	21,397,971	55,558,133	44,201,687	24,198,767	89,701,483	55,023,743	34,677,839
Commercial health insurance	41,436,950	1,888,759	7,887,668	8,153,308	5,286,818	18,220,677	10,914,256	7,306,295
Traditional fee-for-service health plan (not BCBS)	11,324,999	754,503	3,111,194	2,211,733	1,247,428	4,000,411	2,469,560	1,530,654
Preferred-provider health plan (not BCBS)	30,111,951	1,134,257	4,776,166	5,941,829	4,039,261	14,220,266	8,444,696	5,775,641
Blue Cross, Blue Shield	74,385,959	4,766,299	17,311,831	13,917,610	7,385,535	31,004,576	20,115,806	10,888,874
Traditional fee-for-service health plan	13,274,254	964,078	2,975,630	2,309,119	913,395	6,112,347	3,915,598	2,196,836
Preferred-provider health plan	30,120,511	1,763,305	5,925,071	5,574,855	3,206,695	13,651,055	9,072,579	4,578,347
Health maintenance organization	23,271,216	1,242,273	5,864,684	4,631,679	2,349,468	9,183,343	5,682,298	3,501,160
Commercial Medicare supplement	6,630,401	780,013	2,273,778	1,247,761	814,618	1,513,819	1,027,293	486,224
Other BCBS health insurance	1,089,577	16,630	272,669	153,941	101,359	544,382	418,274	126,173
Health maintenance plans (HMOs)	39,059,691	2,865,108	8,352,283	7,349,111	4,648,062	15,845,630	9,305,529	6,539,957
Medicare payments	45,082,325	7,857,612	13,615,247	8,656,724	3,690,637	11,262,667	6,407,322	4,855,226
Medicare prescription drug premium	7,667,395	1,484,625	2,035,309	1,648,972	553,408	1,944,804	1,111,703	833,334
Commercial Medicare supplements and other health insurance	19,195,390	2,020,995	4,961,334	3,312,907	2,047,327	6,853,136	4,290,489	2,562,683
Commercial Medicare supplement (not BCBS)	12,271,500	1,659,486	3,838,618	2,192,458	977,180	3,603,891	2,282,115	1,321,984
Other health insurance (not BCBS)	6,923,890	361,509	1,122,716	1,120,703	1,070,147	3,249,245	2,008,374	1,240,834
Long-term care insurance	8,228,692	514,412	1,394,461	1,163,055	587,109	4,569,993	2,878,638	1,691,336
MEDICAL SERVICES	93,872,393	7,170,923	18,853,871	17,817,878	11,309,492	38,714,863	23,114,221	15,594,068
Physician's services	21,938,288	1,785,425	4,127,000	4,192,427	2,222,413	9,610,622	6,007,910	3,602,800
Dental services	34,933,727	1,976,755	5,964,508	6,686,174	4,589,441	15,716,668	9,075,408	6,641,057
Eye care services	4,538,071	258,820	939,397	763,620	602,087	1,974,450	1,197,527	776,583
Service by professionals other than physician	6,925,113	557,198	1,294,020	1,071,756	635,529	3,366,349	1,582,555	1,783,808
Lab tests, X-rays	5,866,107	324,696	1,207,444	1,186,388	678,784	2,468,433	1,658,477	809,878
Hospital room and services	15,787,252	2,089,292	4,092,800	2,957,600	2,150,881	4,497,359	2,893,728	1,603,581
Care in convalescent or nursing home	1,262,002	35,360	776,412	286,579	33,055	130,074	76,629	53,516
Other medical services	2,162,034	143,538	451,675	534,356	253,204	778,589	455,763	322,711
DRUGS	59,805,680	6,506,515	14,108,823	11,565,630	7,426,079	20,062,089	12,866,515	7,221,775
Nonprescription drugs	11,320,108	1,099,866	2,470,654	2,327,633	1,304,241	4,046,734	2,549,961	1,499,650
Nonprescription vitamins	6,351,587	640,673	891,025	1,460,794	592,144	2,701,158	1,523,139	1,201,338
Prescription drugs	42,135,209	4,765,976	10,747,452	7,777,204	5,529,693	13,314,198	8,793,415	4,520,922
MEDICAL SUPPLIES	16,390,127	1,365,790	3,489,849	3,011,365	1,603,412	6,853,136	3,828,360	3,035,831
Eyeglasses and contact lenses	7,768,893	558,329	1,536,803	1,386,232	788,019	3,499,758	2,057,416	1,442,630
Hearing aids	2,065,427	220,070	597,406	476,280	115,692	655,185	239,552	415,723
Topicals and dressings	4,975,858	375,879	919,679	824,993	548,502	2,237,562	1,330,507	918,392
Adult diapers	350,964	65,714	95,511	55,287	39,123	98,204	62,482	35,857
Medical equipment for general use	465,913	54,412	163,909	75,576	24,533	146,750	47,156	99,752
Supportive and convalescent medical equipment	494,039	48,438	126,629	97,640	63,656	157,497	75,921	81,419
Rental of medical equipment	127,178	17,438	20,951	40,070	6,327	41,505	10,846	30,734
Rental of supportive and convalescent medical equipment	143,076	25,511	28,653	55,033	17,431	15,935	4,716	11,323

Note: Numbers may not add to total because of rounding and missing subcategories.
Source: Calculations by New Strategist based on the Bureau of Labor Statistics' 2011 Consumer Expenditure Survey

Table 7.28 Health Care: Market shares by education, 2011

(percentage of total annual out-of-pocket spending on health care accounted for by consumer unit educational attainment groups, 2011)

	total consumer units	less than high school graduate	high school graduate	some college	associate's degree	bachelor's degree or more		
						total	bachelor's degree	graduate degree
Share of total consumer units	100.0%	13.2%	25.2%	20.7%	10.6%	30.3%	19.3%	11.0%
Share of total before-tax income	100.0	6.8	18.3	17.2	10.6	47.1	27.5	19.6
Share of total spending	100.0	8.0	20.1	18.9	10.8	42.0	25.2	16.8
Share of health care spending	100.0	9.0	22.7	18.9	11.0	38.3	23.4	14.9
HEALTH INSURANCE	100.0	9.1	23.6	18.8	10.3	38.2	23.4	14.8
Commercial health insurance	100.0	4.6	19.0	19.7	12.8	44.0	26.3	17.6
Traditional fee-for-service health plan (not BCBS)	100.0	6.7	27.5	19.5	11.0	35.3	21.8	13.5
Preferred-provider health plan (not BCBS)	100.0	3.8	15.9	19.7	13.4	47.2	28.0	19.2
Blue Cross, Blue Shield	100.0	6.4	23.3	18.7	9.9	41.7	27.0	14.6
Traditional fee-for-service health plan	100.0	7.3	22.4	17.4	6.9	46.0	29.5	16.5
Preferred-provider health plan	100.0	5.9	19.7	18.5	10.6	45.3	30.1	15.2
Health maintenance organization	100.0	5.3	25.2	19.9	10.1	39.5	24.4	15.0
Commercial Medicare supplement	100.0	11.8	34.3	18.8	12.3	22.8	15.5	7.3
Other BCBS health insurance	100.0	1.5	25.0	14.1	9.3	50.0	38.4	11.6
Health maintenance plans (HMOs)	100.0	7.3	21.4	18.8	11.9	40.6	23.8	16.7
Medicare payments	100.0	17.4	30.2	19.2	8.2	25.0	14.2	10.8
Medicare prescription drug premium	100.0	19.4	26.5	21.5	7.2	25.4	14.5	10.9
Commercial Medicare supplements and other health insurance	100.0	10.5	25.8	17.3	10.7	35.7	22.4	13.4
Commercial Medicare supplement (not BCBS)	100.0	13.5	31.3	17.9	8.0	29.4	18.6	10.8
Other health insurance (not BCBS)	100.0	5.2	16.2	16.2	15.5	46.9	29.0	17.9
Long-term care insurance	100.0	6.3	16.9	14.1	7.1	55.5	35.0	20.6
MEDICAL SERVICES	100.0	7.6	20.1	19.0	12.0	41.2	24.6	16.6
Physician's services	100.0	8.1	18.8	19.1	10.1	43.8	27.4	16.4
Dental services	100.0	5.7	17.1	19.1	13.1	45.0	26.0	19.0
Eye care services	100.0	5.7	20.7	16.8	13.3	43.5	26.4	17.1
Service by professionals other than physician	100.0	8.0	18.7	15.5	9.2	48.6	22.9	25.8
Lab tests, X-rays	100.0	5.5	20.6	20.2	11.6	42.1	28.3	13.8
Hospital room and services	100.0	13.2	25.9	18.7	13.6	28.5	18.3	10.2
Care in convalescent or nursing home	100.0	2.8	61.5	22.7	2.6	10.3	6.1	4.2
Other medical services	100.0	6.6	20.9	24.7	11.7	36.0	21.1	14.9
DRUGS	100.0	10.9	23.6	19.3	12.4	33.5	21.5	12.1
Nonprescription drugs	100.0	9.7	21.8	20.6	11.5	35.7	22.5	13.2
Nonprescription vitamins	100.0	10.1	14.0	23.0	9.3	42.5	24.0	18.9
Prescription drugs	100.0	11.3	25.5	18.5	13.1	31.6	20.9	10.7
MEDICAL SUPPLIES	100.0	8.3	21.3	18.4	9.8	41.8	23.4	18.5
Eyeglasses and contact lenses	100.0	7.2	19.8	17.8	10.1	45.0	26.5	18.6
Hearing aids	100.0	10.7	28.9	23.1	5.6	31.7	11.6	20.1
Topicals and dressings	100.0	7.6	18.5	16.6	11.0	45.0	26.7	18.5
Adult diapers	100.0	18.7	27.2	15.8	11.1	28.0	17.8	10.2
Medical equipment for general use	100.0	11.7	35.2	16.2	5.3	31.5	10.1	21.4
Supportive and convalescent medical equipment	100.0	9.8	25.6	19.8	12.9	31.9	15.4	16.5
Rental of medical equipment	100.0	13.7	16.5	31.5	5.0	32.6	8.5	24.2
Rental of supportive and convalescent medical equipment	100.0	17.8	20.0	38.5	12.2	11.1	3.3	7.9

Note: Numbers may not add to total because of rounding.
Source: Calculations by New Strategist based on the Bureau of Labor Statistics' 2011 Consumer Expenditure Survey

CHAPTER 8

Spending on Housing: Household Operations, 2011

Americans spend a large portion of their income on housing. Housing costs—which include shelter, utilities, and all household operations ranging from household services and housekeeping supplies to furniture and equipment—absorbed 33.8 percent of average household expenditures in 2011, down from 34.4 percent in 2010 but up from 32.4 percent in 2000. Average household spending on nearly every subcategory of household operations increased between 2000 and 2006 (when overall household spending peaked), then declined between 2006 and 2011. Spending on housekeeping supplies, for example, rose 13 percent in the earlier time period and fell 14 percent in the latter, after adjusting for inflation. Average spending on household services—a category that includes day care—is an exception to the pattern, however, increasing 18 percent between 2000 and 2006 and by another 6 percent between 2006 and 2011. Spending on household furnishings and equipment fell in both time periods and was 25 percent lower in 2011 than in 2000.

Overall housing costs are highest for householders aged 35 to 44, at an average of $19,979 in 2011. This age group spends the most on household services ($1,494 in 2011) because of day care. Average household spending on home furnishings and equipment peaks in the 45-to-54 age group—at $1,693 in 2011. Householders aged 55 to 64 spent the most on housekeeping supplies ($722). Those under age 25 spend significantly more than average on infants' furniture.

Households with incomes of $100,000 or more spent an enormous average of $30,212 on housing and related services in 2011, almost twice the $16,803 spent by the average household. The most-affluent households spend far more than average on just about every category of household operations. The 18 percent of households in this segment account for 70 percent of spending on babysitting and child care services in the home, 61 percent of spending on floor coverings, and 60 percent of spending on housekeeping services.

Among household types, married couples with children under age 6 spend the most on housing, $25,009 on average in 2011. Behind this figure is their relatively large household size and the high cost of housing for recent homebuyers—many married couples with young children are new homeowners. Married couples with preschoolers spent an average of $2,136 on day care centers in 2011.

Asian households outspend the average household by 24 percent on housing, while Hispanic and black households spend less than average. Asian households spend more than twice the average on babysitting in the own home and computer software, among other things. Hispanics spend 93 percent more than average on babysitting in another home, 48 percent more than average on infants' furniture, 43 percent more than average on soaps and detergents. Blacks outspend the average on babysitting in another home, soaps and detergents, and home security system service fees, among other things.

Households in the Northeast and West spend the most on housing—over $19,000 on average in 2011—because of the high cost of housing in parts of those regions. Households in the Northeast spend over twice the average on reupholstering, furniture repair, and floor coverings.. Midwestern households are the biggest spenders on water softening services, sofas, and sewing machines. Southern households spend the most on termite and pest control products and services and on home security system service fees. Households in the West spend over twice the average on delivery services.

Not surprisingly, college graduates (who dominate the nation's affluent households) spend the most on housing, an average of $23,123 in 2011. They spend far more than the average household on almost every category of household operations. They spend more than twice the average on babysitting in the own home, floor coverings, and housekeeping services, but they spend only about three-quarters of the average amount on power tools.

Table 8.1 Housing: Household Operations: Average spending by age, 2011

(average annual spending of consumer units on household services, supplies, furnishings, and equipment, by age of consumer unit reference person, 2011)

	total consumer units	under 25	25 to 34	35 to 44	45 to 54	55 to 64	65 to 74	75+
Number of consumer units (in 000s)	122,287	7,743	20,463	21,699	24,821	21,688	14,079	11,794
Average number of persons per consumer unit	2.5	2.1	2.9	3.3	2.8	2.1	1.9	1.6
Average before-tax income of consumer units	$63,685.00	$27,514.00	$58,179.00	$77,376.00	$78,519.00	$75,517.00	$52,521.00	$32,144.00
Average spending of consumer units, total	49,704.88	29,911.52	48,097.39	57,271.07	58,050.42	53,615.86	44,645.56	32,688.34
Housing, average spending	**16,803.03**	**10,281.56**	**17,026.09**	**19,979.07**	**18,781.64**	**17,172.91**	**15,104.82**	**12,046.03**
HOUSEHOLD SERVICES	**1,122.18**	**505.05**	**1,359.06**	**1,493.76**	**968.74**	**958.07**	**951.54**	**1,260.99**
Personal services	**398.27**	**174.23**	**804.03**	**783.39**	**187.74**	**68.77**	**110.35**	**525.46**
Babysitting and child care in own home	51.23	20.06	102.27	132.32	35.72	0.95	4.23	15.19
Babysitting and child care in someone else's home	26.87	39.34	86.87	40.55	12.00	0.66	0.46	0.39
Care for elderly, invalids, handicapped, etc.	67.89	–	4.12	4.53	12.77	33.72	91.56	490.27
Day care centers, nurseries, and preschools	251.30	114.83	610.61	605.02	127.12	32.43	11.44	16.85
Other household services	**723.92**	**330.81**	**555.02**	**710.37**	**781.00**	**889.30**	**841.19**	**735.52**
Housekeeping services	105.26	7.10	31.90	101.49	98.91	153.94	140.31	185.90
Gardening, lawn care service	118.65	16.82	39.55	74.24	114.77	168.30	193.88	231.53
Water-softening service	4.87	1.19	1.89	5.13	6.76	5.49	7.63	3.55
Nonclothing laundry and dry cleaning, sent out	14.71	9.72	10.87	17.82	15.75	21.97	10.86	7.44
Nonclothing laundry and dry cleaning, coin-operated	4.40	4.93	6.61	5.61	4.40	3.27	2.54	2.26
Termite and pest control services	20.61	2.15	11.24	18.25	21.98	27.10	31.10	26.05
Home security system service fee	25.65	5.65	17.26	27.59	27.43	33.64	27.55	29.12
Other home services	15.98	1.07	5.49	8.28	16.85	27.77	24.38	24.59
Termite and pest control products	3.57	0.50	2.15	3.41	3.69	4.28	5.06	4.99
Moving, storage, and freight express	52.88	39.24	60.48	48.29	48.59	58.21	62.00	45.45
Appliance repair, including at service center	16.62	0.67	7.87	15.31	15.28	26.54	22.65	22.06
Reupholstering and furniture repair	5.75	0.70	0.52	3.93	7.34	9.89	11.83	3.23
Repairs and rentals of lawn and garden equipment, hand and power tools, etc.	9.29	1.76	4.58	7.28	11.90	9.60	17.03	10.81
Appliance rental	2.01	2.78	2.57	2.61	3.40	0.64	1.02	0.20
Rental of office equipment for nonbusiness use	1.06	0.70	0.68	1.60	1.63	0.98	0.54	0.54
Repair of computer systems for nonbusiness use	6.51	2.20	5.56	5.63	9.69	5.97	7.17	6.07
Computer information services	313.76	223.87	345.62	363.35	367.02	331.22	272.31	131.57
Installation of computer	0.51	–	0.19	0.26	0.56	0.51	1.84	0.14
HOUSEKEEPING SUPPLIES	**614.74**	**268.46**	**420.47**	**701.55**	**691.16**	**721.69**	**695.47**	**568.16**
Laundry and cleaning supplies	**145.06**	**82.23**	**116.99**	**169.58**	**166.63**	**150.68**	**148.49**	**130.13**
Soaps and detergents	78.49	49.74	66.18	95.37	91.27	79.09	67.75	71.87
Other laundry cleaning products	66.57	32.49	50.81	74.20	75.35	71.59	80.74	58.26
Other household products	**339.58**	**140.62**	**231.69**	**406.68**	**367.89**	**402.44**	**379.19**	**312.37**
Cleansing and toilet tissue, paper towels, and napkins	114.81	64.98	92.03	143.03	128.18	117.57	105.12	113.10
Miscellaneous household products	134.12	58.74	104.59	174.59	151.73	146.74	135.41	97.75
Lawn and garden supplies	90.65	16.90	35.07	89.06	87.98	138.13	138.66	101.52
Postage and stationery	**130.09**	**45.61**	**71.78**	**125.29**	**156.65**	**168.57**	**167.79**	**125.67**
Stationery, stationery supplies, giftwrap	67.56	27.12	40.38	71.67	80.00	77.61	86.88	67.21
Postage	55.22	16.66	26.57	49.75	66.50	76.95	72.47	56.72
Delivery services	7.32	1.82	4.83	3.87	10.14	14.01	8.44	1.74
HOUSEHOLD FURNISHINGS AND EQUIPMENT	**1,513.98**	**857.71**	**1,470.87**	**1,650.48**	**1,692.88**	**1,685.41**	**1,710.51**	**848.75**
Household textiles	**109.14**	**36.69**	**95.57**	**129.54**	**107.39**	**106.03**	**182.90**	**66.22**
Bathroom linens	20.16	10.63	12.90	35.00	18.99	13.36	29.94	16.03
Bedroom linens	59.00	10.86	61.44	70.59	56.66	56.51	99.94	26.48
Kitchen and dining room linens	5.95	2.51	2.31	4.11	6.72	8.30	12.47	4.57
Curtains and draperies	11.30	5.79	8.21	8.48	15.68	10.67	19.40	7.73
Slipcovers and decorative pillows	3.52	2.82	3.73	5.02	3.45	3.95	2.52	1.38
Sewing materials for household items	8.07	3.14	4.90	5.02	5.10	12.30	17.94	9.15
Other linens	1.13	0.93	2.08	1.32	0.79	0.94	0.69	0.88
Furniture	**357.94**	**260.13**	**453.62**	**404.15**	**349.72**	**419.49**	**314.26**	**127.42**
Mattresses and springs	61.72	43.41	76.51	73.65	55.31	65.96	73.27	18.08
Other bedroom furniture	70.06	72.77	113.83	102.80	49.25	69.01	32.20	23.06
Sofas	92.81	73.76	118.27	101.83	100.46	105.09	72.59	30.04
Living room chairs	36.12	13.39	24.24	28.88	48.29	49.91	37.81	31.94
Living room tables	11.87	8.21	16.66	12.66	11.00	14.92	10.79	2.08

	total consumer units	under 25	25 to 34	35 to 44	45 to 54	55 to 64	65 to 74	75+
Kitchen and dining room furniture	$27.45	$13.69	$36.54	$28.26	$26.30	$35.19	$28.52	$6.16
Infants' furniture	8.23	12.81	19.52	7.06	4.87	6.21	5.00	2.45
Outdoor furniture	18.70	6.19	12.21	15.43	23.09	30.35	23.83	7.36
Wall units, cabinets, and other furniture	30.97	15.91	35.84	33.58	31.15	42.86	30.26	6.25
Floor coverings	**19.98**	**4.65**	**11.37**	**23.59**	**21.45**	**27.97**	**30.84**	**7.64**
Floor coverings, nonpermanent	19.61	4.65	11.37	23.59	21.43	25.90	30.84	7.62
Major appliances	**193.93**	**81.95**	**159.65**	**219.44**	**208.76**	**245.80**	**214.32**	**128.82**
Dishwashers (built-in), garbage disposals, range hoods	14.60	1.65	5.52	20.55	18.28	17.95	15.36	13.16
Refrigerators and freezers	52.96	15.97	39.51	60.33	47.66	71.58	68.53	45.37
Washing machines	34.00	19.75	34.81	35.70	44.62	34.37	35.74	13.67
Clothes dryers	24.93	18.59	31.33	25.38	29.74	22.10	24.62	12.65
Cooking stoves, ovens	30.51	5.18	21.17	42.60	24.59	43.28	34.38	25.43
Microwave ovens	8.96	6.14	7.36	10.71	8.29	12.05	8.03	7.22
Window air conditioners	4.82	2.03	4.62	3.76	4.60	8.75	4.29	2.89
Electric floor-cleaning equipment	16.06	12.35	12.84	17.09	16.22	23.92	16.13	7.34
Sewing machines	2.43	0.30	0.80	1.14	6.26	2.50	2.18	1.09
Miscellaneous household appliances	4.21	–	1.09	2.18	7.73	9.28	3.56	–
Small appliances and miscellaneous housewares	**89.34**	**76.88**	**76.83**	**92.68**	**98.48**	**89.25**	**123.90**	**54.88**
Housewares	54.84	32.36	49.04	57.21	60.75	55.07	81.76	31.45
Plastic dinnerware	2.47	2.38	3.15	3.24	2.58	2.55	1.58	0.68
China and other dinnerware	5.34	1.77	8.35	4.13	4.73	4.13	10.54	2.01
Flatware	2.96	2.36	2.42	4.25	3.43	3.01	3.02	0.81
Glassware	6.56	6.60	7.10	4.74	7.81	5.76	11.30	2.30
Silver serving pieces	1.43	0.63	1.07	1.49	2.04	1.44	2.03	0.49
Other serving pieces	1.42	0.63	1.51	1.70	1.02	1.65	2.38	0.58
Nonelectric cookware	14.94	7.11	7.61	13.96	18.63	14.71	30.47	9.79
Tableware, nonelectric kitchenware	19.71	10.88	17.84	23.69	20.51	21.81	20.44	14.79
Small appliances	34.50	44.52	27.80	35.46	37.73	34.19	42.13	23.43
Small electric kitchen appliances	24.50	18.23	23.81	24.47	26.03	27.07	29.44	16.02
Portable heating and cooling equipment	10.00	26.29	3.98	10.99	11.70	7.12	12.69	7.41
Miscellaneous household equipment	**743.64**	**397.41**	**673.83**	**781.09**	**907.07**	**796.87**	**844.29**	**463.77**
Window coverings	15.87	2.54	14.17	27.11	14.68	16.55	17.33	6.40
Infants' equipment	14.49	16.44	20.17	34.99	11.34	5.75	2.92	1.48
Laundry and cleaning equipment	17.33	8.73	14.80	20.90	17.50	18.79	23.56	10.49
Outdoor equipment	34.43	7.01	22.72	16.75	26.27	42.49	117.98	11.83
Lamps and lighting fixtures	29.29	18.18	9.91	16.95	65.45	28.50	28.72	19.77
Household decorative items	117.20	35.61	103.78	155.04	121.37	132.72	109.38	94.05
Telephones and accessories	45.56	20.30	31.00	51.81	55.47	54.86	34.31	50.66
Lawn and garden equipment	65.62	–	29.63	40.32	125.23	73.46	111.08	25.93
Power tools	38.18	23.41	44.54	39.40	46.17	27.77	44.35	29.66
Office furniture for home use	5.83	4.56	4.55	6.38	9.94	6.78	2.51	1.39
Hand tools	15.55	12.29	31.05	10.57	7.32	16.37	14.61	15.78
Indoor plants and fresh flowers	46.92	11.01	30.26	38.00	59.70	62.55	60.93	43.50
Closet and storage items	16.85	4.91	24.04	21.53	14.52	16.69	15.75	9.26
Rental of furniture	6.16	11.66	14.31	3.09	2.74	1.16	6.05	10.55
Luggage	6.84	–	3.97	12.32	3.18	6.08	6.02	16.41
Computers and computer hardware for nonbusiness use	152.35	147.05	173.02	169.79	191.08	152.99	116.49	48.01
Portable memory	4.17	4.91	5.05	5.23	4.87	3.99	2.46	1.06
Computer software	14.33	13.53	18.66	14.35	20.45	12.21	8.40	5.39
Computer accessories	12.15	6.53	8.42	12.93	14.41	16.06	15.51	4.92
Personal digital assistants	6.27	7.41	7.36	7.48	8.09	5.59	4.21	1.32
Internet services away from home	7.03	5.16	8.68	9.36	7.45	7.07	4.98	2.57
Telephone answering devices	0.61	0.53	0.34	0.44	1.13	0.32	0.95	0.43
Business equipment for home use	4.05	1.41	2.23	3.62	6.07	5.61	3.73	2.98
Other hardware	11.34	–	10.53	11.10	13.99	9.74	14.57	14.19
Smoke alarms	1.97	1.14	1.12	1.44	1.97	3.55	2.52	1.37
Other household appliances	7.96	4.53	7.18	6.75	9.43	9.47	9.75	5.81
Miscellaneous household equipment and parts	43.13	28.01	29.44	41.46	43.87	58.15	63.95	26.60

Note: Subcategories may not add to total because some are not shown. "–" means sample is too small to make a reliable estimate.
Source: Bureau of Labor Statistics, unpublished tables from the 2011 Consumer Expenditure Survey

Table 8.2 Housing: Household Operations: Indexed spending by age, 2011

(indexed average annual spending of consumer units on household services, supplies, furnishings, and equipment, by age of consumer unit reference person, 2011; index definition: an index of 100 is the average for all consumer units; an index of 125 means that spending by consumer units in that group is 25 percent above the average for all consumer units; an index of 75 indicates spending that is 25 percent below the average for all consumer units)

	total consumer units	under 25	25 to 34	35 to 44	45 to 54	55 to 64	65 to 74	75+
Average spending of consumer units, total	$49,705	$29,912	$48,097	$57,271	$58,050	$53,616	$44,646	$32,688
Average spending of consumer units, index	100	60	97	115	117	108	90	66
Housing, spending index	**100**	**61**	**101**	**119**	**112**	**102**	**90**	**72**
HOUSEHOLD SERVICES	**100**	**45**	**121**	**133**	**86**	**85**	**85**	**112**
Personal services	**100**	**44**	**202**	**197**	**47**	**17**	**28**	**132**
Babysitting and child care in own home	100	39	200	258	70	2	8	30
Babysitting and child care in someone else's home	100	146	323	151	45	2	2	1
Care for elderly, invalids, handicapped, etc.	100	–	6	7	19	50	135	722
Day care centers, nurseries, and preschools	100	46	243	241	51	13	5	7
Other household services	**100**	**46**	**77**	**98**	**108**	**123**	**116**	**102**
Housekeeping services	100	7	30	96	94	146	133	177
Gardening, lawn care service	100	14	33	63	97	142	163	195
Water-softening service	100	24	39	105	139	113	157	73
Nonclothing laundry and dry cleaning, sent out	100	66	74	121	107	149	74	51
Nonclothing laundry and dry cleaning, coin-operated	100	112	150	128	100	74	58	51
Termite and pest control services	100	10	55	89	107	131	151	126
Home security system service fee	100	22	67	108	107	131	107	114
Other home services	100	7	34	52	105	174	153	154
Termite and pest control products	100	14	60	96	103	120	142	140
Moving, storage, and freight express	100	74	114	91	92	110	117	86
Appliance repair, including at service center	100	4	47	92	92	160	136	133
Reupholstering and furniture repair	100	12	9	68	128	172	206	56
Repairs and rentals of lawn and garden equipment, hand and power tools, etc.	100	19	49	78	128	103	183	116
Appliance rental	100	138	128	130	169	32	51	10
Rental of office equipment for nonbusiness use	100	66	64	151	154	92	51	51
Repair of computer systems for nonbusiness use	100	34	85	86	149	92	110	93
Computer information services	100	71	110	116	117	106	87	42
Installation of computer	100	–	37	51	110	100	361	27
HOUSEKEEPING SUPPLIES	**100**	**44**	**68**	**114**	**112**	**117**	**113**	**92**
Laundry and cleaning supplies	**100**	**57**	**81**	**117**	**115**	**104**	**102**	**90**
Soaps and detergents	100	63	84	122	116	101	86	92
Other laundry cleaning products	100	49	76	111	113	108	121	88
Other household products	**100**	**41**	**68**	**120**	**108**	**119**	**112**	**92**
Cleansing and toilet tissue, paper towels, and napkins	100	57	80	125	112	102	92	99
Miscellaneous household products	100	44	78	130	113	109	101	73
Lawn and garden supplies	100	19	39	98	97	152	153	112
Postage and stationery	**100**	**35**	**55**	**96**	**120**	**130**	**129**	**97**
Stationery, stationery supplies, giftwrap	100	40	60	106	118	115	129	99
Postage	100	30	48	90	120	139	131	103
Delivery services	100	25	66	53	139	191	115	24
HOUSEHOLD FURNISHINGS AND EQUIPMENT	**100**	**57**	**97**	**109**	**112**	**111**	**113**	**56**
Household textiles	**100**	**34**	**88**	**119**	**98**	**97**	**168**	**61**
Bathroom linens	100	53	64	174	94	66	149	80
Bedroom linens	100	18	104	120	96	96	169	45
Kitchen and dining room linens	100	42	39	69	113	139	210	77
Curtains and draperies	100	51	73	75	139	94	172	68
Slipcovers and decorative pillows	100	80	106	143	98	112	72	39
Sewing materials for household items	100	39	61	62	63	152	222	113
Other linens	100	82	184	117	70	83	61	78
Furniture	**100**	**73**	**127**	**113**	**98**	**117**	**88**	**36**
Mattresses and springs	100	70	124	119	90	107	119	29
Other bedroom furniture	100	104	162	147	70	99	46	33
Sofas	100	79	127	110	108	113	78	32
Living room chairs	100	37	67	80	134	138	105	88
Living room tables	100	69	140	107	93	126	91	18

	total consumer units	under 25	25 to 34	35 to 44	45 to 54	55 to 64	65 to 74	75+
Kitchen and dining room furniture	100	50	133	103	96	128	104	22
Infants' furniture	100	156	237	86	59	75	61	30
Outdoor furniture	100	33	65	83	123	162	127	39
Wall units, cabinets, and other furniture	100	51	116	108	101	138	98	20
Floor coverings	**100**	**23**	**57**	**118**	**107**	**140**	**154**	**38**
Floor coverings, nonpermanent	100	24	58	120	109	132	157	39
Major appliances	**100**	**42**	**82**	**113**	**108**	**127**	**111**	**66**
Dishwashers (built-in), garbage disposals, range hoods	100	11	38	141	125	123	105	90
Refrigerators and freezers	100	30	75	114	90	135	129	86
Washing machines	100	58	102	105	131	101	105	40
Clothes dryers	100	75	126	102	119	89	99	51
Cooking stoves, ovens	100	17	69	140	81	142	113	83
Microwave ovens	100	69	82	120	93	134	90	81
Window air conditioners	100	42	96	78	95	182	89	60
Electric floor-cleaning equipment	100	77	80	106	101	149	100	46
Sewing machines	100	12	33	47	258	103	90	45
Miscellaneous household appliances	100	–	26	52	184	220	85	–
Small appliances and miscellaneous housewares	**100**	**86**	**86**	**104**	**110**	**100**	**139**	**61**
Housewares	100	59	89	104	111	100	149	57
Plastic dinnerware	100	96	128	131	104	103	64	28
China and other dinnerware	100	33	156	77	89	77	197	38
Flatware	100	80	82	144	116	102	102	27
Glassware	100	101	108	72	119	88	172	35
Silver serving pieces	100	44	75	104	143	101	142	34
Other serving pieces	100	44	106	120	72	116	168	41
Nonelectric cookware	100	48	51	93	125	98	204	66
Tableware, nonelectric kitchenware	100	55	91	120	104	111	104	75
Small appliances	100	129	81	103	109	99	122	68
Small electric kitchen appliances	100	74	97	100	106	110	120	65
Portable heating and cooling equipment	100	263	40	110	117	71	127	74
Miscellaneous household equipment	**100**	**53**	**91**	**105**	**122**	**107**	**114**	**62**
Window coverings	100	16	89	171	93	104	109	40
Infants' equipment	100	113	139	241	78	40	20	10
Laundry and cleaning equipment	100	50	85	121	101	108	136	61
Outdoor equipment	100	20	66	49	76	123	343	34
Lamps and lighting fixtures	100	62	34	58	223	97	98	67
Household decorative items	100	30	89	132	104	113	93	80
Telephones and accessories	100	45	68	114	122	120	75	111
Lawn and garden equipment	100	–	45	61	191	112	169	40
Power tools	100	61	117	103	121	73	116	78
Office furniture for home use	100	78	78	109	170	116	43	24
Hand tools	100	79	200	68	47	105	94	101
Indoor plants and fresh flowers	100	23	64	81	127	133	130	93
Closet and storage items	100	29	143	128	86	99	93	55
Rental of furniture	100	189	232	50	44	19	98	171
Luggage	100	–	58	180	46	89	88	240
Computers and computer hardware for nonbusiness use	100	97	114	111	125	100	76	32
Portable memory	100	118	121	125	117	96	59	25
Computer software	100	94	130	100	143	85	59	38
Computer accessories	100	54	69	106	119	132	128	40
Personal digital assistants	100	118	117	119	129	89	67	21
Internet services away from home	100	73	123	133	106	101	71	37
Telephone answering devices	100	87	56	72	185	52	156	70
Business equipment for home use	100	35	55	89	150	139	92	74
Other hardware	100	–	93	98	123	86	128	125
Smoke alarms	100	58	57	73	100	180	128	70
Other household appliances	100	57	90	85	118	119	122	73
Miscellaneous household equipment and parts	100	65	68	96	102	135	148	62

Note: "–" means sample is too small to make a reliable estimate.
Source: Calculations by New Strategist based on the Bureau of Labor Statistics' 2011 Consumer Expenditure Survey

Table 8.3 Housing: Household Operations: Total spending by age, 2011

(total annual spending on household services, supplies, furnishings, and equipment, by consumer unit age groups, 2011; consumer units and dollars in thousands)

	total consumer units	under 25	25 to 34	35 to 44	45 to 54	55 to 64	65 to 74	75+
Number of consumer units	122,287	7,743	20,463	21,699	24,821	21,688	14,079	11,794
Total spending of all consumer units	$6,078,260,661	$231,604,899	$984,216,892	$1,242,724,948	$1,440,869,475	$1,162,820,772	$628,564,839	$385,526,282
Housing, total spending	2,054,792,130	79,610,119	348,404,880	433,525,840	466,179,086	372,446,072	212,660,761	142,070,878
HOUSEHOLD SERVICES	**137,228,026**	**3,910,602**	**27,810,445**	**32,413,098**	**24,045,096**	**20,778,622**	**13,396,732**	**14,872,116**
Personal services	**48,703,243**	**1,349,063**	**16,452,866**	**16,998,780**	**4,659,895**	**1,491,484**	**1,553,618**	**6,197,275**
Babysitting and child care in own home	6,264,763	155,325	2,092,751	2,871,212	886,606	20,604	59,554	179,151
Babysitting and child care in someone else's home	3,285,852	304,610	1,777,621	879,894	297,852	14,314	6,476	4,600
Care for elderly, invalids, handicapped, etc.	8,302,064	–	84,308	98,296	316,964	731,319	1,289,073	5,782,244
Day care centers, nurseries, and preschools	30,730,723	889,129	12,494,912	13,128,329	3,155,246	703,342	161,064	198,729
Other household services	**88,526,005**	**2,561,462**	**11,357,374**	**15,414,319**	**19,385,201**	**19,287,138**	**11,843,114**	**8,674,723**
Housekeeping services	12,871,930	54,975	652,770	2,202,232	2,455,045	3,338,651	1,975,424	2,192,505
Gardening, lawn care service	14,509,353	130,237	809,312	1,610,934	2,848,706	3,650,090	2,729,637	2,730,665
Water-softening service	595,538	9,214	38,675	111,316	167,790	119,067	107,423	41,869
Nonclothing laundry and dry cleaning, sent out	1,798,842	75,262	222,433	386,676	390,931	476,485	152,898	87,747
Nonclothing laundry and dry cleaning, coin-operated	538,063	38,173	135,260	121,731	109,212	70,920	35,761	26,654
Termite and pest control services	2,520,335	16,647	230,004	396,007	545,566	587,745	437,857	307,234
Home security system service fee	3,136,662	43,748	353,191	598,675	680,840	729,584	387,876	343,441
Other home services	1,954,146	8,285	112,342	179,668	418,234	602,276	343,246	290,014
Termite and pest control products	436,565	3,872	43,995	73,994	91,589	92,825	71,240	58,852
Moving, storage, and freight express	6,466,537	303,835	1,237,602	1,047,845	1,206,052	1,262,458	872,898	536,037
Appliance repair, including at service center	2,032,410	5,188	161,044	332,212	379,265	575,600	318,889	260,176
Reupholstering and furniture repair	703,150	5,420	10,641	85,277	182,186	214,494	166,555	38,095
Repairs and rentals of lawn and garden equipment, hand and power tools, etc.	1,136,046	13,628	93,721	157,969	295,370	208,205	239,765	127,493
Appliance rental	245,797	21,526	52,590	56,634	84,391	13,880	14,361	2,359
Rental of office equipment for nonbusiness use	129,624	5,420	13,915	34,718	40,458	21,254	7,603	6,369
Repair of computer systems for nonbusiness use	796,088	17,035	113,774	122,165	240,515	129,477	100,946	71,590
Computer information services	38,368,769	1,733,425	7,072,422	7,884,332	9,109,803	7,183,499	3,833,852	1,551,737
Installation of computer	62,366	–	3,888	5,642	13,900	11,061	25,905	1,651
HOUSEKEEPING SUPPLIES	**75,174,710**	**2,078,686**	**8,604,078**	**15,222,933**	**17,155,282**	**15,652,013**	**9,791,522**	**6,700,879**
Laundry and cleaning supplies	**17,738,952**	**636,707**	**2,393,966**	**3,679,716**	**4,135,923**	**3,267,948**	**2,090,591**	**1,534,753**
Soaps and detergents	9,598,307	385,137	1,354,241	2,069,434	2,265,413	1,715,304	953,852	847,635
Other laundry cleaning products	8,140,646	251,570	1,039,725	1,610,066	1,870,262	1,552,644	1,136,738	687,118
Other household products	**41,526,219**	**1,088,821**	**4,741,072**	**8,824,549**	**9,131,398**	**8,728,119**	**5,338,616**	**3,684,092**
Cleansing and toilet tissue, paper towels, and napkins	14,039,770	503,140	1,883,210	3,103,608	3,181,556	2,549,858	1,479,984	1,333,901
Miscellaneous household products	16,401,132	454,824	2,140,225	3,788,428	3,766,090	3,182,497	1,906,437	1,152,864
Lawn and garden supplies	11,085,317	130,857	717,637	1,932,513	2,183,752	2,995,763	1,952,194	1,197,327
Postage and stationery	**15,908,316**	**353,158**	**1,468,834**	**2,718,668**	**3,888,210**	**3,655,946**	**2,362,315**	**1,482,152**
Stationery, stationery supplies, giftwrap	8,261,710	209,990	826,296	1,555,167	1,985,680	1,683,206	1,223,184	792,675
Postage	6,752,688	128,998	543,702	1,079,525	1,650,597	1,668,892	1,020,305	668,956
Delivery services	895,141	14,092	98,836	83,975	251,685	303,849	118,827	20,522
HOUSEHOLD FURNISHINGS AND EQUIPMENT	**185,140,072**	**6,641,249**	**30,098,413**	**35,813,766**	**42,018,974**	**36,553,172**	**24,082,270**	**10,010,158**
Household textiles	**13,346,403**	**284,091**	**1,955,649**	**2,810,888**	**2,665,527**	**2,299,579**	**2,575,049**	**780,999**
Bathroom linens	2,465,306	82,308	263,973	759,465	471,351	289,752	421,525	189,058
Bedroom linens	7,214,933	84,089	1,257,247	1,531,732	1,406,358	1,225,589	1,407,055	312,305
Kitchen and dining room linens	727,608	19,435	47,270	89,183	166,797	180,010	175,565	53,899
Curtains and draperies	1,381,843	44,832	168,001	184,008	389,193	231,411	273,133	91,168
Slipcovers and decorative pillows	430,450	21,835	76,327	108,929	85,632	85,668	35,479	16,276
Sewing materials for household items	986,856	24,313	100,269	108,929	126,587	266,762	252,577	107,915
Other linens	138,184	7,201	42,563	28,643	19,609	20,387	9,715	10,379
Furniture	**43,771,409**	**2,014,187**	**9,282,426**	**8,769,651**	**8,680,400**	**9,097,899**	**4,424,467**	**1,502,791**
Mattresses and springs	7,547,554	336,124	1,565,624	1,598,131	1,372,850	1,430,540	1,031,568	213,236
Other bedroom furniture	8,567,427	563,458	2,329,303	2,230,657	1,222,434	1,496,689	453,344	271,970
Sofas	11,349,456	571,124	2,420,159	2,209,609	2,493,518	2,279,192	1,021,995	354,292
Living room chairs	4,417,006	103,679	496,023	626,667	1,198,606	1,082,448	532,327	376,700
Living room tables	1,451,547	63,570	340,914	274,709	273,031	323,585	151,912	24,532

	total consumer units	under 25	25 to 34	35 to 44	45 to 54	55 to 64	65 to 74	75+
Kitchen and dining room furniture	$3,356,778	$106,002	$747,718	$613,214	$652,792	$763,201	$401,533	$72,651
Infants' furniture	1,006,422	99,188	399,438	153,195	120,878	134,682	70,395	28,895
Outdoor furniture	2,286,767	47,929	249,853	334,816	573,117	658,231	335,503	86,804
Wall units, cabinets, and other furniture	3,787,228	123,191	733,394	728,652	773,174	929,548	426,031	73,713
Floor coverings	**2,443,294**	**36,005**	**232,664**	**511,879**	**532,410**	**606,613**	**434,196**	**90,106**
Floor coverings, nonpermanent	2,398,048	36,005	232,664	511,879	531,914	561,719	434,196	89,870
Major appliances	**23,715,118**	**634,539**	**3,266,918**	**4,761,629**	**5,181,632**	**5,330,910**	**3,017,411**	**1,519,303**
Dishwashers (built-in), garbage disposals, range hoods	1,785,390	12,776	112,956	445,914	453,728	389,300	216,253	155,209
Refrigerators and freezers	6,476,320	123,656	808,493	1,309,101	1,182,969	1,552,427	964,834	535,094
Washing machines	4,157,758	152,924	712,317	774,654	1,107,513	745,417	503,183	161,224
Clothes dryers	3,048,615	143,942	641,106	550,721	738,177	479,305	346,625	149,194
Cooking stoves, ovens	3,730,976	40,109	433,202	924,377	610,348	938,657	484,036	299,921
Microwave ovens	1,095,692	47,542	150,608	232,396	205,766	261,340	113,054	85,153
Window air conditioners	589,423	15,718	94,539	81,588	114,177	189,770	60,399	34,085
Electric floor-cleaning equipment	1,963,929	95,626	262,745	370,836	402,597	518,777	227,094	86,568
Sewing machines	297,157	2,323	16,370	24,737	155,379	54,220	30,692	12,855
Miscellaneous household appliances	514,828	–	22,305	47,304	191,866	201,265	50,121	–
Small appliances and miscellaneous housewares	**10,925,121**	**595,282**	**1,572,172**	**2,011,063**	**2,444,372**	**1,935,654**	**1,744,388**	**647,255**
Housewares	6,706,219	250,563	1,003,506	1,241,400	1,507,876	1,194,358	1,151,099	370,921
Plastic dinnerware	302,049	18,428	64,458	70,305	64,038	55,304	22,245	8,020
China and other dinnerware	653,013	13,705	170,866	89,617	117,403	89,571	148,393	23,706
Flatware	361,970	18,273	49,520	92,221	85,136	65,281	42,519	9,553
Glassware	802,203	51,104	145,287	102,853	193,852	124,923	159,093	27,126
Silver serving pieces	174,870	4,878	21,895	32,332	50,635	31,231	28,580	5,779
Other serving pieces	173,648	4,878	30,899	36,888	25,317	35,785	33,508	6,841
Nonelectric cookware	1,826,968	55,053	155,723	302,918	462,415	319,030	428,987	115,463
Tableware, nonelectric kitchenware	2,410,277	84,244	365,060	514,049	509,079	473,015	287,775	174,433
Small appliances	4,218,902	344,718	568,871	769,447	936,496	741,513	593,148	276,333
Small electric kitchen appliances	2,996,032	141,155	487,224	530,975	646,091	587,094	414,486	188,940
Portable heating and cooling equipment	1,222,870	203,563	81,443	238,472	290,406	154,419	178,663	87,394
Miscellaneous household equipment	**90,937,505**	**3,077,146**	**13,788,583**	**16,948,872**	**22,514,384**	**17,282,517**	**11,886,759**	**5,469,703**
Window coverings	1,940,695	19,667	289,961	588,260	364,372	358,936	243,989	75,482
Infants' equipment	1,771,939	127,295	412,739	759,248	281,470	124,706	41,111	17,455
Laundry and cleaning equipment	2,119,234	67,596	302,852	453,509	434,368	407,518	331,701	123,719
Outdoor equipment	4,210,341	54,278	464,919	363,458	652,048	921,523	1,661,040	139,523
Lamps and lighting fixtures	3,581,786	140,768	202,788	367,798	1,624,534	618,108	404,349	233,167
Household decorative items	14,332,036	275,728	2,123,650	3,364,213	3,012,525	2,878,431	1,539,961	1,109,226
Telephones and accessories	5,571,396	157,183	634,353	1,124,225	1,376,821	1,189,804	483,050	597,484
Lawn and garden equipment	8,024,473	–	606,319	874,904	3,108,334	1,593,200	1,563,895	305,818
Power tools	4,668,918	181,264	911,422	854,941	1,145,986	602,276	624,404	349,810
Office furniture for home use	712,933	35,308	93,107	138,440	246,721	147,045	35,338	16,394
Hand tools	1,901,563	95,161	635,376	229,358	181,690	355,033	205,694	186,109
Indoor plants and fresh flowers	5,737,706	85,250	619,210	824,562	1,481,814	1,356,584	857,833	513,039
Closet and storage items	2,060,536	38,018	491,931	467,179	360,401	361,973	221,744	109,212
Rental of furniture	753,288	90,283	292,826	67,050	68,010	25,158	85,178	124,427
Luggage	836,443	–	81,238	267,332	78,931	131,863	84,756	193,540
Computers and computer hardware for nonbusiness use	18,630,424	1,138,608	3,540,508	3,684,273	4,742,797	3,318,047	1,640,063	566,230
Portable memory	509,937	38,018	103,338	113,486	120,878	86,535	34,634	12,502
Computer software	1,752,373	104,763	381,840	311,381	507,589	264,810	118,264	63,570
Computer accessories	1,485,787	50,562	172,298	280,568	357,671	348,309	218,365	58,026
Personal digital assistants	766,739	57,376	150,608	162,309	200,802	121,236	59,273	15,568
Internet services away from home	859,678	39,954	177,619	203,103	184,916	153,334	70,113	30,311
Telephone answering devices	74,595	4,104	6,957	9,548	28,048	6,940	13,375	5,071
Business equipment for home use	495,262	10,918	45,632	78,550	150,663	121,670	52,515	35,146
Other hardware	1,386,735	–	215,475	240,859	347,246	211,241	205,131	167,357
Smoke alarms	240,905	8,827	22,919	31,247	48,897	76,992	35,479	16,158
Other household appliances	973,405	35,076	146,924	146,468	234,062	205,385	137,270	68,523
Miscellaneous household equipment and parts	5,274,238	216,881	602,431	899,641	1,088,897	1,261,157	900,352	313,720

Note: Numbers may not add to total because of rounding and missing subcategories. "–" means sample is vvtoo small to make a reliable estimate.
Source: Calculations by New Strategist based on the Bureau of Labor Statistics' 2011 Consumer Expenditure Survey

Table 8.4 Housing: Household Operations: Market shares by age, 2011

(percentage of total annual spending on household services, supplies, furnishings, and equipment accounted for by consumer unit age groups, 2011)

	total consumer units	under 25	25 to 34	35 to 44	45 to 54	55 to 64	65 to 74	75+
Share of total consumer units	100.0%	6.3%	16.7%	17.7%	20.3%	17.7%	11.5%	9.6%
Share of total before-tax income	100.0	2.7	15.3	21.6	25.0	21.0	9.5	4.9
Share of total spending	100.0	3.8	16.2	20.4	23.7	19.1	10.3	6.3
Share of housing spending	100.0	3.9	17.0	21.1	22.7	18.1	10.3	6.9
HOUSEHOLD SERVICES	**100.0**	**2.8**	**20.3**	**23.6**	**17.5**	**15.1**	**9.8**	**10.8**
Personal services	**100.0**	**2.8**	**33.8**	**34.9**	**9.6**	**3.1**	**3.2**	**12.7**
Babysitting and child care in own home	100.0	2.5	33.4	45.8	14.2	0.3	1.0	2.9
Babysitting and child care in someone else's home	100.0	9.3	54.1	26.8	9.1	0.4	0.2	0.1
Care for elderly, invalids, handicapped, etc.	100.0	–	1.0	1.2	3.8	8.8	15.5	69.6
Day care centers, nurseries, and preschools	100.0	2.9	40.7	42.7	10.3	2.3	0.5	0.6
Other household services	**100.0**	**2.9**	**12.8**	**17.4**	**21.9**	**21.8**	**13.4**	**9.8**
Housekeeping services	100.0	0.4	5.1	17.1	19.1	25.9	15.3	17.0
Gardening, lawn care service	100.0	0.9	5.6	11.1	19.6	25.2	18.8	18.8
Water-softening service	100.0	1.5	6.5	18.7	28.2	20.0	18.0	7.0
Nonclothing laundry and dry cleaning, sent out	100.0	4.2	12.4	21.5	21.7	26.5	8.5	4.9
Nonclothing laundry and dry cleaning, coin-operated	100.0	7.1	25.1	22.6	20.3	13.2	6.6	5.0
Termite and pest control services	100.0	0.7	9.1	15.7	21.6	23.3	17.4	12.2
Home security system service fee	100.0	1.4	11.3	19.1	21.7	23.3	12.4	10.9
Other home services	100.0	0.4	5.7	9.2	21.4	30.8	17.6	14.8
Termite and pest control products	100.0	0.9	10.1	16.9	21.0	21.3	16.3	13.5
Moving, storage, and freight express	100.0	4.7	19.1	16.2	18.7	19.5	13.5	8.3
Appliance repair, including at service center	100.0	0.3	7.9	16.3	18.7	28.3	15.7	12.8
Reupholstering and furniture repair	100.0	0.8	1.5	12.1	25.9	30.5	23.7	5.4
Repairs and rentals of lawn and garden equipment, hand and power tools, etc.	100.0	1.2	8.2	13.9	26.0	18.3	21.1	11.2
Appliance rental	100.0	8.8	21.4	23.0	34.3	5.6	5.8	1.0
Rental of office equipment for nonbusiness use	100.0	4.2	10.7	26.8	31.2	16.4	5.9	4.9
Repair of computer systems for nonbusiness use	100.0	2.1	14.3	15.3	30.2	16.3	12.7	9.0
Computer information services	100.0	4.5	18.4	20.5	23.7	18.7	10.0	4.0
Installation of computer	100.0	–	6.2	9.0	22.3	17.7	41.5	2.6
HOUSEKEEPING SUPPLIES	**100.0**	**2.8**	**11.4**	**20.3**	**22.8**	**20.8**	**13.0**	**8.9**
Laundry and cleaning supplies	**100.0**	**3.6**	**13.5**	**20.7**	**23.3**	**18.4**	**11.8**	**8.7**
Soaps and detergents	100.0	4.0	14.1	21.6	23.6	17.9	9.9	8.8
Other laundry cleaning products	100.0	3.1	12.8	19.8	23.0	19.1	14.0	8.4
Other household products	**100.0**	**2.6**	**11.4**	**21.3**	**22.0**	**21.0**	**12.9**	**8.9**
Cleansing and toilet tissue, paper towels, and napkins	100.0	3.6	13.4	22.1	22.7	18.2	10.5	9.5
Miscellaneous household products	100.0	2.8	13.0	23.1	23.0	19.4	11.6	7.0
Lawn and garden supplies	100.0	1.2	6.5	17.4	19.7	27.0	17.6	10.8
Postage and stationery	**100.0**	**2.2**	**9.2**	**17.1**	**24.4**	**23.0**	**14.8**	**9.3**
Stationery, stationery supplies, giftwrap	100.0	2.5	10.0	18.8	24.0	20.4	14.8	9.6
Postage	100.0	1.9	8.1	16.0	24.4	24.7	15.1	9.9
Delivery services	100.0	1.6	11.0	9.4	28.1	33.9	13.3	2.3
HOUSEHOLD FURNISHINGS AND EQUIPMENT	**100.0**	**3.6**	**16.3**	**19.3**	**22.7**	**19.7**	**13.0**	**5.4**
Household textiles	**100.0**	**2.1**	**14.7**	**21.1**	**20.0**	**17.2**	**19.3**	**5.9**
Bathroom linens	100.0	3.3	10.7	30.8	19.1	11.8	17.1	7.7
Bedroom linens	100.0	1.2	17.4	21.2	19.5	17.0	19.5	4.3
Kitchen and dining room linens	100.0	2.7	6.5	12.3	22.9	24.7	24.1	7.4
Curtains and draperies	100.0	3.2	12.2	13.3	28.2	16.7	19.8	6.6
Slipcovers and decorative pillows	100.0	5.1	17.7	25.3	19.9	19.9	8.2	3.8
Sewing materials for household items	100.0	2.5	10.2	11.0	12.8	27.0	25.6	10.9
Other linens	100.0	5.2	30.8	20.7	14.2	14.8	7.0	7.5
Furniture	**100.0**	**4.6**	**21.2**	**20.0**	**19.8**	**20.8**	**10.1**	**3.4**
Mattresses and springs	100.0	4.5	20.7	21.2	18.2	19.0	13.7	2.8
Other bedroom furniture	100.0	6.6	27.2	26.0	14.3	17.5	5.3	3.2
Sofas	100.0	5.0	21.3	19.5	22.0	20.1	9.0	3.1
Living room chairs	100.0	2.3	11.2	14.2	27.1	24.5	12.1	8.5
Living room tables	100.0	4.4	23.5	18.9	18.8	22.3	10.5	1.7

	total consumer units	under 25	25 to 34	35 to 44	45 to 54	55 to 64	65 to 74	75+
Kitchen and dining room furniture	100.0%	3.2%	22.3%	18.3%	19.4%	22.7%	12.0%	2.2%
Infants' furniture	100.0	9.9	39.7	15.2	12.0	13.4	7.0	2.9
Outdoor furniture	100.0	2.1	10.9	14.6	25.1	28.8	14.7	3.8
Wall units, cabinets, and other furniture	100.0	3.3	19.4	19.2	20.4	24.5	11.2	1.9
Floor coverings	**100.0**	**1.5**	**9.5**	**21.0**	**21.8**	**24.8**	**17.8**	**3.7**
Floor coverings, nonpermanent	100.0	1.5	9.7	21.3	22.2	23.4	18.1	3.7
Major appliances	**100.0**	**2.7**	**13.8**	**20.1**	**21.8**	**22.5**	**12.7**	**6.4**
Dishwashers (built-in), garbage disposals, range hoods	100.0	0.7	6.3	25.0	25.4	21.8	12.1	8.7
Refrigerators and freezers	100.0	1.9	12.5	20.2	18.3	24.0	14.9	8.3
Washing machines	100.0	3.7	17.1	18.6	26.6	17.9	12.1	3.9
Clothes dryers	100.0	4.7	21.0	18.1	24.2	15.7	11.4	4.9
Cooking stoves, ovens	100.0	1.1	11.6	24.8	16.4	25.2	13.0	8.0
Microwave ovens	100.0	4.3	13.7	21.2	18.8	23.9	10.3	7.8
Window air conditioners	100.0	2.7	16.0	13.8	19.4	32.2	10.2	5.8
Electric floor-cleaning equipment	100.0	4.9	13.4	18.9	20.5	26.4	11.6	4.4
Sewing machines	100.0	0.8	5.5	8.3	52.3	18.2	10.3	4.3
Miscellaneous household appliances	100.0	–	4.3	9.2	37.3	39.1	9.7	–
Small appliances and miscellaneous housewares	**100.0**	**5.4**	**14.4**	**18.4**	**22.4**	**17.7**	**16.0**	**5.9**
Housewares	100.0	3.7	15.0	18.5	22.5	17.8	17.2	5.5
Plastic dinnerware	100.0	6.1	21.3	23.3	21.2	18.3	7.4	2.7
China and other dinnerware	100.0	2.1	26.2	13.7	18.0	13.7	22.7	3.6
Flatware	100.0	5.0	13.7	25.5	23.5	18.0	11.7	2.6
Glassware	100.0	6.4	18.1	12.8	24.2	15.6	19.8	3.4
Silver serving pieces	100.0	2.8	12.5	18.5	29.0	17.9	16.3	3.3
Other serving pieces	100.0	2.8	17.8	21.2	14.6	20.6	19.3	3.9
Nonelectric cookware	100.0	3.0	8.5	16.6	25.3	17.5	23.5	6.3
Tableware, nonelectric kitchenware	100.0	3.5	15.1	21.3	21.1	19.6	11.9	7.2
Small appliances	100.0	8.2	13.5	18.2	22.2	17.6	14.1	6.5
Small electric kitchen appliances	100.0	4.7	16.3	17.7	21.6	19.6	13.8	6.3
Portable heating and cooling equipment	100.0	16.6	6.7	19.5	23.7	12.6	14.6	7.1
Miscellaneous household equipment	**100.0**	**3.4**	**15.2**	**18.6**	**24.8**	**19.0**	**13.1**	**6.0**
Window coverings	100.0	1.0	14.9	30.3	18.8	18.5	12.6	3.9
Infants' equipment	100.0	7.2	23.3	42.8	15.9	7.0	2.3	1.0
Laundry and cleaning equipment	100.0	3.2	14.3	21.4	20.5	19.2	15.7	5.8
Outdoor equipment	100.0	1.3	11.0	8.6	15.5	21.9	39.5	3.3
Lamps and lighting fixtures	100.0	3.9	5.7	10.3	45.4	17.3	11.3	6.5
Household decorative items	100.0	1.9	14.8	23.5	21.0	20.1	10.7	7.7
Telephones and accessories	100.0	2.8	11.4	20.2	24.7	21.4	8.7	10.7
Lawn and garden equipment	100.0	–	7.6	10.9	38.7	19.9	19.5	3.8
Power tools	100.0	3.9	19.5	18.3	24.5	12.9	13.4	7.5
Office furniture for home use	100.0	5.0	13.1	19.4	34.6	20.6	5.0	2.3
Hand tools	100.0	5.0	33.4	12.1	9.6	18.7	10.8	9.8
Indoor plants and fresh flowers	100.0	1.5	10.8	14.4	25.8	23.6	15.0	8.9
Closet and storage items	100.0	1.8	23.9	22.7	17.5	17.6	10.8	5.3
Rental of furniture	100.0	12.0	38.9	8.9	9.0	3.3	11.3	16.5
Luggage	100.0	–	9.7	32.0	9.4	15.8	10.1	23.1
Computers and computer hardware for nonbusiness use	100.0	6.1	19.0	19.8	25.5	17.8	8.8	3.0
Portable memory	100.0	7.5	20.3	22.3	23.7	17.0	6.8	2.5
Computer software	100.0	6.0	21.8	17.8	29.0	15.1	6.7	3.6
Computer accessories	100.0	3.4	11.6	18.9	24.1	23.4	14.7	3.9
Personal digital assistants	100.0	7.5	19.6	21.2	26.2	15.8	7.7	2.0
Internet services away from home	100.0	4.6	20.7	23.6	21.5	17.8	8.2	3.5
Telephone answering devices	100.0	5.5	9.3	12.8	37.6	9.3	17.9	6.8
Business equipment for home use	100.0	2.2	9.2	15.9	30.4	24.6	10.6	7.1
Other hardware	100.0	–	15.5	17.4	25.0	15.2	14.8	12.1
Smoke alarms	100.0	3.7	9.5	13.0	20.3	32.0	14.7	6.7
Other household appliances	100.0	3.6	15.1	15.0	24.0	21.1	14.1	7.0
Miscellaneous household equipment and parts	100.0	4.1	11.4	17.1	20.6	23.9	17.1	5.9

Note: Numbers may not add to total because of rounding. "–" means sample is too small to make a reliable estimate.
Source: Calculations by New Strategist based on the Bureau of Labor Statistics' 2011 Consumer Expenditure Survey

Table 8.5 Housing: Household Operations: Average spending by income, 2011

(average annual spending on household services, supplies, furnishings, and equipment, by before-tax income of consumer units, 2011)

	total consumer units	under $20,000	$20,000– $39,999	$40,000– $49,999	$50,000– $69,999	$70,000– $79,999	$80,000– $99,999	$100,000 or more
Number of consumer units (in 000s)	122,287	26,342	27,788	11,347	17,376	7,385	10,456	21,593
Average number of persons per consumer unit	2.5	1.8	2.3	2.6	2.7	2.8	3.0	3.2
Average before-tax income of consumer units	$63,685.00	$10,491.66	$29,658.14	$44,698.00	$59,306.00	$74,742.00	$89,108.00	$169,776.00
Average spending of consumer units, total	49,704.88	22,142.36	33,453.66	40,306.19	50,034.03	57,976.69	65,389.80	97,728.22
Housing, average spending	**16,803.03**	**8,830.55**	**12,538.47**	**14,562.10**	**16,888.03**	**19,178.04**	**20,926.38**	**30,211.87**
HOUSEHOLD SERVICES	**1,122.18**	**442.56**	**730.40**	**837.02**	**933.57**	**1,379.47**	**1,381.30**	**2,543.43**
Personal services	**398.27**	**128.96**	**233.19**	**239.20**	**268.66**	**567.82**	**546.07**	**997.56**
Babysitting and child care in own home	51.23	11.94	12.64	12.61	21.51	23.81	51.18	202.45
Babysitting and child care in someone else's home	26.87	7.62	23.32	22.33	27.92	21.40	26.89	58.31
Care for elderly, invalids, handicapped, etc.	67.89	66.58	100.24	49.09	48.59	165.26	26.14	40.19
Day care centers, nurseries, and preschools	251.30	42.21	94.43	154.11	170.96	354.54	441.87	696.38
Other household services	**723.92**	**313.60**	**497.21**	**597.83**	**664.91**	**811.64**	**835.23**	**1,545.87**
Housekeeping services	105.26	32.04	42.30	63.15	47.99	96.28	77.78	360.19
Gardening, lawn care service	118.65	51.03	76.56	89.39	86.00	124.11	110.35	299.13
Water-softening service	4.87	3.29	3.04	5.58	6.62	4.64	5.19	7.27
Nonclothing laundry and dry cleaning, sent out	14.71	2.96	7.13	7.92	10.47	16.29	16.14	42.79
Nonclothing laundry and dry cleaning, coin-operated	4.40	5.41	6.83	3.74	3.30	2.04	4.39	2.05
Termite and pest control services	20.61	7.44	11.36	16.01	17.97	20.13	25.94	50.74
Home security system service fee	25.65	9.88	14.94	16.48	22.31	33.02	32.47	60.37
Other home services	15.98	5.89	11.49	13.21	17.27	12.20	21.04	33.33
Termite and pest control products	3.57	1.30	2.14	2.92	3.05	3.74	4.62	8.35
Moving, storage, and freight express	52.88	28.13	53.61	32.24	52.77	42.28	50.58	97.80
Appliance repair, including at service center	16.62	6.36	10.42	16.57	16.13	22.96	20.85	33.31
Reupholstering and furniture repair	5.75	1.36	1.95	4.30	5.65	1.27	4.57	19.44
Repairs and rentals of lawn and garden equipment, hand and power tools, etc.	9.29	6.55	5.67	9.69	7.36	9.13	10.85	17.92
Appliance rental	2.01	3.00	1.60	3.91	2.85	1.46	0.44	0.61
Rental of office equipment for nonbusiness use	1.06	0.73	1.53	0.45	1.53	0.69	0.26	1.49
Repair of computer systems for nonbusiness use	6.51	3.15	5.30	7.81	6.04	10.40	6.52	10.52
Computer information services	313.76	140.85	240.83	304.19	357.13	410.93	442.51	493.12
Installation of computer	0.51	–	0.50	0.28	0.46	0.05	0.72	0.69
HOUSEKEEPING SUPPLIES	**614.74**	**337.31**	**435.62**	**529.66**	**625.81**	**679.55**	**755.44**	**1,082.68**
Laundry and cleaning supplies	**145.06**	**97.88**	**115.06**	**141.91**	**154.50**	**159.44**	**184.18**	**203.42**
Soaps and detergents	78.49	61.11	62.67	70.96	87.14	79.97	95.77	104.72
Other laundry cleaning products	66.57	36.77	52.39	70.95	67.37	79.47	88.41	98.70
Other household products	**339.58**	**167.76**	**238.52**	**273.56**	**333.65**	**390.85**	**397.90**	**643.42**
Cleansing and toilet tissue, paper towels, and napkins	114.81	72.13	90.13	100.85	121.57	132.81	137.08	176.04
Miscellaneous household products	134.12	57.66	96.15	95.94	123.99	171.64	154.59	270.65
Lawn and garden supplies	90.65	37.96	52.24	76.78	88.10	86.40	106.24	196.73
Postage and stationery	**130.09**	**71.67**	**82.04**	**114.19**	**137.65**	**129.26**	**173.36**	**235.85**
Stationery, stationery supplies, giftwrap	67.56	28.27	47.56	50.83	71.97	73.38	90.47	126.93
Postage	55.22	39.69	31.20	62.28	57.91	54.09	79.40	85.41
Delivery services	7.32	4.68	3.29	1.08	7.77	1.79	3.49	23.52
HOUSEHOLD FURNISHINGS AND EQUIPMENT	**1,513.98**	**538.85**	**962.37**	**1,099.93**	**1,700.56**	**1,959.37**	**2,004.80**	**3,032.11**
Household textiles	**109.14**	**49.14**	**64.68**	**107.55**	**106.37**	**155.03**	**144.83**	**202.70**
Bathroom linens	20.16	11.12	13.66	23.60	19.58	14.30	22.93	37.52
Bedroom linens	59.00	25.57	31.49	60.24	55.22	95.84	85.38	106.97
Kitchen and dining room linens	5.95	2.87	4.43	6.19	9.35	3.72	5.12	9.62
Curtains and draperies	11.30	3.03	7.33	9.79	7.70	21.03	16.65	24.28
Slipcovers and decorative pillows	3.52	1.88	1.90	2.13	2.22	6.73	4.61	7.75
Sewing materials for household items	8.07	3.69	5.51	4.58	11.15	11.46	8.30	14.83
Other linens	1.13	0.99	0.37	1.02	1.15	1.94	1.84	1.73
Furniture	**357.94**	**140.15**	**207.89**	**259.70**	**310.36**	**390.71**	**433.17**	**859.03**
Mattresses and springs	61.72	19.73	35.87	44.92	61.43	87.53	80.19	137.52
Other bedroom furniture	70.06	38.34	42.33	49.15	59.73	90.08	65.25	159.25
Sofas	92.81	38.86	57.77	63.19	75.39	87.30	114.82	224.55
Living room chairs	36.12	11.99	26.56	24.65	25.90	50.88	36.16	87.02
Living room tables	11.87	5.49	4.62	8.36	10.93	9.40	16.18	30.36

	total consumer units	under $20,000	$20,000– $39,999	$40,000– $49,999	$50,000– $69,999	$70,000– $79,999	$80,000– $99,999	$100,000 or more
Kitchen and dining room furniture	$27.45	$10.00	$15.90	$19.38	$18.04	$21.93	$61.62	$60.78
Infants' furniture	8.23	3.07	5.38	11.35	9.36	8.67	10.53	14.39
Outdoor furniture	18.70	2.36	3.95	21.37	20.49	12.23	18.60	57.02
Wall units, cabinets, and other furniture	30.97	10.32	15.51	17.33	29.09	22.70	29.82	88.14
Floor coverings	**19.98**	**6.33**	**5.01**	**9.47**	**14.19**	**12.59**	**18.29**	**69.44**
Floor coverings, nonpermanent	19.61	5.40	5.01	9.43	14.19	12.59	16.35	69.44
Major appliances	**193.93**	**72.94**	**116.92**	**156.62**	**228.96**	**239.46**	**318.86**	**355.95**
Dishwashers (built-in), garbage disposals, range hoods	14.60	3.56	4.68	11.10	16.48	21.30	15.52	39.29
Refrigerators and freezers	52.96	19.78	32.65	33.49	74.99	84.99	70.68	92.54
Washing machines	34.00	12.66	22.37	26.18	39.46	40.78	63.56	58.04
Clothes dryers	24.93	9.07	17.84	23.57	34.11	20.01	37.34	42.42
Cooking stoves, ovens	30.51	9.50	12.97	23.97	27.25	17.36	74.95	67.74
Microwave ovens	8.96	5.82	5.77	7.76	8.99	9.57	12.29	15.65
Window air conditioners	4.82	2.45	6.49	7.20	3.48	8.12	5.00	4.22
Electric floor-cleaning equipment	16.06	5.94	11.09	14.13	20.50	33.56	22.35	23.24
Sewing machines	2.43	0.62	1.09	1.21	1.95	1.36	4.23	6.99
Miscellaneous household appliances	4.21	–	1.09	7.73	1.24	2.38	12.94	5.73
Small appliances and miscellaneous housewares	**89.34**	**34.57**	**64.13**	**57.93**	**91.64**	**80.52**	**119.41**	**186.93**
Housewares	54.84	16.45	39.43	33.87	56.63	54.70	75.10	116.29
Plastic dinnerware	2.47	1.53	1.61	2.26	2.48	2.29	4.66	3.86
China and other dinnerware	5.34	1.97	2.97	0.70	2.62	4.16	4.55	17.59
Flatware	2.96	0.96	1.68	2.36	2.54	6.03	2.76	6.78
Glassware	6.56	1.41	3.97	3.80	6.42	4.15	11.28	15.55
Silver serving pieces	1.43	0.45	0.89	0.62	1.56	1.76	3.18	2.58
Other serving pieces	1.42	0.20	0.84	1.17	1.87	1.77	1.70	3.19
Nonelectric cookware	14.94	4.78	12.66	8.80	24.05	15.97	16.52	23.29
Tableware, nonelectric kitchenware	19.71	5.15	14.83	14.16	15.07	18.58	30.44	43.44
Small appliances	34.50	18.12	24.70	24.06	35.01	25.83	44.31	70.64
Small electric kitchen appliances	24.50	12.21	16.49	15.36	26.65	21.60	32.83	49.83
Portable heating and cooling equipment	10.00	–	8.21	8.71	8.36	4.22	11.48	20.81
Miscellaneous household equipment	**743.64**	**235.71**	**503.74**	**508.66**	**949.04**	**1,081.05**	**970.24**	**1,358.05**
Window coverings	15.87	1.53	7.70	4.47	7.59	22.62	16.08	54.12
Infants' equipment	14.49	2.64	11.79	9.50	16.99	14.06	7.11	35.10
Laundry and cleaning equipment	17.33	8.04	12.35	12.82	19.50	19.16	26.21	29.63
Outdoor equipment	34.43	4.08	56.74	20.69	36.06	16.97	39.11	48.13
Lamps and lighting fixtures	29.29	10.65	20.73	24.95	36.35	11.55	17.24	69.22
Household decorative items	117.20	33.97	50.53	71.65	183.64	218.35	155.88	209.28
Telephones and accessories	45.56	15.12	34.88	46.18	43.96	50.21	65.99	81.02
Lawn and garden equipment	65.62	6.09	18.27	21.64	140.95	259.00	108.04	71.41
Power tools	38.18	19.70	34.65	41.89	80.40	19.96	68.04	18.19
Office furniture for home use	5.83	1.62	1.92	3.77	6.55	4.04	6.82	16.62
Hand tools	15.55	5.02	25.47	6.44	24.18	13.02	19.32	10.42
Indoor plants and fresh flowers	46.92	17.98	27.24	37.54	41.76	49.32	65.15	107.01
Closet and storage items	16.85	11.05	14.39	6.75	13.57	13.50	19.85	33.42
Rental of furniture	6.16	4.97	10.20	3.44	6.83	0.83	0.07	8.05
Luggage	6.84	4.01	10.02	2.79	4.25	6.99	7.10	10.40
Computers and computer hardware for nonbusiness use	152.35	49.53	81.11	105.52	153.85	207.43	175.16	362.98
Portable memory	4.17	1.80	2.94	3.71	5.80	6.19	5.14	6.39
Computer software	14.33	5.97	6.57	6.78	22.31	26.57	16.38	26.89
Computer accessories	12.15	3.51	7.36	10.56	11.57	22.05	17.70	24.08
Personal digital assistants	6.27	1.78	3.51	2.27	6.38	8.37	10.08	14.78
Internet services away from home	7.03	4.08	5.24	8.25	8.26	10.88	10.34	8.36
Telephone answering devices	0.61	0.32	0.93	0.45	0.43	0.43	0.38	1.01
Business equipment for home use	4.05	1.59	3.30	1.97	4.15	4.09	5.64	8.23
Other hardware	11.34	3.73	9.99	11.45	10.98	24.34	20.37	13.78
Smoke alarms	1.97	0.72	2.77	0.83	1.82	2.35	2.00	3.03
Other household appliances	7.96	4.50	5.91	5.29	11.17	3.94	12.49	12.85
Miscellaneous household equipment and parts	43.13	17.00	34.41	34.54	48.24	43.58	69.39	70.21

Note: Subcategories may not add to total because some are not shown. "–" means sample is too small to make a reliable estimate.
Source: Bureau of Labor Statistics, unpublished tables from the 2011 Consumer Expenditure Survey; calculations by New Strategist

Table 8.6 Housing: Household Operations: Indexed spending by income, 2011

(indexed average annual spending of consumer units on household services, supplies, furnishings, and equipment, by before-tax income of consumer unit, 2011; index definition: an index of 100 is the average for all consumer units; an index of 125 means that spending by consumer units in that group is 25 percent above the average for all consumer units; an index of 75 indicates spending that is 25 percent below the average for all consumer units)

	total consumer units	under $20,000	$20,000–$39,999	$40,000–$49,999	$50,000–$69,999	$70,000–$79,999	$80,000–$99,999	$100,000 or more
Average spending of consumer units, total	$49,705	$22,142	$33,454	$40,306	$50,034	$57,977	$65,390	$97,728
Average spending of consumer units, index	100	45	67	81	101	117	132	197
Housing, spending index	**100**	**53**	**75**	**87**	**101**	**114**	**125**	**180**
HOUSEHOLD SERVICES	**100**	**39**	**65**	**75**	**83**	**123**	**123**	**227**
Personal services	**100**	**32**	**59**	**60**	**67**	**143**	**137**	**250**
Babysitting and child care in own home	100	23	25	25	42	46	100	395
Babysitting and child care in someone else's home	100	28	87	83	104	80	100	217
Care for elderly, invalids, handicapped, etc.	100	98	148	72	72	243	39	59
Day care centers, nurseries, and preschools	100	17	38	61	68	141	176	277
Other household services	**100**	**43**	**69**	**83**	**92**	**112**	**115**	**214**
Housekeeping services	100	30	40	60	46	91	74	342
Gardening, lawn care service	100	43	65	75	72	105	93	252
Water-softening service	100	68	62	115	136	95	107	149
Nonclothing laundry and dry cleaning, sent out	100	20	48	54	71	111	110	291
Nonclothing laundry and dry cleaning, coin-operated	100	123	155	85	75	46	100	47
Termite and pest control services	100	36	55	78	87	98	126	246
Home security system service fee	100	39	58	64	87	129	127	235
Other home services	100	37	72	83	108	76	132	209
Termite and pest control products	100	36	60	82	85	105	129	234
Moving, storage, and freight express	100	53	101	61	100	80	96	185
Appliance repair, including at service center	100	38	63	100	97	138	125	200
Reupholstering and furniture repair	100	24	34	75	98	22	79	338
Repairs and rentals of lawn and garden equipment, hand and power tools, etc.	100	70	61	104	79	98	117	193
Appliance rental	100	149	80	195	142	73	22	30
Rental of office equipment for nonbusiness use	100	68	144	42	144	65	25	141
Repair of computer systems for nonbusiness use	100	48	81	120	93	160	100	162
Computer information services	100	45	77	97	114	131	141	157
Installation of computer	100	–	99	55	90	10	141	135
HOUSEKEEPING SUPPLIES	**100**	**55**	**71**	**86**	**102**	**111**	**123**	**176**
Laundry and cleaning supplies	**100**	**67**	**79**	**98**	**107**	**110**	**127**	**140**
Soaps and detergents	100	78	80	90	111	102	122	133
Other laundry cleaning products	100	55	79	107	101	119	133	148
Other household products	**100**	**49**	**70**	**81**	**98**	**115**	**117**	**189**
Cleansing and toilet tissue, paper towels, and napkins	100	63	79	88	106	116	119	153
Miscellaneous household products	100	43	72	72	92	128	115	202
Lawn and garden supplies	100	42	58	85	97	95	117	217
Postage and stationery	**100**	**55**	**63**	**88**	**106**	**99**	**133**	**181**
Stationery, stationery supplies, giftwrap	100	42	70	75	107	109	134	188
Postage	100	72	56	113	105	98	144	155
Delivery services	100	64	45	15	106	24	48	321
HOUSEHOLD FURNISHINGS AND EQUIPMENT	**100**	**36**	**64**	**73**	**112**	**129**	**132**	**200**
Household textiles	**100**	**45**	**59**	**99**	**97**	**142**	**133**	**186**
Bathroom linens	100	55	68	117	97	71	114	186
Bedroom linens	100	43	53	102	94	162	145	181
Kitchen and dining room linens	100	48	74	104	157	63	86	162
Curtains and draperies	100	27	65	87	68	186	147	215
Slipcovers and decorative pillows	100	53	54	61	63	191	131	220
Sewing materials for household items	100	46	68	57	138	142	103	184
Other linens	100	87	32	90	102	172	163	153
Furniture	**100**	**39**	**58**	**73**	**87**	**109**	**121**	**240**
Mattresses and springs	100	32	58	73	100	142	130	223
Other bedroom furniture	100	55	60	70	85	129	93	227
Sofas	100	42	62	68	81	94	124	242
Living room chairs	100	33	74	68	72	141	100	241
Living room tables	100	46	39	70	92	79	136	256

	total consumer units	under $20,000	$20,000– $39,999	$40,000– $49,999	$50,000– $69,999	$70,000– $79,999	$80,000– $99,999	$100,000 or more
Kitchen and dining room furniture	100	36	58	71	66	80	224	221
Infants' furniture	100	37	65	138	114	105	128	175
Outdoor furniture	100	13	21	114	110	65	99	305
Wall units, cabinets, and other furniture	100	33	50	56	94	73	96	285
Floor coverings	**100**	**32**	**25**	**47**	**71**	**63**	**92**	**348**
Floor coverings, nonpermanent	100	28	26	48	72	64	83	354
Major appliances	**100**	**38**	**60**	**81**	**118**	**123**	**164**	**184**
Dishwashers (built-in), garbage disposals, range hoods	100	24	32	76	113	146	106	269
Refrigerators and freezers	100	37	62	63	142	160	133	175
Washing machines	100	37	66	77	116	120	187	171
Clothes dryers	100	36	72	95	137	80	150	170
Cooking stoves, ovens	100	31	43	79	89	57	246	222
Microwave ovens	100	65	64	87	100	107	137	175
Window air conditioners	100	51	135	149	72	168	104	88
Electric floor-cleaning equipment	100	37	69	88	128	209	139	145
Sewing machines	100	26	45	50	80	56	174	288
Miscellaneous household appliances	100	–	26	184	29	57	307	136
Small appliances and miscellaneous housewares	**100**	**39**	**72**	**65**	**103**	**90**	**134**	**209**
Housewares	100	30	72	62	103	100	137	212
Plastic dinnerware	100	62	65	91	100	93	189	156
China and other dinnerware	100	37	56	13	49	78	85	329
Flatware	100	33	57	80	86	204	93	229
Glassware	100	22	61	58	98	63	172	237
Silver serving pieces	100	32	63	43	109	123	222	180
Other serving pieces	100	14	59	82	132	125	120	225
Nonelectric cookware	100	32	85	59	161	107	111	156
Tableware, nonelectric kitchenware	100	26	75	72	76	94	154	220
Small appliances	100	53	72	70	101	75	128	205
Small electric kitchen appliances	100	50	67	63	109	88	134	203
Portable heating and cooling equipment	100	–	82	87	84	42	115	208
Miscellaneous household equipment	**100**	**32**	**68**	**68**	**128**	**145**	**130**	**183**
Window coverings	100	10	49	28	48	143	101	341
Infants' equipment	100	18	81	66	117	97	49	242
Laundry and cleaning equipment	100	46	71	74	113	111	151	171
Outdoor equipment	100	12	165	60	105	49	114	140
Lamps and lighting fixtures	100	36	71	85	124	39	59	236
Household decorative items	100	29	43	61	157	186	133	179
Telephones and accessories	100	33	77	101	96	110	145	178
Lawn and garden equipment	100	9	28	33	215	395	165	109
Power tools	100	52	91	110	211	52	178	48
Office furniture for home use	100	28	33	65	112	69	117	285
Hand tools	100	32	164	41	155	84	124	67
Indoor plants and fresh flowers	100	38	58	80	89	105	139	228
Closet and storage items	100	66	85	40	81	80	118	198
Rental of furniture	100	81	166	56	111	13	1	131
Luggage	100	59	147	41	62	102	104	152
Computers and computer hardware for nonbusiness use	100	33	53	69	101	136	115	238
Portable memory	100	43	70	89	139	148	123	153
Computer software	100	42	46	47	156	185	114	188
Computer accessories	100	29	61	87	95	181	146	198
Personal digital assistants	100	28	56	36	102	133	161	236
Internet services away from home	100	58	75	117	117	155	147	119
Telephone answering devices	100	53	152	74	70	70	62	166
Business equipment for home use	100	39	82	49	102	101	139	203
Other hardware	100	33	88	101	97	215	180	122
Smoke alarms	100	36	141	42	92	119	102	154
Other household appliances	100	57	74	66	140	49	157	161
Miscellaneous household equipment and parts	100	39	80	80	112	101	161	163

Note: "–" means sample is too small to make a reliable estimate.
Source: Calculations by New Strategist based on the Bureau of Labor Statistics' 2011 Consumer Expenditure Survey

Table 8.7 Housing: Household Operations: Total spending by income, 2011

(total annual spending on household services, supplies, furnishings, and equipment, by before-tax income group of consumer units, 2011; consumer units and dollars in thousands)

	total consumer units	under $20,000	$20,000–$39,999	$40,000–$49,999	$50,000–$69,999	$70,000–$79,999	$80,000–$99,999	$100,000 or more
Number of consumer units	122,287	26,342	27,788	11,347	17,376	7,385	10,456	21,593
Total spending of all consumer units	$6,078,260,661	$583,273,961	$929,610,260	$457,354,338	$869,391,305	$428,157,856	$683,715,749	$2,110,245,454
Housing, total spending	2,054,792,130	232,614,372	348,419,011	165,236,149	293,446,409	141,629,825	218,806,229	652,364,909
HOUSEHOLD SERVICES	**137,228,026**	**11,657,997**	**20,296,370**	**9,497,666**	**16,221,712**	**10,187,386**	**14,442,873**	**54,920,284**
Personal services	**48,703,243**	**3,397,124**	**6,479,829**	**2,714,202**	**4,668,236**	**4,193,351**	**5,709,708**	**21,540,313**
Babysitting and child care in own home	6,264,763	314,534	351,264	143,086	373,758	175,837	535,138	4,371,503
Babysitting and child care in someone else's home	3,285,852	200,797	647,895	253,379	485,138	158,039	281,162	1,259,088
Care for elderly, invalids, handicapped, etc.	8,302,064	1,753,837	2,785,529	557,024	844,300	1,220,445	273,320	867,823
Day care centers, nurseries, and preschools	30,730,723	1,112,013	2,623,988	1,748,686	2,970,601	2,618,278	4,620,193	15,036,933
Other household services	**88,526,005**	**8,260,955**	**13,816,541**	**6,783,577**	**11,553,476**	**5,993,961**	**8,733,165**	**33,379,971**
Housekeeping services	12,871,930	844,098	1,175,488	716,563	833,874	711,028	813,268	7,777,583
Gardening, lawn care service	14,509,353	1,344,102	2,127,356	1,014,308	1,494,336	916,552	1,153,820	6,459,114
Water-softening service	595,538	86,771	84,473	63,316	115,029	34,266	54,267	156,981
Nonclothing laundry and dry cleaning, sent out	1,798,842	77,913	198,087	89,868	181,927	120,302	168,760	923,964
Nonclothing laundry and dry cleaning, coin-operated	538,063	142,541	189,732	42,438	57,341	15,065	45,902	44,266
Termite and pest control services	2,520,335	196,044	315,582	181,665	312,247	148,660	271,229	1,095,629
Home security system service fee	3,136,662	260,368	415,166	186,999	387,659	243,853	339,506	1,303,569
Other home services	1,954,146	155,029	319,215	149,894	300,084	90,097	219,994	719,695
Termite and pest control products	436,565	34,319	59,415	33,133	52,997	27,620	48,307	180,302
Moving, storage, and freight express	6,466,537	741,004	1,489,728	365,827	916,932	312,238	528,864	2,111,795
Appliance repair, including at service center	2,032,410	167,647	289,673	188,020	280,275	169,560	218,008	719,263
Reupholstering and furniture repair	703,150	35,845	54,259	48,792	98,174	9,379	47,784	419,768
Repairs and rentals of lawn and garden equipment, hand and power tools, etc.	1,136,046	172,480	157,649	109,952	127,887	67,425	113,448	386,947
Appliance rental	245,797	78,994	44,537	44,367	49,522	10,782	4,601	13,172
Rental of office equipment for nonbusiness use	129,624	19,122	42,462	5,106	26,585	5,096	2,719	32,174
Repair of computer systems for nonbusiness use	796,088	82,904	147,224	88,620	104,951	76,804	68,173	227,158
Computer information services	38,368,769	3,710,306	6,692,240	3,451,644	6,205,491	3,034,718	4,626,885	10,647,940
Installation of computer	62,366	–	13,988	3,177	7,993	369	7,528	14,899
HOUSEKEEPING SUPPLIES	**75,174,710**	**8,885,488**	**12,105,039**	**6,010,052**	**10,874,075**	**5,018,477**	**7,898,881**	**23,378,309**
Laundry and cleaning supplies	**17,738,952**	**2,578,449**	**3,197,279**	**1,610,253**	**2,684,592**	**1,177,464**	**1,925,786**	**4,392,448**
Soaps and detergents	9,598,307	1,609,813	1,741,571	805,183	1,514,145	590,578	1,001,371	2,261,219
Other laundry cleaning products	8,140,646	968,577	1,455,841	805,070	1,170,621	586,886	924,415	2,131,229
Other household products	**41,526,219**	**4,419,030**	**6,627,972**	**3,104,085**	**5,797,502**	**2,886,427**	**4,160,442**	**13,893,368**
Cleansing and toilet tissue, paper towels, and napkins	14,039,770	1,900,058	2,504,514	1,144,345	2,112,400	980,802	1,433,308	3,801,232
Miscellaneous household products	16,401,132	1,518,886	2,671,827	1,088,631	2,154,450	1,267,561	1,616,393	5,844,145
Lawn and garden supplies	11,085,317	999,982	1,451,775	871,223	1,530,826	638,064	1,110,845	4,247,991
Postage and stationery	**15,908,316**	**1,888,036**	**2,279,644**	**1,295,714**	**2,391,806**	**954,585**	**1,812,652**	**5,092,709**
Stationery, stationery supplies, giftwrap	8,261,710	744,630	1,321,477	576,768	1,250,551	541,911	945,954	2,740,799
Postage	6,752,688	1,045,625	866,861	706,691	1,006,244	399,455	830,206	1,844,258
Delivery services	895,141	123,346	91,317	12,255	135,012	13,219	36,491	507,867
HOUSEHOLD FURNISHINGS AND EQUIPMENT	**185,140,072**	**14,194,388**	**26,742,340**	**12,480,906**	**29,548,931**	**14,469,947**	**20,962,189**	**65,472,351**
Household textiles	**13,346,403**	**1,294,521**	**1,797,234**	**1,220,370**	**1,848,285**	**1,144,897**	**1,514,342**	**4,376,901**
Bathroom linens	2,465,306	292,953	379,533	267,789	340,222	105,606	239,756	810,169
Bedroom linens	7,214,933	673,605	874,945	683,543	959,503	707,778	892,733	2,309,803
Kitchen and dining room linens	727,608	75,540	123,105	70,238	162,466	27,472	53,535	207,725
Curtains and draperies	1,381,843	79,706	203,603	111,087	133,795	155,307	174,092	524,278
Slipcovers and decorative pillows	430,450	49,531	52,857	24,169	38,575	49,701	48,202	167,346
Sewing materials for household items	986,856	97,085	153,024	51,969	193,742	84,632	86,785	320,224
Other linens	138,184	26,026	10,166	11,574	19,982	14,327	19,239	37,356
Furniture	**43,771,409**	**3,691,899**	**5,776,956**	**2,946,816**	**5,392,815**	**2,885,393**	**4,529,226**	**18,549,035**
Mattresses and springs	7,547,554	519,684	996,695	509,707	1,067,408	646,409	838,467	2,969,469
Other bedroom furniture	8,567,427	1,009,841	1,176,197	557,705	1,037,868	665,241	682,254	3,438,685
Sofas	11,349,456	1,023,548	1,605,292	717,017	1,309,977	644,711	1,200,558	4,848,708
Living room chairs	4,417,006	315,869	738,110	279,704	450,038	375,749	378,089	1,879,023
Living room tables	1,451,547	144,599	128,511	94,861	189,920	69,419	169,178	655,563

	total consumer units	under $20,000	$20,000–$39,999	$40,000–$49,999	$50,000–$69,999	$70,000–$79,999	$80,000–$99,999	$100,000 or more
Kitchen and dining room furniture	$3,356,778	$263,312	$441,709	$219,905	$313,463	$161,953	$644,299	$1,312,423
Infants' furniture	1,006,422	80,954	149,385	128,788	162,639	64,028	110,102	310,723
Outdoor furniture	2,286,767	62,270	109,665	242,485	356,034	90,319	194,482	1,231,233
Wall units, cabinets, and other furniture	3,787,228	271,849	431,103	196,644	505,468	167,640	311,798	1,903,207
Floor coverings	**2,443,294**	**166,839**	**139,355**	**107,456**	**246,565**	**92,977**	**191,240**	**1,499,418**
Floor coverings, nonpermanent	2,398,048	142,287	139,222	107,002	246,565	92,977	170,956	1,499,418
Major appliances	**23,715,118**	**1,921,483**	**3,248,990**	**1,777,167**	**3,978,409**	**1,768,412**	**3,334,000**	**7,686,028**
Dishwashers (built-in), garbage disposals, range hoods	1,785,390	93,667	130,014	125,952	286,356	157,301	162,277	848,389
Refrigerators and freezers	6,476,320	521,025	907,314	380,011	1,303,026	627,651	739,030	1,998,216
Washing machines	4,157,758	333,445	621,703	297,064	685,657	301,160	664,583	1,253,258
Clothes dryers	3,048,615	238,870	495,787	267,449	592,695	147,774	390,427	915,975
Cooking stoves, ovens	3,730,976	250,142	360,424	271,988	473,496	128,204	783,677	1,462,710
Microwave ovens	1,095,692	153,385	160,455	88,053	156,210	70,674	128,504	337,930
Window air conditioners	589,423	64,582	180,469	81,698	60,468	59,966	52,280	91,122
Electric floor-cleaning equipment	1,963,929	156,370	308,291	160,333	356,208	247,841	233,692	501,821
Sewing machines	297,157	16,386	30,391	13,730	33,883	10,044	44,229	150,935
Miscellaneous household appliances	514,828	–	30,289	87,712	21,546	17,576	135,301	123,728
Small appliances and miscellaneous housewares	**10,925,121**	**910,660**	**1,782,133**	**657,332**	**1,592,337**	**594,640**	**1,248,551**	**4,036,379**
Housewares	6,706,219	433,331	1,095,713	384,323	984,003	403,960	785,246	2,511,050
Plastic dinnerware	302,049	40,342	44,614	25,644	43,092	16,912	48,725	83,349
China and other dinnerware	653,013	51,801	82,423	7,943	45,525	30,722	47,575	379,821
Flatware	361,970	25,360	46,568	26,779	44,135	44,532	28,859	146,401
Glassware	802,203	37,206	110,289	43,119	111,554	30,648	117,944	335,771
Silver serving pieces	174,870	11,934	24,843	7,035	27,107	12,998	33,250	55,710
Other serving pieces	173,648	5,319	23,271	13,276	32,493	13,071	17,775	68,882
Nonelectric cookware	1,826,968	125,876	351,700	99,854	417,893	117,938	172,733	502,901
Tableware, nonelectric kitchenware	2,410,277	135,624	412,004	160,674	261,856	137,213	318,281	938,000
Small appliances	4,218,902	477,329	686,420	273,009	608,334	190,755	463,305	1,525,330
Small electric kitchen appliances	2,996,032	321,752	458,294	174,290	463,070	159,516	343,270	1,075,979
Portable heating and cooling equipment	1,222,870	–	228,126	98,832	145,263	31,165	120,035	449,350
Miscellaneous household equipment	**90,937,505**	**6,209,036**	**13,997,817**	**5,771,765**	**16,490,519**	**7,983,554**	**10,144,829**	**29,324,374**
Window coverings	1,940,695	40,427	213,922	50,721	131,884	167,049	168,132	1,168,613
Infants' equipment	1,771,939	69,566	327,534	107,797	295,218	103,833	74,342	757,914
Laundry and cleaning equipment	2,119,234	211,729	343,281	145,469	338,832	141,497	274,052	639,801
Outdoor equipment	4,210,341	107,487	1,576,813	234,769	626,579	125,323	408,934	1,039,271
Lamps and lighting fixtures	3,581,786	280,557	576,032	283,108	631,618	85,297	180,261	1,494,667
Household decorative items	14,332,036	894,852	1,404,067	813,013	3,190,929	1,612,515	1,629,881	4,518,983
Telephones and accessories	5,571,396	398,295	969,272	524,004	763,849	370,801	689,991	1,749,465
Lawn and garden equipment	8,024,473	160,320	507,748	245,549	2,449,147	1,912,715	1,129,666	1,541,956
Power tools	4,668,918	519,032	962,973	475,326	1,397,030	147,405	711,426	392,777
Office furniture for home use	712,933	42,596	53,279	42,778	113,813	29,835	71,310	358,876
Hand tools	1,901,563	132,138	707,802	73,075	420,152	96,153	202,010	224,999
Indoor plants and fresh flowers	5,737,706	473,555	756,993	425,966	725,622	364,228	681,208	2,310,667
Closet and storage items	2,060,536	290,960	399,800	76,592	235,792	99,698	207,552	721,638
Rental of furniture	753,288	130,901	283,576	39,034	118,678	6,130	732	173,824
Luggage	836,443	105,620	278,517	31,658	73,848	51,621	74,238	224,567
Computers and computer hardware for nonbusiness use	18,630,424	1,304,841	2,253,900	1,197,335	2,673,298	1,531,871	1,831,473	7,837,827
Portable memory	509,937	47,361	81,592	42,097	100,781	45,713	53,744	137,979
Computer software	1,752,373	157,196	182,464	76,933	387,659	196,219	171,269	580,636
Computer accessories	1,485,787	92,529	204,549	119,824	201,040	162,839	185,071	519,959
Personal digital assistants	766,739	46,780	97,498	25,758	110,859	61,812	105,396	319,145
Internet services away from home	859,678	107,506	145,667	93,613	143,526	80,349	108,115	180,517
Telephone answering devices	74,595	8,545	25,837	5,106	7,472	3,176	3,973	21,809
Business equipment for home use	495,262	41,823	91,781	22,354	72,110	30,205	58,972	177,710
Other hardware	1,386,735	98,138	277,657	129,923	190,788	179,751	212,989	297,552
Smoke alarms	240,905	18,920	77,018	9,418	31,624	17,355	20,912	65,427
Other household appliances	973,405	118,599	164,120	60,026	194,090	29,097	130,595	277,470
Miscellaneous household equipment and parts	5,274,238	447,749	956,128	391,925	838,218	321,838	725,542	1,516,045

Note: Numbers may not add to total because of rounding and missing subcategories. "–" means sample is too small to make a reliable estimate.
Source: Calculations by New Strategist based on the Bureau of Labor Statistics' 2011 Consumer Expenditure Survey

Table 8.8 Housing: Household Operations: Market shares by income, 2011

(percentage of total annual spending on household services, supplies, furnishings, and equipment accounted for by before-tax income group of consumer units, 2011)

	total consumer units	under $20,000	$20,000– $39,999	$40,000– $49,999	$50,000– $69,999	$70,000– $79,999	$80,000– $99,999	$100,000 or more
Share of total consumer units	100.0%	21.5%	22.7%	9.3%	14.2%	6.0%	8.6%	17.7%
Share of total before-tax income	100.0	3.5	10.6	6.5	13.2	7.1	12.0	47.1
Share of total spending	100.0	9.6	15.3	7.5	14.3	7.0	11.2	34.7
Share of housing spending	100.0	11.3	17.0	8.0	14.3	6.9	10.6	31.7
HOUSEHOLD SERVICES	100.0	8.5	14.8	6.9	11.8	7.4	10.5	40.0
Personal services	100.0	7.0	13.3	5.6	9.6	8.6	11.7	44.2
Babysitting and child care in own home	100.0	5.0	5.6	2.3	6.0	2.8	8.5	69.8
Babysitting and child care in someone else's home	100.0	6.1	19.7	7.7	14.8	4.8	8.6	38.3
Care for elderly, invalids, handicapped, etc.	100.0	21.1	33.6	6.7	10.2	14.7	3.3	10.5
Day care centers, nurseries, and preschools	100.0	3.6	8.5	5.7	9.7	8.5	15.0	48.9
Other household services	100.0	9.3	15.6	7.7	13.1	6.8	9.9	37.7
Housekeeping services	100.0	6.6	9.1	5.6	6.5	5.5	6.3	60.4
Gardening, lawn care service	100.0	9.3	14.7	7.0	10.3	6.3	8.0	44.5
Water-softening service	100.0	14.6	14.2	10.6	19.3	5.8	9.1	26.4
Nonclothing laundry and dry cleaning, sent out	100.0	4.3	11.0	5.0	10.1	6.7	9.4	51.4
Nonclothing laundry and dry cleaning, coin-operated	100.0	26.5	35.3	7.9	10.7	2.8	8.5	8.2
Termite and pest control services	100.0	7.8	12.5	7.2	12.4	5.9	10.8	43.5
Home security system service fee	100.0	8.3	13.2	6.0	12.4	7.8	10.8	41.6
Other home services	100.0	7.9	16.3	7.7	15.4	4.6	11.3	36.8
Termite and pest control products	100.0	7.9	13.6	7.6	12.1	6.3	11.1	41.3
Moving, storage, and freight express	100.0	11.5	23.0	5.7	14.2	4.8	8.2	32.7
Appliance repair, including at service center	100.0	8.2	14.3	9.3	13.8	8.3	10.7	35.4
Reupholstering and furniture repair	100.0	5.1	7.7	6.9	14.0	1.3	6.8	59.7
Repairs and rentals of lawn and garden equipment, hand and power tools, etc.	100.0	15.2	13.9	9.7	11.3	5.9	10.0	34.1
Appliance rental	100.0	32.1	18.1	18.1	20.1	4.4	1.9	5.4
Rental of office equipment for nonbusiness use	100.0	14.8	32.8	3.9	20.5	3.9	2.1	24.8
Repair of computer systems for nonbusiness use	100.0	10.4	18.5	11.1	13.2	9.6	8.6	28.5
Computer information services	100.0	9.7	17.4	9.0	16.2	7.9	12.1	27.8
Installation of computer	100.0	–	22.4	5.1	12.8	0.6	12.1	23.9
HOUSEKEEPING SUPPLIES	100.0	11.8	16.1	8.0	14.5	6.7	10.5	31.1
Laundry and cleaning supplies	100.0	14.5	18.0	9.1	15.1	6.6	10.9	24.8
Soaps and detergents	100.0	16.8	18.1	8.4	15.8	6.2	10.4	23.6
Other laundry cleaning products	100.0	11.9	17.9	9.9	14.4	7.2	11.4	26.2
Other household products	100.0	10.6	16.0	7.5	14.0	7.0	10.0	33.5
Cleansing and toilet tissue, paper towels, and napkins	100.0	13.5	17.8	8.2	15.0	7.0	10.2	27.1
Miscellaneous household products	100.0	9.3	16.3	6.6	13.1	7.7	9.9	35.6
Lawn and garden supplies	100.0	9.0	13.1	7.9	13.8	5.8	10.0	38.3
Postage and stationery	100.0	11.9	14.3	8.1	15.0	6.0	11.4	32.0
Stationery, stationery supplies, giftwrap	100.0	9.0	16.0	7.0	15.1	6.6	11.4	33.2
Postage	100.0	15.5	12.8	10.5	14.9	5.9	12.3	27.3
Delivery services	100.0	13.8	10.2	1.4	15.1	1.5	4.1	56.7
HOUSEHOLD FURNISHINGS AND EQUIPMENT	100.0	7.7	14.4	6.7	16.0	7.8	11.3	35.4
Household textiles	100.0	9.7	13.5	9.1	13.8	8.6	11.3	32.8
Bathroom linens	100.0	11.9	15.4	10.9	13.8	4.3	9.7	32.9
Bedroom linens	100.0	9.3	12.1	9.5	13.3	9.8	12.4	32.0
Kitchen and dining room linens	100.0	10.4	16.9	9.7	22.3	3.8	7.4	28.5
Curtains and draperies	100.0	5.8	14.7	8.0	9.7	11.2	12.6	37.9
Slipcovers and decorative pillows	100.0	11.5	12.3	5.6	9.0	11.5	11.2	38.9
Sewing materials for household items	100.0	9.8	15.5	5.3	19.6	8.6	8.8	32.4
Other linens	100.0	18.8	7.4	8.4	14.5	10.4	13.9	27.0
Furniture	100.0	8.4	13.2	6.7	12.3	6.6	10.3	42.4
Mattresses and springs	100.0	6.9	13.2	6.8	14.1	8.6	11.1	39.3
Other bedroom furniture	100.0	11.8	13.7	6.5	12.1	7.8	8.0	40.1
Sofas	100.0	9.0	14.1	6.3	11.5	5.7	10.6	42.7
Living room chairs	100.0	7.2	16.7	6.3	10.2	8.5	8.6	42.5
Living room tables	100.0	10.0	8.9	6.5	13.1	4.8	11.7	45.2

	total consumer units	under $20,000	$20,000– $39,999	$40,000– $49,999	$50,000– $69,999	$70,000– $79,999	$80,000– $99,999	$100,000 or more
Kitchen and dining room furniture	100.0%	7.8%	13.2%	6.6%	9.3%	4.8%	19.2%	39.1%
Infants' furniture	100.0	8.0	14.8	12.8	16.2	6.4	10.9	30.9
Outdoor furniture	100.0	2.7	4.8	10.6	15.6	3.9	8.5	53.8
Wall units, cabinets, and other furniture	100.0	7.2	11.4	5.2	13.3	4.4	8.2	50.3
Floor coverings	**100.0**	**6.8**	**5.7**	**4.4**	**10.1**	**3.8**	**7.8**	**61.4**
Floor coverings, nonpermanent	100.0	5.9	5.8	4.5	10.3	3.9	7.1	62.5
Major appliances	**100.0**	**8.1**	**13.7**	**7.5**	**16.8**	**7.5**	**14.1**	**32.4**
Dishwashers (built-in), garbage disposals, range hoods	100.0	5.2	7.3	7.1	16.0	8.8	9.1	47.5
Refrigerators and freezers	100.0	8.0	14.0	5.9	20.1	9.7	11.4	30.9
Washing machines	100.0	8.0	15.0	7.1	16.5	7.2	16.0	30.1
Clothes dryers	100.0	7.8	16.3	8.8	19.4	4.8	12.8	30.0
Cooking stoves, ovens	100.0	6.7	9.7	7.3	12.7	3.4	21.0	39.2
Microwave ovens	100.0	14.0	14.6	8.0	14.3	6.5	11.7	30.8
Window air conditioners	100.0	11.0	30.6	13.9	10.3	10.2	8.9	15.5
Electric floor-cleaning equipment	100.0	8.0	15.7	8.2	18.1	12.6	11.9	25.6
Sewing machines	100.0	5.5	10.2	4.6	11.4	3.4	14.9	50.8
Miscellaneous household appliances	100.0	–	5.9	17.0	4.2	3.4	26.3	24.0
Small appliances and miscellaneous housewares	**100.0**	**8.3**	**16.3**	**6.0**	**14.6**	**5.4**	**11.4**	**36.9**
Housewares	100.0	6.5	16.3	5.7	14.7	6.0	11.7	37.4
Plastic dinnerware	100.0	13.4	14.8	8.5	14.3	5.6	16.1	27.6
China and other dinnerware	100.0	7.9	12.6	1.2	7.0	4.7	7.3	58.2
Flatware	100.0	7.0	12.9	7.4	12.2	12.3	8.0	40.4
Glassware	100.0	4.6	13.7	5.4	13.9	3.8	14.7	41.9
Silver serving pieces	100.0	6.8	14.2	4.0	15.5	7.4	19.0	31.9
Other serving pieces	100.0	3.1	13.4	7.6	18.7	7.5	10.2	39.7
Nonelectric cookware	100.0	6.9	19.3	5.5	22.9	6.5	9.5	27.5
Tableware, nonelectric kitchenware	100.0	5.6	17.1	6.7	10.9	5.7	13.2	38.9
Small appliances	100.0	11.3	16.3	6.5	14.4	4.5	11.0	36.2
Small electric kitchen appliances	100.0	10.7	15.3	5.8	15.5	5.3	11.5	35.9
Portable heating and cooling equipment	100.0	–	18.7	8.1	11.9	2.5	9.8	36.7
Miscellaneous household equipment	**100.0**	**6.8**	**15.4**	**6.3**	**18.1**	**8.8**	**11.2**	**32.2**
Window coverings	100.0	2.1	11.0	2.6	6.8	8.6	8.7	60.2
Infants' equipment	100.0	3.9	18.5	6.1	16.7	5.9	4.2	42.8
Laundry and cleaning equipment	100.0	10.0	16.2	6.9	16.0	6.7	12.9	30.2
Outdoor equipment	100.0	2.6	37.5	5.6	14.9	3.0	9.7	24.7
Lamps and lighting fixtures	100.0	7.8	16.1	7.9	17.6	2.4	5.0	41.7
Household decorative items	100.0	6.2	9.8	5.7	22.3	11.3	11.4	31.5
Telephones and accessories	100.0	7.1	17.4	9.4	13.7	6.7	12.4	31.4
Lawn and garden equipment	100.0	2.0	6.3	3.1	30.5	23.8	14.1	19.2
Power tools	100.0	11.1	20.6	10.2	29.9	3.2	15.2	8.4
Office furniture for home use	100.0	6.0	7.5	6.0	16.0	4.2	10.0	50.3
Hand tools	100.0	6.9	37.2	3.8	22.1	5.1	10.6	11.8
Indoor plants and fresh flowers	100.0	8.3	13.2	7.4	12.6	6.3	11.9	40.3
Closet and storage items	100.0	14.1	19.4	3.7	11.4	4.8	10.1	35.0
Rental of furniture	100.0	17.4	37.6	5.2	15.8	0.8	0.1	23.1
Luggage	100.0	12.6	33.3	3.8	8.8	6.2	8.9	26.8
Computers and computer hardware for nonbusiness use	100.0	7.0	12.1	6.4	14.3	8.2	9.8	42.1
Portable memory	100.0	9.3	16.0	8.3	19.8	9.0	10.5	27.1
Computer software	100.0	9.0	10.4	4.4	22.1	11.2	9.8	33.1
Computer accessories	100.0	6.2	13.8	8.1	13.5	11.0	12.5	35.0
Personal digital assistants	100.0	6.1	12.7	3.4	14.5	8.1	13.7	41.6
Internet services away from home	100.0	12.5	16.9	10.9	16.7	9.3	12.6	21.0
Telephone answering devices	100.0	11.5	34.6	6.8	10.0	4.3	5.3	29.2
Business equipment for home use	100.0	8.4	18.5	4.5	14.6	6.1	11.9	35.9
Other hardware	100.0	7.1	20.0	9.4	13.8	13.0	15.4	21.5
Smoke alarms	100.0	7.9	32.0	3.9	13.1	7.2	8.7	27.2
Other household appliances	100.0	12.2	16.9	6.2	19.9	3.0	13.4	28.5
Miscellaneous household equipment and parts	100.0	8.5	18.1	7.4	15.9	6.1	13.8	28.7

Note: Numbers may not add to total because of rounding. "–" means sample is too small to make a reliable estimate.
Source: Calculations by New Strategist based on the Bureau of Labor Statistics' 2011 Consumer Expenditure Survey

Table 8.9 Housing: Household Operations: Average spending by high-income consumer units, 2011

(average annual spending on household services, supplies, furnishings, and equipment, by before-tax income of high-income consumer units, 2011)

	total consumer units	$100,000 or more	$100,000–$119,999	$120,000–$149,999	$150,000 or more
Number of consumer units (in 000s)	122,287	21,593	7,045	6,107	8,440
Average number of persons per consumer unit	2.5	3.2	3.2	3.1	3.2
Average before-tax income of consumer units	$63,685.00	$169,776.00	$108,549.00	$133,318.00	$247,261.00
Average spending of consumer units, total	49,704.88	97,728.22	76,496.41	87,239.44	123,056.38
Housing, average spending	**16,803.03**	**30,211.87**	**23,660.02**	**27,420.06**	**37,700.47**
HOUSEHOLD SERVICES	**1,122.18**	**2,543.43**	**1,731.88**	**2,034.81**	**3,589.27**
Personal services	**398.27**	**997.56**	**751.30**	**796.04**	**1,348.93**
Babysitting and child care in own home	51.23	202.45	92.14	64.83	394.10
Babysitting and child care in someone else's home	26.87	58.31	61.81	48.95	62.16
Care for elderly, invalids, handicapped, etc.	67.89	40.19	44.32	82.21	6.32
Day care centers, nurseries, and preschools	251.30	696.38	552.46	600.04	886.22
Other household services	**723.92**	**1,545.87**	**980.58**	**1,238.77**	**2,240.33**
Housekeeping services	105.26	360.19	113.67	189.52	689.44
Gardening, lawn care service	118.65	299.13	145.33	212.83	489.95
Water-softening service	4.87	7.27	7.64	5.75	8.06
Nonclothing laundry and dry cleaning, sent out	14.71	42.79	26.66	41.15	57.85
Nonclothing laundry and dry cleaning, coin-operated	4.40	2.05	2.53	2.26	1.51
Termite and pest control services	20.61	50.74	26.45	55.37	67.66
Home security system service fee	25.65	60.37	46.64	49.71	79.54
Other home services	15.98	33.33	21.80	23.86	49.80
Termite and pest control products	3.57	8.35	3.87	10.81	10.32
Moving, storage, and freight express	52.88	97.80	59.57	69.81	149.95
Appliance repair, including at service center	16.62	33.31	27.21	24.58	44.71
Reupholstering and furniture repair	5.75	19.44	6.69	8.52	37.98
Repairs and rentals of lawn and garden equipment, hand and power tools, etc.	9.29	17.92	12.94	24.48	17.34
Appliance rental	2.01	0.61	0.35	0.03	1.23
Rental of office equipment for nonbusiness use	1.06	1.49	0.25	1.23	2.71
Repair of computer systems for nonbusiness use	6.51	10.52	9.56	12.78	9.68
Computer information services	313.76	493.12	466.39	505.08	506.77
Installation of computer	0.51	0.69	0.33	0.98	0.78
HOUSEKEEPING SUPPLIES	**614.74**	**1,082.68**	**1,064.77**	**1,026.16**	**1,138.15**
Laundry and cleaning supplies	**145.06**	**203.42**	**199.30**	**187.19**	**218.46**
Soaps and detergents	78.49	104.72	98.23	96.99	115.78
Other laundry cleaning products	66.57	98.70	101.06	90.20	102.68
Other household products	**339.58**	**643.42**	**664.88**	**638.54**	**628.37**
Cleansing and toilet tissue, paper towels, and napkins	114.81	176.04	188.01	166.68	172.35
Miscellaneous household products	134.12	270.65	257.31	239.32	304.33
Lawn and garden supplies	90.65	196.73	219.56	232.54	151.69
Postage and stationery	**130.09**	**235.85**	**200.60**	**200.44**	**291.32**
Stationery, stationery supplies, giftwrap	67.56	126.93	115.32	123.09	139.65
Postage	55.22	85.41	77.35	74.56	100.02
Delivery services	7.32	23.52	7.92	2.79	51.65
HOUSEHOLD FURNISHINGS AND EQUIPMENT	**1,513.98**	**3,032.11**	**2,413.63**	**2,687.73**	**3,797.28**
Household textiles	**109.14**	**202.70**	**183.45**	**143.07**	**261.50**
Bathroom linens	20.16	37.52	26.95	39.18	45.47
Bedroom linens	59.00	106.97	109.15	63.98	135.53
Kitchen and dining room linens	5.95	9.62	6.96	4.62	15.46
Curtains and draperies	11.30	24.28	18.17	17.14	34.56
Slipcovers and decorative pillows	3.52	7.75	6.28	5.09	10.89
Sewing materials for household items	8.07	14.83	14.65	11.83	17.14
Other linens	1.13	1.73	1.29	1.22	2.46
Furniture	**357.94**	**859.03**	**663.13**	**681.81**	**1,150.78**
Mattresses and springs	61.72	137.52	80.93	122.79	195.42
Other bedroom furniture	70.06	159.25	95.76	146.82	221.24
Sofas	92.81	224.55	231.88	144.92	276.05
Living room chairs	36.12	87.02	62.96	51.48	132.82
Living room tables	11.87	30.36	20.50	22.80	44.07

	total consumer units	$100,000 or more	$100,000–$119,999	$120,000–$149,999	$150,000 or more
Kitchen and dining room furniture	$27.45	$60.78	$40.63	$61.84	$76.83
Infants' furniture	8.23	14.39	13.01	6.88	20.97
Outdoor furniture	18.70	57.02	39.24	39.97	84.20
Wall units, cabinets, and other furniture	30.97	88.14	78.22	84.31	99.18
Floor coverings	**19.98**	**69.44**	**30.06**	**30.08**	**130.79**
Floor coverings, nonpermanent	19.61	69.44	30.06	30.08	130.79
Major appliances	**193.93**	**355.95**	**260.57**	**349.25**	**440.54**
Dishwashers (built-in), garbage disposals, range hoods	14.60	39.29	29.56	33.95	51.28
Refrigerators and freezers	52.96	92.54	92.18	76.09	104.75
Washing machines	34.00	58.04	33.52	70.84	69.26
Clothes dryers	24.93	42.42	22.23	52.38	52.06
Cooking stoves, ovens	30.51	67.74	43.15	62.12	92.30
Microwave ovens	8.96	15.65	13.60	13.23	19.12
Window air conditioners	4.82	4.22	6.59	0.06	5.25
Electric floor-cleaning equipment	16.06	23.24	17.39	31.19	22.36
Sewing machines	2.43	6.99	0.59	2.73	15.41
Miscellaneous household appliances	4.21	5.73	1.46	6.63	8.77
Small appliances and miscellaneous housewares	**89.34**	**186.93**	**184.71**	**165.09**	**203.61**
Housewares	54.84	116.29	105.50	84.34	148.08
Plastic dinnerware	2.47	3.86	3.89	2.36	4.92
China and other dinnerware	5.34	17.59	14.97	12.16	23.69
Flatware	2.96	6.78	2.60	7.93	9.43
Glassware	6.56	15.55	13.97	12.41	19.13
Silver serving pieces	1.43	2.58	2.81	0.78	3.66
Other serving pieces	1.42	3.19	2.08	3.09	4.19
Nonelectric cookware	14.94	23.29	19.85	8.87	36.48
Tableware, nonelectric kitchenware	19.71	43.44	45.34	36.73	46.56
Small appliances	34.50	70.64	79.20	80.75	55.53
Small electric kitchen appliances	24.50	49.83	34.87	60.38	54.69
Portable heating and cooling equipment	10.00	20.81	44.34	20.38	0.84
Miscellaneous household equipment	**743.64**	**1,358.05**	**1,091.71**	**1,318.43**	**1,610.07**
Window coverings	15.87	54.12	31.67	33.97	87.43
Infants' equipment	14.49	35.10	28.84	17.41	53.03
Laundry and cleaning equipment	17.33	29.63	31.42	28.50	28.87
Outdoor equipment	34.43	48.13	47.28	21.65	67.62
Lamps and lighting fixtures	29.29	69.22	102.00	62.04	46.04
Household decorative items	117.20	209.28	143.87	293.76	205.85
Telephones and accessories	45.56	81.02	96.19	54.06	87.04
Lawn and garden equipment	65.62	71.41	81.07	59.85	71.26
Power tools	38.18	18.19	12.55	12.50	27.07
Office furniture for home use	5.83	16.62	4.85	13.99	28.36
Hand tools	15.55	10.42	9.13	7.02	13.94
Indoor plants and fresh flowers	46.92	107.01	73.65	84.78	150.93
Closet and storage items	16.85	33.42	32.32	28.82	37.63
Rental of furniture	6.16	8.05	0.80	17.54	7.24
Luggage	6.84	10.40	5.93	11.55	13.43
Computers and computer hardware for nonbusiness use	152.35	362.98	233.26	373.06	463.95
Portable memory	4.17	6.39	6.13	6.75	6.35
Computer software	14.33	26.89	21.12	25.73	32.54
Computer accessories	12.15	24.08	18.30	28.22	25.92
Personal digital assistants	6.27	14.78	13.55	9.68	19.50
Internet services away from home	7.03	8.36	9.47	7.98	7.71
Telephone answering devices	0.61	1.01	0.59	1.07	1.33
Business equipment for home use	4.05	8.23	3.28	8.91	11.86
Other hardware	11.34	13.78	13.81	15.81	12.33
Smoke alarms	1.97	3.03	3.06	2.08	3.67
Other household appliances	7.96	12.85	12.35	12.14	13.76
Miscellaneous household equipment and parts	43.13	70.21	53.03	77.62	79.76

Note: Subcategories may not add to total because some are not shown.
Source: Bureau of Labor Statistics, unpublished tables from the 2011 Consumer Expenditure Survey; calculations by New Strategist

Table 8.10 Housing: Household Operations: Indexed spending by high-income consumer units, 2011

(indexed average annual spending of high-income consumer units on household services, supplies, furnishings, and equipment, by before-tax income of consumer unit, 2011; index definition: an index of 100 is the average for all consumer units; an index of 125 means that spending by consumer units in that group is 25 percent above the average for all consumer units; an index of 75 indicates spending that is 25 percent below the average for all consumer units)

	total consumer units	$100,000 or more	$100,000–$119,999	$120,000–$149,999	$150,000 or more
Average spending of consumer units, total	$49,705	$97,728	$76,496	$87,239	$123,056
Average spending of consumer units, index	100	197	154	176	248
Housing, spending index	100	180	141	163	224
HOUSEHOLD SERVICES	100	227	154	181	320
Personal services	100	250	189	200	339
Babysitting and child care in own home	100	395	180	127	769
Babysitting and child care in someone else's home	100	217	230	182	231
Care for elderly, invalids, handicapped, etc.	100	59	65	121	9
Day care centers, nurseries, and preschools	100	277	220	239	353
Other household services	100	214	135	171	309
Housekeeping services	100	342	108	180	655
Gardening, lawn care service	100	252	122	179	413
Water-softening service	100	149	157	118	166
Nonclothing laundry and dry cleaning, sent out	100	291	181	280	393
Nonclothing laundry and dry cleaning, coin-operated	100	47	58	51	34
Termite and pest control services	100	246	128	269	328
Home security system service fee	100	235	182	194	310
Other home services	100	209	136	149	312
Termite and pest control products	100	234	108	303	289
Moving, storage, and freight express	100	185	113	132	284
Appliance repair, including at service center	100	200	164	148	269
Reupholstering and furniture repair	100	338	116	148	661
Repairs and rentals of lawn and garden equipment, hand and power tools, etc.	100	193	139	264	187
Appliance rental	100	30	17	1	61
Rental of office equipment for nonbusiness use	100	141	24	116	256
Repair of computer systems for nonbusiness use	100	162	147	196	149
Computer information services	100	157	149	161	162
Installation of computer	100	135	65	192	153
HOUSEKEEPING SUPPLIES	100	176	173	167	185
Laundry and cleaning supplies	100	140	137	129	151
Soaps and detergents	100	133	125	124	148
Other laundry cleaning products	100	148	152	135	154
Other household products	100	189	196	188	185
Cleansing and toilet tissue, paper towels, and napkins	100	153	164	145	150
Miscellaneous household products	100	202	192	178	227
Lawn and garden supplies	100	217	242	257	167
Postage and stationery	100	181	154	154	224
Stationery, stationery supplies, giftwrap	100	188	171	182	207
Postage	100	155	140	135	181
Delivery services	100	321	108	38	706
HOUSEHOLD FURNISHINGS AND EQUIPMENT	100	200	159	178	251
Household textiles	100	186	168	131	240
Bathroom linens	100	186	134	194	226
Bedroom linens	100	181	185	108	230
Kitchen and dining room linens	100	162	117	78	260
Curtains and draperies	100	215	161	152	306
Slipcovers and decorative pillows	100	220	178	145	309
Sewing materials for household items	100	184	182	147	212
Other linens	100	153	114	108	218
Furniture	100	240	185	190	322
Mattresses and springs	100	223	131	199	317
Other bedroom furniture	100	227	137	210	316
Sofas	100	242	250	156	297
Living room chairs	100	241	174	143	368
Living room tables	100	256	173	192	371

	total consumer units	$100,000 or more	$100,000– $119,999	$120,000– $149,999	$150,000 or more
Kitchen and dining room furniture	100	221	148	225	280
Infants' furniture	100	175	158	84	255
Outdoor furniture	100	305	210	214	450
Wall units, cabinets, and other furniture	100	285	253	272	320
Floor coverings	**100**	**348**	**150**	**151**	**655**
Floor coverings, nonpermanent	100	354	153	153	667
Major appliances	**100**	**184**	**134**	**180**	**227**
Dishwashers (built-in), garbage disposals, range hoods	100	269	202	233	351
Refrigerators and freezers	100	175	174	144	198
Washing machines	100	171	99	208	204
Clothes dryers	100	170	89	210	209
Cooking stoves, ovens	100	222	141	204	303
Microwave ovens	100	175	152	148	213
Window air conditioners	100	88	137	1	109
Electric floor-cleaning equipment	100	145	108	194	139
Sewing machines	100	288	24	112	634
Miscellaneous household appliances	100	136	35	157	208
Small appliances and miscellaneous housewares	**100**	**209**	**207**	**185**	**228**
Housewares	100	212	192	154	270
Plastic dinnerware	100	156	157	96	199
China and other dinnerware	100	329	280	228	444
Flatware	100	229	88	268	319
Glassware	100	237	213	189	292
Silver serving pieces	100	180	197	55	256
Other serving pieces	100	225	146	218	295
Nonelectric cookware	100	156	133	59	244
Tableware, nonelectric kitchenware	100	220	230	186	236
Small appliances	100	205	230	234	161
Small electric kitchen appliances	100	203	142	246	223
Portable heating and cooling equipment	100	208	443	204	8
Miscellaneous household equipment	**100**	**183**	**147**	**177**	**217**
Window coverings	100	341	200	214	551
Infants' equipment	100	242	199	120	366
Laundry and cleaning equipment	100	171	181	164	167
Outdoor equipment	100	140	137	63	196
Lamps and lighting fixtures	100	236	348	212	157
Household decorative items	100	179	123	251	176
Telephones and accessories	100	178	211	119	191
Lawn and garden equipment	100	109	124	91	109
Power tools	100	48	33	33	71
Office furniture for home use	100	285	83	240	486
Hand tools	100	67	59	45	90
Indoor plants and fresh flowers	100	228	157	181	322
Closet and storage items	100	198	192	171	223
Rental of furniture	100	131	13	285	118
Luggage	100	152	87	169	196
Computers and computer hardware for nonbusiness use	100	238	153	245	305
Portable memory	100	153	147	162	152
Computer software	100	188	147	180	227
Computer accessories	100	198	151	232	213
Personal digital assistants	100	236	216	154	311
Internet services away from home	100	119	135	114	110
Telephone answering devices	100	166	97	175	218
Business equipment for home use	100	203	81	220	293
Other hardware	100	122	122	139	109
Smoke alarms	100	154	155	106	186
Other household appliances	100	161	155	153	173
Miscellaneous household equipment and parts	100	163	123	180	185

Source: Calculations by New Strategist based on the Bureau of Labor Statistics' 2011 Consumer Expenditure Survey

Table 8.11 Housing: Household Operations: Total spending by high-income consumer units, 2011

(total annual spending on household services, supplies, furnishings, and equipment, by before-tax income group of high-income consumer units, 2011; consumer units and dollars in thousands)

	total consumer units	$100,000 or more	$100,000– $119,999	$120,000– $149,999	$150,000 or more
Number of consumer units	122,287	21,593	7,045	6,107	8,440
Total spending of all consumer units	$6,078,260,661	$2,110,245,454	$538,917,208	$532,771,260	$1,038,595,847
Housing, total spending	2,054,792,130	652,364,909	166,684,841	167,454,306	318,191,967
HOUSEHOLD SERVICES	**137,228,026**	**54,920,284**	**12,201,095**	**12,426,585**	**30,293,439**
Personal services	**48,703,243**	**21,540,313**	**5,292,909**	**4,861,416**	**11,384,969**
Babysitting and child care in own home	6,264,763	4,371,503	649,126	395,917	3,326,204
Babysitting and child care in someone else's home	3,285,852	1,259,088	435,451	298,938	524,630
Care for elderly, invalids, handicapped, etc.	8,302,064	867,823	312,234	502,056	53,341
Day care centers, nurseries, and preschools	30,730,723	15,036,933	3,892,081	3,664,444	7,479,697
Other household services	**88,526,005**	**33,379,971**	**6,908,186**	**7,565,168**	**18,908,385**
Housekeeping services	12,871,930	7,777,583	800,805	1,157,399	5,818,874
Gardening, lawn care service	14,509,353	6,459,114	1,023,850	1,299,753	4,135,178
Water-softening service	595,538	156,981	53,824	35,115	68,026
Nonclothing laundry and dry cleaning, sent out	1,798,842	923,964	187,820	251,303	488,254
Nonclothing laundry and dry cleaning, coin-operated	538,063	44,266	17,824	13,802	12,744
Termite and pest control services	2,520,335	1,095,629	186,340	338,145	571,050
Home security system service fee	3,136,662	1,303,569	328,579	303,579	671,318
Other home services	1,954,146	719,695	153,581	145,713	420,312
Termite and pest control products	436,565	180,302	27,264	66,017	87,101
Moving, storage, and freight express	6,466,537	2,111,795	419,671	426,330	1,265,578
Appliance repair, including at service center	2,032,410	719,263	191,694	150,110	377,352
Reupholstering and furniture repair	703,150	419,768	47,131	52,032	320,551
Repairs and rentals of lawn and garden equipment, hand and power tools, etc.	1,136,046	386,947	91,162	149,499	146,350
Appliance rental	245,797	13,172	2,466	183	10,381
Rental of office equipment for nonbusiness use	129,624	32,174	1,761	7,512	22,872
Repair of computer systems for nonbusiness use	796,088	227,158	67,350	78,047	81,699
Computer information services	38,368,769	10,647,940	3,285,718	3,084,524	4,277,139
Installation of computer	62,366	14,899	2,325	5,985	6,583
HOUSEKEEPING SUPPLIES	**75,174,710**	**23,378,309**	**7,501,305**	**6,266,759**	**9,605,986**
Laundry and cleaning supplies	**17,738,952**	**4,392,448**	**1,404,069**	**1,143,169**	**1,843,802**
Soaps and detergents	9,598,307	2,261,219	692,030	592,318	977,183
Other laundry cleaning products	8,140,646	2,131,229	711,968	550,851	866,619
Other household products	**41,526,219**	**13,893,368**	**4,684,080**	**3,899,564**	**5,303,443**
Cleansing and toilet tissue, paper towels, and napkins	14,039,770	3,801,232	1,324,530	1,017,915	1,454,634
Miscellaneous household products	16,401,132	5,844,145	1,812,749	1,461,527	2,568,545
Lawn and garden supplies	11,085,317	4,247,991	1,546,800	1,420,122	1,280,264
Postage and stationery	**15,908,316**	**5,092,709**	**1,413,227**	**1,224,087**	**2,458,741**
Stationery, stationery supplies, giftwrap	8,261,710	2,740,799	812,429	751,711	1,178,646
Postage	6,752,688	1,844,258	544,931	455,338	844,169
Delivery services	895,141	507,867	55,796	17,039	435,926
HOUSEHOLD FURNISHINGS AND EQUIPMENT	**185,140,072**	**65,472,351**	**17,004,023**	**16,413,967**	**32,049,043**
Household textiles	**13,346,403**	**4,376,901**	**1,292,405**	**873,728**	**2,207,060**
Bathroom linens	2,465,306	810,169	189,863	239,272	383,767
Bedroom linens	7,214,933	2,309,803	768,962	390,726	1,143,873
Kitchen and dining room linens	727,608	207,725	49,033	28,214	130,482
Curtains and draperies	1,381,843	524,278	128,008	104,674	291,686
Slipcovers and decorative pillows	430,450	167,346	44,243	31,085	91,912
Sewing materials for household items	986,856	320,224	103,209	72,246	144,662
Other linens	138,184	37,356	9,088	7,451	20,762
Furniture	**43,771,409**	**18,549,035**	**4,671,751**	**4,163,814**	**9,712,583**
Mattresses and springs	7,547,554	2,969,469	570,152	749,879	1,649,345
Other bedroom furniture	8,567,427	3,438,685	674,629	896,630	1,867,266
Sofas	11,349,456	4,848,708	1,633,595	885,026	2,329,862
Living room chairs	4,417,006	1,879,023	443,553	314,388	1,121,001
Living room tables	1,451,547	655,563	144,423	139,240	371,951

	total consumer units	$100,000 or more	$100,000– $119,999	$120,000– $149,999	$150,000 or more
Kitchen and dining room furniture	$3,356,778	$1,312,423	$286,238	$377,657	$648,445
Infants' furniture	1,006,422	310,723	91,655	42,016	176,987
Outdoor furniture	2,286,767	1,231,233	276,446	244,097	710,648
Wall units, cabinets, and other furniture	3,787,228	1,903,207	551,060	514,881	837,079
Floor coverings	**2,443,294**	**1,499,418**	**211,773**	**183,699**	**1,103,868**
Floor coverings, nonpermanent	2,398,048	1,499,418	211,773	183,699	1,103,868
Major appliances	**23,715,118**	**7,686,028**	**1,835,716**	**2,132,870**	**3,718,158**
Dishwashers (built-in), garbage disposals, range hoods	1,785,390	848,389	208,250	207,333	432,803
Refrigerators and freezers	6,476,320	1,998,216	649,408	464,682	884,090
Washing machines	4,157,758	1,253,258	236,148	432,620	584,554
Clothes dryers	3,048,615	915,975	156,610	319,885	439,386
Cooking stoves, ovens	3,730,976	1,462,710	303,992	379,367	779,012
Microwave ovens	1,095,692	337,930	95,812	80,796	161,373
Window air conditioners	589,423	91,122	46,427	366	44,310
Electric floor-cleaning equipment	1,963,929	501,821	122,513	190,477	188,718
Sewing machines	297,157	150,935	4,157	16,672	130,060
Miscellaneous household appliances	514,828	123,728	10,286	40,489	74,019
Small appliances and miscellaneous housewares	**10,925,121**	**4,036,379**	**1,301,282**	**1,008,205**	**1,718,468**
Housewares	6,706,219	2,511,050	743,248	515,064	1,249,795
Plastic dinnerware	302,049	83,349	27,405	14,413	41,525
China and other dinnerware	653,013	379,821	105,464	74,261	199,944
Flatware	361,970	146,401	18,317	48,429	79,589
Glassware	802,203	335,771	98,419	75,788	161,457
Silver serving pieces	174,870	55,710	19,796	4,763	30,890
Other serving pieces	173,648	68,882	14,654	18,871	35,364
Nonelectric cookware	1,826,968	502,901	139,843	54,169	307,891
Tableware, nonelectric kitchenware	2,410,277	938,000	319,420	224,310	392,966
Small appliances	4,218,902	1,525,330	557,964	493,140	468,673
Small electric kitchen appliances	2,996,032	1,075,979	245,659	368,741	461,584
Portable heating and cooling equipment	1,222,870	449,350	312,375	124,461	7,090
Miscellaneous household equipment	**90,937,505**	**29,324,374**	**7,691,097**	**8,051,652**	**13,588,991**
Window coverings	1,940,695	1,168,613	223,115	207,455	737,909
Infants' equipment	1,771,939	757,914	203,178	106,323	447,573
Laundry and cleaning equipment	2,119,234	639,801	221,354	174,050	243,663
Outdoor equipment	4,210,341	1,039,271	333,088	132,217	570,713
Lamps and lighting fixtures	3,581,786	1,494,667	718,590	378,878	388,578
Household decorative items	14,332,036	4,518,983	1,013,564	1,793,992	1,737,374
Telephones and accessories	5,571,396	1,749,465	677,659	330,144	734,618
Lawn and garden equipment	8,024,473	1,541,956	571,138	365,504	601,434
Power tools	4,668,918	392,777	88,415	76,338	228,471
Office furniture for home use	712,933	358,876	34,168	85,437	239,358
Hand tools	1,901,563	224,999	64,321	42,871	117,654
Indoor plants and fresh flowers	5,737,706	2,310,667	518,864	517,751	1,273,849
Closet and storage items	2,060,536	721,638	227,694	176,004	317,597
Rental of furniture	753,288	173,824	5,636	107,117	61,106
Luggage	836,443	224,567	41,777	70,536	113,349
Computers and computer hardware for nonbusiness use	18,630,424	7,837,827	1,643,317	2,278,277	3,915,738
Portable memory	509,937	137,979	43,186	41,222	53,594
Computer software	1,752,373	580,636	148,790	157,133	274,638
Computer accessories	1,485,787	519,959	128,924	172,340	218,765
Personal digital assistants	766,739	319,145	95,460	59,116	164,580
Internet services away from home	859,678	180,517	66,716	48,734	65,072
Telephone answering devices	74,595	21,809	4,157	6,534	11,225
Business equipment for home use	495,262	177,710	23,108	54,413	100,098
Other hardware	1,386,735	297,552	97,291	96,552	104,065
Smoke alarms	240,905	65,427	21,558	12,703	30,975
Other household appliances	973,405	277,470	87,006	74,139	116,134
Miscellaneous household equipment and parts	5,274,238	1,516,045	373,596	474,025	673,174

Note: Numbers may not add to total because of rounding and missing subcategories.
Source: Calculations by New Strategist based on the Bureau of Labor Statistics' 2011 Consumer Expenditure Survey

Table 8.12 Housing: Household Operations: Market shares by high-income consumer units, 2011

(percentage of total annual spending on shelter and utilities accounted for by before-tax income group of high-income consumer units, 2011)

	total consumer units	$100,000 or more	$100,000–$119,999	$120,000–$149,999	$150,000 or more
Share of total consumer units	100.0%	17.7%	5.8%	5.0%	6.9%
Share of total before-tax income	100.0	47.1	9.8	10.5	26.8
Share of total spending	100.0	34.7	8.9	8.8	17.1
Share of housing spending	100.0	31.7	8.1	8.1	15.5
HOUSEHOLD SERVICES	100.0	40.0	8.9	9.1	22.1
Personal services	100.0	44.2	10.9	10.0	23.4
Babysitting and child care in own home	100.0	69.8	10.4	6.3	53.1
Babysitting and child care in someone else's home	100.0	38.3	13.3	9.1	16.0
Care for elderly, invalids, handicapped, etc.	100.0	10.5	3.8	6.0	0.6
Day care centers, nurseries, and preschools	100.0	48.9	12.7	11.9	24.3
Other household services	100.0	37.7	7.8	8.5	21.4
Housekeeping services	100.0	60.4	6.2	9.0	45.2
Gardening, lawn care service	100.0	44.5	7.1	9.0	28.5
Water-softening service	100.0	26.4	9.0	5.9	11.4
Nonclothing laundry and dry cleaning, sent out	100.0	51.4	10.4	14.0	27.1
Nonclothing laundry and dry cleaning, coin-operated	100.0	8.2	3.3	2.6	2.4
Termite and pest control services	100.0	43.5	7.4	13.4	22.7
Home security system service fee	100.0	41.6	10.5	9.7	21.4
Other home services	100.0	36.8	7.9	7.5	21.5
Termite and pest control products	100.0	41.3	6.2	15.1	20.0
Moving, storage, and freight express	100.0	32.7	6.5	6.6	19.6
Appliance repair, including at service center	100.0	35.4	9.4	7.4	18.6
Reupholstering and furniture repair	100.0	59.7	6.7	7.4	45.6
Repairs and rentals of lawn and garden equipment, hand and power tools, etc.	100.0	34.1	8.0	13.2	12.9
Appliance rental	100.0	5.4	1.0	0.1	4.2
Rental of office equipment for nonbusiness use	100.0	24.8	1.4	5.8	17.6
Repair of computer systems for nonbusiness use	100.0	28.5	8.5	9.8	10.3
Computer information services	100.0	27.8	8.6	8.0	11.1
Installation of computer	100.0	23.9	3.7	9.6	10.6
HOUSEKEEPING SUPPLIES	100.0	31.1	10.0	8.3	12.8
Laundry and cleaning supplies	100.0	24.8	7.9	6.4	10.4
Soaps and detergents	100.0	23.6	7.2	6.2	10.2
Other laundry cleaning products	100.0	26.2	8.7	6.8	10.6
Other household products	100.0	33.5	11.3	9.4	12.8
Cleansing and toilet tissue, paper towels, and napkins	100.0	27.1	9.4	7.3	10.4
Miscellaneous household products	100.0	35.6	11.1	8.9	15.7
Lawn and garden supplies	100.0	38.3	14.0	12.8	11.5
Postage and stationery	100.0	32.0	8.9	7.7	15.5
Stationery, stationery supplies, giftwrap	100.0	33.2	9.8	9.1	14.3
Postage	100.0	27.3	8.1	6.7	12.5
Delivery services	100.0	56.7	6.2	1.9	48.7
HOUSEHOLD FURNISHINGS AND EQUIPMENT	100.0	35.4	9.2	8.9	17.3
Household textiles	100.0	32.8	9.7	6.5	16.5
Bathroom linens	100.0	32.9	7.7	9.7	15.6
Bedroom linens	100.0	32.0	10.7	5.4	15.9
Kitchen and dining room linens	100.0	28.5	6.7	3.9	17.9
Curtains and draperies	100.0	37.9	9.3	7.6	21.1
Slipcovers and decorative pillows	100.0	38.9	10.3	7.2	21.4
Sewing materials for household items	100.0	32.4	10.5	7.3	14.7
Other linens	100.0	27.0	6.6	5.4	15.0
Furniture	100.0	42.4	10.7	9.5	22.2
Mattresses and springs	100.0	39.3	7.6	9.9	21.9
Other bedroom furniture	100.0	40.1	7.9	10.5	21.8
Sofas	100.0	42.7	14.4	7.8	20.5
Living room chairs	100.0	42.5	10.0	7.1	25.4
Living room tables	100.0	45.2	9.9	9.6	25.6

	total consumer units	$100,000 or more	$100,000– $119,999	$120,000– $149,999	$150,000 or more
Kitchen and dining room furniture	100.0%	39.1%	8.5%	11.3%	19.3%
Infants' furniture	100.0	30.9	9.1	4.2	17.6
Outdoor furniture	100.0	53.8	12.1	10.7	31.1
Wall units, cabinets, and other furniture	100.0	50.3	14.6	13.6	22.1
Floor coverings	**100.0**	**61.4**	**8.7**	**7.5**	**45.2**
Floor coverings, nonpermanent	100.0	62.5	8.8	7.7	46.0
Major appliances	**100.0**	**32.4**	**7.7**	**9.0**	**15.7**
Dishwashers (built-in), garbage disposals, range hoods	100.0	47.5	11.7	11.6	24.2
Refrigerators and freezers	100.0	30.9	10.0	7.2	13.7
Washing machines	100.0	30.1	5.7	10.4	14.1
Clothes dryers	100.0	30.0	5.1	10.5	14.4
Cooking stoves, ovens	100.0	39.2	8.1	10.2	20.9
Microwave ovens	100.0	30.8	8.7	7.4	14.7
Window air conditioners	100.0	15.5	7.9	0.1	7.5
Electric floor-cleaning equipment	100.0	25.6	6.2	9.7	9.6
Sewing machines	100.0	50.8	1.4	5.6	43.8
Miscellaneous household appliances	100.0	24.0	2.0	7.9	14.4
Small appliances and miscellaneous housewares	**100.0**	**36.9**	**11.9**	**9.2**	**15.7**
Housewares	100.0	37.4	11.1	7.7	18.6
Plastic dinnerware	100.0	27.6	9.1	4.8	13.7
China and other dinnerware	100.0	58.2	16.2	11.4	30.6
Flatware	100.0	40.4	5.1	13.4	22.0
Glassware	100.0	41.9	12.3	9.4	20.1
Silver serving pieces	100.0	31.9	11.3	2.7	17.7
Other serving pieces	100.0	39.7	8.4	10.9	20.4
Nonelectric cookware	100.0	27.5	7.7	3.0	16.9
Tableware, nonelectric kitchenware	100.0	38.9	13.3	9.3	16.3
Small appliances	100.0	36.2	13.2	11.7	11.1
Small electric kitchen appliances	100.0	35.9	8.2	12.3	15.4
Portable heating and cooling equipment	100.0	36.7	25.5	10.2	0.6
Miscellaneous household equipment	**100.0**	**32.2**	**8.5**	**8.9**	**14.9**
Window coverings	100.0	60.2	11.5	10.7	38.0
Infants' equipment	100.0	42.8	11.5	6.0	25.3
Laundry and cleaning equipment	100.0	30.2	10.4	8.2	11.5
Outdoor equipment	100.0	24.7	7.9	3.1	13.6
Lamps and lighting fixtures	100.0	41.7	20.1	10.6	10.8
Household decorative items	100.0	31.5	7.1	12.5	12.1
Telephones and accessories	100.0	31.4	12.2	5.9	13.2
Lawn and garden equipment	100.0	19.2	7.1	4.6	7.5
Power tools	100.0	8.4	1.9	1.6	4.9
Office furniture for home use	100.0	50.3	4.8	12.0	33.6
Hand tools	100.0	11.8	3.4	2.3	6.2
Indoor plants and fresh flowers	100.0	40.3	9.0	9.0	22.2
Closet and storage items	100.0	35.0	11.1	8.5	15.4
Rental of furniture	100.0	23.1	0.7	14.2	8.1
Luggage	100.0	26.8	5.0	8.4	13.6
Computers and computer hardware for nonbusiness use	100.0	42.1	8.8	12.2	21.0
Portable memory	100.0	27.1	8.5	8.1	10.5
Computer software	100.0	33.1	8.5	9.0	15.7
Computer accessories	100.0	35.0	8.7	11.6	14.7
Personal digital assistants	100.0	41.6	12.5	7.7	21.5
Internet services away from home	100.0	21.0	7.8	5.7	7.6
Telephone answering devices	100.0	29.2	5.6	8.8	15.0
Business equipment for home use	100.0	35.9	4.7	11.0	20.2
Other hardware	100.0	21.5	7.0	7.0	7.5
Smoke alarms	100.0	27.2	8.9	5.3	12.9
Other household appliances	100.0	28.5	8.9	7.6	11.9
Miscellaneous household equipment and parts	100.0	28.7	7.1	9.0	12.8

Note: Numbers may not add to total because of rounding.
Source: Calculations by New Strategist based on the Bureau of Labor Statistics' 2011 Consumer Expenditure Survey

Table 8.13 Housing: Household Operations: Average spending by household type, 2011

(average annual spending of consumer units on household services, supplies, furnishings, and equipment, by type of consumer unit, 2011)

	total married couples	married couples, no children	married couples with children				single parent with child under age 18	single person
			total	oldest child under age 6	oldest child aged 6 to 17	oldest child aged 18 or older		
Number of consumer units (in 000s)	60,144	25,270	29,097	5,825	14,661	8,612	6,956	36,110
Average number of persons per consumer unit	3.2	2.0	4.0	3.5	4.2	3.9	2.9	1.0
Average before-tax income of consumer units	$86,700.00	$78,823.00	$93,677.00	$91,014.00	$93,029.00	$96,583.00	$37,188.00	$34,540.00
Average spending of consumer units, total	63,971.54	57,658.24	69,724.22	65,947.61	70,708.52	70,411.85	37,553.05	30,613.18
Housing, average spending	20,663.77	18,328.52	22,787.75	25,008.84	23,158.39	20,648.26	14,563.03	11,456.22
HOUSEHOLD SERVICES	1,451.39	1,021.10	1,890.51	3,678.98	1,659.66	1,074.11	1,185.04	692.37
Personal services	549.23	69.17	997.40	2,816.83	767.97	157.30	683.43	166.26
Babysitting and child care in own home	86.18	1.90	164.16	464.00	139.29	3.69	85.26	5.22
Babysitting and child care in someone else's home	35.58	1.22	69.47	209.38	46.13	14.56	67.62	2.66
Care for elderly, invalids, handicapped, etc.	38.69	54.54	30.62	6.23	5.79	89.38	–	138.40
Day care centers, nurseries, and preschools	387.79	9.66	732.83	2,136.11	576.55	49.68	530.55	18.88
Other household services	902.16	951.93	893.11	862.15	891.69	916.81	501.62	526.11
Housekeeping services	142.22	176.77	130.77	122.75	156.20	92.91	63.37	78.69
Gardening, lawn care service	148.78	188.50	124.89	107.80	118.42	147.46	53.32	107.32
Water-softening service	6.55	5.49	8.20	7.18	7.44	10.19	3.14	2.92
Nonclothing laundry and dry cleaning, sent out	19.96	14.78	22.76	20.01	21.92	25.79	2.77	10.17
Nonclothing laundry and dry cleaning, coin-operated	3.22	1.85	3.98	4.33	3.77	4.12	7.40	3.62
Termite and pest control services	28.60	34.20	24.66	25.06	24.19	25.20	10.46	12.63
Home security system service fee	34.73	36.89	35.63	39.89	36.93	30.53	12.15	16.62
Other home services	18.75	23.25	16.26	10.13	15.36	21.92	6.21	13.06
Termite and pest control products	4.64	5.17	4.38	4.14	4.06	5.08	2.05	2.53
Moving, storage, and freight express	53.76	57.31	52.23	78.69	33.92	65.52	38.53	44.75
Appliance repair, including at service center	24.10	26.81	22.33	20.61	25.03	18.89	6.84	9.19
Reupholstering and furniture repair	9.08	8.87	10.71	1.05	7.06	23.46	2.11	2.81
Repairs and rentals of lawn and garden equipment, hand and power tools, etc.	12.70	14.72	10.86	8.67	10.93	12.23	2.95	7.87
Appliance rental	2.07	0.92	2.71	2.50	1.71	4.53	5.55	0.76
Rental of office equipment for nonbusiness use	1.21	1.50	0.74	–	0.16	2.25	1.64	0.72
Repair of computer systems for nonbusiness use	7.62	6.85	8.36	5.97	8.44	9.85	5.85	4.94
Computer information services	382.43	346.73	411.44	394.50	415.20	416.50	277.27	204.94
Installation of computer	0.62	0.58	0.51	0.48	0.61	0.37	–	0.49
HOUSEKEEPING SUPPLIES	825.52	800.29	860.12	833.98	851.49	889.81	392.16	348.17
Laundry and cleaning supplies	188.20	172.08	200.16	168.71	209.55	202.58	138.02	75.94
Soaps and detergents	98.55	80.08	112.58	95.50	115.61	117.38	90.30	39.71
Other laundry cleaning products	89.65	92.00	87.58	73.21	93.94	85.20	47.72	36.23
Other household products	459.54	439.35	494.80	500.01	467.98	536.97	196.30	188.81
Cleansing and toilet tissue, paper towels, and napkins	142.22	116.83	165.41	138.21	149.33	208.26	91.44	67.77
Miscellaneous household products	185.40	161.75	215.09	204.02	212.84	225.29	88.62	73.51
Lawn and garden supplies	131.92	160.77	114.30	157.78	105.80	103.42	16.24	47.54
Postage and stationery	177.79	188.86	165.16	165.26	173.97	150.26	57.84	83.42
Stationery, stationery supplies, giftwrap	91.40	87.33	95.93	72.67	106.53	91.57	31.88	46.32
Postage	75.76	87.66	64.44	81.03	62.84	57.51	21.44	35.17
Delivery services	10.63	13.87	4.79	11.56	4.60	1.17	4.53	1.93
HOUSEHOLD FURNISHINGS AND EQUIPMENT	2,066.75	2,029.47	2,118.34	1,935.50	2,182.37	2,129.22	1,114.88	858.99
Household textiles	141.46	144.10	138.45	159.41	124.34	151.30	139.68	70.57
Bathroom linens	24.19	23.33	25.75	22.48	30.47	19.72	33.95	15.17
Bedroom linens	75.22	72.85	75.34	113.61	56.96	84.14	91.81	37.43
Kitchen and dining room linens	8.39	10.49	6.50	5.17	6.26	7.68	0.64	4.72
Curtains and draperies	16.24	14.44	16.76	9.95	16.75	21.38	6.69	5.93
Slipcovers and decorative pillows	4.50	3.88	5.45	1.93	5.35	8.02	2.49	2.12
Sewing materials for household items	11.46	17.52	7.33	4.33	7.57	8.97	1.45	4.78
Other linens	1.46	1.60	1.30	1.96	1.00	1.39	2.64	0.44
Furniture	472.46	436.90	511.79	484.33	537.06	487.33	347.33	212.95
Mattresses and springs	85.29	82.09	88.55	110.92	76.38	94.13	53.40	31.87
Other bedroom furniture	79.46	67.85	89.98	106.57	105.65	52.09	114.10	49.13
Sofas	122.81	101.29	143.58	96.03	154.88	156.50	103.60	51.23
Living room chairs	52.82	56.21	45.58	28.33	40.37	66.12	17.59	20.95
Living room tables	15.56	13.99	17.58	16.27	20.46	13.58	6.51	9.60

	total married couples	married couples, no children	married couples with children				single parent with child under age 18	single person
			total	oldest child under age 6	oldest child aged 6 to 17	oldest child aged 18 or older		
Kitchen and dining room furniture	$35.86	$34.21	$39.95	$32.19	$52.61	$23.66	$15.16	$17.09
Infants' furniture	11.30	9.77	12.64	36.17	6.67	6.90	6.27	2.29
Outdoor furniture	27.86	29.84	29.31	18.18	30.27	35.19	4.07	11.20
Wall units, cabinets, and other furniture	41.49	41.66	44.61	39.68	49.77	39.16	26.63	19.59
Floor coverings	**29.23**	**36.90**	**22.66**	**14.08**	**20.88**	**31.50**	**12.39**	**11.96**
Floor coverings, nonpermanent	28.89	36.89	22.66	14.08	20.88	31.50	12.39	11.28
Major appliances	**271.41**	**275.09**	**274.93**	**266.58**	**292.97**	**249.35**	**162.56**	**91.50**
Dishwashers (built-in), garbage disposals, range hoods	22.62	23.54	24.23	13.81	29.62	22.09	4.10	6.24
Refrigerators and freezers	73.68	81.39	66.39	73.58	66.55	61.24	43.34	24.01
Washing machines	45.70	46.68	46.31	49.25	47.64	42.02	41.38	16.05
Clothes dryers	32.89	30.86	36.18	49.31	36.72	26.38	28.83	11.06
Cooking stoves, ovens	48.98	47.48	52.64	44.38	59.62	46.32	19.54	10.28
Microwave ovens	10.96	11.58	10.60	7.88	10.14	13.24	9.21	6.42
Window air conditioners	5.32	5.02	5.09	2.63	7.35	2.89	3.87	3.31
Electric floor-cleaning equipment	20.85	20.42	20.22	20.97	17.57	24.22	8.97	9.43
Sewing machines	3.83	2.59	5.28	1.19	8.60	2.38	3.32	0.47
Miscellaneous household appliances	6.04	4.97	7.40	1.85	9.13	7.69	–	4.02
Small appliances and miscellaneous housewares	**121.49**	**137.96**	**110.05**	**108.77**	**106.01**	**117.93**	**50.63**	**54.67**
Housewares	78.40	88.11	72.87	79.02	67.99	77.68	24.77	29.20
Plastic dinnerware	2.96	2.01	4.06	4.47	3.54	4.67	2.24	1.64
China and other dinnerware	8.76	11.44	7.11	15.65	6.40	3.35	2.08	1.72
Flatware	3.31	2.98	3.86	1.14	5.42	3.03	3.39	2.79
Glassware	8.38	8.84	8.67	12.56	4.36	13.69	4.12	3.48
Silver serving pieces	2.23	1.51	2.88	1.61	2.80	3.74	0.64	0.78
Other serving pieces	1.90	2.34	1.68	2.12	1.52	1.65	0.50	0.83
Nonelectric cookware	22.09	26.27	18.92	11.16	16.69	27.17	3.83	7.78
Tableware, nonelectric kitchenware	28.77	32.73	25.69	30.30	27.25	20.40	7.97	10.18
Small appliances	43.10	49.85	37.19	29.75	38.02	40.24	25.86	25.47
Small electric kitchen appliances	31.21	36.14	27.94	26.19	28.35	28.43	16.02	16.48
Portable heating and cooling equipment	11.89	13.71	9.24	3.56	9.68	11.81	9.84	8.99
Miscellaneous household equipment	**1,030.69**	**998.50**	**1,060.47**	**902.32**	**1,101.11**	**1,091.81**	**402.29**	**417.33**
Window coverings	25.94	18.25	36.04	22.95	40.04	38.07	4.10	6.28
Infants' equipment	21.78	9.27	34.11	107.11	16.71	21.11	11.17	5.03
Laundry and cleaning equipment	24.01	24.24	25.11	21.92	26.00	25.47	10.90	10.39
Outdoor equipment	59.13	75.79	38.45	23.50	41.79	41.48	3.08	11.94
Lamps and lighting fixtures	40.39	65.97	17.32	16.94	14.72	21.92	11.23	12.20
Household decorative items	153.46	138.15	169.41	134.09	177.28	176.65	126.36	64.63
Telephones and accessories	64.56	55.73	70.53	51.75	76.57	71.25	4.94	19.13
Lawn and garden equipment	106.92	99.82	107.89	89.43	104.98	123.50	14.50	24.17
Power tools	40.83	42.81	42.88	34.44	56.94	24.10	8.40	41.78
Office furniture for home use	7.28	7.80	7.75	2.63	6.48	13.36	3.15	4.49
Hand tools	17.11	18.70	15.98	10.48	22.28	8.54	11.82	16.04
Indoor plants and fresh flowers	64.14	72.14	60.00	42.49	63.00	66.72	19.29	30.08
Closet and storage items	22.88	19.67	26.29	21.17	34.62	15.22	8.09	13.21
Rental of furniture	6.16	8.68	4.58	7.61	4.90	1.99	3.53	5.15
Luggage	9.17	7.87	11.35	1.07	13.61	13.50	1.19	6.72
Computers and computer hardware for nonbusiness use	207.78	169.54	238.80	185.74	238.45	275.29	95.31	77.38
Portable memory	5.31	4.79	5.69	5.05	5.63	6.24	3.32	2.67
Computer software	16.84	15.44	17.57	16.66	18.44	16.70	8.78	10.91
Computer accessories	17.70	19.30	16.79	13.32	17.54	17.87	6.38	6.44
Personal digital assistants	10.25	10.35	10.64	10.06	14.03	5.26	2.21	2.55
Internet services away from home	7.91	8.20	8.10	11.19	6.25	9.16	6.77	4.65
Telephone answering devices	0.68	0.62	0.68	0.10	1.22	0.17	0.89	0.38
Business equipment for home use	5.99	6.58	5.52	4.05	6.59	4.69	2.78	1.66
Other hardware	14.81	13.10	17.92	9.99	22.63	14.58	5.84	7.31
Smoke alarms	2.57	3.32	2.04	2.43	2.27	1.39	0.73	1.45
Other household appliances	10.80	12.17	8.52	10.47	7.62	8.74	9.61	4.66
Miscellaneous household equipment and parts	63.61	66.47	58.41	41.44	59.12	67.03	17.38	23.89

Note: Average spending figures for total consumer units can be found on Average Spending by Age and Average Spending by Region tables. Subcategories may not add to total because some are not shown.
 "–" means sample is too small to make a reliable estimate.
Source: Bureau of Labor Statistics, unpublished tables from the 2011 Consumer Expenditure Survey

Table 8.14 Housing: Household Operations: Indexed spending by household type, 2011

(indexed average annual spending of consumer units on household services, supplies, furnishings, and equipment, by type of consumer unit, 2011; index definition: an index of 100 is the average for all consumer units; an index of 125 means that spending by consumer units in that group is 25 percent above the average for all consumer units; an index of 75 indicates spending that is 25 percent below the average for all consumer units)

	total married couples	married couples, no children	married couples with children				single parent with child under age 18	single person
			total	oldest child under age 6	oldest child aged 6 to 17	oldest child aged 18 or older		
Average spending of consumer units, total	$63,972	$57,658	$69,724	$65,948	$70,709	$70,412	$37,553	$30,613
Average spending of consumer units, index	129	116	140	133	142	142	76	62
Housing, spending index	123	109	136	149	138	123	87	68
HOUSEHOLD SERVICES	**129**	**91**	**168**	**328**	**148**	**96**	**106**	**62**
Personal services	**138**	**17**	**250**	**707**	**193**	**39**	**172**	**42**
Babysitting and child care in own home	168	4	320	906	272	7	166	10
Babysitting and child care in someone else's home	132	5	259	779	172	54	252	10
Care for elderly, invalids, handicapped, etc.	57	80	45	9	9	132	–	204
Day care centers, nurseries, and preschools	154	4	292	850	229	20	211	8
Other household services	**125**	**131**	**123**	**119**	**123**	**127**	**69**	**73**
Housekeeping services	135	168	124	117	148	88	60	75
Gardening, lawn care service	125	159	105	91	100	124	45	90
Water-softening service	134	113	168	147	153	209	64	60
Nonclothing laundry and dry cleaning, sent out	136	100	155	136	149	175	19	69
Nonclothing laundry and dry cleaning, coin-operated	73	42	90	98	86	94	168	82
Termite and pest control services	139	166	120	122	117	122	51	61
Home security system service fee	135	144	139	156	144	119	47	65
Other home services	117	145	102	63	96	137	39	82
Termite and pest control products	130	145	123	116	114	142	57	71
Moving, storage, and freight express	102	108	99	149	64	124	73	85
Appliance repair, including at service center	145	161	134	124	151	114	41	55
Reupholstering and furniture repair	158	154	186	18	123	408	37	49
Repairs and rentals of lawn and garden equipment, hand and power tools, etc.	137	158	117	93	118	132	32	85
Appliance rental	103	46	135	124	85	225	276	38
Rental of office equipment for nonbusiness use	114	142	70	–	15	212	155	68
Repair of computer systems for nonbusiness use	117	105	128	92	130	151	90	76
Computer information services	122	111	131	126	132	133	88	65
Installation of computer	122	114	100	94	120	73	–	96
HOUSEKEEPING SUPPLIES	**134**	**130**	**140**	**136**	**139**	**145**	**64**	**57**
Laundry and cleaning supplies	**130**	**119**	**138**	**116**	**144**	**140**	**95**	**52**
Soaps and detergents	126	102	143	122	147	150	115	51
Other laundry cleaning products	135	138	132	110	141	128	72	54
Other household products	**135**	**129**	**146**	**147**	**138**	**158**	**58**	**56**
Cleansing and toilet tissue, paper towels, and napkins	124	102	144	120	130	181	80	59
Miscellaneous household products	138	121	160	152	159	168	66	55
Lawn and garden supplies	146	177	126	174	117	114	18	52
Postage and stationery	**137**	**145**	**127**	**127**	**134**	**116**	**44**	**64**
Stationery, stationery supplies, giftwrap	135	129	142	108	158	136	47	69
Postage	137	159	117	147	114	104	39	64
Delivery services	145	189	65	158	63	16	62	26
HOUSEHOLD FURNISHINGS AND EQUIPMENT	**137**	**134**	**140**	**128**	**144**	**141**	**74**	**57**
Household textiles	**130**	**132**	**127**	**146**	**114**	**139**	**128**	**65**
Bathroom linens	120	116	128	112	151	98	168	75
Bedroom linens	127	123	128	193	97	143	156	63
Kitchen and dining room linens	141	176	109	87	105	129	11	79
Curtains and draperies	144	128	148	88	148	189	59	52
Slipcovers and decorative pillows	128	110	155	55	152	228	71	60
Sewing materials for household items	142	217	91	54	94	111	18	59
Other linens	129	142	115	173	88	123	234	39
Furniture	**132**	**122**	**143**	**135**	**150**	**136**	**97**	**59**
Mattresses and springs	138	133	143	180	124	153	87	52
Other bedroom furniture	113	97	128	152	151	74	163	70
Sofas	132	109	155	103	167	169	112	55
Living room chairs	146	156	126	78	112	183	49	58
Living room tables	131	118	148	137	172	114	55	81

	total married couples	married couples, no children	married couples with children				single parent with child under age 18	single person
			total	oldest child under age 6	oldest child aged 6 to 17	oldest child aged 18 or older		
Kitchen and dining room furniture	131	125	146	117	192	86	55	62
Infants' furniture	137	119	154	439	81	84	76	28
Outdoor furniture	149	160	157	97	162	188	22	60
Wall units, cabinets, and other furniture	134	135	144	128	161	126	86	63
Floor coverings	**146**	**185**	**113**	**70**	**105**	**158**	**62**	**60**
Floor coverings, nonpermanent	147	188	116	72	106	161	63	58
Major appliances	**140**	**142**	**142**	**137**	**151**	**129**	**84**	**47**
Dishwashers (built-in), garbage disposals, range hoods	155	161	166	95	203	151	28	43
Refrigerators and freezers	139	154	125	139	126	116	82	45
Washing machines	134	137	136	145	140	124	122	47
Clothes dryers	132	124	145	198	147	106	116	44
Cooking stoves, ovens	161	156	173	145	195	152	64	34
Microwave ovens	122	129	118	88	113	148	103	72
Window air conditioners	110	104	106	55	152	60	80	69
Electric floor-cleaning equipment	130	127	126	131	109	151	56	59
Sewing machines	158	107	217	49	354	98	137	19
Miscellaneous household appliances	143	118	176	44	217	183	–	95
Small appliances and miscellaneous housewares	**136**	**154**	**123**	**122**	**119**	**132**	**57**	**61**
Housewares	143	161	133	144	124	142	45	53
Plastic dinnerware	120	81	164	181	143	189	91	66
China and other dinnerware	164	214	133	293	120	63	39	32
Flatware	112	101	130	39	183	102	115	94
Glassware	128	135	132	191	66	209	63	53
Silver serving pieces	156	106	201	113	196	262	45	55
Other serving pieces	134	165	118	149	107	116	35	58
Nonelectric cookware	148	176	127	75	112	182	26	52
Tableware, nonelectric kitchenware	146	166	130	154	138	104	40	52
Small appliances	125	144	108	86	110	117	75	74
Small electric kitchen appliances	127	148	114	107	116	116	65	67
Portable heating and cooling equipment	119	137	92	36	97	118	98	90
Miscellaneous household equipment	**139**	**134**	**143**	**121**	**148**	**147**	**54**	**56**
Window coverings	163	115	227	145	252	240	26	40
Infants' equipment	150	64	235	739	115	146	77	35
Laundry and cleaning equipment	139	140	145	126	150	147	63	60
Outdoor equipment	172	220	112	68	121	120	9	35
Lamps and lighting fixtures	138	225	59	58	50	75	38	42
Household decorative items	131	118	145	114	151	151	108	55
Telephones and accessories	142	122	155	114	168	156	11	42
Lawn and garden equipment	163	152	164	136	160	188	22	37
Power tools	107	112	112	90	149	63	22	109
Office furniture for home use	125	134	133	45	111	229	54	77
Hand tools	110	120	103	67	143	55	76	103
Indoor plants and fresh flowers	137	154	128	91	134	142	41	64
Closet and storage items	136	117	156	126	205	90	48	78
Rental of furniture	100	141	74	124	80	32	57	84
Luggage	134	115	166	16	199	197	17	98
Computers and computer hardware for nonbusiness use	136	111	157	122	157	181	63	51
Portable memory	127	115	136	121	135	150	80	64
Computer software	118	108	123	116	129	117	61	76
Computer accessories	146	159	138	110	144	147	53	53
Personal digital assistants	163	165	170	160	224	84	35	41
Internet services away from home	113	117	115	159	89	130	96	66
Telephone answering devices	111	102	111	16	200	28	146	62
Business equipment for home use	148	162	136	100	163	116	69	41
Other hardware	131	116	158	88	200	129	51	64
Smoke alarms	130	169	104	123	115	71	37	74
Other household appliances	136	153	107	132	96	110	121	59
Miscellaneous household equipment and parts	147	154	135	96	137	155	40	55

Note: Spending index for total consumer units is 100. "–" means sample is too small to make a reliable estimate.
Source: Calculations by New Strategist based on the Bureau of Labor Statistics' 2011 Consumer Expenditure Survey

Table 8.15 Housing: Household Operations: Total spending by household type, 2011

(total annual spending on household services, supplies, furnishings, and equipment, by consumer unit type, 2011; consumer units and dollars in thousands)

	total married couples	married couples, no children	married couples with children total	oldest child under age 6	oldest child aged 6 to 17	oldest child aged 18 or older	single parent with child under age 18	single person
Number of consumer units	60,144	25,270	29,097	5,825	14,661	8,612	6,956	36,110
Total spending of all consumer units	$3,847,504,302	$1,457,023,725	$2,028,765,629	$384,144,828	$1,036,657,612	$606,386,852	$261,219,016	$1,105,441,930
Housing, total spending	1,242,801,783	463,161,700	663,055,162	145,676,493	339,525,156	177,822,815	101,300,437	413,684,104
HOUSEHOLD SERVICES	87,292,400	25,803,197	55,008,169	21,430,059	24,332,275	9,250,235	8,243,138	25,001,481
Personal services	33,032,889	1,747,926	29,021,348	16,408,035	11,259,208	1,354,668	4,753,939	6,003,649
Babysitting and child care in own home	5,183,210	48,013	4,776,564	2,702,800	2,042,131	31,778	593,069	188,494
Babysitting and child care in someone else's home	2,139,924	30,829	2,021,369	1,219,639	676,312	125,391	470,365	96,053
Care for elderly, invalids, handicapped, etc.	2,326,971	1,378,226	890,950	36,290	84,887	769,741	–	4,997,624
Day care centers, nurseries, and preschools	23,323,242	244,108	21,323,155	12,442,841	8,452,800	427,844	3,690,506	681,757
Other household services	54,259,511	24,055,271	25,986,822	5,022,024	13,073,067	7,895,568	3,489,269	18,997,832
Housekeeping services	8,553,680	4,466,978	3,805,015	715,019	2,290,048	800,141	440,802	2,841,496
Gardening, lawn care service	8,948,224	4,763,395	3,633,924	627,935	1,736,156	1,269,926	370,894	3,875,325
Water-softening service	393,943	138,732	238,595	41,824	109,078	87,756	21,842	105,441
Nonclothing laundry and dry cleaning, sent out	1,200,474	373,491	662,248	116,558	321,369	222,103	19,268	367,239
Nonclothing laundry and dry cleaning, coin-operated	193,664	46,750	115,806	25,222	55,272	35,481	51,474	130,718
Termite and pest control services	1,720,118	864,234	717,532	145,975	354,650	217,022	72,760	456,069
Home security system service fee	2,088,801	932,210	1,036,726	232,359	541,431	262,924	84,515	600,148
Other home services	1,127,700	587,528	473,117	59,007	225,193	188,775	43,197	471,597
Termite and pest control products	279,068	130,646	127,445	24,116	59,524	43,749	14,260	91,358
Moving, storage, and freight express	3,233,341	1,448,224	1,519,736	458,369	497,301	564,258	268,015	1,615,923
Appliance repair, including at service center	1,449,470	677,489	649,736	120,053	366,965	162,681	47,579	331,851
Reupholstering and furniture repair	546,108	224,145	311,629	6,116	103,507	202,038	14,677	101,469
Repairs and rentals of lawn and garden equipment, hand and power tools, etc.	763,829	371,974	315,993	50,503	160,245	105,325	20,520	284,186
Appliance rental	124,498	23,248	78,853	14,563	25,070	39,012	38,606	27,444
Rental of office equipment for nonbusiness use	72,774	37,905	21,532	–	2,346	19,377	11,408	25,999
Repair of computer systems for nonbusiness use	458,297	173,100	243,251	34,775	123,739	84,828	40,693	178,383
Computer information services	23,000,870	8,761,867	11,971,670	2,297,963	6,087,247	3,586,898	1,928,690	7,400,383
Installation of computer	37,289	14,657	14,839	2,796	8,943	3,186	–	17,694
HOUSEKEEPING SUPPLIES	49,650,075	20,223,328	25,026,912	4,857,934	12,483,695	7,663,044	2,727,865	12,572,419
Laundry and cleaning supplies	11,319,101	4,348,462	5,824,056	982,736	3,072,213	1,744,619	960,067	2,742,193
Soaps and detergents	5,927,191	2,023,622	3,275,740	556,288	1,694,958	1,010,877	628,127	1,433,928
Other laundry cleaning products	5,391,910	2,324,840	2,548,315	426,448	1,377,254	733,742	331,940	1,308,265
Other household products	27,638,574	11,102,375	14,397,196	2,912,558	6,861,055	4,624,386	1,365,463	6,817,929
Cleansing and toilet tissue, paper towels, and napkins	8,553,680	2,952,294	4,812,935	805,073	2,189,327	1,793,535	636,057	2,447,175
Miscellaneous household products	11,150,698	4,087,423	6,258,474	1,188,417	3,120,447	1,940,197	616,441	2,654,446
Lawn and garden supplies	7,934,196	4,062,658	3,325,787	919,069	1,551,134	890,653	112,965	1,716,669
Postage and stationery	10,693,002	4,772,492	4,805,661	962,640	2,550,574	1,294,039	402,335	3,012,296
Stationery, stationery supplies, giftwrap	5,497,162	2,206,829	2,791,275	423,303	1,561,836	788,601	221,757	1,672,615
Postage	4,556,509	2,215,168	1,875,011	472,000	921,297	495,276	149,137	1,269,989
Delivery services	639,331	350,495	139,375	67,337	67,441	10,076	31,511	69,692
HOUSEHOLD FURNISHINGS AND EQUIPMENT	124,302,612	51,284,707	61,637,339	11,274,288	31,995,727	18,336,843	7,755,105	31,018,129
Household textiles	8,507,970	3,641,407	4,028,480	928,563	1,822,949	1,302,996	971,614	2,548,283
Bathroom linens	1,454,883	589,549	749,248	130,946	446,721	169,829	236,156	547,789
Bedroom linens	4,524,032	1,840,920	2,192,168	661,778	835,091	724,614	638,630	1,351,597
Kitchen and dining room linens	504,608	265,082	189,131	30,115	91,778	66,140	4,452	170,439
Curtains and draperies	976,739	364,899	487,666	57,959	245,572	184,125	46,536	214,132
Slipcovers and decorative pillows	270,648	98,048	158,579	11,242	78,436	69,068	17,320	76,553
Sewing materials for household items	689,250	442,730	213,281	25,222	110,984	77,250	10,086	172,606
Other linens	87,810	40,432	37,826	11,417	14,661	11,971	18,364	15,888
Furniture	28,415,634	11,040,463	14,891,554	2,821,222	7,873,837	4,196,886	2,416,027	7,689,625
Mattresses and springs	5,129,682	2,074,414	2,576,539	646,109	1,119,807	810,648	371,450	1,150,826
Other bedroom furniture	4,779,042	1,714,570	2,618,148	620,770	1,548,935	448,599	793,680	1,774,084
Sofas	7,386,285	2,559,598	4,177,747	559,375	2,270,696	1,347,778	720,642	1,849,915
Living room chairs	3,176,806	1,420,427	1,326,241	165,022	591,865	569,425	122,356	756,505
Living room tables	935,841	353,527	511,525	94,773	299,964	116,951	45,284	346,656

	total married couples	married couples, no children	married couples with children				single parent with child under age 18	single person
			total	oldest child under age 6	oldest child aged 6 to 17	oldest child aged 18 or older		
Kitchen and dining room furniture	$2,156,764	$864,487	$1,162,425	$187,507	$771,315	$203,760	$105,453	$617,120
Infants' furniture	679,627	246,888	367,786	210,690	97,789	59,423	43,614	82,692
Outdoor furniture	1,675,612	754,057	852,833	105,899	443,788	303,056	28,311	404,432
Wall units, cabinets, and other furniture	2,495,375	1,052,748	1,298,017	231,136	729,678	337,246	185,238	707,395
Floor coverings	**1,758,009**	**932,463**	**659,338**	**82,016**	**306,122**	**271,278**	**86,185**	**431,876**
Floor coverings, nonpermanent	1,737,560	932,210	659,338	82,016	306,122	271,278	86,185	407,321
Major appliances	**16,323,683**	**6,951,524**	**7,999,638**	**1,552,829**	**4,295,233**	**2,147,402**	**1,130,767**	**3,304,065**
Dishwashers (built-in), garbage disposals, range hoods	1,360,457	594,856	705,020	80,443	434,259	190,239	28,520	225,326
Refrigerators and freezers	4,431,410	2,056,725	1,931,750	428,604	975,690	527,399	301,473	867,001
Washing machines	2,748,581	1,179,604	1,347,482	286,881	698,450	361,876	287,839	579,566
Clothes dryers	1,978,136	779,832	1,052,729	287,231	538,352	227,185	200,541	399,377
Cooking stoves, ovens	2,945,853	1,199,820	1,531,666	258,514	874,089	398,908	135,920	371,211
Microwave ovens	659,178	292,627	308,428	45,901	148,663	114,023	64,065	231,826
Window air conditioners	319,966	126,855	148,104	15,320	107,758	24,889	26,920	119,524
Electric floor-cleaning equipment	1,254,002	516,013	588,341	122,150	257,594	208,583	62,395	340,517
Sewing machines	230,352	65,449	153,632	6,932	126,085	20,497	23,094	16,972
Miscellaneous household appliances	363,270	125,592	215,318	10,776	133,855	66,226	–	145,162
Small appliances and miscellaneous housewares	**7,306,895**	**3,486,249**	**3,202,125**	**633,585**	**1,554,213**	**1,015,613**	**352,182**	**1,974,134**
Housewares	4,715,290	2,226,540	2,120,298	460,292	996,801	668,980	172,300	1,054,412
Plastic dinnerware	178,026	50,793	118,134	26,038	51,900	40,218	15,581	59,220
China and other dinnerware	526,861	289,089	206,880	91,161	93,830	28,850	14,468	62,109
Flatware	199,077	75,305	112,314	6,641	79,463	26,094	23,581	100,747
Glassware	504,007	223,387	252,271	73,162	63,922	117,898	28,659	125,663
Silver serving pieces	134,121	38,158	83,799	9,378	41,051	32,209	4,452	28,166
Other serving pieces	114,274	59,132	48,883	12,349	22,285	14,210	3,478	29,971
Nonelectric cookware	1,328,581	663,843	550,515	65,007	244,692	233,988	26,641	280,936
Tableware, nonelectric kitchenware	1,730,343	827,087	747,502	176,498	399,512	175,685	55,439	367,600
Small appliances	2,592,206	1,259,710	1,082,117	173,294	557,411	346,547	179,882	919,722
Small electric kitchen appliances	1,877,094	913,258	812,970	152,557	415,639	244,839	111,435	595,093
Portable heating and cooling equipment	715,112	346,452	268,856	20,737	141,918	101,708	68,447	324,629
Miscellaneous household equipment	**61,989,819**	**25,232,095**	**30,856,496**	**5,256,014**	**16,143,374**	**9,402,668**	**2,798,329**	**15,069,786**
Window coverings	1,560,135	461,178	1,048,656	133,684	587,026	327,859	28,520	226,771
Infants' equipment	1,309,936	234,253	992,499	623,916	244,985	181,799	77,699	181,633
Laundry and cleaning equipment	1,444,057	612,545	730,626	127,684	381,186	219,348	75,820	375,183
Outdoor equipment	3,556,315	1,915,213	1,118,780	136,888	612,683	357,226	21,424	431,153
Lamps and lighting fixtures	2,429,216	1,667,062	503,960	98,676	215,810	188,775	78,116	440,542
Household decorative items	9,229,698	3,491,051	4,929,323	781,074	2,599,102	1,521,310	878,960	2,333,789
Telephones and accessories	3,882,897	1,408,297	2,052,211	301,444	1,122,593	613,605	34,363	690,784
Lawn and garden equipment	6,430,596	2,522,451	3,139,275	520,930	1,539,112	1,063,582	100,862	872,779
Power tools	2,455,680	1,081,809	1,247,679	200,613	834,797	207,549	58,430	1,508,676
Office furniture for home use	437,848	197,106	225,502	15,320	95,003	115,056	21,911	162,134
Hand tools	1,029,064	472,549	464,970	61,046	326,647	73,546	82,220	579,204
Indoor plants and fresh flowers	3,857,636	1,822,978	1,745,820	247,504	923,643	574,593	134,181	1,086,189
Closet and storage items	1,376,095	497,061	764,960	123,315	507,564	131,075	56,274	477,013
Rental of furniture	370,487	219,344	133,264	44,328	71,839	17,138	24,555	185,967
Luggage	551,520	198,875	330,251	6,233	199,536	116,262	8,278	242,659
Computers and computer hardware for nonbusiness use	12,496,720	4,284,276	6,948,364	1,081,936	3,495,915	2,370,797	662,976	2,794,192
Portable memory	319,365	121,043	165,562	29,416	82,541	53,739	23,094	96,414
Computer software	1,012,825	390,169	511,234	97,045	270,349	143,820	61,074	393,960
Computer accessories	1,064,549	487,711	488,539	77,589	257,154	153,896	44,379	232,548
Personal digital assistants	616,476	261,545	309,592	58,600	205,694	45,299	15,373	92,081
Internet services away from home	475,739	207,214	235,686	65,182	91,631	78,886	47,092	167,912
Telephone answering devices	40,898	15,667	19,786	583	17,886	1,464	6,191	13,722
Business equipment for home use	360,263	166,277	160,615	23,591	96,616	40,390	19,338	59,943
Other hardware	890,733	331,037	521,418	58,192	331,778	125,563	40,623	263,964
Smoke alarms	154,570	83,896	59,358	14,155	33,280	11,971	5,078	52,360
Other household appliances	649,555	307,536	247,906	60,988	111,717	75,269	66,847	168,273
Miscellaneous household equipment and parts	3,825,760	1,679,697	1,699,556	241,388	866,758	577,262	120,895	862,668

Note: Total spending figures for total consumer units can be found on Total Spending by Age and Total Spending by Region tables. Spending by type of consumer unit does not add to total because not all types of consumer units are shown. Numbers may not add to category total because of rounding and missing subcategories. "–" means sample is too small to make a reliable estimate.

Source: Calculations by New Strategist based on the Bureau of Labor Statistics' 2011 Consumer Expenditure Survey

Table 8.16 Housing: Household Operations: Market shares by household type, 2011

(percentage of total annual spending on household services, supplies, furnishings, and equipment accounted for by types of consumer units, 2011)

	total married couples	married couples, no children	married couples with children				single parent with child under age 18	single person
			total	oldest child under age 6	oldest child aged 6 to 17	oldest child aged 18 or older		
Share of total consumer units	49.2%	20.7%	23.8%	4.8%	12.0%	7.0%	5.7%	29.5%
Share of total before-tax income	67.0	25.6	35.0	6.8	17.5	10.7	3.3	16.0
Share of total spending	63.3	24.0	33.4	6.3	17.1	10.0	4.3	18.2
Share of housing spending	**60.5**	**22.5**	**32.3**	**7.1**	**16.5**	**8.7**	**4.9**	**20.1**
HOUSEHOLD SERVICES	**63.6**	**18.8**	**40.1**	**15.6**	**17.7**	**6.7**	**6.0**	**18.2**
Personal services	**67.8**	**3.6**	**59.6**	**33.7**	**23.1**	**2.8**	**9.8**	**12.3**
Babysitting and child care in own home	82.7	0.8	76.2	43.1	32.6	0.5	9.5	3.0
Babysitting and child care in someone else's home	65.1	0.9	61.5	37.1	20.6	3.8	14.3	2.9
Care for elderly, invalids, handicapped, etc.	28.0	16.6	10.7	0.4	1.0	9.3	–	60.2
Day care centers, nurseries, and preschools	75.9	0.8	69.4	40.5	27.5	1.4	12.0	2.2
Other household services	**61.3**	**27.2**	**29.4**	**5.7**	**14.8**	**8.9**	**3.9**	**21.5**
Housekeeping services	66.5	34.7	29.6	5.6	17.8	6.2	3.4	22.1
Gardening, lawn care service	61.7	32.8	25.0	4.3	12.0	8.8	2.6	26.7
Water-softening service	66.1	23.3	40.1	7.0	18.3	14.7	3.7	17.7
Nonclothing laundry and dry cleaning, sent out	66.7	20.8	36.8	6.5	17.9	12.3	1.1	20.4
Nonclothing laundry and dry cleaning, coin-operated	36.0	8.7	21.5	4.7	10.3	6.6	9.6	24.3
Termite and pest control services	68.2	34.3	28.5	5.8	14.1	8.6	2.9	18.1
Home security system service fee	66.6	29.7	33.1	7.4	17.3	8.4	2.7	19.1
Other home services	57.7	30.1	24.2	3.0	11.5	9.7	2.2	24.1
Termite and pest control products	63.9	29.9	29.2	5.5	13.6	10.0	3.3	20.9
Moving, storage, and freight express	50.0	22.4	23.5	7.1	7.7	8.7	4.1	25.0
Appliance repair, including at service center	71.3	33.3	32.0	5.9	18.1	8.0	2.3	16.3
Reupholstering and furniture repair	77.7	31.9	44.3	0.9	14.7	28.7	2.1	14.4
Repairs and rentals of lawn and garden equipment, hand and power tools, etc.	67.2	32.7	27.8	4.4	14.1	9.3	1.8	25.0
Appliance rental	50.7	9.5	32.1	5.9	10.2	15.9	15.7	11.2
Rental of office equipment for nonbusiness use	56.1	29.2	16.6	–	1.8	14.9	8.8	20.1
Repair of computer systems for nonbusiness use	57.6	21.7	30.6	4.4	15.5	10.7	5.1	22.4
Computer information services	59.9	22.8	31.2	6.0	15.9	9.3	5.0	19.3
Installation of computer	59.8	23.5	23.8	4.5	14.3	5.1	–	28.4
HOUSEKEEPING SUPPLIES	**66.0**	**26.9**	**33.3**	**6.5**	**16.6**	**10.2**	**3.6**	**16.7**
Laundry and cleaning supplies	**63.8**	**24.5**	**32.8**	**5.5**	**17.3**	**9.8**	**5.4**	**15.5**
Soaps and detergents	61.8	21.1	34.1	5.8	17.7	10.5	6.5	14.9
Other laundry cleaning products	66.2	28.6	31.3	5.2	16.9	9.0	4.1	16.1
Other household products	**66.6**	**26.7**	**34.7**	**7.0**	**16.5**	**11.1**	**3.3**	**16.4**
Cleansing and toilet tissue, paper towels, and napkins	60.9	21.0	34.3	5.7	15.6	12.8	4.5	17.4
Miscellaneous household products	68.0	24.9	38.2	7.2	19.0	11.8	3.8	16.2
Lawn and garden supplies	71.6	36.6	30.0	8.3	14.0	8.0	1.0	15.5
Postage and stationery	**67.2**	**30.0**	**30.2**	**6.1**	**16.0**	**8.1**	**2.5**	**18.9**
Stationery, stationery supplies, giftwrap	66.5	26.7	33.8	5.1	18.9	9.5	2.7	20.2
Postage	67.5	32.8	27.8	7.0	13.6	7.3	2.2	18.8
Delivery services	71.4	39.2	15.6	7.5	7.5	1.1	3.5	7.8
HOUSEHOLD FURNISHINGS AND EQUIPMENT	**67.1**	**27.7**	**33.3**	**6.1**	**17.3**	**9.9**	**4.2**	**16.8**
Household textiles	**63.7**	**27.3**	**30.2**	**7.0**	**13.7**	**9.8**	**7.3**	**19.1**
Bathroom linens	59.0	23.9	30.4	5.3	18.1	6.9	9.6	22.2
Bedroom linens	62.7	25.5	30.4	9.2	11.6	10.0	8.9	18.7
Kitchen and dining room linens	69.4	36.4	26.0	4.1	12.6	9.1	0.6	23.4
Curtains and draperies	70.7	26.4	35.3	4.2	17.8	13.3	3.4	15.5
Slipcovers and decorative pillows	62.9	22.8	36.8	2.6	18.2	16.0	4.0	17.8
Sewing materials for household items	69.8	44.9	21.6	2.6	11.2	7.8	1.0	17.5
Other linens	63.5	29.3	27.4	8.3	10.6	8.7	13.3	11.5
Furniture	**64.9**	**25.2**	**34.0**	**6.4**	**18.0**	**9.6**	**5.5**	**17.6**
Mattresses and springs	68.0	27.5	34.1	8.6	14.8	10.7	4.9	15.2
Other bedroom furniture	55.8	20.0	30.6	7.2	18.1	5.2	9.3	20.7
Sofas	65.1	22.6	36.8	4.9	20.0	11.9	6.3	16.3
Living room chairs	71.9	32.2	30.0	3.7	13.4	12.9	2.8	17.1
Living room tables	64.5	24.4	35.2	6.5	20.7	8.1	3.1	23.9

	total married couples	married couples, no children	married couples with children				single parent with child under age 18	single person
			total	oldest child under age 6	oldest child aged 6 to 17	oldest child aged 18 or older		
Kitchen and dining room furniture	64.3%	25.8%	34.6%	5.6%	23.0%	6.1%	3.1%	18.4%
Infants' furniture	67.5	24.5	36.5	20.9	9.7	5.9	4.3	8.2
Outdoor furniture	73.3	33.0	37.3	4.6	19.4	13.3	1.2	17.7
Wall units, cabinets, and other furniture	65.9	27.8	34.3	6.1	19.3	8.9	4.9	18.7
Floor coverings	**72.0**	**38.2**	**27.0**	**3.4**	**12.5**	**11.1**	**3.5**	**17.7**
Floor coverings, nonpermanent	72.5	38.9	27.5	3.4	12.8	11.3	3.6	17.0
Major appliances	**68.8**	**29.3**	**33.7**	**6.5**	**18.1**	**9.1**	**4.8**	**13.9**
Dishwashers (built-in), garbage disposals, range hoods	76.2	33.3	39.5	4.5	24.3	10.7	1.6	12.6
Refrigerators and freezers	68.4	31.8	29.8	6.6	15.1	8.1	4.7	13.4
Washing machines	66.1	28.4	32.4	6.9	16.8	8.7	6.9	13.9
Clothes dryers	64.9	25.6	34.5	9.4	17.7	7.5	6.6	13.1
Cooking stoves, ovens	79.0	32.2	41.1	6.9	23.4	10.7	3.6	9.9
Microwave ovens	60.2	26.7	28.1	4.2	13.6	10.4	5.8	21.2
Window air conditioners	54.3	21.5	25.1	2.6	18.3	4.2	4.6	20.3
Electric floor-cleaning equipment	63.9	26.3	30.0	6.2	13.1	10.6	3.2	17.3
Sewing machines	77.5	22.0	51.7	2.3	42.4	6.9	7.8	5.7
Miscellaneous household appliances	70.6	24.4	41.8	2.1	26.0	12.9	–	28.2
Small appliances and miscellaneous housewares	**66.9**	**31.9**	**29.3**	**5.8**	**14.2**	**9.3**	**3.2**	**18.1**
Housewares	70.3	33.2	31.6	6.9	14.9	10.0	2.6	15.7
Plastic dinnerware	58.9	16.8	39.1	8.6	17.2	13.3	5.2	19.6
China and other dinnerware	80.7	44.3	31.7	14.0	14.4	4.4	2.2	9.5
Flatware	55.0	20.8	31.0	1.8	22.0	7.2	6.5	27.8
Glassware	62.8	27.8	31.4	9.1	8.0	14.7	3.6	15.7
Silver serving pieces	76.7	21.8	47.9	5.4	23.5	18.4	2.5	16.1
Other serving pieces	65.8	34.1	28.2	7.1	12.8	8.2	2.0	17.3
Nonelectric cookware	72.7	36.3	30.1	3.6	13.4	12.8	1.5	15.4
Tableware, nonelectric kitchenware	71.8	34.3	31.0	7.3	16.6	7.3	2.3	15.3
Small appliances	61.4	29.9	25.6	4.1	13.2	8.2	4.3	21.8
Small electric kitchen appliances	62.7	30.5	27.1	5.1	13.9	8.2	3.7	19.9
Portable heating and cooling equipment	58.5	28.3	22.0	1.7	11.6	8.3	5.6	26.5
Miscellaneous household equipment	**68.2**	**27.7**	**33.9**	**5.8**	**17.8**	**10.3**	**3.1**	**16.6**
Window coverings	80.4	23.8	54.0	6.9	30.2	16.9	1.5	11.7
Infants' equipment	73.9	13.2	56.0	35.2	13.8	10.3	4.4	10.3
Laundry and cleaning equipment	68.1	28.9	34.5	6.0	18.0	10.4	3.6	17.7
Outdoor equipment	84.5	45.5	26.6	3.3	14.6	8.5	0.5	10.2
Lamps and lighting fixtures	67.8	46.5	14.1	2.8	6.0	5.3	2.2	12.3
Household decorative items	64.4	24.4	34.4	5.4	18.1	10.6	6.1	16.3
Telephones and accessories	69.7	25.3	36.8	5.4	20.1	11.0	0.6	12.4
Lawn and garden equipment	80.1	31.4	39.1	6.5	19.2	13.3	1.3	10.9
Power tools	52.6	23.2	26.7	4.3	17.9	4.4	1.3	32.3
Office furniture for home use	61.4	27.6	31.6	2.1	13.3	16.1	3.1	22.7
Hand tools	54.1	24.9	24.5	3.2	17.2	3.9	4.3	30.5
Indoor plants and fresh flowers	67.2	31.8	30.4	4.3	16.1	10.0	2.3	18.9
Closet and storage items	66.8	24.1	37.1	6.0	24.6	6.4	2.7	23.1
Rental of furniture	49.2	29.1	17.7	5.9	9.5	2.3	3.3	24.7
Luggage	65.9	23.8	39.5	0.7	23.9	13.9	1.0	29.0
Computers and computer hardware for nonbusiness use	67.1	23.0	37.3	5.8	18.8	12.7	3.6	15.0
Portable memory	62.6	23.7	32.5	5.8	16.2	10.5	4.5	18.9
Computer software	57.8	22.3	29.2	5.5	15.4	8.2	3.5	22.5
Computer accessories	71.6	32.8	32.9	5.2	17.3	10.4	3.0	15.7
Personal digital assistants	80.4	34.1	40.4	7.6	26.8	5.9	2.0	12.0
Internet services away from home	55.3	24.1	27.4	7.6	10.7	9.2	5.5	19.5
Telephone answering devices	54.8	21.0	26.5	0.8	24.0	2.0	8.3	18.4
Business equipment for home use	72.7	33.6	32.4	4.8	19.5	8.2	3.9	12.1
Other hardware	64.2	23.9	37.6	4.2	23.9	9.1	2.9	19.0
Smoke alarms	64.2	34.8	24.6	5.9	13.8	5.0	2.1	21.7
Other household appliances	66.7	31.6	25.5	6.3	11.5	7.7	6.9	17.3
Miscellaneous household equipment and parts	72.5	31.8	32.2	4.6	16.4	10.9	2.3	16.4

Note: Market share for total consumer units is 100.0%. Market shares by type of consumer unit do not add to total because not all types of consumer units are shown. "–" means sample is too small to make a reliable estimate.
Source: Calculations by New Strategist based on the Bureau of Labor Statistics' 2011 Consumer Expenditure Survey

Table 8.17 Housing: Household Operations: Average spending by race and Hispanic origin, 2011

(average annual spending of consumer units on household services, supplies, furnishings, and equipment, by race and Hispanic origin of consumer unit reference person, 2011)

	total consumer units	Asian	black	Hispanic	non-Hispanic white and other
Number of consumer units (in 000s)	122,287	5,048	15,118	15,222	92,163
Average number of persons per consumer unit	2.5	2.7	2.6	3.4	2.4
Average before-tax income of consumer units	$63,685.00	$85,415.00	$45,552.00	$49,966.00	$68,907.00
Average spending of consumer units, total	49,704.88	60,136.04	36,643.75	42,085.98	53,055.68
Housing, average spending	16,803.03	20,833.57	13,984.57	15,647.65	17,449.43
HOUSEHOLD SERVICES	**1,122.18**	**1,592.70**	**809.64**	**755.03**	**1,232.98**
Personal services	**398.27**	**807.93**	**306.80**	**319.23**	**425.96**
Babysitting and child care in own home	51.23	135.14	37.11	48.41	53.90
Babysitting and child care in someone else's home	26.87	31.43	35.57	51.80	21.26
Care for elderly, invalids, handicapped, etc.	67.89	170.67	2.43	3.57	89.09
Day care centers, nurseries, and preschools	251.30	470.69	231.69	215.05	260.48
Other household services	**723.92**	**784.78**	**502.84**	**435.80**	**807.02**
Housekeeping services	105.26	133.91	18.14	26.40	132.33
Gardening, lawn care service	118.65	146.70	65.44	54.13	137.82
Water-softening service	4.87	2.93	7.11	1.57	5.03
Nonclothing laundry and dry cleaning, sent out	14.71	7.54	18.64	12.67	14.39
Nonclothing laundry and dry cleaning, coin-operated	4.40	7.05	7.50	11.16	2.79
Termite and pest control services	20.61	20.09	12.52	7.31	24.09
Home security system service fee	25.65	29.11	42.87	14.72	24.60
Other home services	15.98	15.03	6.29	8.33	18.79
Termite and pest control products	3.57	4.00	2.18	1.58	4.11
Moving, storage, and freight express	52.88	37.73	37.78	16.68	61.30
Appliance repair, including at service center	16.62	8.25	11.67	6.97	19.03
Reupholstering and furniture repair	5.75	0.12	0.96	1.40	7.24
Repairs and rentals of lawn and garden equipment, hand and power tools, etc.	9.29	3.79	3.64	2.29	11.35
Appliance rental	2.01	1.16	1.48	1.14	2.24
Rental of office equipment for nonbusiness use	1.06	0.05	1.28	1.25	0.99
Repair of computer systems for nonbusiness use	6.51	3.34	4.67	6.81	6.77
Computer information services	313.76	349.48	260.32	260.86	331.22
Installation of computer	0.51	0.01	0.38	0.46	0.54
HOUSEKEEPING SUPPLIES	**614.74**	**392.79**	**425.55**	**535.59**	**656.12**
Laundry and cleaning supplies	**145.06**	**107.65**	**155.04**	**194.84**	**136.47**
Soaps and detergents	78.49	65.83	93.63	112.06	71.13
Other laundry cleaning products	66.57	41.82	61.41	82.78	65.34
Other household products	**339.58**	**211.43**	**194.21**	**254.91**	**374.69**
Cleansing and toilet tissue, paper towels, and napkins	114.81	89.75	99.33	128.58	114.93
Miscellaneous household products	134.12	93.91	72.48	94.71	149.62
Lawn and garden supplies	90.65	27.77	22.40	31.61	110.14
Postage and stationery	**130.09**	**73.72**	**76.29**	**85.84**	**144.96**
Stationery, stationery supplies, giftwrap	67.56	26.91	23.03	52.76	76.65
Postage	55.22	39.38	48.21	30.74	59.90
Delivery services	7.32	7.43	5.06	2.34	8.41
HOUSEHOLD FURNISHINGS AND EQUIPMENT	**1,513.98**	**1,300.17**	**937.54**	**1,128.51**	**1,665.99**
Household textiles	**109.14**	**69.31**	**52.46**	**72.97**	**123.65**
Bathroom linens	20.16	14.84	19.17	24.61	19.61
Bedroom linens	59.00	37.65	18.59	30.43	69.68
Kitchen and dining room linens	5.95	3.99	1.26	4.95	6.82
Curtains and draperies	11.30	4.71	7.95	7.28	12.50
Slipcovers and decorative pillows	3.52	2.35	2.49	2.72	3.81
Sewing materials for household items	8.07	4.82	1.11	1.76	10.24
Other linens	1.13	0.95	1.89	1.22	0.99
Furniture	**357.94**	**381.17**	**306.38**	**309.52**	**374.05**
Mattresses and springs	61.72	83.37	32.96	52.41	67.91
Other bedroom furniture	70.06	118.16	79.70	51.69	71.36
Sofas	92.81	79.13	90.07	91.66	93.46
Living room chairs	36.12	26.97	26.47	20.42	40.20
Living room tables	11.87	19.10	8.13	8.76	12.98

	total consumer units	Asian	black	Hispanic	non-Hispanic white and other
Kitchen and dining room furniture	$27.45	$18.93	$39.61	$38.21	$23.80
Infants' furniture	8.23	5.36	5.76	12.17	7.97
Outdoor furniture	18.70	4.47	4.54	7.19	22.88
Wall units, cabinets, and other furniture	30.97	25.67	19.16	27.01	33.50
Floor coverings	**19.98**	**10.76**	**9.67**	**7.41**	**23.77**
Floor coverings, nonpermanent	19.61	10.76	9.67	6.04	23.50
Major appliances	**193.93**	**152.86**	**152.02**	**128.17**	**211.37**
Dishwashers (built-in), garbage disposals, range hoods	14.60	15.47	5.71	2.79	17.98
Refrigerators and freezers	52.96	49.88	33.61	32.72	59.56
Washing machines	34.00	23.55	30.88	36.64	33.99
Clothes dryers	24.93	14.37	26.32	21.81	25.16
Cooking stoves, ovens	30.51	26.99	29.56	10.50	33.89
Microwave ovens	8.96	11.62	6.99	9.90	9.11
Window air conditioners	4.82	0.61	6.17	6.00	4.40
Electric floor-cleaning equipment	16.06	8.51	10.25	6.86	18.52
Sewing machines	2.43	1.45	0.58	0.82	2.99
Miscellaneous household appliances	4.21	–	1.44	–	5.28
Small appliances and miscellaneous housewares	**89.34**	**83.21**	**39.30**	**60.62**	**101.83**
Housewares	54.84	45.78	21.97	39.79	62.45
Plastic dinnerware	2.47	1.86	2.76	2.67	2.39
China and other dinnerware	5.34	4.96	3.28	2.35	6.10
Flatware	2.96	3.72	2.69	2.55	3.23
Glassware	6.56	10.54	1.41	5.44	7.55
Silver serving pieces	1.43	2.18	0.79	0.62	1.65
Other serving pieces	1.42	0.87	0.43	0.85	1.68
Nonelectric cookware	14.94	11.03	5.78	15.34	16.28
Tableware, nonelectric kitchenware	19.71	10.63	4.81	9.97	23.57
Small appliances	34.50	37.42	17.33	20.83	39.39
Small electric kitchen appliances	24.50	23.71	15.47	18.58	26.95
Portable heating and cooling equipment	10.00	13.71	1.86	2.25	12.44
Miscellaneous household equipment	**743.64**	**602.87**	**377.71**	**549.82**	**831.32**
Window coverings	15.87	19.28	15.30	9.25	17.02
Infants' equipment	14.49	17.42	10.97	15.93	14.76
Laundry and cleaning equipment	17.33	8.33	11.32	19.52	17.96
Outdoor equipment	34.43	4.54	8.47	16.30	41.19
Lamps and lighting fixtures	29.29	3.51	6.31	20.01	34.34
Household decorative items	117.20	39.22	50.24	68.94	134.74
Telephones and accessories	45.56	28.80	41.21	40.76	46.79
Lawn and garden equipment	65.62	23.56	6.65	8.34	83.48
Power tools	38.18	27.28	10.45	64.11	38.47
Office furniture for home use	5.83	5.45	4.15	5.24	6.33
Hand tools	15.55	15.55	7.03	27.54	15.00
Indoor plants and fresh flowers	46.92	31.89	19.13	29.82	54.22
Closet and storage items	16.85	3.72	4.51	8.38	20.03
Rental of furniture	6.16	1.21	6.90	12.69	4.94
Luggage	6.84	12.77	3.92	12.81	6.58
Computers and computer hardware for nonbusiness use	152.35	230.31	102.84	106.21	168.00
Portable memory	4.17	5.02	3.88	4.20	4.21
Computer software	14.33	29.96	8.46	10.13	15.96
Computer accessories	12.15	12.09	8.41	5.40	13.85
Personal digital assistants	6.27	17.76	5.36	8.28	6.18
Internet services away from home	7.03	9.05	4.19	8.07	7.31
Telephone answering devices	0.61	0.74	0.50	0.80	0.59
Business equipment for home use	4.05	6.01	2.73	2.75	4.49
Other hardware	11.34	0.69	0.59	5.21	13.94
Smoke alarms	1.97	1.17	1.22	0.88	2.26
Other household appliances	7.96	8.79	4.54	5.16	8.98
Miscellaneous household equipment and parts	43.13	37.61	28.04	32.21	47.02

Note: "Asian" and "black" include Hispanics and non-Hispanics who identify themselves as being of the respective race alone. "Hispanic" includes people of any race who identify themselves as Hispanic. "Other" includes people who identify themselves as non-Hispanic and as Alaska Native, American Indian, Asian (who are also included in the "Asian" column), or Native Hawaiian or other Pacific Islander, as well as non-Hispanics reporting more than one race. Subcategories may not add to total because some are not shown. "–" means sample is too small to make a reliable estimate.
Source: Bureau of Labor Statistics, unpublished tables from the 2011 Consumer Expenditure Survey

Table 8.18 Housing: Household Operations: Indexed spending by race and Hispanic origin, 2011

(indexed average annual spending of consumer units on household services, supplies, furnishings, and equipment, by race and Hispanic origin of consumer unit reference person, 2011; index definition: an index of 100 is the average for all consumer units; an index of 125 means that spending by consumer units in that group is 25 percent above the average for all consumer units; an index of 75 indicates spending that is 25 percent below the average for all consumer units)

	total consumer units	Asian	black	Hispanic	non-Hispanic white and other
Average spending of consumer units, total	$49,705	$60,136	$36,644	$42,086	$53,056
Average spending of consumer units, index	100	121	74	85	107
Housing, spending index	100	124	83	93	104
HOUSEHOLD SERVICES	100	142	72	67	110
Personal services	100	203	77	80	107
Babysitting and child care in own home	100	264	72	94	105
Babysitting and child care in someone else's home	100	117	132	193	79
Care for elderly, invalids, handicapped, etc.	100	251	4	5	131
Day care centers, nurseries, and preschools	100	187	92	86	104
Other household services	100	108	69	60	111
Housekeeping services	100	127	17	25	126
Gardening, lawn care service	100	124	55	46	116
Water-softening service	100	60	146	32	103
Nonclothing laundry and dry cleaning, sent out	100	51	127	86	98
Nonclothing laundry and dry cleaning, coin-operated	100	160	170	254	63
Termite and pest control services	100	97	61	35	117
Home security system service fee	100	113	167	57	96
Other home services	100	94	39	52	118
Termite and pest control products	100	112	61	44	115
Moving, storage, and freight express	100	71	71	32	116
Appliance repair, including at service center	100	50	70	42	115
Reupholstering and furniture repair	100	2	17	24	126
Repairs and rentals of lawn and garden equipment, hand and power tools, etc.	100	41	39	25	122
Appliance rental	100	58	74	57	111
Rental of office equipment for nonbusiness use	100	5	121	118	93
Repair of computer systems for nonbusiness use	100	51	72	105	104
Computer information services	100	111	83	83	106
Installation of computer	100	2	75	90	106
HOUSEKEEPING SUPPLIES	100	64	69	87	107
Laundry and cleaning supplies	100	74	107	134	94
Soaps and detergents	100	84	119	143	91
Other laundry cleaning products	100	63	92	124	98
Other household products	100	62	57	75	110
Cleansing and toilet tissue, paper towels, and napkins	100	78	87	112	100
Miscellaneous household products	100	70	54	71	112
Lawn and garden supplies	100	31	25	35	122
Postage and stationery	100	57	59	66	111
Stationery, stationery supplies, giftwrap	100	40	34	78	113
Postage	100	71	87	56	108
Delivery services	100	102	69	32	115
HOUSEHOLD FURNISHINGS AND EQUIPMENT	100	86	62	75	110
Household textiles	100	64	48	67	113
Bathroom linens	100	74	95	122	97
Bedroom linens	100	64	32	52	118
Kitchen and dining room linens	100	67	21	83	115
Curtains and draperies	100	42	70	64	111
Slipcovers and decorative pillows	100	67	71	77	108
Sewing materials for household items	100	60	14	22	127
Other linens	100	84	167	108	88
Furniture	100	106	86	86	105
Mattresses and springs	100	135	53	85	110
Other bedroom furniture	100	169	114	74	102
Sofas	100	85	97	99	101
Living room chairs	100	75	73	57	111
Living room tables	100	161	68	74	109

	total consumer units	Asian	black	Hispanic	non-Hispanic white and other
Kitchen and dining room furniture	100	69	144	139	87
Infants' furniture	100	65	70	148	97
Outdoor furniture	100	24	24	38	122
Wall units, cabinets, and other furniture	100	83	62	87	108
Floor coverings	**100**	**54**	**48**	**37**	**119**
Floor coverings, nonpermanent	100	55	49	31	120
Major appliances	**100**	**79**	**78**	**66**	**109**
Dishwashers (built-in), garbage disposals, range hoods	100	106	39	19	123
Refrigerators and freezers	100	94	63	62	112
Washing machines	100	69	91	108	100
Clothes dryers	100	58	106	87	101
Cooking stoves, ovens	100	88	97	34	111
Microwave ovens	100	130	78	110	102
Window air conditioners	100	13	128	124	91
Electric floor-cleaning equipment	100	53	64	43	115
Sewing machines	100	60	24	34	123
Miscellaneous household appliances	100	–	34	–	125
Small appliances and miscellaneous housewares	**100**	**93**	**44**	**68**	**114**
Housewares	100	83	40	73	114
Plastic dinnerware	100	75	112	108	97
China and other dinnerware	100	93	61	44	114
Flatware	100	126	91	86	109
Glassware	100	161	21	83	115
Silver serving pieces	100	152	55	43	115
Other serving pieces	100	61	30	60	118
Nonelectric cookware	100	74	39	103	109
Tableware, nonelectric kitchenware	100	54	24	51	120
Small appliances	100	108	50	60	114
Small electric kitchen appliances	100	97	63	76	110
Portable heating and cooling equipment	100	137	19	23	124
Miscellaneous household equipment	**100**	**81**	**51**	**74**	**112**
Window coverings	100	121	96	58	107
Infants' equipment	100	120	76	110	102
Laundry and cleaning equipment	100	48	65	113	104
Outdoor equipment	100	13	25	47	120
Lamps and lighting fixtures	100	12	22	68	117
Household decorative items	100	33	43	59	115
Telephones and accessories	100	63	90	89	103
Lawn and garden equipment	100	36	10	13	127
Power tools	100	71	27	168	101
Office furniture for home use	100	93	71	90	109
Hand tools	100	100	45	177	96
Indoor plants and fresh flowers	100	68	41	64	116
Closet and storage items	100	22	27	50	119
Rental of furniture	100	20	112	206	80
Luggage	100	187	57	187	96
Computers and computer hardware for nonbusiness use	100	151	68	70	110
Portable memory	100	120	93	101	101
Computer software	100	209	59	71	111
Computer accessories	100	100	69	44	114
Personal digital assistants	100	283	85	132	99
Internet services away from home	100	129	60	115	104
Telephone answering devices	100	121	82	131	97
Business equipment for home use	100	148	67	68	111
Other hardware	100	6	5	46	123
Smoke alarms	100	59	62	45	115
Other household appliances	100	110	57	65	113
Miscellaneous household equipment and parts	100	87	65	75	109

Note: "Asian" and "black" include Hispanics and non-Hispanics who identify themselves as being of the respective race alone. "Hispanic" includes people of any race who identify themselves as Hispanic. "Other" includes people who identify themselves as non-Hispanic and as Alaska Native, American Indian, Asian (who are also included in the "Asian" column), or Native Hawaiian or other Pacific Islander, as well as non-Hispanics reporting more than one race. "–" means sample is too small to make a reliable estimate.
Source: Calculations by New Strategist based on the Bureau of Labor Statistics' 2011 Consumer Expenditure Survey

(total annual spending on household services, supplies, furnishings, and equipment, by consumer unit race and Hispanic origin groups, 2011; consumer units and dollars in thousands)

	total consumer units	Asian	black	Hispanic	non-Hispanic white and other
Number of consumer units	122,287	5,048	15,118	15,222	92,163
Total spending of all consumer units	$6,078,260,661	$303,566,730	$553,980,213	$640,632,788	$4,889,770,636
Housing, total spending	2,054,792,130	105,167,861	211,418,729	238,188,528	1,608,191,817
HOUSEHOLD SERVICES	**$137,228,026**	**$8,039,950**	**$12,240,138**	**$11,493,067**	**$113,635,136**
Personal services	**48,703,243**	**4,078,431**	**4,638,202**	**4,859,319**	**39,257,751**
Babysitting and child care in own home	6,264,763	682,187	561,029	736,897	4,967,586
Babysitting and child care in someone else's home	3,285,852	158,659	537,747	788,500	1,959,385
Care for elderly, invalids, handicapped, etc.	8,302,064	861,542	36,737	54,343	8,210,802
Day care centers, nurseries, and preschools	30,730,723	2,376,043	3,502,689	3,273,491	24,006,618
Other household services	**88,526,005**	**3,961,569**	**7,601,935**	**6,633,748**	**74,377,384**
Housekeeping services	12,871,930	675,978	274,241	401,861	12,195,930
Gardening, lawn care service	14,509,353	740,542	989,322	823,967	12,701,905
Water-softening service	595,538	14,791	107,489	23,899	463,580
Nonclothing laundry and dry cleaning, sent out	1,798,842	38,062	281,800	192,863	1,326,226
Nonclothing laundry and dry cleaning, coin-operated	538,063	35,588	113,385	169,878	257,135
Termite and pest control services	2,520,335	101,414	189,277	111,273	2,220,207
Home security system service fee	3,136,662	146,947	648,109	224,068	2,267,210
Other home services	1,954,146	75,871	95,092	126,799	1,731,743
Termite and pest control products	436,565	20,192	32,957	24,051	378,790
Moving, storage, and freight express	6,466,537	190,461	571,158	253,903	5,649,592
Appliance repair, including at service center	2,032,410	41,646	176,427	106,097	1,753,862
Reupholstering and furniture repair	703,150	606	14,513	21,311	667,260
Repairs and rentals of lawn and garden equipment, hand and power tools, etc.	1,136,046	19,132	55,030	34,858	1,046,050
Appliance rental	245,797	5,856	22,375	17,353	206,445
Rental of office equipment for nonbusiness use	129,624	252	19,351	19,028	91,241
Repair of computer systems for nonbusiness use	796,088	16,860	70,601	103,662	623,944
Computer information services	38,368,769	1,764,175	3,935,518	3,970,811	30,526,229
Installation of computer	62,366	50	5,745	7,002	49,768
HOUSEKEEPING SUPPLIES	**75,174,710**	**1,982,804**	**6,433,465**	**8,152,751**	**60,469,988**
Laundry and cleaning supplies	**17,738,952**	**543,417**	**2,343,895**	**2,965,854**	**12,577,485**
Soaps and detergents	9,598,307	332,310	1,415,498	1,705,777	6,555,554
Other laundry cleaning products	8,140,646	211,107	928,396	1,260,077	6,021,930
Other household products	**41,526,219**	**1,067,299**	**2,936,067**	**3,880,240**	**34,532,554**
Cleansing and toilet tissue, paper towels, and napkins	14,039,770	453,058	1,501,671	1,957,245	10,592,294
Miscellaneous household products	16,401,132	474,058	1,095,753	1,441,676	13,789,428
Lawn and garden supplies	11,085,317	140,183	338,643	481,167	10,150,833
Postage and stationery	**15,908,316**	**372,139**	**1,153,352**	**1,306,656**	**13,359,948**
Stationery, stationery supplies, giftwrap	8,261,710	135,842	348,168	803,113	7,064,294
Postage	6,752,688	198,790	728,839	467,924	5,520,564
Delivery services	895,141	37,507	76,497	35,619	775,091
HOUSEHOLD FURNISHINGS AND EQUIPMENT	**185,140,072**	**6,563,258**	**14,173,730**	**17,178,179**	**153,542,636**
Household textiles	**13,346,403**	**349,877**	**793,090**	**1,110,749**	**11,395,955**
Bathroom linens	2,465,306	74,912	289,812	374,613	1,807,316
Bedroom linens	7,214,933	190,057	281,044	463,205	6,421,918
Kitchen and dining room linens	727,608	20,142	19,049	75,349	628,552
Curtains and draperies	1,381,843	23,776	120,188	110,816	1,152,038
Slipcovers and decorative pillows	430,450	11,863	37,644	41,404	351,141
Sewing materials for household items	986,856	24,331	16,781	26,791	943,749
Other linens	138,184	4,796	28,573	18,571	91,241
Furniture	**43,771,409**	**1,924,146**	**4,631,853**	**4,711,513**	**34,473,570**
Mattresses and springs	7,547,554	420,852	498,289	797,785	6,258,789
Other bedroom furniture	8,567,427	596,472	1,204,905	786,825	6,576,752
Sofas	11,349,456	399,448	1,361,678	1,395,249	8,613,554
Living room chairs	4,417,006	136,145	400,173	310,833	3,704,953
Living room tables	1,451,547	96,417	122,909	133,345	1,196,276

	total consumer units	Asian	black	Hispanic	non-Hispanic white and other
Kitchen and dining room furniture	$3,356,778	$95,559	$598,824	$581,633	$2,193,479
Infants' furniture	1,006,422	27,057	87,080	185,252	734,539
Outdoor furniture	2,286,767	22,565	68,636	109,446	2,108,689
Wall units, cabinets, and other furniture	3,787,228	129,582	289,661	411,146	3,087,461
Floor coverings	**2,443,294**	**54,316**	**146,191**	**112,795**	**2,190,715**
Floor coverings, nonpermanent	2,398,048	54,316	146,191	91,941	2,165,831
Major appliances	**23,715,118**	**771,637**	**2,298,238**	**1,951,004**	**19,480,493**
Dishwashers (built-in), garbage disposals, range hoods	1,785,390	78,093	86,324	42,469	1,657,091
Refrigerators and freezers	6,476,320	251,794	508,116	498,064	5,489,228
Washing machines	4,157,758	118,880	466,844	557,734	3,132,620
Clothes dryers	3,048,615	72,540	397,906	331,992	2,318,821
Cooking stoves, ovens	3,730,976	136,246	446,888	159,831	3,123,404
Microwave ovens	1,095,692	58,658	105,675	150,698	839,605
Window air conditioners	589,423	3,079	93,278	91,332	405,517
Electric floor-cleaning equipment	1,963,929	42,958	154,960	104,423	1,706,859
Sewing machines	297,157	7,320	8,768	12,482	275,567
Miscellaneous household appliances	514,828	–	21,770	–	486,621
Small appliances and miscellaneous housewares	**10,925,121**	**420,044.08**	**594,137**	**922,758**	**9,384,958**
Housewares	6,706,219	231,097	332,142	605,683	5,755,579
Plastic dinnerware	302,049	9,389	41,726	40,643	220,270
China and other dinnerware	653,013	25,038	49,587	35,772	562,194
Flatware	361,970	18,779	40,667	38,816	297,686
Glassware	802,203	53,206	21,316	82,808	695,831
Silver serving pieces	174,870	11,005	11,943	9,438	152,069
Other serving pieces	173,648	4,392	6,501	12,939	154,834
Nonelectric cookware	1,826,968	55,679	87,382	233,505	1,500,414
Tableware, nonelectric kitchenware	2,410,277	53,660	72,718	151,763	2,172,282
Small appliances	4,218,902	188,896	261,995	317,074	3,630,301
Small electric kitchen appliances	2,996,032	119,688	233,875	282,825	2,483,793
Portable heating and cooling equipment	1,222,870	69,208	28,119	34,250	1,146,508
Miscellaneous household equipment	**90,937,505**	**3,043,288**	**5,710,220**	**8,369,360**	**76,616,945**
Window coverings	1,940,695	97,325	231,305	140,804	1,568,614
Infants' equipment	1,771,939	87,936	165,844	242,486	1,360,326
Laundry and cleaning equipment	2,119,234	42,050	171,136	297,133	1,655,247
Outdoor equipment	4,210,341	22,918	128,049	248,119	3,796,194
Lamps and lighting fixtures	3,581,786	17,718	95,395	304,592	3,164,877
Household decorative items	14,332,036	197,983	759,528	1,049,405	12,418,043
Telephones and accessories	5,571,396	145,382	623,013	620,449	4,312,307
Lawn and garden equipment	8,024,473	118,931	100,535	126,951	7,693,767
Power tools	4,668,918	137,709	157,983	975,882	3,545,511
Office furniture for home use	712,933	27,512	62,740	79,763	583,392
Hand tools	1,901,563	78,496	106,280	419,214	1,382,445
Indoor plants and fresh flowers	5,737,706	160,981	289,207	453,920	4,997,078
Closet and storage items	2,060,536	18,779	68,182	127,560	1,846,025
Rental of furniture	753,288	6,108	104,314	193,167	455,285
Luggage	836,443	64,463	59,263	194,994	606,433
Computers and computer hardware for nonbusiness use	18,630,424	1,162,605	1,554,735	1,616,729	15,483,384
Portable memory	509,937	25,341	58,658	63,932	388,006
Computer software	1,752,373	151,238	127,898	154,199	1,470,921
Computer accessories	1,485,787	61,030	127,142	82,199	1,276,458
Personal digital assistants	766,739	89,652	81,032	126,038	569,567
Internet services away from home	859,678	45,684	63,344	122,842	673,712
Telephone answering devices	74,595	3,736	7,559	12,178	54,376
Business equipment for home use	495,262	30,338	41,272	41,861	413,812
Other hardware	1,386,735	3,483	8,920	79,307	1,284,752
Smoke alarms	240,905	5,906	18,444	13,395	208,288
Other household appliances	973,405	44,372	68,636	78,546	827,624
Miscellaneous household equipment and parts	5,274,238	189,855	423,909	490,301	4,333,504

Note: "Asian" and "black" include Hispanics and non-Hispanics who identify themselves as being of the respective race alone. "Hispanic" includes people of any race who identify themselves as Hispanic. "Other" includes people who identify themselves as non-Hispanic and as Alaska Native, American Indian, Asian (who are also included in the "Asian" column), or Native Hawaiian or other Pacific Islander, as well as non-Hispanics reporting more than one race. Numbers may not add to total because of rounding and missing subcategories. "–" means sample is too small to make a reliable estimate.
Source: Calculations by New Strategist based on the Bureau of Labor Statistics' 2011 Consumer Expenditure Survey

Table 8.20 Housing: Household Operations: Market shares by race and Hispanic origin, 2011

(percentage of total annual spending on household services, supplies, furnishings, and equipment accounted for by consumer unit race and Hispanic origin groups, 2011)

	total consumer units	Asian	black	Hispanic	non-Hispanic white and other
Share of total consumer units	100.0%	4.1%	12.4%	12.4%	75.4%
Share of total before-tax income	100.0	5.5	8.8	9.8	81.5
Share of total spending	100.0	5.0	9.1	10.5	80.4
Share of housing spending	100.0	5.1	10.3	11.6	78.3
HOUSEHOLD SERVICES	**100.0**	**5.9**	**8.9**	**8.4**	**82.8**
Personal services	**100.0**	**8.4**	**9.5**	**10.0**	**80.6**
Babysitting and child care in own home	100.0	10.9	9.0	11.8	79.3
Babysitting and child care in someone else's home	100.0	4.8	16.4	24.0	59.6
Care for elderly, invalids, handicapped, etc.	100.0	10.4	0.4	0.7	98.9
Day care centers, nurseries, and preschools	100.0	7.7	11.4	10.7	78.1
Other household services	**100.0**	**4.5**	**8.6**	**7.5**	**84.0**
Housekeeping services	100.0	5.3	2.1	3.1	94.7
Gardening, lawn care service	100.0	5.1	6.8	5.7	87.5
Water-softening service	100.0	2.5	18.0	4.0	77.8
Nonclothing laundry and dry cleaning, sent out	100.0	2.1	15.7	10.7	73.7
Nonclothing laundry and dry cleaning, coin-operated	100.0	6.6	21.1	31.6	47.8
Termite and pest control services	100.0	4.0	7.5	4.4	88.1
Home security system service fee	100.0	4.7	20.7	7.1	72.3
Other home services	100.0	3.9	4.9	6.5	88.6
Termite and pest control products	100.0	4.6	7.5	5.5	86.8
Moving, storage, and freight express	100.0	2.9	8.8	3.9	87.4
Appliance repair, including at service center	100.0	2.0	8.7	5.2	86.3
Reupholstering and furniture repair	100.0	0.1	2.1	3.0	94.9
Repairs and rentals of lawn and garden equipment, hand and power tools, etc.	100.0	1.7	4.8	3.1	92.1
Appliance rental	100.0	2.4	9.1	7.1	84.0
Rental of office equipment for nonbusiness use	100.0	0.2	14.9	14.7	70.4
Repair of computer systems for nonbusiness use	100.0	2.1	8.9	13.0	78.4
Computer information services	100.0	4.6	10.3	10.3	79.6
Installation of computer	100.0	0.1	9.2	11.2	79.8
HOUSEKEEPING SUPPLIES	**100.0**	**2.6**	**8.6**	**10.8**	**80.4**
Laundry and cleaning supplies	**100.0**	**3.1**	**13.2**	**16.7**	**70.9**
Soaps and detergents	100.0	3.5	14.7	17.8	68.3
Other laundry cleaning products	100.0	2.6	11.4	15.5	74.0
Other household products	**100.0**	**2.6**	**7.1**	**9.3**	**83.2**
Cleansing and toilet tissue, paper towels, and napkins	100.0	3.2	10.7	13.9	75.4
Miscellaneous household products	100.0	2.9	6.7	8.8	84.1
Lawn and garden supplies	100.0	1.3	3.1	4.3	91.6
Postage and stationery	**100.0**	**2.3**	**7.2**	**8.2**	**84.0**
Stationery, stationery supplies, giftwrap	100.0	1.6	4.2	9.7	85.5
Postage	100.0	2.9	10.8	6.9	81.8
Delivery services	100.0	4.2	8.5	4.0	86.6
HOUSEHOLD FURNISHINGS AND EQUIPMENT	**100.0**	**3.5**	**7.7**	**9.3**	**82.9**
Household textiles	**100.0**	**2.6**	**5.9**	**8.3**	**85.4**
Bathroom linens	100.0	3.0	11.8	15.2	73.3
Bedroom linens	100.0	2.6	3.9	6.4	89.0
Kitchen and dining room linens	100.0	2.8	2.6	10.4	86.4
Curtains and draperies	100.0	1.7	8.7	8.0	83.4
Slipcovers and decorative pillows	100.0	2.8	8.7	9.6	81.6
Sewing materials for household items	100.0	2.5	1.7	2.7	95.6
Other linens	**100.0**	**3.5**	**20.7**	**13.4**	**66.0**
Furniture	100.0	4.4	10.6	10.8	78.8
Mattresses and springs	100.0	5.6	6.6	10.6	82.9
Other bedroom furniture	100.0	7.0	14.1	9.2	76.8
Sofas	100.0	3.5	12.0	12.3	75.9
Living room chairs	100.0	3.1	9.1	7.0	83.9
Living room tables	100.0	6.6	8.5	9.2	82.4

	total consumer units	Asian	black	Hispanic	non-Hispanic white and other
Kitchen and dining room furniture	100.0%	2.8%	17.8%	17.3%	65.3%
Infants' furniture	100.0	2.7	8.7	18.4	73.0
Outdoor furniture	100.0	1.0	3.0	4.8	92.2
Wall units, cabinets, and other furniture	100.0	3.4	7.6	10.9	81.5
Floor coverings	**100.0**	**2.2**	**6.0**	**4.6**	**89.7**
Floor coverings, nonpermanent	100.0	2.3	6.1	3.8	90.3
Major appliances	**100.0**	**3.3**	**9.7**	**8.2**	**82.1**
Dishwashers (built-in), garbage disposals, range hoods	100.0	4.4	4.8	2.4	92.8
Refrigerators and freezers	100.0	3.9	7.8	7.7	84.8
Washing machines	100.0	2.9	11.2	13.4	75.3
Clothes dryers	100.0	2.4	13.1	10.9	76.1
Cooking stoves, ovens	100.0	3.7	12.0	4.3	83.7
Microwave ovens	100.0	5.4	9.6	13.8	76.6
Window air conditioners	100.0	0.5	15.8	15.5	68.8
Electric floor-cleaning equipment	100.0	2.2	7.9	5.3	86.9
Sewing machines	100.0	2.5	3.0	4.2	92.7
Miscellaneous household appliances	100.0	–	4.2	–	94.5
Small appliances and miscellaneous housewares	**100.0**	**3.8**	**5.4**	**8.4**	**85.9**
Housewares	100.0	3.4	5.0	9.0	85.8
Plastic dinnerware	100.0	3.1	13.8	13.5	72.9
China and other dinnerware	100.0	3.8	7.6	5.5	86.1
Flatware	100.0	5.2	11.2	10.7	82.2
Glassware	100.0	6.6	2.7	10.3	86.7
Silver serving pieces	100.0	6.3	6.8	5.4	87.0
Other serving pieces	100.0	2.5	3.7	7.5	89.2
Nonelectric cookware	100.0	3.0	4.8	12.8	82.1
Tableware, nonelectric kitchenware	100.0	2.2	3.0	6.3	90.1
Small appliances	100.0	4.5	6.2	7.5	86.0
Small electric kitchen appliances	100.0	4.0	7.8	9.4	82.9
Portable heating and cooling equipment	100.0	5.7	2.3	2.8	93.8
Miscellaneous household equipment	**100.0**	**3.3**	**6.3**	**9.2**	**84.3**
Window coverings	100.0	5.0	11.9	7.3	80.8
Infants' equipment	100.0	5.0	9.4	13.7	76.8
Laundry and cleaning equipment	100.0	2.0	8.1	14.0	78.1
Outdoor equipment	100.0	0.5	3.0	5.9	90.2
Lamps and lighting fixtures	100.0	0.5	2.7	8.5	88.4
Household decorative items	100.0	1.4	5.3	7.3	86.6
Telephones and accessories	100.0	2.6	11.2	11.1	77.4
Lawn and garden equipment	100.0	1.5	1.3	1.6	95.9
Power tools	100.0	2.9	3.4	20.9	75.9
Office furniture for home use	100.0	3.9	8.8	11.2	81.8
Hand tools	100.0	4.1	5.6	22.0	72.7
Indoor plants and fresh flowers	100.0	2.8	5.0	7.9	87.1
Closet and storage items	100.0	0.9	3.3	6.2	89.6
Rental of furniture	100.0	0.8	13.8	25.6	60.4
Luggage	100.0	7.7	7.1	23.3	72.5
Computers and computer hardware for nonbusiness use	100.0	6.2	8.3	8.7	83.1
Portable memory	100.0	5.0	11.5	12.5	76.1
Computer software	100.0	8.6	7.3	8.8	83.9
Computer accessories	100.0	4.1	8.6	5.5	85.9
Personal digital assistants	100.0	11.7	10.6	16.4	74.3
Internet services away from home	100.0	5.3	7.4	14.3	78.4
Telephone answering devices	100.0	5.0	10.1	16.3	72.9
Business equipment for home use	100.0	6.1	8.3	8.5	83.6
Other hardware	100.0	0.3	0.6	5.7	92.6
Smoke alarms	100.0	2.5	7.7	5.6	86.5
Other household appliances	100.0	4.6	7.1	8.1	85.0
Miscellaneous household equipment and parts	100.0	3.6	8.0	9.3	82.2

Note: "Asian" and "black" include Hispanics and non-Hispanics who identify themselves as being of the respective race alone. "Hispanic" includes people of any race who identify themselves as Hispanic. "Other" includes people who identify themselves as non-Hispanic and as Alaska Native, American Indian, Asian (who are also included in the "Asian" column), or Native Hawaiian or other Pacific Islander, as well as non-Hispanics reporting more than one race. "–" means sample is too small to make a reliable estimate.
Source: Calculations by New Strategist based on the Bureau of Labor Statistics' 2011 Consumer Expenditure Survey

(average annual spending of consumer units on household services, supplies, furnishings, and equipment, by region in which consumer unit lives, 2011)

	total consumer units	Northeast	Midwest	South	West
Number of consumer units (in 000s)	122,287	22,538	27,107	44,901	27,741
Average number of persons per consumer unit	2.5	2.4	2.4	2.5	2.6
Average before-tax income of consumer units	$63,685.00	$71,733.00	$60,897.00	$58,780.00	$67,810.00
Average spending of consumer units, total	49,704.88	54,547.45	47,191.54	45,698.60	54,745.43
Housing, average spending	**16,803.03**	**19,557.15**	**14,925.78**	**14,968.44**	**19,372.69**
HOUSEHOLD SERVICES	**1,122.18**	**1,267.11**	**934.32**	**967.27**	**1,438.83**
Personal services	**398.27**	**499.07**	**333.62**	**281.56**	**568.44**
Babysitting and child care in own home	51.23	97.14	30.37	26.90	73.71
Babysitting and child care in someone else's home	26.87	29.41	29.12	21.69	30.98
Care for elderly, invalids, handicapped, etc.	67.89	59.12	68.62	16.57	157.39
Day care centers, nurseries, and preschools	251.30	311.38	205.44	216.05	304.35
Other household services	**723.92**	**768.05**	**600.70**	**685.71**	**870.39**
Housekeeping services	105.26	114.78	64.01	80.52	177.87
Gardening, lawn care service	118.65	138.27	77.07	119.81	141.46
Water-softening service	4.87	4.34	5.97	5.12	3.81
Nonclothing laundry and dry cleaning, sent out	14.71	19.88	10.39	16.02	12.61
Nonclothing laundry and dry cleaning, coin-operated	4.40	10.32	3.03	2.44	4.07
Termite and pest control services	20.61	14.38	9.33	32.07	18.17
Home security system service fee	25.65	18.98	17.87	34.47	24.40
Other home services	15.98	19.59	17.17	10.26	21.15
Termite and pest control products	3.57	2.55	1.76	5.52	3.00
Moving, storage, and freight express	52.88	37.32	39.93	49.96	82.90
Appliance repair, including at service center	16.62	16.07	17.77	15.11	18.39
Reupholstering and furniture repair	5.75	12.19	5.49	3.07	5.09
Repairs and rentals of lawn and garden equipment, hand and power tools, etc.	9.29	11.84	11.43	9.44	4.88
Appliance rental	2.01	1.88	2.15	2.24	1.61
Rental of office equipment for nonbusiness use	1.06	1.36	0.67	1.25	0.90
Repair of computer systems for nonbusiness use	6.51	8.31	7.17	4.57	7.54
Computer information services	313.76	332.18	308.11	293.55	337.04
Installation of computer	0.51	0.56	0.63	0.17	0.90
HOUSEKEEPING SUPPLIES	**614.74**	**640.74**	**644.76**	**567.06**	**642.18**
Laundry and cleaning supplies	**145.06**	**134.47**	**155.55**	**141.52**	**149.12**
Soaps and detergents	78.49	74.49	77.85	77.44	84.14
Other laundry cleaning products	66.57	59.98	77.70	64.08	64.98
Other household products	**339.58**	**384.63**	**364.95**	**311.16**	**324.19**
Cleansing and toilet tissue, paper towels, and napkins	114.81	133.38	105.67	115.48	107.62
Miscellaneous household products	134.12	143.67	148.18	116.80	140.84
Lawn and garden supplies	90.65	107.58	111.10	78.87	75.74
Postage and stationery	**130.09**	**121.65**	**124.25**	**114.38**	**168.86**
Stationery, stationery supplies, giftwrap	67.56	64.00	72.34	57.88	81.69
Postage	55.22	54.17	49.85	48.84	72.00
Delivery services	7.32	3.48	2.07	7.66	15.17
HOUSEHOLD FURNISHINGS AND EQUIPMENT	**1,513.98**	**1,520.31**	**1,451.11**	**1,426.83**	**1,714.02**
Household textiles	**109.14**	**101.83**	**98.52**	**94.77**	**149.41**
Bathroom linens	20.16	18.86	14.70	18.27	29.83
Bedroom linens	59.00	47.42	53.69	52.48	84.62
Kitchen and dining room linens	5.95	5.23	5.79	5.80	6.94
Curtains and draperies	11.30	16.35	11.72	8.93	10.62
Slipcovers and decorative pillows	3.52	6.38	2.36	3.35	2.60
Sewing materials for household items	8.07	6.86	9.52	4.96	12.69
Other linens	1.13	0.73	0.73	0.98	2.10
Furniture	**357.94**	**355.86**	**369.83**	**359.96**	**344.76**
Mattresses and springs	61.72	68.57	57.93	57.89	66.07
Other bedroom furniture	70.06	58.05	58.80	89.77	58.94
Sofas	92.81	88.51	110.04	90.24	83.64
Living room chairs	36.12	44.30	45.53	31.31	28.03
Living room tables	11.87	11.35	11.39	10.80	14.51

	total consumer units	Northeast	Midwest	South	West
Kitchen and dining room furniture	$27.45	$32.18	$28.23	$21.78	$32.03
Infants' furniture	8.23	10.35	6.94	7.88	8.34
Outdoor furniture	18.70	14.66	20.08	20.51	17.68
Wall units, cabinets, and other furniture	30.97	27.90	30.88	29.78	35.50
Floor coverings	**19.98**	**40.53**	**23.57**	**12.40**	**12.06**
Floor coverings, nonpermanent	19.61	40.52	23.55	11.86	11.33
Major appliances	**193.93**	**183.65**	**183.13**	**199.36**	**204.14**
Dishwashers (built-in), garbage disposals, range hoods	14.60	18.82	10.68	12.99	17.62
Refrigerators and freezers	52.96	45.25	57.26	51.72	57.03
Washing machines	34.00	27.66	28.91	39.57	35.10
Clothes dryers	24.93	21.43	20.77	31.19	21.73
Cooking stoves, ovens	30.51	28.37	27.47	29.15	37.41
Microwave ovens	8.96	9.14	7.52	9.74	8.95
Window air conditioners	4.82	8.97	2.95	5.78	1.76
Electric floor-cleaning equipment	16.06	17.06	16.50	16.07	14.82
Sewing machines	2.43	1.76	6.59	1.15	0.96
Miscellaneous household appliances	4.21	5.18	3.31	1.62	8.61
Small appliances and miscellaneous housewares	**89.34**	**93.30**	**87.46**	**69.75**	**120.17**
Housewares	54.84	57.73	51.47	45.82	70.73
Plastic dinnerware	2.47	3.09	1.71	2.62	2.50
China and other dinnerware	5.34	6.70	5.01	4.57	5.82
Flatware	2.96	3.56	2.74	2.26	3.84
Glassware	6.56	4.98	7.01	4.54	10.73
Silver serving pieces	1.43	1.76	1.68	0.97	1.66
Other serving pieces	1.42	1.70	1.24	1.40	1.42
Nonelectric cookware	14.94	17.48	12.10	12.58	19.62
Tableware, nonelectric kitchenware	19.71	18.44	19.98	16.89	25.14
Small appliances	34.50	35.57	35.99	23.94	49.44
Small electric kitchen appliances	24.50	24.34	22.71	21.22	31.69
Portable heating and cooling equipment	10.00	11.23	13.28	2.72	17.75
Miscellaneous household equipment	**743.64**	**745.13**	**688.60**	**690.58**	**883.49**
Window coverings	15.87	8.20	8.87	17.00	27.10
Infants' equipment	14.49	21.13	17.53	10.75	12.15
Laundry and cleaning equipment	17.33	17.20	19.66	15.74	17.74
Outdoor equipment	34.43	19.85	23.26	54.26	24.79
Lamps and lighting fixtures	29.29	31.54	31.71	16.02	46.98
Household decorative items	117.20	118.80	120.17	94.31	150.77
Telephones and accessories	45.56	39.77	37.47	50.70	49.90
Lawn and garden equipment	65.62	96.42	54.33	68.02	47.67
Power tools	38.18	21.01	33.02	36.78	59.79
Office furniture for home use	5.83	3.84	8.00	4.62	7.26
Hand tools	15.55	4.46	19.33	19.11	14.97
Indoor plants and fresh flowers	46.92	67.57	44.54	33.18	54.73
Closet and storage items	16.85	15.11	14.48	13.97	25.42
Rental of furniture	6.16	2.95	4.44	9.55	4.95
Luggage	6.84	3.61	4.62	8.34	9.21
Computers and computer hardware for nonbusiness use	152.35	162.68	134.08	134.97	189.94
Portable memory	4.17	3.28	4.86	3.48	5.31
Computer software	14.33	13.37	12.83	10.81	22.26
Computer accessories	12.15	11.62	12.59	11.28	13.56
Personal digital assistants	6.27	5.56	6.58	5.81	7.31
Internet services away from home	7.03	8.99	7.38	5.35	7.81
Telephone answering devices	0.61	0.93	0.51	0.50	0.61
Business equipment for home use	4.05	3.91	3.25	3.70	5.49
Other hardware	11.34	11.21	16.15	8.46	11.39
Smoke alarms	1.97	1.80	2.47	1.91	1.70
Other household appliances	7.96	8.02	9.58	6.12	9.32
Miscellaneous household equipment and parts	43.13	40.39	35.04	44.37	51.42

Note: Subcategories may not add to total because some are not shown.
Source: Bureau of Labor Statistics, unpublished tables from the 2011 Consumer Expenditure Survey

Table 8.22 Housing: Household Operations: Indexed spending by region, 2011

(indexed average annual spending of consumer units on household services, supplies, furnishings, and equipment, by region in which consumer unit lives, 2011; index definition: an index of 100 is the average for all consumer units; an index of 125 means that spending by consumer units in that group is 25 percent above the average for all consumer units; an index of 75 indicates spending that is 25 percent below the average for all consumer units)

	total consumer units	Northeast	Midwest	South	West
Average spending of consumer units, total	$49,705	$54,547	$47,192	$45,699	$54,745
Average spending of consumer units, index	100	110	95	92	110
Housing, spending index	**100**	**116**	**89**	**89**	**115**
HOUSEHOLD SERVICES	**100**	**113**	**83**	**86**	**128**
Personal services	**100**	**125**	**84**	**71**	**143**
Babysitting and child care in own home	100	190	59	53	144
Babysitting and child care in someone else's home	100	109	108	81	115
Care for elderly, invalids, handicapped, etc.	100	87	101	24	232
Day care centers, nurseries, and preschools	100	124	82	86	121
Other household services	**100**	**106**	**83**	**95**	**120**
Housekeeping services	100	109	61	76	169
Gardening, lawn care service	100	117	65	101	119
Water-softening service	100	89	123	105	78
Nonclothing laundry and dry cleaning, sent out	100	135	71	109	86
Nonclothing laundry and dry cleaning, coin-operated	100	235	69	55	93
Termite and pest control services	100	70	45	156	88
Home security system service fee	100	74	70	134	95
Other home services	100	123	107	64	132
Termite and pest control products	100	71	49	155	84
Moving, storage, and freight express	100	71	76	94	157
Appliance repair, including at service center	100	97	107	91	111
Reupholstering and furniture repair	100	212	95	53	89
Repairs and rentals of lawn and garden equipment, hand and power tools, etc.	100	127	123	102	53
Appliance rental	100	94	107	111	80
Rental of office equipment for nonbusiness use	100	128	63	118	85
Repair of computer systems for nonbusiness use	100	128	110	70	116
Computer information services	100	106	98	94	107
Installation of computer	100	110	124	33	176
HOUSEKEEPING SUPPLIES	**100**	**104**	**105**	**92**	**104**
Laundry and cleaning supplies	**100**	**93**	**107**	**98**	**103**
Soaps and detergents	100	95	99	99	107
Other laundry cleaning products	100	90	117	96	98
Other household products	**100**	**113**	**107**	**92**	**95**
Cleansing and toilet tissue, paper towels, and napkins	100	116	92	101	94
Miscellaneous household products	100	107	110	87	105
Lawn and garden supplies	100	119	123	87	84
Postage and stationery	**100**	**94**	**96**	**88**	**130**
Stationery, stationery supplies, giftwrap	100	95	107	86	121
Postage	100	98	90	88	130
Delivery services	100	48	28	105	207
HOUSEHOLD FURNISHINGS AND EQUIPMENT	**100**	**100**	**96**	**94**	**113**
Household textiles	**100**	**93**	**90**	**87**	**137**
Bathroom linens	100	94	73	91	148
Bedroom linens	100	80	91	89	143
Kitchen and dining room linens	100	88	97	97	117
Curtains and draperies	100	145	104	79	94
Slipcovers and decorative pillows	100	181	67	95	74
Sewing materials for household items	100	85	118	61	157
Other linens	100	65	65	87	186
Furniture	**100**	**99**	**103**	**101**	**96**
Mattresses and springs	100	111	94	94	107
Other bedroom furniture	100	83	84	128	84
Sofas	100	95	119	97	90
Living room chairs	100	123	126	87	78
Living room tables	100	96	96	91	122

	total consumer units	Northeast	Midwest	South	West
Kitchen and dining room furniture	100	117	103	79	117
Infants' furniture	100	126	84	96	101
Outdoor furniture	100	78	107	110	95
Wall units, cabinets, and other furniture	100	90	100	96	115
Floor coverings	**100**	**203**	**118**	**62**	**60**
Floor coverings, nonpermanent	100	207	120	60	58
Major appliances	**100**	**95**	**94**	**103**	**105**
Dishwashers (built-in), garbage disposals, range hoods	100	129	73	89	121
Refrigerators and freezers	100	85	108	98	108
Washing machines	100	81	85	116	103
Clothes dryers	100	86	83	125	87
Cooking stoves, ovens	100	93	90	96	123
Microwave ovens	100	102	84	109	100
Window air conditioners	100	186	61	120	37
Electric floor-cleaning equipment	100	106	103	100	92
Sewing machines	100	72	271	47	40
Miscellaneous household appliances	100	123	79	38	205
Small appliances and miscellaneous housewares	**100**	**104**	**98**	**78**	**135**
Housewares	100	105	94	84	129
Plastic dinnerware	100	125	69	106	101
China and other dinnerware	100	125	94	86	109
Flatware	100	120	93	76	130
Glassware	100	76	107	69	164
Silver serving pieces	100	123	117	68	116
Other serving pieces	100	120	87	99	100
Nonelectric cookware	100	117	81	84	131
Tableware, nonelectric kitchenware	100	94	101	86	128
Small appliances	100	103	104	69	143
Small electric kitchen appliances	100	99	93	87	129
Portable heating and cooling equipment	100	112	133	27	178
Miscellaneous household equipment	**100**	**100**	**93**	**93**	**119**
Window coverings	100	52	56	107	171
Infants' equipment	100	146	121	74	84
Laundry and cleaning equipment	100	99	113	91	102
Outdoor equipment	100	58	68	158	72
Lamps and lighting fixtures	100	108	108	55	160
Household decorative items	100	101	103	80	129
Telephones and accessories	100	87	82	111	110
Lawn and garden equipment	100	147	83	104	73
Power tools	100	55	86	96	157
Office furniture for home use	100	66	137	79	125
Hand tools	100	29	124	123	96
Indoor plants and fresh flowers	100	144	95	71	117
Closet and storage items	100	90	86	83	151
Rental of furniture	100	48	72	155	80
Luggage	100	53	68	122	135
Computers and computer hardware for nonbusiness use	100	107	88	89	125
Portable memory	100	79	117	83	127
Computer software	100	93	90	75	155
Computer accessories	100	96	104	93	112
Personal digital assistants	100	89	105	93	117
Internet services away from home	100	128	105	76	111
Telephone answering devices	100	152	84	82	100
Business equipment for home use	100	97	80	91	136
Other hardware	100	99	142	75	100
Smoke alarms	100	91	125	97	86
Other household appliances	100	101	120	77	117
Miscellaneous household equipment and parts	100	94	81	103	119

Source: Calculations by New Strategist based on the Bureau of Labor Statistics' 2011 Consumer Expenditure Survey

Table 8.23 Housing: Household Operations: Total spending by region, 2011

(total annual spending on household services, supplies, furnishings, and equipment, by region in which consumer units live, 2011; consumer units and dollars in thousands)

	total consumer units	Northeast	Midwest	South	West
Number of consumer units	122,287	22,538	27,107	44,901	27,741
Total spending of all consumer units	$6,078,260,661	$1,229,390,428	$1,279,221,075	$2,051,912,839	$1,518,692,974
Housing, total spending	2,054,792,130	440,779,047	404,593,118	672,097,924	537,417,793
HOUSEHOLD SERVICES	137,228,026	28,558,125	25,326,612	43,431,390	39,914,583
Personal services	48,703,243	11,248,040	9,043,437	12,642,326	15,769,094
Babysitting and child care in own home	6,264,763	2,189,341	823,240	1,207,837	2,044,789
Babysitting and child care in someone else's home	3,285,852	662,843	789,356	973,903	859,416
Care for elderly, invalids, handicapped, etc.	8,302,064	1,332,447	1,860,082	744,010	4,366,156
Day care centers, nurseries, and preschools	30,730,723	7,017,882	5,568,862	9,700,861	8,442,973
Other household services	88,526,005	17,310,311	16,283,175	30,789,065	24,145,489
Housekeeping services	12,871,930	2,586,912	1,735,119	3,615,429	4,934,292
Gardening, lawn care service	14,509,353	3,116,329	2,089,136	5,379,589	3,924,242
Water-softening service	595,538	97,815	161,829	229,893	105,693
Nonclothing laundry and dry cleaning, sent out	1,798,842	448,055	281,642	719,314	349,814
Nonclothing laundry and dry cleaning, coin-operated	538,063	232,592	82,134	109,558	112,906
Termite and pest control services	2,520,335	324,096	252,908	1,439,975	504,054
Home security system service fee	3,136,662	427,771	484,402	1,547,737	676,880
Other home services	1,954,146	441,519	465,427	460,684	586,722
Termite and pest control products	436,565	57,472	47,708	247,854	83,223
Moving, storage, and freight express	6,466,537	841,118	1,082,383	2,243,254	2,299,729
Appliance repair, including at service center	2,032,410	362,186	481,691	678,454	510,157
Reupholstering and furniture repair	703,150	274,738	148,817	137,846	141,202
Repairs and rentals of lawn and garden equipment, hand and power tools, etc.	1,136,046	266,850	309,833	423,865	135,376
Appliance rental	245,797	42,371	58,280	100,578	44,663
Rental of office equipment for nonbusiness use	129,624	30,652	18,162	56,126	24,967
Repair of computer systems for nonbusiness use	796,088	187,291	194,357	205,198	209,167
Computer information services	38,368,769	7,486,673	8,351,938	13,180,689	9,349,827
Installation of computer	62,366	12,621	17,077	7,633	24,967
HOUSEKEEPING SUPPLIES	75,174,710	14,440,998	17,477,509	25,461,561	17,814,715
Laundry and cleaning supplies	17,738,952	3,030,685	4,216,494	6,354,390	4,136,738
Soaps and detergents	9,598,307	1,678,856	2,110,280	3,477,133	2,334,128
Other laundry cleaning products	8,140,646	1,351,829	2,106,214	2,877,256	1,802,610
Other household products	41,526,219	8,668,791	9,892,700	13,971,395	8,993,355
Cleansing and toilet tissue, paper towels, and napkins	14,039,770	3,006,118	2,864,397	5,185,167	2,985,486
Miscellaneous household products	16,401,132	3,238,034	4,016,715	5,244,437	3,907,042
Lawn and garden supplies	11,085,317	2,424,638	3,011,588	3,541,342	2,101,103
Postage and stationery	15,908,316	2,741,748	3,368,045	5,135,776	4,684,345
Stationery, stationery supplies, giftwrap	8,261,710	1,442,432	1,960,920	2,598,870	2,266,162
Postage	6,752,688	1,220,883	1,351,284	2,192,965	1,997,352
Delivery services	895,141	78,432	56,111	343,942	420,831
HOUSEHOLD FURNISHINGS AND EQUIPMENT	185,140,072	34,264,747	39,335,239	64,066,094	47,548,629
Household textiles	13,346,403	2,295,045	2,670,582	4,255,268	4,144,783
Bathroom linens	2,465,306	425,067	398,473	820,341	827,514
Bedroom linens	7,214,933	1,068,752	1,455,375	2,356,404	2,347,443
Kitchen and dining room linens	727,608	117,874	156,950	260,426	192,523
Curtains and draperies	1,381,843	368,496	317,694	400,966	294,609
Slipcovers and decorative pillows	430,450	143,792	63,973	150,418	72,127
Sewing materials for household items	986,856	154,611	258,059	222,709	352,033
Other linens	138,184	16,453	19,788	44,003	58,256
Furniture	43,771,409	8,020,373	10,024,982	16,162,564	9,563,987
Mattresses and springs	7,547,554	1,545,431	1,570,309	2,599,319	1,832,848
Other bedroom furniture	8,567,427	1,308,331	1,593,892	4,030,763	1,635,055
Sofas	11,349,456	1,994,838	2,982,854	4,051,866	2,320,257
Living room chairs	4,417,006	998,433	1,234,182	1,405,850	777,580
Living room tables	1,451,547	255,806	308,749	484,931	402,522

	total consumer units	Northeast	Midwest	South	West
Kitchen and dining room furniture	$3,356,778	$725,273	$765,231	$977,944	$888,544
Infants' furniture	1,006,422	233,268	188,123	353,820	231,360
Outdoor furniture	2,286,767	330,407	544,309	920,920	490,461
Wall units, cabinets, and other furniture	3,787,228	628,810	837,064	1,337,152	984,806
Floor coverings	**2,443,294**	**913,465**	**638,912**	**556,772**	**334,556**
Floor coverings, nonpermanent	2,398,048	913,240	638,370	532,526	314,306
Major appliances	**23,715,118**	**4,139,104**	**4,964,105**	**8,951,463**	**5,663,048**
Dishwashers (built-in), garbage disposals, range hoods	1,785,390	424,165	289,503	583,264	488,796
Refrigerators and freezers	6,476,320	1,019,845	1,552,147	2,322,280	1,582,069
Washing machines	4,157,758	623,401	783,663	1,776,733	973,709
Clothes dryers	3,048,615	482,989	563,012	1,400,462	602,812
Cooking stoves, ovens	3,730,976	639,403	744,629	1,308,864	1,037,791
Microwave ovens	1,095,692	205,997	203,845	437,336	248,282
Window air conditioners	589,423	202,166	79,966	259,528	48,824
Electric floor-cleaning equipment	1,963,929	384,498	447,266	721,559	411,122
Sewing machines	297,157	39,667	178,635	51,636	26,631
Miscellaneous household appliances	514,828	116,747	89,724	72,740	238,850
Small appliances and miscellaneous housewares	**10,925,121**	**2,102,795**	**2,370,778**	**3,131,845**	**3,333,636**
Housewares	6,706,219	1,301,119	1,395,197	2,057,364	1,962,121
Plastic dinnerware	302,049	69,642	46,353	117,641	69,353
China and other dinnerware	653,013	151,005	135,806	205,198	161,453
Flatware	361,970	80,235	74,273	101,476	106,525
Glassware	802,203	112,239	190,020	203,851	297,661
Silver serving pieces	174,870	39,667	45,540	43,554	46,050
Other serving pieces	173,648	38,315	33,613	62,861	39,392
Nonelectric cookware	1,826,968	393,964	327,995	564,855	544,278
Tableware, nonelectric kitchenware	2,410,277	415,601	541,598	758,378	697,409
Small appliances	4,218,902	801,677	975,581	1,074,930	1,371,515
Small electric kitchen appliances	2,996,032	548,575	615,600	952,799	879,112
Portable heating and cooling equipment	1,222,870	253,102	359,981	122,131	492,403
Miscellaneous household equipment	**90,937,505**	**16,793,740**	**18,665,880**	**31,007,733**	**24,508,896**
Window coverings	1,940,695	184,812	240,439	763,317	751,781
Infants' equipment	1,771,939	476,228	475,186	482,686	337,053
Laundry and cleaning equipment	2,119,234	387,654	532,924	706,742	492,125
Outdoor equipment	4,210,341	447,379	630,509	2,436,328	687,699
Lamps and lighting fixtures	3,581,786	710,849	859,563	719,314	1,303,272
Household decorative items	14,332,036	2,677,514	3,257,448	4,234,613	4,182,511
Telephones and accessories	5,571,396	896,336	1,015,699	2,276,481	1,384,276
Lawn and garden equipment	8,024,473	2,173,114	1,472,723	3,054,166	1,322,413
Power tools	4,668,918	473,523	895,073	1,651,459	1,658,634
Office furniture for home use	712,933	86,546	216,856	207,443	201,400
Hand tools	1,901,563	100,519	523,978	858,058	415,283
Indoor plants and fresh flowers	5,737,706	1,522,893	1,207,346	1,489,815	1,518,265
Closet and storage items	2,060,536	340,549	392,509	627,267	705,176
Rental of furniture	753,288	66,487	120,355	428,805	137,318
Luggage	836,443	81,362	125,234	374,474	255,495
Computers and computer hardware for nonbusiness use	18,630,424	3,666,482	3,634,507	6,060,288	5,269,126
Portable memory	509,937	73,925	131,740	156,255	147,305
Computer software	1,752,373	301,333	347,783	485,380	617,515
Computer accessories	1,485,787	261,892	341,277	506,483	376,168
Personal digital assistants	766,739	125,311	178,364	260,875	202,787
Internet services away from home	859,678	202,617	200,050	240,220	216,657
Telephone answering devices	74,595	20,960	13,825	22,451	16,922
Business equipment for home use	495,262	88,124	88,098	166,134	152,298
Other hardware	1,386,735	252,651	437,778	379,862	315,970
Smoke alarms	240,905	40,568	66,954	85,761	47,160
Other household appliances	973,405	180,755	259,685	274,794	258,546
Miscellaneous household equipment and parts	5,274,238	910,310	949,829	1,992,257	1,426,442

Note: Numbers may not add to total because of rounding and missing subcategories.
Source: Calculations by New Strategist based on the Bureau of Labor Statistics' 2011 Consumer Expenditure Survey

Table 8.24 Housing: Household Operations: Market shares by region, 2011

(percentage of total annual spending on household services, supplies, furnishings, and equipment accounted for by consumer units by region of residence, 2011)

	total consumer units	Northeast	Midwest	South	West
Share of total consumer units	100.0%	18.4%	22.2%	36.7%	22.7%
Share of total before-tax income	100.0	20.8	21.2	33.9	24.2
Share of total spending	100.0	20.2	21.0	33.8	25.0
Share of housing spending	100.0	21.5	19.7	32.7	26.2
HOUSEHOLD SERVICES	**100.0**	**20.8**	**18.5**	**31.6**	**29.1**
Personal services	**100.0**	**23.1**	**18.6**	**26.0**	**32.4**
Babysitting and child care in own home	100.0	34.9	13.1	19.3	32.6
Babysitting and child care in someone else's home	100.0	20.2	24.0	29.6	26.2
Care for elderly, invalids, handicapped, etc.	100.0	16.0	22.4	9.0	52.6
Day care centers, nurseries, and preschools	100.0	22.8	18.1	31.6	27.5
Other household services	**100.0**	**19.6**	**18.4**	**34.8**	**27.3**
Housekeeping services	100.0	20.1	13.5	28.1	38.3
Gardening, lawn care service	100.0	21.5	14.4	37.1	27.0
Water-softening service	100.0	16.4	27.2	38.6	17.7
Nonclothing laundry and dry cleaning, sent out	100.0	24.9	15.7	40.0	19.4
Nonclothing laundry and dry cleaning, coin-operated	100.0	43.2	15.3	20.4	21.0
Termite and pest control services	100.0	12.9	10.0	57.1	20.0
Home security system service fee	100.0	13.6	15.4	49.3	21.6
Other home services	100.0	22.6	23.8	23.6	30.0
Termite and pest control products	100.0	13.2	10.9	56.8	19.1
Moving, storage, and freight express	100.0	13.0	16.7	34.7	35.6
Appliance repair, including at service center	100.0	17.8	23.7	33.4	25.1
Reupholstering and furniture repair	100.0	39.1	21.2	19.6	20.1
Repairs and rentals of lawn and garden equipment, hand and power tools, etc.	100.0	23.5	27.3	37.3	11.9
Appliance rental	100.0	17.2	23.7	40.9	18.2
Rental of office equipment for nonbusiness use	100.0	23.6	14.0	43.3	19.3
Repair of computer systems for nonbusiness use	100.0	23.5	24.4	25.8	26.3
Computer information services	100.0	19.5	21.8	34.4	24.4
Installation of computer	100.0	20.2	27.4	12.2	40.0
HOUSEKEEPING SUPPLIES	**100.0**	**19.2**	**23.2**	**33.9**	**23.7**
Laundry and cleaning supplies	**100.0**	**17.1**	**23.8**	**35.8**	**23.3**
Soaps and detergents	100.0	17.5	22.0	36.2	24.3
Other laundry cleaning products	100.0	16.6	25.9	35.3	22.1
Other household products	**100.0**	**20.9**	**23.8**	**33.6**	**21.7**
Cleansing and toilet tissue, paper towels, and napkins	100.0	21.4	20.4	36.9	21.3
Miscellaneous household products	100.0	19.7	24.5	32.0	23.8
Lawn and garden supplies	100.0	21.9	27.2	31.9	19.0
Postage and stationery	**100.0**	**17.2**	**21.2**	**32.3**	**29.4**
Stationery, stationery supplies, giftwrap	100.0	17.5	23.7	31.5	27.4
Postage	100.0	18.1	20.0	32.5	29.6
Delivery services	100.0	8.8	6.3	38.4	47.0
HOUSEHOLD FURNISHINGS AND EQUIPMENT	**100.0**	**18.5**	**21.2**	**34.6**	**25.7**
Household textiles	**100.0**	**17.2**	**20.0**	**31.9**	**31.1**
Bathroom linens	100.0	17.2	16.2	33.3	33.6
Bedroom linens	100.0	14.8	20.2	32.7	32.5
Kitchen and dining room linens	100.0	16.2	21.6	35.8	26.5
Curtains and draperies	100.0	26.7	23.0	29.0	21.3
Slipcovers and decorative pillows	100.0	33.4	14.9	34.9	16.8
Sewing materials for household items	100.0	15.7	26.1	22.6	35.7
Other linens	100.0	11.9	14.3	31.8	42.2
Furniture	**100.0**	**18.3**	**22.9**	**36.9**	**21.8**
Mattresses and springs	100.0	20.5	20.8	34.4	24.3
Other bedroom furniture	100.0	15.3	18.6	47.0	19.1
Sofas	100.0	17.6	26.3	35.7	20.4
Living room chairs	100.0	22.6	27.9	31.8	17.6
Living room tables	100.0	17.6	21.3	33.4	27.7

	total consumer units	Northeast	Midwest	South	West
Kitchen and dining room furniture	100.0%	21.6%	22.8%	29.1%	26.5%
Infants' furniture	100.0	23.2	18.7	35.2	23.0
Outdoor furniture	100.0	14.4	23.8	40.3	21.4
Wall units, cabinets, and other furniture	100.0	16.6	22.1	35.3	26.0
Floor coverings	**100.0**	**37.4**	**26.1**	**22.8**	**13.7**
Floor coverings, nonpermanent	100.0	38.1	26.6	22.2	13.1
Major appliances	**100.0**	**17.5**	**20.9**	**37.7**	**23.9**
Dishwashers (built-in), garbage disposals, range hoods	100.0	23.8	16.2	32.7	27.4
Refrigerators and freezers	100.0	15.7	24.0	35.9	24.4
Washing machines	100.0	15.0	18.8	42.7	23.4
Clothes dryers	100.0	15.8	18.5	45.9	19.8
Cooking stoves, ovens	100.0	17.1	20.0	35.1	27.8
Microwave ovens	100.0	18.8	18.6	39.9	22.7
Window air conditioners	100.0	34.3	13.6	44.0	8.3
Electric floor-cleaning equipment	100.0	19.6	22.8	36.7	20.9
Sewing machines	100.0	13.3	60.1	17.4	9.0
Miscellaneous household appliances	100.0	22.7	17.4	14.1	46.4
Small appliances and miscellaneous housewares	**100.0**	**19.2**	**21.7**	**28.7**	**30.5**
Housewares	100.0	19.4	20.8	30.7	29.3
Plastic dinnerware	100.0	23.1	15.3	38.9	23.0
China and other dinnerware	100.0	23.1	20.8	31.4	24.7
Flatware	100.0	22.2	20.5	28.0	29.4
Glassware	100.0	14.0	23.7	25.4	37.1
Silver serving pieces	100.0	22.7	26.0	24.9	26.3
Other serving pieces	100.0	22.1	19.4	36.2	22.7
Nonelectric cookware	100.0	21.6	18.0	30.9	29.8
Tableware, nonelectric kitchenware	100.0	17.2	22.5	31.5	28.9
Small appliances	100.0	19.0	23.1	25.5	32.5
Small electric kitchen appliances	100.0	18.3	20.5	31.8	29.3
Portable heating and cooling equipment	100.0	20.7	29.4	10.0	40.3
Miscellaneous household equipment	**100.0**	**18.5**	**20.5**	**34.1**	**27.0**
Window coverings	100.0	9.5	12.4	39.3	38.7
Infants' equipment	100.0	26.9	26.8	27.2	19.0
Laundry and cleaning equipment	100.0	18.3	25.1	33.3	23.2
Outdoor equipment	100.0	10.6	15.0	57.9	16.3
Lamps and lighting fixtures	100.0	19.8	24.0	20.1	36.4
Household decorative items	100.0	18.7	22.7	29.5	29.2
Telephones and accessories	100.0	16.1	18.2	40.9	24.8
Lawn and garden equipment	100.0	27.1	18.4	38.1	16.5
Power tools	100.0	10.1	19.2	35.4	35.5
Office furniture for home use	100.0	12.1	30.4	29.1	28.2
Hand tools	100.0	5.3	27.6	45.1	21.8
Indoor plants and fresh flowers	100.0	26.5	21.0	26.0	26.5
Closet and storage items	100.0	16.5	19.0	30.4	34.2
Rental of furniture	100.0	8.8	16.0	56.9	18.2
Luggage	100.0	9.7	15.0	44.8	30.5
Computers and computer hardware for nonbusiness use	100.0	19.7	19.5	32.5	28.3
Portable memory	100.0	14.5	25.8	30.6	28.9
Computer software	100.0	17.2	19.8	27.7	35.2
Computer accessories	100.0	17.6	23.0	34.1	25.3
Personal digital assistants	100.0	16.3	23.3	34.0	26.4
Internet services away from home	100.0	23.6	23.3	27.9	25.2
Telephone answering devices	100.0	28.1	18.5	30.1	22.7
Business equipment for home use	100.0	17.8	17.8	33.5	30.8
Other hardware	100.0	18.2	31.6	27.4	22.8
Smoke alarms	100.0	16.8	27.8	35.6	19.6
Other household appliances	100.0	18.6	26.7	28.2	26.6
Miscellaneous household equipment and parts	100.0	17.3	18.0	37.8	27.0

Note: Numbers may not add to total because of rounding.
Source: Calculations by New Strategist based on the Bureau of Labor Statistics' 2011 Consumer Expenditure Survey

Table 8.25 Housing: Household Operations: Average spending by education, 2011

(average annual spending of consumer units on household services, supplies, furnishings, and equipment, by education of consumer unit reference person, 2011)

	total consumer units	less than high school graduate	high school graduate	some college	associate's degree	bachelor's degree or more total	bachelor's degree	graduate degree
Number of consumer units (in 000s)	122,287	16,146	30,810	25,361	12,912	37,058	23,578	13,480
Average number of persons per consumer unit	2.5	2.8	2.5	2.3	2.6	2.5	2.5	2.4
Average before-tax income of consumer units	$63,685.00	$32,564.00	$46,370.00	$52,965.00	$63,664.00	$98,983.00	$90,962.00	$113,013.00
Average spending of consumer units, total	49,704.88	29,950.97	39,704.28	45,355.33	50,819.44	68,902.95	65,051.01	75,731.40
Housing, average spending	**16,803.03**	**10,842.52**	**13,570.62**	**15,258.75**	**16,744.07**	**23,122.85**	**21,702.15**	**25,620.91**
HOUSEHOLD SERVICES	**1,122.18**	**432.49**	**713.98**	**1,005.72**	**1,068.87**	**1,859.09**	**1,654.20**	**2,217.49**
Personal services	**398.27**	**141.22**	**201.08**	**336.65**	**357.17**	**730.69**	**624.25**	**916.87**
Babysitting and child care in own home	51.23	17.43	16.00	21.83	26.55	123.98	65.05	227.06
Babysitting and child care in someone else's home	26.87	28.14	18.77	22.18	17.38	39.56	31.48	53.69
Care for elderly, invalids, handicapped, etc.	67.89	41.80	54.59	104.94	13.00	84.09	74.07	101.62
Day care centers, nurseries, and preschools	251.30	53.67	110.27	187.35	300.25	481.37	452.92	531.13
Other household services	**723.92**	**291.26**	**512.90**	**669.08**	**711.70**	**1,128.40**	**1,029.95**	**1,300.62**
Housekeeping services	105.26	26.56	32.74	82.01	57.48	232.40	186.28	313.08
Gardening, lawn care service	118.65	33.72	76.98	89.06	85.57	222.07	205.95	250.28
Water-softening service	4.87	2.84	5.27	3.68	6.18	5.77	6.33	4.81
Nonclothing laundry and dry cleaning, sent out	14.71	4.93	8.96	13.52	9.13	25.40	23.56	29.01
Nonclothing laundry and dry cleaning, coin-operated	4.40	8.07	4.02	3.90	4.10	3.55	3.75	3.22
Termite and pest control services	20.61	6.94	11.69	18.59	21.19	35.17	28.52	46.82
Home security system service fee	25.65	11.79	17.65	21.45	28.14	40.36	36.24	47.58
Other home services	15.98	10.46	8.77	11.62	15.91	27.39	22.53	35.89
Termite and pest control products	3.57	1.52	1.84	3.08	3.83	6.13	4.59	8.83
Moving, storage, and freight express	52.88	16.62	40.63	57.29	73.40	68.69	60.09	83.72
Appliance repair, including at service center	16.62	8.13	11.49	16.39	17.32	24.50	22.74	27.57
Reupholstering and furniture repair	5.75	1.26	1.82	8.85	3.58	9.60	6.35	15.28
Repairs and rentals of lawn and garden equipment, hand and power tools, etc.	9.29	4.13	12.18	8.20	8.05	10.31	8.14	14.11
Appliance rental	2.01	1.27	4.35	1.45	2.27	0.68	0.60	0.82
Rental of office equipment for nonbusiness use	1.06	0.92	1.02	0.64	1.08	1.44	1.62	1.12
Repair of computer systems for nonbusiness use	6.51	1.58	3.96	7.09	9.42	9.36	10.78	6.87
Computer information services	313.76	150.35	269.33	321.59	358.72	400.88	395.72	409.91
Installation of computer	0.51	0.17	0.16	0.66	0.49	0.85	0.56	1.34
HOUSEKEEPING SUPPLIES	**614.74**	**429.20**	**535.98**	**550.54**	**692.34**	**762.17**	**745.64**	**794.55**
Laundry and cleaning supplies	**145.06**	**142.35**	**144.30**	**133.90**	**167.88**	**146.58**	**147.62**	**144.53**
Soaps and detergents	78.49	87.14	77.65	71.83	90.10	76.53	78.64	72.39
Other laundry cleaning products	66.57	55.21	66.65	62.07	77.78	70.05	68.99	72.15
Other household products	**339.58**	**211.23**	**293.90**	**308.75**	**390.86**	**426.64**	**427.31**	**425.34**
Cleansing and toilet tissue, paper towels, and napkins	114.81	105.88	111.67	106.13	136.14	119.39	119.03	120.09
Miscellaneous household products	134.12	72.02	114.71	113.67	173.00	173.20	172.94	173.70
Lawn and garden supplies	90.65	33.33	67.52	88.95	81.73	134.06	135.34	131.55
Postage and stationery	**130.09**	**75.62**	**97.78**	**107.89**	**133.60**	**188.95**	**170.71**	**224.67**
Stationery, stationery supplies, giftwrap	67.56	32.69	51.49	55.50	70.86	99.87	93.51	112.32
Postage	55.22	39.61	43.00	49.17	54.30	74.82	71.98	80.38
Delivery services	7.32	3.32	3.29	3.22	8.44	14.26	–	–
HOUSEHOLD FURNISHINGS AND EQUIPMENT	**1,513.98**	**669.47**	**1,114.40**	**1,431.14**	**1,733.71**	**2,169.35**	**1,965.70**	**2,535.09**
Household textiles	**109.14**	**66.86**	**78.17**	**98.89**	**91.51**	**162.74**	**140.30**	**206.49**
Bathroom linens	20.16	14.11	13.38	16.98	25.33	28.14	27.80	28.82
Bedroom linens	59.00	39.76	42.93	54.66	37.66	88.41	69.72	125.02
Kitchen and dining room linens	5.95	2.28	5.72	4.46	5.35	8.65	6.24	13.37
Curtains and draperies	11.30	4.42	7.13	10.45	8.69	19.26	18.90	19.89
Slipcovers and decorative pillows	3.52	1.65	2.49	4.19	2.35	5.14	5.08	5.23
Sewing materials for household items	8.07	3.91	6.10	7.21	9.69	11.56	11.16	12.26
Other linens	1.13	0.74	0.42	0.93	2.43	1.58	1.39	1.90
Furniture	**357.94**	**167.36**	**270.18**	**318.87**	**395.96**	**527.44**	**471.16**	**625.88**
Mattresses and springs	61.72	21.65	53.04	65.93	58.52	84.65	85.24	83.60
Other bedroom furniture	70.06	36.89	46.98	62.71	81.49	104.76	94.24	123.17
Sofas	92.81	55.92	70.57	77.44	98.58	135.88	120.14	163.42
Living room chairs	36.12	21.29	33.13	26.16	32.44	53.15	40.81	74.74
Living room tables	11.87	2.91	7.90	8.04	11.12	21.98	18.31	28.39

	total consumer units	less than high school graduate	high school graduate	some college	associate's degree	bachelor's degree or more total	bachelor's degree	graduate degree
Kitchen and dining room furniture	$27.45	$12.45	$21.63	$22.04	$31.74	$41.04	$35.18	$51.29
Infants' furniture	8.23	4.87	7.91	7.07	7.37	11.06	10.19	12.58
Outdoor furniture	18.70	3.09	7.74	15.08	43.24	28.53	21.03	41.65
Wall units, cabinets, and other furniture	30.97	8.29	21.28	34.40	31.45	46.40	46.03	47.04
Floor coverings	**19.98**	**4.98**	**11.28**	**8.24**	**10.00**	**45.28**	**33.33**	**66.19**
Floor coverings, nonpermanent	19.61	3.72	10.46	8.24	10.00	45.28	33.33	66.19
Major appliances	**193.93**	**101.65**	**145.33**	**208.62**	**254.81**	**242.83**	**198.96**	**319.92**
Dishwashers (built-in), garbage disposals, range hoods	14.60	3.36	6.69	12.05	17.01	27.00	17.95	42.82
Refrigerators and freezers	52.96	26.03	42.69	68.99	70.07	56.31	45.98	74.38
Washing machines	34.00	21.49	25.84	29.46	58.71	40.71	34.24	52.01
Clothes dryers	24.93	16.33	19.20	24.44	40.61	28.32	26.28	31.88
Cooking stoves, ovens	30.51	15.17	23.58	30.16	32.26	42.58	31.71	61.57
Microwave ovens	8.96	6.15	7.14	10.12	8.43	11.08	9.83	13.28
Window air conditioners	4.82	5.13	4.82	5.46	3.28	4.82	6.48	1.90
Electric floor-cleaning equipment	16.06	6.98	12.13	19.61	22.51	18.62	17.90	19.88
Sewing machines	2.43	1.01	1.18	1.95	0.78	4.98	1.94	10.29
Miscellaneous household appliances	4.21	–	1.02	5.74	1.17	8.28	6.58	11.61
Small appliances and miscellaneous housewares	**89.34**	**36.84**	**67.44**	**83.33**	**88.18**	**131.66**	**124.76**	**144.37**
Housewares	54.84	24.05	39.97	48.70	55.08	82.16	73.28	99.35
Plastic dinnerware	2.47	1.46	2.23	2.59	3.03	2.85	3.01	2.56
China and other dinnerware	5.34	1.55	3.27	3.71	7.28	8.80	7.33	11.68
Flatware	2.96	1.12	2.30	2.09	3.56	4.71	4.05	5.87
Glassware	6.56	3.88	2.67	6.34	4.92	11.27	11.10	11.61
Silver serving pieces	1.43	0.38	1.14	1.46	1.42	2.03	1.81	2.45
Other serving pieces	1.42	0.50	0.75	1.01	1.86	2.52	2.01	3.41
Nonelectric cookware	14.94	4.94	12.63	16.10	9.88	21.35	19.13	25.70
Tableware, nonelectric kitchenware	19.71	10.21	14.97	15.41	23.14	28.63	24.84	36.07
Small appliances	34.50	12.80	27.47	34.64	33.10	49.49	51.48	45.02
Small electric kitchen appliances	24.50	10.95	17.98	25.36	27.52	34.18	31.42	39.02
Portable heating and cooling equipment	10.00	1.84	9.49	9.27	5.58	15.31	20.07	6.00
Miscellaneous household equipment	**743.64**	**291.78**	**542.00**	**713.19**	**893.25**	**1,059.40**	**997.19**	**1,172.24**
Window coverings	15.87	2.67	7.07	11.79	12.28	32.97	18.10	58.99
Infants' equipment	14.49	9.85	10.85	13.41	29.33	15.02	12.02	20.89
Laundry and cleaning equipment	17.33	9.20	16.12	17.92	18.21	20.64	19.83	22.23
Outdoor equipment	34.43	16.21	57.91	24.33	24.91	32.27	22.38	51.65
Lamps and lighting fixtures	29.29	12.09	12.73	37.20	42.34	39.42	46.62	25.34
Household decorative items	117.20	38.57	78.23	91.48	165.14	178.31	171.47	191.72
Telephones and accessories	45.56	15.76	59.67	37.42	62.07	45.47	51.42	33.83
Lawn and garden equipment	65.62	21.96	16.74	61.28	98.98	112.44	118.44	100.67
Power tools	38.18	10.85	21.84	85.35	47.26	27.81	24.30	34.70
Office furniture for home use	5.83	1.14	2.58	7.00	4.97	10.06	8.97	11.97
Hand tools	15.55	3.56	10.70	31.89	13.57	13.88	9.51	22.43
Indoor plants and fresh flowers	46.92	17.63	36.24	38.32	49.00	73.74	66.99	85.53
Closet and storage items	16.85	10.79	12.12	13.28	14.57	25.85	27.30	23.01
Rental of furniture	6.16	4.93	10.22	2.47	9.20	4.78	0.65	11.99
Luggage	6.84	3.03	4.18	1.54	15.94	10.85	11.20	10.17
Computers and computer hardware for nonbusiness use	152.35	45.92	93.21	148.52	148.87	251.72	245.22	263.09
Portable memory	4.17	1.54	2.59	3.80	5.25	6.49	6.05	7.27
Computer software	14.33	4.39	5.69	10.06	23.29	25.64	20.02	35.49
Computer accessories	12.15	2.88	7.43	10.51	15.62	20.02	18.25	23.12
Personal digital assistants	6.27	2.25	3.65	4.25	5.11	12.00	11.21	13.38
Internet services away from home	7.03	4.05	6.87	6.88	6.85	8.62	8.80	8.30
Telephone answering devices	0.61	0.41	0.49	0.83	0.50	0.68	0.76	0.54
Business equipment for home use	4.05	1.86	2.68	4.20	4.06	6.03	6.18	5.75
Other hardware	11.34	3.77	11.15	7.26	10.31	17.26	11.22	29.08
Smoke alarms	1.97	1.11	1.80	1.46	4.26	2.03	1.69	2.62
Other household appliances	7.96	2.28	9.21	4.44	8.47	11.64	11.00	12.76
Miscellaneous household equipment and parts	43.13	42.56	39.22	33.44	48.22	51.05	45.37	62.18

Note: Subcategories may not add to total because some are not shown. "–" means sample is too small to make a reliable estimate.
Source: Bureau of Labor Statistics, unpublished tables from the 2011 Consumer Expenditure Survey

Table 8.26 Housing: Household Operations: Indexed spending by education, 2011

(indexed average annual spending of consumer units on household services, supplies, furnishings, and equipment, by education of consumer unit reference person, 2011; index definition: an index of 100 is the average for all consumer units; an index of 125 means that spending by consumer units in that group is 25 percent above the average for all consumer units; an index of 75 indicates spending that is 25 percent below the average for all consumer units)

	total consumer units	less than high school graduate	high school graduate	some college	associate's degree	bachelor's degree or more total	bachelor's degree	graduate degree
Average spending of consumer units, total	$49,705	$29,951	$39,704	$45,355	$50,819	$68,903	$65,051	$75,731
Average spending of consumer units, index	100	60	80	91	102	139	131	152
Housing, spending index	100	65	81	91	100	138	129	152
HOUSEHOLD SERVICES	100	39	64	90	95	166	147	198
Personal services	100	35	50	85	90	183	157	230
Babysitting and child care in own home	100	34	31	43	52	242	127	443
Babysitting and child care in someone else's home	100	105	70	83	65	147	117	200
Care for elderly, invalids, handicapped, etc.	100	62	80	155	19	124	109	150
Day care centers, nurseries, and preschools	100	21	44	75	119	192	180	211
Other household services	100	40	71	92	98	156	142	180
Housekeeping services	100	25	31	78	55	221	177	297
Gardening, lawn care service	100	28	65	75	72	187	174	211
Water-softening service	100	58	108	76	127	118	130	99
Nonclothing laundry and dry cleaning, sent out	100	34	61	92	62	173	160	197
Nonclothing laundry and dry cleaning, coin-operated	100	183	91	89	93	81	85	73
Termite and pest control services	100	34	57	90	103	171	138	227
Home security system service fee	100	46	69	84	110	157	141	185
Other home services	100	65	55	73	100	171	141	225
Termite and pest control products	100	43	52	86	107	172	129	247
Moving, storage, and freight express	100	31	77	108	139	130	114	158
Appliance repair, including at service center	100	49	69	99	104	147	137	166
Reupholstering and furniture repair	100	22	32	154	62	167	110	266
Repairs and rentals of lawn and garden equipment, hand and power tools, etc.	100	44	131	88	87	111	88	152
Appliance rental	100	63	216	72	113	34	30	41
Rental of office equipment for nonbusiness use	100	87	96	60	102	136	153	106
Repair of computer systems for nonbusiness use	100	24	61	109	145	144	166	106
Computer information services	100	48	86	102	114	128	126	131
Installation of computer	100	33	31	129	96	167	110	263
HOUSEKEEPING SUPPLIES	100	70	87	90	113	124	121	129
Laundry and cleaning supplies	100	98	99	92	116	101	102	100
Soaps and detergents	100	111	99	92	115	98	100	92
Other laundry cleaning products	100	83	100	93	117	105	104	108
Other household products	100	62	87	91	115	126	126	125
Cleansing and toilet tissue, paper towels, and napkins	100	92	97	92	119	104	104	105
Miscellaneous household products	100	54	86	85	129	129	129	130
Lawn and garden supplies	100	37	74	98	90	148	149	145
Postage and stationery	100	58	75	83	103	145	131	173
Stationery, stationery supplies, giftwrap	100	48	76	82	105	148	138	166
Postage	100	72	78	89	98	135	130	146
Delivery services	100	45	45	44	115	195	–	–
HOUSEHOLD FURNISHINGS AND EQUIPMENT	100	44	74	95	115	143	130	167
Household textiles	100	61	72	91	84	149	129	189
Bathroom linens	100	70	66	84	126	140	138	143
Bedroom linens	100	67	73	93	64	150	118	212
Kitchen and dining room linens	100	38	96	75	90	145	105	225
Curtains and draperies	100	39	63	92	77	170	167	176
Slipcovers and decorative pillows	100	47	71	119	67	146	144	149
Sewing materials for household items	100	48	76	89	120	143	138	152
Other linens	100	65	37	82	215	140	123	168
Furniture	100	47	75	89	111	147	132	175
Mattresses and springs	100	35	86	107	95	137	138	135
Other bedroom furniture	100	53	67	90	116	150	135	176
Sofas	100	60	76	83	106	146	129	176
Living room chairs	100	59	92	72	90	147	113	207
Living room tables	100	25	67	68	94	185	154	239

	total consumer units	less than high school graduate	high school graduate	some college	associate's degree	bachelor's degree or more total	bachelor's degree	graduate degree
Kitchen and dining room furniture	100	45	79	80	116	150	128	187
Infants' furniture	100	59	96	86	90	134	124	153
Outdoor furniture	100	17	41	81	231	153	112	223
Wall units, cabinets, and other furniture	100	27	69	111	102	150	149	152
Floor coverings	**100**	**25**	**56**	**41**	**50**	**227**	**167**	**331**
Floor coverings, nonpermanent	100	19	53	42	51	231	170	338
Major appliances	**100**	**52**	**75**	**108**	**131**	**125**	**103**	**165**
Dishwashers (built-in), garbage disposals, range hoods	100	23	46	83	117	185	123	293
Refrigerators and freezers	100	49	81	130	132	106	87	140
Washing machines	100	63	76	87	173	120	101	153
Clothes dryers	100	66	77	98	163	114	105	128
Cooking stoves, ovens	100	50	77	99	106	140	104	202
Microwave ovens	100	69	80	113	94	124	110	148
Window air conditioners	100	106	100	113	68	100	134	39
Electric floor-cleaning equipment	100	43	76	122	140	116	111	124
Sewing machines	100	42	49	80	32	205	80	423
Miscellaneous household appliances	100	–	24	136	28	197	156	276
Small appliances and miscellaneous housewares	**100**	**41**	**75**	**93**	**99**	**147**	**140**	**162**
Housewares	100	44	73	89	100	150	134	181
Plastic dinnerware	100	59	90	105	123	115	122	104
China and other dinnerware	100	29	61	69	136	165	137	219
Flatware	100	38	78	71	120	159	137	198
Glassware	100	59	41	97	75	172	169	177
Silver serving pieces	100	27	80	102	99	142	127	171
Other serving pieces	100	35	53	71	131	177	142	240
Nonelectric cookware	100	33	85	108	66	143	128	172
Tableware, nonelectric kitchenware	100	52	76	78	117	145	126	183
Small appliances	100	37	80	100	96	143	149	130
Small electric kitchen appliances	100	45	73	104	112	140	128	159
Portable heating and cooling equipment	100	18	95	93	56	153	201	60
Miscellaneous household equipment	**100**	**39**	**73**	**96**	**120**	**142**	**134**	**158**
Window coverings	100	17	45	74	77	208	114	372
Infants' equipment	100	68	75	93	202	104	83	144
Laundry and cleaning equipment	100	53	93	103	105	119	114	128
Outdoor equipment	100	47	168	71	72	94	65	150
Lamps and lighting fixtures	100	41	43	127	145	135	159	87
Household decorative items	100	33	67	78	141	152	146	164
Telephones and accessories	100	35	131	82	136	100	113	74
Lawn and garden equipment	100	33	26	93	151	171	180	153
Power tools	100	28	57	224	124	73	64	91
Office furniture for home use	100	20	44	120	85	173	154	205
Hand tools	100	23	69	205	87	89	61	144
Indoor plants and fresh flowers	100	38	77	82	104	157	143	182
Closet and storage items	100	64	72	79	86	153	162	137
Rental of furniture	100	80	166	40	149	78	11	195
Luggage	100	44	61	23	233	159	164	149
Computers and computer hardware for nonbusiness use	100	30	61	97	98	165	161	173
Portable memory	100	37	62	91	126	156	145	174
Computer software	100	31	40	70	163	179	140	248
Computer accessories	100	24	61	87	129	165	150	190
Personal digital assistants	100	36	58	68	81	191	179	213
Internet services away from home	100	58	98	98	97	123	125	118
Telephone answering devices	100	67	80	136	82	111	125	89
Business equipment for home use	100	46	66	104	100	149	153	142
Other hardware	100	33	98	64	91	152	99	256
Smoke alarms	100	56	91	74	216	103	86	133
Other household appliances	100	29	116	56	106	146	138	160
Miscellaneous household equipment and parts	100	99	91	78	112	118	105	144

Note: "–" means sample is too small to make a reliable estimate.
Source: Calculations by New Strategist based on the Bureau of Labor Statistics' 2011 Consumer Expenditure Survey

Table 8.27 Housing: Household Operations: Total spending by education, 2011

(total annual spending on household services, supplies, furnishings, and equipment, by consumer unit educational attainment group, 2011; consumer units and dollars in thousands)

	total consumer units	less than high school graduate	high school graduate	some college	associate's degree	bachelor's degree or more total	bachelor's degree	graduate degree
Number of consumer units	122,287	16,146	30,810	25,361	12,912	37,058	23,578	13,480
Total spending of all consumer units	$6,078,260,661	$483,588,362	$1,223,288,867	$1,150,256,524	$656,180,609	$2,553,405,521	$1,533,772,714	$1,020,859,272
Housing, total spending	2,054,792,130	175,063,328	418,110,802	386,977,159	216,199,432	856,886,575	511,693,293	345,369,867
HOUSEHOLD SERVICES	137,228,026	6,982,984	21,997,724	25,506,065	13,801,249	68,894,157	39,002,728	29,891,765
Personal services	48,703,243	2,280,138	6,195,275	8,537,781	4,611,779	27,077,910	14,718,567	12,359,408
Babysitting and child care in own home	6,264,763	281,425	492,960	553,631	342,814	4,594,451	1,533,749	3,060,769
Babysitting and child care in someone else's home	3,285,852	454,348	578,304	562,507	224,411	1,466,014	742,235	723,741
Care for elderly, invalids, handicapped, etc.	8,302,064	674,903	1,681,918	2,661,383	167,856	3,116,207	1,746,422	1,369,838
Day care centers, nurseries, and preschools	30,730,723	866,556	3,397,419	4,751,383	3,876,828	17,838,609	10,678,948	7,159,632
Other household services	88,526,005	4,702,684	15,802,449	16,968,538	9,189,470	41,816,247	24,284,161	17,532,358
Housekeeping services	12,871,930	428,838	1,008,719	2,079,856	742,182	8,612,279	4,392,110	4,220,318
Gardening, lawn care service	14,509,353	544,443	2,371,754	2,258,651	1,104,880	8,229,470	4,855,889	3,373,774
Water-softening service	595,538	45,855	162,369	93,328	79,796	213,825	149,249	64,839
Nonclothing laundry and dry cleaning, sent out	1,798,842	79,600	276,058	342,881	117,887	941,273	555,498	391,055
Nonclothing laundry and dry cleaning, coin-operated	538,063	130,298	123,856	98,908	52,939	131,556	88,418	43,406
Termite and pest control services	2,520,335	112,053	360,169	471,461	273,605	1,303,330	672,445	631,134
Home security system service fee	3,136,662	190,361	543,797	543,993	363,344	1,495,661	854,467	641,378
Other home services	1,954,146	168,887	270,204	294,695	205,430	1,015,019	531,212	483,797
Termite and pest control products	436,565	24,542	56,690	78,112	49,453	227,166	108,223	119,028
Moving, storage, and freight express	6,466,537	268,347	1,251,810	1,452,932	947,741	2,545,514	1,416,802	1,128,546
Appliance repair, including at service center	2,032,410	131,267	354,007	415,667	223,636	907,921	536,164	371,644
Reupholstering and furniture repair	703,150	20,344	56,074	224,445	46,225	355,757	149,720	205,974
Repairs and rentals of lawn and garden equipment, hand and power tools, etc.	1,136,046	66,683	375,266	207,960	103,942	382,068	191,925	190,203
Appliance rental	245,797	20,505	134,024	36,773	29,310	25,199	14,147	11,054
Rental of office equipment for nonbusiness use	129,624	14,854	31,426	16,231	13,945	53,364	38,196	15,098
Repair of computer systems for nonbusiness use	796,088	25,511	122,008	179,809	121,631	346,863	254,171	92,608
Computer information services	38,368,769	2,427,551	8,298,057	8,155,844	4,631,793	14,855,811	9,330,286	5,525,587
Installation of computer	62,366	2,745	4,930	16,738	6,327	31,499	13,204	18,063
HOUSEKEEPING SUPPLIES	75,174,710	6,929,863	16,513,544	13,962,245	8,939,494	28,244,496	17,580,700	10,710,534
Laundry and cleaning supplies	17,738,952	2,298,383	4,445,883	3,395,838	2,167,667	5,431,962	3,480,584	1,948,264
Soaps and detergents	9,598,307	1,406,962	2,392,397	1,821,681	1,163,371	2,836,049	1,854,174	975,817
Other laundry cleaning products	8,140,646	891,421	2,053,487	1,574,157	1,004,295	2,595,913	1,626,646	972,582
Other household products	41,526,219	3,410,520	9,055,059	7,830,209	5,046,784	15,810,425	10,075,115	5,733,583
Cleansing and toilet tissue, paper towels, and napkins	14,039,770	1,709,538	3,440,553	2,691,563	1,757,840	4,424,355	2,806,489	1,618,813
Miscellaneous household products	16,401,132	1,162,835	3,534,215	2,882,785	2,233,776	6,418,446	4,077,579	2,341,476
Lawn and garden supplies	11,085,317	538,146	2,080,291	2,255,861	1,055,298	4,967,995	3,191,047	1,773,294
Postage and stationery	15,908,316	1,220,961	3,012,602	2,736,198	1,725,043	7,002,109	4,025,000	3,028,552
Stationery, stationery supplies, giftwrap	8,261,710	527,813	1,586,407	1,407,536	914,944	3,700,982	2,204,779	1,514,074
Postage	6,752,688	639,543	1,324,830	1,247,000	701,122	2,772,680	1,697,144	1,083,522
Delivery services	895,141	53,605	101,365	81,662	108,977	528,447	–	–
HOUSEHOLD FURNISHINGS AND EQUIPMENT	185,140,072	10,809,263	34,334,664	36,295,142	22,385,664	80,391,772	46,347,275	34,173,013
Household textiles	13,346,403	1,079,522	2,408,418	2,507,949	1,181,577	6,030,819	3,307,993	2,783,485
Bathroom linens	2,465,306	227,820	412,238	430,630	327,061	1,042,812	655,468	388,494
Bedroom linens	7,214,933	641,965	1,322,673	1,386,232	486,266	3,276,298	1,643,858	1,685,270
Kitchen and dining room linens	727,608	36,813	176,233	113,110	69,079	320,552	147,127	180,228
Curtains and draperies	1,381,843	71,365	219,675	265,022	112,205	713,737	445,624	268,117
Slipcovers and decorative pillows	430,450	26,641	76,717	106,263	30,343	190,478	119,776	70,500
Sewing materials for household items	986,856	63,131	187,941	182,853	125,117	428,390	263,130	165,265
Other linens	138,184	11,948	12,940	23,586	31,376	58,552	32,773	25,612
Furniture	43,771,409	2,702,195	8,324,246	8,086,862	5,112,636	19,545,872	11,109,010	8,436,862
Mattresses and springs	7,547,554	349,561	1,634,162	1,672,051	755,610	3,136,960	2,009,789	1,126,928
Other bedroom furniture	8,567,427	595,626	1,447,454	1,590,388	1,052,199	3,882,196	2,221,991	1,660,332
Sofas	11,349,456	902,884	2,174,262	1,963,956	1,272,865	5,035,441	2,832,661	2,202,902
Living room chairs	4,417,006	343,748	1,020,735	663,444	418,865	1,969,633	962,218	1,007,495
Living room tables	1,451,547	46,985	243,399	203,902	143,581	814,535	431,713	382,697

	total consumer units	less than high school graduate	high school graduate	some college	associate's degree	bachelor's degree or more total	bachelor's degree	graduate degree
Kitchen and dining room furniture	$3,356,778	$201,018	$666,420	$558,956	$409,827	$1,520,860	$829,474	$691,389
Infants' furniture	1,006,422	78,631	243,707	179,302	95,161	409,861	240,260	169,578
Outdoor furniture	2,286,767	49,891	238,469	382,444	558,315	1,057,265	495,845	561,442
Wall units, cabinets, and other furniture	3,787,228	133,850	655,637	872,418	406,082	1,719,491	1,085,295	634,099
Floor coverings	**2,443,294**	**80,407**	**347,537**	**208,975**	**129,120**	**1,677,986**	**785,855**	**892,241**
Floor coverings, nonpermanent	2,398,048	60,063	322,273	208,975	129,120	1,677,986	785,855	892,241
Major appliances	**23,715,118**	**1,641,241**	**4,477,617**	**5,290,812**	**3,290,107**	**8,998,794**	**4,691,079**	**4,312,522**
Dishwashers (built-in), garbage disposals, range hoods	1,785,390	54,251	206,119	305,600	219,633	1,000,566	423,225	577,214
Refrigerators and freezers	6,476,320	420,280	1,315,279	1,749,655	904,744	2,086,736	1,084,116	1,002,642
Washing machines	4,157,758	346,978	796,130	747,135	758,064	1,508,631	807,311	701,095
Clothes dryers	3,048,615	263,664	591,552	619,823	524,356	1,049,483	619,630	429,742
Cooking stoves, ovens	3,730,976	244,935	726,500	764,888	416,541	1,577,930	747,658	829,964
Microwave ovens	1,095,692	99,298	219,983	256,653	108,848	410,603	231,772	179,014
Window air conditioners	589,423	82,829	148,504	138,471	42,351	178,620	152,785	25,612
Electric floor-cleaning equipment	1,963,929	112,699	373,725	497,329	290,649	690,020	422,046	267,982
Sewing machines	297,157	16,307	36,356	49,454	10,071	184,549	45,741	138,709
Miscellaneous household appliances	514,828	–	31,426	145,572	15,107	306,840	155,143	156,503
Small appliances and miscellaneous housewares	**10,925,121**	**594,819**	**2,077,826**	**2,113,332**	**1,138,580**	**4,879,056**	**2,941,591**	**1,946,108**
Housewares	6,706,219	388,311	1,231,476	1,235,081	711,193	3,044,685	1,727,796	1,339,238
Plastic dinnerware	302,049	23,573	68,706	65,685	39,123	105,615	70,970	34,509
China and other dinnerware	653,013	25,026	100,749	94,089	93,999	326,110	172,827	157,446
Flatware	361,970	18,084	70,863	53,004	45,967	174,543	95,491	79,128
Glassware	802,203	62,646	82,263	160,789	63,527	417,644	261,716	156,503
Silver serving pieces	174,870	6,135	35,123	37,027	18,335	75,228	42,676	33,026
Other serving pieces	173,648	8,073	23,108	25,615	24,016	93,386	47,392	45,967
Nonelectric cookware	1,826,968	79,761	389,130	408,312	127,571	791,188	451,047	346,436
Tableware, nonelectric kitchenware	2,410,277	164,851	461,226	390,813	298,784	1,060,971	585,678	486,224
Small appliances	4,218,902	206,669	846,351	878,505	427,387	1,834,000	1,213,795	606,870
Small electric kitchen appliances	2,996,032	176,799	553,964	643,155	355,338	1,266,642	740,821	525,990
Portable heating and cooling equipment	1,222,870	29,709	292,387	235,096	72,049	567,358	473,210	80,880
Miscellaneous household equipment	**90,937,505**	**4,711,080**	**16,699,020**	**18,087,212**	**11,533,644**	**39,259,245**	**23,511,746**	**15,801,795**
Window coverings	1,940,695	43,110	217,827	299,006	158,559	1,221,802	426,762	795,185
Infants' equipment	1,771,939	159,038	334,289	340,091	378,709	556,611	283,408	281,597
Laundry and cleaning equipment	2,119,234	148,543	496,657	454,469	235,128	764,877	467,552	299,660
Outdoor equipment	4,210,341	261,727	1,784,207	617,033	321,638	1,195,862	527,676	696,242
Lamps and lighting fixtures	3,581,786	195,205	392,211	943,429	546,694	1,460,826	1,099,206	341,583
Household decorative items	14,332,036	622,751	2,410,266	2,320,024	2,132,288	6,607,812	4,042,920	2,584,386
Telephones and accessories	5,571,396	254,461	1,838,433	949,009	801,448	1,685,027	1,212,381	456,028
Lawn and garden equipment	8,024,473	354,566	515,759	1,554,122	1,278,030	4,166,802	2,792,578	1,357,032
Power tools	4,668,918	175,184	672,890	2,164,561	610,221	1,030,583	572,945	467,756
Office furniture for home use	712,933	18,406	79,490	177,527	64,173	372,803	211,495	161,356
Hand tools	1,901,563	57,480	329,667	808,762	175,216	514,365	224,227	302,356
Indoor plants and fresh flowers	5,737,706	284,654	1,116,554	971,834	632,688	2,732,657	1,579,490	1,152,944
Closet and storage items	2,060,536	174,215	373,417	336,794	188,128	957,949	643,679	310,175
Rental of furniture	753,288	79,600	314,878	62,642	118,790	177,137	15,326	161,625
Luggage	836,443	48,922	128,786	39,056	205,817	402,079	264,074	137,092
Computers and computer hardware for nonbusiness use	18,630,424	741,424	2,871,800	3,766,616	1,922,209	9,328,240	5,781,797	3,546,453
Portable memory	509,937	24,865	79,798	96,372	67,788	240,506	142,647	98,000
Computer software	1,752,373	70,881	175,309	255,132	300,720	950,167	472,032	478,405
Computer accessories	1,485,787	46,500	228,918	266,544	201,685	741,901	430,299	311,658
Personal digital assistants	766,739	36,329	112,457	107,784	65,980	444,696	264,309	180,362
Internet services away from home	859,678	65,391	211,665	174,484	88,447	319,440	207,486	111,884
Telephone answering devices	74,595	6,620	15,097	21,050	6,456	25,199	17,919	7,279
Business equipment for home use	495,262	30,032	82,571	106,516	52,423	223,460	145,712	77,510
Other hardware	1,386,735	60,870	343,532	184,121	133,123	639,621	264,545	391,998
Smoke alarms	240,905	17,922	55,458	37,027	55,005	75,228	39,847	35,318
Other household appliances	973,405	36,813	283,760	112,603	109,365	431,355	259,358	172,005
Miscellaneous household equipment and parts	5,274,238	687,174	1,208,368	848,072	622,617	1,891,811	1,069,734	838,186

Note: Numbers may not add to total because of rounding and missing subcategories. "–" means sample is too small to make a reliable estimate.
Source: Calculations by New Strategist based on the Bureau of Labor Statistics' 2011 Consumer Expenditure Survey

Table 8.28 Housing: Household Operations: Market shares by education, 2011

(percentage of total annual spending on household services, supplies, furnishings, and equipment accounted for by consumer unit educational attainment groups, 2011)

	total consumer units	less than high school graduate	high school graduate	some college	associate's degree	bachelor's degree or more total	bachelor's degree	graduate degree
Share of total consumer units	100.0%	13.2%	25.2%	20.7%	10.6%	30.3%	19.3%	11.0%
Share of total before-tax income	100.0	6.8	18.3	17.2	10.6	47.1	27.5	19.6
Share of total spending	100.0	8.0	20.1	18.9	10.8	42.0	25.2	16.8
Share of housing spending	100.0	8.5	20.3	18.8	10.5	41.7	24.9	16.8
HOUSEHOLD SERVICES	100.0	5.1	16.0	18.6	10.1	50.2	28.4	21.8
Personal services	100.0	4.7	12.7	17.5	9.5	55.6	30.2	25.4
Babysitting and child care in own home	100.0	4.5	7.9	8.8	5.5	73.3	24.5	48.9
Babysitting and child care in someone else's home	100.0	13.8	17.6	17.1	6.8	44.6	22.6	22.0
Care for elderly, invalids, handicapped, etc.	100.0	8.1	20.3	32.1	2.0	37.5	21.0	16.5
Day care centers, nurseries, and preschools	100.0	2.8	11.1	15.5	12.6	58.0	34.8	23.3
Other household services	100.0	5.3	17.9	19.2	10.4	47.2	27.4	19.8
Housekeeping services	100.0	3.3	7.8	16.2	5.8	66.9	34.1	32.8
Gardening, lawn care service	100.0	3.8	16.3	15.6	7.6	56.7	33.5	23.3
Water-softening service	100.0	7.7	27.3	15.7	13.4	35.9	25.1	10.9
Nonclothing laundry and dry cleaning, sent out	100.0	4.4	15.3	19.1	6.6	52.3	30.9	21.7
Nonclothing laundry and dry cleaning, coin-operated	100.0	24.2	23.0	18.4	9.8	24.4	16.4	8.1
Termite and pest control services	100.0	4.4	14.3	18.7	10.9	51.7	26.7	25.0
Home security system service fee	100.0	6.1	17.3	17.3	11.6	47.7	27.2	20.4
Other home services	100.0	8.6	13.8	15.1	10.5	51.9	27.2	24.8
Termite and pest control products	100.0	5.6	13.0	17.9	11.3	52.0	24.8	27.3
Moving, storage, and freight express	100.0	4.1	19.4	22.5	14.7	39.4	21.9	17.5
Appliance repair, including at service center	100.0	6.5	17.4	20.5	11.0	44.7	26.4	18.3
Reupholstering and furniture repair	100.0	2.9	8.0	31.9	6.6	50.6	21.3	29.3
Repairs and rentals of lawn and garden equipment, hand and power tools, etc.	100.0	5.9	33.0	18.3	9.1	33.6	16.9	16.7
Appliance rental	100.0	8.3	54.5	15.0	11.9	10.3	5.8	4.5
Rental of office equipment for nonbusiness use	100.0	11.5	24.2	12.5	10.8	41.2	29.5	11.6
Repair of computer systems for nonbusiness use	100.0	3.2	15.3	22.6	15.3	43.6	31.9	11.6
Computer information services	100.0	6.3	21.6	21.3	12.1	38.7	24.3	14.4
Installation of computer	100.0	4.4	7.9	26.8	10.1	50.5	21.2	29.0
HOUSEKEEPING SUPPLIES	100.0	9.2	22.0	18.6	11.9	37.6	23.4	14.2
Laundry and cleaning supplies	100.0	13.0	25.1	19.1	12.2	30.6	19.6	11.0
Soaps and detergents	100.0	14.7	24.9	19.0	12.1	29.5	19.3	10.2
Other laundry cleaning products	100.0	11.0	25.2	19.3	12.3	31.9	20.0	11.9
Other household products	100.0	8.2	21.8	18.9	12.2	38.1	24.3	13.8
Cleansing and toilet tissue, paper towels, and napkins	100.0	12.2	24.5	19.2	12.5	31.5	20.0	11.5
Miscellaneous household products	100.0	7.1	21.5	17.6	13.6	39.1	24.9	14.3
Lawn and garden supplies	100.0	4.9	18.8	20.3	9.5	44.8	28.8	16.0
Postage and stationery	100.0	7.7	18.9	17.2	10.8	44.0	25.3	19.0
Stationery, stationery supplies, giftwrap	100.0	6.4	19.2	17.0	11.1	44.8	26.7	18.3
Postage	100.0	9.5	19.6	18.5	10.4	41.1	25.1	16.0
Delivery services	100.0	6.0	11.3	9.1	12.2	59.0	–	–
HOUSEHOLD FURNISHINGS AND EQUIPMENT	100.0	5.8	18.5	19.6	12.1	43.4	25.0	18.5
Household textiles	100.0	8.1	18.0	18.8	8.9	45.2	24.8	20.9
Bathroom linens	100.0	9.2	16.7	17.5	13.3	42.3	26.6	15.8
Bedroom linens	100.0	8.9	18.3	19.2	6.7	45.4	22.8	23.4
Kitchen and dining room linens	100.0	5.1	24.2	15.5	9.5	44.1	20.2	24.8
Curtains and draperies	100.0	5.2	15.9	19.2	8.1	51.7	32.2	19.4
Slipcovers and decorative pillows	100.0	6.2	17.8	24.7	7.0	44.3	27.8	16.4
Sewing materials for household items	100.0	6.4	19.0	18.5	12.7	43.4	26.7	16.7
Other linens	100.0	8.6	9.4	17.1	22.7	42.4	23.7	18.5
Furniture	100.0	6.2	19.0	18.5	11.7	44.7	25.4	19.3
Mattresses and springs	100.0	4.6	21.7	22.2	10.0	41.6	26.6	14.9
Other bedroom furniture	100.0	7.0	16.9	18.6	12.3	45.3	25.9	19.4
Sofas	100.0	8.0	19.2	17.3	11.2	44.4	25.0	19.4
Living room chairs	100.0	7.8	23.1	15.0	9.5	44.6	21.8	22.8
Living room tables	100.0	3.2	16.8	14.0	9.9	56.1	29.7	26.4

	total consumer units	less than high school graduate	high school graduate	some college	associate's degree	bachelor's degree or more		
						total	bachelor's degree	graduate degree
Kitchen and dining room furniture	100.0%	6.0%	19.9%	16.7%	12.2%	45.3%	24.7%	20.6%
Infants' furniture	100.0	7.8	24.2	17.8	9.5	40.7	23.9	16.8
Outdoor furniture	100.0	2.2	10.4	16.7	24.4	46.2	21.7	24.6
Wall units, cabinets, and other furniture	100.0	3.5	17.3	23.0	10.7	45.4	28.7	16.7
Floor coverings	**100.0**	**3.3**	**14.2**	**8.6**	**5.3**	**68.7**	**32.2**	**36.5**
Floor coverings, nonpermanent	100.0	2.5	13.4	8.7	5.4	70.0	32.8	37.2
Major appliances	**100.0**	**6.9**	**18.9**	**22.3**	**13.9**	**37.9**	**19.8**	**18.2**
Dishwashers (built-in), garbage disposals, range hoods	100.0	3.0	11.5	17.1	12.3	56.0	23.7	32.3
Refrigerators and freezers	100.0	6.5	20.3	27.0	14.0	32.2	16.7	15.5
Washing machines	100.0	8.3	19.1	18.0	18.2	36.3	19.4	16.9
Clothes dryers	100.0	8.6	19.4	20.3	17.2	34.4	20.3	14.1
Cooking stoves, ovens	100.0	6.6	19.5	20.5	11.2	42.3	20.0	22.2
Microwave ovens	100.0	9.1	20.1	23.4	9.9	37.5	21.2	16.3
Window air conditioners	100.0	14.1	25.2	23.5	7.2	30.3	25.9	4.3
Electric floor-cleaning equipment	100.0	5.7	19.0	25.3	14.8	35.1	21.5	13.6
Sewing machines	100.0	5.5	12.2	16.6	3.4	62.1	15.4	46.7
Miscellaneous household appliances	100.0	–	6.1	28.3	2.9	59.6	30.1	30.4
Small appliances and miscellaneous housewares	**100.0**	**5.4**	**19.0**	**19.3**	**10.4**	**44.7**	**26.9**	**17.8**
Housewares	100.0	5.8	18.4	18.4	10.6	45.4	25.8	20.0
Plastic dinnerware	100.0	7.8	22.7	21.7	13.0	35.0	23.5	11.4
China and other dinnerware	100.0	3.8	15.4	14.4	14.4	49.9	26.5	24.1
Flatware	100.0	5.0	19.6	14.6	12.7	48.2	26.4	21.9
Glassware	100.0	7.8	10.3	20.0	7.9	52.1	32.6	19.5
Silver serving pieces	100.0	3.5	20.1	21.2	10.5	43.0	24.4	18.9
Other serving pieces	100.0	4.6	13.3	14.8	13.8	53.8	27.3	26.5
Nonelectric cookware	100.0	4.4	21.3	22.3	7.0	43.3	24.7	19.0
Tableware, nonelectric kitchenware	100.0	6.8	19.1	16.2	12.4	44.0	24.3	20.2
Small appliances	100.0	4.9	20.1	20.8	10.1	43.5	28.8	14.4
Small electric kitchen appliances	100.0	5.9	18.5	21.5	11.9	42.3	24.7	17.6
Portable heating and cooling equipment	100.0	2.4	23.9	19.2	5.9	46.4	38.7	6.6
Miscellaneous household equipment	**100.0**	**5.2**	**18.4**	**19.9**	**12.7**	**43.2**	**25.9**	**17.4**
Window coverings	100.0	2.2	11.2	15.4	8.2	63.0	22.0	41.0
Infants' equipment	100.0	9.0	18.9	19.2	21.4	31.4	16.0	15.9
Laundry and cleaning equipment	100.0	7.0	23.4	21.4	11.1	36.1	22.1	14.1
Outdoor equipment	100.0	6.2	42.4	14.7	7.6	28.4	12.5	16.5
Lamps and lighting fixtures	100.0	5.4	11.0	26.3	15.3	40.8	30.7	9.5
Household decorative items	100.0	4.3	16.8	16.2	14.9	46.1	28.2	18.0
Telephones and accessories	100.0	4.6	33.0	17.0	14.4	30.2	21.8	8.2
Lawn and garden equipment	100.0	4.4	6.4	19.4	15.9	51.9	34.8	16.9
Power tools	100.0	3.8	14.4	46.4	13.1	22.1	12.3	10.0
Office furniture for home use	100.0	2.6	11.1	24.9	9.0	52.3	29.7	22.6
Hand tools	100.0	3.0	17.3	42.5	9.2	27.0	11.8	15.9
Indoor plants and fresh flowers	100.0	5.0	19.5	16.9	11.0	47.6	27.5	20.1
Closet and storage items	100.0	8.5	18.1	16.3	9.1	46.5	31.2	15.1
Rental of furniture	100.0	10.6	41.8	8.3	15.8	23.5	2.0	21.5
Luggage	100.0	5.8	15.4	4.7	24.6	48.1	31.6	16.4
Computers and computer hardware for nonbusiness use	100.0	4.0	15.4	20.2	10.3	50.1	31.0	19.0
Portable memory	100.0	4.9	15.6	18.9	13.3	47.2	28.0	19.2
Computer software	100.0	4.0	10.0	14.6	17.2	54.2	26.9	27.3
Computer accessories	100.0	3.1	15.4	17.9	13.6	49.9	29.0	21.0
Personal digital assistants	100.0	4.7	14.7	14.1	8.6	58.0	34.5	23.5
Internet services away from home	100.0	7.6	24.6	20.3	10.3	37.2	24.1	13.0
Telephone answering devices	100.0	8.9	20.2	28.2	8.7	33.8	24.0	9.8
Business equipment for home use	100.0	6.1	16.7	21.5	10.6	45.1	29.4	15.7
Other hardware	100.0	4.4	24.8	13.3	9.6	46.1	19.1	28.3
Smoke alarms	100.0	7.4	23.0	15.4	22.8	31.2	16.5	14.7
Other household appliances	100.0	3.8	29.2	11.6	11.2	44.3	26.6	17.7
Miscellaneous household equipment and parts	100.0	13.0	22.9	16.1	11.8	35.9	20.3	15.9

Note: Numbers may not add to total because of rounding. "–" means sample is too small to make a reliable estimate.
Source: Calculations by New Strategist based on the Bureau of Labor Statistics' 2011 Consumer Expenditure Survey

CHAPTER 9

Spending on Housing: Shelter and Utilities, 2011

Housing is by far Americans' biggest expense. In 2011, housing costs, which include shelter, utilities, and household operations, absorbed 33.8 percent of average household expenditures, down from 34.4 percent in 2010 but up from 32.4 percent in 2000. Average household spending on shelter rose 16 percent between 2000 and 2006, after adjusting for inflation, then fell 9 percent between 2006 and 2011. Spending on mortgage interest, one of the shelter categories, grew 21 percent in the former time period, then fell by 24 percent in the latter time period as the housing market collapsed and some families lost their home.

Overall housing costs are highest for householders aged 35 to 44, at an average of $19,979 in 2011. This age group spends much more than any other on mortgage interest—$4,711 on average in 2011. Second in spending on mortgage interest are householders aged 45 to 54, who devoted an average of $4,024 to this item. Spending on maintenance and repair services for owned homes is greatest among householders aged 65 to 74. Householders under age 35 spend the most on rent.

Households with incomes of $100,000 or more spent an enormous $30,212 on housing and related services in 2011, almost twice the $16,803 spent by the average household. They devoted $7,270 to mortgage interest alone. The most-affluent households account for only 18 percent of all households but are responsible for one-third of spending in the shelter category, including 41 percent of the spending on owned dwellings, 43 percent of the spending on mortgage interest, and 57 percent of the spending on owned vacation homes.

Among household types, married couples with children under age 6 spend the most on housing, $25,009 on average in 2011. Behind this figure is their relatively large household size and the high cost of housing for recent homebuyers—many married couples with young children are new homeowners. This household type spends over twice as much as the average household on mortgage interest. Married couples without children at home (most of them empty-nesters) spend two-and-one-half times the average on owned vacation homes and 85 percent more than average for lodging on trips.

Asian households outspend the average household by 24 percent on housing, while Hispanic and black households spend less than average. Asians spend 39 percent more than average on mortgage interest, in part because many live in California, where housing costs are high. Blacks spend 40 percent more than the average household on rent, while Hispanics and Asians spend 60 and 63 percent more, respectively. Hispanics spend 16 percent more than average on cellular telephone service and nearly three times the average on phone cards.

Households in the Northeast and West spend the most on housing—over $19,000 on average in 2011—because of the high cost of housing in parts of those regions. Northeastern households spend 63 percent more than average on property taxes. Western households spend 36 percent more than the average household on mortgage interest and 43 percent more on rent. Households in the South spend 24 percent more than average on electricity.

Not surprisingly, college graduates (who dominate the nation's affluent households) spend the most on housing, an average of $23,123 in 2011. They spend far more than the average household on almost every shelter category. They spend two-thirds more than average on mortgage interest and twice the average on lodging on trips and owned vacation homes.

Table 9.1 Housing: Shelter and Utilities: Average spending by age, 2011

(average annual spending of consumer units on shelter and utilities, by age of consumer unit reference person, 2011)

	total consumer units	under 25	25 to 34	35 to 44	45 to 54	55 to 64	65 to 74	75+
Number of consumer units (in 000s)	122,287	7,743	20,463	21,699	24,821	21,688	14,079	11,794
Average number of persons per consumer unit	2.5	2.1	2.9	3.3	2.8	2.1	1.9	1.6
Average before-tax income of consumer units	$63,685.00	$27,514.00	$58,179.00	$77,376.00	$78,519.00	$75,517.00	$52,521.00	$32,144.00
Average spending of consumer units, total	49,704.88	29,911.52	48,097.39	57,271.07	58,050.42	53,615.86	44,645.56	32,688.34
Housing, average spending	**16,803.03**	**10,281.56**	**17,026.09**	**19,979.07**	**18,781.64**	**17,172.91**	**15,104.82**	**12,046.03**
SHELTER	**9,825.36**	**6,732.11**	**10,479.90**	**12,068.47**	**11,111.31**	**9,754.66**	**7,965.78**	**6,237.08**
Owned dwellings*	**6,147.89**	**1,276.69**	**4,825.99**	**7,843.85**	**7,773.67**	**7,001.95**	**5,802.32**	**3,939.48**
Mortgage interest and charges	3,183.73	739.68	3,207.11	4,873.45	4,236.08	3,244.47	2,007.96	716.09
Mortgage interest	3,020.32	734.20	3,157.51	4,711.38	4,024.25	2,981.46	1,789.20	600.15
Interest paid, home equity loan	61.79	2.46	30.31	66.96	89.73	90.67	62.45	33.09
Interest paid, home equity line of credit	101.63	3.02	19.29	95.11	122.09	172.34	156.30	82.84
Property taxes	1,844.51	305.86	1,071.75	1,929.79	2,299.56	2,301.39	2,243.30	1,764.58
Maintenance, repairs, insurance, other expenses	1,119.64	231.15	547.12	1,040.61	1,238.03	1,456.08	1,551.06	1,458.82
Homeowner's insurance	351.98	58.43	180.45	308.02	427.00	460.15	479.68	413.92
Ground rent	48.15	21.49	48.57	31.87	46.96	50.96	84.65	48.63
Maintenance and repair services	555.93	130.18	215.74	555.89	602.20	734.91	784.45	726.44
Painting and papering	61.73	10.58	18.11	75.39	43.33	85.35	125.27	65.24
Plumbing and water heating	65.34	7.45	32.64	64.95	53.66	89.01	101.01	99.30
Heat, air conditioning, electrical work	109.51	60.25	54.92	102.92	147.51	110.10	152.75	116.01
Roofing and gutters	92.49	35.37	27.28	65.14	91.99	159.57	149.50	103.08
Other repair and maintenance services	168.24	11.04	56.18	137.65	212.26	219.91	206.20	289.19
Repair, replacement of hard-surface flooring	56.91	5.02	25.90	109.11	51.27	69.18	45.48	51.73
Repair of built-in appliances	1.71	0.47	0.71	0.73	2.18	1.79	4.23	1.89
Maintenance and repair materials	74.55	12.25	57.37	82.72	101.14	101.62	66.28	34.38
Paints, wallpaper, and supplies	13.69	1.24	15.03	13.40	20.24	20.03	7.08	2.52
Tools, equipment for painting, wallpapering	1.47	0.13	1.61	1.44	2.17	2.15	0.76	0.27
Plumbing supplies and equipment	6.43	3.24	6.33	5.99	10.55	4.21	7.94	3.07
Electrical supplies, heating and cooling equipment	3.44	3.17	1.29	4.05	5.90	3.01	2.26	3.21
Hard-surface flooring, repair and replacement	11.88	2.52	9.42	18.70	13.21	9.12	16.18	6.85
Roofing and gutters	5.22	0.65	1.96	5.59	1.85	11.88	11.19	0.94
Plaster, paneling, siding, windows, doors, screens, awnings	15.77	0.88	10.56	14.59	24.26	26.83	6.56	9.48
Patio, walk, fence, driveway, masonry, brick, and stucco materials	1.78	0.01	0.91	1.04	3.63	3.26	0.54	0.71
Miscellaneous supplies and equipment	14.88	0.41	10.25	17.92	19.32	21.14	13.78	7.31
Material for insulation, other maintenance and repair	14.88	0.41	10.25	17.92	19.32	21.14	13.78	7.31
Property management and security	88.48	8.54	44.59	61.78	60.57	107.57	134.59	234.82
Property management	60.24	6.67	37.23	49.08	43.79	78.49	87.58	124.33
Management and upkeep services for security	28.23	1.86	7.36	12.70	16.78	29.08	47.01	110.48
Parking	0.55	0.27	0.40	0.33	0.17	0.86	1.43	0.63
Rented dwellings	**3,029.49**	**5,110.69**	**5,338.39**	**3,714.31**	**2,582.10**	**1,783.96**	**1,234.17**	**1,772.42**
Rent	2,905.25	4,966.62	5,191.86	3,565.73	2,469.22	1,676.30	1,137.82	1,656.99
Rent as pay	83.62	113.27	101.87	99.28	78.26	63.62	62.13	77.37
Maintenance, insurance, and other expenses	40.62	30.81	44.66	49.30	34.62	44.04	34.22	38.05
Tenant's insurance	13.09	17.78	20.74	14.76	11.32	10.17	6.95	10.10
Maintenance and repair services	15.82	5.77	11.94	13.50	6.50	29.28	16.70	27.23
Maintenance and repair materials	11.71	7.26	11.98	21.04	16.80	4.59	10.57	0.72
Other lodging	**647.99**	**344.73**	**315.52**	**510.31**	**755.53**	**968.75**	**929.29**	**525.17**
Owned vacation homes	261.96	40.60	76.70	178.49	212.06	506.32	430.43	336.79
Mortgage interest and charges	84.79	5.83	46.40	101.59	92.79	130.55	99.22	54.14
Property taxes	116.71	24.46	20.78	52.31	89.78	261.98	195.80	157.26
Maintenance, insurance, and other expenses	60.46	10.31	9.52	24.59	29.49	113.79	135.40	125.39
Housing while attending school	71.40	207.13	16.15	14.32	184.56	71.92	18.67	7.04
Lodging on trips	314.62	97.00	222.67	317.50	358.91	390.51	480.20	181.33

	total consumer units	under 25	25 to 34	35 to 44	45 to 54	55 to 64	65 to 74	75+
UTILITIES, FUELS, AND PUBLIC SERVICES	**$3,726.76**	**$1,918.24**	**$3,295.80**	**$4,064.81**	**$4,317.56**	**$4,053.08**	**$3,781.51**	**$3,131.05**
Natural gas	**419.64**	**172.48**	**340.65**	**457.65**	**481.09**	**461.12**	**434.10**	**426.12**
Electricity	**1,422.95**	**756.54**	**1,256.50**	**1,555.14**	**1,600.90**	**1,555.08**	**1,498.25**	**1,198.72**
Fuel oil and other fuels	**156.83**	**19.45**	**77.48**	**113.64**	**174.50**	**196.62**	**229.31**	**267.26**
Fuel oil	89.23	7.68	38.83	64.26	109.48	96.14	129.35	172.93
Coal, wood, and other fuels	9.36	3.29	4.21	9.71	10.17	10.71	17.01	8.31
Bottled gas	58.24	8.49	34.44	39.67	54.86	89.77	82.95	86.02
Telephone services	**1,226.44**	**776.63**	**1,219.09**	**1,393.92**	**1,501.77**	**1,275.24**	**1,059.93**	**755.91**
Residential telephone and pay phones	380.95	83.98	193.50	340.09	434.68	478.89	526.72	509.12
Cellular phone service	825.71	678.99	1,002.70	1,028.65	1,046.39	778.12	517.01	233.17
Phone cards	8.84	7.21	12.65	10.91	9.73	6.82	5.14	5.73
Voice over IP	10.94	6.44	10.24	14.26	10.97	11.41	11.06	7.89
Water and other public services	**500.91**	**193.13**	**402.09**	**544.46**	**559.30**	**565.02**	**559.93**	**483.05**
Water and sewerage maintenance	376.69	154.49	307.56	421.50	424.08	421.18	407.05	342.26
Trash and garbage collection	121.02	38.64	94.00	121.01	130.76	140.00	145.09	137.87
Septic tank cleaning	3.20	–	0.53	1.95	4.45	3.85	7.79	2.92

See Appendix B for information about mortgage principal reduction.
Note: Subcategories may not add to total because some are not shown. "–" means sample is too small to make a reliable estimate.
Source: Bureau of Labor Statistics, unpublished tables from the 2011 Consumer Expenditure Survey

Table 9.2 Housing: Shelter and Utilities: Indexed spending by age, 2011

(indexed average annual spending of consumer units on shelter and utilities, by age of consumer unit reference person, 2011; index definition: an index of 100 is the average for all consumer units; an index of 125 means that spending by consumer units in that group is 25 percent above the average for all consumer units; an index of 75 indicates spending that is 25 percent below the average for all consumer units)

	total consumer units	under 25	25 to 34	35 to 44	45 to 54	55 to 64	65 to 74	75+
Average spending of consumer units, total	$49,705	$29,912	$48,097	$57,271	$58,050	$53,616	$44,646	$32,688
Average spending of consumer units, index	100	60	97	115	117	108	90	66
Housing, spending index	100	61	101	119	112	102	90	72
SHELTER	100	69	107	123	113	99	81	63
Owned dwellings*	100	21	78	128	126	114	94	64
Mortgage interest and charges	100	23	101	153	133	102	63	22
Mortgage interest	100	24	105	156	133	99	59	20
Interest paid, home equity loan	100	4	49	108	145	147	101	54
Interest paid, home equity line of credit	100	3	19	94	120	170	154	82
Property taxes	100	17	58	105	125	125	122	96
Maintenance, repairs, insurance, other expenses	100	21	49	93	111	130	139	130
Homeowner's insurance	100	17	51	88	121	131	136	118
Ground rent	100	45	101	66	98	106	176	101
Maintenance and repair services	100	23	39	100	108	132	141	131
Painting and papering	100	17	29	122	70	138	203	106
Plumbing and water heating	100	11	50	99	82	136	155	152
Heat, air conditioning, electrical work	100	55	50	94	135	101	139	106
Roofing and gutters	100	38	29	70	99	173	162	111
Other repair and maintenance services	100	7	33	82	126	131	123	172
Repair, replacement of hard-surface flooring	100	9	46	192	90	122	80	91
Repair of built-in appliances	100	27	42	43	127	105	247	111
Maintenance and repair materials	100	16	77	111	136	136	89	46
Paints, wallpaper, and supplies	100	9	110	98	148	146	52	18
Tools, equipment for painting, wallpapering	100	9	110	98	148	146	52	18
Plumbing supplies and equipment	100	50	98	93	164	65	123	48
Electrical supplies, heating and cooling equipment	100	92	38	118	172	88	66	93
Hard-surface flooring, repair and replacement	100	21	79	157	111	77	136	58
Roofing and gutters	100	12	38	107	35	228	214	18
Plaster, paneling, siding, windows, doors, screens, awnings	100	6	67	93	154	170	42	60
Patio, walk, fence, driveway, masonry, brick, and stucco materials	100	1	51	58	204	183	30	40
Miscellaneous supplies and equipment	100	3	69	120	130	142	93	49
Material for insulation, other maintenance and repair	100	3	69	120	130	142	93	49
Property management and security	100	10	50	70	68	122	152	265
Property management	100	11	62	81	73	130	145	206
Management and upkeep services for security	100	7	26	45	59	103	167	391
Parking	100	49	73	60	31	156	260	115
Rented dwellings	100	169	176	123	85	59	41	59
Rent	100	171	179	123	85	58	39	57
Rent as pay	100	135	122	119	94	76	74	93
Maintenance, insurance, and other expenses	100	76	110	121	85	108	84	94
Tenant's insurance	100	136	158	113	86	78	53	77
Maintenance and repair services	100	36	75	85	41	185	106	172
Maintenance and repair materials	100	62	102	180	143	39	90	6
Other lodging	100	53	49	79	117	150	143	81
Owned vacation homes	100	15	29	68	81	193	164	129
Mortgage interest and charges	100	7	55	120	109	154	117	64
Property taxes	100	21	18	45	77	224	168	135
Maintenance, insurance, and other expenses	100	17	16	41	49	188	224	207
Housing while attending school	100	290	23	20	258	101	26	10
Lodging on trips	100	31	71	101	114	124	153	58

	total consumer units	under 25	25 to 34	35 to 44	45 to 54	55 to 64	65 to 74	75+
UTILITIES, FUELS, AND PUBLIC SERVICES	**100**	**51**	**88**	**109**	**116**	**109**	**101**	**84**
Natural gas	**100**	**41**	**81**	**109**	**115**	**110**	**103**	**102**
Electricity	**100**	**53**	**88**	**109**	**113**	**109**	**105**	**84**
Fuel oil and other fuels	**100**	**12**	**49**	**72**	**111**	**125**	**146**	**170**
Fuel oil	100	9	44	72	123	108	145	194
Coal, wood, and other fuels	100	35	45	104	109	114	182	89
Bottled gas	100	15	59	68	94	154	142	148
Telephone services	**100**	**63**	**99**	**114**	**122**	**104**	**86**	**62**
Residential telephone and pay phones	100	22	51	89	114	126	138	134
Cellular phone service	100	82	121	125	127	94	63	28
Phone cards	100	82	143	123	110	77	58	65
Voice over IP	100	59	94	130	100	104	101	72
Water and other public services	**100**	**39**	**80**	**109**	**112**	**113**	**112**	**96**
Water and sewerage maintenance	100	41	82	112	113	112	108	91
Trash and garbage collection	100	32	78	100	108	116	120	114
Septic tank cleaning	100	–	17	61	139	120	243	91

See Appendix B for information about mortgage principal reduction.
Note: "–" means sample is too small to make a reliable estimate.
Source: Calculations by New Strategist based on the Bureau of Labor Statistics' 2011 Consumer Expenditure Survey

Table 9.3 Housing: Shelter and Utilities: Total spending by age, 2011

(total annual spending on shelter and utilities, by consumer unit age groups, 2011; consumer units and dollars in thousands)

	total consumer units	under 25	25 to 34	35 to 44	45 to 54	55 to 64	65 to 74	75+
Number of consumer units	122,287	7,743	20,463	21,699	24,821	21,688	14,079	11,794
Total spending of all consumer units	$6,078,260,661	$231,604,899	$984,216,892	$1,242,724,948	$1,440,869,475	$1,162,820,772	$628,564,839	$385,526,282
Housing, total spending	**2,054,792,130**	**79,610,119**	**348,404,880**	**433,525,840**	**466,179,086**	**372,446,072**	**212,660,761**	**142,070,878**
SHELTER	**1,201,513,798**	**52,126,728**	**214,450,194**	**261,873,731**	**275,793,826**	**211,559,066**	**112,150,217**	**73,560,122**
Owned dwellings*	**751,807,024**	**9,885,411**	**98,754,233**	**170,203,701**	**192,950,263**	**151,858,292**	**81,690,863**	**46,462,227**
Mortgage interest and charges	389,328,791	5,727,342	65,627,092	105,748,992	105,143,742	70,366,065	28,270,069	8,445,565
Mortgage interest	369,345,872	5,684,911	64,612,127	102,232,235	99,885,909	64,661,904	25,190,147	7,078,169
Interest paid, home equity loan	7,556,114	19,048	620,234	1,452,965	2,227,188	1,966,451	879,234	390,263
Interest paid, home equity line of credit	12,428,028	23,384	394,731	2,063,792	3,030,396	3,737,710	2,200,548	977,015
Property taxes	225,559,594	2,368,274	21,931,220	41,874,513	57,077,379	49,912,546	31,583,421	20,811,457
Maintenance, repairs, insurance, other expenses	136,917,417	1,789,794	11,195,717	22,580,196	30,729,143	31,579,463	21,837,374	17,205,323
Homeowner's insurance	43,042,578	452,423	3,692,548	6,683,726	10,598,567	9,979,733	6,753,415	4,881,772
Ground rent	5,888,119	166,397	993,888	691,547	1,165,594	1,105,220	1,191,787	573,542
Maintenance and repair services	67,983,012	1,007,984	4,414,688	12,062,257	14,947,206	15,938,728	11,044,272	8,567,633
Painting and papering	7,548,777	81,921	370,585	1,635,888	1,075,494	1,851,071	1,763,676	769,441
Plumbing and water heating	7,990,233	57,685	667,912	1,409,350	1,331,895	1,930,449	1,422,120	1,171,144
Heat, air conditioning, electrical work	13,391,649	466,516	1,123,828	2,233,261	3,661,346	2,387,849	2,150,567	1,368,222
Roofing and gutters	11,310,325	273,870	558,231	1,413,473	2,283,284	3,460,754	2,104,811	1,215,726
Other repair and maintenance services	20,573,565	85,483	1,149,611	2,986,867	5,268,505	4,769,408	2,903,090	3,410,707
Repair, replacement of hard-surface flooring	6,959,353	38,870	529,992	2,367,578	1,272,573	1,500,376	640,313	610,104
Repair of built-in appliances	209,111	3,639	14,529	15,840	54,110	38,822	59,554	22,291
Maintenance and repair materials	9,116,496	94,852	1,173,962	1,794,941	2,510,396	2,203,935	933,156	405,478
Paints, wallpaper, and supplies	1,674,109	9,601	307,559	290,767	502,377	434,411	99,679	29,721
Tools, equipment for painting, wallpapering	179,762	1,007	32,945	31,247	53,862	46,629	10,700	3,184
Plumbing supplies and equipment	786,305	25,087	129,531	129,977	261,862	91,306	111,787	36,208
Electrical supplies, heating and cooling equipment	420,667	24,545	26,397	87,881	146,444	65,281	31,819	37,859
Hard-surface flooring, repair and replacement	1,452,770	19,512	192,761	405,771	327,885	197,795	227,798	80,789
Roofing and gutters	638,338	5,033	40,107	121,297	45,919	257,653	157,544	11,086
Plaster, paneling, siding, windows, doors, screens, awnings	1,928,466	6,814	216,089	316,588	602,157	581,889	92,358	111,807
Patio, walk, fence, driveway, masonry, brick, and stucco materials	217,671	77	18,621	22,567	90,100	70,703	7,603	8,374
Miscellaneous supplies and equipment	1,819,631	3,175	209,746	388,846	479,542	458,484	194,009	86,214
Material for insulation, other maintenance and repair	1,819,631	3,175	209,746	388,846	479,542	458,484	194,009	86,214
Property management and security	10,819,954	66,125	912,445	1,340,564	1,503,408	2,332,978	1,894,893	2,769,467
Property management	7,366,569	51,646	761,837	1,064,987	1,086,912	1,702,291	1,233,039	1,466,348
Management and upkeep services for security	3,452,162	14,402	150,608	275,577	416,496	630,687	661,854	1,303,001
Parking	67,258	2,091	8,185	7,161	4,220	18,652	20,133	7,430
Rented dwellings	**370,467,244**	**39,572,073**	**109,239,475**	**80,596,813**	**64,090,304**	**38,690,524**	**17,375,879**	**20,903,921**
Rent	355,274,307	38,456,539	106,241,031	77,372,775	61,288,510	36,355,594	16,019,368	19,542,540
Rent as pay	10,225,639	877,050	2,084,566	2,154,277	1,942,491	1,379,791	874,728	912,502
Maintenance, insurance, and other expenses	4,967,298	238,562	913,878	1,069,761	859,303	955,140	481,783	448,762
Tenant's insurance	1,600,737	137,671	424,403	320,277	280,974	220,567	97,849	119,119
Maintenance and repair services	1,934,580	44,677	244,328	292,937	161,337	635,025	235,119	321,151
Maintenance and repair materials	1,431,981	56,214	245,147	456,547	416,993	99,548	148,815	8,492
Other lodging	**79,240,753**	**2,669,244**	**6,456,486**	**11,073,217**	**18,753,010**	**21,010,250**	**13,083,474**	**6,193,855**
Owned vacation homes	32,034,303	314,366	1,569,512	3,873,055	5,263,541	10,981,068	6,060,024	3,972,101
Mortgage interest and charges	10,368,715	45,142	949,483	2,204,401	2,303,141	2,831,368	1,396,918	638,527
Property taxes	14,272,116	189,394	425,221	1,135,075	2,228,429	5,681,822	2,756,668	1,854,724
Maintenance, insurance, and other expenses	7,393,472	79,830	194,808	533,578	731,971	2,467,878	1,906,297	1,478,850
Housing while attending school	8,731,292	1,603,808	330,477	310,730	4,580,964	1,559,801	262,855	83,030
Lodging on trips	38,473,936	751,071	4,556,496	6,889,433	8,908,505	8,469,381	6,760,736	2,138,606

	total consumer units	under 25	25 to 34	35 to 44	45 to 54	55 to 64	65 to 74	75+
UTILITIES, FUELS, AND PUBLIC SERVICES	$455,734,300	$14,852,932	$67,441,955	$88,202,312	$107,166,157	$87,903,199	$53,239,879	$36,927,604
Natural gas	51,316,517	1,335,513	6,970,721	9,930,547	11,941,135	10,000,771	6,111,694	5,025,659
Electricity	174,008,287	5,857,889	25,711,760	33,744,983	39,735,939	33,726,575	21,093,862	14,137,704
Fuel oil and other fuels	19,178,270	150,601	1,585,473	2,465,874	4,331,265	4,264,295	3,228,455	3,152,064
Fuel oil	10,911,669	59,466	794,578	1,394,378	2,717,403	2,085,084	1,821,119	2,039,536
Coal, wood, and other fuels	1,144,606	25,474	86,149	210,697	252,430	232,278	239,484	98,008
Bottled gas	7,121,995	65,738	704,746	860,799	1,361,680	1,946,932	1,167,853	1,014,520
Telephone services	149,977,668	6,013,446	24,946,239	30,246,670	37,275,433	27,657,405	14,922,754	8,915,203
Residential telephone and pay phones	46,585,233	650,257	3,959,591	7,379,613	10,789,192	10,386,166	7,415,691	6,004,561
Cellular phone service	100,973,599	5,257,420	20,518,250	22,320,676	25,972,446	16,875,867	7,278,984	2,750,007
Phone cards	1,081,017	55,827	258,857	236,736	241,508	147,912	72,366	67,580
Voice over IP	1,337,820	49,865	209,541	309,428	272,286	247,460	155,714	93,055
Water and other public services	61,254,781	1,495,406	8,227,968	11,814,238	13,882,385	12,254,154	7,883,254	5,697,092
Water and sewerage maintenance	46,064,290	1,196,216	6,293,600	9,146,129	10,526,090	9,134,552	5,730,857	4,036,614
Trash and garbage collection	14,799,173	299,190	1,923,522	2,625,796	3,245,594	3,036,320	2,042,722	1,626,039
Septic tank cleaning	391,318	–	10,845	42,313	110,453	83,499	109,675	34,438

See Appendix B for information about mortgage principal reduction.
Note: Numbers may not add to total because of rounding and missing subcategories. "–" means sample is too small to make a reliable estimate.
Source: Calculations by New Strategist based on the Bureau of Labor Statistics' 2011 Consumer Expenditure Survey

Table 9.4 Housing: Shelter and Utilities: Market shares by age, 2011

(percentage of total annual spending on shelter and utilities accounted for by consumer unit age groups, 2011)

	total consumer units	under 25	25 to 34	35 to 44	45 to 54	55 to 64	65 to 74	75+
Share of total consumer units	100.0%	6.3%	16.7%	17.7%	20.3%	17.7%	11.5%	9.6%
Share of total before-tax income	100.0	2.7	15.3	21.6	25.0	21.0	9.5	4.9
Share of total spending	100.0	3.8	16.2	20.4	23.7	19.1	10.3	6.3
Share of housing spending	100.0	3.9	17.0	21.1	22.7	18.1	10.3	6.9
SHELTER	100.0	4.3	17.8	21.8	23.0	17.6	9.3	6.1
Owned dwellings*	100.0	1.3	13.1	22.6	25.7	20.2	10.9	6.2
Mortgage interest and charges	100.0	1.5	16.9	27.2	27.0	18.1	7.3	2.2
Mortgage interest	100.0	1.5	17.5	27.7	27.0	17.5	6.8	1.9
Interest paid, home equity loan	100.0	0.3	8.2	19.2	29.5	26.0	11.6	5.2
Interest paid, home equity line of credit	100.0	0.2	3.2	16.6	24.4	30.1	17.7	7.9
Property taxes	100.0	1.0	9.7	18.6	25.3	22.1	14.0	9.2
Maintenance, repairs, insurance, other expenses	100.0	1.3	8.2	16.5	22.4	23.1	15.9	12.6
Homeowner's insurance	100.0	1.1	8.6	15.5	24.6	23.2	15.7	11.3
Ground rent	100.0	2.8	16.9	11.7	19.8	18.8	20.2	9.7
Maintenance and repair services	100.0	1.5	6.5	17.7	22.0	23.4	16.2	12.6
Painting and papering	100.0	1.1	4.9	21.7	14.2	24.5	23.4	10.2
Plumbing and water heating	100.0	0.7	8.4	17.6	16.7	24.2	17.8	14.7
Heat, air conditioning, electrical work	100.0	3.5	8.4	16.7	27.3	17.8	16.1	10.2
Roofing and gutters	100.0	2.4	4.9	12.5	20.2	30.6	18.6	10.7
Other repair and maintenance services	100.0	0.4	5.6	14.5	25.6	23.2	14.1	16.6
Repair, replacement of hard-surface flooring	100.0	0.6	7.6	34.0	18.3	21.6	9.2	8.8
Repair of built-in appliances	100.0	1.7	6.9	7.6	25.9	18.6	28.5	10.7
Maintenance and repair materials	100.0	1.0	12.9	19.7	27.5	24.2	10.2	4.4
Paints, wallpaper, and supplies	100.0	0.6	18.4	17.4	30.0	25.9	6.0	1.8
Tools, equipment for painting, wallpapering	100.0	0.6	18.3	17.4	30.0	25.9	6.0	1.8
Plumbing supplies and equipment	100.0	3.2	16.5	16.5	33.3	11.6	14.2	4.6
Electrical supplies, heating and cooling equipment	100.0	5.8	6.3	20.9	34.8	15.5	7.6	9.0
Hard-surface flooring, repair and replacement	100.0	1.3	13.3	27.9	22.6	13.6	15.7	5.6
Roofing and gutters	100.0	0.8	6.3	19.0	7.2	40.4	24.7	1.7
Plaster, paneling, siding, windows, doors, screens, awnings	100.0	0.4	11.2	16.4	31.2	30.2	4.8	5.8
Patio, walk, fence, driveway, masonry, brick, and stucco materials	100.0	0.0	8.6	10.4	41.4	32.5	3.5	3.8
Miscellaneous supplies and equipment	100.0	0.2	11.5	21.4	26.4	25.2	10.7	4.7
Material for insulation, other maintenance and repair	100.0	0.2	11.5	21.4	26.4	25.2	10.7	4.7
Property management and security	100.0	0.6	8.4	12.4	13.9	21.6	17.5	25.6
Property management	100.0	0.7	10.3	14.5	14.8	23.1	16.7	19.9
Management and upkeep services for security	100.0	0.4	4.4	8.0	12.1	18.3	19.2	37.7
Parking	100.0	3.1	12.2	10.6	6.3	27.7	29.9	11.0
Rented dwellings	100.0	10.7	29.5	21.8	17.3	10.4	4.7	5.6
Rent	100.0	10.8	29.9	21.8	17.3	10.2	4.5	5.5
Rent as pay	100.0	8.6	20.4	21.1	19.0	13.5	8.6	8.9
Maintenance, insurance, and other expenses	100.0	4.8	18.4	21.5	17.3	19.2	9.7	9.0
Tenant's insurance	100.0	8.6	26.5	20.0	17.6	13.8	6.1	7.4
Maintenance and repair services	100.0	2.3	12.6	15.1	8.3	32.8	12.2	16.6
Maintenance and repair materials	100.0	3.9	17.1	31.9	29.1	7.0	10.4	0.6
Other lodging	100.0	3.4	8.1	14.0	23.7	26.5	16.5	7.8
Owned vacation homes	100.0	1.0	4.9	12.1	16.4	34.3	18.9	12.4
Mortgage interest and charges	100.0	0.4	9.2	21.3	22.2	27.3	13.5	6.2
Property taxes	100.0	1.3	3.0	8.0	15.6	39.8	19.3	13.0
Maintenance, insurance, and other expenses	100.0	1.1	2.6	7.2	9.9	33.4	25.8	20.0
Housing while attending school	100.0	18.4	3.8	3.6	52.5	17.9	3.0	1.0
Lodging on trips	100.0	2.0	11.8	17.9	23.2	22.0	17.6	5.6

	total consumer units	under 25	25 to 34	35 to 44	45 to 54	55 to 64	65 to 74	75+
UTILITIES, FUELS, AND PUBLIC SERVICES	**100.0%**	**3.3%**	**14.8%**	**19.4%**	**23.5%**	**19.3%**	**11.7%**	**8.1%**
Natural gas	**100.0**	**2.6**	**13.6**	**19.4**	**23.3**	**19.5**	**11.9**	**9.8**
Electricity	**100.0**	**3.4**	**14.8**	**19.4**	**22.8**	**19.4**	**12.1**	**8.1**
Fuel oil and other fuels	**100.0**	**0.8**	**8.3**	**12.9**	**22.6**	**22.2**	**16.8**	**16.4**
Fuel oil	100.0	0.5	7.3	12.8	24.9	19.1	16.7	18.7
Coal, wood, and other fuels	100.0	2.2	7.5	18.4	22.1	20.3	20.9	8.6
Bottled gas	100.0	0.9	9.9	12.1	19.1	27.3	16.4	14.2
Telephone services	**100.0**	**4.0**	**16.6**	**20.2**	**24.9**	**18.4**	**9.9**	**5.9**
Residential telephone and pay phones	100.0	1.4	8.5	15.8	23.2	22.3	15.9	12.9
Cellular phone service	100.0	5.2	20.3	22.1	25.7	16.7	7.2	2.7
Phone cards	100.0	5.2	23.9	21.9	22.3	13.7	6.7	6.3
Voice over IP	100.0	3.7	15.7	23.1	20.4	18.5	11.6	7.0
Water and other public services	**100.0**	**2.4**	**13.4**	**19.3**	**22.7**	**20.0**	**12.9**	**9.3**
Water and sewerage maintenance	100.0	2.6	13.7	19.9	22.9	19.8	12.4	8.8
Trash and garbage collection	100.0	2.0	13.0	17.7	21.9	20.5	13.8	11.0
Septic tank cleaning	100.0	–	2.8	10.8	28.2	21.3	28.0	8.8

*See Appendix B for information about mortgage principal reduction.
Note: Numbers may not add to total because of rounding. "–" means sample is too small to make a reliable estimate.
Source: Calculations by New Strategist based on the Bureau of Labor Statistics' 2011 Consumer Expenditure Survey

Table 9.5 Housing: Shelter and Utilities: Average spending by income, 2011

(average annual spending on shelter and utilities, by before-tax income of consumer units, 2011)

	total consumer units	under $20,000	$20,000–$39,999	$40,000–$49,999	$50,000–$69,999	$70,000–$79,999	$80,000–$99,999	$100,000 or more
Number of consumer units (in 000s)	122,287	26,342	27,788	11,347	17,376	7,385	10,456	21,593
Average number of persons per consumer unit	2.5	1.8	2.3	2.6	2.7	2.8	3.0	3.2
Average before-tax income of consumer units	$63,685.00	$10,491.66	$29,658.14	$44,698.00	$59,306.00	$74,742.00	$89,108.00	$169,776.00
Average spending of consumer units, total	49,704.88	22,142.36	33,453.66	40,306.19	50,034.03	57,976.69	65,389.80	97,728.22
Housing, average spending	**16,803.03**	**8,830.55**	**12,538.47**	**14,562.10**	**16,888.03**	**19,178.04**	**20,926.38**	**30,211.87**
SHELTER	**9,825.36**	**5,180.22**	**7,253.71**	**8,429.22**	**9,628.04**	**10,886.76**	**12,247.34**	**18,158.32**
Owned dwellings*	6,147.89	1,653.68	3,242.65	4,590.48	6,238.43	7,675.62	9,122.28	14,152.13
Mortgage interest and charges	3,183.73	589.43	1,352.07	2,275.33	3,400.77	4,339.06	5,118.58	7,676.49
Mortgage interest	3,020.32	543.49	1,270.69	2,137.94	3,248.17	4,168.48	4,902.54	7,269.74
Interest paid, home equity loan	61.79	17.90	37.22	63.02	60.84	61.32	80.49	138.15
Interest paid, home equity line of credit	101.63	28.03	44.15	74.36	91.76	109.26	135.55	268.61
Property taxes	1,844.51	647.30	1,099.48	1,433.16	1,768.17	2,105.60	2,493.26	4,138.00
Maintenance, repairs, insurance, other expenses	1,119.64	416.96	791.09	881.99	1,069.49	1,230.96	1,510.45	2,337.63
Homeowner's insurance	351.98	137.28	250.65	295.87	355.18	465.21	507.54	657.15
Ground rent	48.15	59.22	79.62	59.43	46.41	20.49	23.79	10.86
Maintenance and repair services	555.93	157.08	332.34	387.39	508.52	557.78	750.31	1,362.21
Painting and papering	61.73	14.67	38.81	44.92	54.41	35.13	30.15	187.74
Plumbing and water heating	65.34	27.16	49.56	62.56	87.84	77.32	68.03	110.20
Heat, air conditioning, electrical work	109.51	27.25	52.90	44.55	110.78	105.31	205.53	270.79
Roofing and gutters	92.49	20.11	64.36	73.11	76.98	150.91	118.84	206.90
Other repair and maintenance services	168.24	45.95	102.34	144.05	132.36	138.10	175.93	450.41
Repair, replacement of hard-surface flooring	56.91	21.23	23.11	16.77	45.27	49.81	150.60	131.46
Repair of built-in appliances	1.71	0.99	1.28	1.43	0.87	1.19	1.23	4.72
Maintenance and repair materials	74.55	16.35	36.01	68.06	74.44	91.46	145.82	158.36
Paints, wallpaper, and supplies	13.69	2.83	10.32	8.62	13.48	11.57	29.95	26.95
Tools, equipment for painting, wallpapering	1.47	0.31	1.11	0.93	1.45	1.24	3.22	2.89
Plumbing supplies and equipment	6.43	1.63	3.18	5.57	10.98	6.56	15.73	9.47
Electrical supplies, heating and cooling equipment	3.44	0.92	1.76	1.82	4.17	10.32	8.58	4.44
Hard-surface flooring, repair and replacement	11.88	4.33	1.31	21.72	13.19	11.88	29.08	20.11
Roofing and gutters	5.22	0.70	2.18	11.77	5.10	6.63	3.97	11.58
Plaster, paneling, siding, windows, doors, screens, awnings	15.77	4.73	6.79	9.07	11.17	17.78	30.03	42.69
Patio, walk, fence, driveway, masonry, brick, and stucco materials	1.78	0.03	0.25	0.32	1.67	1.68	0.92	7.22
Miscellaneous supplies and equipment	14.88	3.83	9.11	8.24	13.22	23.80	24.33	33.00
Material for insulation, other maintenance and repair	14.88	3.83	9.11	8.24	13.22	23.80	24.33	33.00
Property management and security	88.48	46.91	91.70	70.70	84.25	95.64	82.75	148.12
Property management	60.24	31.48	58.60	48.86	61.87	73.83	54.87	100.09
Management and upkeep services for security	28.23	15.44	33.10	21.84	22.38	21.80	27.89	48.03
Parking	0.55	–	0.77	0.54	0.68	0.39	0.23	0.94
Rented dwellings	**3,029.49**	**3,336.47**	**3,727.39**	**3,475.71**	**2,922.58**	**2,711.10**	**2,364.14**	**2,039.45**
Rent	2,905.25	3,092.66	3,604.98	3,381.52	2,827.70	2,570.52	2,292.08	1,999.63
Rent as pay	83.62	215.63	86.23	58.74	54.03	19.01	26.82	5.70
Maintenance, insurance, and other expenses	40.62	28.18	36.18	35.45	40.86	121.57	45.24	34.11
Tenant's insurance	13.09	9.25	13.87	16.63	16.00	11.99	11.58	13.67
Maintenance and repair services	15.82	15.03	16.00	5.43	15.76	37.62	22.69	11.29
Maintenance and repair materials	11.71	3.90	6.31	13.39	9.09	71.97	10.97	9.15
Other lodging	**647.99**	**190.07**	**283.69**	**363.03**	**467.02**	**500.04**	**760.92**	**1,966.74**
Owned vacation homes	261.96	62.19	110.22	164.88	180.92	175.95	278.46	838.59
Mortgage interest and charges	84.79	11.14	25.70	44.03	47.86	52.53	92.84	308.98
Property taxes	116.71	35.58	50.53	95.21	66.99	99.80	113.66	359.41
Maintenance, insurance, and other expenses	60.46	15.48	34.00	25.63	66.07	23.62	71.96	170.20
Housing while attending school	71.40	65.05	36.37	10.63	21.11	32.76	35.27	227.38
Lodging on trips	314.62	62.83	137.09	187.52	264.99	291.33	447.19	900.78

	total consumer units	under $20,000	$20,000– $39,999	$40,000– $49,999	$50,000– $69,999	$70,000– $79,999	$80,000– $99,999	$100,000 or more
UTILITIES, FUELS, AND PUBLIC SERVICES	**$3,726.76**	**$2,331.60**	**$3,156.36**	**$3,666.27**	**$4,000.06**	**$4,272.90**	**$4,537.50**	**$5,395.33**
Natural gas	**419.64**	**250.99**	**346.81**	**379.71**	**426.59**	**461.64**	**522.14**	**670.47**
Electricity	**1,422.95**	**1,001.21**	**1,257.03**	**1,432.51**	**1,515.68**	**1,600.39**	**1,662.19**	**1,894.81**
Fuel oil and other fuels	**156.83**	**90.23**	**115.18**	**142.26**	**158.31**	**169.39**	**187.01**	**279.24**
Fuel oil	89.23	50.39	65.47	63.33	82.02	88.65	125.91	169.04
Coal, wood, and other fuels	9.36	6.76	6.89	15.37	9.77	16.84	7.69	10.46
Bottled gas	58.24	33.08	42.82	63.55	66.52	63.90	53.41	99.74
Telephone services	**1,226.44**	**693.97**	**1,025.18**	**1,240.29**	**1,375.51**	**1,450.60**	**1,550.37**	**1,774.25**
Residential telephone and pay phones	380.95	290.55	335.04	371.84	398.06	415.58	428.55	506.44
Cellular phone service	825.71	390.21	671.95	851.43	957.59	1,014.48	1,099.28	1,238.19
Phone cards	8.84	8.41	11.38	9.79	10.61	6.64	6.81	5.90
Voice over IP	10.94	4.80	6.80	7.22	9.24	13.90	15.73	23.72
Water and other public services	**500.91**	**295.19**	**412.17**	**471.50**	**523.97**	**590.88**	**615.79**	**776.57**
Water and sewerage maintenance	376.69	229.06	313.57	357.88	391.06	445.00	449.00	577.95
Trash and garbage collection	121.02	65.13	96.91	110.74	129.16	142.63	158.44	193.57
Septic tank cleaning	3.20	1.00	1.70	2.88	3.75	3.25	8.34	5.04

See Appendix B for information about mortgage principal reduction.
Note: Subcategories may not add to total because some are not shown. "–" means sample is too small to make a reliable estimate.
Source: Bureau of Labor Statistics, unpublished tables from the 2011 Consumer Expenditure Survey; calculations by New Strategist

Table 9.6 Housing: Shelter and Utilities: Indexed spending by income, 2011

(indexed average annual spending of consumer units on shelter and utilities, by before-tax income of consumer unit, 2011; index definition: an index of 100 is the average for all consumer units; an index of 125 means that spending by consumer units in that group is 25 percent above the average for all consumer units; an index of 75 indicates spending that is 25 percent below the average for all consumer units)

	total consumer units	under $20,000	$20,000–$39,999	$40,000–$49,999	$50,000–$69,999	$70,000–$79,999	$80,000–$99,999	$100,000 or more
Average spending of consumer units, total	$49,705	$22,142	$33,454	$40,306	$50,034	$57,977	$65,390	$97,728
Average spending of consumer units, index	100	45	67	81	101	117	132	197
Housing, spending index	**100**	**53**	**75**	**87**	**101**	**114**	**125**	**180**
SHELTER	**100**	**53**	**74**	**86**	**98**	**111**	**125**	**185**
Owned dwellings*	**100**	**27**	**53**	**75**	**101**	**125**	**148**	**230**
Mortgage interest and charges	100	19	42	71	107	136	161	241
Mortgage interest	100	18	42	71	108	138	162	241
Interest paid, home equity loan	100	29	60	102	98	99	130	224
Interest paid, home equity line of credit	100	28	43	73	90	108	133	264
Property taxes	100	35	60	78	96	114	135	224
Maintenance, repairs, insurance, other expenses	100	37	71	79	96	110	135	209
Homeowner's insurance	100	39	71	84	101	132	144	187
Ground rent	100	123	165	123	96	43	49	23
Maintenance and repair services	100	28	60	70	91	100	135	245
Painting and papering	100	24	63	73	88	57	49	304
Plumbing and water heating	100	42	76	96	134	118	104	169
Heat, air conditioning, electrical work	100	25	48	41	101	96	188	247
Roofing and gutters	100	22	70	79	83	163	128	224
Other repair and maintenance services	100	27	61	86	79	82	105	268
Repair, replacement of hard-surface flooring	100	37	41	29	80	88	265	231
Repair of built-in appliances	100	58	75	84	51	70	72	276
Maintenance and repair materials	100	22	48	91	100	123	196	212
Paints, wallpaper, and supplies	100	21	75	63	98	85	219	197
Tools, equipment for painting, wallpapering	100	21	76	63	99	84	219	197
Plumbing supplies and equipment	100	25	49	87	171	102	245	147
Electrical supplies, heating and cooling equipment	100	27	51	53	121	300	249	129
Hard-surface flooring, repair and replacement	100	36	11	183	111	100	245	169
Roofing and gutters	100	13	42	225	98	127	76	222
Plaster, paneling, siding, windows, doors, screens, awnings	100	30	43	58	71	113	190	271
Patio, walk, fence, driveway, masonry, brick, and stucco materials	100	2	14	18	94	94	52	406
Miscellaneous supplies and equipment	100	26	61	55	89	160	164	222
Material for insulation, other maintenance and repair	100	26	61	55	89	160	164	222
Property management and security	100	53	104	80	95	108	94	167
Property management	100	52	97	81	103	123	91	166
Management and upkeep services for security	100	55	117	77	79	77	99	170
Parking	100	–	139	98	124	71	42	171
Rented dwellings	**100**	**110**	**123**	**115**	**96**	**89**	**78**	**67**
Rent	100	106	124	116	97	88	79	69
Rent as pay	100	258	103	70	65	23	32	7
Maintenance, insurance, and other expenses	100	69	89	87	101	299	111	84
Tenant's insurance	100	71	106	127	122	92	88	104
Maintenance and repair services	100	95	101	34	100	238	143	71
Maintenance and repair materials	100	33	54	114	78	615	94	78
Other lodging	**100**	**29**	**44**	**56**	**72**	**77**	**117**	**304**
Owned vacation homes	100	24	42	63	69	67	106	320
Mortgage interest and charges	100	13	30	52	56	62	109	364
Property taxes	100	30	43	82	57	86	97	308
Maintenance, insurance, and other expenses	100	26	56	42	109	39	119	282
Housing while attending school	100	91	51	15	30	46	49	318
Lodging on trips	100	20	44	60	84	93	142	286

	total consumer units	under $20,000	$20,000– $39,999	$40,000– $49,999	$50,000– $69,999	$70,000– $79,999	$80,000– $99,999	$100,000 or more
UTILITIES, FUELS, AND PUBLIC SERVICES	**100**	**63**	**85**	**98**	**107**	**115**	**122**	**145**
Natural gas	**100**	**60**	**83**	**90**	**102**	**110**	**124**	**160**
Electricity	**100**	**70**	**88**	**101**	**107**	**112**	**117**	**133**
Fuel oil and other fuels	**100**	**58**	**73**	**91**	**101**	**108**	**119**	**178**
Fuel oil	100	56	73	71	92	99	141	189
Coal, wood, and other fuels	100	72	74	164	104	180	82	112
Bottled gas	100	57	74	109	114	110	92	171
Telephone services	**100**	**57**	**84**	**101**	**112**	**118**	**126**	**145**
Residential telephone and pay phones	100	76	88	98	104	109	112	133
Cellular phone service	100	47	81	103	116	123	133	150
Phone cards	100	95	129	111	120	75	77	67
Voice over IP	100	44	62	66	84	127	144	217
Water and other public services	**100**	**59**	**82**	**94**	**105**	**118**	**123**	**155**
Water and sewerage maintenance	100	61	83	95	104	118	119	153
Trash and garbage collection	100	54	80	92	107	118	131	160
Septic tank cleaning	100	31	53	90	117	102	261	158

See Appendix B for information about mortgage principal reduction.
Note: "–" means sample is too small to make a reliable estimate.
Source: Calculations by New Strategist based on the Bureau of Labor Statistics' 2011 Consumer Expenditure Survey

Table 9.7 Housing: Shelter and Utilities: Total spending by income, 2011

(total annual spending on shelter and utilities, by before-tax income group of consumer units, 2011; consumer units and dollars in thousands)

	total consumer units	under $20,000	$20,000–$39,999	$40,000–$49,999	$50,000–$69,999	$70,000–$79,999	$80,000–$99,999	$100,000 or more
Number of consumer units	122,287	26,342	27,788	11,347	17,376	7,385	10,456	21,593
Total spending of all consumer units	$6,078,260,661	$583,273,961	$929,610,260	$457,354,338	$869,391,305	$428,157,856	$683,715,749	$2,110,245,454
Housing, total spending	2,054,792,130	232,614,372	348,419,011	165,236,149	293,446,409	141,629,825	218,806,229	652,364,909
SHELTER	**1,201,513,798**	**136,457,464**	**201,566,110**	**95,646,359**	**167,296,823**	**80,398,723**	**128,058,187**	**392,092,604**
Owned dwellings*	**751,807,024**	**43,561,277**	**90,106,676**	**52,088,177**	**108,398,960**	**56,684,454**	**95,382,560**	**305,586,943**
Mortgage interest and charges	389,328,791	15,526,707	37,571,351	25,818,170	59,091,780	32,043,958	53,519,872	165,758,449
Mortgage interest	369,345,872	14,316,717	35,310,064	24,259,205	56,440,202	30,784,225	51,260,958	156,975,496
Interest paid, home equity loan	7,556,114	471,647	1,034,187	715,088	1,057,156	452,848	841,603	2,983,073
Interest paid, home equity line of credit	12,428,028	738,262	1,226,967	843,763	1,594,422	806,885	1,417,311	5,800,096
Property taxes	225,559,594	17,051,143	30,552,413	16,262,067	30,723,722	15,549,856	26,069,527	89,351,834
Maintenance, repairs, insurance, other expenses	136,917,417	10,983,531	21,982,766	10,007,941	18,583,458	9,090,640	15,793,265	50,476,445
Homeowner's insurance	43,042,578	3,616,347	6,965,145	3,357,237	6,171,608	3,435,576	5,306,838	14,189,840
Ground rent	5,888,119	1,559,916	2,212,448	674,352	806,420	151,319	248,748	234,500
Maintenance and repair services	67,983,012	4,137,781	9,235,176	4,395,714	8,836,044	4,119,205	7,845,241	29,414,201
Painting and papering	7,548,777	386,401	1,078,371	509,707	945,428	259,435	315,248	4,053,870
Plumbing and water heating	7,990,233	715,453	1,377,169	709,868	1,526,308	571,008	711,322	2,379,549
Heat, air conditioning, electrical work	13,391,649	717,752	1,469,858	505,509	1,924,913	777,714	2,149,022	5,847,168
Roofing and gutters	11,310,325	529,812	1,788,308	829,579	1,337,604	1,114,470	1,242,591	4,467,592
Other repair and maintenance services	20,573,565	1,210,437	2,843,853	1,634,535	2,299,887	1,019,869	1,839,524	9,725,703
Repair, replacement of hard-surface flooring	6,959,353	559,327	642,256	190,289	786,612	367,847	1,574,674	2,838,616
Repair of built-in appliances	209,111	26,197	35,495	16,226	15,117	8,788	12,861	101,919
Maintenance and repair materials	9,116,496	430,604	1,000,573	772,277	1,293,469	675,432	1,524,694	3,419,467
Paints, wallpaper, and supplies	1,674,109	74,659	286,886	97,811	234,228	85,444	313,157	581,931
Tools, equipment for painting, wallpapering	179,762	8,067	30,850	10,553	25,195	9,157	33,668	62,404
Plumbing supplies and equipment	786,305	42,951	88,432	63,203	190,788	48,446	164,473	204,486
Electrical supplies, heating and cooling equipment	420,667	24,120	48,843	20,652	72,458	76,213	89,712	95,873
Hard-surface flooring, repair and replacement	1,452,770	114,004	36,498	246,457	229,189	87,734	304,060	434,235
Roofing and gutters	638,338	18,483	60,675	133,554	88,618	48,963	41,510	250,047
Plaster, paneling, siding, windows, doors, screens, awnings	1,928,466	124,516	188,646	102,917	194,090	131,305	313,994	921,805
Patio, walk, fence, driveway, masonry, brick, and stucco materials	217,671	790	6,950	3,631	29,018	12,407	9,620	155,901
Miscellaneous supplies and equipment	1,819,631	100,879	253,083	93,499	229,711	175,763	254,394	712,569
Material for insulation, other maintenance and repair	1,819,631	100,879	253,083	93,499	229,711	175,763	254,394	712,569
Property management and security	10,819,954	1,235,812	2,548,127	802,233	1,463,928	706,301	865,234	3,198,355
Property management	7,366,569	829,214	1,628,283	554,414	1,075,053	545,235	573,721	2,161,243
Management and upkeep services for security	3,452,162	406,653	919,844	247,818	388,875	160,993	291,618	1,037,112
Parking	67,258	–	21,297	6,127	11,816	2,880	2,405	20,297
Rented dwellings	**370,467,244**	**87,889,293**	**103,576,642**	**39,438,881**	**50,782,750**	**20,021,474**	**24,719,448**	**44,037,844**
Rent	355,274,307	81,466,920	100,175,179	38,370,107	49,134,115	18,983,290	23,965,988	43,178,011
Rent as pay	10,225,639	5,680,120	2,396,137	666,523	938,825	140,389	280,430	123,080
Maintenance, insurance, and other expenses	4,967,298	742,252	1,005,326	402,251	709,983	897,794	473,029	736,537
Tenant's insurance	1,600,737	243,746	385,476	188,701	278,016	88,546	121,080	295,176
Maintenance and repair services	1,934,580	395,804	444,590	61,614	273,846	277,824	237,247	243,785
Maintenance and repair materials	1,431,981	102,703	175,393	151,936	157,948	531,498	114,702	197,576
Other lodging	**79,240,753**	**5,006,763**	**7,883,071**	**4,119,301**	**8,114,940**	**3,692,795**	**7,956,180**	**42,467,817**
Owned vacation homes	32,034,303	1,638,283	3,062,925	1,870,893	3,143,666	1,299,391	2,911,578	18,107,674
Mortgage interest and charges	10,368,715	293,347	714,026	499,608	831,615	387,934	970,735	6,671,805
Property taxes	14,272,116	937,184	1,404,020	1,080,348	1,164,018	737,023	1,188,429	7,760,740
Maintenance, insurance, and other expenses	7,393,472	407,702	944,879	290,824	1,148,032	174,434	752,414	3,675,129
Housing while attending school	8,731,292	1,713,436	1,010,517	120,619	366,807	241,933	368,783	4,909,816
Lodging on trips	38,473,936	1,655,045	3,809,496	2,127,789	4,604,466	2,151,472	4,675,819	19,450,543

	total consumer units	under $20,000	$20,000– $39,999	$40,000– $49,999	$50,000– $69,999	$70,000– $79,999	$80,000– $99,999	$100,000 or more
UTILITIES, FUELS, AND PUBLIC SERVICES	$455,734,300	$61,418,927	$87,709,019	$41,601,166	$69,505,043	$31,555,367	$47,444,100	$116,501,361
Natural gas	51,316,517	6,611,645	9,637,179	4,308,569	7,412,428	3,409,211	5,459,496	14,477,459
Electricity	174,008,287	26,373,930	34,930,374	16,254,691	26,336,456	11,818,880	17,379,859	40,914,632
Fuel oil and other fuels	19,178,270	2,376,837	3,200,541	1,614,224	2,750,795	1,250,945	1,955,377	6,029,629
Fuel oil	10,911,669	1,327,266	1,819,168	718,606	1,425,180	654,680	1,316,515	3,650,081
Coal, wood, and other fuels	1,144,606	178,140	191,453	174,403	169,764	124,363	80,407	225,863
Bottled gas	7,121,995	871,358	1,189,920	721,102	1,155,852	471,902	558,455	2,153,686
Telephone services	149,977,668	18,280,566	28,487,715	14,073,571	23,900,862	10,712,681	16,210,669	38,311,380
Residential telephone and pay phones	46,585,233	7,653,613	9,310,222	4,219,268	6,916,691	3,069,058	4,480,919	10,935,559
Cellular phone service	100,973,599	10,279,028	18,672,197	9,661,176	16,639,084	7,491,935	11,494,072	26,736,237
Phone cards	1,081,017	221,443	316,194	111,087	184,359	49,036	71,205	127,399
Voice over IP	1,337,820	126,563	188,969	81,925	160,554	102,652	164,473	512,186
Water and other public services	61,254,781	7,775,872	11,453,354	5,350,111	9,104,503	4,363,649	6,438,700	16,768,476
Water and sewerage maintenance	46,064,290	6,033,843	8,713,380	4,060,864	6,795,059	3,286,325	4,694,744	12,479,674
Trash and garbage collection	14,799,173	1,715,777	2,692,834	1,256,567	2,244,284	1,053,323	1,656,649	4,179,757
Septic tank cleaning	391,318	26,257	47,140	32,679	65,160	24,001	87,203	108,829

*See Appendix B for information about mortgage principal reduction.
Note: Numbers may not add to total because of rounding and missing subcategories. "–" means sample is too small to make a reliable estimate.
Source: Calculations by New Strategist based on the Bureau of Labor Statistics' 2011 Consumer Expenditure Survey

Table 9.8 Housing: Shelter and Utilities: Market shares by income, 2011

(percentage of total annual spending on shelter and utilities accounted for by before-tax income group of consumer units, 2011)

	total consumer units	under $20,000	$20,000–$39,999	$40,000–$49,999	$50,000–$69,999	$70,000–$79,999	$80,000–$99,999	$100,000 or more
Share of total consumer units	100.0%	21.5%	22.7%	9.3%	14.2%	6.0%	8.6%	17.7%
Share of total before-tax income	100.0	3.5	10.6	6.5	13.2	7.1	12.0	47.1
Share of total spending	100.0	9.6	15.3	7.5	14.3	7.0	11.2	34.7
Share of housing spending	100.0	11.3	17.0	8.0	14.3	6.9	10.6	31.7
SHELTER	100.0	11.4	16.8	8.0	13.9	6.7	10.7	32.6
Owned dwellings*	100.0	5.8	12.0	6.9	14.4	7.5	12.7	40.6
Mortgage interest and charges	100.0	4.0	9.7	6.6	15.2	8.2	13.7	42.6
Mortgage interest	100.0	3.9	9.6	6.6	15.3	8.3	13.9	42.5
Interest paid, home equity loan	100.0	6.2	13.7	9.5	14.0	6.0	11.1	39.5
Interest paid, home equity line of credit	100.0	5.9	9.9	6.8	12.8	6.5	11.4	46.7
Property taxes	100.0	7.6	13.5	7.2	13.6	6.9	11.6	39.6
Maintenance, repairs, insurance, other expenses	100.0	8.0	16.1	7.3	13.6	6.6	11.5	36.9
Homeowner's insurance	100.0	8.4	16.2	7.8	14.3	8.0	12.3	33.0
Ground rent	100.0	26.5	37.6	11.5	13.7	2.6	4.2	4.0
Maintenance and repair services	100.0	6.1	13.6	6.5	13.0	6.1	11.5	43.3
Painting and papering	100.0	5.1	14.3	6.8	12.5	3.4	4.2	53.7
Plumbing and water heating	100.0	9.0	17.2	8.9	19.1	7.1	8.9	29.8
Heat, air conditioning, electrical work	100.0	5.4	11.0	3.8	14.4	5.8	16.0	43.7
Roofing and gutters	100.0	4.7	15.8	7.3	11.8	9.9	11.0	39.5
Other repair and maintenance services	100.0	5.9	13.8	7.9	11.2	5.0	8.9	47.3
Repair, replacement of hard-surface flooring	100.0	8.0	9.2	2.7	11.3	5.3	22.6	40.8
Repair of built-in appliances	100.0	12.5	17.0	7.8	7.2	4.2	6.2	48.7
Maintenance and repair materials	100.0	4.7	11.0	8.5	14.2	7.4	16.7	37.5
Paints, wallpaper, and supplies	100.0	4.5	17.1	5.8	14.0	5.1	18.7	34.8
Tools, equipment for painting, wallpapering	100.0	4.5	17.2	5.9	14.0	5.1	18.7	34.7
Plumbing supplies and equipment	100.0	5.5	11.2	8.0	24.3	6.2	20.9	26.0
Electrical supplies, heating and cooling equipment	100.0	5.7	11.6	4.9	17.2	18.1	21.3	22.8
Hard-surface flooring, repair and replacement	100.0	7.8	2.5	17.0	15.8	6.0	20.9	29.9
Roofing and gutters	100.0	2.9	9.5	20.9	13.9	7.7	6.5	39.2
Plaster, paneling, siding, windows, doors, screens, awnings	100.0	6.5	9.8	5.3	10.1	6.8	16.3	47.8
Patio, walk, fence, driveway, masonry, brick, and stucco materials	100.0	0.4	3.2	1.7	13.3	5.7	4.4	71.6
Miscellaneous supplies and equipment	100.0	5.5	13.9	5.1	12.6	9.7	14.0	39.2
Material for insulation, other maintenance and repair	100.0	5.5	13.9	5.1	12.6	9.7	14.0	39.2
Property management and security	100.0	11.4	23.6	7.4	13.5	6.5	8.0	29.6
Property management	100.0	11.3	22.1	7.5	14.6	7.4	7.8	29.3
Management and upkeep services for security	100.0	11.8	26.6	7.2	11.3	4.7	8.4	30.0
Parking	100.0	–	31.7	9.1	17.6	4.3	3.6	30.2
Rented dwellings	100.0	23.7	28.0	10.6	13.7	5.4	6.7	11.9
Rent	100.0	22.9	28.2	10.8	13.8	5.3	6.7	12.2
Rent as pay	100.0	55.5	23.4	6.5	9.2	1.4	2.7	1.2
Maintenance, insurance, and other expenses	100.0	14.9	20.2	8.1	14.3	18.1	9.5	14.8
Tenant's insurance	100.0	15.2	24.1	11.8	17.4	5.5	7.6	18.4
Maintenance and repair services	100.0	20.5	23.0	3.2	14.2	14.4	12.3	12.6
Maintenance and repair materials	100.0	7.2	12.2	10.6	11.0	37.1	8.0	13.8
Other lodging	100.0	6.3	9.9	5.2	10.2	4.7	10.0	53.6
Owned vacation homes	100.0	5.1	9.6	5.8	9.8	4.1	9.1	56.5
Mortgage interest and charges	100.0	2.8	6.9	4.8	8.0	3.7	9.4	64.3
Property taxes	100.0	6.6	9.8	7.6	8.2	5.2	8.3	54.4
Maintenance, insurance, and other expenses	100.0	5.5	12.8	3.9	15.5	2.4	10.2	49.7
Housing while attending school	100.0	19.6	11.6	1.4	4.2	2.8	4.2	56.2
Lodging on trips	100.0	4.3	9.9	5.5	12.0	5.6	12.2	50.6

	total consumer units	under $20,000	$20,000—$39,999	$40,000—$49,999	$50,000—$69,999	$70,000—$79,999	$80,000—$99,999	$100,000 or more
UTILITIES, FUELS, AND PUBLIC SERVICES	**100.0%**	**13.5%**	**19.2%**	**9.1%**	**15.3%**	**6.9%**	**10.4%**	**25.6%**
Natural gas	**100.0**	**12.9**	**18.8**	**8.4**	**14.4**	**6.6**	**10.6**	**28.2**
Electricity	**100.0**	**15.2**	**20.1**	**9.3**	**15.1**	**6.8**	**10.0**	**23.5**
Fuel oil and other fuels	**100.0**	**12.4**	**16.7**	**8.4**	**14.3**	**6.5**	**10.2**	**31.4**
Fuel oil	100.0	12.2	16.7	6.6	13.1	6.0	12.1	33.5
Coal, wood, and other fuels	100.0	15.6	16.7	15.2	14.8	10.9	7.0	19.7
Bottled gas	100.0	12.2	16.7	10.1	16.2	6.6	7.8	30.2
Telephone services	**100.0**	**12.2**	**19.0**	**9.4**	**15.9**	**7.1**	**10.8**	**25.5**
Residential telephone and pay phones	100.0	16.4	20.0	9.1	14.8	6.6	9.6	23.5
Cellular phone service	100.0	10.2	18.5	9.6	16.5	7.4	11.4	26.5
Phone cards	100.0	20.5	29.2	10.3	17.1	4.5	6.6	11.8
Voice over IP	100.0	9.5	14.1	6.1	12.0	7.7	12.3	38.3
Water and other public services	**100.0**	**12.7**	**18.7**	**8.7**	**14.9**	**7.1**	**10.5**	**27.4**
Water and sewerage maintenance	100.0	13.1	18.9	8.8	14.8	7.1	10.2	27.1
Trash and garbage collection	100.0	11.6	18.2	8.5	15.2	7.1	11.2	28.2
Septic tank cleaning	100.0	6.7	12.0	8.4	16.7	6.1	22.3	27.8

*See Appendix B for information about mortgage principal reduction.
Note: Numbers may not add to total because of rounding. "–" means sample is too small to make a reliable estimate.
Source: Calculations by New Strategist based on the Bureau of Labor Statistics' 2011 Consumer Expenditure Survey

Table 9.9 Housing: Shelter and Utilities: Average spending by high-income consumer units, 2011

(average annual spending on shelter and utilities, by before-tax income of consumer units, 2011)

	total consumer units	$100,000 or more	$100,000–$119,999	$120,000–$149,999	$150,000 or more
Number of consumer units (in 000s)	122,287	21,593	7,045	6,107	8,440
Average number of persons per consumer unit	2.5	3.2	3.2	3.1	3.2
Average before-tax income of consumer units	$63,685.00	$169,776.00	$108,549.00	$133,318.00	$247,261.00
Average spending of consumer units, total	49,704.88	97,728.22	76,496.41	87,239.44	123,056.38
Housing, average spending	16,803.03	30,211.87	23,660.02	27,420.06	37,700.47
SHELTER	9,825.36	18,158.32	13,546.26	16,545.72	23,174.76
Owned dwellings*	6,147.89	14,152.13	10,538.74	12,841.18	18,116.73
Mortgage interest and charges	3,183.73	7,676.49	5,992.98	6,947.62	9,609.08
Mortgage interest	3,020.32	7,269.74	5,702.57	6,578.32	9,078.12
Interest paid, home equity loan	61.79	138.15	113.59	115.88	174.76
Interest paid, home equity line of credit	101.63	268.61	176.82	253.42	356.20
Property taxes	1,844.51	4,138.00	2,879.57	3,644.95	5,545.15
Maintenance, repairs, insurance, other expenses	1,119.64	2,337.63	1,666.18	2,248.61	2,962.49
Homeowner's insurance	351.98	657.15	526.65	592.65	812.74
Ground rent	48.15	10.86	15.97	9.22	7.78
Maintenance and repair services	555.93	1,362.21	883.23	1,392.62	1,740.00
Painting and papering	61.73	187.74	132.48	136.39	271.01
Plumbing and water heating	65.34	110.20	96.59	67.65	152.34
Heat, air conditioning, electrical work	109.51	270.79	195.38	336.02	286.53
Roofing and gutters	92.49	206.90	159.30	143.43	292.54
Other repair and maintenance services	168.24	450.41	205.24	539.52	590.59
Repair, replacement of hard-surface flooring	56.91	131.46	91.66	162.53	142.21
Repair of built-in appliances	1.71	4.72	2.59	7.08	4.78
Maintenance and repair materials	74.55	158.36	105.33	146.47	211.22
Paints, wallpaper, and supplies	13.69	26.95	38.31	24.08	19.54
Tools, equipment for painting, wallpapering	1.47	2.89	4.11	2.59	2.10
Plumbing supplies and equipment	6.43	9.47	8.72	4.09	14.00
Electrical supplies, heating and cooling equipment	3.44	4.44	4.37	2.82	5.67
Hard-surface flooring, repair and replacement	11.88	20.11	19.53	17.97	22.15
Roofing and gutters	5.22	11.58	5.11	1.01	24.64
Plaster, paneling, siding, windows, doors, screens, awnings	15.77	42.69	4.23	50.48	69.15
Patio, walk, fence, driveway, masonry, brick, and stucco materials	1.78	7.22	3.12	11.11	7.83
Miscellaneous supplies and equipment	14.88	33.00	17.84	32.31	46.14
Material for insulation, other maintenance and repair	14.88	33.00	17.84	32.31	46.14
Property management and security	88.48	148.12	134.73	107.00	189.04
Property management	60.24	100.09	103.16	77.35	113.98
Management and upkeep services for security	28.23	48.03	31.57	29.66	75.06
Parking	0.55	0.94	0.27	0.65	1.72
Rented dwellings	3,029.49	2,039.45	2,112.33	2,101.38	1,933.80
Rent	2,905.25	1,999.63	2,076.35	2,066.22	1,887.42
Rent as pay	83.62	5.70	11.59	2.49	3.12
Maintenance, insurance, and other expenses	40.62	34.11	24.40	32.66	43.25
Tenant's insurance	13.09	13.67	14.56	8.30	16.82
Maintenance and repair services	15.82	11.29	7.15	8.40	16.83
Maintenance and repair materials	11.71	9.15	2.69	15.96	9.61
Other lodging	647.99	1,966.74	895.19	1,603.16	3,124.24
Owned vacation homes	261.96	838.59	294.86	669.79	1,414.57
Mortgage interest and charges	84.79	308.98	78.22	271.04	529.05
Property taxes	116.71	359.41	149.74	258.67	607.30
Maintenance, insurance, and other expenses	60.46	170.20	66.89	140.07	278.22
Housing while attending school	71.40	227.38	72.06	163.06	403.56
Lodging on trips	314.62	900.78	528.28	770.30	1,306.11

	total consumer units	$100,000 or more	$100,000– $119,999	$120,000– $149,999	$150,000 or more
UTILITIES, FUELS, AND PUBLIC SERVICES	**$3,726.76**	**$5,395.33**	**$4,903.48**	**$5,125.64**	**$6,001.01**
Natural gas	**419.64**	**670.47**	**602.95**	**598.42**	**778.96**
Electricity	**1,422.95**	**1,894.81**	**1,709.70**	**1,760.44**	**2,146.53**
Fuel oil and other fuels	**156.83**	**279.24**	**227.98**	**266.97**	**330.90**
Fuel oil	89.23	169.04	140.02	164.53	196.52
Coal, wood, and other fuels	9.36	10.46	16.33	6.73	8.26
Bottled gas	58.24	99.74	71.63	95.71	126.11
Telephone services	**1,226.44**	**1,774.25**	**1,672.55**	**1,734.21**	**1,888.11**
Residential telephone and pay phones	380.95	506.44	452.61	467.61	579.47
Cellular phone service	825.71	1,238.19	1,186.24	1,240.90	1,279.61
Phone cards	8.84	5.90	6.24	6.83	4.95
Voice over IP	10.94	23.72	27.47	18.88	24.09
Water and other public services	**500.91**	**776.57**	**690.30**	**765.60**	**856.51**
Water and sewerage maintenance	376.69	577.95	523.91	572.81	626.79
Trash and garbage collection	121.02	193.57	164.47	187.62	222.16
Septic tank cleaning	3.20	5.04	1.92	5.17	7.56

*See Appendix B for information about mortgage principal reduction.
Note: Subcategories may not add to total because some are not shown.
Source: Bureau of Labor Statistics, unpublished tables from the 2011 Consumer Expenditure Survey

Table 9.10 Housing: Shelter and Utilities: Indexed spending by high-income consumer units, 2011

(indexed average annual spending of high-income consumer units on shelter and utilities, by before-tax income of consumer unit, 2011; index definition: an index of 100 is the average for all consumer units; an index of 125 means that spending by consumer units in that group is 25 percent above the average for all consumer units; an index of 75 indicates spending that is 25 percent below the average for all consumer units)

	total consumer units	$100,000 or more	$100,000– $119,999	$120,000– $149,999	$150,000 or more
Average spending of consumer units, total	$49,705	$97,728	$76,496	$87,239	$123,056
Average spending of consumer units, index	100	197	154	176	248
Housing, spending index	**100**	**180**	**141**	**163**	**224**
SHELTER	**100**	**185**	**138**	**168**	**236**
Owned dwellings*	**100**	**230**	**171**	**209**	**295**
Mortgage interest and charges	100	241	188	218	302
Mortgage interest	100	241	189	218	301
Interest paid, home equity loan	100	224	184	188	283
Interest paid, home equity line of credit	100	264	174	249	350
Property taxes	100	224	156	198	301
Maintenance, repairs, insurance, other expenses	100	209	149	201	265
Homeowner's insurance	100	187	150	168	231
Ground rent	100	23	33	19	16
Maintenance and repair services	100	245	159	251	313
Painting and papering	100	304	215	221	439
Plumbing and water heating	100	169	148	104	233
Heat, air conditioning, electrical work	100	247	178	307	262
Roofing and gutters	100	224	172	155	316
Other repair and maintenance services	100	268	122	321	351
Repair, replacement of hard-surface flooring	100	231	161	286	250
Repair of built-in appliances	100	276	151	414	280
Maintenance and repair materials	100	212	141	196	283
Paints, wallpaper, and supplies	100	197	280	176	143
Tools, equipment for painting, wallpapering	100	197	280	176	143
Plumbing supplies and equipment	100	147	136	64	218
Electrical supplies, heating and cooling equipment	100	129	127	82	165
Hard-surface flooring, repair and replacement	100	169	164	151	186
Roofing and gutters	100	222	98	19	472
Plaster, paneling, siding, windows, doors, screens, awnings	100	271	27	320	438
Patio, walk, fence, driveway, masonry, brick, and stucco materials	100	406	175	624	440
Miscellaneous supplies and equipment	100	222	120	217	310
Material for insulation, other maintenance and repair	100	222	120	217	310
Property management and security	100	167	152	121	214
Property management	100	166	171	128	189
Management and upkeep services for security	100	170	112	105	266
Parking	100	171	49	118	313
Rented dwellings	**100**	**67**	**70**	**69**	**64**
Rent	100	69	71	71	65
Rent as pay	100	7	14	3	4
Maintenance, insurance, and other expenses	100	84	60	80	106
Tenant's insurance	100	104	111	63	128
Maintenance and repair services	100	71	45	53	106
Maintenance and repair materials	100	78	23	136	82
Other lodging	**100**	**304**	**138**	**247**	**482**
Owned vacation homes	100	320	113	256	540
Mortgage interest and charges	100	364	92	320	624
Property taxes	100	308	128	222	520
Maintenance, insurance, and other expenses	100	282	111	232	460
Housing while attending school	100	318	101	228	565
Lodging on trips	100	286	168	245	415

	total consumer units	$100,000 or more	$100,000– $119,999	$120,000– $149,999	$150,000 or more
UTILITIES, FUELS, AND PUBLIC SERVICES	100	145	132	138	161
Natural gas	100	160	144	143	186
Electricity	100	133	120	124	151
Fuel oil and other fuels	100	178	145	170	211
Fuel oil	100	189	157	184	220
Coal, wood, and other fuels	100	112	174	72	88
Bottled gas	100	171	123	164	217
Telephone services	100	145	136	141	154
Residential telephone and pay phones	100	133	119	123	152
Cellular phone service	100	150	144	150	155
Phone cards	100	67	71	77	56
Voice over IP	100	217	251	173	220
Water and other public services	100	155	138	153	171
Water and sewerage maintenance	100	153	139	152	166
Trash and garbage collection	100	160	136	155	184
Septic tank cleaning	100	158	60	162	236

*See Appendix B for information about mortgage principal reduction.
Source: Calculations by New Strategist based on the Bureau of Labor Statistics' 2011 Consumer Expenditure Survey

Table 9.11 Housing: Shelter and Utilities: Total spending by high-income consumer units, 2011

(total annual spending on shelter and utilities, by before-tax income group of high-income consumer units, 2011; consumer units and dollars in thousands)

	total consumer units	$100,000 or more	$100,000– $119,999	$120,000– $149,999	$150,000 or more
Number of consumer units	122,287	21,593	7,045	6,107	8,440
Total spending of all consumer units	$6,078,260,661	$2,110,245,454	$538,917,208	$532,771,260	$1,038,595,847
Housing, total spending	2,054,792,130	652,364,909	166,684,841	167,454,306	318,191,967
SHELTER	1,201,513,798	392,092,604	95,433,402	101,044,712	195,594,974
Owned dwellings*	751,807,024	305,586,943	74,245,423	78,421,086	152,905,201
Mortgage interest and charges	389,328,791	165,758,449	42,220,544	42,429,115	81,100,635
Mortgage interest	369,345,872	156,975,496	40,174,606	40,173,800	76,619,333
Interest paid, home equity loan	7,556,114	2,983,073	800,242	707,679	1,474,974
Interest paid, home equity line of credit	12,428,028	5,800,096	1,245,697	1,547,636	3,006,328
Property taxes	225,559,594	89,351,834	20,286,571	22,259,710	46,801,066
Maintenance, repairs, insurance, other expenses	136,917,417	50,476,445	11,738,238	13,732,261	25,003,416
Homeowner's insurance	43,042,578	14,189,840	3,710,249	3,619,314	6,859,526
Ground rent	5,888,119	234,500	112,509	56,307	65,663
Maintenance and repair services	67,983,012	29,414,201	6,222,355	8,504,730	14,685,600
Painting and papering	7,548,777	4,053,870	933,322	832,934	2,287,324
Plumbing and water heating	7,990,233	2,379,549	680,477	413,139	1,285,750
Heat, air conditioning, electrical work	13,391,649	5,847,168	1,376,452	2,052,074	2,418,313
Roofing and gutters	11,310,325	4,467,592	1,122,269	875,927	2,469,038
Other repair and maintenance services	20,573,565	9,725,703	1,445,916	3,294,849	4,984,580
Repair, replacement of hard-surface flooring	6,959,353	2,838,616	645,745	992,571	1,200,252
Repair of built-in appliances	209,111	101,919	18,247	43,238	40,343
Maintenance and repair materials	9,116,496	3,419,467	742,050	894,492	1,782,697
Paints, wallpaper, and supplies	1,674,109	581,931	269,894	147,057	164,918
Tools, equipment for painting, wallpapering	179,762	62,404	28,955	15,817	17,724
Plumbing supplies and equipment	786,305	204,486	61,432	24,978	118,160
Electrical supplies, heating and cooling equipment	420,667	95,873	30,787	17,222	47,855
Hard-surface flooring, repair and replacement	1,452,770	434,235	137,589	109,743	186,946
Roofing and gutters	638,338	250,047	36,000	6,168	207,962
Plaster, paneling, siding, windows, doors, screens, awnings	1,928,466	921,805	29,800	308,281	583,626
Patio, walk, fence, driveway, masonry, brick, and stucco materials	217,671	155,901	21,980	67,849	66,085
Miscellaneous supplies and equipment	1,819,631	712,569	125,683	197,317	389,422
Material for insulation, other maintenance and repair	1,819,631	712,569	125,683	197,317	389,422
Property management and security	10,819,954	3,198,355	949,173	653,449	1,595,498
Property management	7,366,569	2,161,243	726,762	472,376	961,991
Management and upkeep services for security	3,452,162	1,037,112	222,411	181,134	633,506
Parking	67,258	20,297	1,902	3,970	14,517
Rented dwellings	370,467,244	44,037,844	14,881,365	12,833,128	16,321,272
Rent	355,274,307	43,178,011	14,627,886	12,618,406	15,929,825
Rent as pay	10,225,639	123,080	81,652	15,206	26,333
Maintenance, insurance, and other expenses	4,967,298	736,537	171,898	199,455	365,030
Tenant's insurance	1,600,737	295,176	102,575	50,688	141,961
Maintenance and repair services	1,934,580	243,785	50,372	51,299	142,045
Maintenance and repair materials	1,431,981	197,576	18,951	97,468	81,108
Other lodging	79,240,753	42,467,817	6,306,614	9,790,498	26,368,586
Owned vacation homes	32,034,303	18,107,674	2,077,289	4,090,408	11,938,971
Mortgage interest and charges	10,368,715	6,671,805	551,060	1,655,241	4,465,182
Property taxes	14,272,116	7,760,740	1,054,918	1,579,698	5,125,612
Maintenance, insurance, and other expenses	7,393,472	3,675,129	471,240	855,407	2,348,177
Housing while attending school	8,731,292	4,909,816	507,663	995,807	3,406,046
Lodging on trips	38,473,936	19,450,543	3,721,733	4,704,222	11,023,568

	total consumer units	$100,000 or more	$100,000– $119,999	$120,000– $149,999	$150,000 or more
UTILITIES, FUELS, AND PUBLIC SERVICES	**$455,734,300**	**$116,501,361**	**$34,545,017**	**$31,302,283**	**$50,648,524**
Natural gas	**51,316,517**	**14,477,459**	**4,247,783**	**3,654,551**	**6,574,422**
Electricity	**174,008,287**	**40,914,632**	**12,044,837**	**10,751,007**	**18,116,713**
Fuel oil and other fuels	**19,178,270**	**6,029,629**	**1,606,119**	**1,630,386**	**2,792,796**
Fuel oil	10,911,669	3,650,081	986,441	1,004,785	1,658,629
Coal, wood, and other fuels	1,144,606	225,863	115,045	41,100	69,714
Bottled gas	7,121,995	2,153,686	504,633	584,501	1,064,368
Telephone services	**149,977,668**	**38,311,380**	**11,783,115**	**10,590,820**	**15,935,648**
Residential telephone and pay phones	46,585,233	10,935,559	3,188,637	2,855,694	4,890,727
Cellular phone service	100,973,599	26,736,237	8,357,061	7,578,176	10,799,908
Phone cards	1,081,017	127,399	43,961	41,711	41,778
Voice over IP	1,337,820	512,186	193,526	115,300	203,320
Water and other public services	**61,254,781**	**16,768,476**	**4,863,164**	**4,675,519**	**7,228,944**
Water and sewerage maintenance	46,064,290	12,479,674	3,690,946	3,498,151	5,290,108
Trash and garbage collection	14,799,173	4,179,757	1,158,691	1,145,795	1,875,030
Septic tank cleaning	391,318	108,829	13,526	31,573	63,806

See Appendix B for information about mortgage principal reduction.
Note: Numbers may not add to total because of rounding and missing subcategories.
Source: Calculations by New Strategist based on the Bureau of Labor Statistics' 2011 Consumer Expenditure Survey

(percentage of total annual spending on shelter and utilities accounted for by before-tax income group of high-income consumer units, 2011)

	total consumer units	$100,000 or more	$100,000– $119,999	$120,000– $149,999	$150,000 or more
Share of total consumer units	100.0%	17.7%	5.8%	5.0%	6.9%
Share of total before-tax income	100.0	47.1	9.8	10.5	26.8
Share of total spending	100.0	34.7	8.9	8.8	17.1
Share of housing spending	**100.0**	**31.7**	**8.1**	**8.1**	**15.5**
SHELTER	**100.0**	**32.6**	**7.9**	**8.4**	**16.3**
Owned dwellings*	**100.0**	**40.6**	**9.9**	**10.4**	**20.3**
Mortgage interest and charges	100.0	42.6	10.8	10.9	20.8
Mortgage interest	100.0	42.5	10.9	10.9	20.7
Interest paid, home equity loan	100.0	39.5	10.6	9.4	19.5
Interest paid, home equity line of credit	100.0	46.7	10.0	12.5	24.2
Property taxes	100.0	39.6	9.0	9.9	20.7
Maintenance, repairs, insurance, other expenses	100.0	36.9	8.6	10.0	18.3
Homeowner's insurance	100.0	33.0	8.6	8.4	15.9
Ground rent	100.0	4.0	1.9	1.0	1.1
Maintenance and repair services	100.0	43.3	9.2	12.5	21.6
Painting and papering	100.0	53.7	12.4	11.0	30.3
Plumbing and water heating	100.0	29.8	8.5	5.2	16.1
Heat, air conditioning, electrical work	100.0	43.7	10.3	15.3	18.1
Roofing and gutters	100.0	39.5	9.9	7.7	21.8
Other repair and maintenance services	100.0	47.3	7.0	16.0	24.2
Repair, replacement of hard-surface flooring	100.0	40.8	9.3	14.3	17.2
Repair of built-in appliances	100.0	48.7	8.7	20.7	19.3
Maintenance and repair materials	100.0	37.5	8.1	9.8	19.6
Paints, wallpaper, and supplies	100.0	34.8	16.1	8.8	9.9
Tools, equipment for painting, wallpapering	100.0	34.7	16.1	8.8	9.9
Plumbing supplies and equipment	100.0	26.0	7.8	3.2	15.0
Electrical supplies, heating and cooling equipment	100.0	22.8	7.3	4.1	11.4
Hard-surface flooring, repair and replacement	100.0	29.9	9.5	7.6	12.9
Roofing and gutters	100.0	39.2	5.6	1.0	32.6
Plaster, paneling, siding, windows, doors, screens, awnings	100.0	47.8	1.5	16.0	30.3
Patio, walk, fence, driveway, masonry, brick, and stucco materials	100.0	71.6	10.1	31.2	30.4
Miscellaneous supplies and equipment	100.0	39.2	6.9	10.8	21.4
Material for insulation, other maintenance and repair	100.0	39.2	6.9	10.8	21.4
Property management and security	100.0	29.6	8.8	6.0	14.7
Property management	100.0	29.3	9.9	6.4	13.1
Management and upkeep services for security	100.0	30.0	6.4	5.2	18.4
Parking	100.0	30.2	2.8	5.9	21.6
Rented dwellings	**100.0**	**11.9**	**4.0**	**3.5**	**4.4**
Rent	100.0	12.2	4.1	3.6	4.5
Rent as pay	100.0	1.2	0.8	0.1	0.3
Maintenance, insurance, and other expenses	100.0	14.8	3.5	4.0	7.3
Tenant's insurance	100.0	18.4	6.4	3.2	8.9
Maintenance and repair services	100.0	12.6	2.6	2.7	7.3
Maintenance and repair materials	100.0	13.8	1.3	6.8	5.7
Other lodging	**100.0**	**53.6**	**8.0**	**12.4**	**33.3**
Owned vacation homes	100.0	56.5	6.5	12.8	37.3
Mortgage interest and charges	100.0	64.3	5.3	16.0	43.1
Property taxes	100.0	54.4	7.4	11.1	35.9
Maintenance, insurance, and other expenses	100.0	49.7	6.4	11.6	31.8
Housing while attending school	100.0	56.2	5.8	11.4	39.0
Lodging on trips	100.0	50.6	9.7	12.2	28.7

	total consumer units	$100,000 or more	$100,000– $119,999	$120,000– $149,999	$150,000 or more
UTILITIES, FUELS, AND PUBLIC SERVICES	**100.0%**	**25.6%**	**7.6%**	**6.9%**	**11.1%**
Natural gas	**100.0**	**28.2**	**8.3**	**7.1**	**12.8**
Electricity	**100.0**	**23.5**	**6.9**	**6.2**	**10.4**
Fuel oil and other fuels	**100.0**	**31.4**	**8.4**	**8.5**	**14.6**
Fuel oil	100.0	33.5	9.0	9.2	15.2
Coal, wood, and other fuels	100.0	19.7	10.1	3.6	6.1
Bottled gas	100.0	30.2	7.1	8.2	14.9
Telephone services	**100.0**	**25.5**	**7.9**	**7.1**	**10.6**
Residential telephone and pay phones	100.0	23.5	6.8	6.1	10.5
Cellular phone service	100.0	26.5	8.3	7.5	10.7
Phone cards	100.0	11.8	4.1	3.9	3.9
Voice over IP	100.0	38.3	14.5	8.6	15.2
Water and other public services	**100.0**	**27.4**	**7.9**	**7.6**	**11.8**
Water and sewerage maintenance	100.0	27.1	8.0	7.6	11.5
Trash and garbage collection	100.0	28.2	7.8	7.7	12.7
Septic tank cleaning	100.0	27.8	3.5	8.1	16.3

*See Appendix B for information about mortgage principal reduction.
Note: Numbers may not add to total because of rounding.
Source: Calculations by New Strategist based on the Bureau of Labor Statistics' 2011 Consumer Expenditure Survey

Table 9.13 Housing: Shelter and Utilities: Average spending by household type, 2011

(average annual spending of consumer units on shelter and utilities, by type of consumer unit, 2011)

	total married couples	married couples, no children	married couples with children				single parent with child under age 18	single person
			total	oldest child under age 6	oldest child aged 6 to 17	oldest child aged 18 or older		
Number of consumer units (in 000s)	60,144	25,270	29,097	5,825	14,661	8,612	6,956	36,110
Average number of persons per consumer unit	3.2	2.0	4.0	3.5	4.2	3.9	2.9	1.0
Average before-tax income of consumer units	$86,700.00	$78,823.00	$93,677.00	$91,014.00	$93,029.00	$96,583.00	$37,188.00	$34,540.00
Average spending of consumer units, total	63,971.54	57,658.24	69,724.22	65,947.61	70,708.52	70,411.85	37,553.05	30,613.18
Housing, average spending	**20,663.77**	**18,328.52**	**22,787.75**	**25,008.84**	**23,158.39**	**20,648.26**	**14,563.03**	**11,456.22**
SHELTER	**11,779.93**	**10,404.40**	**13,121.52**	**14,570.91**	**13,609.11**	**11,311.04**	**8,425.78**	**7,176.31**
Owned dwellings*	**8,620.42**	**7,622.10**	**9,646.13**	**10,294.59**	**9,974.31**	**8,648.80**	**3,404.52**	**3,438.19**
Mortgage interest and charges	4,591.26	3,340.50	5,694.09	6,808.28	5,944.07	4,514.85	1,967.20	1,479.62
Mortgage interest	4,359.91	3,131.01	5,435.14	6,601.09	5,698.81	4,197.61	1,910.30	1,376.06
Interest paid, home equity loan	86.68	84.10	93.04	94.68	94.67	89.16	20.05	37.66
Interest paid, home equity line of credit	144.68	125.39	165.91	112.51	150.59	228.09	36.85	65.90
Property taxes	2,564.70	2,557.62	2,658.48	2,411.88	2,747.92	2,673.03	929.72	1,127.50
Maintenance, repairs, insurance, other expenses	1,464.46	1,723.97	1,293.56	1,074.43	1,282.31	1,460.92	507.60	831.08
Homeowner's insurance	469.31	513.46	435.79	357.07	436.95	487.06	151.51	239.10
Ground rent	39.53	45.67	29.94	50.16	21.28	31.03	22.12	58.26
Maintenance and repair services	766.54	939.55	660.04	519.39	639.13	790.78	272.94	358.48
Painting and papering	89.69	123.86	67.57	68.71	80.23	45.24	30.63	34.66
Plumbing and water heating	87.68	116.44	73.31	89.57	28.98	137.79	39.47	49.03
Heat, air conditioning, electrical work	156.14	194.65	132.30	115.86	145.38	121.16	44.86	65.36
Roofing and gutters	135.07	198.98	85.42	52.93	89.85	99.86	42.23	39.33
Other repair and maintenance services	213.69	245.90	199.33	58.72	185.39	318.19	71.83	139.37
Repair, replacement of hard-surface flooring	81.83	56.89	100.24	131.88	106.76	67.75	43.73	29.44
Repair of built-in appliances	2.45	2.83	1.86	1.73	2.54	0.79	0.19	1.28
Maintenance and repair materials	114.40	111.18	120.81	94.31	134.78	114.95	34.28	30.26
Paints, wallpaper, and supplies	19.48	19.17	19.71	21.06	17.18	23.11	7.47	5.55
Tools, equipment for painting, wallpapering	2.09	2.06	2.12	2.26	1.85	2.48	0.80	0.60
Plumbing supplies and equipment	9.17	6.90	10.07	6.45	6.78	18.11	1.08	2.42
Electrical supplies, heating and cooling equipment	5.10	4.40	6.47	2.32	9.25	4.55	0.33	1.51
Hard-surface flooring, repair and replacement	17.75	18.28	16.62	8.80	21.13	14.21	10.07	5.47
Roofing and gutters	8.33	12.51	2.81	3.29	3.49	1.33	6.70	1.58
Plaster, paneling, siding, windows, doors, screens, awnings	27.16	22.38	35.92	32.28	50.07	14.28	0.10	5.47
Patio, walk, fence, driveway, masonry, brick, and stucco materials	3.29	3.52	3.40	2.28	1.81	6.88	0.01	0.33
Miscellaneous supplies and equipment	22.02	21.95	23.70	15.57	23.22	30.00	7.72	7.32
Material for insulation, other maintenance and repair	22.02	21.95	23.70	15.57	23.22	30.00	7.72	7.32
Property management and security	74.12	113.23	46.63	52.99	49.88	36.78	26.71	144.40
Property management	51.44	75.31	34.96	46.02	36.13	25.50	18.38	96.35
Management and upkeep services for security	22.67	37.92	11.67	6.97	13.76	11.28	8.33	48.05
Parking	0.56	0.89	0.35	0.51	0.30	0.32	0.04	0.58
Rented dwellings	**2,144.57**	**1,470.72**	**2,649.37**	**3,608.03**	**2,792.27**	**1,757.64**	**4,850.93**	**3,443.27**
Rent	2,065.04	1,416.08	2,556.23	3,489.79	2,683.14	1,708.70	4,511.79	3,284.68
Rent as pay	48.16	23.60	60.55	93.24	70.42	21.64	302.24	113.28
Maintenance, insurance, and other expenses	31.37	31.04	32.59	25.00	38.71	27.30	36.90	45.30
Tenant's insurance	10.64	9.54	12.29	12.18	12.42	12.13	10.36	15.62
Maintenance and repair services	12.55	13.73	12.22	11.42	12.37	12.51	22.49	22.93
Maintenance and repair materials	8.19	7.77	8.09	1.40	13.93	2.67	4.05	6.75
Other lodging	**1,014.94**	**1,311.58**	**826.02**	**668.29**	**842.54**	**904.59**	**170.32**	**294.85**
Owned vacation homes	437.44	645.47	281.60	334.51	301.01	212.75	16.43	94.92
Mortgage interest and charges	147.91	184.95	120.38	160.84	120.30	93.15	0.63	23.13
Property taxes	192.36	288.16	114.20	122.06	126.05	88.72	12.27	50.38
Maintenance, insurance, and other expenses	97.17	172.36	47.01	51.61	54.66	30.88	3.52	21.40
Housing while attending school	97.77	83.76	122.28	–	84.24	269.73	12.79	56.01
Lodging on trips	479.72	582.35	422.15	333.78	457.28	422.11	141.10	143.93

	total married couples	married couples, no children	married couples with children				single parent with child under age 18	single person
			total	oldest child under age 6	oldest child aged 6 to 17	oldest child aged 18 or older		
UTILITIES, FUELS, AND PUBLIC SERVICES	$4,540.17	$4,073.26	$4,797.27	$3,989.47	$4,855.76	$5,244.09	$3,445.17	$2,380.38
Natural gas	505.28	452.05	541.51	443.50	558.14	579.50	370.72	283.78
Electricity	1,712.61	1,563.09	1,783.36	1,484.14	1,809.05	1,942.03	1,427.66	927.21
Fuel oil and other fuels	198.43	212.07	184.75	141.66	185.37	212.86	63.40	112.66
Fuel oil	107.63	104.83	108.78	80.42	111.14	123.96	44.96	67.41
Coal, wood, and other fuels	11.09	12.84	9.21	3.29	10.75	10.58	6.49	6.81
Bottled gas	79.72	94.41	66.76	57.95	63.48	78.31	11.95	38.43
Telephone services	1,498.32	1,275.23	1,640.25	1,377.47	1,636.28	1,824.77	1,164.65	745.35
Residential telephone and pay phones	463.04	492.71	435.40	281.63	435.94	538.48	260.14	289.52
Cellular phone service	1,010.67	765.50	1,175.43	1,064.17	1,169.66	1,260.50	891.13	444.64
Phone cards	9.51	6.25	10.58	14.24	9.56	9.83	6.66	6.09
Voice over IP	15.10	10.76	18.85	17.42	21.12	15.95	6.72	5.10
Water and other public services	625.54	570.83	647.39	542.70	666.93	684.93	418.74	311.38
Water and sewerage maintenance	468.43	418.79	491.06	403.11	503.07	530.12	330.39	226.03
Trash and garbage collection	152.17	146.53	152.82	135.11	161.05	150.77	88.34	83.84
Septic tank cleaning	4.94	5.51	3.51	4.49	2.80	4.04	–	1.50

*See Appendix B for information about mortgage principal reduction.
Note: Average spending figures for total consumer units can be found on Average Spending by Age and Average Spending by Region tables. Subcategories may not add to total because some are not shown.
"–" means sample is too small to make a reliable estimate.
Source: Bureau of Labor Statistics, unpublished tables from the 2011 Consumer Expenditure Survey

Table 9.14 Housing: Shelter and Utilities: Indexed spending by household type, 2011

(indexed average annual spending of consumer units on shelter and utilities, by type of consumer unit, 2011; index definition: an index of 100 is the average for all consumer units; an index of 125 means that spending by consumer units in that group is 25 percent above the average for all consumer units; an index of 75 indicates spending that is 25 percent below the average for all consumer units)

	total married couples	married couples, no children	married couples with children total	oldest child under age 6	oldest child aged 6 to 17	oldest child aged 18 or older	single parent with child under age 18	single person
Average spending of consumer units, total	$63,972	$57,658	$69,724	$65,948	$70,709	$70,412	$37,553	$30,613
Average spending of consumer units, index	129	116	140	133	142	142	76	62
Housing, spending index	123	109	136	149	138	123	87	68
SHELTER	120	106	134	148	139	115	86	73
Owned dwellings*	140	124	157	167	162	141	55	56
Mortgage interest and charges	144	105	179	214	187	142	62	46
Mortgage interest	144	104	180	219	189	139	63	46
Interest paid, home equity loan	140	136	151	153	153	144	32	61
Interest paid, home equity line of credit	142	123	163	111	148	224	36	65
Property taxes	139	139	144	131	149	145	50	61
Maintenance, repairs, insurance, other expenses	131	154	116	96	115	130	45	74
Homeowner's insurance	133	146	124	101	124	138	43	68
Ground rent	82	95	62	104	44	64	46	121
Maintenance and repair services	138	169	119	93	115	142	49	64
Painting and papering	145	201	109	111	130	73	50	56
Plumbing and water heating	134	178	112	137	44	211	60	75
Heat, air conditioning, electrical work	143	178	121	106	133	111	41	60
Roofing and gutters	146	215	92	57	97	108	46	43
Other repair and maintenance services	127	146	118	35	110	189	43	83
Repair, replacement of hard-surface flooring	144	100	176	232	188	119	77	52
Repair of built-in appliances	143	165	109	101	149	46	11	75
Maintenance and repair materials	153	149	162	127	181	154	46	41
Paints, wallpaper, and supplies	142	140	144	154	125	169	55	41
Tools, equipment for painting, wallpapering	142	140	144	154	126	169	54	41
Plumbing supplies and equipment	143	107	157	100	105	282	17	38
Electrical supplies, heating and cooling equipment	148	128	188	67	269	132	10	44
Hard-surface flooring, repair and replacement	149	154	140	74	178	120	85	46
Roofing and gutters	160	240	54	63	67	25	128	30
Plaster, paneling, siding, windows, doors, screens, awnings	172	142	228	205	318	91	1	35
Patio, walk, fence, driveway, masonry, brick, and stucco materials	185	198	191	128	102	387	1	19
Miscellaneous supplies and equipment	148	148	159	105	156	202	52	49
Material for insulation, other maintenance and repair	148	148	159	105	156	202	52	49
Property management and security	84	128	53	60	56	42	30	163
Property management	85	125	58	76	60	42	31	160
Management and upkeep services for security	80	134	41	25	49	40	30	170
Parking	102	162	64	93	55	58	7	105
Rented dwellings	71	49	87	119	92	58	160	114
Rent	71	49	88	120	92	59	155	113
Rent as pay	58	28	72	112	84	26	361	135
Maintenance, insurance, and other expenses	77	76	80	62	95	67	91	112
Tenant's insurance	81	73	94	93	95	93	79	119
Maintenance and repair services	79	87	77	72	78	79	142	145
Maintenance and repair materials	70	66	69	12	119	23	35	58
Other lodging	157	202	127	103	130	140	26	46
Owned vacation homes	167	246	107	128	115	81	6	36
Mortgage interest and charges	174	218	142	190	142	110	1	27
Property taxes	165	247	98	105	108	76	11	43
Maintenance, insurance, and other expenses	161	285	78	85	90	51	6	35
Housing while attending school	137	117	171	–	118	378	18	78
Lodging on trips	152	185	134	106	145	134	45	46

	total married couples	married couples, no children	married couples with children				single parent with child under age 18	single person
			total	oldest child under age 6	oldest child aged 6 to 17	oldest child aged 18 or older		
UTILITIES, FUELS, AND PUBLIC SERVICES	**122**	**109**	**129**	**107**	**130**	**141**	**92**	**64**
Natural gas	**120**	**108**	**129**	**106**	**133**	**138**	**88**	**68**
Electricity	**120**	**110**	**125**	**104**	**127**	**136**	**100**	**65**
Fuel oil and other fuels	**127**	**135**	**118**	**90**	**118**	**136**	**40**	**72**
Fuel oil	121	117	122	90	125	139	50	76
Coal, wood, and other fuels	118	137	98	35	115	113	69	73
Bottled gas	137	162	115	100	109	134	21	66
Telephone services	**122**	**104**	**134**	**112**	**133**	**149**	**95**	**61**
Residential telephone and pay phones	122	129	114	74	114	141	68	76
Cellular phone service	122	93	142	129	142	153	108	54
Phone cards	108	71	120	161	108	111	75	69
Voice over IP	138	98	172	159	193	146	61	47
Water and other public services	**125**	**114**	**129**	**108**	**133**	**137**	**84**	**62**
Water and sewerage maintenance	124	111	130	107	134	141	88	60
Trash and garbage collection	126	121	126	112	133	125	73	69
Septic tank cleaning	154	172	110	140	88	126	–	47

See Appendix B for information about mortgage principal reduction.
Note: Spending Index for total consumer units is 100. "–" means sample is too small to make a reliable estimate.
Source: Calculations by New Strategist based on the Bureau of Labor Statistics' 2011 Consumer Expenditure Survey

Table 9.15 Housing: Shelter and Utilities: Total spending by household type, 2011

(total annual spending on shelter and utilities, by consumer unit type, 2011; consumer units and dollars in thousands)

	total married couples	married couples, no children	married couples with children				single parent with child under age 18	single person
			total	oldest child under age 6	oldest child aged 6 to 17	oldest child aged 18 or older		
Number of consumer units	60,144	25,270	29,097	5,825	14,661	8,612	6,956	36,110
Total spending of all consumer units	$3,847,504,302	$1,457,023,725	$2,028,765,629	$384,144,828	$1,036,657,612	$606,386,852	$261,219,016	$1,105,441,930
Housing, total spending	1,242,801,783	463,161,700	663,055,162	145,676,493	339,525,156	177,822,815	101,300,437	413,684,104
SHELTER	708,492,110	262,919,188	381,796,867	84,875,551	199,523,162	97,410,676	58,609,726	259,136,554
Owned dwellings*	518,466,540	192,610,467	280,673,445	59,965,987	146,233,359	74,483,466	23,681,841	124,153,041
Mortgage interest and charges	276,136,741	84,414,435	165,680,937	39,658,231	87,146,010	38,881,888	13,683,843	53,429,078
Mortgage interest	262,222,427	79,120,623	158,146,269	38,451,349	83,550,253	36,149,817	13,288,047	49,689,527
Interest paid, home equity loan	5,213,282	2,125,207	2,707,185	551,511	1,387,957	767,846	139,468	1,359,903
Interest paid, home equity line of credit	8,701,634	3,168,605	4,827,483	655,371	2,207,800	1,964,311	256,329	2,379,649
Property taxes	154,251,317	64,631,057	77,353,793	14,049,201	40,287,255	23,020,134	6,467,132	40,714,025
Maintenance, repairs, insurance, other expenses	88,078,482	43,564,722	37,638,715	6,258,555	18,799,947	12,581,443	3,530,866	30,010,299
Homeowner's insurance	28,226,181	12,975,134	12,680,182	2,079,933	6,406,124	4,194,561	1,053,904	8,633,901
Ground rent	2,377,492	1,154,081	871,164	292,182	311,986	267,230	153,867	2,103,769
Maintenance and repair services	46,102,782	23,742,429	19,205,184	3,025,447	9,370,285	6,810,197	1,898,571	12,944,713
Painting and papering	5,394,315	3,129,942	1,966,084	400,236	1,176,252	389,607	213,062	1,251,573
Plumbing and water heating	5,273,426	2,942,439	2,133,101	521,745	424,876	1,186,647	274,553	1,770,473
Heat, air conditioning, electrical work	9,390,884	4,918,806	3,849,533	674,885	2,131,416	1,043,430	312,046	2,360,150
Roofing and gutters	8,123,650	5,028,225	2,485,466	308,317	1,317,291	859,994	293,752	1,420,206
Other repair and maintenance services	12,852,171	6,213,893	5,799,905	342,044	2,718,003	2,740,252	499,649	5,032,651
Repair, replacement of hard-surface flooring	4,921,584	1,437,610	2,916,683	768,201	1,565,208	583,463	304,186	1,063,078
Repair of built-in appliances	147,353	71,514	54,120	10,077	37,239	6,803	1,322	46,221
Maintenance and repair materials	6,880,474	2,809,519	3,515,209	549,356	1,976,010	989,949	238,452	1,092,689
Paints, wallpaper, and supplies	1,171,605	484,426	573,502	122,675	251,876	199,023	51,961	200,411
Tools, equipment for painting, wallpapering	125,701	52,056	61,686	13,165	27,123	21,358	5,565	21,666
Plumbing supplies and equipment	551,520	174,363	293,007	37,571	99,402	155,963	7,512	87,386
Electrical supplies, heating and cooling equipment	306,734	111,188	188,258	13,514	135,614	39,185	2,295	54,526
Hard-surface flooring, repair and replacement	1,067,556	461,936	483,592	51,260	309,787	122,377	70,047	197,522
Roofing and gutters	501,000	316,128	81,763	19,164	51,167	11,454	46,605	57,054
Plaster, paneling, siding, windows, doors, screens, awnings	1,633,511	565,543	1,045,164	188,031	734,076	122,979	696	197,522
Patio, walk, fence, driveway, masonry, brick, and stucco materials	197,874	88,950	98,930	13,281	26,536	59,251	70	11,916
Miscellaneous supplies and equipment	1,324,371	554,677	689,599	90,695	340,428	258,360	53,700	264,325
Material for insulation, other maintenance and repair	1,324,371	554,677	689,599	90,695	340,428	258,360	53,700	264,325
Property management and security	4,457,873	2,861,322	1,356,793	308,667	731,291	316,749	185,795	5,214,284
Property management	3,093,807	1,903,084	1,017,231	268,067	529,702	219,606	127,851	3,479,199
Management and upkeep services for security	1,363,464	958,238	339,562	40,600	201,735	97,143	57,943	1,735,086
Parking	33,681	22,490	10,184	2,971	4,398	2,756	278	20,944
Rented dwellings	128,983,018	37,165,094	77,088,719	21,016,775	40,937,470	15,136,796	33,743,069	124,336,480
Rent	124,199,766	35,784,342	74,378,624	20,328,027	39,337,516	14,715,324	31,384,011	118,609,795
Rent as pay	2,896,535	596,372	1,761,823	543,123	1,032,428	186,364	2,102,381	4,090,541
Maintenance, insurance, and other expenses	1,886,717	784,381	948,271	145,625	567,527	235,108	256,676	1,635,783
Tenant's insurance	639,932	241,076	357,602	70,949	182,090	104,464	72,064	564,038
Maintenance and repair services	754,807	346,957	355,565	66,522	181,357	107,736	156,440	828,002
Maintenance and repair materials	492,579	196,348	235,395	8,155	204,228	22,994	28,172	243,743
Other lodging	61,042,551	33,143,627	24,034,704	3,892,789	12,352,479	7,790,329	1,184,746	10,647,034
Owned vacation homes	26,309,391	16,311,027	8,193,715	1,948,521	4,413,108	1,832,203	114,287	3,427,561
Mortgage interest and charges	8,895,899	4,673,687	3,502,697	936,893	1,763,718	802,208	4,382	835,224
Property taxes	11,569,300	7,281,803	3,322,877	711,000	1,848,019	764,057	85,350	1,819,222
Maintenance, insurance, and other expenses	5,844,192	4,355,537	1,367,850	300,628	801,370	265,939	24,485	772,754
Housing while attending school	5,880,279	2,116,615	3,557,981	–	1,235,043	2,322,915	88,967	2,022,521
Lodging on trips	28,852,280	14,715,985	12,283,299	1,944,269	6,704,182	3,635,211	981,492	5,197,312

	total married couples	married couples, no children	married couples with children				single parent with child under age 18	single person
			total	oldest child under age 6	oldest child aged 6 to 17	oldest child aged 18 or older		
UTILITIES, FUELS, AND PUBLIC SERVICES	**$273,063,984**	**$102,931,280**	**$139,586,165**	**$23,238,663**	**$71,190,297**	**$45,162,103**	**$23,964,603**	**$85,955,522**
Natural gas	**30,389,560**	**11,423,304**	**15,756,316**	**2,583,388**	**8,182,891**	**4,990,654**	**2,578,728**	**10,247,296**
Electricity	**103,003,216**	**39,499,284**	**51,890,426**	**8,645,116**	**26,522,482**	**16,724,762**	**9,930,803**	**33,481,553**
Fuel oil and other fuels	**11,934,374**	**5,359,009**	**5,375,671**	**825,170**	**2,717,710**	**1,833,150**	**441,010**	**4,068,153**
Fuel oil	6,473,299	2,649,054	3,165,172	468,447	1,629,424	1,067,544	312,742	2,434,175
Coal, wood, and other fuels	666,997	324,467	267,983	19,164	157,606	91,115	45,144	245,909
Bottled gas	4,794,680	2,385,741	1,942,516	337,559	930,680	674,406	83,124	1,387,707
Telephone services	**90,114,958**	**32,225,062**	**47,726,354**	**8,023,763**	**23,989,501**	**15,714,919**	**8,101,305**	**26,914,589**
Residential telephone and pay phones	27,849,078	12,450,782	12,668,834	1,640,495	6,391,316	4,637,390	1,809,534	10,454,567
Cellular phone service	60,785,736	19,344,185	34,201,487	6,198,790	17,148,385	10,855,426	6,198,700	16,055,950
Phone cards	571,969	157,938	307,846	82,948	140,159	84,656	46,327	219,910
Voice over IP	908,174	271,905	548,478	101,472	309,640	137,361	46,744	184,161
Water and other public services	**37,622,478**	**14,424,874**	**18,837,107**	**3,161,228**	**9,777,861**	**5,898,617**	**2,912,755**	**11,243,932**
Water and sewerage maintenance	28,173,254	10,582,823	14,288,373	2,348,116	7,375,509	4,565,393	2,298,193	8,161,943
Trash and garbage collection	9,152,112	3,702,813	4,446,604	787,016	2,361,154	1,298,431	614,493	3,027,462
Septic tank cleaning	297,111	139,238	102,130	26,154	41,051	34,792	–	54,165

See Appendix B for information about mortgage principal reduction.

Note: Total spending figures for total consumer units can be found on Total Spending by Age and Total Spending by Region tables. Spending by type of consumer unit does not add to total because not all types of consumer units are shown. Numbers may not add to category total because of rounding and missing subcategories. "–" means sample is too small to make a reliable estimate.

Source: Calculations by New Strategist based on the Bureau of Labor Statistics' 2011 Consumer Expenditure Survey

Table 9.16 Housing: Shelter and Utilities: Market shares by household type, 2011

(percentage of total annual spending on shelter and utilities accounted for by types of consumer units, 2011)

	total married couples	married couples, no children	married couples with children				single parent with child under age 18	single person
			total	oldest child under age 6	oldest child aged 6 to 17	oldest child aged 18 or older		
Share of total consumer units	49.2%	20.7%	23.8%	4.8%	12.0%	7.0%	5.7%	29.5%
Share of total before-tax income	67.0	25.6	35.0	6.8	17.5	10.7	3.3	16.0
Share of total spending	63.3	24.0	33.4	6.3	17.1	10.0	4.3	18.2
Share of housing spending	60.5	22.5	32.3	7.1	16.5	8.7	4.9	20.1
SHELTER	59.0	21.9	31.8	7.1	16.6	8.1	4.9	21.6
Owned dwellings*	69.0	25.6	37.3	8.0	19.5	9.9	3.1	16.5
Mortgage interest and charges	70.9	21.7	42.6	10.2	22.4	10.0	3.5	13.7
Mortgage interest	71.0	21.4	42.8	10.4	22.6	9.8	3.6	13.5
Interest paid, home equity loan	69.0	28.1	35.8	7.3	18.4	10.2	1.8	18.0
Interest paid, home equity line of credit	70.0	25.5	38.8	5.3	17.8	15.8	2.1	19.1
Property taxes	68.4	28.7	34.3	6.2	17.9	10.2	2.9	18.1
Maintenance, repairs, insurance, other expenses	64.3	31.8	27.5	4.6	13.7	9.2	2.6	21.9
Homeowner's insurance	65.6	30.1	29.5	4.8	14.9	9.7	2.4	20.1
Ground rent	40.4	19.6	14.8	5.0	5.3	4.5	2.6	35.7
Maintenance and repair services	67.8	34.9	28.2	4.5	13.8	10.0	2.8	19.0
Painting and papering	71.5	41.5	26.0	5.3	15.6	5.2	2.8	16.6
Plumbing and water heating	66.0	36.8	26.7	6.5	5.3	14.9	3.4	22.2
Heat, air conditioning, electrical work	70.1	36.7	28.7	5.0	15.9	7.8	2.3	17.6
Roofing and gutters	71.8	44.5	22.0	2.7	11.6	7.6	2.6	12.6
Other repair and maintenance services	62.5	30.2	28.2	1.7	13.2	13.3	2.4	24.5
Repair, replacement of hard-surface flooring	70.7	20.7	41.9	11.0	22.5	8.4	4.4	15.3
Repair of built-in appliances	70.5	34.2	25.9	4.8	17.8	3.3	0.6	22.1
Maintenance and repair materials	75.5	30.8	38.6	6.0	21.7	10.9	2.6	12.0
Paints, wallpaper, and supplies	70.0	28.9	34.3	7.3	15.0	11.9	3.1	12.0
Tools, equipment for painting, wallpapering	69.9	29.0	34.3	7.3	15.1	11.9	3.1	12.1
Plumbing supplies and equipment	70.1	22.2	37.3	4.8	12.6	19.8	1.0	11.1
Electrical supplies, heating and cooling equipment	72.9	26.4	44.8	3.2	32.2	9.3	0.5	13.0
Hard-surface flooring, repair and replacement	73.5	31.8	33.3	3.5	21.3	8.4	4.8	13.6
Roofing and gutters	78.5	49.5	12.8	3.0	8.0	1.8	7.3	8.9
Plaster, paneling, siding, windows, doors, screens, awnings	84.7	29.3	54.2	9.8	38.1	6.4	0.0	10.2
Patio, walk, fence, driveway, masonry, brick, and stucco materials	90.9	40.9	45.4	6.1	12.2	27.2	0.0	5.5
Miscellaneous supplies and equipment	72.8	30.5	37.9	5.0	18.7	14.2	3.0	14.5
Material for insulation, other maintenance and repair	72.8	30.5	37.9	5.0	18.7	14.2	3.0	14.5
Property management and security	41.2	26.4	12.5	2.9	6.8	2.9	1.7	48.2
Property management	42.0	25.8	13.8	3.6	7.2	3.0	1.7	47.2
Management and upkeep services for security	39.5	27.8	9.8	1.2	5.8	2.8	1.7	50.3
Parking	50.1	33.4	15.1	4.4	6.5	4.1	0.4	31.1
Rented dwellings	34.8	10.0	20.8	5.7	11.1	4.1	9.1	33.6
Rent	35.0	10.1	20.9	5.7	11.1	4.1	8.8	33.4
Rent as pay	28.3	5.8	17.2	5.3	10.1	1.8	20.6	40.0
Maintenance, insurance, and other expenses	38.0	15.8	19.1	2.9	11.4	4.7	5.2	32.9
Tenant's insurance	40.0	15.1	22.3	4.4	11.4	6.5	4.5	35.2
Maintenance and repair services	39.0	17.9	18.4	3.4	9.4	5.6	8.1	42.8
Maintenance and repair materials	34.4	13.7	16.4	0.6	14.3	1.6	2.0	17.0
Other lodging	77.0	41.8	30.3	4.9	15.6	9.8	1.5	13.4
Owned vacation homes	82.1	50.9	25.6	6.1	13.8	5.7	0.4	10.7
Mortgage interest and charges	85.8	45.1	33.8	9.0	17.0	7.7	0.0	8.1
Property taxes	81.1	51.0	23.3	5.0	12.9	5.4	0.6	12.7
Maintenance, insurance, and other expenses	79.0	58.9	18.5	4.1	10.8	3.6	0.3	10.5
Housing while attending school	67.3	24.2	40.7	–	14.1	26.6	1.0	23.2
Lodging on trips	75.0	38.2	31.9	5.1	17.4	9.4	2.6	13.5

	total married couples	married couples, no children	married couples with children				single parent with child under age 18	single person
			total	oldest child under age 6	oldest child aged 6 to 17	oldest child aged 18 or older		
UTILITIES, FUELS, AND PUBLIC SERVICES	**59.9%**	**22.6%**	**30.6%**	**5.1%**	**15.6%**	**9.9%**	**5.3%**	**18.9%**
Natural gas	**59.2**	**22.3**	**30.7**	**5.0**	**15.9**	**9.7**	**5.0**	**20.0**
Electricity	**59.2**	**22.7**	**29.8**	**5.0**	**15.2**	**9.6**	**5.7**	**19.2**
Fuel oil and other fuels	**62.2**	**27.9**	**28.0**	**4.3**	**14.2**	**9.6**	**2.3**	**21.2**
Fuel oil	59.3	24.3	29.0	4.3	14.9	9.8	2.9	22.3
Coal, wood, and other fuels	58.3	28.3	23.4	1.7	13.8	8.0	3.9	21.5
Bottled gas	67.3	33.5	27.3	4.7	13.1	9.5	1.2	19.5
Telephone services	**60.1**	**21.5**	**31.8**	**5.3**	**16.0**	**10.5**	**5.4**	**17.9**
Residential telephone and pay phones	59.8	26.7	27.2	3.5	13.7	10.0	3.9	22.4
Cellular phone service	60.2	19.2	33.9	6.1	17.0	10.8	6.1	15.9
Phone cards	52.9	14.6	28.5	7.7	13.0	7.8	4.3	20.3
Voice over IP	67.9	20.3	41.0	7.6	23.1	10.3	3.5	13.8
Water and other public services	**61.4**	**23.5**	**30.8**	**5.2**	**16.0**	**9.6**	**4.8**	**18.4**
Water and sewerage maintenance	61.2	23.0	31.0	5.1	16.0	9.9	5.0	17.7
Trash and garbage collection	61.8	25.0	30.0	5.3	16.0	8.8	4.2	20.5
Septic tank cleaning	75.9	35.6	26.1	6.7	10.5	8.9	–	13.8

*See Appendix B for information about mortgage principal reduction.

Note: Market share for total consumer units is 100.0%. Market shares by type of consumer unit do not add to total because not all types of consumer units are shown. "–" means sample is too small to make a reliable estimate.

Source: Calculations by New Strategist based on the Bureau of Labor Statistics' 2011 Consumer Expenditure Survey

(average annual spending of consumer units on shelter and utilities, by race and Hispanic origin of consumer unit reference person, 2011)

	total consumer units	Asian	black	Hispanic	non-Hispanic white and other
Number of consumer units (in 000s)	122,287	5,048	15,118	15,222	92,163
Average number of persons per consumer unit	2.5	2.7	2.6	3.4	2.4
Average before-tax income of consumer units	$63,685.00	$85,415.00	$45,552.00	$49,966.00	$68,907.00
Average spending of consumer units, total	49,704.88	60,136.04	36,643.75	42,085.98	53,055.68
Housing, average spending	**16,803.03**	**20,833.57**	**13,984.57**	**15,647.65**	**17,449.43**
SHELTER	**9,825.36**	**14,269.23**	**8,111.34**	**9,766.31**	**10,121.69**
Owned dwellings*	**6,147.89**	**8,209.47**	**3,651.42**	**4,712.77**	**6,790.75**
Mortgage interest and charges	3,183.73	4,348.21	2,151.43	2,813.68	3,412.26
Mortgage interest	3,020.32	4,212.02	2,092.14	2,759.66	3,214.04
Interest paid, home equity loan	61.79	35.57	35.10	26.16	71.90
Interest paid, home equity line of credit	101.63	100.63	24.19	27.86	126.32
Property taxes	1,844.51	2,523.42	930.41	1,202.24	2,100.10
Maintenance, repairs, insurance, other expenses	1,119.64	1,337.83	569.58	696.85	1,278.39
Homeowner's insurance	351.98	291.77	200.73	207.62	400.13
Ground rent	48.15	21.98	7.87	58.18	52.99
Maintenance and repair services	555.93	819.08	276.38	317.84	640.71
Painting and papering	61.73	105.27	38.84	38.81	69.12
Plumbing and water heating	65.34	67.44	35.47	26.75	77.08
Heat, air conditioning, electrical work	109.51	65.05	45.52	32.07	132.54
Roofing and gutters	92.49	196.42	53.80	29.81	108.97
Other repair and maintenance services	168.24	236.23	64.53	141.16	189.47
Repair, replacement of hard-surface flooring	56.91	144.97	37.10	48.87	61.51
Repair of built-in appliances	1.71	3.70	1.12	0.38	2.02
Maintenance and repair materials	74.55	34.78	33.05	71.02	81.79
Paints, wallpaper, and supplies	13.69	13.10	6.09	14.34	14.82
Tools, equipment for painting, wallpapering	1.47	1.41	0.65	1.54	1.59
Plumbing supplies and equipment	6.43	6.33	3.39	3.41	7.41
Electrical supplies, heating and cooling equipment	3.44	1.15	2.54	2.58	3.72
Hard-surface flooring, repair and replacement	11.88	0.82	7.49	23.38	10.67
Roofing and gutters	5.22	0.86	4.64	3.00	5.67
Plaster, paneling, siding, windows, doors, screens, awnings	15.77	0.59	2.40	12.68	18.43
Patio, walk, fence, driveway, masonry, brick, and stucco materials	1.78	0.29	0.26	0.61	2.22
Miscellaneous supplies and equipment	14.88	10.22	5.59	9.49	17.26
Material for insulation, other maintenance and repair	14.88	10.22	5.59	9.49	17.26
Property management and security	88.48	170.00	51.36	41.91	102.10
Property management	60.24	107.66	43.31	29.50	68.01
Management and upkeep services for security	28.23	62.34	8.05	12.41	34.09
Parking	0.55	0.22	0.19	0.27	0.66
Rented dwellings	**3,029.49**	**4,842.70**	**4,268.23**	**4,805.87**	**2,543.29**
Rent	2,905.25	4,724.86	4,055.21	4,657.73	2,437.81
Rent as pay	83.62	78.46	177.29	125.84	61.08
Maintenance, insurance, and other expenses	40.62	39.38	35.73	22.30	44.39
Tenant's insurance	13.09	13.68	13.99	8.12	13.75
Maintenance and repair services	15.82	22.66	13.12	9.05	17.37
Maintenance and repair materials	11.71	3.04	8.62	5.13	13.27
Other lodging	**647.99**	**1,217.05**	**191.68**	**247.66**	**787.65**
Owned vacation homes	261.96	567.43	88.16	97.01	317.12
Mortgage interest and charges	84.79	263.68	56.69	57.66	93.70
Property taxes	116.71	228.70	22.00	31.80	146.00
Maintenance, insurance, and other expenses	60.46	75.06	9.48	7.55	77.42
Housing while attending school	71.40	258.06	16.07	18.76	89.01
Lodging on trips	314.62	391.56	87.44	131.89	381.53

	total consumer units	Asian	black	Hispanic	non-Hispanic white and other
UTILITIES, FUELS, AND PUBLIC SERVICES	**$3,726.76**	**$3,278.67**	**$3,700.51**	**$3,462.22**	**$3,772.65**
Natural gas	**419.64**	**436.23**	**428.98**	**349.96**	**429.27**
Electricity	**1,422.95**	**1,034.70**	**1,497.25**	**1,283.35**	**1,433.26**
Fuel oil and other fuels	**156.83**	**61.56**	**67.12**	**41.53**	**190.22**
Fuel oil	89.23	37.39	39.04	27.53	107.44
Coal, wood, and other fuels	9.36	0.44	3.51	0.11	11.83
Bottled gas	58.24	23.74	24.57	13.89	70.95
Telephone services	**1,226.44**	**1,228.98**	**1,242.29**	**1,288.14**	**1,213.61**
Residential telephone and pay phones	380.95	299.25	402.28	292.61	391.83
Cellular phone service	825.71	887.24	812.58	958.33	806.15
Phone cards	8.84	21.01	12.77	25.03	5.51
Voice over IP	10.94	21.48	14.66	12.17	10.12
Water and other public services	**500.91**	**517.19**	**464.87**	**499.24**	**506.30**
Water and sewerage maintenance	376.69	373.76	385.51	379.67	374.21
Trash and garbage collection	121.02	140.53	78.48	118.20	128.21
Septic tank cleaning	3.20	2.91	0.88	1.37	3.88

*See Appendix B for information about mortgage principal reduction.
Note: "Asian" and "black" include Hispanics and non-Hispanics who identify themselves as being of the respective race alone. "Hispanic" includes people of any race who identify themselves as Hispanic. "Other" includes people who identify themselves as non-Hispanic and as Alaska Native, American Indian, Asian (who are also included in the "Asian" column), or Native Hawaiian or other Pacific Islander, as well as non-Hispanics reporting more than one race. Subcategories may not add to total because some are not shown.
Source: Bureau of Labor Statistics, unpublished tables from the 2011 Consumer Expenditure Survey

Table 9.18 Housing: Shelter and Utilities: Indexed spending by race and Hispanic origin, 2011

(indexed average annual spending of consumer units on shelter and utilities, by race and Hispanic origin of consumer unit reference person, 2011; index definition: an index of 100 is the average for all consumer units; an index of 125 means that spending by consumer units in that group is 25 percent above the average for all consumer units; an index of 75 indicates spending that is 25 percent below the average for all consumer units)

	total consumer units	Asian	black	Hispanic	non-Hispanic white and other
Average spending of consumer units, total	$49,705	$60,136	$36,644	$42,086	$53,056
Average spending of consumer units, index	100	121	74	85	107
Housing, spending index	100	124	83	93	104
SHELTER	100	145	83	99	103
Owned dwellings*	100	134	59	77	110
Mortgage interest and charges	100	137	68	88	107
Mortgage interest	100	139	69	91	106
Interest paid, home equity loan	100	58	57	42	116
Interest paid, home equity line of credit	100	99	24	27	124
Property taxes	100	137	50	65	114
Maintenance, repairs, insurance, other expenses	100	119	51	62	114
Homeowner's insurance	100	83	57	59	114
Ground rent	100	46	16	121	110
Maintenance and repair services	100	147	50	57	115
Painting and papering	100	171	63	63	112
Plumbing and water heating	100	103	54	41	118
Heat, air conditioning, electrical work	100	59	42	29	121
Roofing and gutters	100	212	58	32	118
Other repair and maintenance services	100	140	38	84	113
Repair, replacement of hard-surface flooring	100	255	65	86	108
Repair of built-in appliances	100	216	65	22	118
Maintenance and repair materials	100	47	44	95	110
Paints, wallpaper, and supplies	100	96	44	105	108
Tools, equipment for painting, wallpapering	100	96	44	105	108
Plumbing supplies and equipment	100	98	53	53	115
Electrical supplies, heating and cooling equipment	100	33	74	75	108
Hard-surface flooring, repair and replacement	100	7	63	197	90
Roofing and gutters	100	16	89	57	109
Plaster, paneling, siding, windows, doors, screens, awnings	100	4	15	80	117
Patio, walk, fence, driveway, masonry, brick, and stucco materials	100	16	15	34	125
Miscellaneous supplies and equipment	100	69	38	64	116
Material for insulation, other maintenance and repair	100	69	38	64	116
Property management and security	100	192	58	47	115
Property management	100	179	72	49	113
Management and upkeep services for security	100	221	29	44	121
Parking	100	40	35	49	120
Rented dwellings	100	160	141	159	84
Rent	100	163	140	160	84
Rent as pay	100	94	212	150	73
Maintenance, insurance, and other expenses	100	97	88	55	109
Tenant's insurance	100	105	107	62	105
Maintenance and repair services	100	143	83	57	110
Maintenance and repair materials	100	26	74	44	113
Other lodging	100	188	30	38	122
Owned vacation homes	100	217	34	37	121
Mortgage interest and charges	100	311	67	68	111
Property taxes	100	196	19	27	125
Maintenance, insurance, and other expenses	100	124	16	12	128
Housing while attending school	100	361	23	26	125
Lodging on trips	100	124	28	42	121

	total consumer units	Asian	black	Hispanic	non-Hispanic white and other
UTILITIES, FUELS, AND PUBLIC SERVICES	**100**	**88**	**99**	**93**	**101**
Natural gas	**100**	**104**	**102**	**83**	**102**
Electricity	**100**	**73**	**105**	**90**	**101**
Fuel oil and other fuels	**100**	**39**	**43**	**26**	**121**
Fuel oil	100	42	44	31	120
Coal, wood, and other fuels	100	5	38	1	126
Bottled gas	100	41	42	24	122
Telephone services	**100**	**100**	**101**	**105**	**99**
Residential telephone and pay phones	100	79	106	77	103
Cellular phone service	100	107	98	116	98
Phone cards	100	238	144	283	62
Voice over IP	100	196	134	111	93
Water and other public services	**100**	**103**	**93**	**100**	**101**
Water and sewerage maintenance	100	99	102	101	99
Trash and garbage collection	100	116	65	98	106
Septic tank cleaning	100	91	28	43	121

*See Appendix B for information about mortgage principal reduction.
Note: "Asian" and "black" include Hispanics and non-Hispanics who identify themselves as being of the respective race alone. "Hispanic" includes people of any race who identify themselves as Hispanic. "Other" includes people who identify themselves as non-Hispanic and as Alaska Native, American Indian, Asian (who are also included in the "Asian" column), or Native Hawaiian or other Pacific Islander, as well as non-Hispanics reporting more than one race.
Source: Calculations by New Strategist based on the Bureau of Labor Statistics' 2011 Consumer Expenditure Survey

Table 9.19 Housing: Shelter and Utilities: Total spending by race and Hispanic origin, 2011

(total annual spending on shelter and utilities, by race and Hispanic origin groups, 2011; consumer units and dollars in thousands)

	total consumer units	Asian	black	Hispanic	non-Hispanic white and other
Number of consumer units	122,287	5,048	15,118	15,222	92,163
Total spending of all consumer units	$6,078,260,661	$303,566,730	$553,980,213	$640,632,788	$4,889,770,636
Housing, total spending	2,054,792,130	105,167,861	211,418,729	238,188,528	1,608,191,817
SHELTER	1,201,513,798	72,031,073	122,627,238	148,662,771	932,845,315
Owned dwellings*	751,807,024	41,441,405	55,202,168	71,737,785	625,855,892
Mortgage interest and charges	389,328,791	21,949,764	32,525,319	42,829,837	314,484,118
Mortgage interest	369,345,872	21,262,277	31,628,973	42,007,545	296,215,569
Interest paid, home equity loan	7,556,114	179,557	530,642	398,208	6,626,520
Interest paid, home equity line of credit	12,428,028	507,980	365,704	424,085	11,642,030
Property taxes	225,559,594	12,738,224	14,065,938	18,300,497	193,551,516
Maintenance, repairs, insurance, other expenses	136,917,417	6,753,366	8,610,910	10,607,451	117,820,258
Homeowner's insurance	43,042,578	1,472,855	3,034,636	3,160,392	36,877,181
Ground rent	5,888,119	110,955	118,979	885,616	4,883,717
Maintenance and repair services	67,983,012	4,134,716	4,178,313	4,838,160	59,049,756
Painting and papering	7,548,777	531,403	587,183	590,766	6,370,307
Plumbing and water heating	7,990,233	340,437	536,235	407,189	7,103,924
Heat, air conditioning, electrical work	13,391,649	328,372	688,171	488,170	12,215,284
Roofing and gutters	11,310,325	991,528	813,348	453,768	10,043,002
Other repair and maintenance services	20,573,565	1,192,489	975,565	2,148,738	17,462,124
Repair, replacement of hard-surface flooring	6,959,353	731,809	560,878	743,899	5,668,946
Repair of built-in appliances	209,111	18,678	16,932	5,784	186,169
Maintenance and repair materials	9,116,496	175,569	499,650	1,081,066	7,538,012
Paints, wallpaper, and supplies	1,674,109	66,129	92,069	218,283	1,365,856
Tools, equipment for painting, wallpapering	179,762	7,118	9,827	23,442	146,539
Plumbing supplies and equipment	786,305	31,954	51,250	51,907	682,928
Electrical supplies, heating and cooling equipment	420,667	5,805	38,400	39,273	342,846
Hard-surface flooring, repair and replacement	1,452,770	4,139	113,234	355,890	983,379
Roofing and gutters	638,338	4,341	70,148	45,666	522,564
Plaster, paneling, siding, windows, doors, screens, awnings	1,928,466	2,978	36,283	193,015	1,698,564
Patio, walk, fence, driveway, masonry, brick, and stucco materials	217,671	1,464	3,931	9,285	204,602
Miscellaneous supplies and equipment	1,819,631	51,591	84,510	144,457	1,590,733
Material for insulation, other maintenance and repair	1,819,631	51,591	84,510	144,457	1,590,733
Property management and security	10,819,954	858,160	776,460	637,954	9,409,842
Property management	7,366,569	543,468	654,761	449,049	6,268,006
Management and upkeep services for security	3,452,162	314,692	121,700	188,905	3,141,837
Parking	67,258	1,111	2,872	4,110	60,828
Rented dwellings	370,467,244	24,445,950	64,527,101	73,154,953	234,397,236
Rent	355,274,307	23,851,093	61,306,665	70,899,966	224,675,883
Rent as pay	10,225,639	396,066	2,680,270	1,915,536	5,629,316
Maintenance, insurance, and other expenses	4,967,298	198,790	540,166	339,451	4,091,116
Tenant's insurance	1,600,737	69,057	211,501	123,603	1,267,241
Maintenance and repair services	1,934,580	114,388	198,348	137,759	1,600,871
Maintenance and repair materials	1,431,981	15,346	130,317	78,089	1,223,003
Other lodging	79,240,753	6,143,668	2,897,818	3,769,881	72,592,187
Owned vacation homes	32,034,303	2,864,387	1,332,803	1,476,686	29,226,731
Mortgage interest and charges	10,368,715	1,331,057	857,039	877,701	8,635,673
Property taxes	14,272,116	1,154,478	332,596	484,060	13,455,798
Maintenance, insurance, and other expenses	7,393,472	378,903	143,319	114,926	7,135,259
Housing while attending school	8,731,292	1,302,687	242,946	285,565	8,203,429
Lodging on trips	38,473,936	1,976,595	1,321,918	2,007,630	35,162,949

	total consumer units	Asian	black	Hispanic	non-Hispanic white and other
UTILITIES, FUELS, AND PUBLIC SERVICES	**$455,734,300**	**$16,550,726**	**$55,944,310**	**$52,701,913**	**$347,698,742**
Natural gas	**51,316,517**	**2,202,089**	**6,485,320**	**5,327,091**	**39,562,811**
Electricity	**174,008,287**	**5,223,166**	**22,635,426**	**19,535,154**	**132,093,541**
Fuel oil and other fuels	**19,178,270**	**310,755**	**1,014,720**	**632,170**	**17,531,246**
Fuel oil	10,911,669	188,745	590,207	419,062	9,901,993
Coal, wood, and other fuels	1,144,606	2,221	53,064	1,674	1,090,288
Bottled gas	7,121,995	119,840	371,449	211,434	6,538,965
Telephone services	**149,977,668**	**6,203,891**	**18,780,940**	**19,608,067**	**111,849,938**
Residential telephone and pay phones	46,585,233	1,510,614	6,081,669	4,454,109	36,112,228
Cellular phone service	100,973,599	4,478,788	12,284,584	14,587,699	74,297,202
Phone cards	1,081,017	106,058	193,057	381,007	507,818
Voice over IP	1,337,820	108,431	221,630	185,252	932,690
Water and other public services	**61,254,781**	**2,610,775**	**7,027,905**	**7,599,431**	**46,662,127**
Water and sewerage maintenance	46,064,290	1,886,740	5,828,140	5,779,337	34,488,316
Trash and garbage collection	14,799,173	709,395	1,186,461	1,799,240	11,816,218
Septic tank cleaning	391,318	14,690	13,304	20,854	357,592

*See Appendix B for information about mortgage principal reduction.
Note: "Asian" and "black" include Hispanics and non-Hispanics who identify themselves as being of the respective race alone. "Hispanic" includes people of any race who identify themselves as Hispanic. "Other" includes people who identify themselves as non-Hispanic and as Alaska Native, American Indian, Asian (who are also included in the "Asian" column), or Native Hawaiian or other Pacific Islander, as well as non-Hispanics reporting more than one race. Numbers may not add to total because of rounding and missing subcategories.
Source: Calculations by New Strategist based on the Bureau of Labor Statistics' 2011 Consumer Expenditure Survey

Table 9.20 Housing: Shelter and Utilities: Market shares by race and Hispanic origin, 2011

(percentage of total annual spending on shelter and utilities accounted for by consumer unit race and Hispanic origin groups, 2011)

	total consumer units	Asian	black	Hispanic	non-Hispanic white and other
Share of total consumer units	100.0%	4.1%	12.4%	12.4%	75.4%
Share of total before-tax income	100.0	5.5	8.8	9.8	81.5
Share of total spending	100.0	5.0	9.1	10.5	80.4
Share of housing spending	100.0	5.1	10.3	11.6	78.3
SHELTER	100.0	6.0	10.2	12.4	77.6
Owned dwellings*	100.0	5.5	7.3	9.5	83.2
Mortgage interest and charges	100.0	5.6	8.4	11.0	80.8
Mortgage interest	100.0	5.8	8.6	11.4	80.2
Interest paid, home equity loan	100.0	2.4	7.0	5.3	87.7
Interest paid, home equity line of credit	100.0	4.1	2.9	3.4	93.7
Property taxes	100.0	5.6	6.2	8.1	85.8
Maintenance, repairs, insurance, other expenses	100.0	4.9	6.3	7.7	86.1
Homeowner's insurance	100.0	3.4	7.1	7.3	85.7
Ground rent	100.0	1.9	2.0	15.0	82.9
Maintenance and repair services	100.0	6.1	6.1	7.1	86.9
Painting and papering	100.0	7.0	7.8	7.8	84.4
Plumbing and water heating	100.0	4.3	6.7	5.1	88.9
Heat, air conditioning, electrical work	100.0	2.5	5.1	3.6	91.2
Roofing and gutters	100.0	8.8	7.2	4.0	88.8
Other repair and maintenance services	100.0	5.8	4.7	10.4	84.9
Repair, replacement of hard-surface flooring	100.0	10.5	8.1	10.7	81.5
Repair of built-in appliances	100.0	8.9	8.1	2.8	89.0
Maintenance and repair materials	100.0	1.9	5.5	11.9	82.7
Paints, wallpaper, and supplies	100.0	4.0	5.5	13.0	81.6
Tools, equipment for painting, wallpapering	100.0	4.0	5.5	13.0	81.5
Plumbing supplies and equipment	100.0	4.1	6.5	6.6	86.9
Electrical supplies, heating and cooling equipment	100.0	1.4	9.1	9.3	81.5
Hard-surface flooring, repair and replacement	100.0	0.3	7.8	24.5	67.7
Roofing and gutters	100.0	0.7	11.0	7.2	81.9
Plaster, paneling, siding, windows, doors, screens, awnings	100.0	0.2	1.9	10.0	88.1
Patio, walk, fence, driveway, masonry, brick, and stucco materials	100.0	0.7	1.8	4.3	94.0
Miscellaneous supplies and equipment	100.0	2.8	4.6	7.9	87.4
Material for insulation, other maintenance and repair	100.0	2.8	4.6	7.9	87.4
Property management and security	100.0	7.9	7.2	5.9	87.0
Property management	100.0	7.4	8.9	6.1	85.1
Management and upkeep services for security	100.0	9.1	3.5	5.5	91.0
Parking	100.0	1.7	4.3	6.1	90.4
Rented dwellings	100.0	6.6	17.4	19.7	63.3
Rent	100.0	6.7	17.3	20.0	63.2
Rent as pay	100.0	3.9	26.2	18.7	55.1
Maintenance, insurance, and other expenses	100.0	4.0	10.9	6.8	82.4
Tenant's insurance	100.0	4.3	13.2	7.7	79.2
Maintenance and repair services	100.0	5.9	10.3	7.1	82.8
Maintenance and repair materials	100.0	1.1	9.1	5.5	85.4
Other lodging	100.0	7.8	3.7	4.8	91.6
Owned vacation homes	100.0	8.9	4.2	4.6	91.2
Mortgage interest and charges	100.0	12.8	8.3	8.5	83.3
Property taxes	100.0	8.1	2.3	3.4	94.3
Maintenance, insurance, and other expenses	100.0	5.1	1.9	1.6	96.5
Housing while attending school	100.0	14.9	2.8	3.3	94.0
Lodging on trips	100.0	5.1	3.4	5.2	91.4

	total consumer units	Asian	black	Hispanic	non-Hispanic white and other
UTILITIES, FUELS, AND PUBLIC SERVICES	**100.0%**	**3.6%**	**12.3%**	**11.6%**	**76.3%**
Natural gas	**100.0**	**4.3**	**12.6**	**10.4**	**77.1**
Electricity	**100.0**	**3.0**	**13.0**	**11.2**	**75.9**
Fuel oil and other fuels	**100.0**	**1.6**	**5.3**	**3.3**	**91.4**
Fuel oil	100.0	1.7	5.4	3.8	90.7
Coal, wood, and other fuels	100.0	0.2	4.6	0.1	95.3
Bottled gas	100.0	1.7	5.2	3.0	91.8
Telephone services	**100.0**	**4.1**	**12.5**	**13.1**	**74.6**
Residential telephone and pay phones	100.0	3.2	13.1	9.6	77.5
Cellular phone service	100.0	4.4	12.2	14.4	73.6
Phone cards	100.0	9.8	17.9	35.2	47.0
Voice over IP	100.0	8.1	16.6	13.8	69.7
Water and other public services	**100.0**	**4.3**	**11.5**	**12.4**	**76.2**
Water and sewerage maintenance	100.0	4.1	12.7	12.5	74.9
Trash and garbage collection	100.0	4.8	8.0	12.2	79.8
Septic tank cleaning	100.0	3.8	3.4	5.3	91.4

See Appendix B for information about mortgage principal reduction.

Note: "Asian" and "black" include Hispanics and non-Hispanics who identify themselves as being of the respective race alone. "Hispanic" includes people of any race who identify themselves as Hispanic. "Other" includes people who identify themselves as non-Hispanic and as Aluska Native, American Indian, Asian (who are also included in the "Asian" column), or Native Hawaiian or other Pacific Islander, as well as non-Hispanics reporting more than one race.

Source: Calculations by New Strategist based on the Bureau of Labor Statistics' 2011 Consumer Expenditure Survey

Table 9.21 Housing: Shelter and Utilities: Average spending by region, 2011

(average annual spending of consumer units on shelter and utilities, by region in which consumer unit lives, 2011)

	total consumer units	Northeast	Midwest	South	West
Number of consumer units (in 000s)	122,287	22,538	27,107	44,901	27,741
Average number of persons per consumer unit	2.5	2.4	2.4	2.5	2.6
Average before-tax income of consumer units	$63,685.00	$71,733.00	$60,897.00	$58,780.00	$67,810.00
Average spending of consumer units, total	49,704.88	54,547.45	47,191.54	45,698.60	54,745.43
Housing, average spending	**16,803.03**	**19,557.15**	**14,925.78**	**14,968.44**	**19,372.69**
SHELTER	**9,825.36**	**12,032.84**	**8,409.13**	**8,109.77**	**12,192.55**
Owned dwellings*	**6,147.89**	**7,642.33**	**5,691.41**	**5,109.80**	**7,060.01**
Mortgage interest and charges	3,183.73	3,305.02	2,632.22	2,740.75	4,341.08
Mortgage interest	3,020.32	3,097.94	2,493.07	2,620.40	4,119.74
Interest paid, home equity loan	61.79	97.57	71.14	38.26	61.65
Interest paid, home equity line of credit	101.63	109.51	68.01	82.09	159.69
Property taxes	1,844.51	2,999.56	1,935.54	1,339.74	1,634.18
Maintenance, repairs, insurance, other expenses	1,119.64	1,337.75	1,123.64	1,029.31	1,084.74
Homeowner's insurance	351.98	378.27	365.40	359.86	304.76
Ground rent	48.15	50.18	50.72	35.82	63.95
Maintenance and repair services	555.93	653.21	581.42	495.49	549.82
Painting and papering	61.73	60.60	43.29	58.50	85.88
Plumbing and water heating	65.34	67.73	55.40	62.08	78.39
Heat, air conditioning, electrical work	109.51	91.96	108.32	115.53	115.20
Roofing and gutters	92.49	135.21	123.12	67.60	68.12
Other repair and maintenance services	168.24	232.25	196.63	130.08	150.27
Repair, replacement of hard-surface flooring	56.91	64.50	52.48	60.65	49.02
Repair of built-in appliances	1.71	0.95	2.17	1.05	2.94
Maintenance and repair materials	74.55	86.79	79.80	70.56	65.94
Paints, wallpaper, and supplies	13.69	9.99	11.94	13.88	18.10
Tools, equipment for painting, wallpapering	1.47	1.07	1.28	1.49	1.94
Plumbing supplies and equipment	6.43	9.60	6.68	5.79	4.63
Electrical supplies, heating and cooling equipment	3.44	2.62	6.24	2.41	3.03
Hard-surface flooring, repair and replacement	11.88	7.69	13.95	10.88	14.86
Roofing and gutters	5.22	8.17	9.51	3.79	0.95
Plaster, paneling, siding, windows, doors, screens, awnings	15.77	20.21	14.44	19.70	7.08
Patio, walk, fence, driveway, masonry, brick, and stucco materials	1.78	1.07	2.04	1.94	1.85
Miscellaneous supplies and equipment	14.88	26.36	13.71	10.68	13.50
Material for insulation, other maintenance and repair	14.88	26.36	13.71	10.68	13.50
Property management and security	88.48	168.48	45.93	67.05	99.75
Property management	60.24	136.06	32.38	35.89	65.30
Management and upkeep services for security	28.23	32.42	13.55	31.16	34.45
Parking	0.55	0.82	0.39	0.54	0.53
Rented dwellings	**3,029.49**	**3,567.28**	**2,153.07**	**2,505.48**	**4,297.07**
Rent	2,905.25	3,391.69	2,064.27	2,391.87	4,162.72
Rent as pay	83.62	130.98	54.93	75.95	85.58
Maintenance, insurance, and other expenses	40.62	44.61	33.87	37.65	48.77
Tenant's insurance	13.09	12.92	13.81	12.13	14.08
Maintenance and repair services	15.82	16.64	10.93	14.82	21.55
Maintenance and repair materials	11.71	15.05	9.12	10.70	13.14
Other lodging	**647.99**	**823.23**	**564.65**	**494.50**	**835.47**
Owned vacation homes	261.96	378.95	194.95	205.82	323.25
Mortgage interest and charges	84.79	91.09	56.60	66.75	136.42
Property taxes	116.71	172.60	88.23	94.71	134.71
Maintenance, insurance, and other expenses	60.46	115.26	50.12	44.35	52.12
Housing while attending school	71.40	72.71	80.44	31.91	125.44
Lodging on trips	314.62	371.57	289.26	256.77	386.78

	total consumer units	Northeast	Midwest	South	West
UTILITIES, FUELS, AND PUBLIC SERVICES	**$3,726.76**	**$4,096.16**	**$3,486.47**	**$3,897.50**	**$3,385.11**
Natural gas	**419.64**	**595.57**	**599.81**	**242.77**	**386.91**
Electricity	**1,422.95**	**1,338.04**	**1,224.52**	**1,763.49**	**1,134.66**
Fuel oil and other fuels	**156.83**	**487.42**	**120.63**	**69.82**	**64.46**
Fuel oil	89.23	411.02	20.29	21.71	4.44
Coal, wood, and other fuels	9.36	19.38	10.10	4.06	9.07
Bottled gas	58.24	57.02	90.24	44.05	50.94
Telephone services	**1,226.44**	**1,290.98**	**1,135.83**	**1,276.22**	**1,181.96**
Residential telephone and pay phones	380.95	435.15	348.34	395.90	344.59
Cellular phone service	825.71	817.15	777.70	861.75	821.24
Phone cards	8.84	12.09	6.11	8.19	9.90
Voice over IP	10.94	26.58	3.67	10.38	6.23
Water and other public services	**500.91**	**384.15**	**405.69**	**545.20**	**617.12**
Water and sewerage maintenance	376.69	283.91	295.63	432.69	440.62
Trash and garbage collection	121.02	96.15	106.72	109.20	174.32
Septic tank cleaning	3.20	4.08	3.34	3.31	2.18

See Appendix B for information about mortgage principal reduction.
Note: Subcategories may not add to total because some are not shown.
Source: Bureau of Labor Statistics, unpublished tables from the 2011 Consumer Expenditure Survey

Table 9.22 Housing: Shelter and Utilities: Indexed spending by region, 2011

(indexed average annual spending of consumer units on shelter and utilities, by region in which consumer unit lives, 2011; index definition: an index of 100 is the average for all consumer units; an index of 125 means that spending by consumer units in that group is 25 percent above the average for all consumer units; an index of 75 indicates spending that is 25 percent below the average for all consumer units)

	total consumer units	Northeast	Midwest	South	West
Average spending of consumer units, total	$49,705	$60,136	$36,644	$42,086	$53,056
Average spending of consumer units, index	100	121	74	85	107
Housing, spending index	**100**	**124**	**83**	**93**	**104**
SHELTER	**100**	**145**	**83**	**99**	**103**
Owned dwellings*	**100**	**134**	**59**	**77**	**110**
Mortgage interest and charges	100	137	68	88	107
Mortgage interest	100	139	69	91	106
Interest paid, home equity loan	100	58	57	42	116
Interest paid, home equity line of credit	100	99	24	27	124
Property taxes	100	137	50	65	114
Maintenance, repairs, insurance, other expenses	100	119	51	62	114
Homeowner's insurance	100	83	57	59	114
Ground rent	100	46	16	121	110
Maintenance and repair services	100	147	50	57	115
Painting and papering	100	171	63	63	112
Plumbing and water heating	100	103	54	41	118
Heat, air conditioning, electrical work	100	59	42	29	121
Roofing and gutters	100	212	58	32	118
Other repair and maintenance services	100	140	38	84	113
Repair, replacement of hard-surface flooring	100	255	65	86	108
Repair of built-in appliances	100	216	65	22	118
Maintenance and repair materials	100	47	44	95	110
Paints, wallpaper, and supplies	100	96	44	105	108
Tools, equipment for painting, wallpapering	100	96	44	105	108
Plumbing supplies and equipment	100	98	53	53	115
Electrical supplies, heating and cooling equipment	100	33	74	75	108
Hard-surface flooring, repair and replacement	100	7	63	197	90
Roofing and gutters	100	16	89	57	109
Plaster, paneling, siding, windows, doors, screens, awnings	100	4	15	80	117
Patio, walk, fence, driveway, masonry, brick, and stucco materials	100	16	15	34	125
Miscellaneous supplies and equipment	100	69	38	64	116
Material for insulation, other maintenance and repair	100	69	38	64	116
Property management and security	100	192	58	47	115
Property management	100	179	72	49	113
Management and upkeep services for security	100	221	29	44	121
Parking	100	40	35	49	120
Rented dwellings	**100**	**160**	**141**	**159**	**84**
Rent	100	163	140	160	84
Rent as pay	100	94	212	150	73
Maintenance, insurance, and other expenses	100	97	88	55	109
Tenant's insurance	100	105	107	62	105
Maintenance and repair services	100	143	83	57	110
Maintenance and repair materials	100	26	74	44	113
Other lodging	**100**	**188**	**30**	**38**	**122**
Owned vacation homes	100	217	34	37	121
Mortgage interest and charges	100	311	67	68	111
Property taxes	100	196	19	27	125
Maintenance, insurance, and other expenses	100	124	16	12	128
Housing while attending school	100	361	23	26	125
Lodging on trips	100	124	28	42	121

	total consumer units	Northeast	Midwest	South	West
UTILITIES, FUELS, AND PUBLIC SERVICES	**100**	**88**	**99**	**93**	**101**
Natural gas	**100**	**104**	**102**	**83**	**102**
Electricity	**100**	**73**	**105**	**90**	**101**
Fuel oil and other fuels	**100**	**39**	**43**	**26**	**121**
Fuel oil	100	42	44	31	120
Coal, wood, and other fuels	100	5	38	1	126
Bottled gas	100	41	42	24	122
Telephone services	**100**	**100**	**101**	**105**	**99**
Residential telephone and pay phones	100	79	106	77	103
Cellular phone service	100	107	98	116	98
Phone cards	100	238	144	283	62
Voice over IP	100	196	134	111	93
Water and other public services	**100**	**103**	**93**	**100**	**101**
Water and sewerage maintenance	100	99	102	101	99
Trash and garbage collection	100	116	65	98	106
Septic tank cleaning	100	91	28	43	121

*See Appendix B for information about mortgage principal reduction.
Source: Calculations by New Strategist based on the Bureau of Labor Statistics' 2011 Consumer Expenditure Survey

Table 9.23 Housing: Shelter and Utilities: Total spending by region, 2011

(total annual spending on shelter and utilities, by region in which consumer units live, 2011; consumer units and dollars in thousands)

	total consumer units	Northeast	Midwest	South	West
Number of consumer units	122,287	22,538	27,107	44,901	27,741
Total spending of all consumer units	$6,078,260,661	$1,229,390,428	$1,279,221,075	$2,051,912,839	$1,518,692,974
Housing, total spending	2,054,792,130	440,779,047	404,593,118	672,097,924	537,417,793
SHELTER	1,201,513,798	271,196,148	227,946,287	364,136,783	338,233,530
Owned dwellings*	751,807,024	172,242,834	154,277,051	229,435,130	195,851,737
Mortgage interest and charges	389,328,791	74,488,541	71,351,588	123,062,416	120,425,900
Mortgage interest	369,345,872	69,821,372	67,579,648	117,658,580	114,285,707
Interest paid, home equity loan	7,556,114	2,199,033	1,928,392	1,717,912	1,710,233
Interest paid, home equity line of credit	12,428,028	2,468,136	1,843,547	3,685,923	4,429,960
Property taxes	225,559,594	67,604,083	52,466,683	60,155,666	45,333,787
Maintenance, repairs, insurance, other expenses	136,917,417	30,150,210	30,458,509	46,217,048	30,091,772
Homeowner's insurance	43,042,578	8,525,449	9,904,898	16,158,074	8,454,347
Ground rent	5,888,119	1,130,957	1,374,867	1,608,354	1,774,037
Maintenance and repair services	67,983,012	14,722,047	15,760,552	22,247,996	15,252,557
Painting and papering	7,548,777	1,365,803	1,173,462	2,626,709	2,382,397
Plumbing and water heating	7,990,233	1,526,499	1,501,728	2,787,454	2,174,617
Heat, air conditioning, electrical work	13,391,649	2,072,594	2,936,230	5,187,413	3,195,763
Roofing and gutters	11,310,325	3,047,363	3,337,414	3,035,308	1,889,717
Other repair and maintenance services	20,573,565	5,234,451	5,330,049	5,840,722	4,168,640
Repair, replacement of hard-surface flooring	6,959,353	1,453,701	1,422,575	2,723,246	1,359,864
Repair of built-in appliances	209,111	21,411	58,822	47,146	81,559
Maintenance and repair materials	9,116,496	1,956,073	2,163,139	3,168,215	1,829,242
Paints, wallpaper, and supplies	1,674,109	225,155	323,658	623,226	502,112
Tools, equipment for painting, wallpapering	179,762	24,116	34,697	66,902	53,818
Plumbing supplies and equipment	786,305	216,365	181,075	259,977	128,441
Electrical supplies, heating and cooling equipment	420,667	59,050	169,148	108,211	84,055
Hard-surface flooring, repair and replacement	1,452,770	173,317	378,143	488,523	412,231
Roofing and gutters	638,338	184,135	257,788	170,175	26,354
Plaster, paneling, siding, windows, doors, screens, awnings	1,928,466	455,493	391,425	884,550	196,406
Patio, walk, fence, driveway, masonry, brick, and stucco materials	217,671	24,116	55,298	87,108	51,321
Miscellaneous supplies and equipment	1,819,631	594,102	371,637	479,543	374,504
Material for insulation, other maintenance and repair	1,819,631	594,102	371,637	479,543	374,504
Property management and security	10,819,954	3,797,202	1,245,025	3,010,612	2,767,165
Property management	7,366,569	3,066,520	877,725	1,611,497	1,811,487
Management and upkeep services for security	3,452,162	730,682	367,300	1,399,115	955,677
Parking	67,258	18,481	10,572	24,247	14,703
Rented dwellings	370,467,244	80,399,357	58,363,268	112,498,557	119,205,019
Rent	355,274,307	76,441,909	55,956,167	107,397,355	115,478,016
Rent as pay	10,225,639	2,952,027	1,488,988	3,410,231	2,374,075
Maintenance, insurance, and other expenses	4,967,298	1,005,420	918,114	1,690,523	1,352,929
Tenant's insurance	1,600,737	291,191	374,348	544,649	390,593
Maintenance and repair services	1,934,580	375,032	296,280	665,433	597,819
Maintenance and repair materials	1,431,981	339,197	247,216	480,441	364,517
Other lodging	79,240,753	18,553,958	15,305,968	22,203,545	23,176,773
Owned vacation homes	32,034,303	8,540,775	5,284,510	9,241,524	8,967,278
Mortgage interest and charges	10,368,715	2,052,986	1,534,256	2,997,142	3,784,427
Property taxes	14,272,116	3,890,059	2,391,651	4,252,574	3,736,990
Maintenance, insurance, and other expenses	7,393,472	2,597,730	1,358,603	1,991,359	1,445,861
Housing while attending school	8,731,292	1,638,738	2,180,487	1,432,791	3,479,831
Lodging on trips	38,473,936	8,374,445	7,840,971	11,529,230	10,729,664

	total consumer units	Northeast	Midwest	South	West
UTILITIES, FUELS, AND PUBLIC SERVICES	**$455,734,300**	**$92,319,254**	**$94,507,742**	**$175,001,648**	**$93,906,337**
Natural gas	**51,316,517**	**13,422,957**	**16,259,050**	**10,900,616**	**10,733,270**
Electricity	**174,008,287**	**30,156,746**	**33,193,064**	**79,182,464**	**31,476,603**
Fuel oil and other fuels	**19,178,270**	**10,985,472**	**3,269,917**	**3,134,988**	**1,788,185**
Fuel oil	10,911,669	9,263,569	550,001	974,801	123,170
Coal, wood, and other fuels	1,144,606	436,786	273,781	182,298	251,611
Bottled gas	7,121,995	1,285,117	2,446,136	1,977,889	1,413,127
Telephone services	**149,977,668**	**29,096,107**	**30,788,944**	**57,303,554**	**32,788,752**
Residential telephone and pay phones	46,585,233	9,807,411	9,442,452	17,776,306	9,559,271
Cellular phone service	100,973,599	18,416,927	21,081,114	38,693,437	22,782,019
Phone cards	1,081,017	272,484	165,624	367,739	274,636
Voice over IP	1,337,820	599,060	99,483	466,072	172,826
Water and other public services	**61,254,781**	**8,657,973**	**10,997,039**	**24,480,025**	**17,119,526**
Water and sewerage maintenance	46,064,290	6,398,764	8,013,642	19,428,214	12,223,239
Trash and garbage collection	14,799,173	2,167,029	2,892,859	4,903,189	4,835,811
Septic tank cleaning	391,318	91,955	90,537	148,622	60,475

See Appendix B for information about mortgage principal reduction.
Note: Numbers may not add to total because of rounding and missing subcategories.
Source: Calculations by New Strategist based on the Bureau of Labor Statistics' 2011 Consumer Expenditure Survey

Table 9.24 Housing: Shelter and Utilities: Market shares by region, 2011

(percentage of total annual spending on shelter and utilities accounted for by consumer units by region of residence, 2011)

	total consumer units	Northeast	Midwest	South	West
Share of total consumer units	100.0%	18.4%	22.2%	36.7%	22.7%
Share of total before-tax income	100.0	20.8	21.2	33.9	24.2
Share of total spending	100.0	20.2	21.0	33.8	25.0
Share of housing spending	100.0	21.5	19.7	32.7	26.2
SHELTER	100.0	22.6	19.0	30.3	28.2
Owned dwellings*	100.0	22.9	20.5	30.5	26.1
Mortgage interest and charges	100.0	19.1	18.3	31.6	30.9
Mortgage interest	100.0	18.9	18.3	31.9	30.9
Interest paid, home equity loan	100.0	29.1	25.5	22.7	22.6
Interest paid, home equity line of credit	100.0	19.9	14.8	29.7	35.6
Property taxes	100.0	30.0	23.3	26.7	20.1
Maintenance, repairs, insurance, other expenses	100.0	22.0	22.2	33.8	22.0
Homeowner's insurance	100.0	19.8	23.0	37.5	19.6
Ground rent	100.0	19.2	23.3	27.3	30.1
Maintenance and repair services	100.0	21.7	23.2	32.7	22.4
Painting and papering	100.0	18.1	15.5	34.8	31.6
Plumbing and water heating	100.0	19.1	18.8	34.9	27.2
Heat, air conditioning, electrical work	100.0	15.5	21.9	38.7	23.9
Roofing and gutters	100.0	26.9	29.5	26.8	16.7
Other repair and maintenance services	100.0	25.4	25.9	28.4	20.3
Repair, replacement of hard-surface flooring	100.0	20.9	20.4	39.1	19.5
Repair of built-in appliances	100.0	10.2	28.1	22.5	39.0
Maintenance and repair materials	100.0	21.5	23.7	34.8	20.1
Paints, wallpaper, and supplies	100.0	13.4	19.3	37.2	30.0
Tools, equipment for painting, wallpapering	100.0	13.4	19.3	37.2	29.9
Plumbing supplies and equipment	100.0	27.5	23.0	33.1	16.3
Electrical supplies, heating and cooling equipment	100.0	14.0	40.2	25.7	20.0
Hard-surface flooring, repair and replacement	100.0	11.9	26.0	33.6	28.4
Roofing and gutters	100.0	28.8	40.4	26.7	4.1
Plaster, paneling, siding, windows, doors, screens, awnings	100.0	23.6	20.3	45.9	10.2
Patio, walk, fence, driveway, masonry, brick, and stucco materials	100.0	11.1	25.4	40.0	23.6
Miscellaneous supplies and equipment	100.0	32.6	20.4	26.4	20.6
Material for insulation, other maintenanace and repair	100.0	32.6	20.4	26.4	20.6
Property management and security	100.0	35.1	11.5	27.8	25.6
Property management	100.0	41.6	11.9	21.9	24.6
Management and upkeep services for security	100.0	21.2	10.6	40.5	27.7
Parking	100.0	27.5	15.7	36.1	21.9
Rented dwellings	100.0	21.7	15.8	30.4	32.2
Rent	100.0	21.5	15.8	30.2	32.5
Rent as pay	100.0	28.9	14.6	33.3	23.2
Maintenance, insurance, and other expenses	100.0	20.2	18.5	34.0	27.2
Tenant's insurance	100.0	18.2	23.4	34.0	24.4
Maintenance and repair services	100.0	19.4	15.3	34.4	30.9
Maintenance and repair materials	100.0	23.7	17.3	33.6	25.5
Other lodging	100.0	23.4	19.3	28.0	29.2
Owned vacation homes	100.0	26.7	16.5	28.8	28.0
Mortgage interest and charges	100.0	19.8	14.8	28.9	36.5
Property taxes	100.0	27.3	16.8	29.8	26.2
Maintenance, insurance, and other expenses	100.0	35.1	18.4	26.9	19.6
Housing while attending school	100.0	18.8	25.0	16.4	39.9
Lodging on trips	100.0	21.8	20.4	30.0	27.9

	total consumer units	Northeast	Midwest	South	West
UTILITIES, FUELS, AND PUBLIC SERVICES	**100.0%**	**20.3%**	**20.7%**	**38.4%**	**20.6%**
Natural gas	**100.0**	**26.2**	**31.7**	**21.2**	**20.9**
Electricity	**100.0**	**17.3**	**19.1**	**45.5**	**18.1**
Fuel oil and other fuels	**100.0**	**57.3**	**17.1**	**16.3**	**9.3**
Fuel oil	100.0	84.9	5.0	8.9	1.1
Coal, wood, and other fuels	100.0	38.2	23.9	15.9	22.0
Bottled gas	100.0	18.0	34.3	27.8	19.8
Telephone services	**100.0**	**19.4**	**20.5**	**38.2**	**21.9**
Residential telephone and pay phones	100.0	21.1	20.3	38.2	20.5
Cellular phone service	100.0	18.2	20.9	38.3	22.6
Phone cards	100.0	25.2	15.3	34.0	25.4
Voice over IP	100.0	44.8	7.4	34.8	12.9
Water and other public services	**100.0**	**14.1**	**18.0**	**40.0**	**27.9**
Water and sewerage maintenance	100.0	13.9	17.4	42.2	26.5
Trash and garbage collection	100.0	14.6	19.5	33.1	32.7
Septic tank cleaning	100.0	23.5	23.1	38.0	15.5

See Appendix B for information about mortgage principal reduction.
Note: Numbers may not add to total because of rounding.
Source: Calculations by New Strategist based on the Bureau of Labor Statistics' 2011 Consumer Expenditure Survey

Table 9.25 Housing: Shelter and Utilities: Average spending by education, 2011

(average annual spending of consumer units on shelter and utilities, by education of consumer unit reference person, 2011)

	total consumer units	less than high school graduate	high school graduate	some college	associate's degree	bachelor's degree or more		
						total	bachelor's degree	graduate degree
Number of consumer units (in 000s)	122,287	16,146	30,810	25,361	12,912	37,058	23,578	13,480
Average number of persons per consumer unit	2.5	2.8	2.5	2.3	2.6	2.5	2.5	2.4
Average before-tax income of consumer units	$63,685.00	$32,564.00	$46,370.00	$52,965.00	$63,664.00	$98,983.00	$90,962.00	$113,013.00
Average spending of consumer units, total	49,704.88	29,950.97	39,704.28	45,355.33	50,819.44	68,902.95	65,051.01	75,731.40
Housing, average spending	**16,803.03**	**10,842.52**	**13,570.62**	**15,258.75**	**16,744.07**	**23,122.85**	**21,702.15**	**25,620.91**
SHELTER	**9,825.36**	**6,237.62**	**7,584.71**	**8,786.89**	**9,280.81**	**14,151.83**	**13,245.46**	**15,737.25**
Owned dwellings*	**6,147.89**	**2,650.69**	**4,442.68**	**5,008.03**	**5,903.68**	**9,954.47**	**9,192.49**	**11,287.31**
Mortgage interest and charges	3,183.73	1,238.24	2,230.21	2,637.24	3,079.67	5,234.39	4,902.47	5,814.98
Mortgage interest	3,020.32	1,169.75	2,093.93	2,481.01	2,929.80	4,997.43	4,692.62	5,530.60
Interest paid, home equity loan	61.79	19.41	57.51	64.07	53.55	85.11	74.95	102.88
Interest paid, home equity line of credit	101.63	49.08	78.77	92.16	96.32	151.86	134.91	181.49
Property taxes	1,844.51	845.38	1,373.39	1,463.00	1,665.83	2,994.87	2,707.83	3,496.96
Maintenance, repairs, insurance, other expenses	1,119.64	567.08	839.08	907.79	1,158.19	1,725.20	1,582.19	1,975.37
Homeowner's insurance	351.98	234.68	308.48	300.47	342.83	477.69	439.42	544.64
Ground rent	48.15	90.40	61.29	45.57	62.77	15.49	22.10	3.92
Maintenance and repair services	555.93	196.84	368.36	406.24	548.94	973.20	888.29	1,121.73
Painting and papering	61.73	7.51	47.59	49.57	33.26	115.33	77.36	181.75
Plumbing and water heating	65.34	24.46	46.15	43.57	63.81	114.54	118.28	108.01
Heat, air conditioning, electrical work	109.51	47.10	65.60	74.44	124.24	192.08	167.73	234.69
Roofing and gutters	92.49	21.27	87.63	75.70	122.14	128.72	138.70	111.26
Other repair and maintenance services	168.24	77.90	89.58	127.28	147.28	308.34	285.23	348.77
Repair, replacement of hard-surface flooring	56.91	18.22	31.14	33.97	57.57	110.67	97.68	133.40
Repair of built-in appliances	1.71	0.38	0.67	1.71	0.65	3.52	3.32	3.86
Maintenance and repair materials	74.55	23.99	64.93	70.71	99.88	98.37	97.41	100.05
Paints, wallpaper, and supplies	13.69	4.06	12.54	18.74	16.35	14.46	13.67	15.83
Tools, equipment for painting, wallpapering	1.47	0.44	1.35	2.01	1.76	1.55	1.47	1.70
Plumbing supplies and equipment	6.43	3.40	7.84	3.75	7.40	8.06	7.36	9.28
Electrical supplies, heating and cooling equipment	3.44	1.50	2.79	4.87	4.02	3.64	4.10	2.83
Hard-surface flooring, repair and replacement	11.88	3.29	12.51	9.60	21.90	13.16	13.02	13.40
Roofing and gutters	5.22	2.90	5.36	3.57	5.03	7.31	11.43	0.11
Plaster, paneling, siding, windows, doors, screens, awnings	15.77	1.16	13.77	13.11	20.32	24.02	22.55	26.59
Patio, walk, fence, driveway, masonry, brick, and stucco materials	1.78	0.36	0.92	3.01	3.58	1.64	1.45	1.98
Miscellaneous supplies and equipment	14.88	6.88	7.84	12.06	19.51	24.54	22.36	28.34
Material for insulation, other maintenance and repair	14.88	6.88	7.84	12.06	19.51	24.54	22.36	28.34
Property management and security	88.48	21.07	35.81	84.28	103.29	159.35	134.03	203.63
Property management	60.24	15.53	24.17	57.00	65.28	110.19	95.29	136.26
Management and upkeep services for security	28.23	5.54	11.64	27.29	38.01	49.16	38.74	67.38
Parking	0.55	0.11	0.21	0.51	0.46	1.10	0.93	1.39
Rented dwellings	**3,029.49**	**3,440.59**	**2,845.42**	**3,279.01**	**2,944.81**	**2,862.15**	**2,925.75**	**2,750.92**
Rent	2,905.25	3,209.29	2,754.48	3,125.54	2,817.25	2,778.03	2,841.99	2,666.15
Rent as pay	83.62	195.75	69.37	101.40	69.07	39.51	36.77	44.29
Maintenance, insurance, and other expenses	40.62	35.55	21.56	52.06	58.49	44.61	46.98	40.48
Tenant's insurance	13.09	6.62	9.81	15.08	13.82	17.02	16.26	18.33
Maintenance and repair services	15.82	7.74	7.41	24.13	13.57	21.43	23.38	18.01
Maintenance and repair materials	11.71	21.19	4.34	12.85	31.10	6.17	7.34	4.13
Other lodging	**647.99**	**146.34**	**296.61**	**499.85**	**432.32**	**1,335.21**	**1,127.22**	**1,699.02**
Owned vacation homes	261.96	63.18	125.33	176.51	173.11	551.59	460.72	710.55
Mortgage interest and charges	84.79	14.45	35.19	55.85	61.52	184.60	152.82	240.20
Property taxes	116.71	21.23	59.83	86.86	66.55	243.49	214.07	294.95
Maintenance, insurance, and other expenses	60.46	27.50	30.31	33.80	45.04	123.50	93.83	175.40
Housing while attending school	71.40	6.41	17.70	102.61	24.97	139.20	121.33	170.44
Lodging on trips	314.62	76.75	153.58	220.73	234.24	644.42	545.17	818.03

	total consumer units	less than high school graduate	high school graduate	some college	associate's degree	bachelor's degree or more		
						total	bachelor's degree	graduate degree
UTILITIES, FUELS, AND PUBLIC SERVICES	$3,726.76	$3,073.74	$3,621.55	$3,484.46	$3,968.35	$4,180.41	$4,091.15	$4,336.53
Natural gas	419.64	318.20	374.75	375.64	385.61	543.11	516.57	589.54
Electricity	1,422.95	1,284.65	1,457.84	1,327.41	1,519.44	1,485.98	1,477.48	1,500.84
Fuel oil and other fuels	156.83	121.61	168.33	121.79	148.93	189.34	163.06	235.33
Fuel oil	89.23	43.42	97.13	76.98	67.21	118.67	97.64	155.46
Coal, wood, and other fuels	9.36	12.01	12.09	9.46	7.92	6.37	7.03	5.21
Bottled gas	58.24	66.18	59.12	35.35	73.80	64.30	58.39	74.65
Telephone services	1,226.44	946.93	1,167.33	1,200.34	1,350.52	1,371.98	1,354.00	1,403.43
Residential telephone and pay phones	380.95	346.13	376.25	345.16	388.31	421.97	402.71	455.66
Cellular phone service	825.71	578.51	770.76	839.02	948.58	927.19	932.26	918.30
Phone cards	8.84	17.16	9.95	5.57	6.48	7.35	5.81	10.05
Voice over IP	10.94	5.13	10.38	10.60	7.15	15.48	13.22	19.42
Water and other public services	500.91	402.36	453.29	459.28	563.85	589.99	580.04	607.39
Water and sewerage maintenance	376.69	308.80	349.59	345.32	412.09	437.93	431.55	449.10
Trash and garbage collection	121.02	91.48	101.17	111.66	146.11	148.05	143.85	155.40
Septic tank cleaning	3.20	2.08	2.52	2.31	5.65	4.01	4.65	2.89

See Appendix B for information about mortgage principal reduction.
Note: Subcategories may not add to total because some are not shown.
Source: Bureau of Labor Statistics, unpublished tables from the 2011 Consumer Expenditure Survey

Table 9.26 Housing: Shelter and Utilities: Indexed spending by education, 2011

(indexed average annual spending of consumer units on shelter and utilities, by education of consumer unit reference person, 2011; index definition: an index of 100 is the average for all consumer units; an index of 125 means that spending by consumer units in that group is 25 percent above the average for all consumer units; an index of 75 indicates spending that is 25 percent below the average for all consumer units)

	total consumer units	less than high school graduate	high school graduate	some college	associate's degree	bachelor's degree or more total	bachelor's degree	graduate degree
Average spending of consumer units, total	$49,705	$29,951	$39,704	$45,355	$50,819	$68,903	$65,051	$75,731
Average spending of consumer units, index	100	60	80	91	102	139	131	152
Housing, spending index	100	65	81	91	100	138	129	152
SHELTER	**100**	**63**	**77**	**89**	**94**	**144**	**135**	**160**
Owned dwellings*	**100**	**43**	**72**	**81**	**96**	**162**	**150**	**184**
Mortgage interest and charges	100	39	70	83	97	164	154	183
Mortgage interest	100	39	69	82	97	165	155	183
Interest paid, home equity loan	100	31	93	104	87	138	121	166
Interest paid, home equity line of credit	100	48	78	91	95	149	133	179
Property taxes	100	46	74	79	90	162	147	190
Maintenance, repairs, insurance, other expenses	100	51	75	81	103	154	141	176
Homeowner's insurance	100	67	88	85	97	136	125	155
Ground rent	100	188	127	95	130	32	46	8
Maintenance and repair services	100	35	66	73	99	175	160	202
Painting and papering	100	12	77	80	54	187	125	294
Plumbing and water heating	100	37	71	67	98	175	181	165
Heat, air conditioning, electrical work	100	43	60	68	113	175	153	214
Roofing and gutters	100	23	95	82	132	139	150	120
Other repair and maintenance services	100	46	53	76	88	183	170	207
Repair, replacement of hard-surface flooring	100	32	55	60	101	194	172	234
Repair of built-in appliances	100	22	39	100	38	206	194	226
Maintenance and repair materials	100	32	87	95	134	132	131	134
Paints, wallpaper, and supplies	100	30	92	137	119	106	100	116
Tools, equipment for painting, wallpapering	100	30	92	137	120	105	100	116
Plumbing supplies and equipment	100	53	122	58	115	125	114	144
Electrical supplies, heating and cooling equipment	100	44	81	142	117	106	119	82
Hard-surface flooring, repair and replacement	100	28	105	81	184	111	110	113
Roofing and gutters	100	56	103	68	96	140	219	2
Plaster, paneling, siding, windows, doors, screens, awnings	100	7	87	83	129	152	143	169
Patio, walk, fence, driveway, masonry, brick, and stucco materials	100	20	52	169	201	92	81	111
Miscellaneous supplies and equipment	100	46	53	81	131	165	150	190
Material for insulation, other maintenance and repair	100	46	53	81	131	165	150	190
Property management and security	100	24	40	95	117	180	151	230
Property management	100	26	40	95	108	183	158	226
Management and upkeep services for security	100	20	41	97	135	174	137	239
Parking	100	20	38	93	84	200	169	253
Rented dwellings	**100**	**114**	**94**	**108**	**97**	**94**	**97**	**91**
Rent	100	110	95	108	97	96	98	92
Rent as pay	100	234	83	121	83	47	44	53
Maintenance, insurance, and other expenses	100	88	53	128	144	110	116	100
Tenant's insurance	100	51	75	115	106	130	124	140
Maintenance and repair services	100	49	47	153	86	135	148	114
Maintenance and repair materials	100	181	37	110	266	53	63	35
Other lodging	**100**	**23**	**46**	**77**	**67**	**206**	**174**	**262**
Owned vacation homes	100	24	48	67	66	211	176	271
Mortgage interest and charges	100	17	42	66	73	218	180	283
Property taxes	100	18	51	74	57	209	183	253
Maintenance, insurance, and other expenses	100	45	50	56	74	204	155	290
Housing while attending school	100	9	25	144	35	195	170	239
Lodging on trips	100	24	49	70	74	205	173	260

	total consumer units	less than high school graduate	high school graduate	some college	associate's degree	bachelor's degree or more		
						total	bachelor's degree	graduate degree
UTILITIES, FUELS, AND PUBLIC SERVICES	**100**	**82**	**97**	**93**	**106**	**112**	**110**	**116**
Natural gas	**100**	**76**	**89**	**90**	**92**	**129**	**123**	**140**
Electricity	**100**	**90**	**102**	**93**	**107**	**104**	**104**	**105**
Fuel oil and other fuels	**100**	**78**	**107**	**78**	**95**	**121**	**104**	**150**
Fuel oil	100	49	109	86	75	133	109	174
Coal, wood, and other fuels	100	128	129	101	85	68	75	56
Bottled gas	100	114	102	61	127	110	100	128
Telephone services	**100**	**77**	**95**	**98**	**110**	**112**	**110**	**114**
Residential telephone and pay phones	100	91	99	91	102	111	106	120
Cellular phone service	100	70	93	102	115	112	113	111
Phone cards	100	194	113	63	73	83	66	114
Voice over IP	100	47	95	97	65	141	121	178
Water and other public services	**100**	**80**	**90**	**92**	**113**	**118**	**116**	**121**
Water and sewerage maintenance	100	82	93	92	109	116	115	119
Trash and garbage collection	100	76	84	92	121	122	119	128
Septic tank cleaning	100	65	79	72	177	125	145	90

See Appendix B for information about mortgage principal reduction.
Source: Calculations by New Strategist based on the Bureau of Labor Statistics' 2011 Consumer Expenditure Survey

Table 9.27 Housing: Shelter and Utilities: Total spending by education, 2011

(total annual spending on shelter and utilities, by consumer unit educational attainment group, 2011; consumer units and dollars in thousands)

	total consumer units	less than high school graduate	high school graduate	some college	associate's degree	bachelor's degree or more total	bachelor's degree	graduate degree
Number of consumer units	122,287	16,146	30,810	25,361	12,912	37,058	23,578	13,480
Total spending of all consumer units	$6,078,260,661	$483,588,362	$1,223,288,867	$1,150,256,524	$656,180,609	$2,553,405,521	$1,533,772,714	$1,020,859,272
Housing, total spending	2,054,792,130	175,063,328	418,110,802	386,977,159	216,199,432	856,886,575	511,693,293	345,369,867
SHELTER	1,201,513,798	100,712,613	233,684,915	222,844,317	119,833,819	524,438,516	312,301,456	212,138,130
Owned dwellings*	751,807,024	42,798,041	136,878,971	127,008,649	76,228,316	368,892,749	216,740,529	152,152,939
Mortgage interest and charges	389,328,791	19,992,623	68,712,770	66,883,044	39,764,699	193,976,025	115,590,438	78,385,930
Mortgage interest	369,345,872	18,886,784	64,513,983	62,920,895	37,829,578	185,194,761	110,642,594	74,552,488
Interest paid, home equity loan	7,556,114	313,394	1,771,883	1,624,879	691,438	3,154,006	1,767,171	1,386,822
Interest paid, home equity line of credit	12,428,028	792,446	2,426,904	2,337,270	1,243,684	5,627,628	3,180,908	2,446,485
Property taxes	225,559,594	13,649,505	42,314,146	37,103,143	21,509,197	110,983,892	63,845,216	47,139,021
Maintenance, repairs, insurance, other expenses	136,917,417	9,156,074	25,852,055	23,022,462	14,954,549	63,932,462	37,304,876	26,627,988
Homeowner's insurance	43,042,578	3,789,143	9,504,269	7,620,220	4,426,621	17,702,236	10,360,645	7,341,747
Ground rent	5,888,119	1,459,598	1,888,345	1,155,701	810,486	574,028	521,074	52,842
Maintenance and repair services	67,983,012	3,178,179	11,349,172	10,302,653	7,087,913	36,064,846	20,944,102	15,120,920
Painting and papering	7,548,777	121,256	1,466,248	1,257,145	429,453	4,273,899	1,823,994	2,449,990
Plumbing and water heating	7,990,233	394,931	1,421,882	1,104,979	823,915	4,244,623	2,788,806	1,455,975
Heat, air conditioning, electrical work	13,391,649	760,477	2,021,136	1,887,873	1,604,187	7,118,101	3,954,738	3,163,621
Roofing and gutters	11,310,325	343,425	2,699,880	1,919,828	1,577,072	4,770,106	3,270,269	1,499,785
Other repair and maintenance services	20,573,565	1,257,773	2,759,960	3,227,948	1,901,679	11,426,464	6,725,153	4,701,420
Repair, replacement of hard-surface flooring	6,959,353	294,180	959,423	861,513	743,344	4,101,209	2,303,099	1,798,232
Repair of built-in appliances	209,111	6,135	20,643	43,367	8,393	130,444	78,279	52,033
Maintenance and repair materials	9,116,496	387,343	2,000,493	1,793,276	1,289,651	3,645,395	2,296,733	1,348,674
Paints, wallpaper, and supplies	1,674,109	65,553	386,357	475,265	211,111	535,859	322,311	213,388
Tools, equipment for painting, wallpapering	179,762	7,104	41,594	50,976	22,725	57,440	34,660	22,916
Plumbing supplies and equipment	786,305	54,896	241,550	95,104	95,549	298,687	173,534	125,094
Electrical supplies, heating and cooling equipment	420,667	24,219	85,960	123,508	51,906	134,891	96,670	38,148
Hard-surface flooring, repair and replacement	1,452,770	53,120	385,433	243,466	282,773	487,683	306,986	180,632
Roofing and gutters	638,338	46,823	165,142	90,539	64,947	270,894	269,497	1,483
Plaster, paneling, siding, windows, doors, screens, awnings	1,928,466	18,729	424,254	332,483	262,372	890,133	531,684	358,433
Patio, walk, fence, driveway, masonry, brick, and stucco materials	217,671	5,813	28,345	76,337	46,225	60,775	34,188	26,690
Miscellaneous supplies and equipment	1,819,631	111,084	241,550	305,854	251,913	909,403	527,204	382,023
Material for insulation, other maintenance and repair	1,819,631	111,084	241,550	305,854	251,913	909,403	527,204	382,023
Property management and security	10,819,954	340,196	1,103,306	2,137,425	1,333,680	5,905,192	3,160,159	2,744,932
Property management	7,366,569	250,747	744,678	1,445,577	842,895	4,083,421	2,246,748	1,836,785
Management and upkeep services for security	3,452,162	89,449	358,628	692,102	490,785	1,821,771	913,412	908,282
Parking	67,258	1,776	6,470	12,934	5,940	40,764	21,928	18,737
Rented dwellings	370,467,244	55,551,766	87,667,390	83,158,973	38,023,387	106,065,555	68,983,334	37,082,402
Rent	355,274,307	51,817,196	84,865,529	79,266,820	36,376,332	102,948,236	67,008,440	35,939,702
Rent as pay	10,225,639	3,160,580	2,137,290	2,571,605	891,832	1,464,162	866,963	597,029
Maintenance, insurance, and other expenses	4,967,298	573,990	664,264	1,320,294	755,223	1,653,157	1,107,694	545,670
Tenant's insurance	1,600,737	106,887	302,246	382,444	178,444	630,727	383,378	247,088
Maintenance and repair services	1,934,580	124,970	228,302	611,961	175,216	794,153	551,254	242,775
Maintenance and repair materials	1,431,981	342,134	133,715	325,889	401,563	228,648	173,063	55,672
Other lodging	79,240,753	2,362,806	9,138,554	12,676,696	5,582,116	49,480,212	26,577,593	22,902,790
Owned vacation homes	32,034,303	1,020,104	3,861,417	4,476,470	2,235,196	20,440,822	10,862,856	9,578,214
Mortgage interest and charges	10,368,715	233,310	1,084,204	1,416,412	794,346	6,840,907	3,603,190	3,237,896
Property taxes	14,272,116	342,780	1,843,362	2,202,856	859,294	9,023,252	5,047,342	3,975,926
Maintenance, insurance, and other expenses	7,393,472	444,015	933,851	857,202	581,556	4,576,663	2,212,324	2,364,392
Housing while attending school	8,731,292	103,496	545,337	2,602,292	322,413	5,158,474	2,860,719	2,297,531
Lodging on trips	38,473,936	1,239,206	4,731,800	5,597,934	3,024,507	23,880,916	12,854,018	11,027,044

	total consumer units	less than high school graduate	high school graduate	some college	associate's degree	bachelor's degree or more		
						total	bachelor's degree	graduate degree
UTILITIES, FUELS, AND PUBLIC SERVICES	$455,734,300	$49,628,606	$111,579,956	$88,369,390	$51,239,335	$154,917,634	$96,461,135	$58,456,424
Natural gas	51,316,517	5,137,657	11,546,048	9,526,606	4,978,996	20,126,570	12,179,687	7,946,999
Electricity	174,008,287	20,741,959	44,916,050	33,664,445	19,619,009	55,067,447	34,836,023	20,231,323
Fuel oil and other fuels	19,178,270	1,963,515	5,186,247	3,088,716	1,922,984	7,016,562	3,844,629	3,172,248
Fuel oil	10,911,669	701,059	2,992,575	1,952,290	867,816	4,397,673	2,302,156	2,095,601
Coal, wood, and other fuels	1,144,606	193,913	372,493	239,915	102,263	236,059	165,753	70,231
Bottled gas	7,121,995	1,068,542	1,821,487	896,511	952,906	2,382,829	1,376,719	1,006,282
Telephone services	149,977,668	15,289,132	35,965,437	30,441,823	17,437,914	50,842,835	31,924,612	18,918,236
Residential telephone and pay phones	46,585,233	5,588,615	11,592,263	8,753,603	5,013,859	15,637,364	9,495,096	6,142,297
Cellular phone service	100,973,599	9,340,622	23,747,116	21,278,386	12,248,065	34,359,807	21,980,826	12,378,684
Phone cards	1,081,017	277,065	306,560	141,261	83,670	272,376	136,988	135,474
Voice over IP	1,337,820	82,829	319,808	268,827	92,321	573,658	311,701	261,782
Water and other public services	61,254,781	6,496,505	13,965,865	11,647,800	7,280,431	21,863,849	13,676,183	8,187,617
Water and sewerage maintenance	46,064,290	4,985,885	10,770,868	8,757,661	5,320,906	16,228,810	10,175,086	6,053,868
Trash and garbage collection	14,799,173	1,477,036	3,117,048	2,831,809	1,886,572	5,486,437	3,391,695	2,094,792
Septic tank cleaning	391,318	33,584	77,641	58,584	72,953	148,603	109,638	38,957

*See Appendix B for information about mortgage principal reduction.
Note: Numbers may not add to total because of rounding and missing subcategories.
Source: Calculations by New Strategist based on the Bureau of Labor Statistics' 2011 Consumer Expenditure Survey

Table 9.28 Housing: Shelter and Utilities: Market shares by education, 2011

(percentage of total annual spending on shelter and utilities accounted for by consumer unit educational attainment groups, 2011)

| | total consumer units | less than high school graduate | high school graduate | some college | associate's degree | bachelor's degree or more | | |
						total	bachelor's degree	graduate degree
Share of total consumer units	100.0%	13.2%	25.2%	20.7%	10.6%	30.3%	19.3%	11.0%
Share of total before-tax income	100.0	6.8	18.3	17.2	10.6	47.1	27.5	19.6
Share of total spending	100.0	8.0	20.1	18.9	10.8	42.0	25.2	16.8
Share of housing spending	100.0	8.5	20.3	18.8	10.5	41.7	24.9	16.8
SHELTER	100.0	8.4	19.4	18.5	10.0	43.6	26.0	17.7
Owned dwellings*	100.0	5.7	18.2	16.9	10.1	49.1	28.8	20.2
Mortgage interest and charges	100.0	5.1	17.6	17.2	10.2	49.8	29.7	20.1
Mortgage interest	100.0	5.1	17.5	17.0	10.2	50.1	30.0	20.2
Interest paid, home equity loan	100.0	4.1	23.4	21.5	9.2	41.7	23.4	18.4
Interest paid, home equity line of credit	100.0	6.4	19.5	18.8	10.0	45.3	25.6	19.7
Property taxes	100.0	6.1	18.8	16.4	9.5	49.2	28.3	20.9
Maintenance, repairs, insurance, other expenses	100.0	6.7	18.9	16.8	10.9	46.7	27.2	19.4
Homeowner's insurance	100.0	8.8	22.1	17.7	10.3	41.1	24.1	17.1
Ground rent	100.0	24.8	32.1	19.6	13.8	9.7	8.8	0.9
Maintenance and repair services	100.0	4.7	16.7	15.2	10.4	53.0	30.8	22.2
Painting and papering	100.0	1.6	19.4	16.7	5.7	56.6	24.2	32.5
Plumbing and water heating	100.0	4.9	17.8	13.8	10.3	53.1	34.9	18.2
Heat, air conditioning, electrical work	100.0	5.7	15.1	14.1	12.0	53.2	29.5	23.6
Roofing and gutters	100.0	3.0	23.9	17.0	13.9	42.2	28.9	13.3
Other repair and maintenance services	100.0	6.1	13.4	15.7	9.2	55.5	32.7	22.9
Repair, replacement of hard-surface flooring	100.0	4.2	13.8	12.4	10.7	58.9	33.1	25.8
Repair of built-in appliances	100.0	2.9	9.9	20.7	4.0	62.4	37.4	24.9
Maintenance and repair materials	100.0	4.2	21.9	19.7	14.1	40.0	25.2	14.8
Paints, wallpaper, and supplies	100.0	3.9	23.1	28.4	12.6	32.0	19.3	12.7
Tools, equipment for painting, wallpapering	100.0	4.0	23.1	28.4	12.6	32.0	19.3	12.7
Plumbing supplies and equipment	100.0	7.0	30.7	12.1	12.2	38.0	22.1	15.9
Electrical supplies, heating and cooling equipment	100.0	5.8	20.4	29.4	12.3	32.1	23.0	9.1
Hard-surface flooring, repair and replacement	100.0	3.7	26.5	16.8	19.5	33.6	21.1	12.4
Roofing and gutters	100.0	7.3	25.9	14.2	10.2	42.4	42.2	0.2
Plaster, paneling, siding, windows, doors, screens, awnings	100.0	1.0	22.0	17.2	13.6	46.2	27.6	18.6
Patio, walk, fence, driveway, masonry, brick, and stucco materials	100.0	2.7	13.0	35.1	21.2	27.9	15.7	12.3
Miscellaneous supplies and equipment	100.0	6.1	13.3	16.8	13.8	50.0	29.0	21.0
Material for insulation, other maintenance and repair	100.0	6.1	13.3	16.8	13.8	50.0	29.0	21.0
Property management and security	100.0	3.1	10.2	19.8	12.3	54.6	29.2	25.4
Property management	100.0	3.4	10.1	19.6	11.4	55.4	30.5	24.9
Management and upkeep services for security	100.0	2.6	10.4	20.0	14.2	52.8	26.5	26.3
Parking	100.0	2.6	9.6	19.2	8.8	60.6	32.6	27.9
Rented dwellings	100.0	15.0	23.7	22.4	10.3	28.6	18.6	10.0
Rent	100.0	14.6	23.9	22.3	10.2	29.0	18.9	10.1
Rent as pay	100.0	30.9	20.9	25.1	8.7	14.3	8.5	5.8
Maintenance, insurance, and other expenses	100.0	11.6	13.4	26.6	15.2	33.3	22.3	11.0
Tenant's insurance	100.0	6.7	18.9	23.9	11.1	39.4	24.0	15.4
Maintenance and repair services	100.0	6.5	11.8	31.6	9.1	41.1	28.5	12.5
Maintenance and repair materials	100.0	23.9	9.3	22.8	28.0	16.0	12.1	3.9
Other lodging	100.0	3.0	11.5	16.0	7.0	62.4	33.5	28.9
Owned vacation homes	100.0	3.2	12.1	14.0	7.0	63.8	33.9	29.9
Mortgage interest and charges	100.0	2.3	10.5	13.7	7.7	66.0	34.8	31.2
Property taxes	100.0	2.4	12.9	15.4	6.0	63.2	35.4	27.9
Maintenance, insurance, and other expenses	100.0	6.0	12.6	11.6	7.9	61.9	29.9	32.0
Housing while attending school	100.0	1.2	6.2	29.8	3.7	59.1	32.8	26.3
Lodging on trips	100.0	3.2	12.3	14.5	7.9	62.1	33.4	28.7

	total consumer units	less than high school graduate	high school graduate	some college	associate's degree	bachelor's degree or more		
						total	bachelor's degree	graduate degree
UTILITIES, FUELS, AND PUBLIC SERVICES	**100.0%**	**10.9%**	**24.5%**	**19.4%**	**11.2%**	**34.0%**	**21.2%**	**12.8%**
Natural gas	**100.0**	**10.0**	**22.5**	**18.6**	**9.7**	**39.2**	**23.7**	**15.5**
Electricity	**100.0**	**11.9**	**25.8**	**19.3**	**11.3**	**31.6**	**20.0**	**11.6**
Fuel oil and other fuels	**100.0**	**10.2**	**27.0**	**16.1**	**10.0**	**36.6**	**20.0**	**16.5**
Fuel oil	100.0	6.4	27.4	17.9	8.0	40.3	21.1	19.2
Coal, wood, and other fuels	100.0	16.9	32.5	21.0	8.9	20.6	14.5	6.1
Bottled gas	100.0	15.0	25.6	12.6	13.4	33.5	19.3	14.1
Telephone services	**100.0**	**10.2**	**24.0**	**20.3**	**11.6**	**33.9**	**21.3**	**12.6**
Residential telephone and pay phones	100.0	12.0	24.9	18.8	10.8	33.6	20.4	13.2
Cellular phone service	100.0	9.3	23.5	21.1	12.1	34.0	21.8	12.3
Phone cards	100.0	25.6	28.4	13.1	7.7	25.2	12.7	12.5
Voice over IP	100.0	6.2	23.9	20.1	6.9	42.9	23.3	19.6
Water and other public services	**100.0**	**10.6**	**22.8**	**19.0**	**11.9**	**35.7**	**22.3**	**13.4**
Water and sewerage maintenance	100.0	10.8	23.4	19.0	11.6	35.2	22.1	13.1
Trash and garbage collection	100.0	10.0	21.1	19.1	12.7	37.1	22.9	14.2
Septic tank cleaning	100.0	8.6	19.8	15.0	18.6	38.0	28.0	10.0

See Appendix B for information about mortgage principal reduction.
Note: Numbers may not add to total because of rounding.
Source: Calculations by New Strategist based on the Bureau of Labor Statistics' 2011 Consumer Expenditure Survey

Spending on Personal Care, Reading, Education, and Tobacco, 2011

The average household spent 14 percent less on personal care products and services in 2011 than in 2000, after adjusting for inflation. Spending on reading material fell by a stomach-churning 40 percent during those years as the Internet cut household spending on print. Spending on education rose 27 percent as college tuition soared. The average household spent 16 percent less on tobacco in 2011 than in 2000 as smoking declined in popularity.

Spending on personal care products and services is highest among householders aged 35 to 44, at $736 in 2011. The biggest spenders on reading material are householders aged 65 to 74. The 21 percent of households headed by people aged 65 or older account for 43 percent of spending on newspaper and magazine subscriptions, spending about twice as much as the average household on this item. Average household spending on college tuition is well more than twice the average among householders under age 25, who are most likely to be paying their way through college. Householders aged 45 to 54 (the parents of college students) spend nearly twice the average on college tuition.

Households with incomes of $100,000 or more spend nearly twice the average on personal care products and services. This high-income group spends twice the average on reading material and over two-and-one-half times the average on education. Households with incomes of $100,000 or more spend less than average only on vocational and technical school costs, cigarettes, and smoking accessories.

By household type, spending on education is highest among married couples with adult children at home, who spend an average of $2,978 in 2011, because many have children in college. Married couples with children spend more than other household types on personal care products and services because their households are larger. Married couples without children at home (most of them older empty-nesters) spend the most on reading material, whereas tobacco spending is highest among couples with adult children at home.

Average household spending on personal care products and services does not vary much by racial and ethnic characteristics. Black householders spend four times the average on wigs and hairpieces. Asian spending on college tuition is more than two times the average. Non-Hispanic white householders spend 19 percent more than average on reading material and 13 percent more than average on tobacco.

Households in the Northeast spend 21 percent more than average on newspaper and magazine subscriptions, while households in the South spend 26 percent less than average on this item. Households in the West spend the most on books (40 percent more than average) and on digital book readers (31 percent). Spending on cigarettes is 25 percent below average in the West and slightly above average in the other three regions. Household spending on education is 54 percent above average in the Northeast and 35 percent below average in the South.

College graduates spend more than other households on personal care products and services, reading material, and education. They spend well more than twice the average on test preparation and tutoring services and almost twice the average on books. Householders with a high school diploma and no further education spend the most on tobacco—49 percent more than the average household.

Table 10.1 Personal Care, Reading, Education, and Tobacco: Average spending by age, 2011

(average annual spending of consumer units on personal care, reading, education, and tobacco products, by age of consumer unit reference person, 2011)

	total consumer units	under 25	25 to 34	35 to 44	45 to 54	55 to 64	65 to 74	75+
Number of consumer units (in 000s)	122,287	7,743	20,463	21,699	24,821	21,688	14,079	11,794
Average number of persons per consumer unit	2.5	2.1	2.9	3.3	2.8	2.1	1.9	1.6
Average before-tax income of consumer units	$63,685.00	$27,514.00	$58,179.00	$77,376.00	$78,519.00	$75,517.00	$52,521.00	$32,144.00
Average spending of consumer units, total	49,704.88	29,911.52	48,097.39	57,271.07	58,050.42	53,615.86	44,645.56	32,688.34
PERSONAL CARE PRODUCTS AND SERVICES	**634.26**	**323.63**	**569.62**	**735.94**	**709.21**	**695.42**	**608.52**	**517.38**
Personal care products	**351.90**	**196.88**	**322.72**	**437.42**	**396.56**	**371.20**	**296.77**	**276.90**
Hair care products	67.88	41.36	57.86	91.52	74.53	76.19	64.54	33.05
Hair accessories	7.60	4.12	8.90	10.33	6.98	7.40	7.18	4.62
Wigs and hairpieces	3.77	7.76	3.48	2.72	4.94	3.40	4.14	1.35
Oral hygiene products	34.69	12.66	29.45	39.35	38.21	36.24	37.07	36.48
Shaving products	16.40	10.73	20.81	21.92	18.31	12.83	15.29	5.86
Cosmetics, perfume, and bath products	170.49	97.53	154.76	213.73	192.55	191.25	127.00	129.02
Deodorants, feminine hygiene, miscellaneous products	37.05	18.90	39.76	44.02	41.52	30.80	22.55	49.92
Electric personal care appliances	14.01	3.82	7.71	13.83	19.53	13.09	18.99	16.59
Personal care services	**282.36**	**126.75**	**246.91**	**298.52**	**312.65**	**324.23**	**311.76**	**240.48**
READING	**115.42**	**44.89**	**74.42**	**100.18**	**112.77**	**148.72**	**163.39**	**148.15**
Newspaper and magazine subscriptions	40.35	6.06	10.82	21.80	33.24	57.42	78.78	85.90
Newspapers and magazines, nonsubscription	12.10	5.30	9.04	10.04	12.08	16.80	17.21	10.92
Books	48.58	26.04	42.47	50.99	50.37	60.11	61.45	29.14
Digital book readers	12.83	7.48	12.08	17.34	17.08	14.40	5.94	5.71
EDUCATION	**1,050.71**	**2,253.40**	**1,048.87**	**818.25**	**1,879.29**	**866.12**	**261.83**	**229.06**
College tuition	714.56	1,873.03	768.59	288.57	1,358.81	654.23	162.53	58.12
Elementary and high school tuition	136.92	11.18	86.30	253.81	258.68	66.96	9.25	116.99
Vocational and technical school tuition	6.29	4.38	10.52	12.03	5.93	4.47	0.86	0.18
Other school tuition, books, and supplies	50.30	40.49	41.67	88.96	54.27	48.79	30.22	18.97
Test preparation, tutoring services	10.85	13.22	6.43	18.63	20.29	5.70	4.23	0.19
Books and supplies for college	62.55	273.28	70.27	34.66	94.88	37.40	9.19	4.05
Books and supplies for elementary and high school	16.57	3.41	16.29	38.42	23.77	8.02	2.52	2.80
Books and supplies for vocational and technical schools	0.64	0.24	2.00	0.06	0.51	0.67	0.52	–
Books and supplies for day care and nursery	0.44	2.11	0.51	0.77	0.19	0.21	–	0.05
Miscellaneous school expenses and supplies	51.59	32.06	46.28	82.34	61.97	39.67	42.51	27.71
TOBACCO PRODUCTS AND SMOKING SUPPLIES	**350.57**	**256.17**	**378.14**	**342.85**	**465.05**	**400.66**	**288.59**	**119.70**
Cigarettes	322.07	232.32	343.47	309.59	432.36	374.22	261.52	111.09
Other tobacco products	25.56	21.87	30.85	30.19	29.52	22.60	25.15	7.85
Smoking accessories	2.74	1.98	2.65	3.07	3.17	3.83	1.92	0.77

Note: Subcategories may not add to total because some are not shown. "–" means sample is too small to make a reliable estimate.
Source: Bureau of Labor Statistics, unpublished tables from the 2011 Consumer Expenditure Survey

Table 10.2 Personal Care, Reading, Education, and Tobacco: Indexed spending by age, 2011

(indexed average annual spending of consumer units on personal care, reading, education, and tobacco products, by age of consumer unit reference person, 2011; index definition: an index of 100 is the average for all consumer units; an index of 125 means that spending by consumer units in that group is 25 percent above the average for all consumer units; an index of 75 indicates spending that is 25 percent below the average for all consumer units)

	total consumer units	under 25	25 to 34	35 to 44	45 to 54	55 to 64	65 to 74	75+
Average spending of consumer units, total	$49,705	$29,912	$48,097	$57,271	$58,050	$53,616	$44,646	$32,688
Average spending of consumer units, index	100	60	97	115	117	108	90	66
PERSONAL CARE PRODUCTS AND SERVICES	100	51	90	116	112	110	96	82
Personal care products	100	56	92	124	113	105	84	79
Hair care products	100	61	85	135	110	112	95	49
Hair accessories	100	54	117	136	92	97	94	61
Wigs and hairpieces	100	206	92	72	131	90	110	36
Oral hygiene products	100	36	85	113	110	104	107	105
Shaving products	100	65	127	134	112	78	93	36
Cosmetics, perfume, and bath products	100	57	91	125	113	112	74	76
Deodorants, feminine hygiene, miscellaneous products	100	51	107	119	112	83	61	135
Electric personal care appliances	100	27	55	99	139	93	136	118
Personal care services	100	45	87	106	111	115	110	85
READING	100	39	64	87	98	129	142	128
Newspaper and magazine subscriptions	100	15	27	54	82	142	195	213
Newspapers and magazines, nonsubscription	100	44	75	83	100	139	142	90
Books	100	54	87	105	104	124	126	60
Digital book readers	100	58	94	135	133	112	46	45
EDUCATION	100	214	100	78	179	82	25	22
College tuition	100	262	108	40	190	92	23	8
Elementary and high school tuition	100	8	63	185	189	49	7	85
Vocational and technical school tuition	100	70	167	191	94	71	14	3
Other school tuition, books, and supplies	100	80	83	177	108	97	60	38
Test preparation, tutoring services	100	122	59	172	187	53	39	2
Books and supplies for college	100	437	112	55	152	60	15	6
Books and supplies for elementary and high school	100	21	98	232	143	48	15	17
Books and supplies for vocational and technical schools	100	38	313	9	80	105	81	–
Books and supplies for day care and nursery	100	480	116	175	43	48	–	11
Miscellaneous school expenses and supplies	100	62	90	160	120	77	82	54
TOBACCO PRODUCTS AND SMOKING SUPPLIES	100	73	108	98	133	114	82	34
Cigarettes	100	72	107	96	134	116	81	34
Other tobacco products	100	86	121	118	115	88	98	31
Smoking accessories	100	72	97	112	116	140	70	28

Note: "–" means sample is too small to make a reliable estimate.
Source: Calculations by New Strategist based on the Bureau of Labor Statistics' 2011 Consumer Expenditure Survey

Table 10.3 Personal Care, Reading, Education, and Tobacco: Total spending by age, 2011

(total annual spending on personal care, reading, education, and tobacco products, by consumer unit age groups, 2011; consumer units and dollars in thousands)

	total consumer units	under 25	25 to 34	35 to 44	45 to 54	55 to 64	65 to 74	75+
Number of consumer units	122,287	7,743	20,463	21,699	24,821	21,688	14,079	11,794
Total spending of all consumer units	$6,078,260,661	$231,604,899	$984,216,892	$1,242,724,948	$1,440,869,475	$1,162,820,772	$628,564,839	$385,526,282
PERSONAL CARE PRODUCTS AND SERVICES	77,561,753	2,505,867	11,656,134	15,969,162	17,603,301	15,082,269	8,567,353	6,101,980
Personal care products	43,032,795	1,524,442	6,603,819	9,491,577	9,843,016	8,050,586	4,178,225	3,265,759
Hair care products	8,300,842	320,250	1,183,989	1,985,892	1,849,909	1,652,409	908,659	389,792
Hair accessories	929,381	31,901	182,121	224,151	173,251	160,491	101,087	54,488
Wigs and hairpieces	461,022	60,086	71,211	59,021	122,616	73,739	58,287	15,922
Oral hygiene products	4,242,136	98,026	602,635	853,856	948,410	785,973	521,909	430,245
Shaving products	2,005,507	83,082	425,835	475,642	454,473	278,257	215,268	69,113
Cosmetics, perfume, and bath products	20,848,711	755,175	3,166,854	4,637,727	4,779,284	4,147,830	1,788,033	1,521,662
Deodorants, feminine hygiene, miscellaneous products	4,530,733	146,343	813,609	955,190	1,030,568	667,990	317,481	588,756
Electric personal care appliances	1,713,241	29,578	157,770	300,097	484,754	283,896	267,360	195,662
Personal care services	34,528,957	981,425	5,052,519	6,477,585	7,760,286	7,031,900	4,389,269	2,836,221
READING	14,114,366	347,583	1,522,856	2,173,806	2,799,064	3,225,439	2,300,368	1,747,281
Newspaper and magazine subscriptions	4,934,280	46,923	221,410	473,038	825,050	1,245,325	1,109,144	1,013,105
Newspapers and magazines, nonsubscription	1,479,673	41,038	184,986	217,858	299,838	364,358	242,300	128,790
Books	5,940,702	201,628	869,064	1,106,432	1,250,234	1,303,666	865,155	343,677
Digital book readers	1,568,942	57,918	247,193	376,261	423,943	312,307	83,629	67,344
EDUCATION	128,488,174	17,448,076	21,463,027	17,755,207	46,645,857	18,784,411	3,686,305	2,701,534
College tuition	87,381,399	14,502,871	15,727,657	6,261,680	33,727,023	14,188,940	2,288,260	685,467
Elementary and high school tuition	16,743,536	86,567	1,765,957	5,507,423	6,420,696	1,452,228	130,231	1,379,780
Vocational and technical school tuition	769,185	33,914	215,271	261,039	147,189	96,945	12,108	2,123
Other school tuition, books, and supplies	6,151,036	313,514	852,693	1,930,343	1,347,036	1,058,158	425,467	223,732
Test preparation, tutoring services	1,326,814	102,362	131,577	404,252	503,618	123,622	59,554	2,241
Books and supplies for college	7,649,052	2,116,007	1,437,935	752,087	2,355,016	811,131	129,386	47,766
Books and supplies for elementary and high school	2,026,296	26,404	333,342	833,676	589,995	173,938	35,479	33,023
Books and supplies for vocational and technical schools	78,264	1,858	40,926	1,302	12,659	14,531	7,321	–
Books and supplies for day care and nursery	53,806	16,338	10,436	16,708	4,716	4,554	–	590
Miscellaneous school expenses and supplies	6,308,786	248,241	947,028	1,786,696	1,538,157	860,363	598,498	326,812
TOBACCO PRODUCTS AND SMOKING SUPPLIES	42,870,154	1,983,524	7,737,879	7,439,502	11,543,006	8,689,514	4,063,059	1,411,742
Cigarettes	39,384,974	1,798,854	7,028,427	6,717,793	10,731,608	8,116,083	3,681,940	1,310,195
Other tobacco products	3,125,656	169,339	631,284	655,093	732,716	490,149	354,087	92,583
Smoking accessories	335,066	15,331	54,227	66,616	78,683	83,065	27,032	9,081

Note: Numbers may not add to total because of rounding and missing subcategories. "–" means sample is too small to make a reliable estimate.
Source: Calculations by New Strategist based on the Bureau of Labor Statistics' 2011 Consumer Expenditure Survey

Table 10.4 Personal Care, Reading, Education, and Tobacco: Market shares by age, 2011

(percentage of total annual spending on personal care, reading, education, and tobacco products accounted for by consumer unit age groups, 2011)

	total consumer units	under 25	25 to 34	35 to 44	45 to 54	55 to 64	65 to 74	75+
Share of total consumer units	100.0%	6.3%	16.7%	17.7%	20.3%	17.7%	11.5%	9.6%
Share of total before-tax income	100.0	2.7	15.3	21.6	25.0	21.0	9.5	4.9
Share of total spending	100.0	3.8	16.2	20.4	23.7	19.1	10.3	6.3
PERSONAL CARE PRODUCTS AND SERVICES	100.0	3.2	15.0	20.6	22.7	19.4	11.0	7.9
Personal care products	100.0	3.5	15.3	22.1	22.9	18.7	9.7	7.6
Hair care products	100.0	3.9	14.3	23.9	22.3	19.9	10.9	4.7
Hair accessories	100.0	3.4	19.6	24.1	18.6	17.3	10.9	5.9
Wigs and hairpieces	100.0	13.0	15.4	12.8	26.6	16.0	12.6	3.5
Oral hygiene products	100.0	2.3	14.2	20.1	22.4	18.5	12.3	10.1
Shaving products	100.0	4.1	21.2	23.7	22.7	13.9	10.7	3.4
Cosmetics, perfume, and bath products	100.0	3.6	15.2	22.2	22.9	19.9	8.6	7.3
Deodorants, feminine hygiene, miscellaneous products	100.0	3.2	18.0	21.1	22.7	14.7	7.0	13.0
Electric personal care appliances	100.0	1.7	9.2	17.5	28.3	16.6	15.6	11.4
Personal care services	100.0	2.8	14.6	18.8	22.5	20.4	12.7	8.2
READING	100.0	2.5	10.8	15.4	19.8	22.9	16.3	12.4
Newspaper and magazine subscriptions	100.0	1.0	4.5	9.6	16.7	25.2	22.5	20.5
Newspapers and magazines, nonsubscription	100.0	2.8	12.5	14.7	20.3	24.6	16.4	8.7
Books	100.0	3.4	14.6	18.6	21.0	21.9	14.6	5.8
Digital book readers	100.0	3.7	15.8	24.0	27.0	19.9	5.3	4.3
EDUCATION	100.0	13.6	16.7	13.8	36.3	14.6	2.9	2.1
College tuition	100.0	16.6	18.0	7.2	38.6	16.2	2.6	0.8
Elementary and high school tuition	100.0	0.5	10.5	32.9	38.3	8.7	0.8	8.2
Vocational and technical school tuition	100.0	4.4	28.0	33.9	19.1	12.6	1.6	0.3
Other school tuition, books, and supplies	100.0	5.1	13.9	31.4	21.9	17.2	6.9	3.6
Test preparation, tutoring services	100.0	7.7	9.9	30.5	38.0	9.3	4.5	0.2
Books and supplies for college	100.0	27.7	18.8	9.8	30.8	10.6	1.7	0.6
Books and supplies for elementary and high school	100.0	1.3	16.5	41.1	29.1	8.6	1.8	1.6
Books and supplies for vocational and technical schools	100.0	2.4	52.3	1.7	16.2	18.6	9.4	–
Books and supplies for day care and nursery	100.0	30.4	19.4	31.1	8.8	8.5	–	1.1
Miscellaneous school expenses and supplies	100.0	3.9	15.0	28.3	24.4	13.6	9.5	5.2
TOBACCO PRODUCTS AND SMOKING SUPPLIES	100.0	4.6	18.0	17.4	26.9	20.3	9.5	3.3
Cigarettes	100.0	4.6	17.8	17.1	27.2	20.6	9.3	3.3
Other tobacco products	100.0	5.4	20.2	21.0	23.4	15.7	11.3	3.0
Smoking accessories	100.0	4.6	16.2	19.9	23.5	24.8	8.1	2.7

Note: Numbers may not add to total because of rounding and missing subcategories. "–" means sample is too small to make a reliable estimate.
Source: Calculations by New Strategist based on the Bureau of Labor Statistics' 2011 Consumer Expenditure Survey

Table 10.5 Personal Care, Reading, Education, and Tobacco: Average spending by income, 2011

(average annual spending on personal care, reading, education, and tobacco products, by before-tax income of consumer units, 2011)

	total consumer units	under $20,000	$20,000–$39,999	$40,000–$49,999	$50,000–$69,999	$70,000–$79,999	$80,000–$99,999	$100,000 or more
Number of consumer units (in 000s)	122,287	26,342	27,788	11,347	17,376	7,385	10,456	21,593
Average number of persons per consumer unit	2.5	1.8	2.3	2.6	2.7	2.8	3.0	3.2
Average before-tax income of consumer units	$63,685.00	$10,491.66	$29,658.14	$44,698.00	$59,306.00	$74,742.00	$89,108.00	$169,776.00
Average spending of consumer units, total	49,704.88	22,142.36	33,453.66	40,306.19	50,034.03	57,976.69	65,389.80	97,728.22
PERSONAL CARE PRODUCTS AND SERVICES	**634.26**	**274.48**	**420.83**	**519.45**	**620.29**	**828.67**	**828.33**	**1,235.55**
Personal care products	**351.90**	**159.94**	**242.18**	**299.11**	**362.11**	**472.42**	**455.37**	**632.09**
Hair care products	67.88	31.97	45.54	76.66	66.21	80.77	69.24	127.27
Hair accessories	7.60	3.50	5.76	5.50	7.34	12.41	13.51	11.44
Wigs and hairpieces	3.77	4.29	2.44	3.01	2.28	6.35	3.51	5.70
Oral hygiene products	34.69	19.60	27.30	26.72	38.16	45.66	42.10	54.22
Shaving products	16.40	5.76	9.18	9.93	21.85	25.25	28.09	27.71
Cosmetics, perfume, and bath products	170.49	68.93	115.14	131.84	177.53	226.20	215.79	328.23
Deodorants, feminine hygiene, miscellaneous products	37.05	23.67	28.73	30.18	35.50	42.25	63.14	52.47
Electric personal care appliances	14.01	2.73	8.10	15.28	13.23	33.52	19.99	25.06
Personal care services	**282.36**	**114.54**	**178.65**	**220.35**	**258.18**	**356.25**	**372.96**	**603.46**
READING	**115.42**	**50.46**	**74.06**	**88.86**	**131.51**	**123.20**	**151.28**	**228.40**
Newspaper and magazine subscriptions	40.35	20.47	31.96	30.70	42.65	39.11	48.14	75.26
Newspapers and magazines, nonsubscription	12.10	6.97	9.49	10.44	15.36	12.31	12.87	19.50
Books	48.58	19.75	26.03	36.75	52.75	51.96	66.37	105.82
Digital book readers	12.83	3.27	4.17	10.96	14.13	19.82	23.91	27.82
EDUCATION	**1,050.71**	**758.74**	**483.41**	**539.29**	**629.97**	**755.96**	**1,117.20**	**2,808.82**
College tuition	714.56	610.67	341.79	321.85	420.60	413.67	792.49	1,829.15
Elementary and high school tuition	136.92	7.77	27.20	71.94	49.79	64.62	93.50	585.68
Vocational and technical school tuition	6.29	–	4.24	4.98	8.88	9.80	8.33	4.09
Other school tuition, books, and supplies	50.30	13.70	23.07	37.98	29.39	133.29	54.86	122.71
Test preparation, tutoring services	10.85	6.77	2.22	5.85	13.26	0.84	13.69	29.70
Books and supplies for college	62.55	84.42	39.92	33.84	40.28	41.02	69.16	102.18
Books and supplies for elementary and high school	16.57	7.52	10.86	15.50	17.77	19.65	13.70	34.88
Books and supplies for vocational and technical schools	0.64	–	0.34	0.48	0.51	0.48	0.43	0.27
Books and supplies for day care and nursery	0.44	0.43	0.29	0.34	0.06	2.42	0.18	0.64
Miscellaneous school expenses and supplies	51.59	18.77	33.50	46.54	49.43	70.17	70.87	99.53
TOBACCO PRODUCTS AND SMOKING SUPPLIES	**350.57**	**319.11**	**369.80**	**416.28**	**391.62**	**402.38**	**400.57**	**254.52**
Cigarettes	322.07	293.99	348.93	381.72	360.80	367.86	366.50	222.06
Other tobacco products	25.56	22.52	18.19	29.57	27.75	33.35	31.79	29.18
Smoking accessories	2.74	2.59	2.68	4.98	3.07	1.17	2.28	2.16

Note: Subcategories may not add to total because some are not shown. "–" means sample is too small to make a reliable estimate.
Source: Bureau of Labor Statistics, unpublished tables from the 2011 Consumer Expenditure Survey; calculations by New Strategist

Table 10.6 Personal Care, Reading, Education, and Tobacco: Indexed spending by income, 2011

(indexed average annual spending of consumer units on personal care, reading, education, and tobacco products, by before-tax income of consumer unit, 2011; index definition: an index of 100 is the average for all consumer units; an index of 125 means that spending by consumer units in that group is 25 percent above the average for all consumer units; an index of 75 indicates spending that is 25 percent below the average for all consumer units)

	total consumer units	under $20,000	$20,000– $39,999	$40,000– $49,999	$50,000– $69,999	$70,000– $79,999	$80,000– $99,999	$100,000 or more
Average spending of consumer units, total	$49,705	$22,142	$33,454	$40,306	$50,034	$57,977	$65,390	$97,728
Average spending of consumer units, index	100	45	67	81	101	117	132	197
PERSONAL CARE PRODUCTS AND SERVICES	100	43	66	82	98	131	131	195
Personal care products	100	45	69	85	103	134	129	180
Hair care products	100	47	67	113	98	119	102	187
Hair accessories	100	46	76	72	97	163	178	151
Wigs and hairpieces	100	114	65	80	60	168	93	151
Oral hygiene products	100	56	79	77	110	132	121	156
Shaving products	100	35	56	61	133	154	171	169
Cosmetics, perfume, and bath products	100	40	68	77	104	133	127	193
Deodorants, feminine hygiene, miscellaneous products	100	64	78	81	96	114	170	142
Electric personal care appliances	100	19	58	109	94	239	143	179
Personal care services	100	41	63	78	91	126	132	214
READING	100	44	64	77	114	107	131	198
Newspaper and magazine subscriptions	100	51	79	76	106	97	119	187
Newspapers and magazines, nonsubscription	100	58	78	86	127	102	106	161
Books	100	41	54	76	109	107	137	218
Digital book readers	100	25	32	85	110	154	186	217
EDUCATION	100	72	46	51	60	72	106	267
College tuition	100	85	48	45	59	58	111	256
Elementary and high school tuition	100	6	20	53	36	47	68	428
Vocational and technical school tuition	100	–	67	79	141	156	132	65
Other school tuition, books, and supplies	100	27	46	76	58	265	109	244
Test preparation, tutoring services	100	62	20	54	122	8	126	274
Books and supplies for college	100	135	64	54	64	66	111	163
Books and supplies for elementary and high school	100	45	66	94	107	119	83	211
Books and supplies for vocational and technical schools	100	–	53	75	80	75	67	42
Books and supplies for day care and nursery	100	97	66	77	14	550	41	145
Miscellaneous school expenses and supplies	100	36	65	90	96	136	137	193
TOBACCO PRODUCTS AND SMOKING SUPPLIES	100	91	105	119	112	115	114	73
Cigarettes	100	91	108	119	112	114	114	69
Other tobacco products	100	88	71	116	109	130	124	114
Smoking accessories	100	95	98	182	112	43	83	79

Note: "–" means sample is too small to make a reliable estimate.
Source: Calculations by New Strategist based on the Bureau of Labor Statistics' 2011 Consumer Expenditure Survey

Table 10.7 Personal Care, Reading, Education, and Tobacco: Total spending by income, 2011

(total annual spending on personal care, reading, education, and tobacco products, by before-tax income group of consumer units, 2011; consumer units and dollars in thousands)

	total consumer units	under $20,000	$20,000–$39,999	$40,000–$49,999	$50,000–$69,999	$70,000–$79,999	$80,000–$99,999	$100,000 or more
Number of consumer units	122,287	26,342	27,788	11,347	17,376	7,385	10,456	21,593
Total spending of all consumer units	$6,078,260,661	$583,273,961	$929,610,260	$457,354,338	$869,391,305	$428,157,856	$683,715,749	$2,110,245,454
PERSONAL CARE PRODUCTS AND SERVICES	77,561,753	7,230,225	11,694,063	5,894,199	10,778,159	6,119,728	8,661,018	26,679,231
Personal care products	43,032,795	4,213,122	6,729,735	3,394,001	6,292,023	3,488,822	4,761,349	13,648,719
Hair care products	8,300,842	842,261	1,265,331	869,861	1,150,465	596,486	723,973	2,748,141
Hair accessories	929,381	92,152	160,140	62,409	127,540	91,648	141,261	247,024
Wigs and hairpieces	461,022	112,878	67,706	34,154	39,617	46,895	36,701	123,080
Oral hygiene products	4,242,136	516,281	758,677	303,192	663,068	337,199	440,198	1,170,772
Shaving products	2,005,507	151,672	255,221	112,676	379,666	186,471	293,709	598,342
Cosmetics, perfume, and bath products	20,848,711	1,815,868	3,199,394	1,495,988	3,084,761	1,670,487	2,256,300	7,087,470
Deodorants, feminine hygiene, miscellaneous products	4,530,733	623,617	798,249	342,452	616,848	312,016	660,192	1,132,985
Electric personal care appliances	1,713,241	71,933	225,018	173,382	229,884	247,545	209,015	541,121
Personal care services	34,528,957	3,017,103	4,964,328	2,500,311	4,486,136	2,630,906	3,899,670	13,030,512
READING	14,114,366	1,329,228	2,058,049	1,008,294	2,285,118	909,832	1,581,784	4,931,841
Newspaper and magazine subscriptions	4,934,280	539,283	888,188	348,353	741,086	288,827	503,352	1,625,089
Newspapers and magazines, nonsubscription	1,479,673	183,572	263,685	118,463	266,895	90,909	134,569	421,064
Books	5,940,702	520,222	723,255	417,002	916,584	383,725	693,965	2,284,971
Digital book readers	1,568,942	86,014	115,827	124,363	245,523	146,371	250,003	600,717
EDUCATION	128,488,174	19,986,628	13,432,935	6,119,324	10,946,359	5,582,765	11,681,443	60,650,850
College tuition	87,381,399	16,086,397	9,497,538	3,652,032	7,308,346	3,054,953	8,286,275	39,496,836
Elementary and high school tuition	16,743,536	204,725	755,712	816,303	865,151	477,219	977,636	12,646,588
Vocational and technical school tuition	769,185	–	117,830	56,508	154,299	72,373	87,098	88,315
Other school tuition, books, and supplies	6,151,036	360,778	640,954	430,959	510,681	984,347	573,616	2,649,677
Test preparation, tutoring services	1,326,814	178,263	61,630	66,380	230,406	6,203	143,143	641,312
Books and supplies for college	7,649,052	2,223,718	1,109,277	383,982	699,905	302,933	723,137	2,206,373
Books and supplies for elementary and high school	2,026,296	197,996	301,664	175,879	308,772	145,115	143,247	753,164
Books and supplies for vocational and technical schools	78,264	–	9,479	5,447	8,862	3,545	4,496	5,830
Books and supplies for day care and nursery	53,806	11,223	8,059	3,858	1,043	17,872	1,882	13,820
Miscellaneous school expenses and supplies	6,308,786	494,374	930,792	528,089	858,896	518,205	741,017	2,149,151
TOBACCO PRODUCTS AND SMOKING SUPPLIES	42,870,154	8,405,884	10,276,139	4,723,529	6,804,789	2,971,576	4,188,360	5,495,850
Cigarettes	39,384,974	7,744,222	9,696,110	4,331,377	6,269,261	2,716,646	3,832,124	4,794,942
Other tobacco products	3,125,656	593,319	505,534	335,531	482,184	246,290	332,396	630,084
Smoking accessories	335,066	68,288	74,494	56,508	53,344	8,640	23,840	46,641

Note: Numbers may not add to total because of rounding and missing subcategories. "–" means sample is too small to make a reliable estimate
Source: Calculations by New Strategist based on the Bureau of Labor Statistics' 2011 Consumer Expenditure Survey

Table 10.8 Personal Care, Reading, Education, and Tobacco: Market shares by income, 2011

(percentage of total annual spending on personal care, reading, education, and tobacco products accounted for by before-tax income group of consumer units, 2011)

	total consumer units	under $20,000	$20,000–$39,999	$40,000–$49,999	$50,000–$69,999	$70,000–$79,999	$80,000–$99,999	$100,000 or more
Share of total consumer units	100.0%	21.5%	22.7%	9.3%	14.2%	6.0%	8.6%	17.7%
Share of total before-tax income	100.0	3.5	10.6	6.5	13.2	7.1	12.0	47.1
Share of total spending	100.0	9.6	15.3	7.5	14.3	7.0	11.2	34.7
PERSONAL CARE PRODUCTS AND SERVICES	100.0	9.3	15.1	7.6	13.9	7.9	11.2	34.4
Personal care products	100.0	9.8	15.6	7.9	14.6	8.1	11.1	31.7
Hair care products	100.0	10.1	15.2	10.5	13.9	7.2	8.7	33.1
Hair accessories	100.0	9.9	17.2	6.7	13.7	9.9	15.2	26.6
Wigs and hairpieces	100.0	24.5	14.7	7.4	8.6	10.2	8.0	26.7
Oral hygiene products	100.0	12.2	17.9	7.1	15.6	7.9	10.4	27.6
Shaving products	100.0	7.6	12.7	5.6	18.9	9.3	14.6	29.8
Cosmetics, perfume, and bath products	100.0	8.7	15.3	7.2	14.8	8.0	10.8	34.0
Deodorants, feminine hygiene, miscellaneous products	100.0	13.8	17.6	7.6	13.6	6.9	14.6	25.0
Electric personal care appliances	100.0	4.2	13.1	10.1	13.4	14.4	12.2	31.6
Personal care services	100.0	8.7	14.4	7.2	13.0	7.6	11.3	37.7
READING	100.0	9.4	14.6	7.1	16.2	6.4	11.2	34.9
Newspaper and magazine subscriptions	100.0	10.9	18.0	7.1	15.0	5.9	10.2	32.9
Newspapers and magazines, nonsubscription	100.0	12.4	17.8	8.0	18.0	6.1	9.1	28.5
Books	100.0	8.8	12.2	7.0	15.4	6.5	11.7	38.5
Digital book readers	100.0	5.5	7.4	7.9	15.6	9.3	15.9	38.3
EDUCATION	100.0	15.6	10.5	4.8	8.5	4.3	9.1	47.2
College tuition	100.0	18.4	10.9	4.2	8.4	3.5	9.5	45.2
Elementary and high school tuition	100.0	1.2	4.5	4.9	5.2	2.9	5.8	75.5
Vocational and technical school tuition	100.0	–	15.3	7.3	20.1	9.4	11.3	11.5
Other school tuition, books, and supplies	100.0	5.9	10.4	7.0	8.3	16.0	9.3	43.1
Test preparation, tutoring services	100.0	13.4	4.6	5.0	17.4	0.5	10.8	48.3
Books and supplies for college	100.0	29.1	14.5	5.0	9.2	4.0	9.5	28.8
Books and supplies for elementary and high school	100.0	9.8	14.9	8.7	15.2	7.2	7.1	37.2
Books and supplies for vocational and technical schools	100.0	52.4	12.1	7.0	11.3	4.5	5.7	7.4
Books and supplies for day care and nursery	100.0	–	15.0	7.2	1.9	33.2	3.5	25.7
Miscellaneous school expenses and supplies	100.0	7.8	14.8	8.4	13.6	8.2	11.7	34.1
TOBACCO PRODUCTS AND SMOKING SUPPLIES	100.0	19.6	24.0	11.0	15.9	6.9	9.8	12.8
Cigarettes	100.0	19.7	24.6	11.0	15.9	6.9	9.7	12.2
Other tobacco products	100.0	19.0	16.2	10.7	15.4	7.9	10.6	20.2
Smoking accessories	100.0	20.4	22.2	16.9	15.9	2.6	7.1	13.9

Note: Numbers may not add to total because of rounding. "–" means sample is too small to make a reliable estimate.
Source: Calculations by New Strategist based on the Bureau of Labor Statistics' 2011 Consumer Expenditure Survey

Table 10.9 Personal Care, Reading, Education, and Tobacco: Average spending by high-income consumer units, 2011

(average annual spending on personal care, reading, education, and tobacco products, by before-tax income of high-income consumer units, 2011)

	total consumer units	$100,000 or more	$100,000–$119,999	$120,000–$149,999	$150,000 or more
Number of consumer units (in 000s)	122,287	21,593	7,045	6,107	8,440
Average number of persons per consumer unit	2.5	3.2	3.2	3.1	3.2
Average before-tax income of consumer units	$63,685.00	$169,776.00	$108,549.00	$133,318.00	$247,261.00
Average spending of consumer units, total	49,704.88	97,728.22	76,496.41	87,239.44	123,056.38
PERSONAL CARE PRODUCTS AND SERVICES	**634.26**	**1,235.55**	**996.99**	**1,053.65**	**1,566.70**
Personal care products	**351.90**	**632.09**	**540.64**	**503.65**	**801.77**
Hair care products	67.88	127.27	114.22	101.00	157.12
Hair accessories	7.60	11.44	12.60	11.46	10.43
Wigs and hairpieces	3.77	5.70	0.66	3.48	11.52
Oral hygiene products	34.69	54.22	44.83	46.31	67.92
Shaving products	16.40	27.71	22.35	21.08	37.02
Cosmetics, perfume, and bath products	170.49	328.23	267.68	254.14	432.88
Deodorants, feminine hygiene, miscellaneous products	37.05	52.47	60.69	57.00	42.17
Electric personal care appliances	14.01	25.06	17.61	9.17	42.72
Personal care services	**282.36**	**603.46**	**456.35**	**550.01**	**764.93**
READING	**115.42**	**228.40**	**169.16**	**213.58**	**288.57**
Newspaper and magazine subscriptions	40.35	75.26	56.35	74.47	91.60
Newspapers and magazines, nonsubscription	12.10	19.50	17.49	19.94	20.86
Books	48.58	105.82	77.04	91.49	140.23
Digital book readers	12.83	27.82	18.27	27.67	35.89
EDUCATION	**1,050.71**	**2,808.82**	**1,728.60**	**1,721.77**	**4,497.48**
College tuition	714.56	1,829.15	1,155.04	1,114.57	2,908.85
Elementary and high school tuition	136.92	585.68	292.67	272.22	1,057.06
Vocational and technical school tuition	6.29	4.09	5.35	4.50	2.73
Other school tuition, books, and supplies	50.30	122.71	83.08	116.08	160.60
Test preparation, tutoring services	10.85	29.70	10.31	25.84	48.67
Books and supplies for college	62.55	102.18	77.76	72.88	143.75
Books and supplies for elementary and high school	16.57	34.88	26.99	24.80	48.75
Books and supplies for vocational and technical schools	0.64	0.27	–	0.23	0.52
Books and supplies for day care and nursery	0.44	0.64	0.65	0.58	0.68
Miscellaneous school expenses and supplies	51.59	99.53	76.74	90.07	125.87
TOBACCO PRODUCTS AND SMOKING SUPPLIES	**350.57**	**254.52**	**356.43**	**249.24**	**173.15**
Cigarettes	322.07	222.06	314.39	222.64	144.57
Other tobacco products	25.56	29.18	35.56	25.22	26.72
Smoking accessories	2.74	2.16	3.15	1.38	1.86

Note: Subcategories may not add to total because some are not shown. "–" means sample is too small to make a reliable estimate.
Source: Bureau of Labor Statistics, unpublished tables from the 2011 Consumer Expenditure Survey

Table 10.10 Personal Care, Reading, Education, and Tobacco: Indexed spending by high-income consumer units, 2011

(indexed average annual spending of high-income consumer units on personal care, reading, education, and tobacco products, by before-tax income of consumer unit, 2011; index definition: an index of 100 is the average for all consumer units; an index of 125 means that spending by consumer units in that group is 25 percent above the average for all consumer units; an index of 75 indicates spending that is 25 percent below the average for all consumer units)

	total consumer units	$100,000 or more	$100,000–$119,999	$120,000–$149,999	$150,000 or more
Average spending of consumer units, total	$49,705	$97,728	$76,496	$87,239	$123,056
Average spending of consumer units, index	100	197	154	176	248
PERSONAL CARE PRODUCTS AND SERVICES	**100**	**195**	**157**	**166**	**247**
Personal care products	**100**	**180**	**154**	**143**	**228**
Hair care products	100	187	168	149	231
Hair accessories	100	151	166	151	137
Wigs and hairpieces	100	151	18	92	306
Oral hygiene products	100	156	129	133	196
Shaving products	100	169	136	129	226
Cosmetics, perfume, and bath products	100	193	157	149	254
Deodorants, feminine hygiene, miscellaneous products	100	142	164	154	114
Electric personal care appliances	100	179	126	65	305
Personal care services	**100**	**214**	**162**	**195**	**271**
READING	**100**	**198**	**147**	**185**	**250**
Newspaper and magazine subscriptions	100	187	140	185	227
Newspapers and magazines, nonsubscription	100	161	145	165	172
Books	100	218	159	188	289
Digital book readers	100	217	142	216	280
EDUCATION	**100**	**267**	**165**	**164**	**428**
College tuition	100	256	162	156	407
Elementary and high school tuition	100	428	214	199	772
Vocational and technical school tuition	100	65	85	72	43
Other school tuition, books, and supplies	100	244	165	231	319
Test preparation, tutoring services	100	274	95	238	449
Books and supplies for college	100	163	124	117	230
Books and supplies for elementary and high school	100	211	163	150	294
Books and supplies for vocational and technical schools	100	42	–	36	81
Books and supplies for day care and nursery	100	145	148	132	155
Miscellaneous school expenses and supplies	100	193	149	175	244
TOBACCO PRODUCTS AND SMOKING SUPPLIES	**100**	**73**	**102**	**71**	**49**
Cigarettes	100	69	98	69	45
Other tobacco products	100	114	139	99	105
Smoking accessories	100	79	115	50	68

Note: "–" means sample is too small to make a reliable estimate.
Source: Calculations by New Strategist based on the Bureau of Labor Statistics' 2011 Consumer Expenditure Survey

Table 10.11 Personal Care, Reading, Education, and Tobacco: Total spending by high-income consumer units, 2011

(total annual spending on personal care, reading, education, and tobacco products, by before-tax income group of high-income consumer units, 2011; consumer units and dollars in thousands)

	total consumer units	$100,000 or more	$100,000–$119,999	$120,000–$149,999	$150,000 or more
Number of consumer units	122,287	21,593	7,045	6,107	8,440
Total spending of all consumer units	$6,078,260,661	$2,110,245,454	$538,917,208	$532,771,260	$1,038,595,847
PERSONAL CARE PRODUCTS AND SERVICES	**77,561,753**	**26,679,231**	**7,023,795**	**6,434,641**	**13,222,948**
Personal care products	**43,032,795**	**13,648,719**	**3,808,809**	**3,075,791**	**6,766,939**
Hair care products	8,300,842	2,748,141	804,680	616,807	1,326,093
Hair accessories	929,381	247,024	88,767	69,986	88,029
Wigs and hairpieces	461,022	123,080	4,650	21,252	97,229
Oral hygiene products	4,242,136	1,170,772	315,827	282,815	573,245
Shaving products	2,005,507	598,342	157,456	128,736	312,449
Cosmetics, perfume, and bath products	20,848,711	7,087,470	1,885,806	1,552,033	3,653,507
Deodorants, feminine hygiene, miscellaneous products	4,530,733	1,132,985	427,561	348,099	355,915
Electric personal care appliances	1,713,241	541,121	124,062	56,001	360,557
Personal care services	**34,528,957**	**13,030,512**	**3,214,986**	**3,358,911**	**6,456,009**
READING	**14,114,366**	**4,931,841**	**1,191,732**	**1,304,333**	**2,435,531**
Newspaper and magazine subscriptions	4,934,280	1,625,089	396,986	454,788	773,104
Newspapers and magazines, nonsubscription	1,479,673	421,064	123,217	121,774	176,058
Books	5,940,702	2,284,971	542,747	558,729	1,183,541
Digital book readers	1,568,942	600,717	128,712	168,981	302,912
EDUCATION	**128,488,174**	**60,650,850**	**12,177,987**	**10,514,849**	**37,958,731**
College tuition	87,381,399	39,496,836	8,137,257	6,806,679	24,550,694
Elementary and high school tuition	16,743,536	12,646,588	2,061,860	1,662,448	8,921,586
Vocational and technical school tuition	769,185	88,315	37,691	27,482	23,041
Other school tuition, books, and supplies	6,151,036	2,649,677	585,299	708,901	1,355,464
Test preparation, tutoring services	1,326,814	641,312	72,634	157,805	410,775
Books and supplies for college	7,649,052	2,206,373	547,819	445,078	1,213,250
Books and supplies for elementary and high school	2,026,296	753,164	190,145	151,454	411,450
Books and supplies for vocational and technical schools	78,264	5,830	–	1,405	4,389
Books and supplies for day care and nursery	53,806	13,820	4,579	3,542	5,739
Miscellaneous school expenses and supplies	6,308,786	2,149,151	540,633	550,057	1,062,343
TOBACCO PRODUCTS AND SMOKING SUPPLIES	**42,870,154**	**5,495,850**	**2,511,049**	**1,522,109**	**1,461,386**
Cigarettes	39,384,974	4,794,942	2,214,878	1,359,662	1,220,171
Other tobacco products	3,125,656	630,084	250,520	154,019	225,517
Smoking accessories	335,066	46,641	22,192	8,428	15,698

Note: Numbers may not add to total because of rounding and missing subcategories. "–" means sample is too small to make a reliable estimate.
Source: Calculations by New Strategist based on the Bureau of Labor Statistics' 2011 Consumer Expenditure Survey

Table 10.12 Personal Care, Reading, Education, and Tobacco: Market shares by high-income consumer units, 2011

(percentage of total annual spending on personal care, reading, education, and tobacco products accounted for by before-tax income group of high-income consumer units, 2011)

	total consumer units	$100,000 or more	$100,000–$119,999	$120,000–$149,999	$150,000 or more
Share of total consumer units	100.0%	17.7%	5.8%	5.0%	6.9%
Share of total before-tax income	100.0	47.1	9.8	10.5	26.8
Share of total spending	100.0	34.7	8.9	8.8	17.1
PERSONAL CARE PRODUCTS AND SERVICES	100.0	34.4	9.1	8.3	17.0
Personal care products	100.0	31.7	8.9	7.1	15.7
Hair care products	100.0	33.1	9.7	7.4	16.0
Hair accessories	100.0	26.6	9.6	7.5	9.5
Wigs and hairpieces	100.0	26.7	1.0	4.6	21.1
Oral hygiene products	100.0	27.6	7.4	6.7	13.5
Shaving products	100.0	29.8	7.9	6.4	15.6
Cosmetics, perfume, and bath products	100.0	34.0	9.0	7.4	17.5
Deodorants, feminine hygiene, miscellaneous products	100.0	25.0	9.4	7.7	7.9
Electric personal care appliances	100.0	31.6	7.2	3.3	21.0
Personal care services	100.0	37.7	9.3	9.7	18.7
READING	100.0	34.9	8.4	9.2	17.3
Newspaper and magazine subscriptions	100.0	32.9	8.0	9.2	15.7
Newspapers and magazines, nonsubscription	100.0	28.5	8.3	8.2	11.9
Books	100.0	38.5	9.1	9.4	19.9
Digital book readers	100.0	38.3	8.2	10.8	19.3
EDUCATION	100.0	47.2	9.5	8.2	29.5
College tuition	100.0	45.2	9.3	7.8	28.1
Elementary and high school tuition	100.0	75.5	12.3	9.9	53.3
Vocational and technical school tuition	100.0	11.5	4.9	3.6	3.0
Other school tuition, books, and supplies	100.0	43.1	9.5	11.5	22.0
Test preparation, tutoring services	100.0	48.3	5.5	11.9	31.0
Books and supplies for college	100.0	28.8	7.2	5.8	15.9
Books and supplies for elementary and high school	100.0	37.2	9.4	7.5	20.3
Books and supplies for vocational and technical schools	100.0	7.4	–	1.8	5.6
Books and supplies for day care and nursery	100.0	25.7	8.5	6.6	10.7
Miscellaneous school expenses and supplies	100.0	34.1	8.6	8.7	16.8
TOBACCO PRODUCTS AND SMOKING SUPPLIES	100.0	12.8	5.9	3.6	3.4
Cigarettes	100.0	12.2	5.6	3.5	3.1
Other tobacco products	100.0	20.2	8.0	4.9	7.2
Smoking accessories	100.0	13.9	6.6	2.5	4.7

Note: Numbers may not add to total because of rounding. "–" means sample is too small to make a reliable estimate.
Source: Calculations by New Strategist based on the Bureau of Labor Statistics' 2011 Consumer Expenditure Survey

Table 10.13 Personal Care, Reading, Education, and Tobacco: Average spending by household type, 2011

(average annual spending of consumer units on personal care, reading, education, and tobacco products, by type of consumer unit, 2011)

	total married couples	married couples, no children	married couples with children				single parent with child under age 18	single person
			total	oldest child under age 6	oldest child aged 6 to 17	oldest child aged 18 or older		
Number of consumer units (in 000s)	60,144	25,270	29,097	5,825	14,661	8,612	6,956	36,110
Average number of persons per consumer unit	3.2	2.0	4.0	3.5	4.2	3.9	2.9	1.0
Average before-tax income of consumer units	$86,700.00	$78,823.00	$93,677.00	$91,014.00	$93,029.00	$96,583.00	$37,188.00	$34,540.00
Average spending of consumer units, total	63,971.54	57,658.24	69,724.22	65,947.61	70,708.52	70,411.85	37,553.05	30,613.18
PERSONAL CARE PRODUCTS AND SERVICES	**819.33**	**761.27**	**883.97**	**707.37**	**914.93**	**938.14**	**547.53**	**387.73**
Personal care products	453.42	381.71	521.27	383.32	549.26	554.35	312.52	213.09
Hair care products	89.56	70.95	96.74	59.27	106.99	101.18	55.78	34.53
Hair accessories	10.04	7.39	12.54	18.05	13.68	7.43	5.96	4.27
Wigs and hairpieces	4.50	5.12	3.56	1.06	2.20	7.57	9.64	1.14
Oral hygiene products	45.14	40.39	49.55	48.36	51.90	46.29	26.92	20.33
Shaving products	22.98	17.84	29.20	24.52	33.13	25.28	7.90	8.90
Cosmetics, perfume, and bath products	214.26	177.64	256.46	193.06	263.28	281.74	171.84	111.01
Deodorants, feminine hygiene, miscellaneous products	45.11	40.28	49.18	27.54	51.61	57.65	28.78	27.22
Electric personal care appliances	21.82	22.10	24.03	11.45	26.47	27.21	5.70	5.69
Personal care services	365.91	379.56	362.70	324.05	365.67	383.79	235.01	174.64
READING	**148.30**	**177.09**	**131.82**	**106.75**	**136.10**	**141.47**	**52.31**	**90.16**
Newspaper and magazine subscriptions	53.68	77.39	36.56	22.55	35.54	47.79	8.21	32.04
Newspapers and magazines, nonsubscription	14.16	15.89	12.38	7.47	13.02	14.61	6.02	10.17
Books	61.05	66.32	61.67	56.06	63.47	62.42	25.71	39.69
Digital book readers	18.21	14.87	21.19	20.67	24.07	16.66	12.38	4.82
EDUCATION	**1,340.26**	**715.80**	**1,904.08**	**728.88**	**1,739.40**	**2,978.16**	**552.83**	**781.55**
College tuition	866.98	573.73	1,149.31	441.95	700.85	2,391.24	78.05	618.06
Elementary and high school tuition	224.42	8.70	403.20	104.32	653.78	178.76	235.11	35.52
Vocational and technical school tuition	4.50	4.08	3.29	0.37	1.06	9.06	6.20	8.09
Other school tuition, books, and supplies	63.00	32.29	89.69	31.51	121.52	74.85	101.68	27.44
Test preparation, tutoring services	14.14	1.08	25.12	4.51	39.20	15.09	14.49	5.42
Books and supplies for college	66.60	44.72	88.01	47.76	48.06	183.24	23.59	61.05
Books and supplies for elementary and high school	24.51	2.65	43.03	7.36	66.92	26.50	41.22	2.53
Books and supplies for vocational and technical schools	0.32	0.46	0.22	0.03	0.10	0.56	0.03	1.17
Books and supplies for day care and nursery	0.68	0.70	0.65	3.04	0.09	–	0.94	0.11
Miscellaneous school expenses and supplies	75.11	47.38	101.57	88.04	107.83	98.87	51.52	22.16
TOBACCO PRODUCTS AND SMOKING SUPPLIES	**341.84**	**292.92**	**319.97**	**204.16**	**312.15**	**411.45**	**322.31**	**255.43**
Cigarettes	307.96	261.49	285.02	179.60	275.17	373.11	309.16	236.25
Other tobacco products	30.77	28.41	31.47	23.13	32.49	35.36	10.32	17.07
Smoking accessories	3.12	3.02	3.48	1.42	4.48	2.98	2.82	2.11

Note: Average spending figures for total consumer units can be found on Average Spending by Age and Average Spending by Region tables. Subcategories may not add to total because some are not shown.
"–" means sample is too small to make a reliable estimate.
Source: Bureau of Labor Statistics, unpublished tables from the 2011 Consumer Expenditure Survey

Table 10.14 Personal Care, Reading, Education, and Tobacco: Indexed spending by household type, 2011

(indexed average annual spending of consumer units on personal care, reading, education, and tobacco products, by type of consumer unit, 2011; index definition: an index of 100 is the average for all consumer units; an index of 125 means that spending by consumer units in that group is 25 percent above the average for all consumer units; an index of 75 indicates spending that is 25 percent below the average for all consumer units)

	total married couples	married couples, no children	married couples with children				single parent with child under age 18	single person
			total	oldest child under age 6	oldest child aged 6 to 17	oldest child aged 18 or older		
Average spending of consumer units, total	$63,972	$57,658	$69,724	$65,948	$70,709	$70,412	$37,553	$30,613
Average spending of consumer units, index	129	116	140	133	142	142	76	62
PERSONAL CARE PRODUCTS AND SERVICES	129	120	139	112	144	148	86	61
Personal care products	129	108	148	109	156	158	89	61
Hair care products	132	105	143	87	158	149	82	51
Hair accessories	132	97	165	238	180	98	78	56
Wigs and hairpieces	119	136	94	28	58	201	256	30
Oral hygiene products	130	116	143	139	150	133	78	59
Shaving products	140	109	178	150	202	154	48	54
Cosmetics, perfume, and bath products	126	104	150	113	154	165	101	65
Deodorants, feminine hygiene, miscellaneous products	122	109	133	74	139	156	78	73
Electric personal care appliances	156	158	172	82	189	194	41	41
Personal care services	130	134	128	115	130	136	83	62
READING	128	153	114	92	118	123	45	78
Newspaper and magazine subscriptions	133	192	91	56	88	118	20	79
Newspapers and magazines, nonsubscription	117	131	102	62	108	121	50	84
Books	126	137	127	115	131	128	53	82
Digital book readers	142	116	165	161	188	130	96	38
EDUCATION	128	68	181	69	166	283	53	74
College tuition	121	80	161	62	98	335	11	86
Elementary and high school tuition	164	6	294	76	477	131	172	26
Vocational and technical school tuition	72	65	52	6	17	144	99	129
Other school tuition, books, and supplies	125	64	178	63	242	149	202	55
Test preparation, tutoring services	130	10	232	42	361	139	134	50
Books and supplies for college	106	71	141	76	77	293	38	98
Books and supplies for elementary and high school	148	16	260	44	404	160	249	15
Books and supplies for vocational and technical schools	50	72	34	5	16	88	5	183
Books and supplies for day care and nursery	155	159	148	691	20	–	214	25
Miscellaneous school expenses and supplies	146	92	197	171	209	192	100	43
TOBACCO PRODUCTS AND SMOKING SUPPLIES	98	84	91	58	89	117	92	73
Cigarettes	96	81	88	56	85	116	96	73
Other tobacco products	120	111	123	90	127	138	40	67
Smoking accessories	114	110	127	52	164	109	103	77

Note: Spending index for total consumer units is 100. "–" means sample is too small to make a reliable estimate.
Source: Calculations by New Strategist based on the Bureau of Labor Statistics' 2011 Consumer Expenditure Survey

Table 10.15 Personal Care, Reading, Education, and Tobacco: Total spending by household type, 2011

(total annual spending on personal care, reading, education, and tobacco products, by consumer unit type, 2011; consumer units and dollars in thousands)

	total married couples	married couples, no children	married couples with children				single parent with child under age 18	single person
			total	oldest child under age 6	oldest child aged 6 to 17	oldest child aged 18 or older		
Number of consumer units	60,144	25,270	29,097	5,825	14,661	8,612	6,956	36,110
Total spending of all consumer units	$3,847,504,302	$1,457,023,725	$2,028,765,629	$384,144,828	$1,036,657,612	$606,386,852	$261,219,016	$1,105,441,930
PERSONAL CARE PRODUCTS AND SERVICES	**49,277,784**	**19,237,293**	**25,720,875**	**4,120,430**	**13,413,789**	**8,079,262**	**3,808,619**	**14,000,930**
Personal care products	**27,270,492**	**9,645,812**	**15,167,393**	**2,232,839**	**8,052,701**	**4,774,062**	**2,173,889**	**7,694,680**
Hair care products	5,386,497	1,792,907	2,814,844	345,248	1,568,580	871,362	388,006	1,246,878
Hair accessories	603,846	186,745	364,876	105,141	200,562	63,987	41,458	154,190
Wigs and hairpieces	270,648	129,382	103,585	6,175	32,254	65,193	67,056	41,165
Oral hygiene products	2,714,900	1,020,655	1,441,756	281,697	760,906	398,649	187,256	734,116
Shaving products	1,382,109	450,817	849,632	142,829	485,719	217,711	54,952	321,379
Cosmetics, perfume, and bath products	12,886,453	4,488,963	7,462,217	1,124,575	3,859,948	2,426,345	1,195,319	4,008,571
Deodorants, feminine hygiene, miscellaneous products	2,713,096	1,017,876	1,430,990	160,421	756,654	496,482	200,194	982,914
Electric personal care appliances	1,312,342	558,467	699,201	66,696	388,077	234,333	39,649	205,466
Personal care services	**22,007,291**	**9,591,481**	**10,553,482**	**1,887,591**	**5,361,088**	**3,305,199**	**1,634,730**	**6,306,250**
READING	**8,919,355**	**4,475,064**	**3,835,567**	**621,819**	**1,995,362**	**1,218,340**	**363,868**	**3,255,678**
Newspaper and magazine subscriptions	3,228,530	1,955,645	1,063,786	131,354	521,052	411,567	57,109	1,156,964
Newspapers and magazines, nonsubscription	851,639	401,540	360,221	43,513	190,886	125,821	41,875	367,239
Books	3,671,791	1,675,906	1,794,412	326,550	930,534	537,561	178,839	1,433,206
Digital book readers	1,095,222	375,765	616,565	120,403	352,890	143,476	86,115	174,050
EDUCATION	**80,608,597**	**18,088,266**	**55,403,016**	**4,245,726**	**25,501,343**	**25,647,914**	**3,845,485**	**28,221,771**
College tuition	52,143,645	14,498,157	33,441,473	2,574,359	10,275,162	20,593,359	542,916	22,318,147
Elementary and high school tuition	13,497,516	219,849	11,731,910	607,664	9,585,069	1,539,481	1,635,425	1,282,627
Vocational and technical school tuition	270,648	103,102	95,729	2,155	15,541	78,025	43,127	292,130
Other school tuition, books, and supplies	3,789,072	815,968	2,609,710	183,546	1,781,605	644,608	707,286	990,858
Test preparation, tutoring services	850,436	27,292	730,917	26,271	574,711	129,955	100,792	195,716
Books and supplies for college	4,005,590	1,130,074	2,560,827	278,202	704,608	1,578,063	164,092	2,204,516
Books and supplies for elementary and high school	1,474,129	66,966	1,252,044	42,872	981,114	228,218	286,726	91,358
Books and supplies for vocational and technical schools	19,246	11,624	6,401	175	1,466	4,823	209	42,249
Books and supplies for day care and nursery	40,898	17,689	18,913	17,708	1,319	–	6,539	3,972
Miscellaneous school expenses and supplies	4,517,416	1,197,293	2,955,382	512,833	1,580,896	851,468	358,373	800,198
TOBACCO PRODUCTS AND SMOKING SUPPLIES	**20,559,625**	**7,402,088**	**9,310,167**	**1,189,232**	**4,576,431**	**3,543,407**	**2,241,988**	**9,223,577**
Cigarettes	18,521,946	6,607,852	8,293,227	1,046,170	4,034,267	3,213,223	2,150,517	8,530,988
Other tobacco products	1,850,631	717,921	915,683	134,732	476,336	304,520	71,786	616,398
Smoking accessories	187,649	76,315	101,258	8,272	65,681	25,664	19,616	76,192

Note: Total spending figures for total consumer units can be found in Total Spending by Age and Total Spending by Region tables. Spending by type of consumer unit does not add to total because not all types of consumer units are shown. Numbers may not add to category total because of rounding and missing subcategories. "–" means sample is too small to make a reliable estimate.
Source: Calculations by New Strategist based on the Bureau of Labor Statistics' 2011 Consumer Expenditure Survey

Table 10.16 Personal Care, Reading, Education, and Tobacco: Market shares by household type, 2011

(percentage of total annual spending on personal care, reading, education, and tobacco products accounted for by types of consumer units, 2011)

	total married couples	married couples, no children	married couples with children				single parent with child under age 18	single person
			total	oldest child under age 6	oldest child aged 6 to 17	oldest child aged 18 or older		
Share of total consumer units	49.2%	20.7%	23.8%	4.8%	12.0%	7.0%	5.7%	29.5%
Share of total before-tax income	67.0	25.6	35.0	6.8	17.5	10.7	3.3	16.0
Share of total spending	63.3	24.0	33.4	6.3	17.1	10.0	4.3	18.2
PERSONAL CARE PRODUCTS AND SERVICES	**63.5**	**24.8**	**33.2**	**5.3**	**17.3**	**10.4**	**4.9**	**18.1**
Personal care products	**63.4**	**22.4**	**35.2**	**5.2**	**18.7**	**11.1**	**5.1**	**17.9**
Hair care products	64.9	21.6	33.9	4.2	18.9	10.5	4.7	15.0
Hair accessories	65.0	20.1	39.3	11.3	21.6	6.9	4.5	16.6
Wigs and hairpieces	58.7	28.1	22.5	1.3	7.0	14.1	14.5	8.9
Oral hygiene products	64.0	24.1	34.0	6.6	17.9	9.4	4.4	17.3
Shaving products	68.9	22.5	42.4	7.1	24.2	10.9	2.7	16.0
Cosmetics, perfume, and bath products	61.8	21.5	35.8	5.4	18.5	11.6	5.7	19.2
Deodorants, feminine hygiene, miscellaneous products	59.9	22.5	31.6	3.5	16.7	11.0	4.4	21.7
Electric personal care appliances	76.6	32.6	40.8	3.9	22.7	13.7	2.3	12.0
Personal care services	**63.7**	**27.8**	**30.6**	**5.5**	**15.5**	**9.6**	**4.7**	**18.3**
READING	**63.2**	**31.7**	**27.2**	**4.4**	**14.1**	**8.6**	**2.6**	**23.1**
Newspaper and magazine subscriptions	65.4	39.6	21.6	2.7	10.6	8.3	1.2	23.4
Newspapers and magazines, nonsubscription	57.6	27.1	24.3	2.9	12.9	8.5	2.8	24.8
Books	61.8	28.2	30.2	5.5	15.7	9.0	3.0	24.1
Digital book readers	69.8	24.0	39.3	7.7	22.5	9.1	5.5	11.1
EDUCATION	**62.7**	**14.1**	**43.1**	**3.3**	**19.8**	**20.0**	**3.0**	**22.0**
College tuition	59.7	16.6	38.3	2.9	11.8	23.6	0.6	25.5
Elementary and high school tuition	80.6	1.3	70.1	3.6	57.2	9.2	9.8	7.7
Vocational and technical school tuition	35.2	13.4	12.4	0.3	2.0	10.1	5.6	38.0
Other school tuition, books, and supplies	61.6	13.3	42.4	3.0	29.0	10.5	11.5	16.1
Test preparation, tutoring services	64.1	2.1	55.1	2.0	43.3	9.8	7.6	14.8
Books and supplies for college	52.4	14.8	33.5	3.6	9.2	20.6	2.1	28.8
Books and supplies for elementary and high school	72.7	3.3	61.8	2.1	48.4	11.3	14.2	4.5
Books and supplies for vocational and technical schools	24.6	14.9	8.2	0.2	1.9	6.2	0.3	54.0
Books and supplies for day care and nursery	76.0	32.9	35.2	32.9	2.5	–	12.2	7.4
Miscellaneous school expenses and supplies	71.6	19.0	46.8	8.1	25.1	13.5	5.7	12.7
TOBACCO PRODUCTS AND SMOKING SUPPLIES	**48.0**	**17.3**	**21.7**	**2.8**	**10.7**	**8.3**	**5.2**	**21.5**
Cigarettes	47.0	16.8	21.1	2.7	10.2	8.2	5.5	21.7
Other tobacco products	59.2	23.0	29.3	4.3	15.2	9.7	2.3	19.7
Smoking accessories	56.0	22.8	30.2	2.5	19.6	7.7	5.9	22.7

Note: Market share for total consumer units is 100.0%. Market shares by type of consumer unit do not add to total because not all types of consumer units are shown. "–" means sample is too small to make a reliable estimate.
Source: Calculations by New Strategist based on the Bureau of Labor Statistics' 2011 Consumer Expenditure Survey

Table 10.17 Personal Care, Reading, Education, and Tobacco: Average spending by race and Hispanic origin, 2011

(average annual spending of consumer units on personal care, reading, education, and tobacco products, by race and Hispanic origin of consumer unit reference person, 2011)

	total consumer units	Asian	black	Hispanic	non-Hispanic white and other
Number of consumer units (in 000s)	122,287	5,048	15,118	15,222	92,163
Average number of persons per consumer unit	2.5	2.7	2.6	3.4	2.4
Average before-tax income of consumer units	$63,685.00	$85,415.00	$45,552.00	$49,966.00	$68,907.00
Average spending of consumer units, total	49,704.88	60,136.04	36,643.75	42,085.98	53,055.68
PERSONAL CARE PRODUCTS AND SERVICES	**634.26**	**602.38**	**533.15**	**611.19**	**654.29**
Personal care products	**351.90**	**362.05**	**239.02**	**382.17**	**365.04**
Hair care products	67.88	65.95	39.81	71.32	71.66
Hair accessories	7.60	9.92	9.69	7.48	7.26
Wigs and hairpieces	3.77	0.03	15.14	0.59	2.42
Oral hygiene products	34.69	29.52	31.06	37.77	34.86
Shaving products	16.40	9.50	8.56	20.01	17.15
Cosmetics, perfume, and bath products	170.49	179.66	99.73	194.31	177.70
Deodorants, feminine hygiene, miscellaneous products	37.05	59.33	29.16	36.34	38.45
Electric personal care appliances	14.01	8.14	5.87	14.35	15.54
Personal care services	**282.36**	**240.33**	**294.13**	**229.02**	**289.25**
READING	**115.42**	**110.7**	**48.44**	**46.00**	**137.78**
Newspaper and magazine subscriptions	40.35	25.59	15.97	10.06	49.28
Newspapers and magazines, nonsubscription	12.10	11.57	7.45	7.30	13.63
Books	48.58	57.16	17.53	22.40	57.97
Digital book readers	12.83	16.41	7.49	6.24	14.85
EDUCATION	**1,050.71**	**2,267.29**	**479.18**	**623.96**	**1,212.44**
College tuition	714.56	1,721.35	279.28	401.18	836.09
Elementary and high school tuition	136.92	258.06	66.32	80.62	157.47
Vocational and technical school tuition	6.29	0.06	8.69	4.14	6.23
Other school tuition, books, and supplies	50.30	58.04	29.28	30.07	56.99
Test preparation, tutoring services	10.85	36.88	2.75	10.33	12.25
Books and supplies for college	62.55	119.24	43.04	37.47	69.92
Books and supplies for elementary and high school	16.57	30.71	17.12	17.39	16.30
Books and supplies for vocational and technical schools	0.64	0.19	0.47	0.31	0.72
Books and supplies for day care and nursery	0.44	0.26	0.47	0.62	0.40
Miscellaneous school expenses and supplies	51.59	42.48	31.76	41.84	56.07
TOBACCO PRODUCTS AND SMOKING SUPPLIES	**350.57**	**151.71**	**259.78**	**164.09**	**395.75**
Cigarettes	322.07	148.47	241.33	155.37	362.40
Other tobacco products	25.56	2.86	15.44	6.77	30.27
Smoking accessories	2.74	0.37	3.02	1.94	2.81

Note: "Asian" and "black" include Hispanics and non-Hispanics who identify themselves as being of the respective race alone. "Hispanic" includes people of any race who identify themselves as Hispanic. "Other" includes people who identify themselves as non-Hispanic and as Alaska Native, American Indian, Asian (who are also included in the "Asian" column), or Native Hawaiian or other Pacific Islander, as well as non-Hispanics reporting more than one race. Subcategories may not add to total because some are not shown.
Source: Bureau of Labor Statistics, unpublished tables from the 2011 Consumer Expenditure Survey

Table 10.18 Personal Care, Reading, Education, and Tobacco: Indexed spending by race and Hispanic origin, 2011

(indexed average annual spending of consumer units on personal care, reading, education, and tobacco products, by race and Hispanic origin of consumer unit reference person, 2011; index definition: an index of 100 is the average for all consumer units; an index of 125 means that spending by consumer units in that group is 25 percent above the average for all consumer units; an index of 75 indicates spending that is 25 percent below the average for all consumer units)

	total consumer units	Asian	black	Hispanic	non-Hispanic white and other
Average spending of consumer units, total	$49,705	$60,136	$36,644	$42,086	$53,056
Average spending of consumer units, index	100	121	74	85	107
PERSONAL CARE PRODUCTS AND SERVICES	100	95	84	96	103
Personal care products	100	103	68	109	104
Hair care products	100	97	59	105	106
Hair accessories	100	131	128	98	96
Wigs and hairpieces	100	1	402	16	64
Oral hygiene products	100	85	90	109	100
Shaving products	100	58	52	122	105
Cosmetics, perfume, and bath products	100	105	58	114	104
Deodorants, feminine hygiene, miscellaneous products	100	160	79	98	104
Electric personal care appliances	100	58	42	102	111
Personal care services	100	85	104	81	102
READING	100	96	42	40	119
Newspaper and magazine subscriptions	100	63	40	25	122
Newspapers and magazines, nonsubscription	100	96	62	60	113
Books	100	118	36	46	119
Digital book readers	100	128	58	49	116
EDUCATION	100	216	46	59	115
College tuition	100	241	39	56	117
Elementary and high school tuition	100	188	48	59	115
Vocational and technical school tuition	100	1	138	66	99
Other school tuition, books, and supplies	100	115	58	60	113
Test preparation, tutoring services	100	340	25	95	113
Books and supplies for college	100	191	69	60	112
Books and supplies for elementary and high school	100	185	103	105	98
Books and supplies for vocational and technical schools	100	30	73	48	113
Books and supplies for day care and nursery	100	59	107	141	91
Miscellaneous school expenses and supplies	100	82	62	81	109
TOBACCO PRODUCTS AND SMOKING SUPPLIES	100	43	74	47	113
Cigarettes	100	46	75	48	113
Other tobacco products	100	11	60	26	118
Smoking accessories	100	14	110	71	103

Note: "Asian" and "black" include Hispanics and non-Hispanics who identify themselves as being of the respective race alone. "Hispanic" includes people of any race who identify themselves as Hispanic. "Other" includes people who identify themselves as non-Hispanic and as Alaska Native, American Indian, Asian (who are also included in the "Asian" column), or Native Hawaiian or other Pacific Islander, as well as non-Hispanics reporting more than one race.
Source: Calculations by New Strategist based on the Bureau of Labor Statistics' 2011 Consumer Expenditure Survey

Table 10.19 Personal Care, Reading, Education, and Tobacco: Total spending by race and Hispanic origin, 2011

(total annual spending on personal care, reading, education, and tobacco products, by consumer unit race and Hispanic origin groups, 2011; consumer units and dollars in thousands)

	total consumer units	Asian	black	Hispanic	non-Hispanic white and other
Number of consumer units	122,287	5,048	15,118	15,222	92,163
Total spending of all consumer units	$6,078,260,661	$303,566,730	$553,980,213	$640,632,788	$4,889,770,636
PERSONAL CARE PRODUCTS AND SERVICES	**77,561,753**	**3,040,814**	**8,060,162**	**9,303,534**	**60,301,329**
Personal care products	**43,032,795**	**1,827,628**	**3,613,504**	**5,817,392**	**33,643,182**
Hair care products	8,300,842	332,916	601,848	1,085,633	6,604,401
Hair accessories	929,381	50,076	146,493	113,861	669,103
Wigs and hairpieces	461,022	151	228,887	8,981	223,034
Oral hygiene products	4,242,136	149,017	469,565	574,935	3,212,802
Shaving products	2,005,507	47,956	129,410	304,592	1,580,595
Cosmetics, perfume, and bath products	20,848,711	906,924	1,507,718	2,957,787	16,377,365
Deodorants, feminine hygiene, miscellaneous products	4,530,733	299,498	440,841	553,167	3,543,667
Electric personal care appliances	1,713,241	41090.7	88,743	218,436	1,432,213
Personal care services	**34,528,957**	**1,213,186**	**4,446,657**	**3,486,142**	**26,658,148**
READING	**14,114,366**	**558,915**	**732,316**	**700,212**	**12,698,218**
Newspaper and magazine subscriptions	4,934,280	129,178	241,434	153,133	4,541,793
Newspapers and magazines, nonsubscription	1,479,673	58,405	112,629	111,121	1,256,182
Books	5,940,702	288,544	265,019	340,973	5,342,689
Digital book readers	1,568,942	82,838	113,234	94,985	1,368,621
EDUCATION	**128,488,174**	**11,445,280**	**7,244,243**	**9,497,919**	**111,742,108**
College tuition	87,381,399	8,689,375	4,222,155	6,106,762	77,056,563
Elementary and high school tuition	16,743,536	1,302,687	1,002,626	1,227,198	14,512,908
Vocational and technical school tuition	769,185	303	131,375	63,019	574,175
Other school tuition, books, and supplies	6,151,036	292,986	442,655	457,726	5,252,369
Test preparation, tutoring services	1,326,814	186,170	41,575	157,243	1,128,997
Books and supplies for college	7,649,052	601,924	650,679	570,368	6,444,037
Books and supplies for elementary and high school	2,026,296	155,024	258,820	264,711	1,502,257
Books and supplies for vocational and technical schools	78,264	959	7,105	4,719	66,357
Books and supplies for day care and nursery	53,806	1,312	7,105	9,438	36,865
Miscellaneous school expenses and supplies	6,308,786	214,439	480,148	636,888	5,167,579
TOBACCO PRODUCTS AND SMOKING SUPPLIES	**42,870,154**	**765,832**	**3,927,354**	**2,497,778**	**36,473,507**
Cigarettes	39,384,974	749,477	3,648,427	2,365,042	33,399,871
Other tobacco products	3,125,656	14,437	233,422	103,053	2,789,774
Smoking accessories	335,066	1,868	45,656	29,531	258,978

Note: "Asian" and "black" include Hispanics and non-Hispanics who identify themselves as being of the respective race alone. "Hispanic" includes people of any race who identify themselves as Hispanic. "Other" includes people who identify themselves as non-Hispanic and as Alaska Native, American Indian, Asian (who are also included in the "Asian" column), or Native Hawaiian or other Pacific Islander, as well as non-Hispanics reporting more than one race. Numbers may not add to total because of rounding and missing subcategories.
Source: Calculations by New Strategist based on the Bureau of Labor Statistics' 2011 Consumer Expenditure Survey

Table 10.20 Personal Care, Reading, Education, and Tobacco: Market shares by race and Hispanic origin, 2011

(percentage of total annual spending on personal care, reading, education, and tobacco products accounted for by consumer unit race and Hispanic origin groups, 2011)

	total consumer units	Asian	black	Hispanic	non-Hispanic white and other
Share of total consumer units	100.0%	4.1%	12.4%	12.4%	75.4%
Share of total before-tax income	100.0	5.5	8.8	9.8	81.5
Share of total spending	100.0	5.0	9.1	10.5	80.4
PERSONAL CARE PRODUCTS AND SERVICES	100.0	3.9	10.4	12.0	77.7
Personal care products	100.0	4.2	8.4	13.5	78.2
Hair care products	100.0	4.0	7.3	13.1	79.6
Hair accessories	100.0	5.4	15.8	12.3	72.0
Wigs and hairpieces	100.0	0.0	49.6	1.9	48.4
Oral hygiene products	100.0	3.5	11.1	13.6	75.7
Shaving products	100.0	2.4	6.5	15.2	78.8
Cosmetics, perfume, and bath products	100.0	4.4	7.2	14.2	78.6
Deodorants, feminine hygiene, miscellaneous products	100.0	6.6	9.7	12.2	78.2
Electric personal care appliances	100.0	2.4	5.2	12.7	83.6
Personal care services	100.0	3.5	12.9	10.1	77.2
READING	100.0	4.0	5.2	5.0	90.0
Newspaper and magazine subscriptions	100.0	2.6	4.9	3.1	92.0
Newspapers and magazines, nonsubscription	100.0	3.9	7.6	7.5	84.9
Books	100.0	4.9	4.5	5.7	89.9
Digital book readers	100.0	5.3	7.2	6.1	87.2
EDUCATION	100.0	8.9	5.6	7.4	87.0
College tuition	100.0	9.9	4.8	7.0	88.2
Elementary and high school tuition	100.0	7.8	6.0	7.3	86.7
Vocational and technical school tuition	100.0	0.0	17.1	8.2	74.6
Other school tuition, books, and supplies	100.0	4.8	7.2	7.4	85.4
Test preparation, tutoring services	100.0	14.0	3.1	11.9	85.1
Books and supplies for college	100.0	7.9	8.5	7.5	84.2
Books and supplies for elementary and high school	100.0	7.7	12.8	13.1	74.1
Books and supplies for vocational and technical schools	100.0	1.2	9.1	6.0	84.8
Books and supplies for day care and nursery	100.0	2.4	13.2	17.5	68.5
Miscellaneous school expenses and supplies	100.0	3.4	7.6	10.1	81.9
TOBACCO PRODUCTS AND SMOKING SUPPLIES	100.0	1.8	9.2	5.8	85.1
Cigarettes	100.0	1.9	9.3	6.0	84.8
Other tobacco products	100.0	0.5	7.5	3.3	89.3
Smoking accessories	100.0	0.6	13.6	8.8	77.3

Note: "Asian" and "black" include Hispanics and non-Hispanics who identify themselves as being of the respective race alone. "Hispanic" includes people of any race who identify themselves as Hispanic. "Other" includes people who identify themselves as non-Hispanic and as Alaska Native, American Indian, Asian (who are also included in the "Asian" column), or Native Hawaiian or other Pacific Islander, as well as non-Hispanics reporting more than one race.
Source: Calculations by New Strategist based on the Bureau of Labor Statistics' 2011 Consumer Expenditure Survey

Table 10.21 Personal Care, Reading, Education, and Tobacco: Average spending by region, 2011

(average annual spending of consumer units on personal care, reading, education, and tobacco products, by region in which consumer unit lives, 2011)

	total consumer units	Northeast	Midwest	South	West
Number of consumer units (in 000s)	122,287	22,538	27,107	44,901	27,741
Average number of persons per consumer unit	2.5	2.4	2.4	2.5	2.6
Average before-tax income of consumer units	$63,685.00	$71,733.00	$60,897.00	$58,780.00	$67,810.00
Average spending of consumer units, total	49,704.88	54,547.45	47,191.54	45,698.60	54,745.43
PERSONAL CARE PRODUCTS AND SERVICES	634.26	626.76	581.51	606.38	738.67
Personal care products	351.90	299.75	328.10	336.12	444.71
Hair care products	67.88	52.00	59.68	69.77	86.02
Hair accessories	7.60	6.06	7.33	8.56	7.56
Wigs and hairpieces	3.77	3.59	3.29	4.63	2.98
Oral hygiene products	34.69	35.61	34.97	31.24	39.38
Shaving products	16.40	16.76	11.74	18.48	17.35
Cosmetics, perfume, and bath products	170.49	144.79	154.68	157.50	228.92
Deodorants, feminine hygiene, miscellaneous products	37.05	30.53	36.64	36.89	43.09
Electric personal care appliances	14.01	10.40	19.78	9.05	19.40
Personal care services	282.36	327.01	253.41	270.26	293.96
READING	115.42	129.84	123.22	87.98	140.42
Newspaper and magazine subscriptions	40.35	48.65	47.96	30.00	42.92
Newspapers and magazines, nonsubscription	12.10	19.26	10.30	9.31	12.54
Books	48.58	48.82	47.34	37.12	68.10
Digital book readers	12.83	13.11	10.59	11.55	16.85
EDUCATION	1,050.71	1,620.31	1,094.54	680.24	1,144.69
College tuition	714.56	1,214.40	767.64	375.79	804.93
Elementary and high school tuition	136.92	216.31	100.56	127.14	123.75
Vocational and technical school tuition	6.29	5.53	11.71	4.44	4.58
Other school tuition, books, and supplies	50.30	41.02	51.51	45.72	64.07
Test preparation, tutoring services	10.85	18.69	6.84	6.81	14.96
Books and supplies for college	62.55	62.02	89.86	43.85	66.57
Books and supplies for elementary and high school	16.57	11.49	16.36	19.93	15.45
Books and supplies for vocational and technical schools	0.64	0.13	1.71	0.35	0.49
Books and supplies for day care and nursery	0.44	0.35	0.65	0.41	0.34
Miscellaneous school expenses and supplies	51.59	50.35	47.70	55.80	49.54
TOBACCO PRODUCTS AND SMOKING SUPPLIES	350.57	356.06	363.94	391.06	267.53
Cigarettes	322.07	331.13	336.78	358.23	241.80
Other tobacco products	25.56	20.26	25.24	29.77	23.35
Smoking accessories	2.74	4.67	1.92	3.05	1.47

Note: Subcategories may not add to total because some are not shown.
Source: Bureau of Labor Statistics, unpublished tables from the 2011 Consumer Expenditure Survey

Table 10.22 Personal Care, Reading, Education, and Tobacco: Indexed spending by region, 2011

(indexed average annual spending of consumer units on personal care, reading, education, and tobacco products, by region in which consumer unit lives, 2011; index definition: an index of 100 is the average for all consumer units; an index of 125 means that spending by consumer units in that group is 25 percent above the average for all consumer units; an index of 75 indicates spending that is 25 percent below the average for all consumer units)

	total consumer units	Northeast	Midwest	South	West
Average spending of consumer units, total	$49,705	$54,547	$47,192	$45,699	$54,745
Average spending of consumer units, index	100	110	95	92	110
PERSONAL CARE PRODUCTS AND SERVICES	100	99	92	96	116
Personal care products	100	85	93	96	126
Hair care products	100	77	88	103	127
Hair accessories	100	80	96	113	99
Wigs and hairpieces	100	95	87	123	79
Oral hygiene products	100	103	101	90	114
Shaving products	100	102	72	113	106
Cosmetics, perfume, and bath products	100	85	91	92	134
Deodorants, feminine hygiene, miscellaneous products	100	82	99	100	116
Electric personal care appliances	100	74	141	65	138
Personal care services	100	116	90	96	104
READING	100	112	107	76	122
Newspaper and magazine subscriptions	100	121	119	74	106
Newspapers and magazines, nonsubscription	100	159	85	77	104
Books	100	100	97	76	140
Digital book readers	100	102	83	90	131
EDUCATION	100	154	104	65	109
College tuition	100	170	107	53	113
Elementary and high school tuition	100	158	73	93	90
Vocational and technical school tuition	100	88	186	71	73
Other school tuition, books, and supplies	100	82	102	91	127
Test preparation, tutoring services	100	172	63	63	138
Books and supplies for college	100	99	144	70	106
Books and supplies for elementary and high school	100	69	99	120	93
Books and supplies for vocational and technical schools	100	20	267	55	77
Books and supplies for day care and nursery	100	80	148	93	77
Miscellaneous school expenses and supplies	100	98	92	108	96
TOBACCO PRODUCTS AND SMOKING SUPPLIES	100	102	104	112	76
Cigarettes	100	103	105	111	75
Other tobacco products	100	79	99	116	91
Smoking accessories	100	170	70	111	54

Source: Calculations by New Strategist based on the Bureau of Labor Statistics' 2011 Consumer Expenditure Survey

Table 10.23 Personal Care, Reading, Education, and Tobacco: Total spending by region, 2011

(total annual spending on personal care, reading, education, and tobacco products, by region in which consumer units live, 2011; consumer units and dollars in thousands)

	total consumer units	Northeast	Midwest	South	West
Number of consumer units	122,287	22,538	27,107	44,901	27,741
Total spending of all consumer units	$6,078,260,661	$1,229,390,428	$1,279,221,075	$2,051,912,839	$1,518,692,974
PERSONAL CARE PRODUCTS AND SERVICES	**77,561,753**	**14,125,917**	**15,762,992**	**27,227,068**	**20,491,444**
Personal care products	**43,032,795**	**6,755,766**	**8,893,807**	**15,092,124**	**12,336,700**
Hair care products	8,300,842	1,171,976	1,617,746	3,132,743	2,386,281
Hair accessories	929,381	136,580	198,694	384,353	209,722
Wigs and hairpieces	461,022	80,911	89,182	207,892	82,668
Oral hygiene products	4,242,136	802,578	947,932	1,402,707	1,092,441
Shaving products	2,005,507	377,737	318,236	829,770	481,306
Cosmetics, perfume, and bath products	20,848,711	3,263,277	4,192,911	7,071,908	6,350,470
Deodorants, feminine hygiene, miscellaneous products	4,530,733	688,085	993,200	1,656,398	1,195,360
Electric personal care appliances	1,713,241	234,395	536,176	406,354	538,175
Personal care services	**34,528,957**	**7,370,151**	**6,869,185**	**12,134,944**	**8,154,744**
READING	**14,114,366**	**2,926,334**	**3,340,125**	**3,950,390**	**3,895,391**
Newspaper and magazine subscriptions	4,934,280	1,096,474	1,300,052	1,347,030	1,190,644
Newspapers and magazines, nonsubscription	1,479,673	434,082	279,202	418,028	347,872
Books	5,940,702	1,100,305	1,283,245	1,666,725	1,889,162
Digital book readers	1,568,942	295,473	287,063	518,607	467,436
EDUCATION	**128,488,174**	**36,518,547**	**29,669,696**	**30,543,456**	**31,754,845**
College tuition	87,381,399	27,370,147	20,808,417	16,873,347	22,329,563
Elementary and high school tuition	16,743,536	4,875,195	2,725,880	5,708,713	3,432,949
Vocational and technical school tuition	769,185	124,635	317,423	199,360	127,054
Other school tuition, books, and supplies	6,151,036	924,509	1,396,282	2,052,874	1,777,366
Test preparation, tutoring services	1,326,814	421,235	185,412	305,776	415,005
Books and supplies for college	7,649,052	1,397,807	2,435,835	1,968,909	1,846,718
Books and supplies for elementary and high school	2,026,296	258,962	443,471	894,877	428,598
Books and supplies for vocational and technical schools	78,264	2,930	46,353	15,715	13,593
Books and supplies for day care and nursery	53,806	7,888	17,620	18,409	9,432
Miscellaneous school expenses and supplies	6,308,786	1,134,788	1,293,004	2,505,476	1,374,289
TOBACCO PRODUCTS AND SMOKING SUPPLIES	**42,870,154**	**8,024,880**	**9,865,322**	**17,558,985**	**7,421,550**
Cigarettes	39,384,974	7,463,008	9,129,095	16,084,885	6,707,774
Other tobacco products	3,125,656	456,620	684,181	1,336,703	647,752
Smoking accessories	335,066	105,252	52,045	136,948	40,779

Note: Numbers may not add to total because of rounding and missing subcategories.
Source: Calculations by New Strategist based on the Bureau of Labor Statistics' 2011 Consumer Expenditure Survey

Table 10.24 Personal Care, Reading, Education, and Tobacco: Market shares by region, 2011

(percentage of total annual spending on personal care, reading, education, and tobacco products accounted for by consumer units by region of residence, 2011)

	total consumer units	Northeast	Midwest	South	West
Share of total consumer units	100.0%	18.4%	22.2%	36.7%	22.7%
Share of total before-tax income	100.0	20.8	21.2	33.9	24.2
Share of total spending	100.0	20.2	21.0	33.8	25.0
PERSONAL CARE PRODUCTS AND SERVICES	**100.0**	**18.2**	**20.3**	**35.1**	**26.4**
Personal care products	**100.0**	**15.7**	**20.7**	**35.1**	**28.7**
Hair care products	100.0	14.1	19.5	37.7	28.7
Hair accessories	100.0	14.7	21.4	41.4	22.6
Wigs and hairpieces	100.0	17.6	19.3	45.1	17.9
Oral hygiene products	100.0	18.9	22.3	33.1	25.8
Shaving products	100.0	18.8	15.9	41.4	24.0
Cosmetics, perfume, and bath products	100.0	15.7	20.1	33.9	30.5
Deodorants, feminine hygiene, miscellaneous products	100.0	15.2	21.9	36.6	26.4
Electric personal care appliances	100.0	13.7	31.3	23.7	31.4
Personal care services	**100.0**	**21.3**	**19.9**	**35.1**	**23.6**
READING	**100.0**	**20.7**	**23.7**	**28.0**	**27.6**
Newspaper and magazine subscriptions	100.0	22.2	26.3	27.3	24.1
Newspapers and magazines, nonsubscription	100.0	29.3	18.9	28.3	23.5
Books	100.0	18.5	21.6	28.1	31.8
Digital book readers	100.0	18.8	18.3	33.1	29.8
EDUCATION	**100.0**	**28.4**	**23.1**	**23.8**	**24.7**
College tuition	100.0	31.3	23.8	19.3	25.6
Elementary and high school tuition	100.0	29.1	16.3	34.1	20.5
Vocational and technical school tuition	100.0	16.2	41.3	25.9	16.5
Other school tuition, books, and supplies	100.0	15.0	22.7	33.4	28.9
Test preparation, tutoring services	100.0	31.7	14.0	23.0	31.3
Books and supplies for college	100.0	18.3	31.8	25.7	24.1
Books and supplies for elementary and high school	100.0	12.8	21.9	44.2	21.2
Books and supplies for vocational and technical schools	100.0	3.7	59.2	20.1	17.4
Books and supplies for day care and nursery	100.0	14.7	32.7	34.2	17.5
Miscellaneous school expenses and supplies	100.0	18.0	20.5	39.7	21.8
TOBACCO PRODUCTS AND SMOKING SUPPLIES	**100.0**	**18.7**	**23.0**	**41.0**	**17.3**
Cigarettes	100.0	18.9	23.2	40.8	17.0
Other tobacco products	100.0	14.6	21.9	42.8	20.7
Smoking accessories	100.0	31.4	15.5	40.9	12.2

Note: Numbers may not add to total because of rounding.
Source: Calculations by New Strategist based on the Bureau of Labor Statistics' 2011 Consumer Expenditure Survey

Table 10.25 Personal Care, Reading, Education, and Tobacco: Average spending by education, 2011

(average annual spending of consumer units on personal care, reading, education, and tobacco products, by education of consumer unit reference person, 2011)

	total consumer units	less than high school graduate	high school graduate	some college	associate's degree	bachelor's degree or more		
						total	bachelor's degree	graduate degree
Number of consumer units (in 000s)	122,287	16,146	30,810	25,361	12,912	37,058	23,578	13,480
Average number of persons per consumer unit	2.5	2.8	2.5	2.3	2.6	2.5	2.5	2.4
Average before-tax income of consumer units	$63,685.00	$32,564.00	$46,370.00	$52,965.00	$63,664.00	$98,983.00	$90,962.00	$113,013.00
Average spending of consumer units, total	49,704.88	29,950.97	39,704.28	45,355.33	50,819.44	68,902.95	65,051.01	75,731.40
PERSONAL CARE PRODUCTS AND SERVICES	**634.26**	**366.76**	**478.94**	**572.88**	**661.69**	**900.50**	**851.11**	**992.18**
Personal care products	**351.90**	**225.83**	**270.77**	**330.87**	**376.97**	**468.04**	**443.85**	**515.65**
Hair care products	67.88	53.48	53.95	67.05	59.36	87.45	79.54	102.94
Hair accessories	7.60	2.65	6.16	6.58	6.23	11.68	9.25	16.42
Wigs and hairpieces	3.77	3.01	3.34	4.04	7.03	3.14	4.19	1.29
Oral hygiene products	34.69	26.92	31.24	31.64	35.26	42.08	41.38	43.46
Shaving products	16.40	10.33	13.30	15.24	13.30	22.84	22.03	24.45
Cosmetics, perfume, and bath products	170.49	88.91	124.00	150.75	209.73	237.53	225.32	261.42
Deodorants, feminine hygiene, miscellaneous products	37.05	34.35	33.99	32.38	37.42	43.36	38.70	52.50
Electric personal care appliances	14.01	6.18	4.79	23.18	8.64	19.97	23.44	13.16
Personal care services	**282.36**	**140.93**	**208.17**	**242.01**	**284.72**	**432.46**	**407.26**	**476.53**
READING	**115.42**	**40.43**	**69.56**	**94.59**	**115.87**	**200.36**	**171.94**	**250.71**
Newspaper and magazine subscriptions	40.35	17.34	31.21	31.87	36.43	65.13	54.80	83.20
Newspapers and magazines, nonsubscription	12.10	7.00	10.92	10.45	14.12	15.71	14.92	17.10
Books	48.58	9.61	20.13	40.96	46.15	95.24	82.56	117.44
Digital book readers	12.83	1.56	7.28	11.31	19.18	21.18	19.66	23.85
EDUCATION	**1,050.71**	**252.46**	**380.11**	**1,109.38**	**966.26**	**1,942.78**	**1,900.49**	**2,018.83**
College tuition	714.56	161.21	251.62	769.23	608.59	1,340.05	1,348.66	1,324.99
Elementary and high school tuition	136.92	18.17	29.59	110.31	137.00	296.07	279.25	325.49
Vocational and technical school tuition	6.29	6.27	5.18	10.51	3.73	5.21	3.34	8.49
Other school tuition, books, and supplies	50.30	7.60	22.19	37.16	82.79	89.95	73.00	119.58
Test preparation, tutoring services	10.85	2.88	5.88	4.36	4.65	25.07	23.25	28.26
Books and supplies for college	62.55	15.58	23.38	112.68	60.11	82.12	78.05	89.24
Books and supplies for elementary and high school	16.57	12.72	11.97	14.63	13.01	24.63	24.56	24.76
Books and supplies for vocational and technical schools	0.64	0.18	0.23	1.93	0.05	0.52	0.66	0.26
Books and supplies for day care and nursery	0.44	0.26	0.15	0.35	0.36	0.85	1.27	0.10
Miscellaneous school expenses and supplies	51.59	27.59	29.93	48.23	55.96	78.32	68.44	97.68
TOBACCO PRODUCTS AND SMOKING SUPPLIES	**350.57**	**399.62**	**521.06**	**384.10**	**386.38**	**151.98**	**183.05**	**97.49**
Cigarettes	322.07	372.31	484.62	349.57	352.20	135.71	164.22	85.84
Other tobacco products	25.56	25.86	32.50	31.54	31.62	13.45	15.38	10.07
Smoking accessories	2.74	1.44	3.95	2.99	2.56	2.18	2.49	1.58

Note: Subcategories may not add to total because some are not shown.
Source: Bureau of Labor Statistics, unpublished tables from the 2011 Consumer Expenditure Survey

Table 10.26 Personal Care, Reading, Education, and Tobacco: Indexed spending by education, 2011

(indexed average annual spending of consumer units on personal care, reading, education, and tobacco products, by education of consumer unit reference person, 2011; index definition: an index of 100 is the average for all consumer units; an index of 125 means that spending by consumer units in that group is 25 percent above the average for all consumer units; an index of 75 indicates spending that is 25 percent below the average for all consumer units)

	total consumer units	less than high school graduate	high school graduate	some college	associate's degree	bachelor's degree or more		
						total	bachelor's degree	graduate degree
Average spending of consumer units, total	$49,705	$29,951	$39,704	$45,355	$50,819	$68,903	$65,051	$75,731
Average spending of consumer units, index	100	60	80	91	102	139	131	152
PERSONAL CARE PRODUCTS AND SERVICES	100	58	76	90	104	142	134	156
Personal care products	100	64	77	94	107	133	126	147
Hair care products	100	79	79	99	87	129	117	152
Hair accessories	100	35	81	87	82	154	122	216
Wigs and hairpieces	100	80	89	107	186	83	111	34
Oral hygiene products	100	78	90	91	102	121	119	125
Shaving products	100	63	81	93	81	139	134	149
Cosmetics, perfume, and bath products	100	52	73	88	123	139	132	153
Deodorants, feminine hygiene, miscellaneous products	100	93	92	87	101	117	104	142
Electric personal care appliances	100	44	34	165	62	143	167	94
Personal care services	100	50	74	86	101	153	144	169
READING	100	35	60	82	100	174	149	217
Newspaper and magazine subscriptions	100	43	77	79	90	161	136	206
Newspapers and magazines, nonsubscription	100	58	90	86	117	130	123	141
Books	100	20	41	84	95	196	170	242
Digital book readers	100	12	57	88	149	165	153	186
EDUCATION	100	24	36	106	92	185	181	192
College tuition	100	23	35	108	85	188	189	185
Elementary and high school tuition	100	13	22	81	100	216	204	238
Vocational and technical school tuition	100	100	82	167	59	83	53	135
Other school tuition, books, and supplies	100	15	44	74	165	179	145	238
Test preparation, tutoring services	100	27	54	40	43	231	214	260
Books and supplies for college	100	25	37	180	96	131	125	143
Books and supplies for elementary and high school	100	77	72	88	79	149	148	149
Books and supplies for vocational and technical schools	100	28	36	302	8	81	103	41
Books and supplies for day care and nursery	100	59	34	80	82	193	289	23
Miscellaneous school expenses and supplies	100	53	58	93	108	152	133	189
TOBACCO PRODUCTS AND SMOKING SUPPLIES	100	114	149	110	110	43	52	28
Cigarettes	100	116	150	109	109	42	51	27
Other tobacco products	100	101	127	123	124	53	60	39
Smoking accessories	100	53	144	109	93	80	91	58

Source: Calculations by New Strategist based on the Bureau of Labor Statistics' 2011 Consumer Expenditure Survey

Table 10.27 Personal Care, Reading, Education, and Tobacco: Total spending by education, 2011

(total annual spending on personal care, reading, education, and tobacco products, by consumer unit educational attainment group, 2011; consumer units and dollars in thousands)

	total consumer units	less than high school graduate	high school graduate	some college	associate's degree	bachelor's degree or more total	bachelor's degree	graduate degree
Number of consumer units	122,287	16,146	30,810	25,361	12,912	37,058	23,578	13,480
Total spending of all consumer units	$6,078,260,661	$483,588,362	$1,223,288,867	$1,150,256,524	$656,180,609	$2,553,405,521	$1,533,772,714	$1,020,859,272
PERSONAL CARE PRODUCTS AND SERVICES	**77,561,753**	**5,921,707**	**14,756,141**	**14,528,810**	**8,543,741**	**33,370,729**	**20,067,472**	**13,374,586**
Personal care products	**43,032,795**	**3,646,251**	**8,342,424**	**8,391,194**	**4,867,437**	**17,344,626**	**10,465,095**	**6,950,962**
Hair care products	8,300,842	863,488	1,662,200	1,700,455	766,456	3,240,722	1,875,394	1,387,631
Hair accessories	929,381	42,787	189,790	166,875	80,442	432,837	218,097	221,342
Wigs and hairpieces	461,022	48,599	102,905	102,458	90,771	116,362	98,792	17,389
Oral hygiene products	4,242,136	434,650	962,504	802,422	455,277	1,559,401	975,658	585,841
Shaving products	2,005,507	166,788	409,773	386,502	171,730	846,405	519,423	329,586
Cosmetics, perfume, and bath products	20,848,711	1,435,541	3,820,440	3,823,171	2,708,034	8,802,387	5,312,595	3,523,942
Deodorants, feminine hygiene, miscellaneous products	4,530,733	554,615	1,047,232	821,189	483,167	1,606,835	912,469	707,700
Electric personal care appliances	1,713,241	99,782	147,580	587,868	111,560	740,048	552,668	177,397
Personal care services	**34,528,957**	**2,275,456**	**6,413,718**	**6,137,616**	**3,676,305**	**16,026,103**	**9,602,376**	**6,423,624**
READING	**14,114,366**	**652,783**	**2,143,144**	**2,398,897**	**1,496,113**	**7,424,941**	**4,054,001**	**3,379,571**
Newspaper and magazine subscriptions	4,934,280	279,972	961,580	808,255	470,384	2,413,588	1,292,074	1,121,536
Newspapers and magazines, nonsubscription	1,479,673	113,022	336,445	265,022	182,317	582,181	351,784	230,508
Books	5,940,702	155,163	620,205	1,038,787	595,889	3,529,404	1,946,600	1,583,091
Digital book readers	1,568,942	25,188	224,297	286,833	247,652	784,888	463,543	321,498
EDUCATION	**128,488,174**	**4,076,219**	**11,711,189**	**28,134,986**	**12,476,349**	**71,995,541**	**44,809,753**	**27,213,828**
College tuition	87,381,399	2,602,897	7,752,412	19,508,442	7,858,114	49,659,573	31,798,705	17,860,865
Elementary and high school tuition	16,743,536	293,373	911,668	2,797,572	1,768,944	10,971,762	6,584,157	4,387,605
Vocational and technical school tuition	769,185	101,235	159,596	266,544	48,162	193,072	78,751	114,445
Other school tuition, books, and supplies	6,151,036	122,710	683,674	942,415	1,068,984	3,333,367	1,721,194	1,611,938
Test preparation, tutoring services	1,326,814	46,500	181,163	110,574	60,041	929,044	548,189	380,945
Books and supplies for college	7,649,052	251,555	720,338	2,857,677	776,140	3,043,203	1,840,263	1,202,955
Books and supplies for elementary and high school	2,026,296	205,377	368,796	371,031	167,985	912,739	579,076	333,765
Books and supplies for vocational and technical schools	78,264	2,906	7,086	48,947	646	19,270	15,561	3,505
Books and supplies for day care and nursery	53,806	4,198	4,622	8,876	4,648	31,499	29,944	1,348
Miscellaneous school expenses and supplies	6,308,786	445,468	922,143	1,223,161	722,556	2,902,383	1,613,678	1,316,726
TOBACCO PRODUCTS AND SMOKING SUPPLIES	**42,870,154**	**6,452,265**	**16,053,859**	**9,741,160**	**4,988,939**	**5,632,075**	**4,315,953**	**1,314,165**
Cigarettes	39,384,974	6,011,317	14,931,142	8,865,445	4,547,606	5,029,141	3,871,979	1,157,123
Other tobacco products	3,125,656	417,536	1,001,325	799,886	408,277	498,430	362,630	135,744
Smoking accessories	335,066	23,250	121,700	75,829	33,055	80,786	58,709	21,298

Note: Numbers may not add to total because of rounding and missing subcategories.
Source: Calculations by New Strategist based on the Bureau of Labor Statistics' 2011 Consumer Expenditure Survey

Table 10.28 Personal Care, Reading, Education, and Tobacco: Market shares by education, 2011

(percentage of total annual spending on personal care, reading, education, and tobacco products accounted for by consumer unit educational attainment groups, 2011)

	total consumer units	less than high school graduate	high school graduate	some college	associate's degree	bachelor's degree or more total	bachelor's degree	graduate degree
Share of total consumer units	100.0%	13.2%	25.2%	20.7%	10.6%	30.3%	19.3%	11.0%
Share of total before-tax income	100.0	6.8	18.3	17.2	10.6	47.1	27.5	19.6
Share of total spending	100.0	8.0	20.1	18.9	10.8	42.0	25.2	16.8
PERSONAL CARE PRODUCTS AND SERVICES	**100.0**	**7.6**	**19.0**	**18.7**	**11.0**	**43.0**	**25.9**	**17.2**
Personal care products	**100.0**	**8.5**	**19.4**	**19.5**	**11.3**	**40.3**	**24.3**	**16.2**
Hair care products	100.0	10.4	20.0	20.5	9.2	39.0	22.6	16.7
Hair accessories	100.0	4.6	20.4	18.0	8.7	46.6	23.5	23.8
Wigs and hairpieces	100.0	10.5	22.3	22.2	19.7	25.2	21.4	3.8
Oral hygiene products	100.0	10.2	22.7	18.9	10.7	36.8	23.0	13.8
Shaving products	100.0	8.3	20.4	19.3	8.6	42.2	25.9	16.4
Cosmetics, perfume, and bath products	100.0	6.9	18.3	18.3	13.0	42.2	25.5	16.9
Deodorants, feminine hygiene, miscellaneous products	100.0	12.2	23.1	18.1	10.7	35.5	20.1	15.6
Electric personal care appliances	100.0	5.8	8.6	34.3	6.5	43.2	32.3	10.4
Personal care services	**100.0**	**6.6**	**18.6**	**17.8**	**10.6**	**46.4**	**27.8**	**18.6**
READING	**100.0**	**4.6**	**15.2**	**17.0**	**10.6**	**52.6**	**28.7**	**23.9**
Newspaper and magazine subscriptions	100.0	5.7	19.5	16.4	9.5	48.9	26.2	22.7
Newspapers and magazines, nonsubscription	100.0	7.6	22.7	17.9	12.3	39.3	23.8	15.6
Books	100.0	2.6	10.4	17.5	10.0	59.4	32.8	26.6
Digital book readers	100.0	1.6	14.3	18.3	15.8	50.0	29.5	20.5
EDUCATION	**100.0**	**3.2**	**9.1**	**21.9**	**9.7**	**56.0**	**34.9**	**21.2**
College tuition	100.0	3.0	8.9	22.3	9.0	56.8	36.4	20.4
Elementary and high school tuition	100.0	1.8	5.4	16.7	10.6	65.5	39.3	26.2
Vocational and technical school tuition	100.0	13.2	20.7	34.7	6.3	25.1	10.2	14.9
Other school tuition, books, and supplies	100.0	2.0	11.1	15.3	17.4	54.2	28.0	26.2
Test preparation, tutoring services	100.0	3.5	13.7	8.3	4.5	70.0	41.3	28.7
Books and supplies for college	100.0	3.3	9.4	37.4	10.1	39.8	24.1	15.7
Books and supplies for elementary and high school	100.0	10.1	18.2	18.3	8.3	45.0	28.6	16.5
Books and supplies for vocational and technical schools	100.0	3.7	9.1	62.5	0.8	24.6	19.9	4.5
Books and supplies for day care and nursery	100.0	7.8	8.6	16.5	8.6	58.5	55.7	2.5
Miscellaneous school expenses and supplies	100.0	7.1	14.6	19.4	11.5	46.0	25.6	20.9
TOBACCO PRODUCTS AND SMOKING SUPPLIES	**100.0**	**15.1**	**37.4**	**22.7**	**11.6**	**13.1**	**10.1**	**3.1**
Cigarettes	100.0	15.3	37.9	22.5	11.5	12.8	9.8	2.9
Other tobacco products	100.0	13.4	32.0	25.6	13.1	15.9	11.6	4.3
Smoking accessories	100.0	6.9	36.3	22.6	9.9	24.1	17.5	6.4

Note: Numbers may not add to total because of rounding.
Source: Calculations by New Strategist based on the Bureau of Labor Statistics' 2011 Consumer Expenditure Survey

CHAPTER 11

Spending on Transportation, 2011

Transportation is the second-largest household expenditure category after housing. The average household devoted $8,293 to transportation in 2011, or 16.6 percent of its budget. This is down considerably from 19.5 percent of the budget in 2000. Spending trends in the transportation category have been mixed during the past decade. While average household spending on vehicle purchases declined by a stunning 40 percent between 2000 and 2011, gasoline spending climbed 57 percent. Spending on leased and rented vehicles fell 40 percent during the time span, while spending on public transportation declined 7 percent.

Householders aged 35 to 44 spend the most on transportation—$9,700 in 2011, or 17 percent more than the average household. These householders also spend the most on new cars—22 percent above average. Spending on public transportation peaks in the 45-to-54 age group at 21 percent above average, and the same households spend the most on ship fares (61 percent above average).

Households with incomes of $100,000 or more spent 87 percent more than average on transportation in 2011. They spend over two-and-one-half times the average on new cars and trucks, and their spending on airline fares is nearly triple the average. They also spend three times the average on auto rentals while traveling.

Married couples with children aged 18 or older at home have the highest transportation expenses because they have the most vehicles. In 2011 this household type spent 40 percent more than average on vehicle insurance and 60 percent more than average on gasoline. Married couples without children at home (most of them empty-nesters) spend 93 percent more than average on intercity train fares, 48 percent more than average on airline fares, and 46 percent more than average on ship fares.

Blacks and Hispanics spend less than the average household on transportation, but on some categories their spending is above average. Hispanics spend 70 percent more than average on towing charges and 22 percent more than average on truck lease payments, while blacks spend two-thirds more than average on auto rentals. Asians, the most-affluent racial or ethnic group, spend 69 percent more than average on new cars, three times the average on airline fares, and four times the average on auto rentals. Especially Asians, but also Hispanics and blacks, spend far more than the average household on mass transit.

Households in the Northeast spent the most on transportation in 2011, $8,435, but regional differences in total spending on transportation are small enough to be insignificant. By category, striking differences emerge. Northeastern households spend three times the average on mass transit and two-and-one-half times the average on taxi fares and limousine service in their home city. Southern households spend the most on gasoline, $2,605 on average, whereas Midwesterners spend the most on gasoline on trips. Households in the West spend the most on airline fares, 51 percent more than average.

Because they dominate affluent households, college graduates spend 29 percent more than average on transportation—$10,662 on average in 2011. College graduates spend twice the average on public transportation. Representing 30 percent of all households, they control 68 percent of household spending on auto rentals on trips, 66 percent of spending on ship fares, and 64 percent of spending on airline fares.

Table 11.1 Transportation: Average spending by age, 2011

(average annual spending of consumer units on transportation, by age of consumer unit reference person, 2011)

	total consumer units	under 25	25 to 34	35 to 44	45 to 54	55 to 64	65 to 74	75+
Number of consumer units (in 000s)	122,287	7,743	20,463	21,699	24,821	21,688	14,079	11,794
Average number of persons per consumer unit	2.5	2.1	2.9	3.3	2.8	2.1	1.9	1.6
Average before-tax income of consumer units	$63,685.00	$27,514.00	$58,179.00	$77,376.00	$78,519.00	$75,517.00	$52,521.00	$32,144.00
Average spending of consumer units, total	49,704.88	29,911.52	48,097.39	57,271.07	58,050.42	53,615.86	44,645.56	32,688.34
Transportation, average spending	**8,292.79**	**5,473.59**	**8,860.04**	**9,699.72**	**9,504.58**	**8,991.06**	**6,962.22**	**4,309.43**
VEHICLE PURCHASES	**2,668.56**	**2,068.48**	**3,202.59**	**3,433.87**	**2,624.12**	**2,952.82**	**1,857.52**	**1,266.96**
Cars and trucks, new	**1,265.45**	**609.93**	**1,243.12**	**1,628.72**	**1,118.55**	**1,671.47**	**1,190.27**	**718.44**
New cars	583.32	312.21	485.24	711.76	644.30	589.70	607.34	526.44
New trucks	682.12	297.72	757.88	916.95	474.24	1,081.77	582.93	192.01
Cars and trucks, used	**1,338.96**	**1,430.75**	**1,855.41**	**1,714.86**	**1,450.82**	**1,211.85**	**621.95**	**545.31**
Used cars	683.11	825.73	750.03	774.72	792.05	684.57	416.06	391.64
Used trucks	655.85	605.02	1,105.38	940.14	658.76	527.28	205.89	153.67
Other vehicles	**64.16**	**27.80**	**104.06**	**90.29**	**54.76**	**69.50**	**45.30**	**3.20**
Used motorcycles	33.47	27.80	76.96	31.80	47.61	18.12	–	3.20
GASOLINE AND MOTOR OIL	**2,654.56**	**1,840.17**	**2,726.08**	**3,188.47**	**3,269.89**	**2,713.13**	**2,218.20**	**1,201.05**
Gasoline	2,450.87	1,727.40	2,538.27	2,960.14	3,024.34	2,497.49	1,967.90	1,121.16
Diesel fuel	51.75	33.63	47.88	70.38	75.54	43.11	40.09	15.82
Gasoline on trips	139.24	69.87	127.23	143.55	153.76	158.60	199.82	59.25
Motor oil	11.29	8.56	11.42	12.95	14.70	12.33	8.37	4.22
Motor oil on trips	1.41	0.71	1.29	1.45	1.55	1.60	2.02	0.60
OTHER VEHICLE EXPENSES	**2,453.57**	**1,264.64**	**2,401.88**	**2,564.55**	**2,984.66**	**2,745.85**	**2,343.37**	**1,581.48**
Vehicle finance charges	**232.60**	**128.00**	**301.93**	**328.26**	**269.48**	**224.27**	**143.70**	**48.83**
Automobile finance charges	96.18	64.90	124.67	121.33	115.31	91.10	62.84	29.87
Truck finance charges	115.73	61.32	160.76	172.13	135.38	102.40	62.08	16.73
Motorcycle and plane finance charges	4.27	1.44	4.78	7.15	8.40	2.28	0.04	–
Other vehicle finance charges	16.42	0.33	11.72	27.65	10.39	28.49	18.74	2.23
Maintenance and repairs	**804.93**	**455.78**	**717.67**	**856.09**	**976.51**	**949.64**	**820.47**	**448.50**
Coolant, additives, brake and transmission fluids	4.45	4.04	4.81	5.23	5.17	4.37	4.54	1.16
Tires—purchased, replaced, installed	144.02	77.82	150.38	162.66	164.59	165.20	136.49	68.95
Parts, equipment, and accessories	46.06	27.54	56.10	50.08	48.61	62.45	30.57	16.36
Vehicle audio equipment	2.28	3.58	4.84	1.11	3.27	1.24	0.63	0.94
Vehicle products and cleaning services	11.00	5.02	5.06	10.34	21.57	9.56	14.07	3.61
Vehicle video equipment	1.16	0.17	1.12	1.13	2.28	0.83	1.32	–
Miscellaneous auto repair, servicing	91.82	61.73	63.09	78.30	112.78	102.40	130.79	78.75
Body work and painting	23.31	9.19	20.44	18.60	25.42	35.52	21.95	20.93
Clutch and transmission repair	32.80	9.75	23.83	39.09	52.07	38.15	30.98	3.76
Drive shaft and rear-end repair	8.08	5.65	8.25	10.54	7.93	10.14	7.54	2.01
Brake work	59.49	30.36	56.16	57.58	75.61	76.44	56.49	26.35
Repair to steering or front-end	21.09	12.85	17.23	29.52	21.85	24.13	20.88	10.77
Repair to engine cooling system	21.72	9.77	19.45	19.50	29.53	21.66	24.83	17.57
Motor tune-up	50.56	19.49	41.04	51.48	65.61	65.49	47.13	30.76
Lube, oil change, and oil filters	77.42	44.04	80.01	85.76	87.33	84.33	78.02	45.19
Front-end alignment, wheel balance, rotation	19.10	15.31	13.53	19.39	23.46	26.57	18.21	8.92
Shock absorber replacement	4.99	5.25	5.87	3.69	5.29	6.13	5.70	2.08
Tire repair and other repair work	50.44	31.96	35.66	64.41	61.02	55.50	52.42	28.51
Vehicle air conditioning repair	14.61	3.04	14.00	17.73	14.82	16.53	18.75	8.55
Exhaust system repair	12.82	15.22	9.17	13.12	13.76	18.71	12.44	4.67
Electrical system repair	29.91	23.25	25.07	24.71	40.30	36.95	29.89	17.42
Motor repair, replacement	63.11	40.73	52.59	81.84	70.00	71.98	59.38	35.28
Auto repair service policy	14.69	0.01	9.95	10.28	24.25	15.40	17.47	15.98

	total consumer units	under 25	25 to 34	35 to 44	45 to 54	55 to 64	65 to 74	75+
Vehicle insurance	$983.31	$504.82	$957.31	$920.36	$1,200.85	$1,088.80	$950.33	$828.55
Vehicle rental, leases, licenses, other charges	432.73	176.04	424.96	459.84	537.82	483.15	428.88	255.60
Leased and rented vehicles	199.69	50.35	205.95	209.97	251.67	217.14	198.64	127.72
Rented vehicles	32.40	6.41	30.78	31.38	41.47	40.33	39.52	11.99
Auto rental	7.01	1.92	7.92	6.15	9.86	6.99	6.45	5.04
Auto rental on trips	19.17	3.26	14.07	20.36	23.78	28.23	21.83	6.71
Truck rental	1.87	0.74	2.38	3.05	2.30	1.40	1.42	0.09
Truck rental on trips	4.16	0.48	5.72	1.75	5.52	3.38	9.82	0.14
Leased vehicles	167.29	43.95	175.17	178.59	210.20	176.81	159.12	115.73
Car lease payments	95.87	28.28	91.04	96.60	117.48	99.15	123.31	63.00
Truck lease payments	56.46	15.10	58.23	71.60	78.00	67.10	31.07	18.16
Vehicle registration, state	103.38	50.02	96.82	111.72	120.44	123.15	108.69	55.86
Vehicle registration, local	8.95	2.64	8.89	9.49	10.94	11.59	7.25	5.19
Driver's license	9.05	6.94	11.00	8.28	10.12	9.94	7.59	6.32
Vehicle inspection	11.75	6.36	11.10	12.35	15.66	11.16	12.79	6.89
Parking fees	38.16	36.26	43.10	41.79	48.74	36.54	29.43	15.30
Parking fees in home city, excluding residence	32.02	34.11	37.53	34.25	40.87	29.57	23.25	13.37
Parking fees on trips	6.14	2.15	5.57	7.55	7.87	6.97	6.18	1.93
Tolls	30.34	13.08	28.89	40.77	43.12	31.43	21.22	7.01
Tolls on trips	4.34	2.50	3.96	4.31	5.55	4.93	5.04	1.84
Towing charges	4.13	4.56	5.05	5.42	3.80	4.22	2.70	2.08
Global positioning services	1.87	0.35	0.85	1.40	2.79	3.10	2.09	1.05
Automobile service clubs	21.07	2.96	9.36	14.33	24.99	29.94	33.42	26.33
PUBLIC TRANSPORTATION	516.10	300.31	529.49	512.82	625.91	579.26	543.13	259.94
Airline fares	341.68	145.22	343.01	352.73	396.98	387.61	401.97	175.20
Intercity bus fares	10.67	9.83	10.21	7.55	11.17	10.63	15.71	10.77
Intracity mass transit fares	75.09	103.29	97.45	72.67	97.53	79.51	25.21	26.41
Local transportation on trips	19.63	12.29	16.84	18.90	20.91	22.40	27.90	12.98
Taxi fares and limousine service	14.47	18.62	26.38	10.04	17.40	10.37	2.39	13.94
Intercity train fares	15.91	6.55	14.34	14.99	15.75	18.77	26.94	8.39
Ship fares	35.74	3.02	21.05	30.77	57.67	49.23	42.99	12.25
School bus	2.90	1.50	0.20	5.16	8.49	0.74	–	–

Note: Subcategories may not add to total because some are not shown. "–" means sample is too small to make a reliable estimate.
Source: Bureau of Labor Statistics, unpublished tables from the 2011 Consumer Expenditure Survey

Table 11.2 Transportation: Indexed spending by age, 2011

(indexed average annual spending of consumer units on transportation, by age of consumer unit reference person, 2011; index definition: an index of 100 is the average for all consumer units; an index of 125 means that spending by consumer units in that group is 25 percent above the average for all consumer units; an index of 75 indicates spending that is 25 percent below the average for all consumer units)

	total consumer units	under 25	25 to 34	35 to 44	45 to 54	55 to 64	65 to 74	75+
Average spending of consumer units, total	$49,705	$29,912	$48,097	$57,271	$58,050	$53,616	$44,646	$32,688
Average spending of consumer units, index	100	60	97	115	117	108	90	66
Transportation, spending index	**100**	**66**	**107**	**117**	**115**	**108**	**84**	**52**
VEHICLE PURCHASES	100	78	120	129	98	111	70	47
Cars and trucks, new	100	48	98	129	88	132	94	57
New cars	100	54	83	122	110	101	104	90
New trucks	100	44	111	134	70	159	85	28
Cars and trucks, used	100	107	139	128	108	91	46	41
Used cars	100	121	110	113	116	100	61	57
Used trucks	100	92	169	143	100	80	31	23
Other vehicles	100	43	162	141	85	108	71	5
Used motorcycles	100	83	230	95	142	54	–	10
GASOLINE AND MOTOR OIL	100	69	103	120	123	102	84	45
Gasoline	100	70	104	121	123	102	80	46
Diesel fuel	100	65	93	136	146	83	77	31
Gasoline on trips	100	50	91	103	110	114	144	43
Motor oil	100	76	101	115	130	109	74	37
Motor oil on trips	100	50	91	103	110	113	143	43
OTHER VEHICLE EXPENSES	100	52	98	105	122	112	96	64
Vehicle finance charges	100	55	130	141	116	96	62	21
Automobile finance charges	100	67	130	126	120	95	65	31
Truck finance charges	100	53	139	149	117	88	54	14
Motorcycle and plane finance charges	100	34	112	167	197	53	1	–
Other vehicle finance charges	100	2	71	168	63	174	114	14
Maintenance and repairs	100	57	89	106	121	118	102	56
Coolant, additives, brake and transmission fluids	100	91	108	118	116	98	102	26
Tires—purchased, replaced, installed	100	54	104	113	114	115	95	48
Parts, equipment, and accessories	100	60	122	109	106	136	66	36
Vehicle audio equipment	100	157	212	49	143	54	28	41
Vehicle products and cleaning services	100	46	46	94	196	87	128	33
Vehicle video equipment	100	15	97	97	197	72	114	–
Miscellaneous auto repair, servicing	100	67	69	85	123	112	142	86
Body work and painting	100	39	88	80	109	152	94	90
Clutch and transmission repair	100	30	73	119	159	116	94	11
Drive shaft and rear-end repair	100	70	102	130	98	125	93	25
Brake work	100	51	94	97	127	128	95	44
Repair to steering or front-end	100	61	82	140	104	114	99	51
Repair to engine cooling system	100	45	90	90	136	100	114	81
Motor tune-up	100	39	81	102	130	130	93	61
Lube, oil change, and oil filters	100	57	103	111	113	109	101	58
Front-end alignment, wheel balance, rotation	100	80	71	102	123	139	95	47
Shock absorber replacement	100	105	118	74	106	123	114	42
Tire repair and other repair work	100	63	71	128	121	110	104	57
Vehicle air conditioning repair	100	21	96	121	101	113	128	59
Exhaust system repair	100	119	72	102	107	146	97	36
Electrical system repair	100	78	84	83	135	124	100	58
Motor repair, replacement	100	65	83	130	111	114	94	56
Auto repair service policy	100	0	68	70	165	105	119	109

	total consumer units	under 25	25 to 34	35 to 44	45 to 54	55 to 64	65 to 74	75+
Vehicle insurance	**100**	**51**	**97**	**94**	**122**	**111**	**97**	**84**
Vehicle rental, leases, licenses, other charges	**100**	**41**	**98**	**106**	**124**	**112**	**99**	**59**
Leased and rented vehicles	100	25	103	105	126	109	99	64
Rented vehicles	100	20	95	97	128	124	122	37
Auto rental	100	27	113	88	141	100	92	72
Auto rental on trips	100	17	73	106	124	147	114	35
Truck rental	100	40	127	163	123	75	76	5
Truck rental on trips	100	12	138	42	133	81	236	3
Leased vehicles	100	26	105	107	126	106	95	69
Car lease payments	100	29	95	101	123	103	129	66
Truck lease payments	100	27	103	127	138	119	55	32
Vehicle registration, state	100	48	94	108	117	119	105	54
Vehicle registration, local	100	29	99	106	122	129	81	58
Driver's license	100	77	122	91	112	110	84	70
Vehicle inspection	100	54	94	105	133	95	109	59
Parking fees	100	95	113	110	128	96	77	40
Parking fees in home city, excluding residence	100	107	117	107	128	92	73	42
Parking fees on trips	100	35	91	123	128	114	101	31
Tolls	100	43	95	134	142	104	70	23
Tolls on trips	100	58	91	99	128	114	116	42
Towing charges	100	110	122	131	92	102	65	50
Global positioning services	100	19	45	75	149	166	112	56
Automobile service clubs	100	14	44	68	119	142	159	125
PUBLIC TRANSPORTATION	**100**	**58**	**103**	**99**	**121**	**112**	**105**	**50**
Airline fares	100	43	100	103	116	113	118	51
Intercity bus fares	100	92	96	71	105	100	147	101
Intracity mass transit fares	100	138	130	97	130	106	34	35
Local transportation on trips	100	63	86	96	107	114	142	66
Taxi fares and limousine service	100	129	182	69	120	72	17	96
Intercity train fares	100	41	90	94	99	118	169	53
Ship fares	100	8	59	86	161	138	120	34
School bus	100	52	7	178	293	26	–	–

Note: "–" means sample is too small to make a reliable estimate.
Source: Calculations by New Strategist based on the Bureau of Labor Statistics' 2011 Consumer Expenditure Survey

Table 11.3 Transportation: Total spending by age, 2011

(total annual spending on transportation, by consumer unit age groups, 2011; consumer units and dollars in thousands)

	total consumer units	under 25	25 to 34	35 to 44	45 to 54	55 to 64	65 to 74	75+
Number of consumer units	122,287	7,743	20,463	21,699	24,821	21,688	14,079	11,794
Total spending of all consumer units	$6,078,260,661	$231,604,899	$984,216,892	$1,242,724,948	$1,440,869,475	$1,162,820,772	$628,564,839	$385,526,282
Transportation, total spending	1,014,100,411	42,382,007	181,302,999	210,474,224	235,913,180	194,998,109	98,021,095	50,825,417
VEHICLE PURCHASES	326,330,197	16,016,241	65,534,599	74,511,545	65,133,283	64,040,760	26,152,024	14,942,526
Cars and trucks, new	154,748,084	4,722,688	25,437,965	35,341,595	27,763,530	36,250,841	16,757,811	8,473,281
New cars	71,332,453	2,417,442	9,929,466	15,444,480	15,992,170	12,789,414	8,550,740	6,208,833
New trucks	83,414,408	2,305,246	15,508,498	19,896,898	11,771,111	23,461,428	8,207,071	2,264,566
Cars and trucks, used	163,737,402	11,078,297	37,967,255	37,210,747	36,010,803	26,282,603	8,756,434	6,431,386
Used cars	83,535,473	6,393,627	15,347,864	16,810,649	19,659,473	14,846,954	5,857,709	4,619,002
Used trucks	80,201,929	4,684,670	22,619,391	20,400,098	16,351,082	11,435,649	2,898,725	1,812,384
Other vehicles	7,845,934	215,255	2,129,380	1,959,203	1,359,198	1,507,316	637,779	37,741
Used motorcycles	4,092,946	215,255	1,574,832	690,028	1,181,728	392,987	–	37,741
GASOLINE AND MOTOR OIL	324,618,179	14,248,436	55,783,775	69,186,611	81,161,940	58,842,363	31,230,038	14,165,184
Gasoline	299,709,540	13,375,258	51,940,619	64,232,078	75,067,143	54,165,563	27,706,064	13,222,961
Diesel fuel	6,328,352	260,397	979,768	1,527,176	1,874,978	934,970	564,427	186,581
Gasoline on trips	17,027,242	541,003	2,603,507	3,114,891	3,816,477	3,439,717	2,813,266	698,795
Motor oil	1,380,620	66,280	233,687	281,002	364,869	267,413	117,841	49,771
Motor oil on trips	172,425	5,498	26,397	31,464	38,473	34,701	28,440	7,076
OTHER VEHICLE EXPENSES	300,039,715	9,792,108	49,149,670	55,648,170	74,082,246	59,551,995	32,992,306	18,651,975
Vehicle finance charges	28,443,956	991,104	6,178,394	7,122,914	6,688,763	4,863,968	2,023,152	575,901
Automobile finance charges	11,761,564	502,521	2,551,122	2,632,740	2,862,110	1,975,777	884,724	352,287
Truck finance charges	14,152,275	474,801	3,289,632	3,735,049	3,360,267	2,220,851	874,024	197,314
Motorcycle and plane finance charges	522,165	11,150	97,813	155,148	208,496	49,449	563	–
Other vehicle finance charges	2,007,953	2,555	239,826	599,977	257,890	617,891	263,840	26,301
Maintenance and repairs	98,432,475	3,529,105	14,685,681	18,576,297	24,237,955	20,595,792	11,551,397	5,289,609
Coolant, additives, brake and transmission fluids	544,177	31,282	98,427	113,486	128,325	94,777	63,919	13,681
Tires—purchased, replaced, installed	17,611,774	602,560	3,077,226	3,529,559	4,085,288	3,582,858	1,921,643	813,196
Parts, equipment, and accessories	5,632,539	213,242	1,147,974	1,086,686	1,206,549	1,354,416	430,395	192,950
Vehicle audio equipment	278,814	27,720	99,041	24,086	81,165	26,893	8,870	11,086
Vehicle products and cleaning services	1,345,157	38,870	103,543	224,368	535,389	207,337	198,092	42,576
Vehicle video equipment	141,853	1,316	22,919	24,520	56,592	18,001	18,584	–
Miscellaneous auto repair, servicing	11,228,392	477,975	1,291,011	1,699,032	2,799,312	2,220,851	1,841,392	928,778
Body work and painting	2,850,510	71,158	418,264	403,601	630,950	770,358	309,034	246,848
Clutch and transmission repair	4,011,014	75,494	487,633	848,214	1,292,429	827,397	436,167	44,345
Drive shaft and rear-end repair	988,079	43,748	168,820	228,707	196,831	219,916	106,156	23,706
Brake work	7,274,854	235,077	1,149,202	1,249,428	1,876,716	1,657,831	795,323	310,772
Repair to steering or front-end	2,579,033	99,498	352,577	640,554	542,339	523,331	293,970	127,021
Repair to engine cooling system	2,656,074	75,649	398,005	423,131	732,964	469,762	349,582	207,221
Motor tune-up	6,182,831	150,911	839,802	1,117,065	1,628,506	1,420,347	663,543	362,783
Lube, oil change, and oil filters	9,467,460	341,002	1,637,245	1,860,906	2,167,618	1,828,949	1,098,444	532,971
Front-end alignment, wheel balance, rotation	2,335,682	118,545	276,864	420,744	582,301	576,250	256,379	105,202
Shock absorber replacement	610,212	40,651	120,118	80,069	131,303	132,947	80,250	24,532
Tire repair and other repair work	6,168,156	247,466	729,711	1,397,633	1,514,577	1,203,684	738,021	336,247
Vehicle air conditioning repair	1,786,613	23,539	286,482	384,723	367,847	358,503	263,981	100,839
Exhaust system repair	1,567,719	117,848	187,646	284,691	341,537	405,782	175,143	55,078
Electrical system repair	3,657,604	180,025	513,007	536,182	1,000,286	801,372	420,821	205,451
Motor repair, replacement	7,717,533	315,372	1,076,149	1,775,846	1,737,470	1,561,102	836,011	416,092
Auto repair service policy	1,796,396	77	203,607	223,066	601,909	333,995	245,960	188,468

	total consumer units	under 25	25 to 34	35 to 44	45 to 54	55 to 64	65 to 74	75+
Vehicle insurance	$120,246,030	$3,908,821	$19,589,435	$19,970,892	$29,806,298	$23,613,894	$13,379,696	$9,771,919
Vehicle rental, leases, licenses, other charges	52,917,254	1,363,078	8,695,956	9,978,068	13,349,230	10,478,557	6,038,202	3,014,546
Leased and rented vehicles	24,419,491	389,860	4,214,355	4,556,139	6,246,701	4,709,332	2,796,653	1,506,330
Rented vehicles	3,962,099	49,633	629,851	680,915	1,029,327	874,677	556,402	141,410
Auto rental	857,232	14,867	162,067	133,449	244,735	151,599	90,810	59,442
Auto rental on trips	2,344,242	25,242	287,914	441,792	590,243	612,252	307,345	79,138
Truck rental	228,677	5,730	48,702	66,182	57,088	30,363	19,992	1,061
Truck rental on trips	508,714	3,717	117,048	37,973	137,012	73,305	138,256	1,651
Leased vehicles	20,457,392	340,305	3,584,504	3,875,224	5,217,374	3,834,655	2,240,250	1,364,920
Car lease payments	11,723,655	218,972	1,862,952	2,096,123	2,915,971	2,150,365	1,736,081	743,022
Truck lease payments	6,904,324	116,919	1,191,560	1,553,648	1,936,038	1,455,265	437,435	214,179
Vehicle registration, state	12,642,030	387,305	1,981,228	2,424,212	2,989,441	2,670,877	1,530,247	658,813
Vehicle registration, local	1,094,469	20,442	181,916	205,924	271,542	251,364	102,073	61,211
Driver's license	1,106,697	53,736	225,093	179,668	251,189	215,579	106,860	74,538
Vehicle inspection	1,436,872	49,245	227,139	267,983	388,697	242,038	180,070	81,261
Parking fees	4,666,472	280,761	881,955	906,801	1,209,776	792,480	414,345	180,448
Parking fees in home city, excluding residence	3,915,630	264,114	767,976	743,191	1,014,434	641,314	327,337	157,686
Parking fees on trips	750,842	16,647	113,979	163,827	195,341	151,165	87,008	22,762
Tolls	3,710,188	101,278	591,176	884,668	1,070,282	681,654	298,756	82,676
Tolls on trips	530,726	19,358	81,033	93,523	137,757	106,922	70,958	21,701
Towing charges	505,045	35,308	103,338	117,609	94,320	91,523	38,013	24,532
Global positioning services	228,677	2,710	17,394	30,379	69,251	67,233	29,425	12,384
Automobile service clubs	2,576,587	22,919	191,534	310,947	620,277	649,339	470,520	310,536
PUBLIC TRANSPORTATION	63,112,321	2,325,300	10,834,954	11,127,681	15,535,712	12,562,991	7,646,727	3,065,732
Airline fares	41,783,022	1,124,438	7,019,014	7,653,888	9,853,441	8,406,486	5,659,336	2,066,309
Intercity bus fares	1,304,802	76,114	208,927	163,827	277,251	230,543	221,181	127,021
Intracity mass transit fares	9,182,531	799,774	1,994,119	1,576,866	2,420,792	1,724,413	354,932	311,480
Local transportation on trips	2,400,494	95,161	344,597	410,111	519,007	485,811	392,804	153,086
Taxi fares and limousine service	1,769,493	144,175	539,814	217,858	431,885	224,905	33,649	164,408
Intercity train fares	1,945,586	50,717	293,439	325,268	390,931	407,084	379,288	98,952
Ship fares	4,370,537	23,384	430,746	667,678	1,431,427	1,067,700	605,256	144,477
School bus	354,632	11,615	4,093	111,967	210,730	16,049	–	–

Note: Numbers may not add to total because of rounding and missing subcategories. "–" means sample is too small to make a reliable estimate.
Source: Calculations by New Strategist based on the Bureau of Labor Statistics' 2011 Consumer Expenditure Survey

Table 11.4 Transportation: Market shares by age, 2011

(percentage of total annual spending on transportation accounted for by consumer unit age groups, 2011)

	total consumer units	under 25	25 to 34	35 to 44	45 to 54	55 to 64	65 to 74	75+
Share of total consumer units	100.0%	6.3%	16.7%	17.7%	20.3%	17.7%	11.5%	9.6%
Share of total before-tax income	100.0	2.7	15.3	21.6	25.0	21.0	9.5	4.9
Share of total spending	100.0	3.8	16.2	20.4	23.7	19.1	10.3	6.3
Share of transportation spending	100.0	4.2	17.9	20.8	23.3	19.2	9.7	5.0
VEHICLE PURCHASES	100.0	4.9	20.1	22.8	20.0	19.6	8.0	4.6
Cars and trucks, new	100.0	3.1	16.4	22.8	17.9	23.4	10.8	5.5
New cars	100.0	3.4	13.9	21.7	22.4	17.9	12.0	8.7
New trucks	100.0	2.8	18.6	23.9	14.1	28.1	9.8	2.7
Cars and trucks, used	100.0	6.8	23.2	22.7	22.0	16.1	5.3	3.9
Used cars	100.0	7.7	18.4	20.1	23.5	17.8	7.0	5.5
Used trucks	100.0	5.8	28.2	25.4	20.4	14.3	3.6	2.3
Other vehicles	100.0	2.7	27.1	25.0	17.3	19.2	8.1	0.5
Used motorcycles	100.0	5.3	38.5	16.9	28.9	9.6	–	0.9
GASOLINE AND MOTOR OIL	100.0	4.4	17.2	21.3	25.0	18.1	9.6	4.4
Gasoline	100.0	4.5	17.3	21.4	25.0	18.1	9.2	4.4
Diesel fuel	100.0	4.1	15.5	24.1	29.6	14.8	8.9	2.9
Gasoline on trips	100.0	3.2	15.3	18.3	22.4	20.2	16.5	4.1
Motor oil	100.0	4.8	16.9	20.4	26.4	19.4	8.5	3.6
Motor oil on trips	100.0	3.2	15.3	18.2	22.3	20.1	16.5	4.1
OTHER VEHICLE EXPENSES	100.0	3.3	16.4	18.5	24.7	19.8	11.0	6.2
Vehicle finance charges	100.0	3.5	21.7	25.0	23.5	17.1	7.1	2.0
Automobile finance charges	100.0	4.3	21.7	22.4	24.3	16.8	7.5	3.0
Truck finance charges	100.0	3.4	23.2	26.4	23.7	15.7	6.2	1.4
Motorcycle and plane finance charges	100.0	2.1	18.7	29.7	39.9	9.5	0.1	–
Other vehicle finance charges	100.0	0.1	11.9	29.9	12.8	30.8	13.1	1.3
Maintenance and repairs	100.0	3.6	14.9	18.9	24.6	20.9	11.7	5.4
Coolant, additives, brake and transmission fluids	100.0	5.7	18.1	20.9	23.6	17.4	11.7	2.5
Tires—purchased, replaced, installed	100.0	3.4	17.5	20.0	23.2	20.3	10.9	4.6
Parts, equipment, and accessories	100.0	3.8	20.4	19.3	21.4	24.0	7.6	3.4
Vehicle audio equipment	100.0	9.9	35.5	8.6	29.1	9.6	3.2	4.0
Vehicle products and cleaning services	100.0	2.9	7.7	16.7	39.8	15.4	14.7	3.2
Vehicle video equipment	100.0	0.9	16.2	17.3	39.9	12.7	13.1	–
Miscellaneous auto repair, servicing	100.0	4.3	11.5	15.1	24.9	19.8	16.4	8.3
Body work and painting	100.0	2.5	14.7	14.2	22.1	27.0	10.8	8.7
Clutch and transmission repair	100.0	1.9	12.2	21.1	32.2	20.6	10.9	1.1
Drive shaft and rear-end repair	100.0	4.4	17.1	23.1	19.9	22.3	10.7	2.4
Brake work	100.0	3.2	15.8	17.2	25.8	22.8	10.9	4.3
Repair to steering or front-end	100.0	3.9	13.7	24.8	21.0	20.3	11.4	4.9
Repair to engine cooling system	100.0	2.8	15.0	15.9	27.6	17.7	13.2	7.8
Motor tune-up	100.0	2.4	13.6	18.1	26.3	23.0	10.7	5.9
Lube, oil change, and oil filters	100.0	3.6	17.3	19.7	22.9	19.3	11.6	5.6
Front-end alignment, wheel balance, rotation	100.0	5.1	11.9	18.0	24.9	24.7	11.0	4.5
Shock absorber replacement	100.0	6.7	19.7	13.1	21.5	21.8	13.2	4.0
Tire repair and other repair work	100.0	4.0	11.8	22.7	24.6	19.5	12.0	5.5
Vehicle air conditioning repair	100.0	1.3	16.0	21.5	20.6	20.1	14.8	5.6
Exhaust system repair	100.0	7.5	12.0	18.2	21.8	25.9	11.2	3.5
Electrical system repair	100.0	4.9	14.0	14.7	27.3	21.9	11.5	5.6
Motor repair, replacement	100.0	4.1	13.9	23.0	22.5	20.2	10.8	5.4
Auto repair service policy	100.0	0.0	11.3	12.4	33.5	18.6	13.7	10.5

	total consumer units	under 25	25 to 34	35 to 44	45 to 54	55 to 64	65 to 74	75+
Vehicle insurance	**100.0%**	**3.3%**	**16.3%**	**16.6%**	**24.8%**	**19.6%**	**11.1%**	**8.1%**
Vehicle rental, leases, licenses, other charges	**100.0**	**2.6**	**16.4**	**18.9**	**25.2**	**19.8**	**11.4**	**5.7**
Leased and rented vehicles	100.0	1.6	17.3	18.7	25.6	19.3	11.5	6.2
Rented vehicles	100.0	1.3	15.9	17.2	26.0	22.1	14.0	3.6
Auto rental	100.0	1.7	18.9	15.6	28.5	17.7	10.6	6.9
Auto rental on trips	100.0	1.1	12.3	18.8	25.2	26.1	13.1	3.4
Truck rental	100.0	2.5	21.3	28.9	25.0	13.3	8.7	0.5
Truck rental on trips	100.0	0.7	23.0	7.5	26.9	14.4	27.2	0.3
Leased vehicles	100.0	1.7	17.5	18.9	25.5	18.7	11.0	6.7
Car lease payments	100.0	1.9	15.9	17.9	24.9	18.3	14.8	6.3
Truck lease payments	100.0	1.7	17.3	22.5	28.0	21.1	6.3	3.1
Vehicle registration, state	100.0	3.1	15.7	19.2	23.6	21.1	12.1	5.2
Vehicle registration, local	100.0	1.9	16.6	18.8	24.8	23.0	9.3	5.6
Driver's license	100.0	4.9	20.3	16.2	22.7	19.5	9.7	6.7
Vehicle inspection	100.0	3.4	15.8	18.7	27.1	16.8	12.5	5.7
Parking fees	100.0	6.0	18.9	19.4	25.9	17.0	8.9	3.9
Parking fees in home city, excluding residence	100.0	6.7	19.6	19.0	25.9	16.4	8.4	4.0
Parking fees on trips	100.0	2.2	15.2	21.8	26.0	20.1	11.6	3.0
Tolls	100.0	2.7	15.9	23.8	28.8	18.4	8.1	2.2
Tolls on trips	100.0	3.6	15.3	17.6	26.0	20.1	13.4	4.1
Towing charges	100.0	7.0	20.5	23.3	18.7	18.1	7.5	4.9
Global positioning services	100.0	1.2	7.6	13.3	30.3	29.4	12.9	5.4
Automobile service clubs	100.0	0.9	7.4	12.1	24.1	25.2	18.3	12.1
PUBLIC TRANSPORTATION	**100.0**	**3.7**	**17.2**	**17.6**	**24.6**	**19.9**	**12.1**	**4.9**
Airline fares	100.0	2.7	16.8	18.3	23.6	20.1	13.5	4.9
Intercity bus fares	100.0	5.8	16.0	12.6	21.2	17.7	17.0	9.7
Intracity mass transit fares	100.0	8.7	21.7	17.2	26.4	18.8	3.9	3.4
Local transportation on trips	100.0	4.0	14.4	17.1	21.6	20.2	16.4	6.4
Taxi fares and limousine service	100.0	8.1	30.5	12.3	24.4	12.7	1.9	9.3
Intercity train fares	100.0	2.6	15.1	16.7	20.1	20.9	19.5	5.1
Ship fares	100.0	0.5	9.9	15.3	32.8	24.4	13.8	3.3
School bus	100.0	3.3	1.2	31.6	59.4	4.5	–	–

Note: Numbers may not add to total because of rounding. "–" means sample is too small to make a reliable estimate.
Source: Calculations by New Strategist based on the Bureau of Labor Statistics' 2011 Consumer Expenditure Survey

Table 11.5 Transportation: Average spending by income, 2011

(average annual spending on transportation, by before-tax income of consumer units, 2011)

	total consumer units	under $20,000	$20,000– $39,999	$40,000– $49,999	$50,000– $69,999	$70,000– $79,999	$80,000– $99,999	$100,000 or more
Number of consumer units (in 000s)	122,287	26,342	27,788	11,347	17,376	7,385	10,456	21,593
Average number of persons per consumer unit	2.5	1.8	2.3	2.6	2.7	2.8	3.0	3.2
Average before-tax income of consumer units	$63,685.00	$10,491.66	$29,658.14	$44,698.00	$59,306.00	$74,742.00	$89,108.00	$169,776.00
Average spending of consumer units, total	49,704.88	22,142.36	33,453.66	40,306.19	50,034.03	57,976.69	65,389.80	97,728.22
Transportation, average spending	**8,292.79**	**3,290.69**	**5,499.22**	**7,128.10**	**9,010.06**	**9,804.47**	**12,185.29**	**15,537.96**
VEHICLE PURCHASES	**2,668.56**	**850.31**	**1,491.85**	**1,957.32**	**2,878.68**	**3,094.94**	**4,454.80**	**5,594.94**
Cars and trucks, new	**1,265.45**	**428.66**	**460.65**	**572.93**	**1,231.11**	**1,955.14**	**1,910.46**	**3,327.50**
New cars	583.32	293.92	308.75	315.95	659.99	904.76	662.52	1,331.46
New trucks	682.12	134.74	151.90	256.98	571.12	1,050.38	1,247.94	1,996.04
Cars and trucks, used	**1,338.96**	**539.15**	**1,000.98**	**1,368.43**	**1,603.11**	**1,106.58**	**2,468.39**	**2,054.12**
Used cars	683.11	299.32	516.89	644.82	701.56	503.12	1,251.96	1,156.58
Used trucks	655.85	239.83	484.09	723.60	901.54	603.46	1,216.43	897.54
Other vehicles	**64.16**	**22.41**	**30.22**	**15.97**	**44.45**	**33.21**	**75.95**	**213.31**
Used motorcycles	33.47	–	17.93	15.97	44.23	33.21	53.83	72.51
GASOLINE AND MOTOR OIL	**2,654.56**	**1,247.89**	**2,103.40**	**2,679.27**	**2,960.58**	**3,345.10**	**3,612.33**	**4,120.71**
Gasoline	2,450.87	1,172.24	1,959.78	2,495.80	2,717.79	3,069.89	3,327.85	3,767.93
Diesel fuel	51.75	22.51	40.18	40.95	65.19	80.16	78.57	74.46
Gasoline on trips	139.24	46.19	91.12	130.35	162.37	178.16	188.28	263.70
Motor oil	11.29	6.48	11.40	10.86	13.59	15.10	15.73	11.96
Motor oil on trips	1.41	0.47	0.92	1.32	1.64	1.80	1.90	2.66
OTHER VEHICLE EXPENSES	**2,453.57**	**1,010.69**	**1,670.74**	**2,148.60**	**2,762.23**	**2,937.25**	**3,457.79**	**4,396.94**
Vehicle finance charges	**232.60**	**47.44**	**135.42**	**218.17**	**257.18**	**373.82**	**376.22**	**453.51**
Automobile finance charges	96.18	21.65	70.68	93.55	106.32	143.65	146.45	172.56
Truck finance charges	115.73	22.61	56.75	115.23	138.12	193.08	202.87	218.82
Motorcycle and plane finance charges	4.27	0.73	1.27	5.05	4.30	4.59	5.83	11.17
Other vehicle finance charges	16.42	2.47	6.72	4.33	8.43	32.51	21.07	50.97
Maintenance and repairs	**804.93**	**321.58**	**562.34**	**691.19**	**903.16**	**991.32**	**1,149.15**	**1,448.76**
Coolant, additives, brake and transmission fluids	4.45	2.93	5.15	5.73	5.01	5.31	5.14	3.64
Tires—purchased, replaced, installed	144.02	58.77	101.55	123.53	161.57	185.32	235.12	241.10
Parts, equipment, and accessories	46.06	18.14	34.33	55.09	50.29	63.76	93.83	57.87
Vehicle audio equipment	2.28	0.41	1.13	1.94	1.64	3.65	2.60	6.25
Vehicle products and cleaning services	11.00	5.60	8.49	4.31	7.55	7.54	15.22	25.45
Vehicle video equipment	1.16	0.14	0.57	0.33	0.78	1.35	1.88	3.61
Miscellaneous auto repair, servicing	91.82	38.45	69.05	53.95	98.13	88.52	115.86	183.09
Body work and painting	23.31	8.94	18.86	25.40	27.54	31.35	27.88	37.09
Clutch and transmission repair	32.80	11.68	14.31	32.30	39.69	50.49	50.22	62.62
Drive shaft and rear-end repair	8.08	3.56	6.59	3.32	8.47	10.45	27.94	7.27
Brake work	59.49	22.77	42.36	48.20	73.76	74.13	69.17	111.08
Repair to steering or front-end	21.09	6.42	18.61	16.47	25.96	18.83	28.52	37.89
Repair to engine cooling system	21.72	10.94	14.82	18.39	24.99	30.73	15.07	43.01
Motor tune-up	50.56	16.07	27.96	41.39	55.27	67.35	61.71	111.62
Lube, oil change, and oil filters	77.42	31.28	60.30	67.84	88.26	103.20	104.85	129.95
Front-end alignment, wheel balance, rotation	19.10	6.32	15.56	19.76	16.73	23.03	29.63	34.38
Shock absorber replacement	4.99	2.20	1.69	5.16	8.79	3.74	14.36	5.38
Tire repair and other repair work	50.44	22.20	33.02	40.65	55.08	67.38	58.48	99.01
Vehicle air conditioning repair	14.61	4.10	10.35	12.34	15.83	11.53	26.18	28.55
Exhaust system repair	12.82	5.74	8.59	16.22	16.03	5.72	20.52	21.23
Electrical system repair	29.91	15.90	24.22	33.11	37.15	32.02	30.81	45.64
Motor repair, replacement	63.11	25.97	39.31	63.38	72.60	65.99	90.91	116.85
Auto repair service policy	14.69	4.05	5.53	2.39	12.06	39.96	23.24	36.20

	total consumer units	under $20,000	$20,000–$39,999	$40,000–$49,999	$50,000–$69,999	$70,000–$79,999	$80,000–$99,999	$100,000 or more
Vehicle insurance	$983.31	$500.16	$700.69	$891.95	$1,204.24	$1,105.40	$1,366.84	$1,502.99
Vehicle rental, leases, licenses, other charges	432.73	141.51	272.29	347.28	397.64	466.70	565.58	991.68
Leased and rented vehicles	199.69	42.94	115.93	155.95	177.65	181.17	272.02	510.74
Rented vehicles	32.40	9.59	12.66	29.47	25.05	33.09	48.12	85.24
Auto rental	7.01	3.85	5.11	8.40	9.01	7.70	11.31	8.65
Auto rental on trips	19.17	3.73	6.23	14.65	11.68	17.53	28.49	59.11
Truck rental	1.87	0.56	0.36	2.17	1.50	0.87	3.24	5.39
Truck rental on trips	4.16	–	0.96	4.12	2.86	6.99	4.52	11.38
Leased vehicles	167.29	33.35	103.26	126.48	152.60	148.08	223.90	425.51
Car lease payments	95.87	27.62	55.08	58.54	91.79	90.30	109.03	250.04
Truck lease payments	56.46	2.07	41.24	41.08	45.32	50.17	90.64	145.09
Vehicle registration, state	103.38	47.35	78.03	97.61	108.21	137.78	133.66	177.08
Vehicle registration, local	8.95	3.21	5.19	7.58	7.49	14.32	14.57	18.13
Driver's license	9.05	6.72	8.20	10.16	8.98	7.25	10.96	12.16
Vehicle inspection	11.75	5.60	9.69	9.56	12.32	13.03	14.32	20.89
Parking fees	38.16	13.87	19.99	20.99	26.09	35.72	44.87	107.51
Parking fees in home city, excluding residence	32.02	12.39	17.95	16.90	21.52	29.03	35.99	89.60
Parking fees on trips	6.14	1.48	2.04	4.08	4.57	6.68	8.88	17.91
Tolls	30.34	6.88	12.97	17.39	25.62	41.98	36.47	84.98
Tolls on trips	4.34	1.50	2.29	2.94	3.61	4.70	6.81	10.48
Towing charges	4.13	2.79	3.30	5.02	5.65	2.89	3.36	5.92
Global positioning services	1.87	0.89	0.63	1.26	1.21	2.88	3.94	4.39
Automobile service clubs	21.07	9.92	16.08	18.83	20.82	24.98	24.62	39.40
PUBLIC TRANSPORTATION	516.10	181.79	233.23	342.91	408.58	427.18	660.36	1,425.38
Airline fares	341.68	91.03	137.61	222.47	278.64	301.45	466.80	976.65
Intercity bus fares	10.67	6.26	7.95	6.84	10.81	9.34	11.65	21.44
Intracity mass transit fares	75.09	56.68	54.68	68.04	66.37	61.95	78.74	137.27
Local transportation on trips	19.63	5.73	8.35	12.19	15.89	17.09	24.73	56.46
Taxi fares and limousine service	14.47	12.52	10.15	8.23	6.53	5.46	12.33	35.51
Intercity train fares	15.91	3.68	5.27	11.44	12.67	17.54	30.94	41.65
Ship fares	35.74	5.47	6.35	12.98	16.78	13.41	34.03	146.19
School bus	2.90	–	2.88	0.73	0.89	0.95	1.15	10.21

Note: Subcategories may not add to total because some are not shown. "–" means sample is too small to make a reliable estimate.
Source: Bureau of Labor Statistics, unpublished tables from the 2011 Consumer Expenditure Survey; calculations by New Strategist

Table 11.6 Transportation: Indexed spending by income, 2011

(indexed average annual spending of consumer units on transportation, by before-tax income of consumer unit, 2011; index definition: an index of 100 is the average for all consumer units; an index of 125 means that spending by consumer units in that group is 25 percent above the average for all consumer units; an index of 75 indicates spending that is 25 percent below the average for all consumer units)

	total consumer units	under $20,000	$20,000– $39,999	$40,000– $49,999	$50,000– $69,999	$70,000– $79,999	$80,000– $99,999	$100,000 or more
Average spending of consumer units, total	$49,705	$22,142	$33,454	$40,306	$50,034	$57,977	$65,390	$97,728
Average spending of consumer units, index	100	45	67	81	101	117	132	197
Transportation, spending index	100	40	66	86	109	118	147	187
VEHICLE PURCHASES	100	32	56	73	108	116	167	210
Cars and trucks, new	100	34	36	45	97	155	151	263
New cars	100	50	53	54	113	155	114	228
New trucks	100	20	22	38	84	154	183	293
Cars and trucks, used	100	40	75	102	120	83	184	153
Used cars	100	44	76	94	103	74	183	169
Used trucks	100	37	74	110	137	92	185	137
Other vehicles	100	35	47	25	69	52	118	332
Used motorcycles	100	–	54	48	132	99	161	217
GASOLINE AND MOTOR OIL	100	47	79	101	112	126	136	155
Gasoline	100	48	80	102	111	125	136	154
Diesel fuel	100	43	78	79	126	155	152	144
Gasoline on trips	100	33	65	94	117	128	135	189
Motor oil	100	57	101	96	120	134	139	106
Motor oil on trips	100	33	65	94	116	128	135	189
OTHER VEHICLE EXPENSES	100	41	68	88	113	120	141	179
Vehicle finance charges	100	20	58	94	111	161	162	195
Automobile finance charges	100	23	73	97	111	149	152	179
Truck finance charges	100	20	49	100	119	167	175	189
Motorcycle and plane finance charges	100	17	30	118	101	107	137	262
Other vehicle finance charges	100	15	41	26	51	198	128	310
Maintenance and repairs	100	40	70	86	112	123	143	180
Coolant, additives, brake and transmission fluids	100	66	116	129	113	119	116	82
Tires—purchased, replaced, installed	100	41	71	86	112	129	163	167
Parts, equipment, and accessories	100	39	75	120	109	138	204	126
Vehicle audio equipment	100	18	50	85	72	160	114	274
Vehicle products and cleaning services	100	51	77	39	69	69	138	231
Vehicle video equipment	100	12	49	28	67	116	162	311
Miscellaneous auto repair, servicing	100	42	75	59	107	96	126	199
Body work and painting	100	38	81	109	118	134	120	159
Clutch and transmission repair	100	36	44	98	121	154	153	191
Drive shaft and rear-end repair	100	44	82	41	105	129	346	90
Brake work	100	38	71	81	124	125	116	187
Repair to steering or front-end	100	30	88	78	123	89	135	180
Repair to engine cooling system	100	50	68	85	115	141	69	198
Motor tune-up	100	32	55	82	109	133	122	221
Lube, oil change, and oil filters	100	40	78	88	114	133	135	168
Front-end alignment, wheel balance, rotation	100	33	81	103	88	121	155	180
Shock absorber replacement	100	44	34	103	176	75	288	108
Tire repair and other repair work	100	44	65	81	109	134	116	196
Vehicle air conditioning repair	100	28	71	84	108	79	179	195
Exhaust system repair	100	45	67	127	125	45	160	166
Electrical system repair	100	53	81	111	124	107	103	153
Motor repair, replacement	100	41	62	100	115	105	144	185
Auto repair service policy	100	28	38	16	82	272	158	246

	total consumer units	under $20,000	$20,000–$39,999	$40,000–$49,999	$50,000–$69,999	$70,000–$79,999	$80,000–$99,999	$100,000 or more
Vehicle insurance	**100**	**51**	**71**	**91**	**122**	**112**	**139**	**153**
Vehicle rental, leases, licenses, other charges	**100**	**33**	**63**	**80**	**92**	**108**	**131**	**229**
Leased and rented vehicles	100	22	58	78	89	91	136	256
Rented vehicles	100	30	39	91	77	102	149	263
Auto rental	100	55	73	120	129	110	161	123
Auto rental on trips	100	19	33	76	61	91	149	308
Truck rental	100	30	19	116	80	47	173	288
Truck rental on trips	100	–	23	99	69	168	109	274
Leased vehicles	100	20	62	76	91	89	134	254
Car lease payments	100	29	57	61	96	94	114	261
Truck lease payments	100	4	73	73	80	89	161	257
Vehicle registration, state	100	46	75	94	105	133	129	171
Vehicle registration, local	100	36	58	85	84	160	163	203
Driver's license	100	74	91	112	99	80	121	134
Vehicle inspection	100	48	82	81	105	111	122	178
Parking fees	100	36	52	55	68	94	118	282
Parking fees in home city, excluding residence	100	39	56	53	67	91	112	280
Parking fees on trips	100	24	33	66	74	109	145	292
Tolls	100	23	43	57	84	138	120	280
Tolls on trips	100	35	53	68	83	108	157	241
Towing charges	100	68	80	122	137	70	81	143
Global positioning services	100	48	34	67	65	154	211	235
Automobile service clubs	100	47	76	89	99	119	117	187
PUBLIC TRANSPORTATION	**100**	**35**	**45**	**66**	**79**	**83**	**128**	**276**
Airline fares	100	27	40	65	82	88	137	286
Intercity bus fares	100	59	74	64	101	88	109	201
Intracity mass transit fares	100	75	73	91	88	83	105	183
Local transportation on trips	100	29	43	62	81	87	126	288
Taxi fares and limousine service	100	87	70	57	45	38	85	245
Intercity train fares	100	23	33	72	80	110	194	262
Ship fares	100	15	18	36	47	38	95	409
School bus	100	–	99	25	31	33	40	352

Note: "–" means sample is too small to make a reliable estimate.
Source: Calculations by New Strategist based on the Bureau of Labor Statistics' 2011 Consumer Expenditure Survey

Table 11.7 Transportation: Total spending by income, 2011

(total annual spending on transportation, by before-tax income group of consumer units, 2011; consumer units and dollars in thousands)

	total consumer units	under $20,000	$20,000–$39,999	$40,000–$49,999	$50,000–$69,999	$70,000–$79,999	$80,000–$99,999	$100,000 or more
Number of consumer units	122,287	26,342	27,788	11,347	17,376	7,385	10,456	21,593
Total spending of all consumer units	$6,078,260,661	$583,273,961	$929,610,260	$457,354,338	$869,391,305	$428,157,856	$683,715,749	$2,110,245,454
Transportation, total spending	**1,014,100,411**	**86,683,356**	**152,812,308**	**80,882,551**	**156,558,803**	**72,406,011**	**127,409,392**	**335,511,170**
VEHICLE PURCHASES	**326,330,197**	**22,398,959**	**41,455,512**	**22,209,710**	**50,019,944**	**22,856,132**	**46,579,389**	**120,811,539**
Cars and trucks, new	**154,748,084**	**11,291,795**	**12,800,502**	**6,501,037**	**21,391,767**	**14,438,709**	**19,975,770**	**71,850,708**
New cars	71,332,453	7,742,320	8,579,454	3,585,085	11,467,986	6,681,653	6,927,309	28,750,216
New trucks	83,414,408	3,549,395	4,221,048	2,915,952	9,923,781	7,757,056	13,048,461	43,100,492
Cars and trucks, used	**163,737,402**	**14,202,165**	**27,815,306**	**15,527,575**	**27,855,639**	**8,172,093**	**25,809,486**	**44,354,613**
Used cars	83,535,473	7,884,583	14,363,405	7,316,773	12,190,307	3,715,541	13,090,494	24,974,032
Used trucks	80,201,929	6,317,659	13,451,901	8,210,689	15,665,159	4,456,552	12,718,992	19,380,581
Other vehicles	**7,845,934**	**590,219**	**839,838**	**181,212**	**772,363**	**245,256**	**794,133**	**4,606,003**
Used motorcycles	4,092,946	–	498,374	181,212	768,540	245,256	562,846	1,565,708
GASOLINE AND MOTOR OIL	**324,618,179**	**32,871,957**	**58,449,180**	**30,401,677**	**51,443,038**	**24,703,564**	**37,770,522**	**88,978,491**
Gasoline	299,709,540	30,879,097	54,458,485	28,319,843	47,224,319	22,671,138	34,796,000	81,360,912
Diesel fuel	6,328,352	592,879	1,116,491	464,660	1,132,741	591,982	821,528	1,607,815
Gasoline on trips	17,027,242	1,216,732	2,532,072	1,479,081	2,821,341	1,315,712	1,968,656	5,694,074
Motor oil	1,380,620	170,817	316,769	123,228	236,140	111,514	164,473	258,252
Motor oil on trips	172,425	12,304	25,653	14,978	28,497	13,293	19,866	57,437
OTHER VEHICLE EXPENSES	**300,039,715**	**26,623,692**	**46,426,633**	**24,380,164**	**47,996,508**	**21,691,591**	**36,154,652**	**94,943,125**
Vehicle finance charges	**28,443,956**	**1,249,795**	**3,763,122**	**2,475,575**	**4,468,760**	**2,760,661**	**3,933,756**	**9,792,641**
Automobile finance charges	11,761,564	570,216	1,963,926	1,061,512	1,847,416	1,060,855	1,531,281	3,726,088
Truck finance charges	14,152,275	595,542	1,577,035	1,307,515	2,399,973	1,425,896	2,121,209	4,724,980
Motorcycle and plane finance charges	522,165	19,199	35,215	57,302	74,717	33,897	60,958	241,194
Other vehicle finance charges	2,007,953	64,998	186,800	49,133	146,480	240,086	220,308	1,100,595
Maintenance and repairs	**98,432,475**	**8,471,073**	**15,626,203**	**7,842,933**	**15,693,308**	**7,320,898**	**12,015,512**	**31,283,075**
Coolant, additives, brake and transmission fluids	544,177	77,116	143,146	65,018	87,054	39,214	53,744	78,599
Tires—purchased, replaced, installed	17,611,774	1,548,073	2,821,764	1,401,695	2,807,440	1,368,588	2,458,415	5,206,072
Parts, equipment, and accessories	5,632,539	477,920	953,927	625,106	873,839	470,868	981,086	1,249,587
Vehicle audio equipment	278,814	10,786	31,522	22,013	28,497	26,955	27,186	134,956
Vehicle products and cleaning services	1,345,157	147,401	236,039	48,906	131,189	55,683	159,140	549,542
Vehicle video equipment	141,853	3,688	15,701	3,745	13,553	9,970	19,657	77,951
Miscellaneous auto repair, servicing	11,228,392	1,012,826	1,918,702	612,171	1,705,107	653,720	1,211,432	3,953,462
Body work and painting	2,850,510	235,563	524,116	288,214	478,535	231,520	291,513	800,884
Clutch and transmission repair	4,011,014	307,626	397,672	366,508	689,653	372,869	525,100	1,352,154
Drive shaft and rear-end repair	988,079	93,811	183,187	37,672	147,175	77,173	292,141	156,981
Brake work	7,274,854	599,746	1,177,008	546,925	1,281,654	547,450	723,242	2,398,550
Repair to steering or front-end	2,579,033	168,991	517,078	186,885	451,081	139,060	298,205	818,159
Repair to engine cooling system	2,656,074	288,272	411,904	208,671	434,226	226,941	157,572	928,715
Motor tune-up	6,182,831	423,310	776,916	469,652	960,372	497,380	645,240	2,410,211
Lube, oil change, and oil filters	9,467,460	823,865	1,675,570	769,780	1,533,606	762,132	1,096,312	2,806,010
Front-end alignment, wheel balance, rotation	2,335,682	166,556	432,307	224,217	290,700	170,077	309,811	742,367
Shock absorber replacement	610,212	58,044	46,869	58,551	152,735	27,620	150,148	116,170
Tire repair and other repair work	6,168,156	584,807	917,534	461,256	957,070	497,601	611,467	2,137,923
Vehicle air conditioning repair	1,786,613	108,000	287,639	140,022	275,062	85,149	273,738	616,480
Exhaust system repair	1,567,719	151,280	238,793	184,048	278,537	42,242	214,557	458,419
Electrical system repair	3,657,604	418,914	672,943	375,699	645,518	236,468	322,149	985,505
Motor repair, replacement	7,717,533	684,000	1,092,223	719,173	1,261,498	487,336	950,555	2,523,142
Auto repair service policy	1,796,396	106,670	153,788	27,119	209,555	295,105	242,997	781,667

	total consumer units	under $20,000	$20,000–$39,999	$40,000–$49,999	$50,000–$69,999	$70,000–$79,999	$80,000–$99,999	$100,000 or more
Vehicle insurance	$120,246,030	$13,175,185	$19,470,872	$10,120,957	$20,924,874	$8,163,379	$14,291,679	$32,454,063
Vehicle rental, leases, licenses, other charges	52,917,254	3,727,662	7,566,425	3,940,586	6,909,393	3,446,580	5,913,704	21,413,346
Leased and rented vehicles	24,419,491	1,131,067	3,221,367	1,769,565	3,086,846	1,337,940	2,844,241	11,028,409
Rented vehicles	3,962,099	252,686	351,808	334,396	435,269	244,370	503,143	1,840,587
Auto rental	857,232	101,437	142,043	95,315	156,558	56,865	118,257	186,779
Auto rental on trips	2,344,242	98,165	173,133	166,234	202,952	129,459	297,891	1,276,362
Truck rental	228,677	14,752	9,961	24,623	26,064	6,425	33,877	116,386
Truck rental on trips	508,714	–	26,804	46,750	49,695	51,621	47,261	245,728
Leased vehicles	20,457,392	878,518	2,869,426	1,435,169	2,651,578	1,093,571	2,341,098	9,188,037
Car lease payments	11,723,655	727,556	1,530,657	664,253	1,594,943	666,866	1,140,018	5,399,114
Truck lease payments	6,904,324	54,455	1,145,903	466,135	787,480	370,505	947,732	3,132,928
Vehicle registration, state	12,642,030	1,247,374	2,168,253	1,107,581	1,880,257	1,017,505	1,397,549	3,823,688
Vehicle registration, local	1,094,469	84,686	144,316	86,010	130,146	105,753	152,344	391,481
Driver's license	1,106,697	177,078	227,749	115,286	156,036	53,541	114,598	262,571
Vehicle inspection	1,436,872	147,568	269,216	108,477	214,072	96,227	149,730	451,078
Parking fees	4,666,472	365,435	555,404	238,174	453,340	263,792	469,161	2,321,463
Parking fees in home city, excluding residence	3,915,630	326,427	498,698	191,764	373,932	214,387	376,311	1,934,733
Parking fees on trips	750,842	39,085	56,706	46,296	79,408	49,332	92,849	386,731
Tolls	3,710,188	181,120	360,442	197,324	445,173	310,022	381,330	1,834,973
Tolls on trips	530,726	39,512	63,521	33,360	62,727	34,710	71,205	226,295
Towing charges	505,045	73,577	91,748	56,962	98,174	21,343	35,132	127,831
Global positioning services	228,677	23,403	17,513	14,297	21,025	21,269	41,197	94,793
Automobile service clubs	2,576,587	261,302	446,751	213,664	361,768	184,477	257,427	850,764
PUBLIC TRANSPORTATION	63,112,321	4,788,748	6,480,982	3,891,000	7,099,486	3,154,724	6,904,724	30,778,230
Airline fares	41,783,022	2,398,014	3,823,881	2,524,367	4,841,649	2,226,208	4,880,861	21,088,803
Intercity bus fares	1,304,802	164,992	220,787	77,613	187,835	68,976	121,812	462,954
Intracity mass transit fares	9,182,531	1,492,964	1,519,351	772,050	1,153,245	457,501	823,305	2,964,071
Local transportation on trips	2,400,494	150,849	231,991	138,320	276,105	126,210	258,577	1,219,141
Taxi fares and limousine service	1,769,493	329,832	282,150	93,386	113,465	40,322	128,922	766,767
Intercity train fares	1,945,586	96,930	146,544	129,810	220,154	129,533	323,509	899,348
Ship fares	4,370,537	144,123	176,586	147,284	291,569	99,033	355,818	3,156,681
School bus	354,632	–	80,115	8,283	15,465	7,016	12,024	220,465

Note: Numbers may not add to total because of rounding and missing subcategories. "–" means sample is too small to make a reliable estimate.
Source: Calculations by New Strategist based on the Bureau of Labor Statistics' 2011 Consumer Expenditure Survey

Table 11.8 Transportation: Market shares by income, 2011

(percentage of total annual spending on transportation accounted for by before-tax income group of consumer units, 2011)

	total consumer units	under $20,000	$20,000–$39,999	$40,000–$49,999	$50,000–$69,999	$70,000–$79,999	$80,000–$99,999	$100,000 or more
Share of total consumer units	100.0%	21.5%	22.7%	9.3%	14.2%	6.0%	8.6%	17.7%
Share of total before-tax income	100.0	3.5	10.6	6.5	13.2	7.1	12.0	47.1
Share of total spending	100.0	9.6	15.3	7.5	14.3	7.0	11.2	34.7
Share of transportation spending	100.0	8.5	15.1	8.0	15.4	7.1	12.6	33.1
VEHICLE PURCHASES	100.0	6.9	12.7	6.8	15.3	7.0	14.3	37.0
Cars and trucks, new	100.0	7.3	8.3	4.2	13.8	9.3	12.9	46.4
New cars	100.0	10.9	12.0	5.0	16.1	9.4	9.7	40.3
New trucks	100.0	4.3	5.1	3.5	11.9	9.3	15.6	51.7
Cars and trucks, used	100.0	8.7	17.0	9.5	17.0	5.0	15.8	27.1
Used cars	100.0	9.4	17.2	8.8	14.6	4.4	15.7	29.9
Used trucks	100.0	7.9	16.8	10.2	19.5	5.6	15.9	24.2
Other vehicles	100.0	7.5	10.7	2.3	9.8	3.1	10.1	58.7
Used motorcycles	100.0	–	12.2	4.4	18.8	6.0	13.8	38.3
GASOLINE AND MOTOR OIL	100.0	10.1	18.0	9.4	15.8	7.6	11.6	27.4
Gasoline	100.0	10.3	18.2	9.4	15.8	7.6	11.6	27.1
Diesel fuel	100.0	9.4	17.6	7.3	17.9	9.4	13.0	25.4
Gasoline on trips	100.0	7.1	14.9	8.7	16.6	7.7	11.6	33.4
Motor oil	100.0	12.4	22.9	8.9	17.1	8.1	11.9	18.7
Motor oil on trips	100.0	7.1	14.9	8.7	16.5	7.7	11.5	33.3
OTHER VEHICLE EXPENSES	100.0	8.9	15.5	8.1	16.0	7.2	12.0	31.6
Vehicle finance charges	100.0	4.4	13.2	8.7	15.7	9.7	13.8	34.4
Automobile finance charges	100.0	4.8	16.7	9.0	15.7	9.0	13.0	31.7
Truck finance charges	100.0	4.2	11.1	9.2	17.0	10.1	15.0	33.4
Motorcycle and plane finance charges	100.0	3.7	6.7	11.0	14.3	6.5	11.7	46.2
Other vehicle finance charges	100.0	3.2	9.3	2.4	7.3	12.0	11.0	54.8
Maintenance and repairs	100.0	8.6	15.9	8.0	15.9	7.4	12.2	31.8
Coolant, additives, brake and transmission fluids	100.0	14.2	26.3	11.9	16.0	7.2	9.9	14.4
Tires—purchased, replaced, installed	100.0	8.8	16.0	8.0	15.9	7.8	14.0	29.6
Parts, equipment, and accessories	100.0	8.5	16.9	11.1	15.5	8.4	17.4	22.2
Vehicle audio equipment	100.0	3.9	11.3	7.9	10.2	9.7	9.8	48.4
Vehicle products and cleaning services	100.0	11.0	17.5	3.6	9.8	4.1	11.8	40.9
Vehicle video equipment	100.0	2.6	11.1	2.6	9.6	7.0	13.9	55.0
Miscellaneous auto repair, servicing	100.0	9.0	17.1	5.5	15.2	5.8	10.8	35.2
Body work and painting	100.0	8.3	18.4	10.1	16.8	8.1	10.2	28.1
Clutch and transmission repair	100.0	7.7	9.9	9.1	17.2	9.3	13.1	33.7
Drive shaft and rear-end repair	100.0	9.5	18.5	3.8	14.9	7.8	29.6	15.9
Brake work	100.0	8.2	16.2	7.5	17.6	7.5	9.9	33.0
Repair to steering or front-end	100.0	6.6	20.0	7.2	17.5	5.4	11.6	31.7
Repair to engine cooling system	100.0	10.9	15.5	7.9	16.3	8.5	5.9	35.0
Motor tune-up	100.0	6.8	12.6	7.6	15.5	8.0	10.4	39.0
Lube, oil change, and oil filters	100.0	8.7	17.7	8.1	16.2	8.1	11.6	29.6
Front-end alignment, wheel balance, rotation	100.0	7.1	18.5	9.6	12.4	7.3	13.3	31.8
Shock absorber replacement	100.0	9.5	7.7	9.6	25.0	4.5	24.6	19.0
Tire repair and other repair work	100.0	9.5	14.9	7.5	15.5	8.1	9.9	34.7
Vehicle air conditioning repair	100.0	6.0	16.1	7.8	15.4	4.8	15.3	34.5
Exhaust system repair	100.0	9.6	15.2	11.7	17.8	2.7	13.7	29.2
Electrical system repair	100.0	11.5	18.4	10.3	17.6	6.5	8.8	26.9
Motor repair, replacement	100.0	8.9	14.2	9.3	16.3	6.3	12.3	32.7
Auto repair service policy	100.0	5.9	8.6	1.5	11.7	16.4	13.5	43.5

	total consumer units	under $20,000	$20,000– $39,999	$40,000– $49,999	$50,000– $69,999	$70,000– $79,999	$80,000– $99,999	$100,000 or more
Vehicle insurance	100.0%	11.0%	16.2%	8.4%	17.4%	6.8%	11.9%	27.0%
Vehicle rental, leases, licenses, other charges	100.0	7.0	14.3	7.4	13.1	6.5	11.2	40.5
Leased and rented vehicles	100.0	4.6	13.2	7.2	12.6	5.5	11.6	45.2
Rented vehicles	100.0	6.4	8.9	8.4	11.0	6.2	12.7	46.5
Auto rental	100.0	11.8	16.6	11.1	18.3	6.6	13.8	21.8
Auto rental on trips	100.0	4.2	7.4	7.1	8.7	5.5	12.7	54.4
Truck rental	100.0	6.5	4.4	10.8	11.4	2.8	14.8	50.9
Truck rental on trips	100.0	–	5.3	9.2	9.8	10.1	9.3	48.3
Leased vehicles	100.0	4.3	14.0	7.0	13.0	5.3	11.4	44.9
Car lease payments	100.0	6.2	13.1	5.7	13.6	5.7	9.7	46.1
Truck lease payments	100.0	0.8	16.6	6.8	11.4	5.4	13.7	45.4
Vehicle registration, state	100.0	9.9	17.2	8.8	14.9	8.0	11.1	30.2
Vehicle registration, local	100.0	7.7	13.2	7.9	11.9	9.7	13.9	35.8
Driver's license	100.0	16.0	20.6	10.4	14.1	4.8	10.4	23.7
Vehicle inspection	100.0	10.3	18.7	7.5	14.9	6.7	10.4	31.4
Parking fees	100.0	7.8	11.9	5.1	9.7	5.7	10.1	49.7
Parking fees in home city, excluding residence	100.0	8.3	12.7	4.9	9.5	5.5	9.6	49.4
Parking fees on trips	100.0	5.2	7.6	6.2	10.6	6.6	12.4	51.5
Tolls	100.0	4.9	9.7	5.3	12.0	8.4	10.3	49.5
Tolls on trips	100.0	7.4	12.0	6.3	11.8	6.5	13.4	42.6
Towing charges	100.0	14.6	18.2	11.3	19.4	4.2	7.0	25.3
Global positioning services	100.0	10.2	7.7	6.3	9.2	9.3	18.0	41.5
Automobile service clubs	100.0	10.1	17.3	8.3	14.0	7.2	10.0	33.0
PUBLIC TRANSPORTATION	100.0	7.6	10.3	6.2	11.2	5.0	10.9	48.8
Airline fares	100.0	5.7	9.2	6.0	11.6	5.3	11.7	50.5
Intercity bus fares	100.0	12.6	16.9	5.9	14.4	5.3	9.3	35.5
Intracity mass transit fares	100.0	16.3	16.5	8.4	12.6	5.0	9.0	32.3
Local transportation on trips	100.0	6.3	9.7	5.8	11.5	5.3	10.8	50.8
Taxi fares and limousine service	100.0	18.6	15.9	5.3	6.4	2.3	7.3	43.3
Intercity train fares	100.0	5.0	7.5	6.7	11.3	6.7	16.6	46.2
Ship fares	100.0	3.3	4.0	3.4	6.7	2.3	8.1	72.2
School bus	100.0	–	22.6	2.3	4.4	2.0	3.4	62.2

Note: Numbers may not add to total because of rounding. "–" means sample is too small to make a reliable estimate.
Source: Calculations by New Strategist based on the Bureau of Labor Statistics' 2011 Consumer Expenditure Survey

Table 11.9 Transportation: Average spending by high-income consumer units, 2011

(average annual spending on transportation, by before-tax income of high-income consumer units, 2011)

	total consumer units	$100,000 or more	$100,000–$119,999	$120,000–$149,999	$150,000 or more
Number of consumer units (in 000s)	122,287	21,593	7,045	6,107	8,440
Average number of persons per consumer unit	2.5	3.2	3.2	3.1	3.2
Average before-tax income of consumer units	$63,685.00	$169,776.00	$108,549.00	$133,318.00	$247,261.00
Average spending of consumer units, total	49,704.88	97,728.22	76,496.41	87,239.44	123,056.38
Transportation, average spending	**8,292.79**	**15,537.96**	**13,961.85**	**14,273.57**	**17,755.53**
VEHICLE PURCHASES	**2,668.56**	**5,594.94**	**4,966.03**	**4,878.06**	**6,638.58**
Cars and trucks, new	**1,265.45**	**3,327.50**	**2,792.41**	**2,967.50**	**4,034.62**
New cars	583.32	1,331.46	1,043.26	1,209.94	1,659.95
New trucks	682.12	1,996.04	1,749.14	1,757.56	2,374.67
Cars and trucks, used	**1,338.96**	**2,054.12**	**1,933.93**	**1,715.11**	**2,399.73**
Used cars	683.11	1,156.58	1,030.11	1,016.46	1,363.52
Used trucks	655.85	897.54	903.82	698.64	1,036.22
Other vehicles	**64.16**	**213.31**	**239.69**	**195.45**	**204.23**
Used motorcycles	33.47	72.51	172.58	22.07	25.49
GASOLINE AND MOTOR OIL	**2,654.56**	**4,120.71**	**3,920.54**	**4,149.55**	**4,266.92**
Gasoline	2,450.87	3,767.93	3,600.99	3,793.12	3,889.05
Diesel fuel	51.75	74.46	62.76	76.12	83.03
Gasoline on trips	139.24	263.70	238.59	267.41	281.96
Motor oil	11.29	11.96	15.79	10.19	10.03
Motor oil on trips	1.41	2.66	2.41	2.70	2.85
OTHER VEHICLE EXPENSES	**2,453.57**	**4,396.94**	**4,238.99**	**3,972.77**	**4,823.05**
Vehicle finance charges	**232.60**	**453.51**	**441.76**	**456.80**	**460.94**
Automobile finance charges	96.18	172.56	181.62	180.57	159.19
Truck finance charges	115.73	218.82	205.81	231.87	220.24
Motorcycle and plane finance charges	4.27	11.17	11.63	7.38	13.53
Other vehicle finance charges	16.42	50.97	42.69	36.99	67.98
Maintenance and repairs	**804.93**	**1,448.76**	**1,307.99**	**1,342.60**	**1,641.98**
Coolant, additives, brake and transmission fluids	4.45	3.64	3.42	2.96	4.30
Tires—purchased, replaced, installed	144.02	241.10	178.87	268.43	273.26
Parts, equipment, and accessories	46.06	57.87	53.39	55.40	63.39
Vehicle audio equipment	2.28	6.25	1.77	10.85	6.65
Vehicle products and cleaning services	11.00	25.45	38.63	23.27	15.62
Vehicle video equipment	1.16	3.61	3.45	3.01	4.17
Miscellaneous auto repair, servicing	91.82	183.09	182.59	137.30	215.94
Body work and painting	23.31	37.09	32.47	38.12	40.20
Clutch and transmission repair	32.80	62.62	59.82	31.44	87.52
Drive shaft and rear-end repair	8.08	7.27	5.80	9.64	6.77
Brake work	59.49	111.08	98.31	114.33	119.38
Repair to steering or front-end	21.09	37.89	26.27	48.91	39.63
Repair to engine cooling system	21.72	43.01	48.85	33.20	45.23
Motor tune-up	50.56	111.62	67.35	90.30	164.00
Lube, oil change, and oil filters	77.42	129.95	121.63	129.12	137.51
Front-end alignment, wheel balance, rotation	19.10	34.38	37.80	30.30	34.47
Shock absorber replacement	4.99	5.38	10.97	2.88	2.51
Tire repair and other repair work	50.44	99.01	93.03	99.99	103.28
Vehicle air conditioning repair	14.61	28.55	27.02	16.85	38.28
Exhaust system repair	12.82	21.23	26.67	17.33	19.51
Electrical system repair	29.91	45.64	51.03	25.77	55.52
Motor repair, replacement	63.11	116.85	111.98	129.80	111.55
Auto repair service policy	14.69	36.20	26.84	23.40	53.27

	total consumer units	$100,000 or more	$100,000– $119,999	$120,000– $149,999	$150,000 or more
Vehicle insurance	$983.31	$1,502.99	$1,834.11	$1,343.20	$1,330.67
Vehicle rental, leases, licenses, other charges	432.73	991.68	655.14	830.16	1,389.45
Leased and rented vehicles	199.69	510.74	269.37	372.41	812.29
Rented vehicles	32.40	85.24	53.09	58.77	131.22
Auto rental	7.01	8.65	4.68	5.33	14.37
Auto rental on trips	19.17	59.11	23.26	43.55	100.29
Truck rental	1.87	5.39	4.08	4.68	7.00
Truck rental on trips	4.16	11.38	19.15	5.20	9.37
Leased vehicles	167.29	425.51	216.29	313.65	681.07
Car lease payments	95.87	250.04	92.21	184.95	428.87
Truck lease payments	56.46	145.09	99.72	104.11	212.60
Vehicle registration, state	103.38	177.08	162.99	172.55	192.13
Vehicle registration, local	8.95	18.13	14.99	19.04	20.09
Driver's license	9.05	12.16	14.24	13.41	9.53
Vehicle inspection	11.75	20.89	18.09	18.73	24.79
Parking fees	38.16	107.51	65.09	98.55	149.39
Parking fees in home city, excluding residence	32.02	89.60	55.81	80.78	124.17
Parking fees on trips	6.14	17.91	9.28	17.76	25.22
Tolls	30.34	84.98	59.42	74.62	113.81
Tolls on trips	4.34	10.48	6.22	13.33	11.97
Towing charges	4.13	5.92	9.25	6.05	3.05
Global positioning services	1.87	4.39	3.27	5.83	4.27
Automobile service clubs	21.07	39.40	32.21	35.64	48.12
PUBLIC TRANSPORTATION	516.10	1,425.38	836.29	1,273.20	2,026.98
Airline fares	341.68	976.65	568.41	839.77	1,416.45
Intercity bus fares	10.67	21.44	13.67	19.92	29.02
Intracity mass transit fares	75.09	137.27	91.12	133.10	178.82
Local transportation on trips	19.63	56.46	27.73	60.95	77.19
Taxi fares and limousine service	14.47	35.51	36.18	23.21	43.65
Intercity train fares	15.91	41.65	38.08	40.02	45.80
Ship fares	35.74	146.19	61.10	147.78	216.06
School bus	2.90	10.21	–	8.45	19.99

Note: Subcategories may not add to total because some are not shown. "–" means sample is too small to make a reliable estimate.
Source: Bureau of Labor Statistics, unpublished tables from the 2011 Consumer Expenditure Survey

Table 11.10 Transportation: Indexed spending by high-income consumer units, 2011

(indexed average annual spending of high-income consumer units on transportation, by before-tax income of consumer unit, 2011; index definition: an index of 100 is the average for all consumer units; an index of 125 means that spending by consumer units in that group is 25 percent above the average for all consumer units; an index of 75 indicates spending that is 25 percent below the average for all consumer units)

	total consumer units	$100,000 or more	$100,000– $119,999	$120,000– $149,999	$150,000 or more
Average spending of consumer units, total	$49,705	$97,728	$76,496	$87,239	$123,056
Average spending of consumer units, index	100	197	154	176	248
Transportation, spending index	**100**	**187**	**168**	**172**	**214**
VEHICLE PURCHASES	**100**	**210**	**186**	**183**	**249**
Cars and trucks, new	**100**	**263**	**221**	**235**	**319**
New cars	100	228	179	207	285
New trucks	100	293	256	258	348
Cars and trucks, used	**100**	**153**	**144**	**128**	**179**
Used cars	100	169	151	149	200
Used trucks	100	137	138	107	158
Other vehicles	**100**	**332**	**374**	**305**	**318**
Used motorcycles	100	217	516	66	76
GASOLINE AND MOTOR OIL	**100**	**155**	**148**	**156**	**161**
Gasoline	100	154	147	155	159
Diesel fuel	100	144	121	147	160
Gasoline on trips	100	189	171	192	202
Motor oil	100	106	140	90	89
Motor oil on trips	100	189	171	191	202
OTHER VEHICLE EXPENSES	**100**	**179**	**173**	**162**	**197**
Vehicle finance charges	**100**	**195**	**190**	**196**	**198**
Automobile finance charges	100	179	189	188	166
Truck finance charges	100	189	178	200	190
Motorcycle and plane finance charges	100	262	272	173	317
Other vehicle finance charges	100	310	260	225	414
Maintenance and repairs	**100**	**180**	**162**	**167**	**204**
Coolant, additives, brake and transmission fluids	100	82	77	67	97
Tires—purchased, replaced, installed	100	167	124	186	190
Parts, equipment, and accessories	100	126	116	120	138
Vehicle audio equipment	100	274	78	476	292
Vehicle products and cleaning services	100	231	351	212	142
Vehicle video equipment	100	311	297	259	359
Miscellaneous auto repair, servicing	100	199	199	150	235
Body work and painting	100	159	139	164	172
Clutch and transmission repair	100	191	182	96	267
Drive shaft and rear-end repair	100	90	72	119	84
Brake work	100	187	165	192	201
Repair to steering or front-end	100	180	125	232	188
Repair to engine cooling system	100	198	225	153	208
Motor tune-up	100	221	133	179	324
Lube, oil change, and oil filters	100	168	157	167	178
Front-end alignment, wheel balance, rotation	100	180	198	159	180
Shock absorber replacement	100	108	220	58	50
Tire repair and other repair work	100	196	184	198	205
Vehicle air conditioning repair	100	195	185	115	262
Exhaust system repair	100	166	208	135	152
Electrical system repair	100	153	171	86	186
Motor repair, replacement	100	185	177	206	177
Auto repair service policy	100	246	183	159	363

	total consumer units	$100,000 or more	$100,000–$119,999	$120,000–$149,999	$150,000 or more
Vehicle insurance	100	153	187	137	135
Vehicle rental, leases, licenses, other charges	100	229	151	192	321
Leased and rented vehicles	100	256	135	186	407
Rented vehicles	100	263	164	181	405
Auto rental	100	123	67	76	205
Auto rental on trips	100	308	121	227	523
Truck rental	100	288	218	250	374
Truck rental on trips	100	274	460	125	225
Leased vehicles	100	254	129	187	407
Car lease payments	100	261	96	193	447
Truck lease payments	100	257	177	184	377
Vehicle registration, state	100	171	158	167	186
Vehicle registration, local	100	203	167	213	224
Driver's license	100	134	157	148	105
Vehicle inspection	100	178	154	159	211
Parking fees	100	282	171	258	391
Parking fees in home city, excluding residence	100	280	174	252	388
Parking fees on trips	100	292	151	289	411
Tolls	100	280	196	246	375
Tolls on trips	100	241	143	307	276
Towing charges	100	143	224	146	74
Global positioning services	100	235	175	312	228
Automobile service clubs	100	187	153	169	228
PUBLIC TRANSPORTATION	100	276	162	247	393
Airline fares	100	286	166	246	415
Intercity bus fares	100	201	128	187	272
Intracity mass transit fares	100	183	121	177	238
Local transportation on trips	100	288	141	310	393
Taxi fares and limousine service	100	245	250	160	302
Intercity train fares	100	262	239	252	288
Ship fares	100	409	171	413	605
School bus	100	352	–	291	689

Note: "–" means sample is too small to make a reliable estimate.
Source: Calculations by New Strategist based on the Bureau of Labor Statistics' 2011 Consumer Expenditure Survey

Table 11.11 Transportation: Total spending by high-income consumer units, 2011

(total annual spending on transportation, by before-tax income group of high-income consumer units, 2011; consumer units and dollars in thousands)

	total consumer units	$100,000 or more	$100,000–$119,999	$120,000–$149,999	$150,000 or more
Number of consumer units	122,287	21,593	7,045	6,107	8,440
Total spending of all consumer units	$6,078,260,661	$2,110,245,454	$538,917,208	$532,771,260	$1,038,595,847
Transportation, total spending	1,014,100,411	335,511,170	98,361,233	87,168,692	149,856,673
VEHICLE PURCHASES	326,330,197	120,811,539	34,985,681	29,790,312	56,029,615
Cars and trucks, new	154,748,084	71,850,708	19,672,528	18,122,523	34,052,193
New cars	71,332,453	28,750,216	7,349,767	7,389,104	14,009,978
New trucks	83,414,408	43,100,492	12,322,691	10,733,419	20,042,215
Cars and trucks, used	163,737,402	44,354,613	13,624,537	10,474,177	20,253,721
Used cars	83,535,473	24,974,032	7,257,125	6,207,521	11,508,109
Used trucks	80,201,929	19,380,581	6,367,412	4,266,594	8,745,697
Other vehicles	7,845,934	4,606,003	1,688,616	1,193,613	1,723,701
Used motorcycles	4,092,946	1,565,708	1,215,826	134,781	215,136
GASOLINE AND MOTOR OIL	324,618,179	88,978,491	27,620,204	25,341,302	36,012,805
Gasoline	299,709,540	81,360,912	25,368,975	23,164,584	32,823,582
Diesel fuel	6,328,352	1,607,815	442,144	464,865	700,773
Gasoline on trips	17,027,242	5,694,074	1,680,867	1,633,073	2,379,742
Motor oil	1,380,620	258,252	111,241	62,230	84,653
Motor oil on trips	172,425	57,437	16,978	16,489	24,054
OTHER VEHICLE EXPENSES	300,039,715	94,943,125	29,863,685	24,261,706	40,706,542
Vehicle finance charges	28,443,956	9,792,641	3,112,199	2,789,678	3,890,334
Automobile finance charges	11,761,564	3,726,088	1,279,513	1,102,741	1,343,564
Truck finance charges	14,152,275	4,724,980	1,449,931	1,416,030	1,858,826
Motorcycle and plane finance charges	522,165	241,194	81,933	45,070	114,193
Other vehicle finance charges	2,007,953	1,100,595	300,751	225,898	573,751
Maintenance and repairs	98,432,475	31,283,075	9,214,790	8,199,258	13,858,311
Coolant, additives, brake and transmission fluids	544,177	78,599	24,094	18,077	36,292
Tires—purchased, replaced, installed	17,611,774	5,206,072	1,260,139	1,639,302	2,306,314
Parts, equipment, and accessories	5,632,539	1,249,587	376,133	338,328	535,012
Vehicle audio equipment	278,814	134,956	12,470	66,261	56,126
Vehicle products and cleaning services	1,345,157	549,542	272,148	142,110	131,833
Vehicle video equipment	141,853	77,951	24,305	18,382	35,195
Miscellaneous auto repair, servicing	11,228,392	3,953,462	1,286,347	838,491	1,822,534
Body work and painting	2,850,510	800,884	228,751	232,799	339,288
Clutch and transmission repair	4,011,014	1,352,154	421,432	192,004	738,669
Drive shaft and rear-end repair	988,079	156,981	40,861	58,871	57,139
Brake work	7,274,854	2,398,550	692,594	698,213	1,007,567
Repair to steering or front-end	2,579,033	818,159	185,072	298,693	334,477
Repair to engine cooling system	2,656,074	928,715	344,148	202,752	381,741
Motor tune-up	6,182,831	2,410,211	474,481	551,462	1,384,160
Lube, oil change, and oil filters	9,467,460	2,806,010	856,883	788,536	1,160,584
Front-end alignment, wheel balance, rotation	2,335,682	742,367	266,301	185,042	290,927
Shock absorber replacement	610,212	116,170	77,284	17,588	21,184
Tire repair and other repair work	6,168,156	2,137,923	655,396	610,639	871,683
Vehicle air conditioning repair	1,786,613	616,480	190,356	102,903	323,083
Exhaust system repair	1,567,719	458,419	187,890	105,834	164,664
Electrical system repair	3,657,604	985,505	359,506	157,377	468,589
Motor repair, replacement	7,717,533	2,523,142	788,899	792,689	941,482
Auto repair service policy	1,796,396	781,667	189,088	142,904	449,599

	total consumer units	$100,000 or more	$100,000– $119,999	$120,000– $149,999	$150,000 or more
Vehicle insurance	$120,246,030	$32,454,063	$12,921,305	$8,202,922	$11,230,855
Vehicle rental, leases, licenses, other charges	52,917,254	21,413,346	4,615,461	5,069,787	11,726,958
Leased and rented vehicles	24,419,491	11,028,409	1,897,712	2,274,308	6,855,728
Rented vehicles	3,962,099	1,840,587	374,019	358,908	1,107,497
Auto rental	857,232	186,779	32,971	32,550	121,283
Auto rental on trips	2,344,242	1,276,362	163,867	265,960	846,448
Truck rental	228,677	116,386	28,744	28,581	59,080
Truck rental on trips	508,714	245,728	134,912	31,756	79,083
Leased vehicles	20,457,392	9,188,037	1,523,763	1,915,461	5,748,231
Car lease payments	11,723,655	5,399,114	649,619	1,129,490	3,619,663
Truck lease payments	6,904,324	3,132,928	702,527	635,800	1,794,344
Vehicle registration, state	12,642,030	3,823,688	1,148,265	1,053,763	1,621,577
Vehicle registration, local	1,094,469	391,481	105,605	116,277	169,560
Driver's license	1,106,697	262,571	100,321	81,895	80,433
Vehicle inspection	1,436,872	451,078	127,444	114,384	209,228
Parking fees	4,666,472	2,321,463	458,559	601,845	1,260,852
Parking fees in home city, excluding residence	3,915,630	1,934,733	393,181	493,323	1,047,995
Parking fees on trips	750,842	386,731	65,378	108,460	212,857
Tolls	3,710,188	1,834,973	418,614	455,704	960,556
Tolls on trips	530,726	226,295	43,820	81,406	101,027
Towing charges	505,045	127,831	65,166	36,947	25,742
Global positioning services	228,677	94,793	23,037	35,604	36,039
Automobile service clubs	2,576,587	850,764	226,919	217,653	406,133
PUBLIC TRANSPORTATION	63,112,321	30,778,230	5,891,663	7,775,432	17,107,711
Airline fares	41,783,022	21,088,803	4,004,448	5,128,475	11,954,838
Intercity bus fares	1,304,802	462,954	96,305	121,651	244,929
Intracity mass transit fares	9,182,531	2,964,071	641,940	812,842	1,509,241
Local transportation on trips	2,400,494	1,219,141	195,358	372,222	651,484
Taxi fares and limousine service	1,769,493	766,767	254,888	141,743	368,406
Intercity train fares	1,945,586	899,348	268,274	244,402	386,552
Ship fares	4,370,537	3,156,681	430,450	902,492	1,823,546
School bus	354,632	220,465	–	51,604	168,716

Note: Numbers may not add to total because of rounding and missing subcategories. "–" means sample is too small to make a reliable estimate.
Source: Calculations by New Strategist based on the Bureau of Labor Statistics' 2011 Consumer Expenditure Survey

Table 11.12 Transportation: Market shares by high-income consumer units, 2011

(percentage of total annual spending on transportation accounted for by before-tax income group of high-income consumer units, 2011)

	total consumer units	$100,000 or more	$100,000–$119,999	$120,000–$149,999	$150,000 or more
Share of total consumer units	100.0%	17.7%	5.8%	5.0%	6.9%
Share of total before-tax income	100.0	47.1	9.8	10.5	26.8
Share of total spending	100.0	34.7	8.9	8.8	17.1
Share of transportation spending	100.0	33.1	9.7	8.6	14.8
VEHICLE PURCHASES	100.0	37.0	10.7	9.1	17.2
Cars and trucks, new	100.0	46.4	12.7	11.7	22.0
New cars	100.0	40.3	10.3	10.4	19.6
New trucks	100.0	51.7	14.8	12.9	24.0
Cars and trucks, used	100.0	27.1	8.3	6.4	12.4
Used cars	100.0	29.9	8.7	7.4	13.8
Used trucks	100.0	24.2	7.9	5.3	10.9
Other vehicles	100.0	58.7	21.5	15.2	22.0
Used motorcycles	100.0	38.3	29.7	3.3	5.3
GASOLINE AND MOTOR OIL	100.0	27.4	8.5	7.8	11.1
Gasoline	100.0	27.1	8.5	7.7	11.0
Diesel fuel	100.0	25.4	7.0	7.3	11.1
Gasoline on trips	100.0	33.4	9.9	9.6	14.0
Motor oil	100.0	18.7	8.1	4.5	6.1
Motor oil on trips	100.0	33.3	9.8	9.6	14.0
OTHER VEHICLE EXPENSES	100.0	31.6	10.0	8.1	13.6
Vehicle finance charges	100.0	34.4	10.9	9.8	13.7
Automobile finance charges	100.0	31.7	10.9	9.4	11.4
Truck finance charges	100.0	33.4	10.2	10.0	13.1
Motorcycle and plane finance charges	100.0	46.2	15.7	8.6	21.9
Other vehicle finance charges	100.0	54.8	15.0	11.3	28.6
Maintenance and repairs	100.0	31.8	9.4	8.3	14.1
Coolant, additives, brake and transmission fluids	100.0	14.4	4.4	3.3	6.7
Tires—purchased, replaced, installed	100.0	29.6	7.2	9.3	13.1
Parts, equipment, and accessories	100.0	22.2	6.7	6.0	9.5
Vehicle audio equipment	100.0	48.4	4.5	23.8	20.1
Vehicle products and cleaning services	100.0	40.9	20.2	10.6	9.8
Vehicle video equipment	100.0	55.0	17.1	13.0	24.8
Miscellaneous auto repair, servicing	100.0	35.2	11.5	7.5	16.2
Body work and painting	100.0	28.1	8.0	8.2	11.9
Clutch and transmission repair	100.0	33.7	10.5	4.8	18.4
Drive shaft and rear-end repair	100.0	15.9	4.1	6.0	5.8
Brake work	100.0	33.0	9.5	9.6	13.8
Repair to steering or front-end	100.0	31.7	7.2	11.6	13.0
Repair to engine cooling system	100.0	35.0	13.0	7.6	14.4
Motor tune-up	100.0	39.0	7.7	8.9	22.4
Lube, oil change, and oil filters	100.0	29.6	9.1	8.3	12.3
Front-end alignment, wheel balance, rotation	100.0	31.8	11.4	7.9	12.5
Shock absorber replacement	100.0	19.0	12.7	2.9	3.5
Tire repair and other repair work	100.0	34.7	10.6	9.9	14.1
Vehicle air conditioning repair	100.0	34.5	10.7	5.8	18.1
Exhaust system repair	100.0	29.2	12.0	6.8	10.5
Electrical system repair	100.0	26.9	9.8	4.3	12.8
Motor repair, replacement	100.0	32.7	10.2	10.3	12.2
Auto repair service policy	100.0	43.5	10.5	8.0	25.0

	total consumer units	$100,000 or more	$100,000–$119,999	$120,000–$149,999	$150,000 or more
Vehicle insurance	100.0%	27.0%	10.7%	6.8%	9.3%
Vehicle rental, leases, licenses, other charges	100.0	40.5	8.7	9.6	22.2
Leased and rented vehicles	100.0	45.2	7.8	9.3	28.1
Rented vehicles	100.0	46.5	9.4	9.1	28.0
Auto rental	100.0	21.8	3.8	3.8	14.1
Auto rental on trips	100.0	54.4	7.0	11.3	36.1
Truck rental	100.0	50.9	12.6	12.5	25.8
Truck rental on trips	100.0	48.3	26.5	6.2	15.5
Leased vehicles	100.0	44.9	7.4	9.4	28.1
Car lease payments	100.0	46.1	5.5	9.6	30.9
Truck lease payments	100.0	45.4	10.2	9.2	26.0
Vehicle registration, state	100.0	30.2	9.1	8.3	12.8
Vehicle registration, local	100.0	35.8	9.6	10.6	15.5
Driver's license	100.0	23.7	9.1	7.4	7.3
Vehicle inspection	100.0	31.4	8.9	8.0	14.6
Parking fees	100.0	49.7	9.8	12.9	27.0
Parking fees in home city, excluding residence	100.0	49.4	10.0	12.6	26.8
Parking fees on trips	100.0	51.5	8.7	14.4	28.3
Tolls	100.0	49.5	11.3	12.3	25.9
Tolls on trips	100.0	42.6	8.3	15.3	19.0
Towing charges	100.0	25.3	12.9	7.3	5.1
Global positioning services	100.0	41.5	10.1	15.6	15.8
Automobile service clubs	100.0	33.0	8.8	8.4	15.8
PUBLIC TRANSPORTATION	100.0	48.8	9.3	12.3	27.1
Airline fares	100.0	50.5	9.6	12.3	28.6
Intercity bus fares	100.0	35.5	7.4	9.3	18.8
Intracity mass transit fares	100.0	32.3	7.0	8.9	16.4
Local transportation on trips	100.0	50.8	8.1	15.5	27.1
Taxi fares and limousine service	100.0	43.3	14.4	8.0	20.8
Intercity train fares	100.0	46.2	13.8	12.6	19.9
Ship fares	100.0	72.2	9.8	20.6	41.7
School bus	100.0	62.2	–	14.6	47.6

Note: Numbers may not add to total because of rounding. "–" means sample is too small to make a reliable estimate.
Source: Calculations by New Strategist based on the Bureau of Labor Statistics' 2011 Consumer Expenditure Survey

Table 11.13 Transportation: Average spending by household type, 2011

(average annual spending of consumer units on transportation, by type of consumer unit, 2011)

	total married couples	married couples, no children	married couples with children				single parent with child under age 18	single person
			total	oldest child under age 6	oldest child aged 6 to 17	oldest child aged 18 or older		
Number of consumer units (in 000s)	60,144	25,270	29,097	5,825	14,661	8,612	6,956	36,110
Average number of persons per consumer unit	3.2	2.0	4.0	3.5	4.2	3.9	2.9	1.0
Average before-tax income of consumer units	$86,700.00	$78,823.00	$93,677.00	$91,014.00	$93,029.00	$96,583.00	$37,188.00	$34,540.00
Average spending of consumer units, total	63,971.54	57,658.24	69,724.22	65,947.61	70,708.52	70,411.85	37,553.05	30,613.18
Transportation, average spending	**10,971.74**	**9,474.06**	**12,181.55**	**10,697.52**	**12,217.87**	**13,120.11**	**5,471.45**	**4,367.45**
VEHICLE PURCHASES	**3,608.74**	**2,792.96**	**4,301.88**	**3,562.37**	**4,381.58**	**4,666.42**	**1,394.29**	**1,234.71**
Cars and trucks, new	**1,847.62**	**1,557.39**	**2,133.53**	**1,829.78**	**2,085.39**	**2,420.95**	**333.91**	**582.49**
New cars	747.20	637.73	845.78	463.56	788.46	1,201.92	249.85	389.24
New trucks	1,100.41	919.65	1,287.75	1,366.22	1,296.93	1,219.04	84.07	193.25
Cars and trucks, used	**1,682.99**	**1,158.17**	**2,074.27**	**1,724.93**	**2,135.83**	**2,205.78**	**1,027.84**	**628.88**
Used cars	835.52	646.71	941.75	695.68	831.02	1,296.69	410.08	373.66
Used trucks	847.47	511.47	1,132.53	1,029.25	1,304.80	909.09	617.76	255.22
Other vehicles	**78.14**	**77.40**	**94.08**	**7.66**	**160.36**	**39.68**	**32.53**	**23.34**
Used motorcycles	33.90	21.73	51.12	7.66	75.10	39.68	27.84	23.34
GASOLINE AND MOTOR OIL	**3,471.71**	**2,923.12**	**3,852.23**	**3,205.11**	**3,921.09**	**4,172.74**	**2,118.58**	**1,399.05**
Gasoline	3,186.47	2,610.38	3,580.94	2,989.08	3,611.23	3,929.73	2,019.37	1,284.17
Diesel fuel	71.53	73.01	69.80	51.86	83.15	59.20	10.72	31.11
Gasoline on trips	196.73	224.30	183.77	153.83	209.21	160.70	82.15	77.46
Motor oil	14.99	13.17	15.87	8.79	15.37	21.49	5.51	5.52
Motor oil on trips	1.99	2.27	1.86	1.55	2.11	1.62	0.83	0.78
OTHER VEHICLE EXPENSES	**3,204.13**	**3,055.69**	**3,318.72**	**3,296.61**	**3,168.07**	**3,588.26**	**1,636.01**	**1,417.54**
Vehicle finance charges	**329.81**	**247.62**	**391.12**	**452.47**	**382.94**	**363.55**	**144.03**	**98.50**
Automobile finance charges	121.31	96.57	135.11	143.77	118.57	157.41	69.63	53.18
Truck finance charges	174.51	115.99	220.74	287.17	218.04	180.40	69.60	37.08
Motorcycle and plane finance charges	4.86	2.90	6.51	4.04	8.22	5.28	1.78	3.99
Other vehicle finance charges	29.14	32.16	28.76	17.49	38.11	20.47	3.03	4.25
Maintenance and repairs	**1,041.48**	**981.48**	**1,104.56**	**932.98**	**1,158.89**	**1,123.95**	**519.92**	**500.43**
Coolant, additives, brake and transmission fluids	5.40	3.94	6.00	4.43	6.43	6.34	2.76	2.31
Tires—purchased, replaced, installed	191.93	175.69	209.06	186.52	222.74	200.99	86.21	83.41
Parts, equipment, and accessories	55.97	47.88	61.08	68.62	57.28	62.44	27.97	22.82
Vehicle audio equipment	3.60	2.33	4.79	11.43	1.48	5.93	0.83	1.09
Vehicle products and cleaning services	15.96	20.08	12.45	4.96	13.52	14.99	1.80	4.67
Vehicle video equipment	2.03	1.10	2.84	1.59	3.67	2.27	–	0.18
Miscellaneous auto repair, servicing	117.41	127.75	110.84	76.34	103.24	143.64	37.00	69.41
Body work and painting	32.81	27.96	38.12	41.88	34.71	41.37	7.07	14.38
Clutch and transmission repair	37.49	37.94	36.56	20.23	44.56	33.97	52.55	21.09
Drive shaft and rear-end repair	10.15	11.87	9.88	13.77	7.13	11.94	7.21	5.11
Brake work	76.97	73.69	78.92	59.83	80.14	89.77	32.56	37.50
Repair to steering or front-end	25.27	22.12	29.34	15.14	38.61	23.14	19.86	14.59
Repair to engine cooling system	27.62	23.79	28.34	26.07	28.23	30.05	21.38	12.21
Motor tune-up	72.51	73.74	72.50	44.06	81.86	75.80	25.87	26.23
Lube, oil change, and oil filters	99.77	94.32	104.29	105.79	103.87	103.97	57.85	48.67
Front-end alignment, wheel balance, rotation	25.68	23.54	27.67	21.29	31.96	24.68	10.83	12.41
Shock absorber replacement	6.03	5.34	6.54	5.89	8.87	3.03	1.09	3.06
Tire repair and other repair work	59.67	58.49	63.23	62.78	60.75	67.76	39.71	41.36
Vehicle air conditioning repair	20.72	18.42	24.13	25.10	27.24	18.19	13.69	7.59
Exhaust system repair	15.20	13.98	17.67	11.09	20.85	16.69	8.95	9.29
Electrical system repair	35.32	31.59	37.62	29.95	35.13	47.05	18.99	20.72
Motor repair, replacement	81.30	65.43	97.45	83.31	116.35	74.83	44.24	34.21
Auto repair service policy	22.67	20.50	25.27	12.92	30.27	25.10	1.50	8.11

	total married couples	married couples, no children	married couples with children				single parent with child under age 18	single person
			total	oldest child under age 6	oldest child aged 6 to 17	oldest child aged 18 or older		
Vehicle insurance	$1,242.85	$1,243.66	$1,202.99	$1,248.27	$1,083.85	$1,377.47	$698.57	$573.61
Vehicle rental, leases, licenses, other charges	**589.99**	**582.93**	**620.05**	**662.89**	**542.39**	**723.28**	**273.49**	**245.00**
Leased and rented vehicles	279.99	282.02	298.60	335.77	240.78	371.88	122.56	107.40
Rented vehicles	43.00	46.26	41.79	42.57	43.03	39.16	17.29	20.08
Auto rental	7.92	9.63	6.91	5.86	6.76	7.87	5.39	5.96
Auto rental on trips	27.70	32.88	26.14	24.20	30.63	19.80	9.48	9.66
Truck rental	2.60	1.52	3.20	10.16	0.57	2.98	1.56	0.92
Truck rental on trips	4.45	1.98	5.08	0.04	5.07	8.51	0.86	3.46
Leased vehicles	236.99	235.76	256.81	293.20	197.75	332.72	105.27	87.32
Car lease payments	125.55	138.45	126.27	106.34	91.46	199.00	58.39	64.36
Truck lease payments	88.07	76.03	107.38	129.19	97.61	109.25	33.33	15.95
Vehicle registration, state	139.77	140.56	140.88	141.94	135.22	149.78	66.86	54.87
Vehicle registration, local	12.14	12.51	11.45	12.73	7.72	16.93	6.34	4.59
Driver's license	10.87	10.89	10.69	8.73	10.70	11.98	10.90	6.38
Vehicle inspection	15.93	12.41	18.29	16.72	15.67	23.81	7.78	6.79
Parking fees	47.28	46.28	52.09	62.20	50.27	48.36	20.27	29.58
Parking fees in home city, excluding residence	38.34	36.76	43.19	53.03	39.81	42.30	14.50	26.55
Parking fees on trips	8.94	9.52	8.90	9.17	10.46	6.06	5.77	3.03
Tolls	43.33	32.60	51.84	61.66	48.81	50.34	22.04	12.92
Tolls on trips	6.14	6.22	6.24	5.87	6.67	5.76	2.39	2.36
Towing charges	4.49	3.42	4.86	2.66	4.61	6.76	5.63	2.15
Global positioning services	2.90	3.42	2.31	1.22	2.18	3.28	–	0.99
Automobile service clubs	27.15	32.59	22.81	13.39	19.75	34.39	8.72	16.97
PUBLIC TRANSPORTATION	**687.16**	**702.30**	**708.72**	**633.43**	**747.13**	**692.69**	**322.57**	**316.15**
Airline fares	479.10	505.41	478.95	500.13	518.47	397.33	181.68	196.60
Intercity bus fares	12.71	15.74	10.91	5.87	10.60	14.86	6.06	9.32
Intracity mass transit fares	75.41	61.91	86.18	53.99	76.07	125.15	74.63	52.99
Local transportation on trips	26.46	31.12	24.14	19.30	21.24	32.37	11.82	14.49
Taxi fares and limousine service	12.26	5.25	20.40	4.70	17.91	33.71	10.16	19.41
Intercity train fares	21.37	30.65	16.10	8.17	18.42	17.52	5.06	10.92
Ship fares	57.95	52.23	68.52	33.23	80.98	71.16	13.14	11.15
School bus	1.89	–	3.52	8.04	3.45	0.57	20.02	1.27

Note: Average spending figures for total consumer units can be found on Average Spending by Age and Average Spending by Region tables. Subcategories may not add to total because some are not shown. "–" means sample is too small to make a reliable estimate.
Source: Bureau of Labor Statistics, unpublished tables from the 2011 Consumer Expenditure Survey

Table 11.14 Transportation: Indexed spending by household type, 2011

(indexed average annual spending of consumer units on transportation, by type of consumer unit, 2011; index definition: an index of 100 is the average for all consumer units; an index of 125 means that spending by consumer units in that group is 25 percent above the average for all consumer units; an index of 75 indicates spending that is 25 percent below the average for all consumer units)

	total married couples	married couples, no children	married couples with children				single parent with child under age 18	single person
			total	oldest child under age 6	oldest child aged 6 to 17	oldest child aged 18 or older		
Average spending of consumer units, total	$63,972	$57,658	$69,724	$65,948	$70,709	$70,412	$37,553	$30,613
Average spending of consumer units, index	129	116	140	133	142	142	76	62
Transportation, spending index	**132**	**114**	**147**	**129**	**147**	**158**	**66**	**53**
VEHICLE PURCHASES	**135**	**105**	**161**	**133**	**164**	**175**	**52**	**46**
Cars and trucks, new	**146**	**123**	**169**	**145**	**165**	**191**	**26**	**46**
New cars	128	109	145	79	135	206	43	67
New trucks	·161	135	189	200	190	179	12	28
Cars and trucks, used	**126**	**86**	**155**	**129**	**160**	**165**	**77**	**47**
Used cars	122	95	138	102	122	190	60	55
Used trucks	129	78	173	157	199	139	94	39
Other vehicles	**122**	**121**	**147**	**12**	**250**	**62**	**51**	**36**
Used motorcycles	101	65	153	23	224	119	83	70
GASOLINE AND MOTOR OIL	**131**	**110**	**145**	**121**	**148**	**157**	**80**	**53**
Gasoline	130	107	146	122	147	160	82	52
Diesel fuel	138	141	135	100	161	114	21	60
Gasoline on trips	141	161	132	110	150	115	59	56
Motor oil	133	117	141	78	136	190	49	49
Motor oil on trips	141	161	132	110	150	115	59	55
OTHER VEHICLE EXPENSES	**131**	**125**	**135**	**134**	**129**	**146**	**67**	**58**
Vehicle finance charges	**142**	**106**	**168**	**195**	**165**	**156**	**62**	**42**
Automobile finance charges	126	100	140	149	123	164	72	55
Truck finance charges	151	100	191	248	188	156	60	32
Motorcycle and plane finance charges	114	68	152	95	193	124	42	93
Other vehicle finance charges	177	196	175	107	232	125	18	26
Maintenance and repairs	**129**	**122**	**137**	**116**	**144**	**140**	**65**	**62**
Coolant, additives, brake and transmission fluids	121	89	135	100	144	142	62	52
Tires—purchased, replaced, installed	133	122	145	130	155	140	60	58
Parts, equipment, and accessories	122	104	133	149	124	136	61	50
Vehicle audio equipment	158	102	210	501	65	260	36	48
Vehicle products and cleaning services	145	183	113	45	123	136	16	42
Vehicle video equipment	175	95	245	137	316	196	–	16
Miscellaneous auto repair, servicing	128	139	121	83	112	156	40	76
Body work and painting	141	120	164	180	149	177	30	62
Clutch and transmission repair	114	116	111	62	136	104	160	64
Drive shaft and rear-end repair	126	147	122	170	88	148	89	63
Brake work	129	124	133	101	135	151	55	63
Repair to steering or front-end	120	105	139	72	183	110	94	69
Repair to engine cooling system	127	110	130	120	130	138	98	56
Motor tune-up	143	146	143	87	162	150	51	52
Lube, oil change, and oil filters	129	122	135	137	134	134	75	63
Front-end alignment, wheel balance, rotation	134	123	145	111	167	129	57	65
Shock absorber replacement	121	107	131	118	178	61	22	61
Tire repair and other repair work	118	116	125	124	120	134	79	82
Vehicle air conditioning repair	142	126	165	172	186	125	94	52
Exhaust system repair	119	109	138	87	163	130	70	72
Electrical system repair	118	106	126	100	117	157	63	69
Motor repair, replacement	129	104	154	132	184	119	70	54
Auto repair service policy	154	140	172	88	206	171	10	55

	total married couples	married couples, no children	married couples with children				single parent with child under age 18	single person
			total	oldest child under age 6	oldest child aged 6 to 17	oldest child aged 18 or older		
Vehicle insurance	**126**	**126**	**122**	**127**	**110**	**140**	**71**	**58**
Vehicle rental, leases, licenses, other charges	**136**	**135**	**143**	**153**	**125**	**167**	**63**	**57**
Leased and rented vehicles	140	141	150	168	121	186	61	54
Rented vehicles	133	143	129	131	133	121	53	62
Auto rental	113	137	99	84	96	112	77	85
Auto rental on trips	144	172	136	126	160	103	49	50
Truck rental	139	81	171	543	30	159	83	49
Truck rental on trips	107	48	122	1	122	205	21	83
Leased vehicles	142	141	154	175	118	199	63	52
Car lease payments	131	144	132	111	95	208	61	67
Truck lease payments	156	135	190	229	173	193	59	28
Vehicle registration, state	135	136	136	137	131	145	65	53
Vehicle registration, local	136	140	128	142	86	189	71	51
Driver's license	120	120	118	96	118	132	120	70
Vehicle inspection	136	106	156	142	133	203	66	58
Parking fees	124	121	137	163	132	127	53	78
Parking fees in home city, excluding residence	120	115	135	166	124	132	45	83
Parking fees on trips	146	155	145	149	170	99	94	49
Tolls	143	107	171	203	161	166	73	43
Tolls on trips	141	143	144	135	154	133	55	54
Towing charges	109	83	118	64	112	164	136	52
Global positioning services	155	183	124	65	117	175	–	53
Automobile service clubs	129	155	108	64	94	163	41	81
PUBLIC TRANSPORTATION	**133**	**136**	**137**	**123**	**145**	**134**	**63**	**61**
Airline fares	140	148	140	146	152	116	53	58
Intercity bus fares	119	148	102	55	99	139	57	87
Intracity mass transit fares	100	82	115	72	101	167	99	71
Local transportation on trips	135	159	123	98	108	165	60	74
Taxi fares and limousine service	85	36	141	32	124	233	70	134
Intercity train fares	134	193	101	51	116	110	32	69
Ship fares	162	146	192	93	227	199	37	31
School bus	65	–	121	277	119	20	690	44

Note: Spending index for total consumer units is 100. "–" means sample is too small to make a reliable estimate.
Source: Calculations by New Strategist based on the Bureau of Labor Statistics' 2011 Consumer Expenditure Survey

Table 11.15 Transportation: Total spending by household type, 2011

(total annual spending on transportation, by consumer unit type, 2011; consumer units and dollars in thousands)

	total married couples	married couples, no children	married couples with children				single parent with child under age 18	single person
			total	oldest child under age 6	oldest child aged 6 to 17	oldest child aged 18 or older		
Number of consumer units	60,144	25,270	29,097	5,825	14,661	8,612	6,956	36,110
Total spending of all consumer units	$3,847,504,302	$1,457,023,725	$2,028,765,629	$384,144,828	$1,036,657,612	$606,386,852	$261,219,016	$1,105,441,930
Transportation, total spending	659,884,331	239,409,496	354,446,560	62,313,054	179,126,192	112,990,387	38,059,406	157,708,620
VEHICLE PURCHASES	217,044,059	70,578,099	125,171,802	20,750,805	64,238,344	40,187,209	9,698,681	44,585,378
Cars and trucks, new	111,123,257	39,355,245	62,079,322	10,658,469	30,573,903	20,849,221	2,322,678	21,033,714
New cars	44,939,597	16,115,437	24,609,661	2,700,237	11,559,612	10,350,935	1,737,957	14,055,456
New trucks	66,183,059	23,239,556	37,469,662	7,958,232	19,014,291	10,498,372	584,791	6,978,258
Cars and trucks, used	101,221,751	29,266,956	60,355,034	10,047,717	31,313,404	18,996,177	7,149,655	22,708,857
Used cars	50,251,515	16,342,362	27,402,100	4,052,336	12,183,584	11,167,094	2,852,516	13,492,863
Used trucks	50,970,236	12,924,847	32,953,225	5,995,381	19,129,673	7,829,083	4,297,139	9,215,994
Other vehicles	4,699,652	1,955,898	2,737,446	44,620	2,351,038	341,724	226,279	842,807
Used motorcycles	2,038,882	549,117	1,487,439	44,620	1,101,041	341,724	193,655	842,807
GASOLINE AND MOTOR OIL	208,802,526	73,867,242	112,088,336	18,669,766	57,487,100	35,935,637	14,736,842	50,519,696
Gasoline	191,647,052	65,964,303	104,194,611	17,411,391	52,944,243	33,842,835	14,046,738	46,371,379
Diesel fuel	4,302,100	1,844,963	2,030,971	302,085	1,219,062	509,830	74,568	1,123,382
Gasoline on trips	11,832,129	5,668,061	5,347,156	896,060	3,067,228	1,383,948	571,435	2,797,081
Motor oil	901,559	332,806	461,769	51,202	225,340	185,072	38,328	199,327
Motor oil on trips	119,687	57,363	54,120	9,029	30,935	13,951	5,773	28,166
OTHER VEHICLE EXPENSES	192,709,195	77,217,286	96,564,796	19,202,753	46,447,074	30,902,095	11,380,086	51,187,369
Vehicle finance charges	19,836,093	6,257,357	11,380,419	2,635,638	5,614,283	3,130,893	1,001,873	3,556,835
Automobile finance charges	7,296,069	2,440,324	3,931,296	837,460	1,738,355	1,355,615	484,346	1,920,330
Truck finance charges	10,495,729	2,931,067	6,422,872	1,672,765	3,196,684	1,553,605	484,138	1,338,959
Motorcycle and plane finance charges	292,300	73,283	189,421	23,533	120,513	45,471	12,382	144,079
Other vehicle finance charges	1,752,596	812,683	836,830	101,879	558,731	176,288	21,077	153,468
Maintenance and repairs	62,638,773	24,802,000	32,139,382	5,434,609	16,990,486	9,679,457	3,616,564	18,070,527
Coolant, additives, brake and transmission fluids	324,778	99,564	174,582	25,805	94,270	54,600	19,199	83,414
Tires—purchased, replaced, installed	11,543,438	4,439,686	6,083,019	1,086,479	3,265,591	1,730,926	599,677	3,011,935
Parts, equipment, and accessories	3,366,260	1,209,928	1,777,245	399,712	839,782	537,733	194,559	824,030
Vehicle audio equipment	216,518	58,879	139,375	66,580	21,698	51,069	5,773	39,360
Vehicle products and cleaning services	959,898	507,422	362,258	28,892	198,217	129,094	12,521	168,634
Vehicle video equipment	122,092	27,797	82,635	9,262	53,806	19,549	–	6,500
Miscellaneous auto repair, servicing	7,061,507	3,228,243	3,225,111	444,681	1,513,602	1,237,028	257,372	2,506,395
Body work and painting	1,973,325	706,549	1,109,178	243,951	508,883	356,278	49,179	519,262
Clutch and transmission repair	2,254,799	958,744	1,063,786	117,840	653,294	292,550	365,538	761,560
Drive shaft and rear-end repair	610,462	299,955	287,478	80,210	104,533	102,827	50,153	184,522
Brake work	4,629,284	1,862,146	2,296,335	348,510	1,174,933	773,099	226,487	1,354,125
Repair to steering or front-end	1,519,839	558,972	853,706	88,191	566,061	199,282	138,146	526,845
Repair to engine cooling system	1,661,177	601,173	824,609	151,858	413,880	258,791	148,719	440,903
Motor tune-up	4,361,041	1,863,410	2,109,533	256,650	1,200,149	652,790	179,952	947,165
Lube, oil change, and oil filters	6,000,567	2,383,466	3,034,526	616,227	1,522,838	895,390	402,405	1,757,474
Front-end alignment, wheel balance, rotation	1,544,498	594,856	805,114	124,014	468,566	212,544	75,333	448,125
Shock absorber replacement	362,668	134,942	190,294	34,309	130,043	26,094	7,582	110,497
Tire repair and other repair work	3,588,792	1,478,042	1,839,803	365,694	890,656	583,549	276,223	1,493,510
Vehicle air conditioning repair	1,246,184	465,473	702,111	146,208	399,366	156,652	95,228	274,075
Exhaust system repair	914,189	353,275	514,144	64,599	305,682	143,734	62,256	335,462
Electrical system repair	2,124,286	798,279	1,094,629	174,459	515,041	405,195	132,094	748,199
Motor repair, replacement	4,889,707	1,653,416	2,835,503	485,281	1,705,807	644,436	307,733	1,235,323
Auto repair service policy	1,363,464	518,035	735,281	75,259	443,788	216,161	10,434	292,852

	total married couples	married couples, no children	married couples with children				single parent with child under age 18	single person
			total	oldest child under age 6	oldest child aged 6 to 17	oldest child aged 18 or older		
Vehicle insurance	$74,749,970	$31,427,288	$35,003,400	$7,271,173	$15,890,325	$11,862,772	$4,859,253	$20,713,057
Vehicle rental, leases, licenses, other charges	**35,484,359**	**14,730,641**	**18,041,595**	**3,861,334**	**7,951,980**	**6,228,887**	**1,902,396**	**8,846,950**
Leased and rented vehicles	16,839,719	7,126,645	8,688,364	1,955,860	3,530,076	3,202,631	852,527	3,878,214
Rented vehicles	2,586,192	1,168,990	1,215,964	247,970	630,863	337,246	120,269	725,089
Auto rental	476,340	243,350	201,060	34,135	99,108	67,776	37,493	215,216
Auto rental on trips	1,665,989	830,878	760,596	140,965	449,066	170,518	65,943	348,823
Truck rental	156,374	38,410	93,110	59,182	8,357	25,664	10,851	33,221
Truck rental on trips	267,641	50,035	147,813	233	74,331	73,288	5,982	124,941
Leased vehicles	14,253,527	5,957,655	7,472,401	1,707,890	2,899,213	2,865,385	732,258	3,153,125
Car lease payments	7,551,079	3,498,632	3,674,078	619,431	1,340,895	1,713,788	406,161	2,324,040
Truck lease payments	5,296,882	1,921,278	3,124,436	752,532	1,431,060	940,861	231,843	575,955
Vehicle registration, state	8,406,327	3,551,951	4,099,185	826,801	1,982,460	1,289,905	465,078	1,981,356
Vehicle registration, local	730,148	316,128	333,161	74,152	113,183	145,801	44,101	165,745
Driver's license	653,765	275,190	311,047	50,852	156,873	103,172	75,820	230,382
Vehicle inspection	958,094	313,601	532,184	97,394	229,738	205,052	54,118	245,187
Parking fees	2,843,608	1,169,496	1,515,663	362,315	737,008	416,476	140,998	1,068,134
Parking fees in home city, excluding residence	2,305,921	928,925	1,256,699	308,900	583,654	364,288	100,862	958,721
Parking fees on trips	537,687	240,570	258,963	53,415	153,354	52,189	40,136	109,413
Tolls	2,606,040	823,802	1,508,388	359,170	715,603	433,528	153,310	466,541
Tolls on trips	369,284	157,179	181,565	34,193	97,789	49,605	16,625	85,220
Towing charges	270,047	86,423	141,411	15,495	67,587	58,217	39,162	77,637
Global positioning services	174,418	86,423	67,214	7,107	31,961	28,247	–	35,749
Automobile service clubs	1,632,910	823,549	663,703	77,997	289,555	296,167	60,656	612,787
PUBLIC TRANSPORTATION	**41,328,551**	**17,747,121**	**20,621,626**	**3,689,730**	**10,953,673**	**5,965,446**	**2,243,797**	**11,416,177**
Airline fares	28,814,990	12,771,711	13,936,008	2,913,257	7,601,289	3,421,806	1,263,766	7,099,226
Intercity bus fares	764,430	397,750	317,448	34,193	155,407	127,974	42,153	336,545
Intracity mass transit fares	4,535,459	1,564,466	2,507,579	314,492	1,115,262	1,077,792	519,126	1,913,469
Local transportation on trips	1,591,410	786,402	702,402	112,423	311,400	278,770	82,220	523,234
Taxi fares and limousine service	737,365	132,668	593,579	27,378	262,579	290,311	70,673	700,895
Intercity train fares	1,285,277	774,526	468,462	47,590	270,056	150,882	35,197	394,321
Ship fares	3,485,345	1,319,852	1,993,726	193,565	1,187,248	612,830	91,402	402,627
School bus	113,672	–	102,421	46,833	50,580	4,909	139,259	45,860

Note: Total spending figures for total consumer units can be found on Total Spending by Age and Total Spending by Region tables. Spending by type of consumer unit does not add to total because not all types of consumer units are shown. Numbers may not add to category total because of rounding and missing subcategories. "–" means sample is too small to make a reliable estimate.
Source: Calculations by New Strategist based on the Bureau of Labor Statistics' 2011 Consumer Expenditure Survey

Table 11.16 Transportation: Market shares by household type, 2011

(percentage of total annual spending on transportation accounted for by types of consumer units, 2011)

	total married couples	married couples, no children	married couples with children				single parent with child under age 18	single person
			total	oldest child under age 6	oldest child aged 6 to 17	oldest child aged 18 or older		
Share of total consumer units	49.2%	20.7%	23.8%	4.8%	12.0%	7.0%	5.7%	29.5%
Share of total before-tax income	67.0	25.6	35.0	6.8	17.5	10.7	3.3	16.0
Share of total spending	63.3	24.0	33.4	6.3	17.1	10.0	4.3	18.2
Share of transportation spending	65.1	23.6	35.0	6.1	17.7	11.1	3.8	15.6
VEHICLE PURCHASES	**66.5**	**21.6**	**38.4**	**6.4**	**19.7**	**12.3**	**3.0**	**13.7**
Cars and trucks, new	**71.8**	**25.4**	**40.1**	**6.9**	**19.8**	**13.5**	**1.5**	**13.6**
New cars	63.0	22.6	34.5	3.8	16.2	14.5	2.4	19.7
New trucks	79.3	27.9	44.9	9.5	22.8	12.6	0.7	8.4
Cars and trucks, used	**61.8**	**17.9**	**36.9**	**6.1**	**19.1**	**11.6**	**4.4**	**13.9**
Used cars	60.2	19.6	32.8	4.9	14.6	13.4	3.4	16.2
Used trucks	63.6	16.1	41.1	7.5	23.9	9.8	5.4	11.5
Other vehicles	**59.9**	**24.9**	**34.9**	**0.6**	**30.0**	**4.4**	**2.9**	**10.7**
Used motorcycles	49.8	13.4	36.3	1.1	26.9	8.3	4.7	20.6
GASOLINE AND MOTOR OIL	**64.3**	**22.8**	**34.5**	**5.8**	**17.7**	**11.1**	**4.5**	**15.6**
Gasoline	63.9	22.0	34.8	5.8	17.7	11.3	4.7	15.5
Diesel fuel	68.0	29.2	32.1	4.8	19.3	8.1	1.2	17.8
Gasoline on trips	69.5	33.3	31.4	5.3	18.0	8.1	3.4	16.4
Motor oil	65.3	24.1	33.4	3.7	16.3	13.4	2.8	14.4
Motor oil on trips	69.4	33.3	31.4	5.2	17.9	8.1	3.3	16.3
OTHER VEHICLE EXPENSES	**64.2**	**25.7**	**32.2**	**6.4**	**15.5**	**10.3**	**3.8**	**17.1**
Vehicle finance charges	**69.7**	**22.0**	**40.0**	**9.3**	**19.7**	**11.0**	**3.5**	**12.5**
Automobile finance charges	62.0	20.7	33.4	7.1	14.8	11.5	4.1	16.3
Truck finance charges	74.2	20.7	45.4	11.8	22.6	11.0	3.4	9.5
Motorcycle and plane finance charges	56.0	14.0	36.3	4.5	23.1	8.7	2.4	27.6
Other vehicle finance charges	87.3	40.5	41.7	5.1	27.8	8.8	1.0	7.6
Maintenance and repairs	**63.6**	**25.2**	**32.7**	**5.5**	**17.3**	**9.8**	**3.7**	**18.4**
Coolant, additives, brake and transmission fluids	59.7	18.3	32.1	4.7	17.3	10.0	3.5	15.3
Tires—purchased, replaced, installed	65.5	25.2	34.5	6.2	18.5	9.8	3.4	17.1
Parts, equipment, and accessories	59.8	21.5	31.6	7.1	14.9	9.5	3.5	14.6
Vehicle audio equipment	77.7	21.1	50.0	23.9	7.8	18.3	2.1	14.1
Vehicle products and cleaning services	71.4	37.7	26.9	2.1	14.7	9.6	0.9	12.5
Vehicle video equipment	86.1	19.6	58.3	6.5	37.9	13.8	–	4.6
Miscellaneous auto repair, servicing	62.9	28.8	28.7	4.0	13.5	11.0	2.3	22.3
Body work and painting	69.2	24.8	38.9	8.6	17.9	12.5	1.7	18.2
Clutch and transmission repair	56.2	23.9	26.5	2.9	16.3	7.3	9.1	19.0
Drive shaft and rear-end repair	61.8	30.4	29.1	8.1	10.6	10.4	5.1	18.7
Brake work	63.6	25.6	31.6	4.8	16.2	10.6	3.1	18.6
Repair to steering or front-end	58.9	21.7	33.1	3.4	21.9	7.7	5.4	20.4
Repair to engine cooling system	62.5	22.6	31.0	5.7	15.6	9.7	5.6	16.6
Motor tune-up	70.5	30.1	34.1	4.2	19.4	10.6	2.9	15.3
Lube, oil change, and oil filters	63.4	25.2	32.1	6.5	16.1	9.5	4.3	18.6
Front-end alignment, wheel balance, rotation	66.1	25.5	34.5	5.3	20.1	9.1	3.2	19.2
Shock absorber replacement	59.4	22.1	31.2	5.6	21.3	4.3	1.2	18.1
Tire repair and other repair work	58.2	24.0	29.8	5.9	14.4	9.5	4.5	24.2
Vehicle air conditioning repair	69.8	26.1	39.3	8.2	22.4	8.8	5.3	15.3
Exhaust system repair	58.3	22.5	32.8	4.1	19.5	9.2	4.0	21.4
Electrical system repair	58.1	21.8	29.9	4.8	14.1	11.1	3.6	20.5
Motor repair, replacement	63.4	21.4	36.7	6.3	22.1	8.4	4.0	16.0
Auto repair service policy	75.9	28.8	40.9	4.2	24.7	12.0	0.6	16.3

	total married couples	married couples, no children	married couples with children				single parent with child under age 18	single person
			total	oldest child under age 6	oldest child aged 6 to 17	oldest child aged 18 or older		
Vehicle insurance	62.2%	26.1%	29.1%	6.0%	13.2%	9.9%	4.0%	17.2%
Vehicle rental, leases, licenses, other charges	**67.1**	**27.8**	**34.1**	**7.3**	**15.0**	**11.8**	**3.6**	**16.7**
Leased and rented vehicles	69.0	29.2	35.6	8.0	14.5	13.1	3.5	15.9
Rented vehicles	65.3	29.5	30.7	6.3	15.9	8.5	3.0	18.3
Auto rental	55.6	28.4	23.5	4.0	11.6	7.9	4.4	25.1
Auto rental on trips	71.1	35.4	32.4	6.0	19.2	7.3	2.8	14.9
Truck rental	68.4	16.8	40.7	25.9	3.7	11.2	4.7	14.5
Truck rental on trips	52.6	9.8	29.1	0.0	14.6	14.4	1.2	24.6
Leased vehicles	69.7	29.1	36.5	8.3	14.2	14.0	3.6	15.4
Car lease payments	64.4	29.8	31.3	5.3	11.4	14.6	3.5	19.8
Truck lease payments	76.7	27.8	45.3	10.9	20.7	13.6	3.4	8.3
Vehicle registration, state	66.5	28.1	32.4	6.5	15.7	10.2	3.7	15.7
Vehicle registration, local	66.7	28.9	30.4	6.8	10.3	13.3	4.0	15.1
Driver's license	59.1	24.9	28.1	4.6	14.2	9.3	6.9	20.8
Vehicle inspection	66.7	21.8	37.0	6.8	16.0	14.3	3.8	17.1
Parking fees	60.9	25.1	32.5	7.8	15.8	8.9	3.0	22.9
Parking fees in home city, excluding residence	58.9	23.7	32.1	7.9	14.9	9.3	2.6	24.5
Parking fees on trips	71.6	32.0	34.5	7.1	20.4	7.0	5.3	14.6
Tolls	70.2	22.2	40.7	9.7	19.3	11.7	4.1	12.6
Tolls on trips	69.6	29.6	34.2	6.4	18.4	9.3	3.1	16.1
Towing charges	53.5	17.1	28.0	3.1	13.4	11.5	7.8	15.4
Global positioning services	76.3	37.8	29.4	3.1	14.0	12.4	–	15.6
Automobile service clubs	63.4	32.0	25.8	3.0	11.2	11.5	2.4	23.8
PUBLIC TRANSPORTATION	**65.5**	**28.1**	**32.7**	**5.8**	**17.4**	**9.5**	**3.6**	**18.1**
Airline fares	69.0	30.6	33.4	7.0	18.2	8.2	3.0	17.0
Intercity bus fares	58.6	30.5	24.3	2.6	11.9	9.8	3.2	25.8
Intracity mass transit fares	49.4	17.0	27.3	3.4	12.1	11.7	5.7	20.8
Local transportation on trips	66.3	32.8	29.3	4.7	13.0	11.6	3.4	21.8
Taxi fares and limousine service	41.7	7.5	33.5	1.5	14.8	16.4	4.0	39.6
Intercity train fares	66.1	39.8	24.1	2.4	13.9	7.8	1.8	20.3
Ship fares	79.7	30.2	45.6	4.4	27.2	14.0	2.1	9.2
School bus	32.1	–	28.9	13.2	14.3	1.4	39.3	12.9

Note: Market share for total consumer units is 100.0%. Market shares by type of consumer unit do not add to total because not all types of consumer units are shown. "–" means sample is too small to make a reliable estimate.
Source: Calculations by New Strategist based on the Bureau of Labor Statistics' 2011 Consumer Expenditure Survey

Table 11.17 Transportation: Average spending by race and Hispanic origin, 2011

(average annual spending by consumer units on transportation, by race and Hispanic origin of consumer unit reference person, 2011)

	total consumer units	Asian	black	Hispanic	non-Hispanic white and other
Number of consumer units (in 000s)	122,287	5,048	15,118	15,222	92,163
Average number of persons per consumer unit	2.5	2.7	2.6	3.4	2.4
Average before-tax income of consumer units	$63,685.00	$85,415.00	$45,552.00	$49,966.00	$68,907.00
Average spending of consumer units, total	49,704.88	60,136.04	36,643.75	42,085.98	53,055.68
Transportation, average spending	**8,292.79**	**10,280.77**	**5,944.33**	**7,519.87**	**8,798.32**
VEHICLE PURCHASES	**2,668.56**	**3,450.05**	**1,607.94**	**2,207.70**	**2,918.51**
Cars and trucks, new	**1,265.45**	**2,341.53**	**634.30**	**691.00**	**1,464.04**
New cars	583.32	984.82	388.28	314.67	661.48
New trucks	682.12	1,356.71	246.01	376.33	802.56
Cars and trucks, used	**1,338.96**	**1,100.14**	**959.41**	**1,510.69**	**1,372.67**
Used cars	683.11	894.95	661.32	759.56	675.41
Used trucks	655.85	205.19	298.09	751.13	697.25
Other vehicles	**64.16**	**8.38**	**14.24**	**6.01**	**81.80**
Used motorcycles	33.47	8.38	0.88	3.87	43.63
GASOLINE AND MOTOR OIL	**2,654.56**	**2,282.87**	**2,220.52**	**2,721.26**	**2,713.80**
Gasoline	2,450.87	2,185.85	2,133.22	2,582.06	2,480.77
Diesel fuel	51.75	4.24	15.96	34.07	60.42
Gasoline on trips	139.24	85.55	63.54	90.22	159.50
Motor oil	11.29	6.37	7.16	14.00	11.50
Motor oil on trips	1.41	0.86	0.64	0.91	1.61
OTHER VEHICLE EXPENSES	**2,453.57**	**3,075.34**	**1,833.07**	**2,173.54**	**2,595.55**
Vehicle finance charges	**232.60**	**168.40**	**193.88**	**215.50**	**241.53**
Automobile finance charges	96.18	82.99	109.36	89.27	95.14
Truck finance charges	115.73	85.41	74.55	116.61	122.15
Motorcycle and plane finance charges	4.27	–	1.26	3.04	4.96
Other vehicle finance charges	16.42	–	8.71	6.58	19.28
Maintenance and repairs	**804.93**	**717.20**	**587.27**	**638.15**	**866.65**
Coolant, additives, brake and transmission fluids	4.45	3.92	4.38	5.85	4.22
Tires—purchased, replaced, installed	144.02	106.87	91.32	121.39	156.24
Parts, equipment, and accessories	46.06	35.96	24.87	46.17	49.41
Vehicle audio equipment	2.28	0.24	0.23	1.70	2.71
Vehicle products and cleaning services	11.00	7.34	7.99	7.23	12.01
Vehicle video equipment	1.16	1.91	–	–	1.54
Miscellaneous auto repair, servicing	91.82	58.21	57.57	59.33	101.86
Body work and painting	23.31	25.86	18.13	16.69	25.39
Clutch and transmission repair	32.80	48.83	27.47	29.07	34.39
Drive shaft and rear-end repair	8.08	10.96	4.12	7.19	8.86
Brake work	59.49	53.94	50.51	43.83	63.63
Repair to steering or front-end	21.09	14.10	14.09	8.97	24.20
Repair to engine cooling system	21.72	16.57	21.89	19.63	21.99
Motor tune-up	50.56	76.63	41.22	45.33	52.95
Lube, oil change, and oil filters	77.42	81.83	57.33	70.80	81.71
Front-end alignment, wheel balance, rotation	19.10	18.78	13.98	11.65	21.13
Shock absorber replacement	4.99	1.91	4.08	3.69	5.36
Tire repair and other repair work	50.44	45.10	45.83	30.03	54.49
Vehicle air conditioning repair	14.61	7.08	12.69	13.39	15.09
Exhaust system repair	12.82	11.12	13.75	7.04	13.59
Electrical system repair	29.91	17.98	27.12	25.35	31.16
Motor repair, replacement	63.11	49.59	40.95	55.51	67.86
Auto repair service policy	14.69	22.47	7.77	8.34	16.88

	total consumer units	Asian	black	Hispanic	non-Hispanic white and other
Vehicle insurance	$983.31	$1,608.12	$767.40	$933.93	$1,023.17
Vehicle rental, leases, licenses, other charges	432.73	581.62	284.52	385.96	464.21
Leased and rented vehicles	199.69	272.95	133.59	175.71	214.02
Rented vehicles	32.40	72.92	29.89	10.88	36.29
Auto rental	7.01	28.02	11.59	4.38	6.68
Auto rental on trips	19.17	31.27	14.14	3.37	22.56
Truck rental	1.87	11.47	0.54	1.42	2.16
Truck rental on trips	4.16	2.15	3.62	1.68	4.65
Leased vehicles	167.29	200.03	103.71	164.83	177.73
Car lease payments	95.87	118.89	82.31	75.07	101.30
Truck lease payments	56.46	75.08	20.01	69.00	60.24
Vehicle registration, state	103.38	111.44	63.67	102.02	109.96
Vehicle registration, local	8.95	14.60	7.06	8.08	9.38
Driver's license	9.05	11.80	9.52	6.32	9.50
Vehicle inspection	11.75	13.20	7.74	13.84	12.08
Parking fees	38.16	79.66	23.35	24.86	42.82
Parking fees in home city, excluding residence	32.02	71.57	20.92	21.13	35.69
Parking fees on trips	6.14	8.09	2.43	3.73	7.13
Tolls	30.34	50.68	20.50	34.11	31.34
Tolls on trips	4.34	5.02	2.33	3.16	4.88
Towing charges	4.13	4.09	3.55	7.04	3.73
Global positioning services	1.87	0.58	0.87	1.15	2.15
Automobile service clubs	21.07	17.59	12.33	9.67	24.34
PUBLIC TRANSPORTATION	516.10	1,472.51	282.80	417.37	570.46
Airline fares	341.68	1,050.88	132.25	236.66	392.86
Intercity bus fares	10.67	25.25	5.32	12.03	11.32
Intracity mass transit fares	75.09	231.61	118.27	109.27	62.79
Local transportation on trips	19.63	51.63	4.87	14.87	22.81
Taxi fares and limousine service	14.47	39.57	5.65	13.72	15.93
Intercity train fares	15.91	23.66	6.43	7.87	18.76
Ship fares	35.74	46.58	9.08	19.93	42.80
School bus	2.90	3.33	0.92	3.02	3.20

Note: "Asian" and "black" include Hispanics and non-Hispanics who identify themselves as being of the respective race alone. "Hispanic" includes people of any race who identify themselves as Hispanic. "Other" includes people who identify themselves as non-Hispanic and as Alaska Native, American Indian, Asian (who are also included in the "Asian" column), or Native Hawaiian or other Pacific Islander, as well as non-Hispanics reporting more than one race. Subcategories may not add to total because some are not shown. "–" means sample is too small to make a reliable estimate.
Source: Bureau of Labor Statistics, unpublished tables from the 2011 Consumer Expenditure Survey

(indexed average annual spending of consumer units on transportation, by race and Hispanic origin of consumer unit reference person, 2011; index definition: an index of 100 is the average for all consumer units; an index of 125 means that spending by consumer units in that group is 25 percent above the average for all consumer units; an index of 75 indicates spending that is 25 percent below the average for all consumer units)

	total consumer units	Asian	black	Hispanic	non-Hispanic white and other
Average spending of consumer units, total	$49,705	$60,136	$36,644	$42,086	$53,056
Average spending of consumer units, index	100	121	74	85	107
Transportation, spending index	100	124	72	91	106
VEHICLE PURCHASES	100	129	60	83	109
Cars and trucks, new	100	185	50	55	116
New cars	100	169	67	54	113
New trucks	100	199	36	55	118
Cars and trucks, used	100	82	72	113	103
Used cars	100	131	97	111	99
Used trucks	100	31	45	115	106
Other vehicles	100	13	22	9	127
Used motorcycles	100	25	3	12	130
GASOLINE AND MOTOR OIL	100	86	84	103	102
Gasoline	100	89	87	105	101
Diesel fuel	100	8	31	66	117
Gasoline on trips	100	61	46	65	115
Motor oil	100	56	63	124	102
Motor oil on trips	100	61	45	65	114
OTHER VEHICLE EXPENSES	100	125	75	89	106
Vehicle finance charges	100	72	83	93	104
Automobile finance charges	100	86	114	93	99
Truck finance charges	100	74	64	101	106
Motorcycle and plane finance charges	100	–	30	71	116
Other vehicle finance charges	100	–	53	40	117
Maintenance and repairs	100	89	73	79	108
Coolant, additives, brake and transmission fluids	100	88	98	131	95
Tires—purchased, replaced, installed	100	74	63	84	108
Parts, equipment, and accessories	100	78	54	100	107
Vehicle audio equipment	100	11	10	75	119
Vehicle products and cleaning services	100	67	73	66	109
Vehicle video equipment	100	165	–	–	133
Miscellaneous auto repair, servicing	100	63	63	65	111
Body work and painting	100	111	78	72	109
Clutch and transmission repair	100	149	84	89	105
Drive shaft and rear-end repair	100	136	51	89	110
Brake work	100	91	85	74	107
Repair to steering or front-end	100	67	67	43	115
Repair to engine cooling system	100	76	101	90	101
Motor tune-up	100	152	82	90	105
Lube, oil change, and oil filters	100	106	74	91	106
Front-end alignment, wheel balance, rotation	100	98	73	61	111
Shock absorber replacement	100	38	82	74	107
Tire repair and other repair work	100	89	91	60	108
Vehicle air conditioning repair	100	48	87	92	103
Exhaust system repair	100	87	107	55	106
Electrical system repair	100	60	91	85	104
Motor repair, replacement	100	79	65	88	108
Auto repair service policy	100	153	53	57	115

	total consumer units	Asian	black	Hispanic	non-Hispanic white and other
Vehicle insurance	**100**	**164**	**78**	**95**	**104**
Vehicle rental, leases, licenses, other charges	**100**	**134**	**66**	**89**	**107**
Leased and rented vehicles	100	137	67	88	107
Rented vehicles	100	225	92	34	112
Auto rental	100	400	165	62	95
Auto rental on trips	100	163	74	18	118
Truck rental	100	613	29	76	116
Truck rental on trips	100	52	87	40	112
Leased vehicles	100	120	62	99	106
Car lease payments	100	124	86	78	106
Truck lease payments	100	133	35	122	107
Vehicle registration, state	100	108	62	99	106
Vehicle registration, local	100	163	79	90	105
Driver's license	100	130	105	70	105
Vehicle inspection	100	112	66	118	103
Parking fees	100	209	61	65	112
Parking fees in home city, excluding residence	100	224	65	66	111
Parking fees on trips	100	132	40	61	116
Tolls	100	167	68	112	103
Tolls on trips	100	116	54	73	112
Towing charges	100	99	86	170	90
Global positioning services	100	31	47	61	115
Automobile service clubs	100	83	59	46	116
PUBLIC TRANSPORTATION	**100**	**285**	**55**	**81**	**111**
Airline fares	100	308	39	69	115
Intercity bus fares	100	237	50	113	106
Intracity mass transit fares	100	308	158	146	84
Local transportation on trips	100	263	25	76	116
Taxi fares and limousine service	100	273	39	95	110
Intercity train fares	100	149	40	49	118
Ship fares	100	130	25	56	120
School bus	100	115	32	104	110

Note: "Asian" and "black" include Hispanics and non-Hispanics who identify themselves as being of the respective race alone. "Hispanic" includes people of any race who identify themselves as Hispanic. "Other" includes people who identify themselves as non-Hispanic and as Alaska Native, American Indian, Asian (who are also included in the "Asian" column), or Native Hawaiian or other Pacific Islander, as well as non-Hispanics reporting more than one race. "–" means sample is too small to make a reliable estimate.
Source: Calculations by New Strategist based on the Bureau of Labor Statistics' 2011 Consumer Expenditure Survey

Table 11.19 Transportation: Total spending by race and Hispanic origin, 2011

(total annual spending on transportation, by consumer unit race and Hispanic origin groups, 2011; consumer units and dollars in thousands)

	total consumer units	Asian	black	Hispanic	non-Hispanic white and other
Number of consumer units	122,287	5,048	15,118	15,222	92,163
Total spending of all consumer units	$6,078,260,661	$303,566,730	$553,980,213	$640,632,788	$4,889,770,636
Transportation, total spending	1,014,100,411	51,897,327	89,866,381	114,467,461	810,879,566
VEHICLE PURCHASES	326,330,197	17,415,852	24,308,837	33,605,609	268,978,637
Cars and trucks, new	154,748,084	11,820,043	9,589,347	10,518,402	134,930,319
New cars	71,332,453	4,971,371	5,870,017	4,789,907	60,963,981
New trucks	83,414,408	6,848,672	3,719,179	5,728,495	73,966,337
Cars and trucks, used	163,737,402	5,553,507	14,504,360	22,995,723	126,509,385
Used cars	83,535,473	4,517,708	9,997,836	11,562,022	62,247,812
Used trucks	80,201,929	1,035,799	4,506,525	11,433,701	64,260,652
Other vehicles	7,845,934	42,302	215,280	91,484	7,538,933
Used motorcycles	4,092,946	42,302	13,304	58,909	4,021,072
GASOLINE AND MOTOR OIL	324,618,179	11,523,928	33,569,821	41,423,020	250,111,949
Gasoline	299,709,540	11,034,171	32,250,020	39,304,117	228,635,206
Diesel fuel	6,328,352	21,404	241,283	518,614	5,568,488
Gasoline on trips	17,027,242	431,856	960,598	1,373,329	14,699,999
Motor oil	1,380,620	32,156	108,245	213,108	1,059,875
Motor oil on trips	172,425	4,341	9,676	13,852	148,382
OTHER VEHICLE EXPENSES	300,039,715	15,524,316	27,712,352	33,085,626	239,213,675
Vehicle finance charges	28,443,956	850,083	2,931,078	3,280,341	22,260,129
Automobile finance charges	11,761,564	418,934	1,653,304	1,358,868	8,768,388
Truck finance charges	14,152,275	431,150	1,127,047	1,775,037	11,257,710
Motorcycle and plane finance charges	522,165	–	19,049	46,275	457,128
Other vehicle finance charges	2,007,953	–	131,678	100,161	1,776,903
Maintenance and repairs	98,432,475	3,620,426	8,878,348	9,713,919	79,873,064
Coolant, additives, brake and transmission fluids	544,177	19,788	66,217	89,049	388,928
Tires—purchased, replaced, installed	17,611,774	539,480	1,380,576	1,847,799	14,399,547
Parts, equipment, and accessories	5,632,539	181,526	375,985	702,800	4,553,774
Vehicle audio equipment	278,814	1,212	3,477	25,877	249,762
Vehicle products and cleaning services	1,345,157	37,052	120,793	110,055	1,106,878
Vehicle video equipment	141,853	9,642	–	–	141,931
Miscellaneous auto repair, servicing	11,228,392	293,844	870,343	903,121	9,387,723
Body work and painting	2,850,510	130,541	274,089	254,055	2,340,019
Clutch and transmission repair	4,011,014	246,494	415,291	442,504	3,169,486
Drive shaft and rear-end repair	988,079	55,326	62,286	109,446	816,564
Brake work	7,274,854	272,289	763,610	667,180	5,864,332
Repair to steering or front-end	2,579,033	71,177	213,013	136,541	2,230,345
Repair to engine cooling system	2,656,074	83,645	330,933	298,808	2,026,664
Motor tune-up	6,182,831	386,828	623,164	690,013	4,880,031
Lube, oil change, and oil filters	9,467,460	413,078	866,715	1,077,718	7,530,639
Front-end alignment, wheel balance, rotation	2,335,682	94,801	211,350	177,336	1,947,404
Shock absorber replacement	610,212	9,642	61,681	56,169	493,994
Tire repair and other repair work	6,168,156	227,665	692,858	457,117	5,021,962
Vehicle air conditioning repair	1,786,613	35,740	191,847	203,823	1,390,740
Exhaust system repair	1,567,719	56,134	207,873	107,163	1,252,495
Electrical system repair	3,657,604	90,763	410,000	385,878	2,871,799
Motor repair, replacement	7,717,533	250,330	619,082	844,973	6,254,181
Auto repair service policy	1,796,396	113,429	117,467	126,951	1,555,711

	total consumer units	Asian	black	Hispanic	non-Hispanic white and other
Vehicle insurance	$120,246,030	$8,117,790	$11,601,553	$14,216,282	$94,298,417
Vehicle rental, leases, licenses, other charges	52,917,254	2,936,018	4,301,373	5,875,083	42,782,986
Leased and rented vehicles	24,419,491	1,377,852	2,019,614	2,674,658	19,724,725
Rented vehicles	3,962,099	368,100	451,877	165,615	3,344,595
Auto rental	857,232	141,445	175,218	66,672	615,649
Auto rental on trips	2,344,242	157,851	213,769	51,298	2,079,197
Truck rental	228,677	57,901	8,164	21,615	199,072
Truck rental on trips	508,714	10,853	54,727	25,573	428,558
Leased vehicles	20,457,392	1,009,751	1,567,888	2,509,042	16,380,130
Car lease payments	11,723,655	600,157	1,244,363	1,142,716	9,336,112
Truck lease payments	6,904,324	379,004	302,511	1,050,318	5,551,899
Vehicle registration, state	12,642,030	562,549	962,563	1,552,948	10,134,243
Vehicle registration, local	1,094,469	73,701	106,733	122,994	864,489
Driver's license	1,106,697	59,566	143,923	96,203	875,549
Vehicle inspection	1,436,872	66,634	117,013	210,672	1,113,329
Parking fees	4,666,472	402,124	353,005	378,419	3,946,420
Parking fees in home city, excluding residence	3,915,630	361,285	316,269	321,641	3,289,297
Parking fees on trips	750,842	40,838	36,737	56,778	657,122
Tolls	3,710,188	255,833	309,919	519,222	2,888,388
Tolls on trips	530,726	25,341	35,225	48,102	449,755
Towing charges	505,045	20,646	53,669	107,163	343,768
Global positioning services	228,677	2,928	13,153	17,505	198,150
Automobile service clubs	2,576,587	88,794	186,405	147,197	2,243,247
PUBLIC TRANSPORTATION	63,112,321	7,433,230	4,275,370	6,353,206	52,575,305
Airline fares	41,783,022	5,304,842	1,999,356	3,602,439	36,207,156
Intercity bus fares	1,304,802	127,462	80,428	183,121	1,043,285
Intracity mass transit fares	9,182,531	1,169,167	1,788,006	1,663,308	5,786,915
Local transportation on trips	2,400,494	260,628	73,625	226,351	2,102,238
Taxi fares and limousine service	1,769,493	199,749	85,417	208,846	1,468,157
Intercity train fares	1,945,586	119,436	97,209	119,797	1,728,978
Ship fares	4,370,537	235,136	137,271	303,374	3,944,576
School bus	354,632	16,810	13,909	45,970	294,922

Note: "Asian" and "black" include Hispanics and non-Hispanics who identify themselves as being of the respective race alone. "Hispanic" includes people of any race who identify themselves as Hispanic. "Other" includes people who identify themselves as non-Hispanic and as Alaska Native, American Indian, Asian (who are also included in the "Asian" column), or Native Hawaiian or other Pacific Islander, as well as non-Hispanics reporting more than one race. Numbers may not add to total because of rounding and missing subcategories. "–" means sample is too small to make a reliable estimate.
Source: Calculations by New Strategist based on the Bureau of Labor Statistics' 2011 Consumer Expenditure Survey

Table 11.20 Transportation: Market shares by race and Hispanic origin, 2011

(percentage of total annual spending on transportation accounted for by consumer unit race and Hispanic origin groups, 2011)

	total consumer units	Asian	black	Hispanic	non-Hispanic white and other
Share of total consumer units	100.0%	4.1%	12.4%	12.4%	75.4%
Share of total before-tax income	100.0	5.5	8.8	9.8	81.5
Share of total spending	100.0	5.0	9.1	10.5	80.4
Share of transportation spending	100.0	5.1	8.9	11.3	80.0
VEHICLE PURCHASES	100.0	5.3	7.4	10.3	82.4
Cars and trucks, new	100.0	7.6	6.2	6.8	87.2
New cars	100.0	7.0	8.2	6.7	85.5
New trucks	100.0	8.2	4.5	6.9	88.7
Cars and trucks, used	100.0	3.4	8.9	14.0	77.3
Used cars	100.0	5.4	12.0	13.8	74.5
Used trucks	100.0	1.3	5.6	14.3	80.1
Other vehicles	100.0	0.5	2.7	1.2	96.1
Used motorcycles	100.0	1.0	0.3	1.4	98.2
GASOLINE AND MOTOR OIL	100.0	3.5	10.3	12.8	77.0
Gasoline	100.0	3.7	10.8	13.1	76.3
Diesel fuel	100.0	0.3	3.8	8.2	88.0
Gasoline on trips	100.0	2.5	5.6	8.1	86.3
Motor oil	100.0	2.3	7.8	15.4	76.8
Motor oil on trips	100.0	2.5	5.6	8.0	86.1
OTHER VEHICLE EXPENSES	100.0	5.2	9.2	11.0	79.7
Vehicle finance charges	100.0	3.0	10.3	11.5	78.3
Automobile finance charges	100.0	3.6	14.1	11.6	74.6
Truck finance charges	100.0	3.0	8.0	12.5	79.5
Motorcycle and plane finance charges	100.0	–	3.6	8.9	87.5
Other vehicle finance charges	100.0	–	6.6	5.0	88.5
Maintenance and repairs	100.0	3.7	9.0	9.9	81.1
Coolant, additives, brake and transmission fluids	100.0	3.6	12.2	16.4	71.5
Tires—purchased, replaced, installed	100.0	3.1	7.8	10.5	81.8
Parts, equipment, and accessories	100.0	3.2	6.7	12.5	80.8
Vehicle audio equipment	100.0	0.4	1.2	9.3	89.6
Vehicle products and cleaning services	100.0	2.8	9.0	8.2	82.3
Vehicle video equipment	100.0	6.8	–	–	100.1
Miscellaneous auto repair, servicing	100.0	2.6	7.8	8.0	83.6
Body work and painting	100.0	4.6	9.6	8.9	82.1
Clutch and transmission repair	100.0	6.1	10.4	11.0	79.0
Drive shaft and rear-end repair	100.0	5.6	6.3	11.1	82.6
Brake work	100.0	3.7	10.5	9.2	80.6
Repair to steering or front-end	100.0	2.8	8.3	5.3	86.5
Repair to engine cooling system	100.0	3.1	12.5	11.2	76.3
Motor tune-up	100.0	6.3	10.1	11.2	78.9
Lube, oil change, and oil filters	100.0	4.4	9.2	11.4	79.5
Front-end alignment, wheel balance, rotation	100.0	4.1	9.0	7.6	83.4
Shock absorber replacement	100.0	1.6	10.1	9.2	81.0
Tire repair and other repair work	100.0	3.7	11.2	7.4	81.4
Vehicle air conditioning repair	100.0	2.0	10.7	11.4	77.8
Exhaust system repair	100.0	3.6	13.3	6.8	79.9
Electrical system repair	100.0	2.5	11.2	10.6	78.5
Motor repair, replacement	100.0	3.2	8.0	10.9	81.0
Auto repair service policy	100.0	6.3	6.5	7.1	86.6

	total consumer units	Asian	black	Hispanic	non-Hispanic white and other
Vehicle insurance	**100.0%**	**6.8%**	**9.6%**	**11.8%**	**78.4%**
Vehicle rental, leases, licenses, other charges	**100.0**	**5.5**	**8.1**	**11.1**	**80.8**
Leased and rented vehicles	100.0	5.6	8.3	11.0	80.8
Rented vehicles	100.0	9.3	11.4	4.2	84.4
Auto rental	100.0	16.5	20.4	7.8	71.8
Auto rental on trips	100.0	6.7	9.1	2.2	88.7
Truck rental	100.0	25.3	3.6	9.5	87.1
Truck rental on trips	100.0	2.1	10.8	5.0	84.2
Leased vehicles	100.0	4.9	7.7	12.3	80.1
Car lease payments	100.0	5.1	10.6	9.7	79.6
Truck lease payments	100.0	5.5	4.4	15.2	80.4
Vehicle registration, state	100.0	4.4	7.6	12.3	80.2
Vehicle registration, local	100.0	6.7	9.8	11.2	79.0
Driver's license	100.0	5.4	13.0	8.7	79.1
Vehicle inspection	100.0	4.6	8.1	14.7	77.5
Parking fees	100.0	8.6	7.6	8.1	84.6
Parking fees in home city, excluding residence	100.0	9.2	8.1	8.2	84.0
Parking fees on trips	100.0	5.4	4.9	7.6	87.5
Tolls	100.0	6.9	8.4	14.0	77.9
Tolls on trips	100.0	4.8	6.6	9.1	84.7
Towing charges	100.0	4.1	10.6	21.2	68.1
Global positioning services	100.0	1.3	5.8	7.7	86.7
Automobile service clubs	100.0	3.4	7.2	5.7	87.1
PUBLIC TRANSPORTATION	**100.0**	**11.8**	**6.8**	**10.1**	**83.3**
Airline fares	100.0	12.7	4.8	8.6	86.7
Intercity bus fares	100.0	9.8	6.2	14.0	80.0
Intracity mass transit fares	100.0	12.7	19.5	18.1	63.0
Local transportation on trips	100.0	10.9	3.1	9.4	87.6
Taxi fares and limousine service	100.0	11.3	4.8	11.8	83.0
Intercity train fares	100.0	6.1	5.0	6.2	88.9
Ship fares	100.0	5.4	3.1	6.9	90.3
School bus	100.0	4.7	3.9	13.0	83.2

Note: "Asian" and "black" include Hispanics and non-Hispanics who identify themselves as being of the respective race alone. "Hispanic" includes people of any race who identify themselves as Hispanic. "Other" includes people who identify themselves as non-Hispanic and as Alaska Native, American Indian, Asian (who are also included in the "Asian" column), or Native Hawaiian or other Pacific Islander, as well as non-Hispanics reporting more than one race. "–" means sample is too small to make a reliable estimate.
Source: Calculations by New Strategist based on the Bureau of Labor Statistics' 2011 Consumer Expenditure Survey

Table 11.21 Transportation: Average spending by region, 2011

(average annual spending of consumer units on transportation, by region in which consumer unit lives, 2011)

	total consumer units	Northeast	Midwest	South	West
Number of consumer units (in 000s)	122,287	22,538	27,107	44,901	27,741
Average number of persons per consumer unit	2.5	2.4	2.4	2.5	2.6
Average before-tax income of consumer units	$63,685.00	$71,733.00	$60,897.00	$58,780.00	$67,810.00
Average spending of consumer units, total	49,704.88	54,547.45	47,191.54	45,698.60	54,745.43
Transportation, average spending	8,292.79	8,434.59	8,113.81	8,264.36	8,399.34
VEHICLE PURCHASES	2,668.56	2,675.29	2,805.37	2,736.21	2,419.93
Cars and trucks, new	1,265.45	1,416.85	1,255.04	1,289.82	1,113.16
New cars	583.32	828.23	515.89	589.50	440.25
New trucks	682.12	588.62	739.15	700.33	672.90
Cars and trucks, used	1,338.96	1,161.43	1,464.02	1,403.15	1,257.07
Used cars	683.11	636.91	662.42	745.01	640.67
Used trucks	655.85	524.53	801.60	658.14	616.41
Other vehicles	64.16	97.01	86.31	43.24	49.70
Used motorcycles	33.47	26.96	56.61	12.83	49.56
GASOLINE AND MOTOR OIL	2,654.56	2,509.99	2,632.30	2,793.68	2,568.61
Gasoline	2,450.87	2,373.06	2,402.28	2,605.20	2,311.77
Diesel fuel	51.75	20.80	50.99	51.10	78.69
Gasoline on trips	139.24	107.24	167.39	124.23	162.04
Motor oil	11.29	7.81	9.95	11.89	14.47
Motor oil on trips	1.41	1.08	1.69	1.25	1.64
OTHER VEHICLE EXPENSES	2,453.57	2,519.02	2,222.74	2,400.27	2,713.01
Vehicle finance charges	232.60	198.37	220.37	267.49	215.90
Automobile finance charges	96.18	89.41	84.82	111.69	87.67
Truck finance charges	115.73	100.71	111.40	136.63	98.32
Motorcycle and plane finance charges	4.27	1.16	5.67	5.15	4.02
Other vehicle finance charges	16.42	7.09	18.48	14.02	25.88
Maintenance and repairs	804.93	822.58	759.02	718.98	975.11
Coolant, additives, brake and transmission fluids	4.45	4.20	3.65	4.43	5.47
Tires—purchased, replaced, installed	144.02	149.88	129.32	130.64	175.29
Parts, equipment, and accessories	46.06	35.32	48.13	37.86	66.03
Vehicle audio equipment	2.28	2.54	1.24	2.31	3.03
Vehicle products and cleaning services	11.00	10.83	8.26	12.00	12.24
Vehicle video equipment	1.16	1.49	1.42	0.70	1.37
Miscellaneous auto repair, servicing	91.82	78.35	95.55	78.14	121.79
Body work and painting	23.31	32.44	16.40	20.43	27.30
Clutch and transmission repair	32.80	29.99	29.31	37.18	31.42
Drive shaft and rear-end repair	8.08	10.33	9.29	6.52	7.59
Brake work	59.49	93.55	54.64	44.95	60.08
Repair to steering or front-end	21.09	31.10	26.40	14.71	18.10
Repair to engine cooling system	21.72	24.61	19.90	17.73	27.62
Motor tune-up	50.56	44.52	41.43	37.51	85.53
Lube, oil change, and oil filters	77.42	70.23	76.21	80.23	79.89
Front-end alignment, wheel balance, rotation	19.10	20.36	23.95	17.84	15.39
Shock absorber replacement	4.99	6.94	6.07	3.10	5.39
Tire repair and other repair work	50.44	48.68	46.29	48.27	59.42
Vehicle air conditioning repair	14.61	9.85	11.76	20.71	11.37
Exhaust system repair	12.82	22.24	14.20	9.25	9.60
Electrical system repair	29.91	33.36	31.62	24.39	34.35
Motor repair, replacement	63.11	54.02	51.99	54.10	95.96
Auto repair service policy	14.69	7.74	11.99	15.98	20.89

	total consumer units	Northeast	Midwest	South	West
Vehicle insurance	$983.31	$869.81	$847.90	$1,097.62	$1,023.06
Vehicle rental, leases, licenses, other charges	432.73	628.27	395.45	316.19	498.94
Leased and rented vehicles	199.69	333.04	179.06	142.98	203.29
Rented vehicles	32.40	25.51	27.10	28.52	49.45
Auto rental	7.01	3.72	4.46	9.31	8.44
Auto rental on trips	19.17	18.99	16.50	13.89	30.47
Truck rental	1.87	1.80	1.69	1.39	2.90
Truck rental on trips	4.16	0.73	3.95	3.90	7.59
Leased vehicles	167.29	307.53	151.97	114.46	153.84
Car lease payments	95.87	151.06	91.68	72.72	92.60
Truck lease payments	56.46	111.62	51.61	31.73	56.44
Vehicle registration, state	103.38	60.15	122.99	75.08	165.16
Vehicle registration, local	8.95	4.79	8.60	13.05	6.04
Driver's license	9.05	12.53	8.94	7.67	8.57
Vehicle inspection	11.75	26.00	1.93	10.37	11.98
Parking fees	38.16	68.06	38.03	21.64	40.75
Parking fees in home city, excluding residence	32.02	60.03	32.37	16.41	34.22
Parking fees on trips	6.14	8.03	5.66	5.23	6.53
Tolls	30.34	73.26	9.87	24.17	25.47
Tolls on trips	4.34	9.13	3.70	3.10	3.10
Towing charges	4.13	3.57	4.56	3.77	4.74
Global positioning services	1.87	2.64	2.27	1.37	1.67
Automobile service clubs	21.07	35.10	15.51	13.00	28.16
PUBLIC TRANSPORTATION	516.10	730.29	453.40	334.20	697.79
Airline fares	341.68	368.18	312.03	238.39	516.32
Intercity bus fares	10.67	11.02	11.42	7.83	14.25
Intracity mass transit fares	75.09	228.16	35.05	27.65	66.63
Local transportation on trips	19.63	19.30	21.05	13.70	28.11
Taxi fares and limousine service	14.47	36.07	18.85	4.71	8.48
Intercity train fares	15.91	17.57	14.59	13.21	20.23
Ship fares	35.74	47.21	39.82	22.63	43.67
School bus	2.90	2.78	0.59	6.08	0.11

Note: Subcategories may not add to total because some are not shown.
Source: Bureau of Labor Statistics, unpublished tables from the 2011 Consumer Expenditure Survey

Table 11.22 Transportation: Indexed spending by region, 2011

(indexed average annual spending of consumer units on transportation, by region in which consumer unit lives, 2011; index definition: an index of 100 is the average for all consumer units; an index of 125 means that spending by consumer units in that group is 25 percent above the average for all consumer units; an index of 75 indicates spending that is 25 percent below the average for all consumer units)

	total consumer units	Northeast	Midwest	South	West
Average spending of consumer units, total	$49,705	$54,547	$47,192	$45,699	$54,745
Average spending of consumer units, index	100	110	95	92	110
Transportation, spending index	100	102	98	100	101
VEHICLE PURCHASES	100	100	105	103	91
Cars and trucks, new	100	112	99	102	88
New cars	100	142	88	101	75
New trucks	100	86	108	103	99
Cars and trucks, used	100	87	109	105	94
Used cars	100	93	97	109	94
Used trucks	100	80	122	100	94
Other vehicles	100	151	135	67	77
Used motorcycles	100	81	169	38	148
GASOLINE AND MOTOR OIL	100	95	99	105	97
Gasoline	100	97	98	106	94
Diesel fuel	100	40	99	99	152
Gasoline on trips	100	77	120	89	116
Motor oil	100	69	88	105	128
Motor oil on trips	100	77	120	89	116
OTHER VEHICLE EXPENSES	100	103	91	98	111
Vehicle finance charges	100	85	95	115	93
Automobile finance charges	100	93	88	116	91
Truck finance charges	100	87	96	118	85
Motorcycle and plane finance charges	100	27	133	121	94
Other vehicle finance charges	100	43	113	85	158
Maintenance and repairs	100	102	94	89	121
Coolant, additives, brake and transmission fluids	100	94	82	100	123
Tires—purchased, replaced, installed	100	104	90	91	122
Parts, equipment, and accessories	100	77	104	82	143
Vehicle audio equipment	100	111	54	101	133
Vehicle products and cleaning services	100	98	75	109	111
Vehicle video equipment	100	128	122	60	118
Miscellaneous auto repair, servicing	100	85	104	85	133
Body work and painting	100	139	70	88	117
Clutch and transmission repair	100	91	89	113	96
Drive shaft and rear-end repair	100	128	115	81	94
Brake work	100	157	92	76	101
Repair to steering or front-end	100	147	125	70	86
Repair to engine cooling system	100	113	92	82	127
Motor tune-up	100	88	82	74	169
Lube, oil change, and oil filters	100	91	98	104	103
Front-end alignment, wheel balance, rotation	100	107	125	93	81
Shock absorber replacement	100	139	122	62	108
Tire repair and other repair work	100	97	92	96	118
Vehicle air conditioning repair	100	67	80	142	78
Exhaust system repair	100	173	111	72	75
Electrical system repair	100	112	106	82	115
Motor repair, replacement	100	86	82	86	152
Auto repair service policy	100	53	82	109	142

	total consumer units	Northeast	Midwest	South	West
Vehicle insurance	100	88	86	112	104
Vehicle rental, leases, licenses, other charges	100	145	91	73	115
Leased and rented vehicles	100	167	90	72	102
Rented vehicles	100	79	84	88	153
Auto rental	100	53	64	133	120
Auto rental on trips	100	99	86	72	159
Truck rental	100	96	90	74	155
Truck rental on trips	100	18	95	94	182
Leased vehicles	100	184	91	68	92
Car lease payments	100	158	96	76	97
Truck lease payments	100	198	91	56	100
Vehicle registration, state	100	58	119	73	160
Vehicle registration, local	100	54	96	146	67
Driver's license	100	138	99	85	95
Vehicle inspection	100	221	16	88	102
Parking fees	100	178	100	57	107
Parking fees in home city, excluding residence	100	187	101	51	107
Parking fees on trips	100	131	92	85	106
Tolls	100	241	33	80	84
Tolls on trips	100	210	85	71	71
Towing charges	100	86	110	91	115
Global positioning services	100	141	121	73	89
Automobile service clubs	100	167	74	62	134
PUBLIC TRANSPORTATION	100	142	88	65	135
Airline fares	100	108	91	70	151
Intercity bus fares	100	103	107	73	134
Intracity mass transit fares	100	304	47	37	89
Local transportation on trips	100	98	107	70	143
Taxi fares and limousine service	100	249	130	33	59
Intercity train fares	100	110	92	83	127
Ship fares	100	132	111	63	122
School bus	100	96	20	210	4

Source: Calculations by New Strategist based on the Bureau of Labor Statistics' 2011 Consumer Expenditure Survey

Table 11.23 Transportation: Total spending by region, 2011

(total annual spending on transportation, by region in which consumer units live, 2011; consumer units and dollars in thousands)

	total consumer units	Northeast	Midwest	South	West
Number of consumer units	122,287	22,538	27,107	44,901	27,741
Total spending of all consumer units	$6,078,260,661	$1,229,390,428	$1,279,221,075	$2,051,912,839	$1,518,692,974
Transportation, total spending	**1,014,100,411**	**190,098,789**	**219,941,048**	**371,078,028**	**233,006,091**
VEHICLE PURCHASES	**326,330,197**	**60,295,686**	**76,045,165**	**122,858,565**	**67,131,278**
Cars and trucks, new	**154,748,084**	**31,932,965**	**34,020,369**	**57,914,208**	**30,880,172**
New cars	71,332,453	18,666,648	13,984,230	26,469,140	12,212,975
New trucks	83,414,408	13,266,318	20,036,139	31,445,517	18,666,919
Cars and trucks, used	**163,737,402**	**26,176,309**	**39,685,190**	**63,002,838**	**34,872,379**
Used cars	83,535,473	14,354,678	17,956,219	33,451,694	17,772,826
Used trucks	80,201,929	11,821,857	21,728,971	29,551,144	17,099,830
Other vehicles	**7,845,934**	**2,186,411**	**2,339,605**	**1,941,519**	**1,378,728**
Used motorcycles	4,092,946	607,624	1,534,527	576,080	1,374,844
GASOLINE AND MOTOR OIL	**324,618,179**	**56,570,155**	**71,353,756**	**125,439,026**	**71,255,810**
Gasoline	299,709,540	53,484,026	65,118,604	116,976,085	64,130,812
Diesel fuel	6,328,352	468,790	1,382,186	2,294,441	2,182,939
Gasoline on trips	17,027,242	2,416,975	4,537,441	5,578,051	4,495,152
Motor oil	1,380,620	176,022	269,715	533,873	401,412
Motor oil on trips	172,425	24,341	45,811	56,126	45,495
OTHER VEHICLE EXPENSES	**300,039,715**	**56,773,673**	**60,251,813**	**107,774,523**	**75,261,610**
Vehicle finance charges	**28,443,956**	**4,470,863**	**5,973,570**	**12,010,568**	**5,989,282**
Automobile finance charges	11,761,564	2,015,123	2,299,216	5,014,993	2,432,053
Truck finance charges	14,152,275	2,269,802	3,019,720	6,134,824	2,727,495
Motorcycle and plane finance charges	522,165	26,144	153,697	231,240	111,519
Other vehicle finance charges	2,007,953	159,794	500,937	629,512	717,937
Maintenance and repairs	**98,432,475**	**18,539,308**	**20,574,755**	**32,282,921**	**27,050,527**
Coolant, additives, brake and transmission fluids	544,177	94,660	98,941	198,911	151,743
Tires—purchased, replaced, installed	17,611,774	3,377,995	3,505,477	5,865,867	4,862,720
Parts, equipment, and accessories	5,632,539	796,042	1,304,660	1,699,952	1,831,738
Vehicle audio equipment	278,814	57,247	33,613	103,721	84,055
Vehicle products and cleaning services	1,345,157	244,087	223,904	538,812	339,550
Vehicle video equipment	141,853	33,582	38,492	31,431	38,005
Miscellaneous auto repair, servicing	11,228,392	1,765,852	2,590,074	3,508,564	3,378,576
Body work and painting	2,850,510	731,133	444,555	917,327	757,329
Clutch and transmission repair	4,011,014	675,915	794,506	1,669,419	871,622
Drive shaft and rear-end repair	988,079	232,818	251,824	292,755	210,554
Brake work	7,274,854	2,108,430	1,481,126	2,018,300	1,666,679
Repair to steering or front-end	2,579,033	700,932	715,625	660,494	502,112
Repair to engine cooling system	2,656,074	554,660	539,429	796,095	766,206
Motor tune-up	6,182,831	1,003,392	1,123,043	1,684,237	2,372,688
Lube, oil change, and oil filters	9,467,460	1,582,844	2,065,824	3,602,407	2,216,228
Front-end alignment, wheel balance, rotation	2,335,682	458,874	649,213	801,034	426,934
Shock absorber replacement	610,212	156,414	164,539	139,193	149,524
Tire repair and other repair work	6,168,156	1,097,150	1,254,783	2,167,371	1,648,370
Vehicle air conditioning repair	1,786,613	221,999	318,778	929,900	315,415
Exhaust system repair	1,567,719	501,245	384,919	415,334	266,314
Electrical system repair	3,657,604	751,868	857,123	1,095,135	952,903
Motor repair, replacement	7,717,533	1,217,503	1,409,293	2,429,144	2,662,026
Auto repair service policy	1,796,396	174,444	325,013	717,518	579,509

	total consumer units	Northeast	Midwest	South	West
Vehicle insurance	$120,246,030	$19,603,778	$22,984,025	$49,284,236	$28,380,707
Vehicle rental, leases, licenses, other charges	52,917,254	14,159,949	10,719,463	14,197,247	13,841,095
Leased and rented vehicles	24,419,491	7,506,056	4,853,779	6,419,945	5,639,468
Rented vehicles	3,962,099	574,944	734,600	1,280,577	1,371,792
Auto rental	857,232	83,841	120,897	418,028	234,134
Auto rental on trips	2,344,242	427,997	447,266	623,675	845,268
Truck rental	228,677	40,568	45,811	62,412	80,449
Truck rental on trips	508,714	16,453	107,073	175,114	210,554
Leased vehicles	20,457,392	6,931,111	4,119,451	5,139,368	4,267,675
Car lease payments	11,723,655	3,404,590	2,485,170	3,265,201	2,568,817
Truck lease payments	6,904,324	2,515,692	1,398,992	1,424,709	1,565,702
Vehicle registration, state	12,642,030	1,355,661	3,333,890	3,371,167	4,581,704
Vehicle registration, local	1,094,469	107,957	233,120	585,958	167,556
Driver's license	1,106,697	282,401	242,337	344,391	237,740
Vehicle inspection	1,436,872	585,988	52,317	465,623	332,337
Parking fees	4,666,472	1,533,936	1,030,879	971,658	1,130,446
Parking fees in home city, excluding residence	3,915,630	1,352,956	877,454	736,825	949,297
Parking fees on trips	750,842	180,980	153,426	234,832	181,149
Tolls	3,710,188	1,651,134	267,546	1,085,257	706,563
Tolls on trips	530,726	205,772	100,296	139,193	85,997
Towing charges	505,045	80,461	123,608	169,277	131,492
Global positioning services	228,677	59,500	61,533	61,514	46,327
Automobile service clubs	2,576,587	791,084	420,430	583,713	781,187
PUBLIC TRANSPORTATION	63,112,321	16,459,276	12,290,314	15,005,914	19,357,392
Airline fares	41,783,022	8,298,041	8,458,197	10,703,949	14,323,233
Intercity bus fares	1,304,802	248,369	309,562	351,575	395,309
Intracity mass transit fares	9,182,531	5,142,270	950,100	1,241,513	1,848,383
Local transportation on trips	2,400,494	434,983	570,602	615,144	779,800
Taxi fares and limousine service	1,769,493	812,946	510,967	211,484	235,244
Intercity train fares	1,945,586	395,993	395,491	593,142	561,200
Ship fares	4,370,537	1,064,019	1,079,401	1,016,110	1,211,449
School bus	354,632	62,656	15,993	272,998	3,052

Note: Numbers may not add to total because of rounding and missing subcategories.
Source: Calculations by New Strategist based on the Bureau of Labor Statistics' 2011 Consumer Expenditure Survey

Table 11.24 Transportation: Market shares by region, 2011

(percentage of total annual spending on transportation accounted for by consumer units by region of residence, 2011)

	total consumer units	Northeast	Midwest	South	West
Share of total consumer units	100.0%	18.4%	22.2%	36.7%	22.7%
Share of total before-tax income	100.0	20.8	21.2	33.9	24.2
Share of total spending	100.0	20.2	21.0	33.8	25.0
Share of transportation spending	100.0	18.7	21.7	36.6	23.0
VEHICLE PURCHASES	100.0	18.5	23.3	37.6	20.6
Cars and trucks, new	100.0	20.6	22.0	37.4	20.0
New cars	100.0	26.2	19.6	37.1	17.1
New trucks	100.0	15.9	24.0	37.7	22.4
Cars and trucks, used	100.0	16.0	24.2	38.5	21.3
Used cars	100.0	17.2	21.5	40.0	21.3
Used trucks	100.0	14.7	27.1	36.8	21.3
Other vehicles	100.0	27.9	29.8	24.7	17.6
Used motorcycles	100.0	14.8	37.5	14.1	33.6
GASOLINE AND MOTOR OIL	100.0	17.4	22.0	38.6	22.0
Gasoline	100.0	17.8	21.7	39.0	21.4
Diesel fuel	100.0	7.4	21.8	36.3	34.5
Gasoline on trips	100.0	14.2	26.6	32.8	26.4
Motor oil	100.0	12.7	19.5	38.7	29.1
Motor oil on trips	100.0	14.1	26.6	32.6	26.4
OTHER VEHICLE EXPENSES	100.0	18.9	20.1	35.9	25.1
Vehicle finance charges	100.0	15.7	21.0	42.2	21.1
Automobile finance charges	100.0	17.1	19.5	42.6	20.7
Truck finance charges	100.0	16.0	21.3	43.3	19.3
Motorcycle and plane finance charges	100.0	5.0	29.4	44.3	21.4
Other vehicle finance charges	100.0	8.0	24.9	31.4	35.8
Maintenance and repairs	100.0	18.8	20.9	32.8	27.5
Coolant, additives, brake and transmission fluids	100.0	17.4	18.2	36.6	27.9
Tires—purchased, replaced, installed	100.0	19.2	19.9	33.3	27.6
Parts, equipment, and accessories	100.0	14.1	23.2	30.2	32.5
Vehicle audio equipment	100.0	20.5	12.1	37.2	30.1
Vehicle products and cleaning services	100.0	18.1	16.6	40.1	25.2
Vehicle video equipment	100.0	23.7	27.1	22.2	26.8
Miscellaneous auto repair, servicing	100.0	15.7	23.1	31.2	30.1
Body work and painting	100.0	25.6	15.6	32.2	26.6
Clutch and transmission repair	100.0	16.9	19.8	41.6	21.7
Drive shaft and rear-end repair	100.0	23.6	25.5	29.6	21.3
Brake work	100.0	29.0	20.4	27.7	22.9
Repair to steering or front-end	100.0	27.2	27.7	25.6	19.5
Repair to engine cooling system	100.0	20.9	20.3	30.0	28.8
Motor tune-up	100.0	16.2	18.2	27.2	38.4
Lube, oil change, and oil filters	100.0	16.7	21.8	38.1	23.4
Front-end alignment, wheel balance, rotation	100.0	19.6	27.8	34.3	18.3
Shock absorber replacement	100.0	25.6	27.0	22.8	24.5
Tire repair and other repair work	100.0	17.8	20.3	35.1	26.7
Vehicle air conditioning repair	100.0	12.4	17.8	52.0	17.7
Exhaust system repair	100.0	32.0	24.6	26.5	17.0
Electrical system repair	100.0	20.6	23.4	29.9	26.1
Motor repair, replacement	100.0	15.8	18.3	31.5	34.5
Auto repair service policy	100.0	9.7	18.1	39.9	32.3

	total consumer units	Northeast	Midwest	South	West
Vehicle insurance	**100.0%**	**16.3%**	**19.1%**	**41.0%**	**23.6%**
Vehicle rental, leases, licenses, other charges	**100.0**	**26.8**	**20.3**	**26.8**	**26.2**
Leased and rented vehicles	100.0	30.7	19.9	26.3	23.1
Rented vehicles	100.0	14.5	18.5	32.3	34.6
Auto rental	100.0	9.8	14.1	48.8	27.3
Auto rental on trips	100.0	18.3	19.1	26.6	36.1
Truck rental	100.0	17.7	20.0	27.3	35.2
Truck rental on trips	100.0	3.2	21.0	34.4	41.4
Leased vehicles	100.0	33.9	20.1	25.1	20.9
Car lease payments	100.0	29.0	21.2	27.9	21.9
Truck lease payments	100.0	36.4	20.3	20.6	22.7
Vehicle registration, state	100.0	10.7	26.4	26.7	36.2
Vehicle registration, local	100.0	9.9	21.3	53.5	15.3
Driver's license	100.0	25.5	21.9	31.1	21.5
Vehicle inspection	100.0	40.8	3.6	32.4	23.1
Parking fees	100.0	32.9	22.1	20.8	24.2
Parking fees in home city, excluding residence	100.0	34.6	22.4	18.8	24.2
Parking fees on trips	100.0	24.1	20.4	31.3	24.1
Tolls	100.0	44.5	7.2	29.3	19.0
Tolls on trips	100.0	38.8	18.9	26.2	16.2
Towing charges	100.0	15.9	24.5	33.5	26.0
Global positioning services	100.0	26.0	26.9	26.9	20.3
Automobile service clubs	100.0	30.7	16.3	22.7	30.3
PUBLIC TRANSPORTATION	**100.0**	**26.1**	**19.5**	**23.8**	**30.7**
Airline fares	100.0	19.9	20.2	25.6	34.3
Intercity bus fares	100.0	19.0	23.7	26.9	30.3
Intracity mass transit fares	100.0	56.0	10.3	13.5	20.1
Local transportation on trips	100.0	18.1	23.8	25.6	32.5
Taxi fares and limousine service	100.0	45.9	28.9	12.0	13.3
Intercity train fares	100.0	20.4	20.3	30.5	28.8
Ship fares	100.0	24.3	24.7	23.2	27.7
School bus	100.0	17.7	4.5	77.0	0.9

Note: Numbers may not add to total because of rounding.
Source: Calculations by New Strategist based on the Bureau of Labor Statistics' 2011 Consumer Expenditure Survey

Table 11.25 Transportation: Average spending by education, 2011

(average annual spending of consumer units on transportation, by education of consumer unit reference person, 2011)

	total consumer units	less than high school graduate	high school graduate	some college	associate's degree	bachelor's degree or more total	bachelor's degree	graduate degree
Number of consumer units (in 000s)	122,287	16,146	30,810	25,361	12,912	37,058	23,578	13,480
Average number of persons per consumer unit	2.5	2.8	2.5	2.3	2.6	2.5	2.5	2.4
Average before-tax income of consumer units	$63,685.00	$32,564.00	$46,370.00	$52,965.00	$63,664.00	$98,983.00	$90,962.00	$113,013.00
Average spending of consumer units, total	49,704.88	29,950.97	39,704.28	45,355.33	50,819.44	68,902.95	65,051.01	75,731.40
Transportation, average spending	**8,292.79**	**4,858.71**	**7,119.63**	**8,060.95**	**8,964.12**	**10,661.61**	**10,564.91**	**10,813.13**
VEHICLE PURCHASES	**2,668.56**	**1,231.38**	**2,258.41**	**2,563.91**	**3,123.42**	**3,548.87**	**3,612.83**	**3,436.99**
Cars and trucks, new	1,265.45	205.64	886.76	1,161.45	1,261.93	2,114.43	2,083.16	2,169.13
New cars	583.32	103.81	395.92	525.54	683.07	952.84	879.15	1,081.73
New trucks	682.12	101.83	490.85	635.91	578.86	1,161.59	1,204.01	1,087.41
Cars and trucks, used	1,338.96	983.94	1,326.11	1,328.22	1,779.10	1,358.30	1,471.62	1,160.09
Used cars	683.11	442.47	608.21	674.61	988.07	749.77	808.53	647.00
Used trucks	655.85	541.46	717.90	653.61	791.03	608.53	663.09	513.09
Other vehicles	64.16	41.80	45.53	74.24	82.39	76.14	58.05	107.77
Used motorcycles	33.47	37.37	33.62	38.28	66.74	16.76	1.59	43.29
GASOLINE AND MOTOR OIL	**2,654.56**	**2,006.04**	**2,551.55**	**2,613.10**	**3,020.72**	**2,923.55**	**2,934.42**	**2,904.55**
Gasoline	2,450.87	1,890.14	2,373.53	2,408.53	2,778.58	2,674.26	2,692.17	2,642.95
Diesel fuel	51.75	49.08	64.19	57.57	67.98	32.93	37.45	25.02
Gasoline on trips	139.24	53.03	99.52	134.39	159.14	206.23	193.48	228.52
Motor oil	11.29	13.25	13.31	11.26	13.42	8.05	9.36	5.76
Motor oil on trips	1.41	0.54	1.01	1.36	1.61	2.08	1.95	2.31
OTHER VEHICLE EXPENSES	**2,453.57**	**1,387.79**	**2,060.92**	**2,533.31**	**2,465.70**	**3,158.32**	**3,192.21**	**3,081.66**
Vehicle finance charges	**232.60**	**110.37**	**205.65**	**247.98**	**318.29**	**267.89**	**283.19**	**241.13**
Automobile finance charges	96.18	45.48	77.05	108.24	121.83	116.97	120.04	111.59
Truck finance charges	115.73	58.60	112.22	120.15	154.26	127.08	131.51	119.33
Motorcycle and plane finance charges	4.27	1.69	3.19	7.87	5.20	3.52	4.35	2.08
Other vehicle finance charges	16.42	4.60	13.19	11.72	37.00	20.32	27.29	8.13
Maintenance and repairs	**804.93**	**427.18**	**634.33**	**787.05**	**859.02**	**1,098.93**	**1,082.36**	**1,127.85**
Coolant, additives, brake and transmission fluids	4.45	5.58	5.50	4.44	5.67	2.66	2.48	2.97
Tires—purchased, replaced, installed	144.02	90.03	114.88	151.56	160.69	180.81	175.77	189.62
Parts, equipment, and accessories	46.06	29.36	48.43	60.10	53.50	39.15	40.49	36.81
Vehicle audio equipment	2.28	0.85	2.43	1.71	2.12	3.22	4.42	1.11
Vehicle products and cleaning services	11.00	7.13	8.60	9.84	10.23	15.33	9.29	27.15
Vehicle video equipment	1.16	0.08	0.67	0.73	1.49	2.21	1.54	3.39
Miscellaneous auto repair, servicing	91.82	32.10	53.66	90.28	100.95	142.08	148.47	129.56
Body work and painting	23.31	5.94	16.15	27.89	25.95	32.77	29.73	38.07
Clutch and transmission repair	32.80	12.56	37.11	21.83	39.02	43.38	31.17	64.75
Drive shaft and rear-end repair	8.08	3.77	9.36	7.10	8.59	9.38	9.77	8.69
Brake work	59.49	26.55	48.71	57.71	54.95	85.59	80.22	94.98
Repair to steering or front-end	21.09	7.17	15.77	24.57	20.31	29.47	33.22	22.91
Repair to engine cooling system	21.72	13.48	15.71	21.15	21.97	30.61	32.43	27.43
Motor tune-up	50.56	26.91	29.83	37.85	59.00	83.86	86.28	79.62
Lube, oil change, and oil filters	77.42	45.60	68.47	72.87	83.44	99.73	98.00	102.78
Front-end alignment, wheel balance, rotation	19.10	11.35	15.14	18.51	19.16	26.17	27.53	23.78
Shock absorber replacement	4.99	1.38	4.24	3.02	8.92	7.15	8.17	5.38
Tire repair and other repair work	50.44	27.26	30.66	46.15	59.89	76.62	77.19	75.62
Vehicle air conditioning repair	14.61	5.51	12.93	12.16	14.49	21.68	23.09	19.21
Exhaust system repair	12.82	9.25	9.02	11.03	8.81	20.16	21.86	17.19
Electrical system repair	29.91	25.07	26.74	26.25	23.07	39.53	36.88	44.16
Motor repair, replacement	63.11	37.73	48.19	63.46	59.37	87.64	83.16	95.48
Auto repair service policy	14.69	2.52	12.09	16.85	17.44	19.73	21.18	17.20

	total consumer units	less than high school graduate	high school graduate	some college	associate's degree	bachelor's degree or more		
						total	bachelor's degree	graduate degree
Vehicle insurance	$983.31	$646.88	$929.66	$1,128.94	$884.42	$1,087.81	$1,170.44	$925.98
Vehicle rental, leases, licenses, other charges	432.73	203.35	291.28	369.35	403.96	703.68	656.22	786.70
Leased and rented vehicles	199.69	87.18	118.10	158.90	169.19	355.08	334.35	391.36
Rented vehicles	32.40	6.93	14.14	25.03	26.40	65.81	54.39	85.80
Auto rental	7.01	2.36	4.00	5.40	7.39	12.51	9.12	18.44
Auto rental on trips	19.17	2.74	6.29	15.15	10.04	42.97	37.52	52.49
Truck rental	1.87	0.26	1.17	2.00	2.35	2.91	3.16	2.49
Truck rental on trips	4.16	1.56	2.69	1.93	6.63	7.19	4.59	11.73
Leased vehicles	167.29	80.25	103.95	133.88	142.79	289.27	279.96	305.56
Car lease payments	95.87	45.82	67.21	69.06	88.89	162.28	155.73	173.75
Truck lease payments	56.46	28.46	31.76	43.83	30.82	106.79	104.89	110.10
Vehicle registration, state	103.38	66.72	89.95	96.43	117.06	130.52	122.68	144.23
Vehicle registration, local	8.95	4.64	6.97	8.72	6.63	13.44	13.20	13.87
Driver's license	9.05	6.83	8.07	8.97	12.02	9.86	9.32	10.79
Vehicle inspection	11.75	8.09	11.39	10.43	12.62	14.23	13.57	15.40
Parking fees	38.16	7.16	13.18	30.18	30.58	80.55	69.28	100.24
Parking fees in home city, excluding residence	32.02	6.38	10.32	25.62	26.44	67.58	58.75	83.01
Parking fees on trips	6.14	0.77	2.86	4.56	4.14	12.97	10.54	17.23
Tolls	30.34	8.68	17.06	26.73	23.40	55.71	55.17	56.67
Tolls on trips	4.34	1.17	2.67	3.78	3.89	7.67	6.42	9.86
Towing charges	4.13	2.90	4.49	3.93	4.33	4.43	3.93	5.32
Global positioning services	1.87	0.69	1.87	1.30	3.06	2.37	1.95	3.11
Automobile service clubs	21.07	9.31	17.55	19.97	21.19	29.82	26.36	35.87
PUBLIC TRANSPORTATION	516.10	233.49	248.74	350.63	354.28	1,030.87	825.46	1,389.93
Airline fares	341.68	106.06	155.72	212.16	250.59	719.33	563.81	991.37
Intercity bus fares	10.67	7.17	5.34	10.38	8.25	17.66	15.94	20.67
Intracity mass transit fares	75.09	73.19	49.06	63.09	46.65	115.68	103.83	136.40
Local transportation on trips	19.63	10.00	8.78	15.79	14.54	37.26	29.62	50.62
Taxi fares and limousine service	14.47	25.86	5.63	6.24	4.46	25.72	26.94	23.32
Intercity train fares	15.91	3.95	6.74	14.46	12.48	30.94	20.88	48.54
Ship fares	35.74	6.43	17.05	25.72	16.77	77.53	61.96	104.77
School bus	2.90	0.84	0.41	2.80	0.52	6.76	2.49	14.23

Note: Subcategories may not add to total because some are not shown.
Source: Bureau of Labor Statistics, unpublished tables from the 2011 Consumer Expenditure Survey

Table 11.26 Transportation: Indexed spending by education, 2011

(indexed average annual spending of consumer units on transportation, by education of consumer unit reference person, 2011; index definition: an index of 100 is the average for all consumer units; an index of 125 means that spending by consumer units in that group is 25 percent above the average for all consumer units; an index of 75 indicates spending that is 25 percent below the average for all consumer units)

	total consumer units	less than high school graduate	high school graduate	some college	associate's degree	bachelor's degree or more total	bachelor's degree	graduate degree
Average spending of consumer units, total	$49,705	$29,951	$39,704	$45,355	$50,819	$68,903	$65,051	$75,731
Average spending of consumer units, index	100	60	80	91	102	139	131	152
Transportation, spending index	100	59	86	97	108	129	127	130
VEHICLE PURCHASES	100	46	85	96	117	133	135	129
Cars and trucks, new	100	16	70	92	100	167	165	171
New cars	100	18	68	90	117	163	151	185
New trucks	100	15	72	93	85	170	177	159
Cars and trucks, used	100	73	99	99	133	101	110	87
Used cars	100	65	89	99	145	110	118	95
Used trucks	100	83	109	100	121	93	101	78
Other vehicles	100	65	71	116	128	119	90	168
Used motorcycles	100	112	100	114	199	50	5	129
GASOLINE AND MOTOR OIL	100	76	96	98	114	110	111	109
Gasoline	100	77	97	98	113	109	110	108
Diesel fuel	100	95	124	111	131	64	72	48
Gasoline on trips	100	38	71	97	114	148	139	164
Motor oil	100	117	118	100	119	71	83	51
Motor oil on trips	100	38	72	96	114	148	138	164
OTHER VEHICLE EXPENSES	100	57	84	103	100	129	130	126
Vehicle finance charges	100	47	88	107	137	115	122	104
Automobile finance charges	100	47	80	113	127	122	125	116
Truck finance charges	100	51	97	104	133	110	114	103
Motorcycle and plane finance charges	100	40	75	184	122	82	102	49
Other vehicle finance charges	100	28	80	71	225	124	166	50
Maintenance and repairs	100	53	79	98	107	137	134	140
Coolant, additives, brake and transmission fluids	100	125	124	100	127	60	56	67
Tires—purchased, replaced, installed	100	63	80	105	112	126	122	132
Parts, equipment, and accessories	100	64	105	130	116	85	88	80
Vehicle audio equipment	100	37	107	75	93	141	194	49
Vehicle products and cleaning services	100	65	78	89	93	139	84	247
Vehicle video equipment	100	7	58	63	128	191	133	292
Miscellaneous auto repair, servicing	100	35	58	98	110	155	162	141
Body work and painting	100	25	69	120	111	141	128	163
Clutch and transmission repair	100	38	113	67	119	132	95	197
Drive shaft and rear-end repair	100	47	116	88	106	116	121	108
Brake work	100	45	82	97	92	144	135	160
Repair to steering or front-end	100	34	75	117	96	140	158	109
Repair to engine cooling system	100	62	72	97	101	141	149	126
Motor tune-up	100	53	59	75	117	166	171	157
Lube, oil change, and oil filters	100	59	88	94	108	129	127	133
Front-end alignment, wheel balance, rotation	100	59	79	97	100	137	144	125
Shock absorber replacement	100	28	85	61	179	143	164	108
Tire repair and other repair work	100	54	61	91	119	152	153	150
Vehicle air conditioning repair	100	38	89	83	99	148	158	131
Exhaust system repair	100	72	70	86	69	157	171	134
Electrical system repair	100	84	89	88	77	132	123	148
Motor repair, replacement	100	60	76	101	94	139	132	151
Auto repair service policy	100	17	82	115	119	134	144	117

	total consumer units	less than high school graduate	high school graduate	some college	associate's degree	bachelor's degree or more		
						total	bachelor's degree	graduate degree
Vehicle insurance	100	66	95	115	90	111	119	94
Vehicle rental, leases, licenses, other charges	100	47	67	85	93	163	152	182
Leased and rented vehicles	100	44	59	80	85	178	167	196
Rented vehicles	100	21	44	77	81	203	168	265
Auto rental	100	34	57	77	105	178	130	263
Auto rental on trips	100	14	33	79	52	224	196	274
Truck rental	100	14	63	107	126	156	169	133
Truck rental on trips	100	38	65	46	159	173	110	282
Leased vehicles	100	48	62	80	85	173	167	183
Car lease payments	100	48	70	72	93	169	162	181
Truck lease payments	100	50	56	78	55	189	186	195
Vehicle registration, state	100	65	87	93	113	126	119	140
Vehicle registration, local	100	52	78	97	74	150	147	155
Driver's license	100	75	89	99	133	109	103	119
Vehicle inspection	100	69	97	89	107	121	115	131
Parking fees	100	19	35	79	80	211	182	263
Parking fees in home city, excluding residence	100	20	32	80	83	211	183	259
Parking fees on trips	100	13	47	74	67	211	172	281
Tolls	100	29	56	88	77	184	182	187
Tolls on trips	100	27	62	87	90	177	148	227
Towing charges	100	70	109	95	105	107	95	129
Global positioning services	100	37	100	70	164	127	104	166
Automobile service clubs	100	44	83	95	101	142	125	170
PUBLIC TRANSPORTATION	100	45	48	68	69	200	160	269
Airline fares	100	31	46	62	73	211	165	290
Intercity bus fares	100	67	50	97	77	166	149	194
Intracity mass transit fares	100	97	65	84	62	154	138	182
Local transportation on trips	100	51	45	80	74	190	151	258
Taxi fares and limousine service	100	179	39	43	31	178	186	161
Intercity train fares	100	25	42	91	78	194	131	305
Ship fares	100	18	48	72	47	217	173	293
School bus	100	29	14	97	18	233	86	491

Source: Calculations by New Strategist based on the Bureau of Labor Statistics' 2011 Consumer Expenditure Survey

Table 11.27 Transportation: Total spending by education, 2011

(total annual spending on transportation, by consumer unit educational attainment group, 2011; consumer units and dollars in thousands)

	total consumer units	less than high school graduate	high school graduate	some college	associate's degree	bachelor's degree or more total	bachelor's degree	graduate degree
Number of consumer units	122,287	16,146	30,810	25,361	12,912	37,058	23,578	13,480
Total spending of all consumer units	$6,078,260,661	$483,588,362	$1,223,288,867	$1,150,256,524	$656,180,609	$2,553,405,521	$1,533,772,714	$1,020,859,272
Transportation, total spending	1,014,100,411	78,448,732	219,355,800	204,433,753	115,744,717	395,097,943	249,099,448	145,760,992
VEHICLE PURCHASES	326,330,197	19,881,861	69,581,612	65,023,322	40,329,599	131,514,024	85,183,306	46,330,625
Cars and trucks, new	154,748,084	3,320,263	27,321,076	29,455,533	16,294,040	78,356,547	49,116,746	29,239,872
New cars	71,332,453	1,676,116	12,198,295	13,328,220	8,819,800	35,310,345	20,728,599	14,581,720
New trucks	83,414,408	1,644,147	15,123,089	16,127,314	7,474,240	43,046,202	28,388,148	14,658,287
Cars and trucks, used	163,737,402	15,886,695	40,857,449	33,684,987	22,971,739	50,335,881	34,697,856	15,638,013
Used cars	83,535,473	7,144,121	18,738,950	17,108,784	12,757,960	27,784,977	19,063,520	8,721,560
Used trucks	80,201,929	8,742,413	22,118,499	16,576,203	10,213,779	22,550,905	15,634,336	6,916,453
Other vehicles	7,845,934	674,903	1,402,779	1,882,801	1,063,820	2,821,596	1,368,703	1,452,740
Used motorcycles	4,092,946	603,376	1,035,832	970,819	861,747	621,092	37,489	583,549
GASOLINE AND MOTOR OIL	324,618,179	32,389,522	78,613,256	66,270,829	39,003,537	108,340,916	69,187,755	39,153,334
Gasoline	299,709,540	30,518,200	73,128,459	61,082,729	35,877,025	99,102,727	63,475,984	35,626,966
Diesel fuel	6,328,352	792,446	1,977,694	1,460,033	877,758	1,220,320	882,996	337,270
Gasoline on trips	17,027,242	856,222	3,066,211	3,408,265	2,054,816	7,642,471	4,561,871	3,080,450
Motor oil	1,380,620	213,935	410,081	285,565	173,279	298,317	220,690	77,645
Motor oil on trips	172,425	8,719	31,118	34,491	20,788	77,081	45,977	31,139
OTHER VEHICLE EXPENSES	300,039,715	22,407,257	63,496,945	64,247,275	31,837,118	117,041,023	75,265,927	41,540,777
Vehicle finance charges	28,443,956	1,782,034	6,336,077	6,289,021	4,109,760	9,927,468	6,677,054	3,250,432
Automobile finance charges	11,761,564	734,320	2,373,911	2,745,075	1,573,069	4,334,674	2,830,303	1,504,233
Truck finance charges	14,152,275	946,156	3,457,498	3,047,124	1,991,805	4,709,331	3,100,743	1,608,568
Motorcycle and plane finance charges	522,165	27,287	98,284	199,591	67,142	130,444	102,564	28,038
Other vehicle finance charges	2,007,953	74,272	406,384	297,231	477,744	753,019	643,444	109,592
Maintenance and repairs	98,432,475	6,897,248	19,543,707	19,960,375	11,091,666	40,724,148	25,519,884	15,203,418
Coolant, additives, brake and transmission fluids	544,177	90,095	169,455	112,603	73,211	98,574	58,473	40,036
Tires—purchased, replaced, installed	17,611,774	1,453,624	3,539,453	3,843,713	2,074,829	6,700,457	4,144,305	2,556,078
Parts, equipment, and accessories	5,632,539	474,047	1,492,128	1,524,196	690,792	1,450,821	954,673	496,199
Vehicle audio equipment	278,814	13,724	74,868	43,367	27,373	119,327	104,215	14,963
Vehicle products and cleaning services	1,345,157	115,121	264,966	249,552	132,090	568,099	219,040	365,982
Vehicle video equipment	141,853	1,292	20,643	18,514	19,239	81,898	36,310	45,697
Miscellaneous auto repair, servicing	11,228,392	518,287	1,653,265	2,289,591	1,303,466	5,265,201	3,500,626	1,746,469
Body work and painting	2,850,510	95,907	497,582	707,318	335,066	1,214,391	700,974	513,184
Clutch and transmission repair	4,011,014	202,794	1,143,359	553,631	503,826	1,607,576	734,926	872,830
Drive shaft and rear-end repair	988,079	60,870	288,382	180,063	110,914	347,604	230,357	117,141
Brake work	7,274,854	428,676	1,500,755	1,463,583	709,514	3,171,794	1,891,427	1,280,330
Repair to steering or front-end	2,579,033	115,767	485,874	623,120	262,243	1,092,099	783,261	308,827
Repair to engine cooling system	2,656,074	217,648	484,025	536,385	283,677	1,134,345	764,635	369,756
Motor tune-up	6,182,831	434,489	919,062	959,914	761,808	3,107,684	2,034,310	1,073,278
Lube, oil change, and oil filters	9,467,460	736,258	2,109,561	1,848,056	1,077,377	3,695,794	2,310,644	1,385,474
Front-end alignment, wheel balance, rotation	2,335,682	183,257	466,463	469,432	247,394	969,808	649,102	320,554
Shock absorber replacement	610,212	22,281	130,634	76,590	115,175	264,965	192,632	72,522
Tire repair and other repair work	6,168,156	440,140	944,635	1,170,410	773,300	2,839,384	1,819,986	1,019,358
Vehicle air conditioning repair	1,786,613	88,964	398,373	308,390	187,095	803,417	544,416	258,951
Exhaust system repair	1,567,719	149,351	277,906	279,732	113,755	747,089	515,415	231,721
Electrical system repair	3,657,604	404,780	823,859	665,726	297,880	1,464,903	869,557	595,277
Motor repair, replacement	7,717,533	609,189	1,484,734	1,609,409	766,585	3,247,763	1,960,746	1,287,070
Auto repair service policy	1,796,396	40,688	372,493	427,333	225,185	731,154	499,382	231,856

	total consumer units	less than high school graduate	high school graduate	some college	associate's degree	bachelor's degree or more		
						total	bachelor's degree	graduate degree
Vehicle insurance	$120,246,030	$10,444,524	$28,642,825	$28,631,047	$11,419,631	$40,312,063	$27,596,634	$12,482,210
Vehicle rental, leases, licenses, other charges	**52,917,254**	**3,283,289**	**8,974,337**	**9,367,085**	**5,215,932**	**26,076,973**	**15,472,355**	**10,604,716**
Leased and rented vehicles	24,419,491	1,407,608	3,638,661	4,029,863	2,184,581	13,158,555	7,883,304	5,275,533
Rented vehicles	3,962,099	111,892	435,653	634,786	340,877	2,438,787	1,282,407	1,156,584
Auto rental	857,232	38,105	123,240	136,949	95,420	463,596	215,031	248,571
Auto rental on trips	2,344,242	44,240	193,795	384,219	129,636	1,592,382	884,647	707,565
Truck rental	228,677	4,198	36,048	50,722	30,343	107,839	74,506	33,565
Truck rental on trips	508,714	25,188	82,879	48,947	85,607	266,447	108,223	158,120
Leased vehicles	20,457,392	1,295,717	3,202,700	3,395,331	1,843,704	10,719,768	6,600,897	4,118,949
Car lease payments	11,723,655	739,810	2,070,740	1,751,431	1,147,748	6,013,772	3,671,802	2,342,150
Truck lease payments	6,904,324	459,515	978,526	1,111,573	397,948	3,957,424	2,473,096	1,484,148
Vehicle registration, state	12,642,030	1,077,261	2,771,360	2,445,561	1,511,479	4,836,810	2,892,549	1,944,220
Vehicle registration, local	1,094,469	74,917	214,746	221,148	85,607	498,060	311,230	186,968
Driver's license	1,106,697	110,277	248,637	227,488	155,202	365,392	219,747	145,449
Vehicle inspection	1,436,872	130,621	350,926	264,515	162,949	527,335	319,953	207,592
Parking fees	4,666,472	115,605	406,076	765,395	394,849	2,985,022	1,633,484	1,351,235
Parking fees in home city, excluding residence	3,915,630	103,011	317,959	649,749	341,393	2,504,380	1,385,208	1,118,975
Parking fees on trips	750,842	12,432	88,117	115,646	53,456	480,642	248,512	232,260
Tolls	3,710,188	140,147	525,619	677,900	302,141	2,064,501	1,300,798	763,912
Tolls on trips	530,726	18,891	82,263	95,865	50,228	284,235	151,371	132,913
Towing charges	505,045	46,823	138,337	99,669	55,909	164,167	92,662	71,714
Global positioning services	228,677	11,141	57,615	32,969	39,511	87,827	45,977	41,923
Automobile service clubs	2,576,587	150,319	540,716	506,459	273,605	1,105,070	621,516	483,528
PUBLIC TRANSPORTATION	**63,112,321**	**3,769,930**	**7,663,679**	**8,892,327**	**4,574,463**	**38,201,980**	**19,462,696**	**18,736,256**
Airline fares	41,783,022	1,712,445	4,797,733	5,380,590	3,235,618	26,656,931	13,293,512	13,363,668
Intercity bus fares	1,304,802	115,767	164,525	263,247	106,524	654,444	375,833	278,632
Intracity mass transit fares	9,182,531	1,181,726	1,511,539	1,600,025	602,345	4,286,869	2,448,104	1,838,672
Local transportation on trips	2,400,494	161,460	270,512	400,450	187,740	1,380,781	698,380	682,358
Taxi fares and limousine service	1,769,493	417,536	173,460	158,253	57,588	953,132	635,191	314,354
Intercity train fares	1,945,586	63,777	207,659	366,720	161,142	1,146,575	492,309	654,319
Ship fares	4,370,537	103,819	525,311	652,285	216,534	2,873,107	1,460,893	1,412,300
School bus	354,632	13,563	12,632	71,011	6,714	250,512	58,709	191,820

Note: Numbers may not add to total because of rounding and missing subcategories.
Source: Calculations by New Strategist based on the Bureau of Labor Statistics' 2011 Consumer Expenditure Survey

Table 11.28 Transportation: Market shares by education, 2011

(percentage of total annual spending on transportation accounted for by consumer unit educational attainment groups, 2011)

	total consumer units	less than high school graduate	high school graduate	some college	associate's degree	bachelor's degree or more total	bachelor's degree	graduate degree
Share of total consumer units	100.0%	13.2%	25.2%	20.7%	10.6%	30.3%	19.3%	11.0%
Share of total before-tax income	100.0	6.8	18.3	17.2	10.6	47.1	27.5	19.6
Share of total spending	100.0	8.0	20.1	18.9	10.8	42.0	25.2	16.8
Share of transportation spending	100.0	7.7	21.6	20.2	11.4	39.0	24.6	14.4
VEHICLE PURCHASES	100.0	6.1	21.3	19.9	12.4	40.3	26.1	14.2
Cars and trucks, new	100.0	2.1	17.7	19.0	10.5	50.6	31.7	18.9
New cars	100.0	2.3	17.1	18.7	12.4	49.5	29.1	20.4
New trucks	100.0	2.0	18.1	19.3	9.0	51.6	34.0	17.6
Cars and trucks, used	100.0	9.7	25.0	20.6	14.0	30.7	21.2	9.6
Used cars	100.0	8.6	22.4	20.5	15.3	33.3	22.8	10.4
Used trucks	100.0	10.9	27.6	20.7	12.7	28.1	19.5	8.6
Other vehicles	100.0	8.6	17.9	24.0	13.6	36.0	17.4	18.5
Used motorcycles	100.0	14.7	25.3	23.7	21.1	15.2	0.9	14.3
GASOLINE AND MOTOR OIL	100.0	10.0	24.2	20.4	12.0	33.4	21.3	12.1
Gasoline	100.0	10.2	24.4	20.4	12.0	33.1	21.2	11.9
Diesel fuel	100.0	12.5	31.3	23.1	13.9	19.3	14.0	5.3
Gasoline on trips	100.0	5.0	18.0	20.0	12.1	44.9	26.8	18.1
Motor oil	100.0	15.5	29.7	20.7	12.6	21.6	16.0	5.6
Motor oil on trips	100.0	5.1	18.0	20.0	12.1	44.7	26.7	18.1
OTHER VEHICLE EXPENSES	100.0	7.5	21.2	21.4	10.6	39.0	25.1	13.8
Vehicle finance charges	100.0	6.3	22.3	22.1	14.4	34.9	23.5	11.4
Automobile finance charges	100.0	6.2	20.2	23.3	13.4	36.9	24.1	12.8
Truck finance charges	100.0	6.7	24.4	21.5	14.1	33.3	21.9	11.4
Motorcycle and plane finance charges	100.0	5.2	18.8	38.2	12.9	25.0	19.6	5.4
Other vehicle finance charges	100.0	3.7	20.2	14.8	23.8	37.5	32.0	5.5
Maintenance and repairs	100.0	7.0	19.9	20.3	11.3	41.4	25.9	15.4
Coolant, additives, brake and transmission fluids	100.0	16.6	31.1	20.7	13.5	18.1	10.7	7.4
Tires—purchased, replaced, installed	100.0	8.3	20.1	21.8	11.8	38.0	23.5	14.5
Parts, equipment, and accessories	100.0	8.4	26.5	27.1	12.3	25.8	16.9	8.8
Vehicle audio equipment	100.0	4.9	26.9	15.6	9.8	42.8	37.4	5.4
Vehicle products and cleaning services	100.0	8.6	19.7	18.6	9.8	42.2	16.3	27.2
Vehicle video equipment	100.0	0.9	14.6	13.1	13.6	57.7	25.6	32.2
Miscellaneous auto repair, servicing	100.0	4.6	14.7	20.4	11.6	46.9	31.2	15.6
Body work and painting	100.0	3.4	17.5	24.8	11.8	42.6	24.6	18.0
Clutch and transmission repair	100.0	5.1	28.5	13.8	12.6	40.1	18.3	21.8
Drive shaft and rear-end repair	100.0	6.2	29.2	18.2	11.2	35.2	23.3	11.9
Brake work	100.0	5.9	20.6	20.1	9.8	43.6	26.0	17.6
Repair to steering or front-end	100.0	4.5	18.8	24.2	10.2	42.3	30.4	12.0
Repair to engine cooling system	100.0	8.2	18.2	20.2	10.7	42.7	28.8	13.9
Motor tune-up	100.0	7.0	14.9	15.5	12.3	50.3	32.9	17.4
Lube, oil change, and oil filters	100.0	7.8	22.3	19.5	11.4	39.0	24.4	14.6
Front-end alignment, wheel balance, rotation	100.0	7.8	20.0	20.1	10.6	41.5	27.8	13.7
Shock absorber replacement	100.0	3.7	21.4	12.6	18.9	43.4	31.6	11.9
Tire repair and other repair work	100.0	7.1	15.3	19.0	12.5	46.0	29.5	16.5
Vehicle air conditioning repair	100.0	5.0	22.3	17.3	10.5	45.0	30.5	14.5
Exhaust system repair	100.0	9.5	17.7	17.8	7.3	47.7	32.9	14.8
Electrical system repair	100.0	11.1	22.5	18.2	8.1	40.1	23.8	16.3
Motor repair, replacement	100.0	7.9	19.2	20.9	9.9	42.1	25.4	16.7
Auto repair service policy	100.0	2.3	20.7	23.8	12.5	40.7	27.8	12.9

	total consumer units	less than high school graduate	high school graduate	some college	associate's degree	bachelor's degree or more		
						total	bachelor's degree	graduate degree
Vehicle insurance	100.0%	8.7%	23.8%	23.8%	9.5%	33.5%	23.0%	10.4%
Vehicle rental, leases, licenses, other charges	100.0	6.2	17.0	17.7	9.9	49.3	29.2	20.0
Leased and rented vehicles	100.0	5.8	14.9	16.5	8.9	53.9	32.3	21.6
Rented vehicles	100.0	2.8	11.0	16.0	8.6	61.6	32.4	29.2
Auto rental	100.0	4.4	14.4	16.0	11.1	54.1	25.1	29.0
Auto rental on trips	100.0	1.9	8.3	16.4	5.5	67.9	37.7	30.2
Truck rental	100.0	1.8	15.8	22.2	13.3	47.2	32.6	14.7
Truck rental on trips	100.0	5.0	16.3	9.6	16.8	52.4	21.3	31.1
Leased vehicles	100.0	6.3	15.7	16.6	9.0	52.4	32.3	20.1
Car lease payments	100.0	6.3	17.7	14.9	9.8	51.3	31.3	20.0
Truck lease payments	100.0	6.7	14.2	16.1	5.8	57.3	35.8	21.5
Vehicle registration, state	100.0	8.5	21.9	19.3	12.0	38.3	22.9	15.4
Vehicle registration, local	100.0	6.8	19.6	20.2	7.8	45.5	28.4	17.1
Driver's license	100.0	10.0	22.5	20.6	14.0	33.0	19.9	13.1
Vehicle inspection	100.0	9.1	24.4	18.4	11.3	36.7	22.3	14.4
Parking fees	100.0	2.5	8.7	16.4	8.5	64.0	35.0	29.0
Parking fees in home city, excluding residence	100.0	2.6	8.1	16.6	8.7	64.0	35.4	28.6
Parking fees on trips	100.0	1.7	11.7	15.4	7.1	64.0	33.1	30.9
Tolls	100.0	3.8	14.2	18.3	8.1	55.6	35.1	20.6
Tolls on trips	100.0	3.6	15.5	18.1	9.5	53.6	28.5	25.0
Towing charges	100.0	9.3	27.4	19.7	11.1	32.5	18.3	14.2
Global positioning services	100.0	4.9	25.2	14.4	17.3	38.4	20.1	18.3
Automobile service clubs	100.0	5.8	21.0	19.7	10.6	42.9	24.1	18.8
PUBLIC TRANSPORTATION	100.0	6.0	12.1	14.1	7.2	60.5	30.8	29.7
Airline fares	100.0	4.1	11.5	12.9	7.7	63.8	31.8	32.0
Intercity bus fares	100.0	8.9	12.6	20.2	8.2	50.2	28.8	21.4
Intracity mass transit fares	100.0	12.9	16.5	17.4	6.6	46.7	26.7	20.0
Local transportation on trips	100.0	6.7	11.3	16.7	7.8	57.5	29.1	28.4
Taxi fares and limousine service	100.0	23.6	9.8	8.9	3.3	53.9	35.9	17.8
Intercity train fares	100.0	3.3	10.7	18.8	8.3	58.9	25.3	33.6
Ship fares	100.0	2.4	12.0	14.9	5.0	65.7	33.4	32.3
School bus	100.0	3.8	3.6	20.0	1.9	70.6	16.6	54.1

Note: Numbers may not add to total because of rounding.
Source: Calculations by New Strategist based on the Bureau of Labor Statistics' 2011 Consumer Expenditure Survey

Appendix A
About the Consumer Expenditure Survey

History

The Consumer Expenditure Survey is an ongoing study of the day-to-day spending of American households. In taking the survey, government interviewers collect spending data on products and services as well as the amount and sources of household income, changes in saving and debt, and demographic and economic characteristics of household members. The Bureau of the Census collects data for the Consumer Expenditure Survey under contract with the Bureau of Labor Statistics, which is responsible for analysis and release of the survey data.

Since the late 19th century, the federal government has conducted expenditure surveys about every 10 years. Although the results have been used for a variety of purposes, their primary application is to track consumer prices. Beginning in 1980, the Consumer Expenditure Survey became a continuous survey with annual release of data. The survey is used to update prices for the market basket of products and services used in calculating the Consumer Price Index.

Components of the Consumer Expenditure Survey

The Consumer Expenditure Survey consists of two separate surveys: an interview survey and a diary survey. In the interview portion of the survey, respondents are asked each quarter for five consecutive quarters to report their expenditures for the previous three months. The interview survey records purchases of big-ticket items such as houses, cars, and major appliances as well as recurring expenses such as insurance premiums, utility payments, and rent. It covers about 95 percent of all expenditures.

The diary survey records expenditures on small, frequently purchased items during a two-week period. These detailed records include expenses for food and beverages purchased in grocery stores and at restaurants as well as other items such as tobacco, housekeeping supplies, nonprescription drugs, and personal care products and services. The diary survey is intended to capture expenditures respondents are likely to forget or recall incorrectly over longer periods of time.

The average spending figures shown in this report are the integrated data from both the diary and interview components of the survey. Integrated data provide a more complete accounting of consumer expenditures than either component of the survey is designed to do alone.

Data Collection and Processing

For the interview survey, about 7,000 consumer units are interviewed on a rotating panel basis each quarter for five consecutive quarters. Another 7,000 consumer units keep weekly diaries of spending for two consecutive weeks. Data collection is carried out in 91 areas of the country.

The Bureau of Labor Statistics reviews, audits, and cleanses the data, then weights them to reflect the number and characteristics of all U.S. consumer units. Like any sample survey, the Consumer Expenditure Survey is subject to two major types of error. Nonsampling error occurs when respondents misinterpret questions or interviewers are inconsistent in the way they ask questions or record answers. Respondents may forget items, recall expenses incorrectly, or deliberately give wrong answers. A respondent may remember how much he or she spent at the grocery store but forget the items picked up at a local convenience store. Most surveys of alcohol consumption or spending on alcohol, for example, suffer from underreporting. Mistakes during the various stages of data processing and refinement can also cause nonsampling error.

Sampling error occurs when a sample does not accurately represent the population it is supposed to represent. This kind of error is present in every sample-based survey and is minimized by using a proper sampling procedure. Standard error tables documenting the extent of sampling error in the Consumer Expenditure Survey are available from the Bureau of Labor Statistics at http://www.bls.gov/cex/csxstnderror.htm.

Although the Consumer Expenditure Survey is the best source of information about the spending behavior of American households, it should be treated with caution because of the above problems. Comparisons with consumption data from other sources show that Consumer Expenditure Survey data tend to underestimate expenditures except for rent, fuel, telephone service, furniture, transportation, and personal care services. Despite these problems, the data reveal important spending patterns by demographic segment that can be used to better understand consumer behavior.

Definition of Consumer Unit

The Consumer Expenditure Survey uses the consumer unit as the sampling unit rather than the household, which is the sampling unit used by the Census Bureau. The term "household" is used interchangeably with the term "consumer unit" in this book for convenience, although they are not exactly the same. Some households contain more than one consumer unit.

The Bureau of Labor Statistics defines consumer unit as (1) members of a household who are related by blood, marriage, adoption, or other legal arrangements; (2) a person living alone or sharing a household with others or living as a roomer in a private home or lodging house or in permanent living quarters in a hotel or motel, but who is financially independent; or (3) two or more persons living together who pool their income to make joint expenditure decisions. The bureau defines financial independence in terms of "the three major expenses categories: housing, food, and other living expenses. To be considered financially independent, at least two of the three major expense categories have to be provided by the respondent."

The Census Bureau uses the household as its sampling unit in the decennial census and in the monthly Current Population Survey. The Census Bureau's household "consists of all persons who occupy a housing unit. A house, an apartment or other group of rooms, or a single room is regarded as a housing unit when it is occupied or intended for occupancy as separate living quarters; that is, when the occupants do not live and eat with any other persons in the structure and there is direct access from the outside or through a common hall."

The definition goes on to specify that "a household includes the related family members and all the unrelated persons, if any, such as lodgers, foster children, wards, or employees who share the housing unit. A person living alone in a housing unit or a group of unrelated persons sharing a housing unit as partners is also counted as a household. The count of households excludes group quarters."

Because there can be more than one consumer unit in a household, consumer units outnumber households by several million. Young adults under age 25 head most of the additional consumer units.

For More Information

To find out more about the Consumer Expenditure Survey, contact the specialists at the Bureau of Labor Statistics at (202) 691-6900, or visit the Consumer Expenditure Survey home page at http://www.bls.gov/cex/. The web site includes news releases, technical documentation, and current and historical summary-level data.

Appendix B
Mortgage Principal and Capital Improvements, 2011

The spending statistics reported by the Consumer Expenditure Survey do not include spending on mortgage principal reduction or capital improvements. Because the survey treats home equity as an asset, principal reduction and capital improvements are regarded as asset accumulation rather than expenditures. The table shows the average amount spent by households in 2011 for mortgage principal reduction and capital improvements. Adding these figures to expenditures for the category "owned dwellings" gives a more complete picture of the average amount households devote to housing.

(average annual reduction in mortgage principal and change in capital improvement for owned homes, by age of consumer unit reference person, average before-tax income of consumer unit, type of consumer unit, race and Hispanic origin of consumer unit reference person, region in which consumer unit lives, and educational attainment of consumer unit reference person, 2011)

	total consumer units	under 25	25 to 34	35 to 44	45 to 54	55 to 64	65 or older		
							total	65 to 74	75+
AGE OF REFERENCE PERSON									
Reduction of mortgage principal	$1,606.44	$241.44	$1,152.40	$2,159.98	$2,311.72	$2,072.64	$842.40	$1,200.12	$415.38
Change in capital improvements	748.72	22.39	644.39	918.2	783.79	943.18	709.81	988.66	376.92

	total consumer units	under $20,000	$20,000– to $39,999	$40,000– 49,999	$50,000– 69,999	$70,000– 79,999	$80,000– 99,999	$100,000 or more		
								total	$100,000– $119,999	$120,000– $149,999	$150,000 or more
BEFORE-TAX INCOME OF CONSUMER UNIT										
Reduction of mortgage principal	$1,606.44	$341.70	$658.16	$1,124.15	$1,558.23	$2,075.92	$2,371.60	$4,130.88	$2,989.37	$3,789.48	$5,330.70
Change in capital improvements	748.72	174.91	454.46	282.93	583.79	690.69	1,110.94	2,049.39	794.14	1,699.80	3,350.08

	total consumer units	total married couples	married couples, no children	married couples with children				single parent with child under 18	single person
				total	oldest child under age 6	oldest child 6 to 17	oldest child 18 or older		
TYPE OF CONSUMER UNIT									
Reduction of mortgage principal	$1,606.44	$2,363.30	$1,852.83	$2,776.74	$2,495.38	$2,873.05	$2,803.10	$871.32	$743.67
Change in capital improvements	748.72	1,143.86	1,077.23	1,259.42	1,685.01	1,311.50	882.90	151.13	368.97

	total consumer units	Asian	black	Hispanic	non-Hispanic white and other
RACE/HISPANIC ORIGIN OF REFERENCE PERSON					
Reduction of mortgage principal	$1,606.44	$2,502.20	$1,036.11	$1,079.37	$1,786.84
Change in capital improvements	748.72	905.39	234.30	210.92	920.35

	total consumer units	Northeast	Midwest	South	West
REGION					
Reduction of mortgage principal	$1,606.44	$1,840.47	$1,644.63	$1,339.67	$1,810.80
Change in capital improvements	748.72	953.96	673.18	696.17	740.86

	total consumer units	less than high school graduate	high school graduate	some college	associate's degree	bachelor's degree or more		
						total	bachelor's degree	graduate degree
EDUCATIONAL ATTAINMENT OF REFERENCE PERSON								
Reduction of mortgage principal	$1,606.44	$653.73	$1,126.00	$1,267.86	$1,576.30	$2,663.19	$2,440.14	$3,053.34
Change in capital improvements	748.72	278.94	270.13	695.01	527.69	1,465.08	1,158.96	2,000.54

Source: Bureau of Labor Statistics, 2011 Consumer Expenditure Survey

Appendix C

Percent Reporting Expenditure and Amount Spent, Average Quarter 2011

(percent of consumer units reporting expenditure and amount spent by purchasers during the average quarter, 2011)

	percent reporting expenditure during quarter	average amount spent by purchasers per quarter
FOOD	**99.4%**	**$1,796.38**
Food at home	**98.9**	**1,238.42**
Groceries purchased on trips	10.6	112.24
Food away from home	**81.2**	**691.17**
Meals at restaurants, carry-outs, etc.	77.8	585.19
Food or board at school	1.0	1,054.57
Catered affairs	2.0	661.18
Restaurant food on trips	24.4	242.11
School lunches	7.8	200.52
Meals as pay	1.8	396.29
ALCOHOLIC BEVERAGES	**39.1**	**226.17**
At home	**34.1**	**146.98**
Away from home	**24.5**	**157.03**
Alcoholic beverages at restaurants, bars	17.9	152.21
Alcoholic beverages purchased on trips	12.9	86.63
HOUSING	**99.6**	**3,973.45**
Shelter	**97.7**	**2,513.14**
• Owned dwellings	**65.1**	**2,360.58**
Mortgage interest and charges	41.2	1,930.47
Mortgage interest	38.8	1,947.59
Interest paid, home equity loan	2.7	570.02
Interest paid, home equity line of credit	4.5	560.87
Property taxes	64.1	719.16
Maintenance, repairs, insurance, other expenses	35.1	796.78
Homeowner's insurance	23.1	380.60
Ground rent	1.4	885.11
Maintenance and repair services	13.6	1,021.93
Painting and papering	1.1	1,353.73
Plumbing and water heating	4.0	409.40
Heat, air conditioning, electrical work	5.4	507.93
Roofing and gutters	1.2	1,993.32
Other repair and maintenance services	4.0	1,064.81
Repair/replacement of hard-surface flooring	0.8	1,847.73
Repair of built-in appliances	0.4	122.14
Maintenance and repair materials	5.2	361.19
Paints, wallpaper and supplies	1.8	187.02
Tools/equipment for painting, wallpapering	1.8	20.08
Plumbing supplies and equipment	0.7	232.97
Electrical supplies, heating/cooling equipment	0.4	209.76
Hard-surface flooring, repair and replacement	0.4	724.39
Roofing and gutters	0.2	686.84
Plaster, paneling, siding, windows, doors, screens, awnings	0.7	588.43
Patio, walk, fence, driveway, masonry, brick, and stucco work	0.3	130.88
Miscellaneous supplies and equipment	1.7	221.43
Insulation, other maintenance and repair supplies	1.7	221.43
Property management and security	6.2	359.67
Property management	6.0	253.11
Management and upkeep services for security	1.5	473.66
Parking	0.2	59.78
• Rented dwellings	**33.7**	**2,250.07**
Rent	32.5	2,234.12
Rent as pay	1.3	1,608.08

	percent reporting expenditure during quarter	average amount spent by purchasers per quarter
Maintenance, insurance, and other expenses	5.2%	$193.80
Tenant's insurance	4.0	82.85
Maintenance and repair services	0.7	573.19
Maintenance and repair materials	0.9	311.44
• Other lodging	**18.5**	**874.24**
Owned vacation homes	4.7	1,387.50
Mortgage interest and charges	1.3	1,643.22
Property taxes	4.6	638.46
Maintenance, insurance, and other expenses	1.7	910.54
Housing while attending school	0.9	2,051.72
Lodging on trips	14.6	539.47
Utilities, fuels, public services	**97.8**	**952.36**
Natural gas	48.4	216.71
Electricity	92.0	386.50
Fuel oil and other fuels	8.4	469.55
Fuel oil	3.0	746.07
Coal, wood, and other fuels	0.8	307.89
Bottled gas	5.1	287.18
Telephone services	92.4	331.97
Residential phone service and pay phones	58.9	161.83
Cellular phone service	67.4	306.41
Phone cards	4.1	53.77
Voice over IP	2.1	130.86
Water and other public services	64.1	195.39
Water and sewerage maintenance	58.0	162.34
Trash and garbage collection	39.5	76.58
Septic tank cleaning	0.4	228.57
Household services	**71.8**	**385.34**
Personal services	7.2	1,384.81
Babysitting and child care in own home	1.9	670.55
Babysitting and child care in someone else's home	1.1	633.73
Care for elderly, invalids, handicapped, etc.	0.4	4,243.13
Day care centers, nurseries, and preschools	4.7	1,333.86
Other household services	70.7	250.58
Housekeeping services	5.6	470.75
Gardening, lawn care service	14.8	200.83
Water-softening service	1.3	92.23
Nonclothing laundry and dry cleaning, sent out	0.6	42.74
Nonclothing laundry and dry cleaning, coin-operated	3.8	28.87
Termite/pest control services	4.1	124.76
Home security system service fee	5.0	129.28
Other home services	2.1	191.15
Termite/pest control products	3.2	28.07
Moving, storage, and freight express	2.9	462.24
Appliance repair, including at service center	2.7	155.04
Reupholstering and furniture repair	0.6	256.70
Repairs/rentals of lawn/garden equipment, hand/power tools, etc.	1.5	151.80
Appliance rental	0.3	152.27
Rental of office equipment for nonbusiness use	0.1	220.83
Repair of computer systems for nonbusiness use	1.1	144.03
Computer information services	61.4	127.84
Installation of computer	0.1	98.08
Household furnishings and equipment	**56.7**	**517.98**
Household textiles	18.8	95.09
Bathroom linens	5.8	42.21
Bedroom linens	10.0	89.38
Kitchen and dining room linens	1.9	27.84
Curtains and draperies	2.4	117.22
Slipcovers and decorative pillows	1.3	67.18
Sewing materials for household items	2.6	76.71
Other linens	0.5	60.11

	percent reporting expenditure during quarter	average amount spent by purchasers per quarter
Furniture	11.9%	$751.34
Mattresses and springs	2.0	779.29
Other bedroom furniture	2.5	709.11
Sofas	2.5	913.48
Living room chairs	1.9	470.31
Living room tables	1.2	245.25
Kitchen and dining room furniture	1.3	540.35
Infants' furniture	1.1	188.76
Outdoor furniture	1.7	281.63
Wall units, cabinets, and other furniture	2.8	280.53
Floor coverings	3.0	168.18
Major appliances	8.8	538.98
Dishwashers (built-in), garbage disposals, range hoods (renter)	0.1	292.86
Dishwashers (built-in), garbage disposals, range hoods (owner)	0.6	538.28
Refrigerators, freezers (renter)	0.3	474.17
Refrigerators, freezers (owner)	1.3	881.90
Washing machines (renter)	0.4	392.26
Washing machines (owner)	1.1	646.46
Clothes dryers (renter)	0.4	319.38
Clothes dryers (owner)	0.9	576.16
Cooking stoves, ovens (renter)	0.1	308.93
Cooking stoves, ovens (owner)	0.8	899.38
Microwave ovens (renter)	0.8	76.54
Microwave ovens (owner)	1.0	163.64
Window air conditioners (renter)	0.2	155.56
Window air conditioners (owner)	0.3	280.30
Electric floor-cleaning equipment	2.7	150.37
Sewing machines	0.3	233.65
Small appliances and miscellaneous housewares	17.2	83.41
Housewares	9.7	60.85
Plastic dinnerware	2.7	22.96
China and other dinnerware	2.1	70.24
Flatware	1.3	55.64
Glassware	1.9	28.07
Silver serving pieces	0.1	45.83
Other serving pieces	0.7	50.71
Nonelectric cookware	3.5	62.79
Small appliances	9.7	87.10
Small electric kitchen appliances	8.5	72.49
Portable heating and cooling equipment	1.5	153.17
Miscellaneous household equipment	40.9	292.17
Window coverings	1.5	273.62
Infants' equipment	1.2	124.59
Outdoor equipment	1.8	189.78
Lamps and lighting fixtures	3.2	102.73
Household decorative items	6.3	133.36
Telephones and accessories	6.3	143.54
Lawn and garden equipment	2.8	493.17
Power tools	2.4	169.65
Office furniture for home use	0.8	194.33
Hand tools	2.1	68.81
Indoor plants and fresh flowers	15.9	73.87
Closet and storage items	1.2	66.38
Rental of furniture	0.2	641.67
Luggage	1.5	110.10
Computers and computer hardware, nonbusiness use	7.0	546.45
Portable memory	3.0	35.34
Computer software	2.5	144.46
Computer accessories	3.9	78.69
Personal digital assistants	0.3	461.03
Internet services away from home	1.7	101.01
Telephone answering devices	0.2	76.25
Business equipment for home use	0.9	119.1

	percent reporting expenditure during quarter	average amount spent by purchasers per quarter
Smoke alarms (owner)	0.8%	$55.52
Smoke alarms (renter)	0.2	34.21
Other household appliances (owner)	1.3	136.00
Other household appliances (renter)	0.4	65.91
APPAREL AND SERVICES	**74.5**	**363.31**
Men's apparel	**31.4**	**154.66**
Suits	1.3	360.55
Sport coats and tailored jackets	0.9	154.71
Coats and jackets	4.2	104.86
Underwear	5.6	32.13
Hosiery	4.5	20.09
Nightwear	1.1	37.05
Accessories	3.9	45.99
Sweaters and vests	3.1	83.36
Active sportswear	1.6	56.09
Shirts	17.2	74.46
Pants and shorts	19.1	85.29
Uniforms	0.5	122.12
Costumes	0.3	51.00
Boys' (aged 2 to 15) apparel	**11.8**	**131.93**
Coats and jackets	1.9	69.14
Sweaters	1.0	51.24
Shirts	6.7	65.38
Underwear	2.3	30.24
Nightwear	1.2	32.08
Hosiery	1.5	17.33
Accessories	0.9	31.59
Suits, sport coats, and vests	0.3	75.83
Pants and shorts	8.3	76.33
Uniforms	0.6	105.16
Active sportswear	1.0	35.94
Costumes	0.7	35.21
Women's apparel	**42.1**	**196.31**
Coats and jackets	6.2	94.94
Dresses	8.3	136.75
Sport coats and tailored jackets	0.6	93.44
Sweaters and vests	7.7	72.69
Shirts, blouses, and tops	24.0	79.69
Skirts	3.2	63.32
Pants and shorts	23.0	84.77
Active sportswear	3.5	59.42
Nightwear	4.3	40.70
Undergarments	9.4	48.88
Hosiery	5.5	20.67
Suits	1.1	176.38
Accessories	7.4	79.85
Uniforms	1.0	85.82
Costumes	0.6	54.44
Girls' (aged 2 to 15) apparel	**12.5**	**147.82**
Coats and jackets	2.0	66.41
Dresses and suits	2.5	72.83
Shirts, blouses, and sweaters	7.3	73.49
Skirts, pants, and shorts	7.8	80.46
Active sportswear	1.4	42.99
Underwear and nightwear	3.3	34.62
Hosiery	1.6	19.19
Accessories	1.6	37.18
Uniforms	0.6	116.80
Costumes	0.8	44.41
Children's (under age 2) apparel	**10.1**	**141.12**
Coats, jackets, and snowsuits	0.6	38.11
Outerwear including dresses	3.3	72.62

	percent reporting expenditure during quarter	average amount spent by purchasers per quarter
Underwear	8.4%	$121.54
Nightwear and loungewear	1.0	42.53
Accessories	2.4	46.34
Footwear	**33.3**	**116.50**
Men's	13.6	96.43
Boys'	6.3	69.94
Women's	19.7	87.48
Girls'	6.4	64.85
Other apparel products and services	**36.5**	**143.33**
Material for making clothes	1.0	66.00
Sewing patterns and notions	1.1	22.79
Watches	3.4	202.70
Jewelry	8.1	220.98
Shoe repair and other shoe services	1.1	35.05
Coin-operated apparel laundry and dry cleaning	12.9	76.68
Apparel alteration, repair, and tailoring services	3.0	53.62
Clothing rental	0.3	150.00
Watch and jewelry repair	1.9	71.45
Professional laundry, dry cleaning	14.4	87.22
Clothing storage	0.1	220.83
TRANSPORTATION	**95.2**	**2,125.92**
Vehicle purchases	**5.1**	**13,030.08**
Cars and trucks, new	1.3	24,910.43
New cars	0.6	22,785.94
New trucks	0.6	27,068.25
Cars and trucks, used	3.7	9,120.98
Used cars	2.0	8,371.45
Used trucks	1.7	9,759.67
Other vehicles	0.3	5,940.74
Gasoline and motor oil	**90.5**	**733.38**
Gasoline	89.9	681.48
Diesel fuel	2.2	598.96
Gasoline on trips	20.7	168.16
Motor oil	8.5	33.28
Motor oil on trips	20.7	1.70
Other vehicle expenses	**82.0**	**686.18**
Vehicle finance charges	28.3	205.40
Automobile finance charges	15.1	159.56
Truck finance charges	15.0	192.63
Motorcycle and plane finance charges	0.8	127.08
Other vehicle finance charges	1.3	310.98
Maintenance and repairs	55.5	321.84
Coolant, additives, brake, transmission fluids	5.6	19.94
Tires	8.8	409.61
Vehicle products and cleaning services	5.3	41.21
Parts, equipment, and accessories	9.4	123.16
Vehicle audio equipment	0.2	237.50
Vehicle video equipment	0.2	161.11
Body work and painting	1.1	539.58
Clutch, transmission repair	1.1	725.66
Drive shaft and rear-end repair	0.5	439.13
Brake work	5.3	280.08
Repair to steering or front-end	1.4	387.68
Repair to engine cooling system	2.0	277.04
Motor tune-up	4.6	274.78
Lube, oil change, and oil filters	35.4	54.61
Front-end alignment, wheel balance, rotation	3.1	156.05
Shock absorber replacement	0.3	366.91
Repair tires and other repair work	6.6	192.52
Exhaust system repair	1.0	314.22
Electrical system repair	2.5	302.73

	percent reporting expenditure during quarter	average amount spent by purchasers per quarter
Motor repair, replacement	2.5%	$631.10
Auto repair service policy	0.4	874.40
Vehicle accessories including labor	0.5	198.89
Vehicle air conditioning repair	1.3	285.35
Vehicle insurance	53.8	405.41
Vehicle rental, leases, licenses, other charges	46.2	234.06
Leased and rented vehicles	5.6	894.67
Rented vehicles	2.8	294.55
Auto rental	0.6	273.83
Auto rental, on trips	1.7	280.26
Truck rental	0.2	194.79
Truck rental, on trips	0.2	472.73
Leased vehicles	3.0	1,398.75
Car lease payments	2.1	1,157.85
Truck lease payments	1.2	1,227.39
Vehicle registration, state	18.9	136.75
Vehicle registration, local	1.9	120.95
Driver's license	5.6	40.33
Vehicle inspection	6.9	42.45
Parking fees	13.4	71.35
Parking fees in home city, excluding residence	10.7	74.74
Parking fees, on trips	3.6	42.64
Tolls or electronic toll passes	10.6	71.35
Tolls on trips	6.6	16.34
Towing charges	0.9	117.33
Global positioning services	0.6	79.24
Automobile service clubs	5.7	92.57
Public transportation	**20.0**	**648.29**
Airline fares	10.6	807.37
Intercity bus fares	4.4	60.90
Intracity mass transit fares	8.1	230.90
Local transportation on trips	5.5	56.64
Taxi fares and limousine service on trips	5.5	33.24
Taxi fares and limousine service	3.7	112.20
Intercity train fares	4.1	97.73
Ship fares	2.2	402.48
School bus	0.1	557.69
HEALTH CARE	**79.3**	**984.88**
Health insurance	**64.4**	**746.77**
Commercial health insurance	13.5	627.04
Traditional fee-for-service health plan (not BCBS)	4.2	549.94
Preferred-provider health plan (not BCBS)	9.5	648.00
Blue Cross, Blue Shield	23.0	661.18
Traditional fee-for-service health plan	3.8	716.03
Preferred-provider health plan	9.2	667.87
Health maintenance organization	7.7	617.86
Commercial Medicare supplement	2.4	567.15
Other BCBS health insurance	0.9	244.78
Health maintenance plans (HMOs)	13.6	588.02
Medicare payments	24.3	379.28
Medicare prescription drug premium	8.1	193.04
Commercial Medicare supplements/other health insurance	12.0	327.57
Commercial Medicare supplement (not BCBS)	4.8	527.05
Other health insurance (not BCBS)	7.7	183.59
Long-term care insurance	3.3	511.32
Medical Services	**44.1**	**433.52**
Physician's services	26.8	167.41
Dental services	15.7	455.76
Eye care services	7.9	118.03
Service by professionals other than physician	5.6	251.02
Lab tests, X-rays	6.3	190.36
Hospital room and services	4.9	662.73

	percent reporting expenditure during quarter	average amount spent by purchasers per quarter
Care in convalescent or nursing home	0.2%	$1,720.00
Other medical services	1.8	240.22
Prescription drugs	**44.5**	**193.40**
Medical supplies	**9.9**	**236.17**
Eyeglasses and contact lenses	7.5	211.77
Hearing aids	0.4	1,029.88
Adult diapers	0.7	107.25
Medical equipment for general use	0.9	101.33
Supportive/convalescent medical equipment	0.7	144.29
Rental of medical equipment	0.4	74.29
Rental of supportive, convalescent medical equipment	0.2	121.88
ENTERTAINMENT	**90.8**	**619.63**
Fees and admissions	**46.2**	**315.12**
Recreation expenses on trips	8.1	66.52
Social, recreation, health club membership	13.3	228.79
Fees for participant sports	11.8	185.74
Participant sports on trips	3.7	164.41
Movie, theater, opera, ballet	29.1	99.62
Movie, other admissions on trips	8.3	131.84
Admission to sports events	6.3	182.18
Admission to sports events on trips	8.3	43.92
Fees for recreational lessons	5.8	370.24
Other entertainment services on trips	8.1	66.52
Audio and visual equipment and services	**84.0**	**282.92**
Television sets	4.4	646.16
Cable and satellite television services	73.0	219.41
Satellite radio service	3.2	106.98
Online gaming services	2.0	38.24
VCRs and video disc players	2.1	104.59
Video cassettes, tapes, and discs	11.5	52.48
Video game software	4.5	119.38
Video game hardware and accessories	2.4	204.17
Streamed and downloaded video	3.4	29.17
Applications, games, ringtones for handheld devices	3.7	24.93
Repair of television, radio, and sound equipment	0.5	156.94
Rental of television sets	0.0	200.00
Radios	0.7	76.79
Tape recorders and players	0.1	91.67
Personal digital audio players	1.4	183.75
Sound components and component systems	0.9	240.59
CDs, records, audio tapes	7.4	39.14
Streamed and downloaded audio	7.7	31.11
Rental of VCR, radio, and sound equipment	0.1	90.00
Musical instruments and accessories	1.6	362.18
Rental and repair of musical instruments	0.3	153.85
Rental of video cassettes, tapes, films, and discs	18.2	25.44
Accessories and other sound equipment	1.3	95.64
Satellite dishes	0.2	119.32
Installation of television sets	0.1	193.18
Pets, toys, hobbies, and playground equipment	**40.3**	**236.46**
Pets	30.9	230.38
Pet purchase, supplies, and medicines	25.2	139.89
Pet services	6.1	147.36
Veterinary services	9.4	289.19
Toys, games, arts and crafts, and tricycles	14.9	139.46
Stamp and coin collecting	0.9	293.24
Playground equipment	0.4	226.88
Other entertainment supplies, equipment, services	**21.3**	**394.42**
Unmotored recreational vehicles	0.2	7,568.06
Boat without motor and boat trailers	0.1	1,916.67
Trailer and other attachable campers	0.1	13,219.44

	percent reporting expenditure during quarter	average amount spent by purchasers per quarter
Motorized recreational vehicles	0.2%	$9,567.86
Rental of recreational vehicles	0.6	240.35
Docking and landing fees	0.4	482.43
Sports, recreation, exercise equipment	12.9	231.51
Athletic gear, game tables, exercise equipment	6.7	175.60
Bicycles	2.2	251.38
Camping equipment	1.3	123.69
Hunting and fishing equipment	2.8	220.71
Winter sports equipment	0.4	269.05
Water sports equipment	0.7	189.64
Other sports equipment	1.0	153.88
Rental and repair of miscellaneous sports equipment	0.4	187.14
Photographic equipment, supplies, and services	10.2	132.75
Film	0.9	23.85
Photo processing	6.0	37.48
Repair and rental of photographic equipment	0.1	97.73
Photographic equipment	2.5	267.33
Photographer fees	2.3	189.89
Live entertainment for catered affairs	0.3	609.26
Rental of party supplies for catered affairs	0.6	391.96
PERSONAL CARE PRODUCTS AND SERVICES	**60.7**	**120.91**
Wigs and hairpieces	0.8	116.36
Electric personal care appliances	3.8	47.79
Personal care services	59.4	118.88
READING	**36.9**	**77.16**
Newspaper and magazine subscriptions	16.8	60.19
Newspapers and magazines, nonsubscription	12.5	24.12
Books purchased through book clubs	1.3	71.48
Books not purchased through book clubs	17.6	63.07
Digital book readers	1.3	250.59
EDUCATION	**14.8**	**1,686.55**
College tuition	5.0	3,587.15
Elementary/high school tuition	1.4	2,445.00
Vocational and technical school tuition	0.2	714.77
Test preparation, tutoring services	0.8	352.27
Other school tuition	0.4	674.36
Other school expenses including rentals	3.6	269.26
Books, supplies for college	4.5	346.73
Books, supplies for elementary, high school	3.4	121.48
Books, supplies for vocational and technical schools	0.1	133.33
Books, supplies for day care, nursery school	0.1	78.57
Books, supplies for other schools	0.2	151.14
TOBACCO PRODUCTS AND SMOKING SUPPLIES	**20.3**	**427.90**
Cigarettes	17.8	452.35
Other tobacco products	3.4	189.05
FINANCIAL PRODUCTS AND SERVICES		
Miscellaneous financial products and services	**39.8**	**450.33**
Lottery and gambling losses	11.6	111.68
Legal fees	2.7	1,497.64
Funeral expenses	1.1	1,581.07
Safe deposit box rental	2.1	38.56
Checking accounts, other bank service charges	11.6	48.62
Cemetery lots, vaults, and maintenance fees	0.5	410.58
Accounting fees	5.8	272.75
Finance charges, except mortgage and vehicles	5.6	692.93
Dating services	0.1	84.62
Vacation clubs	0.2	528.26
Expenses for other properties	4.7	650.85
Occupational expenses	6.0	195.45
Credit card memberships	0.8	72.53
Shopping club membership fees	4.0	57.79

	percent reporting expenditure during quarter	average amount spent by purchasers per quarter
Cash contributions	**51.1%**	**$841.91**
Support for college students	3.3	879.73
Alimony expenditures	0.2	5,629.76
Child support expenditures	3.6	1,544.85
Gifts of stocks, bonds and mutual funds to members of other households	0.2	6,804.41
Cash contributions to charities	18.3	294.34
Cash contributions to religious organizations	27.0	600.64
Cash contributions to educational organizations	2.1	299.17
Cash contributions to political organizations	1.3	192.05
Other cash gifts to members of other households	18.9	509.29
Personal insurance and pensions	**82.1**	**1,650.71**
Life and other personal insurance	27.5	288.40
Life, endowment, annuity, other personal insurance	26.3	283.76
Other nonhealth insurance	2.8	167.87
Pensions and Social Security	77.8	1,641.10
Deductions for government retirement	2.7	845.62
Deductions for railroad retirement	0.1	1,579.17
Deductions for private pensions	10.1	1,381.33
Nonpayroll deposit to retirement plans	7.1	1,773.26
Deductions for Social Security	77.6	1,273.84
PERSONAL TAXES	**56.2**	**894.69**
Federal income taxes	49.6	691.01
State and local income taxes	34.6	365.47
Other taxes	15.2	223.63
GIFTS FOR MEMBERS OF OTHER HOUSEHOLDS	**24.1**	**782.76**
Food	**1.1**	**899.56**
Housing	**9.3**	**371.08**
Household textiles	1.3	74.81
Major appliances	0.4	456.58
Small appliances and miscellaneous housewares	1.5	92.35
Miscellaneous household equipment	4.6	134.89
Apparel and services	**11.2**	**228.68**
Males aged 2 or older	4.4	165.56
Females aged 2 or older	5.7	169.00
Children under age 2	3.1	93.95
Jewelry and watches	1.9	180.05
Transportation	**4.8**	**468.80**
Health care	**1.0**	**660.58**
Entertainment	**7.9**	**194.86**
Toys, games, hobbies, and tricycles	4.6	119.92
Education	**1.6**	**3,273.91**
All other gifts	**4.9**	**440.02**

Source: Bureau of Labor Statistics, 2011 Consumer Expenditure Survey

Spending by Product and Service Ranked by Amount Spent, 2011

(average annual spending of consumer units on products and services, ranked by amount spent, 2011)

1.	Deductions for Social Security	$3,955.54
2.	Groceries (also shown by individual category)	3,837.76
3.	Mortgage interest (or rent, $2,905.25)	3,020.32
4.	Vehicle purchases (net outlay)	2,668.56
5.	Gasoline and motor oil	2,654.56
6.	Restaurants (also shown by meal category)	2,195.89
7.	Health insurance	1,922.19
8.	Property taxes	1,844.51
9.	Electricity	1,422.95
10.	Federal income taxes	1,370.41
11.	Dinner at restaurants	1,051.05
12.	Vehicle insurance	983.31
13.	Cellular phone service	825.71
14.	Vehicle maintenance and repairs	804.93
15.	Lunch at restaurants	752.89
16.	College tuition	714.56
17.	Cash contributions to church, religious organizations	649.17
18.	Cable and satellite television services	640.40
19.	Women's apparel	603.77
20.	Deductions for private pensions	556.40
21.	Maintenance and repair services, owner	555.93
22.	State and local income taxes	505.23
23.	Nonpayroll deposit to retirement plans	500.06
24.	Alcoholic beverages	456.43
25.	Natural gas	419.64
26.	Cash gifts to members of other households	384.82
27.	Residential telephone service and pay phones	380.95
28.	Water and sewerage maintenance	376.69
29.	Homeowner's insurance	351.98
30.	Prescription drugs	344.56
31.	Airline fares	341.68
32.	Men's apparel	324.14
33.	Cigarettes	322.07
34.	Life and other personal insurance	317.12
35.	Lodging on trips	314.62
36.	Computer information services	313.76
37.	Dental services	285.67
38.	Personal care services	282.36
39.	Owned vacation homes	261.96
40.	Day care centers, nurseries, and preschools	251.30
41.	Fresh fruits	247.28
42.	Restaurant meals on trips	236.49
43.	Vehicle finance charges	232.60
44.	Breakfast at restaurants	225.86
45.	Child support expenditures	224.93
46.	Fresh vegetables	224.21
47.	Beef	222.60
48.	Cash contributions to charities	215.69
49.	Pet food	182.75
50.	Physician's services	179.40
51.	Cosmetics, perfume, and bath products	170.49
52.	Leased vehicles	167.29
53.	Snacks at restaurants	166.09
54.	Interest paid, home equity loan/line of credit	163.42
55.	Pork	161.95
56.	Movie, theater, amusement park, and other admissions	159.65

57.	Legal fees	$158.75
58.	Finance charges, except mortgage and vehicles	154.94
59.	Poultry	154.49
60.	Computers and computer hardware for nonbusiness use	152.35
61.	Women's footwear	151.99
62.	Prepared foods except frozen, salads, and desserts	147.11
63.	Carbonated drinks	145.49
64.	Laundry and cleaning supplies	145.06
65.	Veterinarian services	142.67
66.	Pet purchase, supplies, and medicines	140.90
67.	Elementary and high school tuition	136.92
68.	Other taxes	135.97
69.	Miscellaneous household products	134.12
70.	Hospital room and services	129.10
71.	Fresh milk, all types	127.38
72.	Cheese	124.74
73.	Fees for participant sports	123.79
74.	Expenses for other properties	122.10
75.	Social, recreation, health club membership	121.90
76.	Trash and garbage collection	121.02
77.	Fish and seafood	120.76
78.	Gardening, lawn care service	118.65
79.	Girls' (aged 2 to 15) apparel	117.43
80.	Household decorative items	117.20
81.	Support for college students	117.18
82.	Toys, games, hobbies, and tricycles	115.02
83.	Cleansing and toilet tissue, paper towels, and napkins	114.81
84.	Television sets	112.69
85.	Vehicle registration	112.33
86.	Beer and ale at home	109.76
87.	Potato chips and other snacks	108.01
88.	Housekeeping services	105.26
89.	Wine at home	104.03
90.	Men's footwear	96.84
91.	Sofas	92.81
92.	Nonprescription drugs	92.57
93.	Ready-to-eat and cooked cereals	91.39
94.	Lawn and garden supplies	90.65
95.	Deductions for government retirement	90.65
96.	Fuel oil	89.23
97.	Lunch meats (cold cuts)	87.67
98.	Candy and chewing gum	86.75
99.	Fees for recreational lessons	85.60
100.	Rent as pay	83.62
101.	Motorized recreational vehicles	80.37
102.	Boys' (aged 2 to 15) apparel	79.63
103.	Babysitting and child care	78.10
104.	Beer and ale at bars, restaurants	76.98
105.	Intracity mass transit fares	75.09
106.	Coffee	75.03
107.	Maintenance and repair materials, owner	74.55
108.	Frozen prepared foods, except meals	74.09
109.	Jewelry	71.95
110.	Housing while attending school	71.40
111.	Bedroom furniture except mattresses and springs	70.06
112.	Children's (under age 2) apparel	68.13
113.	Care for elderly, invalids, handicapped, etc.	67.89
114.	Hair care products	67.88
115.	Funeral expenses	67.67
116.	Stationery, stationery supplies, giftwrap	67.56
117.	Lawn and garden equipment	65.62
118.	Eyeglasses and contact lenses	63.53
119.	Accounting fees	62.95
120.	Books and supplies for college	62.55
121.	School lunches	62.16
122.	Frozen meals	62.14
123.	Mattresses and springs	61.72
124.	Bread, other than white	61.60

125.	Admission to sports events	$60.49
126.	Property management, owner	60.24
127.	Bedroom linens	59.00
128.	Sauces and gravies	58.43
129.	Bottled gas	58.24
130.	Ice cream and related products	57.28
131.	Service by professionals other than physician	56.63
132.	Lottery and gambling losses	56.00
133.	Canned and bottled fruit juice	55.78
134.	Postage	55.22
135.	Unmotored recreational vehicles	54.49
136.	Canned vegetables	54.31
137.	Bottled water	53.48
138.	Refrigerators and freezers	52.96
139.	Biscuits and rolls	52.93
140.	Moving, storage, and freight express	52.88
141.	Catered affairs	52.63
142.	Athletic gear, game tables, exercise equipment	52.52
143.	Nonprescription vitamins	51.94
144.	Miscellaneous personal services	51.94
145.	Other dairy (yogurt, etc.)	50.43
146.	Other alcoholic beverages at bars, restaurants	50.30
147.	School tuition, books, and supplies other than college, vocational/technical, elementary, high school	50.30
148.	Professional laundry, dry cleaning	50.10
149.	Eggs	50.07
150.	Books	48.58
151.	Ground rent	48.15
152.	Lab tests, X-rays	47.97
153.	Food prepared by consumer unit on trips	47.50
154.	Alimony expenditures	47.29
155.	Occupational expenses	47.22
156.	Cookies	46.96
157.	Indoor plants and fresh flowers	46.92
158.	Canned and packaged soups	46.90
159.	Gifts of stocks, bonds, and mutual funds to members of other households	46.27
160.	Telephones and accessories	45.56
161.	White bread	44.93
162.	Alcoholic beverages purchased on trips	44.84
163.	Board (including at school)	43.87
164.	Wine at bars, restaurants	41.96
165.	Topicals and dressings	40.69
166.	Video game hardware and accessories	40.41
167.	Newspaper and magazine subscriptions	40.35
168.	Coin-operated apparel laundry and dry cleaning	39.63
169.	Power tools	38.18
170.	Parking fees	38.16
171.	Cakes and cupcakes	37.81
172.	Eye care services	37.11
173.	Deodorants, feminine hygiene, miscellaneous products	37.05
174.	Nuts	37.01
175.	Boys' footwear	36.67
176.	Crackers	36.63
177.	Prepared salads	36.22
178.	Living room chairs	36.12
179.	Ship fares	35.74
180.	Pet services	35.72
181.	Girls' footwear	35.63
182.	Salt, spices, and other seasonings	35.41
183.	Pasta, cornmeal, and other cereal products	35.26
184.	Frozen vegetables	34.98
185.	Fats and oils	34.84
186.	Oral hygiene products	34.69
187.	Outdoor equipment	34.43
188.	Washing machines	34.00
189.	Video cassettes, tapes, and discs	33.29
190.	Hunting and fishing equipment	33.06

191.	Rented vehicles	$32.40
192.	Salad dressings	31.16
193.	Tea	31.16
194.	Wall units, cabinets, and other furniture	30.97
195.	Cooking stoves, ovens	30.51
196.	Tolls	30.34
197.	Watches	30.27
198.	Lamps and lighting fixtures	29.29
199.	Meals as pay	28.85
200.	Frozen and refrigerated bakery products	28.60
201.	Security services, owner	28.23
202.	Jams, preserves, other sweets	28.14
203.	Baby food	27.80
204.	Kitchen and dining room furniture	27.45
205.	Sound components, equipment, and accessories	26.88
206.	Photographic equipment	26.84
207.	Rice	25.66
208.	Home security system service fee	25.65
209.	Tobacco products other than cigarettes	25.56
210.	Cash contributions to educational institutions	25.37
211.	Clothes dryers	24.93
212.	Noncarbonated fruit-flavored drinks	24.76
213.	Butter	24.64
214.	Small electric kitchen appliances	24.50
215.	Termite and pest control products and services	24.18
216.	Baking needs	23.93
217.	Sugar	23.89
218.	Sweetrolls, coffee cakes, doughnuts	23.86
219.	Frankfurters	23.67
220.	Musical instruments and accessories	22.60
221.	Checking accounts, other bank service charges	22.58
222.	Cream	22.36
223.	Bicycles	21.92
224.	Recreation expenses on trips	21.42
225.	Canned fruits	21.24
226.	Automobile service clubs	21.07
227.	Bathroom linens	20.16
228.	Floor coverings	19.98
229.	Tableware, nonelectric kitchenware	19.71
230.	Local transportation on trips	19.63
231.	Dried vegetables	19.43
232.	Other alcoholic beverages at home	18.97
233.	Outdoor furniture	18.70
234.	Vegetable juices	18.59
235.	Nondairy cream and imitation milk	18.59
236.	Rental of video cassettes, tapes, discs, films	18.54
237.	Laundry and cleaning equipment	17.33
238.	Fresh fruit juice	17.28
239.	Photographer fees	17.09
240.	Hearing aids	16.89
241.	Closet and storage items	16.85
242.	Appliance repair, including at service center	16.62
243.	Books and supplies for elementary and high school	16.57
244.	Shaving products	16.40
245.	Olives, pickles, relishes	16.13
246.	Electric floor-cleaning equipment	16.06
247.	Intercity train fares	15.91
248.	Window coverings	15.87
249.	Maintenance and repair services, renter	15.82
250.	Sports drinks	15.73
251.	Hand tools	15.55
252.	Pies, tarts, turnovers	15.36
253.	Peanut butter	15.25
254.	Prepared desserts	15.03
255.	Nonelectric cookware	14.94
256.	Nonalcoholic beverages (except carbonated, coffee, fruit-flavored drinks, and tea) and ice	14.93
257.	Prepared flour mixes	14.88

258.	Nonclothing laundry and dry cleaning, sent out	$14.71
259.	Dishwashers (built-in), garbage disposals, range hoods	14.60
260.	Infants' equipment	14.49
261.	Taxi fares and limousine service	14.47
262.	Computer software	14.33
263.	Camping equipment	14.09
264.	Electric personal care appliances	14.01
265.	Satellite radio service	13.48
266.	Tenant's insurance	13.09
267.	Digital book readers	12.83
268.	Computer accessories	12.15
269.	Newspapers and magazines, nonsubscription	12.10
270.	Living room tables	11.87
271.	Vehicle inspection	11.75
272.	Maintenance and repair materials, renter	11.71
273.	Compact discs, records, and audio tapes	11.57
274.	Curtains and draperies	11.30
275.	Lamb, organ meats, and others	11.20
276.	Voice over IP	10.94
277.	Test preparation, tutoring services	10.85
278.	Intercity bus fares	10.67
279.	Care in convalescent or nursing home	10.32
280.	Personal digital audio players	10.29
281.	Cash contributions to political organizations	10.14
282.	Portable heating and cooling equipment	10.00
283.	Stamp and coin collecting	9.97
284.	Margarine	9.77
285.	Material for making clothes	9.65
286.	Streamed and downloaded audio	9.62
287.	Whiskey at home	9.60
288.	Coal, wood, and other fuels	9.36
289.	Repairs and rentals of lawn and garden equipment, hand and power tools, etc.	9.29
290.	Shopping club membership fees	9.27
291.	Driver's license	9.05
292.	Microwave ovens	8.96
293.	Photo processing	8.92
294.	Phone cards	8.84
295.	Rental of party supplies for catered affairs	8.78
296.	VCRs and video disc players	8.66
297.	Cemetery lots, vaults, and maintenance fees	8.54
298.	Infants' furniture	8.23
299.	Dried fruits	8.13
300.	Sewing materials for household items	8.07
301.	Sewing patterns and notions	7.88
302.	Flour	7.67
303.	Miscellaneous video equipment	7.67
304.	Hair accessories	7.60
305.	Delivery services	7.32
306.	Docking and landing fees	7.14
307.	Bread and cracker products	7.13
308.	Internet services away from home	7.03
309.	Frozen fruits	6.92
310.	Luggage	6.84
311.	Live entertainment for catered affairs	6.58
312.	Glassware	6.56
313.	Repair of computer systems for nonbusiness use	6.51
314.	Frozen fruit juices	6.40
315.	Apparel alteration, repair, and tailoring services	6.37
316.	Vocational and technical school tuition	6.29
317.	Personal digital assistants	6.27
318.	Rental of furniture	6.16
319.	Kitchen and dining room linens	5.95
320.	Office furniture for home use	5.83
321.	Reupholstering and furniture repair	5.75
322.	Artificial sweeteners	5.61
323.	Rental of recreational vehicles	5.48
324.	Watch and jewelry repair	5.43

325.	China and other dinnerware	$5.34
326.	Water sports equipment	5.31
327.	Global positioning system devices	4.91
328.	Water-softening service	4.87
329.	Vacation clubs	4.86
330.	Window air conditioners	4.82
331.	Winter sports equipment	4.52
332.	Nonclothing laundry and dry cleaning, coin-operated	4.40
333.	Portable memory	4.17
334.	Towing charges	4.13
335.	Business equipment for home use	4.05
336.	Supportive and convalescent medical equipment	4.04
337.	Streamed and downloaded video	3.92
338.	Medical equipment for general use	3.81
339.	Deductions for railroad retirement	3.79
340.	Wigs and hairpieces	3.77
341.	Applications, games, ringtones for handheld devices	3.66
342.	Playground equipment	3.63
343.	Slipcovers and decorative pillows	3.52
344.	Repair of TV, radio, and sound equipment	3.39
345.	Safe deposit box rental	3.27
346.	Septic tank cleaning	3.20
347.	Online gaming services	3.09
348.	Flatware	2.96
349.	School bus	2.90
350.	Adult diapers	2.87
351.	Smoking accessories	2.74
352.	Pinball, electronic video games	2.67
353.	Rental and repair of miscellaneous sports equipment	2.62
354.	Plastic dinnerware	2.47
355.	Sewing machines	2.43
356.	Credit card memberships	2.35
357.	Appliance rental	2.01
358.	Video game software	1.99
359.	Smoke alarms	1.97
360.	Fireworks	1.95
361.	Global positioning services	1.87
362.	Clothing rental	1.68
363.	Rental and repair of musical instruments	1.60
364.	Shoe repair and other shoe services	1.50
365.	Silver serving pieces	1.43
366.	Other serving pieces	1.42
367.	Rental of supportive and convalescent medical equipment	1.17
368.	Rental of office equipment for nonbusiness use	1.06
369.	Clothing storage	1.06
370.	Satellite dishes	1.05
371.	Rental of medical equipment	1.04
372.	Installation of television sets	0.85
373.	Books and supplies for vocational and technical schools	0.64
374.	Telephone answering devices	0.61
375.	Parking at owned home	0.55
376.	Installation of computer	0.51
377.	Portable dishwashers	0.44
378.	Books and supplies for day care and nursery	0.44
379.	Dating services	0.44
380.	Repair and rental of photographic equipment	0.43
381.	Rental of television sets	0.32
382.	Rental of VCR, radio, and sound equipment	0.18

Source: Calculations by New Strategist based on the 2011 Consumer Expenditure Survey

Glossary

age The age of the reference person.

alcoholic beverages Includes beer and ale, wine, whiskey, gin, vodka, rum, and other alcoholic beverages.

annual spending The annual amount spent per household. The Bureau of Labor Statistics calculates the annual average for all households in a segment, not just for those that purchased an item. The averages are calculated by integrating the results of the diary (weekly) and interview (quarterly) portions of the Consumer Expenditure Survey. For items purchased by most households—such as bread—average annual spending figures are a fairly accurate account of actual spending. For products and services purchased by few households during a year's time—such as cars—the average annual amount spent is much less than what purchasers spend.

apparel, accessories, and related services Includes the following:

• *men's and boys' apparel* Includes coats, jackets, sweaters, vests, sport coats, tailored jackets, slacks, shorts and short sets, sportswear, shirts, underwear, nightwear, hosiery, uniforms, and other accessories.

• *women's and girls' apparel* Includes coats, jackets, furs, sport coats, tailored jackets, sweaters, vests, blouses, shirts, dresses, dungarees, culottes, slacks, shorts, sportswear, underwear, nightwear, uniforms, hosiery, and other accessories.

• *infants' apparel* Includes coats, jackets, snowsuits, underwear, diapers, dresses, crawlers, sleeping garments, hosiery, footwear, and other accessories for children.

• *footwear* Includes articles such as shoes, slippers, boots, and other similar items. It excludes footwear for babies and footwear used for sports such as bowling or golf shoes.

• *other apparel products and services* Includes material for making clothes, shoe repair, alterations and sewing patterns and notions, clothing rental, clothing storage, dry cleaning, sent-out laundry, watches, jewelry, and repairs to watches and jewelry.

baby boom Americans born between 1946 and 1964.

cash contributions Includes cash contributed to persons or organizations outside the consumer unit including court-ordered alimony, child support payments, support for college students, and contributions to religious, educational, charitable, or political organizations.

consumer unit (1) All members of a household who are related by blood, marriage, adoption, or other legal arrangements; (2) a person living alone or sharing a household with others or living as a roomer in a private home or lodging house or in permanent living quarters in a hotel or motel, but who is financially independent; or (3) two or more persons living together who pool their income to make joint expenditure decisions. Financial independence is determined by the three major expense categories: housing, food, and other living expenses. To be considered financially independent, at least two of the three major expense categories have to be provided by the respondent. For convenience, called household in the text of this report.

consumer unit, composition of The classification of interview households by type according to (1) relationship of other household members to the reference person; (2) age of the children of the reference person; and (3) combination of relationship to the reference person and age of the children. Stepchildren and adopted children are included with the reference person's own children.

earner A consumer unit member aged 14 or older who worked at least one week during the 12 months prior to the interview date.

education Includes tuition, fees, books, supplies, and equipment for public and private nursery schools, elementary and high schools, colleges and universities, and other schools.

entertainment Includes the following:

• *fees and admissions* Includes fees for participant sports; admissions to sporting events, movies, concerts, plays; health, swimming, tennis, and country club memberships, and other social recreational and fraternal organizations; recreational lessons or instructions; and recreational expenses on trips.

• *audio and visual equipment and services* Includes television sets; radios; cable TV; tape recorders and players; video cassettes, tapes, and discs; video cassette recorders and video disc players; video game hardware and software; personal digital audio players; streaming and downloading audio and video; sound components; CDs, records, and tapes; musical instruments; and rental and repair of TV and sound equipment.

• *pets, toys, hobbies, and playground equipment* Includes pet food, pet services, veterinary expenses, toys, games, hobbies, and playground equipment.

• *other entertainment equipment and services* Includes indoor exercise equipment, athletic shoes, bicycles, trailers, campers, camping equipment, rental of campers and trailers, hunting and fishing equipment, sports equipment, winter sports equipment, water sports equipment, boats, boat motors and boat trailers, rental of boats, landing and docking fees, rental and repair of sports equipment, photographic equipment, film, photo processing, photographer fees, repair and rental of photo equipment, fireworks, pinball and electronic video games.

expenditure The transaction cost including excise and sales taxes of goods and services acquired during the survey period. The full cost of each purchase is recorded even though full payment may not have been made at the date of purchase. Expenditure estimates include gifts. Excluded from expenditures are purchases or portions of purchases directly assignable to business purposes and periodic credit or installment payments on goods and services already acquired.

federal income tax Includes federal income tax withheld in the survey year to pay for income earned in survey year plus additional tax paid in survey year to cover any underpayment or under-withholding of tax in the year prior to the survey.

financial products and services Includes accounting fees, legal fees, union dues, professional dues and fees, other occupational expenses, funerals, cemetery lots, dating services, shopping club memberships, and unclassified fees and personal services.

food Includes the following:

• *food at home* Refers to the total expenditures for food at grocery stores or other food stores during the interview period. It is calculated by multiplying the number of visits to a grocery or other food store by the average amount spent per visit. It excludes the purchase of nonfood items.

• *food away from home* Includes all meals (breakfast, lunch, brunch, and dinner) at restaurants, carry-outs, and vending machines, including tips, plus meals as pay, special catered affairs such as weddings, bar mitzvahs, and confirmations, and meals away from home on trips.

generation X Americans born between 1965 and 1976; also known as the baby-bust generation.

gifts for people in other households Includes gift expenditures for people living in other consumer units. The amount spent on gifts is also included in individual product and service categories.

health care Includes the following:

• *health insurance* Includes health maintenance plans (HMOs), Blue Cross/Blue Shield, commercial health insurance, Medicare, Medicare supplemental insurance, Medicare prescription drug premium, long-term care insurance, and other health insurance.

• *medical services* Includes hospital room and services, physicians' services, services of a practitioner other than a physician, eye and dental care, lab tests, X-rays, nursing, therapy services, care in convalescent or nursing home, and other medical care.

• *drugs* Includes prescription and nonprescription drugs, internal and respiratory over-the-counter drugs.

• *medical supplies* Includes eyeglasses and contact lenses, topicals and dressings, antiseptics, bandages, cotton, first aid kits, contraceptives; medical equipment for general use such as syringes, ice bags, thermometers, vaporizers, heating pads; supportive or convalescent medical equipment such as hearing aids, braces, canes, crutches, and walkers.

Hispanic origin The self-identified Hispanic origin of the consumer unit reference person. All consumer units are included in one of two Hispanic origin groups based on the reference person's Hispanic origin: Hispanic or non-Hispanic. Hispanics may be of any race.

household According to the Census Bureau, all the people who occupy a household. A group of unrelated people who share a housing unit as roommates or unmarried partners is also counted as a household. Households do not include group quarters such as college dormitories, prisons, or nursing homes. A household may contain more than one consumer unit. The terms "household" and "consumer unit" are used interchangeably in this report.

household furnishings and equipment Includes the following:

• *household textiles* Includes bathroom, kitchen, dining room, and other linens, curtains and drapes, slipcovers and decorative pillows, and sewing materials.

• *furniture* Includes living room, dining room, kitchen, bedroom, nursery, porch, lawn, and other outdoor furniture.

• *carpet, rugs, and other floor coverings* Includes installation and replacement of wall-to-wall carpets, room-size rugs, and other soft floor coverings.

• *major appliances* Includes refrigerators, freezers, dishwashers, stoves, ovens, garbage disposals, vacuum cleaners, microwave ovens, air conditioners, sewing machines, washing machines, clothes dryers, and floor-cleaning equipment.

• *small appliances and miscellaneous housewares* Includes small electrical kitchen appliances, portable heating and cooling equipment, china and other dinnerware, flatware, glassware, silver and other serving pieces, nonelectric cookware, and plastic dinnerware. Excludes personal care appliances.

• *miscellaneous household equipment* Includes computer hardware and software, luggage, lamps and other lighting fixtures, window coverings, clocks, lawn mowers and gardening equipment, hand and power tools, telephone answering devices, personal digital assistants, Internet services away from home, office equipment for home use, fresh flowers and house plants, rental of furniture, closet and storage items, household decorative items, infants' equipment, outdoor equipment, smoke alarms, other household appliances, and small miscellaneous furnishing.

household services Includes the following:

• *personal services* Includes baby sitting, day care, and care of elderly and handicapped persons.

• *other household services* Includes computer information services; housekeeping services; gardening and lawn care services; coin-operated laundry and dry-cleaning of household textiles; termite and pest control products; moving, storage, and freight expenses; repair of household appliances and other household equipment; reupholstering and furniture repair; rental and repair of lawn and gardening tools; and rental of other household equipment.

housekeeping supplies Includes soaps, detergents, other laundry cleaning products, cleansing and toilet tissue, paper towels, napkins, and miscellaneous household products; lawn and garden supplies, postage, stationery, stationery supplies, and gift wrap.

housing tenure "Owner" includes households living in their own homes, cooperatives, condominiums, or townhouses. "Renter" includes households paying rent as well as families living rent free in lieu of wages.

income before taxes The total money earnings and selected money receipts accruing to a consumer unit during the 12 months prior to the interview date. Income includes the following components:

• *wages and salaries* Includes total money earnings for all members of the consumer unit aged 14 or older from all jobs, including civilian wages and salaries, Armed Forces pay and allowances, piece-rate payments, commissions, tips, National Guard or Reserve pay (received for training periods), and cash bonuses before deductions for taxes, pensions, union dues, etc.

• *self-employment income* Includes net business and farm income, which consists of net income (gross receipts minus operating expenses) from a profession or unincorporated business or from the operation of a farm by an owner, tenant, or sharecropper. If the business or farm is a partnership, only an appropriate share of net income is recorded. Losses are also recorded.

• *Social Security, private and government retirement* Includes payments by the federal government made under retirement, survivor, and disability insurance programs to retired persons, dependents of deceased insured workers, or to disabled workers; and private pensions or retirement benefits received by retired persons or their survivors, either directly or through an insurance company.

• *interest, dividends, rental income, and other property income* Includes interest income on savings or bonds; payments made by a corporation to its stockholders, periodic receipts from estates or trust funds; net income or loss from the rental of property, real estate, or farms, and net income or loss from roomers or boarders.

• *unemployment and workers' compensation and veterans' benefits* Includes income from unemployment compensation and workers' compensation, and veterans' payments including educational benefits, but excluding military retirement.

• *public assistance, supplemental security income, and food stamps* Includes public assistance or welfare, including money received from job training grants; supplemental security income paid by federal, state, and local welfare agencies to low-income persons who are aged 65 or older, blind, or disabled; and the value of food stamps obtained.

• *regular contributions for support* Includes alimony and child support as well as any regular contributions from persons outside the consumer unit.

• *other income* Includes money income from care of foster children, cash scholarships, fellowships, or stipends not based on working; and meals and rent as pay.

indexed spending Indexed spending figures compare the spending of particular demographic segments with that of the average household. To compute an index, the amount spent on an item by a demographic segment is divided by the amount spent on the item by the average household. That figure is then multiplied by 100. An index of 100 is the average for all households. An index of 132 means average spending by households in a segment is 32 percent above average (100 plus 32). An index of 75 means average spending by households in a segment is 25 percent below average (100 minus 25). Indexed spending figures identify the consumer units that spend the most on a product or service.

life and other personal insurance Includes premiums from whole life and term insurance; endowments; income and other life insurance; mortgage guarantee insurance; mortgage life insurance; premiums for personal life liability, accident and disability; and other nonhealth insurance other than homes and vehicles.

market share The market share is the percentage of total household spending on an item that is accounted for by a demographic segment. Market shares are calculated by dividing a demographic segment's total spending on an item by the total spending of all households on the item. Total spending on an item for all households is calculated by multiplying average spending by the total number of households. Total spending on an item for each demographic segment is calculated by multiplying the segment's average spending by the number of households in the segment. Market shares reveal the demographic segments that account for the largest share of spending on a product or service.

millennial generation Americans born between 1977 and 1994.

occupation The occupation in which the reference person received the most earnings during the survey period. The occupational categories follow those of the Census of Population. Categories shown in the tables include the following:

• *self-employed* Includes all occupational categories; the reference person is self-employed in own business, professional practice, or farm.

• *wage and salary earners, managers and professionals* Includes executives, administrators, managers, and professional specialties such as architects, engineers, natural and social scientists, lawyers, teachers, writers, health diagnosis and treatment workers, entertainers, and athletes.

• *wage and salary earners, technical, sales, and clerical workers* Includes technicians and related support workers; sales representatives, sales workers, cashiers, and sales-related occupations; and administrative support, including clerical.

• *retired* People who did not work either full- or part-time during the survey period.

owner *See* Housing tenure.

pensions and Social Security Includes all Social Security contributions paid by employees; employees' contributions to railroad retirement, government retirement and private pensions programs; retirement programs for self-employed.

personal care Includes products for the hair, oral hygiene products, shaving needs, cosmetics, bath products, suntan lotions, hand creams, electric personal care appliances, incontinence products, other personal care products, personal care services such as hair care services (haircuts, bleaching, tinting, coloring, conditioning treatments, permanents, press, and curls), styling and other services for wigs and hairpieces, body massages or slenderizing treatments, facials, manicures, pedicures, shaves, electrolysis.

quarterly spending Quarterly spending data are collected in the interview portion of the Consumer Expenditure Survey. Quarterly spending tables show the percentage of households that purchased an item during an average quarter, and the amount spent during the quarter on the item by purchasers. Not all items are included in the interview portion of the Consumer Expenditure Survey.

reading Includes subscriptions for newspapers, magazines, and books through book clubs; purchase of single-copy newspapers and magazines, books (hardcopy or electronic format), and digital e-readers.

reference person The first member mentioned by the respondent when asked to "Start with the name of the person or one of the persons who owns or rents the home." It is with respect to this person that the relationship of other consumer unit members is determined. Also called the householder or head of household.

region Consumer units are classified according to their address at the time of their participation in the survey. The four major census regions of the United States are the following state groupings:

• *Northeast* Connecticut, Maine, Massachusetts, New Hampshire, New Jersey, New York, Pennsylvania, Rhode Island, and Vermont.

• *Midwest* Illinois, Indiana, Iowa, Kansas, Michigan, Minnesota, Mississippi, Nebraska, North Dakota, Ohio, South Dakota, and Wisconsin.

• *South* Alabama, Arkansas, Delaware, District of Columbia, Florida, Georgia, Kentucky, Louisiana, Maryland, Mississippi, North Carolina, Oklahoma, South Carolina, Tennessee, Texas, Virginia, and West Virginia.

• *West* Alaska, Arizona, California, Colorado, Hawaii, Idaho, Minnesota, Nevada, New Mexico, Oregon, Utah, Washington, and Wyoming.

renter *See* Housing tenure.

shelter Includes the following:

• *owned dwellings* Includes interest on mortgages, property taxes and insurance, refinancing and prepayment charges, ground rent, expenses for property management and security, homeowner's insurance, fire insurance and extended coverage, landscaping expenses for repairs and maintenance contracted out (including periodic maintenance and service contracts), and expenses of materials for owner-performed repairs and maintenance for dwellings used or maintained by the consumer unit, but not dwellings maintained for business or rent.

• *rented dwellings* Includes rent paid for dwellings, rent received as pay, parking fees, maintenance, and other expenses.

• *other* lodging Includes all expenses for vacation homes, school, college, hotels, motels, cottages, trailer camps, and other lodging while out of town.

• *utilities, fuels, and public services* Includes natural gas, electricity, fuel oil, coal, bottled gas, wood, other fuels; residential telephone service, cell phone service, phone cards; water, garbage, trash collection; sewerage maintenance, septic tank cleaning; and other public services.

size of consumer unit The number of people whose usual place of residence at the time of the interview is in the consumer unit.

state and local income taxes Includes state and local income taxes withheld in the survey year to pay for income earned in survey year plus additional taxes paid in the survey year to cover any underpayment or underwithholding of taxes in the year prior to the survey.

tobacco and smoking supplies Includes cigarettes, cigars, snuff, loose smoking tobacco, chewing tobacco, and smoking accessories such as cigarette or cigar holders, pipes, flints, lighters, pipe cleaners, and other smoking products and accessories.

transportation Includes the following:

• *vehicle purchases (net outlay)* Includes the net outlay (purchase price minus trade-in value) on new and used domestic and imported cars and trucks and other vehicles, including motorcycles and private planes.

• *gasoline and motor oil* Includes gasoline, diesel fuel, and motor oil.

• *other vehicle expenses* Includes vehicle finance charges, maintenance and repairs, vehicle insurance, and vehicle rental licenses and other charges.

• *vehicle finance charges* Includes the dollar amount of interest paid for a loan contracted for the purchase of vehicles described above.

• *maintenance and repairs* Includes tires, batteries, tubes, lubrication, filters, coolant, additives, brake and transmission fluids, oil change, brake adjustment and repair, front-end alignment, wheel balancing, steering repair, shock absorber replacement, clutch and transmission repair, electrical system repair, repair to cooling system, drive train repair, drive shaft and rear-end repair, tire repair, vehicle video equipment, other maintenance and services, and auto repair policies.

• *vehicle insurance* Includes the premium paid for insuring cars, trucks, and other vehicles.

• *vehicle rental, licenses, and other charges* Includes leased and rented cars, trucks, motorcycles, and aircraft, inspection fees, state and local registration, drivers' license fees, parking fees, towing charges, tolls on trips, and global positioning services.

• *public transportation* Includes fares for mass transit, buses, trains, airlines, taxis, private school buses, and fares paid on trips for trains, boats, taxis, buses, and trains.

weekly spending Weekly spending data are collected in the diary portion of the Consumer Expenditure Survey. The data show the percentage of households that purchased an item during the average week, and the amount spent per week on the item by purchasers. Not all items are included in the diary portion of the Consumer Expenditure Survey.

Index

accounting fees, 161–189
admissions
    to entertainment events, 7–44, 103–159
    to movies, theater, opera, ballet, 103–159
    to sporting events, 103–159
air conditioners, window units, 365–421
    maintenance and repair of, 423–479
airline fares, 511–567
    gifts of, 305–333
alarms, smoke, 365–421
alcoholic beverages, 7–44, 191–303. *See also* Beer and ale; Wine; *and* Whiskey.
    at catered affairs, 191–303
    at home, 191–303
    from fast-food restaurants, 191–303
    from full-service restaurants, 191–303
    gifts of, 7–44, 305–333
    purchased on trips, 191–303
alimony, 161–189
amusement park tickets, 103–159
apparel
    boys', 7–44, 45–101
    gifts of, 7–44, 305–333
    girls', 7–44, 45–101
    infants', 7–44, 45–101
    men's, 7–44, 45–101
    repair, 45–101
    shoes, 7–44, 45–101
    shoes, gifts of, 305–333
    women's, 7–44, 45–101
apples, 191–303
appliances
    gifts of, 7–44, 305–333
    kitchen, 365–421
    major, 7–44, 365–421
    personal care, 481–509
    repair, 365–421
    small, 7–44, 365–421
apps for handheld devices, 103–159
artificial sweeteners, 191–303
athletic gear, 103–159
audio
    personal digital players, 103–159
    streamed and downloaded 103–159
    tapes, 103–159
auto rental, 511–567
    on trips, 511–567
automobile service clubs, 511–567
automobiles. *See* Cars *and* Trucks.

baby food, 191–303
babysitting. *See also* Day care centers, nursery schools, and preschools.
    other home, 481–509
    own home, 481–509
bacon, 191 303
bakery products, 7–44, 191–303
    frozen and refrigerated, 191–303
baking needs, 191–303
ballet tickets, 103–159
bananas, 191–303

bank service charges, 161–189
bath products, 481–509
    gifts of, 305–333
bathroom linens, 365–421
bedroom furniture, 365–421
bedroom linens, 365–421
beds. *See* Mattresses and springs.
beef, 7–44, 191–303
beer and ale, 191–303
bicycles, 103–159
biscuits and rolls, 191–303
blouses and tops, 45–101
Blue Cross, Blue Shield. *See* Health insurance.
board, including at school, 191–303
boats, 103–159
bologna, 191–303
books, 481–509
    and supplies for college, 481–509
    and supplies for daycare and nursery school, 481–509
    and supplies for elementary and high school, 481–509
    and supplies for vocational and technical schools, 481–509
boys' apparel, 7–44, 45–101
bread, 191–303
bread and cracker products, 191–303
breakfast and brunch, at restaurants, 191–303
bus fares, intercity, 511–567
business equipment and office furniture for home use, 365–421
butter, 191–303

cabinets, 365–421
cable and satellite television service, 103–159
cafeterias, meals from, 191–303
cakes, 191–303
    gifts of, 305–333
calculators, 365–421
campers, motorized, 103–159
camping equipment, 103–159
candy, 191–303
    gifts of, 305–333
carbonated drinks, 191–303
carpeting, 365–421
cars
    lease payments, 511–567
    new, 7–44, 511–567
    rental, 511–567
    used, 7–44, 511–567
catered affairs, 103–159, 191–303
CDs, 103–159
cellular phone service, 423–479
cemetery lots, vaults, maintenance fees, 161–189
cereal, 7–44, 191–303
chairs, living room, 365–421
charitable contributions, 161–189
checking account service fees, 161–189
cheese, 191–303
chewing gum, 191–303
    gifts of, 305–333
chicken. *See* Poultry.
child care. *See* Babysitting; *and* Day care centers, nursery schools, and preschools.
child support, 161–189

china and other dinnerware, 365–421
cigarettes, 481–509
cleaning services. *See* Housekeeping services.
cleaning supplies. *See* Laundry and cleaning supplies.
cleansing and toilet tissues, 365–421
closet and storage items, 365–421
clothes dryers, 365–421
clothing rental, 45–101
clothing storage, 45–101
clubs
    automobile service, 511–567
    social, recreation, and health, 103–159
coats and jackets, 45–101
coffee, 191–303
coffee cakes, 191–303
colas, 191–303
cold cuts, 191–303
college
    books and supplies, 481–509
    support for students, 161–189
    tuition, 481–509
    tuition, gifts of, 305–333
compact discs, 103–159
computer
    hardware for nonbusiness use, 365–421
    hardware for nonbusiness use, gifts of, 305–333
    information services, 365–421
    installation, 365–421
    repair of systems for nonbusiness use, 365–421
    software for nonbusiness use, 365–421
condiments, 191–303
contact lenses. *See* Eyeglasses and contact lenses.
contributions, cash, 7–44, 161–189
    to charities, 161–189
    to educational organizations, 161–189
    to members of other households, 161–189
    to political organizations, 161–189
    to religious organizations, 161–189
cookies, 191–303
cooking stoves, 365–421
cookware, nonelectric, 365–421
cornmeal, 191–303
cosmetics, 481–509
    gifts of, 305–333
costumes, 45–101
crackers, 191–303
cream
    fresh, 7–44, 191–303
    nondairy, 191–303
credit card memberships, 161–189
cupcakes, 191–303
    gifts of, 305–333
curtains, 365–421

dairy products, 7–44, 191–303
dating services, 161–189
day care, adult, 365–421
day care centers, nursery schools, and preschools, 365–421
    books and supplies for, 481–509
    gifts of, 305–333
decorative items for the home, 365–421
    gifts of, 305–333
delivery services, 365–421
dental, services, 335–363
deodorants, 481–509

desserts, prepared, 191–303
detergents, 365–421
diesel fuel, 511–567
digital book readers, 481–509
dining room
    furniture, 365–421
    linens, 365–421
dinner, at restaurants, 191–303
dinnerware, 365–421
docking and landing fees, 103–159
doctor's services. *See* Physician's services.
donations. *See* Contributions.
doughnuts, 191–303
draperies, 365–421
dresses, 45–101
drinks
    alcoholic, 7–44, 191–303
    fruit juice, canned and bottled, 191–303
    fruit juice, fresh, 191–303
    fruit juice, frozen, 191–303
    fruit-flavored, noncarbonated, 191–303
    nonalcoholic, 7–44, 191–303
driver's license, 511–567
drugs, 7–44
    nonprescription, 335–363
    prescription, 335–363
dry cleaning. *See* Laundry and dry cleaning.
dryers. *See* Clothes dryers.

ebook readers, 481–509
education, 7–44, 481–509. *See also* College; Day care centers,
    nursery schools, and preschools; Elementary school;
    High school; *and* School.
    contributions to, 161–189
    gifts of, 7–44, 305–333
eggs, 7–44, 191–303
electrical work, 423–479
electricity, 7–44, 423–479
    gifts of, renter, 305–333
elementary school
    books and supplies, 481–509
    tuition, 481–509
entertainment, 7–44, 103–159
    gifts of, 7–44, 305–333
equipment
    exercise, 103–159
    fishing, 103–159
    hunting, 103–159
    infants', 365–421
    infants', gifts of, 305–333
    medical, 335–363
    recreational, 103–159
    sound, 7–44, 103–159
    sports, 103–159
    water sports, 103–159
    winter sports, 103–159
eye care services, 335–363
eyeglasses and contact lenses, 335–363

fats and oils, 7–44, 191–303
fees
    accounting, 161–189
    and admissions to entertainment events, 7–44, 103–159
    docking and landing, 103–159
    for recreational lessons, 103–159